THE SPORT AMERICANA©

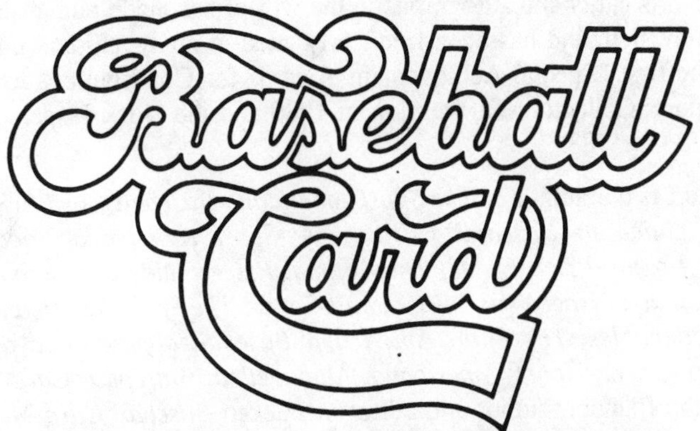

ALPHABETICAL CHECKLIST

NO. 4

By

DR. JAMES BECKETT

 Printed in the U.S.A., 1990. Published by Edgewater Book Company Inc., Box 40238, Cleveland, OH 44140.

ISBN 0-937424-45-5

About the Author

Jim Beckett, the leading authority on sports card values in the United States, maintains a wide range of activities in the world of sports. He possesses one of the finest collections of sports cards and autographs in the world, has made numerous appearances on radio and television, and has been frequently cited in many national publications. He was awarded the first "Special Achievement Award" for Contributions to the Hobby by the National Sports Collectors Convention in 1980 and the "Jock-Jasperson Award" for Hobby Dedication in 1983.

Dr. Beckett is the author of *The Sport Americana Baseball Card Price Guide*; *The Official Price Guide to Baseball Cards*; *The Sport Americana Football, Hockey, Basketball and Boxing Price Guide*; *The Official Price Guide to Football Cards*; *The Official Price Guide to Hockey and Basketball Cards*; *The Sport Americana Price Guide to Baseball Collectibles*; *The Sport Americana Baseball Memorabilia and Autograph Price Guide*; and *The Sport Americana Alphabetical Baseball Card Checklist*. In addition, he is the founder, author and editor of *Beckett Baseball Card Monthly*, *Beckett Basketball Card Magazine* and *Beckett Football Card Magazine*, magazines dedicated to advancing the card collecting hobby.

Jim Beckett received his Ph.D. in Statistics from Southern Methodist University in 1975. He resides in Dallas with his wife Patti and their daughters, Christina, Rebecca and Melissa.

The Sport Americana Baseball Card Alphabetical Checklist No. 4
Table of Contents

Acknowledgements

A great deal of hard work went into this volume, and it could not have been done without a considerable amount of help from many people. Our thanks are extended to each and every one of you.

Those who have worked closely with us on this and many other books, have again proven themselves invaluable -- Mike Aronstein, Frank and Vivian Barning (*Baseball Hobby News*), Chris Benjamin, Rick Benner, Sy Berger (Topps), Cartophilium (Andrew Pywowarczuk), Mike Cramer (Pacific Trading Cards), Jim Dickson, Bill and Diane Dodge, Gervise Ford, Steve Freedman, Craig W. Friedemann, Larry and Jeff Fritsch, Tony Galovich, Georgia Music and Sports (Dick DeCourcy and Floyd Parr), Dick Goddard, Mike and Howard Gordon, Wayne Grove, Bill Haber, Don Harrison (Tenth Inning), Alan Kaye (*Baseball Card News*), Don Lepore, Neil Lewis (Leaf), Lew Lipset, Norman and Ken Liss, Major League Marketing (Dan Shedrick, Tom Day, George Martin), Don McPherson, Andrew Menown, Brian Morris, Paul Mullan and Vincent Murray (Fleer), Ralph Nozaki, Optigraphics (Anne Flavin and Ed Fick), Jack Pollard, Gavin Riley, Alan Rosen (Mr. Mint), John Rumierz, San Diego Sport Collectibles (Bill Goepner and Nacho Arredondo), Mike Schechter, John T. Slater, John Spalding, Sports Collectors Store (Pat Quinn and Don Steinbach), Frank Steele, Murvin Sterling, Lee Temanson, Ed Twombly (New England Bullpen), and Kit Young. Finally we owe a special acknowledgment to Dennis W. Eckes, "Mr. Sport Americana." The success of the *Beckett Price Guides* has always been the result of a team effort.

Many other people have provided checklist verifications, errata and/or background information. We should like to individually thank Ab D Cards (Dale Wesolewski), Jerry Adamic, Dennis Anderson, Gary Blisard, Chris Cauley, Ira Cetron, Chriss Christiansen, Ken Clarke Jr., Richard Davis, Brian DeCaussin, Jamie Doppler, Bob Elliott, Doak Ewing, M.M. Gibson, Pete Green, Hall's Nostalgia, Bill Henderson, Paul Hould, Glenn Ison, Ernest Israel, Steve Kemper, Bob Kershner, Irv Lerner, Chris Liverani, Bob Malanowski, Carl McCaskey, Mike McDonald (Sports Page), Joe Michalowicz, Mike O'Brien, Michael J. Pawlowicz, Mike Perlow, Tom Pfirrmann, Tom Reid, Kent Ritchie, Joe Sak, Gary Sawatzki, Richard A. Shea, Don Tow, Richard Walden, Richard West, Fritz Wisecup, and Robert Zanze.

We have appreciated all of the help we have received over the years from collectors across the country and, indeed, throughout the world. Every year we make active solicitations to individuals and groups for input for a specific edition and we are particularly appreciative of the help (large and small) provided for this volume. While we receive many inquiries, comments, and questions -- and, in fact, each and every one is read and digested -- time constraints prevent us from personally replying to all but a few such letters. We hope that the letters will continue, and that even though no reply is received, you will feel that you are making significant contributions to the hobby through your interest and comments.

Special thanks go the staff of *Beckett Publications* for their help. Editorial Director Fred Reed was very helpful with the editing of the introductory section, the production of the advertising pages, and the supervision of the extensive production support team. He was ably assisted by Jeff Amano, Therese Bellar, Michael Bolduc, Lou Cather, Theo Chen, Susan Elliott, Julie Fulton, Pepper Hastings, Sara Jenks, Jay Johnson, Patricia Jones, Rudy Klancnik, Frances Knight, Omar Mediano, B.A. Murry and Reed Poole. The rest of the overall operations of *Beckett Monthly* were skillfully directed by Claire Backus and Joe Galindo. Working with them were Nancy Barton, Lisa Borden, Chris Calandro, Mary Campana, Paige Crosby, Jan Dickerson, Louise Ebaugh, Mary Gregory, Julie Grove, Beth Hartke, Laura Kelley, Monte King, Debbie Kingsbury, Amy Kirk, Renee MacElvaine, Glen Morante, Ruth Price, Cindy Struble, Mark Whitesell and Jay Yarid. James and Sandi Beane performed several major system programming jobs for us this year in order to help us accomplish our work faster and more accurately. The whole *Beckett Publications* team has my thanks for jobs well done. Thank you, everyone.

I also thank my family, especially my wife, Patti, and daughters, Christina, Rebecca, and Melissa, for putting up with me again.

OLD TIMERS and GROUP PHOTOS

GREAT FOR AUTOGRAPHS

1 to 9 ar $ 3.00 each plus postage & handling
10 to 24 at $ 2.50 each plus postage & handling
25 or more at $ 2.25 each plus postage & handling

NEW LARGER EXPANDED LIST

OLD TIMERS

☐ Aaron, Hank*
☐ Agee, Tommy
☐ Allen, Dick
☐ Alston, Walter*
☐ Aparico, Luis*
☐ Appling, Luke*
☐ Ashburn, Richie
☐ Banks, Ernie*
☐ Bauer, Hank
☐ Bell, Cool Papa
☐ Bench, Johnny*
☐ Berra, Yogi*
☐ Blue, Vida
☐ Bonds, Bobby
☐ Boudreau, Lou*
☐ Brock, Lou*
☐ Buhl, Bob
☐ Bunning, Jim
☐ Burdette, Lew
☐ Campanella, Roy*
☐ Carew, Rod
☐ Carlton, Steve
☐ Cepeda, Orlando
☐ Charboneau, Joe
☐ Crandell, Del
☐ Cueller, Mike
☐ Dandridge, Ray*
☐ Dark, Alvin
☐ Davis, Tommy
☐ DiMaggio, Joe*
☐ Doby, Larry
☐ Doerr, Bobby*
☐ Dropo, Walt
☐ Drysdale, Don*
☐ Erskine, Carl
☐ Face, Elroy
☐ Ferrell, Rick*
☐ Fingers, Rollie
☐ Flanagan, Mike
☐ Friend, Bob
☐ Garvey, Steve
☐ Gehrig, Lou*
☐ Gibson, Bob*
☐ Gomez, Lefty*
☐ Grant, Mud Cat
☐ Groat, Dick
☐ Guidry, Ron
☐ Howard, Ellie
☐ Hubbell, Carl*
☐ Hunter, Catfish*
☐ Irvin, Monte*
☐ Jackson, Reggie
☐ Jenkins, Ferguson
☐ Kaline, Al*
☐ Kell, George*
☐ Killebrew, Harmon*
☐ Kiner, Ralph*
☐ Kluzewski, Ted
☐ Koosman, Jerry
☐ Koufax, Sandy*
☐ Kranepool, Ed
☐ Kubek, Tony
☐ Labine, Clem
☐ Law, Vernon
☐ Lemon, Bob

OLD TIMERS

☐ Lolich, Mickey
☐ Lopat, Eddie
☐ Lopez, Al*
☐ Lyle, Sparky
☐ Mantle, Mickey*
☐ Marichal, Juan*
☐ Marion, Marty
☐ Maris, Roger
☐ Martin, Billy
☐ Mathews, Eddie*
☐ Mays, Willie*
☐ McCovey, Willie*
☐ McDougald, Gil
☐ McGraw, Tug
☐ McLain, Denny
☐ McNally, Dave
☐ Mize, Johnny*
☐ Morgan, Joe
☐ Mueller, Don
☐ Munson, Thurman
☐ Musial, Stan*
☐ Newcomb, Don
☐ Newhouser, Hal
☐ Oliva, Tony
☐ Palmer, Jim
☐ Perez, Tony
☐ Perry, Gaylord
☐ Perry, Jim
☐ Pierce, Billy
☐ Piniella, Lou
☐ Pinson, Vada
☐ Podres, Johnny
☐ Powell, Boog
☐ Reese, Pee Wee*
☐ Rizzuto, Phil
☐ Roberts, Robin*
☐ Robinson, Brooks*
☐ Robinson, Jackie*
☐ Robinson, Frank*
☐ Rosen, Al
☐ Ruth, Babe Player*
☐ Ruth, Babe Retired*
☐ Santo, Ron
☐ Sauer, Hank
☐ Mike Schmidt
☐ Schoendienst, Red*
☐ Score, Herb
☐ Seaver, Tom
☐ Sewell, Joe*
☐ Shantz, Bobby
☐ Sievers, Roy
☐ Slaughter, Enos*
☐ Snider, Duke*
☐ Spahn, Warren*
☐ Stargell, Willie*
☐ Stottlemyre, Mel
☐ Sutter, Bruce
☐ Tresh, Tommy
☐ Virdon, Bill
☐ Walker, Harry
☐ Wilhelm, Hoyt*
☐ Williams, Billy*
☐ Williams, Ted*
☐ Wills, Maury
☐ Wynn, Early*
☐ Yastrzemski, Carl*

*Hall of Fame

GROUPS

☐ 1950 Phillies Team
☐ 1952 Giants Line Up
☐ 1955 Dodgers
☐ 1956 Dodgers
☐ 1961 Yankees Line Up
☐ 1962 Yankees Team
☐ 1963 Dodgers L.A.
☐ 1964 Cardinals Infield
☐ 1964 Yankees Team
☐ 1969 Mets Team
☐ 1973 Mets Team
☐ 1989 Mets Team
☐ Aaron & Mays
☐ Bench & Lasorda
☐ Bench & Perez
☐ Bench & Yastrzemski
☐ Brett & Bo Jackson
☐ Brett & Boggs
☐ Brett & Cal Ripken
☐ Brooks Robinson & Clete Boyer
☐ B. Robinson & Kaline
☐ Cal, Cal Sr. & Billy Ripken
☐ DiMaggio & Feller
☐ Downing, Stottlemyre, Peterson & Ford
☐ Gehrig, Foxx & Ruth
☐ Gehrig, Gehringer, Greenberg & Ruth
☐ Joe & Dom DiMaggio
☐ K. Hernandez & Will Clark
☐ Mantle, DiMaggio, & Williams
☐ Mantle, Houk, Pepitone, B. Robinson & Tresh

GROUPS

☐ Mantle, Maris, Keane & Tresh
☐ Mantle, Maris & Berra
☐ Mantle, Mays & Killebrew
☐ Mantle & Maris
☐ Mantle & Mays
☐ Mattingly, Brett & Boggs
☐ Mattingly & Boggs
☐ Mattingly & Brett
☐ Mattingly & Hernandez
☐ Mattingly & Joyner
☐ Mattingly & Rose
☐ Mattingly & Strawberry
☐ Mattingly & Winfield
☐ McGwire, Canseco & Weiss
☐ McGwire & Joyner
☐ Phil & Joe Niekro
☐ Preacher Roe & Johnny Podres
☐ Roberto, Sandy & Sandy Jr. Alomar
☐ Roberto & Sandy Jr. Alomar
☐ Rose, Morgan, Bench & Perez
☐ Rose & Hernandez
☐ Rose & McGee
☐ Rose & Puckett
☐ Rose & Ryan
☐ Seaver, Cardwell, & Al Jackson
☐ Seaver & Stottlemyre
☐ Strawberry & Davis
☐ Strawberry & Dykstra
☐ Strawberry & McGee
☐ Winfield & Reggie Jackson
☐ Will Clark & Mitchell

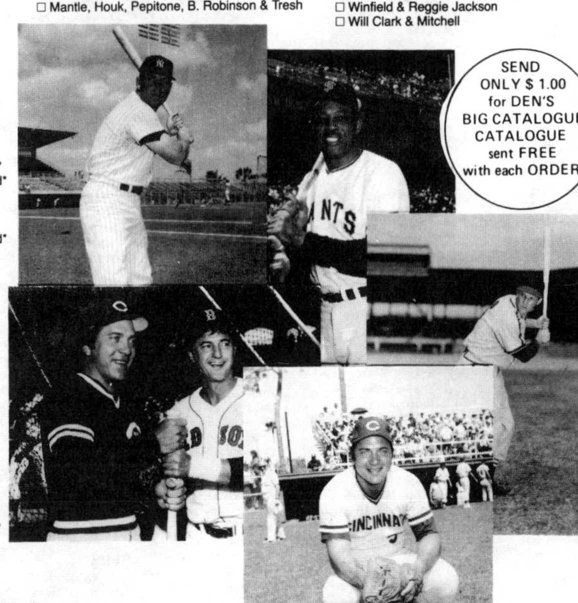

SEND ONLY $ 1.00 for DEN'S BIG CATALOGUE
CATALOGUE sent FREE with each ORDER

NOTE: Most photos are in full color. Some of the older players are in a sepia color as no color negatives are available.

VISA/MASTER CHARGE ACCEPTED

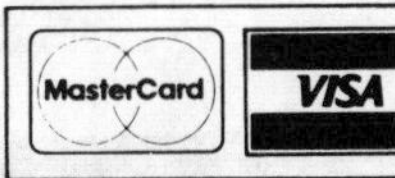

MARYLAND RESIDENTS ADD 5% SALES TAX
CANADIAN ORDERS – BOOKS ONLY
Canadian orders, orders outside the contiguous United States, APO and FPO add 25% additional U.S. FUNDS ONLY

POSTAGE & HANDLING SCHEDULE
$ .01 to $ 20.00 add $ 2.00
$ 20.01 to $ 29.99 add $ 2.50
$ 30.00 to $ 49.99 add $ 3 00
$ 50.00 or more add $ 4.00

To order by VISA/Master Charge, simply place your account number and 4 digit expiration date in your order letter. Also, include your authorized signature with the order. You may order by phone by calling (301) 776-3900 on weekdays between 10:00 am and 5:00 pm Eastern Time. No collect calls are accepted. All VISA/Master Charge orders must be for at least $ 10.00 or more. Specify VISA or Master Card.

DEN'S COLLECTORS DEN

HOME OF SPORT AMERICANA

DEPT. ABC
P.O. BOX 606, LAUREL, MD 20725

ANNOUNCING
The Offical NEW Ultra Clear
BASEBALL CARD ALBUM PAGE
ARCHIVAL
Ultra Pro Page®
NO PVC
The Ultra Pro Page Features:
New! Super Clear plastic made from a special formulation of material to give you a clear glass look. Ultimate in presentation.
New! Super Strong! Resists tearing. Guaranteed not to crack, even in the coldest climates.
New! Non-Slip feature so cards won't fall out.
New! Super Safe! Material contains NO PVC, Plasticizers or harmful chemicals.The pages won't yellow, won't stick and contain ultra-violet barriers for an extra measure of protection.
New! Our High-Tech, fully automatic process guarantees the highest clarity, strongest and safest product available. Additionally, pages are virtually untouched so they remain clean.
Our Prepunched holes are punched clean in each page, saving time and frustration by allowing immediate and hassle-free insertion of the pages into an album.
New specially contoured pages allow for easy flipping in albums.
After 5 Years
A NEW MATERIAL
has been invented with NO PVC
Made in U.S.A.
Prepunched Holes
CALL FOR FREE SAMPLE
1000 Pages For Only 10¢ ea. FREIGHT FREE
Hit a Home Run with the NEW Ultra Pro page - it's the best!
Jose Canseco
Prices Freight Paid
1000-5000 .10
10,000 .09
25,000 .0875
50,000 .085
100,000+ .08
FOR FREE SAMPLE and more information
Call SportsWorld Distribution (213) 679-5000
15926 Figueroa, Los Angeles, CA 90247

Introduction

One of the many problems collectors of baseball cards face is the identification of the many, many thousands of different baseball cards that exist. The best method devised thus far is the checklist. This technique involves breaking down all cards into levels with identifiable characteristics. The most common system begins at the most general level and proceeds to more specific levels. These levels are:

MAKER (Topps, Bowman, Goudey, etc.);

YEAR OF ISSUE;

NUMBER ON CARD (beginning with #1 or the lowest card number and continuing in numerical order until the last or highest card number is reached);

PLAYER ON CARD (corresponding to the particular number on the card); listed alphabetically if the particular year's issue is unnumbered, in which case the NUMBER ON CARD level may not be listed.

The **Sport Americana Baseball Card Price Guide,** the parent book of this one, adds two additional categories to each card's description:

CONDITION (Mint, Very Good-Excellent, Fair-Good);

PRICE (Value of the card in a given condition grade).

The common checklist format is effective for many (possibly most) situations; however, it is not an all-purpose answer to the collector's needs. There are times when neither the common checklist nor the Price Guide provide the right tools for the collector. This alphabetical checklist is intended to fill the void when the common checklist will not suffice.

The theory behind the alphabetical checklist is quite simple: The four levels of the common checklist are reordered. Their hierarchy in the alphabetical checklist is as follows:

PLAYER ON CARD (players are listed alphabetically);

YEAR OF ISSUE;

MAKER (producer or manufacture);

NUMBER ON CARD (not applicable to unnumbered cards).

Simple in design, this restructuring provides the collector with an easy-to-use cross reference to his card collection.

Today's baseball card collecting hobby is no longer dominated by the complete-set collector. While obtaining all cards of all sets still remains the ultimate accomplishment, the sheer numbers, costs, and time involved to obtain them has given rise to large numbers of card collecting specialists. Such specialists collect only cards of particular players or teams (see the **Sport Americana Baseball Card Team Checklist).** The players may be stars, superstars, players from a particular team, players born in a particular place, players with surnames of a particular nationality, or even such

DEALERS WE CARRY IT ALL!

Protecto® Plastic Pages

QTY (Pages)	EACH	PRICE	Shipping & Handling
25		$ 5.95	Postpaid
50		9.50	Postpaid
100		15.95	Postpaid
250		31.95	Postpaid
500	12¢	60.00	SHIPPED
1,000	11.5¢	115.00	FREIGHT
2,000	11¢	220.00	COLLECT
3,000	10.5¢	315.00	
5,000	10¢	500.00	

SIZES AVAILABLE:

9 pocket	1957 to 1983
8 pocket	52-56 Topps
9 pocket	Top Load
6 pocket	Police Sets
4 pocket	Postcards — '64 Giants
2 pocket	5x7 Photos
1 pocket	8x10 Photos
1 pocket	9x11 Photos/Yearbooks
12 pocket	Stickers

Super Sale Protecto® Plastic Pages
1000 $109
POSTPAID
The very best! Guaranteed Safe! 9-Pocket Top or Side Load! 5 to 6 Gauge Heavy!

Poly-Flex Plastic Pages
1000 $99
POSTPAID
Slightly Thinner Page! Safe & Durable! Crystal Clear!

Econoline Plastic Pages
1000 $89
POSTPAID
Best Buy! High Quality! Slightly Clouded! Safe & Durable! Not As Clear!

Baseball Card Boxes

WHOLESALE TO THE PUBLIC

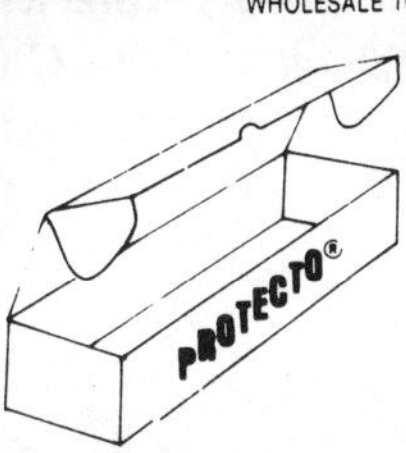

CAL-CARDS INTRODUCES
The Finest Boxes In The World
At The Lowest Prices
Now At Wholesale Prices

Protecto® Indestructo
White Corrugated Boxes • Front Wing Locks • Boxes Secure On Outside • Cannot Damage Cards
(No. of box is amount of cards box holds)
Sizes: ALL SIZES (postpaid) 100 minimum
CC-660 $32.00, CC-726 $33.00, CC-800 $33.00

Protecto® Albums

Deluxe Card Albums

These padded albums have a vinyl pocket on the spine for labeling • Heavy duty design • Durable over-printing and glossed to produce a rich, realistic leather appearance • 2 sizes regular and jumbo • Completely covers sheet • Imprint *"Baseball Card Album"*

Both sizes of **Protecto Albums** are available in Midnight Blue with silver lettering, Burgundy with gold, Black with gold and Brown with silver.
Dealers Call or Write for Special Pricing!

Protecto® CARD-GARDS

INDIVIDUAL CARD PROTECTION

Unconditionally Guaranteed!

WHY PAY MORE!!

Protecto® CARD-GARDS Special Offer

$10.95	$29.00	$39.00
1000 CARD-GARDS	3000 CARD-GARDS	5000 CARD-GARDS

Each **Protecto® CARD-GARDS** Holds 1 Card
Standard size 2⅝x3⅝. Will fit all Topps — 1957 to present. Fleer and Donruss — 1981 to present and most sports & non-sports cards. Slip cards in and out with ease • **Protecto® CARD-GARDS** will protect, preserve your cards from finger marks, dust, scratches, prevent corners from becoming "dog eared" • Use heavy-duty **Protecto® CARD-GARDS** to view, file and store • **Protecto® CARD-GARDS** are made of crystal clear polyethylene • Contains no PVC, and guaranteed not to crack • Packed in quantities of 100 for your convenience • *Dealer inquiries invited.*

Dealers & Stores Write or Call For Pricing

Look

DEALERS-STORES

• All NFL, MLB, NBA Caps, Wool, Wool Blend, Mesh, Twill, Cords • Sized "Pro Caps" • 102 Colleges — Arizona to Yale • All Teams including NHL Pennants and Bumper Strips • Sports Illustrated Posters • Nike Posters • Costacos Posters • Ball Holders • Batting Helmets • All-Pro Wrist Bands • Rawlings Baseballs — National & American Leagues • All Peter David Pins For NFL, MLB, NBA • Topps • Donruss • Fleer • Baseball Cards • Non-Sports Cards • Sports Photos 8x10 • And Much More

Cal-Cards is the largest distributor of sports products at wholesale prices in the United States!

One of the Largest Wholesalers In The Nation!

CAL-CARDS
SUBSIDIARY OF SPORTSWORLD
P.O. BOX 107, GARDENA, CA 90248

213-679-5000

ephemeral common denominators as players who are lefthand throwing switch-hitters born east of the Mississippi below the Mason-Dixon line after 1933. As you can see, the possibilities are endless.

The **Sport Americana Alphabetical Baseball Card Checklist** presents at a glance all the cards issued for a particular player from virtually all the principal baseball card sets. No longer must a collector scan the entire 1957 Topps checklist to determine that the Brooks Robinson card of that year is #328. Nor must one go through four years of Bowman checklists to determine that the Bowman Rookie Card of Willie Mays is #305 in the 1951 series. The alphabetical checklist will show you without the necessity of having the actual card before you.

The concept of an alphabetical baseball card checklist is not new; however, we have attempted to make the current edition of the **Sport Americana Alphabetical Baseball Card Checklist** more complete, easier to use, and more attractive than any previous checklist of this kind. All of the cards of a particular player are listed consecutively below that player's name. There is no need to go to a second or third spot in the book to find that player's cards from another manufacturer or another time period.

Virtually all of the cards contained in any of the editions of the **Sport Americana Baseball Card Price Guide** and **Sport Americana Baseball Collectibles Price Guide** are listed in this book. Many special cards are cross-referenced, as are checklist cards and team cards.

Errata

While a great deal of effort (including many hours of proofreading) has been made to avoid errors of any type, it seems inevitable that some errors, misspellings, and inconsistencies may occur. Please inform the author of any you find, and corrections will be incorporated in the next edition.

How to Collect

Card collecting is a hobby, a leisure pastime. There are no set rules for collecting baseball cards. The amount of time and funds available, and personal tastes, determine the path of a collector's interests. What is presented here is information and ideas that may help you to enjoy this hobby.

Obtaining Cards

Several avenues are open to you to obtain cards. You can purchase current cards in the traditional way at local candy, grocery or drug stores, with bubble gum or other products included. You can also purchase complete recent sets from the many mail order advertisers found in sports publications; e.g., **The Sporting News, Baseball Digest, Street & Smith's Baseball Yearbook, Baseball** magazine, and others. Occasionally, a few older cards and sets are advertised in these same publications. However, most serious card collectors obtain older cards from other collectors or dealers through hobby publications, at sports collectibles shows, or at sports card and memorabilia shops.

Nomenclature

Each hobby has its own language to describe its area of interest. The nomenclature traditionally used for trading cards is derived from the *American Card Catalog*, published in 1960 by Nostalgia Press. That catalog, written by Jefferson Burdick (who is called the "Father of Card Collecting" for his pioneering work), uses letter and number designations for each separate set of cards.

The letter used in the ACC designation refers to the generic type of card. While both sport and non-sport issues are classified in the ACC, we shall confine ourselves to the sport issues. The following list defines the letters and their meanings as used by the American Card Catalog.

(none) or N - 19th Century U.S. Tobacco

B - Blankets

D - Bakery Inserts Including Bread

E - Early Candy and Gum

F - Food Inserts

H - Advertising

M - Periodicals

PC - Postcards

R - Candy and Gum Cards 1930 to Present

T - 20th Century U.S. Tobacco

UO - Gas and Oil Inserts

V - Canadian Candy

W - Exhibits, Strip Cards, Team Issues

Following the letter prefix and an optional hyphen are one-, two-, or three-digit numbers, 1-999. These typically represent the company or entity issuing the cards. In several cases, the ACC number is extended by an additional hyphen and another one- or two-digit numerical suffix. For example, the 1957 Topps regular series baseball card issue carries an ACC designation of R414-11. The "R" indicates a Candy or Gum Card produced since 1930. The "414" is the ACC designation for Topps Chewing Gum baseball card issues, and the "11" is the ACC designation for the 1957 regular issue (Topps' eleventh baseball set).

Store #1
Webb Chapel Village
Shopping Center #231
1-214-243-5271
11-7 Mon-Sat
Closed Sun.

FIRST BASE

231 Webb Chapel Village
Dallas, Texas 75229

Store #2
Audelia Plaza #102
1-214-341-9919
11-6 Mon-Sat
Closed Sun.

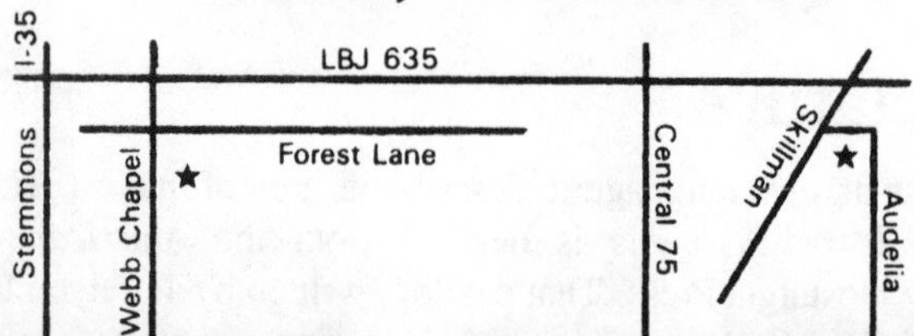

We are located on the southeast corner of Webb Chapel and Forest just 15 minutes from the airport. Our large (1,650-square foot showroom) store is convenient to all parts of Dallas, being only one block south of the LBJ (I-635) Freeway at the Webb Chapel exit. Many collectors and dealers have told us that our store is the most complete they've ever seen. Just look on the opposite page for a few of our offers. We want you for a customer -- please stop in and see for yourself. Also visit our new convenient location in the Audelia Plaza Shopping Center.

FIRST
BASE

Sincerely,

Wayne Grove
Gervise Ford

P.S. We are always interested in buying your cards — let us know what you have.

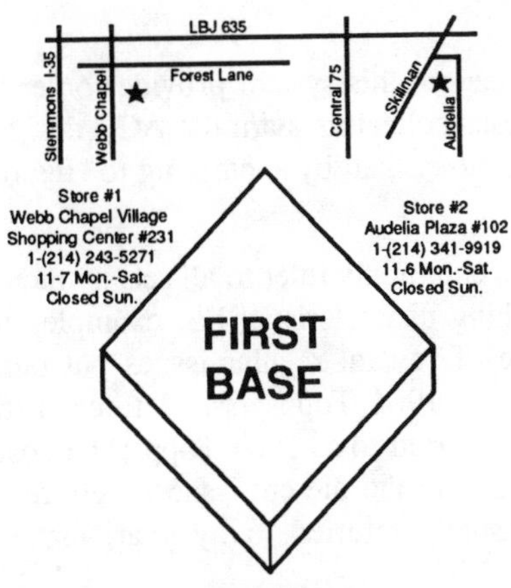

BASEBALL CARD LOTS

Our Choice - No Superstars

1959 Topps 10 diff (f-vg) $10.00
1960 Topps 10 diff (f-vg) 7.50
1961 Topps 10 diff (f-vg) 7.50
1962 Topps 10 diff (f-vg) 7.00
1963 Topps 10 diff (f-vg) 6.50
1964 Topps 10 diff (f-vg) 5.00
1965 Topps 10 diff (f-vg) 5.00
1966 Topps 10 diff (f-vg) 3.50
1967 Topps 10 diff (f-vg) 3.50
1968 Topps 10 diff (f-vg) 3.00

1969 Topps 25 diff (f-vg) 5.95
1970 Topps 25 diff (f-vg) 3.95
1971 Topps 25 diff (f-vg) 3.95
1972 Topps 25 diff (f-vg) 3.95
1973 Topps 25 diff (f-vg) 3.95
1974 Topps 25 diff (f-vg) 3.95
1975 Topps 25 diff (f-vg) 3.95
1976 Topps 25 diff (f-vg) 2.95
1977 Topps 25 diff (f-vg) 2.95

1978 Topps 50 diff (f-vg) 3.95
1979 Topps 50 diff (f-vg) 2.95
1980 Topps 50 diff (f-vg) 2.95

1981 Donruss 50 diff (ex-m) 2.50
1981 Fleer 50 diff (ex-m) 2.50
1982 Fleer 50 diff (ex-m) 2.50

FOOTBALL CARD LOTS

Our Choice - No Superstars

1969 Topps 25 diff (f-vg) $6.95
1970 Topps 25 diff (f-vg) 5.95
1971 Topps 25 diff (f-vg) 4.95
1972 Topps 25 diff (f-vg) 4.95
1973 Topps 25 diff (f-vg) 4.95
1974 Topps 25 diff (f-vg) 2.50
1975 Topps 25 diff (f-vg) 2.50
1976 Topps 25 diff (f-vg) 2.50
1977 Topps 25 diff (f-vg) 2.00

1978 Topps 50 diff (f-vg) 3.00
1979 Topps 50 diff (f-vg) 3.00
1980 Topps 50 diff (f-vg) 2.50

ORDERING INSTRUCTIONS

Offers expire March 1991 while supply lasts. Please include $3.00 per order for postage and handling.

Send orders to:

FIRST BASE
231 Webb Chapel Village
Dallas, Texas 75229
(214) 243-5271

Our current price lists sent free with orders. To receive price lists without ordering send $1.00 or a **large** self addressed stamped (65¢ in stamps) envelope to the above address.

SPECIAL OFFERS

#1: Type Set: One card from each year of Topps baseball 1952 through 1989, our choice of cards, Good to EX, 38 cards for $39.95.

#2: 1987 Fleer Baseball Record Setters - Complete Set of 44 cards — $4.00.

#3: Robert Redford Poster as "The Natural" - $6.95.

#4: 1983 Affiliated Foods Texas Rangers - Complete Set of 28 — $5.00.
Uncut Poster (All 28 cards) — $7.50

#5: 1982 Topps Baseball Stickers (48 Diff.) — $2.50.

#6: 1989 Score "A Year to Remember" Trivia Cards. Complete Set of 56 — $3.95.

#7: 1985 Circle K All-Time Home Run Kings. Complete Set of 33 — $7.95.

#8: 1982 K-Mart Baseball Set of 33 — $2.50.

#9: 50 Diff. Basketball cards - our choice — $5.00.

#10: Super Bowl XX Game Program — $8.00.

#11: 1986 McDonalds Dallas Cowboys Football Card Set of 25 with Herschel Walker — $9.95.

#12: 1986 McDonalds NFL All-Stars Football Card Set of 24 — $3.95.

#13: Dallas Cowboys Police/Safety Sets: 1979 (15) — $14.95, 1980 (14) — $9.95, 1981 (14) — $9.95, 1983 (28) — $9.95.

#14: Dallas Cowboys Media Guides (not issued to the public) 1989 edition $5.00, 1988 edition $5.00, 1987 edition $5.00, 1986 edition $7.50, 1985 edition $7.50.

#15: 1987 Texas Rangers Surf Book (shows pictures of all Rangers cards) — $7.95.

Like other traditional methods of identification, this system provides order to the process of cataloging cards; however, most serious collectors learn the ACC designation of the popular sets by repetition and familiarity, rather than by attempting to "figure out" what they might or should be.

From 1948 forward, collectors and dealers commonly refer to all sets by their year, maker, type of issue, and any other distinguishing characteristic. For example, such a characteristic could be an unusual issue or one of several regular issues put out by a specific maker in a single year. For example, in 1964 Topps issued three distinctly different baseball card sets. The regular issue is referred to as 1964 Topps; the postcard-sized issue is referred to as 1964 Topps Giants; and the die-cut issue is referred to as 1964 Topps Stand-Ups. Regional issues are usually referred to by year, maker, and sometimes by title or theme of the set.

Other Available Literature

With the increase in popularity of the hobby in recent years, there has been a corresponding increase in available literature. Below is a list of the books and periodicals which receive our highest recommendation and which we hope will further advance your knowledge and enjoyment of our great hobby.

The Sport Americana Baseball Card Price Guide by Dr. James Beckett (Twelfth Edition, $14.95, released 1990, published by Edgewater Book Company) -- the authoritative annual price guide to all the most popular baseball cards produced during the past century, 672 pages, illustrated, and priced in three condition grades, with an extensive introduction on the history of baseball cards and collecting.

The Official Price Guide to Baseball Cards by Dr. James Beckett (Tenth Edition, $5.95, released 1990, published by The House of Collectibles) -- an abridgement of the *Sport Americana Price Guide* listed above, in a convenient and economical pocket-size format providing Dr. Beckett's pricing of the major baseball sets since 1948.

The Sport Americana Price Guide to Baseball Collectibles by Dr. James Beckett (Second Edition, $12.95, released 1988, published by Edgewater Book Company) -- the complete guide/checklist with up-to-date values for box cards, coins, labels, Canadian cards, stamps, stickers, pins, etc.

The Sport Americana Football, Hockey, Basketball and Boxing Card Price Guide by Dr. James Beckett (Sixth Edition, $14.95, released 1989, published by Edgewater Book Company) -- the most comprehensive price guide/checklist ever issued on football and other non-baseball sports cards. No serious hobbyist should be without it.

The Official Price Guide to Football Cards by Dr. James Beckett (Ninth Edition, $5.95, released 1989, published by The House of Collectibles) -- an abridgement of the *Sport Americana Price Guide* listed above, in a convenient and economical pocket-size format providing Dr. Beckett's pricing of the major football sets since 1948.

The Official Price Guide to Hockey and Basketball Cards by Dr. James Beckett (First Edition, $5.95, released 1989, published by The House of Collectibles) -- an abridgement of the *Sport Americana Price Guide* listed above, in a convenient and economical pocket-size format providing Dr. Beckett's pricing of the major hockey and basketball sets since 1948.

The Sport Americana Baseball Memorabilia and Autograph Price Guide by Dr. James Beckett and Dennis W. Eckes (First Edition, $8.95, released 1982, co-published by Den's Collectors Den and Edgewater Book Company) -- the most complete book ever produced on baseball memorabilia other than baseball cards. This book presents in an illustrated, logical fashion information on baseball memorabilia and autographs which had been heretofore unavailable to the collector.

The Sport Americana Price Guide to the Non-Sports Cards by Christopher Benjamin and Dennis W. Eckes (Third Edition (Part Two), $12.95, released 1988, published by Edgewater Book Company) -- the definitive guide to all popular non-sports American tobacco and bubble gum cards. In addition to cards, illustrations and prices for wrappers are also included. Part Two covers non-sports cards from 1961 through 1987.

The Sport Americana Baseball Address List by Jack Smalling and Dennis W. Eckes (Fifth Edition, $10.95, released 1988, published by Edgewater Book Company) -- the definitive guide for autograph hunters giving addresses and deceased information for virtually all major league baseball players past and present.

The Sport Americana Baseball Card Team Checklist by Jeff Fritsch and Dennis W. Eckes (Fifth Edition, $12.95, released 1990, published by Edgwater Book Company) -- includes all Topps, Bowman, Donruss, Fleer, Score, Play Ball, Goudey, and Upper Deck cards, with the players portrayed on the cards listed with the teams for whom they played. The book is invaluable to the collector who specializes in an individual team because it is the most complete baseball card team checklist available.

The Encyclopedia of Baseball Cards, Volume I: 19th Century Cards by Lew Lipset ($11.95, released 1983, published by the author) -- everything you ever wanted to know about 19th century cards.

The Encyclopedia of Baseball Cards, Volume II: Early Gum and Candy Cards by Lew Lipset ($10.95, released 1984, published by the author) -- everything you ever wanted to know about Early Candy and Gum cards.

The Encyclopedia of Baseball Cards, Volume III: 20th Century Tobacco Cards, 1909-1932 by Lew Lipset ($12.95, released 1986, published by the author) -- everything you ever wanted to know about old tobacco cards.

Periodicals

Beckett Baseball Card Monthly authored and edited by Dr. James Beckett -- contains the most extensive and accepted monthly price guide, feature articles, "who's hot and who's not" section, convention calendar, and numerous letters to and responses from the editor. Published 12 times annually, it is the hobby's largest paid circulation periodical. **Beckett Football Card Magazine** (eight times a year) and **Beckett Basketball Card Magazine** (six times a year) are both very similar to *Beckett Baseball Card Monthly* in style and content.

History of Baseball Cards

Today's version of the baseball card, with its colorful front and statistical back, is a far cry from its earliest predecessors. The issue remains cloudy as to which was the very first baseball card ever produced, but the institution of baseball cards dates from the latter half of the 19th century, more than 100 years ago. Early issues, generally printed on heavy cardboard, were of poor quality, with photographs, drawings and printing far short of today's standards.

Goodwin & Co., of New York, makers of Gypsy Queen, Old Judge, and other cigarette brands, is considered by many to be the first issuer of baseball and other sports cards. Their issues, predominantly in the 1 1/2" by 2 1/2" size, generally consisted of photographs of baseball players, boxers, wrestlers, and other subjects mounted on stiff cardboard. More than 2,000 different photos of baseball players alone have been identified. These "Old Judges," a collective name commonly used for the Goodwin & Co. cards, were issued from 1886 to 1890 and are treasured parts of many collections today.

Among the other cigarette companies which issued baseball cards that still attract attention today are Allen & Ginter, D. Buchner & Co. (Gold Coin Chewing Tobacco), and P.H. Mayo & Brother. Cards from the first two companies bore colored line drawings, while the Mayos are sepia photographs on black cardboard.

In addition to the small-size cards from this era, several tobacco companies issued cabinet-size baseball cards. These "cabinets" were considerably larger than the small cards, usually about 4 1/4" by 6 1/2", and were printed on heavy stock. Goodwin & Co.'s Old Judge cabinets and the National Tobacco Works' "Newsboy" baseball photos are two that remain popular today.

By 1895 the American Tobacco Company began to dominate its competition. They discontinued baseball card inserts in their cigarette packages (actually slide boxes in those days). The lack of competition in the cigarette market had made these inserts unnecessary. This marked the end of the first era of the baseball card.

At the dawn of the 20th century, few baseball cards were being issued. But once again it was the cigarette companies -- particularly, the American Tobacco Company -- followed to a lesser extent by the candy and gum makers that revived the practice of including baseball cards with their products. The bulk of these cards, identified in the

American Card Catalog (designated hereafter as ACC) as T or E cards for 20th century "Tobacco" or "Early Candy and Gum" issues respectively, were released from 1909 to 1915.

This romantic and popular era of baseball card collecting produced many desirable items. The most outstanding is the fabled T-206 Honus Wagner card. Other perennial favorites among collectors are the T-206 Eddie Plank card, and the T-206 Magee error card. The former was once the second most valuable card and only recently relinquished that position to a more distinctive and aesthetically pleasing Napoleon Lajoie card from the 1933/34 Goudey Gum series. The latter misspells the player's name as "Magie," the most famous and valuable blooper card.

The ingenuity and distinctiveness of this era has yet to be surpassed. Highlights include the T-202 Hassan triple-folders, one of the best looking and the most distinctive cards ever issued; the durable T-201 Mecca double-folders, one of the first sets with players' records on the reverse; the T-3 Turkey Reds, the hobby's most popular cabinet card; the E-145 Cracker Jacks, the only major set containing Federal League player cards; and the T-204 Ramlys, with their distinctive black and white oval photos and ornate gold borders. These are but a few of the varieties issued during this period.

While the American Tobacco Company dominated the field, several other tobacco companies, as well as clothing manufacturers, newspapers and periodicals, game makers, and companies whose identities remain anonymous, also issued cards during this period. In fact, the Collins-McCarthy Candy Company, makers of Zeenuts Pacific Coast League baseball cards, issued cards yearly from 1911 to 1938. Their record for continuous annual card production has been exceeded only by the Topps Chewing Gum Company. The era of the tobacco card issues closed with the onset of World War I, with the exception of the Red Man chewing tobacco sets produced from 1952 to 1955.

The next flurry of card issues broke out in the roaring and prosperous 1920s, the era of the E card. The caramel companies (National Caramel, American Caramel, York Caramel) were the leading distributors of these E cards. In addition, the strip card, a continous strip with several cards divided by dotted lines or other sectioning features, flourished during this time. While the E cards and the strip cards are generally considered less imaginative than the T cards or the recent candy and gum issues, they are still sought after by many advanced collectors.

Another significant event of the 1920s was the introduction of the arcade card. Taking its designation from its issuer, the Exhibit Supply Company of Chicago, it is usually known as the "Exhibit" card. Once a trademark of the penny arcades, amusement parks, and county fairs across the country, Exhibit machines dispensed nearly postcard-size photos on thick stock for one penny. These picture cards bore likenesses of a favorite cowboy, actor, actress, or baseball player. Exhibit Supply and its associated companies produced baseball cards during a longer time span, although discontinuous, than any other manufacturer. Its first cards appeared in 1921, while its last issue was in 1966. In 1979, the Exhibit Supply Company was bought and somewhat revived by a collector/dealer who has since reprinted Exhibit photos of the past.

If the T card period, from 1909 to 1915, can be said to be the "Golden Age" of baseball card collecting, then perhaps the "Silver Age" commenced with the introduction of the Big League Gum series of 239 cards in 1933 (a 240th card was added in 1934). These are the forerunners of today's baseball gum cards, and the Goudey Gum Company of Boston is responsible for their success. This era spanned the period from the Depression days of 1933 to America's formal involvement in World War II in 1941.

Goudey's attractive designs, with full color line drawings on thick card stock, influenced greatly other cards being issued at that time. As a result, the most attractive and popular cards in collecting history were produced in this "Silver Age." The 1933 Goudey Big League Gum series also owes its popularity to the more than 40 Hall of Fame players in the set. These include four cards of Babe Ruth and two of Lou Gehrig. Goudey's reign continued in 1934 when it issued a 96-card set in color, together with the single remaining card from the 1933 series, #106, the Napoleon Lajoie card.

In addition to Goudey, several other bubble gum manufacturers issued baseball cards during this era. DeLong Gum Company issued an extremely attractive set in 1933. National Chicle Company's 192-card "Batter-Up" series of 1934-1936 became the largest die-cut set in card history. In addition, that company offered the popular "Diamond Stars" series during the same period. Other popular sets included the "Tattoo Orbit" set of 60 color cards issued in 1933 and Gum Products' 75-card "Double Play" set, featuring sepia depictions of two players per card.

In 1939 Gum Inc., which later became Bowman Gum, replaced Goudey Gum as the leading baseball card producer. In 1939 and the following year, it issued two important sets of black and white cards. In 1939 its "Play Ball America" set consisted of 162 cards. The larger, 240-card "Play Ball" set of 1940 is still considered by many to be the most attractive black and white cards ever produced. That firm introduced its only color set in 1941, consisting of 72 cards entitled "Play Ball Sports Hall of Fame." Many of these were colored repeats of poses from the black and white 1940 series.

In addition to regular gum cards, many manufacturers distributed premium issues during the 1930s. These premiums were printed on paper or photographic stock, rather than card stock. They were much larger than the regular cards and were sold for a penny across the counter with gum (which was packaged separately from the premium). They were often redeemed at the store or through the mail in exchange for the wrappers of previously purchased gum cards, a la proof-of-purchase box-top premiums today. The gum premiums are scarcer than the card issues of the 1930s and in most cases no manufacturer's name is present.

World War II brought an end to this popular era of card collecting when paper and rubber shortages curtailed the production of bubble gum baseball cards. They were resurrected again in 1948 by the Bowman Gum Company (the direct descendant of Gum, Inc.). This marked the beginning of the modern era of card collecting.

In 1948, Bowman Gum issued a 48-card set in black and white consisting of one card and one slab of gum in every one-cent pack. That same year, the Leaf Gum Company also issued a set of cards. Although rather poor in quality, these cards were issued in color. A squabble over the rights to use players' pictures developed between Bowman and Leaf. Eventually Leaf dropped out of the card market, but not before it had left a lasting heritage to the hobby by issuing some of the rarest cards now in existence. Leaf's baseball card series of 1948-49 contained 98 cards, skip numbered to #168 (not all numbers were printed). Of these 98 cards, 49 are relatively plentiful; however, the other 49 are rare and quite valuable.

Bowman continued its production of cards in 1949 with a color series of 240 cards. Because there are many scarce "high numbers" this series remains the most difficult Bowman regular issue to complete. Although the set was printed in color and commands great interest due to its scarcity, it is considered aesthetically inferior to the Goudey and National Chicle issues of the 1930s. In addition to the regular issue of 1949, Bowman also produced a set of 36 Pacific Coast League players. While this was not a regular issue, it is still prized by collectors. In fact, it has become the most valuable Bowman series.

In 1950 (Bowman's one-year monopoly of the baseball card market), the company began a string of top quality cards which continued until its demise in 1955. The 1950 series was itself something of an oddity because the "low" numbers, rather than the traditional high numbers, were the more difficult cards to obtain.

The year 1951 marked the beginning of the most competitive and perhaps the highest quality period of baseball card production. In that year Topps Chewing Gum Company of Brooklyn entered the market. Topps' 1951 series consisted of two sets of 52 cards each, one set with red backs and the other with blue backs. In addition, Topps also issued 31 insert cards, three of which remain the rarest Topps cards ("Current All-Stars" Konstanty, Roberts, and Stanky). The 1951 Topps cards were unattractive and paled in comparison to the 1951 Bowman issues. However, they were successful, and Topps has continued to produce cards ever since.

Topps issued a larger and much more attractive card in 1952. This larger size became standard for the next five years. (Bowman followed with larger-size baseball cards in 1953.) This 1952 Topps set has become, like the 1933 Goudey series and the T-206 white border series, the classic set of its era. The 407-card set is a collector's dream of scarcities, rarities, errors, and variations. It also contains the first Topps issues of Mickey Mantle and Willie Mays.

As with Bowman and Leaf in the late 1940s, competition over player rights arose. Ensuing court battles occurred between Topps and Bowman. The market split due to stiff competition, and in January, 1956, Topps bought out Bowman. Topps remained relatively unchallenged as the primary producer of baseball cards through 1980. So, the story of major baseball card sets from 1956 through 1980 is by and large the story of Topps' issues with few exceptions. Fleer Gum produced small sets in 1959, 1960, 1961, and 1963, and several cartoon sets in the 1970s, and more recently Kellogg's Cereal and Hostess Cakes issued baseball cards to promote their products.

A court decision in 1980 paved the way for two other large gum companies to enter, or reenter, the baseball card arena. The Fleer Corporation, which had last made photo cards in 1963, and the Donruss Company (then a division of General Mills) secured rights to produce baseball cards of current players, breaking Topps' monopoly. Each company issued major card sets in 1981 with bubble gum products. Then a higher court decision in that year overturned the lower court ruling against Topps. It appeared that Topps had regained its sole position as a producer of baseball cards. Undaunted by the revocation ruling, Fleer and Donruss continued to issue cards in 1982 but without bubble gum or any other edible product. Fleer issued its current player baseball cards with "team logo stickers," while Donruss issued its cards with a piece of a baseball jigsaw puzzle.

Since 1981, these three major baseball card producers have all thrived, sharing relatively equal recognition. Each has steadily increased its involvement in terms of numbers of issues per year. To the delight of collectors, their competition has generated novel, and in some cases exceptional, issues of current major league baseball players. Collectors have also been impressed with the efforts of Score (1988) and Upper Deck (1989), the newest companies to enter the baseball card producing derby. All these major producers have become increasingly aware of the organized collecting market. While the corner candy store remains the major marketplace for card sales, an increasing number of issues have been directed to this organized hobby marketplace. In fact, many of these issues have been distributed exclusively through hobby channels. Although no one can ever say what the future will bring, one can only surmise that the hobby market will play a significant role in future plans of all the major baseball card producers.

The above has been a thumbnail sketch of card collecting from its inception in the 1880s to the present. It is difficult to tell the whole story in just a few pages -- there are several other good sources of information. Serious collectors should subscribe to at least one of the excellent hobby periodicals. We also suggest that collectors attend a sports collectibles convention in their area. Card collecting is still a young and informal hobby. Chances are good that you will run into one or more of the "experts" at such a show. They are usually more than happy to share their knowledge with you.

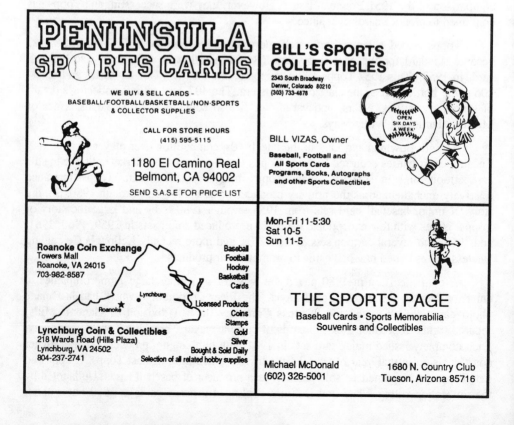

How to Use the Alphabetical Checklist

We are sure you will find this book an invaluable tool in your pursuit of card collecting enjoyment. Because of the large number of different card sets contained in this volume, it is extremely important that you familiarize yourself with the nomenclature used here. **PLEASE READ THE FOLLOWING SECTION BEFORE ATTEMPTING TO USE THE CHECKLISTS.**

Code Meanings

The codes following the players' names give the card sets and numbers within the sets in which the players appeared. Each entry consists of a number/letter combination indicating the particular set (Year, Maker, other set characteristic) followed by a dash, followed by a number/letter combination of the specific card and the type of card (if applicable) within that set. In short, the code before the dash describes the set, while the code after the dash describes the particular card within that set. Cards from unnumbered sets are sometimes listed by set name only.

Tips for Using this Checklist:

Entries for each player are listed in chronological order by year of issue and alphabetically by company within each year. Cards identified by ACC letter designation (rather than year) are listed last.

Some of the people listed herein are NOT baseball players, but are people who appear in the checklisted sets. In addition there are a number of ex-Major League players for whom no cards were produced; many of these players are listed with the designation "No cards."

The majority of the minor league cards were produced primarily by TCMA up through 1985 and by Pro-Cards since 1986. Other producers' cards, such as Larry Fritsch (Midwest League) or Mike Cramer's Pacific Trading cards (PCL) sets are typically so designated.

Codes Used in this Checklist

Code	Example
A&P	76A&P/KC, 76A&P/Milw (A&P)
Ames	1989 Ames 20/20 Club
AmTract	1962 American Tract Society
Armour	1955 Armour Coins
Ault	1986 Ault Foods Blue Jays
B	48B through 55B (Bowman)
BB	58BB through 62BB (Bell Brand)
BeeHive	1961 Bee Hive Starch
Berg	1988 Cubs David Berg
BF#	1916 BF2 Felt Pennants
BK	80BK/PHR (Burger King)
BLChew	1986 Big League Chew

Code	Example
Bohem	1987 Bohemian Padres
Bond	1947 Bond Bread Jackie Robinson
Borden	1984 Borden's Reds
BR	51BR, 52BR (Berk Ross)
Briggs	53Briggs (Briggs Hot Dogs)
BU	35BU (1935 Batter Up)
Buster	1909 Buster Brown Pins
Bz	59Bz through 71Bz (Bazooka)
Cadaco	1989 Cadaco Ellis Game
Cain's	1985 Cain's Tigers Discs
Callahn	50Callahan (1950-1956 Callahan HOF)
CEA	1930 Chicago Evening American pins

Code	Example
Centen	1943 Centennial Flour
ChefBoy	1988 Chef Boyardee
CIGNA	85CIGNA (Phillies)
CircK	85CircK (Circle K)
Citgo	1969 Citgo Metal Coins
CJ	14CJ, 15CJ (Crackerjack)
Class	87Class/Up
Classic	87Classic
Clover	1961-62 Cloverleaf Dairy
Coke	52Coke, 68Coke (Coca Cola)
Conlon	1988 Conlon American All-Stars
Cram	1980 Cramer Legends
Crane	1976 Crane Discs
Crunch	1989 Cap'n Crunch
D#	D301 through D350 (bread issues)
D	81D through 87D (Donruss)
DanDee	54DanDee (1954 DanDee)
Det	1964 Detroit Tiger lids
DF	1959 Darigold Farms
DH	1933 Doubleheader Discs
Dix	37Dix, 52Dix (Dixie Lids)
DL	33DL (1933 Delong)
Domino	1910 Domino Discs
Domino	1988 Domino's Tigers
Dorman	1986 Dorman's Cheese
DP	41DP (1941 Double Play)
Drake	81Drake through 87Drake (Drake)
DS	34DS (1934 Diamond Stars)
Dunkin	1970 Dunkin Donuts Cubs
E#	E90/1 to E300 (candy issues)
EH	66EH (1966 East Hills)
Esskay	54Esskay, 55Esskay (Esskay)
Eureka	49 Eureka stamps
Exh	47Exh (Exhibits)
F	59F through 87F (Fleer)
FanSam	1988 Fantastic Sam's Discs
FB	51FB (Fischer Baking Labels)
FrBauer	1963 French Bauer Caps
French	1988 French Bray Orioles
Frojoy	28FroJoy (1928 Fro Joy)
Fud's	1969 Fud's Photography
FunFood	1984 Fun Foods Pins
G	33G through 41G (Goudey)
Gard	83Gard (Gardner's Brewers)
Gator	86Gator (Gatorade Cubs)
GenMills	1985 General Mills
Glen	53Glen (Glendale)
Gol	1955 Golden Braves stamps
GP	61GP (Golden Press)
Granny	82Granny (Granny Goose)

Code	Example
Hawth	1952 Hawthorne-Mellody pins
HB	82HB/LS (Hillerich/Bradsby)
Helmar	1911 Helmar stamps
HenryH	1960 Henry House Wieners
Hires	58Hires (Hires)
Ho	75Ho through 79Ho (Hostess)
HRDerby	1959 Home Run Derby
Hughes	1940 Hughes Solons
Hunter	53Hunter through 55Hunter (Hunter's)
Hygrade	Hygrade Expos
Icee	76Icee
J	62J, 63J (Jello)
Jay's	1986 Jay's Potato Chip Discs
JB	69JB (Jack in the Box)
JC	53JC through 55JC (Johnston Cookies)
Jiffy	1986 Jiffy Pop Discs
JP	73JP (Johnny Pro)
K	70K through 83K (Kelloggs)
Kahn	55Kahn through 69Kahn
KAS	1986 KAS Cardinals Discs
KayBee	86KayBee
KDKA	68KDKA
Keller	1986 Keller's Phillies
Kelly	1969 Kelly Pins
KingB	1988 King-B Discs
Kitty	1986 Kitty Clover Discs
KMart	82KMart, 87KMart
Kraft	1987 Kraft
L	48L, 60L (Leaf)
L#	L1 Leathers
Lake	60Lake (Lake to Lake)
LaPizza	1971 La Pizza Royale
Laugh	1972 Laughlin Great Feats
Leaf	1985 Leaf Canadian
Lennox	1989 Lennox HSE Astros
M#	M101/4, M116 (periodical issues)
Mara	1989 Marathon Tigers
Master	1988 Master Bread Discs
MB	84MB (Milton Bradley)
McDon	70McDon (McDonalds)
MD	71MD (Milk Duds)
Meadow	1986 Meadow Gold Blank Back
MilSau	1963 Milwaukee Sausage
MnM's	87MnM's
Morrell	59Morrell (Morrell Meats)
Moth	84Mother (Mother's Cookies)
Mother	52Mother (Mother's Cookies)
MP	43MP (MP & Co.)
MSA	76MSA/Disc (Mike Schecter Assoc.)
N#	N28 through N690 (19th century)

Code	Example
Nalley	1983 Nalley's Mariners
NatPhoto	86NatPhoto (Royals)
NB	53NB (Northland Bread Labels)
Nes	84Nestle/792
Nestle	84Nestle/DT
NTea	52NTea (National Tea Labels)
NTF	69NTF (Nabisco Team Flakes)
NuCard	1960 Nu-Card Hi-Lites
NumNum	50NumNum, 52NumNum
NYJour	54NYJour (NY Journal American)
OhHenry	1986 Oh Henry Indians
OldLond	1965 Old London Coins
ONG	1939 Our National Game pins
Orbit	1932-34 Orbit Pins Unnumbered
P	60P through 63P (Post)
Pac	1988 Pacific Eight Men Out
PapaG	1978 Papa Ginos Discs
Panini	Panini stickers
Park	Parkhurst
PB	39PB through 41PB (Play Ball)
Pep	63Pep, 77Pep (Pepsi)
Peters	61Peters (Peter's Meats)
Piedmont	1914 Piedmont stamps
PM#	Pins (PM1, PM10)
Pol	79Pol/Giants (Police/Safety)
Polar	1985 Polaroid Indians
Provigo	1986 Provigo Expos
Quaker	86Quaker Oats
R#	R300-R346 (30's gum issues)
Ralston	84Ralston
Rang	84Rangers
Rangers	83Rangers
Rawl	Rawl (Rawling's)
RedLob	1982 Cubs Red Lobster
Remar	46Remar (Remar Bread)
RFG	55RFG (W605 Robert F. Gould)
RH	54RH (Red Heart)
Rice	Rice Stix
RM	52RM through 55RM (Red Man)
Rodeo	55Rodeo, 56Rodeo (Rodeo Meats)
Royal	49Royal, 52Royal (Royal Desserts)
RoyRog	1983 Roy Rogers Discs
S	86S (Sportflics)
S#	S74 Silks
Salada	1962 Salada Coins
Salem	55Salem (Salem Potato Chips)
Schnucks	1986 Schnucks Cardinals
Score	88Score (Score)
Scrapps	Scrapps
Seven	84SevenUp (Cubs)
Seven	1985 Seven-Eleven Twins
Sf	88Sf (Sportflics)
SFCall	58SFCall (SF Call-Bulletin)
Shirriff	1962 Shirriff coins
SK	33SK (1933 Sport Kings)
SM	53SM through 55SM (Stahl Meyer)
Smok	85Smok/Angles (Smokey Bear)
Sqt	82Sqt (Squirt)
SSPC	76SSPC (1976 SSPC Pure Card)
StarCal	1952 Star Cal decals
Stuart	1983 Stuart Expos
Sugar	62Sugar, 63Sugar (Sugardale)
Sweet	1912 Sweet Caporal pins
SweetCap	1912 Sweet Caporal pins
Swell	48Swell (Swell Sport Thrills)
Swift	57Swift (Swift Meats)
T	51T through 87T (Topps)
Tast	Tastee Freeze discs
TCMA	78TCMA, 79TCMA (TCMA)
TexGold	1986 Texas Gold Reds
Thorn	83Thorn (Apple Valley)
TipTop	47TipTop (TipTop Bread)
Tor	87Tor/Fire (Toronto)
ToysRUs	87ToysRUs
Trans	69Trans, 70Trans (Transogram)
TrueVal	83TrueVal (True Value)
T#	T3 through T227 (Tobacco cards)
UD	1989 Upper Deck
Umpire	1988 Umpire Cards
Union	Union Oil
V#	V100 through V355 (Canadian issues)
W#	W501 through W711 (issued in strips)
Ward's	1934 Ward's Sporties pins
Wendy	85Wendy (Tigers)
West	1984 Doug West Series I
Weston	1974 Weston Expos
WG#	WG1 Card Game 1888
Wheat	35Wheat through 52Wheat (Wheaties)
Wiffle	1978 Wiffle Ball discs
Wilson	54Wilson (Wilson Wieners)
Wool	85Woolwth (Woolworth)
Woolwth	85Woolwth (Woolworth)
Yank	1944 Yankee stamps
YellBase	1956 Yellow Basepath pins
Yueng	28Yueng (Yuenglings)
Zeller	Zeller's Expos

Set Code Suffixes

Code	Example
/A	R303A (Type A)
/A	78BK/A (Astros)
/A	82OrlTw/A (Orlando after season)
/AAS	84D/AAS (Action All-Stars)
/A's	84Moth/A's (Oakland A's)
/AL	American League
/Alb	1969 Topps Stamp albums
/Am	1988 Conlon American All-Stars
/Angels	85Smok/Angels
/AS	86F/AS (All-Stars)
/ASG	1974 Laughlin All-Star Games
/Ast	84Moth/Ast (Astros)
/ATG	63Bz/ATG (All Time Greats)
/Atl	62Kahn/Atl (Atlanta)
/AwardWin	87F/AwardWin (Award Winners)
/B	R303B (Type B)
/B	82OrlTw/B (Orlando before season)
/B	80Penin/B (Peninsula b&w set)
/Back	1988 Topps Sticker Backs
/BB	51T/BB (Blue Backs)
/BB	1988 Fleer Baseball All-Stars
/BC	N172/BC (Brown's Champs)
/Best	Best Cards (Minor League)
/Best	1988 Donruss Baseball's Best
/BHN	Baseball Hobby News
/Big	1988 Topps Big
/Bk	1988 Donruss Mets Team Book
/BK	Burger King
/Black	1974 Laughlin Old Time Black Stars
/Blank	1986 Meadow Gold Blank Back
/blue	T213/blue (blue caption)
/Board	87T/Board (Boardwalk & Baseball)
/Bonus	1989 Donruss Bonus MVP's
/Book	1988 Donruss Mets Team Book
/Box	1983 Topps sticker boxes
/Braves	85Ho/Braves
/Brew	82Pol/Brew (Brewers)
/brown	T213/brown (brown caption)
/Bst	Best Cards (Minor League)
/bucks	62T/bucks (baseball bucks)
/BW	53B/BW (Black and White)
/C	80Penin/C (Peninsula color set)
/Cal	Cal League Minor League cards
/Can	1953 Exhibits Canadian
/Card	1988 Smokey Cardinals
/CAS	51T/CAS (Current All Stars)
/CB	70T/cb (Comic story booklet)
/Cereal	84T/Cereal

Code	Example
/Ch	Chong Minor League cards
/Champs	84D/Champs
/Chong	Chong Minor League cards
/Cloth	1972 Topps Test Cloth
/CM	51T/CM (Connie Mack)
/CMC	Collectors Marketing Corp.
/Coins	1964 Topps coins
Code	Example
/Col	53B/Col (Color)
/Comics	1973 Topps Comics
/Coop	1989 Kahn's Cooperstown
/Cram	Cramer (Minor League)
/Crm	Cramer (Minor League)
/CS	77T/CS (Cloth Stickers)
/DE	69T/DE (Deckle Edge)
/Dec	86S/Dec (Decade Greats)
/decal	69T/decal (decals)
/DH	55T/DH (Double Headers)
/Dice	1961 Topps Dice Game
/Disc	76MSA/Disc
/DKsuper	85D/DKsuper
/Dodg	80Pol/Dodg (Dodgers)
/DT	84Nestle/DT (Dream Team)
/E	65T/E (Embossed)
/Excit	1987 Fleer Exciting Stars
/Ext	1989 Upper Deck Extended
/FamFeat	1972 Fleer Famous Feats
/Fan	1984 Topps Mets Fan Club
/FB	84Shrev/FB (First Base)
/Feder	Grand Slam (Feder)
/FFeat	1972 Fleer Famous Feats
/Fire	87Tor/Fire (Toronto Fire)
/G	68T/G (Game Cards)
/GameWin	87F/GameWin (Game Winners)
/Giants	79Pol/Giants
/GF	1972 Laughlin Great Feats
/GlossRk	87T/Glossy Rookie Jumbo 22
/Gloss22	84T/Gloss22 (All-Stars)
/Gloss40	83T/Gloss40 (Send In Glossy)
/Gloss60	86T/Gloss60 (Send In Glossy)
/GM	71T/GM (Greatest Moments)
/Gov	Rochester Governor's Cup
/GS	Grand Slam (Feder)
/Head	1988 Fleer Headliners
/Hills	1989 Topps Hills Team MVP's
/HL	86D/HL (Highlights)
/Hocus	1956 Topps Hocus Focus
/HOF	48Exh/HOF (Hall of Fame)

Code	Example
/HotRk	1989 Score Hottest 100 Rookies
/HotRook	1989 Score Hottest 100 Rookies
/HotSt	1989 Score Hottest 100 Stars
/HotStar	1989 Score Hottest 100 Stars
/Hottest	87F/Hottest (Hottest Stars)
/HT	81T/HT (Home Team Supers)
/Ind	83Wheat/Ind (Indians)
/Indians	82BK/Indians
/JR	1947 Bond Bread Jackie Robinson
/Jub	1976 Laughlin Diamond Jubilee
/JumboR	1988 Topps Jumbo Rookies
/KC	76A P/KC (Kansas City)
/Kit	1988 CMC Mattingly Kit
/Ko	1988 Kodak Peoria Chiefs
/Kodak	1988 Kodak Peoria Chiefs
Code	Example
/L	1952 Star Cal Large
/Lead	K-Mart Leaders
/Leg	1980 Cramer Legends
/LF	Larry Fritsch (Minor League)
/Lids	1964 Detroit Tiger lids
/Lim	85F/Lim (Limited Edition)
/LL	86F/LL (League Leaders)
/LS	82HB/LS (Louisville Slugger)
/M	75T/M (Mini)
/M	70Trans/M (NY Mets)
/Mar	Mariners
/Mast	Score Scoremasters
/McCror	87F/McCror (McCrory's)
/Mets	1988 Donruss Mets Team Book
/Milk	1986 Meadow Gold Milk
/Milw	76A P/Milw (Milwaukee)
/Mini	86F/Mini
/Minn	1985 Seven-Eleven Twins
/MVP	1989 Donruss Bonus MVP's
/Nat	1988 Conlon National All-Stars
/Neg	1988 Conlon Negro All-Stars
/NL	National League
/num	1932-34 Orbit Pins Numbered
/NWest	Score Nat West Yankees
/OD	87D/OD (Opening Day)
/P	79BK/P (Phillies)
/Padres	84Smok/Padres
/PCL	49B/PCL (Pacific Coast League)
/PHR	80BK/PHR (Pitch, Hit, and Run)
/PI	67T/PI (Paper Insert)
/Pion	1975 Fleer Pioneers
/Pin	1909 Buster Brown Pins
/Pirates	Pittsburgh Pirates
/Pol	Police/safety sets

Code	Example
/PopUp	86D/PopUp
/Post	72T/Post (Posters)
/PP	1967 Topps Test Pirates
/Prem	1949 Leaf Premiums
/Pro	Pro Cards Minor League cards
/Puc	Pucko Minor League cards
/Pucko	Pucko Minor League cards
/R	78BK/R (Rangers)
/RB	51T/RB (Red Backs)
/Rec	1989 Fleer For The Record
/RecSet	87F/RecSet (Record Setters)
/Red	1988 Classic Red
/Reds	1988 Kahn's Reds
/RedSox	1988 Donruss Red Sox Team Book
/Revco	1988 Topps Revco
/RiteAid	1988 Topps Rite-Aid
/RO	66T/RO (Rub Offs)
/Roc	Rock's Dugout Wichita
/Rock	Rock's Dugout Wichita
/Rook	86D/Rook (Rookies)
Code	Example
/Royals	81Pol/Royals
/RSox	Boston Red Sox
/S	69T/S (Supers or Giant Size)
/SC	street clothes
/SDP	84Moth/SDP (S.D. Padres)
/Sea	84Moth/Sea (Seattle)
/SFG	83Moth/SFG (S.F. Giants)
/Slug	86F/Slug (Sluggers vs. Pitchers)
/Sm	PM10 Small
/Smok	Smokey Bear
/SO	63T/SO (Stick Ons, Scratch Offs)
/SP	Sport Pro Minor League sets
/SS	1988 Fleer Superstars
/ST	N172/ST (Spotted Ties)
/St	82F/St (Stickers, Stamps)
/Star	Star Co. Minor League sets
/Stat	1986 Meadow Gold Stat Back
/SU	64T/SU (Stand Ups)
/Sum	Cape Cod Summer League
/Summer	1988 Cape Cod Summer League
/Super	85T/Super
/T	51T/T, 58Hires/T (Team Cards, Test)
/T	78BK/T (Tigers)
/tatt	60T/tatt (tattoo)
/TCMA	TCMA (Minor League)
/Test	1971 Bazooka Numbered Test
/Tips	1982 Post Tips
/TL	1988 Fleer Team Leaders
/Tr	76T/Tr (Traded)

/trans	65T/trans (transfers)
/Tul	63Pep/Tul (Tulsa Oilers)
/Twink	75Ho/Twink (Twinkies)
/U	86F/Update
/UK	88 Topps UK Minis
/un	1932-34 Orbit Pins Unnumbered
/Up	87Classic/Up (Update)
/Update	85F/Update
/WaxBox	1985 Donruss Wax Box Cards
/WBTV	Charlotte TV station
/Wild	1973 Fleer Wildest Plays
/WS	85Coke/WS (White Sox)
/WS	1987 Fleer World Series
/Y	77BK/Y (Yankees)
/YS	1988 Score Young Superstars
/1	1988 Conlon Series 1
/100Ris	1990 Score 100 Rising
/100St	1990 Score 100 Stars
/100Stars	1990 Score 100 Stars
/3/4/500	1980 Laughlin 300/400/500 Club
/3D	68T/3D (three dimensional)
/4	1929-30 Exhibits 4-in-1
/8Men	1988 Pacific Eight Men Out

Individual Card Suffix Codes

Code	Example
a	autograph
A	in action
AGM	assistant gen. mgr.
AS	all-star
bb	batboy
BP	boyhood picture
C	coach
CL	checklist
DK	diamond kings
DR	doctor
FDP	first draft pick
FS	father and son
GC	ground crew
GM	general manager
IA	in action
LL	league leaders
M	multiple or misc.
MG	manager
MV	MVP card
ow	owner
Pz	puzzle
R	rookie
RR	rated rookie
SA	super action
SV	super veteran
T	traded
TC	team checklist
TL	team leader
TR	traded or trainer
tr	trainer
TR	trainer
ump	umpire

Minor League Abbreviations

Code	Example
AAA	AAA All-Stars
Albany	Albany-Colonie A's
Albuq	Albuquerque Dukes
AlexD	Alexandria Dukes
Amari	Amarillo Gold Sox
Ander	Anderson Braves
AppFx	Appleton Foxes
ArkTr	Arkansas Travelers
Ashvl	Asheville Tourists
AubAs	Auburn Astros
Aug	Augusta
Augusta	Augusta
Bakers	Bakersfield Dodgers
Batav	Batavia Trojans
Baton	Baton Rouge Cougars
BBAmer	Baseball America All-Stars
BBCity	Baseball City Royals
Beaum	Beaumont Golden Gators
Beloi	Beloit Brewers
Bend	Bend Phillies
Bill	Billings Mustangs
Billings	Billings Mustangs
BirmB	Birmingham Barons
Bluef	Bluefield Orioles
Bluefield	Bluefield Orioles
Boise	Boise Hawks
Brist	Bristol Red Sox
BuffB	Buffalo Bisons
BurlB	Burlington Bees/Braves
BurlEx	Burlington Expos
BurlR	Burlington Rangers
Butte	Butte Copper Kings
Calg	Calgary Cannons
Calgary	Calgary Cannons
CalLgAS	California Lg. All-Stars
Canton	Canton(-Akron) Indians
CapeCod	Cape Cod Prospects
Cedar	Cedar Rapids Reds
Charl	Charleston Charlies
CharlK	Charlotte Knights
CharlR	Charlotte Rangers
CharO	Charlotte O's
CharR	Charleston Royals

Code	Example
CharRa	Charleston Rainbows
CharRain	Charleston Rainbows
CharWh	Charleston Wheelers
Chatt	Chattanooga Lookouts
CLAS	Carolina League All-Stars
Clearw	Clearwater Phillies
Clint	Clinton Dodgers
Clint	Clinton Giants
Clmbia	Columbia Mets
Cocoa	Cocoa Beach Astros
ColAst	Columbus Astros
ColMud	Columbus Mudcats
ColorSp	Colorado Springs Sky Sox
ColSp	Colorado Springs Sky Sox
Colum	Columbus Clippers
ColumAst	Columbus Astros
Columbia	Columbia Mets
ColumMud	Columbus Mudcats
Cram/PCL	Cramer PCL set
Danvl	Danville Suns
DayBe	Daytona Beach Astros
Denver	Denver Zephyrs
Dubuq	Dubuque Packers
Duned	Dunedin Blue Jays
Durhm	Durham Bulls
EastLAS	Eastern League All-Stars
Edmon	Edmonton Trappers
Elizab	Elizabeth Twins
ElPas	El Paso Diablos
Elmir	Elmira Pioneer Red Sox
Erie	Erie Cardinals/Orioles
Eugene	Eugene Emeralds
Evans	Evansville Triplets
Everett	Everett Giants
Evrt	Everett Giants
Fay	Fayetteville Generals
Fayette	Fayetteville Generals
Freder	Frederick Keys
Fresno	Fresno Giants
FSLAS	Florida St.Lg.All-Stars
FtLaud	Ft. Lauderdale Yankees
FtMyr	Fort Myers Royals
Gasto	Gastonia Rangers
Geneva	Geneva Cubs
GlenF	Glen Falls White Sox
GreatF	Great Falls Dodgers
Green	Greenwood Braves
Greens	Greensboro Hornets
Greenv	Greenville Braves
Greenvl	Greenville Braves
Hagers	Hagerstown Suns

Code	Example
Hamil	Hamilton Redbirds
Harris	Harrisburg Senators
Harrisbg	Harrisburg Senators
Hawai	Hawaii Islanders
Helena	Helena Brewers
Holyo	Holyoke Millers
Huntsvl	Huntsville Stars
Idaho	Idaho Falls Athletics
Indi	Indianapolis Indians
Indianap	Indianapolis Indians
IntLgAS	International Lg.All-Stars
IowaC	Iowa Cubs
Jacks	Jackson Mets
James	Jamestown Expos
Jamestn	Jamestown Expos
Jaxvl	Jacksonville Suns
Keno	Kenosha Twins
Kenosha	Kenosha Twins
Kingspt	Kingsport Mets
Kingst	Kingston Blue Jays
Kinston	Kinston Eagles/Indians
Knoxv	Knoxville Blue Jays
Knoxv	Knoxville Knox Sox
Lafay	Lafayette Drillers
Lakel	Lakeland Tigers
Lakeland	Lakeland Tigers
LasVeg	Las Vegas Stars
LasVegas	Las Vegas Stars
LitFalls	Little Falls Mets
LodiD	Lodi Dodgers
London	London Tigers
Louisvl	Louisville Redbirds
Louvl	Louisville Redbirds
Lynch	Lynchburg Mets
LynnP	Lynn Pirates
LynnS	Lynn Sailors
Macon	Macon Pirates
Madis	Madison Muskies
Martins	Martinsville Phillies
Maine	Maine Guides
Medford	Medford Athletics
Memph	Memphis Chicks
Mia	Miami Marlins/Miracle
Miami	Miami Marlins/Miracle
Miami	Miami Orioles
MidldA	Midland Angels
MidldC	Midland Cubs
MidwLAS	Midwest League All-Stars
Modesto	Modesto A's
Myrtle	Myrtle Beach Blue Jays
Nashua	Nashua Angels

Code	Example
Nashvl	Nashville Sounds
Newar	Newark Co-Pilots
NewBrit	New Britain Red Sox
NiagFls	Niagara Falls Rapids
Ogden	Ogden A's
OkCty	Oklahoma City 89ers
Omaha	Omaha Royals
Oneon	Oneonta Yankees
OrlTw	Orlando Twins
Orlan	Orlando Twins
Osceola	Osceola Astros
PalmSp	Palm Springs Angels
Pawtu	Pawtucket Red Sox
Penin	Peninsula Pilots
Peoria	Peoria Chiefs
Phoen	Phoenix Giants
Pittsf	Pittsfield Cubs
Poca	Pocatello
Pocatel	Pocatello
PortChar	Port Charlotte Rangers
Portl	Portland Beavers
Princet	Princeton Pirates
PrWill	Prince William Pirates
Pulas	Pulaski
Pulaski	Pulaski
QuadC	Quad-City Cubs/Angels
Readg	Reading Phillies
Redwd	Redwood Pioneers
Reno	Reno Silver Sox
Richm	Richmond Braves
River	Riverside Red Wave
Riversi	Riverside Red Wave
RochR	Rochester Red Wings
Rockford	Rockford Expos
Sacra	Sacramento
SALAS	South Atlantic Lg. All-Stars
Salin	Salinas Spurs
Salinas	Salinas Spurs
SanJose	San Jose Bees/Giants
Salem	Salem Pirates
SanBern	San Bernadino Spirit
Saraso	Sarasota White Sox
Savan	Savannah Braves
ScrantWB	Scranton-Wilkes-Barre
ScrWB	Scranton-Wilkes-Barre
Shrev	Shreveport Captains
Shreve	Shreveport Captains
SLAS	Southern League All-Stars
SLCty	Salt Lake City Gulls
SnAnt	San Antonio Brewers
SnBer	San Bernadino Spirit

Code	Example
SnJos	San Jose Missions
SoBend	South Bend White Sox
SoOreg	Southern Oregon
Spart	Spartanburg Phillies
Spoka	Spokane Indians
SpokAT	Spokane All-Time Greats
SpokaAT	Spokane All-Time Greats
Sprin	Springfield Cardinals
StCath	St. Catherines Blue Jays
StLucie	St. Lucie Mets
Stock	Stockton Ports
Stockton	Stockton Ports
StPet	St. Petersburg Cardinals
Sumter	Sumter Braves
Syrac	Syracuse Chiefs
Tacom	Tacoma Tigers
Tacom	Tacoma Tugs
Tampa	Tampa Tarpons
TexLgAS	Texas League All-Stars
Tidew	Tidewater Tides
Tigres	Tigres de Mexico
Toled	Toledo Mud Hens
TriCit	Tri-Cities Triplets
Tucso	Tucson Toros
Tulsa	Tulsa Drillers
Utica	Utica Blue Jays
Vanco	Vancouver Canadians
Ventura	Ventura Gulls
Vermont	Vermont Reds
VeroB	Vero Beach Dodgers
Virgini	Virginia Generals
Visal	Visalia Oaks
Water	Waterbury Reds
Watertn	Watertown Pirates
Watlo	Waterloo Indians
Wausa	Wausau Mets
Wausa	Wausau Timbers
Well	Welland Pirates
Welland	Welland Pirates
WHave	West Haven A's
WHave	West Haven Yankees
Wich	Wichita
Wichi	Wichita Aeros/Pilots
WinHav	Winter Haven Red Sox
WinHaven	Winter Haven Red Sox
WinSal	Winston-Salem Spirits
WinSalem	Winston-Salem Spirits
Wisco	Wisconsin Rapids Twins
Wmspt	Williamsport Tomahawks
WPalm	West Palm Beach Expos
Wythe	Wytheville

Aaron, Henry Louis
(Hank)
54JC-5
54T-128
55B-179
55Gol/Braves-1
55JC-44
55T-47
55T/DH-105
56T-31
56T/Pin-16
56YellBase/Pin-1
57Swift-13
57T-20
58Hires-44
58T-30
58T-351M
58T-418M
58T-488AS
59Armour-1
59Bz
59HRDerby-1
59T-212M
59T-380
59T-467M
59T-561AS
60Armour-1A
60Armour-1B
60Bz-4
60Lake
60MacGregor-1
60NuCard-62
60T-300
60T-566AS
60T/tatt
60T/tatt-1
61NuCard-462
61P-107
61T-415
61T-43LL
61T-484M
61T-577AS
61T/St-37
62Bz
62Exh
62J-149
62P-149
62P/Can-149
62Salada-180
62Shirriff-180
62T-320
62T-394AS
62T/bucks
62T/St-143
63Bz-9
63Exh
63J-152
63P-152
63Salada-24
63T-1LL
63T-242M
63T-390
63T-3LL
63T/SO
64Bz-9
64T-11LL
64T-300
64T-423M
64T-7LL
64T-9LL
64T/Coins-149AS
64T/Coins-83
64T/S-49
64T/St-84
64T/SU
64T/tatt
64Wheat/St-1
65Bz-9
65Kahn
65OldLond-1
65OPC-170
65OPC-2LL
65T-170
65T-2LL
65T/E-59
65T/trans
65T/trans-37
66Bz-30
66Kahn
66T-215LL
66T-500
66T/RO-117
67Bz-30
67Kahn
67OPC/PI-15
67T-242LL
67T-244LL
67T-250
67T/PI-15
67T/Test/SU-20
68Bz-5
68Coke
68Kahn
68OPC-110
68OPC-3LL
68OPC-5LL
68T-110
68T-370AS
68T-3LL
68T-5LL
68T/G-4
68T/Post-9
69Citgo-16
69Kahn
69MB-1
69MLB/St-109
69MLBPA/Pin-31
69NTF
69OPC-100
69T-100
69T/decal
69T/S-34
69T/St-1
69Trans-53
70MB-1
70MLB/St-1
70OPC-462AS
70OPC-500
70OPC-65LL
70T-462AS
70T-500
70T-65LL
70T/S-24
70T/SO
70Trans-4
71Bz
71Bz/Test-23
71MD
71MLB/St-1
71MLB/St-553
71OPC-400
71T-400
71T/Coins-137
71T/S-44
71T/tatt-9
72MB-1
72OPC-299
72OPC-300IA
72OPC-87LL
72OPC-89LL
72T-299
72T-300A
72T-87LL
72T-89LL
72T/Cloth-1
72T/Post-9
73OPC-100
73OPC-1M
73OPC-473LL
73T-100
73T-1LL
73T-473LL
73T/Comics-1
73T/Lids-1
73T/PinUps-1
74Laugh/ASG-72
74OPC-1
74OPC-2M
74OPC-3M
74OPC-4M
74OPC-5M
74OPC-6M
74OPC-7M
74OPC-8M
74OPC-9M
74T-1
74T-2M
74T-332M
74T-3M
74T-4M
74T-5M
74T-6M
74T/DE-57
74T/Puzzles-1
74T/St-1
75Ho-130
75Ho/Twink-130
75OPC-195M
75OPC-1RB
75OPC-660
75T-195MV
75T-1M
75T-660
75T/M-195MV
75T/M-1M
75T/M-660
76A&P/Milw
76Crane-1
76Ho-94
76Laugh/Jub-8
76MSA/Disc
76OPC-1RB
76OPC-550
76SSPC-239
76T-1M
76T-550
79T-412M
79T-413M
80Cram/Leg-7
80Laugh/3/4/5-16
81Pol/Atl-44C
82CJ-1
82KMart-43
83D/HOF-34
83MLBPA/Pin-19
83T/St-1F
84D/Champs-8
85CircK-1
85D/HOF-7
85Woolwth-1
86BLChew-1
86D-602M
86D/AS/WaxBox-PUZ
86D/WaxBox-PUZ
86Leaf-259PUZ
86S/Dec-40
87KMart-1
87Nestle/DT-29
88Pac/Leg-1
89HOF/St-44
89T-663TBC
Exh47
PM10/Sm-1
TCMA78-290
WG10-24
WG9-26

Aaron, Tommie Lee
63T-46
64T-454
65T-567
68T-394
69OPC-128
69T-128
70OPC-278
70T-278
71MLB/St-2
71OPC-717
71T-717
72MB-2
78Richm
82Pol/Atl-23C

Aaron, Wil
75SnAnt
76Wmspt

Aase, Donald William
(Don)
76OPC-597R
76T-597R
77T-472R
78OPC-233
78T-12
79T-368
80OPC-126
80T-239
81D-411
81F-286
81T-601
82D-267
82F-450
82F/St-212
82OPC-199
82T-199
83D-38
83F-76
83T-599
84Smok/Cal-1
85D-255
85F-293
85F/Up-U1
85T-86
85T/Tr-1T
86D-392
86D/HL-12
86F-268
86T-288
87Classic-99
87D-231
87D/AAS-47
87F-461
87F-627M
87F/Excit-1
87F/Mini-1
87F/St-1
87OPC-207
87S-165
87S-194M
87Seven-ME4
87T-766
87T/Mini-38
87T/St-228
88F-553
88French-41
88Score-518
88T-467
89F/Up-100
89Kahn/Mets-49
89Score-524
89T/Tr-1T
89UD-450
90F-196
90Score-377
90T-301
90UD-131

Abarbanel, Mickey
68T-287R

Abare, Bill
89StCath/Pro-2071

Abbaticchio, Ed
12Sweet/Pin-65
D322-14
E254
E270/1
M116
T205
T206

Abbatiello, Pat
87Idaho-26

Abbey, Bert Wood
No Cards.

Abbey, Charles S.
(Charlie)
N300/SC

Abbot, Terry
78Green

Abbott, Frederick H.
(Fred)
E254
E270/1
T206

Abbott, Jim
88T/Tr-1T
89B-39
89Class/Up/2-151
89D/Best-171
89D/Rook-16
89F/Up-11
89Score/Tr-88
89T-573FDP
89T/Big-322
89T/HeadsUp-16
89T/Tr-2T
89UD/Ext-755
90Class-40
90D-108
90F-125
90Score-330
90Score/100Ris-5
90Sf-99
90T-675
90UD-645

Abbott, John
85Elmir-1
86Greens-1
88WinHav/Star-1

Abbott, Kurt
89Medford/Best-27

Abbott, Kyle
89QuadC/GS-13
90Score-673DC
90T-444

Abbott, Leander F.
(Dan)
No Cards.

Abbott, Ody Cleon
No Cards.

Abbott, Paul
86Kenosha-1
87Kenosha-24
88Visal/Cal-165
88Visal/Pro-92
89Orlan/Best-7
89Orlan/Pro-1348
89SLAS-14

Abbott, Terry
89Aug/Pro-515

Abbott, W. Glenn
(Glenn)
74OPC-602R
74T-602R
75OPC-591
75T-591
75T/M-591
76OPC-322
76SSPC-485
76T-322
77Ho-147
77OPC-219
77T-207
78Ho-17
78OPC-92
78T-31
79OPC-263
79T-497
80OPC-92
80T-166
81D-47
81F-615
81OPC-174
81Pol/Mariners-3

81T-699
82D-302
82F-502
82T-336TL
82T-571
84F-74
84Nes/792-356
84OPC-356
84T-356
86Jacks/TCMA-25
88Jacks/GS-5
89Tidew/CMC-26

Abe, Osamu
83SanJose-8

Abel, Sid
51BR-C16

Aber, Albert Julius
(Al)
53T-233
54T-238
55B-24
56T-317
57T-141
D301

Abernathie, William
(Bill)
No Cards.

Abernathy, Talmadge
No Cards.

Abernathy, Ted
57T-293
59T-169
60T-334
64T-64
65T-332
66OPC-2
66T-2
67T-597
68T-264
69MB-2
69T-483
69T/St-21
70T-562
71MLB/St-409
71OPC-187
71T-187
72MB-3
72OPC-519
72T-519
73OPC-22
73T-22

Abernathy, Tom
V355-122

Abernathy, Virgil W.
(Woody)
No Cards.

Aberson, Clifford A.
(Cliff)
48L-136

Ables, Harry Terrell
No Cards.

Abner, Ben
86Macon-1
87Harrisbg-26

Abner, Shawn
85Lynch-25
85T-282FDP
86Jacks/TCMA-19
87LasVegas-2
88D-33
88D/Best-21
88D/Rook-5
88F-576
88Leaf-33RR
88Score-626
88Sf-223
88Smok/Padres-1
89D-323
89LasVeg/CMC-22
89LasVeg/Pro-21
89Score-411
90Score-352
90T-122
90UD-301

Abone, Joseph
80Memph-6
82Wichi-1

Abraham, Brian
77SnJos-23
79Ogden/TCMA-10
80Ogden-9
81WHave-18
82WHave-1

Abraham, Glen
87Everett-10

Abrams, Calvin Ross
(Cal)
51B-152
52B-86
52T-350
53B/Col-160
53NB
53T-98
54B-91
54Esskay
55B-55
55Esskay
89Rini/Dodg-34

Abrams, George Allen
No Cards.

Abrego, Johnny
86D-32
86IowaC-1

Abrell, Thomas
86Sumter-1
87CharWh-26

Abreu, Armand
77Spart

Abreu, Francisco
87DayBe-11

Abreu, Franklin
87Savan-20
88Sprin/Best-21
89StPet/Star-1

Abreu, Joseph L.
(Joe)
No Cards.

Abril, Ernest
(Odie)
85Greens-21
86FSLAS-1
86WinHav-1
87WinHav-15
88WinHav/Star-2
89WinHav/Star-1

Abstein, William H.
(Bill)
C46-86
E104
E254
T201
T206

Acker, James Austin
(Jim)
84D-146
84F-145
84Nes/792-359
84OPC-359
84T-359
84Tor/Fire-1
85F-96
85OPC-101
85T-101
85Tor/Fire-1
86Ault-31
86D-363
86F-50
86OPC-46
86T-569
86Tor/Fire-1
87D-659
87F-509
87Smok/Atl-10
87T-407
88F-531
88OPC-293
88Score-576
88T-678
88T/St-43
89T-244
89UD-52
90D-558
90T-728

Acker, Larry
85Cram/PCL-55
86Tucso-1
87BirmB/Best-8
88Memph/Best-7

Acker, Thomas James
(Tom)
57Kahn
57T-219
58T-149
59Kahn
59T-201
60T-274

Ackerman, John
84Evrt/Cram-27

Ackley, Florian F.
(Fritz)
64T-368R
65T-477R
66Pep/Tul
78TCMA-27

Ackley, John
80Elmir-12

Acosta, Bert
78Newar

Acosta, Carlos
86Tampa-1

Acosta, Cy
73OPC-379
73T-379
74OPC-22
74T-22
75OPC-634
75T-634
75T/M-634

Acosta, Ed
71OPC-343R
71T-343R
72OPC-123
72T-123
73OPC-244
73T-244

Acosta, Jose
87Watertn-17
88Aug/Pro-371
89Aug/Pro-492

Acosta, Oscar
89Gasto/Pro-1025

Acta, Manuel
88Osceola/Star-1
89ColMud/Best-2
89ColMud/Pro-136
89ColMud/Star-1

Adair, Kenneth Jerry
(Jerry)
60L-28
61T-71
62T-449
62T/St-2
63J-61
63P-61
63T-488
64T-22
65OPC-231
65T-231
66T-533
67T-484
68Coke
68T-346
69MB-3
69MLB/St-55
69OPC-159
69T-159
69T/St-181
70MLB/St-217
70OPC-525
70T-525
72MB-4
73OPC-179CO
73T-179C

Adair, James Aubrey
(Jimmy)
No Cards.

Adair, Rick
81Wausa-14
82LynnS-1
83SLCty-8
84Chatt-23
87Watlo-29
89ColrSp/CMC-23
89ColSp/Pro-247

Adamczak, Jim
86Jacks/TCMA-1

Adames, Hernan
88Tampa/Star-1

Adames, Juan
88Wythe/Pro-1997
89Peoria/Ko-16

Adams, Ace Townsend
41DP-138
88Conlon/3-1

Adams, Bob
77Evansvl/TCMA-1

Adams, Bud
88BBCity/Star-1

Adams, Carl Ray
79Newar-15

Adams, Charles B.
(Babe)
21Exh-1
61F-90
80Laugh/FFeat-38
87Conlon/2-7
D322-9
D329-1
D350/2-1
E104
E120
E121/120
E126
E220
E254
E90/1
E96
M101/4-1
M101/5-1
M116
V100
V61-91
W501-84
W514-54
W515-6
W516-18
W573
W575

Adams, Charles Dwight
(Red)
47Signal
49B/PCL-24
53Mother-53
73OPC-569CO
73T-569C
74OPC-144CO
74T-144C

Adams, Craig
77Watlo
81Chatt-20
82Chatt-22

Adams, Daniel Leslie
(Dan)
No Cards.

Adams, Dan
75Lafay

Adams, Daryl
80Penin/C-2

Adams, Earl John
(Sparky)
25Exh-17
26Exh-17
27Exh-9
29Exh/4-13
31Exh/4-15
33DH-1
33Exh/4-8
33G-213
34DS-24
35G-1H
35G-3F
35G-4F
35G-5F

Adams, Elvin Clark
(Buster)
No Cards.

Adams, George
No Cards.

Adams, Gerald
84Newar-20
85Newar-9

Adams, Glenn Charles
76OPC-389
76SSPC-108
76T-389
78T-497
79T-193
80T-604
81D-566
81F-562
82D-431
82F-545
82Syrac-19
82T-519
83OPC-374
83T-574
87Watlo-10MG
88CLAS/Star-21

Adams, Harold Douglas
(Doug)
No Cards.

Adams, Herbert Loren
(Herb)
No Cards.

Adams, James Irvin
(Willie)
No Cards.

Adams, James J.
(Jim)
No Cards.

Adams, John Bertram
(Bert)
11Helmar-153
14CJ-63
15CJ-63
T207

Adams, John
78BurlB
80Holyo-16
83ArkTr-10
84ArkTr-12

Adams, Joseph Edward
(Joe)
No Cards.

Adams, Karl Tutwiler
No Cards.

Adams, Ken
86Cram/PCL-46
88BBCity/Star-2
89BBCity/Star-1

Adams, Lionel
89Idaho/Pro-2012
89Sumter/Pro-1098

Adams, Mike
86Visal-1
87Visal-22

Adams, Pat
82AppFx-27
83AppFx/LF-8
85Cram/PCL-186

87Phoen-21
88WPalm/Star-1
Adams, Ralph
84LitFalls-6
86Lynch-1
Adams, Richard Leroy
(Dick)
No Cards.
Adams, Ricky Lee
78DaytB
80ElPas-21
81Holyo-7
82Holyo-13
84Cram/PCL-104
84D-85
84Nes/792-487
84T-487
85Cram/PCL-188
86Phoen-1
86T-153
Adams, Robert Andrew
(Bob)
No Cards.
Adams, Robert Burd.
(Bob)
No Cards.
Adams, Robert Henry
(Bobby)
48L-54
49Eureka-76
51B-288
52B-166
52T-249
53B/Col-108
53RM-NL2
53T-152
54B-108
54T-123
55B-118
55T-178
56T-287
58T-99
59T-249
Adams, Robert Michael
(Mike)
74OPC-573
74T-573
Adams, Robert Melvin
(Bob)
No Cards.
Adams, Rollo
81Clint-26
Adams, Spencer Dewey
(Spencer)
No Cards.
Adams, Steve
86Watertn-1
87Macon-13
88Salem/Star-1
89Harris/Pro-295
89Harris/Star-1
Adams, Terry
76Cedar
Adamson, John Michael
(Mike)
69OPC-66R
69T-66R
71OPC-362R
71T-362R
Adamson, Wade
80OrlTw-1
Adcock, Joseph Wilbur
(Joe)
51B-323
52B-69
52T-347
53B/Col-151
53JC-17
54B-96
54JC-9
55B-218
55Gol/Braves-2
55JC-9
56T-320
56YellBase/Pin-2
57T-117
58T-325
58T-351M
59T-315
60Lake
60NuCard-33
60T-3
61NuCard-433
61P-104
61T-245
61T/St-38
62J-145
62P-145
62Salada-125
62Shirriff-125
62T-265
62T/bucks
62T/St-144
63F-46
63J-148
63P-148
63Sugar-4
63T-170
67T-563
72Laugh/GF-42
78TCMA-108
78TCMA-73
88Pac/Leg-31
89Swell-6
Exh47
Adderly, Ken
87Miami-18
Addis, Robert Gorden
(Bob)
52T-259
53B/Col-94
53T-157
Adduci, James David
(Jim)
81Louvl-19
82ArkTr-18
84Louvl-19
85Cram/PCL-206
86Vanco-1
87D-495
87Denver-16
88Pol/Brew-14
89F-176
89Score-587
89T-338
Addy, Robert Edward
(Bob)
No Cards.
Adkins, Adrian
89Princet/Star-1
Adkins, Grady Emmett
No Cards.
Adkins, John Dewey
(Dewey)
No Cards.
Adkins, Merle Theron
(Doc)
C46-18
E254
E270/2
T205
T206
Adkins, Richard Earl
(Dick)
No Cards.
Adkins, Steve
87FtLaud-22
87PrWill-20
88PrWill/Star-1
89FtLaud/Star-1
Adkins, Terry
85PrWill-6
Adkinson, Henry Magee
(Henry)
No Cards.
Adler, Marcus
88Fay/Pro-1085
89Lakel/Star-1
Adlesh, David George
(Dave)
67OPC-51R
67T-51R
68T-576
69T-341
Adriance, Dan
86Cram/PCL-190
87Beloi-23
88Beloi/GS-6
89Salin/Cal-124
89Salin/Pro-1818
Afenir, Troy
86ColumAst-1
87ColAst/Pro-4
87ColumAst-4
88ColAst/Best-23
89Huntsvl/Best-3
Agado, David
89Batav/Pro-1926
Agan, Tim
84Toled-19
Agar, Jeff
86Lakel-1
87GlenF-12
Agee, Tommie Lee
65OPC-166R
65T-166R
66OPC-164R
66T-164R
67Bz-2
67OPC/PI-4
67T-455
67T/PI-4
68Bz-15
68Bz-6
68Kahn
68T-465
69MB-4
69MLB/St-163
69T-364
69T/St-61
70K-11
70MLB/St-73
70OPC-307WS
70OPC-50
70T-50
70T/PI-13
70T/S-42
70Trans/M-23
71Bz
71Bz/Test-16
71K-46
71MLB/St-145
71OPC-310
71T-310
71T/Coins-91
71T/tatt-9
72MB-5
72OPC-245
72T-245
72T/S-36
73OPC-420
73T-420
74OPC-630
74T-630
74T/Tr-630T
Agganis, Harry
55T-152
Agler, Joseph Abram
(Joe)
E254
Agnew, Samuel Lester
(Sam)
D328-1
D329-2
D350/2-2
E135-1
M101/4-2
M101/5-2
Agostinelli, Sal
84Savan-22
86StPet-1
87ArkTr-15
88Louvl-5
88Louvl/CMC-21
88Louvl/Pro-424
89Readg/Best-22
89Readg/Pro-654
89Readg/Star-1
Agosto, Juan Roberto
(Woody)
82Edmon-12
84D-208
84F-50
84Nes/792-409
84T-409
84TrueVal/WS-1
85Coke/WS-50
85D-526
85F-506
85T-351
86Coke/WS-50
86D-488
86F-197
86T-657
87T-277
87Tucso-1
88F-437
88Moth/Ast-24
88Pol/Ast-1
88Score-558
88T/Tr-2T
89B-321
89D-354
89F-348
89Lennox/Ast-17
89Moth/Ast-23
89Panini/St-81
89Score-283
89T-559
89UD-251
90D-477
90F-220
90Score-284
90T-181
90UD-450
Aguayo, Carmelo
82Tulsa-14
Aguayo, Luis
79OkCty
80OkCty
82D-622
82F-238
82T-449
83D-546
83Portl-1
83T-252
85D-503
85T-663
86D-503
86F-433
86T-69
87F-169
87F-169
87OPC-18
87T-755
87T-755
88D-185
88F-297
88Score-499
88T-356
88T/Big-226
89B-88
89D-551
89F-249
89Score-436
89T-561
89UD-156
Aguilar, Jose
85Tigres-14
Aguilar, Mark
88Stock/Cal-191
88Stock/Pro-723
89Madis/Star-1
Aguilera, Rick
85Tidew-11
86D-441
86F-74
86KayBee-1
86Leaf-216
86T-599
87Classic-79
87D-620
87F-1
87F/Excit-2
87Leaf-89
87OPC-103
87T-103
88D-446
88D/Mets/Bk-446
88F-127
88Kahn/Mets-15
88Leaf-231
88Score-521
88Score/YS/II-21
88T-434
89D-526
89D/Best-265
89F-27
89Kahn/Mets-38
89Score-327
89T-257
89UD-563
90D-391
90F-365
90Score-519
90T-711
90UD-11
Aguirre, Henry John
(Hank)
57T-96
58T-337
59T-36
60T-546
61T-324
61T/St-144
62T-407
63J-54
63P-54
63Salada-32
63T-257
63T-6LL
64Det/Lids-1
64T-39
64T/Coins-74
64T/St-38
64T/SU
64T/tatt
65T-522
66OPC-113
66T-113
67T-263
68T-553
69OPC-94
69T-94
70T-699
73OPC-81CO
73T-81C
74OPC-354CO
74T-354C
75Tucso-26
78TCMA-225
Ahearn, Charles
(Charlie)
No Cards.
Ahern, Brian
88CapeCod/Sum-30
89Eugene/Best-23
Ahern, Jeff
82Danvi-3

83Redwd-1

Ahr, Jeff
88Hagers/Star-1

Aiello, Talbot
81Wisco-20

Aikens, Willie Mays
75QuadC
77SLCty
78Cr/PCL-20
80OPC-191
80T-368
81Coke
81D-220
81F-43
81OPC-23
81Pol/Royals-1
81T-524
81T/SO-27
81T/St-84
82D-412
82F-404
82F/St-206
82OPC-35
82T-35
82T/St-196
83D-212
83F-104
83OPC-136
83Pol/Royals-1
83T-136
84D-155
84F-341
84F/X-1
84Nes/792-685
84OPC-137
84T-685
84T/St-276
84T/X-1
84Tor/Fire-2
85F-97
85OPC-147
85T-436
85Tor/Fire-2

Ainge, Daniel Rae
(Danny)
78Syrac
80Syrac-20
81D-569
81F-418
81T/Tr-727
82D-638
82F-608
82OPC-125
82T-125

Ainsmith, Edward W.
(Eddie)
D329-3
D350/2-3
E120
E286
M101/4-3
M101/5-3
T207
W572
W573

Aitcheson, Kevin
83Knoxv-15

Aitchison, Raleigh L.
No Cards.

Ake, John Leckie
(John)
No Cards.

Aker, Jack Delane
66T-287
67OPC-110
67T-110
68T-224
69MLB/St-91
69T-612
69T/St-221
70MLB/St-241
70OPC-43
70T-43
71MLB/St-481
71OPC-593
71T-593
72T-769
73OPC-262
73T-262
74OPC-562
74T-562
78TCMA-274
81Tidew-21
82Tidew-19MG
83BuffB-25
84BuffB-18
85Water-22
86OhHenry-CO
87Gator-CO

Akerfelds, Darrel
84Madis/Pol-25
85Huntsvl/BK-32
86Tacom-1
87Tacom-2
88ColSp/CMC-1
88ColSp/Pro-1537
88Score-632
88T-82
89OkCty/CMC-1
89OkCty/Pro-1532
89Smok/R-1

Akers, Albert Earl
(Jerry)
No Cards.

Akers, Howard
86Kinston-1

Akers, Thomas Earnest
(Bill)
No Cards.

Akimoto, Ratoo
87SanJose-14

Akins, Sid
85BurlR-12
85T-390
87Durhm-5
88Richm-16
88Richm/CMC-7
88Richm/Pro-14
89Greenv/Pro-1151

Akins, Tom
88Indi/Pro-525M
89Indi/Pro-1216

Ako, Gerry
80Holyo-23
81ElPas-9
81Vanco-22

Alario, Dave
86Bakers-1

Alba, Gibson
85Syrac-1
86Syrac-1
87BuffB-14
88Louvl-6
88Louvl/CMC-6
88Louvl/Pro-442
89Louvl-7
89Louvl/CMC-1
89Louvl/Pro-1252

Albanese, Joseph P.
(Joe)
No Cards.

Alberro, Hector
87Beloi-20

Albert, August P.
(Gus)
N172

Albert, Richard
(Rick)
83Ander-2
87Richm/TCMA-26
88Sumter/Pro-416

Alberts, Francis Burt
(Butch)
77SLCty
78Syrac
80Syrac-10

Alberts, Frederick J.
(Cy)
No Cards.

Albertson, John
88Idaho/Pro-1839

Alborano, Pete
88CLAS/Star-22
88Virgini/Star-1
89BBCity/Star-2
89Star/Wax-62

Albosta, Edward John
(Ed)
47Signal

Albrecht, Andrew
88CapeCod/Sum-159

Albrecht, Edward A.
(Ed)
No Cards.

Albright, Dave
81CharR-9

Albright, Eric
89NiagFls/Puc-2

Albright, Gilbert
80Clint-25

Albright, Harold John
(Jack)
No Cards.

Albury, Victor
(Vic)
72T-778R
74OPC-605R
74T-605R
75OPC-368
75T-368
75T/M-368
76OPC-336
76SSPC-205
76T-336
77T-536
82Watlo/B-27C
82Watlo/C-3C
83Charl-20
83Watlo/LF-27CO
84Maine-9

Alcala, Jesus
82Oneon-12

Alcala, Julio
86FSLAS-2
86FtMyr-1
87Memph-24
87Memph/Best-5
89Memph/Best-6
89Memph/Pro-1183
89Memph/Star-1

Alcala, Santo
76OPC-589R
76T-589R
77Pep-52
77T-636
78OPC-36
78T-321
81Portl-3

Alcazar, Jorge
86Penin-1
88Vanco/CMC-23
88Vanco/Pro-772

Alcaraz, Angel Luis
(Luis)
69T-437

Alcock, John Forbes
(Scotty)
No Cards.

Alderson, Dale L.
No Cards.

Aldred, Scott
87Fayette-11
88Lakel/Star-1
89London/Pro-1368

Aldrete, Mike
86F/Up-U1
86Phoen-2
87D-450
87F-264
87Moth/SFG-24
87T-71
88D-362
88D/Best-191
88F-76
88Moth/Giants-5
88OPC-351
88Panini/St-426
88RedFoley/St-1
88Score-556
88Score/YS/I-35
88Sf-80
88T-602
88T/Big-119
88T/St-89
89B-368
89D-140
89D/Tr-25
89F-323
89F/Up-95
89OPC-9
89Panini/St-219
89Score-82
89Score/Tr-68
89T-158
89T/St-80
89UD-239
89UD/Ext-738
90Score-220
90T-589
90UD-415

Aldrete, Richard
87Everett-6
88CalLgAS-7
88SanJose/Cal-116
88SanJose/Pro-119
89Shreve/Pro-1847

Aldrich, Jay
83Beloi/LF-8
86ElPas-1
87Denver-4
88D-460
88Denver/CMC-7
88Denver/Pro-1270
88F-155
88Pol/Brew-33
88Score-578
88T-616
89Denver/CMC-1
89Denver/Pro-42

Aldrich, Russell
80Water-20
81Water-18

Aldrich, Tom
88Brist/Pro-1881
89London/Pro-1386

Aldridge, Vic
E120
V61-74
W573

Aleno, Charles
(Chuck)
45Centen-1

Aleshire, Troy
86AubAs-1

Alexander, Charles
(Chuck) 88BurlR/Pro-1785
89Watertn/Star-1

Alexander, Dave
89SLCty-22

Alexander, David Dale
(Dale)
29Exh/4-23
31Exh/4-23
32Orbit/num-27
32Orbit/un-1
33DH-2
33G-221
61F-91
88Conlon/4-1
R300
R305
R308-181
R316

Alexander, Doyle L.
72T-579
73JP
73OPC-109
73T-109
74OPC-282
74T-282
75OPC-491
75T-491
75T/M-491
76OPC-638
76SSPC-374
76T-638
77Ho-140
77T-254
78BK/R-4
78OPC-52
78T-146
79OPC-230
79T-442
80T-67
81D-448
81T-708
81T/Tr-728
82D-96
82F-383
82T-364
82T/Tr-1T
83D-451
83T-512
84D-439
84F-146
84Nes/792-677
84OPC-112
84T-677
84Tor/Fire-3
85D-561
85F-98
85Leaf-134
85OPC-218
85OPC/Post-21
85SpokAT/Cram-1
85T-218
85T/St-365
85Tor/Fire-3
86Ault-33
86D-390
86F-51
86F/LimEd-1
86Leaf-182
86OPC-196
86S-133M
86T-196
86T/Mini-34
86Tor/Fire-2
87D-657
87D/HL-52
87F-510
87OPC-249
87T-686
88D-584
88D/Best-13
88F-51
88F/Mini-21
88F/St-23
88OPC-316
88Pep/T-19
88Pol/T-1
88Score-610
88T-492
88T/Big-34
89B-94
89D-178
89D/AS-12
89D/Best-125
89F-128
89F/BBAS-1

89Mara/Tigers-19
89OPC-77
89Pol/Tigers-19
89RedFoley/St-1
89Score-129
89Sf-211
89T-77
89T/Big-182
89T/St-274
89UD-298
90D-62
90F-599
90Score-237
90T-748
90UD-330

Alexander, Eric
89Bluef/Star-1

Alexander, Gary
88TexLgAS/GS-4
88Tulsa-12
89Tulsa/GS-5

Alexander, Gary Wayne
75Lafay
76Phoen
77Phoen
77T-476R
78OPC-72
78T-624
79Ho-57
79OPC-168
79T-332
80OPC-78
80T-141
81D-200
81F-398
81T-416
81T/Tr-729
82F-475
82T-11

Alexander, Grover C.
14CJ-37
15CJ-37
21Exh-2
25Exh-18
27Exh-29
28Exh-29
29Exh/4-15
40PB-119
48Exh/HOF
48Swell-11
49Leaf/Prem-1
50Call
51T/CM
60Exh/HOF-1
60F-5
61F-2
61GP-2
63Bz/ATG-29
69Bz-2
69Bz/Sm
72F/FFeat-13
72Laugh/GF-41
80Cram/Leg-124
80Laugh/3/4/5-8
80Laugh/FFeat-40
80SSPC/HOF
83D/HOF-23
85Woolwth-2
86Conlon/1-3
87Conlon/2-4
88Conlon/3-2
89HOF/St-72
BF2-81
D327
D328-2
D329-4
D350/2-4
E120
E121/120
E121/80
E122
E126-13
E135-2
E210-44
E220
L1-114
M101/4-4
M101/5-4
R332-19
R332-48
S81-89
T222
V100
V61-69
W501-59
W502-44
W512-2
W514-65
W515-49
W516-9
W572
W573
W575
WG5-1
WG6-1

Alexander, Hugh
No Cards.

Alexander, Jon
88BBCity/Star-3
89BBCity/Star-3

Alexander, Manny
89Bluef/Star-2

Alexander, Matthew
(Matt)
76OPC-382
76SSPC-501
76T-382
77T-644
78T-102
81Portl-4
81T-68
82T-528

Alexander, Pat
78Cedar
81Shrev-23

Alexander, P.
N172

Alexander, Rob
88Madis-1
89Modesto/Cal-270
89Modesto/Ch-7

Alexander, Robert S.
52Park-63
53Exh/Can-34
55Esskay

Alexander, Roberto
82VeroB-1
84Cram/PCL-166

Alexander, Roger
79Richm-12

Alexander, Tim
80Ander-6
83Durhm-27
84Durhm-10

Alexander, Tommy
87Wichi-3
88Jaxvl/Best-9
88Jaxvl/Pro-982

Alexander, Walter E.
(Walt)
D328-3
E135-3

Alexander, William H.
(Nin)
No Cards.

Aleys, Maximo
89Everett/Star-1

Alfaro, Flavio
85Durhm-18
85T-391

Alfaro, Jesus
80Wichi-14
84CharO-19
86ElPas-3
87ElPas-15
87TexLgAS-30
88MidldA/GS-19
89ElPas/GS-20

Alfaro, Jose
74Cedar
75Dubuq

Alfonso, Carlos
75Iowa/TCMA-1
76Indianap-24
82AubAs-18
86Tucso-2MG

Alfonso, Edgar
86QuadC-1
87PalmSp-20
88PalmSp/Cal-96
88QuadC/GS-19
89PalmSp/Cal-44
89PalmSp/Pro-464

Alfonso, Ossie
84Visal-6
85Orlan-14

Alfredson, Tom
86QuadC-2
87PalmSp-19
88MidldA/GS-15
89MidldA/GS-4

Alicea, Edwin
89Greenv/Pro-1156
89Greenv/Star-1
89Greenvl/Best-6

Alicea, Luis
85Anchora-1
86Erie-1
87ArkTr-16
88D/Rook-52
88F/U-U116
88Louvl-7
88Louvl/CMC-20
88Louvl/Pro-436
88Score/Tr-98T
88Smok/Card-24
88T/Tr-3T
89D-466
89F-443
89Louvl-8
89Louvl/CMC-14
89Louvl/Pro-1263
89Panini/St-175
89RedFoley/St-2
89Score-231
89T-261TL
89T-588
89T/St-37
89UD-281

Alicea, Miguel
80Penin/B-4
80Penin/C-6
85Beloi-24
87CharO/WBTV-16
88Edmon/CMC-11
88Edmon/Pro-582
89PalmSp/Cal-55

Allaire, Karl
86ColumAst-2
87ColAst/Pro-14
87ColumAst-14
88Tucso-1
88Tucso/CMC-17
88Tucso/Pro-167

Allanson, Andy
84BuffB-7
85Water-24
86D/Rook-43
86F/Up-U2
86OhHenry-6
86T/Tr-1T
87BuffB-3
87D-95
87F-241
87Gator-6
87Leaf-102
87T-436
87T/GlossRk-1
87T/St-311
87ToysRUs-1
88D-465
88D/Best-5
88F/U-U21
88Gator-6
88Score-586
88T-728
88T/Big-231
89B-83
89D-138
89F-396
89OPC-283
89Panini/St-323
89Score-46
89T-283
89T/Big-311
89T/St-207
89UD-217
90F-483
90Score-452
90T-514
90UD-590

Allard, Brian M.
77Ashev
79Tucso-4
80Charl-5
80T-673R
81Spoka-10
82T-283
83SLCty-6
84Cram/PCL-171
85IntLgAS-43
85Maine-30
86Watlo-1CO
87Wmspt-16
88EastLAS/Pro-50
88Wmspt/Pro-1311
89Keno/Pro-1080

Allcott, Charles
N172

Allen, Bernard Keith
(Bernie)
61Clover-1
62T-596R
63J-2
63P-2
63T-427
64T-455
65OPC-237
65T-237
66T-327
67OPC-118
67T-118
68T-548
69MB-5
69MLB/St-100
69OPC-27
69T-27
69T/St-231
70MLB/St-277
70T-577
71MLB/St-529
71OPC-427
71T-427
72MB-6
72T-644
73OPC-293
73T-293

Allen, Bob
88CapeCod/Sum-157

Allen, Dave
88Batav/Pro-1684

Allen, Edward
83Butte-23
83CharR-10

Allen, Ethan Nathan
(Ethan)
33G-46
34DS-92
35BU-76
35G-1E
35G-3C
35G-5C
35G-6C
R314
R316
V353-46

Allen, Fletcher M.
(Sled)
No Cards.

Allen, Frank Leon
No Cards.

Allen, Greg
78Wisco

Allen, Harold
88Ashvl/Pro-1060
89Osceola/Star-1

Allen, Harold Andrew
(Hank)
67T-569R
68T-426
69MB-6
69T-623
70OPC-14
70T-14
71MLB/St-3
72MB-7

Allen, Hezekiah
No Cards.

Allen, Horace Tanner
No Cards.

Allen, Cyrus Alban
(Jack)
No Cards.

Allen, James
(Jim)
82QuadC-17
83QuadC-18

Allen, James Bradley
(Jamie)
80LynnS-18
81Spoka-31
82SLCty-2
84Cram/PCL-182
84D-267
84F-604
84Nes/792-744
84T-744
84T/St-350

Allen, Jesse Hall
(Pete)
No Cards.

Allen, John Marshall
No Cards.

Allen, John Thomas
(Johnny)
32Orbit/num-103
34G-42
35G-8E
35G-9E
37OPC-122
39Wheat-2
R312
V300
V354-96
W753

Allen, Kim Bryant
(Kim)
75QuadC
78Cr/PCL-15
80Spoka-19
81F-612
81Spoka-27

Allen, Larry
86Penin-2
87CharWh-11

Allen, Lloyd Cecil
71OPC-152R
71T-152R
72OPC-102
72T-102

730PC-267
73T-267
740PC-539
74T-539
76SSPC-140
Allen, Mike
80Buffa-11
80Wichi-13
Allen, Myron Smith
N172
Allen, Neil
78Tidew
80T-94
81Coke
81D-276
81F-322
81F/St-84
810PC-322
81T-322
81T/HT
81T/St-198
82D-506
82F-520
82K-20
820PC-205
82T-205
82T/St-66
83D-98
83F-536
83K-34
830PC-268
83T-575
83T/St-265
83T/X-1
84D-109
84F-318
84Jacks/Smok-1
84Nes/792-435
840PC-183
84T-435
84T/St-147
85D-205
85F-219
850PC-234
85T-731
85T/St-144
86Coke/WS-33
86D-610
86F-98
86F/Up-U3
86T-663
86T/Tr-2T
87Coke/WS-19
87D-507
87F-484
870PC-113
87RedFoley/St-93
87T-113
87T/St-292
88D-597
88T-384
89ColrSp/CMC-6
89D-196
89F-250
89Score-375
89T-61
89UD-567
Allen, Newt
78Laugh/Black-3
Allen, Paul
89Well/Puc-32
Allen, Richard A.
(Richie)
64T-243R
65OldLond-2
65T-460
65T/E-36
65T/trans
65T/trans-38
66Bz-4
660PC-80
66T-80
66T/RO-74
67Bz-4
67T-242LL
67T-244LL
67T-309
67T-450
67T/Test/SU-18
68Bz-14
68Coke
68T-225
68T/G-23
68T/Post-15
69Citgo-17
69MB-7
69MLB/St-172
69MLBPA/Pin-33
69NTF
690PC-6LL
690PC/DE-1
69T-350
69T-6LL
69T/DE-26
69T/decal
69T/S-53
69T/St-71
69Trans-57
70K-33
70MLB/St-133
700PC-40
70T-40
70T/SO
71Bz/Test-44
71K-57
71MLB/St-97
710PC-650
71T-650
71T/S-40
71T/tatt-7
72MB-8
720PC-240
72T-240
73K-26
730PC-310
730PC-62LL
730PC-63LL
73T-310
73T-62LL
73T-63LL
73T/Comics-2
73T/Lids-2
73T/PinUps-2
74K-33
740PC-332AS
740PC-70
74T-332M
74T-70
74T/DE-39
74T/Puzzles-2
74T/St-151
75K-42
750PC-210M
750PC-307LL
750PC-400
75T-210MV
75T-307LL
75T-400
75T/M-210MV
75T/M-307LL
75T/M-400
760PC-455
76SSPC-473
76T-455
82KMart-21
PM10/L-1
Allen, Rick
89Bill/Pro-2045
Allen, Robert
(Bob)
No Cards.
Allen, Robert Earl
No Cards.
Allen, Robert Gilman
(Bob)
N172
Allen, Robert Gray
(Bob)
61T-452
62T-543
63Sugar-33
63T-266
64T-209
66T-538
670PC-24
67T-24
680PC-176
68T-176
Allen, Robert
(Robbie)
82VeroB-15
84Cram/PCL-156
86ElPas-2
87MidldA-23
Allen, Roderick B.
(Rod)
79Knoxv/TCMA-24
82SLCty-3
83SLCty-14
85RochR-10
87BuffB-24
88ColSp/CMC-19
88ColSp/Pro-1545
89F-397
Allen, Ronald F.
(Ron)
No Cards.
Allen, Scott
88BurlR/Pro-1784
Allen, Shane
81QuadC-7
Allen, Sterling
76Baton
Allen, Steve
88Butte-26
89Gasto/Pro-1022
89Gasto/Star-1
Allenson, Gary M.
80T-376
81D-455
81T-128
82Coke/BOS
82D-386
82F-287
820PC-273
82T-686
83D-30
83F-177
83T-472
84D-335
84F-388
84Nes/792-56
840PC-56
84T-56
85F-148
85Syrac-3
85T-259
87Oneon-24
88Oneon/Pro-2064
89Lynch/Star-23
Allenson, Kelvin
88Oneon/Pro-2064
Alley, Leonard Eugene
(Gene)
64T-509R
650PC-121
65T-121
66EH-14
66T-336
67Kahn
67T-283
67T/Test/PP-1
68Kahn
68KDKA-22
680PC-53
68T-368AS
68T-53
68T/G-25
69MB-8
69MLB/St-181
69T-436
69T/St-81
70MLB/St-97
70T-566
71MLB/St-193
710PC-416
71T-416
72MB-9
720PC-286
72T-286
730PC-635
73T-635
Alleyne, Isaac
88James/Pro-1903
Allie, Gair R.
54T-179
55T-59
55T/DH-71
Allietta, Robert G.
(Bob)
760PC-623
76T-623
79Tacom-15
80Tacom-11
Allinger, Bob
83Miami-21
Allison, Arthur A.
(Art)
No Cards.
Allison, Bubba
86Cram/PCL-151
Allison, Dana
89Medford/Best-28
Allison, Douglas L.
(Doug)
No Cards.
Allison, Jamie
88CalLgAS-21
88Reno/Cal-279
89Kinston/Star-1
Allison, Jeff
87Idaho-5
88Mia/Star-1
88SLCty-9
Allison, Jim
83TriCit-12
85BurlR-27
85Utica-1
86DayBe-1
Allison, Mack P.
No Cards.
Allison, Milo Henry
No Cards.
Allison, William R.
(Bob)
59HRDerby-2
59T-116
60Armour-2
60NuCard-66
60T-320
60T/tatt
60T/tatt-2
61NuCard-466
61P-91
61T-355
61T/St-176
62Bz
62J-83
62P-83
62P/Can-83
62Salada-22
62Shirriff-22
62T-180
62T/St-73
63J-7
63P-7
63T-75
64T-10LL
64T-290
64T/Coins-19
64Wheat/St-2
65OldLond-21
650PC-180
65T-180
65T/E-38
65T/trans
65T/trans-1
66T-345
670PC-194
67T-194
67T-334M
68Coke
68T-335
69MB-9
69MLB/St-64
690PC-30
69T-30
69T/St-191
70MLB/St-229
70T-635
72MB-10
78TCMA-26
83MLBPA/Pin-1
89Pac/Leg-165
89Swell-27
Allred, Beau
88CLAS/Star-23
88Kinston/Star-1
89Canton/Best-4
89Canton/Pro-1302
89Canton/Star-1
90D-691
90T-419
Almada, Baldomero M.
(Mel)
35BU-147
39PB-43
40Hughes-1
40PB-71
R313
R314
Almante, Tom
86ArkTr-1
Almaraz, Johnny
88Bill/Pro-1825
89Greens/Pro-431
Almeida, Rafael D.
T207
Almon, William F.
(Bill)
74Hawai
77T-490R
78T-392
79K-53
79T-616
800PC-225
80T-436
81F-332
81T-163
81T/Tr-730
82D-637
82F-335
82F/St-185
820PC-119
82T-521
82T/St-167
83D-356
83F-228
830PC-362
83T-362
83T/X-2
84D-467
84F-436
84Moth/A's-11
84Nes/792-241
840PC-241
84T-241
84T/St-334
85D-589

85F-414
85F/Up-U2
85T-273FDP
85T-607
85T/Tr-2T
86D-479
86F-602
86OPC-48
86T-48
86T/St-131
87D-326
87F-601
87OPC-159
87T-447
87T/Tr-1T
88D-487
88T-787

Aloi, Dave
74Cedar
75Dubuq

Aloma, Luis
51B-231
52T-308
54B-134
54T-57

Alomar, Conde Santos
(Sandy)
65OPC-82R
65T-82R
66T-428
67T-561
68T-541
69JB
69T-283
69T/St-151
70MLB/St-169
70OPC-29
70T-29
71JB
71MLB/St-337
71OPC-745
71T-745
71T/Coins-28
72MB-11
72OPC-253
72T-253
73OPC-123
73T-123
74OPC-347
74T-347
74T/St-141
75OPC-266
75T-266
75T/M-266
76OPC-629
76SSPC-441
76T-269
77T-54
78BK/R-15
78T-533
79T-144
88Smok/Padres-3CO
89B-258M
89T-648M

Alomar, Rafael
61Union

Alomar, Roberto
87TexLgAS-8
87Wichi-4
88D-34RR
88D/Best-42
88D/Rook-35
88F/U-U122
88LasVeg/CMC-20
88LasVeg/Pro-231
88Leaf-34RR
88Score/Tr-105T
88Smok/Padres-2
88T/Tr-4T
89B-458
89Bimbo/Discs-12
89Class-127
89D-246
89D/Best-21
89F-299
89F-630M
89F/Superstar-1
89OPC-206
89Panini/St-191
89RedFoley/St-3
89Score-232
89Score/HotRk-72
89Score/YS/I-28
89Sf-20
89T-206
89T-231TL
89T/Big-102
89T/Gloss60-19
89T/JumboR-1
89T/St-104
89ToysRUs-1
89UD-471
90Class-61
90D-111
90F-149
90Score-12
90Sf-93
90T-517
90UD-346

Alomar, Santos Jr.
(Sandy)
86Beaum-1
87TexLgAS-10
87Wichi-5
88AAA/Pro-20
88LasVeg/CMC-22
88LasVeg/Pro-236
89AAA/Pro-6
89B-258M
89B-454
89Class-79
89D-28RR
89D/Rook-21
89F-300
89F-630M
89LasVeg/CMC-11
89LasVeg/Pro-7
89Panini/St-192
89Score-630M
89Score/YS/II-1
89Sf-223M
89UD-5
90D-30
90F-150
90Score-577
90T-353
90UD-655

Alonso, Julio
77Evansvl/TCMA-2

Alonzo, Ray
83Madis/LF-6

Alou, Felipe Rojas
59T-102
60L-6
60T-287
61T-565
62AmTract-52A
62AmTract-52B
62AmTract-52C
62J-133
62P-133
62P/Can-133
62Salada-130
62Shirriff-130
62T-133
62T/St-193
63J-107
63P-107
63T-270
64T-65
64T/Coins-11
64T/St-62
65T-383
66Kahn
66OPC-96
66T-96
67Kahn
67OPC/Pl-30
67T-240LL
67T-530
67T/Pl-30
68Coke
68Kahn
68OPC-55
68T-55
69MB-10
69MLB/St-110
69MLBPA/Pin-32
69OPC-2LL
69T-2LL
69T-300
69T/DE-17
69T/decal
69T/S-35
69T/St-2
69Trans-51
70MLB/St-253
70OPC-434
70T-434
71K-7
71MLB/St-505
71OPC-495
71T-495
71T/Coins-8
72MB-12
72OPC-263
72T-263
73OPC-650
73T-650
74OPC-485
74T-485
74T/Tr-485T
82D-650
82Wichi-2
84Moth/Giants-19
84Stuart-6CO
85Indianap-2MG
86WPalm-1MG
88FSLAS/Star-2CO
88Pac/Leg-58

Alou, Jesus M. R.
(Jesus)
64T-47R
65T-545
66T-242
66T/RO-3
67T-332
68Coke
68T-452
69MB-11
69MLB/St-136
69OPC-22
69T-22
69T/St-51
70MLB/St-37
70OPC-248
70T-248
71MLB/St-73
71OPC-337
71T-337
72MB-13
72T-716
73OPC-93
73T-93
74OPC-654
74T-654
75OPC-253
75T-253
75T/M-253
76OPC-468
76SSPC-538
76T-468
78BK/A-22
79T-107
80T-593

Alou, Jose
87BurlEx-10
88WPalm/Star-2
89WPalm/Star-1

Alou, Mateo Rojas
(Matty)
61T-327
62T-413
63Salada-25
63T-128
64T-204
65T-318
66EH-18
66OPC-94
66T-94
67Bz-47
67Kahn
67OPC-10
67OPC/Pl-29
67T-10
67T-240LL
67T/Pl-29
67T/Test/PP-2
67T/Test/PP-28
68Bz-2
68Kahn
68KDKA-18
68OPC-1LL
68T-1LL
68T-270
68T/G-1
69Kahn
69MB-12
69MLB/St-182
69OPC-2LL
69T-2LL
69T-490
69T/S-56
69T/St-82
69Trans-58
70K-28
70MLB/St-98
70OPC-30
70OPC-460AS
70T-30
70T-460AS
71K-53
71MLB/St-265
71OPC-720
71T-720
71T/Coins-47
72MB-14
72OPC-395
72T-395
73OPC-132
73T-132
74OPC-430
74T-430
78TCMA-75
88Pac/Leg-37

Alou, Moises
86Watertn-2
87Watertn-27
88Aug/Pro-360
89Salem/Star-1
89Star/Wax-93
90F-650M
90Score-592

Alperman, Charles A.
(Whitey)
C46-7
E270/2
T204
T206

Alpert, George
81Batav-25
82Watlo/B-20
82Watlo/C-27

Alston, Thomas E.
(Tom)
53Mother-24
54Hunter
55B-257
55Hunter

Alston, Walter E.
52Park-66
53Exh/Can-61
55Gol/Dodg-1
56T-8
58T-314M
60BB-18
60Morrell
60T-212
61BB-24
61T-136
62BB-24
62T-217
63T-154
64T-101
65OPC-217MG
65T-217
66OPC-116MG
66T-116
67T-294
68T-472
69OPC-24MG
69T-24
70OPC-242MG
70T-242
71OPC-567MG
71T-567
72T-749
73OPC-569MG
73T-569MG
74OPC-144MG
74T-144MG
75OPC-361MG
75T-361MG
75T/M-361MG
76SSPC-90
76T-46MG
80Cram/Leg-14
87Smok/Dodg-1
88Smok/Dodg-1
89Smok/Dodg-1

Alston, Wendell
(Del)
78Cr/PCL-68
78T-710R
79T-54
79Tacom-19
80T-198
80Tacom-24
81D-322

Altamirano, Porfirio
80OkCty
81OkCty/TCMA-1
83F-153
83Portl-15
83T-432
84IowaC-23
84Nes/792-101
84T-101

Alten, Ernest M.
(Ernie)
No Cards.

Altenberger, Peter
88CapeCod/Sum-48

Altenburg, Jesse H.
No Cards.

Altizer, David Tildon
(Dave)
E254

Altman, George Lee
59T-512
60T-259
61P-195
61T-551
61T/St-1
62J-187
62P-187
62P/Can-187
62Salada-128
62Shirriff-128

62T-240
62T/bucks
62T/St-103
63P-171
63Salada-31
63T-171
63T-357
64Bz-23
64T-95
64T/St-69
64T/SU
65T-528
66OPC-146
66T-146
67OPC-87
67T-87

Altman, John
77Visal

Altobelli, Joseph S.
75IntAS/TCMA-16
77T-211MG
78T-256
79Pol/Giants-6CO
79T-356MG
80Colum-8
83T/X-3
84D-88
84F-643IA
84F/St-125MG
84Nes/792-21MG
84T-21
85T-574
85T/Gloss22-12MG
88Berg/Cubs-CO

Alton, George Wilson
No Cards.

Altrock, Nicholas
(Nick)
61F-3
87Conlon/2-8
88Conlon/5-1
E210-40
E254
R312/M
WG2-1

Alusik, George J.
62T-261
63T-51
64T-431

Alva, John
86Sumter-2
87Durhm-25
88Greenv/Best-6
89Greenv/Pro-1154
89Greenv/Star-2
89Greenvl/Best-7

Alvarado, Arnaldo
75Dubuq

Alvarado, Jose
85Tigres-15

Alvarado, Luis Cesar
70OPC-317R
70T-317R
71OPC-489
71T-489
72T-774
73OPC-627
73T-627
74OPC-462
74T-462

Alvarez, Alex
88CapeCod/Sum-7

Alvarez, Carmelo
82VeroB-16

Alvarez, Chris
86FSLAS-3
86FtLaud-1
87Albany-15
88Colum/CMC-24
88Colum/Pol-13
88Colum/Pro-323
89Colum/Pro-739

Alvarez, Clemente
88Utica/Puc-2
89SoBend/GS-30

Alvarez, David
89Elmir/Puc-1

Alvarez, Javier
89Eugene/Best-15

Alvarez, Jesus O.
(Orlando)
77SLCty

Alvarez, Jose
76Dubuq

Alvarez, Jose Lino
79Savan-12
81Richm-15
82Richm-1
83Richm-1
84Cram/PCL-51
88F/U-U70
88Richm/CMC-8
88Richm/Pro-12
89D-405
89F-585
89Panini/St-31
89T-253
89UD/Ext-734
90D-389
90F-574
90Score-148
90T-782
90UD-634

Alvarez, Mike
81Miami-11
82FtMyr-12
83Omaha-1
84Omaha-19
85FtMyr-27
86FtMyr-2
87AppFx-18
88Savan/Pro-353

Alvarez, Oswaldo
85Tigres-4

Alvarez, Oswaldo G.
(Ossie)
59T-504

Alvarez, Robbie
81Chatt-3
82Miami-12

Alvarez, Rogelio H.
63T-158R

Alvarez, Wilson
88Gasto/Pro-1017

Alvis, Andy
80Batav-20

Alvis, Dave
86Watlo-2
87Watlo-7

Alvis, Roy Maxwell
(Max)
63Sugar-14
63T-228R
64Kahn
64T-545
64T/Coins-48
64T/S-46
64T/St-7
64T/SU
64T/tatt
65Kahn
65OPC-185
65T-185
65T/E-3
65T/trans
65T/trans-2
66Kahn
66T-415
66T/RO-68
67Kahn
67T-520
67T/Test/SU-16
68Bz-9
68Kahn
68T-340
68T/Post-2
69Kahn
69MB-13
69MLB/St-37
69MLBPA/Pin-1
69OPC-145
69T-145
69T/St-161
70McDon-6
70MLB/St-193
70OPC-85
70T-85
72MB-15
78TCMA-83
Exh47

Alvord, William C.
(Billy)
N172

Alyea, Brant Jr.
88Gasto/Pro-1007
88SALAS/GS-16
89StLucie/Star-1

Alyea, Garrabrant R.
(Brant)
66OPC-11R
66T-11R
69OPC-48
69T-48
70OPC-303
70T-303
71MLB/St-457
71OPC-449
71T-449
72MB-16
72OPC-383
72T-383

Amador, Bruce
82Madis-30

Amalfitano, John J.
(Joey)
55B-269
55Gol/Giants-1
55T-144
60T-356
61T-87
62J-144
62P-144
62P/Can-144
62Salada-193
62Shirriff-193
62T-456
62T/St-123
63F-36
63T-199
64T-451
65T-402
73OPC-252CO
73T-252C
74OPC-78CO
74T-78C
76SSPC-629
78TCMA-96
81D-522
81T-676MG
89Smok/Ast-15

Aman, Kevan
77Wausa

Amante, Tom
87StPet-10

Amaral, Rich
86Pittsf-1
87Pittsf-22
88Pittsf/Pro-1362
89BirmB/Best-14
89BirmB/Pro-91

Amaras, Marcos
89Medford/Best-24

Amaro, Ruben
59T-178
61T-103
62J-194
62P-194
62P/Can-194
62Salada-163
62Shirriff-163
62T-284
62T/St-163
63F-50
63T-455
64T-432
65T-419
66OPC-186
66T-186
67T-358
68OPC-138
68T-138
69T-598
76OkCty
78TCMA-28
83Thorn-26C

Amaro, Ruben Jr.
88CalLgAS-32
88PalmSp/Cal-97
88PalmSp/Pro-1434
89Brist/Star-29
89QuadC/Best-30
89QuadC/GS-18

Amaya, Ben
86Chatt-1

Ambler, Wayne H.
39PB-117
41G-7

Ambos, Willie
88SLCty-13
89SanBern/Best-9
89SanBern/Cal-66

Ambrose, Mark
87ElPas-11
88ElPas/Best-15
89Stock/Best-10
89Stock/Cal-159
89Stock/Pro-377

Amelung, Edward
(Ed)
81VeroB-1
83Albuq-19
84Cram/PCL-163
85Cram/PCL-158
86Albuq-1
87Edmon-11
88SanDiegoSt-1

Amerson, Archie
78SnJos-21
79Toled-4

Ames, Doug
86Madis-1
86Madis/Pol-1

Ames, Ken
80Ander-10

Ames, Leon Kessling
(Red)
10Domino-1
11Helmar-120
12Sweet/Pin-106
D328-4
D329-5
D350/2-5
E104
E135-4
E254
E270/1
E270/2
E93
E96
M101/4-5
M101/5-5
M116
S74-79
T202
T205
T206
T213/blue
T215/blue
T215/brown
T3-77
W555
WG3-1

Amole, Morris George
(Doc)
No Cards.

Amor, Vincente A.
No Cards.

Amoros, Edmundo I.
(Sandy)
53Exh/Can-43
55Gol/Dodg-2
55T-75
55T/DH-54
56T-42
56T/Pin-49
57T-201
58T-93
60T-531
89Rini/Dodg-2
PM10/Sm-2

Anaya, Mike
89Star/Wax-22

Ancker, Walter
No Cards.

Anders, Scott
86Peoria-1

Andersen, Larry E.
75OkCty
78T-703R
79Tacom-4
80Port-23
80T-665R
82D-428
82T-52
83D-181
83F-470
83Portl-3
83T-234
85D-570
85F-244
85T-428
86D-355
86F-434
86T-183
87D-640
87F-49
87Moth/Ast-21
87Pol/Ast-1
87T-503
88D-332
88F-438
88Moth/Ast-21
88Pol/Ast-2
88Score-133
88T-342
89B-325
89D-359
89F-349
89Lennox/Ast-18
89Moth/Ast-20
89Score-523
89T-24
89UD-404
90D-359
90F-221
90Score-282
90UD-407

Andersh, Kevin
86Macon-2
89Aug/Pro-512

Anderson, Alfred W.
(Alf)
No Cards.

Anderson, Allan
83Wisco/LF-3
84Visal-20
85Toled-1
86D/Rook-3
86Toled-1
87D-368

87F-533
87Portl-4
87T-336
88F/U-U41
88Portl/Pro-654
88T-101
89B-149
89Class/Up/2-178
89D-419
89D/Best-270
89F-102
89F/LL-1
89OPC-20
89Panini/St-381
89Score-394
89Score/YS/I-34
89Sf-220
89T-672
89T/Mini-60
89UD-85
90D-64
90F-366
90Score-292
90Sf-59
90T-71
90UD-219

Anderson, Andy
88ElPas/Best-16
88Portl/CMC-1

Anderson, Andy Holm
52Park-17

Anderson, Arnold R.
(Red)
No Cards.

Anderson, Bernie
86Lakel-2
87Lakel-10
88GlenF/Pro-928
89London/Pro-1364

Anderson, Brady
85Elmir-2
86FSLAS-4
86WinHav-2
87NewBrit-7
88D/RedSox/Bk-NEW
88D/Rook-14
88Score/Tr-70T
88T/Tr-5T
89B-18
89D-519
89F-606
89French-9
89OPC-161
89Score-563
89Score/YS/I-26
89T-757
89T/JumboR-2
89T/UK-1
89ToysRUs-2
89UD-408
90D-638
90F-172
90Score-33
90T-598
90UD-290

Anderson, Dave
76Cedar
77Cedar

Anderson, David C.
(Dave)
82Albuq-14
84D-642
84Nes/792-376
84Pol/Dodg-10
84T-376
85D-275
85F-366
85T-654
86F-123
86OPC-29
86Pol/Dodg-10
86T-758
87F-436
87Moth/Dodg-17
87Pol/Dodg-4
87T-73
88D-475
88F-508
88Moth/Dodg-17
88OPC-203
88Panini/St-313
88Pol/Dodg-10
88Score-166
88T-456
89D-434
89F-53
89Moth/Dodg-17
89OPC-117
89Pol/Dodg-7
89Score-478
89T-117
89UD-89
90D-486
90Score-238
90T-248
90UD-510

Anderson, David S.
(Dave)
No Cards.

Anderson, Dwain C.
72OPC-268R
72T-268R
73OPC-241
73T-241

Anderson, Ed
88SLCty-30M

Anderson, Edward
76Dubuq
77Cocoa

Anderson, Edward John
(Goat)
No Cards.

Anderson, Eric
82AubAs-6

Anderson, Ferrell J.
No Cards.

Anderson, George A.J.
No Cards.

Anderson, George Lee
(Sparky)
59T-338
60L-125
60T-34
61BeeHive-1
70OPC-181MG
70T-181
71OPC-688MG
71T-688
72OPC-358MG
72T-358
73OPC-296MG
73T-296MG
74OPC-326MG
74T-326MG
75OPC-531MG
75T-531MG
75T/M-531MG
76SSPC-22
76T-104MG
77T-287MG
78T-401
79T-259MG
81D-370
81F-460
81T-666MG
82D-29
83D-533
83T-660
84Nes/792-259MG
84T-259
85F-628M
85F/St-125MG
85Seven-2MG
85T-307
85Wendy-1MG
86D/AAS-58MG
86T-411
86T/Gloss22-1MG
87T-218MG
88Pac/Leg-46
88Pep/T-11MG
88Pol/T-2MG
88T-14
89Mara/Tigers-11
89Pol/Tigers-MG
89T-193MG
90T-609MG

Anderson, Glen
86Cram/PCL-141

Anderson, Greg
76BurlB

Anderson, Harold
(Hal)
No Cards.

Anderson, Harry W.
57T-404
58T-171
59T-85
60T-285
61T-76
PM10/Sm-3

Anderson, James Lea
(Jim)
78Cr/PCL-93
79T-703R
80T-183
81D-165
81F-598
81Pol/Mariners-4
81T-613
82D-181
82F-503
82T-497
83Rangers-46
84Nes/792-353
84Rangers-14
84T-353
85OKCty-6
87Clint-5
88Clint/Pro-703
89Shreve/Pro-1835

Anderson, Jeff
86Penin-3

Anderson, Jesse
81AppFx-1
82AppFx-10
83Albany-1

Anderson, John
84Butte-2
88Martins/Star-1

Anderson, John C.
62T-266

Anderson, John Fred
(Fred)
D328-5
E135-5

Anderson, John Joseph
E107
T204
T206

Anderson, Karl Adam
(Bud)
79Spoka-20
79T-712R
81Chatt-25
82Charl-1
83T-367
83Wheat/Ind-1
84D-590
84F-533
84Maine-8
84Nes/792-497
84T-497

Anderson, Kent
86PalmSp-1
88Edmon/CMC-17
88Edmon/Pro-574
89Edmon/CMC-17
89T/Tr-3T
90D-490
90Score-412
90Score/100Ris-86
90T-16
90UD-691

Anderson, Lawrence D.
(Larry)
76OPC-593R
76SSPC-249
76T-593R
77T-487R

Anderson, Mat
89Bluef/Star-26

Anderson, Michael
87PalmSp-24

Anderson, Michael A.
(Mike)
72OPC-14R
72T-14R
73OPC-147
73T-147
74JP
74OPC-619
74T-619
75OPC-118
75T-118
75T/M-118
76OPC-527
76SSPC-469
76T-527
77T-72
78T-714
79T-102
80OkCty
80T-317
81Portl-5
85Louvl-29

Anderson, Mike
85LitFalls-1
86LitFalls-1
87Columbia-20
88PalmSp/Cal-98
88PalmSp/Pro-1438
89Greens/Pro-428
89Reno/Cal-239

Anderson, Mike
80BurlB-18
82Vanco-22
84Cram/PCL-46

Anderson, Norman C.
(Craig)
62T-593R
63T-59

Anderson, Richard A.
(Rick)
79Jacks-16
81Tidew-26
82Tidew-12
84Tidew-19
85IntLgAS-19
85Tidew-6
86Tidew-1
87F-2
87Omaha-22
87T-594
88Omaha/CMC-1
88Omaha/Pro-1512
89Score-441

Anderson, Richard Lee
(Rick)
76Shrev
77WHave
79Colum-21
80Spoka-20
81Spoka-28
81T-282R

Anderson, Robert Carl
(Bob)
58T-209
59T-447
60T-412
61T-283
61T/St-2
62T-557
63T-379

Anderson, Roy
85Madis-4
85Madis/Pol-1
86Modesto-1
86Modesto-2

Anderson, Scott
82Madis-10
85Tulsa-33
88OkCty/CMC-1
89Indi/CMC-6
89Indi/Pro-1234

Anderson, Steve
83Beloi/LF-12

Anderson, Tim
87Bakers-22

Anderson, Tom
78Watlo

Anderson, Varney S.
N172

Anderson, Walter Carl
No Cards.

Anderson, William
(Bill)
No Cards.

Anderson, William E.
(Bill)
No Cards.

Anderson, Wingo C.
(Wingo)
No Cards.

Andrade, Herberto
88Peoria/Ko-1
89CharWh/Best-13
89CharWh/Pro-1759

Andre, John Edward
No Cards.

Andres, Ernest Henry
(Ernie)
No Cards.

Andrews, Elbert D.
No Cards.

Andrews, Fred
76OkCty
78Tidew

Andrews, George E.
N162
N172
N284
N690
WG1-46

Andrews, Hubert Carl
(Hub)
No Cards.

Andrews, Ivy Paul
32Orbit/num-1
32Orbit/un-2
35BU-106
35BU-115M
36Exh/4-15
R300
R305
R313

Andrews, James Pratt
(Jim)
No Cards.

Andrews, Jeff
87PortChar-12
88Tulsa-9CO
89Tulsa/GS-3

Andrews, John
88SanDiegoSt-2

Andrews, John Richard
No Cards.

Andrews, Michael Jay
(Mike)
67T-314R

67T/Test/RedSox-7
68Coke
68T-502
69MB-14
69MLB/St-10
69OPC-52
69T-52
69T/St-131
70MLB/St-157
70OPC-406
70T-406
71OPC-191
71T-191
72MB-17
72OPC-361
72T-361
73OPC-42
73T-42

Andrews, Nathan H.
(Nate)
No Cards.

Andrews, Robert P.
(Rob)
75IntAS/TCMA-10
76OPC-568
76SSPC-54
76T-568
77T-209
78T-461
79Pol/Giants-21
79T-34
80T-279

Andrews, Stanley J.
(Stan)
41G-24

Andrews, William W.
(Wally)
N172

Andrus, William M.
(Bill)
No Cards.

Andrus, Frederick H.
(Fred)
No Cards.

Andrzejewski, Joe
89Helena/SP-1

Andujar, Joaquin
77T-67
78BK/A-7
78T-158
78T/Zest-1
79OPC-246
79T-471
80K-55
80OPC-324
80T-617
81D-381
81F/St-48
81OPC-329
81T/Tr-731
82D-607
82F-110
82T-533
83D-316
83D/AAS-27
83F-1
83OPC-228
83T-228
83T-561
83T/St-179
84D-181
84F-319
84FunFood/Pin-90
84Nes/792-785
84OPC-371
84T-785
85D-13
85D-449
85D/DKsuper-13
85F-220
85F/St-85
85Leaf-13DK
85OPC-231
85Seven-6C
85T-655
85T/Gloss40-12
85T/St-136
85T/Super-38
86D-231
86F-26
86F/LimEd-2
86F/Up-U4
86KAS/Disc-11
86Moth/A's-4
86Moth/Ast-15
86OPC-150
86S-101
86S-133M
86S-185M
86T-150
86T/Mini-58
86T/St-44
86T/Tr-3T
87D-548
87F-385
87F/Hottest-1
87F/Mini-2
87Leaf-162
87OPC-284
87RedFoley/St-11
87Smok/A's-1
87T-775
87T/St-172
88Moth/Ast-26
88Pol/Ast-3
88Score-193
88T-47
89Score-472
89UD-79

Angelini, Norman S.
(Norm)
73OPC-616R
73T-616R

Angelo, Mark
83Erie-12
84Savan-11

Angero, Jose
87Omaha-2

Angiero, Jose
88BBCity/Star-4
89BBCity/Star-4

Angley, Thomas S.
(Tom)
No Cards.

Anglin, Russ
83Ander-25

Angulo, Ken
83Redwd-2
85MidldA-15

Anicich, Mike
82Jacks-14
82Tidew-25
83MidldC-20

Ankenman, Fred N.
(Pat)
No Cards.

Annee, Tim
89Medford/Best-23

Annis, William P.
(Bill)
N172

Ansley, Willie
89Ashvl/Pro-950
89B-332
89T-607FDP

Anson, Adrian C.
(Cap)
50Callahan
60Exh/HOF-2
60F-44
61F-4
63Bz/ATG-39
69Bz/Sm
75F/Pion-1
80SSPC/HOF
89HOF/St-5
E223
N162
N172
N28
N284
N300/unif
WG1-10

Anthony, Andy
86VeroB-1

Anthony, Dane
82Chatt-8
83Watlo/LF-21

Anthony, Eric
89ColMud/Best-1
89ColMud/Pro-134
89ColMud/Star-2
89SLAS-3
89Star/Wax-1
90Class-70
90D-34
90F-222
90Score-584
90Score/100Ris-45
90Sf-179
90T-608
90UD-28

Anthony, Lee
49B/PCL-1

Anthony, Paul
77Salem

Antigua, Felix
89Aug/Pro-497
89Princet/Star-2

Antolick, Joseph
(Joe)
No Cards.

Antonelli, John A.
(Johnny)
49Eureka-3
50B-74
51B-243
52T-140
53JC-2
53T-106
54B-208
54NYJour
54RM-NL21
54T-119
55Armour-1
55B-124
55Gol/Giants-2
55RM-NL13
56T-138
57T-105
58Hires-50
58Hires/T
58SFCall
58T-152
59Armour-2
59T-377
60Bz-35
60T-572AS
60T-80
60T/tatt
60T/tatt-3
61P-142
61T-115
61T/St-132
83Beloi/LF-6
84Moth/Giants-13
Exh47
PM10/Sm-4
PM10/Sm-5
Rawl

Antonelli, John L.
No Cards.

Antonello, William J.
(Bill)
53T-272
72T/Test-5

Antunez, Martin
82Beloi-23

Anyzeski, Fred
75AppFx

Aparicio, Luis E.
56T-292
56YellBase/Pin-3
57T-7
58T-483AS
58T-85
59T-310
59T-408
59T-560AS
60Bz-22
60L-1
60T-240
60T-559AS
61Bz-35
61P-19
61T-440
61T-574AS
61T/St-120
62Bz
62Exh
62J-49
62P-49
62P/Can-49
62Salada-71
62Shirriff-71
62T-325
62T-469AS
62T/St-22
63Exh
63J-37
63P-37
63Salada-50
63T-205
63T/SO
64T-540
64T/Coins-127AS
64T/Coins-31
64T/S-39
64Wheat/St-3
65T-410
65T/trans
65T/trans-3
66OPC-90
66T-90
67OPC-60
67T-60
68T-310
69Kelly/Pin-1
69MB-15
69MLB/St-28
69MLBPA/Pin-2
69OPC-75
69OPC/DE-2
69T-75
69T/DE-6
69T/decal
69T/S-10
69T/St-152
69Trans-24
70K-22
70MLB/St-181
70OPC-315
70T-315
70T/S-3
70T/SO
71Bz
71Bz/Test-8
71K-19
71MD
71MLB/St-313
71MLB/St-554
71OPC-740
71T-740
71T/Coins-16
71T/GM-51
71T/S-23
71T/tatt-6
72MB-18
72OPC-313
72OPC-314IA
72T-313
72T-314A
72T/Cloth-2IA
73OPC-165
73T-165
74OPC-61
74T-61
74T/St-131
78TCMA-250
84TrueVal/WS-2
84West/1-2
86S/Dec-37M
87Nestle/DT-15
88Pac/Leg-91
89HOF/St-18
Exh47

Apodaca, Robert John
(Bob)
74OPC-608R
74T-608R
75OPC-659
75T-659
75T/M-659
76OPC-16
76SSPC-548
76T-16
77T-225
78T-592
79OPC-98
79T-197
80T-633
82Jacks-23
86Columbia-1CO
87Columbia-2
89Jacks/GS-21

Aponte, Edwin
81LynnS-15
83Watlo/LF-2
84BuffB-19

Aponte, Luis Eduardo
81Pawtu-8
83D-109
83F-178
83T-577
84D-371
84F-389
84F/X-2
84Nes/792-187
84T-187
84T/X-2
84Wheat/Ind-38
85F-437

Aponte, Rick
78DaytB
87AubAs-19

Appier, Kevin
88BBCity/Star-5
89F/Up-35
89Omaha/CMC-4
89Omaha/Pro-1720
90F-100
90Score-625
90Score/100Ris-13
90T-167
90UD-102

Applegate, Fred
No Cards.

Applegate, Russ
85Madis-5
85Madis/Pol-2
86Modesto-3

Appleton, Edward Sam
(Ed)
D328-6
E135-6

Appleton, Peter W.
(Pete)
33G-83
39PB-137
40PB-128

Appling, Lucas B.
(Luke)
31Exh/4-19
34DS-95
34Exh/4-10
34G-27
35BU-124
35G-1I
35G-2F
35G-6F
35G-7F
36Exh/4-10
36Wheat-3
37Exh/4-10
37OPC-115
38Exh/4-10
39Exh
40Wheat-12
41DP-70
48L-59
49B-175
49Royal-16
50B-37
60F-27
60T-461C
80Cram/Leg-22
80SSPC/HOF
83D/HOF-8
84Pol/Atl-55C
88Conlon/AmAS-1
88Pac/Leg-4
89Swell-30
Exh47
PR1-1
R303/A
R303/B
R314
R326-7A
R326-7B
R342-7
R346-10
V300
V354-84
V355-113
WG8-1
Aquedo, Vasquez
87FtMyr-16
Aquino, Luis
86Syrac-2
87D-655
87OPC-301
87Syrac-10
87Syrac/TCMA-1
87T-301
88Omaha/CMC-2
88Omaha/Pro-1520
89D-534
89F-275
89T-266
90D-179
90F-101
90Score-432
90T-707
90UD-274
Aquino, Pedro
87Spoka-20
88Spoka/Pro-1929
Aragon, Angel V. Sr.
No Cards.
Aragon, Angel V. Jr.
(Jack)
No Cards.
Aragon, Joey
86Visal-2
87Visal-19
88Orlan/Best-11
Aragon, Reno
76Dubuq
77Cocoa
Aragon, Steve
82Wisco-23
83Visal/LF-3
84Visal-24
85Orlan-1
86Orlan-1
Arangure, Maurillo
85Tigres-3
Aranzamendi, Jorge
77StPet
79ArkTr-12
80ArkTr-3
81ArkTr-8
82ArkTr-24
83ArkTr-24
Araujo, Andy
86NewBrit-1
87Pawtu-14
87Pawtu/TCMA-1
88Pawtu/CMC-5
88Pawtu/Pro-446
89Pawtu/CMC-8
89Pawtu/Dunkin-23
89Pawtu/Pro-679
Archdeacon, Maurice
No Cards.
Archer, James Peter
(Jimmy)
09Buster/Pin-1
10Domino-2
11Helmar-90
12Sweet/Pin-79A
12Sweet/Pin-79B
14CJ-64
15CJ-64
BF2-62
D328-7
D329-6
D350/2-6
E135-7
E224
E254
E90/3
E91
M101/4-6
M101/5-6
M116
PM1-1
T202
T204
T205
T222
WG4-1
Archer, James William
(Jim)
61T-552
62J-98
62P-98
62Salada-75
62Shirriff-75
62T-433
62T/bucks
62T/St-52
Archibald, Dan
88James/Pro-1920
89James/Pro-2142
Archibald, Jaime
86Columbia-2
87Lynch-9
Archie, George Albert
No Cards.
Arcia, Jose R. Orta
68T-258R
69MB-16
69T-473
69T/St-91
70T-587
71MLB/St-217
71OPC-134
71T-134
72MB-19
73OPC-466
73T-466
Ard, Johnny
89B-153
89Visal/Cal-96
89Visal/Pro-1427
Ardell, Daniel Miers
(Dan)
No Cards.
Ardizoia, Rinaldo J.
(Rugger)
46Remar-20
Ardner, Joseph
N172
Arellanes, Frank J.
E96
M116
T204
T206
Arena, Rich
89Oneon/Pro-2120
Arendas, Dan
87FtLaud-13
88FtLaud/Star-1
Arendas, David
88CapeCod/Sum-100
Arft, Henry Irven
(Hank)
49B-139
51B-173
52B-229
52T-284
53Mother-26
Argo, Billy
88Bakers/Cal-244
89VeroB/Star-1
Arguelles, Fernando
89Salem/Star-2
Arias, Alex
88CharWh/Best-9
88SALAS/GS-13
89Peoria/Ko-17
Arias, Francisco
88Poca/Pro-2078
Arias, Juan
78Salem
Arias, Pedro
88BurlR/Pro-1787
Arias, Rodolfo M.
(Rudy)
59T-537
Arias, Tony
85Madis/Pol-3
86Madis-2
86Madis/Pol-2
88Modesto-19
Arigoni, Scott
82ArkTr-1
83Sprin/LF-9
Ariola, Anthony
88SoOreg/Pro-1696
89Madis/Star-2
89Star/Wax-64
Arlas, Antonio
85Madis-6
Arlett, Russell Loris
(Buzz)
28Exh/PCL-1
31Exh/4-11
WG7-1
Arlich, Donald Louis
(Don)
No Cards.
Arlin, Stephen Ralph
(Steve)
72OPC-78
72T-78
73OPC-294
73T-294
74OPC-406
74T-406
75OPC-159
75T-159
75T/M-159
Arline, James
78Richm
79Richm-23
Armas, Antonio Rafael
(Tony)
77T-492R
78T-298
79T-507
80T-391
81D-239
81Drake-30
81F-575
81F/St-5
81OPC-151
81Sqt-24
81T-629
81T/SO-6
81T/St-116
82D-365
82Drake-1
82F-85
82F/St-128
82Granny
82K-35
82OPC-60
82T-162LL
82T-60
82T/St-224
82T/St-4LL
83D-71
83F-513
83OPC-353
83T-1M
83T-435
83T/St-108
83T/St-191
83T/St-192
83T/X-4
84D-294
84F-390
84F/St-21
84FunFood/Pin-24
84Nes/792-105
84OPC-105
84T-105
84T/Gloss40-20
84T/St-218
85D-249
85Drake-1
85F-149
85F/St-12
85F/St-28
85Leaf-112
85OPC-394
85T-707AS
85T-785
85T/Gloss40-18
85T/St-194
85T/St-209
85T/St-95
85T/Super-10
86D-127
86D-5
86D/DKsuper-5
86F-339
86Leaf-5DK
86OPC-255
86S-140M
86S-61M
86T-255
86T/St-254
86Woolwth-1
87D-498
87F-26
87Moth/A's-21
87OPC-174
87T-535
87T/Board-15
88F-484
88Score-487
88Smok/Angels-5
88T-761
89B-51
89D-580
89F-467
89Panini/St-295
89Score-182
89T-332
89T/Big-99
89UD-212
90D-525
90F-126
90Score-378
90T-603
90UD-58
Armbrister, Edison R.
(Ed)
72OPC-524R
72T-524R
74OPC-601R
74T-601R
75OPC-622R
75T-622R
75T/M-622R
76OPC-652
76SSPC-42
76T-652
77T-203
78Indianap-8
78T-556
Armbrust, Orville M.
No Cards.
Armbruster, Charles
No Cards.
Armbruster, Herman
(Harry)
T206
Armer, Rick
77Wausa
Armstrong, George N.
No Cards.
Armstrong, Howard E.
No Cards.
Armstrong, Jack
88Kahn/Reds-40
88Nashvl/CMC-1
88Nashvl/Pro-484
88Score/Tr-78T
88T/Tr-6T
89Class-97
89D-493
89Panini/St-63
89Score-462
89Score/HotRk-99
89T-317
89UD-257
90D-544
90F-412
90T-642
90UD-684
Armstrong, Kevin
85LitFalls-2
86Columbia-3
87Wichi-2
88River/Cal-206
89SnAnt/Best-6
Armstrong, Michael D.
(Mike)
80Hawai-16
81F-503
82Omaha-1
82T-731
83F-105
83T-219
84D-217
84F-342
84Nes/792-417
84T-417
84T/X-3
85D-602
85F-120
85T-612
86Colum-1
86Colum/Pol-1
87Colum-25
87Colum/Pol-1

Armstrong, William
83Evans-23tr
84Evans-20tr
Arndt, Harry J.
T206
Arndt, Larry
86Madis-3
86Madis/Pol-3
89Tacom/CMC-22
89Tacom/Pro-1557
Arnerich, Ken
82QuadC-18
Arnett, Curt
74Gasto
Arney, Jeff
82Wisco-25
83Visal/LF-2
85Water-14
86Water-1
Arnold, Bryan
88Watertn/Puc-14
Arnold, Chris
72OPC-232R
72T-232R
73OPC-584
73T-584
74OPC-432
74T-432
76SSPC-99
77Phoen
77T-591
Arnold, Gary
88Geneva/Pro-1636
Arnold, Greg
89Pulas/Pro-1912
Arnold, Jeff
84Newar-25
Arnold, Ron
84Albany-2
84Cram/PCL-75
Arnold, Scott
86FSLAS-5
86StPet-2
87ArkTr-13
87TexLgAS-21
88Louvl-8
88TexLgAS/GS-20
89Louvl-9
89Louvl/CMC-2
89Louvl/Pro-1248
Arnold, Sheila
88Geneva/Pro-1660
Arnold, Tim
86FSLAS-6
86WPalm-2
87Jaxvl-2
88Visal/Cal-149
88Visal/Pro-97
89Orlan/Best-8
89Orlan/Pro-1353
Arnold, Tony
84CharO-26
85CharO-8
86RochR-1
88Albuq/CMC-5
88Albuq/Pro-261
89SnAnt/Best-5
Arnovich, Morris
(Morrie)
38Exh/4-6
39PB-46
40PB-97
40Wheat-4
41DP-139
41G-25
41G-25
41PB-57
W711/2
Arnsberg, Brad
84Greens-10
85Albany-1
86Colum-2
86Colum/Pol-2
87Colum-28
87Colum/Pol-2
87Colum/TCMA-1
88F-202
88T-159
89Moth/R-15
89Smok/R-2
90Score/100Ris-72
Arnsberg, Tim
86Ashvl-1
87Osceola-26
Arntzen, Orie Edgar
No Cards.
Arola, Bruce
88Madis-2
89Boise/Pro-1996
Arrigo, Gerald W.
(Jerry)
64T-516R
65OPC-39
65T-39
66T-357
67T-488
68Kahn
68T-302
69Kahn
69OPC-213
69T-213
69T/St-22
70OPC-274
70T-274
72MB-20
78TCMA-64
78TCMA-86
Arrington, Sam
82Amari-23
82Orlan-23
83Visal/LF-4
Arrington, Tom
86BurlEx-1
Arrington, Warren
88Peoria/Ko-2
89Peoria/Ko-23
Arroyd, Freddie
86SanJose-1
Arroyo, Carlos R.
79OkCty
80OkCty
81OkCty/TCMA-2
86Clearw-1CO
87Clearw-15
88Readg/Pro-888
Arroyo, Felipe
80Ander-11
Arroyo, Fernando
76OPC-614
76T-614
78T-607
81T-408
82D-177
82F-546
82T-18
82T-396TL
Arroyo, Hector
81CharR-2
Arroyo, Luis Enrique
56T-64
56T/Pin-45
57T-394
61T-142
61T/St-188
62J-12
62P-12
62P/Can-12
62T-455
63T-569
78TCMA-258
PM10/L-2
Arroyo, Rudolph Jr.
(Rudy)
No Cards.
Arsenault, Ed
75SnAnt
76Wmspt
Arundel, Harry
No Cards.
Arundel, John Thomas
(Tug)
N172
N284
Arvesen, Scott
89Well/Puc-2
Arzola, Richard
86StPet-3
Asadoor, Randy
84Tulsa-18
85Cram/PCL-116
86LasVegas-1
87D-574
87F-650M
87LasVegas-7
87S-158M
Asbe, Daryl
86BurlEx-2
Asbell, Frank
40Hughes-2AS
Asbell, James Marion
(Jim)
No Cards.
Asbell, John
81Watlo-5
Asbjornson, Robert A.
(Asby)
No Cards.
Ascencio, Juan
86Cram/PCL-152
Ash, Kenneth Lowther
(Ken)
No Cards.
Ashburn, Don Richard
(Richie)
49B-214
49Eureka-127
49Lummis
50B-84
51B-186
51BR-A9
51T/BB-3
52B-53
52BR
52Dix
52RM-NL2
52StarCal/L-77A
52T-216
53B/Col-10
53Dix
53NB
53RM-NL3
54B-15
54Dix
54RH
54RM-NL1
54T-45
55B-130
55RFG-22
55RM-NL1
56T-120
56YellBase/Pin-4
57Swift-17
57T-70
58Hires-10
58T-230
59Armour-3
59Bz
59T-300
59T-317M
60Bz-24
60MacGregor-2
60T-305
60T/tatt
60T/tatt-4
60T/tatt-87
61P-192
61T-88
61T/St-3
62J-186
62P-186
62P/Can-186
62Salada-171
62Shirriff-171
62T-213
62T/bucks
63J-197
63P-197
63Salada-27
63T-135
63T/SO
80Cram/Leg-94
85West/2-38
88Pac/Leg-8
89B-I1
89Swell-85
Exh47
PM10/Sm-6
R423-1
Rawl
Ashby, Alan Dean
76OPC-209
76SSPC-514
76T-209
77Ho-124
77OPC-148
77T-564
77T/CS-1
78OPC-76
78T-319
79Ho-142
79OPC-14
79T-36
80OPC-105
80T-187
81Coke
81D-259
81F-64
81OPC-146
81T-696
82D-317
82F-212
82OPC-184
82T-433
82T/St-48
83D-144
83F-445
83OPC-84
83T-774
83T/St-241
84D-539
84F-220
84Moth/Ast-3
84Nes/792-217
84OPC-217
84T-217
84T/St-72
85D-283
85F-343
85Moth/Ast-13
85OPC-29
85T-564
86D-405
86F-292
86OPC-331
86Pol/Ast-8
86T-331
87D-332
87D/OD-17
87F-50
87Moth/Ast-11
87Pol/Ast-21
87T-112
88D-163
88D/Best-8
88F-439
88Moth/Ast-11
88OPC-48
88Panini/St-291
88Pol/Ast-4
88RedFoley/St-2
88Score-73
88Sf-219
88T-48
88T/St-32
89B-327
89D-88
89F-350
89Moth/Ast-10
89OPC-359
89RedFoley/St-4
89Score-366
89T-492
89T/DH-20
89UD-305
Ashby, Andrew
86Cram/PCL-139
87Spart-13
Ashford, Thomas S.
(Tucker)
78T-116
79T-247
80Charl-16
81Colum-2
82Colum-2
82Colum/Pol-12
83Tidew-26
84Nes/792-492
84T-492
88Jacks/GS-4
Ashkinazy, Alan
85Greens-2
86Greens-2
Ashley, Shon
86Beloi-1
87Beloi-4
88CalLgAS-14
88Stock/Cal-194
88Stock/Pro-724
89ElPas/GS-25
Ashman, Mike
82Madis-23
83Albany-11
84Albany-21
85Cram/PCL-136
86Nashua-1
Ashmore, Mitch
82CharR-7
82Omaha-13
84Memph-8
Ashworth, Mike
88BurlR/Pro-1793
89SLCty-28
Asmussen, Thomas W.
(Tom)
No Cards.
Asp, Bryan
89Elizab/Star-1
Aspray, Mike
88Peoria/Ko-3
Aspromonte, Ken
58T-405
59T-424
60T-114
61P-65
61T-176
61T/St-133
62J-19
62P-19
62P/Can-19
62Salada-7A
62Salada-7B
62Shirriff-7
62T-563
63T-464
64T-252
65T/trans-39
72T-784
73OPC-449MG
73T-449MG
74OPC-521MG

74T-521MG
Aspromonte, Robert T.
(Bob)
60T-547
61T-396
62Bz-9
62T-248
62T/St-124
63Exh
63F-37
63J-187
63P-187
63Pep
63T-45
63T/SO
64T-467
64T/Coins-163AS
64T/Coins-84
64T/St-16
64T/SU
65Bz-19
65OPC-175
65T-175
65T/E-61
65T/Trans
66Bz-24
66T-273M
66T-352
66T/RO-12
67Bz-24
67T-274
68Coke
68OPC-95
68T-95
69MB-17
69MLB/St-111
69T-542
69T/St-31
70MLB/St-2
70OPC-529
70T-529
71MLB/St-146
71OPC-469
71T-469
72MB-21
72T-659
89Smok/Ast-16
Exh47
Asselstine, Brian H.
77T-479R
78T-372
79T-529
81D-186
81F-256
81Pol/Atl-30
81T-64
82D-184
82F-428
82T-214
83Phoen/BHN-4
Assenmacher, Paul
84Durhm-20
85Durhm-1
86D/Rook-28
86F/Up-U5
86Pol/Atl-30
86S/Rook-24
86T/Tr-4T
87D-290
87F-511
87Leaf-164
87Smok/Atl-8
87T-132
87T/St-37
87ToysRUs-2
88F-532
88T-266
89B-265
89D-357
89F-586
89Panini/St-33
89Score-373
89T-454
89UD-566
90D-459
90F-25
90T-644
90UD-660
Astroth, Joseph Henry
(Joe)
51B-298
52B-170
52T-290
53B/Col-82
53T-103
54B-131
55B-119
55Rodeo
56Rodeo
56T-106
Astroth, Jon
74Gasto
Atha, Jeff
88James/Pro-1901
Atherton, Charles
No Cards.
Atherton, Keith Rowe
80WHave-16
81WHave-2
82Tacom-23
83Tacom-1
84D-497
84F-437
84Moth/A's-26
84Nes/792-529
84T-529
85D-340
85F-415
85Moth/A's-17
85T-166
86F-410
86Moth/A's-17
86T-353
87D-272
87F-534
87T-52
88D-318
88D/Best-270
88F-1
88Score-613
88T-451
89D-273
89F-103
89F/Up-24
89Score-381
89T-698
89T/Tr-4T
89UD-599
Atilano, Luis
75Clint
Atkins, Francis M.
(Tommy)
E270/2
M116
Atkins, James Curtis
(Jim)
No Cards.
Atkinson, William C.
(Bill)
78OPC-144
78T-43
80OPC-133
80T-415
83AppFx/LF-19C
Atkinson, Hubert B.
(Lefty)
No Cards.
Atkisson, Albert W.
(Al)
No Cards.
Attardi, Jay
76AppFx
Attell, Abe
88Pac/8Men-28M
T3/Box-52
Attreau, Richard G.
(Dick)
No Cards.
Atwell, Gary
75Lafay
Atwell, Maurice D.
(Toby)
52T-356
53B/Col-112
53T-23
54B-123
55B-164
56T-232
Exh47
V362-34
Atwood, William F.
(Bill)
40PB-240
Atz, Jacob Henry
E270/2
T206
Aube, Richard
83CharR-14
Aubrey, Harvey H.
No Cards.
Auchard, Dan
89Kingspt/Star-1
Audain, Miguel
87Penin-13
Auerbach, Frederick
(Rick)
72OPC-153
72T-153
73OPC-427
73T-427
74OPC-289
74T-289
75OPC-588
75T-588
75T/M-588
76OPC-622
76SSPC-74
76T-622
78T-646
79T-174
80T-354
82T-72
Aufdermauer, Bud
85Anchora-44
August, Don
85T-392
86Tucso-3
87Ashvl-20
87Denver-17
88D-602
88Denver/CMC-8
88Denver/Pro-1259
88F/U-U37
88Score/Tr-104T
88T/Tr-7T
89B-130
89D-410
89F-177
89Gard-15
89Panini/St-365
89Pol/Brew-38
89Score-419
89Score/HotRk-83
89Score/YS/II-28
89Sf-131
89T-696
89T/Big-33
89UD-325
90Class-124
90D-617
90Score-144
90T-192
90UD-295
August, Sam
88Osceola/Star-2
89ColMud/Pro-140
Augustine, David R.
(Dave)
74OPC-598R
74T-598R
75OPC-616R
75T-616R
75T/M-616R
78Charl
79Charl-12
81Portl-6
82Portl-18
Augustine, Gerald Lee
(Jerry)
77T-577
78T-133
79T-357
80T-243
81D-445
81F-514
81T-596
82D-332
82F-133
82Pol/Brew
82Pol/Brew-46
82T-46
83F-26
83Pol/Brew-46
83T-424
84F-194
84Nes/792-658
84Pol/Brew-46
84T-658
85RochR-14
Auker, Eldon Leroy
35BU-120
39PB-4
40PB-139
41PB-45
88Conlon/3-3
R309/2
R313
W753
Aulds, Leycester D.
No Cards.
Aulenback, Jim
83AlexD-13
84PrWill-14
Ault, Douglas Reagan
(Doug)
77OPC-202
77T-477R
78OPC-202
78T-267
79OPC-205
79Syrac-15
79T-392
80Syrac-2
81F-424
82Syrac-24
83Knoxv-20
85Syrac-21
86Syrac-3MG
87Syrac-7
87Syrac/TCMA-23
Ausanio, Joe
88Watertn/Puc-2
89Salem/Star-3
Ausmus, Brad
89Oneon/Pro-2110
Aust, Dennis Kay
63Pep/Tul
66OPC-179R
66Pep/Tul
66T-179R
Austin, Frank
52Mother-18
Austin, James
(Bubba)
86Cram/PCL-178
87CharRain-7
88River/Cal-207
88Wichi-25
89ElPas/GS-3
Austin, James Phillip
(Jimmy or Pepper)
10Domino-3
11Helmar-60
12Sweet/Pin-51A
12Sweet/Pin-51B
14CJ-40
15CJ-40
D327
D328-8
D329-7
D350/2-7
E135-8
E220
E224
E254
E286
E94
E97
M101/4-7
M101/5-7
M116
T202
T205
T207
T222
V100
W555
Austin, Pat
87Lakel-18
88GlenF/Pro-914
89Toled/CMC-18
89Toled/Pro-766
90Score-626
Austin, Rick Gerald
71MLB/St-361
71OPC-41
71T-41
76OPC-269
76SSPC-248
76T-269
Austin, Rick
82Orlan-14
83Toled-11
Austin, Terry
81QuadC-12
Auten, Jim
83Memph-16
84MidldC-19
Auth, Bob
86QuadC-3
Autry, Albert Jr.
(Al)
No Cards.
Autry, Bucky
84LitFalls-18
Autry, Gene
61NuCard-414
Autry, Martin Gordon
29Exh/4-20
Autry, William Askew
(Chick)
No Cards.
Averill, Earl D. Jr.
59T-301
60L-110
60T-39
61T-358
62J-80
62P-80
62P/Can-80
62Salada-24A
62Salada-24B
62Shirriff-24
62T-452
63T-139
Averill, Howard Earl
(Earl)
28Exh/PCL-2
29Exh/4-22
31Exh/4-22

32Orbit/num-12
32Orbit/un-3
33DH-3
33Exh/4-11
33G-194
34DS-100
34DS-35
34Exh/4-11
35BU-113
35BU-24
35Exh/4-11
35G-1L
35G-2E
35G-6E
35G-7E
36Exh/4-11
36Wheat
37Exh/4-11
37OPC-103
38Exh/4-11
39Exh
39PB-143
40PB-46
55Salem
60F-71
61F-5
80Cram/Leg-4
86S/Dec-15M
88Conlon/AmAS-2
89Pac/Leg-203
PR1-2
R300
R303/A
R305
R306
R308-160
R310
R311/Gloss
R313
R314
R315-A1
R315-B1
V300
W517-51
WG8-2

Avery, Larry
81BurlB-29
82BurlR-27GM

Avery, Steve
89B-268
89Durhm/Star-1
89Greenvl/Best-28
89Star/Wax-67
89T-784FDP
90D-39
90UD-65

Avila, Roberto G.
(Bobby)
50NumNum
51B-188
52B-167
52NumNum-14
52RM-AL2
52T-257
53B/Col-29
53RM-AL26
54B-68
54DanDee
54RM-AL1
55B-19
55Gol/Ind-1
55RM-AL15
55Salem
56T-132
57T-195
58Hires-33
58T-276
59T-363
60L-59
60T-90

Aviles, Brian Keith
84Durhm-25
87Greenv/Bst-15

Aviles, Ramon Antonio
79OkCty
80T-682R
81F-23
81T-644
82F-239
82OkCty-4
82T-152
83Portl-10
86Readg-1CO
87Spart-11
88Maine/CMC-24
88Maine/Pro-302
89Readg/Best-25
89Readg/Pro-671

Avrea, James Epherium
(Jim)
No Cards.

Ayala, Benigno Felix
(Benny)
75OPC-619R
75T-619R
75T/M-619R
80T-262
81D-236
81F-185
81T-101
82D-581
82F-157
82T-331
83D-331
83F-52
83T-59
84D-270
84Nes/792-443
84T-443
84T/St-22WS
85Polar/Ind-12
85T-624
85T/Tr-3T

Ayala, Eric
80Ander-20

Aydelott, Jacob S.
(Jake)
No Cards.

Ayer, Jack
82ArkTr-20
84Louvl-21
85Louvl-21
86Louisvl-4
87Louvl-3

Ayers, Jim
75Cedar

Ayers, Kevin
86VeroB-2

Ayers, Scott
86WPalm-3
87Jamestn-19

Ayers, William Oscar
(Bill)
47TipTop

Ayers, Yancy Wyatt
(Doc)
No Cards.

Aylward, Jim
88QuadC/GS-22
88Reno/Cal-280
89QuadC/Best-8
89QuadC/GS-27

Aylward, Richard John
(Dick)
No Cards.

Ayoub, Sam
81Richm-25
82Richm-30
83Richm-7
84Richm-22
85Richm-24
86Richm-1TR
87Richm/TCMA-29
88Richm-TR
88Richm/Pro-6
89Richm/CMC-14
89Richm/Ko-TR
89Richm/Pro-820

Ayrault, Bob
89Reno/Cal-240

Azar, Todd
88Wausa/Feder-15
88Wausa/GS-15

Azcue, Jose Joaquin
(Joe)
62T-417
63T-501
64T-199
64T/Coins-110
65Kahn
65T-514
66T-452
67T-336
68Bz-4
68T-443
69JB
69MB-18
69MLB/St-38
69OPC-176
69T-176
69T/St-162
69Trans-1
70MLB/St-170
70OPC-294
70T-294
71MLB/St-338
71OPC-657
71T-657
72MB-22
78TCMA-36

Azocar, Oscar
88Albany/Pro-1347
89Albany/Best-19
89Albany/Pro-332
89Albany/Star-1

Baar, Bryan
89GreatF-19

Babb, Charles Amos
(Charlie)
E254

Babbitt, Gene
47Sunbeam

Babcock, Bill
82AppFx-19

Babcock, Robert E.
(Bob)
77Tucso
78Cr/PCL-106
80Charl-17
81T-41R
82D-565
82T-567
83SLCty-3

Babe, Loren Rolland
No Cards.

Babich, John Charles
(Johnny)
34DS-82
35BU-167
40PB-191
41DP-127
41PB-40
43Centen-1
44Centen-1
48Signal
48Smith-22
R309/2

Babington, Charles P.
(Charlie)
No Cards.

Babitt, Mack Neal II
(Shooty)
80Ogden-21
80WHave-17
82D-556
82F-86
82T-578
82Tacom-28
83Memph-1
84Indianap-14

Baca, Mark A.
88PalmSp/Cal-99
88PalmSp/Pro-1456

Baccioccu, Jack
49Sommer-19

Bach, Jan
78Clint

Bach, Rich
78Clint
80BurlB-16

Bachman, Kent
86WPalm-4

Backman, Lester John
(Les)
M116

Backman, Walter W.
(Wally)
79Jacks-2
80Tidew-4
81F-336
81Tidew-8
83D-618
83F-537
83T-444
83Tidew-3
84Jacks/Smok-2
85D-319
85F-72
85Leaf-79
85OPC-162
85T-677
85T/Mets/Fan-1
85T/St-106
86D-238
86F-75
86OPC-191
86T-191
86T/Mets/Fan-1
86T/St-97
87D-316
87F-3
87Leaf-59
87OPC-48
87S-124
87T-48
87T/St-100
88D-241
88D/Mets/Bk-241
88F-128
88Kahn/Mets-6
88Leaf-202
88OPC-333
88Panini/St-340
88Score-303
88T-333
89B-159
89D-383
89D/Best-186
89D/Tr-10
89F-28
89F/Up-43
89OPC-72
89Score-315
89Score/Tr-34
89T-508
89T/Big-300
89T/Tr-5T
89UD-188
89UD/Ext-732
90D-155
90F-367
90Score-281
90T-218
90UD-158

Backs, Jason
89Spart/Pro-1038
89Spart/Star-1

Backus, Jerry
88Boise/Pro-1618

Bacon, Edgar Suter
(Eddie)
No Cards.

Bacosa, Al
88Idaho/Pro-1848

Bacsik, Michael James
(Mike)
74Gasto
77T-103
77Tucso
78Cr/PCL-43
80T-453

Baczewski, Fred
54B-60
55B-190

Badcock, Tom
75Water

Bader, Arthur Herman
(Art)
No Cards.

Bader, Loren Verne
No Cards.

Badgro, Morris Hiram
(Red)
88Conlon/4-2

Baecht, Edward Joseph
(Ed)
No Cards.

Baehr, Dave
82Idaho-1
83Wisco/LF-25

Baer, Max
33SK-44

Baerga, Carlos
86CharRa-1
87CharRa-2
88TexLgAS/GS-32
88Wichi-15
89LasVeg/CMC-18
89LasVeg/Pro-9

Baerwald, Rudolph
E254
E270

Baez, Angel
81Buffa-17

Baez, Igor
89Greens/Pro-408

Baez, Jesse
79LodiD-9
81Wausa-13
83Wausa/LF-17

Baez, Jose Antonio
75Water
78T-311

Baez, Kevin
88LitFalls/Puc-2
89Clmbia/Best-12
89Clmbia/GS-6

Baez, Pedro
88Madis-3
89Modesto/Cal-267
89Modesto/Ch-8

Bafia, Bob
86WinSal-2
87WinSal-8
88Pittsf/Pro-1363
89CharlK-22

Bagby, James C.J. Jr.
(Jim)
39PB-40
40PB-32
61F-92

Bagby, James C.J. Sr.
(Jim)
21Exh-3
D327
D328-9
E120
E121
E135-9

E220
V100
W501
W572
W575
WG7-2
Baggott, Dave
89SLCty-4GM
Bagiotti, Aldo
81Redwd-10
Bagley, Eugene T.
(Gene)
No Cards.
Bagnall, Jim
83Butte-16
83CharR-4
Bagwell, Jeff
88CapeCod-4
88CapeCod/Sum-57
Bagwell, William M.
(Bill)
No Cards.
Baham, Leon
82Idaho-16
87SanBern-14
88Tampa/Star-2
Bahns, Ed
79AppFx-4
Bahnsen, Stanley R.
(Stan)
670PC-93R
67T-93R
68T-214R
69Citgo-9
69T-380
69T/St-201
70T-568
71MD
71MLB/St-482
710PC-184
71T-184
72T-662
730PC-20
73T-20
740PC-254
74T-254
74T/St-152
750PC-161
75T-161
75T/M-161
760PC-534
76SSPC-486
76T-534
77T-384
780PC-54
78T-97
790PC-244
79T-468
800PC-345
80T-653
81D-452
81F-156
810PC-267
81T-267
82D-392
82F-183
820PC-131
82T-131
83Portl-23
89Swell-39
Bahr, Edson Garfield
(Ed)
No Cards.
Bahret, Frank J.
No Cards.
Baichley, Grover C.
No Cards.
Baier, Marty
82Clint-15
83Clint/LF-7
Bailes, Scott
83AlexD-10
85Nashua-1
86D/Rook-25
86F/Up-U6
86OhHenry-43
86S/Rook-9
86T/Tr-5T
87D-227
87F-242
87Gator-43
870PC-134
87T-585
87ToysRUs-3
88D-104
88D/Best-285
88F-600
88Gator-43
880PC-107
88Panini/St-68
88T-107
88T/St-206
89D-202
89F-398
89Score-424
89T-339
89T/St-217
89UD-209
90D-468
90F-484
90Score-218
90T-784
Bailey, Abraham L.
(Sweetbreads)
No Cards.
Bailey, Ace
33SK-29
Bailey, Arthur Eugene
(Gene)
No Cards.
Bailey, Brandon
86Columbia-4
87Columbia-3
Bailey, Buddy
80Ander-17
82Durhm-23
86Durhm-1MG
87Sumter-10
88BBAmer-30
89Greenv/Pro-1178
89Greenvl/Best-20
89SLAS-23
Bailey, Darryl
77BurlB
78BurlB
79Holyo-22
Bailey, Greg
83TriCit-21
86Tulsa-18
Bailey, Howard Lee
82Evans-1
82Evans-1
82T-261R
84D-212
84Evans-2
84F-75
84Nes/792-284
84T-284
Bailey, James Hopkins
(Jim)
No Cards.
Bailey, Jim
82Idaho-2
Bailey, John Mark
(Mark)
84F/X-3
85D-450
85F-344
85Moth/Ast-17
850PC-64
85T-64
86D-354
86F-293
86Pol/Ast-14
86T-432
86T/St-30
87D-235
87D-429
87Moth/Ast-15
87Pol/Ast-2
87T-197
88Moth/Ast-15
88Pol/Ast-5
88T/Big-248
89Tidew/CMC-29
89Tidew/Pro-1949
Bailey, Lemuel
(King)
No Cards.
Bailey, Lonas Edgar
(Ed)
53T-206
54T-184
55T-69
55T/DH-30
56Kahn
57Kahn
57Swift-5
57T-128
58Kahn
58T-330
58T-386M
58T-490AS
59Kahn
59T-210
60Kahn
60T-411
61Kahn
61T-418
61T/St-13
62J-137
62P-137
62P/Can-137
62Salada-113A
62Salada-113B
62Shirriff-113
62T-459
62T/St-194
63T-368
64T-437
64Wheat/St-4
65T-559
66T-246
78TCMA-173
78TCMA-37
79TCMA-11
84Moth/Giants-17
Exh47
Bailey, Pat
86Cram/PCL-31
87AppFx-19
Bailey, Robert Jr.
89Well/Puc-3
Bailey, Robert S.
(Bob)
63Kahn
63T-228R
64Kahn
64T-91
64T/S-4
65Kahn
65T-412
66EH-7
66Kahn
66T-485
670PC-32
67T-32
68T-580
69Fud's-1
69MLB/St-154
69T-399
69T/St-52
70MLB/St-62
700PC-293
70T-293
71LaPizza-1
71MLB/St-121
710PC-157
71T-157
71T/Coins-59
72MB-23
720PC-493KP
72T-493
72T-526
730PC-505
73T-505
740PC-97
74T-97
74T/St-51
74Weston-3
75Ho-55
750PC-365
75T-365
75T/M-365
760PC-338
76SSPC-333
76T-338
76T/Tr-338T
77T-221
78PapaG/Disc-20
78T-457
790PC-282
79T-549
86Penin-4
87Hawai-26MG
Bailey, Steven John
(Steve)
No Cards.
Bailey, Troy
88Wythe/Pro-2003
Bailey, Vince
79BurlB-18
Bailey, William F.
(Bill)
E254
E90/1
E92
M116
T205
Bailor, Robert M.
(Bob)
76SSPC-386
770PC-48
77T-474R
78Ho-148
78K-39
780PC-148
78T-196
79Ho-105
790PC-259
79T-492
80K-16
800PC-304
80T-581
81F-409
810PC-297
81T-297
81T/Tr-732
82D-308
82F-521
82T-79
83D-506
83F-538
83T-343
83T/St-260
84D-595
84F-580
84F/X-4
84Nes/792-654
84Pol/Dodg-21
84T-654
84T/St-109
84T/X-4
85D-397
85F-367
85T-728
86F-124
86T-522
87Duned-6
88Syrac/CMC-24
88Syrac/Pro-817
89Syrac/CMC-25
89Syrac/Pro-796
Bain, Herbert Loren
(Loren)
No Cards.
Bain, Paul
77Clint
78LodiD
79LodiD-3
Baine, John T.
87Sprin/Best-8
Baine, Tom
86Erie-2
88TexLgAS/GS-16
89Louvl-10
89Louvl/CMC-20
89Louvl/Pro-1265
Baines, Harold D.
78Knoxv
81F-346
810PC-347
81T-347
82D-568
82F-336
82F/St-184
820PC-56
82T-684
83D-143
83F-229
83K-16
830PC-177
83T-177
83T/St-52
84D-58
84D/AAS-11
84F-51
84F/St-4
84FunFood/Pin-110
84Nes/792-434
840PC-197
84T-434
84T/St-242
84TrueVal/WS-3
85Coke/WS-3
85D-58
85D/AAS-58
85Drake-2
85F-507
85F/St-21
85Leaf-231
850PC-249
85Seven-6G
85T-249
85T-275FDP
85T/Gloss40-34
85T/St-234
85T/Super-51
86Coke/WS-3
86D-13
86D-180
86D/AAS-49
86D/DKsuper-13
86Drake-24
86F-198
86F/LimEd-3
86F/Mini-42
86F/Slug-M1
86F/St-1
86Jay's-1
86Leaf-13DK
860PC-65
86S-52M
86S-7
86T-755
86T/Mini-8
86T/St-288
86T/Super-9
87Classic-42
87Coke/WS-2

87D/AAS-25
87D/OD-236
87Drake-22
87F-485
87F-643M
87F/GameWin-1
87F/Hottest-2
87F/Lim-1
87F/Mini-3
87F/St-2
87Ho/St-21
87KayBee-1
87Kraft-13
87Leaf-52
87MnM's-8
87OPC-309
87RedFoley/St-119
87S-153M
87S-171
87Seven-C1
87Smok/AL-4
87T-772
87T/Board-16
87T/Coins-1
87T/Gloss60-14
87T/St-284
88Coke/WS-1
88D-211
88D/AS-12
88D/Best-11
88F-391
88F/Excit-1
88Leaf-157
88OPC-35
88Panini/St-62
88RedFoley/St-3
88Score-590
88Sf-33
88T-35
88T/Big-224
88T/Coins-5
88T/RiteAid-16
88T/St-293
88T/UK-1
89B-72
89Cadaco-1
89Coke/WS-5
89D-148
89D/Best-81
89F-491
89F/Excit-1
89F/Superstar-2
89KMart/DT-22
89OPC-152
89Panini/St-310
89Score-128
89Score/Tr-62
89Sf-157
89T-585
89T/Big-266
89T/Coins-33
89T/Hills-1
89T/St-304
89T/UK-2
89UD-211
89UD-692TC
90Class-69
90D-402
90D-660AS
90F-290
90Score-470
90Sf-125
90T-345
90UD-353

Bair, Charles Douglas
(Doug)
78OPC-229
78T-353
79Ho-3
79OPC-58
79T-126
80OPC-234
80T-449
81D-73
81F-213
81OPC-73
81T-73
82T-262
83D-372
83F-2
83T-627
83T/X-5
84D-369
84F-76
84Nes/792-536
84T-536
85Cain's-1
85D-369
85F-1
85T-744
85Wendy-2
87F-386
87Maine-2
88Syrac/CMC-9
88Syrac/Pro-816
89Syrac/CMC-1
89Syrac/Pro-807
90Score-517

Bair, Rich
84Newar-9

Baird, Albert Wells
(Al)
No Cards.

Baird, Allard
89AppFx/Pro-870

Baird, Chris
85Durhm-19

Baird, Howard D.
(Doug)
D328-10
D329-8
E135-10
M101/4-8

Baird, Robert Allen
(Bob)
No Cards.

Bajus, Mark
80Batav-3
81Batav-1
81Watlo-6

Bakely, Edward Enoch
(Jersey)
No Cards.

Bakenhaster, David L.
(Dave)
64T-479R

Baker, Albert Jones
(Al)
75Clint

Baker, Charles
(Bock)
No Cards.

Baker, Charles
(Charlie)
No Cards.

Baker, Charles
(Joseph)
79Hawai-16
79T-456
80Hawai-1
81F-500
82F-561
82T-253

Baker, Curt
78Wausa

Baker, Darnell
78Cedar

Baker, David Glen
(Dave)
79Syrac-11
80Syrac-17
81Syrac-11
82Syrac-14
83Toled-13
84Toled-20

Baker, Delmar David
(Del)
54T-133
60T-456C
88Conlon/5-2
V355-31

Baker, Derrell
86Indianap-13
87WPalm-7
88Jaxvl/Best-14
88Jaxvl/Pro-968

Baker, Douglas
(Doug)
83BirmB-8
84Evans-13
85T-269
86Nashv-1
87Toled-17
87Toled/TCMA-20
88Portl/CMC-13
88Portl/Pro-647
89Portl/CMC-14
89Portl/Pro-230
90F-368

Baker, Ernest Gould
(Ernie)
No Cards.

Baker, Eugene Walter
(Gene)
52Mother-45
55B-7
56T-142
56YellBase/Pin-5
57T-176
58Hires-65
58Kahn
58T-358
59T-238
60T-539
61T-339
79TCMA-48
Exh47

Baker, Floyd Wilson
47TipTop
48L-153
49B-119
50B-146
51B-87
52T-292
53B/BW-49

Baker, Frank Watts
71OPC-213
71T-213
72OPC-409
72T-409
73JP
74OPC-411
74T-411

Baker, Frank
70T-704
71OPC-689
71T-689

Baker, George F.
No Cards.

Baker, Gerald
86QuadC-4

Baker, Greg
81Shrev-16

Baker, Howard Francis
No Cards.

Baker, Jack Edward
No Cards.

Baker, Jay
88Gasto/Pro-999

Baker, Jesse Eugene
No Cards.

Baker, Jesse Ormond
No Cards.

Baker, Jim
80Utica-4
83Syrac-4
84Syrac-29

Baker, John Franklin
(Home Run)
10Domino-4
11Helmar-52
12Sweet/Pin-40
14CJ-2
15CJ-2
21Exh-4
40PB-177
50Callahan
60Exh/HOF-3
60F-41
61F-1M
61F-6
61GP-21
75F/Pion-16
80Cram/Leg-41
80SSPC/HOF
89Pac/Leg-146
BF2-32
D327
D328-11
D329-9
D350/2-8
E120
E121/80
E122
E135-11
E220
E224
E254
E300
E90/1
E91
E96
L1-120
M101/4-9
M101/5-8
S74-26
S81-95
T201
T202
T205
T206
T208
T213/blue
T215/brown
T227
T3-78
V100
W514-75
W515-15
W573
W575
WG4-2
WG5-2

Baker, John
83Ander-7

Baker, Johnny B.
(Dusty)
71OPC-709R
71Richm
71T-709R
72T-764
73OPC-215
73T-215
73T/Lids-3
74OPC-320
74T-320
74T/St-2
75Ho-117
75OPC-33
75T-33
75T/M-33
76OPC-28
76SSPC-16
76T-28
76T/Tr-28T
77T-146
78Ho-50
78T-668
79OPC-290
79T-562
80OPC-135
80Pol/Dodg-12
80T-255
81D-179
81F-115
81F/St-62
81Pol/Dodg-12
81Sqt-17
81T-495
81T/HT
81T/SO-71
81T/St-182
82D-336
82F-1
82F/St-4
82K-50
82OPC-375
82Pol/Dodg
82Pol/Dodg-12
82T-311TL
82T-375
82T/St-52
83D-462
83F-201
83OPC-220
83Pol/Dodg-12
83Seven-6
83T-220
83T/Gloss-22
83T/Gloss40-22
83T/St-245
84D-226
84D/AAS-47
84F-96
84F/X-5
84Nes/792-40
84OPC-40
84Seven-18W
84T-40
84T/St-80
84T/X-5
85D-445
85F-602
85F/Up-U3
85Moth/A's-15
85OPC-165
85T-165
85T/Tr-4T
86D-467
86F-411
86Leaf-231
86Moth/A's-3
86OPC-31
86T-645
87F-387
87Smok/Dodg-2
87T-565
88Smok/Dodg-21M
88Smok/Dodg-22
89Smok/Dodg-93

Baker, Kenny
79WHave-12
82BirmB-10
83Evans-17
85Omaha-27

Baker, Kerry
84PrWill-32
85Nashua-2
86Nashua-2

Baker, Kirtley
No Cards.

Baker, Mark
83QuadC-6
86ColumAst-3
87ColAst/Pro-13
87ColumAst-13

Baker, Mike
86Elmir-1
87Greens-21
88WinHav/Star-3

89Lynch/Star-1
Baker, Neal Vernon
No Cards.
Baker, Norman Leslie
(Norm)
No Cards.
Baker, Philip
(Phil)
No Cards.
Baker, Rick
(Ricky)
81Chatt-15
82Chatt-7
83MidldC-25
84MidldC-18
Baker, Steven Byrne
(Steve)
80Evansvl/TCMA-12
81Syrac-1
83T/X-6
84Louvl-25
85Indianap-6
Baker, Thomas Calvin
(Tom)
No Cards.
Baker, Thomas Henry
(Tom)
No Cards.
Baker, Tracy Lee
No Cards.
Baker, William
(Bill)
W711/2
49Eureka-177
Bakley, Edward
N172
Balabon, Anthony
86FtLaud-2
Balabon, Rick
87PrWill-9
89SanBern/Best-4
89SanBern/Cal-74
Balas, Mitchell F.
(Mike)
No Cards.
Balaz, John Lawrence
76OPC-539
76T-539
Balboni, Stephen C.
(Steve)
80Nashvl
81Colum-11
82Colum-4
82Colum/Pol-35
82T-83R
83Colum-15
83D-73
83OPC-8
83T-8
84F/X-6
84Nes/792-782
84T-782
84T/X-6
85D-419
85F-196
85Leaf-95
85OPC-152
85T-486
85T/St-271
86D-222
86Drake-20
86F-1
86Kitty/Disc-17
86Leaf-98
86NatPhoto-45
86OPC-164
86S-186M
86T-164
86T/Gloss60-6
86T/Mini-17
86T/St-265
87D-102
87D/OD-199
87F-362
87Leaf-262
87OPC-240
87RedFoley/St-85
87T-240
87T/St-263
88D-424
88F-251
88Score-273
88Score/Tr-46T
88T-638
89D-143
89D/Best-188
89D/Tr-48
89F-538
89F/Up-45
89OPC-336
89Score-353
89Score/NWest-17
89Score/Tr-27
89T-336
89T/St-222
89T/Tr-6T
89UD-111
90D-315
90F-436
90Score-327
90T-716
90UD-497
Balcena, Robert R.
(Bobby)
52Park-20
Baldrick, Bob
83Wausa/LF-22
86Chatt-2
Baldschun, Jack
62T-46
62T/St-164
63T-341
64T-520
64T/Coins-69
64T/St-90
64T/SU
65T-555
65T/E-34
66T-272
67OPC-114
67T-114
70OPC-284
70T-284
78TCMA-104
Baldwin, Brian
88Wausa/Feder-21
88Wausa/GS-21
89SanBern/Best-8
89SanBern/Cal-73
Baldwin, Charles
E223
N172
N403
Scrapp
Baldwin, Clarence G.
(Kid)
N172
Baldwin, Dave
68T-231
69OPC-132
69T-132
70T-613
71MLB/St-433
71OPC-48
71T-48
Baldwin, Frank DeWitt
No Cards.
Baldwin, Henry Clay
No Cards.
Baldwin, Jeff
86Ashvl-2
87Osceola-10
88Osceola/Star-3
89ColMud/Best-13
89ColMud/Pro-135
89ColMud/Star-3
Baldwin, Johnny
83Greens-1
84Nashvl-1
Baldwin, Kirk
89Eugene/Best-3
Baldwin, Marcus E.
(Mark)
E223
N172
Baldwin, O.F.
No Cards.
Baldwin, Reginald C.
(Reggie)
79Charl-4
80T-678R
80Tidew-13
Baldwin, Rickey Alan
(Rick)
76OPC-372
76SSPC-552
76T-372
77T-587
78SnJos-11
Baldwin, Robert H.
(Billy)
76SSPC-370
Baldwin, Tony
88Sumter/Pro-391
89BurlB/Pro-1608
89BurlB/Star-1
Balelo, Nesi
87Chatt/Best-19
88Vermont/Pro-949
Balenti, Michael R.
(Mike)
No Cards.
Bales, Tom
88LitFalls/Puc-3
Bales, Wesley Owen
(Lee)
67OPC-51R
67T-51R
Balfanz, John
88StPet/Star-1
89Reno/Cal-261
Ball, Arthur
(Art)
No Cards.
Ball, Cornelius
(Neal)
10Domino-5
11Helmar-21
12Sweet/Pin-16
T202
T204
T205
T206
T207
T215/brown
Ball, Harry
88CapeCod-19
88CapeCod/Sum-27
Ball, James Chandler
(Jim)
T204
Ball, Jim
77QuadC
Ball, Robert
80Ashev-10
81Tulsa-26
82Tulsa-21
Balla, Gary
77QuadC
Ballanfant, Lee
55B-295ump
Ballanger, Mike
77Jaxvl
Ballard, Dan
78Green
Ballard, Glenn
(Butch)
77Spart
80OrlTw-14
Ballard, Jeff
86Hagers-1
87RochR-25
87RochR/TCMA-1
88D-520
88F-554
88French-34
88RochR-1
88RochR/CMC-1
88RochR/Pro-199
88T-782
89B-7
89D-495
89D/Best-30
89F-607
89French-29
89Panini/St-253
89Score-551
89T-69
89T/St-230
89UD-595
90Class-89
90D-51
90F-173
90Score-349
90Sf-123
90T-296
90T-394AS
90UD-259
Ballard, Tim
82CharR-13
Ballenger, Pelham A.
No Cards.
Baller, Jay Scott
(Jay)
82Readg-1
83Charl-1
83Wheat/Ind-2
84BuffB-9
85IowaC-12
86D-613
86F/Up-U7
86Gator-48
87IowaC-5
88Calg/CMC-5
88Calg/Pro-792
88T-717
89Indi/CMC-7
89Indi/Pro-1231
Ballinger, Mark A.
No Cards.
Ballou, Bill
89Utica/Puc-29
Balmer, Steve
83QuadC-7
Balsley, Darren
86Modesto-4
87Duned-9
88Knoxv/Best-10
89Knoxv/Best-3
89Knoxv/Pro-1137
89Knoxv/Star-5
Balthazar, Doyle
87CharWh-28
87Lakel-8
88Lakel/Star-2
89London/Pro-1384
Baltz, Nick
76Baton
Bamberger, George I.
50Remar
53Mother-38
59T-529
73OPC-136CO
73T-136C
74OPC-306CO
74T-306C
79T-577MG
80T-659MG
83T-246
85Gard-1MG
85Pol/Brew-31MG
85T/Tr-5T
86Pol/Brew-31MG
86T-21
87T-468MG
Bamberger, Harold E.
(Hal)
No Cards.
Ban, Mark
86QuadC-5
Banach, Joe
81Clint-1
Banasiak, Edward
87Elmir-24
87Elmir/Red-24
88WinHav/Star-4
Bancells, Richard
81RochR-20
83RochR-24
Bancroft, David James
(Dave)
21Exh-5
25Exh-1
26Exh-4
27Exh-1
28Exh-5
28Yueng-19
29Exh/4-4
61F-7
89HOF/St-20
89Smok/Dodg-2
BF2-82
D327
D328-12
D329-10
D350/2-9
E120
E121/120
E121/80
E126-52
E135-12
E210
E220
M101/4-10
M101/5-9
V100
V61-73
W501-64
W502-19
W512-1
W514-40
W515-4
W516-30
W572
W573
W575
WG7-3
Bancroft, Frank C.
T204
Bando, Christopher M.
(Chris)
81Charl-8
81T-451R
82D-551
82T-141R
82Wheat/Ind
83D-33
83F-400
83T-227
83Wheat/Ind-3
84D-224
84F-534
84Nes/792-431
84T-431
84Wheat/Ind-23
85D-520
85F-438
85Leaf-39
85OPC-14

85Polar/Ind-23
85T-14
86D-373
86F-579
86OhHenry-23
86OPC-211
86T-594
87D-501
87D/OD-105
87F-243
87Gator-23
87T-322
88D-95
88F-601
88Gator-23
88OPC-51
88Panini/St-71
88Score-172
88T-604
88T/St-209

Bando, Salvatore L.
(Sal)
67OPC-33R
67T-33R
68OPC-146
68T-146
69MLB/St-82
69T-371
69T-556M
69T/St-211
70K-51
70MLB/St-254
70OPC-120
70T-120
70T/S-2
70T/SO
71MLB/St-506
71OPC-285
71T-285
71T/Coins-132
71T/GM-5
71T/S-57
71T/tatt-1
72K-52
72MB-24
72OPC-348KP
72T-348BP
72T-650
73OPC-155
73T-155
73T/Lids-4
74K-51
74OPC-103
74T-103
74T/St-221
75Ho-4
75Ho/Twink-4
75OPC-380
75T-380
75T/M-380
76OPC-90
76SSPC-497
76T-90
77Ho-126
77OPC-145
77T-498
78Ho-94
78OPC-174
78T-265
78Wiffle/Discs-1
79Ho-119
79OPC-283
79T-550
80OPC-363
80T-715
81D-84
81F-510
81OPC-276
81T-623
82D-592
82F-134
87Moth/A's-4
88Pac/Leg-99
89Swell-63

Bandy, Ken
87QuadC-28

Bane, Edward Lee
(Ed)
74OPC-592
74T-592
76SSPC-212
77T-486

Banes, Alan
80Elmir-1

Banes, Dave
82Nashv-1

Baney, Richard Lee
(Dick)
70OPC-88R
70T-88R
74OPC-608R
74T-608R

Bangert, Greg
81Clint-10

Bangston, Pat
88Keno/Pro-1406
88MidwLAS/GS-34
89Orlan/Best-9
89Orlan/Pro-1338

Banister, Jeff
86Watertn-3
87Macon-4
88Harris/Pro-855
89Harris/Pro-306
89Harris/Star-2

Bankhead, Daniel R.
(Dan)
51B-225
52Park-64
79TCMA-159

Bankhead, Sam
78Laugh/Black-31

Bankhead, Scott
85T-393
86D/Rook-36
86F/Up-U8
86Omaha-1
86Omaha/TCMA-25
86S/Rook-39
87F-363
87F/U-U1
87Moth/Sea-13
87T-508
87T/Tr-2T
88D-70
88F-368
88Moth/Sea-13
88OPC-246
88Panini/St-180
88Score-238
88Score/YS/II-37
88T-738
89B-203
89D-463
89D/Best-219
89F-539
89Moth/Sea-13
89OPC-79
89Panini/St-429
89Score-341
89Score/YS/I-42
89T-79
89UD-316
90D-261
90F-505
90Score-555
90Sf-41
90T-213
90UD-561

Bankowski, Chris
81Redwd-27
83Redwd-3

Banks, Darryl
82QuadC-1
83MidldC-12
84MidldC-8

Banks, Dave
86AubAs-2

Banks, Earnest
(Ernie)
54T-94
55B-242
55RFG-26
55T-28
55T/DH-32
56T-15
56T/Pin-5
56YellBase/Pin-6
57T-55
58T-310
58T-482AS
59Armour-4
59Bz
59HRDerby-3
59T-147M
59T-350
59T-469M
59T-559AS
60Armour-3
60Bz-1
60NuCard-20
60T-10
60T-560AS
60T-tatt
60T/tatt-5
61Bz-19
61NuCard-420
61P-191
61T-350
61T-43LL
61T-485MV
61T-575AS
61T/RO
61T/St-4
62Bz
62Exh
62J-188
62P-188
62P/Can-188
62Salada-177A
62Salada-177B
62Shirriff-177
62T-25
62T/bucks
62T/St-104
63Bz-3
63Exh
63J-169
63P-169
63Salada-17
63T-242M
63T-380
63T-3LL
63T/SO
64T-55
64T/Coins-42
64T/St-25
64T/SU
64T/tatt
65OldLond-3
65T-510
65T/E-58
66OPC-110
66T-110
66T/RO
67T-215
68T-355
69Kelly/Pin-2
69MB-19
69MLB/St-118
69MLBPA/Pin-34
69OPC-20
69OPC-6LL
69Sunoco/Pin-1
69T-20
69T-6LL
69T/St-11
69Trans-40
70Dunkin-1
70K-40
70MB-3
70MLB/St-13
70T-630
70T/CB
70Trans-3
71K-50
71MD
71MLB/St-25
71MLB/St-555
71OPC-525
71T-525
71T/GM-36
72MB-25
73OPC-81CO
73T-81C
75OPC-196M
75OPC-197M
75T-196MV
75T-197MV
75T/M-196MV
75T/M-197MV
76Laugh/Jub-2
78TCMA-255
79TCMA-5
80Cram/Leg-33
80Laugh/3/4/5-27
82CJ-14
85CircK-10
85Woolwth-3
86BLChew-9
86S/Dec-29
87Nestle/DT-26
88Pac/Leg-36
89HOF/St-6
Exh47

Banks, George Edward
61Clover-2
63T-564
64T-223
65T-348
66T-488

Banks, William John
(Bill)
No Cards.

Banks, Willie
88Keno/Pro-1380
89Visal/Cal-101
89Visal/Pro-1426

Bankston, Wilborn E.
(Bill)
No Cards.

Banning, Doug
86MidldA-1
87Edmon-7
87MidldA-6

Banning, James M.
(Jim)
N172

Bannister, Alan
77T-559
78K-38
78T-213
79T-134
80OPC-317
80T-608
81T-632
82D-159
82F-359
82T-287
82Wheat/Ind
83D-285
83F-401
83OPC-348
83T-348
83Wheat/Ind-4
84D-154
84F-535
84F/X-7
84Moth/Ast-21
84Nes/792-478
84Rangers-2
84T-478
84T/St-257
84T/X-7
85F-555
85Rangers-5
85T-76
86D-525
86F-556
86T-784
88Rockford-1
89Jaxvl/Best-2
89Jaxvl/Pro-151
89Rockford-1MG

Bannister, Floyd F.
78BK/A-6
78T-39
79OPC-154
79T-306
80OPC-352
80T-699
81D-286
81F-599
81OPC-166
81Pol/Mariners-2
81T-166
81T/St-128
82D-100
82F-504
82T-468
82T/St-234
83D-21DK
83D-50
83F-471
83K-41
83OPC-203
83T-545
83T-706
83T/St-113
83T/St-18
83T/X-7
84D-366
84F-52
84F/St-84
84Nes/792-280
84OPC-280
84T-280
84T/St-247
84TrueVal/WS-4
85Coke/WS-24
85D-379
85F-508
85OPC-354
85T-274FDP
85T-725
86Coke/WS-19
86D-244
86F-199
86Leaf-118
86OPC-64
86T-64
86T/Mini-9
87Coke/WS-12
87D-211
87F-486
87F/McCror-1
87F/St-3
87OPC-356
87T-737
87T/St-286
88D-383
88D/Best-7
88F-392
88OPC-357
88Panini/St-52
88RedFoley/St-4
88Score-622
88Score/Tr-63T
88Smok/Royals-8
88T-357

88T/Big-174
88T/Tr-8T
89B-112
89D-262
89F-276
89OPC-194
89RedFoley/St-5
89Score-249
89Sf-154
89T-638
89T/St-269
89UD-549
90T-116
90UD-695

Bannister, Tim
77BurlB
78BurlB

Bannon, James Henry
(Jimmy)
N300/unif

Bannon, Thomas Edward
(Tom)
No Cards.

Banta, John Kay
(Jack)
49Eureka-28
50B-224
78TCMA-203

Banton, Scott
89Hamil/Star-1

Baranoski, Jim
89Idaho/Pro-2025

Barba, Doug
84Cedar-4

Barba, Michael
82Holyo-1
83ArkTr-6

Barbara, Daniel
89SanBern/Best-7
89SanBern/Cal-76

Barbare, Walter L.
21Exh-6
E120

Barbary, Donald O.
(Red)
No Cards.

Barbe, Jim
(Yogi)
78Ashev
79Tulsa-17

Barbeau, William J.
(Jap)
E91
T206

Barbee, David Monroe
(Dave)
No Cards.

Barber, Charles D.
(Charlie)
No Cards.

Barber, Red
89Rini/Dodg-28M
89Rini/Dodg-29

Barber, Stephen David
(Steve)
60T-514
61P-74
61T-125
61T/St-97
62Salada-11
62Shirriff-11
62T-355
62T-57LL
63Exh
63F-1
63J-64
63P-64
63T-12
64Bz-3
64T-450
64T/Coins-8
64T/St-54
64T/SU
64T/tatt
64Wheat/St-5
65OPC-113
65T-113
66T-477
67OPC-82
67T-82
68T-316
69MB-20
69MLB/St-92
69T-233
69T/St-222
70MLB/St-265
70OPC-224
70T-224
72MB-26
72OPC-333
72T-333
73OPC-36
73T-36
74OPC-631
74T-631
78TCMA-57
Exh47

Barber, Steve Lee
(Steve)
No Cards.

Barber, Tyrus Turner
(Turner)
21Exh-7
E120
E121
E220
V100
W501-60
W573

Barberich, Frank F.
C46-16

Barberie, Bret
88T/Tr-9T
89Star/Wax-32
89T/Big-19
89WPalm/Star-2

Barbieri, James P.
(Jim)
67OPC-76
67T-76

Barbosa, Rafael
84Durhm-11

Barclay, Curtis C.
(Curt)
57T-361
58Hires-70
58SFCall
58T-21
59T-307

Barclay, George O.
No Cards.

Barczi, Scott
87Watertn-7
88Aug/Pro-368
89Salem/Star-4

Bard, Paul Z.
81VeroB-2
82VeroB-12
84CharO-21

Barden, Steve
89Richm/Pro-819

Bardot, Gene
76Wausa

Bare, Raymond Douglas
(Ray)
76OPC-507
76SSPC-613
76T-507
77T-43
78RochR

Barefoot, Mike
89Mia/Star/25-1

Barfield, Jesse Lee
78Duned
82OPC-203R
82T-203R
82T/Tr-2T
83D-595
83F-424
83OPC-257
83T-257
83T/St-307
84D-193
84F-147
84Nes/792-488
84OPC-316
84T-488
84T/St-372
84Tor/Fire-4
85D-195
85F-99
85Leaf-209
85OPC-24
85OPC/Post-20
85T-24
85T/St-362
85Tor/Fire-4
86Ault-29
86D-193
86F-52
86F/Mini-12
86F/St-2
86Leaf-254
86OPC-234
86S-76
86T-593
86T/St-192
86Tor/Fire-3
87Class-58
87D-121
87D/AAS-23
87D/OD-34
87F-219
87F-643M
87F-C2
87F/Excit-3
87F/Lim-2
87F/LL-1
87F/Mini-4
87F/Slug-2
87F/St-4
87F/WaxBox-C2
87Ho/St-1
87KayBee-2
87Kraft-41
87Leaf-127
87OPC-24
87RedFoley/St-3
87S-14
87S-153M
87T-655
87T/Coins-2
87T/Gloss60-35
87T/HL-9
87T/Mini-73
87T/St-184
87Tor/Fire-1
87Tor/Fire-1
87Woolwth-9
88D-442
88D/Best-216
88F-102
88F/RecSet-1
88F/St-70
88Ho/Disc-19
88Leaf-225
88OPC-140
88Panini/St-223
88Score-8
88Sf-13
88T-140
88T/Big-92
88T/Gloss60-2
88T/St-192
88T/St/Backs-46
88Tor/Fire-29
89Ames-1
89B-257
89Class-66
89D-425
89D/Best-132
89D/GrandSlam-11
89F-225
89F/Up-46
89OPC-325
89Panini/St-471
89RedFoley/St-6
89Score-160
89Score/NWest-5
89Score/Tr-22
89Sf-9
89T-325
89T/Tr-7T
89Tor/Fire-29
89UD-149
89UD/Ext-702
90Class-99
90D-74
90F-437
90Score-222
90Sf-10
90T-740
90UD-476

Barfield, John
87PortChar-5
88TexLgAS/GS-17
88Tulsa-14
89OkCty/CMC-2
89OkCty/Pro-1518

Barfoot, Clyde R.
No Cards.

Bargar, Gregory R.
(Greg)
80Memph-5
83Memph-20
84Indianap-13
84Nes/792-474
84OPC-292
84T-474
85Indianap-13
87Louvl-4
88Louvl-9

Barger, Bob
76Wausa

Barger, Eros Bolivar
(Cy)
10Domino-6
11Helmar-82
12Sweet/Pin-69
14CJ-141
14Piedmont/St-1
15CJ-141
M116
S74-48
T202
T205
T206
T207
T213/blue

Barger, Vince
85Durhm-2

Bargerhuff, Brian
83Clint/LF-17
86Chatt-3

Bargfeldt, John
79QuadC-19

Bark, Brian
88CapeCod/Sum-114

Barker, Bob
87Albany-3

Barker, Jeff
78Holyo

Barker, Leonard H.
(Len)
74Gasto
77T-489R
77Tucso
78BK/R-9
78T-634
79OPC-40
79T-94
80T-227
81D-320
81F-408
81OPC-3
81T-432
81T-6LL
81T/St-5
81T/St-72
82D-137
82D-6DK
82F-360
82F/St-200
82K-37
82OPC-360
82T-166LL
82T-360
82T/St-113
82T/St-12
82T/St-178
82Wheat/Ind
83D-111
83F-402
83F-642
83K-33
83OPC-120
83T-120
83T/St-57
83Wheat/Ind-5
84D-443
84F-170
84Nes/792-614
84OPC-309
84Pol/Atl-39
84T-614
85D-165
85F-318
85Ho/Braves-2
85Pol/Atl-39
85T-557
86D-409
86F-507
86Indianap-20
86T-24

Barker, Raymond H.
(Ray)
61T-428
65T-546R
66T-323
67T-583

Barker, Tim
86Tampa-2
87Beloi-17
88Charl/Pro-1221
89GreatF-14

Barkley, Jeff
83Watlo/LF-20
84Maine-15
85Maine-1
85Polar/Ind-49
86T-567

Barkley, Samuel E.
(Sam)
N172
N284
N284/StL

Barlick, Al
55B-265ump

Barling, Glenn
82Clint-6

Barlow, Mike
76SSPC-298
77SLCty
78Cr/PCL-97
78T-429
80Syrac-13
80T-312
81OPC-77
81T-77
82Syrac-1

Barlow, Ricky
86GlenF-1
87Toled-9
87Toled/TCMA-19
89Nashvl-1
89Nashvl/CMC-13
89Nashvl/Pro-1289

Barmes, Bruce R.
No Cards.

Barna, Herbert Paul
(Babe)
No Cards.

Barnard, Jeff
81AppFx-2

Barnard, Steve
85PrWill-11

Barnard, Tom
88Watertn/Puc-32

Barnes, Brian
88CapeCod/Sum-130

Barnes, Charlie
48Sommer-30M

Barnes, Chris
88CapeCod/Sum-115

Barnes, Craig
75Lafay

Barnes, Donald L.
W753

Barnes, Emile Deering
(Red)
No Cards.

Barnes, Everett Duane
(Eppie)
No Cards.

Barnes, Frank
60T-538

Barnes, Jesse L.
25Exh-2
E120
V100
V117-1
W514-120
W516-12
W572
W573
W575

Barnes, John Francis
(Honey)
No Cards.

Barnes, John S.
N172

Barnes, Luther Owen
(Lute)
No Cards.

Barnes, Mike
80Buffa-1

Barnes, Richard
78Knoxv
79Knoxv/TCMA-5
82Edmon-19
84D-608
84Maine-6

Barnes, Roscoe C.
(Ross)
No Cards.

Barnes, Samuel Thomas
(Sam)
No Cards.

Barnes, Virgil
28Exh-17

Barnes, William H.
(Bill)
No Cards.

Barnes, William Henry
(Skeeter)
79Nashvl
80Water-15
81Indianap-29
82Water-13
83Indianap-31
85D-530
86Indianap-16
88BuffB/CMC-23
88BuffB/Pro-1487
89AAA/Pro-15

Barnett, Larry
88Umpire-7
89Umpires-5

Barney, Edmund J.
(Ed)
No Cards.

Barney, Rex
48B-41
49B-61
49Eureka-29
50B-76
51B-153
D305

Barnhart, Clyde Lee
21Exh-8
E120
E126-2
V61-108

Barnhart, Edgar V.
(Ed)
No Cards.

Barnhart, Leslie Earl
(Les)
No Cards.

Barnhart, Rick
79Wausa-13

Barnhart, Victor Dee
(Vic)
No Cards.

Barnhouse, Scott
83Wausa/LF-18

Barnicle, George B.
No Cards.

Barnicle, Ted
76Cedar
79Knoxv/TCMA-21
80GlenF/B-11
80GlenF/C-19

Barnie, William H.
(Billy)
N172

Barnowski, Edward A.
(Ed)
66T-442R
67T-507R

Barns, Jeff
88PalmSp/Cal-100
88PalmSp/Pro-1451
89MidldA/GS-5

Barnwell, Richard
89Oneon/Pro-2117

Barnwell, Rob
87Watertn-21

Barojas, Salome
83D-67
83F-230
84D-570
84F-53
84TrueVal/WS-5
85D-605
85F-482
85Moth/Mar-19

Baron, Sean
88BurlR/Pro-1778

Barone, Richard A.
(Dick)
61Union

Barr, Bob
76Watlo

Barr, Hyder Edward
(Bob)
No Cards.

Barr, James Leland
(Jim)
72OPC-232R
72T-232R
73OPC-387
73T-387
74OPC-233
74T-233
75Ho-13
75Ho/Twink-13
75OPC-107
75T-107
75T/M-107
76OPC-308
76SSPC-92
76T-308
77Ho-83
77OPC-119
77T-609
78OPC-19
78T-62
79T-461
80OPC-275
80T-529
81D-412
81F-287
81T-717
83D-398
83F-252
83T-133
84D-79
84F-365
84Nes/792-282
84T-282

Barr, Robert A.
(Bob)
No Cards.

Barr, Robert M.
(Bob)
No Cards.

Barr, Steven Charles
(Steve)
76OPC-595R
76T-595R

Barr, Tim
78Green
80OrlTw-2

Barragan, Facundo A.
(Cuno)
59DF
62T-66
63T-557

Barragan, Gerry
87Madis-12
88Modesto/Cal-73

Barragan, Jaime
(Jimmy) 88Spart/Pro-1036
88Spart/Star-1
88Spart/Star-17
89Clearw/Star-1

Barranca, German
76Watlo
77Jaxvl
81Indianap-25
83Evans-25
84OKCty-24
85Water-17

Barranco, Vince
88BurlR/Pro-1777

Barrera, Nelson
85BuffB-7

Barrett, Charles H.
39Exh
47TipTop
49B-213
52Park-14

Barrett, Charles
77LodiD

Barrett, Dick
47Centen-1

Barrett, Francis J.
(Frank)
No Cards.

Barrett, James E.
(Jimmy)
E107
T201
WG2-2

Barrett, Jeff
87Indianap-17

Barrett, John Joseph
(Johnny)
No Cards.

Barrett, Kewpie
47Signal

Barrett, Martin F.
(Marty)
No Cards.

Barrett, Martin Glen
(Marty)
81Pawtu-14
83Pawtu-14
84F/X-8
84Nes/792-683
84T-683
85D-127
85F-150
85Leaf-229
85T-298
85T/St-219
86D-294
86F-340
86Leaf-169
86OPC-314
86T-734
86T/St-250
87Classic-61
87D-523
87D/OD-188
87F-27
87F/AwardWin-1
87F/St-5
87F/WS-6
87Leaf-165
87OPC-39
87S-112M
87S-182
87Seven-ME2
87T-39
87T/HL-17
87T/St-18
87Woolwth-17
88D-276
88D/Best-9
88D/RedSox/Bk-276
88F-343
88Leaf-141
88OPC-338
88Panini/St-28
88Score-155
88Sf-157
88T-525
88T/Big-54
88T/St-248
89B-28
89D-184
89D/Best-252
89F-78
89OPC-155
89Panini/St-276
89Score-63
89Sf-198
89T-155
89T/Big-278
89T/St-257
89UD-173
90D-240
90F-266
90Score-15
90T-355
90UD-133

Barrett, Red
49Eureka-4

Barrett, Robert S.
(Bob)
No Cards.

Barrett, Tim
86Indianap-34
87Indianap-9
88Indi/CMC-5
88Indi/Pro-502
89Indi/CMC-1
89Indi/Pro-1229

Barrett, Tom
84Nashvl-2
85Colum-13
85Colum/Pol-1
86Albany/TCMA-5
87Readg-7
88Maine/CMC-16
88Maine/Pro-284
89ScrWB/CMC-11
89ScrWB/Pro-725
89T-653
89T/Big-177
90Score-633

Barrett, Tracey S.
(Dick)
No Cards.

Barrett, William J.
(Bill)
No Cards.

Barretto, Saul M.
87Gasto-6
88Gasto/Pro-1022

Barrick, Andy
88Batav/Pro-1687

Barrilleaux, John
89Oneon/Pro-2099

Barringer, Reggie
85PrWill-20
86PrWill-1
87Salem-23

Barrios, Eugene
85Greens-24

Barrios, Francisco
77T-222
78T-552
79Ho-21
79T-386
80OPC-58
80T-107
81F-352

Barrios, Gregg
86WinHav-3

Barrios, Jose Manuel
76Cedar
80Phoen-17
81Phoen-12
82Phoen

Barron, Anthony
89Star/Wax-26
89VeroB/Star-2

Barron, David Irenus
(Red)
No Cards.

Barros, Ellie
82Danvi-17

Barrow, Ed
50Callahan
60F-23
80SSPC/HOF
89HOF/St-94

Barrow, Mel
79Tucso-22
79Tulsa-21
80Tulsa-11
81Tulsa-6

Barrows, Roland
(Cuke)
No Cards.

Barrs, Stan
88Savan/Pro-349

Barry, John C.
(Shad)
T206

Barry, John Joseph
(Jack)
10Domino-7
11Helmar-53
12Sweet/Pin-41
14CJ-28

14Piedmont/St-2
15CJ-28
88Conlon/3-4
BF2-1
D303
D304
D327
D328-13
D329-11
D350/2-10
E101
E104
E105
E106
E135-13
E254
E270/1
E300
E90/1
E91
M101/4-11
M101/5-10
M116
S74-27
T201
T202
T205
T206
T207
T208
T216
T222

Barry, John
86Clint-1
88Fresno/Cal-10
88Fresno/Pro-1227

Barry, Richard D.
(Rich)
No Cards.

Bartell, Mike
75Clint

Bartell, Richard
(Dick)
29Exh/4-13
31Exh/4-12
32Orbit/num-15
32Orbit/un-4
33DH-4
33Exh/4-6
33G-28
34DS-101
34Exh/4-6
35BU-4
35G-2A
35G-4A
35G-7A
38G-248
38G-272
41DP-56
55B-234
88Conlon/4-3
PM10/Sm-7
R300
R305
R308-158
R309/2
R310
R314
R337-424
V353-28
V355-37

Bartels, Bill
87VeroB-26
85Anchora-2
88Lynch/Star-1

Barthelson, Robert E.
(Bob)
47Sunbeam

Barthold, John F.
No Cards.

Bartholomew, Lester
No Cards.

Bartholow, Bud
83Readg-1

Bartirome, Anthony J.
(Tony)
52T-332
53T-71

Bartley, Boyd Owen
No Cards.

Bartley, Greg
84Chatt-29
86Calgary-1
87Chatt/Best-3

Bartley, William J.
(Bill)
E254

Bartling, Irving H.
(Irv)
No Cards.

Bartolomucci, Tony
86AppFx-1

Barton, Harry Lamb
No Cards.

Barton, Jeff
89Spoka/SP-21

Barton, Ken
76Cedar
77Cedar
81Charl-10

Barton, Larry
40Hughes-3
47Signal

Barton, Robert Wilbur
(Bob)
66T-511R
67T-462
68T-351
69OPC-41
69T-41
70OPC-352
70T-352
71MLB/St-218
71OPC-589
71T-589
72MB-27
72OPC-39
72OPC-40IA
72T-39
72T-40A
73OPC-626
73T-626

Barton, Shawn
86Readg-2
86SanJose-2
87Maine-6
87Maine/TCMA-1
87SanJose-29
88Jacks/GS-19
89Reno/Cal-260
89Tidew/CMC-8
89Tidew/Pro-1969

Barton, Vincent David
(Vince)
No Cards.

Bartosch, David R.
(Dave)
No Cards.

Bartson, Charles F.
(Charlie)
No Cards.

Barun, Barton
82Redwd-24

Basgall, Romanus
(Monty)
49Eureka-152
52T-12
73OPC-569CO
73T-569C
74OPC-144CO
74T-144C

Bashang, Albert C.
(Al)
No Cards.

Bashore, Walter F.
(Walt)
No Cards.

Basinski, Edward F.
(Eddie)
47TipTop
52Mother-6
53Mother-32

Baskette, James B.
(Jim)
No Cards.

Bass, Barry
83BurlR-1
83BurlR/LF-9
84Tulsa-22
85Tulsa-26
87ElPas-27
88ElPas/Best-17

Bass, Bart
77Cedar

Bass, Ed
85FtMyr-1

Bass, Jerry
78Clint
79LodiD-16
82BirmB-18

Bass, John E.
No Cards.

Bass, Kevin
77Newar
78BurlB
79Holyo-5
79T-708R
80Holyo-13
81Vanco-24
82Pol/Brew
82Pol/Brew-26
82Vanco-4
84D-450
84F-221
84Nes/792-538
84T-538
85D-136
85F-345
85F/St-52
85Moth/Ast-22
85T-326
86D-548
86D/HL-21
86F-294
86OPC-52
86Pol/Ast-4
86T-458
86T/St-28
87Classic-17
87D-410
87D/AAS-40
87D/OD-14
87Drake-17
87F-51
87F/Hottest-3
87F/Mini-5
87F/Slug-1
87F/St-6
87Leaf-211
87Moth/Ast-9
87OPC-85
87Pol/Ast-22
87S-117M
87S-175
87T-85
87T/Gloss60-34
87T/Mini-7
87T/St-34
88D-286
88D/Best-38
88F-440
88F/Excit-2
88F/Mini-77
88F/St-85
88Leaf-137
88Moth/Ast-9
88OPC-175
88Panini/St-298
88Pol/Ast-6
88Score-33
88Sf-55
88T-175
88T/Big-77
88T/St-29
89Ames-2
89D-325
89F-351
89Lennox/Ast-5
89Moth/Ast-8
89OPC-102
89Panini/St-91
89Score-226
89Sf-11
89T-646
89T/Big-187
89T/St-14
89UD-425
90D-589
90F-223
90Score-279
90Score/100St-100
90Sf-198
90T-281
90UD-302

Bass, Norm
62T-122
63T-461

Bass, Randy William
79T-707R
82D-439
82F-566
82T-307

Bass, Regan
86DayBe-2

Bass, William Capers
(Doc)
No Cards.

Bassett, Charles E.
(Charley)
N172
N284
WG1-28

Bassett, Matt
84Omaha-29
85Omaha-2

Bassler, John Landis
(Johnny)
21Exh-9
25Exh-89
26Exh-89
27Exh-45
E120
E126-55
V100
V117-10
W572
W573
WG7-4

Basso, Michael A.
86Cram/PCL-167
87CharRa-20
88TexLgAS/GS-23
88Wichi-16
89AubAs/Pro-9
89Wich/Roc-16
89Wich/Roc/HL-12

Bast, Steve
86Elmir-2
87NewBrit-11
89NewBrit/Pro-608
89Pawtu/Dunkin-30

Bastable, John M.
76OkCty

Bastian, Charles J.
(Charlie)
N172
N284
N690
WG1-47

Bastian, John K.
(Jack)
T206

Bastian, Jose
79RochR-17
81Toled-3

Bastian, Robert
81Redwd-1
83Nashua-1
85Cram/PCL-21
86Edmon-1

Batch, Emil Henry
C46-48
T205
T206

Batchelder, Joseph E.
(Joe)
No Cards.

Bateman, John Alvin
63Pep
63T-386R
64T-142
64T/Coins-107
65T-433
66OPC-86
66T-86
67T-231
68Coke
68T-592
69Fud's-2
69MB-21
69MLB/St-155
69OPC-138
69T-138
69T/St-53
70MLB/St-61
70OPC-417
70T-417
71MLB/St-122
71OPC-31
71OPC-628
71T-628
71T/Coins-19
72MB-28
72OPC-5
72T-5

Bates, Billy
86ElPas-4
87Denver-7
88Denver/CMC-17
88Denver/Pro-1271
89AAA/Pro-41
89Denver/CMC-15
89Denver/Pro-38
90Score-608
90Score/100Ris-80

Bates, Charles W.
No Cards.

Bates, Delbert O.
No Cards.

Bates, Eric
89Bill/Pro-2061

Bates, Hubert Edgar
(Buddy)
R314/Can
V355-126

Bates, John William
(Johnny)
10Domino-8
11Helmar-109
12Sweet/Pin-94
E104
E254
E94
M116
S74-97
T202
T204
T205
T206
W555

Bates, Kevin
84Shrev/FB-1
Bates, Raymond
(Ray)
No Cards.
Bates, Richard
(Dick)
No Cards.
Bates, Steve
88Clearw/Star-1
Batesole, Michael
86Bakers-2
87VeroB-15
88VeroB/Star-1
Bathe, Bill
82WHave-10
83Tacom-10
84Cram/PCL-80
85Cram/PCL-148
86D/Rook-41
86F/Up-U9
86Moth/A's-23
87D-281
88AAA/Pro-16
88IowaC/CMC-23
88IowaC/Pro-527
89Phoen/CMC-11
89Phoen/Pro-1495
90D-680
Bathe, Bob
84Albany-23
85Cram/PCL-143
86IowaC-2
Batista, Francisco
82Sprin-24
83ArkTr-20
83StPet-20
Batista, Miguel
86CharRa-2A
86CharRa-2B
Batista, Rafael
No Cards.
Batiste, Chris
89Bluef/Star-3
Batiste, Kevin
87Duned-19
88Knoxv/Best-7
89Knoxv/Best-2
89Knoxv/Pro-1124
89Knoxv/Star-7
90UD-115
Batiste, Kim
88Spart/Pro-1035
88Spart/Star-18
88Spart/Star-2
89Clearw/Star-2
Batsch, William M.
(Bill)
No Cards.
Battam, Lawrence
(Larry)
No Cards.
Battell, Mark
88Hamil/Pro-1725
89Hamil/Star-2
Batten, George B.
No Cards.
Batten, Mark
81Wausa-8
Battey, Earl Jesse
57T-401
58T-364
59T-114
60L-66
60T-328
61Bz-28
61Clover-3
61P-97
61Peters-22
61T-315
61T-582AS
61T/Dice-1
61T/St-177
62Bz
62J-90
62P-90
62P/Can-90
62Salada-19
62Shirriff-19
62T-371
62T/bucks
62T/St-74
63Exh
63J-8
63P-8
63Salada-44
63T-306M
63T-410
64T-90
64T/Coins-101
64T/Coins-136AS
64T/St-71
64T/SU
64Wheat/St-6
65T-490
65T/E-70
66T-240
66T/RO-55
67OPC-15
67T-15
78TCMA-113
88Pac/Leg-35
Exh47
Battin, Joseph V.
(Joe)
No Cards.
Battle, James Milton
(Jim)
No Cards.
Batton, Chris
76Tucso-10
77T-475R
Batts, Matthew Daniel
(Matt)
48L-108
51B-129
52B-216
52T-230
53B/BW-22
53Glen
54B-183
54T-88
55B-161
76Baton/MG
Exh47
Bauer, Alice
52Wheat
Bauer, Dave
89Penin/Star-1
Bauer, Eric
85Spoka/Cram-1
87Wichi-22
88Wichi-33
Bauer, Henry Albert
(Hank)
50B-219
51B-183
51BR-A4
51T/RB-24
52B-65
52BR
52Coke
52T-215
52TipTop
53B/Col-44M
53B/Col-84
53Briggs
53RM-AL2
53SM
54B-129
54DanDee
54NYJour
54RM-AL23
54SM
54T-130
55B-246
55RM-AL22
55SM
55T-166
56T-177
57T-240
58T-9
59T-240
60T-262
61P-90
61T-119M
61T-398
61T/St-156
62T-127M
62T-463
64T-178
65T-323
66T-229
67OPC-1M
67T-1M
67T-534
68T-513
69OPC-124MG
69T-124
79TCMA-22
89Pac/Leg-144
89Swell-82
Exh47
PM10/L-3
Bauer, Mark
85Huntsvl/BK-26
Bauer, Marlene
52Wheat
Bauer, Pete
86LitFalls-2
87Lynch-14
88Clmbia/GS-2
89Jacks/GS-23
Bauer, Phil
76Clint
79AppFx-14
Bauers, Russell
40PB-219
52Park-4
Baum, Jeff
88AppFx/Pro-158
Bauman, Brad
81Shrev-10
Baumann, Charles John
(Paddy)
T207
Baumann, Frank
58T-167
59T-161
60T-306
61P-34
61T-46LL
61T-550
62T-161
63T-381
64T-453
65OPC-161
65T-161
Baumer, James Sloan
(Jim)
61T-292
Baumgardner, George
14CJ-131
15CJ-131
T222
Baumgarten, Ross
79T-704R
80T-138
81D-41
81OPC-328
81T-398
82D-104
82F-337
82OPC-322
82T-563
82T/Tr-3T
83F-302
83T-97
Baumgartner, John E.
No Cards.
Baumholtz, Frank C.
49B-21
52B-195
52T-225
54B-221
54RH
54T-60
55B-227
55T-172
56T-274
Exh47
R423-3
Baur, Al
89Martins/Star-1
Bauta, Ed
61Union
62T-344
63T-336
Bautista, Antonio
77WHave
Bautista, Benny
85Newar-12
87Hagers-6
Bautista, German
86Miami-1
Bautista, Jose
85Lynch-9
88D/Rook-41
88F/U-U1
88French-48
88T/Tr-10T
89B-3
89D-451
89F-608
89French-48
89Score-573
89T-469
89T/St-229
89UD-574
90UD-8
Bautista, Ramon
80Clint-4
82Clint-13
83Clint/LF-8
88Watlo/Pro-676
89Kinston/Star-2
Baxes, Jim
59T-547
60T-318
Baxes, Michael
(Mike)
58T-302
59T-381
Baxter, Jim
88Watlo/Pro-671
89Lakel/Star-2
Baxter, John
No Cards.
Baxter, William
C46-80
Bay, Harry Elbert
E107
T206
T213/brown
WG2-3
Bayer, Chris
86Columbia-5
Bayer, Christopher A.
(Burley)
No Cards.
Bayless, Harry Owen
(Dick)
E254
E270/1
Baylor, Don Edward
71OPC-709R
71T-709R
72OPC-474R
72T-474R
73JP
73OPC-384
73T-384
74OPC-187
74T-187
74T/St-121
75OPC-382
75T-382
75T/M-382
76Ho-118
76OPC-125
76SSPC-394
76T-125
77Ho-129
77OPC-133
77T-462
78OPC-173
78T-48
79Ho-63
79OPC-335
79T-635
80BK/PHR-12
80K-56
80OPC-150
80T-285
81D-413
81F-271
81F/St-122
81K-15
81OPC-309
81T-580
81T/HT
81T/St-51
82D-493
82F-451
82F/St-220
82KMart-35
82OPC-234
82T-415
82T/St-158
83D-493
83Drake-1
83F-77
83K-29
83OPC-105
83T-105
83T/St-40
83T/X-8
84D-152
84Drake-1
84F-119
84F/St-45
84FunFood/Pin-39
84Nes/792-335
84Nes/792-486TL
84OPC-335
84T-335
84T/St-320
85D-173
85D/HL-35
85Drake-3
85F-121
85F/St-49
85Leaf-146
85OPC-70
85T-70
85T/St-311
86D-347
86F-631M
86F-99
86F/St-3
86F/Up-U10
86OPC-184
86S-59M
86T-765
86T/St-300
86T/Tr-6T
86Woolwth-2
87Classic-14
87D-339
87D/OD-186

87F-28
87F/GameWin-2
87F/Hottest-4
87F/Mini-6
87F/St-7
87KayBee-3
87Leaf-232
87OPC-230
87OPC-A
87S-163
87Seven-E2
87T-230
87T-A
87T/Board-17
87T/Gloss60-27
87T/St-252
88Woolwth-1
88Woolwth-29
88D/A's/Bk-NEW
88F-2
88F/St-S1
88F/WS-11
88Moth/A's-8
88OPC-A
88Score-250
88Score/Tr-55T
88T-545
88T/Big-162
88T/St-10
88T/Tr-11T
88T/WaxBox-A
89Ames-3
89F-1
89Score-205
89Smok/Angels-13
89T-673
89UD-601

Bayne, William
E120

Beach, Jackson S.
(Jack)
No Cards.

Beacom, Chris
89StCath/Pro-2085

Beahan, Scott
83Greens-2

Beal, Sally
78Newar-GM

Beal, Tony
86NewBrit-2

Beall, John Woolf
(Johnny)
No Cards.

Beall, Mike
89AppFx/Pro-864

Beall, Robert Brooks
(Bob)
76SSPC-21
79T-222
80Richm-19
81Portl-7

Beals, Bryan
88GreatF-19
89Bakers/Cal-197

Beals, Thomas L.
(Tommy)
No Cards.

Beamesderfer, Kurt
87CharO/WBTV-19

Beamon, Charles Alon.
(Charlie)
59T-192
60HenryH-30

Beamon, Charles Alph.
77SnJos-9
78SnJos-12
79Spoka-6
80Spoka-24
80T-672R
81Syrac-12
82Syrac-15

Beamon, Nick
(Pepper)
79WHave-22M
80WHave-18

Beams, Mike
88Ashvl/Pro-1054
88AubAs/Pro-1962
89Ashvl/Pro-968

Bean, Billy
87Portl-5
88T-267
88Toled/CMC-12
88Toled/Pro-595
89Class-33
89Score/HotRk-19
89Toled/Pro-772

Bean, Joseph William
(Joe)
No Cards.

Bean, Kenneth
88Martins/Star-2
89Martins/Star-2

Beanblossom, Brad
88CapeCod/Sum-147

Beane, William Lamar
(Billy)
82Jacks-19
84Jacks-17
85IntLgAS-7
85Tidew-14
86D-647
86F/Up-U11
87F-535
87T-114
87Toled-26

Beard, Cramer T.
(Ted)
51B-308
52T-150

Beard, Dave
80Ogden-15
81T-96R
81Tacom-24
82F-87
83D-113
83F-514
83Granny-33
83T-102
84D-218
84F-438
84F/X-9
84Moth/Mar-11
84Nes/792-513
84OPC-149
84T-513
84T/St-336
84T/X-8
85F-483
85Maine-2
85T-232
86Richm-2
88Toled/CMC-1
88Toled/Pro-586
89Toled/CMC-10
89Toled/Pro-777

Beard, Mike
76OPC-53
76T-53

Beard, Oliver Perry
(Ollie)
N172

Beard, Ralph
55B-206

Bearden, Gene
46Remar-17
49B-57
50NumNum
51B-284
52B-173
52NTea
52T-229
53Exh/Can-3
55B-93
79TCMA-222
Exh47

Beardman, Larry
84Madis/Pol-24

Beardsley, Chris
89PalmSp/Cal-58

Beare, Gary Ray
78T-516
79OkCty

Bearnarth, Larry
63T-386R
64T-527
65OPC-258
65T-258
66T-464
78TCMA-61
80Memph-8
86Provigo-14CO

Bearse, Kevin
88CLAS/Star-24
88Kinston/Star-2
89Canton/Best-1
89Canton/Pro-1306

Beasley, Bud
46Sunbeam
47Signal
47Sunbeam

Beasley, Chris
86Water-2
87Wmspt-22
89PalmSp/Pro-488

Beasley, Lewis Paige
(Lew)
77Tucso

Beasley, Tony
89Erie/Star-1

Beatin, Ebenezer
N172

Beatle, David
(Dave)
No Cards.

Beattie, Burt
87Kenosha-8

Beattie, Jim
77WHave
79BK/Y-7
79Colum-8
79OPC-86
79T-179
80T-334
81D-166
81Spoka-29
81T-443
82D-478
82T-22
83D-176
83F-472
83OPC-191
83T-675
83T-711
84D-191
84F-605
84Moth/Mar-12
84Nes/792-288
84OPC-288
84T-288
84T/St-346
85D-313
85F-484
85Leaf-85
85Moth/Mar-15
85OPC-303
85T-505
85T/St-334
86D-196
86F-458
86Moth/Mar-27
86T-729
87T-117

Beatty, Aloysius D.
(Des)
No Cards.

Beatty, Blaine
87Hagers-12
88Jacks/GS-15
88TexLgAS/GS-18
89Tidew/CMC-9
89Tidew/Pro-1964
90F-197
90Score-632
90UD-23

Beauchamp, James E.
(Jim)
62Kahn/Atl
63Pep/Tul
64T-492R
65T-409R
66OPC-84R
66T-84R
67T-307
69T-613
71MLB/St-266
71OPC-322
71T-322
72T-594
73OPC-137
73T-137
74OPC-424
74T-424
78Charl
79Charl-2
80Indianap-2MG
81Indianap-2MG
82Syrac-26
83Syrac-1
84Syrac-1
87Greenv/Bst-1MG
87SLAS-22
88Richm-9MG
88Richm/CMC-23
88Richm/Pro-15
89AAA/Pro-53
89Richm/CMC-25MG
89Richm/Ko-9MG
89Richm/Pro-822

Beauchamp, Kash
86Knoxv-1
87Syrac/TCMA-29
88Knoxv/Best-9
89Richm/CMC-23
89Richm/Ko-7
89Richm/Pro-836

Beaumont, Clarence H.
(Ginger)
E107
E254
M116
T206
WG3-2

Beavers, Mark
85Anchora-3
86Cram/PCL-55
87Madis-20
88Modesto/Cal-61
89River/Best-2
89River/Cal-23
89River/Pro-1390

Bechtel, George A.
No Cards.

Beck, Clyde Eugene
29Exh/4-5

Beck, Dion
85Bend/Cram-1
87Readg-8

Beck, Ervin Thomas
(Erve)
E107

Beck, Frederick T.
(Fred)
M116
T205
T206

Beck, Rich
66T-234R

Beck, Rod
88Clint/Pro-695
88MidwLAS/GS-5
89SanJose/Best-2
89SanJose/Cal-209
89SanJose/Pro-459
89SanJose/Star-1
89Star/Wax-82

Beck, Walter
34G-50
40PB-217

Beck, Zinn Bertram
11Helmar-140
D329-12
M101/4-12
S74-42

Beckendorf, Henry W.
(Heinie)
09Buster/Pin-2
M116

Becker, Beals
10Domino-9
11Helmar-121
12Sweet/Pin-107
14CJ-96
14Piedmont/St-3
15CJ-96
E254
S74-80
T202
T205
T206
T207
T213/brown

Becker, Gregory
87StPet-23
88MidwLAS/GS-27
88Sprin/Best-5
89Star/Wax-47
89StPet/Star-2

Becker, Heinz R.
No Cards.

Becker, Joseph Edward
(Joe)
52Park-1
55Gol/Dodg-3
60T-463CO
79TCMA-187

Becker, Martin Henry
(Marty)
No Cards.

Becker, Tim
87FtLaud-1
88Albany/Pro-1341
89Albany/Best-20
89Albany/Pro-315
89Albany/Star-2

Becker, Tom
88LitFalls/Puc-4

Beckert, Glenn Alfred
65T-549R
66T-232
67T-296
68OPC-101
68T-101
69Kelly/Pin-3
69MB-22
69MLB/St-119
69OPC-171
69Sunoco/Pin-2
69T-171
69T/St-12
70Dunkin-2
70K-43
70MLB/St-14
70OPC-480
70T-480
71K-71
71MD
71MLB/St-26

71OPC-390
71T-390
71T/Coins-143
71T/S-50
72K-24
72MB-29
72OPC-45
72OPC-46IA
72OPC-85LL
72T-45
72T-46A
72T-85LL
73OPC-440
73T-440
74McDon
74OPC-241
74T-241
74T/St-11
75Ho-103
75Ho/Twink-103
75OPC-484
75T-484
75T/M-484
89Pac/Leg-142
89Swell-116

Beckley, Jacob Peter
(Jake)
80SSPC/HOF
E107
N172
T206
WG3-3

Beckman, Bernie
83Syrac-2

Beckwith, Joe
78Cr/PCL-36
79Albuq-20
80Albuq-2
80Pol/Dodg-27
80T-679R
81Pol/Dodg-27
81T-231
82Albuq-1
83F-202
83Pol/Dodg-27
84D-337
84F-97
84F/X-10
84Nes/792-454
84T-454
84T/X-9
85D-541
85F-197
85T-77
86F-2
86Syrac-4
86T-562

Beckwith, John
74Laugh/Black-6

Becquer, Julio V.
58T-458
59T-93
60L-43
60T-271
61T-329

Bedell, Howard W.
61T-353
62Salada-217
62Shirriff-217
62T-76

Bedell, Jeff
86FtMyr-3

Bedford, James Elred
(Jim)
No Cards.

Bedrosian, Dave
76Wausa

Bedrosian, Steve
79Savan-14
81Richm-12
82BK/Lids-2
82D-401
82Pol/Atl-32
82T-502R
82T/Tr-4T
83D-173
83F-129
83OPC-157
83Pol/Atl-32
83T-157
84D-565
84F-171
84Nes/792-365
84OPC-365
84Pol/Atl-32
84T-365
84T/St-38
85D-628
85F-319
85Ho/Braves-3
85Leaf-51
85OPC-25
85Pol/Atl-32
85Seven-6S
85T-25
85T/St-23
86CIGNA-11
86D-199
86F-508
86F/Up-U12
86OPC-181
86T-648
86T/St-40
86T/Tr-7T
87D-185
87D/HL-9
87F-170
87F/McCror-3
87F/Slug-M1
87F/St-8
87OPC-233
87RedFoley/St-98
87S-110
87Smok/NL-7
87T-736
87T/Mini-27
87T/St-124
88Woolwth-10
88Class/Blue-222
88D-62
88D/AS-61
88D/Best-16
88F-298
88F-627M
88F/AwardWin-1
88F/Mini-98
88F/SS-1
88F/St-107
88Leaf-82
88MSA/Disc-18
88Nestle-25
88OPC-344
88OPC-B
88Panini/St-351
88Panini/St-440
88Score-161
88Score-656
88Sf-222
88Sf-70
88T-407
88T-440
88T/Big-23
88T/Coins-34
88T/Gloss60-28
88T/Mini-64
88T/Revco-11
88T/St-116
88T/St-6
88T/St/Backs-31
88T/UK-2
88T/WaxBox-B
89B-395
89Class-34
89D-24DK
89D-75
89D/Best-303
89D/DKsuper-24DK
89F-562
89F/BBMVP's-1
89Panini/St-145
89Score-260
89Score/HotSt-29
89Score/Tr-49
89Sf-63
89T-20
89T/Big-137
89T/St-112
89T/Tr-8T
89Tetley/Discs-15
89UD-511
90Class-62
90D-295
90F-50
90Score-379
90Score/100St-31
90Sf-104
90T-310
90UD-618

Beebe, Fred
12Sweet/Pin-95
C46-54
E270/2
M116
T204

Beecher, Edward H.
(Ed)
N284

Beecroft, Mike
82BirmB-6

Beeler, Joseph Sam
(Jodie)
No Cards.

Beeler, Pete
87Tampa-27
88Cedar/Pro-1147
88MidwLAS/GS-8
89Cedar/Star-25
89Chatt/Best-11
89Chatt/GS-4

Beene, Andy
82ElPas-14
84Cram/PCL-26

Beene, Fred
70OPC-121R
70T-121R
71MLB/St-219
73OPC-573
73T-573
74OPC-274
74T-274
75OPC-181
75T-181
75T/M-181
76SSPC-504
79OkCty
80Tidew-14

Beene, Steve
76Watlo
77DaytB

Beer, Darrin
89Geneva/Pro-1863

Beerbower, Dan
76QuadC

Befort, Curt
87Clearw-3

Beggs, Joe
Exh47
W711/2

Begley, James L.
(Jim)
No Cards.

Begue, Roger
82Lynch-18

Behel, Steven A. D.
(Steve)
N172/ST

Behenna, Rick
81Durhm-15
83Pol/Atl-49
84D-346
85Polar/Ind-32

Behney, Mel
72OPC-524R
72T-524R
73OPC-602R
73T-602R

Behnsch, Bobby
87Clearw-7

Behny, Mark
86Erie-3
87Savan-24
88Savan/Pro-339

Behrend, Mike
83Erie-11
84Savan-26

Behrman, Henry
49Eureka-101
50Remar

Beitey, Dan
75Cedar

Bejma, Aloysius Frank
(Ollie)
35BU-55
35BU-93
R312/M

Belan, Lance
86PrWill-2

Belanger, Lee
82Orlan-2
83Visal/LF-1

Belanger, Mark Henry
67T-558R
68Coke
68OPC-118
68T-118
69T-299
69T/St-121
70MLB/St-145
70T-615
71MLB/St-289
71OPC-99
71T-99
72OPC-224WS
72OPC-456
72T-456
73JP
73OPC-253
73T-253
74OPC-329
74T-329
74T/St-122
75OPC-74
75T-74
75T/M-74
76OPC-505
76T-505
77Ho-71
77OPC-154
77T-135
78OPC-125
78T-315
78T-315
79OPC-27
79T-65
80OPC-217
80T-425
81D-472
81F-175
81F/St-39
81T-641
82F-158
82F/St-148
82OPC-42
82Pol/Dodg
82Pol/Dodg-8
82T-776
82T/Tr-5T
83D-514
83T-273

Belardi, Carroll W.
(Wayne)
55B-36
79TCMA-110

Belbru, Juan
89Savan/Pro-356

Belcher, Glenn
87Fayette-27
88Fay/Pro-1080
89Fay/Pro-1568

Belcher, Kevin
88Gasto/Pro-1010
88Gasto/Pro-1004
89Gasto/Star-2

Belcher, Tim
84Madis/Pol-9
85Huntsvl/BK-31
85T-281FDP
87Tacom-21
88D-587
88D/Best-10
88D/Rook-28
88F-509
88Moth/Dodg-23
88Pol/Dodg-49M
88Score/Tr-101T
88T/Tr-12T
89B-336
89Bz-1
89Class-57
89D-203
89D/Best-234
89F-54
89F/Superstar-3
89F/WS-2
89KMart/DT-9
89Moth/Dodg-23
89OPC-177
89Panini/St-21
89Panini/St-95
89Pol/Dodg-25
89Score-418
89Score/HotRk-94
89Score/YS/I-36
89Sf-121
89T-456
89T/Big-145
89T/Gloss60-30
89T/JumboR-3
89T/St-317
89ToysRUs-3
89UD-648
89Woolwth-19
89Woolwth-29
90D-79
90F-389
90F/WaxBox-C2
90Score-126
90T-173
90UD-547

Belcik, Keith
84LitFalls-2

Belden, Ira Allison
No Cards.

Belen, Lance
85PrWill-14
87Harrisbg-11
88Harris/Pro-844

Belen, Mattie
89Bluef/Star-4

Belford, John
89Well/Puc-35M

Belinda, Stan
87Macon-17
88CLAS/Star-3
88Salem/Star-2
89Harris/Pro-305
89Harris/Star-3
90Score-634
90T-354

Belinskas, Dan
86Cedar/TCMA-1
Belinsky, Bo
62T-592R
63T-33
64T-315
65OPC-225
65T-225
66T-506
67T-447
69T-366
89Pac/Leg-130
89Swell-16
Belk, Chuck
79Wisco-20
Bell, Bobby
86PalmSp-2
86PalmSp/Smok-5
87PalmSp-25
88PalmSp/Pro-1459
Bell, Cool Papa
74Laugh/Black-24
80SSPC/HOF
83D/HOF-25
88Conlon/NegAS-1
89Kahn/Coop-1
Bell, David Gus
(Buddy)
73OPC-31
73T-31
74K-10
74OPC-257
74T-257
74T/DE-37
74T/St-161
75Ho-30
75Ho/Twink-30
75OPC-38
75T-38
75T/M-38
76Ho-95
76OPC-358
76OPC-66FS
76SSPC-517
76T-358
76T-66M
77Ho-69
77OPC-86
77Pep-11
77T-590
77T/CS-2
78Ho-15
78OPC-234
78PapaG/Disc-34
78T-280
78Wiffle/Discs-2
79Ho-147
79K-14
79OPC-367
79T-690
80K-53
80OPC-107
80T-190
80T-47
81D-145
81F-625
81F/St-11
81K-64
81MSA/Disc-1
81OPC-66
81T-475
81T/HT
81T/Nat/Super-1
81T/S
81T/SO-21
81T/St-130
82D-23DK
82D-368
82Drake-2
82F-313
82F/St-172
82F/St-239
82K-33
82OPC-50
82T-50
82T/St-238
83D-215
83D/AAS-40
83F-562
83F-632M
83K-12
83OPC-330
83Rangers-25
83T-330
83T-412
83T/Gloss-9
83T/Gloss40-9
83T/St-119
84D-56
84D/AAS-12
84F-413
84FunFood/Pin-76
84Nes/792-37TL
84Nes/792-665
84OPC-347
84Rangers-25
84Seven-11W
84T-665
84T/St-351
85D-56
85D/AAS-11
85F-556
85F/LimEd-1
85F/St-7
85GenMills-13
85Leaf-174
85OPC-176
85Rangers-25
85T-131FS
85T-745
85T/St-347
85T/Super-53
86D-447
86F-172
86F/Mini-37
86OPC-285
86S-151
86T-285
86T/St-139
86TexGold-25
86TrueVal-20
87D-556
87D/OD-196
87F-193
87Kahn-25
87Leaf-169
87OPC-104
87RedFoley/St-38
87S-141
87T-545
87T/Board-21
87T/St-143
88D-206
88F-227
88Jiffy-1
88Leaf-192
88Nestle-30
88OPC-130
88Panini/St-279
88RedFoley/St-5
88Score-99
88Sf-147
88T-130
88T/St-138
88T/Tr-13T
89B-229
89F-352
89Moth/R-9
89OPC-92
89Score-610
89Smok/R-3
89T-461
89T/Big-270
89T/St-18
89UD-112
Bell, David Russell
(Gus)
51B-40
51T/RB-17
52T-170
53B/BW-1
53NB
53T-118
54B-124
54RH
54RM-NL19
55B-243
55Kahn
55RFG-16
55RM-NL23
56Kahn
56T-162
57Kahn
57T-180
58Kahn
58T-75
59Kahn
59T-365
60Kahn
60MacGregor-3
60T-235
60T-352
61Kahn
61P-186
61T-215
61T-25
61T/St-14
62J-120
62P-120
62P/Can-120
62Salada-158A
62Salada-158B
62Shirriff-158
62T-408
62T/St-153
63T-547
64T-534
76OPC-66FS
76T-66M
79TCMA-89
85T-131FS
88Pac/Leg-65
PM10/Sm-8
Bell, Derek
88Myrtle/Pro-1171
88OPC-311
88SALAS/GS-20
89Knoxv/Best-1
89Knoxv/Pro-1149
89Knoxv/Star-1
Bell, Eric
84Newar-2
87D-39RR
87D/Rook-2
87F/U-U2
87Leaf-39RR
87S/Rook-1
87T/Tr-3T
88Class/Red-193
88D-125
88F-555
88OPC-383
88Panini/St-4
88RochR-2
88RochR/CMC-2
88RochR/Pro-194
88Score-101
88Score/YS/II-38
88T-383
88T/St-224
Bell, Fern Lee
No Cards.
Bell, Frank Gustav
No Cards.
Bell, Gary
59Kahn
59T-327
60Kahn
60T-441
61Kahn
61P-58
61T-274
62Kahn
62Salada-213
62Shirriff-213
62Sugar-2
62T-273
62T/bucks
63Sugar-2
63T-129
64T-234
65T-424
66T-525
67T-479
68Coke
68OPC-43
68T-43
69MB-23
69MLB/St-93
69T-377
69T/St-223
89Pac/Leg-213
Bell, George G.
10Domino-10
11Helmar-83
12Sweet/Pin-70A
12Sweet/Pin-70B
D304
E254
E90/1
M116
S74-49
T20
T204
T205
T3-79
Bell, Greg
86WinSal-1
87Pittsf-2
Bell, Herman
34G-52
Bell, Jay
85Visal-8
86Water-4
87BuffB-4
88D-637
88D/Best-61
88F-602
88Gator-16
88T-637
89AAA/Pro-7
89BuffB/CMC-4
89BuffB/Pro-1679
89D-350
89Score-352
89T-144
89UD-489
90D-488
90F-459
90Score-563
90T-523
90UD-517
Bell, Jerry
72OPC-162R
72T-162R
73OPC-92
73T-92
74OPC-261
74T-261
74T/St-191
75SnAnt
Bell, Jorge Antonio
(George)
82D-54
82F-609
82OPC-254
82Syrac-20
82T-254
83Syrac-21
84D-73
84F-148
84FunFood/Pin-113
84Nes/792-278
84OPC-278
84T-278
84Tor/Fire-5
85D-146
85F-100
85F/St-39
85Leaf-248
85OPC-59
85OPC/Post-18
85T-698
85T/St-360
85Tor/Fire-5
86Ault-11
86D-4
86D-71
86D/DKsuper-4
86F-53
86F/Mini-13
86Leaf-4DK
86OPC-338
86OPC-A
86S-102
86T-338
86T-718
86T/Gloss60-47
86T/St-187
86T/Super-10
86T/WaxBox-A
86Tor/Fire-4
87Classic-56
87D-271
87D/OD-39
87F-220
87F/AS-9
87F/AwardWin-2
87F/GameWin-3
87F/McCror-4
87F/Mini-7
87F/Slug-3
87F/St-9
87Ho/St-3
87Kraft-43
87Leaf-184
87OPC-12
87S-51
87S-80M
87T-612AS
87T-681
87T/Coins-3
87T/Gloss60-45
87T/Mini-74
87T/St-193
87Tor/Fire-2
87Tor/Fire-2
88Woolwth-9
88Bz-1
88ChefBoy-4
88Class/Blue-242
88D-656
88D-BC19
88D/AS-6
88D/Best-31
88D/PopUp-6
88F-103
88F-623M
88F/AS-5
88F/AwardWin-2
88F/BB/AS-1
88F/BB/MVP-1
88F/Excit-3
88F/Hottest-1
88F/LL-1
88F/Mini-59
88F/RecSet-2
88F/Slug-1
88F/SS-2
88F/St-71

88F/TL-1
88FanSam-7
88Ho/Disc-22
88KayBee-1
88KMart-1
88Leaf-213CG
88Leaf-214MVP
88Leaf-254
88Nestle-34
88OPC-173
88Panini/St-224
88Panini/St-230M
88RedFoley/St-6
88Score-540
88Score/WaxBox-6
88Sf-4
88T-390
88T-590
88T/Big-15
88T/Coins-1
88T/Gloss22-6
88T/Gloss60-31
88T/Mini-37
88T/Revco-18
88T/RiteAid-26
88T/St-158
88T/St-188
88T/St/Backs-47
88T/UK-3
88Tor/Fire-11
89Ames-4
89B-256
89Class-43
89D-149
89D/Best-272
89F-226
89F/BBAS-2
89F/BBMVP's-2
89F/Heroes-1
89KMart/DT-17
89OPC-50
89Panini/St-472
89RedFoley/St-7
89Score-347
89Score/HotSt-91
89Sf-25
89T-1RB
89T-50
89T/Big-318
89T/Gloss60-27
89T/Mini-75
89T/St-1
89T/St-193
89T/UK-3
89Tor/Fire-11
89UD-255
89Woolwth-7
90Class-84
90D-206
90D/Bon/MVP-BC13
90F-628
90F-76
90Score-286
90Score/100St-27
90Sf-17
90T-170
90UD-127
90UD-95TC

Bell, Juan
87Bakers-7
88BBAmer-23
88SnAnt/Best-24
89B-11
89Class/Up/2-170
89RochR/CMC-21
89RochR/Pro-1658
89UD-20
89UD/Ext-747
90Score-603
90T-724

Bell, Kevin Robert
75AppFx
77T-83
78T-463
79T-662
80OPC-197
80T-379
81D-39
81F-343
81Tacom-25
82Tacom-13

Bell, Lenny
88Peoria/Ko-4
89WinSal/Star-1

Bell, Lester Rowland
(Les)
25Exh-57
26Exh-57
28Yueng-58
E210-58
R309/2
W502-58

Bell, Michael
87Sumter-16
88CLAS/Star-25
88Durhm/Star-1
89Greenv/Pro-1173
89Greenv/Star-3
89Greenvl/Best-4
89Star/Wax-34

Bell, Robert
86Cram/PCL-34

Bell, Ron
77SnJos-20

Bell, Roy Chester
(Beau)
30CEA/Pin-1
37OPC-105
38Exh/4-15
38Wheat-7
39PB-136
40PB-138
V300

Bell, Rudolph Fred
(Rudy)
No Cards.

Bell, Terry
86Chatt-4
87Memph-17
87Memph/Best-23
88Greenv/Best-2
88Richm-14
89Greenv/Pro-1162
89Greenv/Star-4
89Greenvl/Best-19

Bell, Tom
88Fresno/Cal-27
88Fresno/Pro-1248

Bella, John
(Zeke)
59T-254

Bellacetin, Juan
85Tigres-27

Bellaman, Mike
86Water-3
87Wmspt-10

Belle, Joey
88Kinston/Star-3
89Canton/Star-25
89F/Up-25
89Score/Tr-106
90Class-100
90D-390
90F-485
90Score-508
90Score/100Ris-9
90Sf-159
90T-283
90UD-446

Belliard, Rafael
83LynnP-14
87D-538
87D/OD-165
87F-602
87T-541
88F-321
88Score-453
88T-221
88T/Big-175
89F-201
89OPC-119
89Score-379
89T-723
89T/Big-196
89T/St-133
89UD-90
90D-252
90F-460
90Score-520
90T-143
90UD-208

Bellinger, Clayton
89Everett/Star-2

Bellino, Frank
85Newar-25
86Hagers-2
87Hagers-21
88Fresno/Cal-8
89Readg/Best-18
89Readg/Pro-659
89Readg/Star-2

Bellman, John H.
No Cards.

Bello, Duben
88Fay/Pro-1091

Belloir, Robert E.
(Bob)
77T-312
78T-681

Bellver, Juan
86Miami-2

Beltran, Angel
89Well/Puc-4

Beltran, Julio
78DaytB
82Miami-13

Beltre, Esteban
85Utica-12
86WPalm-5
87Jaxvl-11
88Jaxvl/Best-17
88Jaxvl/Pro-991

Beltre, Sergio
79Jacks-9
81Tidew-10

Bemis, Harry Parker
E101
E105
E107
E254
E90/1
E92
M116
T216

Ben, Elijah
83BurlR-12
83BurlR/LF-8

Benavides, Alfredo
89Chatt/Best-12
89Chatt/GS-5

Benavides, Freddie
88Cedar/Pro-1142
89Nashvl-2

Bench, Johnny Lee
68Kahn
68T-247R
69MB-24
69MLB/St-127
69MLBPA/Pin-35
69OPC-95
69T-430AS
69T-95
69T/St-23
70K-58
70MLB/St-25
70OPC-464AS
70T-464AS
70T-660
70T/PI-11
70T/S-8
71Bz
71Bz/Test-29
71MD
71MLB/St-49
71MLB/St-556
71OPC-250
71OPC-64LL
71OPC-66LL
71T-250
71T-64LL
71T-66LL
71T/Coins-149
71T/GM-13
71T/S-32
71T/tatt-11
71T/tatt-11a
72MB-30
72OPC-433
72OPC-434IA
72T-433
72T-434A
73OPC-380
73OPC-62LL
73OPC-63LL
73T-380
73T-62LL
73T-63LL
73T/Comics-3
73T/Lids-5
73T/PinUps-3
74K-28
74OPC-10
74OPC-331AS
74T-10
74T-331M
74T/DE-71
74T/Puzzles-3
74T/St-21
75Ho-83
75K-7
75OPC-208M
75OPC-210M
75OPC-260
75OPC-308LL
75T-208MV
75T-210MV
75T-260
75T-308LL
75T/M-208MV
75T/M-210MV
75T/M-260
75T/M-308LL
76Crane-2
76Ho-22
76Ho/Twink-22
76Icee
76K-36
76MSA/Disc
76OPC-195LL
76OPC-300
76SSPC-31
76T-195LL
76T-300
77Ho-6
77OPC-100
77Pep-44
77T-2LL
77T-3LL
77T-70
78Ho-44
78OPC-50
78T-700
78Wiffle/Discs-3
79Ho-128
79OPC-101
79T-200
79T/Comics-21
80K-52
80OPC-55
80T-100
80T/S-3
81Coke
81D-182
81D-62
81F-196
81F/St-37
81K-65
81MSA/Disc-2
81OPC-286
81Sqt-20
81T-201M
81T-600
81T/HT
81T/Nat/Super-2
81T/S
81T/SO-64
81T/St-160
82Coke/Reds
82D-400
82D-628M
82Drake-3
82F-57
82F/St-17
82K-30
82KMart-18
82KMart-22
82OPC-18
82OPC-304IA
82T-400
82T-401A
82T/St-35
83D-22DK
83D-500
83D/AAS-14
83F-584
83OPC-60
83OPC-61SV
83T-60
83T-61A
83T/St-229
84D-660LLB
84D/Champs-51
84F-462
84F-640IA
84F/St-96
84Nes/792-6HL
84T-6
84T/Gloss22-22
85CircK-22
87KMart-12
87Nestle/DT-30
88Pac/Leg-110
89Kahn/Coop-2
90T-664TBC

Bencomo, Omar
85Kingst-2
87Knoxv-14
88Knoxv/Best-17

Bender, Charles A.
(Chief)
10Domino-11
11Helmar-54
12Sweet/Pin-42A
12Sweet/Pin-42B
14CJ-19
15CJ-19
40PB-172
50Callahan
60F-7
61F-8
61GP-18
63Bz/ATG-11
69Bz/Sm
80Cram/Leg-93
80SSPC/HOF
86Conlon/1-39
BF2-83
D303
D304
D329-13

E101
E102
E103
E104
E105
E106
E107
E224
E286
E90/1
E91
E92
E93
E95
E98
L1-119
M101/4-13
M116
S74-28
S81-94
T201
T202
T204
T205
T206
T207
T208
T213/brown
T215/blue
T227
T3-80
W555
WG2-4
WG5-3
WG6-2

Bendorf, Jerry
82VeroB-17

Bene, Bill
88GreatF-1
89B-340
89Bakers/Cal-184
89T-84FDP

Benedetti, Don
75Cedar

Benedict, Arthur M.
(Art)
No Cards.

Benedict, Bruce Edwin
78Richm
79T-715R
80T-675
81D-208
81F-248
81Pol/Atl-20
81T-108
82BK/Lids-1
82D-375
82F-429
82OPC-168
82Pol/Atl-20
82T-424
82T/St-21
83D-299
83F-130
83OPC-204
83Pol/Atl-20
83T-521
83T/St-151
83T/St-152
83T/St-217
84D-409
84F-172
84Nes/792-255
84OPC-255
84Pol/Atl-20
84T-255
84T/St-34
85D-263
85F-320
85Ho/Braves-4
85Leaf-196
85OPC-335
85Pol/Atl-20
85T-335
85T/St-31
86D-554
86F-509
86OPC-78
86Pol/Atl-20
86T-78
87D-448
87F-512
87Smok/Atl-11
87T-186
88Score-423
88T-652
89B-271
89D-475
89F-587
89OPC-353
89Score-502
89T-778
89T/Big-83
89UD-121
90T-583

Benes, Andy
88T/Tr-14T
89AubAs/Pro-8
89B-448
89T-437FDP
89T/Big-114
89Wich/Roc-30
89Wich/Roc/HL-3
89Wich/Roc/Up-19
89Wich/Roc/Up-5
90Class-120
90D-41
90F-151
90Score-578
90Score/100Ris-69
90Sf-90
90T-193
90UD-55

Benes, Joseph Anthony
(Joe)
82Wausa-7

Benge, Ray
29Exh/4-12
31Exh/4-11
33Exh/4-6
33G-141
34G-24
35BU-11
35BU-99
35G-8A
35G-9A
V354-49
V355-13

Bengough, Bernard O.
(Benny)
29Exh/4-25
33G-1
49Eureka-128
R315-A2
R315-B2
V353-1

Beniquez, Juan Jose
74OPC-647
74T-647
75OPC-601
75T-601
75T/M-601
76OPC-496
76SSPC-406
76T-496
77T-81
78T-238
79BK/Y-22
79T-478
80T-114
81D-518
81F-596
81T-306
81T/Tr-733
82D-587
82F-452
82T-572
83D-640
83F-78
83T-678
84D-207
84F-508
84Nes/792-53
84Smok/Cal-2
84T-53
85D-573
85F-294
85Smok/Cal-14
85T-226
86D-352
86F-148
86F/St-4
86F/Up-U13
86Leaf-156
86OPC-325
86T-325
86T/St-185
86T/Tr-8T
87D-371
87F-462
87F/U-U3
87OPC-173
87T-688
87T/Tr-4T
88F-104
88OPC-77
88OPC-C
88T-541
88T/St-12
88T/WaxBox-C
88Tor/Fire-21
89Bimbo/Discs-8

Benitez, Christian
89Bluef/Star-5

Benitez, Luis
89CharWh/Best-12
89CharWh/Pro-1749
89Geneva/Pro-1870

Benitez, Manuel
86Bakers-3
87VeroB-12

Benjamin, Alfred S.
(Stan)
No Cards.

Benjamin, Mike
88Shreve/Pro-1283
88TexLgAS/GS-11
89Phoen/CMC-16
89Phoen/Pro-1500
90F-51

Benners, Isaac
(Ike)
No Cards.

Bennett, Albert
88Martins/Star-3
89Batav/Pro-1920

Bennett, Brad
82Sprin-23

Bennett, Brian
89Ashvl/Pro-954

Bennett, Charles W.
(Charlie)
N172
N28
N284
N526
Scrapp
WG1-19

Bennett, Chris
89WPalm/Star-3

Bennett, Dave
64T-561R
65T-521R

Bennett, Dennis
63T-56
64T-396
65OPC-147
65T-147
66T-491
67T-206
67T/Test/RedSox-1
78TCMA-93

Bennett, Eric
88CapeCod/Sum-153

Bennett, Herschel E.
No Cards.

Bennett, James Fred
(Red)
No Cards.

Bennett, Jim
82WHave-20
83Tacom-14
84Albany-1
87Memph-25
87Memph/Best-7
89Wausa/GS-17

Bennett, Jose
86Cram/PCL-104
87Wausa-11

Bennett, Joseph R.
(Joe)
No Cards.

Bennett, Justin Titus
(Pug)
No Cards.

Bennett, Keith
86Watlo-3
87Erie-13
87Wmspt-2
88ColSp/Pro-1535
88Watlo/Pro-684

Benoit, Dickens
87Everett-28
89Salin/Cal-137
89Salin/Pro-1827

Benson, Coach
80WHave-23bb

Benson, Randy
76Baton
80Syrac-18

Benson, Steve
80OrlTw-11
83ColumAst-8

Benson, Tom
89Elizab/Star-2

Benson, Vernon A.
(Vern)
53T-205
61Union
73OPC-497CO
73T-497C
74OPC-236CO
74T-236C
78Syrac
79Syrac-2
80Pol/Giants-8C

Bentley, John N.
(Jack)
26Exh-41
27Exh-17
W515-12
WG7-5

Benton, Alfred Lee
(Butch)
76Wausa
79Tidew-8
80Tidew-8
82IowaC-1

Benton, John Alton
50NumNum
52T-374
53Mother-27

Benton, John C.
(Rube)
L1-113
S81-88
T222
W513-69
WG7-6

Benton, Lawrence
25Exh-3
26Exh-1
29Exh/4-9
33G-45
35G-8L
35G-9L
R310
R315-A3
R315-B3
R316
V353-45

Benton, Stanley
(Stan)
No Cards.

Benz, Joseph Louis
15CJ-175
BF2-8
D328-14
D350/2-13
E135-14
E300
M101/5-13
T207

Benza, Brett
82Tulsa-26
83Sprin/LF-10

Benzinger, Todd
86Pawtu-2
87D/Rook-30
87Pawtu-7
87Pawtu/TCMA-13
87S/Rook-44
88Class/Blue-245
88D-297
88D/Best-289
88D/RedSox/Bk-297
88F-344
88F-630M
88Leaf-111
88OPC-96
88Score-546
88Score/YS/I-31
88T-96
88ToysRUs-1
89B-312
89D-358
89D/Best-174
89D/Tr-47
89F-79
89F/Up-83
89K/Reds-25
89OPC-188
89Panini/St-275
89Score-371
89Score/Tr-15
89T-493
89T/Tr-9T
89UD-184
89UD/Ext-785
90D-257
90F-413
90Score-65
90Sf-56
90T-712
90UD-186

Berardino, Dick
79Elmir-21
80Elmir-29
86Pawtu-1CO
87Greens-3

Berardino, John
(Johnny)
47TipTop
51B-245
52T-253
W753

Berberet, Louis J.
(Lou)
56T-329
57T-315

58T-383
59T-96
60L-24
60MacGregor-4
60T-6
61P-43

Berenguer, Juan
78Tidew
79T-721R
79Tacom-6
80Tidew-3
81T-259R
82D-580
82Evans-2
82OPC-107
82OPC/Post-12
82T-437
84D-125
84F-77
84Nes/792-174
84T-174
85Cain's-2
85D-272
85F-2
85T-672
85Wendy-3
86F-221
86Moth/Giants-27
86T-47
86T/Tr-9T
87D-616
87F-265
87F/U-U4
87T-303
87T/Tr-5T
88D-395
88D/Best-298
88F-3
88Master/Disc-3
88T-526
88T/Big-222
89B-152
89D-81
89D/Best-46
89F-104
89OPC-294
89Score-414
89T-294
89T/Big-117
89T/St-291
89UD-232
90D-301
90F-369
90Score-223
90T-709
90UD-440

Berenyi, Bruce
79Indianap-14
80Indianap-9
81T-606R
82Coke/Reds
82F-58
82T-459
83D-103
83F-585
83OPC-139
83T-139
84D-487
84F-463
84Nes/792-297
84OPC-297
84T-297
84T/X-10
85D-625
85F-73
85Indianap-32
85OPC-27
85T-27
85T/Mets/Fan-2
86T-339
87T-582

Berg, Morris
(Moe)
30CEA/Pin-11
33BU-149
33G-158
39PB-103
40PB-30
88Conlon/5-3
R313
R316
V353-84

Berg, Patty
52Wheat

Berg, Rich
88Modesto-4
89Madis/Star-3

Bergamo, August S.
(Augie)
No Cards.

Berge, Jordan
84Cedar-10
86Vermont-1

Berge, Lou
86LitFalls-3

Bergen, Martin
(Marty)
No Cards.

Bergen, William A.
(Bill)
10Domino-12
12Sweet/Pin-71
E101
E105
E300
E92
M116
S74-50
T201
T202
T205
T206
T216
T3-2
WG3-4

Bergendahl, Wray
83Wausa/LF-28
85Lynch-7
86Jacks/TCMA-3

Berger, Carl
28Exh/PCL-3

Berger, Charles
(Heinie)
E254
E270/1
M116
T206

Berger, Clarence E.
No Cards.

Berger, John Henne
(Johnny)
No Cards.

Berger, John Henry
(Tun)
No Cards.

Berger, Joseph August
(Joe)
No Cards.

Berger, Ken
77Spart

Berger, Louis William
(Boze)
35BU-84

Berger, Mike
84PrWill-7
85Nashua-3
86Nashua-3
87Jaxvl-6
88Indi/CMC-20
88Indi/Pro-519
89OkCty/CMC-11
89OkCty/Pro-1515

Berger, Walter Anton
(Wally)
31Exh/4-2
32Orbit/num-51
32Orbit/un-5
33DH-5
33Exh/4-1
33G-98
34DS-108
34DS-25
34Exh/4-1
35BU-1
35BU-172
35Exh/4-1
35Wheat
36Exh/4-1
36G-1
37Exh/4-1
38ONG/Pin-1
39PB-99
40PB-81
88Conlon/3-5
88Conlon/NatAS-1
R300
R305
R309/2
R310
R313
R326-13A
R326-13B
R328-19
R332-12
R342-13
V355-35
W711/1

Bergeron, Gilles
87Jamestn-22

Bergert, Ned
76QuadC
77QuadC

Bergh, John Baptist
No Cards.

Berghammer, Martin A.
(Marty)
No Cards.

Bergman, Alfred Henry
(Al)
No Cards.

Bergman, David Bruce
(Dave)
76SSPC-454
78BK/A-21
78T-705R
79Charl-8
79T-697
81D-139
81F-76
81T-253
81T/Tr-734
82D-146
82T-498
83D-550
83F-253
83Moth/Giants-18
83T-32
84D-624
84F-366
84F/X-11
84Nes/792-522
84T-522
84T/X-11
85Cain's-3
85D-537
85F-3
85OPC-368
85T-368
85Wendy-4
86Cain's-1
86D-471
86F-222
86T-101
87Cain's-4
87Coke/Tigers-9
87D-420
87F-144
87OPC-256
87T-700
88D-373
88F-52
88Pep/T-14
88Pol/T-3
88Score-217
88T-289
89D-389
89F-129
89Mara/Tigers-14
89Pol/Tigers-14
89Score-469
89T-631
89UD-266
90D-445
90F-600
90Score-254
90T-77
90UD-381

Beringer, Carroll
73OPC-486CO
73T-486C
74OPC-119CO
74T-119C

Beringhele, Vince
85VeroB-17

Berkelbach, Francis
No Cards.

Berley, John
V355-118

Berlin, Randy
89Hamil/Star-12

Berman, Gary
86Cram/PCL-150
87Clearw-18
88Readg/Pro-873

Berman, Robert Leon
(Bob)
No Cards.

Bernabe, Sam
85IowaC-18

Bernal, Vic
79Hawai-8

Bernard, Curtis Henry
(Curt)
No Cards.

Bernard, Dwight
78Tidew
79T-721R
79Tidew-6
81Vanco-4
82Pol/Brew
82Pol/Brew-47
83D-28
83F-27
83Gard-2
83T-244
84Cram/PCL-55
86Macon-4
87Kenosha-16
88Keno/Pro-1381
89Orlan/Best-4
89Orlan/Pro-1342

Bernard, Erik
84Albany-16
85Albany-29
86Alban/TCM-12bb

Bernardo, Rick
87PortChar-18
88CharlR/Star-1
89Mia/Star/22-1

Bernardo, Robert
86Wausa-1

Bernazard, Antonio
(Tony)
75WPalm
80OPC-351R
80T-680R
81D-449
81F-168
81OPC-194
81T-413
81T/Tr-735
82D-143
82F-338
82T-206
82T/St-171
83D-482
83F-231
83OPC-369
83T-698
83T/St-49
83T/X-9
84D-240
84F-606
84F/X-12
84Nes/792-41
84OPC-41
84T-41
84T/St-340
84T/X-12
84Wheat/Ind-4
85D-102
85F-439
85OPC-171
85Polar/Ind-4
85T-533
85T/St-252
86D-520
86F-580
86Leaf-249
86OhHenry-4
86OPC-354
86T-354
86T/St-210
87D-377
87D/OD-110
87F-244
87F/GameWin-4
87F/Mini-8
87Gator-4
87OPC-394
87RedFoley/St-105
87S-112M
87S-60
87T-607AS
87T-758
87T/Gloss60-43
87T/St-207
88D-344
88F-275
88OPC-122
88Score-604
88T-122

Bernhard, William H.
E107
T206
T213/brown

Bernhardt, Bill
WG2-5

Bernhardt, Cesar
89SoBend/GS-24

Bernhardt, Juan Ramon
77T-494R
78SnJos-13
78T-698
79OPC-189
79Spoka-24
79T-366

Bernier, Carlos R.
53T-243
54B-171

Bernstine, Pookie
83Watlo/LF-16
84BuffB-23
86IowaC-3
87IowaC-16
88Peoria/Ko-5
89Geneva/Pro-1886
89Peoria/Ko-29

Bero, Albert
48Sommer-30M
Bero, John George
(Johnny)
No Cards.
Berra, Dale Anthony
78Colum
79T-723R
80T-292
81D-153
81F-369
81OPC-147
81T-147
82D-250
82F-476
82T-588
83D-185
83F-303
83OPC-271
83T-433
83T/St-279
84D-430
84F-245
84Nes/792-18
84OPC-18
84T-18
84T/St-136
85D-444
85F-461
85F/Up-U4
85OPC-305
85T-132FS
85T-305
85T/St-133
85T/Tr-6T
86D-295
86F-100
86OPC-366
86T-692
87Tucso-8
88RochR-3
88RochR-3
88RochR/CMC-12
88RochR/Gov-3
88RochR/Pro-193
Berra, Lawrence Peter
(Yogi)
47TipTop
48B-6
49B-60
49MP-117
50B-46
50Drake-24
51B-2
51BR-B4
51T/CAS
51T/RB-1
52B-1
52BR
52NTea
52RM-AL3
52StarCal/L-70C
52T-191
52TipTop
52Wheat
53B/Col-121
53B/Col-44M
53RM-AL3
53T-104
54B-161
54NYJour
54RM-AL20
54T-50
55Armour-2
55B-168
55RM-AL16
55T-198
56T-110
56T/Pin-27
56YellBase/Pin-7
57T-2
57T-407M
58T-370
59T-180
60Bz-8
60NuCard-28
60T-480
60T/tatt
60T/tatt-6
61NuCard-453
61P-1
61T-425
61T-472MV
61T/RO
61T/St-189
62Exh
62J-7
62P-7
62P/Can-7
62Salada-33
62Shirriff-33
62T-360
62T/bucks
62T/St-83
63Exh
63J-17
63P-17
63Salada-62
63T-340
64T-21
65T-470
73OPC-257MG
73T-257MG
74OPC-179MG
74T-179MG
75OPC-189M
75OPC-192M
75OPC-193M
75OPC-421MG
75T-189MV
75T-192MV
75T-193MV
75T-421MG
75T/M-189MV
75T/M-192MV
75T/M-193MV
75T/M-421MG
79TCMA-2
80Cram/Leg-67
81D-351
82D-387
83D/HOF-24
83MLBPA/Pin-2
84T/X-13
85CircK-33
85T-132FS
85T-155
85West/2-31
85Woolwth-4
86S/Dec-31
87Nestle/DT-19
88Pac/Leg-53
89B-I2
D305
Exh47
PM10/L-4
PM10/Sm-10
PM10/Sm-9A
PM10/Sm-9B
R423-5
WG9-1
Berran, Dennis Martin
(Joe)
No Cards.
Berres, Raymond F.
(Ray)
39PB-156
40PB-164
60T-458C
Berringer, John
87Peoria-10
88WinSal/Star-1
Berrios, Hector
87Fayette-1
88GlenF/Pro-935
Berroa, Ed
79Elmir-22
Berroa, Geronimo
85Kingst-21
86Ventura-1
87Knoxv-15
87SLAS-3
88AAA/Pro-36
88D-659
88Syrac/CMC-13
88Syrac/Pro-808
89B-279
89D/Rook-19
89F/Up-72
89Score-632
89Score/HotRk-30
89Score/YS/II-17
89Sf-225M
89T/Big-297
89T/Tr-10T
90Class-83
90D-104
90F-575
90Score-151
90Score/100Ris-36
90T-617
90UD-531
Berry, Allen Kent
(Ken)
65T-368R
66OPC-127
66T-127
67OPC-67
67T-67
68T-485
69MB-25
69MLB/St-29
69T-494
69T/St-153
70MLB/St-182
70OPC-239
70T-239
71JB
71MLB/St-339
71OPC-466
71T-466
72MB-31
72OPC-379
72T-379
73OPC-445
73T-445
74OPC-163
74T-163
75OPC-432
75T-432
75T/M-432
78TCMA-53
82Oneon-4MG
87AppFx-24MG
89BirmB/Best-20
89BirmB/Pro-89
Berry, Charles F.
(Charlie)
31Exh/4-17
33CJ/Pin-1
33Exh/4-10
33Exh/4-9
33G-184
35G-2C
35G-4C
35G-7C
36Exh/4-14
40PB-190
55B-281ump
R313
Berry, Charles Joseph
(Charlie)
No Cards.
Berry, Claude Elzy
No Cards.
Berry, Cornelius John
(Neil)
49B-180
50B-241
51B-213
52B-219
Berry, Joseph H. Jr.
(Joe)
W575
Berry, Joseph H.
(Joe)
No Cards.
Berry, Kirk
85Cedar-14
86FSLAS-7
86Macon-3
86Tampa-3
87Vermont-24
Berry, Mark
87Nashv-1
88Greens/Pro-1575
89Greens/Pro-405
Berry, Sean
86Cram/PCL-38
87FtMyr-7
88BBCity/Star-6
89BBCity/Star-5
Berry, Tony
89Gasto/Pro-1009
89Gasto/Star-3
Berryhill, Damon
86Pittsf-2
87IowaC-15
88Berg/Cubs-9
88D-639
88D/Best-261
88D/Cubs/Bk-639
88D/Rook-31
88F-642
88F/U-U75
88IowaC/CMC-12
88IowaC/Pro-537
88Score/Tr-82T
88T/Tr-15T
89B-288
89Bz-2
89D-275
89D/Best-116
89F-418
89KMart/DT-8
89Mara/Cubs-9
89OPC-6
89Panini/St-52
89Score-336
89Score/HotRk-77
89Score/YS/I-24
89Sf-216
89T-543
89T/Big-60
89T/Gloss60-39
89T/JumboR-4
89T/St-318
89T/St-51
89ToysRUs-4
89UD-455
90D-167
90F-26
90Score-163
90Sf-164
90T-362
90UD-322
Bertaina, Frank
65T-396
66T-579R
68OPC-131
68T-131
69MB-26
69T-554
70T-638
71MLB/St-267
71OPC-422
71T-422
72MB-32
Berte, Harry Thomas
No Cards.
Bertell, Richard G.
(Dick)
61T-441
62T/St-105
63J-176
63P-176
63T-287
64T-424
65OPC-27
65T-27
66T-587
Berthel, Dan
89Erie/Star-2
Berti, Don
83DayBe-14
Bertoia, Reno Peter
54T-131
55T-94
57T-390
58T-232
59T-84
60T-297
61P-95
61Peter-20
61T-392
61T/St-178
Bertolani, Jerry
86Penin-5
87DayBe-22
88BirmB/Best-23
88SLAS-8
89BirmB/Best-12
89BirmB/Pro-100
Bertolotti, Fulvio
78StPet
79ArkTr-15
Bertoni, Jeff
80SLCty-9
81SLCty-16
82Spoka-13
83Evans-13
Bertucio, Charlie
83SanJose-3
Berube, George
87FtLaud-11
Berube, Luc
87Oneon-31
88FtLaud/Star-2
Bescher, Robert Henry
(Bob)
10Domino-13
11Helmar-110
12Sweet/Pin-96
14CJ-110
15CJ-110
D303
D329-15
D350/2-14
E101
E102
E105
E106
E224
E254
E270/2
E90/1
E92
E94
M101/4-15
M101/5-14
M116
S74-72
T202
T205
T206
T207
T216
T3-81
W555

WG5-4
WG6-3
Bessard, Lloyd
79Elmir-1
Besse, Herman
47Signal
49B/PCL-29
Bessent, Don
56T-184
57T-178
58T-401
59T-71
Best, Bill
81CharR-21
82FtMyr-18
84Memph-5
Best, Jayson
89Elizab/Star-3
Best, Jim
83AppFx/LF-6TR
Best, Karl
80LynnS-11
81LynnS-1
82LynnS-2
83SLCty-5
84Cram/PCL-189
85Cram/PCL-76
85F/Up-U5
86D-511
86F-459
86Moth/Mar-19
86S-179M
86T-61
87Calgary-10
87D-198
87F-579
87T-439
88Portl/CMC-2
88Portl/Pro-646
Beswick, James W.
(Jim)
79Hawai-10
79T-725R
80Hawai-8
83Nashua-17
Betances, Marcos
88Brist/Pro-1882
89Fay/Pro-1574
89NiagFls/Puc-3
Betcher, Frank Lyle
No Cards.
Betemit, Manuel
77Newar
78BurlB
Bethea, Steve
89Spoka/SP-25
Bethea, William Lamar
(Bill)
60DF
Bethke, James
65T-533R
Bettencourt, Lawrence
No Cards.
Bettendorf, Dave
88Hagers/Star-2
89Hagers/Best-9
89Hagers/Pro-273
89Hagers/Star-1
Bettendorf, Jeff
83Lynch-4
84Jacks-9
84Moth/A's-25
85Tidew-4
86ColumAst-4
87BirmB/Best-9
87SLAS-21
Betts, Walter
(Huck)
34G-36
E120
V354-83
Betz, Robert
52Park-80
Betzel, Christian
(Bruno)
D328-15
D329-16
D350/2-15
E135-15
M101/4-16
M101/5-15
Beuder, John
88Bakers/Cal-246
Beuder, Mike
83VeroB-1
Beuerlein, John
86Stockton-1
87Denver-14
Beulac, Joe
89SLCty-24
Beumiller
E254
E270/1
Bevacqua, Kurt A.
72OPC-193
72T-193
74OPC-454
74T-454
74T/Tr-454T
76OPC-427
76OPC-564M
76SSPC-233
76T-427
76T-564M
77T-317
77Tucso
78BK/R-16
78T-725
79T-44
80T-584
81F-382
81T-118
82F-477
82T-267
82T/Tr-6T
83F-352
83T-674
84D-80
84F-294
84F/St-43
84Moth/Padres-6
84Nes/792-346
84Smok/Padres-1
84T-346
85D-647
85F-26
85Moth/Padres-14
85T-478
85T/St-16WS
86D-528
86F-315
86T-789
Bevan, Harold Joseph
(Hal)
53B/BW-43
55Rodeo
60HenryH-10
60Union-22
61T-456
Bevenour, Keith
89Watertn/Star-2
Bevens, Floyd
(Bill)
47TipTop
48B-22
60NuCard-3
Beville, Henry Monte
(Monte)
No Cards.
Bevington, Terry
78BurlB
79Holyo-2
80Vanco-6
81BurlB-30
82Beloi-24
84ElPas-12
86Vanco-2MG
87Denver-13
88Vanco/Pro-778
Beyeler, Arnie
87Fayette-19
88Lakel/Star-3
89London/Pro-1371
Beyers, Tom
87VeroB-22
Bezdek, Hugo
W514-83
Bhagwat, Tom
80ElPas-13
Biagini, Greg
87CharO/WBTV-24
87SLAS-24
88CharlK-23
88CharlK/Pep-23
89RochR/CMC-25
89RochR/Pro-1660
Bialas, Dave
82Sprin-2
83Sprin/LF-22
84ArkTr-14
86FSLAS-8MG
86StPet-4MG
87StPet-18
Biancalana, Roland A.
(Buddy)
82Omaha-14
83Omaha-13
85T-387
86D-605
86F-3
86Kitty/Disc-2
86NatPhoto-1
86S-200
86T-99
86T/St-21WS
87D-527
87D/OD-202
87F-364
87Smok/AL-7
87T-554
88Omaha/CMC-20
88Omaha/Pro-1502
88Score-383
Bianchi, Ben
86Visal-3
87Portl-16
89Orlan/Best-10
89Orlan/Pro-1329
Bianchi, Steve
77Ashev
79Tucso-9
Bianco, Robert
75AppFx
Bianco, Ron
86Sumter-3
Bianco, Thomas A.
(Tommy)
76SSPC-250
77Evansvl/TCMA-3
78RochR
79RochR-11
Biasatti, Henry A.
(Hank)
V362-44
Bibby, Jim
72OPC-316R
72T-316R
74OPC-11
74T-11
74T/St-231
75OPC-155
75T-155
75T/M-155
76OPC-324
76T-324
77T-501
78OPC-61
78T-636
79OPC-39
79T-92
80T-229
81Coke
81D-134
81F-370
81F/St-65
81OPC-93
81T-430
81T/SO-105
81T/St-216
81T/St-260
82D-171
82F-478
82F/St-106
82F/St-70
82OPC-170
82T-170
82T/St-86
83T-355
84F-246
84Nes/792-566
84T-566
85Lynch-2
86Lynch-2CO
87Lynch-20
89Lynch/Star-24
Biberdorf, Cam
88GreatF-24
89Bakers/Cal-190
Bible, Mike
89SLCty-21
Bichette, Dante
86PalmSp-3
88Edmon/CMC-23
88Edmon/Pro-576
89Class/Up/2-199
89D-634
89D/Rook-29
89F-468
89Panini/St-283
89T-761
89UD-24
90F-127
90T-43
90UD-688
Bickford, Vern
49B-1
50B-57
51B-42
51FB
52B-48
52T-252
53JC-3
53T-161
54B-176
79TCMA-114
Bickhardt, Eric
89Butte/SP-5
Bicknell, Charlie
49Eureka-129
Bicknell, Greg
89StCath/Pro-2090
Bieger, Philip
87Anchora-1
Bieksha, Steve
88Wausa/Feder-18
88Wausa/GS-18
Bielanin, Ray
89GreatF-11
Bielaski, Oscar
No Cards.
Bielecki, Mike
82Buffa-16
83LynnP-1
84Cram/PCL-131
85D-28
85F-650M
86F-603
86T/Tr-10T
87D-415
87T-394
87Vanco-1
88AAA/Pro-18
88D-484
88D/Cubs/Bk-NEW
88Score-611
88T-436
89D-512
89D/Best-194
89F-419
89Mara/Cubs-36
89T-668
90D-373
90D-9DK
90F-27
90Score-484
90T-114
90UD-359
Bielenberg, Bruce
85IowaC-33
Bienek, Vince
79AppFx-18
80GlenF/B-20
80GlenF/C-11
81GlenF-17
Bierbauer, Louis W.
(Lou)
N172
N690
Biercevicz, Greg
78SnJos-3
79Spoka-21
79T-712R
80Spoka-3
81Spoka-8
81T-282R
82Tidew-17
83Tidew-15
85RochR-30
Bierley, Brad
85Visal-7
86Orlan-2
87Orlan-14
88Portl/CMC-16
88Portl/Pro-639
89Portl/CMC-18
89Portl/Pro-231
Bierscheid, Gene
87Spart-3
Bieser, Steve
89Batav/Pro-1934
Bigbee, Carson Lee
21Exh-10
25Exh-49
26Exh-49
E120
E121/120
E121/80
V61-54
W501
W573
W575
Bigbee, Lyle Randolph
No Cards.
Bigelow, Elliott A.
No Cards.
Biggers, Allan
89Hamil/Star-3
89Savan/Pro-362
Biggerstaff, Kent
78Holyo
79Vanco-22
80Vanco-12
81Portl-27
Biggio, Craig
88F/U-U89
88Score/Tr-103T
88Tucso-2
88Tucso/CMC-15
88Tucso/Pro-166

89Class-51
89D-561
89D/Best-176
89F-353
89Lennox/Ast-24
89Moth/Ast-14
89Panini/St-79
89Score-237
89Score/HotRk-98
89Score/YS/II-33
89T-49
89UD-273
90Class-57
90D-306
90F-224
90Score-275
90Sf-22
90T-157
90T-404AS
90UD-104

Biggs, Doug
88Brist/Pro-1864

Biggus, Bengie
80BurlB-29

Bigham, Craig
88Spoka/Pro-1931

Bigham, David
89Elizab/Star-4

Bigham, Scott
89River/Best-3
89River/Cal-1
89River/Pro-1396

Bignal, George W.
No Cards.

Bigusiak, Mike
76Clint
86SanJose-3

Bilttner, Larry David
72OPC-122
72T-122
73OPC-249
73T-249
75OPC-543
75T-543
75T/M-543
76OPC-238
76SSPC-336
76T-238
77T-64
78T-346
79OPC-224
79T-433
80OPC-334
80T-639
81D-515
81F-314
81T-718
81T/Tr-736
82Coke/Reds
82D-43
82F-59
82T-159
83D-440
83F-586
83Rangers-14
83T-527
83T/X-10
84D-342
84F-414
84Nes/792-283
84T-283
87F/McCror-2

Biko, Tom
80OrlTw-3
82Amari-14

Bilak, Paul
86PalmSp-4TR
86PalmSp/Smok-4
87PalmSp-6

Bilardello, Dann J.
83T/X-11
84D-408
84F-464
84Nes/792-424
84T-424
84T/St-57
85D-243
85T-28
86Provigo-2
86T-253
87F-313
87OPC-217
87T-577
87Vanco-21
88Omaha/CMC-17
88Omaha/Pro-1518
89BuffB/CMC-13
89BuffB/Pro-1677
90T-682

Bilello, John
88Boise/Pro-1605
88Fresno/Cal-18
88Fresno/Pro-1224
89Boise/Pro-1997
89Reno/Cal-241

Bilko, Steven Thomas
(Steve)
51B-265
52T-287
53Hunter
54B-206
54Hunter
54T-116
55B-88
55T-93
55T/DH-117
58T-346
59DF
59T-43
60L-106
60T-396
61T-184
62J-74
62P-74
62P/Can-74
62Salada-17A
62Salada-17B
62Shirriff-17
62T-422
62T/St-63
63J-24
63P-24
79TCMA-177
88MinorLg/Leg-6
Exh47

Bill, Bob
79Newar-4
83TriCit-28
86Tulsa-26TR
88Watertn/Puc-33

Billanueva, Gil
89Reno/Cal-247

Billingham, Jack
68T-228R
69OPC-92
69T-92
70T-701
71MLB/St-74
71OPC-162
71T-162
72T-542
73OPC-89
73T-89
74OPC-158
74T-158
74T/St-22
75OPC-235
75T-235
75T/M-235
76OPC-155
76SSPC-23
76T-155
77Pep-53
77T-512
78BK/T-6
78T-47
79T-388
80T-603
85SpokaAT/Cram-2
87Osceola-18
89Swell-43

Billings, John A.
(Josh)
No Cards.

Billings, Richard A.
(Dick)
71OPC-729
71T-729
72OPC-148
72T-148
73OPC-94
73T-94
74OPC-466
74T-466
76SSPC-288

Billingsley, Rod
89Spoka/SP-3

Billmeyer, Mickey
86Hagers-3
87Miami-11
87PortChar-16
88Mia/Star-2

Billoni, Mike
87BuffB-27
89BuffB/CMC-1

Bingham, Mark
82Danvi-5

Binks, George Eugene
V362-21

Biras, Stephen A.
(Steve)
No Cards.

Birch, Brock
86Cram/PCL-23
87Clint-20

Birchall, A. Judson
(Jud)
No Cards.

Bird, David
89Well/Puc-5

Bird, Doug
74OPC-17
74T-17
75OPC-364
75T-364
75T/M-364
76A&P/KC
76OPC-96
76SSPC-180
76T-96
77OPC-191
77T-556
78T-183
79BK/P-12
79T-664
80T-421
81F-106
81T-516
81T/Tr-737
82D-504
82F-586
82RedLob
82T-273
83D-48
83F-490
83T-759
83T/X-12
84F-391
84Nes/792-82
84T-82

Bird, Frank Zepherin
No Cards.

Bird, Steven
88Kinston/Star-4

Birkbeck, Mike
86Vanco-3
87D-33RR
87D/Rook-19
87F/U-U5
87Leaf-33
87T-229
88D-49
88Pol/Brew-40
88Score-369
88T-692
89B-132
89D-501
89F-178
89Pol/Brew-40
89Score-596
89T-491

Birkofer, Ralph
35BU-90

Birmingham, Joseph L.
(Dode)
10Domino-14
11Helmar-22
12Sweet/Pin-17
14CJ-106
14Piedmont/St-4
15CJ-106
E254
E270/2
E97
M116
T202
T205
T206
T207
W555
WG5-5
WG6-4

Birrell, Bob
79Elmir-24
83Pawtu-1

Birrer, Werner
(Babe)
56T-84

Birriel, Jose
86NewBrit-3
87NewBrit-24
88EastLAS/Pro-19
88NewBrit/Pro-902
89Lynch/Star-2

Birtsas, Tim
82Oneon-8
85F/Up-U6
86D-462
86F-412
86F/St-5
86Leaf-227
86Moth/A's-25
87Tacom-23
88F/U-U82
88Kahn/Reds-48
88Nashvl/CMC-2
88Nashvl/Pro-477
88T-501
89F-152
89K/Reds-48
89Score-454
89T-103
89UD-638
90D-493
90F-414
90Score-408
90T-687
90UD-137

Bisceglia, Dave
81Water-20

Bisceglia, James
86Cram/PCL-90
87QuadC-14
88PalmSp/Pro-1458
89PalmSp/Cal-52

Bischoff, John George
No Cards.

Bishop, Charles
52Park-98
53T-186
55Rodeo
55T-96
55T/DH-110

Bishop, Frank H.
No Cards.

Bishop, James
86Knoxv-2
87Wmspt-8
88Cedar/Pro-1165
89Mia/Star/25-2

Bishop, Max F.
25Exh-105
26Exh-105
29Exh/4-28
33G-61
34DS-6
35G-1G
35G-3E
35G-5E
35G-6E
88Conlon/4-4
R308-187
R315-A4
R315-B4
R316
V353-61

Bishop, Michael D.
(Mike)
77QuadC
80ElPas-12
81SLCty-14
82Spoka-10
83Tidew-6
87Anchora-2

Bishop, Tim
87Oneon-28
88PrWill/Star-2

Bishop, William
N172

Bisland, Rivington M.
No Cards.

Bispo, Randy
86SanJose-4

Bissonette, Del
29Exh/4-4
31Exh/4-4
R314/Can
R316

Bitker, Joe
86Beaum-2
87LasVegas-1
88LasVeg/CMC-1
88LasVeg/Pro-230
89LasVeg/CMC-1
89LasVeg/Pro-4

Bittiger, Jeff
82Jacks-1
83Tidew-13
84Tidew-13
85IntLgAS-20
85Tidew-8
86Portl-1
87Portl-1
88Score/Tr-66T
88Vanco/CMC-1
89B-60
89Score-512
89T-209
89UD-509
89Vanco/CMC-1

Bittmann, Henry
(Red)
No Cards.

Bivens, William E.
87Sprin/Best-10
88Sprin/Best-7
89StPet/Star-3

Bjorkman, George A.
80ArkTr-2

82Louvl-1
83ColumAst-1
84Indianap-20
84Nes/792-116
84T-116
85Indianap-20
85RochR-31

Black, Allen
82QuadC-2

Black, Bob
89Richm/CMC-9

Black, Don
R346-28

Black, Harry
(Bud)
80SanJose
81LynnS-2
83D-322
83F-107
83F-644M
83Omaha-2
83T-238
84D-130
84F-343
84Nes/792-26
84T-26
84T/St-283
85D-100
85F-198
85Leaf-202
85OPC-47
85T-412
85T/St-275
86D-374
86F-4
86Kitty/Disc-7
86Leaf-170
86NatPhoto-40
86OPC-319
86T-697
86T/St-261
87D-404
87F-365
87OPC-315
87T-669
88D-301
88F-252
88OPC-301
88SanDiegoSt-3
88SanDiegoSt-4
88Score-313
88Score/Tr-11T
88Smok/Royals-9
88T-301
88T/Tr-16T
89B-82
89D-556
89OPC-5
89Score-404
89T-509
89T/St-209
89UD-466
90D-556
90F-486
90Score-197
90T-144
90UD-498

Black, Joe
52T-321
53RM-NL4
53T-81
54NYJour
54T-98
55Gol/Dodg-4
55T-156
56Kahn
56T-178
56T/Pin-54
79TCMA-160
89Pac/Leg-177
89Swell-69
PM10/Sm-11
PM10/Sm-12
PM10/Sm-13

Black, John Falconer
(Jack)
No Cards.

Black, John William
(Bill)
No Cards.

Black, Robert B.
(Bob)
No Cards.

Blackaby, Ethan Allan
75Phoen-25
76Phoen
77Phoen
78Cr/PCL-107
79Phoen
80Phoen-24
82Phoen
83Phoen/BHN-26GM

Blackburn, Earl S.
No Cards.

Blackburn, Jackie
85FtMyr-24

Blackburn, James Ray
49B-160
51B-287
79TCMA-259

Blackburn, Ron
58T-459
59T-401
60T-209

Blackburne, Russell
(Lena)
E90/3
M116
T205
T206
T207

Blackerby, George F.
(George)
No Cards.

Blackmon, Tom
80Batav-7
83Knoxv-1

Blackmun, Ben
85Bend/Cram-2

Blackshear, Steve
87Readg-18

Blackwell, Barry
85Anchora-4
89Kinston/Star-3

Blackwell, Ewell
48B-2
48L-39
49Royal-9
50B-63
51B-24
52BR
52RM-NL3
52Royal
52T-344
53T-31
79TCMA-119
D305
Exh47
R346-4

Blackwell, Ewell
49Eureka-77
89Pac/Leg-188

Blackwell, Fred
No Cards.

Blackwell, Larry
86Kenosha-2
87Orlan-26
88Visal/Cal-159
88Visal/Pro-83
89Orlan/Best-11
89Orlan/Pro-1340

Blackwell, Orlando
83Clint/LF-11
84Shrev/FB-2

Blackwell, Timothy P.
(Tim)
76SSPC-415
78OPC-223
78T-449
80T-153
81Coke
81D-559
81F-304
81OPC-43
81T-553
81T/HT
82D-99
82F-587
82Hygrade
82T-374
82T/St-28
82T/Tr-7T
83D-214
83OPC-57
83Stuart-26
83T-57
84Cram/PCL-241C
86Fres/Smok-1MG
88Phoen/CMC-25M

Blackwell, Tom
88Phoen/Pro-53

Blades, Francis R.
(Ray)
21Exh-11
25Exh-58
26Exh-58
28Exh-30
54T-243

Bladt, Richard Alan
74OPC-601R
74T-601R
76SSPC-444

Blaeholder, George
32Orbit/num-9
32Orbit/un-6
33G-16
34DS-13
34G-1F
35G-3D
35G-5D
35G-6D
R305
R314
V353-12
V353-169

Blaemire, Rae Bertram
No Cards.

Blaine, Tom
88ArkTr/GS-8

Blair, Clarence Vick
(Footsie)
No Cards.

Blair, Dennis
75OPC-521
75T-521
75T/M-521
76OPC-642
76SSPC-344
76T-642
77OPC-189
77T-593
78T-466
79Hawai-22
80Hawai-9

Blair, Louis Nathan
(Buddy)
No Cards.

Blair, Paul
65T-473R
66OPC-48
66T-48
67OPC-153WS
67T-319
68Coke
68OPC-135
68T-135
69MB-27
69MLB/St-1
69T-506
70MLB/St-146
70OPC-285
70T-285
71K-35
71MLB/St-290
71OPC-53
71T-53
71T/tatt-6
72MB-33
72T-660
73JP
73OPC-528
73T-528
74OPC-92
74T-92
74T/St-123
75Ho-12
75Ho/Twink-12
75OPC-275
75T-275
75T/M-275
76OPC-473
76SSPC-395
76T-473
77BK/Y-21
77T-313
78BK/Y-22
78T-114
79OPC-304
79T-582
80OPC-149
80T-281
84Evrt/Cram-19
88CalLgAS-4
88SanJose/Cal-117
88SanJose/Pro-109
89Shreve/Pro-1834

Blair, Walter Allan
14CJ-126
14Piedmont/St-5
15CJ-126
T201
T202
T204

Blair, William E.
N172

Blair, Willie
87Duned-22
89Syrac/CMC-6
89Syrac/Pro-805

Blake, Bob
79Wisco-5

Blake, Ed
52T-144

Blake, Harry Cooper
No Cards.

Blake, J. Fred
26Exh-18

Blakely, Dave
85Evrt/Cram-1
86Clint-2
87Visal-10

Blakely, Lincoln H.
(Link)
R314/Can

Blakiston, Robert J.
(Bob)
No Cards.

Blanchard, John Edwin
(Johnny)
59T-117
60L-89
60T-283
61P-18
61T-104
61T/St-190
62J-11
62P-11
62P/Can-11
62T-93
63J-21
63P-21
63T-555
64T-118
65T-388
66T-268
89Swell-92
PM10/L-5
WG10-1
WG9-2

Blanche, Prosper A.
(Al)
35BU-83

Blanco, Damasco
No Cards.

Blanco, Gil
65T-566R
67T-303

Blanco, Oswaldo C.
(Ossie)
No Cards.

Blanco, Romauldo
73Cedar
75Dubuq

Blanding, Fred
(Fritz)
14CJ-109
15CJ-109
T207

Blank, Frank Ignatz
(Coonie)
No Cards.

Blanke, Scott
83Clint/LF-26

Blankenship, Bob
89Bill/Pro-2060

Blankenship, Cliff
E90/1
T204

Blankenship, Kevin
85Durhm-3
87Greenv/Bst-19
88Greenv/Best-16
88SLAS-28
89AAA/Pro-44
89D-658
89IowaC/CMC-7
89IowaC/Pro-1699
89UD/Ext-762
90F-28
90Score-646
90UD-47

Blankenship, Lance
86Cram/PCL-69
87Modesto-10
88AAA/Pro-38
88Tacom/CMC-11
88Tacom/Pro-630
89D-621
89F-2
89Score-641
89Score/HotRk-20
89Tacom/CMC-12
89Tacom/Pro-1539
89UD-15
90F-1
90Score-536
90Score/100Ris-82
90T-132
90UD-687

Blankenship, Ted
26Exh-73
27Exh-37

Blanks, Daryl
88Idaho/Pro-1834
89BurlB/Pro-1621
89BurlB/Star-2

Blanks, Larvell
73OPC-609R
73T-609R
75OPC-394

75T-394
75T/M-394
76OPC-127
76SSPC-8
76T-127
76T/TR-127T
77Pep-6
77T-441
78OPC-213
78T-61
79T-307
80T-656

Blanton, Darrell
(Cy)
34DS-57
35BU-88
35G-8K
35G-9K
37Exh/4-7
38Exh/4-7
R312
R313
R314
V355-3

Blaser, Mark
83Greens-16
85Albany-14
86WPalm-6

Blasingame, Donald L.
(Don)
56T-309
57T-47
58T-199
59Armour-5
59T-491
60T-397
61P-148
61T-294
61T/St-73
62J-117
62P-117
62P/Can-117
62Salada-103
62Shirriff-103
62T-103
63FrBauer-1
63J-126
63Kahn
63P-126
63T-518
64T-327
65OPC-21
65T-21
78TCMA-84
Exh47

Blasingame, Wade
65OPC-44
65T-44
66Kahn
66T-355
67OPC-119
67T-119
68T-507
69MB-28
69T-308
71OPC-79
71T-79
72T-581

Blass, Steve
65OPC-232
65T-232
66EH-28
66T-344
67T-562
67T/Test/PP-4
68KDKA-28
68T-499
69Kahn
69OPC-104
69T-104
69T/S-57
69T/St-83
70OPC-396
70T-396
71MLB/St-194
71OPC-143
71T-143
72K-44
72MB-34
72OPC-229WS
72OPC-320
72T-320
73K-11
73OPC-95
73T-95
74OPC-595
74T-595

Blasucci, Tony
85PrWill-18
86PrWill-3
87DayBe-5
88BirmB/Best-2
89BirmB/Best-10
89BirmB/Pro-94

Blateric, Steve
73OPC-616R
73T-616R

Blatnick, John Louis
(Johnny)
49B-123

Blattner, Robert G.
(Buddy)
40Hughes-4
47TipTop
49Eureka-130

Blauser, Jeff
86Durhm-2
87Richm/TCMA-11
87S/Rook-48
88D-513
88F-533
88Richm-2
88Richm/CMC-22
88Richm/Pro-18
88Score-562
88Score/YS/II-14
89D-592
89F-588
89Panini/St-41
89Score-589
89T-83
89T/Big-317
89UD-132
90Class-123
90D-271
90F-576
90Score-178
90T-251
90UD-406

Blaylock, Gary
59T-539

Blaylock, Marvin E.
(Marv)
55B-292
57T-224

Blaylock, Robert
59T-211
62-Pep/Tul

Blefary, Curtis LeRoy
(Curt)
65OPC-49R
65T-49R
66Bz-28
66T-460
66T/RO-87
67Bz-28
67OPC-180
67T-180
67T-521M
68Coke
68T-312
69MB-29
69MLB/St-137
69T-458
69T/S-44
69T/St-122
70MLB/St-242
70OPC-297
70T-297
71MLB/St-483
71OPC-131
71T-131
72MB-35
72T-691
72T-692A

Blessitt, Isiah
(Ike)
77Holyo

Blevins, Brad
83QuadC-8

Bligh, Edwin Forrest
(Ned)
N172

Bliss, Elmer Ward
No Cards.

Bliss, Howard Frank
No Cards.

Bliss, John J.A.
11Helmar-166
E90/1
M116
T206

Blobaum, Jeff
84Cram/PCL-19

Block, James John
(Bruno)
11Helmar-6
E286
M116
T204
T207

Block, Richard
79Newar-19

Block, Seymour
(Cy)
V362-9

Blocker, Terry
82Jacks-20
84Tidew-20
85IntLgAS-16
85Tidew-19
86Tidew-2
87Tidew-5
87Tidew/TCMA-19
89F-589
89Richm/CMC-17
89Richm/Ko-19
89Score-605
89T-76
89UD-399

Blohm, Pete
89Aug/Pro-516

Blomberg, Ronald Mark
(Ron)
72OPC-203
72T-203
73OPC-462
73T-462
74K-54
74OPC-117
74T-117
74T/DE-60
74T/St-211
75OPC-68
75T-68
75T/M-68
76Ho-38
76Ho/Twink-38
76OPC-354
76SSPC-450
76T-354
77T-543
78Ho-147
78T-506
79OPC-17
79T-42
88T-663TBC

Blomberg, Steve
76Shrev

Blong, Joseph Myles
(Joe)
No Cards.

Blong, Wesley C.
(Wes)
No Cards.

Blood, Ed
33SK-9

Bloodworth, James H.
(Jimmy)
40PB-189
49Eureka-78
51B-185

Bloomfield, Clyde S.
62Pep/Tul
63Pep/Tul
64T-532R

Blosser, Greg
89LittleSun-21
90Score-681DC

Blott, Jack Leonard
No Cards.

Blouin, Gary
86Cram/PCL-45
87FtMyr-3

Blount, Bill
85Spoka/Cram-2
86CharRa-3
87LasVegas-16
88River/Cal-230
88River/Pro-1421

Blowers, Michael
86Jamestn-1
87WPalm-13
88Jaxvl/Best-16
88Jaxvl/Pro-975
89Indi/CMC-14
89Indi/Pro-1221
90D-656
90F-438
90Score-624

Blue, Bird Wayne
(Bert)
No Cards.

Blue, Luzerne Atwell
(Lu)
26Exh-90
28Exh-57
29Exh/4-30
31Exh/4-20
33Exh/4-10
E120
E126-54
R316
V61-5
W517-50
W572
W573

Blue, Vida
70OPC-21R
70T-21R
71MLB/St-507
71OPC-544
71T-544
72K-9
72OPC-169
72OPC-170IA
72OPC-92LL
72OPC-94LL
72OPC-96LL
72T-169
72T-170A
72T-92LL
72T-94LL
72T-96LL
72T/Post-8
73OPC-430
73T-430
74OPC-290
74T-290
74T/St-222
75OPC-209M
75OPC-510
75T-209MV
75T-510
75T/M-209MV
75T/M-510
76Crane-3
76Ho-20
76Ho/Twink-20
76K-47
76MSA/Disc
76OPC-140
76OPC-200LL
76SSPC-481
76T-140
76T-200LL
77Ho-52
77OPC-75
77T-230
77T/CS-4
78OPC-177
78T-680
78Wiffle/Discs-4
79Ho-74
79K-23
79OPC-49
79Pol/Giants-14
79T-110
79T/Comics-33
80BK/PHR-1
80K-42
80OPC-14
80Pol/Giants-14
80T-30
80T/S-59
81D-433
81F-432
81F/St-63
81K-23
81OPC-310
81T-310
81T/SO-108
81T/St-239
82D-222
82D-4DK
82F-384
82F/St-61
82K-63
82KMart-19
82OPC-267
82OPC-82IA
82T-430
82T-431A
82T-576TL
82T/St-111
82T/Tr-8T
83D-34
83D-648M
83F-106
83F-643M
83OPC-178
83T-471TL
83T-570
84Moth/Giants-25
85F/Up-U7
85Moth/Giants-10
86D-509
86F-533
86Leaf-247
86Moth/Giants-10
86S-132M
86S-142M
86S/Dec-63M
86T-770
87D-362
87F-266
87Moth/A's-7
87OPC-260
87RedFoley/St-128
87T-260

89Pac/Leg-198

Blueberg, James
86Cram/PCL-120
87Wausa-2
88CalLgAS-30
88SanBern/Best-15
88SanBern/Cal-47
89SanBern/Best-6

Bluege, Oswald Louis
(Ossie)
25Exh-121
26Exh-121
29Exh/4-31
31Exh/4-32
33G-113
33G-159
34DS-71
35BU-105
36Exh/4-16
61F-93
R313
V353-83
V355-87

Bluege, Otto Adam
No Cards.

Bluestone, Brad
86Erie-4tr
87Sprn/Bst-27tr
88Sprin/Best-27

Bluhm, Bill
87Everett-25
88Watlo/Pro-668
89Reno/Cal-262

Bluhm, Harvey Fred
(Red)
No Cards.

Blum, Brent
86Albany/TCMA-30
87Albany-22
88PrWill/Star-3

Blumberg, Rob
89StCath/Pro-2088

Blume, David
81Wausa-11

Blundin, Barry
88BurlR/Pro-1791

Bluthardt, Jay
88Watertn/Puc-15

Blyleven, Bert
71MLB/St-458
71OPC-26
71T-26
72OPC-515
72T-515
73K-35
73OPC-199
73T-199
74K-46
74OPC-98
74T-98
74T/DE-47
74T/St-201
75Ho-74
75OPC-30
75T-30
75T/M-30
76Ho-116
76K-11
76OPC-204LL
76OPC-235
76SSPC-219
76T-204LL
76T-235
77OPC-101
77T-630
77T/CS-5
78Ho-74
78K-53
78OPC-113
78T-131
78Wiffle/Discs-5
79Ho-133
79OPC-155
79T-308
80K-5
80OPC-238
80T-457
81D-135
81F-383
81OPC-294
81T-554
81T/Tr-738
82D-111
82F-361
82F/St-199
82OPC-164
82T-559TL
82T-685
82T/St-173
82Wheat/Ind
83D-589
83OPC-280
83T-280
83Wheat/Ind-6
84D-129
84D/AAS-45
84D/Champs-42
84F-536
84FunFood/Pin-106
84Nes/792-716LL
84Nes/792-789
84OPC-126
84T-716ATL
84T-789
84T/St-261
84Wheat/Ind-28
85D-224
85D-4
85D/DKsuper-4
85F-440
85F/LimEd-2
85F/St-112
85F/St-81
85F/St-92
85Leaf-4DK
85OPC-355
85Polar/Ind-28
85Seven-7G
85T-355
85T/Gloss40-17
85T/St-247
85T/Super-35
86D-649
86D/AAS-52
86D/HL-31
86F-386
86F/Mini-82
86F/Slug-1
86F/St-6
86Leaf-88
86OPC-272
86Quaker-21
86S-103
86S-142M
86S-64M
86T-445
86T/3D-1
86T/Mini-23
86T/St-279
86T/Super-11
87D-71
87D/OD-226
87F-536
87F/AwardWin-3
87F/Mini-9
87F/St-10
87F/St-S3
87Leaf-100
87OPC-25
87RedFoley/St-101
87S-81
87T-25
87T/Mini-61
87T/St-278
88Woolwth-21
88D-71
88D/Best-18
88F-4
88F/St-41
88Leaf-52
88Master/Disc-1
88OPC-295
88Panini/St-132
88Score-90
88Sf-92
88Smok/Minn-6
88T-295
88T/Big-180
88T/St-20
88T/St-276
89B-41
89D-119
89D/Best-3
89D/Tr-35
89F-105
89F/Up-12
89OPC-204
89Score-215
89Score/Tr-17
89T-555
89T/St-285
89T/Tr-11T
89UD-225
89UD/Ext-712
90Class-142
90D-331
90F-128
90Score-180
90Score/100St-12
90Sf-193
90T-130
90UD-527

Blyth, Robert
(Bert)
82IowaC-14

Blyzka, Michael
54Esskay
54T-152

Boag, Jack
78StPet

Boak, Chester Robert
(Chet)
No Cards.

Boatright, Dennis
83Butte-1

Bobb, Mark Randall
(Randy)
70OPC-429R
70T-429R
71OPC-83R
71T-83R

Boccabella, John D.
64T-192R
66T-482R
67T-578
68T-542
69MB-30
69T-466
70OPC-19
70T-19
71LaPizza-2
71MLB/St-123
71OPC-452
71T-452
72OPC-159
72T-159
73OPC-592
73T-592
74OPC-253
74T-253
74T/St-52
74Weston-12
75OPC-553
75T-553
75T/M-553
78TCMA-291

Bocek, Milton Frank
(Milt)
No Cards.

Bochesa, Greg
86WinHav-4
87NewBrit-13
88NewBrit/Pro-900

Bochte, Bruce Anton
74SLCty
75OPC-392
75T-392
75T/M-392
76OPC-637
76SSPC-200
76T-637
77T-68
78Ho-81
78PapaG/Disc-29
78T-537
79Ho-123
79OPC-231
79T-443
80K-59
80OPC-80
80T-143
80T/S-55
81D-403
81Drake-25
81F-600
81F/St-8
81K-62
81MSA/Disc-3
81OPC-18
81Sqt-31
81T-723
81T/SO-30
81T/St-123
82D-505
82F-505
82F/St-222
82OPC-224
82T-224
82T/St-232
83D-127
83F-473
83OPC-28
83T-28
83T-711
83T/St-111
84F/X-13
84Moth/A's-6
85D-253
85F-416
85Moth/A's-10
85OPC-391
85T-632
85T/St-331
86D-400
86F-413
86F/Mini-86
86F/St-7
86Leaf-189
86Moth/A's-10
86OPC-378
86T-378
86T/St-170
87F-388
87T-496
87T/St-169

Bochy, Bruce Douglas
76Dubuq
77Cocoa
79T-718R
80T-289
81D-20
81F-69
81Tidew-2
82Tidew-6
84Cram/PCL-225
84Nes/792-571
84T-571
85D-505
85Moth/Padres-12
85T-324
86D-551
86T-608
87D-311
87F-411
87T-428
88LasVeg/CMC-21
88LasVeg/Pro-241
88Score-469
88T-31
89River/Best-25
89River/Cal-29CO
89River/Pro-1405
89Spoka/SP-4

Bock, Doug
88AppFx/Pro-157

Bock, Paul
75AppFx
77Clint

Bockewitz, Stan
76Wmspt

Bockhorn, Glen
81Durhm-11
86BuffB-1

Bockman, Joseph E.
(Eddie)
49B-195
49Eureka-153

Bockus, Randy
84Shrev/FB-3
86Phoen-3
87F/U-U6
87Phoen-3
88F/U-U127
88Phoen/CMC-1
88Phoen/Pro-55
89B-96
89T-733
89Toled/CMC-1
89Toled/Pro-769

Boddicker, Mike
80RochR-6
81RochR-1
81T-399R
82RochR-1
84D-123
84F-1
84F-645IA
84F/St-110
84FunFood/Pin-121
84Nes/792-191
84Nes/792-426TL
84Seven-9E
84T-191
84T/St-13
84T/St-375
85D-291
85Drake-34
85F-170
85F/St-80
85F/St-90
85Leaf-109
85OPC-225
85Seven-6E
85T-225
85T-709AS
85T/3D-26
85T/Gloss40-4
85T/St-202
85T/Super-16
86D-47
86D-8
86D/DKsuper-8
86F-269
86F/Mini-57
86Leaf-8DK
86OPC-367
86S-104
86T-575
86T/St-233
87D-125

87D/OD-140
87F-463
87F/LL-2
87F/St-11
87Leaf-76
87OPC-149
87RedFoley/St-40
87S-56
87Seven-ME8
87T-455
87T/St-227
88D-89
88D/Best-317
88F-556
88F/St-1
88F/U-U5
88French-52
88OPC-281
88Panini/St-5
88Score-67
88Sf-146
88T-725
88T/St-231
89B-21
89Class-139
89D-612
89D/Best-297
89F-80
89OPC-71
89Score-549
89Sf-122
89T-71
89T/Big-296
89T/St-261
89UD-542
90D-280
90F-267
90Score-31
90T-652
90UD-652

Boddie, Eric
89Bakers/Cal-193

Boddie, Rodney
88James/Pro-1905

Bodenhamer, Don
74Gasto

Bodie, Frank Stephan
(Ping)
11Helmar-7
14CJ-79
15CJ-79
28Exh/PCL-4
D327
D328-16
E121/80
E122
E135-16
E224
T207
W514-66
W516-3
W575

Bodie, Keith
76Wausa
79Jacks-11
86AubAs-3MG
87Ashvl-4
88FSLAS/Star-3
89Clint/Pro-898

Boeckel, Norman Doxie
(Tony)
E120
V100
V61-80
W572
W573

Boehling, John Joseph
14CJ-72
15CJ-72
D328-17
E135-17

Boehmer, Leonard J.
(Len)
69T-519R

Boelter, Tarry
79Wisco-14

Boemier, Bill
53Mother-63

Boever, Dan
85Cedar-21
88Nashvl/CMC-15
88Nashvl/Pro-476
89Calg/CMC-12
89Calg/Pro-535
89Canton/Best-7
89Canton/Pro-1325
89Canton/Star-3

Boever, Joe
83StPet-1
86Louisvl-6
87Louvl-5
88AAA/Pro-34
88F-534
88Richm-36
88Richm/CMC-9
88Richm/Pro-22
88Score-542
88T-627
89D-168
89T-586
90D-357
90F-577
90Score-81
90T-410
90UD-408

Bogar, Tim
89Jacks/GS-3

Bogart
N172

Bogener, Terrence W.
(Terry)
79Tulsa-15
83D-520
83OKCty-3

Boggess, Dusty
55B-297ump

Boggs, Tommy
77T-328
78T-518
79Richm-22
79T-384
81D-597
81F-267
81Pol/Atl-40
81T-132
82BK/Lids-3
82D-249
82F-430
82T-61
83D-349
83F-131
83T-649
85OKCty-7

Boggs, Wade Anthony
81Pawtu-15
83D-586
83F-179
83T-498
83T/St-308
84D-151
84D-26
84D/AAS-22
84D/Champs-16
84Drake-2
84F-392
84F-630IA
84F/St-11
84F/St-28
84F/St-52
84FunFood/Pin-43
84MiltBrad-1
84Nes/792-131LL
84Nes/792-30
84Nes/792-786TL
84OPC-30
84Ralston-11
84Seven-10E
84T-131LL
84T-30
84T-786TL
84T/Cereal-11
84T/Gloss40-8
84T/St-100
84T/St-216
84T/St/Box-7
84T/Super-7
84T/Super-7
85D-172
85D/AAS-38
85D/HL-49
85F-151
85F/LimEd-3
85F/St-6
85Leaf-179
85OPC-350
85Seven-7E
85Seven-8C
85T-350
85T/St-210
86BK/AP-9
86D-371
86D/AAS-47
86D/AS/WaxBox-PC7
86D/HL-11
86D/HL-13
86Dorman-18
86Drake-27
86F-341
86F-634M
86F-639M
86F/LimEd-4
86F/LL-1
86F/Mini-72
86F/Slug-2
86F/St-8
86F/St-S2
86Jiffy-2
86Leaf-168
86Meadow/Blank-1
86Meadow/Milk-1
86Meadow/Stat-9
86OPC-262
86OPC-B
86Quaker-22
86S-180M
86S-183M
86S-184M
86S-3
86S-75M
86S/Dec-68
86T-510
86T/3D-3
86T/Gloss60-26
86T/Mini-3
86T/St-164
86T/St-247
86T/Super-12
86T/WaxBox-B
86TrueVal-30
86Woolwth-3
87BK-1
87Class/Up-105
87Classic-60
87D-252
87D/AAS-7
87D/HL-14
87D/HL-44
87D/OD-181
87D/PopUp-7
87Drake-16
87F-29
87F-637M
87F/Excit-4
87F/GameWin-5
87F/HL-1
87F/Lim-3
87F/LL-3
87F/Mini-10
87F/Slug-4
87F/St-12
87F/St-S2
87F/WS-2M
87Ho/St-19
87Jiffy-20
87KayBee-4
87KMart-23
87Kraft-7
87Leaf-193
87MnM's-5
87MSA/Discs-13
87OPC-150
87Ralston-3
87RedFoley/St-96
87S-114M
87S-197M
87S-2
87Seven-E5
87Seven-ME6
87T-150
87T-608AS
87T/Board-31
87T/Coins-4
87T/Gloss22-15
87T/Gloss60-18
87T/HL-10
87T/Mini-41
87T/St-148
87T/St-253
87Woolwth-10
88Woolwth-13
88Bz-2
88ChefBoy-22
88Class/Blue-214
88Class/Red-155
88D-153
88D-BC7
88D/AS-31
88D/AS-7
88D/Best-65
88D/PopUp-7
88D/RedSox/Bk-153
88F-345
88F/AS-8
88F/AwardWin-3
88F/BB/AS-2
88F/BB/MVP-2
88F/Excit-4
88F/Hottest-2
88F/LL-2
88F/Mini-4
88F/RecSet-3
88F/Slug-2
88F/SS-3
88F/St-5
88F/TL-2
88FanSam-8
88Jiffy-2
88KayBee-2
88KMart-2
88Leaf-65
88MSA/Disc-1
88Nestle-32
88OPC-200
88Panini/St-228M
88Panini/St-29
88Score-2
88Score/WaxBox-4
88Sf-50
88Sf/Gamewin-3
88T-200
88T-388
88T/Big-32
88T/Coins-4
88T/Gloss22-4
88T/Gloss60-51
88T/Mini-1
88T/Revco-16
88T/RiteAid-14
88T/St-157
88T/St-244
88T/St/Backs-40
88T/UK-4
89B-32
89Bz-3
89Cadaco-2
89Class-102
89Class-2
89D-68
89D/AS-7
89D/Best-140
89D/PopUp-7
89F-633M
89F-81
89F/BBAS-3
89F/BBMVP's-3
89F/Excit-2
89F/Heroes-2
89F/LL-2
89F/Rec-1
89F/Superstar-4
89F/WaxBox-C2
89Holsum/Discs-2
89KayBee-1
89KingB/Discs-3
89KMart/DT-14
89KMart/Lead-1
89Master/Discs-5
89Nissen-2
89OPC-184
89Panini/St-242AS
89Panini/St-245AS
89Panini/St-277
89Panini/St-7
89RedFoley/St-8
89Score-175
89Score-654HL
89Score/HotSt-100
89Score/Mast-17
89Sf-100
89Sf-221M
89T-2RB
89T-399AS
89T-600
89T/Big-241
89T/Coins-32
89T/DH-3
89T/Gloss22-4
89T/Gloss60-5
89T/HeadsUp-11
89T/Hills-2
89T/Mini-45
89T/St-147
89T/St-260
89T/St-9
89T/St/Backs-7
89T/UK-4
89Tetley/Discs-7
89UD-389
89UD-687TC
89Woolwth-8
90Class-26
90D-68
90D-712AS
90D/Preview-11
90F-268
90F-632M
90Score-245
90Score-683DT
90Score-704
90Score/100St-80
90Sf-2
90T-387AS
90T-760
90UD-555

Bohanon, Brian
88CharlR/Star-2

Bohlke, Scott
88Durhm/Star-2

Bohn, Charles
(Charlie)
No Cards.
Bohn, Matt
88CalLgAS-23
Bohne, Sammy Arthur
21Exh-12
E120
V117-20
V61-67
Bohnenkamp, Dave
89Clint/Pro-880
Bohnet, Bob
79Wisco-13
82Holyo-14
Bohnet, John
81Chatt-13
82Charl-2
84BuffB-14
Boisclair, Bruce A.
77T-399
78T-277
79OPC-68
79T-148
80T-654
Boitano, Danny
76OkCty
79Vanco-9
80T-668R
80Vanco-14
81Tidew-27
Bokelman, Dick
53T-204
79TCMA-249
Boken, Robert A.
(Bob)
34G-74
Boland, Edward John
(Ed)
No Cards.
Bolar, Wendell
86Cram/PCL-106
87Wausa-9
88Boise/Pro-1607
Bold, Charles Dickens
(Charlie)
No Cards.
Bolek, Ken
76Clint
78Watlo
83ColumAst-23
86Ashvl-3MG
87Osceola-6
88Watlo/Pro-687
89Kinston/Star-25
Boles, Carl Theodore
63T-428
Boles, John
83AppFx/LF-25MG
85BuffB-1
86Omah/TCM-23MG
86Omaha-2MG
Boley, John Peter
(Joe)
31Exh/4-27
Bolger, James Cyril
(Jim)
55T-179
57T-289
58T-201
59T-29
61Union
Bolick, Frank
88Beloi/GS-4
89Beloi/Star-1
Bolin, Bobby
61T-449
62T-329
63T-106
64T-374
65T-341
66OPC-61
66T-61
67T-252
68Coke
68OPC-169
68T-169
69OPC-8LL
69T-505
69T-8LL
69T/St-101
70McDon-1
70MLB/St-266
70T-574
71MLB/St-314
71OPC-446
71T-446
72MB-36
72OPC-266
72T-266
73OPC-541
73T-541
74OPC-427
74T-427
78TCMA-109
Boling, John
86AppFx-2
87BirmB/Best-12
88BirmB/Best-18
Bolling, Frank Elmore
55B-204
57T-325
58T-95
59T-280
60T-482
61P-41
61T-335
61T/St-145
62J-146
62P-146
62P/Can-146
62Salada-140
62Shirriff-140
62T-130
62T-211M
62T/St-145
63F-44
63J-149
63P-149
63Salada-18
63T-570
64T-115
65Kahn
65OPC-269
65T-269
66Kahn
78TCMA-9
Bolling, John Edward
No Cards.
Bolling, Milton J.
(Milt)
53T-280
54B-130
54T-82
55B-48
55T-91
55T/DH-92
56T-315
57T-131
58T-188
Bollo, Greg
65T-541R
66T-301
78TCMA-30
Bollweg, Donald R.
(Don)
52T-128
54B-115
55B-54
55Rodeo
PM10/Sm-14
Bolster, Bob
80GlenF/B-29bb
80GlenF/C-23bb
Bolt, James
86SanJose-5
Bolton, Cecil G.
No Cards.
Bolton, Tom
80Elmir-2
87Pawtu-12
87Pawtu/TCMA-27
88F-346
88Pawtu/CMC-9
88Pawtu/Pro-452
88T-442
89AAA/Pro-17
89D-539
89Pawtu/CMC-1
89Pawtu/Dunkin-15
89Pawtu/Pro-680
89Score-531
89T-269
89UD-545
90UD-351
Bolton, William C.
(Cliff)
34DS-47
34G-65
R313
R314
V355-133
Bomback, Mark
77Holyo
79Vanco-7
81F-323
81OPC-264
81T-567
81T/Tr-739
82D-559
82F-610
82OPC-307
82T-707
83Syrac-5
84Syrac-23
Bombard, Marc
86FSLAS-9CO
87Tampa-8
88Cedar/Pro-1144
88MidwLAS/GS-15
89ElPas/GS-1
Bombard, Rich
82AubAs-13
83DayBe-3
86ColumAst-5
87Cedar-26
88Chatt/Best-5
89Chatt/Best-8
89Chatt/GS-2
Bomgardner, Rich
89Clmbia/Best-25
89Clmbia/GS-3
Bonacquista, Jeff
87Anchora-3
Bonaparte, Elijah
77Spart
80OkCty
81OkCty/TCMA-3
82Toled-19
83RochR-19
Bonarigo, Nick
43Centen-2
Bonchek, Jeff
88BurlR/Pro-1779
89Mia/Star/25-3
Boncore, Steve
82VeroB-13
83VeroB-14
Bond, Daven
86AubAs-4
87Ashvl-6
88Osceola/Star-4
89Osceola/Star-2
Bond, David
87Spoka-16
88Charl/Pro-1196
89CharRa/Pro-993
Bond, Doug
88Bill/Pro-1809
Bond, Thomas Henry
(Tommy)
No Cards.
Bond, Walter F.
(Walt)
60T-552
61T-334
62Salada-208
62Shirriff-208
63T-493
64T-339
65OPC-109
65T-109
65T/E-50
65T/trans-4
66T-431
67T-224
Bonds, Barry
86D/Rook-11
86F/Up-U14
86S/Rook-13
86T/Tr-11T
87Class/Up-113
87D-361
87D/OD-163
87F-604
87F/Hottest-5
87Leaf-219
87OPC-320
87T-320
87T/Gloss60-30
87T/St-131
87ToysRUs-4
88D-326
88D/Best-17
88F-322
88F/SS-4
88KingB/Disc-11
88Leaf-113
88OPC-267
88Panini/St-376
88RedFoley/St-7
88Score-265
88Score/YS/II-12
88Sf-119
88T-450
88T/Big-89
88T/St-135
88T/UK-5
89Ames-5
89B-426
89Class-117
89D-92
89D/Best-73
89F-202
89F/Heroes-3
89OPC-263
89Panini/St-172
89RedFoley/St-9
89Score-127
89Score/HotSt-31
89Sf-146
89T-620
89T/Big-5
89T/St-127
89T/St/Backs-46
89T/UK-5
89UD-440
90Class-82
90D-126
90F-461
90Score-4
90Score/100St-53
90Sf-143
90T-220
90UD-227
Bonds, Bobby Lee
69MB-31
69T-630
70MLB/St-121
70OPC-425
70T-425
71MLB/St-241
71OPC-295
71T-295
71T/Coins-13
72MB-37
72T-711
72T-712A
73K-8
73OPC-145
73T-145
73T/Lids-6
74K-39
74Laugh/ASG-73
74OPC-30
74T-30
74T/Puzzles-4
74T/St-101
75Ho-145
75OPC-55
75T-55
75T/M-55
76Ho-18
76Ho/Twink-18
76OPC-2RB
76OPC-380
76SSPC-436
76T-380
76T/Tr-380T
77OPC-173
77T-570
78Ho-42
78OPC-206
78T-150
78Wiffle/Discs-6
79OPC-142
79T-285
80BK/PHR-23
80OPC-215
80T-410
81D-71
81F-548
81OPC-223
81T-635
81T/Tr-740
82F-588
82OPC-27
82T-580
84Moth/Giants-12
85Polar/Ind
86OhHenry-CO
87Gator-CO
Bone, George D.
No Cards.
Bone, Pat
82Oneon-10
Bones, Ricardo
86Cram/PCL-163
87CharRa-21
88CalLgAS-41
88River/Cal-208
88River/Pro-1426
89AubAs/Pro-16
89Wich/Roc-10
89Wich/Roc/HL-2
Bongiovanni, Anthony
(Nino)
W711/1
Bonham, Bill
72OPC-29
72T-29
73OPC-328
73T-328
74OPC-528
74T-528
75OPC-85
75T-85
75T/M-85
76OPC-151
76SSPC-303

76T-151
77OPC-95
77T-446
78T-276
79K-31
79OPC-182
79T-354
80OPC-26
80T-47
81F-215
81Indianap-13
81T-712
86AubAs-5CO

Bonham, Ernie
43MP-1
44Yank/St-1
47TipTop
49B-77
49Eureka-154

Boni, Joel
82Madis-2

Bonikowski, Joe
61Clover-4
62T-592R

Bonilla, Bobby
83AlexD-16
86Coke/WS-26
86D/Rook-30
86F/Up-U15
86S/Rook-26
86T/Tr-12T
87D-558
87D/OD-167
87F-605
87T-184
88Class/Blue-236
88D-238
88D/Best-33
88F-323
88F/BB/AS-3
88F/Hottest-3
88F/Mini-103
88F/Slug-3
88F/St-114
88Leaf-188
88OPC-189
88Panini/St-372
88Score-116
88Score/YS/II-9
88Sf-131
88T-681
88T/Big-25
88T/Coins-37
88T/St-129
89B-422
89Cadaco-3
89D-151
89D-2DK
89D/AS-39
89D/Best-33
89D/DKsuper-2DK
89D/PopUp-39
89F-203
89F-637M
89F/AS-1
89F/BBAS-4
89Nissen-15
89OPC-142
89Panini/St-171
89Panini/St-234AS
89RedFoley/St-10
89Score-195
89Score/HotSt-42
89Sf-182
89T-388AS
89T-440
89T/Big-159
89T/Coins-5
89T/DH-15
89T/Gloss22-15
89T/Gloss60-24
89T/Mini-30
89T/St-131
89T/St-158
89T/St/Backs-40
89T/UK-6
89UD-578
90Class-143
90D-290
90D/Bon/MVP-BC16
90F-462
90Score-170
90Score/100St-37
90Sf-195
90T-273
90UD-16TC
90UD-366

Bonilla, George
85Evrt/Cram-2A
85Evrt/Cram-2B
86Clint-3
88Shreve/Pro-1289
89Shreve/Pro-1855

Bonilla, Juan G.
78Watlo
80Tacom-19
82D-220
82F-567
82T-464
83D-346
83F-353
83T-563
84D-234
84F-295
84Nes/792-168
84OPC-168
84T-168
84T/St-152
85Colum-26
85IntLgAS-26
86T/Tr-13T
87F-464
87OPC-131
87T-668

Bonin, Ernest Luther
(Luther)
No Cards.

Bonin, Greg
88Umpire-56
89Umpires-54

Bonine, Eddie
83Tucso-1
84Cram/PCL-64
85Cram/PCL-70

Bonitto, Arturo
77QuadC

Bonk, Thomas
85Greens-5

Bonneau, Rob
88Wythe/Pro-1976

Bonnell, Robert Barry
(Barry)
78Ho-142
78T-242
79T-496
80OPC-331
80T-632
81D-272
81F-413
81OPC-82
81OPC/Post-19
81T-558
82D-432
82F-611
82OPC-99
82T-99
82T/St-251
83D-430
83F-425
83OPC-281
83T-766
83T/St-133
84D-559
84F-149
84F/X-14
84Moth/Mar-2
84Nes/792-302
84OPC-302
84T-302
84T/St-370
84T/X-14
85D-191
85F-485
85Leaf-195
85Moth/Mar-10
85OPC-107
85T-423
85T/St-342
86F-460
86Moth/Mar-10
86OPC-119
86T-119

Bonner, Frank J.
No Cards.

Bonner, Jeffry
89Clint/Pro-892

Bonner, Mark
82Danvi-25
83Redwd-4
85MidldA-5

Bonner, Robert A.
(Bob)
80RochR-1
81RochR-2
82D-610
82T-21R
83F-53
83RochR-14
84RochR-13

Bonura, Henry John
(Zeke)
34DS-65
35BU-141
35BU-65
35Exh/4-10
35G-8B
35G-9B
36Exh/4-10
36G
37Exh/4-10
37OPC-116
37Wheat
38G-252
38G-276
38Wheat
39PB-144
40PB-131
88Conlon/5-4
R312/M
R313
R314
V300
V355-112
WG8-3

Bonura, Tony
86Cram/PCL-93

Booe, Everitt Little
No Cards.

Booker, Greg
84Cram/PCL-218
85F-27
85Moth/Padres-22
85T-262
86LasVegas-2
86T-429
87F/U-U7
87T/Tr-6T
88Coke/Padres-51
88D-311
88F-577
88Score-447
88Smok/Padres-4
88T-727
89Score-417
89T-319
89T/Big-194
89UD-641

Booker, Richard Lee
(Buddy)
No Cards.

Booker, Rod
82OrlTw/A-1
82Toled-12
83ArkTr-19
84Louvl-12
86ArkTr-2
86Louisvl-7
87Louvl-6
88Louvl-10
88T-483
89Louvl-11
89Louvl/CMC-8
89Louvl/Pro-1264
89T/Big-256
89UD-644

Bool, Albert
(Al)
No Cards.

Boone, Danny
79SLCty-23
82D-187
82F-568
82T-407
83Tucso-2
84Cram/PCL-36
85Anchora-5

Boone, Isaac Morgan
(Ike)
87Conlon/2-24
88MinorLg/Leg-3
R314/Can

Boone, Lute Joseph
(Luke)
D350/2-12
M101/5-12

Boone, Raymond Otis
(Ray)
50NumNum
51B-54
51T/RB-23
52B-214
52NumNum-13
52T-55
53B/Col-79
53T-25
54T-77
55RFG-11
55RM-AL1
55T-65
55T/DH-113
56T-6
56T/Hocus-A7
56T/Hocus-B9
56T/Pin-36
57T-102
58T-185
59T-252
60Lake
60T-281
76OPC-67FS
76T-67M
79TCMA-179
85T-133FS

Boone, Robert Raymond
(Bob)
73OPC-613R
73T-613R
74JP
74OPC-131
74T-131
74T/St-71
75OPC-351
75T-351
75T/M-351
76OPC-318
76OPC-67FS
76SSPC-471
76T-318
76T-67M
77OPC-68
77T-545
78Ho-29
78OPC-141
78T-161
79BK/P-2
79Ho-113
79OPC-38
79T-90
80BK/P-2
80OPC-246
80T-470
81Coke
81D-262
81F-4
81F/St-79
81OPC-290
81T-290
81T/HT
81T/St-203
82D-471
82F-240
82OPC-23
82OPC-392IA
82T-615
82T-616A
82T/St-77
82T/Tr-9T
83D-192
83F-79
83OPC-366
83T-765
83T/St-45
84D-158
84F-509
84F-637
84Nes/792-520
84OPC-174
84Smok/Cal-3
84T-520
84T/St-234
85D-230
85F-295
85OPC-348
85Smok/Cal-3
85T-133FS
85T-348
85T/St-228
86D-17
86D-230
86D/DKsuper-17
86F-149
86Leaf-17DK
86OPC-62
86Smok/Cal-3
86T-62
86T/St-179
87D-233
87D/HL-41
87F-73
87F/AwardWin-4
87Leaf-202
87OPC-166
87T-166
87T/St-180
88D-305
88D/Best-3
88F-485
88Leaf-151
88OPC-158
88OPC-D
88Panini/St-39
88Score-63
88Sf-212
88Smok/Angels-9
88T-498
88T/Big-30
88T/St-182
88T/St-5
88T/UK-6
88T/WaxBox-D

89B-119
89Class/Up/2-187
89D-170
89D/Best-263
89D/Tr-5
89F-469
89F/Up-36
89OPC-243
89Panini/St-287
89Score-233
89Score/HotSt-81
89Score/Tr-74
89Sf-40
89Smok/Angels-17
89T-243
89T-404AS
89T/Big-269
89T/St-175
89T/St/Backs-22
89T/Tr-12T
89UD-119
89UD/Ext-767
90D-326
90F-102
90Score-60
90Sf-40
90T-671
90UD-271

Boone, Ron
75Iowa/TCMA-2

Bootay, Kevin
86Salem-1
86Tulsa-16
88TexLgAS/GS-9
88Tulsa-13
89ScrWB/CMC-24
89ScrWB/Pro-713

Booth, Amos Smith
No Cards.

Booth, David
88Poca/Pro-2098
89SanJose/Best-10
89SanJose/Cal-228
89SanJose/Pro-440
89SanJose/Star-2

Booth, Edward H.
(Eddie)
No Cards.

Boozer, John
63T-29R
64T-16
65OPC-184
65T-184
66T-324
68OPC-173
68T-173
69T-599

Boras, Scott
77StPet

Borbon, Ernie
82VeroB-2
83Albuq-21
84Cram/PCL-159

Borbon, Pedro
70OPC-358
70T-358
71OPC-613
71T-613
73OPC-492
73T-492
74OPC-410
74T-410
74T/St-23
75OPC-157
75T-157
75T/M-157
76OPC-77
76SSPC-24
76T-77
77Pep-54
77T-581
78OPC-199
78T-220
79OPC-164
79T-326
80T-627

Borcherding, Mark
89Bill/Pro-2066

Borchers, Rick
79Tacom-3
80Tacom-21
81Chatt-18
82Chatt-20

Borchert, Shane
89Clint/Pro-889

Bordagaray, Stanley
(Frenchy)
36Exh/4-2
36G-3
39PB-75
R312/M
R314
W711/1

Border, Bob
80ElPas-10

Border, Mark
82Idaho-3

Borders, Pat
85Kingst-15
86Knoxv-3
87Knoxv-20
88D/Rook-12
88F/U-U65
88Score/Tr-99T
88T/Tr-17T
88Tor/Fire-10
89D-560
89F-227
89OPC-343
89Panini/St-464
89Score-198
89Score/HotRk-91
89Score/YS/I-11
89T-693
89T/St-191
89Tor/Fire-10
89UD-593
90D-560
90F-77
90Score-288
90Sf-45
90T-191
90UD-112

Bordi, Rich
81Tacom-10
82SLCty-4
82T-531R
83IowaC-1
84SevenUp-42
85D-289
85F-49
85F/Up-U8
85Leaf-166
85T-357
85T/Tr-7T
86D-518
86F-101
86F/Up-U16
86T-94
86T/Tr-14T
87Colum-22
87Colum/Pol-3
87Colum/TCMA-2
87D-213
87F-465
87T-638
88Tacom/CMC-1
88Tacom/Pro-627
89Tacom/CMC-1
89Tacom/Pro-1544

Bordick, Michael
87Modesto-6
88Huntsvl/BK-1
88SLAS-4
89Tacom/CMC-23
89Tacom/Pro-1565

Bordley, Bill
79Phoen
80Phoen-10

Borelli, Dean
88SoOreg/Pro-1705
89Madis/Star-4

Borg, Gary
86Visal-4
87Orlan-16
88Orlan/Best-12
89Stock/Best-18
89Stock/Cal-164
89Stock/Pro-396
89Stock/Star-1

Borgatti, Mike
87Hagers-1
88Virgini/Star-2
89Watlo/Pro-1793
89Watlo/Star-1

Borges, George
83MidldC-15
84PrWill-33

Borges, Jose
89Butte/SP-9

Borgese, Jeff
88CapeCod/Sum-20

Borgmann, Bennie
40Hughes-5

Borgmann, Glenn D.
73OPC-284
73T-284
74OPC-547
74T-547
75OPC-127
75T-127
75T/M-127
76OPC-498
76SSPC-213
76T-498
77T-87
78T-307
79T-431
80T-634
81D-159
81T-716

Boris, Paul
81Colum-7
83T-266
83Toled-1
84Richm-4

Bork, Frank
65T-592
66OPC-123R
66T-123R

Borkowski, Robert V.
(Bob)
52T-328
53T-7
54T-138
55T-74
55T/DH-63

Borland, Scott
83AlexD-4
84PrWill-18
85PrWill-15

Borland, Toby
88Martins/Star-4
89Spart/Pro-1037
89Spart/Star-2

Borland, Tom
60L-26
60T-117
61T-419
89Smok/Ast-6

Borman, Dave
89Utica/Puc-9

Bormann, Mike
83Durhm-16
85Durhm-4

Bornw, Tony
89Tidew/CMC-27

Borom, Edward Jones
(Red)
No Cards.

Boros, Stephen
(Steve)
58T-81
59T-331
61T-348
61T/St-146
62J-16
62P-16
62P/Can-16
62Salada-50
62Shirriff-50
62T-62
62T-72M
62T/St-42
63J-47
63P-47
63T-532
65OPC-102
65T-102
65T-131
78TCMA-88
83Granny-14MG
83T/X-13
84Moth/A's-1MG
84Nes/792-531MG
84T-531
86T/Tr-15T
87T-143MG

Boroski, Stan
83Beloi/LF-28
86FtMyr-4
87FtMyr-2

Borowicz, Ray
88BurlR/Pro-1801

Borowski, Rich
83Idaho-20
84Madis/Pol-23

Borowsky, Erez
83Visal/LF-15
84Visal-3
85Orlan-2

Borowy, Henry
39Exh
44Yank/St-2
49B-134
49Eureka-131
49Lummis
50B-177
51B-250

Borriello, Sebby
82Wisco-13

Borruel, Jeff
78Cedar

Borton, William Baker
(Babe)
No Cards.

Borucki, Ray
80Penin/B-19
80Penin/C-25

Bosch, Donald John
(Don)
68T-572
69Fud's-3
69T-578
70OPC-527
70T-527
72MB-38

Bosco, Mike
89Reno/Cal-253

Bosetti, Richard Alan
(Rick)
76OkCty
78T-710R
79OPC-279
79T-542
80OPC-146
80T-277
80T/S-51
81D-152
81OPC-46
81OPC/Post-18
81T-46
81T/Tr-741
82D-626
82F-88
82T-392
82Tacom-33

Bosio, Chris
83Beloi/LF-27
86Vanco-4
87D-478
87D/Rook-20
87F-338
87S/Rook-2
87T-448
88D-117
88D/Best-295
88F-156
88OPC-137
88Pol/Brew-29
88Score-38
88Score/YS/I-4
88T-137
89B-134
89D-412
89D/Best-109
89F-179
89Pol/Brew-29
89RedFoley/St-11
89Score-243
89T-311
89UD-292
90D-20DK
90D-57
90F-316
90Score-283
90Sf-25
90T-597
90UD-293

Boskie, Shawn
87Peoria-8
89CharlK-17

Bosley, Rich
86Beloi-2

Bosley, Thaddis
(Thad)
75QuadC
77SLCty
78T-619
79T-129
80T-412
81D-162
81F-353
82T-350
83Thorn-20
84IowaC-7
84Nes/792-657
84SevenUp-27
84T-657
85D-388
85SevenUp-27
85T-432
86D-483
86F-361
86Gator-27
86T-512
87D-191
87F-555
87F/U-U8
87T-58
87T/Tr-7T
88D-348
88F-253
88T-247
89UD-591

Bosman, Dick
67T-459R
68T-442
69T-607

70MLB/St-278
70OPC-175
70OPC-68LL
70T-175
70T-68LL
70T/S-22
70T/SO
71MLB/St-530
71OPC-60
71T-60
71T/Coins-70
71T/GM-49
71T/S-7
71T/tatt-1
72MB-39
72OPC-365
72T-365
73OPC-640
73T-640
73T/Lids-7
74OPC-465
74T-465
75Ho-114
75OPC-354
75OPC-7M
75T-354
75T-7M
75T/M-354
75T/M-7M
76OPC-298
76SSPC-483
76T-298
77T-101
86BuffB-2CO
89RochR/CMC-24
89RochR/Pro-1641
89Swell-124

Boss, David
89Hamil/Star-5

Boss, Elmer Harley
(Harley)
No Cards.

Bostick, Henry L.
No Cards.

Bostock, Lyman W.
76OPC-263
76T-263
77Ho-102
77K-16
77OPC-239
77T-531
78Ho-145
78K-46
78T-655

Boston, Daryl L.
82AppFx-24
83GlenF-1
85Coke/WS-8
85D-33
85F/Up-U9
85T/Tr-8T
86BuffB-3
86Coke/WS-8
86D-86
86T-139
87Coke/WS-4
87D-137
87F-487
87T-482
88Coke/WS-2
88F-393
88Score-582
88T-739
89B-70
89Coke/WS-6
89D-455
89F-492
89Panini/St-311
89Score-443
89T-633
89UD-496
90Score-213
90T-524
90UD-529

Boswell, Dave
67T-575
68Coke
68T-322
69T-459
70MLB/St-230
70OPC-325
70OPC-70LL
70T-325
70T-70LL
71MLB/St-459
71OPC-675
71T-675
72MB-40

Boswell, Kenneth G.
69T-402
70OPC-214
70T-214
70Trans/M-22
71MLB/St-147
71OPC-492
71T-492
72MB-41
72OPC-305
72OPC-306IA
72T-305
72T-306A
73OPC-87
73T-87
74OPC-645
74T-645
75OPC-479
75T-479
75T/M-479
76OPC-379
76SSPC-55
76T-279
77T-429

Boswell, Mike
88Peoria/Ko-6

Botelho, Derek
83Omaha-3
84IowaC-xx
85IowaC-13
87Omaha-10
88Louvl-11

Botkin, Alan
88CapeCod/Sum-81

Botkin, Mike
83DayBe-24

Bottarini, John C.
No Cards.

Bottenfield, Kent
87BurlEx-5
88WPalm/Star-3
89Jaxvl/Best-9
89Jaxvl/Pro-163

Bottenfield, Keven
88Boise/Pro-1628

Botting, Ralph
75QuadC
76QuadC
80SLCty-1
80T-663R
81SLCty-2
81T-214R
82Omaha-2

Bottomley, James L.
(Jim)
21Exh-13
25Exh-59
26Exh-59
27Exh-30
29Exh/4-15
31Exh/4-15
33DH-6
33G-44
34DS-59
34Exh/4-4
35BU-115M
35BU-179
35BU-8
35Exh/4-4
35G-1H
35G-1K
35G-3B
35G-3F
35G-4F
35G-5B
35G-6B
40PB-236
60F-45
61F-9
69Bz-7
72F/FFeat-6
72Laugh/GF-13
80Cram/Leg-64
R300
R308-205
R310
R311/Gloss
R315-A5
R315-B5
R316
V117-19
V353-44
V355-85

Bouchee, Edward F.
(Ed)
57T-314
59T-39
60T-347
61T-196
61T/St-5
62J-182
62P-182
62P/Can-182
62Salada-116
62Shirriff-116
62T-497

Boucher, Alexander F.
(Al)
No Cards.

Boucher, Denis
88Myrtle/Pro-1168
88SALAS/GS-23
89Duned/Star-1

Boucher, Medric C.
No Cards.

Boudreau, Jim
84MidldC-4

Boudreau, Louis
(Lou)
39Exh
41DP-132
43MP-2
48L-106
49B-11
49MP-100
50B-94
50NumNum
51B-62
53B/Col-57
55B-89
55Rodeo
56Rodeo
60F-16
61F-94
79TCMA-287
80Cram/Leg-79
83D/HOF-12
86S/Dec-17
88Pac/Leg-106
89Pac/Leg-166
89Swell-80
D305
PM10/Sm-15
PM10/Sm-16
R346-22

Boudreaux, Eric
87Clearw-12
89Readg/Best-19
89Readg/Pro-668

Bouldin, Carl
63T-496R
64T-518

Bourjos, Christopher
(Chris)
77Cedar
79Phoen
80Phoen-11
81RochR-21
81T-502R
83Portl-14

Bourne, Kendrick
86Elmir-3
87Elmir-6
87Elmir/Red-6
88WinHav/Star-5
89Clearw/Star-3

Bournigal, Rafael
89Star/Wax-27
89VeroB/Star-3

Bourque, Patrick D.
(Pat)
73OPC-605R
73T-605R
74OPC-141
74T-141
75OPC-502
75T-502
75T/M-502

Bouton, Jim
62T-592R
63T-401
64T-219M
64T-470
64T-4LL
64T/Coins-138AS
64T/Coins-4
64T/St-45
64Wheat/St-7
65OPC-137WS
65OPC-30
65T-30
65T/E-25
65T/trans-5
66T-276
67T-393
68T-562
78TCMA-77
88Pac/Leg-20
89Swell-66
WG10-2
WG9-3

Bowa, Lawrence Robert
(Larry)
70OPC-539R
70T-539R
71MLB/St-169
71OPC-233
71T-233
71T/tatt-16
72OPC-520
72T-520
73OPC-119
73T-119
74JP
74OPC-255
74T-255
74T/DE-70
74T/St-72
75OPC-420
75T-420
75T/M-420
76Crane-4
76Ho-145
76MSA/Disc
76OPC-145
76SSPC-464
76T-145
77Ho-62
77OPC-17
77T-310
78Ho-71
78K-26
78OPC-68
78T-90
79BK/P-15
79Ho-134
79K-44
79OPC-104
79T-210
80BK/P-7
80K-39
80OPC-330
80T-630
80T/S-34
81Coke
81D-142
81F-2
81F-645
81F/St-20
81F/St-43M
81K-43
81OPC-120
81T-120
81T/HT
81T/St-201
82D-63
82F-241
82F/St-107M
82F/St-56
82OPC-194
82OPC-374IA
82RedLob
82T-515
82T-516A
82T/St-80
82T/Tr-10T
83D-435
83F-491
83OPC-305
83T-305
83Thorn-1
84D-239
84F-486
84FunFood/Pin-126
84Nes/792-705LL
84Nes/792-757
84OPC-346
84SevenUp-1
84T-705
84T-757
84T/St-46
85D-361
85D/HL-7
85F-50
85OPC-56
85SevenUp-1
85T-484
85T/St-45
87Bohem-10MG
87T/Tr-8T
88Coke/Pad-10MG
88T-284

Bowcock, Benjamin J.
(Benny)
No Cards.

Bowden, David Timon
(Tim)
No Cards.

Bowden, James
84Butte-3

Bowden, Mark
81Cedar-22
86Readg-3
87Readg-17
88RochR-2
88RochR-4
88RochR/CMC-4
88RochR/Gov-2
88RochR/Pro-208

Bowden, Steve
85Bend/Cram-3
87Hagers-15

88Fresno/Cal-16
Bowen, Emmons Joseph
(Chick)
No Cards.
Bowen, John
89Erie/Star-3
Bowen, Kenny
88Memph/Best-5
89Memph/Best-8
89Memph/Pro-1207
89Memph/Star-2
Bowen, Ryan
87Ashvl-5
88Osceola/Star-5
89ColMud/Best-18
89ColMud/Pro-126
89ColMud/Star-4
Bowen, Samuel Thomas
(Sam)
78PapaG/Disc-6
81Pawtu-18
Bowens, Samuel Edward
(Sam)
64T-201R
65OPC-188
65T-188
66T-412
67T-491
68OPC-82
68T-82
69MB-32
Bowens, Steve
83Idaho-1
Bowerman, Frank E.
T204
T206
Bowers, Grover Bill
(Billy)
52Park-6
Bowers, Mickey
80LynnS-15
81LynnS-25
82LynnS-18
83Chatt-12
Bowers, Tom
58SFCall
Bowes, Frank M.
No Cards.
Bowie, Jim Jr.
86Cram/PCL-102
87Wausa-15
88CalLgAS-27
88SanBern/Best-16
88SanBern/Cal-30
89Calg/CMC-17
89Calg/Pro-525
Bowlan, Mark
89Hamil/Star-4
Bowlin, Allan
80Elmir-3
Bowlin, Lois Weldon
(Hoss)
No Cards.
Bowling, Stephen S.
(Steve)
79Indianap-20
Bowman, Don
(Gen. Mgr.)
88Pulas/Pro-1771
Bowman, Elmer W.
No Cards.
Bowman, Ernest F.
(Ernie)
62T-231
63T-61
66T-302
Bowman, Joseph Emil
(Joe)
39PB-128
40PB-162
Bowman, Michael
89Brist/Star-1
Bowman, Robert LeRoy
(Bob)
57T-332
58T-415
59T-221
Bowman, Roger
55B-115
Bowman, William G.
(Bill)
No Cards.
Bowman, William
77StPet
Bowser, James H.
(Red)
No Cards.
Bowsfield, Edward
(Ted)
59T-236
60T-382
61T-216
62T-369
62T/St-64
63T-339
64T-447
Box, Newt
80Cedar-2
Boxberger, Rod
83Nashua-2
Boyan, Michael
88CapeCod/Sum-155
Boyce
N172
Boyce, Bob
82Miami-14
Boyce, Randy
78Newar
79BurlB-19
Boyce, Tommy
88SLCty-10
89Keno/Star-1
89Mia/Star/22-2
Boyd, Bob
76QuadC
77QuadC
Boyd, Daryl
86Watertn-4
89WPalm/Star-4
Boyd, Dennis
(Oil Can)
80Elmir-4
83Pawtu-2
84D-457
84F-393
85D-151
85F-152
85T-116
86D-50
86F-342
86F/St-9
86Leaf-35
86OPC-259
86S-152
86T-605
86T/Mini-4
86T/St-249
87Classic-85
87D-51
87F-30
87F/Excit-5
87F/Lim-4
87Leaf-248
87OPC-285
87RedFoley/St-122
87S-47
87Smok/AL-2
87T-285
87T/St-249
88D-462
88D/RedSox/Bk-462
88F-347
88Leaf-252
88Panini/St-20
88Score-121
88T-704
89D-476
89F-82
89OPC-326
89Panini/St-269
89Score-238
89T-326
89UD-415
90D-633
90Score-137
90T-544
90UD-484
Boyd, Frank John
No Cards.
Boyd, Gary Lee
70OPC-7R
70T-7R
Boyd, Jacob Henry
(Jake)
N172
Boyd, Randy
77SnJos-16
Boyd, Robert Richard
(Bob)
53T-257
54B-118
54T-113
57T-26
58Hires-75
58T-279
59T-82
60L-13
60T-207
61T-199
61T/St-157
Boyer, Cletis Leroy
(Clete)
57T-121
59T-251
60L-46
60T-109
61P-11
61T-19
61T/St-191
62Exh
62J-3
62P-3
62P/Can-3
62Salada-80
62Shirriff-80
62T-163M
62T-490
62T/St-84
63Exh
63J-14
63Kahn
63P-14
63T-361
64T-69
65T-475
66OPC-9
66T-9
67T-328
68Bz-1
68Coke
68Kahn
68T-550
69T-489
69T/St-3
70OPC-206
70T-206
71MLB/St-4
71OPC-374
71T-374
72MB-42
78Green
87Colum-3
88Pac/Leg-13
89Swell-94
Exh47
PM10/L-6
WG10-3
WG9-4
Boyer, Cloyd
51B-228
52T-280
53B/Col-115
53Hunters
53T-60
55B-149
55Rodeo
85Syrac-30
88Pulas/Pro-1770
Boyer, Kenton Lloyd
(Ken)
55Hunter
55T-125
56T-14
56T/Pin-46
57Swift-8
57T-122
58T-350
59Bz
59HRDerby-4
59T-325
59T-557AS
60Armour-4
60Bz-9
60L-12
60T-160M
60T-485
61Bz-14
61P-171
61T-375
61T-43LL
61T-573AS
61T/St-85
62Bz
62J-159
62P-159
62P/Can-159
62Salada-167
62Shirriff-167
62T-370
62T-392AS
62T-52LL
62T/bucks
62T/St-183
63F-60
63J-160
63P-160
63Salada-15
63T-375
63T/SO
64Bz-35
64T-11LL
64T-160
64T/Coins-145AS
64T/Coins-25
64T/S-57
64T/St-61
64T/SU
64T/tatt
64Wheat/St-8
65Bz-35
65OldLond-4
65OPC-100
65OPC-135WS
65OPC-6LL
65T-100
65T-6LL
65T/E-47
65T/trans-40
66T-385
66T/RO-41
67Bz-33
67Kahn
67OPC-105
67T-105
68T-259
69MB-33
69T-379
74Laugh/ASG-56
75OPC-202M
75T-202MV
75T/M-202MV
78TCMA-67
79T-192MG
82KMart-6
88Pac/Leg-12
Boylan, Brad
84Cram/PCL-193TR
86Toled-2TR
87Portl-24
88Portl/Pro-648
Boyland, Dorian Scott
78Colum
79Portl-7
80Port-2
80T-683R
81Portl-8
82Phoen
Boyle, Edward J.
(Eddie)
No Cards.
Boyle, Gary
76QuadC
Boyle, Henry J.
N172
N284
WG1-29
Boyle, John Anthony
(Jack)
No Cards.
Boyle, John Bellew
(Jack)
No Cards.
Boyle, Ralph Francis
(Buzz)
R310
Boyles, John
85Cedar-1
86Vermont-2
89Wausa/GS-6
Boyne, Bryan
76Cedar
Braase, John
88GreatF-14
Brabender, Gene
66T-579R
67OPC-22
67T-22
68OPC-163
68T-163
69T-393
70McDon-3
70OPC-289
70T-289
71MLB/St-340
71OPC-666
71T-666
Bracho, Jose
52Park-24
Brack, Gilbert Herman
(Gib)
39PB-127
Braddy, Leonard
84Visal-9
Brader, Tim
88Brist/Pro-1865
89Fay/Pro-1583
Bradford, Charles W.
(Buddy)
68OPC-142R
68T-142R
69MB-34
69OPC-97
69T-97
70MLB/St-183
70OPC-299
70T-299
71MLB/St-362
71OPC-552
71T-552
72MB-43

74OPC-357
74T-357
75OPC-504
75T-504
75T/M-504
76OPC-451
76SSPC-281
76T-451

Bradford, Henry V.
(Vic)
No Cards.

Bradford, Larry
78Richm
79Richm-17
80T-675R
81D-584
81F-265
81Pol/Atl-34
81T-542
82D-553
82F-431
82T-271
83Portl-24

Bradford, Mark
88Batav/Pro-1672

Bradford, Troy
88CapeCod/Sum-103

Bradley, Bert
80WHave-10
81WHave-3
82WHave-2
83Tacom-2
84Cram/PCL-92
85Colum-2
85Colum/Pol-2
87Madis-1
88Madis-4

Bradley, George W.
N172

Bradley, Hugh F.
M116
T207

Bradley, J. Nichols
(Nick)
No Cards.

Bradley, John Thomas
(Jack)
No Cards.

Bradley, Len
80GlenF/C-2
81GlenF-23
82Edmon-17

Bradley, M.
N172

Bradley, Mark
77LodiD
82Albuq-19
83Pol/Dodg-22
84F-581
84Nes/792-316
84T-316

Bradley, Philip Poole
(Phil)
83SLCty-11
84F/X-15
84Moth/Mar-24
84T/X-15
85D-631
85F-486
85Leaf-50
85Moth/Mar-21
85OPC-69
85T-449
86D-191
86D-22
86D/AAS-41
86D/DKsuper-22
86F-461
86F/LimEd-5
86F/Mini-96
86F/St-10
86Leaf-22DK
86Moth/Mar-8
86OPC-305
86S-77
86T-305
86T/Gloss60-54
86T/St-217
86T/Super-13
87D-270
87D/OD-122
87F-580
87F/LL-4
87F/Mini-11
87F/St-13
87Ho/St-29
87Leaf-200
87Moth/Sea-6
87OPC-170
87S-89
87T-525
87T/Mini-70
87T/St-221
88D-243
88D/Best-47
88F-369
88F/U-U107
88OPC-55
88Panini/St-191
88Score-66
88Score/Tr-34T
88Sf-93
88T-55
88T/Mini-33
88T/St-218
88T/Tr-18T
89Ames-6
89B-17
89D-369
89D/Best-198
89D/Tr-41
89F-563
89F/Up-1
89French-16
89OPC-308
89Panini/St-154
89Score-79
89Score/Tr-44
89T-608
89T/St-113
89T/Tr-13T
89UD-229
89UD/Ext-749
90D-259
90F-174
90Score-24
90Score/100St-36
90Sf-95
90T-163
90UD-194

Bradley, Rick
77Phoen
78Cr/PCL-75
79Phoen

Bradley, Scott W.
83Nashvl-1
84Colum-11
84Colum/Pol-2
85D-37
86BuffB-4
86D-396
86T-481
87D-440
87F-581
87F/Lim-5
87Moth/Sea-14
87T-376
87T/St-217
88D-147
88D/Best-24
88F-370
88Leaf-75
88Moth/Sea-14
88OPC-199
88Panini/St-183
88RedFoley/St-8
88Score-151
88T-762
88T/St-222
89B-209
89D-261
89F-540
89Moth/Sea-14
89OPC-279
89Panini/St-432
89Score-324
89T-279
89T/St-225
89UD-226
90D-581
90F-506
90Score-228
90T-593
90UD-383

Bradley, Tom
71OPC-588
71T-588
72OPC-248
72T-248
73OPC-336
73T-336
74OPC-455
74T-455
74T/St-102
75OPC-179
75Phoen-9
75T-179
75T/M-179
76OPC-644
76T-644
76Tucso-35

Bradley, Wayne
75Cedar

Bradley, William J.
(Bill)
E107
E90/1
E97
T206
T213/blue
W555
WG2-6

Bradshaw, Dallas C.
No Cards.

Bradshaw, George T.
No Cards.

Bradshaw, Kevin
87Lakel-7
88GlenF/Pro-934
89Toled/CMC-19
89Toled/Pro-783

Brady, Brian
86MidldA-2
87MidldA-5
88Edmon/CMC-16
88Edmon/Pro-572

Brady, Clifford F.
(Cliff)
No Cards.

Brady, Dave
83Redwd-6

Brady, James J.
56T-126

Brady, Jim
77Salem

Brady, Lawrence
86Watertn-5

Brady, Mike
89Myrtle/Pro-1476

Brady, Pat
89Salin/Cal-138
89Salin/Pro-1815

Brady, Robert Jay
(Bob)
No Cards.

Brady, Stephen A.
(Steve)
E223
N172/ST

Bragan, Peter
89Jaxvl/Best-23

Bragan, Robert R.
(Bobby)
47TipTop
53Mother-4
59DF
60T-463CO
63T-73
64T-506
65T-346
66T-476

Braggs, Glenn
86S/Rook-21
86Vanco-5
87D-337
87D/OD-52
87F-339
87T-622
88D-240
88D/Best-15
88F-157
88OPC-263
88Panini/St-127
88Pol/Brew-26
88Score-59
88Score/YS/II-2
88T-263
88T/St-197
89B-145
89Class/Up/2-169
89D-103
89D/Best-277
89F-180
89Gard-12
89OPC-271
89Panini/St-375
89Pol/Brew-26
89Score-147
89Sf-29
89T-718
89T/Big-204
89T/St-196
89UD-504
90D-264
90F-317
90Score-105
90T-88
90UD-456

Brahms, Russ
82QuadC-3

Brain, David Leonard
(Dave)
T206

Brainerd, Frederick
(Fred)
No Cards.

Brake, Greg
85Madis/Pol-4

Brakeley, Bill
89Helena/SP-9

Braley, Jeff
89Brist/Star-2

Brame, Ervin Beckham
(Erv)
No Cards.

Bramhall, Arthur W.
(Art)
No Cards.

Branca, Ralph
47TipTop
49B-194
49Eureka-30
50B-59
51B-56
51FB
51T/BB-20
52B-96
52T-274
52TipTop
53B/BW-52
53Exh/Can-8
79TCMA-32
89Rini/Dodg-7
89Smok/Dodg-51
D305
Exh47
R423-4

Brancato, Albert
(Al)
41DP-48
41PB-43

Branch, Roy
80Spoka-7

Brand, Ronald George
(Ron)
64T-326
65OPC-212
65T-212
66T-394
68Coke
68T-317
69T-549
70MLB/St-63
70OPC-221
70T-221
71MLB/St-124
71OPC-304
71T-304
72MB-44
72T-773
78TCMA-41

Brandon, Darrell
66T-456R
67OPC-117
67T-117
67T/Test/RedSox-2
68Coke
68OPC-26
68T-26
69MB-35
69T-301
72OPC-283
72T-283
73OPC-326
73T-326

Brandt, Ed
(Dutch/Lefty)
33DH-7
33G-50
34Exh/4-1
34T-5
35BU-107
35BU-2
35Exh/4-1
35G-1J
35G-2E
35G-3A
35G-4A
35G-4E
35G-5A
35G-7E
36Exh/4-2
R306
R328-28
V353-50
V354-62

Brandt, John George
(Jackie)
59T-297
60T-53
61P-76
61T-515
61T/RO-27
61T/St-98
62J-31
62P-31
62P/Can-31
62Salada-53A
62Salada-53B

62Shirriff-53
62T-165
62T/bucks
62T/St-3
63J-58
63P-58
63T-65
64T-399
65OPC-33
65T-33
66T-383
67OPC-142
67T-142
78TCMA-33
Exh47

Brandt, Randy
77Salem

Brannan, Otis Owen
No Cards.

Brannon, Cliff
89Hamil/Star-6

Branom, Edgar Dudley
(Dudley)
No Cards.

Bransfield, William
(Kitty)
12Sweet/Pin-124
E104
E254
E270/1
E90/1
E97
M116
T204
T205
T206
T3-82
W555

Branson, Jeff
88T/Tr-19T
89Cedar/Best-1
89Cedar/Pro-928
89Cedar/Star-1
89T/Big-69

Brant, Marshall Lee
78Tidew
79Tidew-13
80Colum-20
81Colum-13
82Colum-6
82Colum/Pol-33
83Colum-16

Brantley, Cliff
88Clearw/Star-2
89Readg/Best-11
89Readg/Pro-662

Brantley, Jeff
86Shrev-1
87Phoen-28
87Shrev-13
88Phoen/CMC-5
88Phoen/Pro-78
89D/Rook-41
89F/Up-127
89Moth/Giants-17
89Score/Tr-101
89T/Tr-14T
90D-466
90F-52
90Score-371
90Score/100Ris-22
90T-703
90UD-358

Brantley, Mickey
84Chatt-26
85Cram/PCL-88
86Calgary-2
86F-651M
86S/Rook-45
87D-656
87D/Rook-27
87F-582
87Moth/Sea-15
87T-347
88D-610
88D/Best-80
88F-371
88F/Excit-5
88F/Mini-51
88Leaf-258
88Moth/Sea-15
88Panini/St-192
88Score-213
88Score/YS/II-15
88T-687
89D-212
89F-541
89Moth/Sea-7
89OPC-369
89Panini/St-439
89Score-89
89Sf-6
89T-568
89T/Big-38
89T/St-219
89UD-550

Brashear, Robert N.
(Kitty)
No Cards.

Brashear, Roy Parks
T206

Brassil, Tom
85Beaum-14
86Beaum-3
87Wichi-19
88LasVeg/CMC-23
88LasVeg/Pro-238
89Spoka/SP-13

Bratcher, Joseph W.
(Joe)
No Cards.

Bratchi, Frederick O.
(Fred)
No Cards.

Bratlien, Erik
88Batav/Pro-1673
89Batav/Pro-1941
89Readg/Star-3

Braun, Bart
81Redwd-29

Braun, John Paul
65OPC-82R
65T-82R

Braun, Randy
83DayBe-17
86Calgary-3
87Calgary-15
88Jaxvl/Best-21
88Jaxvl/Pro-976
88SLAS-20
89Indi/CMC-16
89Indi/Pro-1213

Braun, Stephen R.
(Steve)
72OPC-244
72T-244
73OPC-16
73T-16
74OPC-321
74T-321
74T/St-202
75K-41
75OPC-273
75T-273
75T/M-273
76Ho-96
76OPC-183
76SSPC-221
76T-183
77Ho-134
77OPC-123
77T-606
77T/CS-6
78T-422
79T-502
80T-9
81F-427
82D-418
82F-111
82T-316
83F-3
83T-734
84F-320
84F/St-42
84Nes/792-227
84T-227
85F-221
85F/St-51
85T-152
86D-534
86F-27
86KAS/Disc-4
86Louisvl-5
86T-631
88Louvl-4

Bravo, Angel Alfonso
(Angel)
70OPC-283
70T-283
71MLB/St-50
71OPC-538
71T-538

Bravo, Luis
79Wisco-17
83Albany-17

Braxton, Glenn
86AppFx-3
87Penin-16
89Utica/Puc-2

Bray, Clarence W.
(Buster)
No Cards.

Bray, Scott
89SLCty-23

Brazell, Don
78Wausa

Brazill, Frank Leo
(Frank)
V100

Brazle, Alpha
47TipTop
49B-126
49Eureka-178
50B-126
51B-157
52B-134
52T-228
53B/Col-140
53Hunter
54B-142
54Hunter
55B-230

Breadon, Sam
W754

Bream, Sidney Eugene
(Sid)
82VeroB-18
83Albuq-15
84Cram/PCL-149
85D-470
85T-253
86D-566
86F-604
86T-589
87D-79
87D/OD-168
87F-606
87F/Excit-6
87F/Mini-12
87F/Slug-5
87F/St-14
87Leaf-239
87OPC-35
87T-35
87T/St-126
88D-188
88D/Best-45
88F-324
88F/Excit-6
88F/St-113
88OPC-304
88Panini/St-370
88Score-260
88Sf-98
88T-478
88T/Big-205
88T/St-130
89B-419
89D-252
89D/Best-89
89F-204
89OPC-126
89Score-48
89T-126
89T/Big-106
89T/Mini-31
89T/St-125
89UD-556
90D-329
90F-463
90Score-423
90T-622
90UD-250

Breaux, Greg
88Martins/Star-5

Breazeale, James Leo
(Jim)
73OPC-33
73T-33
79AppFx-17
83Miami-25

Brecheen, Harry
48L-158
49B-158
49Eureka-179
50B-90
51B-86
51FB
51T/BB-28
52B-176
52T-263
53Exh/Can-14
54Esskay
54T-203
55Esskay
55T-113
55T/DH-74
56T-229
60L-132
60T-455C
79TCMA-166
D305
Exh47
R423-8

Brecht, Mike
83Phoen/BHN-17

Breckinridge
N172/PCL

Breeden, Daniel R.
(Danny)
69T-536R
70OPC-36R
70T-36R
71MLB/St-27

Breeden, Harold Noel
(Hal)
72T-684
73OPC-173
73T-173
74OPC-297
74T-297
75OPC-341
75T-341
75T/M-341
76SSPC-329

Breeden, Joe
89Memph/Best-25
89Memph/Pro-1193

Breeden, Scott
82IowaC-26
83IowaC-27
85Cedar-32
86TexGold-CO
88Kahn/Reds-CO

Breeding, Marvin E.
(Marv)
60T-525
61P-77
61T-321
61T/St-99
62J-28
62P-28
62P/Can-28
62Salada-65A
62Salada-65B
62Shirriff-65
62T-6
63T-149

Breedlove, Larry R.
87Sprin/Best-21

Breen, Dick
C46-88

Breining, Fred
78Colum
80Phoen-9
82D-186
82F-385
82T-144
83D-503
83F-254
83Moth/Giants-7
83T-747
84D-387
84F-367
84F/X-16
84Nes/792-428
84Stuart-35
84T-428
84T/X-16
85F-392
85Indianap-10
85OPC-36
85T-36
86Nashv-2

Breitenbucher, Karl
89Clint/Pro-888

Breitenstein, Ted
T206
T213/brown

Bremer, Bernard
85Albany-28

Bremer, Herbert F.
(Herb)
No Cards.

Bremigan, Nick
88Umpire-19
89Umpires-15

Brenegan, Olaf Selmer
(Sam)
No Cards.

Brenly, Robert Earl
(Bob)
77Cedar
81Phoen-4
82D-574
82T-171R
83D-377
83F-255
83Moth/Giants-6
83T-494
84D-616
84F-368
84Nes/792-378
84T-378
84T/St-174
85D-187
85D-26
85D/DKsuper-26
85F-603
85Leaf-26DK

85Moth/Giants-7
85OPC-215
85T-215
85T/Gloss40-3
85T/St-158
86D-323
86F-534
86Leaf-194
86Moth/Giants-5
86OPC-307
86T-625
86T/St-92
87D-485
87D/OD-95
87F-267
87Moth/SFG-4
87OPC-125
87T-125
87T/St-87
88D-189
88F-77
88Moth/Giants-4
88OPC-69
88Panini/St-419
88Score-134
88T-703
88T/Big-143
88T/St-92
89B-249
89D-453
89OPC-52
89Score-395
89T-52
89Tor/Fire-9
89UD-479

Brennan, Addison
14CJ-115
15CJ-115

Brennan, James A.
(Jim)
N172

Brennan, James D.
32Orbit/num-92
35BU-178

Brennan, Thomas M.
(Tom)
75OkCty
77Watlo
79Tacom-5
80Tacom-12
81Charl-1
81T-451R
82T-141R
82Wheat/Ind
83F-403
83T-524
84D-102
84F-537
84Nes/792-662
84T-662
84TrueVal/WS-6

Brennan, Tom
80Wausa-1
81Wausa-5
83GlenF-12

Brennan, William
85VeroB-15
87Albuq/Pol-5
88Albuq/CMC-6
88Albuq/Pro-250
89Albuq/CMC-1
89Albuq/Pro-65
89D-589
89Score-622
89Score/HotRk-9
89UD-16

Brennen, James
87DayBe-9

Brenzel, William R.
(Bill)
No Cards.

Bresnahan, Dave
86Watlo-4
87Wmspt-14

Bresnahan, Roger P.
10Domino-15
11Helmar-167
12Sweet/Pin-145A
12Sweet/Pin-145B
14CJ-17
15CJ-17
48Exh/HOF
50Callahan
60Exh/HOF-4
60F-8
61F-10
75F/Pion-7
80Cram/Leg-102
80SSPC/HOF
89HOF/St-55
D303
D350/2-16
E103
E106
E254
E270/2
E90/1
E91
E98
L1-129
M101/5-16
M116
S74-117
S81-104
T201
T202
T204
T205
T206
T207
T213/blue
T215/blue
T216
T222
T3-4
WG3-5
WG5-6
WG6-5

Bressler, Raymond B.
(Rube)
25Exh-25
26Exh-25
27Exh-13
W514-28

Bressoud, Edward F.
(Ed)
58SFCall
58T-263
59T-19
60T-253
61P-152
61T-203
61T/St-74
62Salada-182A
62Salada-182B
62Shirriff-182
62T-504
63J-78
63P-78
63T-188
64T-352
65T-525
66T-516
67OPC-121
67T-121
78TCMA-164
78TCMA-39
PM10/Sm-17

Breton, John F.
(Jim)
No Cards.

Brett, George Howard
75OPC-228
75T-228
75T/M-228
76A&P/KC
76Ho-114
76OPC-19
76SSPC-167
76T-19
77Ho-36
77K-6
77OPC-170
77OPC-1LL
77OPC-261RB
77Pep-32
77T-1LL
77T-231M
77T-580
77T-631M
77T/CS-7
78Ho-27
78OPC-215
78PapaG/Disc-36
78T-100
78Wiffle/Discs-7
79Ho-68
79K-50
79OPC-167
79T-330
79T/Comics-9
80BK/PHR-13
80K-9
80OPC-235
80T-450
80T/S-14
81Coke
81D-100
81D-491
81Drake-5
81F-28
81F-655M
81F/St-116
81K-8
81MSA/Disc-4
81OPC-113
81Pol/Royals-2
81Sqt-1
81T-1LL
81T-700
81T/Nat/Super-3
81T/S
81T/SO-1
81T/St-243
81T/St-82
81T/St-9
82D-15DK
82D-34
82Drake-4
82F-405
82F/St-202
82K-3
82KMart-38
82OPC-200
82OPC-201IA
82OPC-261AS
82Sqt-3
82T-200
82T-201A
82T-549
82T-96TL
82T/St-133
82T/St-190
83D-338
83D/AAS-42
83F-108
83K-4
83OPC-3
83OPC-388AS
83Pol/Royals-2
83T-388
83T-600
83T/Gloss-31
83T/Gloss40-31
84D-53
84D/AAS-55
84D/Champs-15
84Drake-3
84F-344
84F-638IA
84F/St-36
84FunFood/Pin-6
84MiltBrad-2
84Nes/792-399AS
84Nes/792-500
84Nes/792-710LL
84Nestle/DT-3
84OPC-212
84OPC-223AS 84Ralston-13
84Seven-5C
84Seven-5E
84Seven-5W
84T-399
84T-500
84T-710
84T/Cereal-13
84T/Gloss22-4
84T/Gloss40-12
84T/St-198
84T/St-275
84T/Super-13
84T/Super-13
85D-53
85D/AAS-26
85D/HL-11
85D/HL-25
85Drake-4
85F-199
85F/LimEd-4
85GenMills-14
85Leaf-176
85OPC-100
85Seven-2C
85Seven-2E
85Seven-2G
85T-100
85T-703AS
85T/3D-4
85T/Gloss22-15
85T/St-188
85T/St-268
85T/Super-46
86BK/AP-20
86D-53
86D/AAS-12
86D/HL-3
86D/PopUp-12
86Dorman-1
86Drake-14
86F-5
86F-634M
86F/AS-3
86F/LimEd-6
86F/LL-2
86F/Mini-1
86F/Slug-3
86F/St-11
86F/WaxBox-C2
86Jiffy-4
86Kitty/Disc-20
86Leaf-42
86Meadow/Blank-2
86Meadow/Milk-2
86Meadow/Stat-1
86NatPhoto-5
86OPC-300
86OPC-C
86Quaker-23
86S-1
86S-180M
86S-186M
86S-52M
86S-63M
86S/Dec-64
86T-300
86T-714
86T/3D-5
86T/Gloss22-4
86T/Gloss60-18
86T/Mini-18
86T/St-157
86T/St-16ALCS
86T/St-23
86T/St-256
86T/St-3
86T/Super-14
86T/WaxBox-C
86TrueVal-17
86Woolwth-4
87Class-47
87D-15DK
87D-54
87D/AAS-27
87D/DKsuper-15
87D/OD-206
87Drake-14
87F-366
87F-C3
87F/GameWin-6
87F/Hottest-6
87F/LL-5
87F/McCror-5
87F/Mini-13
87F/RecSet-1
87F/Slug-6
87F/St-15
87F/WaxBox-C3
87Ho/St-24
87Jiffy-5
87KayBee-5
87KMart-24
87Kraft-21
87Leaf-15DK
87Leaf-96
87MnM's-14
87OPC-126
87RedFoley/St-111
87S-114M
87S-197M
87S-5
87T-400
87T/Board-13
87T/Coins-5
87T/Gloss60-31
87T/Mini-57
87T/St-254
88Class/Blue-248
88D-102
88D/Best-39
88F-254
88F/BB/AS-4
88F/Hottest-4
88F/St-30
88FanSam-2
88KingB/Disc-7
88KMart-3
88Leaf-93
88OPC-312
88Panini/St-104
88Score-11
88Sf-150
88Smok/Royals-20
88T-700
88T/Big-157
88T/Gloss60-53
88T/St-259
88T/St/Backs-41
88T/UK-7
89B-121
89Cadaco-4
89Class-47
89Crunch-9
89D-204
89D/AS-11
89D/Best-7
89D/MVP-BC7
89F-277
89F/BBMVP's-4
89F/Superstar-5

89F/WaxBox-C3
89KayBee-2
89KMart/Lead-5
89Master/Discs-9
89OPC-200
89Panini/St-355
89Ralston-9
89RedFoley/St-12
89Score-75
89Score/HotSt-4
89Score/Mast-11
89Sf-64
89T-200
89T/Big-46
89T/Coins-34
89T/Gloss60-14
89T/Hills-3
89T/Mini-54
89T/St-270
89T/St/Backs-1
89T/UK-7
89T/WaxBox-A
89Tastee/Discs-1
89UD-215
89UD-689TC
90D-144
90F-103
90F-621
90Score-140
90Score/100St-76
90Sf-214
90T-60
90UD-124

Brett, Kenneth Alvin
(Ken)
69T-476R
71MLB/St-315
71OPC-89
71T-89
72MB-45
72OPC-517
72T-517
73OPC-444
73T-444
74OPC-237
74T-237
75K-52
75OPC-250
75T-250
75T/M-250
76OPC-401
76SSPC-569
76T-401
76T/Tr-401T
77Ho-65
77OPC-21
77T-157
77T-631M
78T-682
79T-557
80Pol/Dodg-34
80T-521
81T-47
82D-364
82F-406
82T-397
85Utica-24

Breuer, Marvin
44Yank/St-3

Brevell, Ron
(Bubba)
86Kinston-2
88Mia/Star-3

Brewer, Anthony Bruce
(Tony)
83Albuq-20
84Cram/PCL-161
85Cram/PCL-152
85D-31

Brewer, Chet
78Laugh/Black-23

Brewer, Jim
61T-317
61T/St-6
62T-191
63T-309
64T-553
65T-416
66OPC-158
66T-158
67OPC-31
67T-31
68T-298
69MB-36
69T-241
70T-571
71MLB/St-98
71OPC-549
71T-549
72MB-46
72OPC-151
72T-151
73OPC-126
73T-126
74K-14
74OPC-189
74T-189
75OPC-163
75T-163
75T/M-163
76OPC-459
76T-459
78TCMA-243
87Smok/Dodg-3
88Smok/Dodg-14
89Smok/Dodg-79

Brewer, John H.
48Sommer-2
49B/PCL-8
49Sommer-2

Brewer, Marvin
40PB-183

Brewer, Mike
84Omaha-9
85Maine-26
86Omaha-3
86Omaha/TCMA-13

Brewer, Omar
88CharlR/Star-3

Brewer, Rodney
88Sprin/Best-19
89ArkTr/GS-3

Brewer, Tom
55B-178
55T-83
55T/DH-128
56T-34
57T-112
58T-220
59T-346M
59T-55
60T-439
61P-50
61T-434
61T/St-108
62Salada-4
62Shirriff-4
Exh47

Brewington, Mike
89Well/Puc-6

Brewster, Charles L.
(Charlie)
No Cards.

Brewster, Rich
76QuadC
77QuadC
80ElPas-20

Brian, Braden
87Jamestn-17

Brickell, Fritz D.
(Fritzie)
61BeeHive-2
61T-333

Brickell, George F.
(Fred)
33G-38
35G-1E
35G-3C
35G-5C
35G-6C
V353-38

Brickhouse, Jack
89Pac/Leg-209

Brickley, Geroge V.
No Cards.

Brideweser, James E.
(Jim)
53B/Col-136
55B-151
57T-382

Bridges, Everett L.
(Rocky)
52T-239
53B/BW-32
54B-156
55B-136
56T-324
57T-294
58T-274
59T-318
60L-31
60T-22
61T-508
62J-75
62P-75
62P/Can-75
75Phoen-1
76Phoen
77Phoen
78Cr/PCL-50
79Phoen
80Phoen-22
81Phoen-25
82Phoen
84Evrt/Cram-28MG
86PrWill-4MG
87Vanco-8
88BuffB/CMC-25
88BuffB/Polar-1
88BuffB/Pro-1478
89Salem/Star-25
V362-1

Bridges, Jason
88Oneon/Pro-2045
89PrWill/Star-1

Bridges, Jim
85BurlR-28

Bridges, Marshall
58Union
78TCMA-48
WG9-5

Bridges, Thomas
33G-199
34DS-5
34G-44
35BU-81
35BU-9
35G-1D
35G-2D
35G-6D
35G-7D
35Wheat
37OPC-133
37Wheat
38Exh/4-12
38Wheat
39PB-104
41PB-65
61F-95
88Conlon/AmAS-3
R308-177
R313
R314
V300
V354-87
V355-33

Bridges-Clements, Tony
88BBCity/Star-9
89Memph/Best-7
89Memph/Pro-1202
89Memph/Star-3

Bridwell, Albert H.
(Al)
10Domino-16
11Helmar-77
12Sweet/Pin-108
14CJ-42
14Piedmont/St-6
15CJ-42
D303
E101
E104
E105
E106
E254
E90/1
E91
E92
E98
M116
S74-81
T201
T202
T204
T205
T206
T213/blue
T215/brown
T216
T3-83

Brief, Anthony V.
(Bunny)
No Cards.

Brier, Coe
83Wisco/LF-1

Briggs, Daniel Lee
(Dan)
77T-592
79T-77
80T-352
82OPC-102
82T-102
82T/Tr-11T
84Colum-5
84Colum/Pol-3
85Colum-14
85Colum/Pol-3
85IntLgAS-33

Briggs, David
88Spoka/Pro-1938
89CharRa/Pro-994

Briggs, Grant
No Cards.

Briggs, John Edward
64T-482R
65OPC-163
65T-163
66T-359
67T-268
68T-284
69MB-37
69MLB/St-173
69OPC-73
69T-73
69T/St-72
70MLB/St-85
70T-564
71MLB/St-170
71OPC-297
71T-297
72MB-47
72OPC-197
72T-197
73OPC-71
73T-71
74OPC-218
74T-218
74T/St-192
75K-16
75OPC-123
75T-123
75T/M-123
76OPC-373
76T-373

Briggs, John T.
59T-177
60T-376

Briggs, Kenny
83Wausa/LF-29

Bright, Don
74Gasto
78Cr/PCL-86

Bright, Harry James
59T-523
60T-277
61T-447
62T-551
63J-95
63P-95
63T-304
64T-259
65T-584
76Tucso-23
78TCMA-214
85Durhm-14
WG9-6

Bright, Tom
77AppFx

Briles, Nelson
65T-431R
66T-243
67T-404
68OPC-153WS 68T-540
69MB-38
69MLB/St-208
69OPC-60
69T-60
69T/St-111
70MLB/St-134
70OPC-435
70T-435
71MLB/St-195
71OPC-257
71T-257
72MB-48
72OPC-227WS 72T-605
73OPC-303
73T-303
74OPC-123
74T-123
74T/St-81
74T/Tr-123T
75OPC-495
75T-495
75T/M-495
76OPC-569
76SSPC-159
76T-569
77T-174
78T-717
79T-262
89Swell-79

Briley, Greg
86Cram/PCL-107
87Chatt/Best-17
88Calg/CMC-13
88Calg/Pro-799
88Score/Tr-74T
89F/Up-57
89Score/HotRk-54
89T-781
89T/Big-247
89UD/Ext-770
90Class-54
90D-463
90F-507
90Score-303
90Score/100Ris-60
90Sf-43

90T-288
90UD-455

Brilinski, Tyler
86Modesto-5
88Tacom/CMC-12
88Tacom/Pro-617
89Tacom/CMC-13
89Tacom/Pro-1561

Brill, Clint
83Ander-26

Brill, Tim
78Watlo
79Savan-6

Brill, Todd
88Oneon/Pro-2042

Bringhurst, Stewart
78Wausa

Brink, Brad
87Clearw-23
88Maine/CMC-5
88Maine/Pro-289
89ScrWB/Pro-721

Brink, Craig
88Oneon/Pro-2051

Brinker, William H.
(Bill)
No Cards.

Brinkman, Charles E.
(Chuck)
71OPC-13R
71T-13R
72T-786
73OPC-404
73T-404
74OPC-641
74T-641

Brinkman, Edwin A.
(Ed)
63T-479
64T-46
64T/Coins-108
64T/S-27
65T-417
66T-251
67T-311
68OPC-49
68T-49
69MB-39
69MLB/St-101
69OPC-153
69T-153
69T/St-232
70MLB/St-279
70T-711
71MLB/St-385
71OPC-389
71T-389
71T/Coins-46
72MB-49
72T-535
73OPC-5
73T-5
74OPC-138
74T-138
74T/St-171
75OPC-439
75T-439
75T/M-439
76SSPC-447
82BirmB-24

Brinkman, Greg
84Butte-8
88Vermont/Pro-957
89Orlan/Best-30
89Visal/Pro-1428

Brinkman, Joe
88Umpire-15
89Umpires-13

Brinkopf, Leon C.
No Cards.

Brinson, Hugh
86Ventura-2
87Duned-5
88Knoxv/Best-24

Briody, Charles F.
(Fatty)
No Cards.

Brisbin, Steve
75QuadC

Brisco, Jamie
83Erie-9
84Savan-13
86Stockton-2
87ElPas-10
88ElPas/Best-4

Briskey, Dick
45Centen-2

Brissie, Lou
48L-31
49B-41
49Royal-8
50B-48
50Drake-4
51B-155
51T/BB-31
52B-79
52NTea
52NumNum-1
52Royal
52T-270
52TipTop
Exh47

Bristol, Dave
67OPC-21MG
67T-21
68OPC-148MG
68T-148
69T-234
70McDon-5
70T-556
71OPC-637MG 71T-637
72T-602
73OPC-377CO
73T-377C
74OPC-531CO
74T-531C
76T-631MG
77T-442MG
79Pol/SFG-1MG
80Pol/SFG-1MG
80T-499MG
81D-436
81T-686MG

Bristow, George
No Cards.

Brito, Bernardo
81Batav-20
81Watlo-31
83Watlo/LF-17
86Water-5
87Wmspt-23
88Orlan/Best-28
88SLAS-13
89Portl/CMC-21
89Portl/Pro-212

Brito, Jorge
88Modesto-17
88Modesto/Cal-68
89Modesto/Cal-282

Brito, Jose Oscar
80Water-12
81Indianap-11
81Louvl-14
82Louisvl-3
85CharO-26
85RochR-15

Brito, Luis
89Martins/Star-3

Brito, Mario
87Jamestn-20
88MidwLAS/GS-45
88Rockford-3
89Rockford-2

Britt, Bob
88Spart/Pro-1046

Britt, Doug
78Charl
81Buffa-3
82DayBe-10

Britt, Patrick
87Modesto-21

Brittain, August S.
(Gus)
No Cards.

Britton, James Alan
64T-94R
68OPC-76R
68T-76R
69OPC-154
69T-154
70T-646
71OPC-699
71T-699
72MB-50

Britton, Jimmy W.
72OPC-351R
72T-351R

Britton, Stephen G.
(Gil)
No Cards.

Brizzolara, Tony
79Richm-25
80OPC-86
80Richm-7
80T-156
81Richm-2
82Richm-2
83Richm-2
84Richm-9
85IntLgAS-11
85Richm-1
86BuffB-5

Broaca, Johnny
35BU-192

Broadfoot, Scott
87Erie-15
88StPet/Star-2
89Sprin/Best-6

Broas, Rick
77Newar

Broberg, Pete
72OPC-64
72T-64
73K-41
73OPC-162
73T-162
74OPC-425
74T-425
75OPC-542
75T-542
75T/M-542
76A&P/Milw
76Ho-74
76OPC-39
76SSPC-245
76T-39
77Ho-145
77OPC-55
77T-409
78T-722
79OPC-301
79T-578

Brocail, Doug
87CharRa-23
88Charl/Pro-1211
89AubAs/Pro-13
89Wich/Roc-28

Brock, Don
88Poca/Pro-2073
89SanJose/Best-6
89SanJose/Cal-210
89SanJose/Pro-442
89SanJose/Star-3

Brock, Gregory Allen
(Greg)
82Albuq-15
83D-579
83F-203
83Pol/Dodg-17
83Seven-12
83T/X-14
84D-296
84F-98
84Nes/792-555
84OPC-242
84Pol/Dodg-9
84T-555
84T/St-376YS
85F-368
85OPC-242
85T-753
86D-296
86F-125
86OPC-368
86Pol/Dodg-9
86T-368
86T/St-67
87D/OD-50
87F-437
87F/U-U9
87OPC-26
87T-26
87T/St-68
87T/Tr-9T
88D-337
88D/Best-71
88F-158
88Leaf-148
88OPC-212
88Panini/St-121
88Pol/Brew-9
88Score-234
88Sf-184
88T-212
88T/Big-217
89B-143
89D-57
89D/Best-239
89F-181
89Gard-11
89OPC-163
89Panini/St-371
89Pol/Brew-9
89Score-307
89T-517
89T/Big-100
89T/St-201
89UD-543
90D-293
90F-318
90Score-485
90T-139
90UD-514

Brock, John Roy
No Cards.

Brock, Louis Clark
(Lou)
62T-387
63T-472
64T-29
64T/Coins-97
65T-540
66OPC-125
66T-125
67OPC-63M
67T-285
67T-63M
68Bz-15
68OPC-151WS
68T-372AS
68T-520
69Kelly/Pin-4
69MB-40
69MLB/St-209
69MLBPA/Pin-36
69NTF
69OPC-165WS
69OPC-85
69T-428AS
69T-85
69T/St-112
69Trans-31
70K-44
70MB-2
70MLB/St-135
70OPC-330
70T-330
70T/PI-4
70T/S-11
71K-17
71MD
71MLB/St-268
71OPC-625
71T-625
71T/Coins-87
71T/GM-27
71T/S-25
72K-48
72MB-51
72OPC-200
72T-200
73K-40
73OPC-320
73OPC-64LL
73T-320
73T-64LL
73T/Lids-8
74OPC-204LL
74OPC-60
74T-204LL
74T-60
74T/DE-20
74T/St-111
75Ho-23
75Ho/Twink-23
75K-39
75OPC-2RB
75OPC-309LL
75OPC-540
75T-2M
75T-309LL
75T-540
75T/M-2M
75T/M-309LL
75T/M-540
76Crane-5
76Ho-7
76Ho/Twink-7
76K-40
76Laugh/Jub-14
76MSA/Disc
76OPC-10
76OPC-197LL
76SSPC-275
76T-10
76T-197LL
77Ho-32
77OPC-51
77T-355
77T/CS-8
78K-7
78OPC-204
78OPC-236RB 78T-1M
78Wiffle/Discs-8
79OPC-350
79T-415M
79T-665
80T-1M
85West/2-28
85Woolwth-5
86S/Dec-59
87KMart-13
89Kahn/Coop-3
89T-662TBC

Brock, Norman
86FSLAS-10
86Osceola-1
87ColAst/Pro-24
87ColumAst-24

88ColAst/Best-27
89Cedar/Best-18
89Cedar/Pro-938
89Cedar/Star-2

Brocker, John
(Gene)
49Sommer-26

Brockett, Lew
11Helmar-39
C46-55
E254
E270/1

Brocki, Mike
87SanBern-16
88SanBern/Best-26
88SanBern/Cal-40
89Wmspt/Pro-629

Brockil, Dave
86Cram/PCL-162

Brocklander, Fred
88Umpire-38
89Umpires-36

Brockway, Kevin
86Cram/PCL-188

Broderick, Matthew T.
(Matt)
No Cards.

Broderick, Stan
83QuadC-24

Brodie, Walter Scott
(Steve)
No Cards.

Brodowski, Dick
52T-404
53T-69
54T-221
55T-171
56T-157
59Kahn
59T-371

Broersma, Eric
82Orlan/B-3
82OrlTw/A-13
83Orlan-19
83Toled-26
84Toled-17
85Toled-2
86Toled-3
87Tacom-11

Broglio, Ernie
59T-296
60L-41
60T-16
61Bz-16
61P-179
61T-420
61T-451M
61T-45LL
61T-47LL
61T-49LL
62J-164
62P-164
62P/Can-164
62Salada-132
62Shirriff-132
62T-507
63J-165
63P-165
63T-313
64T-59
64T/Coins-95
64T/St-77
64T/SU
65T-565
66T-423
78TCMA-18

Brogna, Dennis
81Watlo-3
83MidldC-6
84MidldC-13

Brogna, Ricco
88Brist/Pro-1885
89B-102
89Lakel/Star-3

Brohamer, John A.
(Jack)
73OPC-181
73T-181
74OPC-586
74T-586
75OPC-552
75T-552
75T/M-552
76OPC-618
76SSPC-518
76T-618
76T/Tr-618T
77T-293
78PapaG/Disc-3
78T-416
79OPC-25
79T-63
80T-349
81F-393
81T-462

Bromby, Scott
88Rockford-2
89Rockford-3

Bronkey, Jeff
87Orlan-21
88Visal/Cal-166
88Visal/Pro-95
89Orlan/Best-12
89Orlan/Pro-1337

Bronkie, Herman C.
No Cards.

Brookens, Thomas D.
(Tom)
77Evansvl/TCMA-4
80T-416
81D-6
81F-473
81T-251
82D-202
82F-263
82OPC-11
82T-753
83D-454
83F-327
83T-119
84D-578
84F-78
84Nes/792-14
84T-14
85Cain's-4
85D-593
85F-4
85T-512
85Wendy-5
86Cain's-2
86D-537
86F-223
86OPC-286
86T-643
87Cain's-1
87Coke/Tigers-17
87D-296
87F-145
87OPC-232
87T-713
88D-107
88F-53
88Panini/St-93
88Pep/T-16
88Pol/T-4
88Score-233
88T-474
89D-508
89D/Tr-53
89F-130
89OPC-342
89Panini/St-340
89Score-269
89Score/NWest-21
89Score/Tr-73
89T-342
89T/St-278
89UD-106
90F-439
90Score-297
90UD-138

Brooks, Billy
87Bakers-6
88Bakers/Cal-250

Brooks, Brian Todd
87CharRa-1
88River/Cal-216
88River/Pro-1410
89Wich/Roc-25
89Wich/Roc/Up-12

Brooks, Craig
81Brist-1

Brooks, Damon
86AubAs-6
87AubAs-5

Brooks, Desi
86Lynch-3
87Lynch-6

Brooks, Eric
89Myrtle/Pro-1460

Brooks, Hubert
(Hubie)
79Jacks-3
80Tidew-15
81T-259R
81T/Tr-742
82D-476
82F-522
82F/St-81
82K-10
82OPC-266
82T-246TL
82T-494
82T/St-68
83D-49
83F-539
83OPC-134
83T-134
83T/St-261
84D-607
84F-582
84Jacks/Smok-3
84Nes/792-368
84OPC-368
84T-368
84T/St-103
85D-197
85F-74
85F/Up-U10
85Leaf-214
85OPC-222
85OPC/Post-5
85T-222
85T/St-104
85T/Tr-9T
86D-55
86D/HL-15
86F-244
86F/LimEd-7
86F/Mini-52
86F/St-12
86Leaf-44
86OPC-308
86Provigo-1
86S-187
86T-555
86T/St-77
86T/Super-15
87D-17DK
87D-88
87D/AAS-48
87D/DKsuper-17
87D/OD-91
87F-314
87F/GameWin-7
87F/LL-6
87F/Mini-14
87F/St-16
87Ho/St-4
87KayBee-6
87Kraft-42
87Leaf-142
87Leaf-17DK
87OPC-3
87RedFoley/St-91
87S-18
87S-197M
87S-79M
87T-650
87T/Coins-27
87T/Gloss60-46
87T/St-76
88D-468
88D/AS-45
88D/Best-12
88F-179
88Ho/Disc-5
88Leaf-257
88OPC-50
88Panini/St-328
88Score-305
88Sf-187
88T-50
88T/Big-81
88T/St-81
88T/St/Backs-10
88T/UK-8
89B-367
89D-220
89D/Best-292
89F-371
89F/BBMVP's-5
89OPC-221
89Panini/St-123
89RedFoley/St-13
89Score-53
89Sf-96
89T-485
89T/Big-301
89T/Mini-21
89T/St-72
89T/UK-8
89UD-122
90Class-129
90D-130
90F-341
90Score-299
90T-745
90UD-197

Brooks, Jerry
88GreatF-11
89Bakers/Cal-203

Brooks, John
25Exh-19

Brooks, Jonathan J.
(Mandy)
No Cards.

Brooks, Kevin
88Virgini/Star-3

Brooks, Michael
75OkCty
75SnAnt
76Baton
82Redwd-1

Brooks, Monte
87Spoka-12
88Charl/Pro-1204
89River/Best-27
89River/Cal-10
89River/Pro-1417

Brooks, Robert
(Bobby)
70OPC-381R
70T-381R
71OPC-633R
71T-633R

Brooks, Rodney
88Hamil/Pro-1740

Brooks, Trey
83MidldC-16
84IowaC-14
85IowaC-3
86IowaC-4

Broome, Kim
89Well/Puc-7

Brosious, Frank
82BurlR-14

Brosius, Scott
88Madis-5
88MidwLAS/GS-50
89Huntsvl/Best-12

Broskie, Sigmund T.
(Siggy)
No Cards.

Brosnan, Jason
89GreatF-10

Brosnan, Jim
55B-229
57T-155
58T-342
59T-194
60L-124
60T-449
61T-513
61T/RO-25
61T/St-15
62J-125
62Kahn
62P-125
62T-2
63T-116

Brosnan, Timothy
N172

Bross, Terry
88LitFalls/Puc-15
89StLucie/Star-2
90D-502

Brottem, Anton C.
(Tony)
No Cards.

Broughton, Cecil C.
(Cal)
N172

Brouhard, Mark Steven
82D-154
82F-135
82Pol/Brew
82Pol/Brew-29
82T-517
83D-532
83F-28
83Gard-3
83T-167
84D-211
84F-195
84Gard-2
84Nes/792-528
84Pol/Brew-29
84T-528
85D-149
85F-576
85Gard-2
85Pol/Brew-29
85T-653
86OPC-21
86T-473

Brouthers, Arthur H.
(Art)
No Cards.

Brouthers, Dennis J.
(Dan)
50Callahan
75F/Pion-6
80SSPC/HOF
89HOF/St-7
89Smok/Dodg-3
N162
N172
N284
N300/unif

Scrapp
WG1-20
Brovia, Joseph John
(Joe)
48Sommer-11
52Mother-51
53Mother-18
Brow, Dennis
88PrWill/Star-4
89PrWill/Star-2
Brow, Steve
87FtLaud-28
Browder, Bubba
88Wythe/Pro-1987
Brower, Bob
83BurlR-13
83BurlR/LF-11
83Tulsa-13
85OKCty-21
86OKCty-1
87D-651
87D/Rook-49
87F/U-U10
87Moth/Rang-18
87S/Rook-3
87Smok/R-26
87T/Tr-10T
88D-346
88F-461
88Moth/R-18
88OPC-252
88RedFoley/St-9
88Score-236
88Smok/R-16
88T-252
88ToysRUs-2
89B-182
89D-411
89F-514
89Score-344
89T-754
89UD-439
Brower, Louis Lester
(Lou)
No Cards.
Brown, Adam
88Bakers/Cal-242
88CalLgAS-48
89SnAnt/Best-10
Brown, Charles E.
(Buster)
E90/1
M116
Brown, Clint
35BU-189
35BU-82
Brown, Craig
83AlexD-19
84PrWill-26
85Nashua-4
86Nashua-4
87Harrisbg-8
Brown, Curt S.
84Colum-15
84Colum/Pol-1
85Colum-3
85Colum/Pol-4
86Indianap-25
87Indianap-13
88CharlK-24
88CharlK/Pep-24
88RochR-4
88RochR/Gov-4
Brown, Curtis Jr.
(Curt)
81Holyo-11
Brown, Dana
88CapeCod/Sum-95
89Batav/Pro-1932
Brown, Daren
89StCath/Pro-2073
Brown, Darrell Wayne
80Evansvl/TCMA-11
84F-556
84Nes/792-193
84T-193
84T/St-311
85D-558
85F-270
85RochR-11
85T-767
85T/St-306
Brown, Dave
78Laugh/Black-27
89Erie/Star-4
Brown, Delos Hight
No Cards.
Brown, Don
87Cedar-22
88Greens/Pro-1572
89Cedar/Star-26
89Chatt/Best-22
89Chatt/GS-6
Brown, Drummond Nicol
No Cards.
Brown, Edward P.
(Ed)
No Cards.
Brown, Edward William
(Eddie)
28Exh-1
E126-44
E126-50
W575
Brown, Edwin Randolph
(Randy)
No Cards.
Brown, Eric
74Cedar
82Idaho-4
Brown, Fred Herbert
No Cards.
Brown, George
WG3-6
Brown, Greg
78Wausa
Brown, Hector Harold
53T-184
54T-172
55B-221
55T-148
57T-194
58Hires-18
58T-394
59T-487
60T-89
61T-218
62T-488
63T-289
64T-56
Brown, Isaac
(Ike)
70OPC-152
70T-152
71MLB/St-387
71OPC-669
71T-669
72OPC-284
72T-284
72T/Cloth-3
73OPC-633
73T-633
74OPC-409
74T-409
Brown, J.B.
83GlenF-2
Brown, Jackie G.
71MLB/St-531
71OPC-591
71T-591
74OPC-89
74T-89
75OPC-316
75T-316
75T/M-316
76OPC-301
76T-301
77OPC-36
77T-147
78Cr/PCL-23
78OPC-126
78T-699
86Hawai-1
87Vanco-2
88BuffB/Pro-1479
89BuffB/CMC-25
89BuffB/Pro-1683
Brown, James D.
(Don)
No Cards.
Brown, James Roberson
(Jimmy)
39PB-132
40PB-112
41DP-146
41PB-12
W754
Brown, Jarvis
87Kenosha-14
88Keno/Pro-1390
88MidwLAS/GS-33
89Visal/Cal-106
89Visal/Pro-1437
Brown, Jeff
85Anchora-6
85FtMyr-14
87SnAnt-12
87VeroB-16
88Bakers/Cal-234
88CalLgAS-46
Brown, Jerald Ray
(Jake)
75Lafay
Brown, Jim
76QuadC
76Wausa
Brown, John C.
(Chris)
80Clint-16
84Cram/PCL-23
85F/Up-U11
85Moth/Giants-18
85T/Tr-10T
86D-553
86F-535
86F/LimEd-8
86F/Mini-108
86F/St-13
86KayBee-2
86Leaf-215
86Moth/Giants-18
86OPC-383
86S-78
86T-383
86T/Gloss60-10
86T/St-311
86T/St-85
87Classic-65
87D-11DK
87D-80
87D/AAS-44
87D/DKsuper-11
87D/OD-100
87F-268
87F/LL-7
87F/Mini-15
87F/RecSet-2
87F/U-U11
87Leaf-11DK
87Leaf-236
87Moth/SFG-5
87OPC-180
87S-115M
87S-13
87T-180
87T/St-86
88Coke/Padres-35
88D-483
88D/Best-77
88F-578
88Leaf-221
88OPC-112
88Panini/St-408
88Score-363
88Smok/Padres-5
88T-568
88T/Big-130
88T/St-111
89B-106
89D-183
89D/Tr-9
89F-301
89Score-369
89T-481
89T/St-103
89UD-193
89UD/Ext-784
Brown, John Lindsay
(Lindsay)
No Cards.
Brown, John
67OPC-72R
Brown, Keith
87Cedar-10
88Chatt/Best-3
89D-115
89F-154
89Nashvl-4
89Nashvl/CMC-2
89Nashvl/Pro-1296
Brown, Ken
88PrWill/Star-5
Brown, Kevin
86Lynch-4
87D-627
87Sumter-7
87Wichi-21
88BBAmer-25
88Tulsa-15
88Wichi-32
89D-613
89D/Best-256
89D/Rook-44
89F-641M
89F/Up-63
89Jacks/GS-26
89Moth/R-18
89Score/Tr-89
89Smok/R-4
89T/Tr-15T
89Tidew/Pro-1962
89UD/Ext-752
90D-343
90F-291
90Score-210
90Score/100Ris-28
90Sf-73
90T-136
90UD-123
Brown, Knock-out
T3/Box-66
Brown, Kurt
86AppFx-4
87Penin-26
88Tampa/Star-3
89Saraso/Star-1
Brown, Larry Lesley
64T-301
65T-468
66OPC-16
66T-16
67OPC-145
67T-145
68Kahn
68T-197
69MB-42
69MLB/St-39
69T-503
69T/St-163
70MLB/St-194
70OPC-391
70T-391
71MLB/St-363
71OPC-539
71T-539
72MB-53
72OPC-279
72T-279
73JP
84Cram/PCL-238
Brown, Larry
78Laugh/Black-2
Brown, Leon
75Phoen-21
Brown, Lewis J.
(Lew)
No Cards.
Brown, Mace
40PB-220
41DP-36
R303/A
R312
Brown, Mark
81Miami-4
83RochR-2
85Toled-3
86T-451
86Toled-4
89Erie/Star-28
Brown, Marty
86Cedar/TCMA-14
87Vermont-5
88AAA/Pro-26
88Nashvl/CMC-18
88Nashvl/Pro-481
89F-645M
89Nashvl-3
89Nashvl/CMC-14
89Nashvl/Pro-1292
89Score/HotRk-70
Brown, Michael C.
(Mike)
81Holyo-8
82Spoka-19
84Cram/PCL-117
84D-42
84F/X-17
84Nes/792-643
84T-643
85D-207
85F-296
85Smok/Cal-4
85T-258
86D-642
86F-605
86F/Mini-117
86Leaf-256
86T-114
87D-168
87F-607
87Richm/TCMA-27
87T-341
89Edmon/CMC-18
89Edmon/Pro-558
Brown, Michael G.
(Mike)
83T/X-15
84D-517
84F-394
84Nes/792-472
84T-472
86Pawtu-3
87Calgary-7
87D-563
87F-583
87T-271
Brown, Mike
86Osceola-2
87Osceola-3

88ColSp/CMC-2
88ColSp/Pro-1526
88Toled/CMC-24
88Toled/Pro-611
89Kinston/Star-26

Brown, Mordecai
10Domino-17
11Helmar-91
12Sweet/Pin-80A
12Sweet/Pin-80B
14CJ-32
14Piedmont/St-7
15CJ-32
50Callahan
60Exh/HOF-5
60F-9
61F-11
63Bz/ATG-13
69Bz/Sm
75F/Pion-23
80Cram/Leg-71
80SSPC/HOF
89HOF/St-60
BF2-63
D329-17
D350/2-23
E103
E270/2
E300
E90/1
E90/3
E91
E93
E96
E98
M101/4-17
M101/5-23
M116
S74-58
T201
T202
T204
T205
T206
T213/blue
T215/blue
T222
T3-1
W555
WG1-1
WG3-7

Brown, Ollie Lee
66T-524R
67OPC-83
67T-83
68T-223
69MLB/St-190
69OPC-149
69T-149
69T/St-92
70K-55
70MLB/St-109
70OPC-130
70T-130
70T/PI-18
70T/S-36
71MLB/St-220
71OPC-505
71T-505
71T/Coins-133
72MB-54
72T-551
72T-552A
73OPC-526
73T-526
74OPC-625
74T-625
75OPC-596
75T-596
75T/M-596
76OPC-223
76SSPC-466
76T-223
77T-84

Brown, Oscar Lee
71MLB/St-5
71OPC-52R
71T-52R
72OPC-516
72T-516
73OPC-312
73T-312

Brown, Paul D.
62T-181
63T-478
64T-319

Brown, Paul
87Elmir-34
88Lynch/Star-2

Brown, Randy
76Wausa

Brown, Reggie
89Helena/SP-3

Brown, Renard
87Stockton-9

Brown, Richard Ernest
(Dick)
58T-456
59T-61
60T-256
61T-192
62J-21
62P-21
62P/Can-21
62Salada-37
62Shirriff-37
62T-438
63J-52
63P-52
63T-112
78TCMA-95

Brown, Rick
86LitFalls-4
87Columbia-12

Brown, Robert M.
34G-81

Brown, Robert W.
(Bobby)
47TipTop
49B-19
50B-101
51B-110
51BR-B6
52B-105
52BR
R346-9

Brown, Rogers Lee
(Bobby)
79Colum-27
80T-670R
81D-469
81F-95
81OPC-107
81T-418
82D-552
82F-30
82T-791
82T/Tr-12T
83T-287
84D-478
84F-296
84Moth/Padres-14
84Nes/792-261
84Smok/Padres-2
84T-261
84T/St-157
85D-383
85F-28
85Moth/Padres-23
85OPC-92
85T-583
85Utica-17
86T-182

Brown, Samuel W.
(Sam)
No Cards.

Brown, Scott
80Indianap-17
81Indianap-19
82F-60
82T-351R
83Omaha-4

Brown, Sid
89Panini/St-169

Brown, Steven E.
80ElPas-16
81SLCty-3
82Spoka-1
85Indianap-24

Brown, Tab
89Pulas/Pro-1899

Brown, Terry
87Beloi-15
89Keno/Pro-1068
89Keno/Star-2

Brown, Thomas D.
76Baton
78SnJos-16
79Tacom-2
80Syrac-8
81Syrac-2

Brown, Thomas Michael
(Tom)
49B-178
49Eureka-31
52B-236
52T-281
53B/Col-42

Brown, Thomas T.
(Tom)
N172
N284
N526

Brown, Thomas William
(Tom)
64T-311

Brown, Timothy
88StCath/Pro-2007
89Myrtle/Pro-1464

Brown, Todd
86Readg-4
86Stockton-3
87ElPas-17
88Denver/CMC-19
88Denver/Pro-1278

Brown, Tom
89Hagers/Best-11
89Hagers/Pro-283

Brown, Tony
87Readg-2
88EastLAS/Pro-31
88Readg/Pro-867
89Tidew/Pro-1974

Brown, Walter G.
(Jumbo)
33G-192
39PB-124
40PB-154

Brown, Willard Jessie
E223
N172
N338/2

Brown, William James
(Gates)
64T-471
65OPC-19
65T-19
66T-362
67OPC-134
67T-134
68T-583
69MB-41
69T-256
70OPC-98
70T-98
71MLB/St-386
71OPC-503
71T-503
72MB-52
72OPC-187
72T-187
73OPC-508
73T-508
74OPC-389
74T-389
75OPC-371
75T-371
75T/M-371
76SSPC-371
88Domino-1

Brown, William Verna
(Bill)
No Cards.

Brown, Winston
61T-391

Brown, Winston
89Sprin/Best-8

Browne, Byron Ellis
66OPC-139R
66T-139R
67T-439
68T-296
70OPC-388
70T-388
71MLB/St-171
71OPC-659
71T-659

Browne, Earl James
No Cards.

Browne, George Edward
E90/3
E91
T206
T3-84

Browne, Jerry
86Tulsa-9A
87Class/Up-146
87D-41RR
87D/OD-170
87D/Rook-29
87F-647M
87F/U-U12
87Leaf-41RR
87Moth/Rang-22
87S/Rook-4
87Smok/R-31
87T/Tr-11T
88D-408
88F-462
88Leaf-236
88Moth/R-22
88OPC-139
88Panini/St-201
88Score-278
88Score/YS/II-13
88Smok/R-15
88T-139
88T/Big-163
88T/JumboR-21
88ToysRUs-3
89B-85
89D-529
89D/Best-280
89D/Tr-44
89F/Up-26
89T-532
89T/Big-236
89T/Tr-16T
89UD-314
90Class-53
90D-138
90F-487
90Score-52
90Sf-111
90T-442
90UD-426

Browne, Prentice A.
(Pidge)
89Smok/Ast-20

Browning, Jim
33SK-41

Browning, Louis R.
(Pete)
N172

Browning, Mike
82Nashv-2
83Nashvl-2
84Cram/PCL-114
86Miami-3
87Miami-15
88Mia/Star-4
89ColMud/Best-17
89ColMud/Pro-122
89ColMud/Star-5

Browning, Tom
83Tampa-5
85D-634
85D/HL-43
85F/Up-U12
85T/Tr-11T
86D-384
86Drake-37
86F-173
86F/Mini-38
86F/Slug-4
86F/St-14
86F/WaxBox-C6
86KayBee-3
86Leaf-179
86S-185M
86S-79
86T-652
86T/Gloss60-49
86T/Mini-40
86T/St-141
86T/St-313
86T/Super-16
86TexGold-32
87Classic-78
87D-63
87D/OD-194
87F-194
87Kahn-32
87Leaf-138
87OPC-65
87T-65
87T/St-137
88D-63
88D/Best-335
88F-228
88Kahn/Reds-32
88Score-132
88T-577
88T/Big-96
89B-306
89Class-126
89D-71
89D/Best-62
89F-153
89F-629M
89K/Reds-32
89OPC-234
89Panini/St-4
89Panini/St-65
89Score-554
89Score-658HL
89Score/HotSt-61
89Sf-180
89Sf-222M
89T-234
89T/Big-14
89T/Gloss60-46
89T/Mini-6
89T/St-141
89T/St-7
89T/St/Backs-61
89UD-617
89Woolwth-9

90D-308
90F-415
90Score-165
90Score/100St-33
90Sf-91
90T-418
90UD-189

Brubaker, Bruce
65T-493R
67T-276

Brubaker, John
89Oneon/Pro-2128

Brubaker, Wilbur L.
(Bill)
34G-4
36G
39PB-130
40PB-166
R314

Brucato, Bob
89CharRa/Pro-973

Bruce, Bob
60T-118
61T-83
62T-419
63Pep
63T-24
64T-282
65OPC-240
65T-240
66OPC-64
66T-64
66T/RO-8
67T-417
89Smok/Ast-1

Bruce, Louis
(Lou)
No Cards.

Brucker, Earle F. Jr.
No Cards.

Brueggemann, Jeff
80Toled-18
83Visal/LF-14GM

Brueggemann, Steve
85LitFalls-3

Bruehl, Darin
89AubAs/Pro-2179

Bruett, Joseph T.
88CapeCod/Sum-168
89Keno/Pro-1074
89Keno/Star-3

Bruggy, Frank Leo
No Cards.

Bruhert, Mike
78Tidew
79T-172
79Tucso-3
82Colum-7
82Colum/Pol-25

Brumfield, Harvey
87Clearw-9
88Readg/Pro-881
89Readg/Best-20
89Readg/Pro-667
89Readg/Star-4

Brumfield, Jacob
87FtMyr-33
88Memph/Best-6
89Memph/Best-3
89Memph/Pro-1188
89Memph/Star-4

Brumley, Mike
66OPC-29
86IowaC-5
87IowaC-13
88AAA/Pro-21
88D-609
88LasVeg/CMC-19
88LasVeg/Pro-235
89D-302
89D/Rook-39
89F-302
89F/Up-30
89Mara/Tigers-12
89T/Big-324
90D-533
90Score/100Ris-88
90T-471
90UD-312

Brumley, Tony Mike
(Mike)
60DF
64T-167R
65T-523
66T-29

Brummer, Glenn Edward
82Louvl-2
82T-561R
83D-418
83F-4
83T-311
84D-138
84F-321
84Nes/792-152
84T-152
85D-290
85Rangers-7
86F-557
86Hawai-2
86T-616

Brummett, Greg
89Everett/Star-26

Brunansky, Thomas A.
(Tom)
80ElPas-17
81SLCty-21
82Spoka-20
82T-653R
82T/Tr-13T
83D-555
83F-607
83OPC-232
83T-232
83T/St-309
83T/St-90
84D-242
84F-557
84FunFood/Pin-130
84Nes/792-447
84OPC-98
84T-447
84T/St-304
85D-364
85F-271
85GenMills-15
85Leaf-36
85OPC-122
85Seven/Minn-7
85T-122
85T/Gloss40-39
85T/St-299
85T/Super-57
86D-192
86D-24
86D/AAS-44
86D/DKsuper-24
86F-387
86F/LimEd-9
86F/Mini-83
86F/St-15
86KayBee-4
86Leaf-24DK
86OPC-392
86S-80
86T-565
86T/St-276
87D-194
87D/OD-222
87F-537
87F/Hottest-7
87F/St-17
87Leaf-244
87OPC-261
87RedFoley/St-75
87S-134
87T-776
87T/St-280
88D-245
88D/Best-19
88F-5
88F/Slug-4
88F/St-42
88F/U-U117
88Master/Disc-12
88OPC-375
88Panini/St-142
88Score-194
88Score/Tr-5T
88Sf-194
88Smok/Card-25
88T-375
88T/Big-211
88T/St-15
88T/St-275
88T/Tr-20T
89B-444
89Class/Up/2-186
89D-112
89D/Best-187
89F-444
89F/Heroes-4
89OPC-60
89Panini/St-187
89RedFoley/St-14
89Score-184
89Sf-161
89Smok/Cards-1
89T-261TL
89T-60
89T/Big-54
89T/Hills-4
89T/St-41
89T/UK-9
89UD-272
90Class-119
90D-399
90F-242
90Score-72
90T-409
90UD-257

Brundage, Dave
87Clearw-20
88Vermont/Pro-951
89Wmspt/Pro-642
89Wmspt/Star-1

Brune, Jim
88Bill/Pro-1804
88Cedar/Pro-1154

Brunelle, Rodney
85Bend/Cram-4
87CharWh-7
88Clearw/Star-3

Brunenkant, Barry
84OKCty-15
85Tulsa-14
86Maine-1
87BuffB-5

Brunet, George
58T-139
63T-538
64T-322
65OPC-242
65T-242
66T-393
67OPC-122
67T-122
68T-347
69MB-43
69MLB/St-19
69MLBPA/Pin-3
69T-645
69T/St-141
70MLB/St-267
70OPC-328
70T-328
71MLB/St-269
71OPC-73
71T-73
72MB-55

Brunner, Tom
79Elmir-26

Bruno, Joe
80Penin/B-15
80Penin/C-21
87Cedar-12
88Chatt/Best-17
88SLAS-37
89Chatt/Best-21
89Chatt/GS-7
89SLAS-18

Bruno, Thomas
77OPC-32
79T-724R

Brunsberg, Arlo A.
No Cards.

Brunson, Eddie
78Newar
80Holyo-7

Brunswick, Mark
85LitFalls-13
86Columbia-6
87Lynch-25

Brunswick, Tom
77Spart

Brush, Robert
(Bob)
No Cards.

Bruske, James
87Kinston-17
88Wmspt/Pro-1323
89Kinston/Star-4

Brusky, Brad
86Cedar/TCMA-2
87Vermont-1
88Cedar/Pro-1156
89Wmspt/Pro-644
89Wmspt/Star-2

Brusstar, Warren
78T-297
79BK/P-9
79T-653
80T-52
81OkCty/TCMA-4
81T-426
82F-242
82T-647
83Thorn-41
84D-442
84F-487
84Nes/792-304
84SevenUp-41
84T-304
85D-533
85F-51
85SevenUp-41
85T-189
86D-555
86F-362
86T-564
87SanJose-21

Brust, Jerry
76QuadC

Bruton, William Haron
(Bill)
53JC-22
53T-214
54B-224
54JC-38
54T-109
55B-11
55Gol/Braves-3
55JC-38
55RFG-15
56T-185
56YellBase/Pin-8
57T-48
58T-355
59T-165
60Lake
60T-37
61P-109
61T-251
61T/St-39
62J-18
62P-18
62P/Can-18
62Salada-92
62Shirriff-92
62T-335
62T/St-43
63J-49
63P-49
63T-437
64Det/Lids-2
64T-98
Exh47
PM10/Sm-18

Bruyette, Edward T.
(Ed)
No Cards.

Bryan, Frank
87SanJose-9
88Fresno/Cal-17
88Fresno/Pro-1222
89PalmSp/Cal-47
89PalmSp/Pro-487

Bryan, William Ronald
(Billy)
63T-236
65OPC-51
65T-51
66T-332
67T-601
68T-498
78TCMA-47

Bryand, Renay
88Spoka/Pro-1941
89CharRa/Pro-996

Bryant, Bobby
79Jacks-19
79Tidew-21

Bryant, Chris
87Idaho-12

Bryant, Clay
74OPC-521CO
74T-521C

Bryant, Derek Roszell
77SnJos-4
80Ogden-4
80T-671R
81Tacom-9

Bryant, Donald Ray
(Don)
69T-499R
70OPC-473
70T-473
74OPC-403CO
74T-403C
77T-597C

Bryant, Erick
89Wausa/GS-25

Bryant, Erwin
81Brist-16

Bryant, Franklin S.
81VeroB-3

Bryant, George
No Cards.

Bryant, James
86Chatt-5
87Chatt/Best-7

Bryant, John
82CharR-5
83CharR-15
86Cedar/TCMA-23
87Vermont-15

Bryant, Mike
80Elmir-25

Bryant, Neil
82Amari-15
83MidldC-5

Bryant, Phil
87Gasto-7
88CharlR/Star-4
89Tulsa/GS-6

Bryant, Ralph
82VeroB-21
83VeroB-22
85Cram/PCL-161
86Albuq-2
87Albuq/Pol-25
87D-587
87F-649M
87F/U-U13
87Pol/Dodg-24
87T/Tr-12T
88F-510

Bryant, Ron
70OPC-433
70T-433
71MLB/St-242
71OPC-621
71T-621
72OPC-185
72OPC-186IA
72T-185
72T-186A
73OPC-298
73T-298
74OPC-104
74OPC-205LL
74T-104
74T-205LL
74T/DE-21
74T/St-103
75OPC-265
75T-265
75T/M-265

Bryant, Scott
90Score-667DC

Bryden, Thomas R.
(T.R.)
82Danvi-4
83Redwd-7
85MidldA-11
87Edmon-21
87T-387
88Portl/CMC-3
88Portl/Pro-663

Brye, Stephen Robert
(Steve)
71OPC-391R
71T-391R
72OPC-28R
72T-28
73OPC-353
73T-353
74OPC-232
74T-232
75OPC-151
75T-151
75T/M-151
76OPC-519
76SSPC-215
76T-519
77T-424
78T-673
79Hawai-12
79T-28

Bryeans, Chris
82CharR-10
83CharR-5

Brynan, Charles
N172

Brzezinski, George
88Geneva/Pro-1657

Bubser, Harold Fred
(Hal)
No Cards.

Buccheri, James
88SoOreg/Pro-1692
89Madis/Star-5
89Star/Wax-65

Bucci, Mike
78Cr/PCL-115
79Tucso-5
80Tacom-13
81Charl-11
82Wausa-12
83Chatt-9
85BurlR-10
86Salem-2MG
87BuffB-26MG
88BurlR/Pro-1786

Buccola, Vic
47Signal
48Smith-16

Bucha, John George
(Johnny)
52T-19
53Glen
54B-215

Buchanan, Bob
81Cedar-23
82Water-7
83Indianap-28
87Tidew-26
87Tidew/TCMA-27
88Omaha/CMC-3
88Omaha/Pro-1514
89Omaha/CMC-1
89Omaha/Pro-1724

Buchanan, Reggie
81Buffa-25

Buchanan, Rob
88Eugene/Best-13
89AppFx/Pro-868
89Eugene/Best-21

Buchek, Gerald Peter
(Jerry)
61Union
62Kahn/Atl
62T-439
64T-314
65T-397
66T-454
67T-574
68T-277
69MB-44

Bucher, James Quinter
(Jim)
R313

Buchheister, Don
(Bucky)
73Cedar
74Cedar
75Cedar
76Cedar
77Cedar
78Cedar
80Cedar-21
81Cedar-20
82Cedar-27
83Cedar-26
84Cedar-19
85Cedar-28
86Cedar/TCMA-27
88Cedar/Pro-1136
89Cedar/Best-24
89Cedar/Pro-931

Buckels, Gary
88MidwLAS/GS-25
88QuadC/GS-28
89MidldA/GS-6

Buckenberger, Albert
N172

Buckholz, Steven
88Watertn/Puc-3

Buckle, Larry
80Cedar-5
82Water-2

Buckley, Brian
81Redwd-2
82Holyo-2
84PrWill-10

Buckley, Joe
89Spoka/SP-7

Buckley, Kevin John
82BurlR-15
83BurlR-2
83BurlR/LF-20
83Tulsa-16
84OKCty-16
84Tulsa-27
85Maine-15
86Maine-2
87LasVegas-8

Buckley, Mike
81QuadC-6

Buckley, Richard D.
(Dick)
N172

Buckley, Troy
88CapeCod/Sum-170

Buckmier, Jim
83AlexD-29
84PrWill-2

Buckner, Jim
79Tidew-10
79Toled-14
80Buffa-5
81Omaha-20

Buckner, William J.
(Bill)
70OPC-286R
70T-286R
71MLB/St-99
71OPC-529R
71T-529R
72OPC-114
72T-114
73OPC-368
73T-368
74OPC-505
74T-505
74T/St-41
75Ho-97
75K-32
75OPC-244
75T-244
75T/M-244
76OPC-253
76SSPC-91
76T-253
77Ho-54
77T-27
78Ho-46
78OPC-127
78T-473
78Wiffle/Discs-10
79Ho-27
79OPC-177
79T-346
80OPC-75
80T-135
81Coke
81D-482
81Drake-13
81F-292
81F/St-29
81MSA/Disc-5
81OPC-202
81Sqt-6
81T-1LL
81T-625
81T/HT
81T/SO-55
81T/St-153
81T/St-17
82D-403
82Drake-5
82F-589
82F/St-96
82K-2
82OPC-124
82RedLob
82T-456TL
82T-760
82T/St-29
83D-14DK
83D-99
83D/AAS-7
83Drake-2
83F-492
83K-59
83OPC-250
83T-250
83T/Gloss-24
83T/Gloss40-24
83T/St-223
83Thorn-22
84D-117
84D/AAS-28
84D/Champs-18
84Drake-4
84F-488
84F/X-18
84FunFood/Pin-100
84Nes/792-545
84OPC-96
84T-545
84T/St-42
84T/Super-14
84T/Super-14
84T/X-17
85D-416
85F-153
85Leaf-254
85OPC-65
85SpokaAT/Cram-3
85T-65
85T/St-214
86D-151
86Drake-17
86F-343
86F/St-16
86Leaf-77
86OPC-239
86S-135M
86S-81
86T-443
86T/St-252
86T/Super-17
86Woolwth-5
87D-462
87D/OD-183
87F-31
87F/Lim-C2
87Leaf-241
87OPC-306
87S-70
87T-764
87T/Board-14
87T/St-250
88D-456
88F-486
88OPC-147
88Score-591
88Score/Tr-36T
88T-147
89F-278
89Score-214
89T/WaxBox-B
89UD-639
90D-474
90Score-396
90UD-252

Bucz, Bruce
88Visal/Cal-171

Budaska, Mark David
79Ogden/TCMA-18
80Ogden-7
81Tacom-13
82T-531R

Buddin, Donald Thomas
(Don)
58T-297
59T-32
60T-520
61P-53
61T-99
62J-59
62P-59
62P/Can-59
62Salada-68A
62Salada-68B
62Shirriff-68
62T-332
89Smok/Ast-19

Budke, Todd
85Visal-17
86Orlan-3

Budnick, Michael
47TipTop

Buechele, Steve
82Tulsa-27
83Tulsa-22
84OKCty-13
85OKCty-17
86D-544
86F-558
86Rangers-22
86T-397
87D-180
87D/OD-179
87F-121
87Moth/Rang-7
87OPC-176
87Smok/R-11
87T-176
87T/St-242
88D-224
88D/Best-312
88F-463
88Moth/R-7
88OPC-2
88Panini/St-204
88Score-306
88Smok/R-12
88T-537
88T/Big-104
88T/St-235
89B-232
89D-174
89D/Best-223
89F-515
89Moth/R-8
89OPC-83
89Panini/St-453
89Score-368
89Smok/R-5
89T-729TL
89T-732
89T/Big-156
89T/St-250
89UD-418
90D-107
90F-292
90Score-221
90T-279
90UD-685

Buelow, Frederick W.
(Fritz)
E107

Bues, Arthur F.
(Art)
No Cards.

Buettemeyer, Kim
80Wichi-3

Buffamoyer, John
75BurlB
77Holyo

Buffinton, Charles G.
(Charlie)
E223
N172
N690

Buffolino, Rocco
88Fresno/Cal-24
88Fresno/Pro-1231

Buford, Bobby
76Clint
Buford, Don Jr.
88Hagers/Star-3
89Hagers/Best-15
89Hagers/Pro-277
89Hagers/Star-2
Buford, Donald Alvin
(Don)
64T-368R
65OPC-81
65T-81
66T-465
67OPC-143M
67T-143M
67T-232
68Coke
68OPC-194
68T-194
69MB-45
69MLB/St-2
69T-478
69T/St-123
70MLB/St-147
70OPC-305WS
70OPC-428
70T-428
71MLB/St-291
71OPC-29
71OPC-328WS
71T-29
72MB-56
72OPC-370
72T-370
73OPC-183
73T-183
86Indianap-29
88French-2CO
Buggs, Michael J.
82AppFx-26
Buggs, Ron
(Doc)
77Newar
78Newar
79BurlB-9
Buhe, Tim
89Kingspt/Star-2
Buheller, Tim
86Elmir-4
87WinHav-1
88Lynch/Star-3
89Lynch/Star-3
Buhl, Bob
53JC-4
54JC-10
54T-210
55B-43
55Gol/Braves-4
55JC-10
56T-244
57T-127
58T-176
59T-347
60Lake
60T-230M
60T-374
61P-103
61T-145
61T/St-40
62J-154
62P-154
62P/Can-154
62Salada-117
62Shirriff-117
62T-458
63T-175
64T-96
65OPC-264
65T-264
66OPC-185
66T-185
67OPC-68
67T-68
89Swell-21
Buhner, Jay
87Colum-19
87Colum/Pol-4
87Colum/TCMA-19
88Class/Blue-244
88Colum/CMC-23
88Colum/Pol-18
88Colum/Pro-329
88D-545
88D/Rook-11
88D/Y/Bk-545
88Score/Tr-95T
88Sf-223
88T/Tr-21T
89B-219
89Bz-4
89Calg/CMC-13
89Calg/Pro-544
89D-581
89D/Best-136
89F-542
89KMart/DT-5
89OPC-223
89Panini/St-440
89Score-530
89Score/YS/I-6
89Sf-89
89T-223
89T/Big-20
89T/Coins-35
89T/Gloss60-9
89T/JumboR-5
89T/St-319
89T/UK-10
89ToysRUs-5
89UD-220
90D-448
90F-508
90Score-521
90T-554
90UD-534
Buice, DeWayne
78Cedar
81WHave-4
82Tacom-1
83Tacom-3
86MidldA-3
87D/Rook-6
87F/U-U14
87S/Rook-26
87T/Tr-13T
88D-58
88F-487
88OPC-396
88Score-376
88Smok/Angels-7
88T-649
88T/JumboR-4
88T/Mini-4
88T/St-180
88ToysRUs-4
89Score-153
89Syrac/CMC-8
89Syrac/Pro-811
89T-147
89UD-147
Buitimea, Martin
85Tigres-5
Buker, Henry L.
(Harry)
No Cards.
Buksa, Ken
88Watertn/Puc-16
Bulkeley, Morgan
50Callahan
80SSPC/HOF
Bullard, George D.
No Cards.
Bullard, Larry
(Rocky)
78Duned
Bullas, Simeon E.
(Sam)
No Cards.
Bulling, Terry C.
(Bud)
78OrlTw
78T-432
79Spoka-23
80Spoka-10
82D-612
82T-98
83D-226
83F-630
83SLCty-15
83T-519
Bullinger, Jim
86Geneva-1
87WinSal-10
88Pittsf/Pro-1367
89CharlK-6
Bullinger, Matt
81Chatt-6
82Jacks-2
Bullock, Eric
82DayBe-12
83ColumAst-9
85Cram/PCL-52
87Tucso-19
88Portl/CMC-17
88Portl/Pro-640
89F-106
Bulls, Dave
86Portl-2
Bumbry, Alonza B.
(Al)
73JP
73OPC-614R
73T-614R
74OPC-137
74T-137
75OPC-358
75T-358
75T/M-358
76OPC-307
76SSPC-396
76T-307
77Ho-90
77OPC-192
77T-626
78T-188
79T-517
80OPC-36
80T-65
81D-355
81F-172
81F/St-30
81OPC-34
81T-425
81T/SO-29
81T/St-35
82D-153
82F-159
82F/St-147
82OPC-265
82T-265
83D-383
83F-54
83OPC-272
83T-655
84D-210
84F-2
84Nes/792-319
84T-319
85D-350
85F-171
85F/Up-U13
85Moth/Padres-25
85T-726
85T/St-205
85T/Tr-12T
86F-316
86T-583
87Elmir-29
87Elmir/Red-29
Bumgarner, Jeff
86Kenosha-3
87ColAst/Pro-25
87ColumAst-25
87Orlan-1
88Portl/CMC-4
88Portl/Pro-659
89Jacks/GS-10
Bumstead, Mark
78StPet
Bunce, Joshua
(Josh)
No Cards.
Bundy, Lorenzo
83AlexD-31
84Cram/PCL-127
89Indi/CMC-17
89Indi/Pro-1223
Bunker, Wally
64T-201R
65OPC-9LL
65T-290
65T-9LL
66T-499
67T-585
68T-489
69MLB/St-56
69OPC-137
69T-137
69T/St-182
70K-70
70MLB/St-218
70OPC-266
70T-266
70T/CB
71MLB/St-410
71OPC-528
71T-528
72MB-57
Bunning, Jim
57T-338
58T-115
59T-149
60L-144
60T-502
61P-39
61T-46LL
61T-490
61T-50LL
61T/St-147
62J-26
62P-26
62P/Can-26
62Salada-13
62Shirriff-13
62T-460
62T-57LL
62T-59LL
62T/bucks
62T/St-44
63J-53
63P-53
63Salada-33
63T-10LL
63T-218M
63T-365
63T-8LL
63T/SO
64T-265
64T-6LL
64T/Coins-93
64T/S-10
64Wheat/St-9
65Bz-21
65OldLond-5
65OPC-20
65T-20
65T/E-17
65T/trans-6
66Bz-31
66T-435
66T/RO-78
67Bz-31
67T-238LL
67T-560
68Bz-7
68KDKA-14
68OPC-11LL
68OPC-7LL
68OPC-9LL
68T-11LL
68T-215
68T-7LL
68T-9LL
69Citgo-20
69MB-46
69MLB/St-183
69OPC-175
69T-175
69T/St-84
70MLB/St-86
70OPC-403
70T-403
71MLB/St-172
71OPC-574
71T-574
71T/Coins-3
71T/GM-43
72MB-58
74Laugh/ASG-61
76Laugh/Jub-10
76OkCty
88Pac/Leg-92
89Swell-7
PM10/L-7
Buonantony, Rich
82QuadC-4
86Louisvl-8
87Louvl-7
88Louvl-12
88Louvl/CMC-7
88Louvl/Pro-445
Burba, Dave
88SanBern/Best-17
88SanBern/Cal-49
89Wmspt/Pro-630
Burbach, Bill
69T-658R
70OPC-167
70T-167
71MLB/St-484
71OPC-683
71T-683
Burbank, Dennis
88CapeCod-6
88CapeCod/Sum-151
Burbrink, Nelson E.
(Nels)
56T-27
Burch, Albert William
(Al)
E254
E270/2
M116
T206
Burch, Ernest W.
N172
N28
Burcham, Tim
86QuadC-6
87PalmSp-21
88MidldA/GS-6
89Edmon/CMC-5
89Edmon/Pro-553
89MidldA/GS-7
Burchart, Larry
69T-597R
70OPC-412
70T-412
Burchell, Fred
C46-14

T204
T206

Burchett, Kerry D.
81ArkTr-10

Burda, Edward Robert
(Bob)
61Union
62Kahn/Atl
69T-392
70OPC-357
70T-357
71OPC-541
71T-541
72T-734

Burden, John
80Wausa-2
81Chatt-2
83Chatt-20
86Chatt-6CO

Burdette, Freddie
64T-408R

Burdette, Lew
52B-244
53B/BW-51
53JC-5
54B-192
54JC-33
54RM-NL24
55B-70
55Gol/Braves-5
55JC-33
56T-219
57T-208
58T-10
58T-289M
59T-440
60Lake
60NuCard-35
60T-230M
60T-70
60T/tatt
60T/tatt-7
61NuCard-408
61NuCard-435
61P-102
61T-320
61T-47LL
62Exh
62J-153
62P-153
62P/Can-153
62Salada-166
62Shirriff-166
62T-380
62T/bucks
62T/St-146
63Exh
63J-155
63P-155
63T-429
64T-523
65OPC-64
65T-64
66T-299
67T-265
73OPC-237CO
73T-237C
78TCMA-276
88Pac/Leg-68
Exh47

Burdette, Ricky
77Spart
80Ashev-24

Burdick, Kevin
87Watertn-11
88Salem/Star-3
89Harris/Pro-297
89Harris/Star-4
89Star/Wax-19

Burdick, Stacey
87Miami-3
89Freder/Star-1

Burdick, William B.
N172

Burdock, John Joseph
(Jack)
N172
N284

Burg, Joseph Peter
(Pete)
No Cards.

Burgess, Bob
89Well/Puc-34

Burgess, Forrest H.
(Smokey)
49Eureka-52
51B-317
52B-112
52T-357
53B/Col-28
53T-10
54B-31
55B-209
55RFG-12
56Kahn
56T-192
57Kahn
57T-228
58Kahn
58T-49
59Kahn
59T-432
60Kahn
60T-393
61Kahn
61P-138
61T-461
61T/St-61
62J-176
62Kahn
62P-176
62P/Can-176
62Salada-114
62Shirriff-114
62T-389
62T/St-173
63F-55
63J-144
63Kahn
63P-144
63T-18M
63T-425
64T-37
65OPC-198
65T-198
66T-354
67T-506
72Laugh/GF-28
78Green
78TCMA-1
88Pulas/Pro-1750
89Pac/Leg-201
89Swell-32

Burgess, Gus
80Elmir-26
83Pawtu-20
84Pawtu-9
85Pawtu-1

Burgess, Thomas R.
(Tommy)
54Hunter
79Richm-15MG
80Charl-1
81Tulsa-20
82Tulsa-22MG
83OKCty-2
84OKCty-3
86Lakel-3MG
87GlenF-3

Burgmeier, Tom
69T-558
70OPC-108
70T-108
71MLB/St-411
71OPC-431
71T-431
72OPC-246
72T-246
73OPC-306
73T-306
75OPC-478
75T-478
75T/M-478
76OPC-87
76SSPC-206
76T-87
77T-398
78PapaG/Disc-16
78T-678
79OPC-272
79T-524
80T-128
81Coke
81D-97
81F-228
81OPC-320
81T-228
81T/HT
82Coke/BOS
82D-361
82F-288
82T-455
83D-235
83F-180
83Granny-39
83OPC-213
83T-213
83T/X-16
84D-522
84F-439
84Moth/A's-18
84Nes/792-33
84OPC-33
84T-33
85D-400
85F-417

Burgo, Dale
88WinHav/Star-6
89Lynch/Star-4

Burgo, William Ross
(Bill)
No Cards.

Burgos, Enrique
87Knoxv-17
88Syrac/Pro-815
89Duned/Star-2

Burgos, John
87Gasto-27
89Savan/Pro-351

Burgos, Paco
87SanJose-17
88CharlR/Star-5

Burich, William Max
(Bill)
No Cards.

Burk, Mack Edwin
57T-91
58T-278

Burkam, Robert
(Bob)
No Cards.

Burke, Curtis
83DayBe-25

Burke, Daniel L.
(Dan)
No Cards.

Burke, Don
86Jamestn-2
87WPalm-12
87WPalm-24

Burke, Edward D.
(Eddie)
33SK-33

Burke, Edward
N566-177

Burke, Frank A.
No Cards.

Burke, Glenn L.
75Water
78T-562
79OPC-78
79T-163

Burke, James Timothy
(Jimmy)
T206
W514-89

Burke, John Patrick
No Cards.

Burke, Kevin
85Newar-24
87Hagers-20

Burke, Leo Patrick
63T-249
64T-557
65OPC-202
65T-202

Burke, Leslie K.
(Les)
No Cards.

Burke, Michael E.
(Mike)
86Bakers-4
87VeroB-25

Burke, Patrick Edward
(Pat)
No Cards.

Burke, Robert J.
33G-71
35G-2C
35G-4C
35G-7C
V354-25

Burke, Steve
77Jaxvl
78T-709R
79Spoka-22

Burke, Tim
82Buffa-15
83Colum-7
83Nashvl-3
84Indianap-23
85F/Up-U14
86D-421
86F-245
86Leaf-198
86OPC-258
86Provigo-17
86T-258
87D-222
87F-315
87Leaf-205
87OPC-132
87T-624
87T/St-78
88D-98
88D/Best-34
88F-180
88F/Mini-87
88F/St-95
88Ho/Disc-2
88Leaf-84
88OPC-14
88Score-187
88T-529
89B-360
89D-274
89D/Best-180
89F-372
89OPC-48
89Panini/St-113
89RedFoley/St-15
89Score-228
89Sf-73
89T-48
89T/St-69
89UD-456
90D-334
90F-342
90Score-127
90Score/100St-34
90Sf-199
90T-195
90UD-515

Burke, Todd
87Visal-18

Burke, Tom
77Charl

Burke, William I.
E254
T206

Burkett, Jesse Cail
50Callahan
80SSPC/HOF
89HOF/St-33
E254
E286
T204
W575

Burkett, John
86Shrev-2
87Shrev-14
87TexLgAS-33
88F-651
88Phoen/CMC-2
88Phoen/Pro-76
89Phoen/CMC-1
89Phoen/Pro-1483

Burkhart, Ken
47TipTop

Burks, Ellis
86NewBrit-4
87D/Rook-5
87F/U-U15
87Pawtu-23
87Pawtu/TCMA-22
87S/Rook-5
87T/Tr-14T
88Class/Blue-229
88D-174
88D/Best-121
88D/RedSox/Bk-174
88F-348
88F-630M
88F/Slug-5
88F/St-6
88Leaf-174
88MSA/Disc-2
88OPC-269
88Panini/St-31
88RedFoley/St-10
88Score-472
88Score/YS/I-37
88Sf-144
88T-269
88T/Big-80
88T/Gloss60-50
88T/JumboR-2
88T/St-250
88T/St-310
88ToysRUs-5
89Ames-7
89Class/Up/2-152
89Class/Up/2-175M
89D-303
89D/Best-9
89D/GrandSlam-12
89F-83
89Nissen-3
89OPC-311
89Panini/St-278
89Score-9
89Score/HotSt-43
89Score/Mast-25
89Sf-191
89T-785
89T/Big-259
89T/HeadsUp-12
89T/St-254
89UD-434

90D-228
90D-23DK
90F-269
90Score-340
90Score/100St-16
90Sf-80
90T-155
90UD-343

Burks, Robert E.
N172

Burleson, Richard P.
(Rick)
75OPC-302
75T-302
75T/M-302
76Ho-44
76Ho/Twink-44
76OPC-29
76SSPC-410
76T-29
77Ho-68
77OPC-237
77T-585
78OPC-37
PapaG/Disc-7
78T-245
79OPC-57
79T-125
80OPC-339
80T-125
80T-645
81D-454
81F-225
81F/St-33
81K-49
81OPC-172
81Sqt-13
81T-455
81T/HT
81T/SO-37
81T/St-52
81T/Tr-743
82D-342
82F-453
82F/St-219
82K-44
82OPC-55
82T-55
82T/St-134
82T/St-157
83D-318
83F-80
83OPC-315
83T-315
84F-510
84Nes/792-735
84OPC-376
84Smok/Cal-4
84T-735
84T/St-238
86Smok/Cal-15
86T/Tr-16T
87D/OD-134
87F-74
87OPC-152
87T-579

Burley, Tony
82Cedar-16
83Tampa-1

Burlingame, Dennis
88SALAS/GS-28
88Sumter/Pro-393
89Durhm/Star-2

Burlingame, Greg
89SanBern/Best-5
89SanBern/Cal-70

Burn
T222

Burnau, Ben
89Wausa/GS-10

Burnett, Hercules H.
No Cards.

Burnett, John H.
(Johnny)
R314/Can

Burnett, John P.
No Cards.

Burnett, Lance
88Poca/Pro-2083

Burnett, Ora
46Remar-9
47Remar-5
47Signal
47Smith-17
49B/PCL-36

Burnette, Wallace
57T-13
58T-69

Burnham, George W.
N172

Burnitz, Jeromy
88CapeCod/Sum-145

Burnos, Jim
83Wisco/LF-20

Burns, Bill
(Sleepy)
88Pac/8Men-17M
88Pac/8Men-18

Burns, Britt
79Knoxv/TCMA-6
81Coke
81D-279
81F-342
81OPC-218
81T-412
81T/HT
81T/St-63
82D-230
82F-339
82F/St-189
82T-44
83D-193
83D-23DK
83F-232
83K-43
83T-541
83T/St-48
84D-424
84F-54
84Nes/792-125
84OPC-125
84T-125
84TrueVal/WS-7
85Coke/WS-40
85D-257
85F-509
85OPC-338
85T-338
86D-58
86F-200
86F/St-17
86OPC-174
86S-105
86T-679
86T/Mini-10
86T/St-292

Burns, Dan
83ElPas-1

Burns, Daren
88Wythe/Pro-1985

Burns, Edward James
(Ed)
11Helmar-111
D327
D328-18
D329-18
D350/2-17
E135-18
E270/2
M101/4-18
M101/5-17

Burns, George Henry
21Exh-14
26Exh-81
27Exh-41
D327
D328-19
D329-19
E120
E121/80
E135-19
E210-9
E220
M101/4-19
V100
W502-9
W514-24
W516-10
W572
W573
W575

Burns, George Joseph
21Exh-15
28Yueng-9
32Orbit/num-64
32Orbit/un-7
D327
D328-20
D329-20
D350/2-18
E120
E121/80
E122
E135-20
E220
M101/4-20
M101/5-18
V100
W515-54
W572
W573
W575

Burns, George
21Exh-16
21Exh-17
80Laugh/FFeat-35
BF2-73
V61-1
V61-70
WG7-7

Burns, Gregory
85Madis-7

Burns, James M.
(Jim)
N172

Burns, James
83StPet-16

Burns, John Irving
(Jack)
33G-198
34DS-75
34Exh/4-15
35BU-18
35BU-191
35Exh/4-15
35G-8C
35G-9C
R305
R326-1A
R326-1B
R342-1

Burns, John Joseph
No Cards.

Burns, Joseph Francis
(Joe)
No Cards.

Burns, Joseph James
(Joe)
No Cards.

Burns, Kerry
83TriCit-4

Burns, Patrick
(Pat)
No Cards.

Burns, Richard Simon
(Dick)
No Cards.

Burns, Thomas E.
(Tom)
80Batav-8
81Batav-2
81Watlo-7
83Wausa/LF-4
85Lynch-11
86Tidew-3

Burns, Thomas P.
(Oyster)
E223
N172
N284
WG1-11

Burns, Todd
85Madis-8
85Madis/Pol-5
86SLAS-18
88F/U-U52
88Score/Tr-106T
88Tacom/CMC-2
88Tacom/Pro-632
89Class/Up/2-171
89D-564
89F-3
89Moth/A's-24
89Panini/St-411
89Score-465
89Score/HotRk-100
89Score/YS/II-4
89Sf-87
89T-174
89T/Big-10
89UD/Ext-718
90D-446
90F-2
90Score-64
90T-369
90UD-689

Burns, William T.
T206
T3-85

Burnside, Pete
58T-211
59T-354
60T-261
61P-46
61T-507
62T-207
63T-19

Burnside, Sheldon
80Indianap-3
81F-220

Burr, Alexander T.
(Alex)
No Cards.

Burrell, Frank Andrew
(Buster)
No Cards.

Burrell, Kevin
85Lynch-14
86Shrev-3
87Phoen-8
88Memph/Best-11
88SLAS-2
89Omaha/CMC-10
89Omaha/Pro-1733

Burress, Davey
76Clint

Burright, Larry
62T-348
63T-174

Burris, Paul Robert
54JC-29

Burris, Ray
74OPC-161
74T-161
75OPC-566
75T-566
75T/M-566
76Ho-60
76Ho/Twink-60
76OPC-51
76T-51
77Ho-67
77OPC-197
77T-190
78T-371
78Wiffle/Discs-9
79OPC-43
79T-98
80T-364
81D-524
81F-328
81OPC-323
81T-654
81T/Tr-744
82D-414
82F-184
82Hygrade
82OPC-227
82T-227
82Zeller-20
83D-36
83F-277
83OPC-12
83Stuart-16
83T-474
84D-331
84F-270
84F/X-19
84Moth/A's-22
84Nes/792-552
84OPC-319
84T-552
84T/X-18
85D-218
85F-418
85F/Up-U15
85Leaf-116
85OPC-238
85Pol/Brew-48
85T-758
85T/St-328
85T/Tr-13T
86D-107
86F-482
86T-106
89Helena/SP-26

Burroughs, Darren
82OkCty-23
83Readg-2
84Cram/PCL-235
86BuffB-6
88Calg/CMC-1
88Calg/Pro-780

Burroughs, Jeffrey A.
(Jeff)
72OPC-191
72T-191
73OPC-489
73T-489
74K-16
74OPC-223
74T-223
74T/DE-48
74T/St-232
75Ho-111
75Ho-94
75K-8
75OPC-212M
75OPC-308LL 75OPC-470
75T-212MV
75T-308LL
75T-470
75T/M-212MV
75T/M-308LL
75T/M-470
76Crane-6
76MSA/Disc
76OPC-360
76SSPC-269
76T-360

77OPC-209
77Pep-58
77T-55
78Ho-61
78K-15
78OPC-134
78T-130
78Wiffle/Discs-11
79Ho-20
79K-12
79OPC-124
79T-245
80OPC-283
80T-545
81D-66
81F-245
81Pol/Mariners-1
81T-20
81T/Tr-745
82D-379
82F-506
82F/St-220
82KMart-25
82OPC-309
82T-440
82T/St-231
82T/Tr-14T
83D-323
83F-515
84D-156
84D/Champs-7
84F-440
84Moth/A's-17
84Nes/792-354
84OPC-354
84T-354
84T/St-329
85D-542
85F/Up-U16
85OPC-91
85T-272FDP
85T-91
85T/Tr-14T
85Tor/Fire-6
86F-54
86OPC-168
86T-168

Burroughs, Kenny
89Utica/Puc-3

Burrus, Maurice L.
(Dick)
25Exh-4
26Exh-3

Burt, Frank J.
No Cards.

Burton, Bob
89Wausa/GS-4

Burton, Chris
89Idaho/Pro-2022

Burton, Ellis N.
59T-231
60T-446
61BeeHive-3
63T-262
64T-269

Burton, Jim
76OPC-471
76SSPC-418
76T-471

Burton, Ken
76Cedar

Burtschy, Ed
55B-120
55Rodeo

Burtt, Dennis
81Brist-21
83Pawtu-3
84Pawtu-5
85IntLgAS-39
85Toled-4
87Albuq/Pol-6
88Albuq/CMC-7
88Albuq/Pro-276
89Albuq/CMC-2
89Albuq/Pro-68

Burwell, Bill
60T-467C

Burwell, Phil
83Erie-17

Busby, James F.
(Jim)
51B-302
52B-68
52BR
52StarCal/L-73F
52T-309
53B/Col-15
53Briggs
53NB
54B-8
54RM-AL2
55B-166
55RFG-8
55RM-AL2
55Salem
56T-330
57T-309
58Hires-68
58Hires/T
58T-28
59T-185
60L-11
60T-232
62Salada-30
62Shirriff-30
73OPC-237CO
73T-237C
74OPC-634CO 74T-634C
77T-597C
79TCMA-66

Busby, Paul Miller
No Cards.

Busby, Steve
73OPC-608R
73T-608R
74OPC-365
74T-365
74T/St-181
75Ho-124
75K-24
75OPC-120
75OPC-7M
75T-120
75T-7M
75T/M-120
75T/M-7M
76A&P/KC
76Ho-71
76K-33
76Laugh/Jub-15
76OPC-260
76SSPC-183
76T-260
78T-336
80T-474
81F-33

Busby, Wayne
89SoBend/GS-23

Busch, Edgar John
(Ed)
No Cards.

Buschorn, Don
65T-577R

Bush, Guy T.
30CEA/Pin-12
32Orbit/num-16
32Orbit/un-8
33G-67
35BU-158
35Exh/4-7
35G-1E
35G-3C
35G-4C
35G-5C
36Exh/4-7
88Conlon/NatAS-2
R305
R306
R308-189
R316
V353-67

Bush, Kalani
89Geneva/Pro-1872

Bush, Leslie Ambrose
(Joe)
15CJ-166
21Exh-18
D328-21
D329-21
D350/2-19
E120
E121/120
E121/80
E126-3
E135-21
E220
M101/4-21
M101/5-19
V61-4
W501-34
W515-27
W572
W575
WG7-8

Bush, Owen Joseph
(Donnie)
09Buster/Pin-3
11Helmar-27
14CJ-122
15CJ-122
21Exh-19
86Indianap-2
BF2-24
D303
D327
D328-22
D329-22
D350/2-20
E106
E135-22
E224
E254
E270/2
E286
E90/1
F61-96
M101/4-22
M101/5-20
M116
T206
T216
T222
W514-30
W575

Bush, Robert Randall
(Randy)
80Toled-8
82OrlTw/A-2
82Toled-20
83T/X-17
84D-513
84F-558
84Nes/792-429
84OPC-84
84T-429
84T/St-314
85D-633
85F-272
85T-692
86F-388
86OPC-214
86T-214
87D-441
87F-538
87T-364
88D-272
88F-6
88F/WS-2
88Master/Disc-7
88Panini/St-450IA 88Score-292
88Smok/Minn-9
88T-73
89B-164
89D-537
89D/Best-214
89F-107
89OPC-288
89Panini/St-391
89Score-212
89T-577
89T/Big-282
89UD-158
90D-199
90F-370
90Score-278
90T-747
90UD-493

Bushelman, John
(Jack)
T207

Bushing, Chris
89Penin/Star-2

Bushong, Albert John
(Doc)
N172
N172/BC
N284
N370
Scrapps

Busick, Warren
86DayBe-3

Buskey, Joseph Henry
(Joe)
No Cards.

Buskey, Michael T.
(Tom)
75OPC-403
75T-403
75T/M-403
76OkCty
76OPC-178
76SSPC-505
76T-178
77T-236
80OPC-265
80T-506
81D-270

Buss, Scott
86Chatt-7
87Kinston-5

Busse, Raymond Edward
(Ray)
72OPC-101R
72T-101R
73OPC-607R
73T-607R
75Iowa/TCMA-3

Bustabad, Juan
83Pawtu-15
84Pawtu-25
85Pawtu-2
87SnAnt-9
88SnAnt/Best-12
89Albuq/CMC-20
89Albuq/Pro-78

Bustillos, Albert
89Star/Wax-28
89VeroB/Star-4

Buszka, John
77Watlo
78Watlo

Butcher, A. Maxwell
40PB-222

Butcher, Henry Joseph
(Hank)
T207

Butcher, John
78Ashev
79Tulsa-16
80Charl-13
81F-635
81T-41R
82T-418
83D-37
83F-563
83Rangers-29
83T-534
84D-220
84F-415
84F/X-20
84Nes/792-299
84T-299
84T/X-19
85D-314
85F-273
85Leaf-71
85OPC-356
85Seven/Minn-5
85T-741
85T/St-305
86D-120
86F-389
86T-638
87F-245
87T-107

Butcher, Matthew
84Visal-17

Butcher, Mike
86Cram/PCL-40
87AppFx-10
88BBCity/Star-7
89MidlA/GS-8

Butera, Brian
80Elmir-35

Butera, Salvatore P.
(Sal)
79Toled-8
81D-530
81F-570
81T-243
82D-532
82F-548
82T-676
83T-67
84Indianap-5
85Indianap-15
86OPC-261
86T-407
86TexGold-22
87F-195
87T-358
88Score-361
88Syrac/CMC-16
88Syrac/Pro-826
88T-772
89Syrac/CMC-11
89Syrac/Pro-802
89Tor/Fire-26

Butka, Edward Luke
(Ed)
No Cards.

Butler, Arthur Edward
(Art)
D329-23
D350/2-21
E90/1
M101/4-23
M101/5-21
T201

Butler, Brett Morgan
80Ander-26
81Richm-8
82BK/Lids-4
82D-275
82Pol/Atl-22
82T-502R
83D-636
83F-132

83Pol/Atl-22
83T-364
84D-141
84F-173
84F/X-21
84Nes/792-77
84T-77
84T/X-20
84Wheat/Ind-2
85D-216
85D/AAS-23
85F-441
85F/St-56
85Leaf-186
85OPC-241
85Polar/Ind-2
85T-637
85T/St-246
86D-102
86D-12
86D/DKsuper-12
86F-581
86F/Mini-114
86F/St-18
86Leaf-12DK 86OhHenry-2
86OPC-149
86S-26
86T-149
86T/Gloss60-52
86T/Mini-12
86T/St-206
86T/Super-18
87Classic-36
87D-219
87D/OD-113
87F-246
87F/Hottest-8
87Gator-2
87Leaf-183
87OPC-197
87RedFoley/St-79
87S-69
87T-723
88D-279
88D/Best-23
88F-603
88F/U-U128
88Moth/Giants-14
88OPC-202
88Panini/St-78
88Score-122
88Score/Tr-3T
88Sf-153
88T-479
88T/Big-166
88T/St-212
88T/Tr-22T
89B-480
89Class-38
89D-217
89D/Best-274
89F-324
89Moth/Giants-5
89OPC-241
89Panini/St-220
89Score-216
89Sf-31
89T-241
89T/Big-62
89T/Coins-6
89T/Mini-39
89T/St-85
89T/UK-11
89UD-218
90D-249
90F-53
90Score-236
90Score/100St-47
90Sf-136
90T-571
90UD-119

Butler, Cecil
62T-239
63T-201

Butler, Chris
89Kingspt/Star-3

Butler, Frank Dean
No Cards.

Butler, Frank E.
No Cards.

Butler, John Albert
No Cards.

Butler, John S.
(Johnny)
C46-46
T206

Butler, John
26Exh-9
27Exh-5

Butler, Mark
83SanJose-11

Butler, Mick
86PalmSp-5
86PalmSp/Smok-17

Butler, Richard H.
(Dick)
No Cards.

Butler, Todd
88BurlR/Pro-1782

Butler, W. J.
(Bill)
69T-619R
70MLB/St-219
70OPC-377
70T-377
71MLB/St-412
71OPC-681
71T-681
72MB-59
75OPC-549
75T-549
75T/M-549
76OPC-619
76SSPC-207
76T-619
78Cr/PCL-1

Butler, Willis E.
(Kid)
No Cards.

Butterfield, Brian
82Nashv-3
87Oneon-14
89Oneon/Pro-2098

Butters, Dave
85PrWill-28

Butters, Tom
63T-299R
64T-74R
65OPC-246
65T-246

Button, Dick
51BR-B17

Butts, David
87Sumter-29
88Durhm/Star-3
89Durhm/Star-3

Butts, Randy
86Erie-5
87StPet-24
88Hamil/Pro-1735

Butts, Tom
82IowaC-29

Butts, Tommy
78Laugh/Black-11

Buxton, Ralph
(Buck)
46Remar-21
47Remar-6
47Signal
47Smith-11
48Signal
48Smith-11
49Remar

Buzas, Joseph John
(Joe)
47Centen-2

Buzhardt, John
59T-118
60T-549
61T-3
61T/St-49
62J-200
62P-200
62P/Can-200
62Salada-129A
62Salada-129B
62Shirriff-129
62T-555
63T-35
64T-323
65T-458
66T-245
67OPC-178
67T-178
68T-403

Buzzard, Buddy
87Kenosha-7

Buzzard, Dale
89James/Pro-2130

Byam, George
V362-47

Byerly, Eldred
(Bud)
52T-161
58T-72
60T-371

Byerly, Rod
89Aug/Pro-518
89Well/Puc-8

Byers , James W.
(Bill)
No Cards.

Byers, John William
C46-74
E254

Byers, Randell
86Beaum-4
87LasVegas-14
88D-605
88F-653
88LasVeg/CMC-13
88LasVeg/Pro-224
89LasVeg/CMC-12
89LasVeg/Pro-6
89Louvl-12
89Louvl/CMC-23
89Louvl/Pro-1245

Byington, John
88CapeCod/Sum-21

Byrd, Felan
76Clint

Byrd, Harry
53B/Col-38
53T-131
54B-49
54NYJour
55B-159
55Esskay
58T-154
79TCMA-172

Byrd, Jeff
78OPC-211
78Syrac
78T-667

Byrd, Jim
89Star/Wax-10
89WinHav/Star-2

Byrd, Leland
77Visal

Byrd, Samuel D.
(Sammy)
32Orbit/num-96
33G-157
35BU-56
35G-2F
35G-4F
35G-7F
R313
R314
V353-86

Byrne, Robert M.
(Bobby)
10Domino-18
11Helmar-154
12Sweet/Pin-133
D322
D328-23
D329-24
D350/2-22
E135-23
E224
E270/2
E300
E94
M101/4-24
M101/5-22
M116
S74-106
T201
T202
T205
T206
T207
T213/blue
T213/brown
T215/blue
T215/brown
T222

Byrne, T.J.
81Holyo-4

Byrne, Thomas Joseph
(Tommy)
44Yank/St-4
51B-73
51BR-D4
51T/BB-35
52B-61
52T-241
53T-123
55B-300
56T-215
57T-108
79TCMA-198

Byrnes, Chris
87Oneon-20

Byrnes, James Joseph
(Jim)
No Cards.

Byrnes, Milton John
(Milt)
No Cards.

Byron, Bill
73F/Wild-20

Byron, Tim
82Oneon-11
85Albany-2

Bystrom, Marty
77Spart
79OkCty
80OkCty
81T-526R
82D-93
82T-416R
83D-93
83F-154
83T-199
84D-259
84F-24
84Nes/792-511
84T-511
85F-122
85T-284
86D-591
86F-102
86T-723
87FtLaud-2
88Maine/CMC-1
88Maine/Pro-292

Caballero, Ed
88Peoria/Ko-7
89WinSal/Star-2

Caballero, Jose
82Miami-8

Caballero, Ralph J.
(Putsy)
49Eureka-132

Cabassa, Carlos
80Penin/B-3
80Penin/C-3

Cabell, Billy
83Clint/LF-4

Cabell, Enos Milton
73OPC-605R
73T-605R
75OPC-247
75T-247
75T/M-247
76OPC-404
76SSPC-61
76T-404
77Ho-94
77T-567
78BK/A-14
78Ho-9
78OPC-44
78T-132
79Ho-70
79OPC-269
79T-515
80BK/PHR-24
80OPC-201
80T-385
81D-138
81F-58
81F/St-36
81OPC-45
81T-45
81T/Tr-746
82D-272
82F-386
82F/St-64
82OPC-311
82T-627
82T/St-105
82T/Tr-15T
83D-202
83F-328
83OPC-225
83T-225
84D-456
84F-79
84F/X-22
84Moth/Ast-11
84Nes/792-482
84T-482
84T/St-273
84T/X-21
85D-110
85F-346
85Leaf-161
85Moth/Ast-10
85T-786
85T/St-61
86D-418
86F-126
86Pol/Dodg-23
86T-197
87F-438
87T-509

Cabello, Bobby
86Cram/PCL-83

Cabrera, Alfredo A.
(Al)
No Cards.

Cabrera, Antonio
(Tony)
86Madis-4
86Madis/Pol-4

Cabrera, Basilio
87Fayette-5
88Lakel/Star-4
89Lakel/Star-4
Cabrera, Carlos
80Utica-3
Cabrera, Francisco
86Ventura-3
87Myrtle-28
88BBAmer-20
88Duned/Star-1
88SLAS-22
89AAA/Pro-16
89F/Up-68
89Syrac/CMC-20
89Syrac/Pro-791
90D-646
90T-254
90UD-64
Cabrera, Fremio
86Wausa-2
Cabrera, Nasusel
88Madis-6
Cabrera, Victor
86CharRa-4
Cacciatore, Frank
88AubAs/Pro-1967
89Tucso/Pro-202
Cacciatore, Paul
76Wausa
77Wausa
79Jacks-10
Cacek, Craig Thomas
78Charl
79Portl-18
80Port-3
81Portl-9
82Spoka-14
Caceres, Edgar
86WPalm-7
87Jaxvl-9
89Saraso/Star-2
Caci, Bob
86Beloi-3
Cadahia, Aurelio
(Chino)
80OrlTw-13
81Toled-11
82Orlan/B-15
82OrlTw/A-3
83Orlan-10
86DayBe-4MG
87Gasto-3
Cadahia, Ben
81CharR-15
82FtMyr-4
86Tulsa-12
Cadaret, Greg
85Huntsvl/BK-34
88D-528
88D/A's/Bk-528
88Modesto-35
88Moth/A's-26
88T-328
89D-479
89F-4
89Moth/A's-20
89Score-340
89Score/Tr-69
89T-552
90D-545
90F-440
90T-659
90UD-549
Cadian, Larry
89Portl/CMC-7
Cadore, Leon
21Exh-20
61T-403M
72F/FFeat-19M
72Laugh/GF-37M
E120
E220
V100
V61-97
W572
Cady, Charles B.
(Charlie)
No Cards.
Cady, Forrest LeRoy
(Hick)
BF2-2
D328-24
D329-25
E135-24
M101/4-25
T205
Cafego, Thomas
(Tom)
No Cards.
Caffie, Joseph C.
(Joe)
58T-182
Caffrey, Bob
85T-394
87WPalm-10
88Jaxvl/Best-25
88Jaxvl/Pro-979
88SLAS-19
Caffyn, Benjamin T.
(Ben)
No Cards.
Cage, Wayne Levell
76Wmspt
78T-706R
79OPC-70
79T-150
79Tacom-26
80T-208
80Tacom-4
Cahill, John F.P.
(Patsy)
N172
N284
Cahill, Mark
80Wausa-3
81LynnS-3
83Chatt-21
Cahill, Thomas H.
(Tom)
No Cards.
Cain, Aaron
81Hawai-9
82Hawai-9
Cain, Bob
50B-236
51B-197
52B-19
52T-349
53B/Col-56
53T-266
54B-195
54T-61
Cain, Cal
86Cedar/TCMA-19
87Cedar-18
Cain, Jerald
83VeroB-23
Cain, John
88Rockford-4
89Rockford-4TR
Cain, Les
69T-324R
71K-29
71MLB/St-388
71OPC-101
71T-101
72T-783
Caines, Arturo
89Brist/Star-3
Cairo, Sergio
89Bluef/Star-6
Caithamer, George T.
No Cards.
Cajide, Al
78DaytB
Cakora, Matthew
88CharWh/Best-17
89CharlK-20
89CharWh/Best-22
89CharWh/Pro-1770
Cala, Craig A.
88CapeCod/Sum-92
Calderon, Ivan
81Wausa-26
82Wausa-10
83Chatt-27
84Cram/PCL-173
85F/Up-U17
85Moth/Mar-26
86D-435
86F-462
86Leaf-204
86Moth/Mar-15
86OPC-382
86T-382
87Coke/WS-14
87D/OD-230
87F-488
87F/Slug-7
87T/Tr-15T
88Coke/WS-3
88D-182
88D-25DK
88D-BC5
88D/Best-25
88D/DKsuper-25DK
88F-394
88F/BB/MVP-4
88F/LL-3
88F/Mini-14
88F/St-14
88Leaf-175
88Leaf-25DK
88OPC-184
88Panini/St-63
88Score-607
88Score/YS/II-22
88Sf-166
88T-184
88T/Big-63
88T/Coins-6
88T/Mini-7
88T/St-285
88T/UK-9
89B-68
89Coke/WS-7
89D-371
89D/Best-193
89F-493
89OPC-101
89RedFoley/St-16
89Score-331
89T-656
89T/Big-289
89T/St-297
89UD-650
90D-294
90F-529
90Score-94
90Sf-167
90T-569
90UD-503
Calderon, Jose
81Buffa-16
84Cram/PCL-207
85Maine-3
87ArkTr-4
87Louvl-8
Calderone, Samuel F.
(Sammy)
53T-260
54JC-42
54T-68
79TCMA-236
Caldwell, Bruce
No Cards.
Caldwell, Earl W.
47TipTop
Caldwell, Ralph M.
(Mike)
73OPC-182
73T-182
74OPC-344
74T-344
75OPC-347
75T-347
75T/M-347
76OPC-157
76SSPC-93
76T-157
77T-452
78T-212
79Ho-14
79OPC-356
79T-651
80OPC-269
80T-515
81D-86
81F-512
81OPC-85
81T-85
81T/St-97
82D-330
82F-136
82OPC-378
82Pol/Brew
82Pol/Brew-48
82T-378
83D-154
83F-29
83Gard-4
83OPC-142
83Pol/Brew-48
83T-142
83T/St-184
83T/St-185
84D-237
84F-196
84Gard-3
84Nes/792-605
84OPC-326
84Pol/Brew-48
84T-605
85D-490
85F-577
85T-419
85T/St-289
Caldwell, Raymond B.
(Ray)
14CJ-129
15CJ-129
D329-27
D350/2-25
M101/4-27
M101/5-25
Caldwell, Rich
84Newar-17
85CharO-19
Calhoun, Brad
77AppFx
Calhoun, Jeff
83ColumAst-13
85F/Up-U18
85Moth/Ast-24
86D-426
86F-295
86Pol/Ast-19
86T-534
87D-578
87F-52
87Maine-14
87Maine/TCMA-2
87T-282
87T/Tr-16T
88D-509
88F-299
88T-38
89UD-33
Calhoun, John Charles
No Cards.
Calhoun, Ray
89GreatF-30
Calhoun, William D.
(Bill)
No Cards.
Calise, Michael S.
80ArkTr-6
81Louvl-21
82Louvl-4
84RochR-5
85Cram/PCL-63
Call, Keith
82Madis-26
83Madis/LF-14
84Nashvl-3
Callaghan, Martin F.
(Marty)
E120
V61-66
W573
Callahan, Ben
82Nashv-4
83Colum-14
83Nashvl-4
Callahan, Edward J.
(Ed)
No Cards.
Callahan, James J.
(Nixey)
10Domino-19
11Helmar-8
12Sweet/Pin-8
14CJ-111
D329-26
D350/2-24
E107
E224
E270/2
E300
M101/4-26
M101/5-24
T207
WG5-7
WG6-6
Callahan, Mike
83DayBe-4
Callahan, Patrick B.
79WHave-6
81Colum-4
82Nashv-5
Callahan, Patrick H.
(Pat)
No Cards.
Callahan, Steve
89Everett/Star-3
Callahan, Wesley L.
(Wes)
No Cards.
Callas, Pete
87CharWh-6
88Clearw/Star-4
Callaway, Frank B.
E120
Calley, Robert
85Visal-10
86Visal-5
Callis, Al
75Clint
Callison, John W.
(Johnny)
59T-119
60L-118
60T-17
61T-434
61T-468
61T/St-50
62Bz
62P/Can-118

62Salada-204
62Shirriff-204
62T-17
62T/St-165
63Bz-15
63Exh
63F-51
63J-179
63P-179
63Salada-26
63T/SO
64Bz-15
64T-135
64T/Coins-50
64T/S-36
64T/St-80
64T/SU
64T/tatt
65Bz-15
65OPC-4LL
65T-310
65T-4LL
65T/E-32
65T/trans-41
66Bz-12
66OPC-52M
66T-230
66T-52M
66T/RO
67Bz-12
67OPC-85
67OPC/PI-14
67T-309M
67T-85
67T/PI-14
68T-415
69MB-47
69MLB/St-174
69MLBPA/Pin-37
69OPC-133
69T-133
69T/St-73
70MLB/St-15
70OPC-375
70T-375
71MLB/St-28
71OPC-12
71T-12
72MB-60
72OPC-364
72T-364
72T/Cloth-4
73OPC-535
73T-535
74Laugh/ASG-64
78TCMA-29
Exh47
PM10/L-8

Calmus, Dick
64T-231
68T-427

Calufetti, Larry
76Wausa

Calvert, Art
87PrWill-8
88FtLaud/Star-3
89Star/Wax-48
89StPet/Star-4

Calvert, Chris
85Visal-12
87Visal-13
88Clearw/Star-5
88Readg/Pro-886
89Readg/Best-21
89Readg/Pro-664
89Readg/Star-5

Calvert, Mark
81Phoen-9
83Phoen/BHN-2
84Cram/PCL-2
85Maine-4

Calvey, Jack
46Sunbeam

Calvo, Jacinto
(Jack)
No Cards.

Calzado, Francis
84Evrt/Cram-23

Calzado, Lorenzo
89Savan/Pro-360

Camacho, Adulfo
85Tigres-18

Camacho, Ernie
81T-96R
84Wheat/Ind-13
85D-129
85F-442
85Polar/Ind-13
85T-739
85T/St-253
86F-582
86OhHenry-13
86T-509
87D-350
87F-247
87Gator-13
87OPC-353
87T-353
87T/St-209
88Moth/Ast-16
88Tucso/Pro-189
89Phoen/CMC-6
89Phoen/Pro-1494

Cambria, Fred
71OPC-27R
71T-27R
72OPC-392R
72T-392R

Camelli, Henry R.
(Hank)
47TipTop

Camelo, Pete
86Jaxvl/TCMA-6
87Jaxvl-4

Cameron, John S.
No Cards.

Cameron, Paul
84CharO-5
85CharO-30
87CharO/WBTV-xx

Camilli, Adolf Louis
(Dolf)
34G-91
35BU-150
36Exh/4-6
36G-5
37Exh/4-6
38Exh/4-2
38Wheat-16
39Exh
39PB-86
40PB-68
40Wheat-11
41DP-20
41PB-51
61F-97
89Smok/Dodg-42
PM10/Sm-19
R302
R312
R313
R314
WG8-4

Camilli, Douglass J.
(Doug)
61Union
62T-594R
63T-196
64T-249
65OPC-77
65T-77
66T-593
67T-551
73OPC-131CO
73T-131C
85Greens-1
86Greens-3MG
87WinHav-24

Camilli, Kevin
86Greens-4
88Fay/Pro-1099

Camilli, Louis Steven
(Lou)
71MLB/St-364
71OPC-612R
71T-612R

Caminiti, Ken
86ColumAst-6
87S/Rook-37
87SLAS-10
88Class/Blue-228
88D-308
88F-441
88OPC-64
88Score-164
88Score/YS/I-29
88Sf-124
88T-64
88T/St-33
88ToysRUs-6
88Tucso-3
88Tucso/CMC-11
88Tucso/Pro-182
89D-542
89D/Best-262
89Lennox/Ast-21
89Moth/Ast-25
89T-369
89T/Big-210
89UD-141
90D-424
90F-225
90Score-76
90Sf-209
90T-531
90UD-122

Camnitz, Samuel H.
(Howard)
10Domino-20
11Helmar-155
12Sweet/Pin-134A
12Sweet/Pin-134B
14CJ-16
14Piedmont/St-8
15CJ-16
D322
E224
E254
E270/1
E90/1
E97
L1-124
M116
S74-107
S81-99
T202
T205
T206
T207
T213/blue
T215/blue
T215/brown
T3-7

Camp, Howard Lee
(Howie)
No Cards.

Camp, Llewellan R.
No Cards.

Camp, Rick
77T-475R
78T-349
79Richm-21
79T-105
81D-197
81F-246
81OPC-87
81Pol/Atl-37
81T-87
81T/St-150
82BK/Lids-5
82D-223
82F-432
82OPC-138
82Pol/Atl-37
82T-637
83D-149
83F-133
83Pol/Atl-37
83T-207
84D-165
84F-174
84Nes/792-597
84OPC-136
84Pol/Atl-37
84T-597
85D-409
85F-321
85Ho/Braves-5
85Leaf-130
85OPC-167
85Pol/Atl-37
85T-491
86D-385
86F-510
86T-319

Camp, Scott
86Osceola-3

Campagno, Steve
82Oneon-9

Campanella, Roy
49B-84
49Eureka-32
50B-75
50Drake-6
51B-31
52B-44
52BR
52StarCal/L-79C
52T-314
52TipTop
52Wheat
53B/Col-46
53Exh/Can-20
53RM-NL5
53SM
53T-27
54B-90
54NYJour
54RM-NL13
54Wilson
55B-22
55Gol/Dodg-5
56T-101
57T-210
57T-400M
58BB
59T-550
60NuCard-29
61NuCard-429
61T-480MV
75OPC-189M
75OPC-191M
75OPC-193M
75T-189MV
75T-191MV
75T-193MV
75T/M-189MV
75T/M-191MV
75T/M-193MV
79TCMA-43
79TCMA-8
80Cram/Leg-90
80SSPC/HOF
83D/HOF-39
83MLBPA/Pin-20
84West/1-22
86S/Dec-33
88Pac/Leg-47
89HOF/St-54
89Rini/Dodg-9
89Smok/Dodg-4
Exh47
PM10/Sm-20A
PM10/Sm-20B
PM10/Sm-21
R423-12

Campaneris, Blanco D.
(Bert)
65OPC-266
65T-266
66Bz-44
66OPC-175
66T-175
66T/RO-108
67Bz-44
67OPC/PI-2
67T-515
67T/PI-2
68OPC-109
68T-109
69MB-48
69MLB/St-83
69T-423AS
69T-495
69T-556M
69T/S-29
69T/St-212
70K-39
70MLB/St-255
70OPC-205
70T-205
70T/PI-23
71Bz
71Bz/Test-31
71MLB/St-508
71OPC-440
71T-440
71T/Coins-64
71T/GM-6
71T/S-31
71T/tatt-7
72MB-61
72OPC-75
72T-75
73OPC-209WS
73OPC-295
73OPC-64LL
73T-295
73T-64
74K-4
74OPC-155
74OPC-335AS
74OPC-474WS
74OPC-478WS
74T-155
74T-335AS
74T/DE-46
74T/St-223
75Ho-28
75Ho/Twink-28
75OPC-170
75T-170
75T/M-170
76Ho-61
76OPC-580
76SSPC-492
76T-580
77Ho-149
77K-2
77OPC-74
77T-373
78BK/R-14
78T-260
78T/Zest-2
78Wiffle/Discs-12
79OPC-326
79T-620
80OPC-264
80T-505

81D-50
81F-280
81T-410
82D-593
82F-454
82T-772
83Colum-17
83T/X-18
84F-120
84Nes/792-139
84Nes/792-711LL
84Nes/792-714LL
84T-139
84T-711
84T-714
87Moth/A's-1
89Pac/Leg-157

Campanis, Alexander
(Al)
No Cards.

Campanis, James A.
(Jim)
67OPC-12R
67T-12R
68T-281
69T-396
70T-671
71MLB/St-196
74OPC-513
74T-513

Campanis, Jim Jr.
88T/Tr-23T
89SanBern/Best-1
89SanBern/Cal-85

Campas, Mike
89Hamil/Star-7

Campau, Charles C.
(Count)
N172

Campbell, Arthur V.
(Vin)
15CJ-168
D322
M116

Campbell, Bill
74OPC-26
74T-26
75OPC-226
75T-226
75T/M-226
76OPC-288
76SSPC-208
76T-288
77OPC-12
77OPC-8LL
77T-166
77T-8LL
78Ho-107
78OPC-87
78OPC-8LL
78PapaG/Disc-22
78T-208LL
78T-545
79OPC-195
79T-375
80T-15
81F-240
81OPC-256
81T-396
82D-487
82F-289
82RedLob
82T-619
82T/Tr-16T
83D-504
83F-493
83T-436
83Thorn-39
84D-555
84F-489
84F/X-23
84Nes/792-787
84T-787
84T/X-22
85D-163
85F-245
85F/Up-U19
85OPC-209
85T-209
85T/Tr-15T
86D-571
86F-28
86F/Up-U17
86T-112
86T/Tr-17T
87F-146
87OPC-362
87T-674
89Pac/Leg-191

Campbell, Bruce D.
35BU-152
41PB-37
R305
R313

Campbell, Clarence
(Soup)
40PB-200
41DP-131

Campbell, Darrin
89Saraso/Star-3

Campbell, David Alan
(Dave)
78T-402
79T-9

Campbell, David W.
(Dave)
69T-324R
70MLB/St-110
70T-639
71MLB/St-221
71OPC-46
71T-46
72OPC-384
72T-384
73OPC-488
73T-488
74OPC-556
74T-556
84Smok/Padres-3

Campbell, Donovan
88Idaho/Pro-1845
89BurlB/Pro-1620
89BurlB/Star-3

Campbell, Greg
83BurlR-28
83BurlR/LF-25TR
84Tulsa-TR
85OKCty-14
86OKCty-2TR

Campbell, James R.
(Jim)
63Pep
63T-373
64T-303

Campbell, Jim
88Memph/Best-10
89F-646M
89Memph/Best-17
89Memph/Pro-1194
89Memph/Star-5
89Smok/Ast-13

Campbell, Joseph Earl
(Joe)
No Cards.

Campbell, Kevin
87VeroB-17
88VeroB/Star-2
89Bakers/Cal-182

Campbell, Marc T.
(Hutch)
No Cards.

Campbell, Mark
82DayBe-17

Campbell, Mike
86Cedar/TCMA-4
87Calgary-14
87Tampa-21
88D-30
88D/Best-163
88D/Rook-2
88F-372
88Leaf-30RR
88Moth/Sea-18
88T-246
89D-497
89F-543
89Moth/Sea-18
89Score-568
89Score/HotRk-86
89Score/YS/II-30
89T-143
89UD-337

Campbell, Paul M.
No Cards.

Campbell, Ronald T.
(Ron)
67T-497

Campbell, Samuel
(Sam)
No Cards.

Campbell, Steve
82Idaho-23

Campbell, William G.
(Gilly)
32Orbit/num-34
32Orbit/un-9
35BU-164
35G-8D
35G-9D

Campbell, William J.
E270/1
T206
T213/blue
T213/brown

Camper, Cardell
78T-711R

Campisi, Sal
70T-716R
71OPC-568
71T-568

Campos, Francisco J.
(Frank)
52T-307
53T-51

Campos, Frank
88CharWh/Best-24
89CharWh/Best-23
89CharWh/Pro-1767

Campusano, Silvestre
86Knoxv-4
87Syrac-1
87Syrac/TCMA-18
88D/Rook-42
88F/U-U66
88Score/Tr-93T
88T/Tr-24T
88Tor/Fire-6
89Class-137
89D-584
89OPC-191
89Score-473
89Syrac/CMC-21
89Syrac/Pro-808
89T-191
89Tor/Fire-6
89UD-45

Campusano, Teo
89AubAs/Pro-2162

Canady, Chuckie
82BurlR-16
83Tulsa-14
84OKCty-17
85OKCty-29

Canale, George
87Stockton-18
88ElPas/Best-5
89Denver/CMC-19
89Denver/Pro-35
90D-699
90F-641
90Score-656
90T-344
90UD-59

Canan, Dick
86Peoria-2
87Peoria-5
89WinSal/Star-3

Canavan, James Edward
(Jimmy)
N172

Cancel, Victor
88Wythe/Pro-1980

Candaele, Casey
85Indianap-25
86Indianap-33
87Class/Up-128
87D-549
87D/Rook-33
87F/U-U16
87S-158M
87S/Rook-6
87T/Tr-17T
88D-179
88D/Best-68
88F-181
88Ho/Disc-12
88Leaf-199
88OPC-87
88Panini/St-329
88RedFoley/St-11
88Score-97
88Score/YS/I-34
88Sf-140
88T-431
88T/Gloss60-60
88T/JumboR-11
88T/St-305
88T/St-77
88ToysRUs-7
89Tucso/CMC-16
89Tucso/Pro-197
89UD-58

Candelari, Rick
89Wausa/GS-21

Candelaria, Al
83Ander-9

Candelaria, John
76Crane-7
76Ho-92
76MSA/Disc
76OPC-317
76SSPC-563
76T-317
77Ho-80
77K-7
77OPC-59
77Pep-63
77T-510
78Ho-104
78K-18
78OPC-221
78OPC-7LL
78T-190
78T-207LL
79Ho-86
79K-34
79OPC-29
79T-70
80OPC-332
80T-635
81Coke
81D-374
81F-375
81OPC-265
81T-265
82D-297
82F-479
82OPC-3
82T-425
83D-549
83F-304
83OPC-127
83T-291TL
83T-755
83T/St-282
84D-357
84F-247
84F/St-57
84FunFood/Pin-50
84Nes/792-330
84OPC-330
84T-330
84T/St-127
85D-430
85F-462
85F/St-98
85Leaf-157
85OPC-50
85T-50
85T/St-123
86D-499
86F-150
86OPC-140
86S-129M
86Smok/Cal-16
86T-140
87D-551
87F-75
87F/AwardWin-5
87F/Lim-C3
87Leaf-242
87OPC-313
87S-148
87Smok/AL-3
87Smok/Cal-1
87T-630
88D-608
88D/Best-20
88D/Y/Bk-NEW
88F/U-U46
88Score-293
88Score/Tr-40T
88T-546
88T/Tr-25T
89B-171
89D-192
89F-251
89OPC-285
89Panini/St-397
89Score-246
89Score/NWest-8
89Sf-202
89T-285
89T/St-306
89UD-248
90T-485

Candelaria, Jorge
88Oneon/Pro-2055
89Boise/Pro-1998
89Reno/Cal-242

Candini, Mario
49Remar
51B-255

Candiotti, Tom
81ElPas-22
84Cram/PCL-32
84D-393
84F-197
84Nes/792-262
84T-262
86F/Up-U18
86OhHenry-49
86T/Tr-18T
87D-342
87D/OD-104
87F-248
87F/Mini-16
87F/St-18
87Gator-49

87Leaf-81
87OPC-296
87T-463
87T/Mini-50
87T/St-211
88D-377
88D/Best-112
88F-604
88Gator-49
88OPC-123
88Panini/St-69
88Score-595
88Sf-37
88T-123
88T/Big-93
89B-80
89D-256
89D/Best-117
89F-399
89Panini/St-317
89RedFoley/St-17
89Score-239
89T-599
89T/Big-267
89T/St-211
89UD-470
90D-256
90F-488
90Score-269
90Sf-126
90T-743
90UD-388

Caneira, John
75QuadC
77SLCty
78Cr/PCL-55

Canestro, Art
88Oneon/Pro-2060
89Oneon/Pro-2104

Cangelosi, John
83AppFx/LF-13
86Coke/WS-44
86D/HL-51
86D/Rook-51
86F/Up-U19
86S/Rook-31
86T/Tr-19T
87D-162
87F-489
87Leaf-251
87OPC-201
87S-157M
87Seven-C3
87T-201
87T/GlossRk-2
87T/Mini-49
87T/St-293
87T/Tr-18T
88D-435
88F-325
88OPC-328
88Panini/St-377
88Score-418
88T-506
89Score-601
89T-592
89UD-67
90D-565
90Score-367
90T-29
90UD-370

Cangemi, Jamie
87Beloi-7
89Stock/Best-6
89Stock/Cal-150
89Stock/Pro-389
89Stock/Star-13

Canino, Carlos
88Geneva/Pro-1655

Cannell, Virgin Wirt
(Rip)
No Cards.

Cannizzaro, Chris Jr.
86Pawtu-4
87Pawtu-27
87Pawtu/TCMA-2
88Pawtu/CMC-15
88Pawtu/Pro-451
89Pawtu/CMC-11
89Pawtu/Dunkin-7
89Pawtu/Pro-686

Cannizzaro, Chris
61T-118
62T-26
65OPC-61
65T-61
66T-497
69OPC-131
69T-131
70OPC-329
70T-329
71MLB/St-222
71OPC-426
71T-426
71T/Coins-109
71T/tatt-6
72T-759
75OPC-355
75T-355
75T/M-355
81Redwd-28
82Redwd-25MG

Cannon, Joseph Jerome
(J.J.)
75Dubuq
78Charl
79Syrac-7
80OPC-118
80T-221
81Syrac-17
82Knoxv-18
86Knoxv-5
87Knoxv-26
89Knoxv/Best-25
89Knoxv/Pro-1129
89Knoxv/Star-24

Cannon, Scott
86Kinston-3

Cannon, Stan
79Wisco-16

Cannon, Tim
83Miami-22

Cano, Jose
83Ander-8
84Durhm-22
87Osceola-27
88Tucso-4
88Tucso/CMC-7
88Tucso/Pro-171
89ColMud/Best-25
90UD-43

Canseco, Jose
83Madis/LF-13
85Huntsvl/BK-44
86D-39
86D/HL-55
86D/Rook-22
86F-649M
86F/LL-3
86F/Mini-87
86F/Slug-5
86F/St-19
86F/Up-U20
86Moth/A's-9
86S-178M
86S/Rook-11
86SLAS-14
86T/Tr-20T
87Class-46
87Class/Up-125
87D-6DK
87D-97
87D-PC12
87D/AAS-21
87D/DKsuper-6
87D/HL-40M
87D/OD-24
87D/WaxBox-PC12
87Drake-4
87F-389
87F-625M
87F-628M
87F-633M
87F/AwardWin-6
87F/Excit-7
87F/GameWin-8
87F/HL-2
87F/Hottest-9
87F/Lim-6
87F/LL-8
87F/McCror-6
87F/Mini-17
87F/RecSet-3
87F/Slug-8
87F/St-131M
87F/St-19
87Ho/St-28
87KayBee-7
87Kraft-35
87Leaf-151
87Leaf-6DK
87MnM's-10
87Moth/A's-26
87Moth/A's-27M
87MSA/Discs-17
87OPC-247
87RedFoley/St-63
87S-80M
87S-90
87Smok/A's-2
87Smok/AL-1
87T-620
87T/Coins-6
87T/Gloss60-59
87T/GlossRk-3
87T/HL-12
87T/Mini-68
87T/St-164
87T/St-304
87ToysRUs-5
87Woolwth-12
88Bz-3
88Class/Red-165
88Class/Red-197M
88D-302
88D/A's/Bk-302
88D/Best-22
88F-276
88F-624M
88F/AwardWin-4
88F/BB/AS-5
88F/BB/MVP-3
88F/Excit-7
88F/Hottest-5
88F/LL-4
88F/Mini-45
88F/RecSet-4
88F/Slug-6
88F/SS-5
88F/St-54
88F/TL-3
88KayBee-3
88KMart-4
88Leaf-138
88Moth/A's-7
88Nestle-37
88OPC-370
88Panini/St-173
88Score-45
88Score/YS/I-30
88Sf-201
88T-370
88T/Big-13
88T/Coins-7
88T/Gloss60-55
88T/Mini-30
88T/St-173
88T/St/Backs-48
88T/UK-10
89Ames-8
89B-201
89Bz-5
89Cadaco-5
89Class-103
89Class-3
89Crunch-1
89D-643M
89D-91
89D/AS-2
89D/AS-30
89D/Best-57
89D/GrandSlam-1
89D/MVP-BC5
89D/PopUp-2
89F-5
89F-628M
89F-634M
89F/AS-2
89F/BBAS-5
89F/BBMVP's-6
89F/Excit-3
89F/Heroes-5
89F/LL-3
89F/Superstar-6
89F/WaxBox-C4
89F/WS-3
89Holsum/Discs-5
89KayBee-3
89KingB/Discs-17
89KMart/DT-18
89Master/Discs-10
89Modesto/Ch-34
89Moth/A's-7
89Moth/ROY's-1
89Moth/ROY's-4M
89Moth/Canseco-1
89Moth/Canseco-2
89Moth/Canseco-3
89Moth/Canseco-4
89Nissen-5
89OPC-389
89Panini/St-238AS
89Panini/St-246
89Panini/St-422
89Panini/St-477
89Panini/St-480
89Panini/St-8
89Ralston-12
89RedFoley/St-18
89Score-1
89Score-582M
89Score-655HL
89Score/HotSt-1
89Score/Mast-40
89Sf-1
89Sf-221M
89T-401AS
89T-500
89T/Big-190
89T/Coins-29
89T/DH-5
89T/Gloss22-6
89T/Gloss60-12
89T/HeadsUp-18
89T/Hills-5
89T/Mini-68
89T/St-11
89T/St-148
89T/St-171
89T/St/Backs-13
89T/UK-12
89Tacom/Pro-1536
89Tetley/Discs-18
89UD-371
89UD-659MVP
89UD-664M
89UD-670TC
89Woolwth-1
89Woolwth-23
90Class-22
90D-125
90F-3
90F-629
90Score-375
90Score/100St-5
90Sf-23
90T-250
90UD-66

Canseco, Ozzie
83Greens-3
87Madis-6
88Madis-7
88MidwLAS/GS-51
89Huntsvl/Best-28
89UD/Ext-756

Cantrell, Dave
89Salin/Cal-129
89Salin/Pro-1826

Cantwell, Ben
33G-139
35BU-96
35G-8L
35G-9L
R308-168
R332-25
V354-14
WG8-5

Cantwell, Rob
88Spoka/Pro-1924
89Watlo/Pro-1780
89Watlo/Star-2

Cantz, Bartholomew L.
(Bart)
N172

Capel, Mike
84MidldC-10
86Pittsf-3
87IowaC-4
88D/Rook-46
88IowaC/CMC-1
88IowaC/Pro-547
89F-643M
89IowaC/CMC-1
89IowaC/Pro-1706
89T-767

Capellan, Carlos
88Keno/Pro-1396
89Visal/Cal-112
89Visal/Pro-1441

Capello, Pete
87AppFx-4
88Virgini/Star-4
89AppFx/Pro-865

Capilla, Doug
78OPC-11
78T-477
80T-628
81D-587
81F-309
81T-136
82T-537
82Wichi-3

Capowski, Jim
78Ashev
79Tulsa-4

Cappadona, Pete
86NewBrit-5

Cappuzzello, George
77Evansvl/TCMA-5
78Indianap-15
79Indianap-16
81Evans-2
82F-264
82T-137
82Tucso-20
83T-422
84Colum-7
84Colum/Pol-4

Capra, Lee
(Buzz)

72OPC-141R
72T-141R
75OPC-105
75OPC-311LL
75T-105
75T-311LL
75T/M-105
75T/M-311LL
76Ho-85
76OPC-153
76SSPC-1
76T-153
77T-432
78T-578
83Ander-6
86AppFx-5CO
87BurlEx-21
88Spart/Pro-1047
88Spart/Star-23
88Spart/Star-7

Capra, Nick Lee
79Tulsa-20
80Tulsa-8
83OKCty-4
84OKCty-11
85OKCty-25
86BuffB-7
87OKCty-23
88Omaha/CMC-12
88Omaha/Pro-1499
89F-279
89Omaha/CMC-19
89Omaha/Pro-1742

Capri, Patrick N.
(Pat)
No Cards.

Caprillo, Matias
85Tigres-25

Capron, Ralph Earl
No Cards.

Caraballo, Felix
88Madis-8
88Modesto-5

Caraballo, Ramon
87Clearw-11
88Clearw/Star-6

Caraballo, Wilmer
85Lynch-21
86Lynch-5
87BirmB/Best-6

Carabello, Nelson
89Well/Puc-9

Caray, Harry
88Peoria/Ko-8

Carballo, Lee
88SLCty-28
88Virgini/Star-5

Carbine, John C.
No Cards.

Carbo, Bernardo
(Bernie)
70OPC-36R
70T-36R
71MLB/St-51
71OPC-478
71T-478
72OPC-463
72T-463
73OPC-171
73T-171
74OPC-621
74T-621
75OPC-379
75T-379
75T/M-379
76OPC-278
76SSPC-411
76T-278
77T-159
78T-524
79T-38
80T-266

Carcione, Tom
88SoOreg/Pro-1699
89Madis/Star-6
89Modesto/Ch-19

Cardenal, Jose
65T-374R
66T-505
66T/RO-80
67OPC-193
67T-193
68OPC-102
68T-102
69MB-49
69MLB/St-40
69T-325
69T/S-15
69T/St-164
69Trans-5
70MLB/St-136
70T-675
71K-26
71MLB/St-270
71OPC-435
71T-435
72MB-62
72OPC-12
72T-12
72T-757TR
73OPC-393
73T-393
74OPC-185
74T-185
74T/DE-55
74T/St-12
75Ho-65
75Ho/Twink-65
75K-29
75OPC-15
75T-15
75T/M-15
76Crane-8
76Ho-37
76Ho/Twink-37
76MSA/Disc
76OPC-430
76T-430
77Ho-85
77OPC-127
77T-610
77T/CS-9
78T-210
79BK/P-18
79T-317
80T-512
81T-473
89Pac/Leg-149
89Swell-61

Cardenas, Leonardo L.
(Leo)
60T-119
61T-244
61T/St-16
62Kahn
62T-381
63FrBauer-2
63J-127
63Kahn
63P-127
63T-203
64Kahn
64T-72
65Kahn
65T-437
66Kahn
66T-370
67Kahn
67OPC/PI-10
67T-325
67T/PI-10
68Kahn
68OPC-23
68T-23
68T-480M
69MB-50
69T-265
70MLB/St-231
70OPC-245
70T-245
71MLB/St-460
71OPC-405
71T-405
71T/Coins-148
71T/tatt-8
72K-30
72MB-63
72T-561
72T-562A
73OPC-522
73T-522
75OPC-518
75T-518
75T/M-518
76OPC-587
76SSPC-261
76T-587
78TCMA-69
83Wisco/LF-15

Cardieri, Ron
82Miami-9

Cardinal, Conrad
(Randy)
63T-562R

Cardoz, Don
78RochR

Cardwell, Buddy
77Wausa

Cardwell, Don
57T-374
58T-372
59T-314
60T-384
61NuCard-410
61P-194
61T-393M
61T-564
62T-495
62T/bucks
62T/St-106
63Sugar-A
63T-575
64T-417
65T-502
66EH-43
66T-235
67T-555
68T-437
69MB-51
69OPC-193
69T-193
70OPC-83
70T-83
72MB-64
78TCMA-89

Cardwood, Alfredo
85Orlan-15
86Visal-6
87WPalm-4

Carew, Rodney Cline
(Rod)
67T-569R
68Bz-13
68Coke
68OPC-80
68T-363AS
68T-80
68T/G-29
69MB-52
69MLB/St-65
69MLBPA/Pin-4
69OPC/DE-3
69T-419AS
69T-510
69T/DE-12
69T/St-192
70K-47
70MB-4
70MLB/St-232
70OPC-290
70OPC-453AS
70OPC-62LL
70T-290
70T-453AS
70T-62LL
70T/PI-16
71MLB/St-461
71OPC-210
71T-210
71T/Coins-24
71T/tatt-15
72MB-65
72T-695
72T-696A
73K-51
73OPC-330
73OPC-61LL
73T-330
73T-61LL
73T/Lids-9
74K-30
74OPC-201LL
74OPC-333AS
74OPC-50
74T-201LL
74T-333M
74T-50
74T/DE-32
74T/DE-36
74T/St-203
75Ho-56
75K-33
75OPC-306LL
75OPC-600
75T-306LL
75T-600
75T/M-306LL
75T/M-600
76Crane-9
76Ho-33
76Ho/Twink-33
76K-48
76MSA/Disc
76OPC-192LL
76OPC-400
76SSPC-214
76T-192LL
76T-400
77Ho-9
77K-53
77OPC-143
77Pep-2
77T-120
77T/CS-10
78Ho-140
78K-29
78OPC-1LL
78OPC-230
78PapaG/Disc-35
78T-201LL
78T-580
78Wiffle/Discs-13
79Ho-38
79K-13
79OPC-151
79T-1LL
79T-300
79T/Comics-11
80BK/PHR-14
80K-60
80OPC-353
80T-700
80T/S-12
81D-169
81D-49
81Drake-2
81F-268
81F/St-40
81K-26
81MSA/Disc-6
81OPC-100
81Sqt-9
81T-100
81T/HT
81T/Nat/Super-4
81T/S
81T/SO-18
81T/St-49
82D-216
82Drake-6
82F-455
82F/St-217
82K-51
82KMart-31
82OPC-187
82OPC-363IA
82OPC-36AS
82T-276TL
82T-500
82T-501A
82T-547
82T/St-131
82T/St-160
83D-8DK
83D-90
83D/AAS-38
83Drake-3
83F-81
83K-1
83OPC-200
83OPC-201SV
83OPC-386AS
83Seven-1
83T-200
83T-201A
83T-386
83T-651
83T/Gloss-29
83T/Gloss40-29
83T/St-39
84D-352
84D/Champs-21
84Drake-5
84F-511
84F/St-103
84F/St-12
84F/St-54
84FunFood/Pin-35
84MiltBrad-3
84Nes/792-276TL
84Nes/792-600
84Nes/792-710LL
84Nes/792-711LL
84OPC-26
84Ralston-17
84Seven-8W
84Smok/Cal-5
84T-600
84T-710
84T-711
84T/Cereal-17
84T/Gloss22-2
84T/Gloss40-26
84T/St-227
84T/St/Box-11
85D-85
85D/HL-31
85F-297
85F/LimEd-5
85Leaf-132
85OPC-300
85Seven-6W
85Smok/Cal-5
85T-300
85T/Gloss22-13
85T/St-184
85T/St-223
86D-280
86F-151
86F-629M

86F/HOF-4
86F/LL-4
86F/St-20
86OPC-371
86S-106
86S-146M
86S-180M
86S-182M
86S-69M
86S-74M
86T-400
86T/Gloss60-16
86T/St-176
86T/St-4
86Woolwth-6
87KMart-14
87Nestle/DT-12
89Smok/Angels-10

Carey, Andrew Arthur
(Andy)
53T-188
54NYJour
54T-105
55T-20
55T/DH-36
56T-12
57T-290
58T-333
59T-45
60T-196
61T-518
61T/St-158
62J-52
62P-52
62P/Can-52
62Salada-86A
62Salada-86B
62Shirriff-86
62T-418
79TCMA-243
PM10/L-9

Carey, Brooks M.
81RochR-3
82Indianap-9

Carey, George C.
(Scoops)
E107
T206

Carey, Jeff
82WHave-3

Carey, Max George
11Helmar-156
14CJ-73
15CJ-73
21Exh-21
25Exh-50
26Exh-50
28Exh-6
28Yueng-32
40PB-178
61F-12
72Laugh/GF-9
80Laugh/FFeat-12
80SSPC/HOF
89HOF/St-38
89Smok/Dodg-5
BF2-90
D327
D329-28
D350/2-26
E120
E121/120
E121/80
E122
E126-32
E126-32
E210-32
E220
M101/4-28
M101/5-26
T206
T207
T213/brown
V100
V61-71
W501-86
W502-32
W514-22
W573
W575

Carey, Pete
86FtMyr-5
87Tampa-2

Carey, Roger J.
No Cards.

Carey, Thomas Francis
(Tom)
35BU-89
39PB-62
40PB-39

Cargo, Robert J.
(Chick)
No Cards.

Cariel, Rafael
76Shrev

Carisch, Frederick B.
(Fred)
No Cards.

Carista, Mike
85Elmir-3
86WinHav-5
87Greens-5
88EastLAS/Pro-20
88NewBrit/Pro-909
89NewBrit/Pro-605

Carl, Frederick E.
(Fred)
No Cards.

Carl, Jeff
83Memph-5

Carleton, James
(Tex)
34G-48
35G-1A
35G-2A
35G-6A
35G-7A
R310
V354-90

Carley, Dave
87Beloi-19

Carlin, James Arthur
(Jim)
No Cards.

Carlin, Mike
89Spart/Pro-1035
89Spart/Star-3

Carlisle, Walter G.
No Cards.

Carlo
C46-85

Carlos, Cisco
68T-287R
69OPC-54
69T-54
70OPC-487
70T-487
72MB-66

Carlos, Gil
84IowaC-20

Carlson, Bill
87Clint-11
88Clint/Pro-700
89SanJose/Best-9
89SanJose/Cal-229
89SanJose/Pro-439
89SanJose/Star-4

Carlson, Hal
R316
V100
W513-75

Carlson, Tom
76Clint

Carlstrom, Albin O.
(Swede)
No Cards.

Carlton, Steve
65T-477R
67OPC-146
67T-146
68T-408
69T-255
70MLB/St-137
70OPC-220
70OPC-67LL
70T-220
70T-67LL
71MLB/St-271
71OPC-55
71T-55
71T/Coins-115
72MB-67
72OPC-420
72OPC-93LL
72T-420
72T-751TR
72T-93LL
73K-7
73OPC-300
73OPC-65LL
73OPC-66LL
73OPC-67LL
73T-300
73T-65LL
73T-66LL
73T-67
73T/Comics-4
73T/Lids-10
73T/PinUps-4
74JP
74OPC-95
74T-95
74T/DE-5
74T/St-73
75Ho-63
75OPC-185
75OPC-312LL
75T-185
75T-312LL
75T/M-185
75T/M-312LL
76Crane-10
76MSA/Disc
76OPC-355
76SSPC-459
76T-355
77Ho-117
77K-57
77OPC-93
77T-110
77T/CS-11
78Ho-49
78K-1
78OPC-170
78OPC-5LL
78T-205LL
78T-540
78Wiffle/Discs-14
79BK/P-4
79Ho-71
79K-18
79OPC-9
79T-25
80BK/P-15
80BK/PHR-2
80K-14
80OPC-113
80T-210
81Coke
81D-481CY
81D-73
81Drake-23
81F-6
81F-660M
81F/St-85
81K-50
81MSA/Disc-7
81OPC-203
81T-202M
81T-5LL
81T-630
81T-6LL
81T/HT
81T/SO-104
81T/St-206
81T/St-25
81T/St-261
81T/St-28
81T/St-29
82D-42
82Drake-7
82F-243
82F-641M
82F/St-240M
82F/St-241M
82F/St-54
82K-27
82OPC-122IA
82OPC-68
82T-1M
82T-480
82T-481A
82T-636TL
82T/St-129
82T/St-75
83D-16DK
83D-219
83D/AAS-24
83F-155
83K-45
83OPC-384AS
83OPC-70
83OPC-71SV
83T-229TL
83T-406AS
83T-70
83T-705LL
83T-706LL
83T-71A
83T/Gloss-36
83T/Gloss40-36
83T/St-203
83T/St-204
83T/St-267
84D-111
84D/AAS-24
84D/Champs-38
84F-25
84F-642
84F/St-101
84F/St-78
84FunFood/Pin-30
84MiltBrad-4
84Nes/792-136LL
84Nes/792-1HL
84Nes/792-395AS
84Nes/792-4HL
84Nes/792-706LL
84Nes/792-707LL
84Nes/792-708LL
84Nes/792-780
84Nestle/DT-21
84OPC-214
84OPC-395AS
84Ralston-16
84Seven-12E
84T-1
84T-136
84T-395
84T-4
84T-706
84T-707
84T-708
84T-780
84T/Cereal-16
84T/Gloss40-27
84T/St-1
84T/St-119
84T/St-15
84T/St-184
84T/St-2
84T/Super-16
84T/Super-16
85CIGNA-12
85D-305
85D/AAS-55
85Drake-35
85F-246
85F/LimEd-6
85Leaf-113
85OPC-360
85Seven-2S
85Seven-3E
85T-360
85T/3D-25
85T/St-112
85T/Super-24
85Woolwth-6
86BK/AP-6
86D-183
86D/HL-35
86F-435
86F/HOF-2
86F/Mini-91
86F/Slug-M2
86F/St-21
86Keller-1
86Leaf-117
86Meadow/Milk-3
86OPC-120
86S-27
86S-70M
86S/Dec-54
86T-120
86T-246M
86T/St-116
87D-617
87F-490
87F-635M
87F/Excit-8
87F/U-U17
87KMart-15
87OPC-271
87OPC-B
87S-200
87T-718
87T-B
87T/HL-1
87T/Tr-19T
87Woolwth-1
88F-7
89Swell-95

Carlucci, Dave
86Bakers-5

Carlucci, Rich
81Water-1
82Indianap-19
83Indianap-16
84RochR-2
86Syrac-6

Carlucci, Tony
83TriCit-14

Carlyle, Hiram Cleo
(Cleo)
No Cards.

Carlyle, Roy Edward
No Cards.

Carman, Don
80Penin/B-11
80Penin/C-5
82OkCty-24
83Readg-3
84Cram/PCL-204
85F/Up-U20
85T/Tr-16T
86CIGNA-2
86D-427
86F-436
86F/St-22

86Leaf-200
86T-532
87D-432
87F-171
87Leaf-174
87OPC-355
87S-108
87T-355
87T/St-122
88D-385
88D/Best-72
88F-300
88Score-401
88T-415
89B-392
89D-396
89F-564
89OPC-154
89Panini/St-146
89Score-222
89T-154
89T/St-121
89UD-409
90D-604
90F-552
90T-731
90UD-420

Carman, George W.
No Cards.

Carmel, Leon James
(Duke)
60T-120
61Union
63T-544R
64T-44
64T/Coins-81
65OPC-261
65T-261
WG10-4

Carmichael, Al
85Lynch-15
86Lynch-6

Carmody, Kevin
89Beloi/Star-2

Carmona, Greg
89StPet/Star-5

Carmona, Williams
89Martins/Star-4

Carnera, Primo
33SK-43
D305

Carnes, Scott
77QuadC
80ElPas-3
81SLCty-17
82Spoka-15

Carnett, Edwin E.
(Eddie)
43Centen-3

Carney, John Joseph
(Jack)
N172

Carney, Patrick J.
(Pat)
No Cards.

Carney, Ron
78Ashev
79Tulsa-18
80Ashev-14
81Tulsa-10

Carney, William John
(Bill)
No Cards.

Carosielli, Marc
88Wythe/Pro-1999

Carpenter, Cris
88D/Rook-50
88Louvl-13
88Louvl/CMC-8
88Louvl/Pro-428
89Class/Up/2-185
89D-39RR
89D/Rook-40
89F/Up-117
89Louvl-13
89Score/Tr-81
89Score/YS/II-37
89T-282
89T/Big-307
89UD-8
90D-634
90F-243
90Score/100Ris-74
90T-443
90UD-523

Carpenter, Doug
84Greens-9
85Albany-20
86FtLaud-3
87Miami-7
89Reno/Cal-254

Carpenter, Glenn
83DayBe-18
86Tucso-4
87Tucso-2
88Tucso-5
88Tucso/CMC-12
88Tucso/Pro-173

Carpenter, John
45Centen-3

Carpenter, Paul
44Centen-2
47Centen-3

Carpenter, Warren W.
(Hick)
N172

Carper, Mark
88CapeCod/Sum-172

Carpin, Frank
66OPC-71
66T-71

Carpio, Jorge
82QuadC-5
84MidldC-6

Carr, Charles Carbitt
(Charlie)
E107
E254
E270/1
E270/2
T206

Carr, Chuck
88MidwLAS/GS-56
88Wausa/Feder-8
88Wausa/GS-8
89Jacks/GS-2

Carr, Ernie
88GreatF-4
89Bakers/Cal-200

Carr, Lewis Smith
(Lew)
No Cards.

Carr, Terence
86Cram/PCL-95
87QuadC-1
88QuadC/GS-9
89Reno/Cal-255

Carrano, Rick
86Miami-4TR

Carranza, Javier
83StPet-2

Carrasco, Carlos
88Bakers/Cal-251
89Reno/Cal-243

Carrasco, Claudio
86Watlo-5
87Watlo-26
88Wmspt/Pro-1320
89QuadC/Best-23
89QuadC/GS-29
89Reno/Cal-259

Carrasco, Ernie
83Erie-22
84Savan-15
86ArkTr-3

Carrasco, Hector
89Kingspt/Star-4

Carrasco, Norman
82Danvi-28
83Redwd-5
85Cram/PCL-22
86Edmon-2
87Edmon-19
88MidldA/GS-25
89Toled/CMC-20
89Toled/Pro-768

Carrasquel, Alfonso
(Chico)
51B-60
51FB
51T/BB-26
52B-41
52BR
52Dix-53
52StarCal/L-73D
52T-251
53B/Col-54
53Exh/Can-4
54B-54
54RM-AL19
55B-173
55RFG-4
55RM-AL23
55Salem
56T-230
57T-67
58Hires-11
58T-55
59T-264
79TCMA-74
Exh47
PM10/Sm-22
R423-9

Carrasquel, Emilio
82BirmB-22

Carraway, Rod
82Watlo/B-14
82Watlo/C-9

Carreno, Amalio
87PrWill-19
88Albany/Pro-1329
89Readg/Star-6

Carreon, Camilo G.
(Cam)
60L-88
60T-121
61T-509
62T-178
62T/St-23
63T-308
64T-421
65T-578
66T-513

Carreon, Mark
83Lynch-14
84Jacks-20
85Tidew-25
86Tidew-4
87Tidew-21
87Tidew/TCMA-20
88AAA/Pro-39
88F-129
88Tidew/CANDL-14
88Tidew/CMC-22
88Tidew/Pro-1588
89B-389
89Class-84
89D/Rook-18
89F-29
89Kahn/Mets-32
89Score/HotRk-16
89Score/Tr-108
89Tidew/CANDL-14
89Tidew/CMC-24
90Class-112
90D-454
90F-198
90Score-363
90Score/100Ris-67
90T-434
90UD-135

Carrick, William
E107

Carrigan, William F.
(Bill)
10Domino-21
11Helmar-1
12Sweet/Pin-1A
12Sweet/Pin-1B
14CJ-27
14Piedmont/St-9
15CJ-27
E95
E97
M116
S74-1
T202
T204
T205
T206
T207
T3-86
WG6-7

Carriger, Rick
87Hagers-18
88Jaxvl/Best-1
88Jaxvl/Pro-988
89Jaxvl/Best-19
89Jaxvl/Pro-168

Carrillo, Matias
86Nashua-5
87Salem-10
88ElPas/Best-12
89Denver/CMC-22
89Denver/Pro-49

Carrion, Jesus
86Osceola-4

Carrion, Leonel
80Memph-12
83Memph-15
84Indianap-3C
86Jaxvl/TCMA-9C

Carrithers, Don
71MLB/St-243
72OPC-76
72T-76
73OPC-651
73T-651
74OPC-361
74T-361
75OPC-438
75T-438
75T/M-438
76OPC-312
76SSPC-348
76T-312
77OPC-18
77T-579
78Cr/PCL-80
78T-113
79Phoen

Carroll, Bob
77Visal

Carroll, Carson
83Orlan-25
83Wisco/LF-7
84Visal-15
86Albany/TCMA-3
87Albany-14

Carroll, Chris
86FtLaud-4
87FtLaud-5

Carroll, Clay
65T-461R
66T-307
67T-219
68Coke
68T-412
69Kahn
69OPC-26
69T-26
70OPC-133
70T-133
71MLB/St-52
71OPC-394
71T-394
72MB-68
72OPC-311
72OPC-312IA
72T-311
72T-312A
73OPC-195
73OPC-68LL
73T-195
73T-68LL
74OPC-111
74T-111
75OPC-345
75T-345
75T/M-345
76K-6
76OPC-211
76SSPC-25
76T-211
76T/Tr-211T
77T-497
78T-615
79Vanco-14

Carroll, Don
88GreatF-12

Carroll, Dorsey Lee
(Dixie)
No Cards.

Carroll, Ed
78Holyo
79Holyo-4
80Holyo-19

Carroll, Edward
(Chick)
No Cards.

Carroll, Frederick H.
(Fred)
N172
N284

Carroll, James
86Cram/PCL-71
87Madis-21

Carroll, Jim
88Madis-9
88Modesto-6
89Clearw/Star-4

Carroll, Joe
78Ashev

Carroll, John E.
(Scrappy)
N172

Carroll, Owen
33DH-8
33G-72
R310
R316
V354-46

Carroll, Patrick
(Pat)
No Cards.

Carroll, Ralph A.
(Doc)
No Cards.

Carroll, Samuel C.
(Cliff)
N172
N284
WG1-55

Carroll, Shadow
C46-39

Carroll, Steve
83IowaC-24
85IowaC-30

Carroll, Thomas E.
(Tommy)

55T-158
56T-139
57T-164
59T-513
Carroll, Thomas M.
75OPC-507
75T-507
75T/M-507
76Indianap-12
76OPC-561
76T-561
Carruth, Jim
76Baton
Carsey, Wilfred
(Kid)
No Cards.
Carsley, Jeff
78Duned
Carson, Henry
83StPet-3
86StPet-5
Carson, Paul
89Martins/Star-5
Carson, Ted
84Savan-23
Carson, Walter Lloyd
(Kit)
R313
Carstensen, Chris
77Newar
78BurlB
Carswell, Frank W.
53Glen
Cartaya, Joel
86Salem-3
87PortChar-21
88Tulsa-16
Cartelli, John
(Doc)
86Modesto-6TR
87Modesto-22
Carter, Andy
88SALAS/GS-27
88Spart/Star-19
88Spart/Star-3
89Clearw/Star-5
Carter, Bruce
86Clearw-2
86Cram/PCL-189
Carter, Conrad P.
W514-45
Carter, Dell
85Elmir-4
Carter, Dennis
87ArkTr-1
88StPet/Star-3
89ArkTr/GS-4
Carter, Dick
60T-466C
Carter, Don
83Memph-7
84BuffB-21
Carter, Dwight
75Clint
Carter, Eddie
87Erie-7
88Savan/Pro-354
89Savan/Pro-358
Carter, Fred
87FtLaud-29
88Reno/Cal-290
89PalmSp/Cal-45
89PalmSp/Pro-479
Carter, Gary Edmund
75IntAS/TCMA-21
75OPC-620R
75T-620R
75T/M-620R
76Ho-62
76K-34
76OPC-441
76SSPC-334
76T-441
77Ho-41
77OPC-45
77T-295
78Ho-146
78OPC-135
78T-120
79Ho-24
79OPC-270
79T-520
80OPC-37
80T-70
80T/S-52
81D-90
81F-142
81F/St-73
81OPC-6
81OPC/Post-8
81T/SO-66
81T/St-184
81T/St-259
82D-114
82D-2DK
82F-185
82F/St-39
82Hygrade
82K-24
82OPC-244
82OPC-344AS
82OPC/Post-16
82Sqt-19
82T-344
82T-730
82T/St-128
82T/St-61
82Zeller-1
82Zeller-13
82Zeller-16
82Zeller-19
82Zeller-6
83D-340
83D/AAS-58
83Drake-4
83F-278
83F-637
83F-638
83K-55
83OPC-314AS
83OPC-370
83Stuart-8
83T-370
83T-404
83T/Gloss-20
83T/Gloss40-20
83T/St-178
83T/St-255
83T/St/Box-2
84D-55
84D/Champs-58
84Drake-6
84F-271
84FunFood/Pin-3
84MiltBrad-5
84Nes/792-393AS
84Nes/792-450
84OPC-366
84OPC-393AS
84Ralston-28
84Seven-15C
84Stuart-15
84Stuart-36AS
84T-393
84T-450
84T/Cereal-28
84T/Gloss22-20
84T/Gloss40-9
84T/St-183FOIL
84T/St-90
84T/Super-18
84T/Super-18
85D-55
85D/AAS-57
85D/HL-21M
85D/HL-47
85Drake-5
85F-393
85F-631IA
85F/St-16
85F/St-26
85F/St-35
85F/Up-U21
85GenMills-1DP
85Leaf-241
85OPC-230
85Seven-9C
85T-230
85T-719AS
85T/3D-5
85T/Gloss22-9
85T/Gloss40-36
85T/Mets/Fan-3
85T/St-180
85T/St-192
85T/St-83
85T/Super-13
85T/Tr-17T
86D-68
86Dorman-3
86Drake-1
86F-76
86F/AS-4
86F/LimEd-10
86F/LL-5
86F/Mini-17
86F/Slug-M3
86F/St-23
86F/WaxBox-C7
86Jiffy-19
86Leaf-63
86OPC-170
86Quaker-4
86S-126M
86S-137M
86S-28
86S/Dec-72M
86T-170
86T-708
86T/3D-2
86T/Gloss60-23
86T/Mets/Fan-2
86T/Mini-50
86T/St-96
86T/Super-19
86TrueVal-16
86Woolwth-7
87BK-2
87Class-5
87D-69
87D/AAS-19
87D/OD-130
87D/PopUp-19
87Drake-20
87F-4
87F-629M
87F-634M
87F/AS-2
87F/AwardWin-7
87F/Excit-9
87F/GameWin-9
87F/Lim-7
87F/Mini-18
87F/St-20
87F/WS-4
87Ho/St-12
87KayBee-8
87KMart-25
87Leaf-109
87MnM's-12
87MSA/Discs-8
87OPC-20
87Ralston-9
87RedFoley/St-110
87S-151M
87S-50
87Seven-E1
87Seven-ME1
87T-20
87T-602AS
87T/Board-11
87T/Coins-28
87T/Gloss22-9
87T/Gloss60-11
87T/HL-25
87T/Mets/Fan-1
87T/Mini-20
87T/St-101
87T/St-14LCS
87T/St-158
87T/St-22WS
87Woolwth-25
88ChefBoy-10
88D-199
88D/AS-41
88D/Best-14
88D/Mets/Bk-199
88D/PopUp-19
88F-130
88F-636M
88F/St-S2
88Jiffy-3
88Kahn/Mets-8
88Leaf-156
88Nestle-26
88OPC-157
88Panini/St-232M
88Panini/St-338
88Score-325
88Score/WxBx-10
88Sf-28
88Sf/Gamewin-14
88T-530
88T/Big-37
88T/Gloss22-20
88T/Gloss60-7
88T/Mets/Fan-8
88T/St-105
88T/St-152
88T/St/Backs-22
88T/UK-11
89B-379
89Cadaco-6
89Class-64
89D-53
89D/AS-41
89D/Best-182
89D/PopUp-41
89F-30
89F/Superstar-7
89Kahn/Mets-8
89KayBee-4
89OPC-324
89Panini/St-136
89Panini/St-228AS
89RedFoley/St-19
89Score-240
89Sf-155
89T-393AS
89T-3RB
89T-680
89T/Big-325
89T/Gloss22-20
89T/Gloss60-17
89T/Mets/Fan-8
89T/St-160
89T/St-2
89T/St-94
89T/St/Backs-55
89UD-390
89Woolwth-10
90D-147
90F-199
90Score-416
90T-790
90UD-168
Carter, Glenn
89QuadC/Best-1
89QuadC/GS-8
Carter, Herbert
82Wisco-10
Carter, Jeff
86Clint-4
87Jamestn-27
88Rockford-5
88Shreve/Pro-1291
89Rockford-5
89Shreve/Pro-1846
89WPalm/Star-5
Carter, Joe
83IowaC-20
83Thorn-33
84D-41
84IowaC-25
84Wheat/Ind-30
85D-616
85F-443
85Polar/Ind-30
85T-694
86D-224
86D/HL-42
86F-583
86OhHenry-30
86OPC-377
86T-377
86T/St-213
87Class/Up-127
87D-156
87D/OD-109
87F-249
87F/AwardWin-8
87F/Lim-8
87F/LL-9
87F/McCror-7
87F/Mini-19
87F/St-21
87Gator-30
87KayBee-9
87Kraft-15
87Leaf-133
87MnM's-16
87OPC-220
87RedFoley/St-27
87S-176
87Smok/AL-5
87T-220
87T/Coins-7
87T/Gloss60-16
87T/Mini-51
87T/St-208
88D-254
88D-BC9
88D/Best-56
88F-605
88F/Mini-18
88F/Slug-7
88F/SS-6
88F/St-18
88Gator-30
88KayBee-4
88Leaf-184
88Nestle-36
88OPC-75
88OPC-I
88Panini/St-72
88Score-80
88Sf-5
88T-75
88T/Big-71
88T/Coins-8
88T/Gloss60-44
88T/RiteAid-17
88T/St-213
88T/St/Backs-49
88T/UK-12
88T/WaxBox-I
89Ames-9
89B-91
89Cadaco-7
89Class-11

89D-83
89D/Best-56
89D/MVP-BC3
89F-400
89F/Excit-4
89F/Heroes-6
89KingB/Discs-8
89OPC-164
89Panini/St-327
89RedFoley/St-20
89Score-213
89Score/HotSt-55
89Score/Mast-34
89Sf-104
89T-420
89T/Big-155
89T/Coins-36
89T/Gloss60-3
89T/Hills-6
89T/St-216
89T/St/Backs-14
89T/UK-13
89UD-190
90Class-138
90D-114
90F-489
90Score-319
90Score/100St-59
90Sf-120
90T-580
90UD-375
90UD-53TC

Carter, John Howard
(Howard)
No Cards.

Carter, Larry
89Salin/Cal-126
89Salin/Pro-1816

Carter, Otis Leonard
(Jackie)
No Cards.

Carter, Richard
87Lakel-13
88Lakel/Star-6
89SanBern/Best-3
89SanBern/Cal-68

Carter, Richie
86PalmSp-6
86PalmSp/Smok-14

Carter, Ron
86Madis-5
86Madis/Pol-5
87SanBern-8

Carter, Steve
87Watertn-10
88Aug/Pro-385
89BuffB/Pro-1665
89D/Rook-8
90T-482
90UD-368

Cartwright, Alan
84ElPas-19
86ElPas-5
87Denver-19
88ElPas/Best-13

Cartwright, Alexander
50Call
80SSPC/HOF
89HOF/St-90

Cartwright, Edward C.
(Ed)
N172
N300/SC

Cartwright, Mark
83Visal/LF-16

Carty, Jorge
77Charl

Carty, Ricardo A.
(Rico)
64T-476R
65Kahn
65OPC-2LL
65T-2LL
65T-305
65T/trans-7
66OPC-153
66T-153
67Kahn
67OPC-35
67T-240LL
67T-35
68Coke
68T-455
69MLB/St-112
69T-590
70MLB/St-3
70OPC-145
70T-145
71Bz
71Bz/Test-28
71MD
71MLB/St-557
71MLB/St-6
71OPC-270
71OPC-62LL
71T-270
71T-62LL
71T/Coins-113
71T/GM-3
71T/S-29
71T/tatt-11
72T-740
73OPC-435
73T-435
75OPC-655
75T-655
75T/M-655
76OPC-156
76SSPC-519
76T-156
77OPC-114
77Pep-9
77T-465
78T-305
79OPC-291
79T-565
80OPC-25
80T-46

Caruthers, Robert Lee
(Bob)
N162
N172
N172/BC
N28
N284
N370
Scrapps

Carver, Billy Paul
87AubAs-6
88Ashvl/Pro-1049
88SALAS/GS-4
89ColMud/Best-23
89Osceola/Star-3

Cary, Chuck
82BirmB-9
83BirmB-14
86F/Up-U21
86Nashv-3
87D-461
87F-147
87Richm/TCMA-1
87T-171
89Colum/CMC-7
89Colum/Pol-1
89Colum/Pro-745
89Score/NWest-27
89T/Tr-17T
89UD-396
90Class-125
90D-429
90Score-393
90T-691
90UD-528

Cary, Jeff
80LynnS-12
81Wausa-15
82Madis-31

Casado, Cancio
89Martins/Star-6

Casagrande,Tom
55T-167

Casale, Jerry
59T-456
60MacGregor-5
60T-38
61T-195
61T/St-169

Casano, Andy
88Watlo/Pro-666
89Kinston/Star-5

Casanova, Ortiz P.
(Paul)
67OPC-115
67T-115
68Bz-1
68T-560
69MB-53
69MLB/St-102
69NTF
69T-486
69T/St-233
70MLB/St-280
70OPC-84
70T-84
71MLB/St-532
71OPC-139
71T-139
71T/Coins-146
72MB-69
72T-591
73OPC-452
73T-452
74OPC-272
74T-272
75OPC-633
75T-633
75T/M-633

Casarotti, Rich
88MidwLAS/GS-17
89Durhm/Star-4
89Star/Wax-68

Cascarella, Joe
35BU-162
W711/1

Case, George W.
39PB-138
40PB-15
41DP-76
41DP-88
41G-16
41PB-69
Exh47
R303/A
R303/B

Casey, Dan
N172
N284
N690
WG1-48

Casey, Dennis Patrick
No Cards.

Casey, Hugh
39PB-151
40PB-148
47TipTop
49B-179
49Eureka-155
80Laugh/FFeat-27
Exh47

Casey, James Peter
(Doc)
E107
T206

Casey, Jas.
WG3-8

Casey, Joie
88SLCty-30M

Casey, Joseph Felix
(Joe)
14CJ-87
15CJ-87
E101
E92

Casey, Orrin Robinson
(Bob)
No Cards.

Casey, Pat
83Beaum-16
84Beaum-16
85Cram/PCL-86
86Calgary-4
87Portl-7

Casey, Tim
86Stockton-4
87ElPas-13
89Huntsvl/Best-14

Cash, David
(Dave)
70OPC-141R
70T-141R
71MLB/St-197
71OPC-582
71T-582
72OPC-125
72T-125
73OPC-397
73T-397
74JP
74OPC-198
74T-198
75Ho-93
75K-48
75OPC-22
75T-22
75T/M-22
76Crane-11
76Ho-40
76Ho/Twink-40
76K-16
76MSA/Disc
76OPC-295
76SSPC-465
76T-295
77Ho-133
77OPC-180
77Pep-66
77T-649
77T/CS-12
78Ho-23
78OPC-18
78T-495
78Wiffle/Discs-15
79OPC-207
79T-395
80OPC-3
80T-14
81D-121
81F-492
81T-707
88Batav/Pro-1663
89ScrWB/CMC-6

Cash, Earl
86Osceola-5
87ColAst/Pro-19
87ColumAst-19

Cash, Johnny
86Durhm-3

Cash, Mike
75Cedar
78Cr/PCL-94

Cash, Norman Dalton
(Norm)
59T-509
60T-488
61P-40
61T-95
61T/St-148
62Bz
62Exh
62J-14
62P-14
62P/Can-14
62Salada-72
62Shirriff-72
62T-250
62T-466AS
62T-51LL
62T-90LL
62T/bucks
62T/St-45
63Exh
63J-46
63P-46
63T-445
63T-4LL
64Bz-20
64Det/Lids-3
64T-331M
64T-425
64T/Coins-79
64T/St-49
64T/SU
64T/tatt
65OPC-153
65T-153
66T-218LL
66T-315
67T-216M
67T-540
68T-256
69MB-54
69MLB/St-46
69OPC-80
69T-80
69T/St-171
70MLB/St-205
70T-611
71MLB/St-389
71OPC-599
71T-599
72MB-70
72OPC-150
72OPC-90LL
72T-90LL
72T-150
73OPC-485
73T-485
74OPC-367
74T-367
74T/St-172
78TCMA-49
83MLBPA/Pin-3
85CircK-25
88Domino-2
Exh47

Cash, Ronald Forrest
(Ron)
74OPC-600R
74T-600R

Cash, Timothy
88VeroB/Star-3

Cash, Todd
86Clint-5

Cashion, Jay Carl
14CJ-62
E270/1

Casian, Larry
88SLAS-29
89Portl/Pro-223

Casillas, Adam
88Greens/Pro-1562
89Cedar/Best-14
89Cedar/Pro-922
89Cedar/Star-3

Caskin, Edward James
(Ed)
No Cards.

Cassady, Harry D.
No Cards.

Cassels, Chris
88Beloi/GS-23
89Stock/Best-19
89Stock/Cal-163
89Stock/Pro-392
89Stock/Star-14
Cassidy, David
89Hamil/Star-9
Cassidy, Howard
79Colum-25
Cassidy, John P.
No Cards.
Cassidy, Joseph P.
(Joe)
No Cards.
Cassidy, Peter F.
(Pete)
T206
Cassini, Jack Dempsey
No Cards.
Castaigne, Arcilio
80Ander-2
Castain, Maurice
83Idaho-26
84Madis/Pol-22
Castaneda, Nick
82AlexD-13
83AlexD-5
84PrWill-31
85Tigres-23
89Omaha/CMC-13
89Omaha/Pro-1722
Casteel, Brent
86WinSal-3
Castello, Brian
89Salin/Cal-149TR
Caster, George
W753
Castiglione, Peter P.
(Pete)
49Eureka-156
50B-201
51B-17
52B-47
52T-260
54B-174
Castillo, Ace
75QuadC
Castillo, Albert
89Kingspt/Star-5
Castillo, Anthony
(Tony)
79Hawai-24
80Hawai-21
85IowaC-1
85Kingst-3
87Duned-12
88Duned/Star-2
89B-244
89D/Rook-12
90D-592
90T-620
90UD-551
Castillo, Axel
88BurlR/Pro-1781
Castillo, Benny
88Brist/Pro-1892
89Fay/Pro-1580
Castillo, Bobby
79Albuq-22
79T-641
80Pol/Dodg-37
81D-298
81F-137
81Pol/Dodg-37
81T-146
82D-236
82F-2
82T-48
82T/Tr-17T
83F-608
83T-327
83T-771TL
84D-436
84F-559
84Nes/792-491
84OPC-329
84T-491
85F-274
85F/Up-U22
85T-588
85T/Tr-18T
86F-127
86T-252
Castillo, Braulio
89Bakers/Cal-202
Castillo, Esteban M.
(Manny)
81Omaha-15
81T-66R
83D-253
83F-474
83T-258
84F-607
84Nes/792-562
84Syrac-24
84T-562
Castillo, Felipe
87Gasto-1
88Gasto/Pro-1008
89Tulsa/GS-7
Castillo, Frank
89WinSal/Star-4
Castillo, Jeff
88GreatF-8
Castillo, Juan
80BurlB-22
80Utica-13
81BurlB-20
83ElPas-10
84ElPas-16
85Cram/PCL-205
86F/Up-U22
86Pol/Brew-3
87D-249
87F/U-U18
87T/Tr-20T
88D-363
88F-159
88OPC-362
88Pol/Brew-3
88Score-429
88T-362
88T/Big-117
89D-530
89T-538
89T/Big-9
89UD-522
Castillo, Luis T.
82Wausa-16
87Stockton-17
88ElPas/Best-8
Castillo, M. Carmelo
(Carmen)
81Chatt-16
82Charl-19
83F-404
84Wheat/Ind-8
85D-590
85F-444
85OPC-184
85Polar/Ind-8
85T-184
85T/St-255
86D-460
86F-584
86OhHenry-8
86T/Tr-21T
87D-588
87F-250
87Gator-8
87T-513
88D-403
88F-606
88Gator-8
88Score-581
88T-341
89D-374
89F-401
89Score-497
89Score/Tr-23
89T-637
89T/Big-91
89T/Tr-18T
89UD-487
90D-554
90F-371
90Score-123
90T-427
90UD-281
Castillo, Martin H.
(Marty)
80Evans-19
81Evans
82Evans-11
82F-265
82T-261R
83Evans-11
84D-247
84Nes/792-303
84T-303
85Cain's-5
85D-394
85F-5
85T-461
85Wendy-6
86T-788
Castillo, Tomas
80Utica-12
Castino, John A.
77Orlan
78OrlTw
80OPC-76
80T-137
81D-488
81Drake-29
81F-554
81F/St-112
81OPC-304
81Sqt-29
81T-304
81T/SO-33
81T/St-99
82D-256
82F-549
82F/St-230
82K-29
82OPC-73
82T-396TL
82T-644
82T/St-209
83D-303
83F-609
83OPC-93
83T-93
83T/St-89
84D-120
84D-4
84D/AAS-7
84F-560
84Nes/792-237
84OPC-237
84T-237
84T/St-307
85OPC-298
85T-452
Castle, Donald Hardy
(Don)
77WHave
Castle, John Francis
No Cards.
Castleberry, Kevin
88CapeCod/Sum-111
Castleman, Clydell
36G
R314
V355-36
Castleman, Foster E.
55Gol/Giants-3
56T-271
57T-237
58T-416
79TCMA-225
Castner, Rodger
87Watertn-2
88Watertn/Puc-4
Castro, Antionio
85Tigres-24
Castro, Bill
76OPC-293
76T-293
77T-528
78T-448
79T-133
80T-303
81D-578
81F-517
81T-271
82Tacom-4
83F-109
Castro, Earnest
89Wausa/GS-3
Castro, Edgar
82Miami-15
Castro, Fidel
88MinorLg/Leg-11
Castro, Frank
85Beaum-15
86Beaum-5
Castro, Genaro
86LitFalls-5
Castro, Guillermo
82DayBe-1
83DayBe-5
Castro, Jose
81OkCty/TCMA-24
82Edmon-2
85BuffB-8
86Syrac-7
87Syrac-18
87Syrac/TCMA-12
88Omaha/CMC-24
88Omaha/Pro-1509
89Omaha/CMC-14
89Omaha/Pro-1731
Castro, Liliano
87Fayette-21
88Fay/Pro-1101
Castro, Louis M.
No Cards.
Castro, Pablo
88StCath/Pro-2012
Cataline, Dan
81QuadC-16
83VeroB-24
Cater, Danny Anderson
64T-482R
65OPC-253
65T-253
66T-398
67OPC-157
67T-157
68T-535
69MB-55
69MLB/St-84
69OPC-1LL
69OPC-44
69T-1LL
69T-44
69T-556M
69T/St-213
69Trans-12
70MLB/St-243
70OPC-437
70T-437
71K-30
71MD
71MLB/St-485
71OPC-358
71T-358
71T/Coins-14
72MB-71
72T-676
73OPC-317
73T-317
74OPC-543
74T-543
75OPC-645
75T-645
75T/M-645
Cates, Eli Eldo
No Cards.
Cates, Tim
83Memph-11
85Indianap-8
Cathcart, Gary
86FtLaud-5
87Albany-9
88Albany/Pro-1335
Cather, Theodore P.
(Ted)
15CJ-145
Cato, Keefe
81Water-2
82Water-3
83Water-1
85Cram/PCL-118
85T-367
86Omaha-4
Cato, Wayne
76Cedar
80Clint-26MG
Caton, James Howard
(Buster)
No Cards.
Catterson, Thomas H.
(Tom)
No Cards.
Caudill, Bill
76ArkTr
80T-103
81D-586
81F-306
81OPC-346
81T-574
81T/St-152
82D-426
82F-590
82T-303
82T/Tr-18T
83D-302
83F-475
83Nalley-5
83OPC-78
83T-78
83T/St-118
84D-118
84F-608
84F/St-76
84F/X-24
84Moth/A's-12
84Nes/792-769
84OPC-299
84T-769
84T/St-345
84T/X-23
85D-96
85F-419
85F/St-100
85F/Up-U23
85Leaf-154
85OPC-275
85OPC/Post-23
85T-685
85T/St-322
85T/Tr-19T
85Tor/Fire-7
86Ault-36
86D-317
86F-55

860PC-207
86T-435
86Tor/Fire-5
87F-221
87Moth/A's-24
870PC-156
87T-733

Caughey, Wayne
79Toled-11
80Albuq-18
81Albuq/TCMA-14
82Portl-12

Cauley, Chris
88Tampa/Star-4
89Saraso/Star-4

Caulfield, John J.
No Cards.

Caulfield, Tom
83Erie-23

Causey, Cecil
(Red)
E120
E121/80
E122
W501-65

Causey, James Wayne
(Wayne)
62Salada-100
62Shirriff-100
62T-496
63T-539
64T-75
64T/Coins-102
64T/Coins-161AAS
64T/Coins-161BAS
64T/S-45
64T/St-87
64T/SU
64T/tatt
65T-425
65T/E-21
65T/trans-8
66T-366
67T-286
68T-522
690PC-33
69T-33
78TCMA-8

Cavalier, Kevin
87Jamestn-26
88WPalm/Star-4

Cavallo, Pablo
77Newar
78Newar

Cavanaugh, John J.
No Cards.

Cavarretta, Phil
35BU-101
39Exh
41DP-104
47TipTop
48L-168
49B-6
49Eureka-53
50B-195
51B-138
52B-126
52StarCal/L-80F
52T-295
52TipTop
53B/Col-30
54T-55
55B-282
74Laugh/ASG-44
76SSPC-617
89Pac/Leg-131
PM10/Sm-23
PR1-3
R312/M
R314
R423-13
V355-54
WG8-6

Caveney, James C.
(Ike or Jimmy)
21Exh-22
E120
V61-116
W573

Cavers, Mike
89Freder/Star-2

Cebuhar, John
88Hamil/Pro-1721
89Hamil/Star-8

Ceccarelli, Art
55Rodeo
58T-191
59T-226
60T-156

Cecchetti, George
81Chatt-14
82Chatt-14
83BuffB-22
84BuffB-2
85Water-20
86Maine-3

Cecchini, Jim
86Jaxvl/TCMA-3

Cecena, Jose
86Readg-5
88D/Rook-6
88F/U-U62
88Moth/R-12
88T/Tr-26T
89F-516
89Score/HotRk-35
89T-683
89UD-560

Cecil, Rex
47Centen-4
49Remar

Cedeno, Andujar
89Ashvl/Pro-952

Cedeno, Cesar
710PC-237
71T-237
71T/S-15
720PC-65
72T-65
73K-13
730PC-290
73T-290
740PC-200
740PC-337AS
74T-200
74T-337M
74T/St-31
75Ho-17
75Ho/Twink-17
750PC-590
75T-590
75T/M-590
76Crane-12
76Ho-47
76Ho/Twink-47
76MSA/Disc
760PC-460
76SSPC-63
76T-460
77Ho-58
770PC-131
77T-90
77T/S-13
78BK/A-18
78Ho-50
780PC-226
78T-650
78Wiffle/Discs-16
79Ho-91
790PC-294
79T-570
80BK/PHR-25
80K-36
800PC-193
80T-370
80T/S-56
81Coke
81D-263
81Drake-20
81F-59
81F/St-35
81K-14
81MSA/Disc-8
810PC-190
81T-191
81T/HT
81T/SO-77
81T/St-167
81T/St-258
82Coke/Reds
82D-118
82F-213
82F/St-41
820PC-48
82T-640
82T/St-47
82T/Tr-19T
83D-43
83F-587
830PC-238
83T-351TL
83T-475
83T/St-231
84D-306
84F-465
84FunFood/Pin-42
84Nes/792-705LL
84Nes/792-725
840PC-191
84T-705
84T-725
84T/St-54
85D-447
85F-531
85Leaf-87
850PC-54
85T-54
85T/St-55
86D-648
86F-29
86Moth/Ast-11
860PC-224
86T-224

Cedeno, Domingo
89Myrtle/Pro-1456

Cedeno, Ramon
88Ashvl/Pro-1053
890sceola/Star-4

Cedeno, Vinicio
86MidldA-4
87MidldA-8
88MidldA/GS-4
89MidldA/GS-9

Centala, Scott
88CapeCod/Sum-123
89Eugene/Best-7

Centeno, Jose
75Clint

Cento, Tony
86AppFx-6
87Penin-28

Cepeda, Octavio
86Macon-5
87Salem-5

Cepeda, Orlando M.
58SFCall
58T-343
59Bz
59T-390
59T-533AS
60Bz-10
60L-128
60T-450
60T/tatt
60T/tatt-8
61P-144
61T-435
61T/St-75
62Bz
62Exh
62J-136
62P-136
62P/Can-136
62Salada-175
62Shirriff-175
62T-390AS
62T-40
62T-401M
62T-54LL
62T/bucks
62T/St-195
63Bz-22
63Exh
63F-64
63J-101
63P-101
63Salada-13
63T-3LL
63T-520
63T/SO
64T-306
64T-390
64T-9LL
64T/Coins-142AS
64T/Coins-63
64T/S-55
64T/St-50
64T/SU
64T/tatt
64Wheat/St-10
65OldLond-6
650PC-4LL
65T-360
65T-4LL
65T/E-45
65T/trans-9
660PC-132
66T-132
670PC-20
670PC/PI-9
67T-20
67T/PI-9
67T/Test/SU-13
68Bz-6
680PC-3LL
68T-200
68T-362AS
68T-3LL
68T/G-32
68T/Post-12
69MB-56
69MLB/St-113
69MLBPA/Pin-38
69T-385
69T/St-113
70MLB/St-4
70T-555
70T/CB
71Bz
71Bz/Test-33
71MD
71MLB/St-7
710PC-605
71T-605
71T/Coins-61
71T/GM-26
71T/tatt-3
72MB-72
720PC-195
72T-195
730PC-545
73T-545
74K-24
740PC-83
74T-83
74T/St-132
750PC-205M
75T-205MV
75T/M-205MV
78TCMA-50
80GlenF/B-26C
80GlenF/C-25C
82KMart-12
83MLBPA/Pin-21
84Moth/Giants-11
85CircK-24
86S/Dec-48M
88Pac/Leg-94
89Swell-8
Exh47
PM10/Sm-24
PM10/Sm-25

Cerame, Mike
89Pulas/Pro-1903

Cerdan, Marcel
D305

Cermak, Edward Hugo
(Ed)
No Cards.

Cerny, Chris
88Bakers/Cal-252
89Boise/Pro-1999

Cerny, Mark
89Bill/Pro-2054

Cerny, Marty
87PortChar-7
88Gasto/Pro-1016
89Mia/Star/22-3
89Mia/Star/25-4

Cerny, Scott
86Cram/PCL-86
87QuadC-24
88CalLgAS-33
88PalmSp/Cal-101
88PalmSp/Pro-1440
89MidldA/GS-10

Cerone, Richard Aldo
(Rick)
76SSPC-516
770PC-76
77T-476R
780PC-129
78T-469
790PC-72
79T-152
800PC-311
80T-591
81D-346
81F-83
81F/St-88
810PC-335
81T-335
81T/HT
81T/SO-28
81T/St-109
81T/St-248
82D-199
82F-31
82F/St-118
82F/St-238M
820PC-45
82T-45
82T/St-218
83D-577
83F-376
830PC-254
83RoyRog/Disc-1
83T-254
84D-492
84F-121
84Nes/792-617
840PC-228
84T-617
85D-274
85F-123
85F/Up-U24
85Ho/Braves-6
850PC-337
85Pol/Atl-5
85T-429

85T/Tr-20T
86D-310
86F-511
86F/Up-U23
86OPC-203
86Pol/Brew-11
86T-747
86T/Tr-22T
87F-340
87T-129
87T/Tr-21T
88D-351
88D/Best-332
88D/RedSox/Bk-NEW
88F-203
88F/U-U6
88Panini/St-151
88Score-486
88Score/Tr-21T
88T-561
88T/Tr-27T
89D-398
89D/Best-308
89F-84
89OPC-96
89Score-396
89T-96
89T/Big-119
89UD-152
90D-305
90F-270
90Score-139
90T-303
90UD-405

Cerqueira, Jeff
88CapeCod/Sum-83

Cerrud, Roberto
80Utica-14

Cerutti, John
83Knoxv-3
84Syrac-31
85Syrac-27
86D/Rook-20
86F/Up-U24
86S/Rook-36
86Syrac-8
86T/Tr-23T
87D-442
87F-222
87Leaf-210
87OPC-282
87T-557
87Tor/Fire-3
87Tor/Fire-3
87ToysRUs-6
88D-321
88F-105
88Leaf-152
88OPC-191
88Score-98
88T-191
88Tor/Fire-55
89B-247
89D-467
89F-228
89OPC-347
89Score-304
89T-347
89Tor/Fire-55
89UD-129
90D-645
90F-78
90Score-429
90Sf-86
90T-211
90UD-485

Cerv, Robert Henry
(Bob)
53T-210
55B-306
56T-288
57T-269
58T-329
59Armour-6
59Bz
59HRDerby-5
59T-100
60Bz-15
60T-415
61P-13
61T-563
61T/St-170
62T-169
79TCMA-162
Exh47

Cesari, Jeff
89Geneva/Pro-1868

Cesario, Jim
83TriCit-23

Cespedes, Teodoro
89Everett/Star-4

Cey, Ronald Charles
(Ron)
72T-761R
73OPC-615R
73T-615R
74OPC-315
74T-315
74T/St-42
75Ho-61
75Ho/Twink-61
75OPC-390
75T-390
75T/M-390
76Crane-13
76Ho-63
76MSA/Disc
76OPC-370
76SSPC-75
76T-370
77Ho-89
77K-18
77OPC-199
77T-50
77T/CS-14
78Ho-93
78K-24
78OPC-130
78T-630
78Wiffle/Discs-17
79Ho-28
79OPC-94
79T-190
80K-19
80OPC-267
80Pol/Dodg-10
80T-510
81D-296
81F-126
81F/St-3
81OPC-260
81Pol/Dodg-10
81T-260
81T/HT
81T/SO-73
81T/St-177
82D-210
82F-3
82F/St-3
82K-46
82OPC-216
82OPC-367IA
82Pol/Dodg
82Pol/Dodg-10
82T-410
82T-411A
82T/St-51
83D-84
83D/AAS-21
83F-204
83OPC-15
83T-15
83T/St-244
83T/X-19
83Thorn-11
84D-361
84Drake-7
84F-490
84FunFood/Pin-89
84Nes/792-357
84OPC-357
84SevenUp-11
84T-357
84T/St-41
85D-320
85Drake-6
85F-52
85F/St-19
85Leaf-84
85OPC-366
85SevenUp-11
85T-768
85T/St-42
86D-198
86F-363
86Gator-11
86OPC-194
86S-150M
86T-669
87F-556
87OPC-322
87OPC-C
87Smok/Dodg-4
87T-767
87T-C
87T/Tr-22T
88Smok/Dodg-15M
88Smok/Dodg-21M
88Smok/Dodg-27
89Smok/Dodg-82

Chacon, Elio R.
60T-543
62T-256
66Pep/Tul

Chacon, Troy
88CapeCod/Sum-183

Chadbourne, Chester
No Cards.

Chadwick, Henry
50Call
80SSPC/HOF

Chadwick, Ray
86Edmon-3
87D-505
88BirmB/Best-4

Chadwick, Robert
86NewBrit-6TR
87NewBrit-9TR
88NewBrit/Pro-893

Chafin, John
88Utica/Puc-14

Chagnon, Leon
R314/Can

Chakales, Bob
52NumNum-9
52T-120
55B-148
57T-261
61BeeHive-4

Chalk, David Lee
(Dave)
74OPC-597R
74T-597R
75Ho-46
75Ho/Twink-46
75OPC-64
75T-64
75T/M-64
76Ho-59
76Ho/Twink-59
76OPC-52
76SSPC-194
76T-52
77T-315
78T-178
79OPC-362
79T-682
80OPC-137
80T-261
81D-101
81F-35
82D-590
82F-407
82T-462

Chalmers, George
D329-29
D350/2-27
M101/4-29
M101/5-27
T207
T222

Chamberlain, Bill
78Wausa

Chamberlain, Craig
80T-417
81Omaha-4
81T-274
82Phoen
83Phoen/BHN-23
88CharlK-12
88CharlK/Pep-12

Chamberlain, Elton
N172

Chamberlain, Joseph
No Cards.

Chamberlain, Tom
78StPet
79ArkTr-19

Chamberlain, Wesley
87Watertn-12
88Aug/Pro-359
89Harris/Pro-296
89Harris/Star-5

Chamberlin, Buck
79Toled-13
80Toled-14
81Toled-2
82Toled-24

Chambers, Albert E.
(Al)
81LynnS-20
82SLCty-5
83D-649
83SLCty-21
84Cram/PCL-188
85Cram/PCL-80
85D-389
85T-277FDP
87ColAst/Pro-1
87ColumAst-1

Chambers, Carl
87Watlo-17

Chambers, Cliff
47Signal
49Eureka-157
50B-202
51B-131
51FB
51T/RB-25
52B-14
52RM-NL4
52StarCal/L-81C
52T-68
53Hunter
54B-126

Chambers, Jeff
89Elizab/Star-31

Chambers, Travis
86Clearw-3
87Maine-19
87Maine/TCMA-3
88Maine/CMC-2
88Maine/Pro-283
89Jaxvl/Best-10
89Jaxvl/Pro-162

Chambliss, Carroll C.
(Chris)
72OPC-142
72T-142
73OPC-11
73T-11
74OPC-384
74T-384
74T/DE-15
74T/St-162
75OPC-585
75T-585
75T/M-585
76Ho-58
76Ho/Twink-58
76OPC-65
76SSPC-434
76T-65
77BK/Y-12
77Ho-98
77K-52
77OPC-49
77T-220
78BK/Y-12
78K-13
78OPC-145
78T-485
78Wiffle/Discs-18
79BK/Y-12
79K-37
79OPC-171
79T-335
80OPC-328
80T-625
81D-219
81F-252
81F/St-81
81OPC-155
81Pol/Atl-10
81T/St-147
82BK/Lids-6
82D-47
82F-433
82F/St-70
82K-52
82OPC-320
82OPC-321IA
82Pol/Atl-10
82T-320
82T-321A
82T/St-17
83D-123
83F-134
83OPC-11
83Pol/Atl-10
83T-792
83T/St-212
84D-537
84D/AAS-29
84F-175
84FunFood/Pin-123
84Nes/792-50
84OPC-50
84Pol/Atl-10
84T-50
84T/St-28
85D-287
85F-322
85Ho/Braves-7
85Leaf-168
85OPC-187
85Pol/Atl-10
85T-518
85T/St-29
86D-618
86F-512
86Pol/Atl-10
86T-293
87F-513
87OPC-204
87T-777
89London/Pro-1378

Champ, Jeff
89Penin/Star-3

Champagne, Boo
86Cram/PCL-44
87FtMyr-8
Champion, Billy
70OPC-149
70T-149
71MLB/St-173
71OPC-323
71T-323
72T-599
73OPC-74
73T-74
74OPC-391
74T-391
75Ho-118
75OPC-256
75T-256
75T/M-256
76OPC-501
76T-501
Champion, Brian
89Durhm/Star-5
89Star/Wax-69
Champion, Keith
88Savan/Pro-337
89Savan/Pro-344
Champion, Kirk
89SoBend/GS-5
Champion, Randall
83StPet-14
87ArkTr-8
Champion, Robert M.
(Mike)
77T-494R
78T-683
79Tacom-14
80Tacom-16
Chance, Dean
62T-194
63Exh
63J-32
63P-32
63T-355
63T-6LL
64T-32
64T/Coins-67
64T/S-16
65Bz-5
65OldLond-22
65OPC-11LL
65OPC-140
65OPC-7LL
65OPC-9LL
65T-11LL
65T-140
65T-7LL
65T-9LL
65T/E-66
65T/trans-10
65T/trans-42
66Bz-25
66T-340
66T/RO-83
67Bz-25
67T-380
67T/Test/SU-12
68Bz-10
68Coke
68OPC-10LL
68OPC-12LL
68T-10
68T-12LL
68T-255
68T/G-16
68T/Post-1
69MB-57
69MLB/St-66
69MLBPA/Pin-5
69T-620
69T/S-21
69T/St-193
70K-67
70MLB/St-195
70T-625
71MLB/St-148
71OPC-36
71T-36
72MB-73
89Smok/Angels-2
89Swell-89
Exh47
Chance, Frank Leroy
10Domino-22
11Helmar-92
12Sweet/Pin-81A
12Sweet/Pin-81BLL
14CJ-99
14Piedmont/St-10
40PB-234
48Exh/HOF
50Callahan
60Exh/HOF-6
60F-50
61F-98
63Bz/ATG-25
69Bz/Sm
73F/Wild-2
80Cram/Leg-84
80SSPC/HOF
D304
D350/2-28
E101
E103
E105
E107
E224
E254
E270/1
E270/2
E286
E90/1
E90/3
E91
E92
E93
E94
E95
E98
M101/5-28
M116
PM1-2
S74-59
T201
T202
T204
T205
T206
T207
T213/blue
T213/brown
T215/blue
T215/brown
T216
T222
T3-47
W555
WG3-9
WG4-3
WG5-8
WG6-8
Chance, Robert
(Bob)
64T-146R
65Bz-18
65OPC-224
65T-224
66T-564
67T-349
69T-523
78TCMA-82
Chance, Tony
86Macon-6
86PrWill-5
87Salem-25
88Harris/Pro-854
89UD-3
Chandler, A.B.
(Happy)
49Eureka-1
50Callahan
80SSPC/HOF
89HOF/St-97
Chandler, Ed
52Mother-63
Chandler, Ken
81Wisco-13
Chandler, Spud
40PB-181
44Yank/St-5
89Pac/Leg-136
Exh47
Chaney, Darrel Lee
69T-624R
70OPC-3
70T-3
71MLB/St-53
71OPC-632
71T-632
72OPC-136
72T-136
73OPC-507
73T-507
74OPC-559
74T-559
75OPC-581
75T-581
75T/M-581
76OPC-259
76SSPC-33
76T-259
76T/Tr-259T
77Ho-57
77OPC-134
77T-384
78T-443
79OPC-91
79T-184
Chaney, Norma
89Well/Puc-35M
Channell, Lester C.
(Les)
No Cards.
Chant, Charles J.
(Charlie)
75Tucso-7
Chanye, Bruce
83MidldC-10
Chapin, Darrin
88FtLaud/Star-4
89Albany/Pro-340
89Albany/Star-3
89Colum/CMC-30
Chaplin, Bert Edgar
(Ed)
No Cards.
Chapman, Calvin Louis
No Cards.
Chapman, Dan
(AGM)
88Stock/Cal-205
88Stock/Pro-751
89Stock/Best-28
89Stock/Cal-174
89Stock/Pro-398
89Stock/Star-23
Chapman, Glenn J.
No Cards.
Chapman, Harry E.
No Cards.
Chapman, John Curtis
(Jack)
No Cards.
Chapman, Kelvin Keith
77Wausa
79Tidew-18
80Tidew-18
81Syrac-13
82Tidew-2
83Tidew-7
84Tidew-27
85D-626
85F-75
85T-751
86T-492
Chapman, Mark
88Beloi/GS-10
88MidwLAS/GS-59
89ElPas/GS-4
Chapman, Nathan
79Colum-22
82Nashv-6
Chapman, Raymond J.
(Ray)
BF2-21
D327
D328-26
D329-30
D350/2-29
E135-26
M101/4-30
M101/5-29
Chapman, Ron
85Albany-15
Chapman, Samuel Blake
(Sam)
40PB-194
41DP-125
41PB-44
48L-26
49B-112
50B-104
51B-9
51T/BB-52
52Mother-33
52NTea
Chapman, William B.
(Ben)
32Orbit/num-99
33G-191
34DS-38
34G-9
35BU-188
35BU-62
37OPC-130
41DP-74
52T-391
88Conlon/3-6
88Conlon/AmAS-4
R303/A
R303/B
R310
R313
R332-40
V300
V354-5l
V355-90
Chappas, Harold Perry
(Harry)
80T-347
Chappell, Laverne A.
(Larry)
No Cards.
Chappelle, William
T206
T213/blue
Charboneau, Joseph
(Joe)
81D-82
81Drake-21
81F-397
81K-54
81OPC-13
81Sqt-32
81T-13
81T/SO-12
81T/St-66
82D-363
82F-362
82F/St-192
82OPC-211
82T-630
82Wheat/Ind
83BuffB-23
84PrWill-15
Charland, Colin
86Cram/PCL-76
87PalmSp-9
88CalLgAS-31
88PalmSp/Cal-85
88PalmSp/Pro-1447
89Edmon/CMC-6
89Edmon/Pro-565
90F-640M
Charles, Edwin
(Ed)
62T-595R
63J-89
63P-89
63T-67
64T-475
64T/Coins-117
64T/St-1
64T/SU
65OPC-35
65T-35
66T-422
66T/RO-106
67OPC-182
67T-182
68T-563
69MB-58
69MLB/St-164
69T-245
69T/St-62
78TCMA-25
Charles, Ezzard
51BR-A13
Charles, Raymond
(Chappy)
M116
T206
T213/brown
Charleston, Oscar
74Laugh/Black-34
88Conlon/NegAS-2
Charlton, Norm
86Vermont-3
87Nashv-2
88Nashvl/CMC-3
88Nashvl/Pro-488
89D-544
89F-155
89K/Reds-37
89Score-646
89Score/YS/II-15
89T-737
89UD/Ext-783
90D-426
90F-416
90Score-248
90T-289
90UD-566
Charno, Joe
88Ashvl/Pro-1055
89Ashvl/Pro-962
Charpia, Reed
89Helena/SP-16
Charry, Stephen
83Madis/LF-2TD
Chartak, Michael G.
(Mike)
No Cards.
Charton, Frank
(Pete)
64T-459R
66T-329
Chase, Dave
80Ander-12
Chase, Harold Homer
(Hal)

10Domino-23
11Helmar-40
12Sweet/Pin-32A
12Sweet/Pin-32B
14Piedmont/St-11
75F/Pion-22
88Conlon/4-5
D303
D304
E101
E102
E103
E106
E254
E270/2
E300
E90/1
E92
E93
E98
M116
S74-20
T201
T202
T205
T206
T213/blue
T213/brown
T216
T3-6
W514-114
W555
WG5-9
WG6-9

Chase, Ken
39PB-59
40PB-19

Chase, Scott
89Oneon/Pro-2107

Chasey, Mark
88Utica/Puc-4
89SoBend/GS-21

Chasteen, Steve
83Idaho-2

Chatham, Charles L.
(Buster)
No Cards.

Chatterton, James M.
(Jim)
No Cards.

Chauncey, Keathel
77Tucso
78Cr/PCL-58
79Tucso-19
80WHave-21
81Toled-19

Chavarria, Oswaldo Q.
(Ossie)
67T-344

Chaves, Rafael
86CharRa-5

Chavez, Harold P.
WG7-9

Chavez, Joe
86Beaum-6TR
88Wichi-TR
89Wich/Roc-TR

Chavez, Pedro
83BirmB-21
86Nashv-4
87GlenF-21
88Toled/CMC-17
88Toled/Pro-601

Chavez, Rafael
88CalLgAS-42
88River/Cal-209
88River/Pro-1429
89AubAs/Pro-25
89Wich/Roc-14

Chavez, Sam
88Cedar/Pro-1160
89SoBend/GS-9

Chech, Charles
E90/1
T204

Checo, Pedro
89Brist/Star-4

Cheek, Carey
86PrWill-6

Cheek, Harry G.
(Harry)
No Cards.

Cheeves, Virgil
(Chief)
E120
E126-23
V61-84

Chelette, Mark
81Wausa-23

Chelini, Dan
83Butte-2

Chelini, Italo
35BU-114

Chenevey, Jim
88Madis-10
88MidwLAS/GS-53

Cheney, Larry
14CJ-89
15CJ-89
D328-27
D329-31
D350/2-30
E135-27
M101/4-31
M101/5-30
WG4-4

Cheney, Tom
57T-359
61T-494
63Exh
63F-27
63J-99
63P-99
78TCMA-85
Exh47
WG9-27

Cherry, Gus
85Omaha-6

Cherry, Michael
85VeroB-23
86VeroB-3

Cherry, Paul
83Sprin/LF-3
86ArkTr-4
87Louvl-9
88Toled/CMC-9
88Toled/Pro-591

Chervinko, Paul
No Cards.

Chesbro, Jack
48Exh/HOF
50Callahan
61F-13
61T-407M
63Bz/ATG-3
69Bz/Sm
72F/FFeat-39
72Laugh/GF-12
79T-416M
80SSPC/HOF
85Woolwth-7
E107
T206
WG2-7

Cheshire, Donnie
78StPet

Chesnes, Bob
49B-13
50B-70

Cheso, Reno
49Sommer-11
53Mother-33

Chestnut, Troy
87Knoxv-7

Chevez, Tony
78RochR
79RochR-19

Chevolek, Tom
80ElPas-5

Chiamparino, Scott
88Huntsvl/BK-2
88Modesto-8
88Modesto/Cal-64

Chicken, San Diego
82D-531
83D-645
84D-651
84Smok/Padres-4

Chiffer, Floyd
81Hawai
83D-44
83F-354
83T-298
85Toled-32
87Richm/TCMA-2

Chikida, Honen
89Salin/Pro-1812

Childers, Jeffrey
85Beaum-1
88Modesto-7
88Wichi-30

Childress, Chip
83Durhm-1
84Durhm-13
85Durhm-20

Childress, Rocky
85Cram/PCL-31
87Tucso-10
88D-554
88F-442
88T-643
88Tucso-6
88Tucso/CMC-8
88Tucso/Pro-181
89Tucso/CMC-1
89Tucso/Pro-194

Childress, Willie J.
87Greenv/Bst-11

Childs, Clarence A.
(Cupid)
N172

Childs, Peter Pierre
(Pete)
No Cards.

Chiles, Pearce Nuget
No Cards.

Chiles, Richard F.
(Rich)
72OPC-56
72T-56
73OPC-617
73T-617
78T-193
79T-498
79Tacom-20

Chimelis, Joel
88SoOreg/Pro-1703
89Modesto/Cal-279
89Modesto/Ch-22

Ching, Maurice
(Mo)
83Greens-17
84Greens-22
86Albany/TCMA-18

Chiozza, Louis Peo
(Lou)
34DS-80
38ONG/Pin-2
39PB-58
40PB-157
41G-3
41G-3

Chipman, Robert
47TipTop
49B-184
49Eureka-54
50B-192
52B-228
52T-388

Chipple, Walter John
(Walt)
No Cards.

Chireno, Manny
87Beloi-24

Chism, Thomas R.
(Tom)
78RochR
79RochR-18
81RochR-4
82RochR-21
83RochR-23

Chiti, Dom
79Savan-1
85CharO-13C
86RochR-2C
87RochR-15C
87RochR/TCMA-25C
88RochR-28
88RochR-5
88RochR/Gov-28
88RochR/Pro-212

Chiti, Harry Dominick
53B/Col-7
55B-304
56T-179
58T-119
59T-79
60T-339
61T-269
61T/St-149
62T-253

Chitren, Steve
87Anchora-4
89Medford/Best-20

Chittum, Nelson
60T-296

Chlupsa, Bob
71OPC-594R
71T-594R

Chmil, Steve
83Durhm-2

Choate, Don
61Union

Chouinard, Felix G.
No Cards.

Chozen, Harry Kenneth
No Cards.

Chris, Mike
80Evans-5
80T-666R
81Evans-3
82Phoen
85Cram/PCL-149

Chrisley, Barbra O.
(Neil)
57T-320
58T-303
59T-189
60L-117
60T-273
62T-308

Christ, Michael
87Chatt/Best-11
88Calg/CMC-6

Christenbury, Lloyd
V100

Christensen, Bruce R.
75Phoen-15
76Phoen

Christensen, Jim
82Toled-13

Christensen, John L.
84Tidew-4
86D-360
86Pawtu-5
86Pawtu-6
86T-287
87Moth/Sea-27
87T/Tr-23T
88Calg/CMC-17
88Calg/Pro-794
88Score-419
88T-413
89F-108
89Portl/CMC-19
89Portl/Pro-214

Christensen, Walter
(Cuckoo)
No Cards.

Christenson, Gary
81Omaha-5

Christenson, Kim
83AppFx/LF-4
84PrWill-25
85Nashua-5

Christenson, Larry
74OPC-587
74T-587
75OPC-551
75T-551
75T/M-551
76OPC-634
76SSPC-460
76T-634
77OPC-194
77T-59
78OPC-17
78T-247
79BK/P-5
79OPC-260
79T-493
80BK/P-16
80OPC-89
80T-161
81F-8
81T-346
82D-219
82F-244
82T-544
83D-345
83F-156
83OPC-286
83T-668
84Nes/792-252
84T-252

Christian, Rick
86Erie-6
87Erie-1
88Hamil/Pro-1724
89StPet/Star-6

Christian, Robert
69OPC-173R
69T-173R
70OPC-51
70T-51

Christiansen, Clay
82Nashv-7
83Colum-9
84Colum-12
84Colum/Pol-5
85Colum-4
85Colum/Pol-5
85D-396
85T-211
86Albany/TCMA-28
86Colum-3
86Colum/Pol-3
88Tucso/Pro-179

Christiansen, Jim
83Tacom-30A

Christianson, Alex
79Wausa-19

Christman, Mark J.
49B-121

Christmas, Stephen R.
(Steve)
80Water-3
81Water-12
82Indianap-22
83Tucso-12

85BuffB-4
86Gator-18
86IowaC-6
Christofferson, Bob
83Tacom-25B
Christopher, Fred
86Cram/PCL-143
87Spart-27
88Clearw/Star-7
89Clearw/Star-6
89Readg/Star-7
Christopher, Joe
61T-82
63T-217
64T-546
65Bz-20
65T-495
65T/E-52
65T/trans-43
66T-343
78TCMA-7
WG10-25
Christopher, Lloyd
43Centen-4
44Centen-3
47Signal
47TipTop
48Signal
48Smith
49Remar
50Remar
Christopher, Mike
86FtLaud-6
87FtLaud-8
88Albany/Pro-1337
89Albany/Best-22
89Albany/Pro-321
89Albany/Star-4
Christy, Al
83Peoria/LF-19
Christy, Claude
53Mother-47
Chue, Jose
80Clint-3
81Clint-7
Chumas, Steve
83Idaho-18
Church, Dan
80Ander-1
Church, Donald
86Cram/PCL-138
Church, Emory
(Bubba)
51B-149
52B-40
52T-323
53B/Col-138
53T-47
55B-273
Exh47
Church, Hiram Lincoln
(Hi)
No Cards.
Churchill, James
82AlexD-16
Churchill, Norman
77Watlo
79QuadC-27
Churchill, Tim
88Martins/Star-6
89Batav/Pro-1919
89Spart/Pro-1053
89Spart/Star-4
Churn, Chuck
59DF
60DF-13
Churry, John
No Cards.
Chylak, Nestar
55B-283ump
Claffone, Lawrence T.
(Larry)
No Cards.
Ciaglo, Paul
88CapeCod/Sum-6
89James/Pro-2135
Ciampa, Mike
80Elmir-27
Cianfrocco, Angelo
87Jamestn-2
Cianfrocco, Archie
88Rockford-6
89Jaxvl/Best-11
89Jaxvl/Pro-160
89Rockford-6
Ciardi, Mark
86Vanco-6
88Denver/CMC-9
88Denver/Pro-1272
88T-417
Cias, Darryl
80WHave-14
81WHave-5
82Tacom-11
83Tacom-9
84Nes/792-159
84T-159
86SanJose-6
Cicero, Joseph F.
No Cards.
Cicione, Mike
84Evrt/Cram-3
Cicotte, Al
57T-398
58T-382
59T-57
60T-473
61T-241
62T-126
89Smok/Ast-2
Cicotte, Eddie
10Domino-24
11Helmar-2
12Sweet/Pin-2
14CJ-94
15CJ-94
87Conlon/2-29
88Pac/8Men-104
88Pac/8Men-14
88Pac/8Men-19
88Pac/8Men-22M
88Pac/8Men-38
88Pac/8Men-58
88Pac/8Men-59
88Pac/8Men-6
D327
D328-28
D329-31
E135-28
E270/1
E286
E94
E95
M101/4-31
M116
S74-2
T201
T202
T204
T205
T206
T207
W514-81
W516-21
Cicotte, Greg
80BurlB-17
Ciczczon, Steve
89ColrSp/CMC-25
Cieslak, Mark
85Cedar-2
Cieslak, Thaddeus W.
(Ted)
No Cards.
Cifarelli, Gerard
89CharRa/Pro-980
Cihocki, Albert J.
(Al)
V362-4
Cihocki, Edward J.
(Ed)
No Cards.
Cijntje, Sherwin
85Newar-13
86Hagers-4
87CharO/WBTV-2
88CharlK-25
88CharlK/Pep-25
88RochR-6
88RochR/CMC-20
88RochR/Pro-198
89Hagers/Best-7
89Hagers/Star-3
89RochR/CMC-15
89RochR/Pro-1632
Cimino, Pete
66T-563R
67OPC-34
67T-34
68OPC-143
68T-143
Cimo, Matt
87CharO/WBTV-15
88RochR-5
88RochR-7
88RochR/CMC-11
88RochR/Gov-5
88RochR/Pro-203
89ScrWB/CMC-14
89ScrWB/Pro-730
Cimoli, Gino Nicholas
52Park-70
57T-319
58BB
58Hires-63
58T-286
59T-418
60Kahn
60L-142
60T-58
61Kahn
61P-136
61T-165
62J-150
62P-150
62P/Can-150
62Salada-148
62Shirriff-148
62T-402
63J-88
63P-88
63T-321
64T-26
65T-569
89Smok/Dodg-62
V362-22
Cina, Randy
88Lynch/Star-4
Cinnella, Doug
87Hagers-29
88FSLAS/Star-4
88WPalm/Star-5
89WPalm/Star-6
Cipolloni, Joe
86Portl-3
87Maine-18
87Maine/TCMA-8
Cipot, Ed
76Wausa
78Tidew
79Tidew-14
80Tidew-7
81Toled-20
Cipres, Mark
83TriCit-6
Ciprian, Francis
88Modesto-18
88Modesto/Cal-78
Cipriani, Frank D.
62T-333
Cirbo, Dennis
78StPet
Cisar, George Joseph
No Cards.
Cisarik, Brian
88Spoka/Pro-1940
89AubAs/Pro-5
89Wich/Roc-32
Cisco, Galen
61Union
62T-301
63T-93
64T-202
64TS-47
65T-364
67T-596
69OPC-211
69T-211
73OPC-593CO
73T-593C
74T-166C
83Stuart-13CO
84Stuart-4CO
88Syrac/CMC-25
88Syrac/Pro-818
89Syrac/Pro-799
Cisco, Jeff
86CharRa-6
Cissell, Chalmer W.
(Bill)
28Exh-37
29Exh/4-19
30CEA/Pin-13
31Exh/4-19
32Orbit/num-23
32Orbit/un-10
33CJ/Pin-2
33G-26
34Exh/4-9
35BU-13
35G-1G
35G-3E
35G-5E
35G-6E
R305
R315-C1
R315-D1
R316
V353-26
W517-5
Ciszczon, Steve
80Tacom-26
83Charl-21TR
85Maine-31
86Maine-4TR
88ColSp/Pro-1539
89ColSp/Pro-250
Ciszkowski, Jeff
84LitFalls-16
86Lynch-7
87Lynch-13
89Stock/Best-11
89Stock/Cal-154
89Stock/Pro-399
89Stock/Star-17
Citarella, Ralph A.
81ArkTr-18
81Louvl-16
82Louvl-5
84Louvl-16
85Cram/PCL-44
85D-504
86Louisvl-9
86Tacom-2
87Hawai-6
Citari, Joe
86Omaha-5
86Omaha/TCMA-14
87Omaha-9
88Omaha/CMC-21
88Omaha/Pro-1519
89Readg/Star-8
Clabaugh, John W.
(Moose)
No Cards.
Clack, Marvin
82AlexD-12
83AlexD-7
Clack, Robert S.
(Bobby)
No Cards.
Claire, David M.
(Danny)
No Cards.
Clancey, William E.
(Bill)
E254
T206
Clancy, Albert H.
No Cards.
Clancy, Jim
78OPC-103DP
78T-496
79OPC-61
79T-131
80OPC-132
80T-249
81F-412
81OPC-19
81OPC/Post-21
81T-19
81T/St-143
82D-227
82F-612
82OPC-28
82T-665
83D-101
83F-426
83OPC-345
83T-345
83T/St-132
84D-119
84D-19
84D/AAS-49
84F-150
84Nes/792-575
84OPC-337
84T-575
84T/St-367
84Tor/Fire-6
85D-439
85F-101
85OPC-188
85T-746
85Tor/Fire-8
86Ault-18
86D-268
86F-56
86Leaf-141
86OPC-213
86T-412
86T-96M
86Tor/Fire-6
87D-639
87D/HL-11
87F-223
87Leaf-90
87OPC-122
87S-189
87T-122
87T/St-189
87Tor/Fire-5
87Tor/Fire-5
88D-74
88D/Best-48
88F-106
88Ho/Disc-13
88Leaf-73
88OPC-54

88Score-530
88Sf-215
88T-54
88T/Big-258
88T/St-184
88Tor/Fire-18
89B-324
89D-267
89D/Best-206
89D/Tr-32
89F-229
89F/Up-88
89Lennox/Ast-7
89Moth/Ast-15
89OPC-219
89Score-538
89Score/Tr-42
89T-219
89T/Tr-19T
89UD-282
90D-69
90F-226
90Score-424
90T-648
90UD-203

Clancy, John William
(Bud)
29Exh/4-19
33G-32
R315-D2
V353-32

Clanton, Ucal
(Uke)
No Cards.

Clapham, Mark
78OrlTw

Clapp, Aaron Bronson
No Cards.

Clapp, John Edgar
No Cards.

Clarey, Douglas W.
(Doug)
77Holyo

Clark, Al
88Umpire-24
89Umpires-22

Clark, Alfred A.
(Allie)
49B-150
50B-233
50NumNum
51B-29
52B-130
52T-278
53B/Col-155

Clark, Alfred Robert
(Fred)
No Cards.

Clark, Bailey Earl
(Earl)
33G-57
40Wheat-4
V354-41

Clark, Bob
84Nes/792-626
86OPC-352

Clark, Bryan
77Salem
78Charl
80Spoka-8
82D-596
82F-507
82SLCty-6
82T-632
83D-603
83F-476
83T-789
84D-562
84F-609
84F/X-26
84Nes/792-22
84T-22
84T/X-25
84Tor/Fire-7
85Maine-5
85OPC-217
85Polar/Ind-43
85T-489
85T/Tr-21T
86BuffB-8
89AAA/Pro-39
89Tacom/CMC-7
89Tacom/Pro-1563

Clark, Casey
77Salem
78Charl

Clark, Chris
81Holyo-9
82Holyo-19
84Cram/PCL-108
85Cram/PCL-18

Clark, Dan
84Butte-4

Clark, Daniel Curran
(Danny)
21Exh-23

Clark, Dave
85Water-15
86Maine-5
87BuffB-6
87D-623
87F-644M
87Gator-12
87S-118M
88D-473
88Gator-25
88Rockford-7
88Score-633
88T-49
89D-585
89F-402
89Rockford-7
89T-574
89UD-517
90D-492
90F-490
90Score-141
90T-339
90UD-449

Clark, Dera
88BBCity/Star-8
89Memph/Best-18
89Memph/Pro-1199
89Memph/Star-6
89Star/Wax-40

Clark, Garry
87Clearw-13
87Spart-7
88Clearw/Star-8

Clark, Glen Ester
No Cards.

Clark, Harry
(Pep)
No Cards.

Clark, Isaiah
86Beloi-4
87Stockton-11
88Modesto-20
89River/Best-29
89River/Cal-9
89River/Pro-1404

Clark, Jack Anthony
75Lafay
76Phoen
77T-488R
78T-384
79Ho-116
79K-40
79OPC-268
79Pol/Giants-22
79T-512
79T/Comics-32
80K-57
80OPC-93
80Pol/Giants-22
80T-167
80T/S-54
81D-315
81Drake-15
81F-433
81F/St-52
81MSA/Disc-9
81OPC-30
81Sqt-18
81T-30
81T/SO-70
81T/St-234
82D-46
82Drake-8
82F-387
82F/St-65
82T-460
82T/St-106
83D-222
83D/AAS-29
83Drake-5
83F-256
83K-48
83Moth/Giants-2
83OPC-210
83T-210
83T/Gloss-32
83T/Gloss40-32
83T/St-162
83T/St-300
84D-65
84D-7
84D/AAS-31
84F-369
84FunFood/Pin-19
84Moth/Giants-7
84Nes/792-690
84OPC-381
84T-690
84T/St-167
85D-65
85D/AAS-30
85F-604
85F/Up-U25
85Leaf-207
85OPC-208
85T-740
85T/St-160
85T/Tr-22T
86D-168
86D/AAS-23
86F-30
86F/LL-6
86F/Mini-6
86F/St-24
86KAS/Disc-9
86Leaf-96
86OPC-350
86Quaker-5
86S-107
86Schnucks-1
86T-350
86T/Gloss60-4
86T/Mini-59
86T/St-50
87Class/Up-148
87D-111
87D/OD-67
87F-289
87F/Lim-C4
87F/Slug-9
87OPC-331
87S-195M
87Smok/Cards-13
87T-520
87T/Board-25
87T/St-52
88Class/Blue-205
88D-15DK
88D-183
88D/AS-33
88D/Best-49
88D/DKsuper-15DK
88D/PopUp-11
88D/Y/Bk-NEW
88F-26
88F/AS-11
88F/BB/AS-6
88F/Excit-8
88F/Mini-39
88F/RecSet-5
88F/SS-7
88F/U-U47
88Jiffy-4
88KayBee-5
88KMart-5
88Leaf-15DK
88Leaf-181
88Nestle-17
88OPC-100
88Panini/St-232M
88Panini/St-388
88RedFoley/St-12
88Score-650
88Score-78
88Score/Tr-1T
88Score/WxBx-11
88Sf-18
88Sf/Gamewin-25
88T-100
88T-397
88T/Big-262
88T/Coins-9
88T/Gloss22-13
88T/Gloss60-41
88T/Mini-69
88T/Revco-4
88T/RiteAid-10
88T/St-150
88T/St-46
88T/St/Backs-1
88T/Tr-28T
88T/UK-13
89B-456
89Class/Up/2-158
89Crunch-14
89D-311
89D/Best-98
89D/Tr-2
89F-252
89F/Up-123
89KayBee-5
89OPC-3
89RedFoley/St-21
89Score-25
89Score/HotSt-27
89Score/Tr-3
89Sf-26
89T-410
89T/Big-240
89T/Coins-7
89T/Gloss60-56
89T/Mini-65
89T/St-308
89T/Tr-20T
89T/UK-14
89UD-346
89UD/Ext-773
90D-128
90F-152
90Score-20
90Sf-28
90T-90
90UD-342

Clark, James Edward
(Jim)
No Cards.

Clark, James Francis
(Jim)
E96

Clark, James
(Jim)
No Cards.

Clark, Jeff
89Pulas/Pro-1910

Clark, Jerald
85Spoka/Cram-3
87Wichi-24
88LasVeg/CMC-12
88LasVeg/Pro-229
89AAA/Pro-49
89B-462
89D-599
89F-642M
89LasVeg/CMC-13
89LasVeg/Pro-10
89Score-644
89Sf-179
89UD-30
90D-593
90Score-660
90UD-624

Clark, John Carroll
(Cap)
No Cards.

Clark, Joshua B.
(Pepper)
T206

Clark, Leroy
76Dubuq

Clark, Mark
87Sumter-11
88Hamil/Pro-1736
89Savan/Pro-370

Clark, Melvin Earl
(Mel)
53B/Col-67
54B-175
55B-41

Clark, Mike J.
53Hunter
53T-193

Clark, Owen F.
(Spider)
No Cards.

Clark, Phil
87Fayette-23
88FSLAS/Star-31
88Lakel/Star-7
89London/Pro-1383

Clark, Philip J.
58T-423
59T-454

Clark, Randy
79QuadC-14

Clark, Rickey
70T-586
71OPC-697
71T-697
72OPC-462
72T-462
73OPC-636
73T-636

Clark, Rob
83Tulsa-4
84OKCty-2
85Tulsa-27
86OKCty-3

Clark, Robert Cale
(Bobby)
76QuadC
79SLCty-12
80SLCty-23
80T-663R
81D-572
81T-288
82D-318
82F-456
82T-74
83D-444
83F-82
83T-184
84D-524
84F-512
84F/X-25

84Gard-4
84Pol/Brew-25
84T-626
84T/X-24
85Cram/PCL-204
85D-481
85F-578
85Gard-3
85T-553
86Edmon-4
86T-452
87Tacom-4

Clark, Robert H.
(Bob)
N172

Clark, Rodney
85Utica-13

Clark, Ronald Bruce
(Ron)
67OPC-137R
67T-137R
68T-589R
69T-561
70OPC-531
70T-531
71MLB/St-509
75IntAS/TCMA-13
76OkCty
82OkCty-6MG
86Clearw-4MG

Clark, Roy
79Tulsa-24M

Clark, Roy
80LynnS-20
81Spoka-6
82SLCty-7

Clark, Royal
No Cards.

Clark, Russell
76Wausa
79Jacks-20
79Tidew-22

Clark, Skip
81Miami-12

Clark, Terry
83ArkTr-3
84Louvl-24
86MidldA-5
87Edmon-22
88Edmon/CMC-1
88Edmon/Pro-569
89AAA/Pro-27
89D-607
89F-470
89OPC-129
89Score-566
89Score/HotRk-89
89T-129
89UD-234

Clark, Tony
86DayBe-5

Clark, Will
86D/HL-1
86D/Rook-32
86F/Slug-6
86F/Up-U25
86Moth/Giants-7
86S/Rook-6
86T/Tr-24T
87BK-3
87D-66
87D/OD-96
87F-269
87F/Excit-10
87F/McCror-8
87F/Slug-M2
87F/St-22
87Leaf-144
87Moth/SFG-2
87OPC-361
87RedFoley/St-50
87S-95
87T-420
87T/St-88
87ToysRUs-7
88Class/Blue-225
88D-204
88D-21DK
88D-BC24
88D/Best-79
88D/DKsuper-21DK
88F-78
88F/AwardWin-5
88F/BB/AS-7
88F/BB/MVP-5
88F/Excit-9
88F/Hottest-6
88F/LL-5
88F/Mini-116
88F/RecSet-6
88F/Slug-8
88F/SS-8
88F/St-126
88F/TL-4
88FanSam-12
88Jiffy-5
88KMart-6
88Leaf-170
88Leaf-21DK
88Moth/Giants-2
88Moth/WClark-1
88Moth/WClark-2
88Moth/WClark-3
88Moth/WClark-4
88MSA/Disc-10
88Nestle-14
88OPC-350
88Panini/St-420
88Score-78
88Score/YS/I-25
88Sf-9
88Sf/Gamewin-4
88T-350
88T/Big-9
88T/Coins-38
88T/RiteAid-12
88T/St-87
88T/UK-14
89B-476
89Cadaco-8
89Class-150
89Class-18
89Class/Up/2-180
89Crunch-19
89D-249
89D/AS-33
89D/Best-23
89D/MVP-BC22
89D/PopUp-33
89F-325
89F-631M
89F-632M
89F/AS-3
89F/BBAS-6
89F/BBMVP's-7
89F/Excit-5
89F/Heroes-7
89F/LL-4
89F/Superstar-8
89F/WaxBox-C6
89KayBee-6
89KingB/Discs-22
89KMart/DT-23
89Moth/Giants-2
89Moth/WClark-1
89Moth/WClark-2
89Moth/WClark-3
89Moth/WClark-4
89OPC-321
89Panini/St-212
89Panini/St-232AS
89RedFoley/St-22
89Score-450
89Score/HotSt-85
89Score/Mast-10
89Sf-170
89T-660
89T/Big-146
89T/Coins-8
89T/DH-13
89T/Gloss22-13
89T/Gloss60-11
89T/HeadsUp-2
89T/Hills-7
89T/Mini-40
89T/St-159
89T/St-88
89T/St/Backs-34
89T/UK-15
89Tetley/Discs-4
89UD-155
89UD-678TC
90Class-150
90Class-6
90Class-87
90D-230
90D-707AS
90D/Preview-12
90F-54
90F-630
90F-637M
90Score-300
90Score-684DT
90Score-699M
90Score/100St-30
90Sf-5
90T-100
90T-397AS
90UD-50M
90UD-556

Clark, William Otis
(Willie)
No Cards.

Clark, William Watson
(Lefty)
32Orbit/num-8
32Orbit/un-11
33DH-9
33G-17
35G-1G
35G-3E
35G-4E
35G-5E
R305
R337-407
V353-17
V355-86

Clark, William Winf.
(Bill)
No Cards.

Clarke, Arthur F.
(Archie)
No Cards.

Clarke, Fred C.
10Domino-25
11Helmar-112
11Helmar-157
12Sweet/Pin-135A
12Sweet/Pin-135B
14CJ-70
14Piedmont/St-12
15CJ-70
48Exh/HOF
50Callahan
63Bz/ATG-26
73F/Wild-21
80SSPC/HOF
86Conlon/1-53
D322
E107
E254
E270/1
E270/2
E300
E90/1
E90/2
E91
E93
E96
E98
M116
S74-108
T201
T205
T206
T3-8
W555
WG3-10
WG5-10
WG6-10

Clarke, Harry Corson
No Cards.

Clarke, Horace M.
66T-547
67OPC-169
67T-169
68T-263
69MB-59
69MLB/St-73
69OPC-87
69T-87
69T/St-202
70MLB/St-244
70T-623
71MLB/St-486
71OPC-715
71T-715
72MB-74
72OPC-387
72T-387
73OPC-198
73T-198
74OPC-529
74T-529

Clarke, Jay Austin
(Nig)
E254
E270/1
E270/2
M116
T202
T206

Clarke, Joshua B.
(Josh)
No Cards.

Clarke, Richard Grey
(Dick)
No Cards.

Clarke, Stan
83Knoxv-2
84Syrac-19
84Tor/Fire-8
85Syrac-4
86Syrac-5
87Calgary-18
88T-556
88Toled/CMC-2
88Toled/Pro-607
89Omaha/CMC-2
89Omaha/Pro-1737

Clarke, Sumpter Mills
No Cards.

Clarke, Thomas A.
(Tommy)
D328-29
D329-33
D350/2-32
E135-29
M101/4-33
M101/5-32
M116
T207

Clarke, Tim
82QuadC-6

Clarke, William H.
N172

Clarke, William Jones
(Boileryard)
E107
E270/2

Clarke, William S.
(Stu)
No Cards.

Clarkin, Mike
86WinHav-6
87NewBrit-1
88NewBrit/Pro-891

Clarkson, James B.
(Buzz)
No Cards.

Clarkson, John Gibson
75F/Pion-26
80SSPC/HOF
E223
N172
N28
N284
N300/unif
N403
WG1-2

Clary, Ellis
60T-470C

Clary, Marty
85Richm-2
86D-36
87Richm/TCMA-3
88F-535
88Richm-32
88Richm/CMC-10
88Richm/Pro-11
89Richm/CMC-1
89Richm/Ko-32
89Richm/Pro-826
90D-381
90F-578
90T-304

Clatterbuck, Don
79Newar-9

Clawson, Chris
86Ashvl-4

Clawson, Ken
87PortChar-1

Clay, Billy
79Newar-17

Clay, Dain Elmer
No Cards.

Clay, Danny
83Wisco/LF-16
85Orlan-16
86Toled-5
87Portl-11
88F/U-U108
88Maine/Pro-297
89ScrWB/Pro-706

Clay, Dave
82Durhm-14
83Durhm-17
85Richm-3
86ElPas-6
87Denver-1

Clay, Frederick C.
(Bill)
No Cards.

Clay, Jeff
81Cedar-21
82Cedar-26
86Salem-4TR

Clay, Ken
78T-89
79OPC-225
79T-434
80T-159
81F-633
81Pol/Mariners-8
81T-305
81T/Tr-747
82F-508
82T-649

Clayton, Kenny
82Beloi-14

82Idaho-22
Clayton, Royal
88CLAS/Star-4
88PrWill/Star-6
89Albany/Best-6
89Albany/Pro-318
89Albany/Star-5
89Star/Wax-96
Clayton, Royce
89B-472
89Clint/Pro-895
Clear, Mark
76QuadC
77QuadC
80T-638
81D-291
81T-12
81T/Tr-748
82Coke/BOS
82D-452
82F-290
82OPC-169
82T-421
82T/St-154
83D-361
83F-181
83F-629M
83OPC-162
83T-162
83T/St-36
84D-611
84F-395
84Nes/792-577
84OPC-148
84T-577
85D-538
85F-154
85Leaf-32
85T-207
86D-493
86F-344
86F/Up-U26
86Pol/Brew-25
86T-349
86T/Tr-25T
87D-355
87F-341
87F/Lim-9
87F/St-23
87OPC-244
87T-640
87T/St-195
88D-372
88F-160
88Pol/Brew-25
88Score-446
88T-742
89B-37
89D-528
89F-182
89Score-430
89T-63
Cleary, Tony
79Elmir-16
86Pawtu-7TR
87Pawtu-15
88Pawtu/CMC-14
88Pawtu/Pro-467
89Pawtu/Dunkin-TR
89Pawtu/Pro-683
Clem, John
86Wausa-3
Clemens, Chester S.
(Chet)
No Cards.
Clemens, Clement L.
(Clem)
No Cards.
Clemens, Douglas H.
(Doug)
67T-489
Clemens, Roger
84F/X-27
84Pawtu-22
85D-273
85F-155
85F/St-123
85Leaf-99
85T-181
86D-172
86D/HL-17
86D/HL-18
86D/HL-26
86D/HL-5
86D/HL-6
86F-345
86F/Mini-73
86F/Slug-7
86OPC-98
86T-661
87BK-4
87Class-84
87Class/Up-114
87D-276
87D-2DK
87D/AAS-8
87D/AS/Wax-PC14
87D/DKsuper-2
87D/PopUp-8
87Drake-31
87F-32
87F-634M
87F-640M
87F/AS-11
87F/AwardWin-9
87F/Excit-11
87F/GameWin-10
87F/Hottest-10
87F/Lim-10
87F/LL-10
87F/McCror-9
87F/Mini-20
87F/RecSet-4
87F/Slug-10
87F/St-24
87F/WS-3
87Jiffy-12
87KayBee-10
87Kraft-45
87Leaf-190
87Leaf-2DK
87MnM's-7
87MSA/Discs-2
87OPC-340
87Ralston-10
87RedFoley/St-70
87S-10
87S-111M
87S-159M
87S-196M
87Seven-E8
87Seven-ME10
87T-1RB
87T-340
87T-614AS
87T/Coins-8
87T/Gloss22-21
87T/Gloss60-5
87T/HL-7
87T/Mini-42
87T/St-154
87T/St-2
87T/St-244
87T/St-3
87Woolwth-7
88Woolwth-11
88Bz-4
88ChefBoy-23
88Class/Blue-217
88Class/Red-158
88D-51
88D/Best-57
88D/RedSox/Bk-51
88F-349
88F/AS-4
88F/AwardWin-6
88F/BB/AS-8
88F/BB/MVP-6
88F/Excit-10
88F/Hottest-7
88F/LL-6
88F/Mini-5
88F/RecSet-7
88F/Slug-9
88F/SS-9
88F/St-7
88F/TL-5
88Jiffy-6
88KingB/Disc-20
88KMart-7
88Leaf-56
88MSA/Disc-9
88Nestle-1
88OPC-70
88Panini/St-21
88RedFoley/St-13
88Score-110
88Score/YS/II-23
88Sf-207
88Sf/Gamewin-20
88T-394
88T-70
88T/Big-118
88T/Coins-2
88T/Gloss60-13
88T/Mini-2
88T/Revco-28
88T/St-251
88T/St/Backs-58
88T/UK-15
89B-26
89Cadaco-9
89Class-119
89Crunch-18
89D-280
89D/AS-14
89D/Best-65
89F-85
89F/BBAS-7
89F/BBMVP's-8
89F/Excit-6
89F/Heroes-8
89F/LL-5
89F/Rec-2
89F/Superstar-9
89Holsum/Discs-16
89KayBee-7
89KMart/DT-20
89Nissen-16
89OPC-121
89Panini/St-249
89Panini/St-270
89Ralston-7
89RedFoley/St-23
89Score-350
89Score/HotSt-90
89Score/Mast-20
89Sf-3
89T-405AS
89T-450
89T/Big-42
89T/Coins-37
89T/DH-9
89T/Gloss60-23
89T/Hills-8
89T/Mini-46
89T/St-259
89T/St/Backs-25
89T/UK-16
89Tetley/Discs-8
89UD-195
90Class-51
90D-184
90F-271
90F-627
90F/WaxBox-C3
90Score-310
90Score/100St-79
90Sf-149
90T-245
90UD-323
90UD-57TC
Clement, Wallace Oaks
(Wally)
E90/1
Clemente, Roberto W.
55T-164
56T-33
57Kahn
57T-76
58Kahn
58T-52
59Kahn
59T-478
59T-543M
60Bz-7
60Kahn
60T-326
61Kahn
61P-132
61T-388
61T-41LL
62Bz-11
62Exh
62J-173
62Kahn
62P-173
62P/Can-173
62Salada-150
62Shirriff-150
62Sugar-B
62T-10
62T-52LL
62T/bucks
62T/St-174
63Bz-14
63Exh
63F-56
63J-143
63Kahn
63P-143
63Salada-23
63T-18M
63T-540
63T/SO
64Bz-14
64Kahn
64T-440
64T-7LL
64T/Coins-150AS
64T/Coins-55
64T/S-11
64T/St-27
64T/SU
64Wheat/St-11
65Bz-14
65MacGregor-1
65OPC-160
65OPC-2LL
65T-160
65T-2LL
65T/E-19
65T/trans-44
66Bz-26
66EH-21
66Kahn
66T-215LL
66T-300
66T/RO-47
67Bz-26
67OPC/PI-11
67T-242LL
67T-400
67T/PI-11
67T/Test/PP-27
67T/Test/PP-6
67T/Test/SU-7
68Bz-12
68Coke
68KDKA-21
68OPC-150
68OPC-1LL
68OPC-3LL
68T-150
68T-1LL
68T-374AS
68T-3LL
68T-480M
68T/3D
68T/G-6
68T/Post-6
69MB-60
69MLB/St-184
69MLBPA/Pin-39
69OPC-50
69OPC/DE-4
69T-50
69T/DE-27
69T/decal
69T/S-58
69T/St-85
69Trans-56
70K-27
70MB-5
70MLB/St-99
70OPC-350
70OPC-61LL
70T-350
70T-61LL
70T/PI-21
70T/S-12
70Trans-5
71Bz
71Bz/Test-38
71K-5
71MLB/St-198
71MLB/St-558
71OPC-630
71T-630
71T/Coins-71
71T/S-37
72K-49
72MB-75
72OPC-226WS
72OPC-309
72OPC-310IA
72T-309
72T-310A
72T/Cloth-6
73OPC-50
73T-50
74Laugh/ASG-62
75OPC-204M
75T-204MV
75T/M-204MV
78TCMA-13
79TCMA-23
80Cram/Leg-50
80Laugh/FFeat-21
82KMart-10
83D/HOF-17
83MLBPA/Pin-22
84West/1-3
86CharRa-7
86S/Dec-43
87D-612PUZ
87D/AS/WaxBox-PUZ
87D/DKsuper-28
87D/WaxBox-PUZ
87KMart-2
87Leaf-163
87Nestle/DT-27
87T-313TBC
89HOF/St-46
89Pac/Leg-135
89Swell-125
Exh47
PM10/Sm-26

Clements, Dave
83Sprin/LF-2
84ArkTr-2
85Louvl-14
86ArkTr-5
Clements, Edward
(Ed)
No Cards.
Clements, John T.
(Jack)
N172
N284
N690
WG1-49
Clements, Pat
85F/Up-U26
85Smok/Cal-22
85T/Tr-23T
86D-600
86F-606
86OPC-283
86T-754
87D-390
87F-608
87T-16
88Colum/CMC-1
88Colum/Pol-1
88Colum/Pro-318
88D-52
88F-204
88Score-389
88T-484
89B-452
89LasVeg/Pro-15
89T-159
90F-153
90T-548
Clements, Wes
83Tucso-14
84Cram/PCL-53
85Beloi-14
87GlenF-5
Clemo, Scott
86Jamestn-3
87Indianap-28
88WPalm/Star-6
Clemons, Lance
72OPC-372R
72T-372R
Clemons, Mark
85Kingst-1
86Orlan-4
87Orlan-10
88Jaxvl/Best-8
88Jaxvl/Pro-977
Clemons, Robert
E270/2
Clemons, Vern
V61-85
Clemons, Verne James
E120
V100
W573
Clendenon, Donn Alvin
62T-86
63Kahn
63T-477
64Kahn
64T-163
64T/Coins-15
64T/St-76
64T/SU
65Kahn
65T-325
65T/E-9
66EH-17
66OPC-99M
66T-375
66T-99M
67T-266M
67T-535
67T/Test/PP-30
67T/Test/PP-7
68KDKA-17
68T-344
69MB-61
69OPC-208
69T-208
69T/decal
69T/St-54
70MLB/St-74
70OPC-280
70OPC-306WS
70T-280
70Trans/M-24
71MLB/St-149
71OPC-115
71T-115
71T/Coins-151
71T/S-4
71T/tatt-6
72MB-76
72T-671
78TCMA-237
Cleveland, Elmer E.
N172
Cleveland, Reggie
70T-716R
71OPC-216R
71T-216R
72OPC-375
72T-375
73OPC-104
73T-104
74OPC-175
74T-175
74T/St-112
74T/Tr-175T
75OPC-32
75T-32
75T/M-32
76OPC-419
76T-419
77OPC-111
77T-613
78BK/R-10
78T-105
79OPC-103
79T-209
80T-394
81D-206
81F-523
81T-576
82D-456
82F-137
82T-737
Clevenger, Tex
58T-31
59T-298
60T-392
61T-291
63T-457
Cleverly, Gary
75SnAnt
Cliburn, Stanley Gene
(Stan)
75QuadC
76QuadC
78Cr/PCL-74
82Portl-10
83LynnP-11
84Cram/PCL-132
85Cram/PCL-242
86Edmon-5M
86Edmon-6
87Richm/TCMA-28
88BuffB/CMC-24
88BuffB/Pro-1480
88Watertn/Puc-31
89Aug/Pro-514
Cliburn, Stewart
77Salem
80Port-13
81Buffa-9
83Nashua-3
84Cram/PCL-113
85Cram/PCL-19
85F/Up-U27
86D-301
86Edmon-5M
86Edmon-7
86F-152
86S-177M
86T-179
87D-530
88Smok/Angels-19
89D-462
89Edmon/CMC-7
89Edmon/Pro-566
89F-471
89Score-445
89T-649
89UD-483
Clift, Harland Benton
36Exh/4-15
37Exh/4-15
37OPC-104
38Exh/4-15
38Wheat
41DP-148
41G-2
41G-2
41PB-66
V300
W753
Clifton, Herman Earl
(Flea)
R314
V355-32
Cline, John
(Monk)
N172
Cline, Steve
75Cedar
81Clint-3
82Clint-3
84Shrev/FB-4CO
88Shreve/Pro-1286
89Shreve/Pro-1837
Cline, Tyrone A.
(Ty)
61T-421
62Kahn
62Sugar-8
62T-362
62T/St-32
63J-74
63P-74
63T-414
64T-171
65OPC-63
65T-63
66T-306
67T-591
68T-469
69MB-62
69MLB/St-156
69T-442
70MLB/St-64
70OPC-164
70T-164
71MLB/St-54
71OPC-199NLCS
71OPC-201
71OPC-319
71T-319
72MB-77
78TCMA-149
78TCMA-191
Clines, Eugene
(Gene)
71OPC-27R
71T-27R
72OPC-152
72T-152
73OPC-333
73T-333
74OPC-172
74T-172
75OPC-575
75T-575
75T/M-575
76OPC-417
76SSPC-543
76T-417
77T-237
78T-639
79T-171
Clingman, William F.
(Billy)
No Cards.
Clinton, James L.
(Jim)
No Cards.
Clinton, Jim
89Butte/SP-11
Clinton, Luciean L.
(Lu)
60T-533
61Union
62T-457
63F-6
63J-82
63P-82
63T-96
64T-526
65OPC-229
65T-229
67T-426
Cloherty, John
76Dubuq
78DaytB
Cloninger, Darin
85Albany-3
Cloninger, Greg
88Sumter/Pro-406
89BurlB/Pro-1601
89BurlB/Star-4
Cloninger, Todd
86Geneva-2
87WinSal-3
Cloninger, Tom
87Oneon-33
Cloninger, Tony
62T-63
63J-157
63P-157
63T-367
64T-575
65Kahn
65T-520
66Bz-27
66Kahn
66OPC-10
66T-10
66T-223LL
66T/RO-116
67Bz-27
67Kahn
67T-396M
67T-490
68Coke
68OPC-93
68T-93
69Kahn
69MLB/St-128
69T-492
70MLB/St-26
70T-705
71MLB/St-55
71OPC-218
71T-218
72T-779
78TCMA-20
88Albany/Pro-1353
Close, Casey
88Colum/CMC-21
88Colum/Pol-19
88Colum/Pro-325
Clossen, Bill
86Durhm-4
87PrWill-15
Closter, Alan
66T-549R
69OPC-114R
69T-114R
72OPC-124R
72T-124R
73OPC-634
73T-634
Clough, Edgar George
(Ed)
No Cards.
Cluck, Bob
74Cedar
75Dubuq
76Dubuq
81Tucso-5
84Cram/PCL-239MG
85Cram/PCL-110MG
Cluff, Paul
89Boise/Pro-2006
Clutterbuck, Bryan
82Beloi-20
83ElPas-15
84ElPas-5
85Cram/PCL-222
86Vanco-7
87D-397
87Denver-23
87F-342
87T-562
89Pol/Brew-48
89T/Tr-21T
90T-264
90UD-239
Clyde, David
74OPC-133
74T-133
74T/St-233
75OPC-12
75T-12
75T/M-12
76Laugh/Jub-19
77Tucso
79T-399
80T-697
Clymer, Otis Edgar
E254
E270/2
T204
Clymer, William J.
T206
Coachman, Pete
86PalmSp-7
86PalmSp/Smok-22
87Edmon-13
88Edmon/CMC-13
88Edmon/Pro-578
89Edmon/CMC-12
89Edmon/Pro-563
Coakley, Andrew
T204
Coan, Gilbert F.
(Gil)
49B-90
50B-54
51B-18
52B-51
52RM-AL4
52T-291
53B/Col-34
53T-133
54B-40
54Esskay
55B-78
55Esskay
R302-114
Coates, Jim
59T-525

60L-35
60T-51
61P-17
61T-531
62T-553
63T-237
67T-401
78TCMA-217
78TCMA-267

Coatney, Rick
81Durhm-16
82Durhm-15

Cobb, Joseph S.
No Cards.

Cobb, Mark
88Spart/Star-20
88Spart/Star-4
89Clearw/Star-7
89Star/Wax-11

Cobb, Tyrus Raymond
(Ty)
09Buster/Pin-4
10Domino-26
11Helmar-28
12Sweet/Pin-22A
12Sweet/Pin-22B
14CJ-30
14Piedmont/St-13
15CJ-30
21Exh-24
25Exh-90
26Exh-91
27Exh-53
28Yueng-27
33SK-1
33SK-1
48Exh/HOF-2
50Callahan
60Exh/HOF-7
60F-42
60NuCard-43
61F-14
61F-1M
61GP-25
61NuCard-443
63Bz/ATG-35
69Bz-1
69Bz-7
69Bz-8
72F/FFeat-15
72K/ATG-15
72K/ATG-15
72Laugh/GF-35
73F/Wild-35M
73OPC-471LL
73OPC-475LL
73T-471LL
73T-475LL
75F/Pion-14
76OPC-346AS
76T-346M
79T-411M
79T-414M
80Cram/Leg-31
80Laugh/3/4/5-4
80Laugh/FFeat-28
80SSPC/HOF
83D/HOF-1
84D/Champs-26
84West/1-8
85Woolwth-8
86Conlon/1-2
86Conlon/1-24
86Conlon/1-41
86Conlon/1-6
87Conlon/2-5
87Nestle/DT-7
88Conlon/4-6
89HOF/St-37
89Pac/Leg-117
89Swell-2
B18
BF2-25
D303
D304
D327
D328-30
D329-38
E101
E102
E103
E105
E106
E120
E121/120
E121/80
E126-17
E135-30
E210-27
E220
E224
E254
E270/1
E270/2
E300
E90/1
E92
E93
E94
E95
E98
L1-127
M101/4-38
M116
PM1-3
R328-14
R423-14
S74-13
S81-102
T201
T202
T205
T206
T213/blue
T213/brown
T215/blue
T215/brown
T216
T227
T3-9
V100
V117-22
V61-30
W501-8
W502-27
W512-3
W514-43
W515-10
W516-6
W555
W572
W573
WG4-5
WG5-11
WG6-11

Coble, David Lamar
(Dave)
No Cards.

Coble, Drew
88Umpire-45
89Umpires-43

Cobleigh, Mike
89Modesto/Ch-5

Cocanower, Jaime
81Vanco-1
82Vanco-20
84F/X-28
84Pol/Brew-47
84T/X-26
85Cram/PCL-210
85D-455
85F-579
85Gard-4
85Pol/Brew-47
85T-576
85T/St-288
86D-393
86F-483
86Pol/Brew-47
86T-277
86T/Tr-24T
87Albuq/Pol-7
87F/McCror-8
87T-423
87T/GlossRk-4

Coccia, Dan
88Martins/Star-7

Cochran, Arnold
81Batav-12
81Watlo-20

Cochran, Dave
84Jacks-21

Cochran, George L.
No Cards.

Cochran, Greg
79Colum-17
80Colum-21
81Colum-12
82Colum-8
82Colum/Pol-27

Cochrane, Dave
87Hawai-13
87S-158M
87Seven-C5
88Calg/CMC-14
88Calg/Pro-785
89Calg/CMC-14
89Calg/Pro-542
90T-491

Cochrane, Gordon S.
(Mickey)
28Exh-53
29Exh/4-27
31Exh/4-28
32Orbit/num-28
32Orbit/un-12
33DH-10
33DL-6
33Exh/4-14
33G-76
34DS-4
34Exh/4-12
34Exh/4-14
34G-2
35BU-25
35Exh/4-12
35G-1D
35G-1J
35G-2D
35G-3A
35G-5A
35G-6A
35G-6D
35G-7D
35Wheat
36Exh/4-12
36G
36Wheat
37Exh/4-12
40PB-180
48Exh/HOF
49Leaf/Prem-2
50Callahan
51T/CMAS
60F-24
60NuCard-19
61F-15
61GP-12
61NuCard-419
63Bz/ATG-34
69Bz/Sm
72K/ATG-4
72K/ATG-4
76OPC-348AS
76T-348M
80Cram/Leg-38
80SSPC/HOF
85West/2-29
86Conlon/1-7
86S/Dec-13
87Nestle/DT-8
88Conlon/3-7
88Conlon/AmAS-5
89HOF/St-56
89Pac/Leg-151
R305
R306
R308-155
R308-186
R309/2
R310
R311/Gloss
R312
R314
R328-12
R332-32
V353-69
V354-59
V355-45
W517-37
W517-54

Cockman, James
(Jim)
No Cards.

Cockrell, Alan
86Shrev-4
87Phoen-15
88Phoen/CMC-19
88Phoen/Pro-68
89Portl/CMC-20
89Portl/Pro-224

Codinach, Antonio
84Visal-19

Codiroli, Chris
82WHave-4
83T/X-20
84D-345
84F-441
84Moth/A's-10
84Nes/792-61
84OPC-61
84T-61
84T/St-330
85D-462
85F-420
85Moth/A's-9
85T-552
85T/St-327
86D-278
86F-414
86Leaf-151
86Moth/A's-15
86OPC-388
86T-433
86T/St-173
87D-226
87F-390
87T-217
89T-6

Cody
N172

Coentopp, Kevin
86Cram/PCL-175

Coffey, John Francis
(Jack)
No Cards.

Coffey, Mike
85Cedar-3
86Elmir-5
87WinHav-11

Coffman, George David
39PB-147
40PB-55
41G-32

Coffman, Jim
82Amari-12

Coffman, Kevin
85Durhm-5
86Durhm-5
87Greenv/Bst-20
87SLAS-19
88D/Rook-49
88F-536
88T/Tr-29T
89B-282
89OPC-44
89T-488

Coffman, Samuel R.
(Dick)
33G-101
35BU-92
35G-1F
35G-3D
35G-5D
35G-6D
39PB-24
40PB-140
V354-23

Coggins, Franklin
68OPC-96R
68T-96R

Coggins, Richard A.
(Rich)
73JP
73OPC-611R
73T-611R
74OPC-353
74T-353
75OPC-167
75T-167
76OPC-572
76SSPC-446
76T-572
76T/M-167

Coghen, Al
77Wausa
78Wausa

Coghill, Dave
80Ander-7

Cogswell, Edward
(Ed)
No Cards.

Cohea, Dave
77Clint
82Albuq-25
83Albuq-24

Cohen, Albert
(Alta)
No Cards.

Cohen, Andrew Howard
(Andy)
33G-52
60T-466C
V353-52

Cohen, Tony
87Macon-23
88Aug/Pro-380

Cohoon, Don
86Wausa-4
88CharWh/Best-18
89WinSal/Star-5

Coin, Mike
85Beloi-5

Coker, Jimmie Goodwin
60T-438
61T-144
63T-456
64T-211
65OPC-192
65T-192
66T-292
67OPC-158
67T-158

Coker, Larry
88Fay/Pro-1084

Colarusso, Sam
88CapeCod/Sum-105

Colavito, Rocco D.
(Rocky)
55Salem

57Swift
57T-212
58T-368
59Bz
59HRDerby-6
59Kahn
59T-166M
59T-420
59T-462M
60Armour-5
60Bz-30
60NuCard-68
60T-260M
60T-400
60T/tatt
60T/tatt-88
60T/tatt-9
61Bz-17
61NuCard-468
61P-36
61T-330
61T-44LL
62Exh
62P-19
62P/Can-19
62Salada-28
62Shirriff-28
62T-20
62T-314M
62T-472AS
62T/bucks
62T/St-46
63Bz-33
63Exh
63J-50
63P-50
63Salada-58
63T-240
63T-4LL
63T/SO
64Bz-33
64T-320
64T/Coins-46
64T/S-9
64T/St-65
64T/SU
64T/tatt
65Bz-33
65OldLond-23
65T-380
65T/E-46
65T/trans-45
66Bz-15
66OPC-150
66T-150
66T-220LL
66T/RO-72
67Bz-15
67OPC-109M
67T-109M
67T-580
68OPC-99
68T-99
73OPC-449CO
73T-449C
79TCMA-216
85CircK-27
89Swell-126
Exh47

Colavito, Steve
88Watlo/Pro-679

Colbern, Michael M.
(Mike)
79T-704R
80T-664R
81T-522
82Richm-22
88Indi/Pro-499M

Colbert, Craig
88Clint/Pro-707
89Shreve/Pro-1844

Colbert, Nathan
(Nate)
66T-596R
69MB-63
69T-408
70MLB/St-111
70OPC-11
70T-11
70T/SO
71K-72
71MLB/St-223
71OPC-235
71T-235
71T/Coins-77
71T/GM-28
71T/S-22
71T/tatt-1
72K-41
72MB-78
72T-571
72T-572A
73K-33
73OPC-340
73T-340
73T/Comics-5
73T/Lids-11
73T/PinUps-5
74K-19
74McDon
74OPC-125
74T/DE-34
74T/M-599
74T/St-91
75Ho-76
75OPC-599
75T-125
75T-599
76Laugh/Jub-16
76OPC-495
76SSPC-330
76T-495
77T-433M
87Wichi-6
88Wichi-17
89River/Best-24
89River/Cal-27CO
89River/Pro-1391

Colbert, Rick
81Brist-10
85Cram/PCL-59
87Louvl-10
88ArkTr/GS-1
89Sprin/Best-27

Colbert, Vince
71MLB/St-365
71OPC-231R
71T-231R
72OPC-84
72T-84

Colborn, Jim
71MLB/St-29
71OPC-38
71T-38
72OPC-386
72T-386
73OPC-408
73T-408
74OPC-75
74T-75
74T/DE-49
74T/St-193
75OPC-305
75T-305
75T/M-305
76A&P/Milw
76OPC-521
76SSPC-226
76T-521
77T-331
78OPC-116
78T-129
79OPC-137

79T-276
85IowaC-29
86IowaC-7CO

Colbrunn, Greg
88MidwLAS/GS-42
88Rockford-8
89Rockford-8
89WPalm/Star-7

Cole, Albert G.
E120
V100
W573

Cole, Alex
86FSLAS-11
86StPet-6
87ArkTr-20
88Louvl-14
88Louvl/CMC-11
88Louvl/Pro-438
89Louvl-14
89Louvl/CMC-21
89Louvl/Pro-1266
89StPet/Star-7
90F-244

Cole, Bert
V61-28

Cole, David
52B-132
53B/BW-38
53JC-6

Cole, Joey
79QuadC-13

Cole, Leonard
(King)
11Helmar-93
E286
E300
E90/3
T201
T207

Cole, Marvin
88Wythe/Pro-1982

Cole, Michael
81Wisco-15

Cole, Richard Roy
(Dick)
52Mother-35
54B-27
54T-84
55B-28
57T-234
58Union

Cole, Robert (Bob)
88Sumter/Pro-392
89BurlB/Pro-1627
89BurlB/Star-5

Cole, Rodger
85Cram/PCL-45
86Indianap-17

Cole, Stewart
89Memph/Best-9
89Memph/Pro-1184
89Memph/Star-7
89Star/Wax-41

Cole, Tim
78Green
79Savan-20
82Richm-3
83Durhm-18

Cole, Victor
89Memph/Best-19
89Memph/Pro-1185
89Memph/Star-8

Cole, Willis Russell
No Cards.

Cole, Winston
76Baton
77Salem

Coleman, Clarence
(Choo Choo)
61T-502
63Exh

63T-27
64T-251
66T-561
89Tidew/CANDL-5
Exh47

Coleman, Curtis H.
(Curt)
No Cards.

Coleman, David Lee
(Dave)
79Toled-17
80Colum-19
81Colum-18

Coleman, DeWayne
86Visal-7
87WinSal-25
88CharWh/Best-19

Coleman, Gerald F.
(Jerry)
49B-225
50B-47
50Drake-26
51B-49
51BR-A6
51T/RB-18
52B-73
52BR
52StarCal/L-70E
52T-237
54B-81
55B-99
55RFG-25
56T-316
57T-192
79TCMA-36
84Smok/Padres-5
Exh47
PM10/L-10
PM10/Sm-27
R423-10

Coleman, Gordon C.
(Gordy)
60HenryH-5
60T-257
60Union-19
61Kahn
61T-194
62J-116
62Kahn
62P-116
62P/Can-116
62Salada-110
62Shirriff-110
62T-508
62T/St-113
63FrBauer-3
63J-125
63Kahn
63P-125
63T-90
64T-577
65Kahn
65T-289
66T-494
67OPC-61
67T-61
Exh47

Coleman, J. Dale
89VeroB/Star-5

Coleman, Joe H.
66T-333R
67OPC-167R
67T-167R
68T-573
69MB-64
69MLB/St-103
69T-246
69T/St-234
70MLB/St-281
70OPC-127
70T-127
71MLB/St-390

71OPC-403
71T-403
72K-18
72MB-79
72OPC-96LL
72T-640
72T-96LL
73K-48
73OPC-120
73T-120
74K-3
74OPC-240
74T-240
74T/DE-53
74T/St-173
75OPC-42
75T-42
75T/M-42
76OPC-456
76OPC-68
76OPC-68FS
76SSPC-358
76T-456
76T-68M
77T-219
78T-554
79OPC-166
79Portl-11
79T-329
80Spoka-5
80T-542
81Spoka-19
83Peor/LF-29MG

Coleman, Joe P.
50B-141
51B-120
53T-279
54Esskay
54NYJour
54T-156
55B-3
55Esskay
55RFG-20
55RM-AL17
55T-162
76T-68M

Coleman, John Francis
E223
N172
N284
WG1-56

Coleman, Ken
89Utica/Puc-4

Coleman, Matthew
89Brist/Star-5

Coleman, Parke Edward
(Ed)
34G-28
35G-8J
35G-9J
V354-76

Coleman, Paul
89LittleSun-10
90Score-662DC
90T-654

Coleman, Raymond L.
(Ray)
50B-250
51B-136
52B-201
52Hawth/Pin-1
52T-211

Coleman, Rickey
85Beaum-2

Coleman, Rico
89Spoka/SP-24

Coleman, Solomon
(Hampton)
53Exh/Can-52
52Park-65

Coleman, Ty
80BurlB-14

Coleman, Vince
84Louvl-20
85D/HL-29M
85D/HL-54
85F/Up-U28
85Louvl-5
85T/Tr-24T
86D-181
86D-651M
86F-31
86F-636M
86F-637M
86F/LimEd-11
86F/LL-7
86F/Mini-7
86F/Slug-M4
86F/St-25
86KAS/Disc-1
86KayBee-5
86Leaf-115
86Leaf-225M
86OPC-370
86OPC-D
86Quaker-3
86S-136M
86S-176M
86S-24
86Schnucks-2
86T-201RB
86T-370
86T-D
86T/Gloss60-21
86T/Mini-60
86T/St-306
86T/St-47
86T/St-5
86T/Super-8
86T/WaxBox-D
87Class-30
87D-263
87D/HL-36
87D/OD-60
87F-290
87F/LL-11
87F/McCror-10
87F/Mini-21
87F/Slug-M3
87F/St-25
87KayBee-11
87Kraft-18
87Leaf-194
87OPC-119
87RedFoley/St-8
87S-152M
87S-199M
87S-65
87Smok/Cards-24
87T-590
87T/Coins-29
87T/Gloss60-38
87T/Mini-32
87T/St-50
88Woolw-2
88Bz-5
88Class/Blue-223
88D-293
88D/Best-44
88F-27
88F-634M
88F/BB/MVP-7
88F/Excit-11
88F/LL-7
88F/Mini-106
88F/St-117
88F/WS-6
88Jiffy-7
88KMart-8
88Leaf-128
88MSA/Disc-11
88OPC-260
88Panini/St-394
88Score-652HL
88Score-68
88Score/YS/II-24
88Sf-221
88Sf-67
88Smok/Card-19
88T-1RB
88T-260
88T/Big-5
88T/Mini-70
88T/Revco-3
88T/St-4
88T/St-47
88T/UK-16
89B-443
89Bz-6
89Cadaco-10
89D-181
89D-19DK
89D/AS-38
89D/Best-19
89D/DKsuper-19DK
89D/PopUp-38
89F-445
89F/BBAS-8
89F/Excit-7
89F/LL-6
89OPC-90
89Panini/St-188
89Panini/St-229AS
89Score-155
89Score/HotSt-86
89Score/Mast-35
89Sf-113
89Smok/Cards-2
89T-90
89T/Big-124
89T/Gloss22-17
89T/Mini-33
89T/St-154
89T/St-43
89UD-253
90Class-105
90D-279
90F-245
90Score-260
90Score/100St-73
90Sf-142
90T-660
90T-6RB
90UD-223
90UD-68TC

Coleman, W. Rip
57T-354
59T-51
60T-179
61BeeHive-5
D301

Coles, Cadwallader R.
(Cad)
T206

Coles, Charles Edward
(Chuck)
59T-120

Coles, Darnell
81Wausa-19
83Chatt-1
84Cram/PCL-190
84D-630
84Moth/Mar-26
85Cram/PCL-96
85D-118
85T-108
86D-557
86F/Up-U27
86T-337
86T/Tr-26T
87Cain's-2
87Coke/Tigers-14
87D-230
87D/OD-215
87F-148
87OPC-388
87Seven-DT1
87T-411
87T/St-271
88D-572
88D/Best-185
88OPC-46
88Score-554
88T-46
88T/Big-255
89B-217
89D-566
89F-544
89Moth/Sea-23
89Score-83
89T-738
89T/Big-133
89UD-339
90D-212
90F-509
90Score-62
90T-232
90UD-311

Colescott, Rob
85LitFalls-15
86LitFalls-6
87Columbia-27
88SALAS/GS-24
88Savan/Pro-335
89Sprin/Best-5

Coletta, Chris
75IntAS/TCMA-12
75IntAS/TCMA-27

Colgan, William H.
(Bill)
No Cards.

Coliver, William J.
(Bill)
No Cards.

Colletti, Manny
82Omaha-15
82OrlTw/A-4

Colley, Jay
88RochR/Pro-220

Collier, Anthony
89GreatF-22

Collins, Allen
86WPalm-8
87WPalm-15
88WPalm/Star-7

Collins, Charles
(Chub)
No Cards.

Collins, Chris
86QuadC-7
87MidldA-4
88MidldA/GS-7

Collins, Cyril Wilson
No Cards.

Collins, Daniel T.
(Dan)
No Cards.

Collins, Dave
83Madis/LF-3DB

Collins, David S.
(Dave)
76OPC-363
76SSPC-191
76T-363
77OPC-248
77T-431
78T-254
79T-622
80T-73
81Coke
81D-185
81F-201
81OPC-175
81T-175
81T/HT
81T/SO-84
81T/St-162
82D-169
82F-61
82F/St-14
82OPC-349
82T-595
82T/St-33
82T/Tr-20T
83D-234
83F-377
83OPC-359
83T-359
83T/X-21
84D-650
84F-151
84Nes/792-733
84OPC-38
84T-733
84Tor/Fire-9
85D-241
85F-102
85F/St-55
85F/Up-U29
85Leaf-172
85Moth/A's-14
85OPC-164
85T-463
85T/St-363
85T/Tr-25T
86Cain's-3
86D-218
86F-415
86F/Up-U28
86OPC-271
86T-271
86T/St-172
86T/Tr-27T
87D-215
87F-149
87T-148
88Kahn/Reds-22
88Score-371
89Score-267
89UD-351

Collins, Don
80Tacom-5
82Sprin-18

Collins, Edw.T. Jr.
(Eddie)
No Cards.

Collins, Edw.T. Sr.
(Eddie)
10Domino-27
11Helmar-55
12Sweet/Pin-43A
12Sweet/Pin-43B
14CJ-7
14Piedmont/St-14
15CJ-7
21Exh-25
25Exh-73
26Exh-74
27Exh-54
33G-42
48Exh/HOF
50Callahan
51T/CM
60Exh/HOF-8
60F-20
61F-16
61GP-28
63Bz/ATG-41
69Bz/Sm
72F/FFeat-18
72K/ATG-10
72K/ATG-10
72Laugh/GF-43
75F/Pion-20
80Cram/Leg-26
80Laugh/FFeat-32
80SSPC/HOF
87Conlon/2-27
88Conlon/5-5
88Pac/8Men-8
88Pac/8Men-99
BF2-9
D303
D304
D327
D328-31
D329-34
E101
E102
E103
E104
E105
E106
E120
E121/120
E121/80
E122
E126-16
E135-31
E210-47
E221
E254
E90/1
E92
E93
E98
L1-125
M101/4-34
M116
R328-1
S74-29
S81-100
T202
T204
T205
T206
T207
T208
T213/blue
T215/blue
T215/brown
T216
V117-4
V353-42
V61-29
W501-38
W514-25
W515-58
W517-52
W555
W572
W573
W575
WG4-6

Collins, Frankie
80GlenF/C-29M

Collins, George H.
(Hub)
N172

Collins, Harry W.
(Rip)
W575

Collins, Hugh
No Cards.

Collins, James Joseph
(Jimmy)
35Wheat
50Callahan
51T/CMAS
60Exh/HOF-9
60F-25
61F-99
63Bz/ATG-23
69Bz/Sm
80SSPC/HOF
89HOF/St-23
E104
E107
E220
E91
E95
R310

T204
T205
T206
T3-87
W555
WG2-8
Collins, James A.
(Rip)
35BU-146
35BU-78
35G-51
88Conlon/NatAS-3
R312
R312/M
R313
V355-18
WG8-7
Collins, John Edgar
(Zip)
No Cards.
Collins, John Francis
(Shano)
11Helmar-9
21Exh-26
88Pac/8Men-98
BF2-10
D327
D328-32
D329-35
D350/2-34
E120
E135-32
M101/4-35
M101/5-34
V100
W572
Collins, Joseph E.
(Joe)
52B-181
52BR
52T-202
53T-9
54NYJour
54T-83
55T-63
55T/DH-65
56T-21
56T/Pin-28
57T-295
79TCMA-21
PM10/L-11
Collins, Kevin M.
65T-581R
69OPC-127
69T-127
70T-707
71OPC-553
71T-553
Collins, Orth Stein
No Cards.
Collins, Patrick T.
26Exh-97
28Exh-49
29Exh/4-1
E126-35
V61-35
Collins, Phil
32Orbit/num-22
32Orbit/un-13
33G-21
35Exh/4-6
R305
V353-21
Collins, Ray
15CJ-169
M116
Collins, Robert J.
(Bob)
No Cards.
Collins, Ron
88Eugene/Best-18
89Eugene/Best-20
Collins, Scott
81Batav-19
Collins, Sean
89Eugene/Best-24
Collins, Sherman
89VeroB/Star-6
Collins, Terry
78Cr/PCL-41
80Albuq-19
82VeroB-26
84Cram/PCL-167
85Cram/PCL-156MG
86Albuq-3MG
87Albuq/Pol-1MG
88AAA/Pro-47
88Albuq/CMC-25
88Albuq/Pro-270
89BuffB/CMC-24
89BuffB/Pro-1668
Collins, Tharon L.
(Pat)
E120
W573
Collins, Tim
85Bend/Cram-5
Collins, Tony
86Geneva-3
86Peoria-3
Collins, William J.
(Bill)
N172
Collins, William S.
(Bill)
No Cards.
Collins, William
C46-34
Collucio, Bob
74T/St-194
Collum, Jack
54B-204
55B-189
57T-268
V362-30
Colman, Frank Lloyd
52Park-9
Colombino, Carlo
86Ashvl-5
87Osceola-4
88ColAst/Best-19
88SLAS-10
89Tucso/CMC-21
89Tucso/Pro-206
Colon, Cris
87PortChar-22
88Gasto/Pro-1005
89Gasto/Pro-1014
89Gasto/Star-4
Colon, David
88Sumter/Pro-411
Colon, Tony
89Geneva/Pro-1875
Colpaert, Dick
73OPC-608R
73T-608R
Colpitt, Mike
87Spart-28
Colson, Bruce
88Cedar/Pro-1145
Colson, Loyd
71OPC-111R
71T-111R
Colston, Frank
87Miami-16
88Wausa/Feder-24
88Wausa/GS-24
Colton, Lawrence
68T-348R
69T-454R
Coluccio, Robert P.
(Bob)
74OPC-124
74T-124
75OPC-456
75T-456
75T/M-456
76OPC-333
76SSPC-150
76T-333
78Charl
Colvard, Benny
88Bill/Pro-1830
89Cedar/Best-19
89Cedar/Pro-916
89Cedar/Star-4
Colzie, Rick
80Batav-22
81Watlo-2
Combe, Geoff
79Indianap-19
80Indianap-7
81Indianap-3
81T-606R
82Edmon-23
82F-62
82T-351R
Combs, Bobby
75AppFx
77AppFx
Combs, Earle Bryan
26Exh-98
28Yueng-21
29Exh/4-25
31Exh/4-25
32Orbit/num-111
33G-103
40PB-124
44Yank/St-6
54T-183
61F-17
80Cram/Leg-105
80SSPC/HOF
R314
R316
R328-5
R332-28
V354-21
W502-21
W513-86
W517-1
Combs, Mark
87SanBern-9
88Fresno/Cal-2
Combs, Merrill R.
48Signal
48Smith-23
52T-18
Combs, Pat
88T/Tr-30T
89B-398
89Clearw/Star-8
89Readg/Pro-676
89Readg/Star-9
89Star/Wax-12
89T/Big-227
90D-44
90F-553
90Score-623
90T-384
Comeau, Drew
88CapeCod/Sum-124
Comer, H. Wayne
69T-346
70McDon-2
70MLB/St-268
70OPC-323
70T-323
88Domino-3
Comer, Steve
79T-463
80T-144
81T-592
82D-341
82F-314
82F/St-177
82T-16
82T/St-242
83D-163
83F-564
83T-353
84Wheat/Ind-31
85T-788
86Maine-6C
88Orlan/Best-7
Comforti, Dave
81Holyo-5M
Comiskey, Charles A.
(Charlie)
14CJ-23
15CJ-23
50Callahan
61F-18
80SSPC/HOF
87Conlon/2-26
88Pac/8Men-24
88Pac/8Men-80
BF2-11
D329-36
D350/2-35
M101/4-36
M101/5-35
N172
N172/BC
N28
N284
N370
Scrapps
Command, James Dalton
(Jim)
No Cards.
Como, George
82Holyo-25
83Nashua-26
85Nashua-28
Comoletti, Glenn
78StPet
Comorosky, Adam A.
31Exh/4-13
33G-77
34G-85
35BU-44
35G-1H
35G-1K
35G-3B
35G-3F
35G-4F
35G-5B
35G-5F
35G-6B
V353-70
Compos, Rafael
89Ashvl/Pro-949
Compres, Fidel
87Watlo-1
Compton, Anna S.
(Pete)
No Cards.
Compton, Kenny
86Fres/Smok-27bb
Compton, Michael Lynn
(Mike)
71MLB/St-174
71OPC-77
71T-77
77Spart
80Water-10
Comstock, Brad
87Everett-27
88Fresno/Cal-25
88Fresno/Pro-1226
Comstock, Keith
77QuadC
80WHave-19
81WHave-6
82Tacom-39
82WHave-5
83BirmB-22
84Toled-16
88F-579
88LasVeg/CMC-2
88LasVeg/Pro-246
88Score-438
88T-778
89LasVeg/CMC-2
89LasVeg/Pro-14
90F-510
Conatser, Clinton A.
(Clint)
49Eureka-5
Concepcion, Carlos
84CharO-6
Concepcion, David E.
(Dave)
71MLB/St-56
71OPC-14
71T-14
72OPC-267
72T-267
72T/Cloth-7
73OPC-554
73T-554
74OPC-435
74T-435
74T/St-24
75Ho-47
75OPC-17
75T-17
75T/M-17
76Ho-128
76Icee
76OPC-48
76SSPC-34
76T-48
77Ho-95
77OPC-258
77Pepsi-47
77T-560
78Ho-108
78OPC-220
78T-180
78Wiffle/Discs-19
79Ho-85
79OPC-234
79T-450
80OPC-117
80T-220
81Coke
81D-181
81F-197
81F/St-15
81K-28
81OPC-83
81T-375
81T/HT
81T/SO-95
81T/St-161
82Coke/Reds
82D-421
82F-63
82F/St-109M
82K-22
82OPC-221IA
82OPC-340AS
82OPC-86
82Sqt-15
82T-340
82T-660
82T-661A
82T/St-124
82T/St-37
83D-148
83D/AAS-47
83F-588
83F-631M
83K-57
83OPC-102
83OPC-32AS
83T-400
83T-720

83T/Gloss-34
83T/Gloss40-34
83T/St-227
84D-121
84D-2
84F-466
84FunFood/Pin-23
84MiltBrad-6
84Nes/792-55
84OPC-55
84Ralston-20
84T-55
84T/Cereal-20
84T/St-56
85D-203
85D/HL-8
85F-532
85Leaf-131
85OPC-21
85T-515
85T/St-48
86D-243
86F-174
86OPC-195
86S-131M
86S-153
86T-366M
86T/St-137
86TexGold-13
87F-196
87Kahn-13
87OPC-193
87RedFoley/St-12
87T-731
88D-329
88F-229
88Kahn/Reds-13
88OPC-336
88Panini/St-275
88Score-210
88Sf-218
88T-422
88T/Big-144
89F-156
89Score-166
89UD-196

Concepcion, Onix
81Omaha-16
83D-516
83F-110
83T-52
84D-95
84F-345
84Nes/792-247
84T-247
85D-155
85F-200
85T-697
86D-252
86F-6
86Kitty/Disc-5
86OPC-163
86T-596

Conde, Ramon Luis
60DF-14
61Union

Cone, David
82CharR-19
84Memph-25
85Omaha-25
86Omaha-6
86Omaha/TCMA-16
87D-502
87D/Rook-35
87S/Rook-39
87T/Tr-24T
88D-653
88D/Best-40
88D/Mets/Bk-653
88F-131
88Kahn/Mets-44
88Score-49
88T-181
88ToysRUs-8
89B-375
89Cadaco-11
89Class-100
89Class-125
89D-388
89D-9DK
89D/AS-44
89D/Best-96
89D/DKsuper-9DK
89F-31
89F-636M
89F/BBAS-9
89F/Excit-8
89F/Heroes-9
89F/LL-7
89F/WaxBox-C7
89Holsum/Discs-19
89Kahn/Mets-44
89Nissen-19
89OPC-384
89Panini/St-129
89RedFoley/St-24
89Score-221
89Score/HotSt-2
89Score/YS/I-9
89Sf-51
89T-710
89T/Gloss60-6
89T/Hills-9
89T/Mets/Fan-44
89T/Mini-24
89T/St-96
89T/St/Backs-58
89T/UK-17
89Tetley/Discs-2
89UD-584
90D-265
90F-200
90Score-430
90Sf-201
90T-30
90UD-224

Confreda, Gene
83Beaum-23
87Ashvl-3
88Ashvl/Pro-1076

Congalton, William M.
(Bunk)
E254
E270/2
T206

Conigliaro, Anthony
(Tony)
64T-287R
65OPC-55
65T-55
65T/trans-11
66Bz-6
66T-218LL
66T-380
66T/RO-113
67Bz-6
67T-280
67T/Test/RSox-3
67T/Test/RSox-30
68Bz-4
68OPC-140
68T-140
69T-330
70OPC-340
70T-340
71Bz/Test-45
71JB
71MLB/St-342
71OPC-105
71OPC-63LL
71T-105
71T-63LL
71T/Coins-142
71T/tatt-10
78TCMA-206
PM10/Sm-28
PM10/Sm-29

Conigliaro, William
(Billy)
69T-628R
70OPC-317R
70T-317R
71MLB/St-316
71OPC-114
71T-114
72MB-80
72OPC-481
72T-481
74OPC-545
74T-545

Conine, Jeff
88BBCity/Star-10
89BBCity/Star-6

Conklin, Chip
82Wausa-28
83Wausa/LF-11
85Huntsvl/BK-17

Conkright, Dan
88BirmB/Best-21

Conlan, John Bertrand
(Jocko)
55B-303ump
80Cram/Leg-59
80SSPC/HOF
88Umpire-63
89HOF/St-98

Conley, Bob
78Watlo

Conley, D. Eugene
53T-215
54JC-22
54T-59
55Gol/Braves-6
55JC-22
55T-81
55T/DH-34
56T-17
56T/Pin-17
57T-28
58T-431
59T-492
60Armour-6
60T-293
61P-124
61T-193
61T/St-119
62T-187
63T-216
64T-571

Conley, Greg
88Spoka/Pro-1922
89CharRa/Pro-974

Conley, Robert Burns
(Bob)
59T-121

Conley, Virgil
83Tampa-2
84Cedar-8
85Cedar-4
86Penin-6
87Penin-27
88Jacks/GS-11

Conlon, Arthur Joseph
(Art)
No Cards.

Conlon, Charles M.
86Conlon/1-59

Conn, Albert Thomas
(Bert)
No Cards.

Conn, Gary
75BurlB
76BurlB
77Holyo

Connally, Fritzie Lee
81QuadC-5
83IowaC-13
84Cram/PCL-224
85F/Up-U30

Connally, George
(Sarge)
33G-27
R337-406
V353-27

Connally, Mervin T.
(Bud)
No Cards.

Connatser, Broadus M.
(Bruce)
No Cards.

Connaughton, Frank H.
No Cards.

Connell, Eugene J.
(Gene)
No Cards.

Connell, Joseph B.
(Joe)
No Cards.

Connell, Peter J.
(Pete)
N172

Connelly, Bill
53T-126

Connelly, Daron
86Cram/PCL-196
87Clint-24
88SanJose/Cal-130
88SanJose/Pro-135

Connelly, David
86Cram/PCL-197

Connelly, Thomas M.
(Tom)
No Cards.

Conner, Greg
88SanJose/Cal-118
88SanJose/Pro-129
89Shreve/Pro-1839

Conner, Jeff
81Holyo-12
82Holyo-3
83Nashua-4
84Evans-18
86Nashv-5

Connolly
89Umpires-63

Connolly, Edward J.
(Ed)
65T-543

Connolly, John M.
(Red)
No Cards.

Connolly, Joseph A.
(Joe)
15CJ-155
D329-37
D350/2-36
M101/4-37
M101/5-36

Connolly, Joseph G.
(Joe)
No Cards. **Connolly, Steve**
88Clint/Pro-696
88MidwLAS/GS-6
89Shreve/Pro-1830

Connolly, Thomas F.
(Blackie)
No Cards.

Connolly, Thomas H.
50Callahan
80SSPC/HOF

Connor, James Matthew
(Jim)
No Cards.

Connor, Joseph F.
(Joe)
No Cards.

Connor, Joseph
(Joe)
No Cards.

Connor, Roger
80SSPC/HOF
89HOF/St-9
E223
N167
N172
N284
N690
WG1-37

Connors, Billy
67T-272R
83Thorn-26CO

Connors, Jeremiah
(Jerry)
No Cards.

Connors, Joseph P.
(Joe)
No Cards.

Connors, Kevin Joseph
(Chuck)
52Mother-4
80Cram/Leg-28
88Pac/Leg-71
89Rini/Dodg-21
V362-2

Connors, Mervyn James
(Merv)
No Cards.

Conquest, Tom
82Idaho-5
83Madis/LF-12

Conroy, Bernard P.
(Ben)
No Cards.

Conroy, Mike
88Stock/Pro-752
89Stock/Best-31M
89Stock/Pro-402M
89Stock/Star-28M

Conroy, Tim
80WHave-22
81WHave-7
84D-340
84F-442
84Moth/A's-24
84Nes/792-156TL
84Nes/792-189
84T-189
85D-156
85F-421
85Moth/A's-16
85T-503
86F/Up-U29
86Schnucks-3
86T/Tr-28T
87F-291
88Louvl-15
88Louvl/CMC-5
88Score-384
88T-658
89Harris/Pro-288
89Harris/Star-6

Conroy, William E.
(Wid)
11Helmar-67
46Sunbeam
E254
E91
M116
T204
T206
T215/brown

Conroy, William F.
(Pep)
No Cards.

Conroy, William G.
(Bill)
No Cards.

Consolo, William A.
(Billy)
54T-195
55T-207
57T-399
58T-148
59T-112
60T-508
61P-100
61Peters-26
61T-504
88Pep/T-CO
89Mara/Tigers-CO
Constable, Jimmy
59T-451
63T-411
Constant, Andres
89Freder/Star-3
Consuegra, Sandy
51B-96
52B-143
53B/Col-89
54B-166
55B-116
55RM-AL25
56T-265
79TCMA-170
Conte, Michael
89Medford/Best-1
Conti, Guy
86Watertn-6CO
88Bakers/Cal-263
89Bakers/Cal-207
Conti, Joe
88CapeCod/Sum-15
Contreras, Frank
82Miami-21
Contreras, Henry
81BurlB-15
Contreras, Joaquin
85LitFalls-22
86Columbia-7
87TexLgAS-16
88Jacks/GS-20
88Tidew/CANDL-15
88Tidew/CMC-17
89Tidew/CMC-16
89Tidew/Pro-1960
Contreras, Nardi
82Edmon-14C
85BuffB-2
87Richm/TCMA-22
88Jaxvl/Best-23
88Jaxvl/Pro-969
88SLAS-40
89Jaxvl/Best-26
89Jaxvl/Pro-173
Converse, Mike
86Cedar/TCMA-3
87Tampa-3
Conway, Jack Clements
No Cards.
Conway, James P.
N172
Conway, John
52Park-96
Conway, Owen S.
No Cards.
Conway, Peter J.
(Pete)
N172
Scrapps
Conway, Richard D.
(Rip)
N172
Conway, William
(Bill)
No Cards.
Conwell, Edward J.
(Ed)
No Cards.
Conyers, Herbert L.
(Herb)
No Cards.
Coogan, Dale Roger
50B-244
52T-87
Coogan, Daniel George
(Dan)
No Cards.
Cook, Andy
88Oneon/Pro-2041
89PrWill/Star-3
Cook, Dennis
86Fresno/Smok-16
87Shrev-4
88Phoen/CMC-3
88Phoen/Pro-80
89D-646
89D/Best-327
89F-652M
89F/Up-104
89Panini/St-207
89Phoen/CMC-3
89Phoen/Pro-1482
89UD/Ext-779
90Class-80
90D-193
90F-554
90Score-545
90Score/100Ris-75
90T-633
90UD-71
Cook, Doug
81CharR-12
83CharR-16
84Memph-12
Cook, Glen
82BurlR-17
83BurlR-3
83BurlR/LF-12
83Tulsa-2
84OKCty-22
85OKCty-8
86OKCty-4
86T-502
87OKCty-14
Cook, James Fitchie
(Jim)
No Cards.
Cook, James
86Kenosha-4
Cook, Jeff
86PrWill-7
87Harrisbg-10
88EastLAS/Pro-13
88Harris/Pro-835
89Harris/Pro-304
89Harris/Star-7
Cook, Kerry
83SanJose-13
86WPalm-9
Cook, Larry
86PalmSp-8
86PalmSp/Smok-11
Cook, Luther Almus
(Doc)
D350/2-37
M101/5-37
Cook, Mike
86MidldA-6
88Edmon/CMC-2
88Edmon/Pro-567
89F-472
Cook, Mitch
83QuadC-9
86ColumAst-7
87ColAst/Pro-9
87ColumAst-9
Cook, Paul
N172
Cook, Raymond C.
(Cliff)
61T-399
62T-41
63T-566
Cook, Ron
71MLB/St-75
71OPC-583
71T-583
72OPC-339
72T-339
72T/Cloth-8
88Fay/Pro-1096
89Lakel/Star-5
Cook, Stan
89Boise/Pro-1982
Cook, Tim
79Holyo-12
81ElPas-20
82Vanco-12
84Beaum-12
Cooke, Allan Lindsey
(Dusty)
35BU-148
W711/1
Cooke, Frederick B.
(Fred)
No Cards.
Cooke, Mitch
82QuadC-7
Coolbaugh, Scott
88TexLgAS/GS-12
88Tulsa-18
89AAA/Pro-26
89OkCty/CMC-21
89OkCty/Pro-1512
90D-43
90F-293
90Score-612
90Score/100Ris-79
90Sf-180
90UD-42
Cooley, Dick Gordon
(Duff)
E107
Cooley, Fred
89Medford/Best-9
Coombs, Cecil L.
(Cecil)
No Cards.
Coombs, Daniel
65T-553R
66T-414
67T-464
68T-547
69T-389
71OPC-126
71T-126
71T/Coins-49
72OPC-91LL
Coombs, John W.
(Jack)
86Conlon/1-40
D350/2-38
E224
E270/2
E286
E98
M101/5-38
M116
T201
T204
Coomer, Ron
88CalLgAS-9
88Modesto-21
88Modesto/Cal-72
Coonan, Bill
86Cram/PCL-58
Cooney, Ed
88CapeCod/Sum-14
Cooney, James E.
26Exh-19
Cooney, James Edward
(Jimmy)
N172
Cooney, John Walter
(Johnny)
39PB-85
40PB-60
41DP-41
41PB-50
54JC-28
55Gol/Braves-7
55JC-28
60T-458C
Cooney, Phillip
(Phil)
No Cards.
Cooney, Terry
88Umpire-21
89Umpires-19
Cooney, William A.
(Bill)
No Cards.
Coons, Wilbur K.
(William)
No Cards.
Cooper, Arley Wilbur
E120
E121/120
E220
W501-80
W514-42
W516-19
W572
W573
Cooper, Bill
86Lakel-4
87GlenF-8
88GlenF/Pro-933
Cooper, Cecil C.
72OPC-79R
72T-79R
74OPC-523
74T-523
75OPC-489
75T-489
75T/M-489
76OPC-78
76SSPC-404
76T-78
77OPC-102
77T-235
78Ho-119
78K-41
78OPC-71
78T-154
79Ho-36
79OPC-163
79T-325
80OPC-52
80T-95
80T/S-33
81D-83
81Drake-16
81F-639
81K-32
81MSA/Disc-10
81OPC-356
81Sqt-30
81T-3LL
81T-555
81T/Nat/Super-5
81T/S
81T/SO-2
81T/St-10
81T/St-13
81T/St-241
81T/St-93
82D-258
82Drake-9
82F-138
82F/St-140
82K-60
82OPC-167
82Pol/Brew-15
82Sqt-1
82T-675
82T-703TL
82T/St-199
83D-106
83D/AAS-19
83Drake-6
83F-30
83Gard-5
83K-28
83OPC-190
83Pol/Brew-15
83T-190
83T/Gloss-15
83T/Gloss40-15
83T/St-173
83T/St-181
83T/St-80
84D-351
84D/Champs-24
84Drake-8
84F-198
84F/St-31
84FunFood/Pin-48
84Gard-5
84MiltBrad-7
84Nes/792-133LL
84Nes/792-420
84Nes/792-710LL
84OPC-43
84Pol/Brew-15
84Ralston-27
84Seven-8C
84T-133
84T-420
84T-710
84T/Cereal-27
84T/Gloss40-34
84T/St-200A
84T/St-291
85D-170
85F-580
85Gard-5
85Leaf-246
85OPC-290
85Pol/Brew-15
85T-290
85T/St-287
86D-170
86D-7
86D/AAS-54
86D/AS/WaxBox-PC9
86D/DKsuper-7
86F-484
86F/LimEd-12
86F/Mini-100
86F/St-26
86Jay's-2
86Leaf-7DK
86OPC-385
86Pol/Brew-15
86S-140M
86S-180M
86S-29
86T-385
86T/St-196
86T/Super-20
86Woolwth-8
87D-363
87F-343
87F/AwardWin-10
87F/Mini-22
87Leaf-230
87OPC-10
87OPC-D
87RedFoley/St-48
87S-169
87T-10
87T-D
87T/Board-6
87T/HL-2
87T/St-198

87Woolwth-2
88F-161
88Score-169
88T-769

Cooper, Claude W.
No Cards.

Cooper, Craig
86Cram/PCL-168
88Wichi-24
89Wich/Roc-34
89Wich/Roc/Up-8

Cooper, Dave
87LakeI-23
88Toled/CMC-8
88Toled/Pro-608
89London/Pro-1362

Cooper, Don
79WHave-3
82F-550
82T-409
82Toled-1
83Syrac-6
84Colum-17
84Colum/Pol-6
85Colum-5
85Colum/Pol-6
86Syrac-9

Cooper, Gary N.
74Gasto
79Savan-2
81Durhm-6

Cooper, Gary
86AubAs-7
87Osceola-21
88ColAst/Best-21
89Tucso/CMC-22
89Tucso/Pro-184

Cooper, Jamie
87Everett-9
88Clint/Pro-715
88MidwLAS/GS-4
89SanJose/Best-3
89SanJose/Cal-230
89SanJose/Pro-458
89SanJose/Star-5
89Star/Wax-83

Cooper, Kent
84Evrt/Cram-7

Cooper, Mark
85Kingst-12

Cooper, Morton
39PB-131
40PB-113
Exh47
PM10/Sm-30
R302
W754

Cooper, Neal
76Dubuq

Cooper, Orge
(Pat)
No Cards.

Cooper, Paul
78DaytB

Cooper, Scott
86Elmir-6
87Greens-10
88CLAS/Star-5
88Lynch/Star-5
89NewBrit/Pro-609
89NewBrit/Star-3
90Score-651

Cooper, Virgil
88Utica/Puc-15
89SoBend/GS-10

Cooper, Wilbur
21Exh-27
V61-57

Cooper, William W.
(Walker)
48B-9
49B-117
49Eureka-79
50B-111
51B-135
52B-208
52T-294
53B/BW-30
53Exh/Can-58
53JC-14
54DanDee
56T-273
57T-380
60T-462C
79TCMA-69
Exh47
R302
R423-11
W754

Coplon, Mitch
82DayBe-2

Copp, Bill
86Watertn-7
87Salem-19
88Harris/Pro-853

Coppell, Shannon
89Clint/Pro-902

Coppenbarger, Frank
77QuadC

Cora, Joey
85Spoka/Cram-4
86Beaum-7
87Bohem-4
87D/OD-147
88AAA/Pro-22
88F-580
88LasVeg/CMC-18
88LasVeg/Pro-234
88Score-420
88T-91
89LasVeg/CMC-14
89LasVeg/Pro-23
90D-538
90F-154
90UD-601

Corbell, Charlie
86Shrev-5
87Phoen-6
88Tacom/CMC-3
88Tacom/Pro-636

Corbett
N284

Corbett, Doug
79Indianap-12
81D-546
81F-555
81F/St-227
81OPC-162
81T-162
81T/St-106
82D-53
82F-551
82OPC-157
82T-560
82T/St-210
82T/Tr-21T
83F-83
83T-27
84Cram/PCL-111
85D-474
85F-298
85Smok/Cal-18
85T-682
86Smok/Cal-8
86T-234
87D-333
87F-76
87T-359

Corbett, Eugene Louis
(Gene)
46Sunbeam

Corbett, Ray
81Cedar-8
82Water-11
83Indianap-15
85RochR-1

Corbett, Sherman
86MidldA-7
87Edmon-18
88F/U-U11
89D-407
89Edmon/CMC-8
89Edmon/Pro-547
89F-473
89T-99
89ToysRUs-6
89UD-464

Corbin, A. Ray
72OPC-66
72T-66
73OPC-411
73T-411
74OPC-296
74T-296
74T/St-204
75OPC-78
75T-78
75T/M-78
76OPC-474
76SSPC-209
76T-474

Corbin, Archie
89Clmbia/Best-5
89Clmbia/GS-7

Corbitt, Claude E.
No Cards.

Corcino, Luis
86BurlEx-3
87FtMyr-22
88Virgini/Star-6

Corcoran, Arthur A.
(Art)
No Cards.

Corcoran, John A.
No Cards.

Corcoran, John H.
No Cards.

Corcoran, Lawrence J.
(Larry)
No Cards.

Corcoran, Lawrence
N172

Corcoran, Lori
83GlenF-23

Corcoran, Michael J.
(Mickey)
C46-49

Corcoran, Thomas W.
(Tommy)
E107
E270/2
N300/unif
WG3-11

Corcoran, Timothy M.
(Tim)
77Evansvl/TCMA-6
78BK/T-20
78T-515
79T-272
81D-367
81Evans-18
81F-479
81T-448
82OkCty-3
83Portl-11
85CIGNA-6
85D-381
85F-247
85T-302
86D-381
86F-437
86T-664
86Tidew-5
87Maine/TCMA-24
88Readg/Pro-887

Cordani, Richard
88CapeCod/Sum-8

Cordero, Will
89WPalm/Star-8

Cordner, Steve
83QuadC-19

Cordoba, Wilfrido
82AlexD-9
83LynnP-2
84PrWill-13

Cordoua, Marty
89Elizab/Star-5

Cordova, Antonio
82QuadC-21
84MidldC-2

Cordova, Rocky
78Clint
79LodiD-7

Corey, Frederick H.
(Fred)
No Cards.

Corey, Mark M.
79RochR-15
79T-701R
80RochR-5
80T-661R
81F-193
81T-399R
82Evans-23
86Jaxvl/TCMA-20
87Indianap-30

Corgan, Charles H.
(Chuck)
No Cards.

Corhan, Roy George
No Cards.

Corkhill, John S.
(Pop)
N172

Corkins, Mike
70T-573R
71MLB/St-224
71OPC-179
71T-179
72T-608
73OPC-461
73T-461
74OPC-546
74T-546

Cormack, Terry
83Durhm-3
84Durhm-6
85Durhm-21

Corman, Dave
85Beaum-20

Cormier, Rheal
89StPet/Star-8

Cormier, Russ
89Medford/Best-21

Cornejo, Mardie
78Tidew

Cornelius, Willie
78Laugh/Black-17

Cornell, Jeff
83Phoen/BHN-7
84Cram/PCL-12
85Cram/PCL-200
85T-514
86IowaC-8

Cornelius, Brian
89NiagFls/Puc-4

Cornutt, Terry
75Lafay
76Phoen
78Cr/PCL-71
79Phoen
80Phoen-8

Corrado, Gary
77Wausa

Corrales, Patrick
(Pat)
65OPC-107R
65T-107R
66OPC-137
66T-137
67OPC-78
67T-78
69T-382
70OPC-507
70T-507
71MLB/St-57
71OPC-293
71T-293
72T-705
72T-706A
73OPC-542
73T-542
74OPC-498
74T-498
79T-499MG
81F-623
83D-626
83T-637
84Nes/792-141MG
84T-141
84Wheat/Ind-18
85Polar/Ind-18MG
85T-119
86OhHenry-7MG
86T-699
87Gator-7MG
87Gator-MG
87T-268MG
88Toled/CMC-25
88Toled/Pro-590

Correa, Edwin
83AppFx/LF-17
86D/Rook-4
86F/Up-U30
86Rangers-18
86S/Rook-2
87Class/Up-143
87D-57
87F-122
87Leaf-145
87Moth/Rang-19
87OPC-334
87Smok/R-22
87T-334
88D-57
88F-464
88Panini/St-196
88Score-523
88Smok/R-18
88T-227
89RedFoley/St-25
89UD-598

Correa, Ramser
89Helena/SP-15

Correia, Rod
88SoOreg/Pro-1702
89Modesto/Cal-277
89Modesto/Ch-23

Correll, Victor C.
(Vic)
75OPC-177
75T-177
75T/M-177
76OPC-608
76SSPC-14
76T-608
77T-364
78Indianap-19
78T-527
79T-281
80T-419
81T-628

Corridan, Phillip
No Cards.

Corriden, John M. Jr.
R346-17

Corriden, John M. Sr.
(Red)
No Cards.

Corridon, Frank
C46-17
E90/1
M116
T205
Corrigan, Larry
75Water
Corsaro, Robby
89Batav/Pro-1945
Corsi, James
83Greens-4
85Greens-16
86NewBrit-7
87Modesto-25
88Tacom/CMC-7
88Tacom/Pro-625
89F-649M
89Score/HotRk-36
89T-292
89Tacom/CMC-2
89Tacom/Pro-1560
90D-422
90F-4
90Score-553
90T-623
90UD-521
Cort, Barry
75BurlB
79Holyo-26
80Holyo-4
Cortazzo, John F.
(Shine)
No Cards.
Cortes, Hernan
89Penin/Star-4
Cortez, Conde
87DayBe-12
Cortez, Dave
87Wichi-18
Corwin, Elmer
(Al)
52B-121
53B/Col-126
53B/Col-149
54B-137
55B-122
55Gol/Giants-4
79TCMA-232
Cosby, Rob
84Evrt/Cram-13A
Coscarart, Joseph M.
(Joe)
No Cards.
Coscarart, Peter J.
(Pete)
36G
39PB-141
40PB-63
49B/PCL-21
89Smok/Dodg-46
R314
Cosey, Donald Ray
(Ray)
79Ogden/TCMA-16
80Ogden-2
Cosgrove, Mike
75Iowa/TCMA-4
75OPC-96
75T-96
75T/M-96
76Ho-96
76OPC-122
76T-122
77T-589
Cosio, Raymundo
78Cedar
Cosman, Jim
66Pep/Tul
67T-384R
70OPC-429R
70T-429R
89Martins/Star-7
Costell, Arnie
75Dubuq
Costello, Bob
83Wisco/LF-14
Costello, Brian
89Salin/Pro-1828
Costello, Daniel F.
(Dan)
D350/2-39
M101/5-39
Costello, Fred
88Ashvl/Pro-1063
89ColMud/Best-16
89ColMud/Pro-129
89ColMud/Star-6
Costello, John
83Erie-18
84Savan-4
85Sprin-5
86StPet-7
87ArkTr-25
88F/U-U118
88Louvl-16
88Louvl/CMC-1
88Louvl/Pro-440
88Score/Tr-107T
89Class-142
89D-518
89F-446
89Panini/St-176
89Score-534
89Score/HotRk-75
89Smok/Cards-3
89T-184
89UD-625
90D-555
90F-246
90Score-347
90T-36
90UD-486
Costello, Mike
86Beaum-8
87Wichi-15
88Wichi-26
89Denver/CMC-5
89Denver/Pro-45
89ElPas/GS-5
Costello, Tim
77Visal
Costner, Kevin
89Durhm/Star-29
Cota, Chris
87DayBe-20
Cota, Francisco
83Miami-4
85Tigres-11
Cota, Tim
87Visal-4
Cote, Brice
80Elmir-5
Cote, Henry Joseph
No Cards.
Cote, Warren Peter
(Pete)
No Cards.
Cotes, Eugenio
77Salem
79Portl-10
79T-723R
Cotter, Edward C.
(Ed)
No Cards.
Cotter, Harvey L.
No Cards.
Cotter, Richard R.
(Dick)
No Cards.
Cotter, Thomas B.
(Tom)
No Cards.
Cottier, Charles K.
(Chuck)
60L-138
60Lake
60T-417
61P-113
61T-13
62J-66
62P-66
62P/Can-66
62Salada-20
62Shirriff-20
62T-27
62T/bucks
62T/St-93
63F-28
63J-98
63P-98
63T-219
64T-397
69T-252
77QuadC
78TCMA-189
85Moth/Mar-1MG
85T-656
86T-141
88Berg/Cubs-CO
Cotto, Hector
88Mia/Star-5
Cotto, Henry
81QuadC-15
83IowaC-21
84SevenUp-28
85D-411
85F-53
85F/Up-U31
85T-267
87Colum-20
87Colum/TCMA-20
87T-174
88D/Best-51
88F-205
88F/U-U58
88Moth/Sea-6
88OPC-172
88Score-368
88Score/Tr-48T
88T-766
88T/Big-125
88T/Tr-31T
89D-109
89F-545
89Moth/Sea-6
89OPC-207
89Panini/St-441
89Score-209
89T-468
89T/Big-160
89T/St-218
89UD-134
90D-644
90F-511
90Score-161
90T-31
90UD-207
Cottrell, Steve
84Evrt/Cram-8
Couch, Richard
77Ashev
Couchee, Mike
82Amari-16
85CharO-31
85Cram/PCL-123
86Tulsa-4CO
88QuadC/GS-2
88SanDiegoSt-5
Coughlin
N172
Coughlin, Red
85Syrac-24
86Syrac-10TR
87Syrac/TCMA-33
88Syrac/Pro-819
Coughlin, William P.
(Bill)
E107
Coughlon, Kevin
82Madis-7
84Madis/Pol-21
Coughtry, James M.
(Marlan)
61Union
62T-595R
Coulon, Johnny
T3/Box-54
Coulson, Robert
T207
Coulson, Steven
77WHave
Coulter, Darrell
88Spart/Pro-1029
88Spart/Star-21
88Spart/Star-5
89Spart/Pro-1042
89Spart/Star-5
Coulter, Roy
75AppFx
76AppFx
Coulter, Thomas Lee
(Tom)
No Cards.
Coumbe, Fred
(Fritz)
D328-33
E135-33
Counts, Rick
78Duned
Courtney, Clinton D.
(Clint)
53B/Col-70
53NB
53T-127
54B-69
54Dix
55B-34
56T-159
57T-51
58T-92
59T-483
60T-344
61T-342
79TCMA-169
Courtney, Ernest E.
(Ernie)
E254
Courtney, Harry
E120
Cousineau, Edward T.
(Dee)
No Cards.
Cousins, Derryl
88Umpire-40
89Umpires-38
Cousy, Bob
51BR-A11
60P
Coveleski, Harry
BF2-26
D327
D328-34
D329-39
D350/2-40
E135-34
M101/4-39
M101/5-40
M116
T206
Coveleski, Stan
21Exh-28
25Exh-122
26Exh-122
28Yueng-57
61F-100
80SSPC/HOF
E120
E121/120
E210-57
E220
E254
E93
T3-88
V100
W501-21
W502-57
W555
W572
W575
Coveney, Jim
89Ashvl/Pro-961
Coveney, John P.
(John)
No Cards.
Coveney, Patrick
86Clearw-5
87DayBe-13
Covington, Clarence
(Sam)
No Cards.
Covington, John W.
(Wes)
57T-283
58T-140
59T-290
59T-565AS
60Lake
60T-158
61P-108
61T-296
61T/St-41
62Salada-105
62Shirriff-105
62T-157
63J-182
63P-182
63T-529
64T-208
65T-583
66OPC-52M
66T-484
78TCMA-132
Covington, William
(Tex)
T207
Cowan, Billy Roland
64T-192R
65OPC-186
65T-186
69T-643
71MLB/St-341
71OPC-614
71T-614
72OPC-19
72T-19
78TCMA-282
Cowan, Ed
77DaytB
Cowens, Alfred Edward
(Al)
75OPC-437
75T-437
75T/M-437
76A&P/KC
76Ho-28
76Ho/Twink-28
76OPC-648
76SSPC-175
76T-648
77T-262
78Ho-67
78K-5
78OPC-143
78T-46
79OPC-258
79T-490
80OPC-174
80T-330
81Coke

81D-369
81F-471
81OPC-123
81T-123
82D-207
82F-266
82OPC-103
82T-575
82T/St-182
82T/Tr-22T
83D-554
83F-477
83Nalley-2
83OPC-193
83T-763
83T/St-115
84D-511
84F-610
84Moth/Mar-19
84Nes/792-622
84T-622
84T/St-344
85D-196
85F-487
85Leaf-239
85Moth/Mar-6
85OPC-224
85T-224
85T/St-333
86D-389
86F-463
86Leaf-184
86Moth/Mar-6
86OPC-92
86T-92

Cowger, Tracy
80Tulsa-18
81Tulsa-2
82Tulsa-12
83OKCty-5
83Tulsa-17

Cowley, Joe
78Green
79Savan-15
82Pol/Atl-38
83Richm-3
83T-288
84Colum-13
84Colum/Pol-7
85D-613
85F-124
85Leaf-58
85T-769
85T/St-318
86BuffB-9
86Coke/WS-40
86D-608
86D/HL-44
86F-103
86F/Up-U31
86T-427
86T/Tr-29T
87D-552
87F-491
87F/LL-12
87Leaf-240
87S-196M
87T-27
87T/St-290

Cox, Boyce
89Brist/Star-31

Cox, Carl
47Signal

Cox, Carl
86VeroB-4

Cox, Dalene
81ArkTr-23M

Cox, Danny
82Sprin-12
83StPet-4
84D-449
85D-571
85F-222
85T-499
86D-382
86F-32
86KAS/Disc-5
86Leaf-177
86OPC-294
86S-108
86Schnucks-4
86T-294
86T/Mini-61
86T/St-48
87D-553
87F-292
87F/Excit-12
87Leaf-160
87OPC-202
87Smok/Cards-6
87T-621
87T/Mini-33
88Woolwth-27
88D-60
88D/Best-75
88F-28
88Leaf-72
88Louvl-17
88OPC-59
88Panini/St-383
88Score-415
88Sf-84
88Smok/Card-2
88T-59
88T/Big-111
89D-348
89F-447
89OPC-158
89Score-613
89T-562
89UD-535
90T-184

Cox, Darren
87Idaho-21

Cox, Darron
88CapeCod/Sum-97
89Bill/Pro-2067

Cox, Doug
87Bakers-13
88VeroB/Star-4

Cox, Elmer Joseph
(Dick)
E120
E126-5
W573

Cox, Frank Bernhardt
No Cards.

Cox, J. Casey
66T-549R
67T-414
68OPC-66
68T-66
69T-383
70OPC-281
70T-281
71MLB/St-533
71OPC-82
71T-82
72MB-81
72OPC-231
72T-231
73OPC-419
73T-419

Cox, James Charles
(Jim)
74T-600R
76SSPC-325

Cox, Jeffrey Linden
(Jeff)
79Ogden/TCMA-12
80Ogden-19
81D-230
81T-133
81Tacom-19
82Evans-14
83Omaha-14
86Vermont-4
87Vanco-3
87Watertn-30
88Aug/Pro-382
89Memph/Best-24
89Memph/Pro-1195

Cox, Jim
74OPC-600R

Cox, Jim
85Elmir-5

Cox, Larry Eugene
76SSPC-596
77T-379
78T-541
79T-489
80OPC-63
80T-116
81D-285
81F-604
81T-249
81T/Tr-749
83QuadC-2
85IowaC-28
86IowaC-9MG
87IowaC-22MG
88Berg/Cubs-CO

Cox, Robbie
76Baton

Cox, Robert Joe
(Bobby)
69MB-65
69T-237
78T-93
79T-302MG
81D-426
81F-247
81Pol/Atl-6MG
81T-675MG
83OPC-34MG
83T-606
84Nes/792-202MG
84OPC-202MG
84T-202
84Tor/Fire-10MG
85OPC-135MG
85T-411
85Tor/Fire-9MG
86OPC-359MG
86T-471

Cox, Terry
71OPC-559R
71T-559R

Cox, William Richard
(Billy)
47TipTop
49B-73
49Eureka-33
50B-194
51B-224
51T/BB-48
52B-152
52Dix
52T-232
53B/BW-60
53NB
54B-26
54NYJour
54RH
54RM-NL2
55B-56
55Esskay
79TCMA-83
PM10/Sm-31
PM10/Sm-32

Cox, William Ted
(Ted)
78T-706R
79T-79
80T-252
81D-283
81F-602
81Spoka-16

Coyle, Joseph
(Rocky)
87Knoxv-6
87Syrac/TCMA-27

Coyne, Toots
No Cards.

Cozzolino, Paul
82VeroB-3

Crabbe, Bruce
86Pittsf-4
87IowaC-12
88IowaC/CMC-13
88IowaC/Pro-550
89IowaC/CMC-14
89IowaC/Pro-1714

Crabtree, Estel C.
V355-134
W754

Craddock, Walt
59T-281

Craft, Harry Francis
39PB-65
40PB-79
55Rodeo
62T-12
63T-491
64T-298
78TCMA-244
89Smok/Ast-27
W711/1
W711/2

Craig, Dean
78Clint
79Wausa-18
82Nashv-8

Craig, Pete
65T-466R
66OPC-11R
66T-11R
67T-459R

Craig, Rodney Paul
79Spoka-5
80T-672R
81Charl-19
81D-288
81F-597
81T-282R
82Wheat/Ind
83Charl-15
83D-515
84Maine-19

Craig, Roger
56T-63
57T-173
58T-194
60BB-15
60L-8
60Morrell
60T-62
61BB-38
61T-543
62Salada-189
62Shirriff-189
62T-183
62T/bucks
62T/St-154
63Exh
63F-47
63J-200
63P-200
63T-197
64T-295
65T-411
66T-543
74OPC-31CO
74T-31C
76SSPC-628
78TCMA-201
79T-479MG
86Moth/SFG-1MG
86T-111
87Moth/SFG-1MG
87T-193MG
88Moth/Giants-1MG
88T-654
89Moth/Giants-1MG
89Pac/Leg-145
89Rini/Dodg-15
89T-744MG
90T-351MG
Exh47

Craig, Tom
82Syrac-25
83Syrac-3
84Syrac-3

Cram, Jerry
71OPC-247R
71T-247R
76SSPC-559
81Omaha-2
82Omaha-26
83Omaha-25
84Omaha-13

Cramer, George
35Exh/4-14

Cramer, Michael J.
(Mike)
75Phoen-26

Cramer, Rob
86Visal-8

Cramer, Roger Maxwell
(Doc)
34G-25
35BU-53
35G-8J
35G-9J
39PB-101
40PB-29
89Pac/Leg-181
R314
V354-74

Cramer, William B.
(Dick)
No Cards.

Crandall, Bob
80Elmir-33

Crandall, Delmar W.
(Del)
50B-56
51B-20
52T-162
53JC-15
53T-197
54B-32
54JC-1
54RM-NL3
54T-12
55Armour-3
55B-217
55Gol/Braves-8
55JC-1
55RM-NL2
57T-133
57T-175
58T-351M
58T-390
59Armour-7
59Bz
59T-425
59T-567AS
60Armour-7
60Bz-36
60Lake
60MacGregor-6
60T-170
60T-568AS
61P-110
61T-390
61T-583AS
61T/Dice-2
61T/St-42
62T-351M

62T-443
62T/St-147
63J-153
63P-153
63Salada-11
63T-460
64T-169
65OPC-68
65T-68
66T-339
73OPC-646MG
73T-646MG
74T-99MG
75OPC-384MG
75T-384MG
75T/M-384MG
78Cr/PCL-30
78TCMA-144
79TCMA-68
80Albuq-23
81Albuq/TCMA-25
82Albuq-24
83Albuq-23
84D-632
84Moth/Mar-1MG
84Nes/792-721MG
84T-721
88Pac/Leg-98
89Swell-132
Exh47
PM10/L-12
WG9-28

Crandall, Ducky
75Lafay

Crandall, James Otis
(Doc)
10Domino-28
11Helmar-122
12Sweet/Pin-109
14CJ-67
15CJ-67
D304
E104
E254
M116
S74-82
T202
T204
T205
T206
T207
T213/blue
T215/blue
T215/brown

Crane, Edward N.
(Cannonball)
N172

Crane, Rich
89GreatF-3

Crane, Samuel Byren
(Sam)
E120

Crane, Samuel N.
(Sam)
N172
N284
Scrapps

Cranston, William
T206

Cravath, Clifford C.
(Gavvy)
14CJ-82
15CJ-82
BF2-84
D327
D328-35
D329-40
D350/2-41
E135-35
E254
E270/1
M101/4-40
M101/5-41
T206
W514-11

Craver, William H.
(Bill)
No Cards.

Crawford, Clifford R.
(Pat)
No Cards.

Crawford, Forrest
No Cards.

Crawford, George
No Cards.

Crawford, Glenn M.
47Remar-25

Crawford, Jack
82Danvi-8
83Peoria/LF-15

Crawford, Jerry
88Umpire-28
89Umpires-26

Crawford, Jim
74OPC-279
74T-279
76OPC-428
76SSPC-47
76T-428
76T/Tr-428T
77T-69
89Gasto/Pro-1015

Crawford, Kenneth D.
(Ken)
No Cards.

Crawford, Rufus
55B-121

Crawford, Samuel Earl
(Sam)
11Helmar-29
14CJ-14
15CJ-14
72F/FFeat-27
80Cram/Leg-55
80SSPC/HOF
87Conlon/2-30
89HOF/St-50
BF2-27
D303
D304
D327
D328-36
E101
E102
E103
E104
E106
E135-36
E90/1
E92
E94
E95
M116
T201
T206
T213/blue
T215/brown
T216
T3-5
W514-95
W555
WG2-9
WG5-12
WG6-12

Crawford, Shag
89Pac/Leg-199

Crawford, Steve
82Coke/BOS
82D-564
82F-291
82T-157
83Pawtu-4
83T-419
84Pawtu-14
85D-395
85F-156
85T-661
86D-416
86F-346
86Leaf-193
86T-91
87D-399
87F-33
87T-589
88F-350
88Score-289
88T-299

Crawford, Willie M.
65T-453R
68T-417
69T-327
70K-26
70OPC-34
70T-34
71MLB/St-100
71OPC-519
71T-519
72T-669
73OPC-639
73T-639
74OPC-480
74T-480
74T/St-43
75OPC-186
75T-186
75T/M-186
76OPC-76
76SSPC-84
76T-76
77T-642
78T-507
78TCMA-157
85SpokAT/Crm-4

Creager, Mack
66Pep/Tul

Creamer, George W.
No Cards.

Credeur, Todd
85Anchora-7
86Ashvl-6
87Osceola-28
88Osceola/Star-6
89ColMud/Best-26
89Osceola/Star-5

Cree, William F.
(Birdie)
10Domino-29
11Helmar-41
12Sweet/Pin-33
E224
M116
T206
T213/blue
T213/brown
T215/blue
T215/brown

Creeden, Patrick F.
(Pat)
No Cards.

Creedon, Cornelius C.
(Connie)
No Cards.

Creegan, Martin
(Marty)
No Cards.

Creel, Keith
82Omaha-3
83D-574
83Omaha-5
84F-346
84Omaha-15
85Maine-6
86Maine-7
87OKCty-7

Creely, August L.
(Gus)
No Cards.

Cregan, Peter James
(Pete)
No Cards.

Creger, Bernard Odell
(Bernie)
47TipTop
No Cards.

Crenshaw, Ken
89Princet/Star-28

Crespi, Frank A.
(Creepy)
41DP-145
W754

Crew, Ken
87Memph-20
87Memph/Best-8
88ColAst/Best-6

Crews, Larry
82Clint-19
84Shrev/FB-5
85Cram/PCL-178

Crews, Tim
81BurlB-10
83ElPas-17
84ElPas-10
86ElPas-7
87Albuq/Pol-8
88Albuq/CMC-8
88Albuq/Pro-264
88D-464
88D/Rook-20
88F-511
88Pol/Dodg-52M
88Score-641
88Sf-224
88T-57
89D-486
89Moth/Dodg-24
89Panini/St-96
89Pol/Dodg-27
89Score-505
89T-22
89UD-611
90D-550
90F-390
90Score-164
90T-551
90UD-670

Crider, Jerry
69T-491R
71OPC-113
71T-113

Criger, Louis
E107
E90/1
M116
T205
T206
T3-89
WG2-10

Crim, Chuck
83Beloi/LF-22
84ElPas-6
85Cram/PCL-220
86Vanco-8
87D/Rook-18
87F/U-U19
87T/Tr-25T
88D-355
88F-162
88Pol/Brew-32
88Score-402
88T-286
89B-136
89D-617
89D/Best-127
89F-183
89OPC-99
89Pol/Brew-32
89Score-272
89T-466
89UD-501
90D-221
90F-319
90Score-108
90T-768
90UD-511

Crimian, Jack
53Hunter
56T-319
57T-297

Cripe, David Gordon
(Dave)
83DayBe-1
86ColumAst-8MG

Criscione, Dave G.
78RochR

Criscola, Anthony P.
(Tony)
47Centen-5

Crisham, Patrick L.
(Pat)
No Cards.

Crisler, Joel
77QuadC
79SLCty-15
80ElPas-11

Crisler, Thomas
81Redwd-3

Crisp, Joseph Shelby
(Joe)
No Cards.

Criss, Dode
E254
M116
T206

Crist, Chester Arthur
(Ches)
No Cards.

Crist, Clark
81LynnS-28
81Wausa-21
82LynnS-10
84Chatt-7

Cristelli, Pat
77SLCty
78Cr/PCL-5

Criswell, Brian
85Madis-9
85Madis/Pol-6
86Madis-6
86Madis/Pol-6
88Huntsvl/BK-3

Criswell, Tim
86Durhm-6
87Durhm-7

Critz, Hugh Melville
(Hughie)
25Exh-26
26Exh-26
28Exh-13
29Exh/4-7
31Exh/4-9
33Exh/4-5
33G-238
33G-3
34G-17
35Exh/4-5
35G-2A
35G-4A
35G-7A
61F-101
87Conlon/2-10
88Conlon/5-6
R316
R332-46
V353-3
V354-72
W517-25
WG7-10

Crockett, Claude
77StPet

Crockett, David S.
(Davey)
No Cards.
Crockett, Rusty
88Peoria/Ko-9
89WinSal/Star-6
Croft, Arthur F.
(Art)
No Cards.
Croft, Henry T.
No Cards.
Croft, Paul
78Wisco
Croghan, John
N172
Crolius, Fred J.
No Cards.
Cromartie, Warren L.
78OPC-117
78T-468
79OPC-32
79T-76
80OPC-102
80T-180
81D-332
81F-142
81F/St-92
81OPC-345
81OPC/Post-5
81T-345
81T/SO-78
81T/St-188
82D-340
82F-186
82F/St-33
82Hygrade
82OPC-61
82OPC-94TL
82OPC/Post-13
82T-526TL
82T-695
82T/St-60
82Zeller-18
82Zeller-7
83D-466
83F-279
83OPC-351
83Stuart-18
83T-495
84F-272
84Nes/792-287
84OPC-287
84T-287
Cromer, Tripp
89Hamil/Star-10
Crompton, Edward
(Ned)
No Cards.
Crompton, Herbert B.
(Herb)
No Cards.
Cromwell, Nate
88Myrtle/Pro-1174
89Duned/Star-3
Cron, Chris
86Durhm-7
87QuadC-23
88CalLgAS-34
88PalmSp/Cal-102
88PalmSp/Pro-1441
89MidldA/GS-11
Crone, Bill
81LynnS-16
82LynnS-11
83SLCty-18
84Cram/PCL-172
85Cram/PCL-93
86Calgary-5
87Tucso-4
Crone, Ray
85Newar-18
Crone, Raymond H.
54JC-20
54T-206
55Gol/Braves-9
55JC-12
55T-149
56T-76
57T-68
58SFCall
58T-272
Cronin, Chuck
47Sunbeam
Cronin, Daniel
(Dan)
No Cards.
Cronin, James John
(Jim)
No Cards.
Cronin, Joseph Edward
(Joe)
31Exh/4-31
33DH-11
33G-109
33G-63
34Exh/4-16
35BU-183
35BU-32
35Exh/4-9
35G-1G
35G-3E
35G-5E
35G-6E
36Exh/4-9
37Exh/4-9
37OPC-124
38Exh/4-9
38ONG/Pin-3
40PB-134
40Wheat-7
41DP-59
41DP-82
41PB-15
61GP-14
80Cram/Leg-39
80SSPC/HOF
83D/HOF-20
86Conlon/1-9
86S/Dec-7
88Conlon/AmAS-6
89HOF/St-19
89Pac/Leg-167
R300
R302
R303/A
R303/B
R306
R308-176
R310
R311/Gloss
R312/M
R313
R314
R328-7
R332-37
V300
V353-63
V355-63
WG8-8
Cronin, William P.
(Bill)
No Cards.
Cronk, Doug
89Gasto/Pro-1013
89Gasto/Star-5
Cronkright, Dan
86Penin-7
Cronkright, Dave
87DayBe-24
Crooks, John Charles
N172
Crooks, Thomas A.
(Tom)
No Cards.
Crosby, Edward C.
(Ed)
71OPC-672
71T-672
73OPC-599
73T-599
76OPC-457
76SSPC-520
76T-457
78SnJos-5
79Spoka-1
Crosby, Ken
76OPC-593R
76SSPC-602
76T-593R
Crosby, Pat
86LitFalls-7
Crosby, Todd
87Spart-15
88Clearw/Star-9
89Star/Wax-49
89StPet/Star-9
Crosetti, Frank P.
33G-217
34DS-86
35BU-182
36G-9
38ONG/Pin-4
41DP-113
44Yank/St-7
47TipTop
52B-252
52T-384
60T-465C
68Bz-13
88Conlon/3-8
R303/A
R311/Leath
R313
R314
R346-24
R423-17
V355-91
WG8-9
Cross, Amos C.
No Cards.
Cross, Bob
79Newar-16
Cross, Clarence
No Cards.
Cross, Frank Atwell
No Cards.
Cross, Jesse
89Myrtle/Pro-1473
Cross, Joffre
(Jeff)
47TipTop
Cross, LaFayette N.
(Lave)
E107
N172
N300/unif
WG2-11
Cross, Leach
T3/Box-69
Cross, Montford M.
(Monte)
E107
T206
WG2-12
Crossin, Frank P.
No Cards.
Crossley, William
N172
Crotty, Joseph P.
(Joe)
N172
N172/ST
Crouch, Bill
41G-27
W754
Crouch, Jack Albert
No Cards.
Crouch, Matt
86BurlEx-4
88Memph/Best-8
89Omaha/CMC-5
89Omaha/Pro-1717
Crouch, Zach
85Greens-9
87NewBrit-2
88Pawtu/CMC-6
88Pawtu/Pro-457
89NewBrit/Pro-612
89NewBrit/Star-4
Croucher, Frank D.
No Cards.
Crough, Bill
41G-27
Crouse, Clyde E.
(Buck)
No Cards.
Crow, Donald Leroy
(Don)
80Albuq-27
81Albuq/TCMA-13
82Albuq-12
Crow, Roger
(Gabby)
79QuadC-4
81QuadC-32
82QuadC-12
83QuadC-1
Crowder, Alvin
33G-122
33G-95
34DS-93
34Exh/4-16
34G-15
35BU-161
35G-1H
35G-3F
35G-5F
35G-6F
61F-102
88Conlon/AmAS-7
R308-185
R310
R312/M
V353-71
V354-65
Crowe, George Daniel
52T-360
53JC-18
53T-3
55JC-39
56T-254
57Kahn
57T-73
58Kahn
58T-12
59T-337
60T-419
61T-52
Crowe, Ron
89Everett/Star-5
Crowell, William
N172
Crowley, Brian
89Butte/SP-8
Crowley, Edgar Jewel
(Ed)
No Cards.
Crowley, John A.
No Cards.
Crowley, Ray
80Memph-11
Crowley, Terrence M.
(Terry)
70OPC-121R
70T-121R
71MLB/St-292
71OPC-453
71T-453
72T-628
73JP
73OPC-302
73T-302
74OPC-648
74T-648
74T/Tr-648T
75OPC-447
75T-447
75T/M-447
76OPC-491
76SSPC-35
76T-491
79T-91
80T-180
81D-507
81F-190
81OPC-342
81T-543
82D-383
82F-160
82T-232
83D-457
83F-55
83T-372
83T/X-22
84Nes/792-732
84OPC-246
84T-732
88French-10CO
Crowley, Terry Jr.
88Salem/Star-4
89Salem/Star-5
Crowley, William M.
N284
Cruise, Walton Edwin
(Walt)
21Exh-29
E120
E220
V100
Crum, George
83BurlR-14
83BurlR/LF-4
85Tulsa-4
86Water-6
Crumling, Eugene Leon
(Gene)
No Cards.
Crump, Arthur Elliott
(Buddy)
No Cards.
Crutcher, Dave
79Tulsa-19
80Tulsa-2
81Tulsa-15
Crutchfield, Jim
78Laugh/Black-35
Cruthers, Charles P.
(Press)
No Cards.
Cruz, Arcadio
77Charl
Cruz, Cirilio Dilan
(Tommy)
78Cr/PCL-105
79Colum-13
Cruz, Georgie
83Memph-2
Cruz, Hector Dilan
(Heity)
76OPC-598R
76T-598R
77T-624
78T-257
79Pol/Giants-9
79T-436
80T-516
81F-206
81T-52
81T/Tr-750

82D-57
82F-214
82OPC-364
82T-663
Cruz, Henry Acosta
76OPC-590R
76SSPC-85
76T-590R
78T-316
Cruz, Ismael
89Martins/Star-8
Cruz, Javier
85Tigres-26
Cruz, Jose Dilan
72OPC-107
72T-107
73OPC-292
73T-292
74OPC-464
74T-464
74T/St-113
75OPC-514
75T-514
75T/M-514
76OPC-321
76SSPC-62
76T-321
77Ho-75
77K-50
77OPC-147
77T-42
78BK/A-17
78Ho-72
78K-16
78OPC-131
78T-625
79Ho-58
79OPC-143
79T-289
80OPC-367
80T-722
81Coke
81D-383
81F-60
81F/St-78
81OPC-105
81T/HT
81T/SO-83
81T/St-169
82D-244
82Drake-10
82F-214
82F/St-50
82OPC-325
82T-325
82T/St-44
83D-41
83F-446
83OPC-327
83T-585
83T/St-242
84F-222
84F/St-24
84F/St-8
84FunFood/Pin-129
84Moth/Ast-8
84Nes/792-422
84Nes/792-66TL
84OPC-189
84Seven-19W
84T-422
84T/St-65
84T/St/Box-13
85D-20
85D-304
85D/DKsuper-20
85Drake-7
85F-347
85Leaf-20DK
85Moth/Ast-4
85OPC-95
85Seven-10C
85T-95
85T/Gloss40-20
85T/St-59
85T/Super-34
86D-60
86D/AAS-19
86F-296
86F/LimEd-13
86F/LL-8
86F/Mini-62
86F/St-27
86Leaf-49
86Moth/Ast-20
86OPC-96
86Pol/Ast-12
86S-30
86T-186M
86T-640
86T/St-26
87D-85
87D/OD-13
87F-53
87F/Lim-11
87F/St-26
87F/St-S4
87Leaf-116
87Moth/Ast-3
87OPC-343
87Pol/Ast-3
87RedFoley/St-95
87S-152M
87S-42
87T-670
87T/St-29
88D/Y/Bk-NEW
88F-443
88Panini/St-299
88Score-28
88T-278
Cruz, Juan
83Madis/LF-21
85MidldA-23
Cruz, Julio Luis
75QuadC
78T-687
79Ho-111
79OPC-305
79T-583
80BK/PHR-26
80OPC-16
80T-32
81D-163
81F-601
81OPC-121
81Pol/Mariners-6
81T-397
81T/St-126
82D-250
82F-509
82F/St-225
82OPC-130
82T-130
82T/St-114
82T/St-235
83D-379
83F-478
83OPC-113
83T-414
83T/St-112
83T/X-23
84D-182
84D-379
84F-55
84F/St-95
84Nes/792-257
84OPC-257
84T-257
84T/St-248
84TrueVal/WS-9
85Coke/WS-12
85D-452
85F-510
85OPC-71
85T-749
85T/St-239
86Coke/WS-12
86D-257
86F-201
86OPC-14
86T-14
87F-492
87OPC-53
87T-790
89Stock/Cal-179CO
Cruz, Luis
83Wisco/LF-19
86Pittsf-5
87WinSal-9
88CLAS/Star-26
88WinSal/Star-2
89CharlK-8
89IowaC/CMC-15
89IowaC/Pro-1692
89NiagFls/Puc-5A
Cruz, Pablo
77Salem
78Salem
Cruz, Rafael
86DayBe-6
87Gasto-13
Cruz, Todd Ruben
80T-492
81Coke
81F-341
81T-571
83D-505
83F-479
83Nalley-4
83OPC-132
83T-132
84D-148
84F-3
84Nes/792-773
84T-773
85F-172
85T-366
87SanBern-20
Cruz, Victor
78Syrac
79T-714R
80OPC-54
80T-99
81D-321
81F-407
81OPC-252
81T-252
81T/Tr-751
82F-480
82T-263
83OKCty-6
84OKCty-20
88Poca/Pro-2089
Csefalvay, John
83ColumAst-3
84Nashvl-4
Cubbage, Michael Lee
(Mike)
75OPC-617R
75T-617R
75T/M-617R
76OPC-615
76T-615
77T-149
78T-219
79OPC-187
79T-362
80OPC-262
80T-503
81D-492
81F-566
81T-657
81T/Tr-752
82F-523
82T-43
82Tidew-26
85Lynch-1
86Jacks/TCMA-24
87Tidew-12
87Tidew/TCMA-23
88AAA/Pro-54
88Tidew/CANDL-3MG
88Tidew/CMC-24
88Tidew/Pro-1586
89Tidew/CMC-21
Cuccinello, Alfred E.
(Al)
No Cards.
Cuccinello, Anthony
(Tony)
33G-99
34DS-55
35BU-79
35Exh/4-2
38Exh/4-1
39Exh
39PB-61
40PB-61
49Eureka-80
55Gol/Ind-3
55Salem
60T-458C
89Pac/Leg-170
89Smok/Dodg-37
R314
Cucjen, Romy
87Shrev-9
88Shreve/Pro-1293
89Louvl-15
89Louvl/CMC-15
89Louvl/Pro-1257
Cudjo, Lavell
89Greens/Pro-406
Cudworth, James A.
(Jim)
N172
Cuellar, Bobby
77Tucso
78Cr/PCL-111
79Tacom-7
80T-665R
80Tacom-6
81Charl-2
84Cram/PCL-192
85Cram/PCL-84
86Wausa-5MG
87Wausa-1
88SanBern/Best-27
88SanBern/Cal-54
89Wmspt/Pro-627
89Wmspt/Star-3
Cuellar, Mike
59T-518
60T-398
65T-337
66T-566
67OPC-97
67T-234LL
67T-97
68Coke
68T-274
69MB-66
69T-453
69T-532M
70MLB/St-148
70OPC-199ALCS
70OPC-68LL
70OPC-70LL
70T-590
70T-68LL
70T-70LL
70T/CB
71K-49
71MLB/St-293
71OPC-170
71OPC-69LL
71T-170
71T-69LL
71T/Coins-150
71T/tatt-16
72K-27
72MB-82
72OPC-70
72T-70
73JP
73K-47
73OPC-470
73T-470
74OPC-560
74T-560
75Ho-42
75OPC-410
75T-410
75T/M-410
76Ho-121
76OPC-285
76SSPC-375
76T-285
77T-162
86Moth/Ast-5
Cuen, Eleno
73Cedar
75Dubuq
81Portl-26
82Buffa-14
Cuervo, Ed
78Wausa
83ColumAst-2
Cuesta, Jamie
89Durhm/Star-6
Cueto, Manuel Melo
No Cards.
Cuevas, Angelo
86Lynch-8
88Jacks/GS-21
88TexLgAS/GS-10
89Jacks/GS-14
Cuevas, Johnny
86Sumter-4
87Durhm-8
88Sumter/Pro-397
89BurlB/Pro-1597
89BurlB/Star-6
Cuevas, Rafael
78Newar
Cuff, John J.
No Cards.
Culberson, Calvain
88Pulas/Pro-1760
89Sumter/Pro-1101
Culberson, Charles
86Fresno/Smok-25
87FtMyr-15
88Memph/Best-17
Culberson, Delbert L.
No Cards.
Culkar, Steve
88Virgini/Star-7
89Hagers/Best-8
89Hagers/Pro-276
89Hagers/Star-4
Cullen, John
(Jack)
63T-54R
66OPC-31
66T-31
Cullen, Mike
85Kingst-4
Cullen, Tim
67OPC-167R
67T-167R
68T-209
69T-586
70K-30
70OPC-49
70T-49
71MLB/St-534
71OPC-566
71T-566

72OPC-461
72T-461
Cullenbine, Roy
W753
Culler, Richard
47TipTop
Cullers, Steve
85BurlR-5
Cullop, Henry Nick
29Exh/4-3
31Exh/4-7
87Conlon/2-11
88Conlon/4-7
W514-59
Culmer, Will
80Penin/B-8
80Penin/C-19
82OkCty-25
83Charl-16
83Wheat/Ind-7
84Maine-14
Culp, Ray
60L-75
63T-29R
64T-412
64T/Coins-35
64T/St-96
64T/SU
64T/tatt
64Wheat/St-12
65T-505
66OPC-4
66T-4
67OPC-168
67T-168
68T-272
69MB-67
69MLB/St-11
69T-391
69T/S-6
69T/St-132
70K-35
70MLB/St-158
70OPC-144
70T-144
71MD
71MLB/St-317
71OPC-660
71T-660
71T/tatt-13
72MB-83
72OPC-2
72T-2
78TCMA-197
Culver, George
65OPC-166R
65T-166R
67T-499R
68T-319
69Kahn
69T-635
70OPC-92
70T-92
71MLB/St-76
71OPC-291
71T-291
72MB-84
72T-732
73OPC-242
73T-242
74OPC-632
74T-632
83Portl-12
84Cram/PCL-215
86Readg-6MG
87Readg-1
88Maine/CMC-23
88Maine/Pro-300
89ScrWB/Pro-724
Culver, Lanell C.
83Tampa-3
84Cedar-16
Cumberland, John
69OPC-114R
69T-114R
71MLB/St-244
71OPC-108
71T-108
72OPC-403
72T-403
83Lynch-13
85Tidew-26
86Tidew-6C
87Tidew-18
87Tidew/TCMA-24
88Tidew/CANDL-2PC
88Tidew/CMC-25
88Tidew/Pro-1579
Cummings, Audelle
89GreatF-8
Cummings, Bob
80Clint-24
84Shrev/FB-6
85Cram/PCL-197
Cummings, Brian
88Batav/Pro-1689
89Batav/Pro-1943
89BurlB/Pro-1618
89BurlB/Star-7
Cummings, Dick
84IowaC-21
85IowaC-25
Cummings, Steve
87Duned-2
88Knoxv/Best-20
88SLAS-27
89Syrac/CMC-7
89Syrac/Pro-803
90D-698
90T-374
Cummings, William
(Candy)
50Callahan
80SSPC/HOF
89HOF/St-64
Cunningham, Bill
86WPalm-10
87Jaxvl-17
Cunningham, Bill
V61-112
Cunningham, Chip
85PrWill-5
Cunningham, Dave
88Ashvl/Pro-1075
89Watlo/Pro-1795
89Watlo/Star-3
Cunningham, Earl
89LittleSun-2
90Score-670DC
90T-134
Cunningham, Ellsworth
N172
Cunningham, Everett
88Butte-27
89Gasto/Pro-1000
89Gasto/Star-6
Cunningham, Glen
51BR-D16
Cunningham, Joseph R.
(Joe)
55T-37
55T/DH-38
57T-304
58T-168
59T-285
60Bz-27
60T-40
60T-562AS
60T/tatt
60T/tatt-10
61P-172
61T-520
62J-195
62P-195
62P/Can-195
62Salada-173A
62Salada-173B
62Shirriff-173
62T-195
63Exh
63J-35
63P-35
63T-100
64T-340
65T-496
65T/E-63
66T-531
79TCMA-105
Exh47
Cunningham, Joseph
87StPet-8
88StPet/Star-4
89Hamil/Star-28
Cunningham, Sean
87BurlEx-25
88Rockford-9
89Jaxvl/Best-22
89Jaxvl/Pro-158
89Rockford-9TR
Cunningham, Troy
89Spoka/SP-17
Cunningham, Wm. A.
E120
W515-1
W573
W575
Cunningham, Wm. J.
E102
E220
T207
Cupples, Michael
85Madis-10
85Madis/Pol-7
86Madis-7
86Madis/Pol-7
87Madis-16
Curbelo, Jorge
82Miami-10
Curley, Tim
89Princet/Star-3
Curnal, Jim
78Cr/PCL-96
Curnow, Bob
88Spoka/Pro-1939
89Watlo/Pro-1777
89Watlo/Star-4
Curran, Bud
88Cedar/Pro-1161
Curran, Dave
80Holyo-22
Curren, Bud
85Cedar-30
Currence, Delaney
(Lafayette)
76SSPC-251
Current, Matt
88Martins/Star-8
89Martins/Star-9
Currie, Brian
89Boise/Pro-2000
Currier, Lenny
86Albuq-4TR
87Albuq/Pol-4TR
88Albuq/Pro-272
Currin, Wes
88Sumter/Pro-395
89Durhm/Star-7
89Star/Wax-70
Curry, Clint
83TriCit-25
Curry, G. Tony
60T-541
61P-120
61T-262
61T/St-51
Curry, Steve
81Richm-17
86NewBrit-8
86Richm-3
87Pawtu-3
87Pawtu/TCMA-3
88AAA/Pro-31
88Pawtu/CMC-7
88Pawtu/Pro-468
88Score/Tr-81T
89BurlB/Pro-1613
89F-86
89Panini/St-267
89Pawtu/CMC-2
89Pawtu/Dunkin-35
89Pawtu/Pro-691
89Score/HotRk-53
89T-471
Curtis, Clinton
(Cliff)
M116
Curtis, Ed
C46-90
Curtis, Irvin
N172
Curtis, Jack P.
61T-533
62T-372
Curtis, John D.
72T-724R
73OPC-143
73T-143
74OPC-373
74T-373
74T/Tr-373T
75OPC-381
75T-381
75T/M-381
76OPC-239
76T-239
77T-324
78T-486
79Pol/Giants-40
79T-649
80T-12
81F-491
81OPC-158
81T-531
81T/St-231
82F-569
82T-219
83D-170
83F-84
83T-777
84F-513
84Nes/792-158
84Smok/Cal-6
84T-158
89Princet/Star-4
Curtis, Mike
86Geneva-4
87WinSal-27
88Harris/Pro-843
Curtwright, Guy
Exh47
Cusack, Rocky
87Lakel-12
88CharlK-13
88CharlK/Pep-13
Cusak, John
88Pac/8Men-12
Cushing, Steve
81Batav-4
81Watlo-32
82Watlo/B-1
82Watlo/C-15
Cushman, Ed
N172
N172/ST
N284
N690
Cusick, Anthony
N172
Cusick, Jack
52B-192
Cutshall, Bill
86Jaxvl/TCMA-24
87Nashv-3
88Orlan/Best-27
Cutshaw, George
21Exh-30
D327
D328-37
E100
E120
E135-37
E220
E99
V100
W573
Cutty, Fran
81CharR-11
82FtMyr-15
Cuyler, Hazen
(Ki-Ki)
25Exh-51
26Exh-51
27Exh-25
29Exh/4-6
30CEA/Pin-2
31Exh/4-6
32Orbit/num-6
32Orbit/un-14
33CJ/Pin-3
33DL-8
33G-23
34DS-31
34G-90
35G-1F
35G-3D
35G-4D
35G-5D
36G
36G-10
38Wheat
60F-75
61F-19
73F/Wild-14
80Cram/Leg-92
80SSPC/HOF
89Smok/Dodg-6
R305
R308-152
R312
R312/M
R314
R332-29
R332-3
V353-23
V355-55
W517-19
WG8-10
Cuyler, Milt
87Fayette-8
88FSLAS/Star-32
88Lakel/Star-8
89Toled/CMC-21
89Toled/Pro-787
90Score-583
90Score/100Ris-84
Cvejdlik, Kent
76Watlo
Cyburt, Phil
78Salem
Cypret, Greg
81Tucso-1
82Tucso-6
83Tucso-15
84Cram/PCL-54
Czajkowski, Jim
87Sumter-19
88Durhm/Star-4
89Durhm/Star-8

Czarnik, Chris
89BurlB/Pro-1617
89BurlB/Star-8
D'Acquisto, John F.
(John)
74OPC-608R
74T-608R
75OPC-372
75T-372
75T/M-372
76OPC-628
76SSPC-94
76T-628
77T-19
79T-506
80T-339
81F-163
81OPC-204
81T-427
82Richm-4
82T-58
83F-516
D'Alessandro, Sal
85Durhm-22
88Greenv/Best-3
D'Amore, Louis
81Clint-14
D'Boever, William
86Jamestn-4
D'Onofrio, Gary
83DayBe-20
D'Vincenzo, Mark
86LitFalls-8
Dabney, Fred
88Utica/Puc-16
89SoBend/GS-11
Dabney, Ty
85Evrt/Cram-3
86Fresno/Smok-19
87Shrev-3
87TexLgAS-32
88Phoen/CMC-22
88Phoen/Pro-72
Daboll, Dennis
65T-561R
Dacko, Mark
82Evans-3
83Evans-1
84Evans-6
Dacosta, Bill
87Oneon-11
88PrWill/Star-7
Dacus, Barry
86PalmSp-9
86PalmSp/Smok-19
87MidldA-28
88Edmon/CMC-10
88Edmon/Pro-568
Dade, Lonnie Paul
(Paul)
78K-14
78OPC-86
78T-662
79OPC-3
79T-13
80OPC-134
80T-254
81T-496
Dafforn, Mike
88Martins/Star-9
89Martins/Star-10
Dagres, Angelo George
(Angie)
No cards.
Dahle, Dave
52Mother-15
Dahlen, William F.
(Bill)
10Domino-30
11Helmar-84
12Sweet/Pin-72
14Piedmont/St-15
E107
E254
E286
E98
M116
N300/SC
S74-51
T202
T205
T206
T3-11
WG3-12
WG5-13
Dahlgren, Ellsworth
(Babe)
39PB-81
40PB-3
41PB-49
Dahse, David
84Newar-4
Dailey, William G.
63T-391
64T-156
Daily, Cornelius F.
(Con)
N172
N284
Daily, Edward M.
(Ed)
E223
N172
N284
N690/2
Dal Canton, John B.
(Bruce)
69T-468R
70OPC-52
70T-52
71MLB/St-413
71OPC-168
71T-168
72T-717
73-487
73OPC-487
74OPC-308
74T-308
75OPC-472
75T-472
75T/M-472
76OPC-486
76T-486
77T-114
79Knoxv/TCMA-18
82Durhm-22
85IntLgAS-23
85Richm-23
86Richm-4
Dale, Emmett Eugene
(Gene)
D329-42
D350/2-43
M101/4-42
M101/5-43
Dale, Phil
86Tampa-4
87Cedar-2
88Chatt/Best-18
89Greens/Pro-427
Dalena, Pete
83Nashvl-5
84Colum-18
84Colum/Pol-8
84Nashvl-5
85Colum-15
85Colum/Pol-7
86Colum-4
86Colum/Pol-4
87Colum-11
87Colum/Pol-5
87Colum/TCMA-12
88Colum/CMC-16
88Colum/Pol-14
88Colum/Pro-321
89AAA/Pro-36
89ColrSp/CMC-12
89ColSp/Pro-235
Daley, Leavitt Leo
(Buddy)
55Salem
58T-222
59T-263
60Armour-8
60Bz-2
60T-8
60T/tatt
60T/tatt-11
61Bz-4
61P-83
61T-422
61T-48LL
61T/St-159
61T/St-201
62Salada-203
62Shirriff-203
62T-376
63T-38
64T-164
65OPC-262
65T-262
78TCMA-257
Exh47
Daley, Peter Harvey
(Pete)
55T-206
57T-388
58T-73
59T-276
60T-108
61T-158
62T/St-94
Daley, William
(Bill)
N172
Dalkowski, Steve
63T-496R
Dallessandro, Dom
41DP-101
49B/PCL-9
Dalrymple, Abner F.
(Abner)
N172
WG1-57
Dalrymple, Clayton E.
(Clay)
60L-143
60T-523
61T-299
61T/St-52
62J-197
62P-197
62P/Can-197
62Salada-141
62Shirriff-141
62T-434
62T/St-166
63F-52
63J-184
63P-184
63T-192
64T-191
65T-372
66T-202
67OPC-53
67T-53
68T-567
69MB-68
69OPC-151
69T-151
69T/St-74
70OPC-319
70T-319
71MLB/St-294
71OPC-617
71T-617
78TCMA-203
PM10/L-13
Dalton, Harry
82Pol/Brew-GM
Dalton, Mike
86Pawtu-8
87Pawtu-16
87Pawtu/TCMA-4
88NewBrit/Pro-896
89NewBrit/Pro-607
89Pawtu/Dunkin-27
Dalton, Rich
78OrlTw
Daly, James J.
(Sun)
N172
Daly, Mark
81Tidew-25
Daly, Thomas Peter
(Tom)
E107
N172
N300/SC
Damian, Len
88IowaC/CMC-2
88IowaC/Pro-544
89IowaC/CMC-2
89IowaC/Pro-1705
Damian, Leonard
86Peoria-4
87Pittsf-13
Damon, John
83Memph-4
Dancy, Bill
80Penin/B-27MG
80Penin/C-12MG
83Readg-23
85Cram/PCL-35MG
87Maine/TCMA-23
89ScrWB/CMC-25
89ScrWB/Pro-1208
Dandridge, Ray
74Laugh/Black-26
87D/HL-18
89HOF/St-26
Danek, Bill
86Peoria-5
87WinSal-5
Danforth, David C.
(Dave)
21Exh-31
E120
E121/120
T207
V61-26
W501-101
W572
W573
Danforth, Perry
77Spoka
Daniel, Clay
85Cedar-5
86Vermont-5
88Harris/Pro-860
Daniel, Dian
81ArkTr-23M
Daniel, Jim
86CharRa-8TR
87CharO/WBTV-11
88CharlK-16
88CharlK/Pep-16
88River/Cal-231
88River/Pro-1412
89River/Best-28
89River/Pro-1407
Daniel, Steve
85BurlR-25
Daniels, Bennie
58T-392
59T-122
60L-7
60T-91
61T-368
62Salada-42
62Shirriff-42
62T-378
62T/bucks
62T/St-95
63T-497
64T-587
65OPC-129
65T-129
78TCMA-145
Daniels, Bernard E.
(Bert)
E270/1
E286
T207
Daniels, Dave
79AppFx-11
82VeroB-4
Daniels, Greg
87Miami-19
Daniels, Harold Jack
(Jack)
53B/Col-83
Daniels, Jerry
87Erie-23
88StPet/Star-5
Daniels, Jim
89River/Cal-28TR
Daniels, Kal
83Cedar-22
83Cedar/LF-17
86D-27
86F-646M
86S/Rook-43
86TexGold-28
87Class/Up-130
87D-142
87D/OD-192
87F-197
87F/LL-13
87Kahn-28
87T-466
87ToysRUs-8
88Class/Red-161
88D-14DK
88D-289
88D/Best-6
88D/DKsuper-14DK
88F-230
88F/AwardWin-7
88F/Mini-72
88F/St-82
88Kahn/Reds-28
88Leaf-14DK
88Leaf-150
88OPC-53
88Panini/St-281
88RedFoley/St-14
88Score-86
88Score/YS/I-39
88Sf-112
88T-622
88T/Big-48
88T/St-139
89Ames-10
89B-314
89Class-74
89D-198
89D/Best-118
89D/MVP-BC18
89F-157
89F/LL-8
89F/Superstar-10
89K/Reds-28
89OPC-45
89Panini/St-75
89RedFoley/St-26
89Score-7
89Score/Tr-48
89Sf-52
89T-45

89T/Big-323
89T/Mini-7
89T/St-144
89UD-160
90D-432
90Score-490
90T-585
90UD-603

Daniels, Lance
89Brist/Star-6

Daniels, Lawrence L.
(Law)
N172

Daniels, Steve
80Cedar-24

Dann, Tom
79Newar-1

Danning, Harry
(Harry)
39PB-18
40PB-93
41DP-25
41DP-91
41PB-7
41Wheat-20
R302
V355-22

Danson, Roger
76BurlB

Dantzler, Shawn
86Clearw-6
87Clearw-10
88Clearw/Star-10

Darby, Mike
86Wausa-6

Darcy, Patrick L.
(Pat)
75OPC-615R
75T-615R
75T/M-615R
76OPC-538
76SSPC-26
76T-538

Dark, Alvin Ralph
(Alvin)
48L-51
49B-67
49Eureka-6
49Royal-18
50B-64
50Drake-20
51B-14
52B-34
52BR
52Royal
52StarCal/L-78B
52T-351
53B/Col-19
53T-109
54B-41
54NYJour
54RH
55B-2
55Gol/Giants-5
56T-148
57T-98
58T-125
59T-502
60T-472
61T-220
62T-322
63T-258
64T-529
66T-433
67T-389
68T-237
69OPC-91MG
69T-91
70OPC-524MG
70T-524
71OPC-397MG
71T-397
75OPC-561MG
75T-561MG
75T/M-561MG
76SSPC-488
78T-467
79TCMA-25
80Cram/Leg-80
87Moth/A's-13
88Pac/Leg-28
89Swell-77
Exh47
PM10/Sm-33
R302-116
R423-20

Darkis, Willie
83Readg-18
84Cram/PCL-211
86GlenF-2

Darling, Dell Conrad
(Dell)
N172
N184

Darling, Gary
89Umpires-58

Darling, Ronald M.
(Ron)
81Tulsa-18
82Tidew-13
83Tidew-1
84D-30
84F/X-29
84T/Mets/Fan-2
84T/X-27
85D-434
85F/St-117
85Leaf-256
85OPC-138
85T-415
85T/St-105
86D-563
86D/AAS-37
86F-77
86F/Mini-18
86F/St-28
86KayBee-6
86Leaf-221
86OPC-225
86S-109
86T-225
86T/Mets/Fan-3
86T/St-98
87BK-6
87D-192
87Drake-28
87F-5
87F/Hottest-11
87F/Lim-C1
87F/Mini-23
87F/St-27
87F/WS-5
87Kraft-28
87Leaf-85
87MSA/Discs-3
87OPC-75
87S-53
87T-75
87T/HL-26
87T/Mets/Fan-2
87T/Mini-21
87T/St-105
87Woolwth-26
88D-6DK
88D-76
88D/Best-41
88D/DKsuper-6DK
88D/Mets/Bk-76
88F-132
88F/Slug-C1
88F/St-100
88Kahn/Mets-12
88Leaf-6DK
88Leaf-78
88OPC-38
88Panini/St-335
88Score-141
88Sf-73
88T-685
88T/Big-85
88T/St-98
89B-372
89D-171
89D/Best-41
89F-32
89Kahn/Mets-12
89OPC-105
89Panini/St-130
89Score-180
89Score/HotSt-71
89Sf-32
89T-105
89T/Big-166
89T/St-100
89UD-159
90D-289
90F-201
90Score-446
90T-330
90UD-241

Darnbrough, William
N172

Darnell, Robert Jack
(Bob)
55B-39
79TCMA-257

Darnell, Steve
76Wausa

Darr, Michael Edward
(Mike)
78Syrac

Darretta, Dave
85BurlR-9

Darrow, Darrell
79SLCty-17

Darrow, George Oliver
(George)
34G-87

Darwin, Arthur B.
(Bobby)
69T-641R
73OPC-228
73T-228
74OPC-527
74T-527
74T/St-205
75Ho-98
75OPC-346
75T-346
75T/M-346
76Ho-31
76Ho/Twink-31
76OPC-63
76SSPC-247
76T-63
77T-617

Darwin, Danny Wayne
78Cr/PCL-81
79T-713R
80T-498
81D-147
81F-632
81OPC-22
81T-22
81T/St-136
82D-231
82F-315
82T-298
82T/St-237
83D-289
83F-565
83Rangers-44
83T-609
83T/St-121
84D-544
84F-416
84Nes/792-377
84Rangers-44
84T-377
84T/St-359
85D-98
85F-557
85F/Up-U32
85OPC-227
85Pol/Brew-18
85T-227
85T/St-352
85T/Tr-26T
86D-149
86F-485
86Leaf-75
86OPC-206
86Pol/Brew-18
86T-519
86T/St-205
87D-508
87F-54
87Moth/Ast-14
87OPC-157
87Pol/Ast-4
87T-157
88D-358
88F-444
88Moth/Ast-14
88Pol/Ast-7
88Score-184
88T-461
89D-390
89F-354
89Lennox/Ast-13
89Moth/Ast-13
89Score-553
89T-719
89UD-97
90D-561
90F-227
90Score-402
90Sf-83
90T-64
90UD-305

Dascenzo, Doug
86WinSal-4
87Pittsf-23
88IowaC/CMC-19
88IowaC/Pro-528
89D-491
89F-420
89IowaC/CMC-20
89IowaC/Pro-1702
89Panini/St-47
89Score-621
89Score/HotRk-4
89Sf-42
89T-149
89UD-10
90T-762
90UD-211

Dascoli, Frank
55B-291ump

Dasso, Francis J.
(Frank)
47Signal

Datz, Jeff
82AubAs-11
83DayBe-15
86ColumAst-9
87ColAst/Pro-2
87ColumAst-2
88Tucso-7
88Tucso/CMC-9
88Tucso/Pro-187
89Toled/CMC-11
89Toled/Pro-761

Daubert, Jacob E.
(Jake)
11Helmar-85
14CJ-143
14Piedmont/St-16
15CJ-143
21Exh-32
75F/Pion-24
87Conlon/2-12
88Pac/8Men-95
BF2-57
D327
D328-38
D329-43
D350/2-44
E120
E121/80
E122
E135-38
E220
E254
E270/1
M101/4-43
M101/5-44
S74-52
T201
T202
T205
T207
V100
V61-99
W501-52
W514-68
W572
W575
WG5-14
WG6-13
WG7-11

Dauer, Richard F.
(Rich)
77T-477R
78T-237
79T-666
80OPC-56
80T-102
81D-232
81F-182
81OPC-314
81T-314
81T/St-36
82D-256
82F-161
82OPC-8
82T-8
82T/St-147
83D-477
83F-57
83OPC-192
83T-579
83T/St-27
84D-114
84F-370
84F-4
84Nes/792-723
84OPC-374
84T-723
84T/St-214
85D-106
85F-173
85OPC-58
85T-494
85T/St-203
86F-270
86OPC-251
86T-251
87SanBer-7
89ColrSp/CMC-24
89ColSp/Pro-242
89SanBer/Best-28M

Daugherty, Jack
86Jaxvl/TCMA-25
87Indianap-10
88Indi/CMC-21
88Indi/Pro-521
89OkCty/CMC-13
89OkCty/Pro-1525
90D-461

90F-294
90Score-564
90Score/100Ris-61
90T-52
90UD-614

Daughterty, Mike
83SanJose-19

Daughtry, Dorian
89SnBer/Best-2
89SnBer/Cal-88

Daulton, Darren
83Readg-11
84Cram/PCL-198
85Cram/PCL-42
85F/Up-U33
86CIGNA-7
86D-477
86F-438
86T-264
87D-262
87F-172
87Maine/TCMA-21
87OPC-57
87T-636
88D-309
88Score-473
88T-468
89D-549
89D/Best-128
89Score-413
89T-187
89UD-448
90D-194
90F-555
90Score-389
90T-542
90UD-418

Dauss, George August
(Hooks)
21Exh-33
25Exh-91
26Exh-92
27Exh-46
88Conlon/5-7
D327
D328-39
E120
E121/120
E121/80
E122
E135-39
V100
V117-11
V61-18
W501-110
W573
W575

Davalillo, Victor J.
(Vic)
63Sugar-24
63T-324R
64Kahn
64T-435
64T/Coins-86
64T/St-100
64T/tatt
65Kahn
65OldLond-24
65OPC-128
65T-128
66Kahn
66T-216LL
66T-325
66T/RO-70
67OPC-69
67T-69
68T-397
69MB-70
69MLB/St-20
69T-275
69T/S-9
69T/St-142
70MLB/St-138
70OPC-256
70T-256
71MLB/St-199
71OPC-4
71T-4
72MB-86
72T-785
73OPC-163
73T-163
74OPC-444
74T-444
78T-539
79T-228
81F-132
WG10-26

DaVanon, Frank G.
(Jerry)
69T-637R
71OPC-32
71T-32
75Iowa/TCMA-5
76OPC-551
76T-551
77T-283

Davenport, Adell
87Anchora-5
89Clint/Pro-882

Davenport, Arthur D.
(Dave)
D327

Davenport, Gary
86Fresno/Smok-2CO

Davenport, James H.
(Jim)
58SFCall
58T-413
59Bz
59T-198
60T-154
61P-149
61T-55
61T/Dice-3
61T/St-76
62J-134
62P-134
62P/Can-134
62Salada-169
62Shirriff-169
62T-9
62T/St-196
63F-65
63J-104
63P-104
63Salada-19
63T-388
64T-82
64T/St-63
65OPC-213
65T-213
66OPC-176
66T-176
67T-441
68Coke
68T-525
69MB-69
69OPC-102
69T-102
69T/St-102
70MLB/St-122
70OPC-378
70T-378
72MB-85
76SSPC-626
78TCMA-131
79Pol/SFG-12
79TCMA-288
80Pol/SFG-12
84Moth/SFG-6
85Moth/SFG-1MG
85T/Tr-27T
89Pac/Leg-118
PM10/Sm-34

Davenport, Neal
86Cedar/TCMA-26
87Tampa-23TR

Davey, Michael Gerard
(Mike)
79Spoka-14
80Port-19

David, Andre
82Orlan/B-16
82OrlTw/A-5
83Toled-19
84Toled-11
85T-43
85Toled-20
86Toled-7
87D-519
87Tidew-24
87Tidew/TCMA-12
88Tidew/CANDL-7
88Tidew/CMC-18
88Tidew/Pro-1596
89ElPas/GS-26

David, Brian
83Wausa/LF-6
86Chatt-8
87Chatt/Best-23

David, Greg
87Duned-20
88Myrtle/Pro-1176
89Myrtle/Pro-1454

Davidsmeier, Dan
82ElPas-5
84Cram/PCL-29
85Cram/PCL-201
86Vanco-9

Davidsmeier, David
87Denver-22

Davidson, Bob
88Umpire-44
89Umpires-42

Davidson, Bobby
86Albany/TCMA-31
87PrWill-3
88Albany/Pro-1334
89Albany/Best-3
89Albany/Pro-327
89Albany/Star-6
89Star/Wax-97

Davidson, Jackie
86Pittsf-6
87IowaC-3
88Pittsf/Pro-1375
89CharlK-19

Davidson, Mark
85Orlan-3
86Toled-6
87D/OD-225
87D/Rook-22
87F/U-U20
88D-519
88F-8
88Score-570
88T-19
89F-109
89Portl/CMC-22
89Portl/Pro-227
89Score-107
89T-451
89T/Big-320
89UD-577
90T-267

Davidson, Mike
88Brist/Pro-1871
89Fay/Pro-1593

Davidson, Randy
78Indianap-24
79Indianap-13
81Cedar-19
82Cedar-25

Davidson, Thomas E.
(Ted)
65OPC-243R
65T-243R
66OPC-89
66T-89
67T-519
68OPC-48
68T-48

Davidson, William J.
M116
T206

Davie, Gerald Lee
(Jerry)
59T-256
60T-301

Davies, Bob
52Wheat

Davila, Vic
83Butte-17

Davin, D.
N172

Davino, Mike
89Utica/Puc-5

Davins, Jim
86Macon-7
87Kenosha-1
88Portl/CMC-10
88Portl/Pro-660
89Portl/CMC-1
89Portl/Pro-211

Davis, Alvin
83Chatt-8
84F/X-30
84FunFood/Pin-37
84Moth/Mar-23
84T/X-28
85D-18
85D-69
85D/AAS-16
85D/DKsuper-18
85Drake-8
85F-488
85F/LimEd-7
85F/St-15
85GenMills-16
85Leaf-18DK
85Moth/Mar-2
85OPC-145
85Seven-7W
85T-145
85T/Gloss40-8
85T/St-332
85T/St-368YS
85T/Super-6
86D-69
86F-464
86F/LL-9
86F/Mini-97
86F/Slug-8
86F/St-29
86KayBee-7
86Leaf-65
86Moth/Mar-2
86OPC-309
86S-31
86S-74M
86T-440
86T/St-218
86TrueVal-21
87D-75
87D/OD-115
87F-584
87F/Excit-13
87F/Mini-24
87F/RecSet-5
87F/St-28
87Kraft-37
87Leaf-118
87Moth/Sea-2
87OPC-235
87RedFoley/St-71
87S-21
87T-235
87T/Coins-9
87T/St-220
88D-193
88D-BC25
88D/Best-107
88F-373
88F/RecSet-8
88F/SS-10
88F/St-59
88KayBee-6
88KingB/Disc-17
88Leaf-196
88Moth/Sea-2
88OPC-349
88Panini/St-185
88Score-83
88Sf-52
88T-785
88T/Big-64
88T/Coins-10
88T/RiteAid-24
88T/St-219
88T/UK-17
89B-215
89Class-81
89D-345
89D/Best-24
89D/MVP-BC25
89F-546
89Moth/Sea-2
89OPC-57
89Panini/St-435
89RedFoley/St-27
89Score-51
89Score/HotSt-78
89Sf-33
89T-687
89T/Big-218
89T/Coins-38
89T/Mini-72
89T/St-227
89T/UK-18
89UD-105
89UD-680TC
90Class-136
90D-109
90D/Bon/MVP-BC9
90F-512
90Score-205
90Score/100St-26
90Sf-112
90T-373
90UD-364

Davis, Arthur W.
(Bill)
65T-546R
66OPC-44R
66T-44R
67T-253R
68T-432R
69T-304R

Davis, Bill
82Idaho-17

Davis, Bo
89Bluef/Star-7

Davis, Brad
85FtMyr-3

Davis, Braz
88CharWh/Best-20
89Peoria/Ko-2P

Davis, Bret
85Anchora-8
86Wausa-7
88James/Pro-1897

Davis, Brian
88Tampa/Star-5
89Utica/Puc-6

Davis, Bryshear B.
(Brock)
63T-553R
71OPC-576R
71T-576R

72OPC-161
72T-161
73OPC-366
73T-366

Davis, Charles T.
(Chili)
78Cedar
82T-171R
82T/Tr-23T
83D-348
83F-257
83Moth/Giants-3
83OPC-115
83T-115
83T/St-319
84D-350
84FunFood/Pin-38
84Nes/792-494
84OPC-367
84T-494
84T/St-171
85D-480
85Drake-9
85F-605
85F/St-10
85Leaf-66
85Moth/Giants-2
85OPC-245
85T-245
85T/St-162
85T/Super-40
86D-6
86D-65
86D/DKsuper-6
86F-536
86F/Mini-109
86Leaf-6DK
86Moth/Giants-2
86S-82
87D-268
87D/AAS-38
87D/OD-97
87F-270
87F/Lim-12
87F/Mini-25
87F/St-29
87Kraft-46
87Leaf-208
87Moth/SFG-3
87OPC-162
87RedFoley/St-76
87S-45
87T-672
87T/St-95
88D-313
88F-79
88F/U-U12
88OPC-15
88Score-605
88Score/Tr-28T
88Sf-172
88Smok/Angels-10
88T-15
88T/Big-235
88T/Tr-32T
89B-50
89Class-80
89D-449
89D/Best-115
89F-474
89F/LL-9
89OPC-103
89Panini/St-296
89RedFoley/St-28
89Score-54
89Sf-129
89T-525
89T/Big-294
89T/St-177
89UD-126
90D-136
90D/Bon/MVP-BC20
90F-129
90Score-326
90Sf-21
90T-765
90UD-38

Davis, Chris
78StPet
79ArkTr-17

Davis, Chuck
86NewBrit-9
87Pawtu-24
87Pawtu/TCMA-5

Davis, Curtis Benton
(Curt)
35BU-97
36Exh/4-6
36Wheat
R314

Davis, Douglas
82BurlR-18
85MidldA-14
86MidldA-8
87MidldA-10
88Edmon/CMC-18
88Edmon/Pro-559
89Edmon/CMC-15
89Edmon/Pro-551

Davis, Eric Keith
(Eric)
82Cedar-20
83Water-15
84Borden-44
85D-325
85F-533
85T-627
86D-164
86D/HL-30
86F-175
86T-28
86TexGold-44
87Class-21
87Class/Up-102
87Class/Up-150M
87D-22DK
87D-265
87D/DKsuper-22
87D/HL-3
87D/HL-8
87D/OD-197
87F-198
87F/AwardWin-11
87F/Excit-14
87F/GameWin-11
87F/Hottest-12
87F/Mini-26
87F/Slug-11
87F/St-132M
87F/St-30
87Ho/St-9
87Kahn-44
87Kraft-10
87Leaf-179
87Leaf-22DK
87MSA/Discs-7
87OPC-228
87S-155M
87S-199M
87S-22
87T-412
87T/Coins-30
87T/Gloss60-44
87T/Mini-4
87T/St-136
88Bz-6
88ChefBoy-2
88Class/Blue-201M
88Class/Blue-213
88Class/Red-154
88D-369
88D-BC2
88D/AS-38
88D/Best-62
88D/PopUp-16
88F-231
88F-637M
88F/AS-7
88F/AwardWin-8
88F/BB/AS-9
88F/BB/MVP-8
88F/Excit-12
88F/Hottest-8
88F/LL-8
88F/Mini-73
88F/RecSet-9
88F/Slug-10
88F/SS-11
88F/St-83
88F/St-S6M
88F/TL-6
88FanSam-14
88Kahn/Reds-44
88KayBee-7
88KingB/Disc-22
88Leaf-149
88MSA/Disc-12
88Nestle-3
88OPC-150
88OPC-J
88Panini/St-235M
88Panini/St-282
88RedFoley/St-15
88Score-10
88Score-649
88Score/WaxBox-15
88Score/YS/II-1
88Sf-10
88Sf/Gamewin-5
88T-150
88T/Big-20
88T/Coins-39
88T/Gloss22-17
88T/Gloss60-16
88T/Mini-46
88T/RiteAid-3
88T/St-141
88T/St-146
88T/St/Backs-14
88T/UK-18
88T/WaxBox-J
89Ames-11
89B-316
89Cadaco-12
89Class-109
89Class-9
89Crunch-13
89D-80
89D/Best-6
89F-158
89F-639M
89F/BBMVP's-9
89F/Excit-9
89F/Heroes-10
89F/LL-10
89F/Superstar-11
89Holsum/Discs-7
89K/Reds-44
89KayBee-8
89Nissen-7
89OPC-330
89Panini/St-76
89RedFoley/St-29
89Score-109
89Score/HotSt-58
89Score/Mast-18
89Sf-69
89T-111TL
89T-330
89T/Big-273
89T/Coins-9
89T/Gloss60-2
89T/HeadsUp-21
89T/Mini-8
89T/St-138
89T/St/Backs-47
89T/UK-19
89Tetley/Discs-11
89UD-410
89UD-688TC
90Class-11
90D-233
90D-695AS
90D/Bon/MVP-BC23
90F-417
90F/WaxBox-C4
90Score-185
90Score/100St-95
90Sf-97
90T-260
90T-402AS
90UD-116

Davis, Frank
(Dixie)
E120
E121/120
V100
V61-36
W501-3
W514-48
W573
W575

Davis, Fred
89Lynch/Star-5

Davis, Geff
86BurlEx-5
87WPalm-27

Davis, George Stacey
(George)
11Helmar-23
E107
E254
E90/1
N142
T206
V355-17

Davis, George Allen
(George)
D350/2-45
M101/5-45

Davis, George Willis
(Kiddo)
33G-236
W711/1

Davis, George
(Storm)
83D-619
83F-56
83T-268
83T/St-310
84D-585
84FunFood/Pin-120
84Nes/792-140
84OPC-140
84T-140
85D-454
85F-174
85Leaf-81
85OPC-73
85T-599
86D-169
86F-271
86Leaf-99
86OPC-179
86T-469
86T/St-231
87Bohem-34
87D-273
87F-466
87F/U-U22
87OPC-349
87T-349
87T/St-230
87T/Tr-26T
88D-595
88D/A's/Bk-595
88D/Best-282
88F-278
88Moth/A's-19
88T-248
89B-192
89D-210
89F-6
89Moth/A's-18
89Panini/St-413
89Score-248
89T-701
89T/Big-121
89UD-153
90D-479
90F-5
90Score-266
90T-606
90UD-292

Davis, George
76Clint

Davis, Gerald Edward
(Gerry)
82Amari-5

Davis, Gerry
88Umpire-52
89Umpires-50

Davis, Glenn
52Wheat

Davis, Glenn Earl
(Glenn)
82DayBe-20
83ColumAst-11
84Cram/PCL-62
85Cram/PCL-65
85F-652M
86D-380
86F-297
86F/Mini-63
86Leaf-175
86OPC-389
86Pol/Ast-22
86S-188
86T-389
86T/Gloss60-59
86T/St-29
86T/St-314
87Class-28
87Class/Up-107
87D-61
87D/AAS-42
87D/OD-16
87F-55
87F-636M
87F/GameWin-12
87F/LL-14
87F/McCror-11
87F/Mini-27
87F/St-31
87F/St-S5
87KayBee-12
87Kraft-36
87Leaf-115
87Moth/Ast-10
87OPC-56
87Pol/Ast-23
87RedFoley/St-43
87S-17
87S-195M
87T-560
87T/Coins-31
87T/Gloss60-4
87T/Mini-8
87T/St-26
88Class/Red-182
88D-184
88D/Best-64
88F-445
88F/Mini-78
88F/Slug-11
88F/SS-12
88F/St-86
88Leaf-186
88Moth/Ast-10
88OPC-159

88Panini/St-292
88Pol/Ast-8
88Score-460
88Sf-102
88T-430
88T/Big-192
88T/St-35
88T/UK-19
89B-331
89Cadaco-13
89Class-17
89Class/Up/2-168
89D-236
89D-25DK
89D/Best-8
89D/DKsuper-25DK
89F-355
89F/BBMVP's-10
89F/Excit-10
89F/Heroes-11
89F/LL-11
89Lennox/Ast-26
89Moth/Ast-9
89OPC-378
89Panini/St-88
89RedFoley/St-30
89Score-164
89Score/HotSt-46
89Sf-137
89T-579TL
89T-765
89T/Big-89
89T/Coins-10
89T/Gloss60-32
89T/Hills-10
89T/St-21
89T/St/Backs-35
89T/UK-20
89UD-443
90Class-71
90D-118
90D/Bon/MVP-BC21
90F-228
90F/WaxBox-C5
90Score-272
90Score/100St-52
90Sf-19
90T-50
90UD-245

Davis, Harry H.
(Harry)
E101
E103
E104
E105
E107
E254
E270/1
E286
E90/1
E91
E92
E94
E96
E97
E98
M116
T206
T207
T208
T213/blue
T215/blue
T215/brown
T216
T222
W555

Davis, Harry
84Evrt/Cram-5
86Fresno/Smok-26
88Shreve/Pro-1299
89Wmspt/Pro-641
89Wmspt/Star-4
WG2-13

Davis, Herman Thomas
(Tommy)
59DF
60T-509
61BB-12
61Morrell
61P-165
61T-168
61T/St-25
62BB-12
62J-105
62P-105
62P/Can-105
62Salada-154A
62Salada-154B
62Shirriff-154
62T-358
63Bz-36
63F-40
63J-117
63P-117
63T-1LL
63T-310
63T/SO
64Bz-36
64T-180
64T-7LL
64T/Coins-153AS
64T/Coins-57
64T/S-43
64T/St-64
64T/SU
64Wheat/St-13
65Bz-36
65T-370
65T/E-49
65T/trans-46
66OPC-75
66T-75
67Bz-37
67Kahn
67T-370
68Bz-10
68T-265
68T/G-10
69MB-72
69MLB/St-94
69OPC-135
69T-135
69T/DE-15
69T/decal
69T/S-32
69T/St-224
70MB-6
70MLB/St-38
70T-559
71OPC-151
71T-151
71T/Coins-93
72MB-87
72OPC-41
72OPC-42IA
72T-41
72T-42A
73JP
74K-43
74OPC-396
74T-396
74T/St-124
75OPC-564
75T-564
75T/M-564
76OPC-149
76SSPC-398
76T-149
77T-362
78TCMA-87
82D-648
87Smok/Dodg-5
88Bakers/Cal-265
88Pac/Leg-83
88Smok/Dodg-8
89Smok/Dodg-70

Davis, I.M.
25Exh-77

Davis, Jacke S.
(Jacke)
62T-521
63T-117

Davis, James Bennett
(Jim)
52Mother-2
53Mother-46
55T-68
55T/DH-28
56T-102
57T-273

Davis, James J.
(Jumbo)
N172

Davis, Jerry
84Cram/PCL-222
85D-162
85F/Up-U34
85Moth/Padres-26
85T/Tr-28T
86D-429
86F-317
86T-323
87Toled-30
87Toled/TCMA-24

Davis, Jody Richard
(Jody)
79Jacks-7
82D-225
82F-592
82RedLob
82T-508
83D-183
83F-494
83T-542
83T/St-226
83Thorn-7
84D-433
84F-491
84FunFood/Pin-51
84Jacks/Smok-4
84Nes/792-73
84OPC-73
84SevenUp-7
84T-73
84T/St-43
85D-76
85D/AAS-54
85F-54
85Leaf-180
85OPC-384
85SevenUp-7
85T-384
85T/St-37
86D-289
86F-364
86F/St-30
86Gator-7
86Jay's-3
86OPC-176
86T-767
86T/St-58
87Berg/Cubs-7
87D-269
87D/AAS-50
87D/OD-72
87F-557
87F/Lim-13
87F/LL-15
87Kraft-6
87Leaf-48
87OPC-270
87RedFoley/St-68
87S-170
87Seven-C2
87Seven-ME3
87Smok/NL-3
87T-270
87T/St-64
88Berg/Cubs-7
88D-119
88D/Cubs/Bk-119
88F-414
88Leaf-69
88OPC-376
88Panini/St-258
88Score-551
88Sf-60
88T-615
88T/St-60
88T/St/Backs-23
89B-270
89D-650
89D/Best-58
89F-421
89OPC-115
89RedFoley/St-31
89Score-173
89Score/Tr-64
89Sf-187
89T-115
89T/Big-3
89T/Tr-22T
89UD-148
89UD/Ext-795
90F-579
90Score-328
90T-453
90UD-429

Davis, Joel
86Coke/WS-52
86D-623
86F-202
86T/Tr-30T
87Coke/WS-26
87D-124
87T-299
88T-511
88Vanco/CMC-2
88Vanco/Pro-763
89ColrSp/CMC-7
89ColSp/Pro-237

Davis, John Humphrey
(John)
52Mother-27
61Union
75OkCty
76Wmspt

Davis, John
83CharR-17
87Omaha-19
88CapeCod/Sum-56
88Coke/WS-5
88D-594
88D/Rook-48
88F-255
88F/U-U15
88Score-636
88Sf-224
88T-672
89Score-608
89T-162
89UD-548
89Vanco/CMC-9
89Vanco/Pro-582

Davis, Kelvin
88Eugene/Best-17

Davis, Kenny
87Visal-15
88Visal/Cal-145
88Visal/Pro-81

Davis, Kevin
83Peoria/LF-3
83Redwd-8
85MidldA-18
87Salem-30
88EastLAS/Pro-14
88Harris/Pro-837
89BirmB/Best-6
89BirmB/Pro-98

Davis, Larry
81Tacom-1
82Tacom-20
83Tacom-22

Davis, Mark
84LitFalls-22
86Kenosha-5
87Penin-1
87Savan-12
88BirmB/Best-14
88Sumter/Pro-396
89BurlB/Pro-1599
89BurlB/Star-9
89Vanco/CMC-22
89Vanco/Pro-585

Davis, Mark William
(Mark)
81OkCty/TCMA-6
82OkCty-12
82T-231R
83Phoen/BHN-20
84D-201
84F-371
84Nes/792-343
84T-343
85D-553
85F-606
85Moth/Giants-20
85T-541
86D-265
86F-537
86Moth/Giants-20
86T-138
86T/St-91
87D-313
87F-271
87F/U-U21
87Moth/SFG-14
87T-21
88Coke/Padres-48
88D-64
88D/Best-98
88F-581
88Score-391
88Smok/Padres-6
88T-482
89B-447
89D-65
89D/AS-46
89D/Best-133
89F-303
89F-635M
89F/BBAS-10
89F/Up-18
89OPC-59
89RedFoley/St-32
89Score-490
89Score/HotSt-62
89Sf-74
89T-59
89T/St-110
89T/St/Backs-64
89UD-268
90D-302
90F-155
90F-631M
90Score-259
90Score/100St-51
90Sf-62
90T-205
90T-407AS
90UD-431

Davis, Michael Dwayne
(Mike)
81D-470
81F-586
81T-364
81Tacom-11
82T-671
82Tacom-34
83Granny-16

83T/X-24
84D-298
84F-443
84Moth/A's-5
84Nes/792-558
84T-558
84T/St-338
85D-223
85D/HL-3
85Moth/A's-7
85T-778
86D-14DK
86D-96
86D/DKsuper-14
86F-416
86F/LimEd-14
86F/Mini-88
86F/St-31
86Leaf-14DK
86Moth/A's-7
86OPC-165
86S-83
86T-165
86T/St-166
87D-133
87D/OD-21
87F-391
87F/McCror-12
87F/Mini-28
87F/St-32
87Smok/A's-3
87T-83
87T/St-168
88D-281
88D/Best-36
88F-277
88Moth/Dodg-12
88OPC-217
88Panini/St-174
88Pol/Dodg-37
88RedFoley/St-16
88Score-211
88Score/Tr-53T
88Sf-206
88T-448
88T/Big-154
88T/St-171
88T/Tr-33T
89Ames-12
89B-352
89D-316
89F-55
89Moth/Dodg-12
89OPC-277
89Panini/St-193
89Panini/St-24
89Pol/Dodg-11
89Score-376
89T-277
89T/Big-225
89UD-146
89Woolwth-32
90D-552
90F-391
90Score-437
90T-697
90UD-258

Davis, Michael
82Tidew-3
83Pawtu-16
84Pawtu-26
84Pawtu-7
85Tidew-23
86Tidew-7
89Kingspt/Star-6

Davis, Odie Ernest
(Odie)
79Tucso-18
80Charl-15
81Charl-16

Davis, Piper
53Mother-54

Davis, Ray
(Peaches)
39PB-123
W711/1

Davis, Richard Earl
(Dick)
77Spoka
79T-474
80T-553
81D-528
81F-527
81T-183
81T/Tr-753
82D-147
82F-245
82T-352
82T/Tr-24T
83D-647
83F-305
83Portl-16
83T-667

Davis, Rick
89Spoka/SP-11

Davis, Robert Edward
(Bob)
61T-246

Davis, Robert John
76OPC-472
76T-472
77T-78
78T-713
80OPC-185
80T-351
81D-30
81F-428
81OPC-221
81SLCty-26
81T-221

Davis, Robert
86FtMyr-6
89Brist/Star-7

Davis, Ronald E.
(Ron)
67T-298
68Coke
68T-21
69T-553

Davis, Ronald Gene
(Ron)
68OPC-21
69MB-71
69MLB/St-185
70MLB/St-100
79Colum-14
80OPC-101
80T-179
81D-467
81F-86
81OPC-16
81T-179
82D-451
82F-32
82F/St-117
82F/St-242M
82OPC-283
82T-2M
82T-635
82T/Tr-25T
83D-228
83F-610
83OPC-380
83T-380
83T/St-94
84D-269
84F-5
84F-561
84F/St-75
84FunFood/Pin-112
84Nes/792-519
84OPC-101
84T-519
84T/St-309

85D-120
85F-275
85F/St-103
85OPC-78
85Seven/Minn-8
85T-430
85T/St-297
86D-364
86F-390
86OPC-265
86T-265
86T/St-281
87Berg/Cubs-39
87D-438
87F-558
87OPC-383
87T-383
89Phoen/Pro-1505

Davis, Russell
89FtLaud/Star-2
89Oneon/Pro-2109

Davis, Sammy
78Watlo

Davis, Stan
77Newar
78Newar
79BurlB-21
81ElPas-6
82Vanco-9
83ElPas-6
84ElPas-14

Davis, Steven K.
86Ault-25
86Tor/Fire-7
87Syrac-21
87Syrac/TCMA-2
88Syrac/CMC-1
88Syrac/Pro-814
89ColrSp/CMC-1
89ColSp/Pro-249
90Score-187
90T-428

Davis, Steven Michael
(Steve)
81Syrac-14
87Tampa-19
88Cedar/Pro-1150

Davis, Ted
78Ashev
79Wausa-20
80Tulsa-4
81Tulsa-8
82Jacks-3
83BirmB-18

Davis, Thomas Oscar
(Tod)
47Signal

Davis, Trench
82Portl-19
84Cram/PCL-139
85Cram/PCL-238
86Hawai-3
87Richm/TCMA-17

Davis, Virgil L.
(Spud)
33G-210
39PB-37
40PB-163
88Conlon/NatAS-4
R314
V355-12
W711/1
WG8-11

Davis, Wallace M.
(Butch)
84D-277
85Omaha-12
85T-49
87Vanco-17
88CharlK-3
88CharlK/Pep-3
89RochR/CMC-22

89RochR/Pro-1652

Davis, Wayne
87Myrtle-20
88Duned/Star-3

Davis, Willie Henry
(Willie)
60DF-8
61BB-3
61T-506
62BB-3
62J-106
62P-106
62P/Can-106
62Salada-161
62Shirriff-161
62T-108
63J-119
63P-119
63Salada-21
63T-229
64T-68
65OldLond-7
65T-435
66T-535
66T/RO-17
67OPC-160
67T-160
68T-208
68T/3D
69MB-73
69MLB/St-145
69MLBPA/Pin-40
69OPC-65
69T-65
69T/S-45
69T/St-41
69Trans-45
70MLB/St-49
70OPC-390
70T-390
70T/PI-3
70T/S-39
70Trans-2
71K-16
71MD
71MLB/St-101
71OPC-585
71T-585
72K-3
72MB-88
72OPC-390
72T-390
72T/Cloth-9
73K-43
73OPC-35
73T-35
73T/Comics-6
73T/Lids-12
73T/PinUps-6
74K-45
74OPC-165
74T-165
74T/DE-42
74T/St-44
74T/Tr-165T
75OPC-10
75T-10
75T/M-10
76OPC-265
76SSPC-279
76T-265
77T-603
78TCMA-24
87Smok/Dodg-6
88Smok/Dodg-12
89Smok/Dodg-77

Davison, Michael Lynn
(Mike)
71MLB/St-245
71OPC-276R
71T-276R

Davison, Scott
89James/Pro-2145

Davisson, Jay
83Readg-4
84Cram/PCL-213
85Cram/PCL-41

Dawley, Bill
79Nashvl
80Indianap-25
81Indianap-28
82Indianap-7
84D-328
84F-223
84F/St-108
84Moth/Ast-22
84Nes/792-248
84OPC-248
84T-248
84T/St-71
85D-354
85F-348
85Moth/Ast-16
85OPC-363
85T-634
86F-298
86F/Up-U32
86Moth/Ast-25
86T-376
87D-628
87F-493
87F/U-U23
87Smok/Cards-9
87T-54
88D-331
88F-29
88Score-328
88T-509
89Tacom/CMC-5
89Tacom/Pro-1555

Dawson, Andre Nolan
(Andre)
77T-473R
78OPC-180
78T-72
79OPC-179
79T-348
80OPC-124
80T-235
81D-212
81F-145
81F/St-123
81OPC-125
81OPC/Post-6
81T-125
81T/SO-90
81T/St-187
82D-88
82F-187
82F/St-35
82Hygrade
82OPC-341
82OPC-379
82OPC/Post-18
82Sqt-17
82T-341
82T-540
82T/St-125
82T/St-57
82Zeller-10
82Zeller-14
82Zeller-4
83D-518
83D/AAS-9
83F-280
83OPC-173AS
83OPC-303
83Stuart-4
83T-402
83T-680
83T/St-164
83T/St-252
84D-97

84D/AAS-18
84Drake-9
84F-273
84F/St-18
84F/St-25
84F/St-33
84FunFood/Pin-22
84MiltBrad-8
84Nes/792-200
84Nes/792-392AS
84Nestle/DT-16
84OPC-200
84OPC-392AS
84Ralston-6
84Seven-1C
84Seven-1E
84Seven-1W
84Stuart-11
84Stuart-36AS
84Stuart-37M
84T-200
84T-392
84T/Cereal-6
84T/Gloss22-18
84T/Gloss40-35
84T/St-181
84T/St-92
84T/Super-20
84T/Super-20
85D-421
85D/HL-41
85F-394
85F/LimEd-8
85GenMills-2
85Leaf-133
85OPC-133
85OPC/Post-9
85Seven-7S
85T-420
85T/St-86
86D-25
86D-87
86D/DKsuper-25
86F-246
86F/Mini-53
86F/St-32
86Leaf-25DK
86OPC-256
86Provigo-9
86S-110
86S-66M
86T-576M
86T-760
86T/St-74
86TrueVal-29
87Berg/Cubs-8
87Class/Up-124
87D-458
87D/HL-28
87D/HL-31
87D/OD-70
87F-316
87F/Hottest-13
87F/Slug-12
87F/St-33
87F/U-U24
87Leaf-212
87OPC-345
87RedFoley/St-13
87S-139
87T-345
87T/Board-10
87T/St-77
87T/Tr-27T
88Woolwth-8
88Berg/Cubs-8
88ChefBoy-18
88Class/Blue-216
88Class/Red-157
88D-269
88D-9DK
88D-BC10
88D/AS-36
88D/Best-225
88D/Cubs/Bk-269
88D/DKsuper-9DK
88D/PopUp-14
88F-415
88F/AS-6
88F/AwardWin-9
88F/BB/AS-10
88F/BB/MVP-9
88F/Excit-13
88F/Hottest-9
88F/LL-9
88F/Mini-67
88F/RecSet-10
88F/Slug-12
88F/SS-13
88F/St-79
88F/TL-7
88FanSam-15
88Jiffy-8
88KayBee-8
88KingB/Disc-14
88KMart-9
88Leaf-126
88Leaf-9DK
88Nestle-9
88OPC-247
88Panini/St-236M
88Panini/St-265
88RedFoley/St-17
88Score-4
88Score/WaxBox-16
88Sf-3
88T-401
88T-500
88T/Big-153
88T/Coins-33
88T/Gloss22-18
88T/Gloss60-1
88T/Mini-43
88T/Revco-2
88T/RiteAid-2
88T/St-148
88T/St-56
88T/St/Backs-13
88T/UK-20
89Ames-13
89B-298
89Cadaco-14
89Class-37
89Crunch-10
89D-167
89D/AS-36
89D/Best-4
89D/MVP-BC8
89D/PopUp-36
89F-422
89F/BBAS-11
89F/BBMVP's-11
89F/Excit-11
89F/Heroes-12
89F/LL-12
89F/Superstar-12
89KayBee-9
89Mara/Cubs-8
89OPC-10
89Panini/St-230AS
89Panini/St-59
89Ralston-2
89RedFoley/St-33
89Score-2
89Score/HotSt-80
89Score/Mast-28
89Sf-95
89T-10
89T-391AS
89T-4RB
89T/Big-120
89T/Coins-11
89T/DH-17
89T/Gloss22-18
89T/Hills-11
89T/Mini-3
89T/St-156
89T/St-5
89T/St-54
89T/St/Backs-48
89T/UK-21
89Tetley/Discs-14
89UD-205
89Woolwth-11
90Class-85
90D-223
90F-29
90Score-265
90Score/100St-74
90Sf-108
90T-140
90UD-357
90UD-73TC

Dawson, David
89Bakers/Cal-180

Dawson, Gary
83Madis/LF-24

Dawson, Larry
88AppFx/Pro-164

Day, Charles F.
(Boots)
70T-654R
71MLB/St-125
71OPC-42
71T-42
72OPC-254
72T-254
73OPC-307
73T-307
74OPC-589
74T-589
74Weston-8
77Evansvl/TCMA-7

Day, Dexter
83Water-16
84Cedar-13

Day, Kevin
89Ashvl/Pro-943

Day, Leon
78Laugh/Black-5

Day, Mike
86WPalm-11

Day, Ned
52Wheat

Day, Paul
88Aug/Pro-388

Day, Randy
86Portl-4
87Syrac/TCMA-31

Day, Steve
77Newar

Dayett, Brian Kelly
(Brian)
79WHave-4
82Nashv-9
83Colum-26
84Colum-4
84Colum/Pol-9
84D-45
85D-152
85F-125
85F/Up-U35
85IowaC-8
85SevenUp-24
85T-534
85T/Tr-29T
86T-284
87Berg/Cubs-24
87D/OD-73
87F/U-U25
87T-369
88D-416
88F-416
88OPC-136
88Score-205
88T-136

Dayley, Kenneth Grant
(Ken)
81Richm-19
82BK/Lids-7
82D-501
82Richm-25
83D-375
83F-135
83Richm-4
83T-314
84D-199
84F-176
84Nes/792-104
84T-104
84T/X-29
86D-303
86F-33
86KAS/Disc-2
86OPC-202
86Schnucks-5
86T-607
87D-357
87F-293
87T-59
88D-357
88D/Best-299
88F-30
88Score-517
88Smok/Card-3
88T-234
89B-428
89D-299
89D/Best-268
89F-448
89OPC-396
89Smok/Cards-4
89T-409
89UD-114
90D-281
90F-247
90Score-556
90T-561
90UD-280

Deabenderfer, Blaine
87Madis-22

Deak, Brian
87Sumter-26
88MidwLAS/GS-16
89Durhm/Star-9
89Star/Wax-71

Deal, Charles Albert
(Charlie)
21Exh-34
D327
D328-40
D329-44
D350/2-46
E121/80
E122
E135-40
E220
M101/4-44
M101/5-46
V100
W514-18
W575

Deal, Ellis Fergason
(Cot)
54Hunter
54T-192
60T-459C
78Colum
79OkCty
81OkCty/TCMA-22
82OkCty-5

Dealey, Patrick E.
(Pat)
N172

Dean, Alfred Lovill
(Chubby)
40PB-193

Dean, Bob
73Cedar
75Dubuq

Dean, Jay Hanna
(Dizzy)
32Orbit/num-14
32Orbit/un-15
33CJ/Pin-4
33G-223
34G-6
34Ward's/Pin-1
35BU-64
35Exh/4-8
35G-1A
35G-2A
35G-6A
35G-7A
35Wheat
36Exh/4-8
37Exh/4-8
38Exh/4-3
38ONG/Pin-5
38Wheat-1
39Exh
50Callahan
60NuCard-14M
61GP-8
61NuCard-476M
74Laugh/ASG-36
80Cram/Leg-12
80Laugh/FFeat-5
80SSPC/HOF
83D/HOF-29
86Conlon/1-10
86S/Dec-14M
88Conlon/4-8
88Conlon/NatAS-5
PM10/Sm-35
PR1-4
R300
R305
R308-202
R310
R311/Gloss
R332-31
R332-35
R423-21
RiceStix
V354-55
V355-19

Dean, Jeff
83Miami-11

Dean, John
77Salem

Dean, Kevin
87WPalm-9
88Jaxvl/Best-13
88Jaxvl/Pro-984
89Indi/CMC-21
89Indi/Pro-1225

Dean, Paul Dee
(Daffy)
35BU-143
35Exh/4-8
35Wheat
36Exh/4-8
39PB-19
40PB-156
60NuCard-14M
61NuCard-476M
88Conlon/3-9
RiceStix

Dean, Roger
85Utica-9

Dean, Tommy Douglas
(Tommy)
69T-641R
70OPC-234
70T-234
71MLB/St-225
71OPC-364
71T-364

DeAngelis, Steve
86Readg-7
87Maine-13
88Readg/Pro-877
89QuadC/Best-29
89QuadC/GS-26
DeArmas, Rollie
87Clearw-19
88Martins/Star-10
Dearse, Ed
46Remar-14
Deasley, Thomas H.
(Pat)
E223
N172
N403
DeBattista, Dan
77Salem
DeBerry, John Herman
(Hank)
25Exh-9
29Exh/4-4
E120
E126-30
R316
V61-101
W572
W573
DeBord, Bob
83CharR-18
DeBottis, Marc
88Syrac/Pro-828
Debus, Jon Eric
81VeroB-4
84Cram/PCL-164
86Albuq-5
87Albuq/Pol-15
88Albuq/CMC-15
88Albuq/Pro-269
89Albuq/CMC-12
89Albuq/Pro-76
DeBusschere, David A.
(Dave)
63T-54R
64T-247
65T-297
78TCMA-246
DeButch, Mike
86Beaum-9
87TexLgAS-1
87Wichi-1
88Wichi-10
89Jacks/GS-19
89Tidew/Pro-1959
Decatur, A.R.
25Exh-10
27Exh-21
DeChavez, Oscar
83Idaho-3
Decillis, Dean
88Lakel/Star-9
89London/Pro-1372
DeCinces, Douglas V.
(Doug)
75OPC-617R
75T-617R
75T/M-617R
76OPC-438
76SSPC-387
76T-438
77Ho-15
77OPC-228
77T-216
78Ho-10
78OPC-192
78T-9
79Ho-54
79OPC-217
79T-421
80OPC-322
80T-615
81D-352
81F-173
81F/St-90
81OPC-188
81T-188
82D-279
82F-162
82F/St-142
82OPC-174
82T-564
82T/St-142
82T/Tr-26T
83D-216
83F-85
83OPC-341
83Seven-7
83T-34
83T/St-155
83T/St-171
83T/St-46
84D-230
84D/AAS-6
84F-514
84FunFood/Pin-73
84Nes/792-790
84OPC-82
84Smok/Cal-7
84T-790
84T/St-229
85D-179
85D-2
85D/AAS-51
85D/DKsuper-2
85F-299
85Leaf-2DK
85OPC-111
85Smok/Cal-6
85T-111
85T/St-222
86D-57
86D/HL-39
86D/WaxBox-PC6
86F-153
86OPC-257
86S-173
86Smok/Cal-6
86T-257
86T/St-178
87D-356
87D/OD-1
87F-77
87F/Hottest-14
87F/Mini-29
87F/St-34
87OPC-22
87S-106
87Seven-W1
87Smok/Cal-17
87T-22
87T/Gloss60-52
87T/St-182
88F-31
88OPC-141
88Score-239
88Sf-185
88T-446
89Smok/Angels-16
Decker, Dee Martin
(Marty)
82OkCty-22
83Portl-18
84Cram/PCL-226
85Cram/PCL-107
Decker, Edward
N172
Decker, George Henry
(Joe)
71MLB/St-30
71OPC-98
71T-98
72T-612
73OPC-311
73T-311
74OPC-469
74T-469
74T/St-206
75Ho-96
75OPC-102
75T-102
75T/M-102
76OPC-636
76SSPC-210
76T-636
78SnJos-6
79Spoka-12
82SLCty-25
83SLCty-10
Decker, Steve
89SanJose/Best-11
89SanJose/Cal-227
89SanJose/Pro-446
89SanJose/Star-6
89Star/Wax-84
DeCordova, David
87StPet-14
DeCosta, Bob
83Visal/LF-8
Dedeaux, Rod
85T-389OLY
Dedmon, Jeffrey L.
(Jeff)
81Durhm-17
82Durhm-16
84T/X-30
85D-554
85F-323
85Richm-4
85T-602
86D-443
86F-513
86Pol/Atl-49
86T-129
87D-314
87F-514
87Smok/Atl-7
87T-373
88D-325
88F-537
88Gator-50
88Score-498
88T-469
89Indi/Pro-1214
Dedos, Felix
87WinHav-2
89WinHav/Star-3
Deer, Robert George
(Rob)
80Clint-20
84Cram/PCL-4
85F-648
85Moth/Giants-25
86F-538
86F/Up-U33
86Pol/Brew-45
86T-249
86T/Tr-31T
87Class-43
87Class/Up-141
87D-274
87D/OD-57
87F-344
87F/Excit-15
87F/Lim-14
87F/Mini-30
87OPC-188
87S-172
87T-547
87T/Coins-10
87T/Gloss60-22
87T/Mini-59
87T/St-194
88D-274
88D/Best-109
88F-163
88F/St-36
88OPC-33
88Panini/St-128
88Pol/Brew-45
88RedFoley/St-18
88Score-95
88Sf-183
88T-33
88T/Big-151
88T/St-198
89B-146
89Class-39
89D-173
89D/Best-71
89F-184
89Gard-4
89OPC-364
89Panini/St-376
89Pol/Brew-45
89RedFoley/St-34
89Score-72
89Sf-111
89T-364
89T-759TL
89T/Big-78
89T/St-202
89UD-442
90D-55
90F-320
90Score-390
90Sf-137
90T-615
90UD-176
Dees, Charles Henry
(Charlie)
64T-159
DeFillippis, Art
76OPC-595R
76T-595R
DeFrancesco, Anthony
85Greens-25
86WinHav-7
87NewBrit-15
88Chatt/Best-7
89Chatt/Best-3
89Chatt/GS-8
DeFreites, Arturo S.
(Art)
76Indianap-4
77Indianap-20
78Indianap-22
80T-677R
Degifico, Vincent
87Elmir-16
87Elmir/Red-16
89WinHav/Star-4
Deguero, Jerry
86Modesto-7
DeHart, Greg
78Newar
79BurlB-20
80BurlB-6
83SanJose-25
DeHart, Rick
87Birm/Bst-28tr
Deiley, Lou
87Ashvl-23
88Osceola/Star-7
Deitz, Tim
86Cedar/TCMA-5
88Chatt/Best-15
89Greenv/Pro-1175
89Greenv/Star-5
89Greenvl/Best-12
Dejak, Tom
78Duned
DeJardin, Bob
88Oneon/Pro-2044
89PrWill/Star-4
DeJesus, Ivan
(Ivan)
74Albuq
76SSPC-76
78OPC-158
78T-152
79Ho-88
79OPC-209
79T-398
80OPC-349
80T-691
81Coke
81D-483
81F-297
81OPC-54
81T-54
81T/HT
81T/SO-94
81T/St-156
82D-14DK
82D-48
82F-593
82F/St-95
82OPC-313
82T-484
82T/St-32
82T/Tr-27T
83D-399
83F-157
83OPC-233
83T-587
83T/St-271
84D-427
84F-26
84Nes/792-279
84OPC-279
84T-279
84T/St-121
85D-204
85F-248
85T-791
85T/Tr-30T
86D-449
86F-34
86T-178
89Toled/Pro-774
89UD-355
DeJesus, Jorge
78Newar
80BurlB-21
DeJesus, Jose
85FtMyr-12
85Tigres-19
86FtMyr-7
87Memph-5
87Memph/Best-9
88BBAmer-14
88Memph/Best-18
89D-558
89F-280
89Omaha/CMC-6
89Omaha/Pro-1735
89UD/Ext-769
90F-104
90Score-587
90Score/100Ris-95
90Sf-131
90T-596
90UD-255
DeJohn, Mark Stephen
(Mark)
80Evans-2
81Evans-13
83Evans-24
87Savan-26
88Sprin/Best-26
Dejulio, Frank
80Cedar-15
DeKraal, Brad
81BurlB-21
82Beloi-22
DeLaCruz, Carlos
87DayBe-6
88Utica/Puc-17
89SoBend/GS-12

DeLaCruz, Francisco
87Spoka-15
DeLaCruz, Gerry
77Clint
DeLaCruz, Hector
87Duned-16
88Knoxv/Best-8
89Syrac/CMC-18
89Syrac/Pro-816
Delahanty, Edward J.
(Ed)
50Callahan
72F/FFeat-38
72Laugh/GF-10
75F/Pion-10
80SSPC/HOF
89HOF/St-31
N142
N172
N300/SC
Delahanty, Frank G.
(Frank)
14CJ-81
15CJ-81
T206
Delahanty, James C.
(Jim)
10Domino-31
11Helmar-30
12Sweet/Pin-23
E104
E107
E254
E300
E91
E93
E96
M116
S74-14
T202
T205
T206
T207
W555
Delahanty, Joseph
C46-67
DeLaHoya, Javier
89LittleSun-13
DeLaHoz, Miguel A.
(Mike)
61T-191
62T-123
63Sugar-8
63T-561
64T-216
65OPC-182
65T-182
66T-346
67T-372
DeLaMata, Fred
87Miami-21
Delancer, Julio
86Kenosha-7
DeLancey, William P.
(Bill)
34DS-81
35Wheat
V355-15
DeLaNuez, Rex
89Elizab/Star-24
Delany, Dennis
79ArkTr-16
81ArkTr-4
DeLao, Mike
85Durhm-17
88Fay/Pro-1105
89London/Pro-1367
DeLaRosa, Benny
77Charl
81Buffa-6
DeLaRosa, Cesar
87Spart-24
88QuadC/GS-23
89PalmSp/Cal-43
89PalmSp/Pro-475
DeLaRosa, Domingo
89Clint/Pro-905
DelaRosa, Francisco
89Freder/Star-4
DeLaRosa, Jesus
75Iowa/TCMA-10
DeLaRosa, Juan
88Myrtle/Pro-1175
89Myrtle/Pro-1458
DeLaRosa, Nelson
82AlexD-25
83AlexD-23
85Nashua-6
Delas, Mickey
88Brist/Pro-1883
89Fay/Pro-1590
DeLeeuw, Karel
76Watlo
DeLeon, Felix
63Pep/Tul
DeLeon, Jesus
87FtMyr-11
88AppFx/Pro-155
88MidwLAS/GS-39
89RedFoley/St-35
DeLeon, John
81Miami-7
DeLeon, Jose
81Buffa-4
82Portl-1
84D-628
84F-248
84Nes/792-581
84T-581
85D-308
85F-463
85OPC-385
85T-385
86D-235
86F-607
86OPC-75
86T-75
87Coke/WS-16
87D-457
87F-494
87T-421
88D-59
88F-395
88F/St-15
88F/U-U119
88OPC-23
88Score-508
88Score/Tr-7T
88Smok/Card-4
88T-634
88T/Big-194
88T/Tr-34T
89B-431
89D-437
89F-449
89OPC-107
89Panini/St-177
89Score-115
89Smok/Cards-5
89T-107
89T/Mini-34
89UD-293
90D-536
90F-248
90Score-309
90Sf-76
90T-257
90UD-697
DeLeon, Julio
87PortChar-20
DeLeon, Luis Antonio
(Luis)
80ArkTr-7
80Tacom-27
81Chatt-4
82Charl-14
82D-588
82T-561R
83Charl-9
83D-296
83F-355
83OPC-323
83T-323
84D-162
84F-297
84Moth/Padres-17
84Nes/792-38
84Smok/Padres-6
84T-38
85D-406
85F-29
85Moth/Padres-11
85T-689
86F-318
86T-286
87RochR-16
87RochR/TCMA-2
88Tucso-8
88Tucso/CMC-10
88Tucso/Pro-174
89Calg/CMC-1
DeLeon, Paulo
73Cedar
74Cedar
75Dubuq
DeLeon, Pedro
86Ashvl-7
88Osceola/Star-8
89PrWill/Star-5
89Star/Wax-88
DeLeon, Pichy
84Maine-11
DeLeon, Rafael
86FtMyr-8
DeLeon, Roberto
89Sumter/Pro-1113
Delgado, Carlos
89StCath/Pro-2077
Delgado, Juan
83DayBe-19
86ColumAst-10
87Osceola-22
Delgado, Luis Felipe
(Luis)
78SnJos-14
Delgado, Pablo
89Geneva/Pro-1879
DelGreco, Robert G.
(Bobby)
52T-353
53T-48
57T-94
60T-486
61T-154
61T/St-53
62Salada-16
62Shirriff-16
62T-548
63J-91
63P-91
63T-282
78TCMA-259
DeLima, Rafael
86Kenosha-8
87Kenosha-6
88BBAmer-15
88Orlan/Best-22
88SLAS-11
89Portl/CMC-23
89Portl/Pro-222
Delkus, Pete
88Keno/Pro-1398
88MidwLAS/GS-35
89Orlan/Best-13
89Orlan/Pro-1331
Dell, Tim
88Batav/Pro-1674
89Spart/Pro-1052
89Spart/Star-6
89Star/Wax-54
Dell, William George
(Wheezer)
D328-41
WG7-12
Deller, Tom
87Anchora-6
89Well/Puc-10
DelliCarri, Joseph
88CapeCod/Sum-16
Delmonte, John
82Lynch-4
DeLoach, Bobby
87Savan-1
89Savan/Pro-346
DeLoach, Lee
89GreatF-16
Delock, Ivan Martin
(Ike)
52B-250
52T-329
55B-276
56T-284
57T-63
58T-328
59T-437
60T-336
61T-268
61T/St-110
62T-201
63T-136
DelOrbe, Chico
75Lafay
DeLosSantos, Alberto
89Princet/Star-5
DeLosSantos, German
75Cedar
76Cedar
DeLosSantos, Luis
86SLAS-9
87Omaha-25
88AAA/Pro-30
88Omaha/CMC-22
88Omaha/Pro-1506
89D-562
89D/Rook-33
89F-646M
89F/Up-37
89Omaha/Pro-1729
89Panini/St-347
89Score-648
89Score/HotRk-52
89UD-12
90Class-9
90F-105
90Score-659
90Score/100Ris-100
90T-452
DeLosSantos, Pedro
89Ashvl/Pro-951
DeLosSantos, Ramon
75Iowa/TCMA-11
84Cram/PCL-76
DelRosario, Manny
83Miami-18
DelRosario, Maximo
85Durhm-6
86Durhm-8
87Greenv/Bst-18
88Greenv/Best-17
89Greenv/Pro-1161
89Greenv/Star-6
89Greenvl/Best-11
DelRosario, Sergio
83Miami-6
Delsing, James Henry
(Jim)
47Signal
51B-279
52B-157
52T-271
53B/BW-44
53Glen
53T-239
54B-55
54RM-AL24
54T-111
55B-274
55T-192
56T-338
59T-386
DeLuca, Kurt
85LitFalls-16
86Columbia-8
Delucchi, Ron
86PrWill-8
DeLucia, Richard
86Cram/PCL-121
88SnBer/Best-8
88SnBer/Cal-50
89Wmspt/Pro-649
89Wmspt/Star-5
DelVecchio, Jim
77Clint
Delyon, Gene
77Holyo
Delzer, Ed
85MidldA-22
86Kinston-4
DeMaestri, Joseph P.
(Joe)
52T-286
54B-147
55B-176
55Rodeo
56Rodeo
56T-161
57T-44
58T-62
59T-64
60L-139
60T-358
61T-116
Demaree, Albert W.
(Al)
14CJ-92
15CJ-92
37Wheat
D329-45
D350/2-47
M101/4-45
M101/5-47
PM1-4
Demaree, Joseph F.
(Frank)
33G-224
35BU-166
38G-244
38G-268
38ONG/Pin-6
39PB-34
40PB-90
41PB-58
WG8-12
DeMars, William L.
(Billy)
50B-252
51B-43
52Park-8
73OPC-486CO
73T-486C
74OPC-119CO
74T-119C
82Zeller-9
83Stuart-11CO
84Stuart-3CO
86TexGold-CO
Dembowski, Steve
79Newar-7

DeMeo, Bob M.
79OkCty
81OkCty/TCMA-21
DeMerit, John Stephen
(John)
61T-501
62Salada-192
62Shirriff-192
62T-4
78TCMA-129
DeMerit, Thomas
88VeroB/Star-5
DeMerritt, Martin
75BurlB
76Dubuq
83Clint/LF-25
86Shrev-6
87Shrev-24
88Phoen/CMC-25M
88Phoen/Pro-67
89Phoen/CMC-7
89Phoen/Pro-1486
Demery, Lawrence C.
(Larry)
75OPC-433
75T-433
75T/M-433
76OPC-563
76SSPC-564
76T-563
77T-607
78T-138
Demeter, Donald Lee
(Don)
58T-244
59T-324
60BB-14
60T-234
61BB-16
61T-23
62J-195
62P-195
62P/Can-195
62Salada-170
62Shirriff-170
62T-146
62T/bucks
62T/St-167
63F-53
63J-180
63P-180
63T-268
64Det/Lids-4
64T-58
64T/Coins-116
65T-429
66OPC-98
66T-98
67T-572
67T/Test/RSox-4
78TCMA-198
79TCMA-237
Demeter, Stephen
(Steve)
61BeeHive-6
77Salem
80Buffa-16
87Salem-29
Demeter, Todd
85Sprin-6
Demmitt, Charles R.
(Ray)
C46-11
D303
E106
E254
E270/1
E90/1
M116
T206
T213/blue
T216
T222
DeMola, Donald John
(Don)
75OPC-391
75T-391
75T/M-391
76OPC-571
76T-571
DeMontreville, Eugene
E107
Demoran, Joe
43Centen-5
44Centen-4
45Centen-4
DeMoss, Bingo
74Laugh/Black-4
Dempsay, Adam
87Lakel-24
88GlenF/Pro-932
Dempsey, Cornelius F.
(Con)
48Sommer-3
49Sommer-4
52T-44
Dempsey, Jack
33SK-17
Dempsey, John Rikard
(Rick)
72T-778R
74OPC-569
74T-569
75OPC-451
75T-451
75T/M-451
76OPC-272
76SSPC-438
76T-272
77T-189
78T-367
79Ho-73
79OPC-312
79T-593
80OPC-51
80T-91
81D-113
81F-177
81OPC-132
81T-615
81T/St-38
82D-77
82F-163
82F/St-146
82OPC-262
82T-489
83D-329
83F-58
83OPC-138
83T-138
83T/St-30
84D-413
84F-6
84F-644
84F/St-115
84Nes/792-272
84OPC-272
84Seven-21E
84T-272
84T/St-213
84T/St-23WS
85D-332
85F-175
85OPC-94
85T-521
85T/St-199
86D-106
86F-272
86OPC-358
86S-147M
86T-358
86T-726M
86T/St-232
87D-294
87F-467
87F/U-U26
87Gator-24
87OPC-28
87RedFoley/St-92
87T-28
87T/St-225
87T/Tr-28T
88Moth/Dodg-15
88Score-262
88Score/Tr-32T
89B-343
89D-432
89Moth/Dodg-15
89Pol/Dodg-10
89Score-556
89T-606
89T/Big-108
89UD/Ext-713
90D-557
90F-392
90Score-414
90T-736
Dempsey, Mark S.
(Mark)
81Shrev-11
82Phoen
83Phoen/BHN-21
Dempsey, Mike
76BurlB
77BurlB
78Holyo
Dempsey, Pat
77Modesto
79Ogden/TCMA-20
80Ogden-22
81T-96R
81Tacom-7
82Tacom-26
84Nashvl-6
85Maine-14
86Toled-8
87Portl-2
Dempster, Kurt
88Bill/Pro-1828
89Bill/Pro-2053
89Greens/Pro-426
DeMuth, Dana
88Umpire-53
89Umpires-51
DeMuth, Don
89Spart/Pro-1056
Denbo, Gary
84Cedar-26
85Cedar-16
86Vermont-6
87Tampa-1
88Cedar/Pro-1143
89Greens/Pro-404
Denby, Darryl
83Lynch-6
84Jacks-19
Denehy, William F.
(Bill)
67T-581R
68T-526
Denevi, Mike
77Jaxvl
Denkenberger, Ralph
88Watertn/Puc-17
Denkinger, Don
88Umpire-8
89Umpires-6
Denman, Brian John
(Brian)
81Brist-7
83Pawtu-5
84Pawtu-24
86Nashv-6
Dennis, Donald Ray
(Don)
63Pep/Tul
66OPC-142
66T-142
67T-259
Dennis, Ed
(Eddie) 78Duned
82Knoxv-16
83Knoxv-16
86Knoxv-6
88StCath/Pro-2014
Denny, Jeremiah D.
(Jerry)
N172
N284
WG1-30
Denny, John Allen
(John)
75OPC-621R
75T-621R
75T/M-621R
76OPC-339
76SSPC-295
76T-339
77Ho-42
77OPC-109
77OPC-7LL
77T-541
77T-7LL
78Ho-129
78T-609
79Ho-1
79T-59
80OPC-242
80T-464
81T-122
82D-572
82F-363
82F/St-194
82T-773
82Wheat/Ind
83D-237
83F-158
83T-211
84D-407
84F-27
84F/St-56
84FunFood/Pin-49
84Nes/792-135LL
84Nes/792-17
84Nes/792-637TL
84Seven-19E
84T-135
84T-17
84T/St-122
84T/St-177
84T/St-19WS
84T/Super-4
84T/Super-4
85CIGNA-13
85D-111
85F-249
85Leaf-228
85OPC-325
85T-325
85T/St-119
86D-204
86F-439
86F/Up-U34
86OPC-268
86S-132M
86S-134M
86S-64M
86T-556
86T/Tr-32T
86TexGold-40
87D-329
87F-199
87OPC-139
87T-644
Denson, Andrew
86Durhm-9
87Greenvl/Best-7
88Greenv/Best-9
88SLAS-17
89Richm/CMC-18
89Richm/Ko-39
89Richm/Pro-847
Dent, Russell Earl
(Bucky)
74OPC-582
74T-582
75OPC-299
75T-299
75T/M-299
76Ho-119
76OPC-154
76SSPC-143
76T-154
77BK/Y-14
77Ho-91
77OPC-122
77T-29
78BK/Y-15
78K-2
78OPC-164
78T-335
79BK/Y-14
79Ho-131
79OPC-254
79T-485
80OPC-33
80T-60
81D-465
81F-80
81F/St-110
81K-7
81MSA/Disc-11
81OPC-164
81T-650
81T/HT
81T/St-110
82D-209
82F-33
82OPC-240
82OPC-241IA
82OPC-298AS
82T-240
82T-241A
82T-550
83F-566
83OPC-279
83Rangers-7
83T-565
83T/St-122
84D-300
84F-417
84Nes/792-331
84OPC-331
84T-331
84T/St-362
87Colum-1
87Colum/Pol-6MG
87Colum/TCMA-23
88Colum/CMC-25
88Colum/Pol-24MG
88Colum/Pol-25MG
88Colum/Pro-306
89AAA/Pro-21
89Colum/CMC-25
89Colum/Pol-25MG
89Colum/Pro-757
89Swell-72
90T-519MG
Dente, Samuel Joseph
(Sam)
50B-107
51B-133
52Hawth/Pin-2
52T-304
53B/Col-137
55Gol/Ind-4
55Salem
DePalo, Jim
79TCMA-82

DePastino, Rich
87Myrtle-22
88Duned/Star-5
89Myrtle/Pro-1628
DePew, Daren
88Boise/Pro-1627
DePrimo, John
85Greens-28
Deriso, Phil
81Batav-8
Derksen, Rob
85Beloi-25
86Stockton-5CO
87Stockton-2
88CalLgAS-18
88Stock/Cal-201
88Stock/Pro-721
89Stock/Best-30
89Stock/Cal-177CO
89Stock/Pro-385
89Stock/Star-25
Dernier, Robert E.
(Bob)
80Readg
81OkCty/TCMA-5
82T-231R
82T/Tr-28T
83D-189
83F-159
83OPC-43
83T-43
83T/St-320
84D-541
84F-28
84F/X-31
84FunFood/Pin-127
84Nes/792-358
84OPC-358
84SevenUp-20
84T-358
84T/X-31
85D-510
85F-55
85Leaf-57
85OPC-334
85SevenUp-20
85T-589
85T/St-38
86D-266
86F-365
86Gator-20
86Jay's-4
86Leaf-139
86OPC-188
86T-188
86T/St-63
87Berg/Cubs-20
87D-146
87D/OD-68
87F-559
87OPC-138
87T-715
88D-392
88F-417
88OPC-183
88Score-451
88Score/Tr-45T
88T-642
89D-430
89F-565
89Panini/St-155
89Score-357
89T-418
89T/Big-265
89UD-340
90T-204
DeRosa, Tom
77Newar
78BurlB
DeRosa, Tony
81Syrac-24tr
Derrick, Claud Lester
(Claud)
T207
Derringer, Paul
34G-84
35BU-190
35Exh/4-4
36Exh/4-4
36G
37Exh/4-4
38Exh/4-4
39Exh
39PB-15
40PB-74
41DP-7
41PB-4
60F-43
61F-20
80Cram/Leg-113
86S/Dec-14M
PR1-5
R303/A
R310
R311/Leath
R313
R314
R326-9A
R326-9B
R342-9
V355-66
W711/1
W711/2
WG8-13
Derrington, Charles
39PB-116
40PB-28
53Mother-60
Derrington, Chas. J.
(Jim)
58T-129
Derryberry, Tim
82RochR-9
Dersin, Eric
86Albany/TCMA-14
Dertli, Chuck
87WinSal-21
DeSa, Joseph
(Joe)
79ArkTr-10
81Louvl-7
82Louvl-6
85Coke/WS-20
86BuffB-10
86D-546
86T-313
DeSalvo, Steve
85FtMyr-22
DeSanto, Tom
79Elmir-27
DeSapio, Jim
88AubAs/Pro-1968
89AubAs/Pro-2172
Desautels, Eugene A.
(Gene)
39PB-116
40PB-28
Desert, Harry
52Park-92
Deshaies, Jim
85Colum-23
85Colum/Pol-8
85IntLgAS-34
86D/HL-45
86D/Rook-34
86F/Up-U35
86Pol/Ast-24
86S/Rook-15
87Class/Up-137
87D-184
87F-56
87F/Mini-31
87Leaf-255
87Moth/Ast-23
87Pol/Ast-19
87S-156M
87T-167
87T-2RB
87T/Gloss60-20
87T/St-1
87ToysRUs-9
88D-85
88D/Best-94
88F-446
88Leaf-96
88Moth/Ast-23
88OPC-24
88Panini/St-287
88Pol/Ast-9
88Score-354
88Sf-190
88T-24
88T/St-27
89B-320
89D-241
89D/Best-120
89F-356
89Lennox/Ast-11
89Moth/Ast-22
89OPC-341
89Score-546
89T-341
89T/Big-29
89UD-76
90D-187
90D-7DK
90F-229
90Score-154
90Sf-32
90T-225
90UD-221
DeShields, Delino
88MidwLAS/GS-44
88OPC-88
88Rockford-10
89Jaxvl/Best-15
89Jaxvl/Pro-152
89Rockford-10
89SLAS-5
90Class-55
90D-42
90F-653
90Score-645
90T-224
Deshong, James B.
(Jimmie)
34G-96
35G-8E
35G-9E
39PB-10
DeSilva, John
89NiagFls/Puc-6
DeSimone, Jerry
81Hawai-7
82Hawai-7
84Cram/PCL-223
DesJardins, Brad
89Watertn/Star-29
Desjarlais, Keith
81AppFx-3
82Edmon-7
83GlenF-13
Dessau, Frank Rolland
(Rube)
C46-61
M116
T206
Dest, Blanch
80WHave-18M
Dest, Vanna
80WHave-18M
Destrade, Orestes
82Oneon-1
85Albany-16
86Colum-5
86Colum/Pol-5
87Colum-12
87Colum/Pol-7
87Colum/TCMA-13
88BuffB/CMC-20
88BuffB/Pro-1486
88Score/Tr-110T
89BuffB/Pro-1687
89T-27
Detherage, Robert W.
(Bob)
75Water
81Omaha-21
Dettore, Thomas A.
(Tom)
75OPC-469
75T-469
75T/M-469
76OPC-126
76T-126
89Princet/Star-27
Deutsch, John
89GreatF-17
Deutsch, Mike
89Freder/Star-5
Devares, Cesar
89Bluef/Star-8
Devereaux, Mike
87SnAnt-10
87TexLgAS-28
88AAA/Pro-1
88Albuq/CMC-18
88Albuq/Pro-252
88D-546
88F-512
88Moth/Dodg-27
88Score-637
89Class/Up/2-181
89D-603
89D/Best-326
89D/Rook-51
89D/Tr-30
89F-56
89F/Up-2
89French-12
89Score/HotRk-11
89Score/YS/II-22
89T/Tr-23T
89UD-68
90D-282
90F-175
90Score-232
90Score/100Ris-90
90Sf-114
90T-127
90UD-681
Devich, John
83Butte-24
Deville, Dan
89Spoka/SP-10
DeVincenzo, Rich
83AppFx/LF-7
Devine, Kevin
86VeroB-5
87VeroB-23
Devine, Paul Adrian
(Adrian)
74OPC-614
74T-614
77T-339
78T-92
79T-257
80T-528
81T-464
Devito, Fred
80WHave-13
Devlin, Arthur M.
(Art)
10Domino-32
11Helmar-123
12Sweet/Pin-110
E101
E103
E254
E91
E92
E94
E95
M116
S74-83
T202
T204
T205
T206
T207
T3-10
W555
Devlin, Bob
84Greens-21
86WPalm-12
87Jaxvl-18
Devlin, James H.
(Tim)
N172
N690
Devlin, Paul
88Lynch/Star-6
89Lynch/Star-6
Devore, Joshua
(Josh)
10Domino-33
11Helmar-124
12Sweet/Pin-111
14CJ-47
15CJ-47
BF2-85
D329-46
E270/2
E300
E94
E97
M101/4-46
M116
S74-84
T202
T205
T206
T207
T213/blue
T215/blue
T215/brown
W555
DeVormer, Albert E.
(Al)
E120
E121/120
W501-105
W513-80
W572
W573
W575
Dewechter, Pat
85Greens-14
Deweerdt, Dan
88Rockford-11
89Rockford-11
Dewey, Mark
87Everett-32
88Clint/Pro-711
89SanJose/Best-7
89SanJose/Cal-211
89SanJose/Pro-448
89SanJose/Star-7
89Star/Wax-85
Dewey, Todd Alan
86Durhm-10
87Greenv/Bst-10
88Richm/CMC-11
88Richm/Pro-4
89Durhm/Star-10
DeWillis, Jeff
88Score-583
DeWitt, William O.
63FrBauer-4

W753
DeWolf, Rob
85Beloi-7
86Stockton-6
87ElPas-6
88ElPas/Best-14
89Wich/Roc-9
89Wich/Roc/Up-15
DeWright, Wayne
78Duned
Dews, Robert
(Bobby)
66Pep/Tul
82Durhm-25MG
85Pol/Atl-53C
DeYoung, Rob
87BurlEx-28
88WPalm/Star-8
89WPalm/Star-9
Diaale, Rob
86Vermont-7
Dial, Bryan
85BurlR-20
86Salem-5
Diaz, Alberto
89Kingspt/Star-7
Diaz, Alex
88Clmbia/GS-14
89StLucie/Star-3
Diaz, Angel
89Helena/SP-2
Diaz, Baudilio Jose
(Bo)
78T-708R
79T-61
80T-483
81D-517
81F-404
81T-362
82D-263
82F-364
82F/St-197
82OPC-258
82T-258
82T/St-176
82T/Tr-29T
83D-147
83F-160
83F-637M
83OPC-175
83T-175
83T-229TL
83T/St-273
84D-137
84F-29
84F/St-118
84Nes/792-535
84OPC-131
84T-535
84T/St-120
85F-250
85OPC-219
85T-737
86D-530
86F-176
86Leaf-258
86OPC-253
86T-639
86TexGold-6
87D-246
87D/HL-21
87D/OD-190
87F-200
87F/Mini-32
87Kahn-6
87OPC-41
87T-41
87T/St-142
88D-186
88D/AS-47
88D/Best-110
88F-232
88Kahn/Reds-6
88Leaf-191
88OPC-265
88Panini/St-273
88Score-206
88Sf-117
88T-265
88T/St-143
89B-307
89D-242
89D/Best-293
89F-159
89K/Reds-6
89OPC-201
89Panini/St-71
89RedFoley/St-36
89Score-187
89T-422
89T/St-135
89UD-169
90D-139
90Score-434
90UD-664
Diaz, Carlos Antonio
(Carlos)
80Spoka-4
81Richm-13
82Richm-5
83D-562
83F-540
84D-600
84F-583
84F/X-32
84Nes/792-524
84Pol/Dodg-27
84T-524
84T/X-32
85F-369
85T-159
86D-348
86F-128
86Pol/Dodg-27
86T-343
87Duned-1
88Knoxv/Best-12
89Knoxv/Best-4
89Knoxv/Pro-1125
89Knoxv/Star-2
Diaz, Derek
85Beloi-23
86ElPas-8
87ElPas-16
Diaz, Eddie
83Watlo/LF-4
Diaz, Edgar
83Beloi/LF-23
86Vanco-10
Diaz, Enrique
80Wausa-15
81Wausa-16
Diaz, Johnny
87Elmir-22
87Elmir/Red-22
88WinHav/Star-7
89Elmir/Puc-2
Diaz, Jorge
83Madis/LF-8
Diaz, Jose
87Myrtle-3
88Duned/Star-4
88FSLAS/Star-33
89Knoxv/Best-5
89Knoxv/Star-3
Diaz, Kiki
88Denver/CMC-18
88Denver/Pro-1256
89Denver/CMC-12
89Denver/Pro-47
Diaz, Mario
80Wausa-14
81LynnS-17
82LynnS-12
84Chatt-25
86Calgary-6
87Calgary-11
88F-649
88Calg/Pro-804
88Moth/Sea-21
89F-547
89Moth/Sea-21
88F/U-U59
89Panini/St-427
89T-309
89UD-318
90T-781
Diaz, Mike
83IowaC-11
85Cram/PCL-50
86S/Rook-50
87D-267
87F-609
87T-469
88D-267
88F-326
88Score-143
88T-567
88OPC-239
88Panini/St-378
89D-655
89F-494
89Score-603
89T-142
89UD-606
Diaz, Rich
83Watlo/LF-25
Diaz, Roberto
78Newar
79BurlB-16
Diaz, Sandy
89Elizab/Star-6
Diaz, Tony
84Butte-9
88Mia/Star-6
89StLucie/Star-4
Diaz, Victor
87Myrtle-23
89BirmB/Best-4
89BirmB/Pro-101
Diaz, William
86Wausa-8
88SnBer/Best-9
88SnBer/Cal-37
89Wmspt/Pro-640
89Wmspt/Star-6
Dibble, Rob
85Cedar-6
87Nashv-4
88F/U-U83
88Nashvl/CMC-4
88Nashvl/Pro-493
88Score/Tr-86T
89B-305
89Class-76
89D-426
89D/Best-334
89F-160
89K/Reds-49
89Score-618
89T-264
89UD-375
90Class-43
90D-189
90F-418
90Score-277
90T-46
90UD-586
DiCeglio, Tom
85Visal-11
86Kenosha-6
Dick, Bill
76BurlB
77BurlB
77Holyo
78BurlB
78Holyo
Dick, Ed
79TCMA-81
Dick, Ralph
88SnBer/Best-14
88SnBer/Cal-53
89SnBer/Best-11
89SnBer/Cal-90MG
Dickerson, Bob
87Oneon-27
88FtLaud/Star-5
89Albany/Best-16
89Albany/Pro-319
89Albany/Star-7
Dickerson, Jim
86Pittsf-7
Dickey, George W.
47TipTop
Dickey, William M.
(Bill)
31Exh/4-25
33Exh/4-13
33G-19
34DS-103
34DS-11
34Exh/4-13
35BU-117
35BU-30
35Exh/4-13
35G-2D
35G-4D
35G-7D
37OPC-119
38Exh/4-13
39Exh
39PB-30
40PB-7
41DP-66
41PB-70
44Yank/St-8
48Swell-6
50Callahan
51B-290
52T-400
60NuCard-34
60T-465C
61GP-27
61NuCard-434
63Bz/ATG-40
80Cram/Leg-44
80SSPC/HOF
83D/HOF-26
86S/Dec-13
88Conlon/AmAS-8
PM10/Sm-36
PR1-6
R300
R302
R303/A
R303/B
R308-161
R310
R312
R314
R328-4
R332-11
R423-22
V300
V353-19
V355-34
WG8-14
Dickman, Dave
89Pulas/Pro-1888
89Sumter/Pro-1100
Dickman, Geo. Emerson
39PB-17
40PB-37
41G-6
Dickman, Mark
85Kingst-5
86Ventura-4
Dickson, James Edward
(Jim)
64T-524R
65T-286R
66T-201
Dickson, Ken
87AubAs-21
88Ashvl/Pro-1050
Dickson, Murry Monroe
(Murry)
49B-8
49Eureka-158
50B-34
51B-167
51T/BB-16
52B-59
52RM-NL5
52T-266
52TipTop
53RM-NL22
54B-111
55B-236
56T-211
57T-71
58T-349
59T-23
Exh47
R423-23
Dickson, Walter R.
(Walt)
T205
Didier, Robert Daniel
(Bob)
69T-611R
70MLB/St-5
70OPC-232
70T-232
71MLB/St-8
71OPC-432
71T-432
73OPC-574
73T-574
74OPC-482
74T-482
75Iowa/TCMA-6
80Vanco-11
81WHave-1
82WHave-26
83Tacom-18
87Tucso-24
88Tucso-9
88Tucso/CMC-24
88Tucso/Pro-190
Didrickson, Babe
33SK-45
Diehl, Charles
52Wheat
Diemido, Chet
87Penin-3
Dierderger, George
78Wisco
79Wisco-4
Diering, Charles E.
(Chuck)
47TipTop
49Eureka-180
50B-179
51B-158
52B-198
52NTea
52T-265
54Esskay
55Esskay
55T-105
55T/DH-2
56T-19
56T/Pin-1
79TCMA-51
Dierker, Lawrence E.
(Larry)
65T-409R
66T-228

67T-498
68T-565
69MLB/St-138
69T-411
69T/St-32
70MLB/St-39
70OPC-15
70T-15
70T/PI-15
70T/S-6
71Bz
71Bz/Test-24
71K-48
71MLB/St-77
71OPC-540
71T-540
71T/Coins-141
71T/GM-32
71T/S-30
71T/tatt-6
72MB-89
72OPC-155
72T-155
73K-53
73OPC-375
73T-375
73T/Lids-13
74OPC-660
74T-660
75OPC-49
75T-49
75T/M-49
76Ho-25
76Ho/Twink-25
76OPC-75
76T-75
77T-350
78T-195
86Moth/Ast-8
89Swell-78

Dietrich, William J.
(Bill)
41G-9
R313

Dietrick, P.J.
(Pat)
85Madis-12
85Madis/Pol-9
86Madis-8
86Madis/Pol-8
88Huntsvl/BK-4
89Tacom/CMC-24
89Tacom/Pro-1553

Dietz, Don
87Vermont-11

Dietz, Richard Allen
(Dick)
62Kahn/Atl
67T-341R
68OPC-104
68T-104
69T-293
69T/St-103
70MLB/St-123
70OPC-135
70T-135
71K-42
71MD
71MLB/St-246
71OPC-545
71T-545
71T/Coins-33
71T/tatt-4
72MB-90
72OPC-295
72OPC-296IA
72T-295
72T-296A
73OPC-442
73T-442
84Moth/Giants-21

Diez, Scott
87Miami-14
88FSLAS/Star-5
88Mia/Star-7

Diggle, Ron
77Spoka
79RochR-14

Diggs, Tony
89Helena/SP-8

DiGioia, John
85Sprin-7
86PalmSp-10
86PalmSp/Smok-7

DiGiovanna, Charlie
55Gol/Dodg-6

Digirolama, Dave
83Butte-3

DiHigo, Martin
74Laugh/Black-29
88Conlon/NegAS-3
89HOF/St-63

DiLauro, Jack Edward
(Jack)
70OPC-382
70T-382
71MLB/St-78
71OPC-677
71T-677

Dilks, Darren
84Indianap-27

Dillard, David Donald
(Don)
59T-123
60T-122
61T-172
63T-298

Dillard, Gordon
87Hagers-25
88CharlK-20
88CharlK/Pep-20
88RochR-6
88RochR/Gov-6
89ScrWB/CMC-7
89ScrWB/Pro-714

Dillard, Harrison
51BR-D18

Dillard, Jay
75Lafay

Dillard, Mike
87Elmir/Red-32

Dillard, Ron
81Miami-1
82Tulsa-18
83BurlR-15
83BurlR/LF-14

Dillard, Stephen B.
75IntAS/TCMA-22
77T-142
78BK/T-16
78T-597
79T-217
80T-452
81D-502
81F-298
81T-78
82D-174
82Edmon-4
82F-594
82T-324

Dillhoefer, William
(Pickles)
W514-71

Dillinger, Robert B.
(Bob)
48L-144
49B-143
50B-105
51B-63
53Mother-61
Exh47
R346-14

Dillman, William H.
(Bill)
67T-558R
68T-466
69OPC-141
69T-141
70OPC-386
70T-386

Dillmore, Phillip
87Kinston-6

Dillon, Frank Edward
(Pop)
E107

Dillon, Stephen E.
(Steve)
64T-556R

Dilone, Miguel Angel
(Miguel)
78T-705R
79Ho-118
79OPC-256
79T-487
80T-541
81D-441
81F-391
81F/St-86
81OPC-141
81T-141
81T/St-67
82D-515
82F-365
82F/St-196
82OPC-77
82T-77
82Wheat/Ind
83D-85
83F-405
83T-303
83Wheat/Ind-8
84Stuart-25
85D-453
85F-395
85Leaf-135
85OPC-178
85T-178

DiMaggio, Dominic P.
(Dom)
41DP-108
41PB-63
47TipTop
48L-75
49B-64
49Royal-4
50B-3
50Drake-33
51BR-A8
51T/RB-20
52BR
52NTea
52RM-AL5
52Royal
52StarCal/L-71F
52T-22
53Exh/Can-23
53RM-AL22
53T-149
D305
Exh47
PM10/Sm-37
PM10/Sm-38
R423-24

DiMaggio, Joseph Paul
(Joe)
37Exh/4-13
37OPC-118
37Wheat
38Exh/4-13
38G-250
38G-274
38ONG/Pin-7
38Wheat
39Exh
39PB-26
40PB-1
40Wheat
41DP-63
41PB-7
41Wheat
48L-1
48Swell-15
50Callahan
51BR-B5
52BR
53Exh/Can-28
60NuCard-38
60NuCard-7
61GP-9
61NuCard-438
61NuCard-467
72Laugh/GF-1
74Laugh/ASG-39
76Laugh/Jub-25
79TCMA-1
80Cram/Leg-5
80SSPC/HOF
83MLBPA/Pin-4
84West/1-5
85CircK-31
86S/Dec-20
88Pac/Leg-100
89HOF/St-39
D305
PM10/Sm-39
PM10/Sm-40
PM10/Sm-41A
PM10/Sm-41B
PM10/Sm-42
PM10/Sm-43
PR1-7
R302
R303/A
R303/B
R311/Leath
R312
R314
R314/M
R326-4A
R326-4B
R342-4
R346-16
R423-25
V300
V355-51

DiMaggio, Vincent P.
(Vince)
38Exh/4-1
41PB-61
47Signal

Dimas, Rodolfo
85Tigres-7

DiMascio, Dan
87GlenF-22
88EastLAS/Pro-6
88GlenF/Pro-931
89Toled/CMC-17
89Toled/Pro-788

DiMichele, Frank
86QuadC-8
87PalmSp-27
88Edmon/Pro-565
88MidldA/GS-8
89MidldA/GS-12

Dimmel, Michael Wayne
(Mike)
75Water
78RochR
80ArkTr-8

Dineen, Kerry Michael
(Kerry)
76SSPC-452
79OkCty

Dinkelmeyer, John
75Clint

Dinneen, William H.
(Bill)
E107
T204
T206
WG2-14

Diorio, Ronald M.
(Ron)
74OPC-599R
74T-599R

DiPietro, Fred
76Clint

DiPino, Frank M.
78BurlB
80Holyo-12
81Vanco-17
82T-333R
82Vanco-16
83T/X-25
84D-502
84F-224
84F/St-72
84Moth/Ast-17
84Nes/792-172
84T-172
84T/St-74
85D-232
85F-349
85Moth/Ast-11
85OPC-376
85T-532
85T/St-66
86D-304
86F-299
86Pol/Ast-25
86T-26
87Berg/Cubs-33
87D-416
87F-560
87OPC-297
87T-662
88Berg/Cubs-33
88D-570
88D/Best-205
88D/Cubs/Bk-570
88F-418
88Score-413
88T-211
89B-434
89D-393
89F-423
89F/Up-118
89Score-146
89Smok/Cards-6
89T-439
89T/Tr-24T
89UD-61
90D-518
90F-249
90Score-462
90T-788
90UD-202

Dipoto, Jerry
89Watertn/Star-3

DiSalvo, Pio
(trainer) 77Evansvl/TCMA-8

Disarcina, Gary
89MidldA/GS-13

Disher, Dan
87Wausa-4
88SnBer/Best-10
88SnBer/Cal-31

Disher, David
86Cram/PCL-122

Distaso, Alec John
(Alec)
69T-602R

Distefano, Benny
83LynnP-19
84Cram/PCL-144
85Cram/PCL-231
85D-166

85T-162
86D-78
86Hawai-4
87D-514
87T-651
88AAA/Pro-4
88BuffB/CMC-11
88BuffB/Polar-6
88BuffB/Pro-1489
89BuffB/CMC-11
89BuffB/Pro-1682
89F-205
89T/Tr-25T
90F-464

Ditmar, Arthur J.
(Art)
55B-90
55Rodeo
56Rodeo
56T-258
57T-132
58T-354
59T-374
60L-78
60MacGregor-7
60T-430
61P-16
61T-46LL
61T-48LL
61T-510
61T/St-192
62J-100
62P-100
62P/Can-100
62Salada-202
62Shirriff-202
62T-246
79TCMA-220

Dittmar, Carl
28Exh/PCL-5

Dittmer, John D.
(Jack)
53JC-19
53T-212
54B-48
54JC-6
54T-53
55B-212
55Gol/Braves-10
55JC-6
57T-282

Ditton, Julian
76Clint

Divison, Julio
75Lafay

Dixon, Andrew
86Cram/PCL-11
88Shreve/Pro-1287

Dixon, Bryan
88StCath/Pro-2030

Dixon, Dan
79Tulsa-7

Dixon, Dee
87Clint-15
89Shreve/Pro-1836

Dixon, Eddie
86WPalm-13
87WPalm-21
88Jaxvl/Best-6
88Jaxvl/Pro-967
89Jaxvl/Best-5
89Jaxvl/Pro-159

Dixon, Hal
55B-309ump

Dixon, John Craig
(Sonny)
53Briggs
55B-211
55Rodeo

Dixon, Ken
84CharO-17
85D-270
85F/Up-U36
85T/Tr-31T
86D-148
86F-273
86T-198
87D-171
87F-468
87T-528
88D-48
88F-557
88Score-411
88T-676

Dixon, Mike
81Watlo-8

Dixon, Rap
74Laugh/Black-2

Dixon, Ronn
82Wausa-14
83Wausa/LF-7

Dixon, Thomas Earl
(Tom)
75Dubuq
79OPC-186
79T-361
80T-513
80Tidew-12
81Tidew-14
82Syrac-2

Dixon, Troy
83BirmB-23

Djakonow, Paul
75Shreve/TCMA-1
76Shrev
80Buffa-10
82Evans-15

Doak, William L.
(Bill)
21Exh-35
21Exh-36
D327
D328-42
D329-47
D350/2-48
E120
E121/120
E121/80
E122
E135-42
E220
M101/4-47
M101/5-48
V100
V61-65
W501-78
W514-51
W572
W573
W575

Dobbek, Daniel J.
(Dan)
59T-124
60T-123
61Peters-24
61T-108
62T-267

Dobbins, Joe
43Centen-6
44Centen-5
45Centen-5

Dobbs, Gary
78Wisco
79Wisco-15

Doberenz, Mark
82Idaho-32
83Idaho-33

Dobernic, Andrew J.
(Jess)
49B-200
49Eureka-81

Dobie, Reggie
85Lynch-5
86Jacks/TCMA-2
87Tidew-3
87Tidew/TCMA-1
88Tidew/Pro-1590
89Calg/CMC-5
89Calg/Pro-528

Dobson, Charles T.
(Chuck)
66T-588R
67T-438
68OPC-62
68T-62
69MB-74
69T-397
70MLB/St-256
70OPC-331
70T-331
71K-32
71MLB/St-510
71OPC-238
71T-238
72MB-91
72OPC-523
72T-523
75OPC-635
75T-635
75T/M-635
77SLCty

Dobson, Joseph Gordon
(Joe)
49B-7
50B-44
51B-36
52Hawth/Pin-3
52T-254
53B/Col-88
53RM-AL15
53T-5
Exh47

Dobson, Patrick E.
(Pat)
67T-526R
68OPC-22
68T-22
69T-231
70MLB/St-112
70OPC-421
70T-421
71MLB/St-295
71OPC-547
71T-547
72MB-92
72OPC-140
72T-140
73OPC-34
73T-34
74OPC-463
74T-463
75OPC-44
75T-44
75T/M-44
76OPC-296
76SSPC-431
76T-296
76T/Tr-296T
77Pep-8
77T-618
78T-575
83Pol/Brew-45C
88Domino-4
88Smok/Padres-7CO

Doby, Lawrence Eugene
(Larry)
48L-138
49B-233
50B-39
50NumNum
51B-151
51T/CAS
52B-115
52BR
52NumNum-18
52RM-AL6
52StarCal/L-74A
52T-243
53B/Col-40
53Exh/Can-11
54B-84
54DanDee
54T-70
55Armour-4
55Gol/Ind-5
55RM-AL18
55Salem
56T-250
56YellBase/Pin-9
57T-85
58Hires-17
58T-424
59T-166
59T-455
73OPC-377CO
73T-377C
74OPC-531CO
74T-531C
79TCMA-27
82CJ-6
88Pac/Leg-102
89Swell-115
Exh47
PM10/Sm-44
PM10/Sm-45
PM10/Sm-46
R302-124
R423-18

Dodd, Bill
88Cedar/Pro-1138
88MidwLAS/GS-11
89Chatt/Best-14
89Chatt/GS-9

Dodd, Daniel
88StCath/Pro-2018
89Myrtle/Pro-1471

Dodd, Lance
82AlexD-8

Dodd, Mike
75Cedar

Dodd, Tim
83Tampa-7
84Cedar-11

Dodd, Tom
86SLAS-12
87CharO/WBTV-8
87SLAS-6
88Omaha/CMC-19
88Omaha/Pro-1505
89Omaha/CMC-11
89Omaha/Pro-1727

Dodd, Tommie
82Nashv-10

Dodig, Jeff
87Idaho-25
88Durhm/Star-5

Dodson, Bo
89Helena/SP-17
89LittleSun-11

Dodson, Pat
84Pawtu-19
85Pawtu-3
86Pawtu-9
87Class-8
87D-44RR
87Leaf-44RR
87Pawt/TCMA-24
87S-118M
87Seven-E11
87T-449
88Pawtu/CMC-16
88Pawtu/Pro-466
88Score-352

Doerr, Robert P.
(Bobby)
38G-258
38G-282
39PB-7
40PB-38
41DP-106
41PB-64
48L-83
49B-23
50B-43
50Drake-13
51T/BB-37
52BR
53Exh/Can-24
74Laugh/ASG-43
83MLBPA/Pin-5
86D/HL-32
88Pac/Leg-73
89HOF/St-11
89Pac/Leg-150
89Swell-110
89T/Gloss22-11
D305
Exh47
R314
Rawl

Doerr, Tim
76Clint

Does, Raymond
89Well/Puc-11

Doescher, Edward
C46-50

Doggett, George
85Lynch-26

Doherty, John Michael
(John)
75OPC-524
75T-524
75T/M-524
89NiagFls/Puc-7

Dohne, Heriberto
88Modesto/Cal-76

Dolan, Cozy
V117-9

Dolan, John
88Elmir-7
89Lynch/Star-7

Dolan, Thomas J.
(Tom)
N172

Dolf, Mike
76Wmspt

Doll, Chris
88Wausa/Feder-4
88Wausa/GS-4

Dombrowski, Rob
89Bill/Pro-2055

Dominguez, Frank
89Reno/Cal-256

Dominguez, Jose
86Orlan-5
88Shreve/Pro-1281
88TexLgAS/GS-19
89Shreve/Pro-1854

Dominico, Ron
84LitFalls-26
85LitFalls-4

Dominquez, Jose
85Visal-22

Donaghue, Ray
77StPet

Donahue, Chuck
86Tampa-5

Donahue, James A.
(Jim)
No Cards.

Donahue, Patrick W.
(Pat)
E107
E91
M116
T204
T205
T206

Donald, Richard Atley
(Atley)

40PB-121
41PB-38
44Yank/St-9

Donaldson, John David
(John)
68T-244
69MB-75
69MLB/St-85
69OPC-217
69T-217
70MLB/St-269
70OPC-418
70T-418
72MB-93
78Laugh/Black-28

Donatelli, Andy
85Utica-18

Donatelli, Augie
55B-313ump

Donlin, Michael J.
(Mike)
11Helmar-158
75F/Pion-25
E107
E90/1
E91
T204
T206
T207
T213/blue
T215/blue
T215/brown
WG3-13

Donnelly, Edward
(Ed)
T207

Donnelly, James B.
(Jim)
N172
N284
WG1-64

Donnelly, Rich
74Gasto
77Tucso
78Cr/PCL-8
79Tucso-8

Donnelly, Sylvester
(Blix)
49B-145
49Eureka-133
50B-176
51B-208

Donnels, Chris
88Clmbia/GS-26
89StLucie/Star-5

Donofrio, Larry
80Ashev-22
81AppFx-13

Donohue, J.A.
E91

Donohue, Jack
N172
N172/ST

Donohue, James A.
(Jim)
N172
N284
N690

Donohue, James T.
(Jim)
60T-124
61T-151
62T-498

Donohue, John F.
(Jiggs)
No Cards.

Donohue, Peter J.
(Pete)
25Exh-27
26Exh-27
E120
R316
V61-77
W517-26
W572

Donohue, Steve
79WHave-19
82Colum-24M

Donohue, Thomas J.
(Tom)
77SLCty
78Cr/PCL-52
80T-454
81D-51
81F-281
81T-621

Donovan, Bret
88CapeCod/Sum-165

Donovan, Gary
77BurlB

Donovan, Jack
81Tucso-25

Donovan, Michael B.
(Mike)
80BurlB-3

Donovan, Patrick J.
(Patsy)
09Buster/Pin-5
11Helmar-31
12Sweet/Pin-24
E107
M116
WG2-15

Donovan, Richard E.
(Dick)
55T-146
56T-18
56T/Pin-32
57T-181
58T-290
59T-5
60L-72
60T-199
61Bz-10
61T-414
61T/St-202
62J-73
62Kahn
62P-73
62P/Can-73
62Sugar-3
62T-15
62T-55LL
62T/St-33
63Bz-10
63F-11
63J-75
63P-75
63Salada-34
63Sugar-3
63T-370
63T-8LL
63T/SO
64Kahn
79TCMA-34
Exh47

Donovan, William E.
(Wild Bill)
87Conlon/2-13
D303
D327
D328-43
D329-48
D350/2-49
E101
E102
E103
E104
E105
E106
E121/80
E122
E254
E300
E90/1
E92
E93
E96
M116
T201
T204
T206
T213/blue
T213/brown
T216
T3-12
V100
W555
W575

Dooin, Charles S.
(Red)
10Domino-34
11Helmar-141
12Sweet/Pin-125A
12Sweet/Pin-125B
14CJ-38
15CJ-38
BF2-74
D303
D329-49
D350/2-50
E101
E103
E104
E105
E106
E224
E270/2
E300
E90/1
E92
E93
E96
E98
L1-126
M101/4-49
M101/5-50
M116
S74-98
S81-101
T201
T202
T205
T206
T207
T215/blue
T215/brown
T216
T3-14
W555
WG3-14
WG5-15
WG6-14

Doolan, Michael J.
(Mickey)
10Domino-35
11Helmar-142
12Sweet/Pin-126A
12Sweet/Pin-126B
14CJ-120
15CJ-120
D303
D329-50
D350/2-51
E101
E104
E105
E106
E224
E254
E270/1
E92
E94
E97
M101/4-50
M101/5-51
M116
S74-99
T202
T205
T206
T213/blue
T213/brown
T215/blue
T215/brown
T216
T3-90
W555
WG3-15

Dooley
N172/PCL

Dooley, Marvin
89Princet/Star-6

Doolittle, James
33SK-28

Dooner, Glenn
82Toled-2

Dophied, Tracy
82AubAs-12

Dopson, John
86Indianap-12
88D/Rook-43
88F/U-U99
88Score/Tr-88T
89B-24
89Class/Up/2-161
89D-392
89D/Best-177
89D/Tr-7
89F-373
89F/Up-8
89OPC-251
89Score-466
89Score/Tr-40
89T-251
89T/Tr-26T
89UD-57
90D-162
90F-272
90Score-331
90T-733
90UD-671

Doran, Bill
82Tucso-7
83T/X-26
84D-580
84F-225
84Moth/Ast-4
84Nes/792-198
84OPC-198
84T-198
84T/St-377
85D-84
85F-350
85Moth/Ast-8
85OPC-299
85T-684
85T/St-68
86D-10
86D-110
86D/DKsuper-10
86F-300
86Leaf-10DK
86OPC-57
86Pol/Ast-5
86T-57
86T/St-25
87D-286
87D/OD-11
87F-57
87Leaf-197
87Moth/Ast-4
87OPC-243
87Pol/Ast-5
87RedFoley/St-69
87S-116M
87S-162
87T-472
87T/Mini-9
87T/St-31
88D-235
88D/Best-120
88F-447
88F/LL-10
88F/St-87
88Leaf-183
88Moth/Ast-4
88Nestle-19
88OPC-166
88Panini/St-295
88Pol/Ast-10
88Score-52
88Sf-48
88T-745
88T/Big-51
88T/St-34
89B-329
89D-306
89D/Best-38
89F-357
89Lennox/Ast-8
89Moth/Ast-4
89OPC-226
89Panini/St-89
89RedFoley/St-37
89Score-21
89Sf-57
89T-226
89T/Big-168
89T/St-16
89T/UK-22
89UD-101
90D-236
90F-230
90Score-182
90Score/100St-8
90T-368
90UD-198

Doran, John F.
(John)
N172

Doran, Mark
86PalmSp-11
87MidldA-21
88Edmon/CMC-24
88Edmon/Pro-570
89MidldA/GS-14

Dorante, Luis
87Elmir-14
87Elmir/Red-14
88Elmir-12
89Elmir/Puc-3

Dorgan, Charles
77Clint

Dorgan, Michael C.
(Mike)
N172
N284
N403
N690

Dorish, Harry
51B-266
52T-303
53T-145
54B-86
54T-110
55B-248
56T-167
80Port-14C

Dorner, Augustus
(Gus)
T204
T206

Dorsett, Brian
85Huntsvl/BK-22
85Madis-11
85Madis/Pol-8
86Tacom-3
87Tacom-22
88F-607

89Colum/CMC-14
89Colum/Pol-2
89Colum/Pro-759
Dorsey, James Edward
(Jim)
75QuadC
79SLCty-14
80SLCty-16
81Pawtu-9
81T-214R
83Pawtu-6
84Pawtu-6
Doss, Dennis
77Watlo
Doss, Greg
88Savan/Pro-357
Doss, Jason
88Wythe/Pro-1998
89CharWh/Best-20
89CharWh/Pro-1765
Doss, Larry
87Jamestn-9
Dostal, Bruce
88Bakers/Cal-247
89VeroB/Star-7
Doster, Zach
87Fayette-7
88Fay/Pro-1090
89Mia/Star/25-5
Dotson, J.
(Gene)
79ArkTr-8
81Louvl-15
Dotson, Larry
81Watlo-25
Dotson, Richard E.
(Rich)
78Knoxv
79Knoxv/TCMA-8
81Coke
81D-280
81F-356
81OPC-138
81T-138
81T/HT
81T/St-62
82D-356
82F-340
82F/St-186
82OPC-257
82T-457
82T/St-166
83D-319
83F-233
83OPC-46
83T-46
84D-180
84F-56
84F/St-62
84Nes/792-216TL
84Nes/792-759
84OPC-24
84T-759
84T/St-241
84TrueVal/WS-10
85Coke/WS-34
85D-3
85D-302
85D/DKsuper-3
85F-511
85Leaf-3DK
85OPC-364
85T-364
85T/St-233
86Coke/WS-34
86D-160
86F-203
86Jay's-5
86OPC-233
86S-133M
86T-156M
86T-612
87Coke/WS-20
87D-383
87D/OD-238
87F-495
87F/Mini-33
87OPC-211
87T-720
88D-124
88D/Best-52
88D/Y/Bk-NEW
88F-396
88F/U-U48
88OPC-209
88Panini/St-53
88Score-480
88Score/Tr-60T
88T-209
88T/St-291
88T/Tr-35T
89D-277
89F-253
89OPC-357
89Panini/St-398
89Score-278
89Score/NWest-23
89Score/Tr-80
89Sf-194
89T-511
89T/St-316
89UD-80
90Score-19
90T-169
Dotter, Gary Richard
(Gary)
65T-421R
Dotterer, Henry John
(Dutch)
58T-396
59T-288
60T-21
61T-332
61T/RO-24
Doty, Sean
89Bill/Pro-2052
Dotzler, Mike
86DayBe-7
87Salem-12
88Orlan/Best-21
89Visal/Cal-105
89Visal/Pro-1438
Doucet, Eric
89Boise/Pro-1983
Dougherty, Jim
88CapeCod/Sum-55
Dougherty, Mark
83Erie-7
86ArkTr-6
87Louvl-11
88Louvl-18
88Louvl/CMC-23
88Louvl/Pro-444
Dougherty, Pat
86BurlEx-6
Dougherty, Patrick H.
(Patsy)
10Domino-36
11Helmar-10
12Sweet/Pin-9
E101
E102
E105
E107
E254
E90/1
E90/3
E92
E94
M116
T201
T205
T206
T215/blue
T215/brown
T216
WG2-16
Doughty, Jamie
85Tulsa-9
86Tulsa-11
Douglas, Charles
(Whammy)
58T-306
59T-431
Douglas, Charles
88Boise/Pro-1624
Douglas, Dave
87Harrisbg-16
Douglas, Phillip B.
(Phil)
E120
E121/120
W501-74
W514-5
W575
Douglas, Preston
88Utica/Puc-27
Douglas, Steve
82Orlan/B-17
82OrlTw/A-6
Douglas, William B.
(Klondike)
E107
Dour, Brian
88CapeCod/Sum-64
89Everett/Star-6
Douthit, Taylor Lee
(Taylor)
29Exh/4-16
31Exh/4-16
33Exh/4-4
33G-40
R316
V353-40
Dovalis, Alex
79Wisco-6
Dovey, Troy
89Ashvl/Pro-956
Dowell, Ken
83Readg-13
84Cram/PCL-210
85Cram/PCL-46
86Portl-5
87F/U-U27
87Maine-16
87Maine/TCMA-10
88Tidew/CANDL-8
88Tidew/CMC-14
88Tidew/Pro-1595
89Tidew/CMC-11
89Tidew/Pro-1963
Dowles, Butch
82Danvi-10
Dowless, Mike
81Water-3
82Indianap-16
83Indianap-23
84Cedar-24
Dowling, David B.
(Dave)
65OPC-116R
65T-116R
66T-482R
67T-272R
Downey, Thomas E.
(Tom)
10Domino-37
11Helmar-143
12Sweet/Pin-97A
12Sweet/Pin-97B
14CJ-107
15CJ-107
E254
M116
S74-73
T201
T205
T206
T207
T213/blue
T3-91
Downing, Alphonso E.
(Al)
62T-219
64T-219M
64T-86
64T/Coins-109
65MacGregor-2
65OPC-11LL
65T-11LL
65T-598
66T-384
67T-308
68Bz-12
68OPC-105
68T-105
69MB-76
69T-292
70T-584
71MLB/St-102
71OPC-182
71T-182
72MB-94
72OPC-460
72OPC-93LL
72T-460
72T-93LL
73OPC-324
73T-324
74OPC-620
74T-620
75OPC-498
75T-498
75T/M-498
76OPC-605
76SSPC-66
76T-605
WG10-5
WG9-7
Downing, Brian Jay
(Brian)
74OPC-601R
74T-601R
75OPC-422
75T-422
75T/M-422
76OPC-23
76SSPC-141
76T-23
77Ho-138
77OPC-246
77T-344
78T-519
79T-71
80OPC-315
80T-602
80T/S-49
81D-410
81F-282
81OPC-263
81T-263
81T/St-50
82D-115
82F-457
82F/St-215
82OPC-158
82T-158
83D-367
83F-86
83OPC-298
83T-442
84D-423
84F-515
84Nes/792-574
84OPC-135
84Smok/Cal-8
84T-574
84T/St-236
85D-158
85F-300
85Leaf-223
85OPC-374
85Smok/Cal-7
85T-374
85T/St-224
86D-108
86F-154
86Leaf-39
86OPC-205
86S-154
86Smok/Cal-7
86T-772
86T/St-183
87D-86
87D/HL-5
87D/OD-9
87F-78
87F/Excit-16
87F/Lim-15
87F/Mini-34
87F/St-35
87OPC-88
87S-161
87Smok/Cal-19
87T-782
87T/St-178
88D-258
88D/Best-27
88F-488
88F/Mini-10
88F/St-11
88Leaf-203
88OPC-331
88Panini/St-46
88RedFoley/St-19
88Score-44
88Sf-181
88Smok/Angels-18
88T-331
88T/Big-78
88T/Mini-5
88T/Revco-23
88T/St-181
89B-53
89D-254
89D/Best-321
89F-475
89OPC-17
89Panini/St-288
89Score-76
89Sf-117
89Smok/Angels-12
89T-17
89T/St-178
89UD-485
90D-10DK
90D-352
90F-130
90Score-26
90Score/100St-46
90Sf-77
90T-635
90UD-146
Downs, Dorley
84PrWill-12
85Nashua-7
86Macon-8
Downs, Jerome Willis
(Red)
T201
T206
Downs, Kelly
82OkCty-21
83Portl-9
84Cram/PCL-201
85Cram/PCL-189
86Phoen-4
87D-573
87F-272
87Moth/SFG-17

87T-438
88Class/Red-194
88D-145
88D/Best-106
88F-80
88Moth/Giants-17
88OPC-187
88Panini/St-415
88Score-27
88Score/YS/I-19
88Sf-203
88T-629
88T/JumboR-19
88ToysRUs-9
89B-465
89D-367
89D/Best-247
89F-326
89Moth/Giants-4
89OPC-361
89Panini/St-209
89Score-124
89Sf-39
89T-361
89T/Big-112
89T/St-81
89UD-476
90D-177
90F-55
90Score-534
90T-17
90UD-699

Downs, Kirk
80BurlB-24

Downs, Ron
88Aug/Pro-378
88SALAS/GS-5
89Salem/Star-6

Doyel, Dan
89Savan/Pro-347

Doyle
N172/PCL

Doyle, Blake
78RochR
79RochR-4
80Indianap-20

Doyle, Brian Reed
(Brian)
78Cr/PCL-14
79T-710R
80Colum-13
80T-582
81F-104
81T-159
81T/Tr-754
82Syrac-16

Doyle, James
M116

Doyle, Jeffrey D.
(Jeff)
81ArkTr-7
81Louvl-11
82Louvl-7

Doyle, John Joseph
(Jack)
E107
N566-178

Doyle, Judd Bruce
(Slow Joe)
T206

Doyle, Lawrence J.
(Larry)
10Domino-38
11Helmar-125
12Sweet/Pin-112A
12Sweet/Pin-112B
14CJ-4
14Piedmont/St-19
15CJ-4
BF2-75
D303
D328-44
D329-51
D350/2-52
E101
E102
E103
E104
E105
E106
E135-44
E224
E254
E270/2
E286
E91
E92
E95
M101/4-51
M101/5-52
M116
S74-85
T201
T202
T205
T206
T207
T213/blue
T215/blue
T215/brown
T216
T3-13
W514-81
W516-13
WG4-7

Doyle, Paul S.
(Paul)
70OPC-277
70T-277
72T-629

Doyle, Rich
82Watlo/B-2
82Watlo/C-23
83BuffB-3
84BuffB-11
85Water-6
86Beaum-10
88SnBer/Best-24
88SnBer/Cal-52
89Calg/CMC-7
89Calg/Pro-541

Doyle, Robert Dennis
(Denny)
70OPC-539R
70T-539R
71MLB/St-175
71OPC-352
71T-352
72T-768
73OPC-424
73T-424
74OPC-552
74T-552
75OPC-187
75T-187
75T/M-187
76Ho-107
76OPC-381
76SSPC-407
76T-381
77Ashev
77T-336
78OPC-111
78T-642

Doyle, Tom
86Columbia-9TR
87Columbia-23
88Jacks/GS-7
88Martins/Star-11

Doyle, William Carl
R313

Dozier, Tom
82Sprin-15
83StPet-5
84Albany-11
85Cram/PCL-145
85Huntsvl/BK-15
86Tacom-4
87Tacom-1
88Greenv/Best-18

Drabek, Doug
85Albany-4
86Colum-6
86Colum/Pol-6
86D/Rook-31
86F/Up-U36
87D-251
87D/HL-32
87F-96
87T-283
87T/Tr-29T
88D-79
88D/Best-73
88F-327
88Leaf-88
88OPC-143
88RedFoley/St-20
88Score-51
88T-591
88T/Big-124
88T/St-134
89B-416
89D-211
89D/Best-17
89F-206
89OPC-37
89Panini/St-161
89Score-117
89Score/HotSt-87
89Score/YS/I-21
89Sf-27
89T-478
89UD-597
90D-92
90F-465
90Score-505
90T-197
90UD-422

Drabowsky, Myron W.
(Moe)
57T-84
58T-135
59T-407
60L-68
60T-349
61T-364
62T-331
64T-42
64T/St-82
64T/tatt-36
65T-439
66T-291
67OPC-125
67OPC-151WS
67T-125
68Coke
68T-242
69MB-77
69MLB/St-57
69T-508
69T/St-183
70MLB/St-220
70T-653
71MLB/St-272
71OPC-685
71T-685
72MB-95
72T-627
78TCMA-121
87Birm/Bst-3C
88BirmB/Best-7
89Pac/Leg-215
89Swell-103
89Vanco/CMC-25
89Vanco/Pro-581

Drago, Richard A.
(Dick)
69T-662R
70OPC-37
70T-37
71MLB/St-414
71OPC-752
71T-752
72K-40
72OPC-205
72T-205
73OPC-392
73T-392
74OPC-113
74T-113
75OPC-333
75T-333
75T/M-333
76OPC-142
76SSPC-422
76T-142
77T-426
78PapaG/Disc-11
78T-567
79OPC-2
79T-12
80T-271
81D-336
81F-239
81OPC-332
81T-647
81T/Tr-755
82F-510
82T-742

Drahman, Brian
87Beloi-10
88Stock/Cal-186
88Stock/Pro-734
89ElPas/GS-6

Drake, Bill
78Laugh/Black-8

Drake, Delos Daniel
(Delos)
T207

Drake, H.P.
78LodiD

Drake, Kevin
74Cedar
75Dubuq

Drake, Sam
88CapeCod/Sum-131
89Helena/SP-22

Drake, Samuel H.
(Sammy)
62T-162

Drake, Solomon L.
(Solly)
57T-159
59T-406

Drake, Tex
85Kingst-26
86Kinston-5bb
89Richm/Pro-819

Draper, Mike
88Oneon/Pro-2059
89PrWill/Star-6

Dravecky, David F.
(Dave)
79BuffB
80Buffa-4
81Hawai-20
82Hawai-20
83F-356
83T-384
84D-551
84D-8
84F-298
84Moth/Padres-11
84Nes/792-290
84Nes/792-366TL
84OPC-290
84Smok/Padres-7
84T-290
84T/St-155
85D-112
85F-30
85Moth/Padres-8
85OPC-32
85T-530
85T/St-154
86D-162
86F-319
86Leaf-92
86OPC-276
86T-735
87Bohem-43
87D-187
87F-412
87F/U-U28
87OPC-62
87T-470
87T/St-107
88D-485
88D/Best-135
88F-81
88F/BB/MVP-10
88F/St-127
88Moth/Giants-9
88Score-564
88T-68
89F-327
89Moth/Giants-9
89T-601
89UD-39
90Score-550
90T-124
90UD-679

Drawdy, Duke
77WHave

Drees, Tom
86Penin-8
87DayBe-4
88BirmB/Best-3
88SLAS-34
89AAA/Pro-29
89Vanco/CMC-10
89Vanco/Pro-588
90F-644
90UD-3

Drell, Tom
88CapeCod-1
88CapeCod/Sum-18

Dressen, Charles W.
(Chuck)
25Exh-28
26Exh-28
40PB-72
49Remar
50Remar
51B-259
52B-188
52T-377
53B/Col-124
53RM-NL1
53T-50
60Lake
60T-213
61T-137
64Det/Lids-5MG
64T-443
65T-538
66OPC-187MG
66T-187
79TCMA-56
87Conlon/2-31
88Conlon/4-9
89Smok/Dodg-59
R312
R316
R346-8

Dressendorfer, Kirk
88CapeCod/Sum-134

Dressler, Robert Alan
(Rob)

75Lafay
75Phoen-11
76OPC-599R
76Phoen
76T-599R
77Phoen
77T-11
78Cram/PCL-57
79Spoka-19
80T-366
81D-405
81OPC-163
81T-508

Drew, Bob
75Lafay
82Madis-24M

Drew, Cameron
86Ashvl-8
87ColAst/Pro-7
87ColumAst-7
87SLAS-7
88Tucso-10
88Tucso/CMC-14
88Tucso/Pro-188
89B-334
89Class-135
89D-30
89F-640M
89Score-643
89Score/HotRk-3
89Sf-225M

Drews, Karl August
(Karl)
49B-188
52T-352
53B/Col-113
53T-59
54B-191

Dreyfuss, Barney
D322

Drezek, Karl
88AppFx/Pro-148
88Eugene/Best-21

Driessen, Daniel
(Dan)
74OPC-341
74T-341
74T/St-25
75OPC-133
75T-133
75T/M-133
76OPC-514
76SSPC-36
76T-514
77OPC-31
77Pep-45
77T-23
78Ho-64
78OPC-84
78T-246
79K-26
79OPC-247
79T-475
80OPC-173
80T-325
81Coke
81D-301
81F-205
81F/St-22
81OPC-14
81T-655
81T/HT
81T/St-164
82Coke/Reds
82D-248
82F-64
82OPC-373
82T-785
83D-274
83F-589
83OPC-165
83T-165
83T/St-228
84D-243
84F-467
84Nes/792-585
84OPC-44
84T-585
84T/St-55
85D-619
85F-396
85Leaf-255
85OPC-285
85OPC/Post-2
85T-285
85T/St-92
86D-641
86F-539
86Leaf-255
86Moth/Giants-14
86T-65
86T/St-89
87Louvl-12
88F/WS-7M

Drill, Lewis L.
(Lew)
E107

Drilling, Robert
49Sommer-20

Driscoll, James B.
(Jim)
71OPC-317R
71T-317R
85Water-19
86Water-7C

Driscoll, Jim
T3/Box-51

Driver, Ron
77Newar
78Holyo
79Holyo-11

Drizmala, Tom
83CharR-19

Drohan, Bill
88Eugene/Best-5
89AppFx/Pro-854

Dromerhauser, Rob
85Newar-17

Dropo, Walter
(Walt)
50B-246
51T/CAS
52B-169
52T-235
53B/Col-45
53Glen
53RM-AL4
53T-121
54B-7
54T-18
55B-285
56T-238
57T-257
58T-338
59T-158
60T-79
61T-489
80Laugh/FFeat-36
89Swell-108
Exh47
R423-19

Droschak, Dave
83Sprin/LF-5

Drott, Richard Fred
(Dick)
58T-80
59T-15
60L-76
60T-27
61T-231
79TCMA-64

Drucke, Louis
10Domino-39
11Helmar-126
12Sweet/Pin-113

Drummond, Tim
86PrWill-9
87Vanco-13
88Tidew/CANDL-18
88Tidew/CMC-4
88Tidew/Pro-1593
89Tidew/CMC-1
89Tidew/Pro-1952
90D-510
90T-713

Drummonds, Lamar
63Pep/Tul

Drumwright, Keith A.
78Charl
79Charl-1
81Tacom-17
82D-616
82F-89
82T-673
82Tacom-29

Drury, Scott
88Batav/Pro-1668

Drysdale, Donald S.
(Don)
57T-18
58BB
58Hires-55
58T-25
59Bz
59Morrell
59T-262M
59T-387
60Armour-9
60Morrell
60P
60T-475
60T-570AS
60T/tatt
60T/tatt-12
61Bz-26
61Morrell
61P-160
61T-260
61T-45LL
61T-49LL
61T/Dice-4
61T/St-26
62BB-53
62J-110
62P-110
62P/Can-110
62T-340
62T-398AS
62T-60LL
62T/bucks
62T/St-133
63Bz-17
63Exh
63F-41
63J-123
63P-123
63Salada-1
63T-360
63T-412M
63T-5LL
63T-7LL
63T-9LL
63T/SO
64T-120
64T-5LL
64T/Coins-34
64T/St-79
64T/SU
65OPC-12LL
65OPC-260
65OPC-8LL
65T-12LL
65T-260
65T-8LL
65T/E-15
65T/trans-47
66Bz-42
66T-223LL
66T-430
66T/RO-16
67Bz-42
67OPC-55
67OPC/PI-16
67T-55
67T/PI-16
67T/Test/SU-11
68Bz-15
68Bz-6
68OPC-145
68T-145
68T/Post-7
69MLBPA/Pin-41
69T-400
69T/decal
69T/S-46
69T/St-42
72Laugh/GF-38
78TCMA-3
82KMart-42
83MLBPA/Pin-23
84West/1-9
87Smok/Dodg-7
88Smok/Dodg-11
89Rini/Dodg-8
89Smok/Dodg-7
Exh47

Drzayich, Emil
80Cedar-4
81Cedar-10

Duant, Rich
86LitFalls-9

Duarte, Luis
80Batav-16
81Watlo

Dube, Greg
87Wmspt-19

DuBeau, Jack
78Watlo

Dubee, Rich
76Watlo
77DaytB
84Memph-2
85Omaha-11
87Memph-11
87Memph/Best-3C
88Omaha/CMC-23
88Omaha/Pro-1494
89Omaha/Pro-1739

Dubiel, Walter John
(Monk)
47Centen-6
49Eureka-55
51B-283
52T-164

DuBois, Brian
86Hagers-5
87Hagers-4
88CLAS/Star-6
88Virgini/Star-8
89Hagers/Best-13
89Hagers/Pro-274
89Hagers/Star-5
90D-38
90F-601
90Score-657
90T-413
90UD-78

Dubuc, Jean J.
(Jean)
15CJ-156
BF2-28
D329-52
D350/2-53
M101/4-52
M101/5-52
T206
T213/blue
T213/brown
T215/blue

Ducey, Rob
86Ventura-5
87D/HL-39
87Syrac-16
87Syrac/TCMA-19
87Tor/Fire-6
87Tor/Fire-6
88F-107
88OPC-106
88Score-629
88Syrac/CMC-14
88Syrac/Pro-825
88T-438
88Tor/Fire-40
89OPC-203
89Panini/St-459
89Score/HotRk-7
89T-203
89T/Big-280
89Tor/Fire-40
89UD/Ext-721
90T-619
90UD-464

Duckworth, James R.
(Jim)
78TCMA-151
78TCMA-23

Duenas, Vernon
88CharWh/Best-11

Duensing, Larry
80Hawai-3
81Hawai-25
82Hawai-25
84Cram/PCL-244tr

Dues, Hal Joseph
(Hal)
79OPC-373
79T-699
81OPC-71
81T-71

Duey, Kody
86Jamestn-5

Duezabou, Mel
47Remar-20
47Signal
47Smith-23
48Signal
48Smith-14
49Remar
50Remar

Duff, Dave
82Jacks-12

Duffalo, Jim
62T-578
63T-567
64T-573
65OPC-159
65T-159
78TCMA-204
78TCMA-249
80Phoen-23
81Shrev-13

Duffee, Charles E.
(Charlie)
N172

Duffy, Allen
86GlenF-3

Duffy, Darrin
86Cram/PCL-72
88Modesto-22
89WinSal/Star-7

Duffy, Frank Thomas
(Frank)
71OPC-164R
71T-164R
72T-607
73OPC-376
73T-376
74OPC-81
74T-81
74T/St-163

75OPC-448
75T-448
75T/M-448
76Ho-115
76OPC-232
76SSPC-521
76T-232
77OPC-253
77Pep-18
77T-542
78PapaG/Disc-17
78T-511
79OPC-47
79T-106

Duffy, Hugh
12Sweet/Pin-10A
12Sweet/Pin-10B
48Exh/HOF
50Callahan
63Bz/ATG-33
69Bz-4
80SSPC/HOF
87Conlon/2-33
E90/1
M116
N172
N300/unif
S74-5
T205
T206
V100
WG3-16

Duffy, John
87GlenF-23
88Toled/CMC-10
88Toled/Pro-596
89Memph/Best-2
89Memph/Pro-1181
89Memph/Star-9

Duffy, Tom
83VeroB-2

Dugan, Joseph Anthony
(Joe)
21Exh-37
21Exh-38
21Exh-39
28Yueng-3
29Exh/4-1
61F-103
88Conlon/5-8
E120
E210-3
E220
V100
W502-3
W513-66
W515-30
W573
WG7-13

Dugas, Augustin J.
(Gus)
R314/Can

Dugas, Shanie
81Watlo-21
82Chatt-13
83BuffB-15
84Maine-23
85Maine-17
87Albuq/Pol-18
88Albuq/CMC-22
88Albuq/Pro-266
89Albuq/CMC-13
89Albuq/Pro-85

Dugdale, Daniel E.
(Dan)
N172

Dugey, Oscar Joseph
(Oscar)
15CJ-60
D329-53
D350/2-54
M101/4-53
M101/5-54

Duggan, Tom
83Wausa/LF-21
86Salem-6

Dugger, Lonnie
81Holyo-13
82Holyo-4

Dugrahm
N172

Duke, Andy
89Bill/Pro-2056

Duke, Doug
87BurlEx-7
88Jaxvl/Best-22
89Jaxvl/Best-6
89Jaxvl/Pro-167

Duke, Ed
86ColumAst-11tr

Duke, Jerome
86Jamestn-6

Duke, Martin F.
N172

Duke, Marvin
V355-116

Duke, Richard
87Idaho-6

Dukes, Jan Noble
(Jan)
70OPC-154R
70T-154R

Dukes, Kevin
82LynnS-3
83Chatt-19

Dukes, Thomas Earl
(Tom)
68OPC-128R
68T-128R
69T-223
71OPC-106
71T-106

Duliba, Robert John
(Bob)
60L-77
60T-401
62Kahn/Atl
62T-149
63T-97
64T-441
66OPC-53
66T-53
67T-599

Dulin, Tim
86Miami-5
87Hagers-10
88CharlK-5
88CharlK/Pep-5
88SLAS-9
89RochR/CMC-20
89RochR/Pro-1646

Dull, Darrell
83Idaho-19

Dull, Mike
87BurlEx-9
88WPalm/Star-9
89Jaxvl/Best-7
89Jaxvl/Pro-164

Dumas, Don
87Savan-21

Dumouchelle, Pat
81Miami-8
84CharO-13

Dumoulin, Dan
77Indianap-13
78Indianap-7
79Indianap-26

Dunbar, Matt
88CapeCod/Sum-65

Dunbar, Thomas Jerome
(Tommy)
82Tulsa-10
83OKCty-7
84D-28
84OKCty-18
84Rangers-13
85D-159
85F/Up-U37
85Rangers-13
85T-102
86D-221
86OKCty-5
86T-559
87Vanco-6
88Greenv/Best-21
89Greenv/Pro-1179
89Greenv/Star-7
89Greenvl/Best-26

Duncan, C.
(Duke)
78Newar
79Holyo-27

Duncan, Chip
87Watertn-6
88Salem/Star-5
89Salem/Star-7

Duncan, David Edwin
(Dave)
64T-528R
68T-261
69OPC-68
69T-68
69T/St-214
70T-678
71MLB/St-511
71OPC-178
71T-178
72OPC-17
72T-17
73OPC-337
73T-337
74OPC-284
74T-284
74T/St-164
75OPC-238
75OPC-626
75T-238
75T/M-238
76OPC-49
76SSPC-383
76T-49
77T-338
87Moth/A's-8

Duncan, Doug
77Visal

Duncan, John
83Wausa/LF-26

Duncan, Lindy
81Tulsa-25

Duncan, Louis Baird
(Pat)
21Exh-40
88Pac/8Men-94
E120
V100
V61-109
W572
WG7-14

Duncan, Mariano
83VeroB-16
85F/Up-U38
85T/Tr-32T
86D-128
86F-129
86F/LL-10
86F/Mini-27
86F/St-33
86KayBee-8
86Leaf-50
86OPC-296
86Pol/Dodg-25
86T-602
87D-253
87D/OD-84
87F-439
87Moth/Dodg-7
87OPC-199
87Pol/Dodg-12
87Seven-W2
87T-199
87T/Mini-13
87T/St-74
88Albuq/CMC-23
88Albuq/Pro-255
88D-155
88F-513
88OPC-181
88Pol/Dodg-25
88Score-321
88T-481
89Moth/Dodg-26
89Pol/Dodg-15
90D-684
90Score-506
90T-234
90UD-430

Duncan, Michael
86Modesto-8
87Modesto-4

Duncan, Rick
78OrlTw

Duncan, Taylor M.
79T-658

Duncan, Tim
80Elmir-20

Duncun, John
86Chatt-9

Dunegan, James W. Jr.
(Jim)
71OPC-121R
71T-121R

Dunlap, Frederick C.
(Fred)
N162
N172
N284
Scrapps
WG1-58

Dunlap, Joe
86Cedar/TCMA-15
87Vermont-10
89Calg/CMC-18
89Calg/Pro-529

Dunlap, Paul
V355-125

Dunleavy, John E.
WG3-17

Dunlop, Harry
73OPC-593CO
73T-593C
74T-166C
84Smok/SDP-8C

Dunn
N172

Dunn, Greg
82Sprin-13
83Sprin/LF-14
85Sprin-8
86Louisvl-10

Dunn, James William
(Jim)
81Shrev-3

Dunn, John Joseph
(Jack)
C46-19
E107
E254
T205
T206

Dunn, Joseph Edward
(Joe)
T205
T206
T213/brown

Dunn, Mike
82Clint-14

Dunn, Ronald Ray
(Ron)
76SSPC-322

Dunn, Steve
88QuadC/GS-10
89Elizab/Star-7
89Keno/Pro-1073
89Keno/Star-4

Dunne, Mike
85T-395
86Louisvl-11
87D/Rook-38
87F/U-U29
87S/Rook-40
87T/Tr-30T
87Vanco-15
88Class/Blue-237
88D-390
88D/Best-89
88F-328
88F/AwardWin-10
88F/BB/MVP-11
88F/Mini-104
88F/RecSet-11
88F/St-115
88Leaf-235
88OPC-224
88Panini/St-367
88Score-432
88Score/YS/I-26
88Sf-171
88T-619
88T/Big-236
88T/Coins-40
88T/Gloss60-19
88T/JumboR-16
88T/Mini-68
88T/RiteAid-9
88T/St-132
88T/St-307
88T/UK-21
88ToysRUs-10
89B-412
89D-269
89F-207
89OPC-165
89Panini/St-162
89Score-285
89T-165
89T/St-130
89UD-518
90T-522

Dunnegan, Steve
82DayBe-11

Dunning, Stephen John
(Steve)
71OPC-294
71T-294
72T-658
73OPC-53
73T-53
78T-647

Dunnum, Rick
88AubAs/Pro-1969
89Ashvl/Pro-964

Dunster, Don
86Osceola-6
87Osceola-19
88ColAst/Best-2

Dunston, Shawon
83QuadC-20
84MidldC-22
85D-39
85F-649
85T-280FDP
86D-311
86F-366
86F/Mini-77
86F/St-34
86Gator-12
86Jay's-6
86KayBee-9
86Leaf-181
86S-155

86T-72
87Berg/Cubs-12
87D-119
87D/OD-76
87F-561
87F/GameWin-13
87F/Mini-35
87F/RecSet-6
87F/St-36
87Leaf-128
87OPC-346
87RedFoley/St-94
87S-79M
87S-98
87Seven-C4
87T-346
87T/St-59
88Berg/Cubs-12
88D-146
88D/Best-37
88D/Cubs/Bk-146
88F-419
88Leaf-70
88OPC-277
88Panini/St-264
88Score-529
88Score/YS/II-18
88Sf-163
88T-695
88T/Big-225
88T/St-65
88T/St/Backs-11
89B-294
89Cadaco-15
89D-137
89D/AS-43
89D/Best-93
89F-424
89KMart/DT-26
89Mara/Cubs-12
89OPC-140
89Panini/St-58
89RedFoley/St-38
89Score-235
89Sf-190
89T-140
89T/Big-233
89T/St-49
89T/St/Backs-43
89UD-107
90D-49
90F-30
90Score-169
90T-415
90UD-231

Dunton, Kevin
86WPalm-14

Dupont, Margaret
51BR-D13

Dupree, Michael D.
(Mike)
77T-491R
79Hawai-19

Duquette, Bryan
83ElPas-5
84ElPas-11
85Cram/PCL-212
86Vanco-11

Duquette, Chuck
88Fay/Pro-1089

Duran, Daniel James
(Dan)
74Gasto
80Charl-12

Duran, Dave
81Holyo-14
82Holyo-5

Duran, Rick
79Holyo-14

Durant, Richard
87Columbia-25
88Clmbia/GS-3

89Stock/Best-7
89Stock/Cal-155
89Stock/Pro-388
89Stock/Star-19

Duren, Rinold George
(Ryne)
58T-296
59T-485
60L-22
60T-204
60T/tatt-13
61P-14
61T-356
62J-81
62P-81
62P/Can-81
62Salada-46A
62Salada-46B
62Shirriff-46
62T-388
63T-17
64T-173
65T-339
79TCMA-135
89Pac/Leg-141

Durham, Donald Gary
(Don)
73OPC-548
73T-548

Durham, Edward Fant
(Ed)
34G-79

Durham, Joseph Vann
(Joe)
58T-96

Durham, Leon
81Coke
81D-427
81F-540
81OPC-321
81T-321
81T/HT
81T/Tr-756
82D-151
82F-595
82F/St-94
82OPC-206
82RedLob
82T-607
82T/St-25
83D-477
83D/AAS-55
83F-495
83K-27
83OPC-125
83T-125
83T-51
83T/St-219
83Thorn-10
84D-5
84D-67
84F-492
84FunFood/Pin-107
84Nes/792-565
84OPC-209
84SevenUp-10
84T-565
84T/St-40
85D-189
85D/AAS-46
85F-56
85Leaf-238
85OPC-330
85Seven-8G
85SevenUp-10
85T-330
85T/Gloss40-11
85T/St-36
86D-320
86F-367
86F/LL-11
86F/Mini-78

86F/St-35
86Gator-10
86Leaf-190
86OPC-58
86S-111
86T-460
86T/St-60
87Berg/Cubs-10
87D-242
87D/OD-74
87F-562
87F/Hottest-15
87Leaf-125
87OPC-290
87RedFoley/St-120
87S-185
87Seven-C6
87T-290
87T/Board-26
87T/St-57
88D-191
88D/Cubs/Bk-191
88F-420
88Kahn/Reds-10
88OPC-65
88Panini/St-259
88Score-378
88T-65
88T/Big-42
88T/St-63
89Louvl-16
89Louvl/CMC-16
89Louvl/Pro-1260
89UD-354

Durham, Louis
E97
T206
W555

Durham, Shane
87Anchora-7

Durkin, Martin
88CapeCod/Sum-128
89Watertn/Star-4

Durnan, Bill
51BR-A17

Durney, Bill
88PalmSp/Cal-115
88PalmSp/Pro-1462

Durocher, Francois
86Osceola-7

Durocher, Leo Ernest
(Leo)
29Exh/4-26
31Exh/4-7
33G-147
34G-7
35BU-156
38Exh/4-2
39PB-6
41DP-142
49Eureka-102
50B-220
51B-233
52B-146
52RM-NL1
52T-315
53B/Col-55
55Gol/Giants-6
67T-481
68T-321
69OPC-147MG
69T-147
70OPC-291MG
70T-291
71OPC-609MG
71T-609
72T-576
73OPC-624MG
73T-624MG
79TCMA-201
80Cram/Leg-40
86Conlon/1-11

88Conlon/3-10
88Pac/Leg-27
89Rini/Dodg-28M
89Rini/Dodg-30
89Smok/Dodg-39
R310
R346-2
V353-74
V354-69
V355-25

Durrman, Jim
81WHave-8
83Albany-9

Duryea, James Whitney
(Jesse)
N172

Dusak, Ervin Frank
(Erv)
47TipTop
51B-310
52T-183
79TCMA-122

Dusan, Gene
75OkCty
77Watlo
79Tacom-24
80Tacom-23
82Jacks-22
86Cedr/TCM-25MG

Dustal, Robert Andrew
(Bob)
63T-299R

Duval, Michael
(Mickey)
79Indianap-27
82Madis-24M

DuVall, Brad
88Hamil/Pro-1722
89B-430
89Sprin/Best-4

Dwyer, James Edward
(Jim)
75OPC-429
75T-429
75T/M-429
76OPC-94
76SSPC-341
76T-94
78T-644
79T-236
80T-577
81D-577
81F-235
81OPC-184
81T-184
81T/Tr-757
82D-64
82F-164
82T-359
83D-583
83F-59
83T-718
84D-454
84F-7
84F/St-117
84Nes/792-473
84T-473
85F-176
85T-56
86D-413
86F-274
86OPC-339
86T-653
87D-418
87F-469
87T-246
88D-459
88F-558
88French-9
88Score-229
88T-521
89D/Best-311

90D-484

Dwyer, John Francis
(Frank)
N172

Dybzinski, Jerome M.
(Jerry)
78Watlo
79Tacom-13
81D-438
81F-399
81OPC-198
81T-198
82D-647
82F-366
82T-512
82Wheat/Ind
83D-576
83F-406
83T-289
83T/X-27
84D-160
84F-57
84Nes/792-619
84T-619
84TrueVal/WS-11
85Cram/PCL-250
85F-512
85T-52
86Calgary-7

Dyce, George
89Nashvl-26VP

Dyck, James Robert
(Jim)
53B/C-111
53NB
53T-177
54B-85
56T-303

Dye, Mark
82Idaho-18

Dye, Scott
80Water-8
81Tidew-15
82Jacks-4
83Tidew-14

Dye, Steve
89Modesto/Cal-269
89Modesto/Ch-9

Dyer, Don Robert
(Duffy)
69T-624R
70T-692
71MLB/St-150
71OPC-136
71T-136
72OPC-127
72T-127
73OPC-493
73T-493
74OPC-536
74T-536
75OPC-538
75T-538
75T/M-538
76OPC-88
76SSPC-581
76T-88
77T-318
78T-637
79T-286
80OPC-232
80T-446
81D-7
81T-196
83Thorn-26CO
86ElPas-9MG
87ElPas-14
88Denver/CMC-25
88Denver/Pro-1264

Dyer, Eddie
49Eureka-181

Dyer, Hal
87CharWh-14
Dyer, John
78Green
Dyer, Linton
88AppFx/Pro-143
89AppFx/Pro-867
Dyer, Mike
87Kenosha-11
88Orlan/Best-9
89Portl/CMC-8
89Portl/Pro-228
90D-642
90F-372
90Score-571
90T-576
90UD-374
Dyes, Andy
78Syrac
79Hawai-5
80Hawai-24
Dygert, James Henry
(Jimmy)
12Sweet/Pin-44
C46-45
E104
E90/1
E97
M116
S74-30
T201
T205
T206
T208
T3-92
W555
Dyke, Bill
89Knoxv/Pro-1120
Dykes, James Joseph
(Jimmy)
21Exh-41
25Exh-106
26Exh-107
29Exh/4-28
31Exh/4-27
32Orbit/num-11
32Orbit/un-16
33DH-12
33DL-18
33G-6
34DS-42
34Ward's/Pin-2
35BU-159
35BU-29
35Exh/4-10
35G-1I
35G-2F
35G-6F
35G-7F
36Exh/4-10
36G
37Exh/4-10
40PB-187
47Signal
51B-226
52B-98
53B/Col-31
54Esskay
60T-214
61Kahn
61T-222
78TCMA-224
87Conlon/2-37
88Conlon/4-10
E120
E210-51
E220
R300
R305
R308-167
R311/Gloss
R314
R316
R337-410
V100
V353-6
V355-1
W517-22
W572
Dykstra, Len
83Lynch-15
84Jacks-18
85Tidew-20
86D-482
86F-78
86OPC-53
86T-53
87Class-2
87D-611
87F-6
87F/McCror-13
87Leaf-88
87OPC-295
87S-58
87Seven-E4
87Seven-ME5
87T-295
87T/HL-23
87T/Mets/Fan-3
87T/St-13
87T/St-21WS
87T/St-98
87Woolwth-23
88D-364
88D/Best-264
88D/Mets/Bk-364
88F-133
88Kahn/Mets-4
88Leaf-135
88OPC-299
88Panini/St-345
88Score-370
88Score/YS/II-19
88Sf-106
88T-655
88T/Big-203
88T/Mini-59
89Class-36
89D-353
89D/Best-159
89F-33
89F/Up-105
89OPC-349
89Panini/St-138
89Score-84
89Score/Tr-28
89Sf-123
89T-435
89T/Big-41
89T/St-90
89T/Tr-27T
89UD-369
90D-313
90F-556
90Score-427
90Sf-156
90T-515
90UD-472
Dyson, Ted
88PalmSp/Cal-103
Dyson, Tim
88PalmSp/Pro-1453
Dzafic, Bernie
88Elmir-5
89WinHav/Star-5
Dziadkowiec, Andy
87Myrtle-27
89Duned/Star-4
Eagar, Brad
87Anchora-8
89Medford/Best-7
Eagar, Steve
86Lakel-5
Eagelston, Chris
86Hagers-6
Eagen, Charles
E254
M116
Eakes, Steven
82Redwd-2
83Redwd-9
Ealy, Thomas
85Evrt/Cram-4
86Clint-6
86Cram/PCL-200
87Clint-12
88Clint/Pro-718
89SanJose/Best-14
89SanJose/Cal-231
89SanJose/Pro-434
89SanJose/Star-8
Eaman, Bob
89London/Pro-1359
Earl, Scottie
83BirmB-17
84Evans-14
85D-491
86Nashv-7
87Toled-1
87Toled/TCMA-10
88Nashvl/CMC-19
88Nashvl/Pro-471
Earle, William
(Billy)
N172
Earley, Arnold Carl
(Arnie)
67T-388
78TCMA-209
Earley, Bill
83IowaC-2
84IowaC-2
85OKCty-30
86Louisvl-12
87Louvl-13
88Wythe/Pro-1989
89CharWh/Best-24
89CharWh/Pro-1754
Earls, Peter
82Tucso-28M
Early, Jacob Willard
(Jake)
48L-61
49B-106
Earnshaw, George L.
(George)
32Orbit/num-38
32Orbit/un-17
33DH-13
34Exh/4-10
34G-41
35G-1I
35G-2F
35G-6F
35G-7F
40PB-233
R305
R306
R308-169
R310
R312/M
R328-29
R332-13
V354-93
W517-8
Easler, Michael A.
(Mike)
75Iowa/TCMA-7
76Tulsa
78Colum
78T-710R
80T-194
81Coke
81D-256
81F-372
81F/St-74
81OPC-92
81T-92
81T/SO-81
81T/St-212
82D-221
82F-481
82K-49
82OPC-235
82T-235
82T/St-84
83D-221
83F-306
83OPC-385
83T-385
84D-444
84F-249
84F/X-33
84Nes/792-589
84OPC-353
84T-589
84T/St-137
84T/X-33
85D-213
85F-157
85F/St-46
85Leaf-206
85OPC-349
85T-686
85T/St-213
86D-395
86F-347
86F/Up-U37
86T-477
86T/St-255
86T/Tr-33T
87D-277
87D/OD-155
87F-97
87F/AS-7
87Leaf-192
87OPC-135
87S-92
87T-135
87T/St-295
88F-206
88OPC-9
88Score-220
88T-741
Easley, Logan
83Greens-5
85Albany-5
86Albany/TCMA-17
88BuffB/CMC-1
88BuffB/Pro-1490
Eason, Greg
80Ashev-26
Easter, Dick
84IowaC-4
Easter, Luscious Luke
(Luke)
50NumNum
51B-258
51T/RB-26
52B-95
52NumNum-12
52T-24
53B/Col-104
53Exh/Can-2
53T-2
54B-116
54DanDee
54T-23
79TCMA-80
88MinorLg/Leg-5
D301
Exh47
PM10/Sm-47
Easterly, James M.
(Jamie)
75OPC-618R
75T-618R
75T/M-618R
76OPC-511
76T-511
78T-264
79Richm-11
79T-684
82D-623
82F-139
82Pol/Brew
82Pol/Brew-28
82T-122
83D-280
83F-31
83Pol/Brew-28
83T-528
83T/X-28
84F-538
84Nes/792-367
84T-367
84T/St-258
85F-445
85Polar/Ind-36
85T-764
86D-582
86F-585
86OhHenry-36
86T-31
87Gator-11
Easterly, Theodore H.
(Ted)
14CJ-117
15CJ-117
T206
T207
Eastman, Doug
88Cedar/Pro-1153
89Cedar/Best-20
89Cedar/Pro-923
89Cedar/Star-5
Eastwick, Rawlins J.
(Rawley)
75OPC-621R
75T-621R
75T/M-621R
76Icee
76OPC-469
76T-469
77OPC-140
77OPC-8LL
77Pep-55
77T-45
77T-8LL
78BK/Y-11
78T-405
79T-271
80T-692
82F-596
82T-117
Eaton, Craig
76Watlo
77DaytB
80SLCty-3
81SLCty-4
82Spoka-2
83Evans-2
84Indianap-8
Eaton, Tom R.
81RochR-5
Eave, Gary
87Durhm-19
88Richm-31
88Richm/CMC-5
88Richm/Pro-26
89Richm/CMC-2
89Richm/Ko-31
89Richm/Pro-828
90D-713
90Score-621
Ebel, Brian
89Hagers/Best-16
89Hagers/Pro-284

Ebel, Dino
89VeroB/Star-8
Eberle, Mike
88CLAS/Star-7
88Hagers/Star-4
89Hagers/Best-12
89Hagers/Pro-270
89Hagers/Star-6
Eberle, Greg
89Peoria/Ko-27MG
Ebersberger, Randy
82Clint-24
Ebert, Scott
88Poca/Pro-2080
89Everett/Star-7
Ebright, Chris
88CapeCod/Sum-33
89Geneva/Pro-1876
Ebright, Hiram C.
(Hi)
N172
Eccles, John
85Anchora-9
87Orlan-4
88CalLgAS-38
88Visal/Cal-150
88Visal/Pro-84
89Orlan/Pro-1351
Eccleston, Tom
86Wausa-9
Echemendia, Idalberto
(Bert)
88James/Pro-1906
89Star/Wax-33
89WPalm/Star-10
Echevarria, Francisco
84Evrt/Cram-17
Echevarria, Robert
87Elmir-7
87Elmir/Red-7
Echols, Tony
76Wausa
Eckersley, Dennis Lee
(Dennis)
76Ho-137
76K-19
76OPC-202LL
76OPC-98
76SSPC-506
76T-202LL
76T-98
77Ho-106
77OPC-15
77Pep-13
77T-525
78Ho-78
78OPC-138
78PapaG/Disc-5
78T-122
78Wiffle/Discs-20
79Ho-145
79K-9
79OPC-16
79T-40
80OPC-169
80T-320
81Coke
81D-96
81F-226
81F/St-34
81OPC-109
81T-620
81T/HT
81T/St-48
82Coke/BOS
82D-30
82F-292
82F/St-165
82OPC-287
82T-490
83D-487
83F-182
83F-629M
83OPC-270
83T-270
83T/St-34
84D-639
84F-396
84F/X-34
84Nes/792-745
84OPC-218
84SevenUp-43
84T-745
84T/St-224
84T/X-34
85D-442
85F-57
85OPC-163
85SevenUp-43
85T-163
86D-239
86F-368
86Gator-43
86Leaf-113
86OPC-199
86S-129M
86T-538
86T/St-62
87D-365
87F-563
87F/U-U30
87OPC-381
87Seven-C8
87T-459
87T/St-63
87T/Tr-31T
88D-349
88D/A's/Bk-349
88D/Best-43
88F-279
88F/Slug-13
88Moth/A's-10
88OPC-72
88Score-104
88T-72
88T/St-170
89B-190
89Cadaco-16
89Class-90
89D-67
89D/AS-16
89D/Best-134
89F-7
89F/AS-4
89F/BBAS-12
89F/Heroes-13
89Moth/A's-10
89OPC-370
89Panini/St-12
89Panini/St-414
89RedFoley/St-39
89Score-276
89Score/HotSt-16
89Sf-101
89Sf-222M
89T-370
89T/DH-11
89T/Gloss60-16
89T/Hills-12
89T/Mini-69
89T/St-167
89T/St/Backs-31
89T/UK-23
89UD-289
89Woolwth-20
90D-210
90F-6
90Score-315
90Sf-170
90T-670
90UD-513
Eckhardt, Tom
89Idaho/Pro-2030
Economy, Scott
88Bill/Pro-1814
89Cedar/Best-9
89Cedar/Pro-921
89Cedar/Star-6
Eddings, Jay
88CharWh/Best-12
89CharWh/Best-21
89CharWh/Pro-1766
89Peoria/Ko-6
Eddins, Glenn Jr.
79Elmir-6
81Brist-18
Eddy, Donald Eugene
(Don)
72OPC-413R
72T-413R
Eddy, Martin
88BurlR/Pro-1775
Eddy, Steven Allen
(Steve)
76QuadC
80SLCty-17
Edelen, Benny Joe
(Joe)
77StPet
80ArkTr-1
82F-65
83Indianap-8
Eden, Edward Michael
(Mike)
75Phoen-16
76Phoen
79RochR-9
80RochR-12
Edens, Tom
83Butte-4
86Jacks/TCMA-4
87Tidew-9
87Tidew/TCMA-2
88Tidew/CANDL-19
88Tidew/CMC-5
88Tidew/Pro-1581
89Tidew/CMC-2
89Tidew/Pro-1956
Edge, Alvin
76BurlB
78BurlB
Edge, Claude Lee Jr.
(Butch)
76BurlB
78Syrac
79Syrac-9
80OPC-329R
80Richm-3
80T-674R
81Richm-11
82Portl-2
Edge, Greg
86Clearw-7
87Readg-4
88EastLAS/Pro-32
88Readg/Pro-880
89ElPas/GS-21
89Readg/Best-16
89Readg/Pro-666
Edgerton, Bill
No Cards.
Ediger, Lance
78Newar
Edler, David Delmar
(Dave)
80Spoka-15
81F-610
81Pol/Mariners-7
82Omaha-16
82T-711
83T-622
Edmonds, Bobby Joe
89Readg/Best-17
89Readg/Pro-673
89Readg/Star-10
Edmonds, Jim
89QuadC/Best-27
89QuadC/GS-6
Edmonds, Stan
82Wausa-4
Edmondson, Paul M.
(Paul)
70OPC-414
70T-414
Eduardo, Hector
77StPet
78StPet
79ArkTr-19
Edwards, Allen
82Madis-17
83Albany-2
Edwards, Bobby
88SLCty-11
Edwards, Charles B.
(Bruce)
47TipTop
48B-43
49B-206
49Eureka-34
50B-165
51B-116
51T/BB-42
52B-88
52NTea
52T-224
89Smok/Dodg-52
D305
Exh47
R346-26
Edwards, David L.
(Dave)
80T-657
81D-595
81F-568
81T-386
81T/Tr-758
82D-247
82T-151
83D-565
83F-357
83T-94
88Poca/Pro-2084
Edwards, Glenn
85Water-5
Edwards, Henry Albert
(Hank)
48L-72
49B-136
49Eureka-56
50B-169
52B-141
52T-176
53T-90
Edwards, Howard R.
(Doc)
62T-594R
63T-296
64T-174
65OPC-239
65T-239
79RochR-10
80RochR-13
81RochR-22
82Charl-23
83Charl-22
84Maine-10
85IntLgAS-24
85Maine-29
86OhHenry-CO
87Gator-CO
88Gator-32MG
88T-374
89T-534MG
Edwards, Jeff
86Ashvl-9
86AubAs-8
87Albuq/Pol-9
87Ashvl-25
87SnBer-3
88ColAst/Best-16
89Canton/Pro-1316
89Canton/Star-4
Edwards, John Alban
(Johnny)
62Kahn
62Salada-191
62Shirriff-191
62T-302
62T/St-114
63FrBauer-5
63J-132
63P-132
63T-178
64Kahn
64T-507
64Wheat/St-14
65Kahn
65MacGregor-3
65T-418
66Kahn
66T-507
67Kahn
67T-202
68T-558
69MLB/St-139
69OPC-186
69T-186
69T/St-33
70MLB/St-40
70OPC-339
70T-339
71MLB/St-79
71OPC-44
71T-44
72MB-96
72OPC-416
72T-416
73OPC-519
73T-519
74OPC-635
74T-635
Edwards, Jovon
86Bakers-6
Edwards, Larry
77BurlB
78BurlB
79BurlB-1
80Ander-5
81GlenF-24
Edwards, Marshall L.
78Holyo
79Vanco-4
80Vanco-19
82F-140
82T-333R
83D-406
83F-32
83Gard-6
83Pol/Brew-16
83T-582
84Cram/PCL-47
84D-490
84Nes/792-167
84T-167
Edwards, Michael L.
(Mike)
75Shreve/TCMA-2
76Shrev
79T-201M
79T-613
80OPC-158
80T-301
81D-497
Edwards, Todd
86Miami-6
Edwards, Wayne
86Penin-9
87DayBe-15
88BirmB/Best-1

89BirmB/Best-21
89BirmB/Pro-110
89SLAS-16
90F-652M

Effrig, Mark
83ElPas-7
84ElPas-1

Egan, Richard Joseph
(Joe)
14Piedmont/St-20
T202
T205
T206

Egan, Richard Wallis
(Dick)
63T-169R
64T-572R
66T-536
67T-539
89Smok/R-6CO

Egan, Thomas Patrick
(Tom)
65T-486R
66T-263
67OPC-147
67T-147
69T-407
70MLB/St-171
70OPC-4
70T-4
71OPC-537
71T-537
72MB-97
72OPC-207
72T-207
73OPC-648
73T-648
75OPC-88
75T-88
75T/M-88
77Wausa-MG

Eggertsen, Todd
86PalmSp-12
86PalmSp/Smok-16
87PalmSp-29
88MidldA/GS-9

Eggleston, Darren
88CharWh/Best-10

Eggleston, Skip
88Geneva/Pro-1639

Egins, Paul C. III
89BurlB/Pro-1625

Egloff, Bruce
87Watlo-15
89Watertn/Star-5

Ehmig, Greg
88SLCty-14

Ehmke, Howard J.
(Howard)
21Exh-42
21Exh-43
25Exh-65
28Exh-54
61F-21
88Conlon/5-9
E120
R316
V100
W573
WG7-15

Ehret, Philip S.
(Red)
N172

Ehrhard, Jim
88FtLaud/Star-6

Ehrhard, Rob
89PrWill/Star-7

Ehrhard, Rod
88Oneon/Pro-2072

Ehrhard, Ron
87Oneon-23

Eichelberger, Juan T.
79Hawai-21
80Hawai-4
81T-478
81T/St-97
82D-442
82F-570
82T-366TL
82T-614
83D-422
83F-358
83OPC-168
83T-168
83T/X-29
84D-398
84F-539
84Nes/792-226
84T-226
86Richm-5
87Richm/TCMA-4
88Richm/CMC-6
88Richm/Pro-10

Eichhorn, Dave
86Albuq-6
87SnAnt-20
88SnAnt/Best-13
89Albuq/CMC-6
89Albuq/Pro-61

Eichhorn, Mark A.
82Syrac-3
83Syrac-7
84Syrac-18
86D/Rook-13
86F/Up-U38
86S/Rook-38
86T/Tr-34T
86Tor/Fire-8
87D-321
87F-224
87F/GameWin-14
87F/Hottest-16
87F/Mini-36
87F/St-37
87Leaf-173CG
87Leaf-229
87OPC-371
87S-194M
87T-371
87T/Gloss60-49
87T/GlossRk-5
87T/St-187
87Tor/Fire-7
87Tor/Fire-7
87ToysRUs-10
88D-121
88F-108
88F/Mini-60
88Ho/Disc-18
88Leaf-74
88OPC-116
88Panini/St-212
88Score-198
88Sf-210
88T-749
88T/Big-208
88T/Revco-30
88Tor/Fire-38
89F-230
89OPC-274
89Richm/Pro-825
89Score-152
89T-274
89T/Big-188
90F-580
90T-513

Eiland, Dave
87Oneon-17
88Albany/Pro-1336
88EastLAS/Pro-1
89Colum/CMC-8
89Colum/Pol-3
89Colum/Pro-750
89D-481
89T-8
90Score-652

Eilers, David Louis
(Dave)
66T-534R
78TCMA-245

Eischen, Joe
89Butte/SP-13

Eisenreich, Charlie
87AppFx-15

Eisenreich, James M.
(Jim)
81Wisco-21
83T-197
87Memph-27
87Memph/Best-21
88D-343
88OPC-348
88Score-456
88Smok/Royals-26
88T-348
89D/Best-306
89F/Up-38
89Score-594
89T/Tr-28T
89UD-44
90D-238
90F-106
90Score-179
90Sf-166
90T-246
90UD-294

Eisenstat, Harry
40PB-204

Eklund, Troy
89Butte/SP-16

Elam, Scott
82Knoxv-2

Elam, Todd
88Batav/Pro-1682
89Spart/Pro-1028
89Spart/Star-7

Elberfeld, Norman A.
(Kid)
12Sweet/Pin-57A
12Sweet/Pin-57B
E107
E254
M116
S74-38
T201
T202
T204
T205
T206
T213/blue
T215/blue
T215/brown
T3-15
WG2-17

Elder, Isaac
89James/Pro-2147

Elders, Mike
76Clint

Eldred, Cal
90Score-669DC

Eldredge, Ted
88SnBer/Best-11
88SnBer/Cal-41
89Wausa/GS-9

Elenes, Larry
74Cedar

Elguezabal, Jose
78SnJos-7

Elia, Lee Constantine
(Lee)
66T-529R
67T-406
68T-561
69T-312
75IntAS/TCMA-26
75IntAS/TCMA-8
79OkCty
82RedLob
83D-614
83T-456
83Thorn-26MG
84Cram/PCL-200MG
87T/Tr-32T
88T-254

Elkin, Rick
80Batav-15
81Batav-11

Ellam, Roy
T206
T213/brown

Eller, Horace Owen
(Hod)
88Pac/8Men-93
W514-38

Ellerbe, Francis R.
(Frank)
E120
V100
V61-51
W573

Elli, Rocky
88Clmbia/GS-4

Ellingsen, H. Bruce
75OkCty
75OPC-288
75T-288
75T/M-288

Elliot, Corey
84Visal-7

Elliot, Lawrence L.
(Larry)
63T-407R
64T-536R
67OPC-23
67T-23

Elliot, Terry
88StPet/Star-6
89StPet/Star-10

Elliott, Clay
79Savan-11

Elliott, Donnie
88Martins/Star-12
89Batav/Pro-1925

Elliott, Glenn
43Centen-7
44Centen-6
45Centen-6
49Eureka-8

Elliott, Harry Lewis
(Harry)
55Hunters
55T-137

Elliott, James Thomas
(Jumbo)
33G-132
V354-6
W513-64

Elliott, John
86Ashvl-10
87Osceola-17
88ColAst/Best-13

Elliott, Mark
78Clint

Elliott, Randy Lee
(Randy)
78T-719R

Elliott, Robert I.
(Bob)
39Exh
48B-1
48L-65
49B-58
49Eureka-7
50B-20
50Drake-35
51B-66
51T/BB-32
52BR
52T-14
53Exh/Can-26
60T-215
D305
R346-38
R423-28

Ellis, Dock Phillip
(Dock)
69T-286
70T-551
71MLB/St-200
71OPC-2
71T-2
71T/Coins-99
72OPC-179
72OPC-180IA
72T-179
72T-180A
73OPC-575
73T-575
74OPC-145
74T-145
74T/St-82
75OPC-385
75T-385
75T/M-385
76OPC-528
76T-528
76T/Tr-528T
77K-4
77OPC-146
77T-71
78BK/R-6
78T-209
79T-691
80OPC-64
80T-117

Ellis, Doug
87Macon-15

Ellis, George W.
(Rube)
E254
E270/1
E286
E90/1
M116
T207

Ellis, John Charles
(John)
70OPC-516R
70T-516R
71MLB/St-487
71OPC-263
71T-263
72OPC-47
72OPC-48IA
72T-47
72T-48A
73OPC-656
74OPC-128
74T-128
74T/St-165
75Ho-54
75OPC-605
75T-605
75T/M-605
76Ho-27
76Ho/Twink-27
76OPC-383
76SSPC-515
76T-383
76T/Tr-383T
77T-36
78BK/R-3
78T-438
79T-539
80T-283
81D-26
82D-642
82F-316
82T-177

T73-656
Ellis, Robert Walter
(Rob)
76SSPC-240
77Spoka
79Tacom-23
80Port-5
Ellis, Rufus
86FSLAS-12
86FtMyr-9
87FtMyr-18
88CharlR/Star-6
Ellis, Samuel Joseph
(Sammy)
63T-29R
64T-33R
65Kahn
65T-507
66Kahn
66T-250
66T/RO
67Kahn
67OPC-176
67T-176
68T-453
69OPC-32
69T-32
78TCMA-293
80Colum-14
81Colum-26
82Colum-24M
Ellis, Tim
88Geneva/Pro-1643
Ellison, Darold
80Batav-18
Ellison, Jeff
76Dubuq
77Cocoa
Ellison, Paul
88Spart/Star-22
88Spart/Star-6
89Spart/Pro-1041
89Spart/Star-8
Ellsworth, Richard C.
(Dick)
60T-125
61T-427
61T/St-7
62T-264
62T/St-107
63T-399
64Bz-28
64T-1LL
64T-220
64T/Coins-56
64T/S-17
64T/St-5
64T/SU
64T/tatt
65OPC-165
65T-165
65T/E-67
66T-447
67T-359
68Coke
68T-406
69MB-78
69MLB/St-12
69T-605
70MLB/St-196
70OPC-59
70T-59
71MLB/St-435
71OPC-309
71T-309
72MB-98
Ellsworth, Steve
86NewBrit-10
87Pawtu-17
87Pawtu/TCMA-6
88D/RedSox/Bk-NEW
88D/Rook-54
88Score/Tr-83T
89Pawtu/CMC-7
89Pawtu/Dunkin-28
89Pawtu/Pro-704
89T-299
Elpin, Ralph
81Watlo-33
82Watlo/B-3
82Watlo/C-12
Elsea, Dottie
89Kingspt/Star-30
Elster, Kevin
84LitFalls-19
85Lynch-19
86Jacks/TCMA-13
87D-635
87F-7
87Tidew-32
87Tidew/TCMA-13
88Class/Red-190
88D-37
88D/Best-70
88D/Mets/Bk-37
88D/Rook-34
88F/U-U104
88Kahn/Mets-21
88Leaf-37RR
88Score-624
88Score/YS/II-40
88Sf/Gamewin-24
88T-8
88T/Mets/Fan-21
89B-383
89Class-75
89D-289
89D/Best-97
89F-34
89Kahn/Mets-21
89Panini/St-127
89Score-130
89Sf-71
89T-356
89T/Big-16
89T/JumboR-6
89Tidew/CANDL-15
89ToysRUs-7
89UD-269
90D-152
90F-202
90Score-443
90Sf-118
90T-734
90UD-187
Elston, Curt
C46-23
Elston, Donald Ray
(Don)
57T-376
58T-363
59T-520
60T-233
61P-200
61T-169
61T/St-8
62J-190
62P-190
62P/Can-190
62Salada-101
62Shirriff-101
62T-446
63T-515
64T-111
65T-436
78TCMA-143
Elston, Guy
82Nashv-11
83Colum-13
84Maine-13
Elvira, Narcisco
88Stock/Cal-183
88Stock/Pro-748
89Stock/Star-6
Elway, John
82Oneon-13
Elwert
E270/2
Embree, Charles W.
(Red)
52Mother-22
Embser, Rich
85Sprin-2
86ArkTr-7
Emery, Calvin Wayne
(Cal)
81Charl-24
89Vanco/CMC-21
89Vanco/Pro-572
Emmerke, R.
N172
Empting, Mike
83Clint/LF-15
Encarcion, Miguel
76BurlB
Encarnacion, Luis
86Water-8
87Wmspt-5
88Memph/Best-12
89Memph/Best-20
89Memph/Pro-1187
89Memph/Star-10
89SLAS-22
Ender, Scott
81Cedar-24
Engel, Bob
88Umpire-5
89Umpires-3
Engel, Steve
86D-510
86IowaC-10
88ArkTr/GS-3
Engelkin, Gary
88Jaxvl/Best-28
88Jaxvl/Pro-990
89James/Pro-2149
Engelmeyer, Bob
77DaytB
Engeln, William
55B-301ump
England, Dave
82ArkTr-23
83ArkTr-25
Engle, Arthur Clyde
(Hack)
10Domino-40
11Helmar-3
12Sweet/Pin-3A
12Sweet/Pin-3B
14Piedmont/St-21
D303
E106
E254
E90/1
M116
T205
T206
T207
T213/brown
T216
Engle, Ralph David
(Dave)
79Toled-7
80Toled-15
81T-328R
82D-102
82F-552
82T-738
83D-646
83T-294
84D-598
84F-562
84Nes/792-463
84T/St-313
85D-72
85F-276
85Leaf-173
85OPC-199
85T-667
85T/St-298
86D-438
86F-391
86F/Up-U39
86T-43
88OPC-196
88Score-617
88T-196
89Pol/Brew-25
Engle, Tom
89Kingspt/Star-8
89LittleSun-3
Englehart, Bill
84Greens-26
English, Elwood G.
(Woody)
28Exh-9
29Exh/4-6
30CEA/Pin-3
31Exh/4-6
32Orbit/num-32A
32Orbit/num-32B
32Orbit/un-18
33Exh/4-3
33G-135
34Exh/4-3
34G-4
35G-1F
35G-3D
35G-4D
35G-5D
37Exh/4-2
R305
R308-156
R308-193
R316
R332-18
V354-11
V354-50
WG8-15
Englishby, Steve
73Cedar
78DaytB
Englund, Tim
86Knoxv-7
87Knoxv-8
Engram, Duane
86Penin-10
Engram, Graylyn
87DayBe-21
Ennis, Alan
84Newar-8
Ennis, Delmar
(Del)
48L-49
49Eureka-134
49Lummis
50B-31
50Drake-21
51B-4
51BR-A10
51T/BB-4
52B-76
52BR
52NTea
52T-223
53B/Col-103
53Exh/Can-60
53RM-N17
54B-127
54Wilson
55B-17
56T-220
57T-260
58T-60
59T-255
79TCMA-18
89Pac/Leg-121
89Swell-19
D305
Exh47
PM10/Sm-48
R302
Enos, Dave
82Readg-13
Enos, Eric
88Batav/Pro-1671
Enright, George A.
(George)
82QuadC-26
84MidldC-15
Enriquez, Martin
82Wausa-15
83Wausa/LF-5
Enyart, Terry Gene
(Terry)
79Ogden/TCMA-1
80Ogden-8
Epley, Daren
89Kinston/Star-6
Eppard, Jim
84Albany-24
86Tacom-5
87Edmon-1
88Edmon/CMC-21
88Edmon/Pro-558
88F-645
88F/U-U13
89Edmon/CMC-14
89Edmon/Pro-548
89F-476
89Score-607
89T-42
89UD-614
Epple, Tom
82Sprin-8
83StPet-6
Epps, Riley
86Salem-7
Epstein, Michael P.
(Mike)
67T-204R
68T-358
69MB-79
69MLB/St-104
69T-461
69T-539M
69T/St-235
69Trans-25
70K-24
70MLB/St-282
70OPC-235
70T-235
70T/CB
71K-34
71MLB/St-535
71OPC-655
71T-655
71T/Coins-126
72MB-99
72T-715
73OPC-38
73T-38
73T/Lids-14
74OPC-650
74T-650
74T/St-142
78TCMA-261
Erardi, Joseph G.
(Joe)
77Holyo
Erautt, Edward L.S.
(Eddie)
49Eureka-82
52Mother-43
52T-171
53T-226
Erautt, Joseph M.
(Joe)
No Cards.

Erb, Gerry
77Newar
Erb, Mike
88PalmSp/Cal-86
88PalmSp/Pro-1443
89QuadC/Best-10
89QuadC/GS-14
Erdahl, Jay Michael
82Wausa-21
Erhardt, Herb
88Oneon/Pro-2046
89FtLaud/Star-3
Ericks, John
89B-433
89Savan/Pro-371
Erickson, Don
89Beloi/Star-3
Erickson, Eric G.
82Clint-22
86Fresn/Smok-14
87Lynch-7
Erickson, Harold J.
(Hal)
53Glen
Erickson, Henry Nels
(Hank)
R314/Can
Erickson, Roger F.
79Ho-94
79OPC-34
79T-81
80T-256
81D-549
81F-561
81OPC-80
81T-434
81T/St-105
82D-303
82F-553
82T-153
82T/St-211
82T/Tr-30T
83F-378
83T-539
87SanJose-23
89Louvl-17
89Louvl/CMC-3
89Louvl/Pro-1242
Erickson, Steve
87Oneon-8
88FtLaud/Star-7
89FtLaud/Star-4
Erickson, Tim
87Wausa-28
Ericson, E.G.
V100
Ericson, Mark
88Keno/Pro-1394
Ermer, Calvin C.
(Cal)
68T-206
70McDon-2
79Toled-3
80Toled-3
81Toled-1
82Toled-23
83Toled-23
84Toled-6
85Toled-26
Erskine, Carl Daniel
(Carl)
51B-260
52B-70
52T-250
53B/Col-12
53Briggs
54B-10
54NYJour
54RH
54RM-NL4
54SM
54Wilson
55B-170
55Gol/Dodg-8
55RM-NL14
55SM
56T-233
57T-252
58T-258
59T-217
60NuCard-69
61NuCard-469
79TCMA-146
88Pac/Leg-75
89Rini/Dodg-23
89Rini/Dodg-25
89Smok/Dodg-60
89Swell-44
PM10/Sm-49
Erwin, Ross Emil
(Tex)
10Domino-41
11Helmar-86
12Sweet/Pin-73
M116
T207
Erwin, Scott
88CapeCod/Sum-78
89Medford/Best-5
Erwin, Terry
75BurlB
Esasky, Nicholas A.
(Nick)
80Water-21
81Indianap-15
82Indianap-4
83Indianap-5
84D-602
84F-468
84Nes/792-192
84OPC-192
84T-192
84T/St-378YS
85D-121
85F-534
85Indianap-35
85OPC-253
85T-779
85T/St-51
86D-286
86F-177
86Leaf-162
86OPC-201
86T-677
86TexGold-12
87D-166
87F-201
87Kahn-12
87OPC-13
87T-13
88D-413
88D/Best-118
88F-233
88Kahn/Reds-12
88Leaf-240
88OPC-364
88Panini/St-274
88Score-163
88T-364
88T/Big-167
88T/St-137
89B-31
89D-189
89D/Best-284
89D/Tr-18
89F-161
89F/Up-9
89OPC-262
89Panini/St-72
89Score-64
89Score/Tr-37
89T-554
89T/Big-316
89T/St-134
89T/Tr-29T
89UD-299
89UD/Ext-757
90D-303
90F-273
90Score-91
90Sf-72
90T-206
90UD-463
Escalera, Carlos
86Beloi-5
86Cram/PCL-30
87AppFx-6
88BBCity/Star-11
88FSLAS/Star-34
89Memph/Best-10
89Memph/Pro-1182
89Memph/Star-11
Escalera, Ruben
87Stockton-14
88CalLgAS-17
88Stock/Cal-200
88Stock/Pro-735
89ElPas/GS-27
Escarrega, Chico E.
(Ernesto)
83D-291
83F-234
Eschen, Jim
77Evansvl/TCMA-9
89Kingspt/Star-26
Escobar, Angel
86Shrev-7
87Phoen-7
88Phoen/CMC-14
88Phoen/Pro-63
89Huntsvl/Best-25
Escobar, John
88Martins/Star-13
89Batav/Pro-1940
Escobar, Jose
80Utica-15
87Syrac-17
87Syrac/TCMA-13
88Knoxv/Best-13
Escobar, Oscar
86Ventura-6
87Myrtle-2
88Salem/Star-6
Escribano, Eddie
83Madis/LF-17
Eskew, Dan
88SoOreg/Pro-1711
89Modesto/Ch-10
Eskins, Mark
88Idaho/Pro-1856
Esmond, James J.
(Jimmy)
E270/2
Espinal, Josue
88SoOreg/Pro-1700
Espinal, Mendy
87Cedar-9
Espinal, Sergio
86Geneva-5
87Peoria-4
88Peoria/Ko-10
Espino, Francisco
88Geneva/Pro-1648
89Geneva/Pro-1860
89Peoria/Ko-3
Espino, Juan
79WHave-24
80Colum-28
81Colum-15
82Colum-23
82Colum/Pol-29
83Colum-3
84D-92
84Maine-17
85Colum-11
85Colum/Pol-9
85IntLgAS-32
86Colum-7
86Colum/Pol-7
87Colum-8
87Colum/Pol-8
87Colum/TCMA-10
87T-239
88Richm-29
88Richm/CMC-20
88Richm/Pro-7
Espinosa, Anulfo A.
(Nino)
77T-376
78T-197
79BK/P-11
79OPC-292
79T-566
80BK/P-17
80OPC-233
80T-447
81F-20
81T-405
89Tidew/CANDL-7
Espinosa, Philip
87Anchora-9
Espinosa, Santiago
86Cram/PCL-98
86QuadC-9
87QuadC-4
Espinoza, Alvaro
82Wisco-7
83Visal/LF-23
84Toled-3
85Toled-15
86Toled-9
87Portl-14
87T-529
88Colum/CMC-15
88Colum/Pol-15
88Colum/Pro-320
89D/Best-161
89F/Up-47
89Score/NWest-3
89T/Tr-30T
90D-245
90F-441
90Score-101
90T-791
90UD-163
Espinoza, Andres
85LitFalls-17
86QuadC-10
87PalmSp-31
Esposito, Nick
83TriCit-9
Esposito, Samuel
(Sammy)
57T-301
58T-425
59T-438
60T-31
61T-323
62T-586
63T-181
Espy, Cecil Edward
(Cecil)
81AppFx-14
82VeroB-22
86Hawai-5
87OKCty-16
88D/Rook-9
88F-465
88Moth/R-13
88Score/Tr-73T
88T/Tr-36T
89B-236
89Bz-7
89Class-143
89D-292
89D/Best-335
89F-517
89KMart/DT-6
89Moth/R-12
89Panini/St-443
89Score-401
89Score/YS/II-10
89Smok/R-7
89T-221
89T/Big-36
89T/Gloss60-59
89T/JumboR-7
89T/St-240
89T/St-320
89ToysRUs-8
89UD-92
90D-260
90F-295
90Score-69
90T-496
90UD-371
Espy, Duane
77Spoka
79BurlB-17
80BurlB-10
84Shrev/FB-7MG
86Phoen-5CO
87Phoen-22
88SanJose/Cal-141
88SanJose/Pro-125
89SanJose/Best-28
89SanJose/Cal-235
89SanJose/Pro-453
Esquer, David
89QuadC/Best-7
89QuadC/GS-25
Esquer, Mercedes
83Knoxv-4
Essegian, Charles A.
(Chuck)
58T-460
59T-278
60BB-11
60T-166
61T-384
62J-45
62P-45
62P/Can-45
62T-379
63J-71
63P-71
63T-103
Esser, Mark Gerald
(Mark)
80GlenF/B-14
80GlenF/C-5
Essian, James Sarkis
(Jim)
76SSPC-142
77T-529
78T-98
79OPC-239
79T-458
80OPC-179
80T-341
81Coke
81D-503
81F-593
81T-178
81T/Tr-759
82D-369
82F-341
82T-269
82T/Tr-31T
83D-478
83T-646
83T/St-117
83T/X-30
83Wheat/Ind-10
84D-629
84F-540
84F/X-35
84Moth/A's-19
84Nes/792-737
84T-737

84T/X-35
85F-423
85T-472
86WinSal-7MG
87Pittsf-4
88EastLAS/Pro-47
88Pittsf/Pro-1360
89CharlK-3

Estalella, Roberto M.
(Bobby)
W753

Esteban, Felipe
87VeroB-21
88VeroB/Star-6

Estelle, Richard H.
(Dick)
65OPC-282R
65T-282R
66T-373R

Estep, Chris
87Anchora-10
88Watertn/Puc-18
89Aug/Pro-499

Estepa, Ramon
81LynnS-21
82LynnS-14
83Chatt-5
84Chatt-3

Estepan, Rafael
80Clint-18

Esterbrook, Thomas J.
(Dude)
E223
N167
N172
N284
N690
WG1-31

Esterday, Henry
N172

Estes, Frank
(Doc)
78OrlTw
80OrlTw-9
81Toled-21
85IntLgAS-8
85Richm-18
86Richm-6
87Syrac-22
87Syrac/TCMA-22

Estes, Joel
86AubAs-9
87Osceola-20
89ColMud/Pro-128
89ColMud/Star-7

Estes, Marc
86Miami-7

Estevez, Juan
88Brist/Pro-1866

Estrada, Charles L.
(Chuck)
60T-126
61Bz-13
61P-73
61T-395
61T-48LL
61T/St-100
62J-36
62P-36
62P/Can-36
62Salada-212
62Shirriff-212
62T-560
62T/bucks
62T/St-4
63T-465
64T-263
65T-378
67T-537
73OPC-549CO
73T-549C
82Charl-24
85Cram/PCL-129
86Tacom-6
87Tacom-12
88Tacom/Pro-623
89Tacom/CMC-9
89Tacom/Pro-1564

Estrada, Eduardo
86NewBrit-11
87NewBrit-25
88EastLAS/Pro-21
88NewBrit/Pro-903
89NewBrit/Star-1
89Pawtu/CMC-23
89Pawtu/Pro-698

Estrada, Jay
87Spoka-5
88Charl/Pro-1213
89River/Best-4
89River/Cal-21
89River/Pro-1409

Estrada, Luis
79AppFx-16
81GlenF-1

Estrada, Manuel
(Manny)
78SnJos-22
79Spoka-25
80LynnS-13
81Spoka-29
82SLCty-23
83SLCty-25
84Butte-1

Estrada, Peter
88Elmir-8
89WinHav/Star-6

Etchandy, Curt
76AppFx

Etchebarren, Andy
66OPC-27R
66T-27R
67T-457
68Coke
68T-204
69MB-80
69MLB/St-3
69T-634
70MLB/St-159
70OPC-213
70T-213
71MLB/St-296
71OPC-501
71T-501
72MB-100
72OPC-26
72T-26
73JP
73OPC-618
73T-618
74OPC-488
74T-488
75OPC-583
75T-583
75T/M-583
76OPC-129
76T-129
77T-454
78T-313
86Pol/Brew-8C

Etchebarren, Ray
84Beaum-24

Etheredge, Jeff
89Batav/Pro-1917

Etheridge, Bobby L.
(Bobby)
68OPC-126
68T-126
69T-604
70OPC-107
70T-107

Etten, Nicholas R.
(Nick)
41DP-123
44Yank/St-10
48Signal
48Smith-4

Ettles, Mark
89NiagFls/Puc-8

Etzweiler, Dan
88Myrtle/Pro-1177

Eubanks, Larry
77Cocoa

Eufemia, Frank
83Visal/LF-11
85Toled-6
86D-513
86F-392
86T-236
86Toled-10

Eusebio, Tony
88Osceola/Star-9
89ColMud/Best-15
89ColMud/Pro-125
89ColMud/Star-8

Evans, Alfred Hubert
(Al)
48L-22
49B-132
50B-144
51B-38
52T-152

Evans, Barry Steven
(Barry)
81F-499
81OPC-72DP
81T-72
82D-271
82F-571
82T-541
83Colum-19
85Maine-18
86Maine-8

Evans, Darrell
70T-621R
72OPC-171
72OPC-172IA
72T-171
72T-172A
73OPC-374
73T-374
74OPC-140
74T-140
74T/DE-2
74T/St-3
75Ho-3
75Ho/Twink-3
75OPC-475
75T-475
75T/M-475
76Ho-24
76Ho/Twink-24
76OPC-81
76SSPC-9
76T-81
77T-571
78T-215
79Ho-64
79OPC-215
79Pol/Giants-41
79T-410
80OPC-81
80Pol/Giants-41
80T-145
81D-192
81F-436
81OPC-69
81T-648
81T/St-235
82D-398
82F-388
82OPC-17
82T-17
82T/St-112
83D-251
83F-258
83Moth/Giants-9
83OPC-329
83T-448
83T/St-305
84D-431
84F-372
84F/St-3
84F/X-36
84FunFood/Pin-117
84Moth/Giants-27
84Nes/792-325
84OPC-325
84T-325
84T/Gloss40-11
84T/St-163
84T/X-36
85Cain's-6
85D-227
85D/HL-51
85F-6
85Leaf-215
85OPC-319
85Seven-3D
85T-792
85Wendy-7
86Cain's-4
86D-369
86F-224
86F/St-36
86OPC-103
86Quaker-24
86S-183M
86S-189
86T-515
86T/3D-7
86T/Gloss60-60
86T/Mini-13
86T/St-165
86T/St-269
86T/Super-21
86Woolwth-9
87Cain's-6
87Coke/Tigers-13
87D-398
87D/OD-210
87F-150
87F/LL-16
87OPC-265
87S-132
87Seven-DT2
87T-265
87T/St-264
88Woolwth-3
88D-250
88D/Best-35
88F-54
88KayBee-9
88KingB/Disc-12
88Leaf-173
88OPC-390
88OPC-E
88Panini/St-441
88Panini/St-89
88Pep/T-41
88Pol/T-5
88Score-75
88Sf-188
88T-630
88T/Big-82
88T/Mini-10
88T/St-265
88T/St-8
88T/WaxBox-E
89B-275
89D-533
89Score-171
89Score/Tr-65
89T/Tr-31T
89T/WaxBox-C
89UD-394
90F-581
90Score-302
90T-55
90UD-143

Evans, Duane
82Lynch-13

Evans, Dwight Michael
(Dwight)
73OPC-614R
73T-614R
74OPC-351
74T-351
75Ho-18
75Ho/Twink-18
75K-38
75OPC-255
75T-255
75T/M-255
76Ho-87
76OPC-575
76SSPC-408
76T-575
77Ho-21
77OPC-259
77T-25
78Ho-54
78PapaG/Disc-24
78T-695
79Ho-33
79K-41
79OPC-73
79T-155
80OPC-210
80T-405
81Coke
81F-232
81OPC-275
81T-275
81T/HT
82Coke/BOS
82D-109
82Drake-11
82Drake-45
82F-293
82F/St-167
82OPC-355
82T-162LL
82T-355
82T/St-135
82T/St-153
82T/St-4LL
83D-452
83D-7DK
83D/AAS-2
83Drake-7
83F-183
83OPC-135
83T-135
84D-395
84F-397
84FunFood/Pin-62
84Nes/792-720
84OPC-244
84T-720
84T/St-219
85D-294
85D/AAS-15
85Drake-10
85F-158
85F/St-40
85Leaf-150
85OPC-271
85Seven-8E
85T-580
85T/St-212
85T/Super-33
86D-249
86Drake-2
86F-348
86F/Mini-74
86Leaf-127
86OPC-60
86S-32
86T-396M

86T-60
86T/Mini-5
86T/St-251
86T/Super-22
86Woolwth-10
87D-129
87D/HL-33
87D/OD-184
87F-34
87F/LL-17
87F/Mini-37
87F/St-38
87F/WS-9M
87Leaf-57
87OPC-368
87S-128
87T-3RB
87T-645
87T/Board-7
87T/HL-21
87T/St-20WS
87T/St-251
87T/St-4
87Woolwth-21
88D-16DK
88D-216
88D/AS-23
88D/Best-84
88D/DKsuper-16DK
88D/RedSox/Bk-216
88F-351
88F-C2
88F/AwardWin-11
88F/BB/MVP-12
88F/LL-11
88F/Mini-6
88F/St-8
88F/WaxBox-C2
88KayBee-10
88Leaf-16DK
88Leaf-171
88OPC-221
88Panini/St-25
88RedFoley/St-21
88Score-65
88Sf-137
88T-470
88T/Big-6
88T/Coins-11
88T/Coins-42
88T/Gloss60-21
88T/Mini-3
88T/Revco-24
88T/St-245
88T/St/Backs-50
88T/UK-22
89B-35
89Class-44
89D-240
89D/Best-121
89F-87
89F/Excit-12
89KayBee-10
89OPC-205
89Panini/St-279
89RedFoley/St-40
89Score-193
89Score/HotSt-8
89Sf-204
89T-205
89T/Big-193
89T/Gloss60-36
89T/Mini-47
89T/St-252
89T/St/Backs-15
89T/UK-24
89UD-366
90Class-77
90D-122
90F-274
90Score-3
90Score/100St-54
90Sf-217
90T-375
90UD-113

Evans, Frank
85Louvl-3

Evans, Freeman
76Clint

Evans, Gary
82Beloi-17

Evans, Jim
77Clint

Evans, Jim
88Umpire-13
89Umpires-11

Evans, John
79BurlB-15
80BurlB-25
81ElPas-21
82Tacom-16

Evans, Louis Richard
10Domino-42
11Helmar-168
12Sweet/Pin-146
14CJ-128
15CJ-128
E254
M116
S74-118
T202
T205
T206
T207
T213/blue

Evans, Mike
82Wausa-22
84Chatt-1
87Erie-17
88Hamil/Pro-1734
89Hamil/Star-29

Evans, Phil
89SLCty-25

Evans, Randy
80GlenF/B-4
80GlenF/C-15
81GlenF-2

Evans, Richard (Dr.)
82IowaC-32

Evans, Rick
(Bubba)
76AppFx
77Charl
78Salem
80Buffa-8

Evans, Rob
87Tidew-29

Evans, Russell Edison
(Red)
39PB-159

Evans, Scott
87Miami-4
88Hagers/Star-5

Evans, Tony
83Tampa-4

Evans, Tory
89SnBer/Cal-65

Evans, Van
85PrWill-25
86Kinston-6

Evans, William L.
(Billy)
21Exh-44UMP
61F-22
80SSPC/HOF
89HOF/St-100

Evaschuk, Brad
88StCath/Pro-2010

Eveline, William
(Billy)
86AppFx-7
87DayBe-18
88Tampa/Star-6
89QuadC/Best-26
89QuadC/GS-30

Everett, Smokey
81Wisco-3
82Orlan-4

Evers, Bill
83Greens-28
86Clint-7CO
87Clint-17
88Clint/Pro-712
89Shreve/Pro-1838

Evers, John Joseph
(Johnny)
10Domino-43
11Helmar-94
12Sweet/Pin-82
14CJ-118
15CJ-118
40PB-174
48Exh/HOF
50Callahan
60Exh/HOF-10
60F-57
61F-23
63Bz/ATG-21
69Bz/Sm
72F/FFeat-7
75F/Pion-17
80SSPC/HOF
BF2-50
D303
D304
D327
D328-45
D329-54
D350/2-55
E101
E102
E105
E106
E121/80
E122
E135-45
E254
E270/1
E90/3
E91
E92
E93
E94
E95
E98
L1-134
M101/4-54
M101/5-55
M116
PM1-5
S74-60
S81-109
T201
T202
T204
T205
T206
T213/blue
T213/brown
T215/blue
T216
V100
W555
W575
WG5-16
WG6-15

Evers, Troy
87FtLaud-4
88Albany/Pro-1340

Evers, Walter Arthur
(Hoot)
47TipTop
48L-78
49B-42
50B-41
51B-23
51FB
51T/CAS
52B-111
52StarCal/L-71H
52StarCal/L-72C
52T-222
53B/Col-25
54B-18
55Esskay
79TCMA-264
Exh47
R302-123

Everson, Gregory
88FSLAS/Star-35
88Lakel/Star-10
89London/Pro-1380

Ewart, Ron
86WinSal-8

Ewing, William
(Buck)
50Callahan
75F/Pion-3
80SSPC/HOF
89HOF/St-57
E223
N172
N284
N29
N300/unif
N338/2
N403
N43
WG1-38

Ewing, Bill
76QuadC
79SLCty-13

Ewing, George L.
(Long Bob)
E103
M116
S74-100
T204
T205
T206
WG3-18

Ewing, Jim
84Evrt/Cram-10B

Ewing, John
(Long John)
N172

Ewing, Samuel James
(Sam)
77OPC-221
78OPC-112
78Syrac
78T-344
79OPC-271
79T-521
81AppFx-28

Ezell, Glenn
86Ventura-7MG
87Knoxv-23
88Omaha/CMC-25
88Omaha/Pro-1503

Faatz, Jay
N172

Fabbro, Arthur
52Park-55
53Exh/Can-45

Faber, Dick
52Mother-28

Faber, Urban
(Red)
21Exh-45
28Yueng-4
30CEA/Pin-14
33G-79
40PB-230
61F-24
80SSPC/HOF
88Pac/8Men-96
89HOF/St-61
BF2-12
D327
D328-46
D329-55
D350/2-56
E120
E121/120
E121/80
E126-6
E135-46
E210-4
E220
M101/4-55
M101/5-56
R316
V100
V353-54
V61-14
W501-48
W502-4
W514-69
W515-60
W572
W573
W575

Faccio, John
89Beloi/Star-4
89Star/Wax-4

Faccio, Luis
85Bend/Cram-6
88PrWill/Star-8
89Sprin/Best-7

Face, Elroy
53T-246
54T-87
56T-13
57Kahn
57T-166
58Hires-59
58Kahn
58T-74
59Kahn
59T-339
59T-425M
60Kahn
60L-16
60T-115M
60T-20
60T/tatt
60T/tatt-14
60T/tatt-89
61Kahn
61P-133
61T-250M
61T-370
61T/St-62
62J-177
62P-177
62P/Can-177
62Salada-174
62Shirriff-174
62T-210
62T-423M
62T/St-175
63F-57
63J-147
63P-147
63T-409
64T-539
65T-347
66EH-26
66T-461
67OPC-49
67T-49
67T/Test/PP-8
68KDKA-26
68T-198
69OPC-207
69T-207
72Laugh/GF-26
78TCMA-5
89Pac/Leg-178

89Swell-51
Faedo, Len
80OrlTw-10
81Charl-12
82T-766R
83F-611
83T-671
84Evans-10
84F-563
84Nes/792-84
84T-84
84T/St-310
Fagan, Pete
87StPet-26
Fagan, William
N172
Fagnano, Phil
88Spart/Pro-1032
Faherty, Sean
83AlexD-18
84PrWill-3
Fahey, Bill
72OPC-334R
72T-334R
73OPC-186
73T-186
74OPC-558
74T-558
75OPC-644
75T-644
75T/M-644
76OPC-436
76SSPC-259
76T-436
77T-511
78Cr/PCL-67
78T-388
80OPC-23
80T-44
81D-361
81F-490
81T-653
81T/Tr-760
82T-286
83D-281
83T-196
85Tulsa-28CO
89T-351TL
Fahr, Gerald
52Park-23
Fahrow, Bryant
75QuadC
Fain, Ferris
48B-21
49B-9
49Royal-24
50B-13
51T/RB-3
52B-154
52BR
52Dix-53
52NTea
52RM-AL7
52Royal
52StarCal/L-76B
52T-21
52TipTop
53T-24
54B-214
54RH
54RM-AL22
54T-27
54Wilson
55T-11
55T/DH-116
Exh47
Fairchild, Glenn
86Watlo-6
87Watlo-25
88Kinston/Star-5
Fairey, Jim
68T-228R
69MLB/St-157
69OPC-117
69T-117
71MLB/St-126
71OPC-474
71T-474
72T-653
73OPC-429
73T-429
85SpokAT/Cram-5
Fairly, Ron
59T-125
60DF-21
60T-321
61T-492
62BB-6
62T-375
62T/St-134
63T-105
64T-490
64T/Coins-54
65OldLond-8
65OPC-196
65T-196
65T/E-2
66Bz-20
66T-330
66T/RO-18
67Bz-20
67OPC-94
67T-94
68T-510
68T/3D
69MB-81
69MLB/St-146
69MLBPA/Pin-42
69OPC-122
69T-122
69T/St-43
70MLB/St-65
70T-690
70T/PI-10
71LaPizza-3
71MLB/St-127
71OPC-315
71T-315
71T/Coins-83
72MB-101
72OPC-405
72T-405
73OPC-125
73T-125
74K-27
74OPC-146
74T-146
74T/St-53
75OPC-270
75T-270
75T/M-270
76OPC-375
76SSPC-276
76T-375
77T-127
78OPC-40
78T-85
79T-580
Falcone, Dave
84CharO-16
85RochR-4
87CharO/WBTV-36
87SLAS-1
Falcone, Pete
76OPC-524
76T-524
76T/Tr-524T
77Ho-24
77OPC-177
77T-205
78T-669
79OPC-36
79T-87
80T-401
81D-395
81F-327
81OPC-117
81T-117
82D-380
82F-524
82T-326
83D-182
83F-541
83Pol/Atl-33
83T-764
83T/X-31
84D-385
84F-177
84Nes/792-521
84OPC-51
84Pol/Atl-33
84T-521
85T-618
Falk, Bibb A.
21Exh-46
25Exh-74
26Exh-75
28Exh-38
29Exh/4-22
31Exh/4-22
39Yueng
61F-104
E120
E121/120
E210-39
V100
V61-15
W501-41
W502-39
W572
W573
W575
Falkenburg, Frederick (Cy)
14CJ-20
15CJ-20
M116
T201
Falkner, Richard
88BurlR/Pro-1773
89Kinston/Star-7
89Star/Wax-75
Fallon, Robert
81GlenF-3
85BuffB-17
85F/Up-U39
Falls, Bobby
86ColumAst-12
Falzone, Jim
87Miami-2
Fannin, Cliff
47TipTop
48L-123
49B-120
50B-106
51B-244
51T/BB-36
52T-285
53T-203
Fanning, Jim
82D-492
82Hygrade
85OPC-267MG
85T-759
Fanning, Steve
88Hamil/Pro-1739
89Savan/Pro-363
Fanok, Harry
62Kahn/Atl
63T-54R
64T-262R
Fanovich, Frank
49Eureka-83
52Park-84
54Esskay
Fansler, Stan
85Nashua-8
86Hawai-7
87Vanco-7
88BuffB/CMC-2
88BuffB/Pro-1469
Fanzone, Carmen
73OPC-139
73T-139
74OPC-484
74T-484
75OPC-363
75T-363
75T/M-363
Faria, Joe
47Smith-25
Faries, Paul
87Spoka-17
88CalLgAS-43
88River/Cal-217
88River/Pro-1422
89AubAs/Pro-18
89Wich/Roc-22
89Wich/Roc/HL-17
89Wich/Roc/Up-3
Fariss, Monty
88Butte-22
88Tulsa-3
89B-233
89T-177FDP
89Tulsa/GS-8
Farkas, Ron
82Indianap-24
Farley, Bob
61Union
62T-426
Farley, Brian
83Erie-10
87Sprin/Best-20
Farmar, Damon
83QuadC-25
87MidldA-14
Farmer, Al
86Salem-8
Farmer, Billy
70OPC-444R
70T-444R
Farmer, Bryan Pierce
87Greenv/Bst-16
88Greenv/Best-13
89Richm/CMC-8
89Richm/Ko-12
89Richm/Pro-834
Farmer, Ed
72OPC-116
72T-116
73OPC-272
73T-272
74OPC-506
74T-506
80T-702
81Coke
81D-40
81F-339
81F/St-114
81OPC-36
81T-37
81T/HT
81T/SO-54
81T/St-64
82D-482
82F-342
82OPC-328
82T-328
82T/Tr-32T
83D-471
83F-161
83T-459
84Cram/PCL-247
86Hawai-8
Farmer, Gordon
88AubAs/Pro-1970
89Ashvl/Pro-953
Farmer, Howard
87Jamestn-24
88MidwLAS/GS-46
88Rockford-12
89Jaxvl/Best-12
89Jaxvl/Pro-155
89Rockford-12
Farmer, Ken
86LitFalls-10
Farmer, Kevin
87Spoka-14
88River/Cal-218
88River/Pro-1408
89River/Best-5
89River/Cal-7
89River/Pro-1412
Farmer, Reggie
87Spoka-11
88Charl/Pro-1216
89Watlo/Pro-1796
89Watlo/Star-5
Farmer, William
N172
Farnsworth, Mark
82CharR-23
83CharR-26
85FtMyr-21
86FtMyr-10TR
87FtMyr-31
Faron, Robert J.
87Sprin/Best-11
88ArkTr/GS-9
Farr, Jim
80Tulsa-7
83OKCty-22
84Cram/PCL-9
Farr, Michael
86Watlo-7
87Kinston-15
88Wmspt/Pro-1307
Farr, Steve
78Charl
80Buffa-7
81Buffa-18
82Buffa-13
84Maine-4
84Wheat/Ind-27
85D-653
85F-446
85T-664
86D-588
86NatPhoto-26
86T/Tr-35T
87D-301
87F-367
87OPC-216
87T-473
87T/St-255
88D-378
88F-256
88Score-466
88Smok/Royals-10
88T-222
89B-114
89D-356
89D/Best-151
89F-281
89OPC-356
89Panini/St-349
89Score-183
89T-507
89T/St-272
89Tastee/Discs-12
89UD-308
90D-356
90F-107
90Score-356
90T-149
90UD-680
Farrar, Sid
N172

N284
N690
WG1-50

Farrell, Charles A.
E107
N172

Farrell, Dick
(Turk)
58Hires-43
58T-76
59T-175
60T-103
61P-115
61T-522
61T/St-54
62Salada-184
62Shirriff-184
62T-304
62T/bucks
62T/St-125
63Bz-8
63Exh
63F-38
63J-192
63P-192
63Pep
63Salada-2
63T-277
63T-9LL
63T/SO
64Bz-8
64T-560
64T/Coins-91
64T/S-22
64T/St-98
64T/SU
65OldLond-9
65OPC-80
65T-80
66T-377
67OPC-190
67T-190
68T-217
69MB-82
69T-531
78TCMA-202
78TCMA-256
86Moth/Ast-1
89Smok/Ast-8
Exh47

Farrell, Edward S.
(Doc)
26Exh-33
29Exh/4-1
33G-148
V353-73

Farrell, John A.
N172
N284

Farrell, John
85Water-21
86Water-9
87BuffB-15
88CapeCod/Sum-76
88Class/Blue-239
88D-42
88D/Best-117
88F-608
88Gator-52
88Leaf-42RR
88Score-620
88Score/YS/I-33
88Sf-132
88T-533
88T/Big-213
89B-74
89D-320
89D/Best-285
89F-403
89OPC-227
89Panini/St-318
89Score-266
89Sf-37
89T-227
89T/Big-135
89T/St-214
89UD-468
90D-232
90F-491
90Score-103
90T-32
90UD-570

Farrell, Mike
76AppFx

Farrow, Doug
82Idaho-6

Farson, George
78Holyo
79Holyo-8
80Penin/C-11C

Farwell, Fred
87Bakers-20

Fascher, Stan
86Ashvl-11
87Osceola-11

Fassero, Jeff
86FSLAS-13
86StPet-8
87ArkTr-6
88ArkTr/GS-5
89Louvl-18
89Louvl/CMC-4
89Louvl/Pro-1246

Fassero, John
85Sprin-9

Fast, Darcy
72OPC-457R
72T-457R

Faszholz, John
55Hunter

Fator, Laverne
33SK-13

Faul, Bill
63T-558R
64T-236
66T-322

Faulk, James
88Rockford-13
89Rockford-13

Faulk, Kelly
80Penin/B-6
80Penin/C-13
82Readg-2
85Colum-6
85Colum/Pol-10
86Colum-8
86Colum/Pol-8
87Indianap-24

Faulkner, Craig
88Hagers/Star-6
89Hagers/Best-14
89Hagers/Pro-266
89Hagers/Star-7

Faust, Nancy
84TrueVal/WS-12
85Coke/WS-org
86Coke/WS-org
87Coke/WS-28
88Coke/WS-6
89Coke/WS-29

Fava, Andres
85Anchora-10

Fazekas, Robert
88CapeCod/Sum-160

Fazio, Ernie
63Pep
78TCMA-215

Fazzini, Frank
86Beloi-6

Fears, Tom
52Wheat

Feder, Mike
76Wausa

Federici, Rick
78Charl
80Buffa-3

Federico, Gustavo
89Helena/SP-14

Federico, Joe
87Anchora-11
88Hamil/Pro-1738
89StPet/Star-11

Federoff, Al
53Mother-62

Fedor, Chris
84Greens-11

Fedor, Fritz
82Beloi-9
83Beloi/LF-24
86BurlEx-7
87Kinston-10

Feeley, James
82Madis-20

Feinburg, Ken
77Cedar
78Cedar

Felda, Brian
75Cedar

Felden, Keith
88Utica/Puc-18
89Mia/Star/25-6

Felder, Mike
83ElPas-9
84ElPas-23
85Cram/PCL-211
86D-634
86Pol/Brew-16
87D-295
87T-352
88D-397
88F-164
88Pol/Brew-16
88Score-388
88T-718
89Pol/Brew-16
89T-263
89UD-252
90D-609
90F-321
90Score-268
90T-159
90UD-178

Felice, Jason
83Tampa-8
86Jacks/TCMA-20
87Tidew-7

Feliciano, Felix
80Utica-5

Felix, Antonio
89Aug/Pro-510

Felix, Junior
87Myrtle-21
88SLAS-24
89D/Best-199
89D/Rook-55
89F/Up-69
89Score/Tr-83
89Syrac/CMC-19
89Syrac/Pro-810
89T/Tr-32T
89UD/Ext-743
90Class-50
90D-70
90F-79
90Score-258
90Score/100Ris-18
90Sf-186
90T-347
90UD-106

Felix, Nick
89Wausa/GS-16

Felix, Paul
83Wisco/LF-6
85Orlan-4
86GlenF-4
87GlenF-19
88Toled/CMC-20
88Toled/Pro-600

Felix, Sanchez
88Knoxv/Best-2

Feliz, Adolfo
81Water-13
82Cedar-15
83Tampa-9
83Water-11

Feller, Bob
37Exh/4-11
37OPC-120
38Dix
38Exh/4-11
38G-264
38G-288
38ONG/Pin-8
38Wheat
39Exh
40Wheat
41DP-78
48B-5
48L-93
48Swell-19
49B-27
50B-6
50NumNum
51B-30
51T/RB-22
51Wheat
52B-43
52BR
52NumNum-5
52RM-AL8
52StarCal/L-74E
52T-88
52Wheat
53B/Col-114
53Exh/Can-17
53T-54
54B-132
54DanDee
54Wilson
55B-134
55Gol/Ind-6
55Salem
56T-200
60F-26
60NuCard-60
61F-25
61NuCard-460
72Laugh/GF-44
79TCMA-28
80Cram/Leg-53
80SSPC/HOF
81Watlo-34
82CJ-10
83D/HOF-36
83MLBPA/Pin-6
84West/1-10
86S/Dec-16
87Nestle/DT-20
88Pac/Leg-101
89HOF/St-62
89Pac/Leg-156
89Swell-75
D305
PM10/Sm-50
PM10/Sm-51
PR1-8
R302-103
R303/A
R303/B
R326-8A
R326-8B
R342-8
R346-43
R423-31
V300

Fellows, Mark
82Madis-14
83Albany-3

Felsch, Oscar
(Happy)
88Pac/8Men-10
88Pac/8Men-109
88Pac/8Men-41
88Pac/8Men-55M
88Pac/8Men-76
D327
D328-47
D329-56
D350/2-57
E135-47
M101/4-56
M101/5-57
W514-3

Felske, John
73OPC-332
73OPC-45
73T-332
77Spoka
79Vanco-20
82Readg-22
83Portl-13
85T/Tr-33T
86T-621
87T-443MG

Felt, Jim
82AlexD-24
83AlexD-22
84PrWill-5

Felt, Rich
82VeroB-5
83VeroB-3

Felton, Fred
88Batav/Pro-1686

Felton, Terry
79Toled-9
80Toled-7
81Toled-4
83D-354
83F-612
83T-181
83Toled-2

Felton, Todd
88Spart/Pro-1043

Fendrick, Dave
74Gasto

Fennell, Mike
82Oneon-14
83Greens-18
85Albany-26

Fennelly, Francis
N172

Fenwick, Bob
72T-679R
73OPC-567
73T-567

Feola, Lawrence
(Larry)
75Clint
87SanJose-22

Ferguson, George
10Domino-44
12Sweet/Pin-66
E254
E270/1
E286
M116
T204
T205
T206

Ferguson, Alex
E126-40

Ferguson, Bruce
78Wausa

Ferguson, Charles
N172
N284
N690

Ferguson, Fergy
83Tampa-10

Ferguson, Greg
88SoOreg/Pro-1708
Ferguson, Jim
82Oneon-15
88Savan/Pro-348
89Savan/Pro-354
Ferguson, Joe
72T-616
73OPC-621
73T-621
74OPC-86
74T-86
74T/DE-67
74T/St-45
75OPC-115
75T-115
75T/M-115
76OPC-329
76SSPC-81
76T-329
77OPC-107
77T-573
78BK/A-2
78Ho-109
78T-226
79T-671
80OPC-29
80Pol/Dodg-13
80T-51
81D-177
81F-124
81Pol/Dodg-13
81T-711
82T-514
83D-604
83F-87
83T-416
87Smok/R-24CO
Ferguson, Mark
83Albany-4
84Greens-19
85Albany-6
Ferguson, Mike
82Cedar-8
Ferlenda, Greg
86Salem-9
86Tulsa-15
88Kinston/Star-6
89Canton/Best-14
89Canton/Star-5
89Kinston/Star-8
Ferm, Ed
88Brist/Pro-1886
Fermin, Felix
84PrWill-16
85Nashua-9
86Hawai-9
87Harrisbg-6
88BuffB/CMC-21
88BuffB/Pro-1465
88D-144
88F-643
88T-547
89D-565
89D/Best-229
89D/Tr-33
89F-208
89F/Up-27
89Score-620
89Score/Tr-78
89T-303
89T/Tr-33T
89UD-88
90D-191
90F-492
90Score-256
90T-722
90UD-409
Fermin, Pompilio
76Clint
Fernandes, Eddie
47Sunbeam
Fernandez, Chris
87Tampa-22
Fernandez, Dan
89SanJose/Best-8
89SanJose/Cal-232
89SanJose/Pro-441
89SanJose/Star-9
Fernandez, Frank
66T-584R
68T-214R
69T-557
70OPC-82
70T-82
71MLB/St-512
71OPC-468
71T-468
72MB-102
Fernandez, Froilan
(Nanny)
47TipTop
49Royal-23
Fernandez, Humberto
(Chico)
55B-270
57T-305
58Hires-16
58Hires/T
58T-348
59T-452
60T-314
61T-112
61T/St-150
62J-17
62P-17
62P/Can-17
62Salada-3
62Shirriff-3
62T-173
63T-278
79TCMA-274
88Cedar/Pro-1141
Fernandez, James
88StPet/Star-7
Fernandez, Joey
89StPet/Star-12
Fernandez, Jose
89Hamil/Star-11
Fernandez, Julio
89Clint/Pro-900
Fernandez, Reynaldo
88Oneon/Pro-2053
88PrWill/Star-9
Fernandez, Sid
82VeroB-6
84D-44
84Tidew-2
85D-563
85F-77
85OPC-390
85T-649
85Tidew-3
86D-625
86F-79
86KayBee-10
86Leaf-242
86T-104
86T/Mini-51
87Class-74
87D-323
87D/AAS-26
87D/HL-4
87F-629M
87F-8
87F/Lim-16
87F/Slug-13
87Leaf-93
87OPC-337
87S-63
87T-570
87T/Mini-22
87T/St-97
88D-118
88D/AS-58
88D/Mets/Bk-118
88F-134
88F/BB/MVP-13
88F/St-101
88Kahn/Mets-50
88Leaf-63
88OPC-30
88Panini/St-336
88RedFoley/St-22
88Score-615
88Sf-177
88T-30
88T/Mets/Fan-50
88T/St-103
88T/St/Backs-28
89B-377
89D-471
89F-35
89Kahn/Mets-50
89OPC-34
89Score-268
89T-790
89T/Big-276
89T/Mini-25
89UD-168
90D-572
90F-203
90Score-18
90Sf-113
90T-480
90UD-261
Fernandez, Tony
82Syrac-17
83Syrac-16
84D-32
84F-152
84Syrac-9
84Tor/Fire-11
85D-390
85F-103
85Leaf-91
85OPC-48
85OPC/Post-16
85T-48
85Tor/Fire-10
86Ault-1
86D-119
86F-57
86F/Mini-14
86F/St-37
86KayBee-11
86Leaf-45
86OPC-241
86S-112
86T-241
86T/St-194
86Tor/Fire-9
87Class-57
87D-72
87D/AAS-35
87D/OD-35
87F-225
87F/AS-3
87F/AwardWin-12
87F/Mini-38
87F/RecSet-7
87F/St-39
87Leaf-106
87OPC-329
87RedFoley/St-29
87S-113M
87S-187
87T-485
87T/Mini-75
87T/St-191
87Tor/Fire-8
87Tor/Fire-8
88Bz-7
88D-12DK
88D-319
88D/AS-25
88D/Best-87
88D/DKsuper-12DK
88F-109
88F-635M
88F/BB/MVP-14
88F/Hottest-10
88F/Mini-61
88F/SS-C3
88F/St-72
88Ho/Disc-21
88Leaf-12DK
88Leaf-133
88OPC-290
88Panini/St-222
88Score-20
88Score-651
88Score/YS/II-6
88Sf-26
88T-290
88T/Big-187
88T/Coins-12
88T/Gloss60-15
88T/St-193
88T/St/Backs-43
88T/UK-23
88Tor/Fire-1
89B-254
89Class-115
89D-206
89D/Best-48
89F-231
89F/Superstar-13
89OPC-170
89Panini/St-470
89RedFoley/St-41
89Score-57
89Score/HotSt-53
89Sf-93
89T-170
89T/Big-157
89T/Coins-39
89T/Gloss60-52
89T/Mini-76
89T/St-189
89T/St/Backs-10
89T/UK-25
89Tor/Fire-1
89UD-139
90D-149
90F-634M
90F-80
90Score-89
90Sf-6
90T-685
90UD-130
Ferran, Alex
89Watertn/Star-6
Ferran, George
86Shrev-8
87Phoen-4
Ferrante, Joe
82DayBe-3
Ferrara, Al
64T-337R
65T-331R
66T-487
67T-557
68T-34
69NTF
69T-452
69T/DE-30
70T-345
70T/CB
71T-214
Ferrara, Al
68OPC-34
69MLB/St-191
69T/St-93
70MLB/St-113
70OPC-345
71MLB/St-226
71OPC-214
71T/Coins-25
72MB-103
Ferrarese, Don
55T-185
56T-266
57T-146
58T-469
59T-247
60T-477
61T-558
62T-547
Ferraro, Carl
86CharRa-9
Ferraro, Mike
68T-539R
69OPC-83
69T-83
72T-613
77WHave
78Cr/PCL-119
83T/X-32
83Wheat/Ind-11MG
Ferraro, Vincent
84Visal-5
Ferrebee, Anthony
87Idaho-2
Ferreira, Arturo J.
(Jose)
85Madis-13
85Madis/Pol-10
Ferreira, Tony
82FtMyr-11
84Omaha-3
85Omaha-10
86Tidew-8
87Calgary-20
88Albany/Pro-1339
Ferreiras, Sal
86PrWill-10
Ferrell, Frank
75Cedar
Ferrell, Rick
31Exh/4-30
33Exh/4-15
33G-197
34DS-48
34Exh/4-9
35BU-10
35BU-126
35Exh/4-9
35G-8G
35G-9G
36Exh/4-9
36G
37Exh/4-9
37OPC-132
38Exh/4-16
39PB-39
40PB-21
61F-105
R310
R312/M
R314
V300
W753
WG8-17
Ferrell, Wes
31Exh/4-21
33CJ/Pin-5
33DH-14
33Exh/4-11
33G-218
34DS-94
34Exh/4-11
35BU-12
35BU-174
35G-8G
35G-9G
37OPC-138
38Exh/4-16
61F-26
88Conlon/3-11

R300
R306
R308-162
R311/Leath
R314
R332-21
V300
V355-40

Ferrer, Sergio
76OkCty
78Tidew
79T-397
80T-619
80Tidew-5
81Indianap-31

Ferretti, Sam
88Watlo/Pro-680
89Canton/Pro-1307
89Kinston/Star-9

Ferreyra, Raul
77Indianap-19
78Indianap-21

Ferrick, Tom
39Exh
51B-182
60T-461C

Ferris, Albert
(Hobe)
E107
E254
E270/1
E270/2
T204
T206
WG2-18

Ferris, Bob
76QuadC
78Cr/PCL-60
79SLCty-10
80SLCty-24
81SLCty-5

Ferris, David
(Boo)
47TipTop
49B-211

Ferro, Bob
83Wisco/LF-11

Ferroni, Frank
81Miami-14

Ferry, John
11Helmar-159
T207

Ferson, Alexander
N172

Ferst, Larry
78Clint

Fessenden, Wallace
N172

Fette, Lou
38Wheat
PR1-9

Fetters, Michael
86Cram/PCL-97
87PalmSp-26
88MidldA/GS-10
89Edmon/CMC-9
90D-35
90F-131
90T-14

Fewster, Wilson
(Chick)
25Exh-81
26Exh-12
27Exh-6
E121/120
E220
W501-120
W575

Fiala, Mike
86Bakers-7

Fiala, Neil
78StPet
79ArkTr-13
82Indianap-29

Fiala, Walter
52Park-67
53Exh/Can-48

Fichman, Mal
79Newar-6
88Boise/Pro-1632

Fick, Barry
85Cedar-7

Fick, Chuck
82WHave-11

Ficklin, Winston
81Watlo-29
82Watlo/B-15
82Watlo/C-19
83Watlo/LF-18
85Water-4
86Water-10
87Wmspt-3
88Portl/CMC-18
88Portl/Pro-652
89IowaC/CMC-21
89IowaC/Pro-1711

Fidler, Andy
89Kingspt/Star-9

Fidrych, Mark
77Ho-46
77K-26
77OPC-115
77OPC-7LL
77Pep-30
77T-265
77T-7LL
77T/CS-15
78BK/T-4
78OPC-235
78PapaG/Disc-32
78T-45
78Wiffle/Discs-21
79Ho-77
79OPC-329
79T-625
80Evans-6
80OPC-231
80T-445
81D-8
81Evans-4
81F-462
81OPC-150
81T-150
83Pawtu-7
88Pac/Leg-62

Fiedler, Mark
86LitFalls-11

Field, Greg
79Portl-3
83Richm-5
84Toled-18

Field, James
E254

Fielder, Cecil
86Ault-23
86D-512
86F-653M
86OPC-386
86T-386
86Tor/Fire-10
87F/U-U31
87OPC-178
87T-178
87Tor/Fire-9
87Tor/Fire-9
88D-565
88F-110
88OPC-21
88Score-399
88T-618
88Tor/Fire-23
89D-442
89F-232
89OPC-224
89Score-120
89T-541
89UD-364

Fields, Bruce
82BirmB-11
83SanJose-14
86Nashv-8
87D-47RR
87Leaf-47RR
87Toled-14
87Toled/TCMA-9
88Moth/Sea-16
89Calg/CMC-19
89Calg/Pro-534
89Score/HotRk-43
89T-556
89UD-238

Fields, John James
N172

Fields, Wilmer
52Park-21

Fiene, Lou
T206

Fiepke, Scott
86Nashua-6

Fierro, John
80Penin/B-24tr
80Penin/C-10tr
86Peoria-6

Fife, Dan
74OPC-421
74T-421

Figuerda, Fernando
87PrWill-22

Figueroa, Alexis
89Watlo/Pro-1774
89Watlo/Star-6

Figueroa, Bienvenido
86Erie-7
87Sprin/Best-22
88ArkTr/GS-6
89Louvl-19
89Louvl/CMC-17
89Louvl/Pro-1262

Figueroa, Ed
75OPC-476
75T-476
75T/M-476
76OPC-27
76SSPC-190
76T-27
76T/Tr-27T
77BK/Y-5
77K-42
77OPC-164
77T-195
78BK/Y-5
78T-365
78T/Zest-3
79BK/Y-11
79OPC-13
79T-35
80OPC-288
80T-555
81F-624
81T-245
81Tacom-32
82Tacom-10

Figueroa, Fernando
88FtLaud/Star-8
89Mia/Star/22-4

Figueroa, Jesus
77WHave
80Wichi-9
81D-556
81T-533

Figueroa, Ray
88Geneva/Pro-1637

Figueroa, Rich
80Clint-23
81Clint-28

Figueroa, Vic
86Modesto-9

Filer, Thomas
79WHave-11
81Colum-24
82IowaC-15
83IowaC-3
83T-508
84IowaC-28
85Syrac-6
86D-439
86F-58
86Leaf-211
86OPC-312
86T-312
86Tor/Fire-11
88Denver/CMC-10
88Denver/Pro-1257
88T/Tr-37T
89F-185
89T-419
90D-687
90F-322

Filippi, James
86AppFx-8
87SnBer-10

Filkey, Bernard
89ArkTr/GS-6

Filkins, Les
81Evans-19
82Evans-19

Fillingim, Dana
21Exh-47
E120

Filson, Pete
82Colum-9
82Colum/Pol-30
82Toled-26
84D-194
84F-564
84Nes/792-568
84T-568
85D-607
85F-277
85T-97
86BuffB-11
86D-436
86F-393
86T-122
87Colum-29
87Colum/Pol-9
87Colum/TCMA-3

Fimple, Jack
81Watlo-18
82VeroB-14
83Albuq-11
84Cram/PCL-146
84D-372
84F-99
84Nes/792-263
84Pol/Dodg-31
84T-263
85Cram/PCL-163
86Albuq-7
87Edmon-23

Finch, Joel
79T-702R
80T-662R
81Pawtu-1

Finch, Steve
77Ashev
79Tulsa-6
81Spoka-11
82SLCty-8
84Cram/PCL-106
85MidldA-13
86Edmon-8

Findlay, Bill
88Gasto/Pro-997

Fine, Tom
89Penin/Star-5

Fine, Tommy
48Sommer-4

Fingers, Bob
87Modesto-18

Fingers, Rollie
69T-597R
70OPC-502
70T-502
71MLB/St-513
71OPC-384
71T-384
72OPC-241
72T-241
73OPC-84
73T-84
74OPC-212
74T-212
75Ho-52
75Ho/Twink-52
75K-55
75OPC-21
75OPC-463WS
75T-21
75T/M-21
76Ho-104
76OPC-405
76SSPC-480
76T-405
77Ho-137
77K-51
77OPC-52
77T-523
78Ho-144
78OPC-201
78OPC-8LL
78T-140
78T-208LL
78Wiffle/Discs-22
79OPC-203
79T-8LL
80BK/PHR-3
80OPC-343
80T-651
81D-2
81F-485
81F/St-47
81OPC-229
81T-229
81T-8LL
81T/St-31M
81T/Tr-761
82D-28
82F-141
82F-644M
82F/St-132
82K-7
82KMart-40
82OPC-176
82OPC-44
82Pol/Brew
82Pol/Brew-34
82Sqt-11
82T-168LL
82T-585
82T-586A
82T/St-16
82T/St-198
83D-2DK
83D-78
83D/AAS-33
83F-33
83Gard-7
83K-2
83OPC-35
83OPC-36SV
83Pol/Brew-34
83T-35
83T-36A
83T/St-79
83T/St/Box-6
84D-LLA
84D/Champs-45

84F-199
84FunFood/Pin-10
84Gard-6
84Nes/792-495
84Nes/792-717LL
84Nes/792-718LL
84OPC-283
84Pol/Brew-34
84T-495
84T-717
84T-718
85D-292
85D/AAS-36
85D/HL-2
85F-581
85Gard-6
85Leaf-190
85OPC-182
85Pol/Brew-34
85T-750
85T/St-285
85Woolwth-10
86D-229
86F-486
86OPC-185
86S-146M
86S-150M
86S-65M
86T-185
86T/St-198
87Moth/A's-10
88Pac/Leg-103

Finigan, Jim
55Armour-5
55RFG-17
55Rodeo
55T-14
55T/DH-50
56Rodeo
56T-22
56T/Pin-12
57T-248
58T-136
59T-47
79TCMA-128

Finigan, Kevin
87BurlEx-13
88James/Pro-1915

Fink, Eric
84PrWill-11

Finken, Steve
88GreatF-15
89Bakers/Cal-205

Finley, Bob
45Centen-7

Finley, Brian
83Beloi/LF-18
86ElPas-10
88Chatt/Best-13

Finley, Chuck
86QuadC-11
87D-407
87F-79
87Smok/Cal-6
87T-446
88D-530
88D/Best-283
88F-489
88Smok/Angels-15
88T-99
88T/Big-254
89B-36
89D-226
89D/Best-333
89F-477
89Score-503
89T-708
89T/Big-76
89UD-632
90D-344
90F-132
90Score-380
90Score/100St-24
90Sf-172
90T-147
90UD-667

Finley, David
88Modesto-23
88Modesto/Cal-70

Finley, Steve
88AAA/Pro-29
88Hagers/Star-7
88RochR-7
88RochR/Gov-7
89B-15
89D/Rook-47
89F/Up-3
89French-10
89RochR/Pro-1639
89Score/Tr-95
89UD/Ext-742
90D-215
90F-176
90Score-339
90Score/100Ris-58
90T-349
90UD-602

Finn, Neal (Mickey)
28Exh/PCL-7
33DH-15

Finney, Lou
40PB-197
41PB-30
R314
V355-64

Fiore, Mike Jr.
88T/Tr-38T
89Sprin/Best-1
89T/Big-8

Fiore, Mike
69T-376R
70T-709
71MLB/St-318
71OPC-287
71T-287
72MB-104
72OPC-199
72T-199
78Colum

Fiore, Tom
86Kenosha-9tr

Fiorillo, Nicholas
80Water-1
82Water-10
83Tampa-27

Fireovid, Steve
81Hawai-13
82Hawai-13
84Cram/PCL-214
85BuffB-18
86Calgary-8
87F-653M
87Syrac-6
87Syrac/TCMA-30
87T-357
88Omaha/CMC-4
88Omaha/Pro-1513
89Omaha/CMC-3
89Omaha/Pro-1718

Firova, Dan
80Spoka-22
86Calgary-9
89UD-32

Fischback, Bruce
86Kinston-7tr

Fischer
N172

Fischer, Brad
82Madis-19
83Madis/LF-31MG
84Madis/Pol-1MG
85Huntsv/BK-25MG
88Tacom/Pro-622
89Tacom/CMC-25
89Tacom/Pro-1551

Fischer, Carl
43Centen-8
44Centen-7
45Centen-8

Fischer, Dan
81Omaha-7
82Omaha-4

Fischer, Hank
63T-554
64T-218
65T-585
66T-381
67T-342
67T/Test/RSox-5

Fischer, Jeff
86FSLAS-14
86WPalm-15
87Indianap-15
88Indi/CMC-6
88Indi/Pro-503
89Albuq/CMC-3
89Albuq/Pro-86
90Score-654

Fischer, Todd
82Idaho-7
83Madis/LF-4
84Albany-12
86Edmon-9

Fischer, Tom
89B-20
89Lynch/Star-8

Fischer, William C.
58T-56
59T-230
60T-76
61T-553
63T-301
64T-409
72Laugh/GF-47

Fischer, William C.
D328-48
D329-57
D350/2-58
E135-48
M101/4-57
M101/5-58
W514-27

Fischetti, Art
75Water

Fischlin, Mike
78Charl
79Charl-6
79T-718R
80Tucso-17
81Charl-13
82Wheat/Ind
83D-489
83F-407
83T-182
83Wheat/Ind-12
84F-541
84Nes/792-689
84T-689
84Wheat/Ind-22
85D-495
85F-447
85Polar/Ind-22
85T-41
86F/Up-U40
86T-283
87F-98
87Richm/TCMA-12
87T-434
88Greenv/Best-23
88Richm-4
89Myrtle/Pro-1465

Fishel, John
86FSLAS-15
86Osceola-8
87ColAst/Pro-12
87ColumAst-12
88F/U-U88
88Tucso-11
88Tucso/CMC-19
88Tucso/Pro-178
89Colum/CMC-18
89Colum/Pol-4
89Colum/Pro-735
89D-443
89F-358
89Panini/St-80
89Score/HotRk-42

Fisher, Brian
77Newar
82Durhm-17
84Richm-20
85Colum-7
85Colum/Pol-11
85F/Up-U40
86D-492
86F-104
86KayBee-12
86S-177M
86T-584
86T/Gloss60-30
86T/St-312
87D-340
87F-99
87F/U-U32
87OPC-316
87T-316
87T/Tr-33T
88D-415
88D/Best-101
88F-329
88Leaf-244
88OPC-193
88Panini/St-368
88Score-130
88T-193
88T/Big-159
89B-415
89D-126
89F-209
89OPC-303
89RedFoley/St-42
89Score-24
89T-423
89UD-69
90Score-547
90T-666
90UD-97

Fisher, Eddie
60T-23
61T-366
63T-223
63T-6LL
64T-66
65T-328
66Bz-47
66OPC-85
66T-222LL
66T-85
66T/RO-22
67T-434
68T-418
69T-315
69T/St-143
70OPC-156
70T-156
71MLB/St-343
71OPC-631
71T-631
72T-689
73OPC-439
73T-439

Fisher, Frederick
(Fritz)
64T-312R
66T-209R

Fisher, Glen
81Shrev-6
82Redwd-20

Fisher, Jack H.
60T-399M
60T-46
61T-463
62T-203
63T-474
64T-422
65OPC-93
65T-93
66T-316
66T/RO-6
67Kahn
67T-533
68T-444
69T-318
70T-684
89Clmbia/Best-23
89Clmbia/GS-2

Fisher, Kyle
89Aug/Pro-521

Fisher, Ray
11Helmar-42
14CJ-102
15CJ-102
88Pac/8Men-92
D328-49
D329-58
D350/2-59
E135-49
M101/4-58
M101/5-59
T205
T207

Fisher, Robert
C46-43

Fisk, Carlton
72OPC-79R
72T-79R
73K-27
73OPC-193
73T-193
73T/Lids-15
74K-5
74OPC-105
74OPC-331AS
74T-105
74T-331M
74T/DE-64
74T/St-133
75Ho-143
75OPC-80
75T-80
75T/M-80
76Crane-14
76Ho-64
76MSA/Disc
76OPC-365
76SSPC-403
76T-365
77Ho-104
77OPC-137
77Pep-22
77T-640
78OPC-210
78PapaG/Disc-25
78T-270
78Wiffle/Discs-23
79Ho-106
79OPC-360
79T-680
80K-41
80OPC-20
80T-40
81D-335
81Drake-32
81F-224
81F/St-58
81MSA/Disc-12
81OPC-116
81T-480
81T/HT
81T/St-46

81T/Tr-762
82D-20DK
82D-495
82Drake-12
82F-343
82F/St-183
82K-25
82OPC-110
82OPC-111IA
82OPC-58AS
82Sqt-8
82T-110
82T-111A
82T-554
82T/St-138
82T/St-170
83D-104
83D/AAS-43
83F-235
83F-638
83K-56
83OPC-20
83OPC-393AS
83T-20
83T-393
83T/Gloss-17
83T/Gloss40-17
83T/St-177
83T/St-54
84D-302
84D/Champs-52
84F-58
84F/St-39
84FunFood/Pin-72
84MiltBrad-9
84Nes/792-216TL
84Nes/792-560
84OPC-127
84Ralston-33
84Seven-12C
84T-560
84T/Cereal-33
84T/Gloss40-40
84T/St-243
84T/Super-15
84T/Super-15
84TrueVal/WS-13
85Coke/WS-72
85D-208
85F-513
85GenMills-17
85Leaf-155
85OPC-49
85T-1RB
85T-770
85T/St-243
86Coke/WS-72
86D-366
86D/AAS-17
86D/PopUp-17
86F-204
86F-643M
86F/LimEd-15
86F/LL-12
86F/Mini-43
86F/St-38
86F/WaxBox-C8
86Jay's-7
86Leaf-163
86Meadow/Blank-3
86Meadow/Stat-13
86OPC-290
86OPC-E
86S-125
86S-67M
86S/Dec-62M
86T-290
86T-719
86T/Gloss22-9
86T/Gloss60-28
86T/Mini-11
86T/St-162
86T/St-286
86T/Super-23
86T/WaxBox-E
87Class-41
87Coke/WS-27
87D-247
87D/OD-232
87F-496
87F/RecSet-8
87Leaf-199
87OPC-164
87RedFoley/St-41
87S-140
87Seven-C7
87T-756
87T/St-288
88Coke/WS-8
88D-260
88D/Best-67
88F-397
88F/AwardWin-12
88KingB/Disc-18
88Leaf-208
88Nestle-38
88OPC-385
88Panini/St-55
88RedFoley/St-23
88Score-592
88Sf-43
88T-385
88T/Big-197
88T/Mini-8
88T/St-290
89B-62
89Cadaco-17
89Coke/WS-8
89D-101
89D-7DK
89D/Best-11
89D/DKsuper-7DK
89F-495
89KayBee-11
89OPC-46
89Panini/St-304
89RedFoley/St-43
89Score-449
89Score/HotSt-39
89Score/Mast-9
89Sf-219
89T-695
89T/Big-24
89T/Coins-40
89T/DH-8
89T/St-299
89T/St/Backs-23
89T/UK-26
89UD-609
90Class-116
90D-58
90D/Bon/MVP-BC19
90F-530
90Score-290
90Score/100St-70
90Sf-204
90T-392AS
90T-420
90UD-367

Fitzgerald, Dave
89Beloi/Star-5

Fitzgerald, Ed
47Signal
47Sunbeam
49B-109
49Eureka-159
50B-178
52B-180
52T-236
53Briggs
54B-168
55B-208
56T-198
57T-367
58T-236
59T-33
60T-423
gerald, Kevin
86Cram/PCL-1

Fitzgerald, Matthew
E254
E270/1

Fitzgerald, Mike P.
85Sprin-11
87ArkTr-21
87TexLgAS-26
88Louvl-19
88Louvl/CMC-18
88Louvl/Pro-427
89Louvl-20
89Louvl/CMC-18
89Louvl/Pro-1259

Fitzgerald, Mike R.
82Tidew-4
83Tidew-2
84D-482
84F/X-37
84T/X-37
85D-238
85F-78
85F/Up-U41
85OPC-104
85OPC/Post-1
85T-104
85T/St-108
85T/St-372YS
85T/Tr-34T
86D-97
86F-247
86Leaf-32
86OPC-313
86Provigo-26
86T-503
87D-345
87F-317
87Leaf-222
87OPC-212
87Smok/NL-14
87T-212
88D-159
88F-182
88Ho/Disc-6
88Leaf-81
88OPC-386
88Panini/St-322
88Score-318
88T-674
88T/St-78
89D-456
89F-374
89OPC-23
89Score-511
89T-23
89UD-133
90D-392
90F-343
90Score-361
90T-484
90UD-558

Fitzmorris, Al
70OPC-241R
70T-241R
71OPC-564
71T-564
72OPC-349
72T-349
72T/Cloth-10
73OPC-643
73T-643
74OPC-191
74T-191
75OPC-24
75T-24
75T/M-24
76A&P/KC
76Ho-8
76Ho/Twink-8
76OPC-144
76SSPC-160
76T-144
77T-449
78T-227
79Hawai-17
79T-638

Fitzpatrick, Dan
84Newar-7
86Beloi-7
87Stockton-6
88CalLgAS-11
88Stock/Cal-187
88Stock/Pro-745
89Stock/Best-12
89Stock/Cal-151
89Stock/Pro-395

Fitzpatrick, Edward
C46-70
T201

Fitzpatrick, Gary
83LynnP-27

Fitzpatrick, John
54T-213

Fitzsimmons, Fred
31Exh/4-10
33Exh/4-5
33G-130
33G-235
35BU-72
35G-8A
35G-9A
39PB-110
40PB-65
41DP-143
52B-234
60T-462C
R315-A6
R315-B6
R316
V354-20
V355-14
WG8-16

Fix, Greg
86Cram/PCL-91
87QuadC-17

Flack, Max
25Exh-60
D329-59
D350/2-60
E120
E121/120
M101/4-59
M101/5-60
V100
W501-117
W573

Flagstead, Ira
21Exh-48
25Exh-66
26Exh-65
27Exh-33
28Exh-33
87Conlon/2-34
E120
E121/120
E210-21
W501-7
W514-1
W573

Flaherty, John
55B-272ump

Flaherty, John
88Elmir-13
89WinHav/Star-7

Flaherty, Patrick
E254

Flammang, Chris
81Spoka-1

Flanagan, James
T206

Flanagan, Mike
76OPC-589R
76T-589R
77T-106
78Ho-134
78OPC-231
78T-341
79K-48
79OPC-76
79T-160
80K-3
80OPC-335
80T-640
81D-234
81F-171
81F/St-56
81K-60
81OPC-10
81T-10
82D-329
82F-165
82F/St-145
82OPC-153
82T-520
82T/St-148
83D-105
83F-60
83OPC-172
83T-445
83T/St-25
84D-169
84F-8
84F/St-63
84Nes/792-295
84OPC-295
84T-295
84T/St-12LCS
84T/St-210
85D-88
85F-177
85Leaf-175
85OPC-46
85T-780
85T/St-207
86D-576
86F-275
86S-57M
86T-365
87D-459
87F-470
87OPC-112
87T-748
88D-636
88D/Best-272
88F/U-U67
88OPC-164
88Score-427
88T-623
88Tor/Fire-46
89B-241
89D-324
89D/Best-316
89F-233
89OPC-139
89RedFoley/St-44
89Score-475
89T-139
89T/Big-243
89T/St-190
89Tor/Fire-46
89UD-385
90D-324
90F-81
90Score-67
90T-78
90UD-483

Flanigan, Thomas
N172

Flannery, John
76QuadC
79Knoxv/TCMA-10
82BirmB-15

Flannery, Kevin
81AppFx-4
82AppFx-21
83Toled-3
Flannery, Tim
80Hawai-19
80T-685R
81F-493
81T-579
82D-61
82F-572
82T-249
83D-472
83F-359
83T-38
84D-202
84F-299
84Moth/Padres-12
84Nes/792-674
84Smok/Padres-9
84T-674
85D-551
85F-31
85Moth/Padres-20
85T-182
86D-383
86F-320
86OPC-387
86T-413
86T/St-112
87Bohem-11
87D-287
87F-413
87OPC-52
87T-763
87T/St-114
88Coke/Padres-11
88D-328
88F-582
88OPC-262
88Panini/St-404
88Score-483
88Smok/Padres-8
88T-513
88T/St-108
89B-457
89D-364
89Score-513
89T-379
89T/Big-174
89UD-603
Flater, John
E254
Fleita, Oneri
89Freder/Star-6
Fleming, Jack
77DaytB
80Tucso-7
Fleming, Keith
87Stockton-20
88Stock/Cal-185
88Stock/Pro-725
89ElPas/GS-7
Fleming, Les
49Eureka-160
Fleming, Paul
82Wisco-8
Fleshman, Richard
77WHave
Fletcher, Arthur
11Helmar-127
21Exh-49
40PB-125
44Yank/St-11
61F-106
87Conlon/2-32
88Conlon/4-11
D304
D327
D328-50
D329-60
D350/2-61
E120
E135-50
E220
M101/4-60
M101/5-61
M116
S74-86
T202
T205
T206
T207
T213/brown
T222
V61-107
W514-14
W516-14
W573
WG4-8
Fletcher, Bob
89GreatF-27
89Saraso/Star-5
Fletcher, Darrin
88SnAnt/Best-15
89Albuq/CMC-18
89Albuq/Pro-58
90Score-622
Fletcher, Don
76Clint
Fletcher, Elburt
39PB-69
40PB-103
41DP-150
41G-26
41PB-62
47TipTop
49Eureka-9
R314
Fletcher, Mitch
80Tulsa-26
Fletcher, Paul
88Martins/Star-14
89Batav/Pro-1921
Fletcher, Scott
82D-554
82IowaC-2
84D-452
84F-59
84Nes/792-364
84T-364
84T/St-250
84TrueVal/WS-14
85Coke/WS-1
85D-330
85F-514
85T-78
85T/St-240
86D-282
86D/HL-28
86F-205
86F/Up-U41
86OPC-187
86Rangers-1
86T-187
86T/Tr-36T
87Class/Up-118
87D-304
87D/OD-171
87F-123
87F/AwardWin-13
87Leaf-226
87Moth/Rang-6
87S-113M
87S-136
87Smok/R-13
87T-462
87T/St-237
88D-11DK
88D-180
88D/Best-32
88D/DKsuper-11DK
88F-466
88F/Mini-54
88F/St-63
88Leaf-11DK
88Leaf-155
88Moth/R-6
88OPC-345
88Panini/St-206
88RedFoley/St-24
88Score-251
88Sf-77
88Smok/R-10
88T-345
88T/Big-19
88T/St-241
89B-230
89Cadaco-18
89D-142
89D/Best-167
89F-518
89F/Superstar-14
89Moth/R-13
89OPC-295
89Panini/St-454
89Score-78
89Score/Tr-47
89Sf-185
89Smok/R-8
89T-295
89T/Big-205
89T/St-246
89UD-420
90D-455
90F-531
90Score-58
90Sf-220
90T-565
90UD-310
Fletcher, Van
(Guy)
46Sunbeam
47Signal
47Sunbeam
Flick, Elmer
80SSPC/HOF
89HOF/St-53
E107
E254
E270/1
M116
T206
WG2-19
Flinn, Geoff
89Butte/SP-15
Flinn, John
79T-701R
81T-659R
81Vanco-21
82RochR-2
83RochR-3
85CharO-24
87CharO/WBTV-25
Flinn, Mike
82Madis-4
Flint, Frank S.
E223
N172
N284
WG1-12
Floethe, Chris
72OPC-268R
72T-268R
Flood, Curt
58T-464
59T-353
60L-141
60T-275
61P-178
61T-438
61T/St-86
62J-166
62P-166
62P/Can-166
62Salada-139
62Shirriff-139
62T-590
63J-162
63P-162
63T-162M
63T-505
64T-103
64T/Coins-65
64T/St-28
64T/tatt
65T-415
66OPC-60
66T-60
67OPC-63M
67T-245
67T-63M
68Bz-11
68OPC-180
68T-180
68T/3D
69Kelly/Pin-5
69MB-83
69MLB/St-210
69MLBPA/Pin-43
69OPC/DE-5
69T-426AS
69T-540
69T/DE-28
69T/S-59
69T/St-114
70K-48
70MLB/St-87
70OPC-360
70T-360
71MLB/St-536
71OPC-535
71T-535
71T/S-41
72MB-105
78TCMA-240
Flood, Thomas J.
N172
Flora, Kevin
88QuadC/GS-5
89QuadC/Best-6
89QuadC/GS-11
Florence, Donald
88WinHav/Star-8
89WinHav/Star-8
Florence, Paul
V355-177
Flores, Adalberto
76BurlB
77BurlB
77Newar
Flores, Alex
87Greens-18
Flores, Gil
77SLCty
78Cr/PCL-40
78T-268
80T-478
80Tidew-6
81Tidew-11
82Tidew-7
83Tidew-22
84Tidew-7
Flores, Jose
85Greens-23
86Greens-5
Flores, Norberto
(Bert)
85VeroB-12
86Bakers-8
Flores, Willi
82Wisco-21
Florie, Bryce
89CharRa/Pro-983
Flower, George
86WPalm-16
Flowers, Bennett
55B-254
Flowers, D'Arcy
(Jake)
29Exh/4-3
31Exh/4-3
33G-151
V353-81
Flowers, Kim
85Evrt/Cram-5A
85Evrt/Cram-5B
87Clint-16
88Fresno/Cal-11
88Fresno/Pro-1223
Flowers, Perry
86Clint-8
Flowers, Willie
78Newar
Floyd, Chris
88Myrtle/Pro-1173
Floyd, Robert
(Bobby)
69T-597R
70OPC-101
70T-101
71MLB/St-415
71OPC-646
71T-646
72OPC-273
72T-273
72T/Cloth-11
74OPC-41
74T-41
80LynnS-4MG
81LynnS-24
82SLCty-24
83SLCty-24
84Cram/PCL-191
85Cram/PCL-78MG
86Lynch-9
Floyd, Stan
77Charl
Floyd, Tony
88SoOreg/Pro-1707
Flynn, Bob
75AppFx
76AppFx
Flynn, David
88CapeCod/Sum-13
Flynn, Errol
88Pulas/Pro-1758
Flynn, John A.
(Jocko)
N172
Flynn, John Anthony
12Sweet/Pin-136
D322
M116
S74-109
T205
Flynn, R. Doug
76OPC-518
76SSPC-37
76T-518
77T-186
78T-453
79Ho-81
79OPC-116
79T-229
80OPC-32
80T-58
81Coke
81D-394
81F-330
81OPC-311
81T-634
81T/HT
81T/SO-93
81T/St-192
82D-427
82F-525
82F/St-87
82OPC-302
82T-302

82T/St-70
82T/Tr-33T
83D-240
83F-282
83OPC-169
83Stuart-7
83T-169
84D-254
84F-274
84Nes/792-749
84OPC-262
84Stuart-29
84T-749
84T/St-97
85D-463
85F-397
85Leaf-257
85OPC-112
85T-554
85T/St-93
86Cain's-5
86T-436

Fobbs, Larry
78LodiD
81Albuq/TCMA-15
82Albuq-16

Fodge, Gene
58T-449

Fogarty, James
N172
N284
N29
N43
N690
WG1-51

Fogg, Kevin
76Baton

Foggie, Cornell
89Watertn/Star-7

Fohl, Lee
V100
V117-5

Folles, Hank
52Park-85
53T-252
55Gol/Ind-7
57T-104
58Hires-71
58Kahn
58T-4
59T-294
60T-77
61T-277
62T-112
63T-326
64T-554

Folt, Jim
83Tulsa-20

Foldman, Harry
(Hal)
49Sommer-29

Foley, Bill
77Newar
78BurlB
79Holyo-3
82ElPas-6

Foley, Jack
83Tampa-11

Foley, Jim
88Modesto-9
89Madis/Star-8

Foley, Joe
87Anchora-12

Foley, Keith
86WPalm-17
88Vermont/Pro-948

Foley, Mark
87Penin-4

Foley, Martin
87Spart-17
88Spart/Pro-1038
88Spart/Star-23
88Spart/Star-7
89Readg/Best-15
89Readg/Pro-672
89Readg/Star-11

Foley, Marvis
77AppFx
78Knoxv
81D-399
81T-646
83D-652
83T-409
84Rangers-30
85D-500
85T-621
89Vanco/CMC-23
89Vanco/Pro-573

Foley, Rick
79SLCty-18
80SLCty-15
81Holyo-15
82Spoka-3

Foley, Thomas
80Water-19
81Indianap-7
82Indianap-20
84D-81
84Nes/792-632
84T-632
85D-569
85F-535
85T-107
86D-549
86F-440
86T-466
87D-504
87F-318
87OPC-78
87T-78
88D-303
88F-183
88Ho/Disc-3
88Leaf-143
88OPC-251
88Score-159
88T-251
89D-342
89D/Best-314
89F-375
89OPC-159
89Panini/St-121
89Score-405
89T-529
89T/Big-261
89UD-441
90D-274
90F-344
90Score-32
90T-341
90UD-489

Folga, Mike
85PrWill-12
87Peoria-26

Foli, Tim
71OPC-83R
71T-83R
72T-707
72T-708A
73OPC-19
73T-19
73T/Lids-16
74OPC-217
74T-217
74T/DE-19
74T/St-54
74Weston-19
75Ho-9
75Ho/Twink-9
75OPC-149
75T-149
75T/M-149
76OPC-397
76SSPC-328
76T-397
77OPC-162
77T-76
78OPC-169
78T-167
79OPC-213
79T-403
80OPC-131
ke
81D-13
81F-379
81OPC-38
82D-376
82F-482
82F/St-75
82OPC-97
82T-618
82T/St-88
82T/Tr-34T
83D-342
83F-88
83OPC-319
83T-738
84D-474
84F-516
84F/X-38
84Nes/792-342
84OPC-342
84T-342
84T/X-38
85F-126
85T-271FDP
85T-456
87Smok/R-29CO

Folkers, Rich
71OPC-648R
71T-648R
73OPC-649
73T-649
74OPC-417
74T-417
75OPC-98
75T-98
75T/M-98
76OPC-611
76SSPC-114
76T-611
77Spoka
77T-372

Followell, Vern
81Evans-14
82Evans-18
85Cram/PCL-57

Fondy, Dee
52B-231
52T-359
53B/BW-5
54B-173
54RH
55B-224
56T-112
57T-42
58Kahn
58T-157
79TCMA-47

Fonseca, Dave
80Clint-13

Fonseca, Lew
29Exh/4-21
31Exh/4-22
32Orbit/num-20
32Orbit/un-19
33DH-16
33G-43
34DS-7
61F-27
R305
R308-184
R310
R316
V353-43
W517-48
WG7-16

Fonsecca, Angel
82Wausa-25

Fontenot, Ray
82Nashv-12
84D-370
84F-122
84Nes/792-19
84T-19
85D-248
85F-127
85F/Up-U42
85SevenUp-31
85T-507
85T/Tr-35T
86D-361
86F-369
86Gator-31
86T-308
87T-124
87Tucso-12

Fontenot, Silton
83Colum-5

Fontes, Brad
88Butte-24
89Keno/Pro-1062
89Keno/Star-5

Fonville, Charlie
84Butte-10

Foor, Jim
72OPC-257R
72T-257R

Foote, Barry
74OPC-603R
74T-603R
75Ho-39
75OPC-229
75T-229
75T/M-229
76OPC-42
76T-42
77OPC-207
77T-612
78T-513
79T-161
80OPC-208
80T-398
81D-558
81F-313
81OPC-305
81T-492
81T/St-154
81T/Tr-763
82D-43
82F-34
82T-706
83T-697
85Albany-23
86Colum-9MG
87Myrtle-7
89Knoxv/Best-28
89Knoxv/Pro-1128
89SLAS-24

Forbes, Andre
78Green

Forbes, Willie
88Charl/Pro-1193

Ford, Curt
83Sprin/LF-6
84ArkTr-16
85Louvl-13
86F-648M
86Louisvl-13
87D-454
87F-294
87Smok/Cards-21
87T-399
88Woolwth-28
88D-417
88F-32
88Panini/St-395
88Score-288
88Smok/Card-20
88T-612
88T/St-23
89B-408
89F-450
89T-132
89UD-309
90D-694
90F-557
90Score-183
90T-39
90UD-490

Ford, Dale
88Umpire-23
89Umpires-21

Ford, Darnell
(Dan)
76OPC-313
76SSPC-216
76T-313
77Ho-121
77OPC-104
77T-555
77T/CS-16
78Ho-18
78OPC-34
78T-275
79OPC-201
79T-385
80OPC-7
80T-20
81D-54
81F-273
81OPC-303
81T-422
82D-468
82F-458
82F/St-216
82OPC-134
82T-134
82T/St-163
82T/Tr-35T
83D-509
83F-61
83OPC-357
83T-683
84D-367
84F-9
84Nes/792-530
84OPC-349
84T-530
84T/St-212
85D-489
85F-178
85T-252
86T-753

Ford, Dave
79RochR-20
80T-661R
81D-552
81F-192
81T-706
82D-597
82F-166
82T-174
83RochR-4
84Cram/PCL-94

Ford, Doug
47Centen-7

Ford, Edward C.
(Whitey)
51B-1
51BR-D5
53B/Col-153
53T-207
54B-177
54NYJour
54RM-AL16
54T-37
55Armour-6
55B-59
55RM-AL3

56T-240
57T-25
58T-320
59Armour-8
59T-430
60Armour-10
60T-35
60T/tatt
60T/tatt-15
61P-6
61T-160
61T-586AS
61T/St-193
62Bz
62Exh
62J-9
62P-9
62P/Can-9
62Salada-8
62Shirriff-8
62T-310
62T-315M
62T-475AS
62T-57LL
62T-59LL
62T/bucks
62T/St-85
63Exh
63J-19
63P-19
63T-446
63T-6LL
64T-380
64T-4LL
64T/Coins-139AS
64T/S-7
64Wheat/St-15
65T-330
66OPC-160
66T-160
66T/RO-60
67OPC-5
67T-5
78TCMA-21
80SSPC/HOF
82CJ-11
83MLBPA/Pin-7
85Woolwth-11
86S/Dec-44
87Nestle/DT-21
89B-I3
89HOF/St-70
89Kahn/Coop-4
89Pac/Leg-210
89Swell-50
Exh47
PM10/L-14
PM10/Sm-52
WG10-6
WG9-8

Ford, Horace E.
29Exh/4-8
31Exh/4-8
33G-24
E120
E126-57
R316
V353-24
V61-111
W573

Ford, Ken
82AlexD-23
83LynnP-20
85Nashua-10
86Nashua-7

Ford, Ondra
86Cram/PCL-33
89AppFx/Pro-859

Ford, Randy
82Knoxv-3

Ford, Rick
76BurlB
77BurlB
77Holyo
78Clint

Ford, Russ
10Domino-45
11Helmar-43
12Sweet/Pin-34A
12Sweet/Pin-34B
14CJ-83
14Piedmont/St-22
15CJ-83
E270/2
E286
E98
L1-115
M116
S74-21
S81-90
T201
T202
T205
T206
T213/blue
T215/blue
T215/brown

Ford, Rusty
86Beaum-11
87LasVegas-9
88Wichi-41

Ford, Ted
71OPC-612R
71T-612R
72OPC-24
72T-24
73OPC-299
73T-299
74OPC-617
74T-617

Fordyce, Brook
89Kingspt/Star-10

Fore, Chuck L.
78Syrac
79Syrac-14
81Syrac-3
83Richm-6

Foreman, Dave
87Anchora-40STAT

Foreman, Francis
N172

Forer, Daniel Lynn
81VeroB-5

Forgeur, Freddy
79QuadC-21

Forgione, Chris
85Visal-9
86Visal-9
87Kenosha-22
88Orlan/Best-16

Forney, Jeff
87Tampa-25
88Cedar/Pro-1151
88MidwLAS/GS-10

Fornieles, Mike
54T-154
55B-266
57T-116
58T-361
59T-473
60T-54
61T-113
62T-512
62T/St-12
63T-28
79TCMA-132

Forrest, Chris
87StPet-15
89Boise/Pro-2001

Forrest, Joel
87Macon-3
88Aug/Pro-381
88Watertn/Puc-5

Forrester, Tom
87Hawai-7
88BirmB/Best-12
89Vanco/CMC-20
89Vanco/Pro-597

Forry, Dewey
75Water

Forsch, Ken
71OPC-102R
71T-102R
72OPC-394
72T-394
73OPC-589
73T-589
74OPC-91
74T-91
75OPC-357
75T-357
75T/M-357
76OPC-357
76SSPC-48
77OPC-78
77T-21
77T-632M
78BK/A-8
78Ho-3
78K-50
78T-181
79Ho-51
79OPC-276
79T-534
80OPC-337
80T-642
81D-141
81F-52
81OPC-269
81T-269
81T/Tr-764
82D-393
82F-459
82F/St-221
82OPC-385
82T-276TL
82T-385
82T/St-159
83D-164
83F-89
83OPC-346
83T-625
84D-280
84F-517
84Nes/792-765
84OPC-193
84Smok/Cal-9
84T-765
84T/St-237
85F-301
85OPC-141
85Smok/Cal-8
85T-442
86F-155
86Moth/Ast-14

Forsch, Robert
75OPC-51
75T-51
75T/M-51
76OPC-426
76SSPC-294
76T-526
77T-381
77T-632M
78OPC-83
78T-58
79K-38
79OPC-117
79T-230
80OPC-279
80T-535
81Coke
81D-69
81F-537
81OPC-140
81T-140
82D-91
82F-112
82F/St-22
82OPC-34
82T-186TL
82T-775
82T/St-90
83D-64
83F-5
83OPC-197
83T-415
83T/St-289
84D-168
84F-322
84F-639
84Nes/792-5
84Nes/792-75
84OPC-75
84T-5
84T-75
84T/St-288A
85F-223
85OPC-137
85T-631
86D-353
86F-35
86KAS/Disc-6
86S-129M
86Schnucks-6
86T-322
86T-66M
87D-540
87F-295
87F/AwardWin-14
87F/St-40
87Leaf-161
87OPC-257
87S-191
87Smok/Cards-7
87T-257
87T/St-47
88D-111
88F-33
88Panini/St-384
88Score-264
88Sf-199
88Smok/Card-5
88T-586
89D-118
89Lennox/Ast-23
89Moth/Ast-11
89Score-525
89T-163
90F-231
90Score-219

Forster, Guillermo
73Cedar
74Cedar

Forster, Terry
72T-539
73OPC-129
73T-129
74OPC-310
74T-310
74T/St-153
75Ho-14
75OPC-137
75OPC-313LL
75T-137
75T-313LL
75T/M-137
75T/M-313LL
76Ho-14
76Ho/Twink-14
76OPC-437
76SSPC-157
76T-437
77T-271
78T-347
79OPC-7
79T-23
80T-605
81Pol/Dodg-51
81T-104
82D-362
82F-4
82Pol/Dodg
82Pol/Dodg-51
82T-444
83D-453
83F-205
83Pol/Atl-51
83T-583
83T/X-33
84F-178
84Nes/792-791
84OPC-109
84Pol/Atl-51
84T-791
85F-324
85Ho/Braves-8
85OPC-248
85Pol/Atl-51
85T-248
86D-432
86F-514
86F/Up-U42
86Leaf-202
86Smok/Cal-23
86T-363
86T/Tr-37T
87F-80
87T-652

Forster, Tom
N172
N284

Fortaleza, Ray
84Greens-2

Fortenberry, Jim
86Clearw-8
86FSLAS-16
87Readg-21

Fortinberry, Bill
80Port-12

Fortugno, Tim
86Cram/PCL-115
88Readg/Pro-876
89Reno/Cal-244
89Stock/Star-7

Fortuna, Mike
89Salem/Star-8
89Well/Puc-12

Fortune, Steve
79Elmir-9

Fosnow, Gerald
65T-529

Fossa, Dick
88CalLgAS-24

Fossas, Tony
80Ashev-7
81Tulsa-16
83Tulsa-3
84OKCty-12
85OKCty-10
86Edmon-10
87Edmon-20
88OkCty/CMC-9
88OkCty/Pro-34
89Denver/CMC-3
89Denver/Pro-55
90D-457
90F-323
90Score-567
90T-34

Fosse, Ray
69T-244R
70OPC-184
70T-184
71K-39
71MD
71MLB/St-366
71OPC-125
71T-125

58T-479AS
59Armour-9
59Bz
59T-30
59T-408M
59T-556AS
60Armour-11
60Bz-25
60NuCard-72
60T-100
60T-429M
60T-555AS
60T/tatt
60T/tatt-16
61NuCard-472
61P-20
61T-30
61T-477MV
61T-570AS
62Exh
62J-47
62P-47
62P/Can-47
62Salada-12
62Shirriff-12
62T-73
62T/bucks
62T/St-24
63Exh
63J-36
63P-36
63T-525
64T-205
64T-81M
64T/S-13
64Wheat/St-16
65T-485
74Laugh/ASG-58
75OPC-197M
75T-197MV
75T/M-197MV
76Laugh/Jub-24
79TCMA-15
80Cram/Leg-68
80Laugh/FFeat-7
83MLBPA/Pin-8
86S/Dec-37M
87Nestle/DT-13
88Pac/Leg-57
Exh47
PM10/Sm-53

Fox, Kenneth
86Jamestn-7

Fox, Mike
87StPet-11
89ArkTr/GS-5

Fox, Terry
61T-459
62T-196
63T-44
64T-387
65T-576
66T-472
67OPC-181
67T-181

Foxen, Bill
M116
S74-61
T202
T205

Foxx, James Emory (Jimmie)
29Exh/4-27
31Exh/4-28
32Orbit/num-18
32Orbit/un-20
33DH-17
33DL-21
33Exh/4-14
33G-154
33G-29
34DS-64
34Exh/4-14
34G-1
34Ward's/Pin-3
35BU-144
35BU-28
35Exh/4-14
35G-1B
35G-2B
35G-6B
35G-7B
35Wheat
36Exh/4-9
36Wheat
37Exh/4-9
37OPC-106
38Dix
38Exh/4-9
38G-249
38G-273
38ONG/Pin-9
38Wheat
39Exh
39Wheat-5
40PB-133
40Wheat-3
41DP-60
41PB-13
41Wheat-14
50Callahan
60F-53
61F-28
61GP-22
72F/FFeat-16
72Laugh/GF-19
73F/Wild-41
74Laugh/ASG-35
80Cram/Leg-16
80Laugh/3/4/5-21
80Laugh/FFeat-23
80SSPC/HOF
83D/HOF-13
85CircK-7
86BLChew-7
86Conlon/1-12
86S/Dec-2
87Nestle/DT-11
88Conlon/5-10
88Conlon/AmAS-9
PR1-10
R300
R302-153
R303/A
R303/B
R305
R306
R308-153
R310
R311/
R311/Gloss
R312/M
R314
R315-A7
R315-B7
R316
R326-12A
R326-12B
R328-23
R337
R342-12
V300
V353-29
V353-85
V354-58
V355-47
W517-21
WG8-19

Foy, Joe
66T-456R
67T-331
67T/Test/RSox-6
68Coke
68T-387
69MB-84
69MLB/St-58
69OPC-93
69T-93
69T/DE-22
69T/decal
69T/S-22
69T/St-184
70MLB/St-75
70OPC-138
70T-138
71MLB/St-537
71OPC-706
71T-706
72MB-106

Foytack, Paul
53Glen
57T-77
58T-282
59T-233
60T-364
61P-62
61T-171
62T-349
63T-327
64T-149

Frailing, Ken
74OPC-605R
74T-605R
75OPC-436
75T-436
75T/M-436
76SSPC-305
78Knoxv

Frame, Michael
89GreatF-2

France, Todd
86Stockton-7TR
87Stockton-5

Franchi, Kevin
86Macon-9
87Salem-1

Francis, Earl
61T-54
62T-252
63T-303
64T-117
78TCMA-226

Francis, Harry
81Redwd-13
82Holyo-20
83Nashua-12

Francis, Todd
83Wausa/LF-14

Francis, Tommy
83Miami-23

Francisco, Rene
89Geneva/Pro-1862

Franco, John
82Albuq-2
84F/X-39
85D-164
85F-536
85F/St-120
85T-417
86D-487
86F-178
86F/St-39
86KayBee-13
86Leaf-240
86OPC-54
86S-156
86T-54
86T/St-142
86TexGold-31
87Class-100
87D-289
87D/AAS-22
87F-202
87F-631M
87F/Lim-17
87F/LL-18
87F/McCror-14
87F/Slug-14
87F/St-41
87Kahn-31
87Leaf-178
87OPC-305
87RedFoley/St-116
87S-192
87T-305
87T/Mini-5
87T/St-138
88D-123
88D/AS-53
88D/Best-54
88F-234
88F-627M
88F/Mini-74
88F/RecSet-12
88F/St-84
88Kahn/Reds-31
88Leaf-79
88Nestle-8
88OPC-341
88Panini/St-271
88Score-535
88Sf-195
88T-730
88T/Big-232
88T/Coins-41
88T/Mini-47
88T/St-142
88T/St/Backs-32
88T/UK-24
89B-301
89Cadaco-19
89D-233
89D/Best-166
89F-162
89F/Heroes-14
89F/LL-13
89K/Reds-31
89OPC-290
89Panini/St-66
89RedFoley/St-45
89Score-575
89Score/HotSt-97
89Sf-176
89T-290
89T/Coins-12
89T/DH-23
89T/Mini-9
89T/St-136
89T/St-4
89T/St/Backs-65
89T/UK-27
89UD-407
89Woolwth-12
90Class-86
90D-124
90D-14DK
90F-419
90F/WaxBox-C7
90Score-273
90Score/100St-49
90Sf-138
90T-120
90UD-139

Franco, Julio
80Penin/B-21
80Penin/C-17
82OkCty-11
83D-525
83T/X-34
83Wheat/Ind-13
84D-216
84F-542
84F/St-111
84Nes/792-48
84OPC-48
84T-48
84T/St-379
84Wheat/Ind-14
85D-94
85F-448
85Leaf-213
85OPC-237
85Polar/Ind-14
85T-237
85T/St-245
86D-216
86F-586
86F/LimEd-16
86F/LL-13
86F/Mini-115
86F/Slug-9
86F/St-40
86KayBee-14
86Leaf-93
86OhHenry-14
86OPC-391
86S-33
86T-391
86T/St-211
87D-131
87D/OD-111
87F-251
87F/LL-19
87F/McCror-15
87F/Mini-39
87F/St-42
87Gator-14
87Leaf-131
87OPC-160
87RedFoley/St-1
87S-84
87T-160
87T/St-210
88Class/Red-187
88D-10DK
88D-156
88D/Best-168
88D/DKsuper-10DK
88F-609
88F/AwardWin-13
88F/BB/AS-11
88F/BB/MVP-15
88F/Excit-14
88F/Hottest-11
88F/LL-12
88F/Mini-19
88F/RecSet-13
88F/St-19
88F/TL-8
88FanSam-10
88Gator-14
88Leaf-10DK 88Leaf-71
88OPC-49
88Panini/St-77
88RedFoley/St-25
88Score-60
88Score/YS/II-7
88Sf-58
88T-683
88T/Big-135
88T/St-207
89B-228
89Cadaco-20
89D-310
89D/Best-32
89D/Tr-31
89F-404
89F/AS-5
89F/Up-64
89KMart/Lead-14
89Master/Discs-11
89Moth/R-3
89OPC-55
89Panini/St-325
89Score-11
89Score/HotSt-36
89Score/Mast-29
89Score/Tr-35
89Sf-149
89Smok/R-9

89T-398AS
89T-55
89T/Big-288
89T/DH-2
89T/St-208
89T/St/Backs-4
89T/Tr-34T
89UD-186
89UD/Ext-793
90Class-67
90D-142
90D-701AS
90D/Bon/MVP-BC14
90F-296
90Score-160
90Score/100St-84
90Sf-158
90T-386AS
90T-550
90UD-103
90UD-82TC

Franco, Matthew
89CharWh/Best-11
89CharWh/Pro-1748

Francois, Manny
85VeroB-5
87VeroB-11
88SnAnt/Best-14
89SnAnt/Best-2

Francona, John
(Tito)
57T-184
58T-316
59T-268
60Kahn
60T-260M
60T-30
60T/tatt
60T/tatt-17
61Kahn
61P-64
61T-503
61T/St-134
62Exh
62J-40
62Kahn
62P-40
62P/Can-40
62Salada-15
62Shirriff-15
62Sugar-9
62T-97
62T/St-34
63Exh
63F-12
63J-64
63P-64
63Sugar-9
63T-248
63T-392M
64T-583
65OPC-256
65T-256
66OPC-163
66T-163
67T-443
68T-527
69MB-85
69T-398
69T/St-4
70MLB/St-257
70T-663
72MB-107
78TCMA-205
78TCMA-231
85T-134FS
89Pac/Leg-133
89Swell-76
Exh47
WG9-29

Francona, Terry
80Memph-13
82D-627
82F-188
82Hygrade
82OPC-118R
82OPC/Post-19
82T-118R
82Zeller-11
82Zeller-5
83D-592
83F-281
83OPC-267
83Stuart-14
83T-267
83T/St-321
84D-463
84F-275
84Nes/792-496
84OPC-89
84Stuart-18
84T-496
85D-132
85F-398
85Leaf-245
85OPC-258
85T-134FS
85T-578
85T/St-88
86D-401
86F-248
86F/Up-U43
86Gator-16
86IowaC-11
86Leaf-191
86OPC-374
86T-374
86T/St-80
86T/Tr-38T
87D/OD-193
87F-564
87Kahn-10
87OPC-294
87T-785
87T/Tr-34T
88ColSp/CMC-20
88ColSp/Pro-1541
88Score-297
88T-686
89Pol/Brew-30
89Score-597
89T-31
89T/Tr-35T
89UD-536
90Score-216
90T-214
90UD-180

Franek, Ken
88CalLgAS-49

Franjul, Miguel
78Clint
79LodiD-15

Frankhouse, Fred
33G-131
34DS-62
35BU-75
35G-2E
35G-4E
35G-7E
39PB-70
V354-19

Franklin, Elliott
76BurlB

Franklin, Glen
80Memph-10
82Water-17
83Indianap-24

Franklin, Jay
89Butte/SP-17

Franklin, Jeff
78Wausa

Franklin, Tony
76Indianap-23
79RochR-7

Franko, Phil
82Wisco-18
83Visal/LF-5

Franks, Herman
52T-385
65OPC-32MG
65T-32
66T-537
67OPC-116MG
67T-116
68T-267
77T-518MG
78T-234
79T-551MG
Rawl

Fraser, Chick
WG3-19

Fraser, Gretchen
52Wheat

Fraser, Will
(Willie)
86PalmSp-13
86PalmSp/Smok-9
87D-40RR
87D/Rook-9
87F-646M
87F/U-U33
87Leaf-40
87S/Rook-27
87Smok/Cal-7
87T/Tr-35T
88D-135
88F-490
88OPC-363
88Score-394
88Smok/Angels-14
88T-363
88T/Big-183
89D-567
89F-478
89Score-157
89T-679
89T/Big-272
89UD-613
90D-587
90F-133
90Score-358
90T-477
90UD-85

Frash, Roger
82Lynch-12

Frassa, Bob
88Brist/Pro-1867

Frazier, Fred
75IntAS/TCMA-15
75IntAS/TCMA-20
77SLCty
78Knoxv

Frazier, George
76BurlB
77Holyo
79T-724R
80T-684R
81D-310
82D-584
82F-35
82T-349
83D-535
83F-379
83T-123
84D-591
84F-123
84F/X-40
84Nes/792-539
84OPC-139
84SevenUp-39
84T-539
84T/X-39
85D-167
85F-58
85OPC-19
85SevenUp-39
85T-19
86D-411
86F-370
86Gator-39
86T-431
87D-564
87F-539
87T-207
88D-443
88F-9
88Score-332
88T-709

Frazier, Joseph F.
55Hunter
55T-89
55T/DH-83
56T-141
60DF-22
76SSPC-610
76T-531MG
77T-259MG
82Louvl-8

Frazier, Keith
45Centen-9

Frazier, Ken
81Clint-18

Frazier, Lou
87Ashvl-7
88Osceola/Star-10
89ColMud/Best-12
89ColMud/Pro-145
89ColMud/Star-10

Frazier, Ron
88CapeCod/Sum-90

Frazier, Shawn
86Sumter-5

Freck
E254

Frederick, Charlie
84CharO-3
85CharO-29
87CharO/WBTV-xx

Frederick, John
34G-47
85Woolwth-12
88Conlon/NatAS-6
R315-A8
R315-B8
V354-85

Fredlund, Jay
79Elmir-2
81Brist-15

Fredymond, Juan
85Durhm-23
86Durhm-11
87Durhm-21
88Sumter/Pro-409

Freeburg, Larry
82Cedar-11

Freed, Daniel
88James/Pro-1899

Freed, Roger
70OPC-477R
70T-477R
71MLB/St-176
71OPC-362R
71T-362R
72OPC-69
72T-69
78T-504
79T-111
80T-418

Freehan, Bill
63T-466R
64Det/Lids-6
64T-407
64T/Coins-87
64T/S-30
64T/St-68
64T/tatt
65T-390
65T/E-41
65T/trans-12
66OPC-145
66T-145
66T/RO-63
67OPC-48
67T-48
68Bz-2
68Coke
68Kahn
68T-375AS
68T-470
68T/G-11
69Kahn
69MB-86
69MLB/St-47
69MLBPA/Pin-6
69NTF
69OPC/DE-6
69T-390
69T-431AS
69T/DE-10
69T/S-18
69T/St-172
70K-57
70MB-7
70MLB/St-206
70OPC-335
70OPC-465AS
70T-335
70T-465AS
70T/CB
70T/S-7
71Bz
71Bz/Test-37
71K-31
71MD
71MLB/St-391
71OPC-575
71T-575
71T/Coins-38
71T/GM-22
71T/S-12
71T/tatt-12
72MB-108
72OPC-120
72T-120
73OPC-460
73T-460
73T/Comics-7
73T/Lids-18
73T/PinUps-7
74OPC-162
74T-162
74T/St-174
75Ho-120
75OPC-397
75T-397
75T/M-397
76Ho-6
76Ho/Twink-6
76OPC-540
76T-540
77T-22
78TCMA-285
86S/Dec-49M
88Domino-5
88Pac/Leg-93
89Swell-106
WG10-27

Freeland, Dean
85Beloi-15
86Clint-9
87Shrev-5
88Shreve/Pro-1285
89Shreve/Pro-1852

Freeman, Clem Jr.
82Water-6
83Tampa-12

Freeman, Herschel
55B-290
56Kahn
56T-242

57Kahn
57T-32
58T-27
79TCMA-120
Freeman, James J.
(Buck)
T204
T206
WG2-20
Freeman, Jimmy
73OPC-610R
73T-610R
Freeman, John
N172
Freeman, Julius
N172
Freeman, LaVell
86ElPas-11
87ElPas-1
87TexLgAS-25
88AAA/Pro-12
88Denver/CMC-20
88Denver/Pro-1277
89Denver/CMC-14
89Denver/Pro-48
89UD/Ext-788
Freeman, Mark
59T-532
79TCMA-265
Freeman, Marty
86GlenF-5
Freeman, Marvin
86Readg-8
87D-576
87F-651
87Maine-12
87Maine/TCMA-4
87Sf/Rook-4
88Maine/CMC-4
88Maine/Pro-279
89D-631
89F-566
89Score/HotRk-34
89ScrWB/CMC-1
89T-634
90T-103
Freeman, Pete
87Watertn-9
88Aug/Pro-367
Freeman, Rick
89Elizab/Star-8
Freese, Gene
55T-205
56T-46
58T-293
59T-472
60L-140
60MacGregor-8
60T-435
60T/tatt
60T/tatt-18
61Kahn
61P-30
61T-175
61T/St-17
62J-118
62Kahn
62P-118
62P/Can-118
62Salada-137
62Shirriff-137
62T-205
62T/St-115
63F-33
63Kahn
63T-133
64T-266
65T-492
66T-319
Freese, George
55B-84

Fregin, Doug
82Toled-27
Fregosi, Jim Jr.
85Sprin-3
86StPet-9
87ArkTr-11
Fregosi, Jim
62T-209
63T-167
64Bz-22
64T-97
64T/Coins-128AS
64T/Coins- 98
64T/S-18
64T/St-60
64T/SU
64T/tatt
65Bz-22
65OldLond-25
65OPC-210
65T-210
65T/E-39
65T/trans-13
66Bz-19
66OPC-5
66T-5
66T/RO-84
67Bz-19
67T-385
67T/Test/SU-9
68Coke
68OPC-170
68T-170
68T-367AS
68T/G-33
68T/Post-4
69Bz-28
69Citgo-7
69JB
69MB-87
69MLB/St-21
69MLBPA/Pin-7
69NTF
69T-365
69T/DE-5
69T/decal
69T/S-7
69T/St-144
69Trans-14
70K-36
70MB-8
70MLB/St-172
70T-570
70T/S-30
70Trans-14
71Bz
71Bz/Test-25
71JB
71K-64
71MD
71MLB/St-344
71OPC-360
71T-360
71T/Coins-136
71T/GM-16
71T/tatt-3
71T/tatt-3a
72MB-109
72OPC-115
72OPC-346KP
72T-115
72T-346BP
72T-755TR
72T/Cloth-13KP
73OPC-525
73T-525
74T-196
74T/St-234
75OPC-339
75T-339
75T/M-339
76OPC-635

76SSPC-262
76T-635
78T-323
78TCMA-170
79T-424MG
81F-274
81Louvl-1
81T-663MG
84Louvl-1
85Louvl-1MG
86Louisvl-1MG
86T/Tr-39T
87Coke/WS-10
87T-318MG
88ArkTr/GS-16
88Coke/WS-7MG
88T-714
89Smok/Angels-3
89T-414MG
89WPalm/Star-11
Freigau, Howard
21Exh-52
25Exh-20
26Exh-20
Freiling, Howard
88VeroB/Star-7
89Jacks/GS-18
Freisleben, Dave
74OPC-599R
74T-599R
75OPC-37
75T-37
75T/M-37
76OPC-217
76SSPC-116
76T-217
77T-407
78T-594
79T-168
80OPC-199
80T-382
89Butte/SP-30
Freitas, Antonio
40Hughes-6
46Sunbeam
47Signal
47Sunbeam
49B/PCL-11
R314
French, Charlie
C46-25
French, Jim
69OPC-199
71MLB/St-538
71OPC-399
French, Larry
34G-29
35BU-132
41DP-1
88Conlon/NatAS-7
V354-79
WG8-20
French, Ray
28Exh/PCL-31
WG7-17
French, Richard J.
66T-333R
69T-199
70T-617
71T-399
French, Steve
84Butte-11
Frew, Mike
85Beloi-16
86Stockton-8
87Stockton-15
Frey, Eric
77Newar
Frey, Jim
73OPC-136CO
73T-136C
74OPC-306CO
/4T-306C

81D-464
81T-667MG
84Nes/792-51MG
84SevenUp- MG
84T-51
85SevenUp-MG
85T-241
86T-231
Frey, Linus
34G-89
35G-1G
35G-3E
35G-4E
35G-5E
39PB-161
40PB-76
41DP-5
R310
R312
R314
W711/1
W711/2
Frey, Steve
85Albany-7
87Albany-23
87FtLaud-3
88Tidew/CANDL-20
88Tidew/CMC-6
88Tidew/Pro-1602
89Indi/CMC-3
89Indi/Pro-1218
90F-649M
90T-91
Frias, Israel
89Bluef/Star-10
Frias, Jesus M.
(Pepe)
73OPC-607R
73T-607R
74OPC-468
74T-468
75OPC-496
75T-496
75T/M-496
76OPC-544
76SSPC-231
76T-544
77OPC-225
77T-199
78OPC-171
78T-654
79OPC-146
79T-294
80OPC-48
80T-87
81F-134
81Pol/Dodg-36
Friberg, A. Bernhardt
26Exh-42
29Exh/4-11
31Exh/4-12
33G-105
V354-10
Fricano, Marion
53T-199
54B-3
54T-124
55B-316
55Rodeo
Frick, Ford
49Eureka-2
59T-1
60F-74
61F-29
80SSPC/HOF
Frick, James
T205
Fridley, Jim
52T-399
53T-187
54Esskay
72T/Test-6

Friedel, Chuck
84LitFalls-5
Friederich, Mike
86ColumAst-13
Friel, Bill
E107
E270/2
Friend, Bob
52B-191
52T-233
53B/Col-16
54B-43
54DanDee
55B-57
56T-221
56YellBase/Pin-10
57Kahn
57T-150
58Hires-24
58Hires/T
58Kahn
58T-315
58T-334
58T-492AS
59Kahn
59T-428M
59T-460
59T-569AS
60Kahn
60L-53
60T-437
61Kahn
61P-125
61T-270
61T-45LL
61T-585AS
61T/St-63
62J-178
62Kahn
62P-178
62P/Can-178
62Salada-157
62Shirriff-157
62T-520
62T/bucks
62T/St-176
63J-145
63Kahn
63P-145
63T-450
64Bz-6
64Kahn
64T-1LL
64T-20
64T/Coins-77
64T/S-28
64T/St-66
64T/SU
64T/tatt
64Wheat/St-17
65Kahn
65OldLond-10
65T-392
66T-519
78TCMA-160
88Pac/Leg-78
89Swell-86
Exh47
Friend, Owen
50B-189
51B-101
52T-160
53Glen
54B-212
55B-256
Frierson, John
83Miami-19
Frierson, Mike
80Wausa-19
Friesen, Rob
87Fayette-26

86Toled-11
87Orlan-25
88Orlan/Best-5
89Orlan/Best-3
89Orlan/Pro-1344

Funk, Art
R314/Can

Funk, Brian
83Water-2
84Cedar-6

Funk, E.
31Exh/4-24

Funk, Frank
61T-362
62Sugar-4
62T-587
63T-476
64T-289
80Penin/B-26C
86Omaha-7CO
86Omaha/TCMA-24
87Omaha-1

Funk, Tom
86ColumAst-14
87Tucso-25
88ColAst/Best-18

Fuqua, David
75Lafay

Furcal, Lorenzo
89Madis/Star-9
89Medford/Best-17

Furch, John
89Utica/Puc-7

Furillo, Carl
48Swell-20
49B-70
49Eureka-35
50B-58
50Drake-18
51B-81
52B-24
52Coke
52TipTop
53B/Col-78
54B-122
54NYJour
55B-169
55Gol/Dodg-9
56T-190
57T-400M
57T-45
58T-417
59Morrell
59T-206
60BB-8
60Morrell
60NuCard-32
60T-408
61NuCard-432
72T/Test-5
79TCMA-43
89Rini/Dodg-14
89Smok/Dodg-58
D305
Exh47
PM10/Sm-54
PM10/Sm-55
PM10/Sm-56
PM10/Sm-57

Furman, Jon
83BirmB-20

Furmanik, Dan
89Clmbia/Best-6
89Clmbia/GS-8

Fuson, Grady
82Idaho-31
83Idaho-31
89Medford/Best-18

Fuson, Robin
78Watlo
82Chatt-18
83BuffB-1
84BuffB-24
85Pawtu-13

Fusselman, Les
52T-378
53Hunter
53T-218

Fye, Chris
89Clint/Pro-885

Fynan, Kevin
88Clearw/Star-11
89Clearw/Star-9

Gabler, Frank
35BU-91

Gabler, John
60L-62

Gables, Kenneth
48Sommers-5
49Sommers-3

Gabriele, Dan
85Elmir-7
86Greens-6
87WinHav-10
88NewBrit/Pro-898
89NewBrit/Pro-604
89NewBrit/Star-6

Gabrielson, Len
63T-253R
64T-198
65OPC-14
65T-14
66T-395
67T-469
68T-357
69MB-89
69MLB/St-147
69T-615
69T/St-44
70MLB/St-50
70OPC-204
70T-204
PM10/Sm-58

Gabrielson, Leonard
43Centen-9

Gaddy, Robert
89Batav/Pro-1928

Gaeckle, Chris
86Greens-7
87Greens-25

Gaedel, Eddie
60NuCard-26
61NuCard-426
73F/Wild-4

Gaeta, Chris
85Newar-19

Gaetti, Gary
80Wisco
82OrlTw/A-7
83D-53
83F-613
83T-431
83T/St-87
84D-314
84F-565
84FunFood/Pin-131
84Nes/792-157
84OPC-157
84T-157
84T/St-306
85D-242
85F-278
85Leaf-145
85OPC-304
85Seven/Minn-9
85T-304
85T/St-302
86D-314
86F-394
86OPC-97
86T-97
86T/St-283
87Class-54
87D-122
87D/OD-219
87F-540
87F/GameWin-15
87F/Mini-40
87F/RecSet-9
87F/St-43
87Leaf-245
87OPC-179
87S-114M
87S-64
87T-710
87T/Gloss60-3
87T/Mini-62
87T/St-279
88Woolwth-18
88Woolwth-22
88Class/Blue-233
88D-194
88D-19DK
88D/Best-46
88D/DKsuper-19DK
88F-10
88F/Hottest-12
88F/LL-13
88F/Mini-34
88F/St-43
88KayBee-11
88Leaf-19DK
88Leaf-200
88Master/Disc-9
88Nestle-4
88OPC-257
88Panini/St-140
88Panini/St-445
88RedFoley/St-26
88Score-62
88Sf-154
88Smok/Minn-2
88T-578
88T/Big-127
88T/Coins-13
88T/RiteAid-31
88T/St-17
88T/St-277
88T/UK-25
89B-158
89Cadaco-21
89Class-41
89D-64
89D/AS-13
89D/Best-102
89F-110
89F/Heroes-15
89Master/Discs-3
89OPC-220
89Panini/St-389
89RedFoley/St-46
89Score-8
89Score/HotSt-21
89Score/Mast-16
89Sf-48
89T-220
89T/Big-264
89T/Gloss60-33
89T/Mini-61
89T/St-289
89T/St/Backs-8
89UD-203
90D-151
90F-373
90Score-145
90Score/100St-22
90Sf-51
90T-630
90UD-454

Gaff, Brent
78Wausa
79Wausa-1
81Tidew-17
82Tidew-20
83D-553
83Tidew-16
84Tidew-8
85F-80
85T-546
86T-18

Gaffney, John H.
N172

Gagliano, Phil
61Union
62Kahn/Atl
64T-568R
65T-503
66T-418
67T-304
68T-479
69T-609
70OPC-143
70T-143
71OPC-302
71T-302
72MB-112
72OPC-472
72T-472
73OPC-69
73T-69
74OPC-622
74T-622

Gagliano, Ralph
65T-501R

Gagliardi, Joe
88CalLgAS-25

Gagne, Greg
82Orlan-8
83Toled-14
84D-39
85F/Up-U43
85T/Tr-36T
86D-558
86F-395
86T-162
87D-395
87D/OD-223
87F-541
87T-558
87T/St-283
88Woolwth-32WS7
88D-441
88D/Best-74
88F-11
88Master/Disc-11
88OPC-343
88Panini/St-141
88Score-214
88Smok/Minn-8
88T-343
88T/Big-58
89B-161
89D-318
89D/Best-158
89F-111
89OPC-19
89Panini/St-390
89Score-159
89T-19
89T-429TL 89T/Big-186
89T/St-288
89UD-166
90D-237
90F-374
90Score-102
90T-448
90UD-217

Gahbrielson, Rick
86Bakers-9CO

Gainer, Delos C.
BF2-3
D328-53
D329-63
D350/2-64
E135-53
M101/4-63
M101/5-64
T207

Gainer, Keith
79Newar-18

Gaines, A. Joe
62T-414
63T-319
64T-364
65T-595
66OPC-122
66T-122

Gaines, Jerry
77Ashev

Gainey, Ty
82DayBe-13
83ColumAst-10
85Cram/PCL-69
86D-31
86Tucso-5
87D-533
87S-118M
87Tucso-23
88D-578
88F-448
89ColrSp/CMC-22
89ColSp/Pro-258

Gainous, Trey
88AppFx/Pro-151

Gakeler, Dan
85Greens-20
86Greens-8
87NewBrit-19
88NewBrit/Pro-904
89Jaxvl/Best-24
89Jaxvl/Pro-157

Galan, Augie
35BU-135
36Exh/4-3
37Exh/4-3
38Exh/4-3
41DP-102
48B-39
49B-230
49Eureka-103
50Remar
53Mother-7
54T-233
89Smok/Dodg-48
Exh47
R312/M
R314
V355-106
WG8-22

Galante, Matt
75BurlB
76BurlB
77Holyo
83Tucso-23
84Cram/PCL-50

Galarraga, Andres
85Indianap-3
86D-33
86D/Rook-7
86F-647M
86F/Up-U44
86Leaf-27RR
86Provigo-10
86S/Rook-27
86T/Tr-40T
87Class-71
87D-303
87D/OD-90
87F-319
87F/Lim-18
87F/Mini-41
87Leaf-221
87OPC-272
87T-272
87T/St-84
88D-282
88D/Best-90
88F-184
88F-C3
88F/LL-14

88F/Mini-88
88F/Slug-14
88F/St-96
88F/TL-9
88F/WaxBox-C3
88Ho/Disc-8
88Leaf-121
88OPC-25
88Panini/St-323
88Score-19
88Score/YS/II-8
88Sf-182
88T-25
88T/Big-55
88T/Gloss60-58
88T/Mini-56
88T/St-79
88T/St/Backs-2
89B-365
89Cadaco-22
89Class-46
89D-130
89D-14DK
89D/AS-45
89D/Best-12
89D/DKsuper-14DK
89D/MVP-BC16
89F-376
89F-638M
89F/BBAS-13
89F/BBMVP's-12
89F/Excit-13
89F/Heroes-16
89F/LL-14
89F/Rec-3
89F/Superstar-15
89F/WaxBox-C8
89KayBee-12
89OPC-93
89Panini/St-119
89Panini/St-224
89RedFoley/St-47
89Score-144
89Score/HotSt-74
89Score/Mast-33
89Sf-139
89T-386AS
89T-590
89T/Big-173
89T/Coins-13
89T/Gloss60-44
89T/Hills-13
89T/Mini-22
89T/St-76
89T/St/Backs-36
89T/UK-28
89UD-115
89UD-677TC
90Class-115
90D-97
90F-345
90Score-25
90Score/100St-14
90Sf-148
90T-720
90UD-356

Galasso, Bob
80T-711R
80Vanco-20
81Spoka-9
82T-598
84Richm-16

Galatzer, Milt
R313

Galbato, Chan
86Jamestn-9

Gale, Rich
76Watlo
77Jaxvl
79OPC-149
79T-298
80T-433
81D-462
81F-40
81OPC-363
81Pol/Royals-3
81T-544
82D-138
82F-408
82OPC-67
82T-67
82T/Tr-38T
83D-172
83F-260
83OPC-243
83T-719
83T/X-35
84D-140
84F-469
84F/X-41
84Nes/792-142
84Pawtu-23
84T-142
84T/X-40
85T-606
89NewBrit/Pro-602
89NewBrit/Star-24

Galehouse, Dennis
40PB-198
47TipTop
61F-107
W753

Galindez, Luis
89Watlo/Pro-1789
89Watlo/Star-8

Galindo, Luis
88Lakel/Star-5
89Lakel/Star-6

Gallagher
N690

Gallagher, Alan
71OPC-224
71T-224
72T-693
72T-694A
78Green
81Durhm-14
82Chatt-23
83BuffB-24

Gallagher, Bob
74OPC-21
74T-21
75OPC-406
75T-406
75T/M-406
76Phoen
76SSPC-608

Gallagher, Dave
80Batav-25
81Watlo-26
82Chatt-17
82Watlo/C-11
83BuffB-19
84Maine-7
85IntLgAS-35
85Maine-27
86Maine-9CO
87Calgary-22
88D/Rook-7
88F/U-U16
88Score/Tr-89T
88Vanco/CMC-24
88Vanco/Pro-771
89B-71
89Bz-8
89Coke/WS-9
89D-384
89D/Best-67
89F-496
89KMart/DT-7
89Panini/St-299
89Score-455
89Score/HotRk-96
89Score/YS/I-4
89Sf-88
89T-156
89T/Big-310
89T/Gloss60-49
89T/JumboR-8
89T/St-295
89T/St-321
89ToysRUs-9
89UD-164
90Class-49
90D-219
90F-532
90Score-115
90Score/100St-56
90Sf-105
90T-612
90UD-328

Gallardo, Luis
87QuadC-31

Galle, Mike
89GreatF-28

Gallego, Mike
82Tacom-30
82WHave-12
84Cram/PCL-81
85Moth/A's-24
86D-156
86T-304
86Tacom-7
88D-379
88D/A's/Bk-379
88Modesto-33
88Moth/A's-22
88Score-428
88T-702
88T/Big-103
89D-422
89F-8
89Moth/A's-23
89Score-537
89T-102
89UD-583
90D-361
90F-7
90Score-323
90T-293
90UD-230

Gallegos, Matt
83Nashvl-6

Gallia, Melvin
(Bert)
D328-54
E135-54
W514-76

Gallo, Ben
81Clint-6

Gallo, Raymond
81BurlB-6
83ElPas-14

Galloway, Clarence E.
(Chick)
21Exh-54
61F-108
E120
E126-15
E210-58
V100
W572
W573

Galloway, Gill
89Bill/Pro-2065

Galloway, Ike
88Batav/Pro-1680

Galloway, Joseph
26Exh-106

Galloway, Troy
85Visal-24
86Orlan-6
87Visal-9

Galvan, Mike
88Utica/Puc-20
89Utica/Puc-8

Galvez, Balvino
86Albuq-8
89Colum/CMC-10
89Colum/Pol-6
89Colum/Pro-748

Galvez, Roberto
78Duned

Galvin, James
(Pud)
75F/Pion-11
80SSPC/HOF
89HOF/St-80
N172
WG1-59

Gamba, Tom J.
87Watlo-8
88Watlo/Pro-673

Gambee, Brad
86Cram/PCL-4
87Everett-29

Gambeski, Mike
83Sprin/LF-23

Gamble, Billy
88Wythe/Pro-2000

Gamble, Fredie
89Brist/Star-8

Gamble, John
74OPC-597R
74T-597R

Gamble, Lee
40PB-208
W711/1

Gamble, Oscar
70T-654R
71MLB/St-178
71OPC-23
71T-23
72OPC-423
72T-423
73OPC-372
73T-372
74OPC-152
74T-152
74T/St-166
75Ho-147
75OPC-213
75T-213
75T/M-213
76OPC-74
76SSPC-526
76T-74
76T/Tr-74T
77T-505
78Ho-100
78T-390
79OPC-132
79T-263
80T-698
81D-229
81F-98
81OPC-139
81T-139
82D-360
82F-36
82OPC-229
82T-472
83D-461
83F-380
83OPC-19
83T-19
84F-124
84Nes/792-512
84OPC-13
84T-512
85Coke/WS-0
85F/Up-U44
85OPC-93
85T-724
85T/Tr-37T

Gamble, Robert
N172

Gamby, Steve
75Clint

Gammage, Mark
82BurlR-19

Ganch, Tim
78Charl

Gandil, Charles
(Chick)
14CJ-39
15CJ-39
88Pac/8Men-106
88Pac/8Men-22M
88Pac/8Men-25
88Pac/8Men-46
88Pac/8Men-48M
88Pac/8Men-9
BF2-22
C46-65
D328-55
D329-64
E135-55
E90/3
M101/4-64
T206
T213/blue
W514-31

Ganley, Robert
E91
T204
T206

Gant, Ronald Edwin
(Ronnie)
86Durhm-12
87Greenv/Bst-13
87SLAS-13
88D-654
88D/Best-2
88D/Rook-47
88F-538
88Richm/CMC-12
88Richm/Pro-3
88Score-647
88T/Big-249
88T/Tr-39T
89B-274
89Bz-9
89Class-35
89D-50
89F-590
89KMart/DT-2
89OPC-196
89Panini/St-42
89Score-372
89Score/HotRk-87
89Score/YS/I-16
89Sf-28
89T-296
89T/Big-43
89T/Gloss60-10
89T/JumboR-9
89T/St-322
89T/St-34
89T/UK-29
89ToysRUs-10
89UD-378
90D-475
90F-582
90T-567
90UD-232

Gantner, Jim
77Spoka
77T-494R
79T-154
80T-374
81D-204
81F-522
81F/St-133
81OPC-122
81T-482
82D-406
82F-142
82OPC-207

82Pol/Brew-17
82T-613
83D-232
83F-34
83Gard-8
83OPC-88
83Pol/Brew-17
83T-88
84D-115
84F-200
84Gard-7
84Nes/792-298
84OPC-298
84Pol/Brew-17
84T-298
84T/St-298
85D-229
85D/AAS-2
85F-582
85Gard-7
85Leaf-217
85OPC-216
85Pol/Brew-17
85T-781
85T/St-295
86D-115
86F-487
86Jay's-8
86Leaf-43
86OPC-51
86Pol/Brew-17
86T-582
86T/St-202
87D-172
87D/OD-53
87F-345
87OPC-108
87Smok/AL-15
87T-108
87T/St-197
88D-214
88D/Best-53
88F-165
88Leaf-161
88OPC-337
88Panini/St-124
88Pol/Brew-17
88Score-197
88Sf-130
88T-337
88T/St-195
89B-141
89D-264
89D/Best-295
89F-186
89Gard-3
89OPC-134
89Panini/St-372
89Pol/Brew-17
89Score-313
89T-671
89T/Big-184
89T/St-203
89UD-274
90D-291
90F-324
90Score-382
90T-417
90UD-218

Ganzel, Charles
N172
N300/unif
N526
Scrapp

Ganzel, John Henry
C46-26
T206

Garagiola, Joe
47TipTop
49Eureka-182
51B-122
52B-27
52T-227
53B/Col-21
54B-141
79TCMA-262
80Cram/Leg-76

Garber, Gene
74OPC-431
74T-431
75OPC-444
75T-444
75T/M-444
76OPC-14
76SSPC-458
76T-14
77T-286
78T-177
79OPC-331
79T-629
80OPC-263
80T-504
81D-77
81F-249
81OPC-307
81Pol/Atl-26
81T-307
81T/SO-42
81T/St-137
82BK/Lids-8
82D-123
82F-434
82F/St-234
82Pol/Atl-26
82T-32
82T/St-245
83D-223
83F-136
83OPC-255
83OPC-256SV
83Pol/Atl-26
83T-255
83T-256A
83T/St-213
84D-287
84F-179
84Nes/792-466
84Nes/792-709LL
84OPC-167
84Pol/Atl-26
84T-466
84T-709
84T/St-35
85F-325
85Ho/Braves-9
85Pol/Atl-26
85T-129
86F-515
86Pol/Atl-26
86T-776
87D-414
87F-515
87F/Excit-17
87F/RecSet-10
87F/St-44
87Leaf-172
87Smok/Atl-9
87T-351
87T/St-40
88D-618
88D/Best-63
88F-257
88OPC-289
88Score-565
88Sf-88
88Smok/Royals-11
88T-597

Garber, Jeff
88Eugene/Best-16
89AppFx/Pro-863

Garbey, Barbaro
81BirmB
82BirmB-2
83Evans-18
84F/X-42
84T/X-41
85Cain's-7
85D-456
85F-7
85F/St-121
85Leaf-121
85OPC-243
85T-243
85T/St-263
85Wendy-8
86D-349
86F-225
86OPC-88
86T-609
88OkCty/CMC-16
88OkCty/Pro-45

Garbould, Bob
44Centen-8

Garces, Maduro
89Hagers/Best-6

Garces, Rich
89Keno/Pro-1076
89Keno/Star-6
89Star/Wax-51

Garces, Robinson
87Lakel-21
88Fay/Pro-1087
89Hagers/Pro-281
89Hagers/Star-8

Garcia, Alfonso
(Kiko)
77T-474R
78T-287
79T-543
80T-37
81D-514
81F-191
81OPC-192
81T-688
81T/Tr-765
82D-476
82F-215
82T-377
83D-569
83F-447
83Portl-25
83T-198
83T/X-36
84D-545
84F-30
84Nes/792-458
84T-458
85T-763

Garcia, Amadeo
89Elizab/Star-26

Garcia, Apolinar
89Madis/Star-10

Garcia, Carlos
88Aug/Pro-365
89Salem/Star-9

Garcia, Cheo
89Keno/Pro-1083
89Keno/Star-7

Garcia, Chidez
89BirmB/Best-9

Garcia, Cornelio
86AppFx-9
88FSLAS/Star-37
88Tampa/Star-7
89BirmB/Pro-102

Garcia, Damaso
76FtLaud
77WHave
78Cr/PCL-49
79Colum-4
81D-269
81F-415
81OPC-233
81OPC/Post-14
81T-488
82D-479
82F-613
82OPC-293
82OPC/Post-2
82T-596
83D-54
83D/AAS-17
83F-427
83OPC-202TL
83OPC-222
83T-202TL
83T-222
83T/St-134
84D-241
84F-153
84Nes/792-124
84OPC-124
84T-124
84T/St-364
84Tor/Fire-12
85D-315
85D/AAS-6
85F-104
85Leaf-65
85OPC-353
85OPC/Post-15
85T-645
85T-702AS
85T/St-357
85Tor/Fire-11
86Ault-7
86D-241
86D/AAS-40
86F-59
86F/LimEd-17
86F/Mini-15
86F/St-41
86Leaf-116
86OPC-45
86S-34
86T-45
86T-713
86T/St-190
86Tor/Fire-12
87D-614
87F-226
87Leaf-92
87OPC-395
87S-183
87Smok/Atl-22
87T-395
87T/St-188
88D-414
88T-241
89T/Big-275
90F-346
90T-432
90UD-649

Garcia, Danny
76Watlo

Garcia, Dave
73OPC-12CO
73T-12C
78T-656
81D-442
81T-665MG
82BK/Ind-1
82BK/Ind-2
82BK/Indians-1
82BK/Indians-2
82D-337
82Wheat/Ind
83Pol/Brew-C
83T-546

Garcia, Edward M.
(Mike)
50B-147
50NumNum
51B-150
51T/RB-40
52B-7
52NumNum-7
52T-272
53B/Col-43
53T-75
54B-100
54DanDee
55B-128
55Gol/Ind-8
55Salem
56T-210
57T-300
58T-196
59T-516
60T-532

Garcia, Frank
80Ashev-23
80Tulsa-12
83StPet-17

Garcia, Joe
75SnAnt

Garcia, Julio
89Princet/Star-26

Garcia, Leo
81AppFx-15
82AppFx-3
83Water-17
87Nashv-5
89Toled/CMC-16
89Toled/Pro-767

Garcia, Leonard
77SLCty
78Cr/PCL-88
79SLCty-23
80SLCty-19
81SLCty-1
86Edmon-12TR

Garcia, Librado
89Beloi/Star-6

Garcia, Longo
89Mia/Star/22-5
89Mia/Star/25-7

Garcia, Manny
89Butte/SP-19

Garcia, Miguel
75BurlB
76Clint
80Ander-22
81Durhm-2
82Durhm-1
86PalmSp-14
86PalmSp/Smok-8
87MidldA-1
89BuffB/CMC-7
89BuffB/Pro-1686
89D-622
89F-647M
90UD-538

Garcia, Mike
89Brist/Star-9

Garcia, Nelson Jose
75OkCty
80ArkTr-17

Garcia, Oscar
89StCath/Pro-2075

Garcia, Pedro
73OPC-609R
73T-609R
74OPC-142
74T-142
74T/St-195
75OPC-147
75T-147
75T/M-147
76OPC-187
76SSPC-234
76T-187
77OPC-166
77T-453
77Watlo

Garcia, Ralph
73OPC-602R
73T-602R

Garcia, Ray
85Utica-19

Garcia, Reggie
88Martins/Star-15
89Spart/Pro-1039
89Spart/Star-9
Garcia, Rene
86Bakers-10
87VeroB-27
Garcia, Rich
88Umpire-22
89Umpires-20
Garcia, Santiago
88Vanco/CMC-13
88Vanco/Pro-764
Garcia, Steve
83Beaum-12
84Beaum-18
85Cram/PCL-115
86LasVegas-3
87LasVegas-20
88Albuq/CMC-24
88Albuq/Pro-249
Garcia, Victor
(Butch)
87Columbia-16
87Peoria-2
88CLAS/Star-27
88PrWill/Star-11
88WinSal/Star-3
89CharlK-7
89FtLaud/Star-5
89Greens/Pro-407
89IowaC/CMC-11
89IowaC/Pro-1693
Garcia, Vinicio U.
(Chico)
54Esskay
Garczyk, Ed
89SLCty-9
Gardella, Mike
88CapeCod/Sum-69
89Oneon/Pro-2103
Gardenhire, Ron
81Tidew-5
82D-649
82T-623R
82T/Tr-39T
83D-175
83F-543
83T-469
83Tidew-20
85D-360
85F-81
85T-144
86T-274
86Tidew-10
87Portl-25
88Keno/Pro-1402
88MidwLAS/GS-36
89Orlan/Best-5
89Orlan/Pro-1355
Gardey, Rudy
88Idaho/Pro-1855
Gardiner, Mike
88Wausa/Feder-25
88Wausa/GS-25
89Wausa/GS-28
Gardner, Art
73Cedar
75Iowa/TCMA-8
78Cr/PCL-2
86Tulsa-5CO
87Gasto-24
Gardner, Bill
88Eugene/Best-19
Gardner, Billy F.
52Park-88
55B-249
55Gol/Giants-7
55T-27
55T/DH-61
57T-17
58Hires-37
58T-105
59T-89
60T-106
61Clover-5
61P-96
61Peters-14
61T-123
61T/St-179
62Salada-211
62Shirriff-211
62T-163M
62T-338
63T-408
82D-591
83T-11
84Nes/792-771MG
84T-771
85T-213
87T/Tr-36T
Gardner, Chuck
77Clint
Gardner, Earl M.
11Helmar-44
M116
T201
T205
T207
Gardner, Floyd(Jelly)
74Laugh/Black-7
Gardner, Franklin W.
N172
Gardner, Glen
88Pulas/Pro-1756
89Sumter/Pro-1097
Gardner, Jeff
86Lynch-10
87TexLgAS-7
88Jacks/GS-10
89Tidew/CMC-20
89Tidew/Pro-1966
Gardner, Jim
(Jimmie)
86Peoria-7
87CharWh-20
Gardner, Jimmie C.
86Geneva-6
Gardner, Jimmie
T3/Box-62
Gardner, John
88CharWh/Best-15
89CharWh/Best-19
89CharWh/Pro-1769
Gardner, Mark
86Jaxvl/TCMA-15
87Indianap-19
88Jaxvl/Best-7
88Jaxvl/Pro-987
89AAA/Pro-10
89Indi/CMC-8
89Indi/Pro-1224
90D-40
90F-646M
90Score-639
90Score/100Ris-66
90T-284
Gardner, Myron
86Watlo-8
88SLCty-20
Gardner, Rob
66T-534R
67T-217
68T-219
71OPC-734
71T-734
72OPC-22
72T-22
73OPC-222
73T-222
Gardner, Scott
82DayBe-4
83Miami-3
Gardner, Vassie
81Charl-20
82Knoxv-19
Gardner, Wes
83Lynch-23
84Tidew-3
85IntLgAS-21
85Tidew-9
88D-634
88D/RedSox/Bk-634
88F-352
88T-189
89B-23
89D-541
89F-88
89Score-412
89T-526
90D-541
90F-275
90Score-348
90T-38
Gardner, William L.
21Exh-55
D327
D328-56
D329-65
D350/2-65
E120
E121/120
E121/80
E135-56
E220
E254
M101/4-65
M101/5-65
M116
V100
W501-24
W575
Garibaldi, Art
40Hughes-7
Garibaldi, Bob
70T-681
71OPC-701
71T-701
Garibaldo, Chris
89AppFx/Pro-862
Gariglio, Robert
81Chatt-1
Garland, Wayne
74OPC-596R
74T-596R
76OPC-414
76SSPC-376
76T-414
77Ho-144
77K-21
77OPC-138
77Pep-14
77T-33
77T/CS-17
78Ho-137
78OPC-15
78T-174
78Wiffle/Discs-25
79T-636
80T-361
81D-440
81F-394
81OPC-272
81T-511
82D-489
82F-367
82T-446
87Nashv-6CO
88Nashvl/CMC-24
88Nashvl/Pro-494
Garman, Mike
71OPC-512R
71T-512R
72OPC-79R
72T-79R
73OPC-616R
73T-616R
75OPC-584
75T-584
75T/M-584
76OPC-34
76SSPC-293
76T-34
77T-302
78T-417
79OPC-88
79Portl-15
79T-181
Garman, Pat
88Gasto/Pro-1014
Garms, Debs
39PB-72
40PB-161
41DP-149
41G-29
41PB-11
Garner, Darrin
86DayBe-8
87Gasto-22
88CharlR/Star-7
88FSLAS/Star-38
89Tulsa/GS-9
Garner, Kevin
88River/Cal-220
88River/Pro-1431
89AubAs/Pro-17
89Wich/Roc-33OF
Garner, Mike
87VeroB-13
88Reno/Cal-277
Garner, Phil
75OPC-623R
75T-623R
75T/M-623R
76OPC-57
76SSPC-495
76T-57
77Ho-11
77OPC-34
77T-261
78Ho-52
78OPC-203
78T-53
79Ho-75
79OPC-200
79T-383
80OPC-65
80T-118
1Coke
81D-372
81F-364
81F/St-71
81K-44
81OPC-99
81T-573
81T/SO-102
81T/St-209
81T/St-253
82D-544
82F-215
82Sqt-13
82T-683
83D-270
83F-448
83OPC-128
83T-478
83T/St-170
83T/St-237
84D-354
84F-226
84Moth/Ast-5
84Nes/792-752
84OPC-119
84T-752
84T/St-63
85D-161
85F-351
85Moth/Ast-3
85OPC-206
85T-206
85T/St-64
86D-527
86F-301
86F/Mini-64
86OPC-83
86Pol/Ast-9
86T-83
86T/St-32
87D-358
87D/OD-12
87F-58
87Moth/A's-16
87Moth/Ast-6
87OPC-304
87Pol/Ast-24
87T-304
87T/St-30
88Moth/Giants-25
88Score-431
88T-174
Garnett, Brad
82AlexD-11
Garr, Ralph
70OPC-172R
70T-172R
71MLB/St-9
71OPC-494R
71T-494R
72K-21
72OPC-260
72OPC-85LL
72T-260
72T-85LL
73K-37
73OPC-15
73T-15
74OPC-570
74T-570
74T/St-4
75Ho-87
75K-35
75OPC-306LL
75OPC-550
75T-306LL
75T-550
75T/M-306LL
75T/M-550
76OPC-410
76SSPC-17
76T-410
76T/Tr-410T
77Ho-108
77K-13
77OPC-77
77Pep-26
77T-133
78K-37
78OPC-195
78PapaG/Disc-37
78T-628
78Wiffle/Discs-26
79OPC-156
79T-309
80OPC-142
80T-272
Garrelts, Scott
80Clint-10
81Shrev-20
83Phoen/BHN-3
84Cram/PCL-5
84D-646
85Moth/Giants-23
85T/Tr-38T
86D-309
86D/AAS-35
86F-540
86F/LL-14
86F/Mini-110
86F/St-42

86Leaf-180
86Moth/Giants-19
86OPC-395
86S-157
86T-395
86T/St-86
87D-116
87F-273
87F/Hottest-17
87F/Mini-42
87F/St-45
87Leaf-75
87Moth/SFG-11
87OPC-37
87RedFoley/St-24
87S-68
87T-475
87T/St-89
88D-80
88D/Best-162
88F-82
88Moth/Giants-11
88OPC-97
88Panini/St-416
88Score-533
88Sf-44
88T-97
88T/Big-240
88T/St-90
89B-467
89D-295
89D/Best-218
89F-328
89Moth/Giants-11
89OPC-214
89RedFoley/St-48
89Score-258
89T-703
89UD-50
90D-217
90F-56
90Score-246
90Sf-39
90T-602
90UD-478

Garrett, Bobby
81WHave-9

Garrett, Eric
83Idaho-15
84Madis/Pol-19

Garrett, Greg
70T-642R
71MLB/St-58
71OPC-377
71T-377

Garrett, H. Adrian
(Pat)
66T-553R
71OPC-576R
71T-576R
74OPC-656
74T-656
76OPC-562
76T-562
82AppFx-31
83GlenF-22
87Omaha-16

Garrett, Lee
80Water-9
81Water-23
82Indianap-31tr
83Indianap-32tr

Garrett, Lynn
81WHave-11
82WHave-21
83Tacom-15

Garrett, R. Wayne
70T-628
71MLB/St-152
71OPC-228
71T-228
72OPC-518
72T-518
73OPC-562
73T-562
74OPC-510
74T-510
74T/St-61
75OPC-111
75T-111
75T/M-111
76OPC-222
76SSPC-539
76T-222
77OPC-117
77T-417
78OPC-198
78T-679
79T-319

Garrett, Steve
80Elmir-6

Garrick, Darren
86SanJose-8

Garrido, Gil
61Union
64T-452R
69T-331R
70OPC-48
70T-48
71MLB/St-10
71OPC-173
71T-173
72T-758
89Sumter/Pro-1094

Garriott, Cece
47Signal

Garrison, Jim
87Watertn-18
88Aug/Pro-369

Garrison, Marv
77LodiD
78LodiD

Garrison, Venoy
75Clint

Garrison, Webster
85Kingst-16
87Duned-15
88SLAS-23
89Knoxv/Best-6
89Knoxv/Pro-1131
89Knoxv/Star-4

Garver, Ned
49B-15
50B-51
51B-172
51FB
51T/BB-18
52B-29
52BR
52StarCal/L-75A
52T-212
52TipTop
53B/Col-47
53Glen
53T-112
54B-39
54T-44
55B-188
56T-189
57T-285
58T-292
59T-245
60T-471
61T-331
61T/St-171
89Pac/Leg-183
PM10/Sm-59

Garvey, Brian
75AppFx

Garvey, Steve
71MLB/St-103
71OPC-341
71T-341
72T-686
73OPC-213
73T-213
74OPC-575
74T-575
75Ho-49
75Ho/Twink-49
75K-17
75OPC-140
75OPC-212M
75OPC-460NLCS
75T-140
75T-212MV
75T/M-140
75T/M-212MV
76Crane-16
76Ho-19
76Ho/Twink-19
76K-54
76MSA/Disc
76OPC-150
76SSPC-77
76T-150
77Ho-35
77K-14
77OPC-255
77Pep-61
77T-400
77T/CS-19
78OPC-190
78T-350
78Wiffle/Discs-27
79Ho-8
79OPC-21
79T-50
79T/Comics-24
80K-31
80OPC-152
80Pol/Dodg-6
80T-290
80T/S-13
81D-176
81D-56
81Drake-11
81F-110
81F-606M
81F/St-1
81K-10
81MSA/Disc-13
81OPC-251
81Pol/Dodg-6
81Sqt-4
81T-530
81T/HT
81T/Nat/Super-6
81T/S
81T/SO-56
81T/St-176
81T/St-252
82D-3DK
82D-84
82Drake-14
82F-5
82F/St-9
82HB/LS
82K-47
82KMart-26
82OPC-179
82OPC-180IA
82P/Tips-1
82P/Tips-12
82Pol/Dodg
82Pol/Dodg-6
82T-179
82T-180A
82T/St-54
83D-488
83F-206
83OPC-198
83T-610
83T/St-243
83T/X-37
84D-63
84D/AAS-38
84D/Champs-56
84Drake-10
84F-300
84F-628
84FunFood/Pin-9
84MiltBrad-10
84Moth/Padres-7
84Nes/792-380
84Nestle/DT-12
84OPC-380
84Ralston-18
84Seven-7W
84Smok/Padres-10
84T-380
84T/Cereal-18
84T/St-156
84T/Super-22
84T/Super-22
85D-307
85Drake-11
85F-32
85F-631IA
85F/LimEd-9
85GenMills-3
85Leaf-94
85Moth/Padres-6
85OPC-177
85Seven-8W
85SpokAT/Cram-7
85T-2RB
85T-450
85T/Gloss22-2
85T/St-1
85T/St-13
85T/St-14
85T/St-149
85T/St-176
85T/St-2
85T/Super-26
86BK/AP-18
86D-63
86D/AAS-3
86D/PopUp-3
86F-321
86F-640M
86F/LL-15
86F/Mini-67
86F/St-43
86F/St-S3
86Jiffy-18
86Leaf-56
86Meadow/Blank-4
86Meadow/Stat-15
86OPC-4
86Quaker-6
86S-137M
86S-35
86S-51M
86S/Dec-61
86T-660
86T/Gloss22-13
86T/Gloss60-38
86T/St-104
86T/St-148
86T/Super-24
86TrueVal-2
87BK-5
87Bohem-6
87Class-27
87D-81
87D/OD-143
87F-414
87F/Excit-18
87F/GameWin-16
87F/McCror-16
87F/Mini-43
87F/St-46
87Kraft-20
87Leaf-114
87MnM's-20
87OPC-100
87Ralston-2
87RedFoley/St-61
87S-40
87Smok/Dodg-8
87Smok/NL-10
87T-100
87T/Board-18
87T/Coins-32
87T/St-115
88Score-225
88Smok/Dodg-15M
88Smok/Dodg-17
88Smok/Dodg-21M
89Smok/Dodg-83

Garvin, Theodore
(Jerry)
78OPC-49
78T-419
79OPC-145
79T-293
80OPC-320
80T-611
81D-150
81F-429
81OPC-124
81T-124
82D-430
82F-614
82OPC-264
82T-768
83D-227
83F-428
83T-358

Garvin, Virgil
E107

Garza, Lonnie
83Redwd-10

Garza, Willie
88Watlo/Pro-670

Gasian, Larry
88Orlan/Best-20

Gaspar, Harry
10Domino-47
11Helmar-114
12Sweet/Pin-99
E254
M116
T201
T202
T205
T206

Gaspar, Rod
70OPC-371
70T-371
71MLB/St-227
71OPC-383
71T-383

Gass, Jeff
83Erie-16

Gassaway, Charles
46Remar-7
47Remar-4
47Signal
47Smith-8
48Signal
48Smith-10
49B/PCL-10
49Remar
50Remar

Gasser, Steve
86Kenosha-10
87Orlan-11
87SLAS-18
88Orlan/Best-23

Gast, Joe
89Penin/Star-6

Gastelum, Macario
87Bakers-3
89Bakers/Cal-185

Gastfield, Ed
N172

Gaston, Alex
E121/120
W501-11
W575
Gaston, Clarence
(Cito)
69MB-90
69T-304R
70T-604
71Bz
71Bz/Test-12
71K-41
71MLB/St-228
71OPC-25
71T-25
71T/Coins-1
71T/tatt-4
72MB-113
72OPC-431
72OPC-432IA
72T-431
72T-432A
73OPC-159
73T-159
74OPC-364SD
74T-364
75OPC-427
75T-427
75T/M-427
76OPC-558
76SSPC-18
76T-558
77T-192
78T-716
79T-208
84Tor/Fire-13CO
85Tor/Fire-12CO
86Tor/Fire-13CO
87Tor/Fire-10
87Tor/Fire-10CO
88Tor/Fire-43CO
89T/Tr-36T
89Tor/Fire-43
90T-201MG
Gaston, John
83Greens-6
Gaston, Milt
33G-65
V353-65
Gastreich, Henry
N172
Gateman, Wareham
88CapeCod-25
Gates, Bryan
87Anchora-34BB
Gates, Eddie
81Evans-20
82Evans-20
Gates, Joe
77Jaxvl
78Knoxv
Gates, Michael
80Memph-9
82Wichi-4
83D-114
83OPC-195
83T-657
84Indianap-29
Gatewood, Aubrey
64T-127R
65T-422
66OPC-42
66T-42
Gatewood, Henry
85VeroB-11
86Visal-10
87Orlan-5
88WinSal/Star-4
Gatlin, Mike
82Oneon-16
Gaton, Frank
75BurlB
76BurlB
Gattis, Jim
89Mia/Star/22-6
Gaudet, Jim
77Jaxvl
79T-707R
80Evans-3
81Omaha-13
82Syrac-11
Gaughan, Hank
82Chatt-25
Gault, Raymond
77Watlo
Gaunt
C46-69
Gausepohl, Dan
81Hawai-8
82Hawai-8
Gavan, John
E120
W573
Gavin, Dave
88Madis-11
89Modesto/Ch-28
89Watlo/Pro-1776
89Watlo/Star-9
Gay, Jeff
86Cram/PCL-78
87QuadC-26
89PalmSp/Cal-34
89PalmSp/Pro-466
Gay, Scott
87FtLaud-17
88FtLaud/Star-9
89Salin/Pro-1823
Gay, Steve
86Lynch-11
Gaylor, Bobby
86Jamestn-10
87BurlEx-18
88WPalm/Star-10
Gaynor, Richard Kent
83Readg-5
84Cram/PCL-212
87BirmB/Best-11
88BirmB/Best-17
Gazzilli, Dan
85Utica-26
Gbur, Paul
79AppFx-25
Gebhard, Bob
72OPC-28R
72T-28R
75IntAS/TCMA-29
Geddes, Jim
73OPC-561
73T-561
Gedeon, Elmer Joe
D327
D328-57
D329-66
D350/2-66
E135-57
M101/4-66
M101/5-66
W514-39
Gedman, Rich
81Pawtu-24
82Coke/BOS
82D-512
82F-294
82T-59
83D-156
83F-184
83T-602
84D-579
84F-398
84Nes/792-498
84OPC-296
84T-498
84T/St-222
85D-457
85F-159
85OPC-18
85T-529
85T/St-217
86D-273
86D/AAS-56
86F-349
86F-643M
86F/LimEd-18
86F/Mini-75
86F/St-44
86Leaf-145
86OPC-375
86S-84
86T-375
86T/St-248
87Class-49
87D-153
87D/AAS-39
87F-35
87F/RecSet-11
87F/WS-9M
87Leaf-254
87OPC-137
87S-149
87S-154M
87T-740
87T/St-247
88D-129
88D/Best-140
88D/RedSox/Bk-129
88F-353
88OPC-245
88Panini/St-24
88Score-241
88T-245
88T/Big-152
88T/St-252
89B-27
89D-162
89F-89
89OPC-178
89Score-345
89T-652
89T/Big-72
89T/St-253
89UD-368
90D-346
90F-276
90Score-173
90T-123
90UD-402
Gee, Steve
82Tucso-28M
Gegan, Fred
87VeroB-9
Gehrig, Henry Louis
(Lou)
25Exh-97
26Exh-99
27Exh-49
28Exh-50
28Yueng-26
29Exh/4-26
31Exh/4-26
33CJ/Pin-7
33DL-7
33G-160
33G-92
34Exh/4-13
34G-37
34G-61
35Exh/4-13
35Wheat
36Exh/4-13
36Wheat
37Exh/4-13
38Exh/4-13
38ONG/Pin-11
39Exh
48Exh/HOF
48Swell-14
49Leaf/Prem-3
50Callahan
51T/CM
60Exh/HOF-11
60F-28
60NuCard-24
61F-31
61GP-16
61NuCard-424
61T-405M
63Bz/ATG-15
69Bz-5
69Bz/Sm
72F/FFeat-5
72K/ATG-13
72K/ATG-13
72Laugh/GF-8
73OPC-472LL
73T-472LL
76Laugh/Jub-28
76OPC-341AS
76T-341M
80Cram/Leg-13
80Laugh/3/4/5-29
80Laugh/FFeat-10
80SSPC/HOF
85CircK-14
85D-635PUZ
85D/HOF-3
85D/WaxBox-PUZ
85Leaf- 635PUZ
85West/2-25
85Woolwth-14
86Conlon/1-1
86Conlon/1-17
86Conlon/1-52
86Conlon/1-57
86S/Dec-10
87Conlon/2-1
87Nestle/DT-1
88Conlon/5-12
88Conlon/AmAS-10
89HOF/St-1
89Pac/Leg-174
89Swell-25
PM10/Sm-60
PR1-11
R310
R315-A10
R315-B10
R316
R328-26
R332-20
R346-29
R423-35
V353-55
V354-92
V355-96
W502-26
W517-35
Gehringer, Charles
26Exh-95
27Exh-47
29Exh/4-23
31Exh/4-23
33DH-20
33DL-5
33Exh/4-12
33G-222
34DS-77
34Exh/4-12
34G-23
34Ward's/Pin-5
35BU-130
35BU-42
35Exh/4-12
35G-1D
35G-2D
35G-6D
35G-7D
36Exh/4-12
36Wheat
37Dix
37Exh/4-12
37OPC-112
37Wheat-4
38Exh/4-12
38G-241
38G-265
38ONG/Pin-10
38Wheat
39Exh
39PB-50
40PB-41
41DP-54
41PB-19
50Callahan
60F-58
61F-32
61GP-10
80SSPC/HOF
83D/HOF-28
84West/1-16
86Conlon/1-43
86S/Dec-12
88Conlon/5-13
88Conlon/AmAS-11
R300
R303/A
R308-183
R310
R311/Leath
R313
R314
R316
V300
V354-57
V355-42
WG8-23
Geiger, Burt
82Albuq-3
83Albuq-2
Geiger, Gary Jr.
87Everett-24
88Fresno/Cal-23
88Fresno/Pro-1229
Geiger, Gary Merle
58T-462
59T-521
60T-184
61T-33
61T/St-111
62J-60
62P-60
62P/Can-60
62Salada-38A
62Salada-38B
62Shirriff-38
62T-117
62T/St-13
63J-81
63P-81
63T-513
64T-93
65T-452
66T-286
67T-566
69T-278
77Evans/TCMA-10CO
Geisel, J. Dave
79T-716R
80T-676R
82D-633
82Syrac-4
84Cram/PCL-175
84D-645
84F-154
84Nes/792-256
84OPC-256
84T-256
85Moth/Mar-22
86OKCty-6
Geishert, Vern
70T-683R

Geiss, Emil
N172
Geist, Pete
86FSLAS-17
86VeroB-6
87VeroB-6
88Duned/Star-7
Geivett, Billy
86PalmSp-15
86PalmSp/Smok-23
87MidldA-3
Gelatt, Dave
85LitFalls-18
86Columbia-10
87Lynch-18
Gelbert, Charles M.
29Exh/4-16
31Exh/4-16
33Exh/4-8
39PB-93
40PB-18
R306
R313
R314
V355-49
Gelfarb, Steve
81WHave-12
82WHave-13
Gelinas, Marc
78Salem
Gellinger, Mike
87DayBe-25
89Utica/Puc-30
Gelnar, John
65OPC-143R
65T-143R
67T-472R
70McDon-4
70OPC-393
70T-393
71MLB/St-436
71OPC-604
71T-604
Gendron, Bob
84Shrev/FB-8
Genewich, Joseph
21Exh-56
25Exh-5
26Exh-5
27Exh-2
Genins, C. Frank
N172
Gentile, Gene
78Charl
81Brist-4
83Pawtu-21
84Albany-3
86Kinston-8
87Harrisbg-21
88Harris/Pro-856
Gentile, Jim
60T-448
61NuCard-401
61P-68
61T-559
61T/St-101
62Bz
62Exh
62J-27
62P-27
62P/Can-27
62Salada-1
62Shirriff-1
62T-290
62T-53LL
62T/bucks
62T/St-5
63Bz-11
63Exh
63J-57
63P-57
63T-260
63T-4LL
63T/SO
64Bz-11
64T-196
64T/S-15
64T/St-75
64T/SU
65T-365
66OPC-45
66T-45
78TCMA-4
85Woolwth-15
Exh47
WG10-28
Gentile, Randy
89Elizab/Star-9
Gentle, Mike
83VeroB-4
Gentleman, J.P.
88Hamil/Pro-1743
Gentleman, Jean
88Savan/Pro-356
Gentry, Gary
69OPC-31R
69T-31R
70OPC-153
70T-153
70Trans/M-23
71MLB/St-153
71OPC-725
71T-725
72OPC-105
72T-105
73OPC-288
73T-288
74OPC-415
74T-415
75OPC-393
75T-393
75T/M-393
George, Andre
88Poca/Pro-2075
George, Chris
89Stock/Best-2
89Stock/Cal-153
89Stock/Pro-391
89Stock/Star-8
George, Don
33SK-40
George, Frankie
77SLCty
George, Leo
82QuadC-14
George, Nattie
84Greens-7
George, Phil
83Butte-5
85FtMyr-11
86FtMyr-11
87Memph-2
87Memph/Best-11
George, Steve
83Greens-7
84Greens-18
86Albany/TCMA-29
George, Thomas
(Lefty)
T207
George, Will
82Miami-1
83Miami-1
87Hagers-3
89Kinston/Star-27
George, William
N172
N338/2
Georger, Joe
80LynnS-17
81LynnS-4
82LynnS-4
86Wausa-10CO
89QuadC/Best-3
89QuadC/GS-3
Gerace, Joanne
88Utica/Puc-29
89Utica/Puc-32
Gerald, Edward
89LittleSun-19
Gerber, Craig
82Redwd-3
83Nashua-13
84Cram/PCL-109
86D-545
86Edmon-13
86F-156
86T-222
88Edmon/Pro-583
88MidldA/GS-24
Gerber, Walter
(Wally)
21Exh-57
25Exh-113
26Exh-117
E120
E220
V61-49
W573
Geren, Bob
83Sprin/LF-13
84ArkTr-11
87Albany-5
88AAA/Pro-9
88Colum/CMC-11
88Colum/Pol-12
88Colum/Pro-303
89Colum/CMC-11
89Colum/Pol-7
89Colum/Pro-758
89D/Rook-11
89F/Up-48
89Score/HotRk-66
89Score/NWest-25
89Score/Tr-93
89T/Tr-37T
90Class-25
90D-395
90F-442
90Score-464
90Score/100Ris-50
90Sf-205
90T-536
90UD-608
Gergen, Bob
83BurlR-16
83BurlR/LF-13
84Tulsa-26
85Tulsa-25
86Tulsa-14
Gerhardt, Allen
83Beaum-22
87Gasto-10
Gerhardt, Bill
83Miami-7
Gerhardt, John
N172
N284
N338/2
Gerhardt, Rusty
84OKCty-5
85OKCty-24
86OKCty-7CO
Gerhart, Ken
84CharO-22
85CharO-1
86RochR-3
87D-30RR
87D/OD-141
87D/Rook-24
87F/U-U34
87Leaf-30
87S/Rook-7
87T/Tr-37T
88D-213
88F-559
88French-38
88OPC-271
88Panini/St-14
88RedFoley/St-27
88Score-58
88T-271
88ToysRUs-11
89F-609
89OPC-192
89Phoen/CMC-20
89Phoen/Pro-1499
89Score-506
89T-598
89UD-426
Gering, Scott
79Elmir-13
Gerlach, Jim
81QuadC-27
83MidldC-21
German, Rene
83QuadC-11
Germann, Mark
86Cedar/TCMA-16
87Vermont-20
88Chatt/Best-10
89Nashvl/CMC-15
89Nashvl/Pro-1275
Germer, Glen
81Durhm-18
Gernert, Dick
52StarCal/L-71G
52T-343
53B/BW-11
54B-146
57T-202
58T-38
59T-13
59T-519M
60T-86
61T-284
61T/St-151
62T-536
62T/bucks
89Smok/Ast-18
Geronimo, Cesar
71OPC-447
71T-447
72T-719
73OPC-156
73T-156
74OPC-181
74T-181
74T/St-26
75Ho-121
75K-50
75OPC-41
75T-41
75T/M-41
76Ho-150
76Icee
76OPC-24
76SSPC-45
76T-24
77Ho-76
77K-40
77OPC-160
77Pep-49
77T-535
78OPC-32
78T-354
79OPC-111
79T-220
80OPC-247
80T-475
81D-305
81T-390
81T/Tr-766
82D-322
82F-409
82T-693
83D-448
83F-112
83T-194
84D-252
84Nes/792-544
84T-544
Gertz, Mike
82Watlo/B-16
82Watlo/C-14
83Watlo/LF-22
Gessler, Harry
(Doc)
14CJ-59
15CJ-59
M116
Gettel, Allen
50Remar
51B-304
52Mother-3
Getter, Kerry
76Clint
Gettler, Chris
88Bakers/Cal-253
Gettman, Jake
C46-40
Getz, Gustave
D328-58
D329-67
D350/2-67
E135-58
E254
E270/2
M101/4-67
M101/5-67
Getzein, Charles
N172
N284
N29
N43
Scrapps
WG1-21
Geyer, Jacob
(Rube)
T213/blue
Gharrley, Joe
W514-109
Gharrity, Edward P.
(Patsy)
E120
E121/120
V100
V61-50
W501-12
W572
W573
W575
WG7-18
Ghelfi, Andrew
86Watlo-9
87Kinston-16
88Wmspt/Pro-1308
Ghelfi, Tony
85Cram/PCL-40
88Wmspt/Pro-1314
89LasVeg/CMC-5
89LasVeg/Pro-1
Giallombardo, Bob
59DF
59T-321
60DF-9
61Union
Giamatti, A.Bartlett
89Wich/Rc/HL-16
90D-716
90T-396
Giannelli, Ray
89Myrtle/Pro-1469
Giannotta, Go
80Evans-13
Giansanti, Ralph
83Ander-21
Gianukakis, John
86Cram/PCL-146

Gibbon, Joe
60T-512
61T-523
62Kahn
62T-448
63Kahn
63T-101
64T-307
65OPC-54
65T-54
66T-457
67T-541
68OPC-32
68T-32
69OPC-158
69T-158
70OPC-517
70T-517
72OPC-382
72T-382
78TCMA-219
Gibbons, Bill
89Clint/Pro-907
Gibbons, John
82Beloi-8
85D-116
85IntLgAS-15
85Tidew-15
86ElPas-12
86Tidew-11
87Chatt/Best-22
87D-626
87Tidew-6
87Tidew/TCMA-10
88Albuq/CMC-20
88Albuq/Pro-260
88Vermont/Pro-950
89OkCty/CMC-12
89OkCty/Pro-1531
Gibbons, Michael
88SLCty-15
Gibbs, Jake
62T-281
64T-281R
65OPC-226R
65T-226R
66OPC-117
66T-117
67T-375
68OPC-89
68T-89
69MB-91
69MLB/St-74
69T-401
69T/St-203
70MLB/St-245
70T-594
71MLB/St-488
71OPC-382
71T-382
72MB-114
WG10-7
WG9-9
Gibbs, James
88Sprin/Best-9
89Medford/Best-4
Gilbert, Pat
89Huntsvl/Best-21
Gibree, Bob
86Wausa-11
Gibson, Frank
25Exh-6
Gibson, George
10Domino-48
11Helmar-160
12Sweet/Pin-137
D303
D322
D329-68
D350/2-68
E101
E103
E105
E106
E121/120
E254
E270/1
E270/2
E90/1
E90/2
E91
E92
E93
E96
M101/4-68
M101/5-68
M116
S74-110
T201
T202
T205
T206
T216
T3-94
V100
W501-88
W514-63
W555
Gibson, Hoot
81Durhm-19
Gibson, J. Russ
67T-547R
68T-297
69MB-92
69OPC-89
69T-89
69T/St-133
70OPC-237
70T-237
71MLB/St-248
71OPC-738
71T-738
72MB-115
72T-643
Gibson, Joel
65T-368R
78TCMA-208
Gibson, Josh
74Laugh/Black-8
80SSPC/HOF
83D/HOF-4
88Conlon/NegAS-5
Gibson, Kirk
81Coke
81F-481
81OPC-315
81T-315
81T/St-78
82D-407
82Drake-15
82F-267
82F/St-161
82K-40
82OPC-105
82Sqt-6
82T-105
82T/St-184
83D-459
83F-329
83OPC-321
83T-430
83T/St-67
84D-593
84F-80
84FunFood/Pin-21
84Nes/792-65
84OPC-65
84T-65
84T/St-272
85Cain's-8
85D-471
85Drake-12
85F-8
85F/St-22
85Leaf-103
85OPC-372
85Seven-13D
85Seven-8S
85T-565
85T/St-11ALCS
85T/St-19WS
85T/St-267
85T/Super-27
85Wendy-9
86BK/AP-13
86Cain's-6
86D-1
86D-125
86D/DKsuper-1
86D/WaxBox-PC4
86Drake-28
86F-226
86F/LimEd-19
86F/Mini-47
86F/Slug-10
86F/St-45
86Leaf-1DK
86OPC-295
86S-21
86T-295
86T/Gloss60-29
86T/St-266
86T/Super-25
86TrueVal-8
87Cain's-9
87Class-9
87Coke/Tigers-1
87D-50
87F-151
87F/GameWin-17
87F/McCror-17
87F/Mini-44
87F/St-47
87Kraft-19
87Leaf-104
87OPC-386
87RedFoley/St-10
87S-48
87Seven-DT3
87T-765
87T/Board-29
87T/Coins-11
87T/Mini-53
87T/St-273
87Toled-28
88D-275
88D/Best-66
88F-55
88F/Mini-82
88F/St-24
88F/U-U93
88Leaf-136
88Moth/Dodg-8
88OPC-201
88Panini/St-95
88Pol/Dodg-23
88Score-525
88Score/Tr-10T
88Sf-111
88T-605
88T/Big-191
88T/St-267
88T/Tr-40T
88T/UK-26
89Ames-14
89B-351
89Bz-10
89Cadaco-23
89Class-120
89Crunch-2
89D-132
89D-15DK
89D/Best-10
89D/DKsuper-15DK
89F-57
89F/BBAS-14
89F/BBMVP's-13
89F/Excit-14
89F/Heroes-17
89F/LL-15
89F/Rec-4
89F/Superstar-16
89F/WaxBox-C10
89F/WS-5
89Holsum/Discs-20
89KayBee-13
89KingB/Discs-1
89Moth/Dodg-8
89OPC-340
89OPC-382
89Panini/St-107
89Panini/St-16
89Panini/St-17
89Panini/St-479
89Pol/Dodg-14
89RedFoley/St-49
89Score-210
89Score-582M
89Score/HotSt-30
89Sf-65
89T-340
89T-396AS
89T/Big-299
89T/Coins-1
89T/DH-24
89T/Gloss60-55
89T/Hills-14
89T/Mini-17
89T/St-66
89T/St/Backs-49
89T/UK-30
89UD-633
89UD-662MVP
89UD-676TC
89Woolwth-2
89Woolwth-24
90D-368
90F-393
90Score-487
90T-150
90UD-264
Gibson, Leighton
N172
N690
Gibson, Paul
80Cedar-18
82BirmB-23
83Orlan-20
86GlenF-6
86Nashv-9
87Toled-10
87Toled/TCMA-17
88D/Rook-19
88F/U-U26
88Pep/T-48
89B-99
89Bz-11
89Class-140
89D-445
89F-131
89KMart/DT-10
89Mara/Tigers-48
89Panini/St-331
89Score-595
89T-583
89T/Big-230
89T/Gloss60-20
89T/JumboR-10
89T/St-323
89ToysRUs-11
89UD-47
90D-657
90F-602
90Score-261
90T-11
90UD-496
Gibson, Robert L.
(Bob L.) 79BurlB-14
82ElPas-21
83Pol/Brew-40
84Cram/PCL-40
84D-246
84F-201
84Nes/792-349
84T-349
85D-393
85Pol/Brew-40
85T/Tr-39T
86D-271
86F-488
86T-499
86Vanco-12
87Tidew-33
87Tidew/TCMA-3
88RochR-8
88RochR/CMC-5
88RochR/Pro-196
Gibson, Robert
(Bob) 59T-514
60T-73
61T-211
62T-530
63F-61
63J-166
63P-166
63Salada-3
63T-415
63T-5LL
63T-9LL
64T-460
64T/Coins-59
64T/S-41
65Bz-23
65OPC-12LL
65OPC-138WS
65T-12LL
65T-320
65T/E-69
65T/trans-14
66Bz-21
66T-225LL
66T-320
66T/RO-39
67Bz-21
67T-210
67T-236LL
68Bz-9
68OPC-100
68OPC-154WS
68T-100
68T-378AS
69Kelly/Pin-6
69MLB/St-211
69MLBPA/Pin-44
69NTF
69OPC-107CL
69OPC-10LL
69OPC-12LL
69OPC-162WS
69OPC-168WS
69OPC-200
69OPC-8LL
69OPC/DE-7
69T-10LL
69T-12LL
69T-200
69T-432AS
69T-8LL
69T/DE-29
69T/decal
69T/S-60
69T/St-115
69Trans-33
70K-71
70MLB/St-139
70OPC-530
70OPC-67LL
70OPC-71LL
70T-530
70T-67LL

70T-71LL
70T/CB
70T/S-33
70Trans-5
71Bz
71Bz/Test-41
71K-51
71MD
71MLB/St-273
71MLB/St-559
71OPC-450
71OPC-70LL
71OPC-72LL
71T-450
71T-70LL
71T-72LL
71T/Coins-63
71T/GM-24
71T/S-48
71T/tatt-15
71T/tatt-15a
72K-26
72OPC-130
72T-130
73K-14
73OPC-190
73T-190
73T/Lids-19
74K-1
74OPC-350
74T-350
74T/DE-3
74T/Puzzles-5
74T/St-114
75Ho-119
75OPC-150
75OPC-206M
75OPC-3RB
75T-150
75T-206MV
75T-3M
75T/M-150
75T/M-206MV
75T/M-3M
78TCMA-60
82KMart-14
82Pol/Atl-45CO
83Pol/Atl-45CO
84Pol/Atl-45CO
86S/Dec-42
87KMart-3
87Nestle/DT-31
88T-664TBC
89Kahn/Coop-5

Gibson, Scott
82AppFx-22
84Visal-22

Gibson, Steve
78Newar
79BurlB-13
80BurlB-1
81BurlB-11

Giddens, Ron
84Cedar-20
86Macon-10

Giddings, Wayne
83Idaho-4
84Madis/Pol-18
85Huntsvl/BK-42

Gideon
BF2-33

Gideon, Brett
86PrWill-11
87Harrisbg-18
88BuffB/CMC-3
88BuffB/Pro-1492
88F-330
89Indi/CMC-5
89Indi/Pro-1230

Gideon, Jim
77T-478R
82Tulsa-9

Gideon, Ron
86Lynch-12
87Lynch-8
88Jacks/GS-1
89StLucie/Star-7

Giel, Paul
55B-125
55Gol/Giants-9
58SFCall
58T-308
59T-9
60T-526
61Clover-6
61Peters-19
61T-374

Gierhan, Sam
78Newar
79BurlB-5

Giesdal, Brent
82Oneon-3

Giesecke, Rob
(Doc)
82VeroB-27
83VeroB-27
85VeroB-24
86VeroB-7TR
87VeroB-18

Gieseke, Mark
89Watlo/Star-30

Giesen, Dan
87Readg-6
88Readg/Pro-874

Gifford, Frank
60P

Giggie, Bob
60Lake

Gigon, Norm
67T-576R

Gil, Carlos
83MidldC-7

Gil, Jose
82Wisco-15

Gil, T. Gus
67T-253R
69T-651
82Danvi-2MG

Gilbert, Andrew
(Andy)
73OPC-252CO
73T-252C
74OPC-78CO
74T-78C

Gilbert, Angelo
80Batav-1
82Idaho-8

Gilbert, Dennis
80ElPas-2
81Holyo-10
82Holyo-21
83Redwd-11

Gilbert, Drew E.
(Buddy)
60HenryH-16
60T-359
60Union-6

Gilbert, Greg
84Evrt/Cram-6A
86Fresno/Smok-7
87Anchora-13
87Idaho-15
88Sumter/Pro-405

Gilbert, Harold
(Tookie)
50B-235
52Mother-31
52T-61

Gilbert, Jeff
83SanJose-21
84CharO-18
85CharO-20

Gilbert, Mark
79QuadC-12
80Water-14
81Water-19
82Water-18
83Indianap-22
85BuffB-13

Gilbert, Pat
86Cram/PCL-59
87Madis-7
88Modesto-26
88Modesto/Cal-79

Gilbert, Robbie
86Cram/PCL-62

Gilbert, Roy
89Freder/Star-7

Gilbert, Shawn
88MidwLAS/GS-32
88Visal/Cal-151
88Visal/Pro-91
89Visal/Cal-104
89Visal/Pro-1439

Gilbert, William
E107
T206

Gilbreath, Rod
74OPC-93
74T-93
75OPC-431
75T-431
75T/M-431
76OPC-306
76SSPC-10
76T-306
77T-126
78T-217
79OPC-296
79T-572
80Port-22
87Idaho-9

Gilchrist, John
88Eugene/Best-24
89Eugene/Best-22

Gilcrease, Doug
84Memph-19
85FtMyr-17

Gile, Don
61T-236
62T-244

Gile, Mark
83TriCit-16
85Tulsa-10

Giles, Brian
81Tidew-4
82Tidew-8
83F-544
83T-548
83T/St-322
84D-563
84F-585
84Jacks/Smok-5
84Nes/792-676
84OPC-324
84T-676
84T/St-111
84Tidew-24
85Pol/Brew-26
87Hawai-8
88Calg/CMC-15
88Calg/Pro-784
89ColrSp/CMC-13
89ColSp/Pro-253

Giles, Troy
87QuadC-2
88QuadC/GS-15
89PalmSp/Cal-32
89PalmSp/Pro-473

Giles, Warren
56T-2
57T-100M
58T-300M
59T-200
60F-73
61F-33
80SSPC/HOF
89HOF/St-92

Gilhooley, Frank
D328-59
E135-59

Gilkey, Otis Bernard
87Sprin/Best-25
88Sprin/Best-13

Gilks, Robert
N172

Gill, Chris
89Bill/Pro-2046

Gill, John
45Centen-10
WG8-24

Gill, Shawn
82Idaho-14
83Madis/LF-11
84Madis/Pol-17

Gill, Turner
87Wmspt-25
88Wmspt/Pro-1312

Gillaspie, Mark
83Beaum-15
84Beaum-5
85IowaC-22
88Memph/Best-13

Gillen, Kevin
76Watlo
77Jaxvl

Gillenwater, Carden
V362-32

Gilles, Bob
83VeroB-15

Gilles, Mark
87Kinston-3
88Kinston/Star-7
89Canton/Best-13
89Canton/Pro-1323
89Canton/Star-7

Gilles, Tom
87AppFx-16
88Keno/Pro-1387
89Knoxv/Best-7
89Knoxv/Pro-1143

Gillespie, John
E120

Gillespie, Patrick
N172
N284
N690

Gillespie, Paul
47Smith-20

Gillespie, Robert
52Mother-21

Gilliam, Darryl
86Bakers-11
86Cram/PCL-199

Gilliam, Ed
78BurlB

Gilliam, James
(Junior)
52Park-68
53T-258
54B-74
54NYJour
54RH
54RM-NL14
54T-35
55Armour-7
55B-98
55Gol/Dodg-10
55T-5
55T/DH-129
56T-280
57Swift-10
57T-115
58BB
58T-215
59Morrell
59T-306
60BB-4
60L-18
60MacGregor-9
60T-255
60T/tatt
60T/tatt-19
61BB-19
61P-158
61T-238
62BB-19
62J-112
62P-112
62P/Can-112
62Salada-201
62Shirriff-201
62T-486
63J-114
63P-114
63T-80
64T-310
64Wheat/St-18
73OPC-569CO
73T-569C
74OPC-144CO
74T-144C
78TCMA-45
79TCMA-290
88Pac/Leg-44
PM10/L-15
PM10/Sm-61
PM10/Sm-62

Gilliam, Keith
85Syrac-7
86Knoxv-8
87Knoxv-13

Gilliam, Melvin
80Ashev-4

Gilligan, Andrew
N172
N284

Gills, Amy
85Anchora-35TR
87Anchora-14TR

Gills, Jack
87Oneon-32

Gillum, K.C.
89Bill/Pro-2042

Gilmartin, Dan
78Newar
79BurlB-10
82Beloi-18

Gilmore, Bill
87AppFx-2

Gilmore, Bob
79Richm-9M

Gilmore, Frank T.
N172

Gilmore, Lenny
88BurlR/Pro-1774

Gilmore, Terry
87Spoka-19
88TexLgAS/GS-29
88Wichi-20
89LasVeg/CMC-4
89LasVeg/Pro-16

Gilmore, Tony
80Utica-16

Gilson, Bob
89London/Pro-1358

Gilson, Hal
66Pep/Tul
68OPC-162R
68T-162R
69OPC-156R
69T-156R

Gimenez, Issac
75Clint

Gimenez, Ray
75Clint

Ging, Adam
85Spoka/Cram-5
87Columbia-8

Gingrich, Gary
76BurlB
77BurlB
Ginsberg, Myron
(Joe)
52T-192
53B/Col-6
53Glen
54B-52
57T-236
58T-67
59T-66
60T-304
61T-79
79TCMA-52
Gioia, Joe
86Cram/PCL-194
Gionfriddo, Al
48Swell-9
V362-24
Giordano, Marc
89Princet/Star-7
Giordano, Mike
83Orlan-21
Girardi, Joe
87WinSal-17
88BBAmer-8
88EastLAS/Pro-25
88Pittsf/Pro-1359
89D/Rook-23
89F-644M
89Mara/Cubs-7
89Score/Tr-84
89UD/Ext-776
90D-404
90F-31
90Score-535
90Score/100Ris-33
90T-12
90UD-304
Giron, Ysidro
86FtLaud-7
87PrWill-17
Gisselman, Bob
82Wausa-31
Githens, John
86Watlo-10
87Watlo-13
88Kinston/Star-8
89Hagers/Best-2
89Hagers/Pro-262
89Hagers/Star-9
Giusti, Dave
62T-509
63T-189
64T-354
65T-524
66T-258
67T-318
68Coke
68OPC-182
68T-182
69MB-93
69OPC-98
69T-98
69T/St-95
70OPC-372
70T-372
71MLB/St-202
71OPC-562
71T-562
72MB-116
72OPC-190
72T-190
73OPC-465
73T-465
74OPC-82
74T-82
74T/St-83
75OPC-53
75T-53
75T/M-53
76OPC-352
76SSPC-565
76T-352
77T-154
89Smok/Ast-3
89Swell-58
Giustino, Gerard
89SLCty-26
Givens, Brian
85LitFalls-5
86Columbia-11A
86Columbia-11B
87Lynch-28
88Jacks/GS-14
89Jacks/GS-27
Givler, Doug
87Chatt/Best-9
88ColAst/Best-7
89ColMud/Best-11
89ColMud/Pro-124
89ColMud/Star-11
Gjesdal, Brent
86Beaum-12
Glabman, Barry
76Dubuq
Gladd, Jim
52Mother-53
53Mother-29
Gladden, Dan
81Shrev-9
82Phoen
83Phoen/BHN-8
84Cram/PCL-17
85D-567
85F-607
85F/St-118
85Leaf-30
85Moth/Giants-3
85T-386
85T/St-166
85T/St-374YS
86D-187
86F-541
86Moth/Giants-3
86OPC-336
86T-678
86T/St-90
87D-189
87D/OD-224
87F-274
87F/U-U36
87OPC-46
87T-46
87T/St-93
87T/Tr-38T
88Woolwth-20
88D-491
88D/Best-130
88F-12
88F/WS-1
88OPC-206
88Panini/St-143
88Score-324
88Smok/Minn-10
88T-502
88T/St-19
88T/St-281
89B-163
89D-391
89D/Best-298
89F-112
89OPC-387
89Panini/St-392
89RedFoley/St-50
89Score-62
89T-426
89T/St-286
89UD-400
90Class-148
90D-182
90D-22DK
90F-375
90Score-61
90Sf-190
90T-298
90UD-238
Gladden, Jeff
81CharR-17
82FtMyr-13
83Clint/LF-28
Gladding, Fred
64T-312R
65OPC-37
65T-37
66T-337
67OPC-192
67T-192
68T-423
69OPC-58
69T-58
70MLB/St-41
70OPC-208
70T-208
71MLB/St-80
71OPC-381
71T-381
72MB-117
72OPC-507
72T-507
73OPC-17
73T-17
78TCMA-158
79Tacom-25
86Ashvl-12CO
87ColAst/Pro-3
87ColumAst-3
88ColAst/Best-20
89ColMud/Best-10
89ColMud/Pro-139
Glade, Fred
WG2-21
Gladu, Mike
88Wythe/Pro-1993
Glanz, Scott
83Peoria/LF-4
Glaser, Gordy
81Charl-3
82Charl-3
83BuffB-4
Glasker, Stephen
86Salem-10
87PortChar-15
Glass, Bobby
77Jaxvl
Glass, Steve
87Idaho-22
89BurlB/Pro-1607
89BurlB/Star-10
Glass, Tim
78Watlo
81Chatt-11
82Chatt-6
83BuffB-11
84BuffB-3
85Water-18
Glasscock, John
(Jack)
75F/Pion-21
86Indianap-5
N162
N172
N284
N300
WG1-32
Glasscock, Larry
83Memph-18
Glaviano, Thomas
49Eureka-183
51B-301
51T/RB-47
52T-56
53T-140
Glavine, Tom
86SLAS-23
87Richm/TCMA-5
88D-644
88F-539
88Score-638
88T-779
88T/St-44
89B-267
89Class/Up/2-159
89D-381
89D/Best-2
89F-591
89Panini/St-34
89Score-442
89Score/YS/II-23
89T-157
89UD-360
90Class-36
90D-145
90F-583
90Score-481
90Sf-34
90T-506
90UD-571
Glazner, Charles
(Whitey)
E120
E121/120
E220
W501-87
W572
W573
W575
Gleason, Harry
E107
Gleason, William G.
N172
N172/BC
N284
N370
Scrapps
Gleason, William J.
(Kid)
88Conlon/5-14
88Pac/8Men-102
88Pac/8Men-23
88Pac/8Men-73
E107
E223
N172
Gleason, William P.
D327
D328-60
E121/120
E121/80
E122
E135-60
V100
W501-39
W514-112
W575
Gleaton, Jerry Don
80T-673R
80Tulsa-1
81T-41R
82T-371
83SLCty-2
84Cram/PCL-186
85BuffB-19
85T-216
86BuffB-12
86T-447
88D-547
88F-258
88Omaha/CMC-5
88Omaha/Pro-1497
88Score-343
88Smok/Royals-7
88T-116
89D-444
89F-282
89Score-423
89T-724
Gleckel, Scott
82OrlTw/A-14
Gleissner, James
82FtMyr-17
Glenn, Edward C.
N172
Glenn, Joe
35BU-87
Glenn, John
62Kahn/Atl
Glenn, Simon
80Elmir-28
Glinatsis, Mike
76Cedar
82Miami-2
Glisson, Robert
86Erie-8
87Sprin/Best-18
88Sprin/Best-1
Globig, Dave
76BurlB
Glossop, Alban
47Signal
49B/PCL-17
Glover, Jeff
86Cram/PCL-68
87Madis-17
88Modesto-10
88Modesto/Cal-60
Glover, Reggie
88Reno/Cal-271
Glover, Terence
88SLCty-23
Glynn, Dennis
86Jacks/TCMA-14
Glynn, Ed
77Evansvl/TCMA-11
77T-487R
79T-343
80T-509
81Charl-4
81T-93
82Charl-4
83Charl-19
83D-537
83F-408
83T-614
83Wheat/Ind-14
84Maine-22
86Tidew-12
87Tidew-15
87Tidew/TCMA-4
Glynn, Gene
84Indianap-22
85Utica-25
86WPalm-18CO
87Jamestn-16
88Rockford-15
89Jaxvl/Best-27
89Jaxvl/Pro-174
89Rockford-15CO
Glynn, William V.
(Bill)
52Mother-56
53T-171
54T-178
55T-39
55T/DH-59
V362-42
Gnacinski, Paul
84Pawtu-8
Gobbo, Michael
85Beloi-8
86Stockton-10
87ElPas-26
Gochnaur, John
E107
Godwin, Glenn
83Madis/LF-25
Goedde, Mike
85Cedar-8
89Bill/Pro-2049

Goedhart, Darrell
89Martins/Star-12
Goergen, Todd
89Batav/Pro-1927
Goetz, Jack
75Dubuq
Goetz, Lawrence
55B-311ump
Goff, Jerry
86Cram/PCL-110
87Wausa-17
88SnBer/Best-12
88SnBer/Cal-33
89Wmspt/Pro-631
89Wmspt/Star-7
Goff, Mike
86Greens-9
88MidwLAS/GS-57
88Wausa/Feder-27
88Wausa/GS-27
89SnBer/Best-24
89SnBer/Cal-72
Goff, Tim
86Cram/PCL-32
87FtMyr-17
Goff, Wally
79Wausa-8
80Penin/B-7
80Penin/C-14
Goggin, Chuck
74OPC-457
74T-457
Gogolewski, Bill
71MLB/St-539
71OPC-559R
71T-559R
72OPC-424
72T-424
73OPC-27
73T-27
74OPC-242
74T-242
Gogolewski, Doug
87Oneon-10
88FtLaud/Star-10
89FtLaud/Star-6
Gohl, Lefty
52Park-78
Gohmann, Ken
86Lakel-6
87Lakel-26
88GlenF/Pro-930
89Saraso/Star-7
Gohr, Greg
90Score-679DC
Goins, Scott
87Everett-3
89SanJose/Best-27
89SanJose/Cal-233
89SanJose/Pro-438
89SanJose/Star-10
Gokey, Steve
87Modesto-8
88Modesto-30
89Modesto/Cal-289CO
89Modesto/Ch-6
Gold, Bret
81Miami-20
Gold, Mark
87Wausa-23
Golden, Brian
89Hamil/Star-16
Golden, Ike
81AppFx-16
Golden, Jim
61T-298
62T-568
63T-297
89Smok/Ast-4
Goldetsky, Larry
80Memph-7
83Memph-6
Goldman, J.
31Exh/4-21
Goldsberry, Gordon
52T-46
53T-200
Goldsby, Walt
N172
Goldstein, David R.
80WHave-20
Goldstein, Ike
87Visal-12
Goldthorn, Burk
82AlexD-15
83LynnP-12
85PrWill-30
86Hawai-10
Goldy, Purnal
63T-516
Goliat, Mike
50B-205
51B-77
51BR-B10
61Union
Gollehon, Chris
88Brist/Pro-1875
89Spoka/SP-20
Goltz, Dave
73OPC-148
73T-148
74OPC-636
74T-636
75OPC-419
75T-419
75T/M-419
76OPC-136
76SSPC-218
76T-136
77Ho-48
77OPC-73
77T-321
78Ho-96
78K-35
78OPC-142
78OPC-5LL
78T-205LL
78T-249
79Ho-16
79OPC-10
79T-27
80OPC-108
80Pol/Dodg-38
80T-193
81F-127
81OPC-289
81Pol/Dodg-38
81T-548
82D-604
82F-6
82Pol/Dodg
82Pol/Dodg-38
82T-674
83F-90
83T-468
Gomez, Art
81Clint-8
Gomez, Dana
87WinHav-30
Gomez, Fabio
88BurlR/Pro-1788
89Watertn/Star-8
Gomez, Henry
88CharWh/Best-14
Gomez, Jorge
80Ashev-3
82BurlR-20
83Tulsa-1
84Tulsa-4
Gomez, Jose L.R.
(Chile)
R313
Gomez, Jose Luis
(Luis)
77T-13
78OPC-121
78T-573
79OPC-128
79T-254
80OPC-95
80T-169
81D-88
81F-253
81Pol/Atl-9
81T-477
82T-372
Gomez, Jose
83Miami-14
Gomez, Juan A.
75Tucso-9
76Tucso-33
Gomez, Leo
87Hagers-5
89Hagers/Best-1
89Hagers/Pro-280
89Hagers/Star-10
Gomez, Marcos
82Beloi-10
Gomez, Miguel
78Duned
Gomez, Orlando
82Tulsa-23
83BurlR-26
83BurlR/LF-27MG
84Tulsa-23
85Tulsa-23MG
86Water-11MG
87BuffB-25
88Gasto/Pro-1009
89Gasto/Pro-1017
Gomez, Pat
87Peoria-13
Gomez, Patrick
88CharWh/Best-13
89WinSal/Star-8
Gomez, Pedro
(Preston)
60DF-10
61Union
69OPC-74
69T-74
70OPC-513MG
70T-513
71OPC-737MG
71T-737
72T-637
73OPC-624CO
73T-624C
74OPC-31MG
74T-31MG
75OPC-487MG
75T-487MG
75T/M-487MG
Gomez, Randy
84Cram/PCL-20
85Cram/PCL-179
86Phoen-6
87Hawai-24
Gomez, Ruben
54NYJour
54T-220
55Gol/Giants-10
55T-71
55T/DH-89
56T-9
56T/Pin-39P
57T-58
58SFCall
58T-335
59T-535
60T-82
61T-377
67T-427
79TCMA-80
PM10/L-16
PM10/Sm-64
Gomez, Steve
86Orlan-7
87Orlan-13
Gomez, Vernon
(Lefty)
32Orbit/num-120
33CJ/Pin-8
33DL-14
33G-216
34Exh/4-13
35BU-23
35BU-86
35Exh/4-13
36Exh/4-13
36G
36Wheat-1
37Exh/4-13
38Exh/4-13
38ONG/Pin-12
39Exh
39PB-48
39Wheat-3
40PB-6
41DP-61
41PB-72
60F-54
61F-34
72Laugh/GF-18
80Cram/Leg-117
80SSPC/HOF
86Conlon/1-45
86S/Dec-9
87Conlon/2-2
88Conlon/5-15
88Conlon/AmAS-12
89HOF/St-76
PM10/Sm-63
PR1-12
R303/A
R303/B
R308-151
R309/2
R310
R312/M
R313
R314
R328-31
V355-56
Gonder, Jesse
63FrBauer-6
63T-29R
64T-457
64T/Coins-43
64T/St-30
64T/SU
65T-423
66EH-20
66T-528
67T-301
67T/Test/PP-10
69T-617
78TCMA-122
78TCMA-238
Goninger, Gerry
89Cedar/Pro-930
Gonring, Doug
87Ashvl-8
Gonsalves, Dennis
83Madis/LF-7
84Madis/Pol-16
Gonzales, Arturo
73Cedar
74Cedar
Gonzales, Ben
89AubAs/Pro-2171
Gonzales, Cliff
85LitFalls-23
Gonzales, Dan
77Evansvl/TCMA-12
80Evans-20
Gonzales, Eddie
87SanJose-25
Gonzales, Fernando
83LynnP-3
Gonzales, Fredi
83Greens-14
84Greens-6
Gonzales, Jose
82ArkTr-13
Gonzales, Julian
85MidldA-25
87SanJose-24
Gonzales, Larry
89QuadC/Best-21
89QuadC/GS-28
Gonzales, Mike
21Exh-58
Gonzales, Orlando
83Tampa-13
Gonzales, Otto
83BurlR-17
Gonzales, Rene C.
83Memph-3
84Indianap-25
85Indianap-11
86Indianap-10
88D-582
88F-560
88French-88
88T-98
88T/Big-209
89D-377
89French-88
89OPC-213
89Score-585
89T-213
89T/Big-87
89T/St-234
90D-401
90Score-118
90T-787
Gonzales, Todd
87Watlo-11
88Kinston/Star-9
89Canton/Best-16
89Canton/Pro-1320
89Canton/Star-8
Gonzalez, Angel
86WinHav-9
87NewBrit-4
88NewBrit/Pro-910
88Pawtu/CMC-17
88Pawtu/Pro-462
89Pawtu/CMC-22
89Pawtu/Dunkin-12
89Pawtu/Pro-684
Gonzalez, Arturo
85Cram/PCL-33
86Portl-6
Gonzalez, Carlos
86FtMyr-12
87AppFx-14
88BBCity/Star-12
89BBCity/Star-7
Gonzalez, Cliff
86LitFalls-12
87Columbia-4
89Saraso/Star-8
Gonzalez, Denio
(Denny)
82Portl-13
84Cram/PCL-130
85Cram/PCL-229
85D-600
86D-410
86F-608
86T-746
88BuffB/CMC-15
88BuffB/Pro-1473
89ColrSp/CMC-14
89ColSp/Pro-248
Gonzalez, Felipe
86Fresno/Smok-5
87Clint-7

Gonzalez, Ferdi
86Albany/TCMA-6
87Albany-20
Gonzalez, Fred
86FtLaud-8
Gonzalez, German
87Kenosha-26
88BBAmer-18
88Orlan/Best-17
88SLAS-30
89D-590
89D/Rook-24
89F-113
89Panini/St-379
89Score/HotRk-49
89T-746
90F-376
90Score-133
90Score/100Ris-81
90T-266
90UD-352
Gonzalez, Gilberto
80Elmir-32
Gonzalez, Henry
84Newar-18
85Newar-10
Gonzalez, Javier
88Clmbia/GS-12
Gonzalez, Joe
88Albuq/CMC-19
Gonzalez, Jose Fern.
(Fernando)
74OPC-649
74T-649
74T/Tr-649T
78Colum
78T-433
79T-531
80SLCty-25
80T-171
81SLCty-18
82AlexD-7
Gonzalez, Jose
86Albuq-9
87Albuq/Pol-26
87D-525
87F-649M
87Pol/Dodg-25
88Albuq/Pro-258
88D-341
88Score-364
89Albuq/CMC-17
89Albuq/Pro-80
89D/Best-260
89Score/HotRk-29
89UD-626
90Class-96
90D-314
90F-394
90Score-368
90T-98
90UD-666
Gonzalez, Juan
76Clint
Gonzalez, Juan
87Gasto-4
88CharlR/Star-8
89Tulsa/GS-10
90D-33
90F-297
90Score-637
90T-331
90UD-72
Gonzalez, Julian
83Peoria/LF-23
Gonzalez, Julio C.
78BK/A-13
78T-389
79T-268
80T-696
81F-73
82D-645
82T-503
83Evans-14
83T-74
Gonzalez, Luis
78Ashev
80Tulsa-14
Gonzalez, Luis
88AubAs/Pro-1973
89Osceola/Star-6
89Star/Wax-15
Gonzalez, Marcos
82Miami-3
87Fayette-20
Gonzalez, Miguel
28Yueng-34
40PB-115
86Conlon/1-14M
D328-61
E121/80
E135-61
E210-34
W502-34
W575
W754
Gonzalez, Mike
75Shreve/TCMA-3
76Shrev
Gonzalez, Orlando
75OkCty
77T-477R
79OkCty
80BurlB-7
80OkCty
81F-585
87Nashv-7
88Mia/Star-8
Gonzalez, Otto
82BurlR-21
83BurlR/LF-17
85Tulsa-35
86DayBe-9
86FSLAS-18
88OkCty/CMC-12
88OkCty/Pro-47
89MidldA/GS-15
Gonzalez, Pedro
63T-537R
64T-581R
65OPC-97
65T-97
66Kahn
66T-266
67T-424
WG10-8
WG9-10
Gonzalez, Ruben
88Wausa/Feder-6
88Wausa/GS-6
89SnBer/Best-23
89SnBer/Cal-82
Gonzalez, Tommy
75Phoen-5
76Phoen
79Phoen
80Phoen-25
81Phoen-26
82Phoen
83Phoen/BHN-28
Gonzalez, Tony
60T-518
61T-93
61T/St-55
62T-534
62T/St-168
63Exh
63J-181
63P-181
63T-32
64T-379
64T/Coins-58
64T/S-14
64T/St-58S6
64T/SU
65OPC-72
65T-72
66T-478
67T-548
68Bz-8
68OPC-1LL
68T-1LL
68T-245
68T/G-20
69MB-94
69MLB/St-192
69T-501
69T/decal
69T/St-94
70MLB/St-6
70OPC-105
70T-105
71MLB/St-345
71OPC-256
71T-256
72MB-118
77Spart/C
82Danvi-13C
Exh47
Gooch, John B.
31Exh/4-8
E120
E126-1
Gooch, Ron
79Tucso-7
79Tulsa-11
80Tulsa-17
81Tulsa-28
Good, Wilbur
D329-69
D350/2-69
M101/4-69
M101/5-69
T205
T206
Goodale, Jeff
89NiagFls/Puc-9
Goodchild, Chris
80Clint-6
Goode, William
14Piedmont/St-24
Gooden, Dwight
83Lynch-10
84F/X-43
84FunFood/Pin-27
84T/X-42
85D-190
85D/AAS-47
85D/HL-32
85D/HL-33
85D/HL-48
85D/WaxBox-PC1
85Drake-36
85F-634IA
85F-82
85F/St-113
85F/St-87
85F/St-95
85Leaf-234
85OPC-41
85Seven-9E
85T-3RB
85T-620
85T/3D-19
85T/Gloss40-38
85T/Mets/Fan-5
85T/St-107
85T/St-280
85T/St-3
85T/St-371M
85T/St-4
85T/Super-7
85Woolwth-16
86BK/AP-17
86D-26
86D-75
86D/AAS-28
86D/DKsuper-26
86D/HL-8
86Dorman-5
86Drake-35
86F-626M
86F-638M
86F-641M
86F-81
86F/AS-10
86F/LimEd-20
86F/LL-16
86F/Mini-19A
86F/Mini-19B
86F/Slug-11
86F/St-132CL
86F/St-46
86Jiffy-20
86KayBee-16
86Leaf-26DK
86Meadow/Blank-5
86Meadow/Milk-4
86Meadow/Stat-3
86OPC-250
86OPC-F
86Quaker-2
86S-100
86S-136M
86S-143M
86S-176M
86S-184M
86S-185M
86S/Dec-75
86S/Rook-47M
86T-202RB
86T-250
86T-709
86T/3D-4
86T/Gloss60-41
86T/Mets/Fan-4
86T/Mini-52
86T/St-6
86T/St-94
86T/Super-4
86T/WaxBox-F
87Class-72
87D-199
87D/AAS-18
87D/PopUp-18
87Drake-26
87F-629M
87F-9
87F-C4
87F/AwardWin-15
87F/Excit-19
87F/GameWin-18
87F/HL-3
87F/Hottest-18
87F/Lim-19
87F/LL-20
87F/McCror-18
87F/Mini-45
87F/RecSet-12
87F/Slug-15
87F/St-48
87F/WaxBox-C4
87F/WS-7
87Jiffy-9
87KayBee-13
87KMart-26
87Leaf-84
87OPC-130
87RedFoley/St-6
87S-100
87S-120M
87S-159M
87Seven-E7
87Seven-ME9
87T-130
87T-603AS
87T/Coins-33
87T/Gloss22-10
87T/Gloss60-51
87T/Mini-23
87T/St-163
87T/St-5
87T/St-6
87T/St-96
87Tidew-31
87Tidew/TCMA-30
88Bz-8
88Class/Red-171
88D-69
88D/Best-96
88D/Mets/Bk-69
88F-135
88F/AwardWin-14
88F/BB/AS-12
88F/BB/MVP-16
88F/Excit-15
88F/Head-5
88F/Hottest-13
88F/LL-15
88F/Mini-92
88F/RecSet-14
88F/Slug-15
88F/SS-14
88F/St-102
88F/TL-10
88Kahn/Mets-16
88KMart-10
88Leaf-48
88MSA/Disc-19
88Nestle-21
88OPC-287
88Panini/St-337
88Score-350
88Score/YS/II-3
88Sf-200
88Sf/Gamewin-9
88T-405
88T-480
88T/Big-11
88T/Gloss60-54
88T/Mets/Fan-16
88T/Mini-60
88T/St-101
88T/St/Backs-25
88T/UK-27
89B-376
89Class-107
89Class-7
89Class/Up/2-189
89Crunch-17
89D-270
89D/AS-40
89D/Best-14
89D/PopUp-40
89F-36
89F-635M
89F/BBAS-15
89F/BBMVP's-14
89F/Excit-15
89F/Heroes-18
89F/LL-16
89F/Superstar-17
89Kahn/Mets-16
89KayBee-14
89KMart/DT-31
89OPC-30
89Panini/St-131
89Panini/St-227AS
89RedFoley/St-51
89Score-200
89Score/HotSt-15
89Score/Mast-26
89Sf-140
89T-30
89T-661TBC84
89T/Big-304
89T/Coins-14
89T/Gloss22-21
89T/Gloss60-37
89T/HeadsUp-3

89T/Mets/Fan-16
89T/Mini-26
89T/St-162
89T/St-99
89T/St/Backs-59
89T/UK-31
89Tetley/Discs-6
89UD-565
90Class-58
90D-171
90F-204
90Score-313
90Score/100St-99
90Sf-145
90T-510
90UD-114
90UD-62TC

Gooden, Maury
85LitFalls-24

Goodenough, Randy
86Cram/PCL-39
87FtMyr-23

Goodfellow, Michael
N172

Goodin, Craig
83CharR-6

Goodin, Rich
83CharR-20

Goodman, Billy
48L-30
49B-39
50B-99
51B-237
51BR-C2
51FB
51T/RB-46
52B-81
52StarCal/L-71E
52T-23
53B/Col-148
53Exh/Can-63
54B-82
55B-126
56T-245
57T-303
58T-225
59T-103
60T-69
61T-247
79TCMA-96
Exh47
PM10/Sm-65

Goodman, Billy
80Ashev-1

Goodman, Ival
35BU-127
35G-8D
35G-9D
38Exh/4-4
41DP-115
R303/A
R303/B
W711/1
W711/2

Goodson, J. Ed
73OPC-197
73T-197
74K-18
74OPC-494
74T-494
74T/St-105
75OPC-322
75T-322
75T/M-322
76OPC-386
76SSPC-588
76T-386
77T-584
78T-586

Goodwin, Danny
77SLCty
79Ogden/TCMA-15
79T-322
80T-362
81D-474
81T-527
82D-305
82F-554
82T-123
82Tacom-14
83Tacom-25A
84Cram/PCL-91
85Cram/PCL-134

Goodwin, David
88Geneva/Pro-1641
89CharWh/Best-18
89CharWh/Pro-1768

Goodwin, Mike
86PrWill-12

Goodwin, Tom
89GreatF-1
90Score-668DC

Goossen, Greg
67T-287R
68T-386
70McDon-5
70OPC-271
70T-271

Gorbould, Bob
45Centen-11

Gorbous, Glen
56T-174

Gordon, Don
83BirmB-2
85Syrac-13
86Ault-39
86Tor/Fire-14
87RochR/TCMA-29
87Syrac-5
87Syrac/TCMA-26
87Syrac/TCMA-4
88ColSp/CMC-3
88ColSp/Pro-1538
88Score/Tr-92T
88T-144
89ColrSp/CMC-2
89ColSp/Pro-260
89F-405
89Score-547

Gordon, Joe
39Exh
41DP-67
41DP-83
41Wheat-21
44Yank/St-12
48L-117
49B-210
49Royal-13
50B-129
50NumNum
52Mother-19
59Kahn
60T-216
61T-224
61T/RO-30
69T-484
86S/Dec-24M
D305
R303/A
R303/B
R423-36

Gordon, Kevin
85PrWill-21
86Nashua-8

Gordon, Sid
47TipTop
48B-27
48L-131
49B-101
49Eureka-104
50B-109
50Drake-16
51B-19
51T/RB-2
52B-60
52Dix
52NTea
52RM-NL6
52T-267
52TipTop
53B/Col-5
53Dix
53JC-23
53NB
53T-117
54B-11
54DanDee
54Dix
55B-163
55RFG-24
79TCMA-67
D305

Gordon, Tom
87FtMyr-25
88AppFx/Pro-149
88MidwLAS/GS-40
89B-115
89Class/Up/2-182
89D-45RR
89D/Best-287
89D/Rook-4
89F-284
89Score-634
89Score/HotRk-68
89Score/Mast-7
89Score/YS/II-2
89T/Tr-38T
89UD/Ext-736
90Class-4
90D-297
90F-108
90Score-472
90Score/100Ris-1
90Sf-30
90T-752
90UD-365

Gore, Arthur
55B-289ump

Gore, George
N172
N284
N338/2
WG1-40

Gore, Kevin
89Geneva/Pro-1865

Gore, Ricky
89Idaho/Pro-2017

Gorin, Charles
54JC-15
55Gol/Braves-11
55JC-15

Gorinski, Bob
78T-386
79Tidew-24

Gorman, Bill
82Omaha-24
83Omaha-23
84Omaha-14
85Omaha-1

Gorman, Mike
86GlenF-7

Gorman, Thomas A.
(Tom)
53B/BW-61
54B-17
55Rodeo
56T-246
57T-87
58T-235
59T-449

Gorman, Thomas P.
(Tom)
80Memph-4
82Wichi-5
83Tidew-11
84Nes/792-774
84T-774
84Tidew-14
85F-83
85T-53
86F-82
86Portl-7
86T-414

Gorman, Tom
55B-293ump

Gorsica, John
47TipTop

Gorski, Gary
86Cram/PCL-82
88Modesto-11
88Modesto/Cal-62
89Modesto/Ch-12

Gorton, Chris
89Hamil/Star-15

Goryl, John
58T-384
59T-77
61Clover-7
62T-558
63T-314
64T-194
78OrlTw
81D-527
81T-669MG
82BK/Ind-3
82BK/Ind-4
82BK/Indians-3
82BK/Indians-4
82Wheat/Ind
83Wheat/Ind-15CO
85Polar/Ind-xx
86OhHenry-CO
87Gator-CO
88Gator-45CO

Goselin, Scott
88Pulas/Pro-1751
89Sumter/Pro-1107

Gosger, Jim
63T-553R
66OPC-114
66T-114
67OPC-17
67T-17
68T-343
69MB-95
69T-482
70T-651
71LaPizza-4
71MLB/St-128
71OPC-284
71T-284
72MB-119

Goshay, Henry Lee
88VeroB/Star-8
89Duned/Star-5

Goslin, Leon
(Goose)
25Exh-123
26Exh-123
27Exh-61
28Exh-61
29Exh/4-31
31Exh/4-29
33CJ/Pin-9
33DH-21
33Exh/4-15
33G-110
33G-168
34Exh/4-12
35BU-85
35Exh/4-12
35G-1H
35G-3F
35G-5F
35G-6F
36Exh/4-12
37Exh/4-12
37OPC-111
40PB-232
48Swell-13
61F-35
80Cram/Leg-104
80SSPC/HOF
87Conlon/2-38
E120
E210-49
R300
R308-173
R309/2
R312/M
R313
R314
R315-A11
R315-B11
R316
R332-27
V300
V355-43
V61-8
W502-49
W517-47
W573

Goss, Howie
62T-598R
63T-364

Gossage, Rich
(Goose)
73OPC-174
73T-174
74OPC-542
74T-542
75OPC-554
75T-554
75T/M-554
76Ho-77
76OPC-180
76OPC-205LL
76SSPC-156
76T-180
76T-205LL
77Ho-128
77T-319
78BK/Y-10
78K-8
78T-70
79BK/Y-10
79Ho-48
79OPC-114
79T-225
79T-8LL
80OPC-77
80T-140
81D-347
81F-89
81F/St-118
81K-41
81MSA/Disc-14
81OPC-48
81T-460
81T/HT
81T/Nat/Super-7
81T/S
81T/St-113
81T/St-251
81T/St-8
82D-283
82F-37
82F/St-116
82K-32
82OPC-117IA
82OPC-286AS
82OPC-396
82T-557
82T-770
82T-771A
82T/St-140
82T/St-217
83D-157
83F-381
83K-10

83OPC-240
83OPC-241SV
83RoyRog/Disc-2
83T-240
83T-241A
83T/Gloss-11
83T/Gloss40-11
83T/St-100
84D-396
84F-125
84F/X-44
84FunFood/Pin-85
84Moth/Padres-2
84Nes/792-670
84Nes/792-718LL
84OPC-121
84Seven-22E
84T-670
84T-718
84T/St-316
84T/X-43
85D-185
85D/AAS-14
85F-33
85F/LimEd-10
85F/St-108
85Leaf-204
85Moth/Padres-5
85OPC-90
85Seven-9W
85T-90
85T/3D-27
85T/Gloss40-19
85T/St-147
85T/Super-49
86D-185
86D-2
86D/AAS-31
86D/DKsuper-2
86F-322
86F/Mini-68
86F/Slug-12
86Leaf-2DK
86Meadow/Stat-20
86OPC-104
86S-190
86S-55M
86T-530
86T/3D-6
86T/Gloss60-56
86T/St-107
86T/Super-26
87Bohem-54
87Class-96
87D-483
87F-415
87F/LL-21
87OPC-380
87RedFoley/St-9
87T-380
87T/St-109
88Berg/Cubs-54
88D-434
88D/Best-26
88D/Cubs/Bk-NEW
88F-583
88F/U-U76
88OPC-170
88Score-331
88Score/Tr-14T
88T-170
88T/Tr-41T
89D-158
89F-425
89Moth/Giants-27
89OPC-162
89Score-223
89T-415
89T/WaxBox-D
89UD-452
90D-678

Gosse, John
80WHave-19

Gotay, Julio
62T-489
63J-161
63P-161
63T-122
65T-552
68Coke
68OPC-41
68T-41
69MB-96

Gotay, Ruben
83ArkTr-2

Gott, James
81ArkTr-17
83D-353
83OPC-62
83T-506
84D-268
84F-155
84Nes/792-9
84OPC-9
84T-9
84Tor/Fire-14
85D-632
85F-105
85F/Up-U45
85Leaf-136
85Moth/Giants-21
85OPC-311
85T-311
85T/Tr-40T
86D-358
86F-542
86Moth/Giants-21
86OPC-106
86T-463
87F/U-U35
87Moth/SFG-19
87T/Tr-39T
88D-606
88D/Best-213
88F/U-U112
88Leaf-253
88Score-320
88T-127
89B-411
89D-362
89F-210
89F/Excit-16
89F/Superstar-18
89OPC-172
89Panini/St-163
89Score-257
89Score/HotSt-98
89Sf-83
89T-752
89T/Mini-41
89UD-539
90D-605
90F-466
90Score-515
90T-292
90UD-89

Goughan, Bob
88RochR-32
88RochR/Gov-32

Gould, Bob
85Madis-14
85Madis/Pol-11
86Madis-9
86Madis/Pol-9
87Modesto-11

Goulding, Rich
77Clint
78LodiD

Gouldrup, Gary
85Elmir-8

Governor, Tony
28Exh/PCL-8

Gowdy, Hank
11Helmar-78
14CJ-138
15CJ-138
21Exh-59
21Exh-60
40PB-82
72F/FFeat-33
87Conlon/2-39
88Conlon/3-12
BF2-51
D327
D328-62
D329-70
D350/2-70
E120
E121/120
E121/80
E122
E135-62
E220
M101/4-70
M101/5-70
R313
T207
V100
W501-90
W514-67
W516-23
W572
W573
W575
W711/1
W711/2

Gozzo, Mauro
(Goose)
84LitFalls-21
86Lynch-13
87Memph-3
87Memph/Best-20
88Memph/Best-16
89Knoxv/Best-8
89Knoxv/Pro-1145
89Knoxv/Star-6
90D-655
90F-82
90Score-610
90Score/100Ris-48
90Sf-168
90T-274

Grabarkewitz, Bill
70OPC-446
70T-446
71K-56
71MD
71MLB/St-104
71OPC-85
71T-85
71T/Coins-21
71T/tatt-5
72T-578
73OPC-301
73T-301
74OPC-214
74T-214
74T/St-74
75OPC-233
75T-233
75T/M-233
75Tucso-8
87Smok/Dodg-9
89Smok/Dodg-76

Graber, Red
61Union

Grabowski, Joe
R310

Grace, Joe
52Mother-5
V355-103
W753

Grace, Mark
86Peoria-8
87Pittsf-10
88Berg/Cubs-17
88D-40
88D/Best-4
88D/Cubs/Bk-40
88D/Rook-1
88F-641
88F/Mini-68
88F/U-U77
88IowaC/CMC-14
88IowaC/Pro-539
88Leaf-40RR
88Peoria/Ko-11
88Peoria/Ko-34M
88Score/Tr-80T
88T/Tr-42T
89B-291
89Bz-12
89Class-13
89Class/Up/2-155
89D-17DK
89D-255
89D/DKsuper-17DK
89F-426
89F/BBMVP's-15
89F/Excit-17
89F/LL-17
89F/Superstar-19
89Holsum/Discs-12
89KMart/DT-1
89Mara/Cubs-17
89Nissen-12
89OPC-297
89Panini/St-55
89Score-362
89Score/HotRk-78
89Score/Mast-22
89Score/YS/I-3
89Sf-15
89T-465
89T/Big-189
89T/Coins-15
89T/Gloss60-29
89T/HeadsUp-15
89T/JumboR-11
89T/St-324
89T/St-50
89ToysRUs-12
89UD-140
90Class-8
90D-577
90F-32
90Score-150
90Score/100St-60
90Sf-15
90T-240
90UD-128

Grace, Michael
87Anchora-15
89SLCty-14

Grace, Mike
77Indianap-12
78Indianap-16
79Indianap-18
80Indianap-4
83ColumAst-4

Grace, Robert Earl
34DS-69
34G-58
35BU-69
R314

Grachen, Tim
83QuadC-12

Grady, Pat
80Batav-26

Graff, Milt
57T-369
58T-192
59T-182

Graff, Stephen
86Erie-9

Graham, George
(Peaches)
11Helmar-95
C46-63
E270/2
E90/1
M116
S74-43
S74-62
T201
T202
T204
T205
T206
T207
T3-95

Graham, Bert
M116

Graham, Brian
83Madis/LF-28
84Albany-6
85Huntsvl/BK-14
87Kinston-11
88EastLAS/Pro-51
88Wmspt/Pro-1313
89Watertn/Star-11

Graham, Bruce
87Everett-33
89Phoen/Pro-1488

Graham, Dan
79Toled-6
80T-669R
81D-233
81F-189
81OPC-161
81T-161
82D-455
82F-167
82RochR-10
82T-37

Graham, Everett
82Clint-10
86Phoen-7
87Shrev-1
88Phoen/CMC-20
88Phoen/Pro-60
89MidldA/GS-16

Graham, Jack
50B-145

Graham, Jeffrey L.
87Sprin/Best-9

Graham, Johnny
88AubAs/Pro-1971
89AubAs/Pro-2177

Graham, Lee
81Pawtu-19
83Pawtu-22
84Pawtu-2
85Richm-19
86Richm-7

Graham, Lew
84LitFalls-23

Graham, Lindsey
74Gasto

Graham, Otto
52Wheat

Graham, Randy
83Greens-8
84Nashvl-8
85Albany-8
86Colum-10
86Colum/Pol-9
87Colum-23
87Colum/Pol-11
87Colum/TCMA-5

Graham, Steve
88Hamil/Pro-1745
89Hamil/Star-13

Graham, William
T206

Grahek, Larry
81CharR-22

Grahovac, Mike
89Everett/Star-8
Gralewski, Bob
88CapeCod-5
88CapeCod/Sum-154
Grammas, Alex
54Hunter
54T-151
55B-186
55Hunter
55T-21
55T/DH-107
56T-37
57T-222
58T-254
59T-6
60T-168
61P-177
61T-64
61T/St-87
62J-168
62P-168
62P/Can-168
62Salada-197
62Shirriff-197
62T-223
63T-416
73OPC-296CO
73T-296C
74OPC-326CO
74T-326C
76SSPC-620
76T-606
77T-51MG
88Pep/T-CO
89Mara/Tigers-CO
Granco, Julio
86Cram/PCL-79
Grandas, Bob
79Ogden/TCMA-25
80Ogden-11
81Tacom-27
82Tacom-35
83Evans-19
Grandquist, Ken
82IowaC-27
83IowaC-29
84IowaC-5
85IowaC-26
Graney, Jack
D327
D328-63
D329-71
D350/2-71
E120
E121/120
E121/80
E135-63
E220
M101/4-71
M101/5-71
T207
W501-112
W573
W575
Grange, Red
33SK-4
Granger, George
R314/Can
Granger, Lee
82Miami-19
83SanJose-4
84RochR-7
85CharO-2
Granger, Wayne
69T-551
70MLB/St-27
70OPC-73
70T-73
71MLB/St-59
71OPC-379
71T-379
72T-545
73OPC-523
73T-523
74OPC-644
74T-644
76OPC-516
76T-516
Grant, Ed
10Domino-49
11Helmar-115
12Sweet/Pin-100
E104
E270/2
E90/1
E94
M116
S74-75
T201
T202
T205
Grant, Bob
77Wausa
Grant, Charles
52Park-10
Grant, Charlie
74Laugh/Black-23
Grant, Frank
74Laugh/Black-17
Grant, Jim
(Mudcat)
58T-394
59Kahn
59T-186
60Kahn
60L-25
60T-14
61Kahn
61P-60
61T-18
61T/St-135
62Kahn
62Salada-26
62Shirriff-26
62T-307
63Sugar-23
63T-227
64Kahn
64T-133
64T/Coins-99
64Wheat/St-19
65T-432
66Bz-37
66OPC-40
66T-224LL
66T-40
66T/RO-3
67T-545
68T-398
69Fud's-4
69MLB/St-158
69T-306
69T/St-55
71MLB/St-201
71OPC-509
71T-509
72MB-120
72OPC-111
72T-111
78TCMA-200
85Durhm-15C
89Pac/Leg-186
89Swell-84
Grant, Ken
86QuadC-12
87PalmSp-7
88QuadC/GS-21
88Visal/Cal-152
88Visal/Pro-86
Grant, Mark
64T/St-37S4
82Clint-23
84Cram/PCL-3
85Cram/PCL-199
85D-601
86Phoen-8
87D-644
87Moth/SFG-26
88Coke/Padres-55PAN
88D-511
88D/Best-133
88F-584
88Smok/Padres-9
88T-752
89F-304
89Score-349
89Score/YS/I-12
89T-178
89T/Big-154
89UD-622
90D-441
90F-156
90Score-466
90T-537
90UD-412
Grant, Tom
82IowaC-3
83IowaC-22
84IowaC-30
85IowaC-9
Grantham, George
25Exh-52
26Exh-52
31Exh/4-14
33CJ/Pin-10
33Exh/4-4
33G-66
R316
V353-66
W513-76
Grapenthin, Dick
84Indianap-16
86LasVegas-4
87Louvl-14
88AAA/Pro-24
88Louvl-20
88Louvl/CMC-2
88Louvl/Pro-426
89Colum/CMC-23
89Colum/Pol-9
89Colum/Pro-747
Graser, Rick
80Wausa-18
Grasso, Newton M.
(Mickey)
49B/PCL-6
51B-205
52B-174
52T-90
53B/Col-77
53Briggs
53T-148
54B-184
Grater, Mark
87Savan-11
88Sprin/Best-2
89StPet/Star-14
Graupmann, Tim
83Wisco/LF-9
84Visal-16
Graven, Tim
79Savan-7
Graves, Chris
87QuadC-22
88QuadC/GS-27
89PalmSp/Cal-40
89PalmSp/Pro-483
Graves, Frank M.
N172
Graves, Joe
83Lynch-20
84Jacks-8
86Jaxvl/TCMA-11
Graves, John
89Butte/SP-21
Graves, Kenley
85Bend/Cram-7
Gray, Dave
64T-572R
Gray, David
88Lynch/Star-7
89Lynch/Star-9
Gray, Dick
58T-146
59T-244
60T-24
Gray, Elliott
89Martins/Star-13
Gray, Gary
77Tucso
78Cr/PCL-38
79Tucso-1
80Tacom-17
81F-402
81T/Tr-767
82F-511
82OPC-78
82SLCty-9
82T-523
82T/St-233
83D-637
83F-480
83T-313
Gray, Jeff
86Vermont-8
87Nashv-8
88Nashvl/CMC-5
88Nashvl/Pro-478
89Nashvl-5
89Nashvl/CMC-3
89Nashvl/Pro-1288
Gray, John L.
55Rodeo
55T-101
55T/DH-48
Gray, Lorenzo
77AppFx
80GlenF/B-22
80GlenF/C-20M
80GlenF/C-26
82Edmon-10
84Maine-12
84Nes/792-163
84T-163
86SanJose-9
Gray, Pete
88MinorLg/Leg-2
Gray, Samuel
25Exh-107
29Exh/4-29
31Exh/4-30
33Exh/4-15
Gray, Scott
86AubAs-10
Gray, Stanley
43Centen-10
44Centen-9
Gray, Steve
89Clint/Pro-899
89Salin/Pro-1802
Gray, Ted
49B-10
50B-210
51B-178
52B-199
52T-86
53B/Col-72
53T-52
54B-71
55B-86
Gray, Terry
77StPet
Gray, William
(Dolly)
11Helmar-68
12Sweet/Pin-58
E90/1
T202
T205
T206
Graybill, Dave
87Jaxvl-15
89PalmSp/Cal-59
Grayner, Paul
82Nashv-13
83Nashvl-7TR
Grayson, Mike
89Beloi/Star-7
Grayston, Joe
85BurlR-1
Grayum, Richie
89Geneva/Pro-1871
Grba, Eli
60T-183
61T-121
62T-96
63T-231
64T-464
65T-203
82Vanco-23
88Vanco/Pro-769
89Reno/Cal-265MG
Grebeck, Craig
87Penin-10
88BirmB/Best-24
89BirmB/Best-17
89BirmB/Pro-111
Greco, George
80Elmir-7
Green, Bob
86FtLaud-9
87FtLaud-6
88Albany/Pro-1331
89Albany/Best-10
89Colum/CMC-20
89Colum/Pol-8
89Colum/Pro-734
Green, Charlie
87Watertn-29
Green, Christopher
82AlexD-6
85Cram/PCL-240
86Edmon-14
87RochR/TCMA-22
Green, Daryl
86Cram/PCL-88
87QuadC-10
88QuadC/GS-13
89Modesto/Cal-271
89Modesto/Ch-11
Green, David A.
80Holyo-14
82Louvl-10
83D-166
83F-6
83T-578
83T/St-323
84D-425
84D-625
84F-323
84Nes/792-362
84OPC-362
84T-362
84T/St-149
85D-303
85F-224
85F/Up-U46
85Leaf-191
85Moth/Giants-17
85OPC-87
85T-87
85T/St-145
85T/Tr-41T
86D-114
86F-543
86OPC-122
86T-727
87Louvl-15
88F-34

88Louvl-21
88Louvl/CMC-14
88Louvl/Pro-421

Green, Dick
65OPC-168
67OPC-54
69MB-97
69T/St-215
70MLB/St-258
70OPC-311
71MLB/St-514
71OPC-258
72MB-121
73OPC-456
74OPC-392
75OPC-91

Green, Don
89Hamil/Star-18

Green, Edward
(Danny)
E107

Green, Elijah
(Pumpsie)
60T-317
61T-454
62Salada-187
62Shirriff-187
62T-153
63T-292
64T-442
65T-588

Green, Fred
60T-272
61T-181

Green, G. Dallas
60L-52
60T-366
61T-359
62Salada-219
62Shirriff-219
62T-111
63T-91
64T-464
65OPC-203
65T-203
78TCMA-187
80BK/P-1MG
81D-415
81T-682MG
89Score/NWest-31
89T-104MG

Green, Gary
85Beaum-18
85T-396
86LasVegas-5
87LasVegas-22
88LasVeg/CMC-17
88LasVeg/Pro-232
89UD/Ext-722

Green, Gene
58T-366
59T-37
60L-82
60T-269
61T-206
62J-72
62P-72
62P/Can-72
62Salada-70
62Shirriff-70
62T-78
63Sugar-10
63T-506

Green, Jeff
83BuffB-8

Green, John
86Geneva-7
86Peoria-9
87Peoria-3
89FtLaud/Star-7

Green, Larry
76Dubuq

Green, Lenny
58T-471
59T-209
60T-99
61Clover-8BOTH
61Peters-15
61T-4
62J-87
62P-87
62P/Can-87
62Salada-69A
62Salada-69B
62Shirriff-69
62T-84
62T/bucks
62T/St-75
63J-6
63P-6
63T-198
64T-386
65T-588
66T-502

Green, Nat
85Bend/Cram-8

Green, Otis
86Syrac-11
87Syrac-15
87Syrac/TCMA-14
88Syrac/CMC-19
88Syrac/Pro-831
89Syrac/CMC-12
89Syrac/Pro-793

Green, Randy
80Ogden-5

Green, Richard
64T-466R
65T-168
66T-545
67T-54
68T-303
69T-515
70T-311
71T-258
72T-780
73T-456
74T-392
75T-91
75T/M-91

Green, Rick
77Visal

Green, Stephen
88Bakers/Cal-248
89VeroB/Star-9

Green, Steve
78Holyo
80OrlTw/B-4
82OrlTw/A-15

Green, Terry
86Osceola-9
87Osceola-25
88ColAst/Best-22

Green, Tom
86Sumter-7

Green, Willie
90Score-682DC

Greenberg, Hank
34DS-54
34G-62
35BU-57
35G-8F
35G-9F
36G
36Wheat
37OPC-107
38Exh/4-12
38G-253
38G-277
38ONG/Pin-13
38Wheat
39Exh
39PB-56
39Wheat-7
40PB-40
41DP-52
41DP-85
41PB-18
41Wheat-16
55Gol/Ind-9
60NuCard-42
61GP-4
61NuCard-442
63Bz-19
80Cram/Leg-30
80SSPC/HOF
83D/HOF-16
85T/Gloss22-22
85West/2-33
86S/Dec-4
89Pac/Leg-195
PR1-13
R302
R303-B
R303/A
R309/2
R311/Gloss
R312
R313
R314
R346-35
R423-38
V300
V355-41

Greenberg, Steve
76Dubuq

Greene, Altar
(Al)
80Evans-8
80T-666R

Greene, Ed
86Beloi-8

Greene, Henry
77DaytB

Greene, Ira Thomas
87Greenv/Bst-23

Greene, James
(Joe)
78Laugh/Black-13

Greene, Jeff
86Sumter-6
87Durhm-22
87Penin-20
88Tampa/Star-8

Greene, Keith
86Cram/PCL-137
87Spart-8

Greene, Steve
77BurlB

Greene, Tommy
88Richm-33
88Richm/CMC-1
88Richm/Pro-2
89AAA/Pro-54
89Richm/CMC-3
89Richm/Ko-33
89Richm/Pro-831
90D-576
90F-584
90Score-640
90Sf-224
90UD-49

Greengrass, Jim
53T-209
54B-28
54T-22
55B-49
56T-275
56YellBase/Pin-12
58Union
Exh47

Greenhalgh, Ted
46Sunbeam

Greenlee, Robert
87SnBer-19

Greenwell, Mike
85IntLgAS-44
85Pawtu-4
86Pawtu-10
86S-178M
87D-585
87D/Rook-4
87F/U-U37
87S/Rook-8
87T-259
88Class/Blue-227
88D-339
88D/Best-177
88D/RedSox/Bk-339
88F-354
88F-630M
88F/Excit-16
88F/Hottest-14
88F/Mini-7
88F/St-9
88Leaf-153
88OPC-274
88Panini/St-32
88Score-175
88Score/YS/I-24
88Sf-118
88T-493
88T/Big-233
88T/Coins-14
88T/Gloss60-20
88T/JumboR-3
88T/St-249
88T/St-312
88ToysRUs-12
89B-34
89Cadaco-24
89Class-149
89D-186
89D-1DK
89D/AS-15
89D/Best-28
89D/DKsuper-1DK
89D/GrandSlam-5
89D/MVP-BC13
89F-90
89F/AS-6
89F/BBAS-16
89F/BBMVP's-16
89F/Excit-18
89F/Heroes-19
89F/LL-18
89F/Superstar-20
89F/WaxBox-C11
89KayBee-15
89Nissen-6
89OPC-374
89Panini/St-280
89Score-659HL
89Score-66
89Score/HotSt-70
89Score/Mast-36
89Sf-143
89Sf-221M
89T-402AS
89T-630
89T/Big-211
89T/Coins-41
89T/DH-6
89T/Gloss60-31
89T/HeadsUp-22
89T/Hills-15
89T/Mini-48
89T/St-255
89T/St/Backs-16
89T/UK-32
89UD-432
90Class-47
90D-66
90D/Bon/MVP-BC17
90F-277
90F-632M
90F/WaxBox-C8
90Score-345
90Score/100St-67
90Sf-50
90T-70
90UD-354

Greenwell, Richard
89LittleSun-12

Greenwood, Bob
55B-42

Greenwood, John
88Pulas/Pro-1753

Greenwood, William
N172

Greer, Brian K.
80T-685R
82Amari-2

Greer, Edward C.
N172
N403

Greer, Ken
88Oneon/Pro-2047
89PrWill/Star-8

Greer, Randy
80Penin/B-14
80Penin/C-20

Gregg, Eric
88Umpire-34
89Umpires-32

Gregg, Hal
47TipTop
49Eureka-161
52T-318

Gregg, Tommy
86Nashua-9
87Harrisbg-19
88BuffB/CMC-12
88BuffB/Pro-1474
88D-203
88F/U-U113
88Score/Tr-69T
89Class/Up/2-192
89D-121
89D/Best-170
89F-592
89Panini/St-32
89T/Tr-39T
89UD/Ext-751
90D-239
90F-585
90Score-78
90T-223
90UD-121

Gregg, Vean
14CJ-29
15CJ-29
T207
W514-33
WG5-17
WG6-16

Gregory, Grover
(Lee)
62Kahn/Atl

Gregory, John
83VeroB-17

Gregory, Paul
47Signal

Gregory, Scott
78Duned

Gregson, Glenn
83MidldC-3
84MidldC-14
87WinSal-12

Gregson, Goose
88GreatF-27
89GreatF-33

Greif, Bill
72OPC-101R
72T-101R
73T-583
74McDon
74OPC-102
74T-102

75OPC-168
75T-168
75T/M-168
76OPC-184
76T-184
77OPC-243
77T-112

Greiner, Dan
W514-80

Greminger, Edward
T206
T213/brown

Grich, Bob
71OPC-193
71T-193
72OPC-338
72T-338
73JP
73K-39
73OPC-418
73T-418
74OPC-109
74T-109
74T/DE-8
74T/St-125
75Ho-72
75K-4
75OPC-225
75T-225
75T/M-225
76Ho-13
76Ho/Twink-13
76OPC-335
76SSPC-388
76T-335
77Ho-131
77K-39
77OPC-28
77Pepsi-25
77T-521
78Ho-62
78OPC-133
78T-18
79Ho-112
79OPC-248
79T-447
80OPC-326
80T-621
81D-289
81F-269
81F/St-50
81OPC-182
81T-182
81T/HT
81T/St-53
82D-90
82F-461
82F/St-218
82K-38
82OPC-284
82T-162LL
82T-284
82T/St-162
82T/St-4LL
83D-468
83F-91
83K-60
83OPC-381
83OPC-387AS
83Seven-11
83T-387
83T-790
83T/St-43
84D-179
84F-518
84Nes/792-315
84OPC-315
84Smok/Cal-10
84T-315
84T/St-228
85D-280
85F-302
85Leaf-88
85OPC-155
85Smok/Cal-12
85T-465
85T/St-230
86D-207
86F-157
86OPC-155
86Smok/Cal-12
86T-155
86T-486M
86T/St-181
86Woolwth-12
87D-456
87F-81
87OPC-4
87RedFoley/St-30
87S-184
87T-677
89Smok/Angels-11

Grief
E270/2

Grief, Bill
73OPC-583
74T/St-92

Grier, Antron
87Erie-12
88Hamil/Pro-1723
88Savan/Pro-355
89Sprin/Best-3

Grier, Dave
80BurlB-5
82ElPas-17

Grier, Mark
79Newar-14

Grieve, Tom
71MLB/St-540
71OPC-167
71T-167
72T-609
73OPC-579
73T-579
74OPC-268
74T-268
75Ho-38
75OPC-234
75T-234
75T/M-234
76Ho-130
76OPC-106
76SSPC-270
76T-106
77Ho-93
77T-403
78T-337
79OPC-138
79T-277
79Tucso-14

Grieve, William
55B-275ump

Griffey, G. Ken
74OPC-598R
74T-598R
75OPC-284
75T-284
75T/M-284
76Crane-17
76Icee
76K-44
76MSA/Disc
76OPC-128
76SSPC-40
76T-128
77Ho-59
77K-49
77OPC-11
77Pep-50
77T-320
78K-4
78OPC-140
78T-80
79Ho-45
79K-39
79OPC-216
79T-420
80OPC-285
80T-550
81Coke
81D-184
81F-199
81F/St-60
81OPC-280
81T-280
81T/HT
81T/SO-91
81T/St-163
82D-634
82F-67
82F/St-16
82OPC-171IA
82OPC-330
82T-621
82T-756TL
82T/St-38
82T/St-38
82T/Tr-40T
83D-486
83F-382
83OPC-110
83RoyRog/Disc-3
83T-110
83T/St-98
84D-613
84D/AAS-21
84D/Champs-25
84F-126
84Nes/792-770
84OPC-306
84T-770
84T/St-317
85D-347
85F-128
85Leaf-193
85OPC-380
85T-380
86D-126
86F-105
86Leaf-48
86OPC-40
86T-40
86T/Tr-41T
87D-513
87D/OD-42
87F-516
87F/Mini-46
87F/St-49
87OPC-114
87Smok/Atl-19
87T-711
88D-202
88D/Best-141
88F-540
88Leaf-165
88OPC-255
88Panini/St-248
88RedFoley/St-28
88Score-390
88Sf-178
88T-443
88T/Big-110
88T/St-38
89B-259FS
89F/Up-84
89K/Reds-30
89Score-609
89T/Tr-40T
90D-469
90F-420
90Score-338
90T-581
90UD-682

Griffey, Ken Jr.
88CalLgAS-26
88SnBer/Best-1
88SnBer/Cal-34
89B-220
89B-259FS
89Class-131
89Class/Up/2-193
89D-33RR
89D/Best-192
89D/Rook-3
89F-548
89Moth/Griffey-1
89Moth/Griffey-2
89Moth/Griffey-3
89Moth/Griffey-4
89Moth/Sea-3
89Score/Mast-30
89Score/Tr-100
89Score/YS/II-18
89T/HeadsUp-5
89T/Tr-41T
89UD-1
90Class-20
90D-365
90D-4DK
90F-513
90F/WaxBox-C10
90Score-560
90Score/100Ris-3
90Sf-7
90T-336
90UD-156
90UD-24TC

Griffin, Alan
75Tucso-21
76Tucso-34
78SnJos-9

Griffin, Alfredo
79T-705R
80OPC-290
80T-558
81D-149
81F-430
81OPC-277
81OPC/Post-15
81T-277
81T/St-140
82D-101
82F-615
82F/St-236
82OPC-148
82T-677
82T/St-252
83D-180
83F-429
83OPC-294
83T-488
83T/St-129
84D-605
84F-156
84Nes/792-76
84OPC-76
84T-76
84T/St-369
84Tor/Fire-15
85D-73
85F-106
85F/Up-U47
85Leaf-230
85Moth/A's-5
85OPC-361
85T-361
85T/St-366
85T/Tr-42T
86D-101
86F-417
86Leaf-34
86Moth/A's-5
86OPC-121
86S-136M
86T-566
86T/St-168
87D-256
87D/OD-28
87F-392
87Leaf-198
87OPC-111
87S-164
87Smok/A's-4
87T-111
87T/St-166
88D-226
88D/Best-92
88F-280
88F/U-U94
88Moth/Dodg-7
88OPC-42
88Panini/St-172
88Pol/Dodg-7
88Score-88
88Score/Tr-37T
88Sf-156
88T-726
88T/Big-247
88T/St-169
88T/Tr-43T
89B-345
89D-79
89D/Best-178
89F-58
89Moth/Dodg-7
89OPC-62
89Pol/Dodg-5
89Score-167
89T-62
89T/St-59
89UD-631
90D-195
90F-395
90Score-156
90T-643
90UD-338

Griffin, Barry
88Boise/Pro-1614

Griffin, Dave
83Ander-20
84Durhm-8
85Durhm-24
87Richm/TCMA-13
88Richm-34
88Richm/CMC-19
88Richm/Pro-20
89Colum/CMC-27
89Toled/CMC-12
89Toled/Pro-785

Griffin, Doug
71OPC-176R
71T-176R
72T-703
72T-704A
73OPC-96
73T-96
74OPC-219
74T-219
75OPC-454
75T-454
75T/M-454
76OPC-654
76SSPC-412
76T-654
77T-191

Griffin, Frankie
83Readg-6

Griffin, Greg
83Knoxv-17

Griffin, Ivy M.
V100

Griffin, Mark
89Star/Wax-29
89VeroB/Star-10

Griffin, Michael
N172
N300/unif

Griffin, Mike
77Ashev
79WHave-17

81Colum-10
81F-107
81T-483
82D-553
82T-146
83OKCty-8
84OKCty-7
85Omaha-13
86Omaha-8
86Omaha/TCMA-15
87RochR-9
87RochR/TCMA-3
88D-494
88F-561
88RochR-8
88RochR-9
88RochR/CMC-7
88RochR/Gov-8
88RochR/Pro-210
89Nashvl-6
89Nashvl/CMC-4
89Nashvl/Pro-1274

Griffin, Terry
88LitFalls/Puc-16
89StLucie/Star-8

Griffin, Tom
69T-614R
70T-578
71MLB/St-81
71OPC-471
71T-471
72MB-122
73OPC-468
73T-468
74OPC-256
74T-256
75OPC-188
75T-188
75T/M-188
76OPC-454
76T-454
77T-39
78T-318
79Pol/Giants-43
79T-291
80Pol/Giants-43
80T-649
81D-75
81F-456
81T-538
82D-474
82F-389
82T-777

Griffin, Ty
88T/Tr-44T
89B-289
89CharlK-14
89Peoria/Ko-1
89T-713FDP
89T/Big-170

Griffith, Clark C.
10Domino-50
11Helmar-69
12Sweet/Pin-101A
12Sweet/Pin-101B
14Piedmont/St-25
48Exh/HOF
50Callahan
60Exh/HOF-12
60F-15
61F-36
63Bz/ATG-37
80Cram/Leg-37
80SSPC/HOF
D329-72
E220
E93
M101/4-72
M116
N172
S74-76
T202
T204
T205
T206
T213/blue
T215/blue
T215/brown
T3-77
W514-41
W555
WG2-22
WG5-18
WG6-17

Griffith, Jeff
87Watertn-22
88Aug/Pro-363

Griffith, Kerry
86Erie-10

Griffith, Robert D.
(Derrell)
65OPC-112
65T-112
66T-573
67T-502

Griffith, Thomas H.
(Tommy)
15CJ-167
D327
D328-64
D329-73
D350/2-72
E120
E121/120
E121/80
E122
E135-64
M101/4-73
M101/5-72
V100
V61-58
W501-106
W515-35
W572
W575

Griffith, Tommy
89Boise/Pro-1984

Griffiths, Brian
89Ashvl/Pro-955

Griggs, Hal
58T-455
59T-434
60L-34
60T-244

Grillone, Dave
86Cram/PCL-94
87QuadC-29

Grilk, Jim
40Hughes-8

Grilli, Guido
66T-558R

Grilli, Steve
76OPC-591R
76T-591R
77T-506
78Syrac
79Syrac-17
81Syrac-4

Grim, Bob
55B-167
55RM-AL5
55T-80
55T/DH-58
56T-52
57T-36
58T-224
59T-423
60L-10
60T-78
62T-564

Grimes, Bob
88CharWh/Best-27
89Peoria/Ko-32TR

Grimes, Burleigh A.
21Exh-61
25Exh-12
26Exh-11
27Exh-7
28Yueng-1
32Orbit/num-26
32Orbit/un-21
33G-64
35G-1F
35G-3D
35G-4D
35G-5D
60F-59
61F-37
80Cram/Leg-51
80SSPC/HOF
83D/HOF-21
89Smok/Dodg-8
E120
E210-1
R305
R308-191
R315-A12
R315-B12
R316
V100
V353-64
V61-89
W502-1
W513-72
W515-16
W572

Grimes, Dave
89Sprin/Best-2

Grimes, John
84Evrt/Cram-25
86Shrev-9
87Shrev-22

Grimes, Lee
87WinSal-14
88CharWh/Best-6

Grimes, Mike
88CapeCod/Sum-122
89Medford/Best-6

Grimes, Oscar Ray
21Exh-62
44Yank/St-13
E120
V61-105
W572
W573

Grimes, Steve
76Cedar
78Holyo

Grimm, Charlie
21Exh-63
25Exh-21
26Exh-21
27Exh-10
29Exh/4-6
30CEA/Pin-4
31Exh/4-6
32Orbit/num-37
32Orbit/un-22
33CJ/Pin-11
33Exh/4-3
33G-51
34Exh/4-3
34G-3
34Ward's/Pin-6
35Exh/4-3
40PB-228
53B/Col-69
53JC-1
54JC-40
55B-298
55Gol/Braves-12
55JC-40
60T-217
80Cram/Leg-75
87Conlon/2-40
88Conlon/4-12
E120
E121/120
E126-19
E220
R300
R305
R332-15
R337-423
V100
V353-51
V354-61
V355-89
W501-82
W575
WG8-25

Grimshaw, Myron
(Moose)
E254
T206

Grimsley, Jason
85Bend/Cram-9
88Clearw/Star-12
89Readg/Best-10
89Readg/Pro-670
89Readg/Star-12
90F-653M
90Score-649
90T-493
90UD-27

Grimsley, Ross
72OPC-99
72T-99
73OPC-357
73T-357
74OPC-59
74T-59
74T/Tr-59T
75K-2
75OPC-458
75T-458
75T/M-458
76OPC-257
76SSPC-377
76T-257
77OPC-47
77T-572
78T-691
79Ho-5
79K-3
79OPC-4
79T-15
79T/Comics-26
80K-1
80OPC-195
80T-375
81F-406
81T-170
84Chatt-8
86Calgary-10C
87Calgary-5
89BurlB/Pro-1614

Grissom, Lee
38Wheat
39PB-2
W711/1

Grissom, Marquis
88James/Pro-1910
89Jaxvl/Best-1
89Jaxvl/Pro-175
90Class-65
90D-36
90F-347
90Score-591
90Score/100Ris-99
90Sf-134
90T-714
90UD-9

Grissom, Marv
54NYJour
55B-123
55Gol/Giants-11
55RM-NL25
56T-301
57T-216
58Hires-64
58SFCall
58T-399
59T-243

Groat, Dick
52T-369
53T-154
54T-43
55T-26
55T/DH-100
56T-24
56T/Hocus-A1
56T/Hocus-B3
56T/Pin-42SS
57Kahn
57T-12
58Hires-21
58Kahn
58T-45
59Kahn
59T-160
60Kahn
60T tattoo
60T-258
60T/tatt-20
61Bz-8
61Kahn
61NuCard-413
61P-129
61T-1
61T-41LL
61T-486MV
61T/Dice-5
61T/St-64
62Exh
62J-172
62Kahn
62P-172
62P/Can-172
62Salada-138
62Shirriff-138
62Sugar-A
62T-270
62T/bucks
62T/St-177
63Exh
63J-139
63Kahn
63P-139
63Salada-16
63T-130
64Bz-2
64T-40
64T-7LL
64T/Coins-147AS
64T/Coins-5
64T/S-19
64T/St-81S9
64T/SU
64T/tatt
64Wheat/St-20
65OldLond-11
65OPC-275
65T-275
65T/trans-15
66OPC-103
66T-103
67T-205
75OPC-198M
75T-198MV
75T/M-198MV
78TCMA-150
85West/2-40
88Pac/Leg-108
89Swell-91
Exh47
WG10-29
WG9-30

Grob, Connie
59DF
Groennert, John
88Bill/Pro-1815
Groh, Don
83Peoria/LF-5
85Cram/PCL-4
Groh, Heinie
15CJ-159
21Exh-64
21Exh-65
25Exh-34
88Pac/8Men-81
D327
D328-65
D329-74
D350/2-73
E120
E121/120
E121/80
E135-65
E220
M101/4-74
M101/5-73
V61-88
W501-67
W514-46
W515-52
W516-2
W572
W573
W575
WG7-19
Gromek, Steve
49B-198
50B-131
50NumNum
51B-115
52B-203
52NumNum-8
52T-258
53B/BW-63
54B-199
55B-203
56T-310
56YellBase/Pin-13
57T-258
79TCMA-133
Exh47
Groninger, Gerry
88Bill/Pro-1803
89Cedar/Best-23
89Cedar/Star-23
Groom, Bob
10Domino-51
11Helmar-70
12Sweet/Pin-59
14CJ-46
14Piedmont/St-26
15CJ-46
D328-66
E135-66
E270/2
E90/1
E91
T202
T205
T206
T213/blue
T215
T3-96
Groom, Buddy
88Tampa/Star-9
89BirmB/Best-24
89BirmB/Pro-109
89SLAS-17
Gross, Bob
87Gasto-5
Gross, Deryk
89Keno/Pro-1064
89Keno/Star-8
Gross, Don
57Kahn
57T-341
58T-172
59T-228
60T-284
Gross, George
78DaytB
80Tucso-10
81Tucso-22
Gross, Greg
75Ho-101
75K-5
75OPC-334
75T-334
75T/M-334
76Ho-90
76K-56
76OPC-171
76SSPC-64
76T-171
77T-614
78Ho-141
78T-397
79OPC-302
79T-579
80BK/P-12
80OPC-364
80T-718
81D-598
81F-18
81T-459
82D-371
82F-246
82T-53
83D-441
83F-162
83T-279
84D-285
84F-31
84Nes/792-613
84T-613
85CIGNA-5
85D-407
85F-251
85F/St-53
85OPC-117
85T-117
86CIGNA-5
86D-163
86F-441
86OPC-302
86T-302
87D-385
87F-173
87OPC-338
87RedFoley/St-20
87T-702
88D-412
88F-302
88Score-386
88T-518
89F-568
89Lennox/Ast-2
89Moth/Ast-12
89Score-125
89T-438
89T/WaxBox-E
89UD-534
Gross, Kevin
83Portl-5
84D-381
84F-32
84Nes/792-332
84T-332
85CIGNA-14
85D-477
85F-252
85T-584
86CIGNA-8
86D-529
86F-442
86T-764
86T/St-119
87D-236
87F-174
87OPC-163
87T-163
88D-113
88D/Best-103
88F-303
88OPC-20
88Score-468
88T-20
88T/St-118
89B-355
89D-194
89D/AS-48
89D/Best-202
89D/MVP-BC12
89D/Tr-3
89F-569
89F/Up-96
89OPC-215
89Panini/St-147
89Score-227
89Score/Tr-39
89Sf-213
89T-215
89T/St-116
89T/Tr-42T
89UD-31
89UD/Ext-719
90D-248
90F-348
90Score-251
90T-465
90UD-468
Gross, Kip
87Lynch-5
88FSLAS/Star-6
89Jacks/GS-22
Gross, Wayne
76Tucso-25
77T-479R
78OPC-106
78T-139
79BK/P-22
79T-528
80OPC-189
80T-363
81D-237
81F-587
81OPC-86
81T-86
81T/St-118
82D-139
82F-90
82F/St-124
82Granny-2
82OPC-303
82T-692
83D-591
83F-517
83Granny-10
83T-233
84D-375
84F-444
84F/X-45
84Nes/792-741
84OPC-263
84T-741
84T/St-333
84T/X-44
85D-228
85F-179
85OPC-233
85T-416
86D-535
86F-276
86OPC-173
86T-173
87Moth/A's-17
Grossman, Bob
75OkCty
75SnAnt
76Wmspt
Grossman, Dave
82Edmon-24
86IowaC-12tr
88IowaC/Pro-531
89IowaC/Pro-1703
Grossman, Jim
87Kinston-8
Grote, Bob
79Jacks-8
Grote, Gerald
64T-226R
65T-504
66T-328
67T-413
68T-582
69MB-98
69MLB/St-165
69OPC-55
69T-55
69T/St-63
70MLB/St-76
70OPC-183
70T-183
70Trans-22
71MLB/St-154
71OPC-278
71T-278
71T/GM-54
72MB-123
72T-655
73OPC-113
73T-113
74OPC-311
74T-311
74T/St-62
75OPC-158
75T-158
75T/M-158
76Ho-78
76OPC-143
76T-143
78T-464
79T-279
Grotewald, Jeff
87Spart-21
88Clearw/Star-13
89Clearw/Star-10
Groth, Bill
52StarCal/L-72F
Groth, Ernest
50Remar
Groth, John
50B-243
51B-249
51T/BB-11
52B-67
52NTea
52RM-AL10
52T-25
52TipTop
53T-36
54B-165
54Wilson
55B-117
56T-279
56YellBase/Pin-14
57T-360
58T-262
59T-164
60L-133
60T-171
79TCMA-38
Exh47
Grout, Ron
79Wisco-7
Grove, George M.
WG7-20
Grove, LeRoy Orval
48L-66
Exh47
Grove, Robert M.
(Lefty)
29Exh/4-27
31Exh/4-28
32Orbit/un-23
33CJ/Pin-12
33DL-23
33Exh/4-14
33G-220
34DS-1
34Exh/4-14
34Exh/4-9
34G-19
35BU-153
35BU-31
35Exh/4-9
35Wheat
36Exh/4-9
36Wheat
37Exh/4-9
37OPC-137
37Wheat-9
38Exh/4-9
38Wheat
39Exh
41DP-105
48Exh/HOF
50Callahan
60F-60
61F-38
61GP-17
72K/ATG-7
72K/ATG-7
72Laugh/GF-16
76OPC-350AS
76T-350M
80Cram/Leg-27
80Laugh/3/4/5-19
80Laugh/FFeat-8
80SSPC/HOF
86Conlon/1-47
86S/Dec-3
88Conlon/4-13
88Conlon/AmAS-13
89HOF/St-74
89Pac/Leg-185
89Swell-15
PR1-14
R300
R305
R306
R308-182
R310
R312/M
R313
R315-A13
R315-B13
R316
R328-27
R332-49
R337-408
R423-39
V300
V354-54
V355-88
W517-39
Grove, Scott
88Pulas/Pro-1752
89Sumter/Pro-1114
Groves, Larry
86Indianap-27
Grovom, Carl
86AubAs-11
87CharWh-15
88Osceola/Star-11
Grow, Lorin
76Indianap-14
Grubb, Cary
88Reno/Cal-281

Grubb, John
(Johnny)
74McDon
74OPC-32SD
74T-32
74T/St-93
75Ho-109
75K-43
75OPC-298
75T-298
75T/M-298
76OPC-422
76SSPC-130
76T-422
77OPC-165
77Pep-10
77T-286
78T-608
79OPC-99
79T-198
80OPC-165
80T-313
81D-148
81F-631
81T-545
82D-467
82F-317
82OPC-193
82T-496
83D-341
83F-567
83T-724
83T/St-123
83T/X-38
84D-90
84F-81
84Nes/792-42
84T-42
85Cain's-9
85D-578
85F-9
85T-643
85Wendy-10
86Cain's-7
86D-615
86F-227
86T-243
87Cain's-12
87Coke/Tigers-18
87D-476
87F-152
87T-384
87T/St-265
88Richm-27
88Score-199
88T-128
89Richm/CMC-24CO
89Richm/Ko-CO

Grubb, Sean
89Hamil/Star-17

Grube, Frank
32Orbit/num-5
32Orbit/un-24
34G-64
35G-8C
35G-9C
R305
W753

Gruber, Henry
N172

Gruber, Kelly
80Batav-21
81Watlo-22
82Chatt-16
83BuffB-16
84Syrac-27
84Tor/Fire-16
85F-645
85IntLgAS-37
85Syrac-22
85Tor/Fire-13
86Ault-17
86D/Rook-16
86Tor/Fire-15
87D-444
87F-227
87OPC-191
87T-458
87Tor/Fire-11
87Tor/Fire-11
88D-244
88D/Best-255
88F-111
88OPC-113
88Panini/St-221
88Score-422
88T-113
88T/Big-134
88Tor/Fire-17
89B-251
89D-113
89D/Best-31
89F-234
89OPC-29
89Panini/St-469
89Score-194
89Score/YS/II-12
89Sf-163
89T-201TL
89T-29
89T/Big-95
89T/St-187
89Tor/Fire-17
89UD-575
90D-113
90D-12DK
90F-83
90Score-425
90Sf-57
90T-505
90UD-111

Grudzinski, Gary
85PrWill-19

Gruff, John
89Richm/Pro-821

Grunard, Dan
86QuadC-13
87PalmSp-8

Grundler, Frank
75Shreve/TCMA-4
76Shrev

Grunhard, Danny
85Anchora-12
88MidldA/GS-16
89MidldA/GS-17

Grunsky, Gary
76Baton

Grunwald, Al
60T-427

Gryskevich, Larry
89Hamil/Star-14

Grzenda, Joe
69OPC-121
69T-121
70T-691
71MLB/St-541
71OPC-518
71T-518
72OPC-13
72T-13

Grzybeck, Ben
77DaytB

Gsellman, Bob
87CharWh-8

Guante, Cecilio
81Portl-10
82Portl-3
83D-423
84D-78
84F-250
84Nes/792-122
84T-122
85D-357
85F-465
85T-457
86D-142
86F-609
86T-668
87D-238
87F-610
87F/U-U38
87OPC-219
87T-219
87T/St-127
87T/Tr-40T
88D/Best-276
88D/Y/Bk-NEW
88T-84
89D-260
89F-519
89Moth/R-23
89Score-439
89Smok/R-10
89T-766
89UD-576
90D-403
90F-298
90Score-438
90T-532

Guarache, Jose
88StCath/Pro-2011

Gubicza, Mark
84F/X-46
84T/X-45
85D-344
85F-201
85OPC-127
85T-127
86D-583
86F-8
86Kitty/Disc-19
86Leaf-226
86NatPhoto-23
86T-644
87D-466
87F-368
87F/Excit-20
87F/Mini-47
87Leaf-238
87OPC-326
87T-326
88D-54
88D/Best-95
88F-259
88F/RecSet-15
88OPC-378
88Score-516
88Smok/Royals-12
88T-507
88T/Big-199
88T/St-262
89B-117
89Cadaco-25
89Class-138
89D-179
89D/AS-18
89D/Best-119
89F-283
89F/BBAS-17
89F/Excit-19
89OPC-379
89Panini/St-350
89Score-291
89Score/HotSt-69
89Score/YS/II-14
89Sf-102
89T-430
89T/Big-26
89T/Mini-55
89T/St-271
89T/St/Backs-26
89T/UK-33
89Tastee/Discs-9
89UD-202
90D-204
90F-109
90F-633M
90Score-121
90T-20
90UD-676

Guenther, Bob
87Myrtle-26

Guercio, Maurice
86FSLAS-19
86FtLaud-10
87Albany-6

Guerra, Fermin
(Mike)
49B-155
50B-157
51B-202

Guerra, Rich
75SnAnt
76Wmspt

Guerrero, Alex
75QuadC

Guerrero, Inocencio
83Durhm-4
87Greenv/Bst-17
88Greenv/Best-4
89Durhm/Star-28

Guerrero, Juan
88Clint/Pro-701
89SanJose/Best-21
89SanJose/Cal-219
89SanJose/Pro-451
89SanJose/Star-11
89Star/Wax-86

Guerrero, Mario
73OPC-607R
73T-607R
74OPC-192
74T-192
75OPC-152
75T-152
75T/M-152
76OPC-499
76SSPC-285
76T-499
77T-628
78T-339
79Ho-78
79K-43
79OPC-131
79T-261
80T-49
81F-591
81T-547

Guerrero, Mike
88Beloi/GS-15
89Beloi/Star-8

Guerrero, Patrick
88StCath/Pro-2038

Guerrero, Pedro
78Cr/PCL-11
79Albuq-16
79T-719R
80Pol/Dodg-28
81Pol/Dodg-28
81T-651
82D-136
82F-7
82F/St-6
82OPC-247
82Pol/Dodg
82Pol/Dodg-28
82T-247
82T/St-55
83D-110
83Drake-9
83F-207
83K-20
83OPC-116
83Pol/Dodg-28
83Seven-4
83T-425
83T-681
83T/St-248
84D-174
84D-24
84D/AAS-17
84Drake-11
84F-100
84F/St-19
84F/St-34
84FunFood/Pin-26
84MiltBrad-11
84Nes/792-306TL
84Nes/792-90
84OPC-90
84Pol/Dodg-28
84Ralston-30
84Seven-14W
84T-90
84T/Cereal-30
84T/Gloss40-25
84T/St-75
84T/Super-24
84T/Super-24
85D-174
85D/AAS-34
85D/HL-19
85Drake-13
85F-370
85Leaf-211
85OPC-34
85Seven-10W
85T-575
85T/St-70
85T/Super-44
86D-174
86Drake-6
86F-130
86F/AS-8
86F/LimEd-21
86F/Mini-28
86F/Slug-13
86F/St-47
86Leaf-105
86Meadow/Blank-6
86Meadow/Stat-18
86OPC-145
86OPC-G
86Pol/Dodg-28
86S-14
86S-148M
86S-181M
86S/Dec-74M
86T-145
86T-706
86T/3D-8
86T/Gloss60-25
86T/Mini-44
86T/St-65
86T/Super-27
86T/WaxBox-G
86TrueVal-1
87BK-7
87Class-39
87D-53
87F-440
87F/Slug-16
87Jiffy-10
87KayBee-14
87Leaf-237
87Moth/Dodg-2
87OPC-360
87Pol/Dodg-14
87RedFoley/St-83
87S-27
87Seven-W4
87Smok/Dodg-10
87T-360
87T/Board-27
87T/St-69
88D-278
88D-BC16
88D/AS-48
88D/Best-122
88F-514

88F-623M
88F/AwardWin-15
88F/Mini-83
88F/Slug-16
88F/St-91
88FanSam-20
88KayBee-12
88KMart-11
88Leaf-101
88Moth/Dodg-2
88Nestle-24
88OPC-111
88Panini/St-314
88Pol/Dodg-28
88RedFoley/St-29
88Score-9
88Sf-97
88Smok/Dodg-28
88T-550
88T/Big-171
88T/Coins-43
88T/Gloss60-24
88T/Mini-52
88T/RiteAid-5
88T/St-75
88T/St/Backs-15
88T/UK-28
89Ames-15
89B-440
89Cadaco-26
89Class-60
89D-418
89D/Best-75
89F-451
89KayBee-16
89KingB/Discs-20
89KMart/DT-33
89KMart/Lead-6
89OPC-68
89Panini/St-183
89RedFoley/St-52
89Score-564
89Score/HotSt-44
89Smok/Cards-7
89Smok/Dodg-94
89T-780
89T/Big-285
89T/Coins-16
89T/St-40
89T/UK-34
89UD-306
90Class-146
90D-63
90D-674AS
90D/Bon/MVP-BC6
90F-250
90F/WaxBox-C11
90Score-13
90Score/100St-61
90Sf-66
90T-610
90UD-244

Guerrero, Ramces
88Idaho/Pro-1844
89Idaho/Pro-2010

Guerrero, Sandy
(Epy)
86Ventura-8
87Stockton-4
88CalLgAS-15
88Stock/Cal-196
88Stock/Pro-727
89ElPas/GS-22

Guerrero, Tony
81Wisco-4
83Orlan-22
85Visal-21

Guetterman, Lee
84Chatt-16
86F/Up-U45
87D-322
87F-585
87T-307
88D-270
88D/Y/Bk-NEW
88F-374
88OPC-382
88Score-323
88Sf-45
88T-656
89D/Best-108
89Score/NWest-24
89T/Tr-43T
90D-127
90F-443
90Score-294
90T-286
90UD-318

Guidry, Ron
76OPC-599R
76T-599R
77BK/Y-11
77T-656
78BK/Y-4
78Ho-25
78PapaG/Disc-28
78T-135
79BK/Y-4
79Ho-89
79K-11
79OPC-264
79T-202M
79T-500
79T-5LL
79T-7LL
79T/Comics-13
80BK/PHR-4
80K-4
80OPC-157
80T-300
80T/S-7
81D-227
81F-88
81F/St-76
81K-45
81OPC-250
81T-250
81T/St-112
82D-548
82D-558M
82F-38
82F/St-120
82K-26
82OPC-10IA
82OPC-9
82Sqt-9
82T-10A
82T-9
83D-17DK
83D-31
83D/AAS-15
83F-383
83OPC-104
83RoyRog/Disc-4
83T-440
83T/St-102
84D-173
84D/AAS-51
84F-127
84FunFood/Pin-96
84MiltBrad-12
84Nes/792-110
84Nes/792-406AS
84Nes/792-486TL
84Nes/792-717LL
84Nestle/DT-10
84OPC-110
84OPC-204AS
84Ralston-31
84Seven-16E
84T-110
84T-406AS
84T-717LL
84T/Cereal-31
84T/Gloss40-14
84T/St-194
84T/St-318
84T/Super-17
85D-214
85F-129
85Leaf-237
85OPC-388
85T-790
85T/St-313
86D-103
86Drake-32
86F-106
86F/Mini-22
86F/Slug-14
86F/St-48
86Leaf-36
86OPC-109
86OPC-H
86S-149M
86S-18
86S-185M
86S-57M
86S/Dec-71
86T-610
86T-721
86T/3D-9
86T/Gloss60-12
86T/Mini-26
86T/St-302
86T/Super-28
86T/WaxBox-H
87Class-68
87D-93
87F-100
87F/AwardWin-16
87Leaf-101
87OPC-375
87RedFoley/St-54
87S-83
87T-375
87T/St-301
88D-175
88D/Y/Bk-175
88F-207
88F/St-S3
88Leaf-180
88OPC-127
88Score-310
88T-535
88T/Big-50
88T/St-296
88T/St/Backs-61
89Score-342
89Score/NWest-28
89T-255
89UD-307

Guiheen
T206

Guillen, Ozzie
83Beaum-2
84Cram/PCL-236
85Coke/WS-13
85D/HL-55
85F/Up-U48
85T/Tr-43T
86Coke/WS-13
86D-208
86F-206
86F/LL-17
86F/Mini-44
86F/St-49
86F/WaxBox-C3
86Jay's-9
86KayBee-16
86Leaf-140
86OPC-254
86Quaker-20
86S-176M
86S-22
86T-254
86T/Gloss60-58
86T/St-294
86T/St-309
86T/Super-7
87Coke/WS-7
87D-87
87D/OD-235
87F-497
87F/AwardWin-17
87F/Mini-48
87F/RecSet-13
87F/St-50
87Kraft-11
87Leaf-117
87OPC-89
87RedFoley/St-67
87S-186
87Seven-C9
87T-89
87T/St-287
88Coke/WS-9
88D-137
88D/Best-81
88F-398
88F/Mini-15
88F/RecSet-16
88F/St-16
88Leaf-59
88Nestle-7
88OPC-296
88Panini/St-61
88Score-603
88Score/YS/I-21
88Sf-14
88T-585
88T/Big-27
88T/St-284
89B-64
89Class/Up/2-175M
89Coke/WS-10
89D-176
89D/Best-137
89D/MVP-BC23
89F-497
89F/BBAS-18
89KingB/Discs-6
89OPC-195
89Panini/St-309
89RedFoley/St-53
89Score-433
89Score/HotSt-51
89Sf-85
89T-195
89T/Big-148
89T/St-303
89T/UK-35
89UD-175
90Class-92
90D-135
90D-15DK
90F-533
90Score-6
90Sf-48
90T-365
90UD-267
90UD-79TC

Guin, Greg
82ArkTr-14
83ArkTr-17
84ArkTr-10

Guindon, Bob
65T-509R

Guinn, Brian
86SLAS-8
87Pittsf-11
88IowaC/CMC-15
88IowaC/Pro-526
89IowaC/CMC-16
89IowaC/Pro-1709

Guinn, Drannon E.
(Skip)
69T-614R
70OPC-316
70T-316
71MLB/St-82
71OPC-741
71T-741

Guinn, Wayne
80Cedar-26

Guintini, Ben
48Sommer-14

Guise, Witt
W711/2

Guisto, Lou
D328-67
E135-67

Gulden, Brad
77LodiD
78Cr/PCL-46
79Colum-1
80Colum-6
80T-670R
81Spoka-30
83Colum-4
85D-365
85F-537
85OPC-251
85T-251
86Moth/Giants-25

Gull, Sterling
80SLCty-20

Gullett, Don
71MLB/St-60
71OPC-124
71T-124
72OPC-157
72T-157
73OPC-595
73T-595
74OPC-385
74T-385
74T/St-27
75Ho-107
75OPC-65
75T-65
75T/M-65
76Crane-18
76Ho-45
76Ho/Twink-45
76Icee
76K-3
76MSA/Disc
76OPC-390
76SSPC-27
76T-390
77BK/Y-6
77Ho-143
77OPC-250
77Pepsi-35
77T-15
78BK/Y-8
78OPC-30
78T-225
78Wiffle/Discs-28
79OPC-64
79T-140
80T-435

Gullickson, Bill
81D-91
81F-150
81OPC-41
81T-203M
81T-578
82D-162
82F-190
82Hygrade
82OPC-172
82OPC-94
82OPC/Post-21
82T-172
82T-526TL
82Zeller-15
83D-288
83F-284
83OPC-31

83Stuart-15
83T-31
84D-401
84F-276
84Nes/792-318
84OPC-318
84Stuart-16
84T-318
84T/St-96
85D-97
85F-399
85Leaf-236
85OPC-143
85T-687
85T/St-91
86D-331
86D/HL-40
86F-249
86F/Up-U46
86OPC-229
86T-229
86T/St-78
86T/Tr-42T
86TexGold-34
87D-369
87F-203
87F/AwardWin-18
87F/Mini-49
87F/RecSet-14
87F/St-51
87Kahn-34
87Smok/NL-4
87T-489
87T/St-140
88D-586
88F-208
88OPC-329
88Score-585
88T-711

Gulliver, Glenn
77Evansvl/TCMA-13
80Evans-21
81Evans-15
82RochR-12
83D-131
83F-62
83RochR-15
83T-293
84RochR-11
85Richm-13
86Hagers-7
86RochR-4
87Hagers-11

Gumbert, Addison
N172

Gumbert, Harry
39PB-54
40PB-86
41DP-27
41DP-92
41PB-26
49B-192
50B-171
W754

Gumbert, Rich
83Greens-9

Gumpert, Dave
82BirmB-5
83Evans-3
84Evans-8
84Nes/792-371
84T-371
85IowaC-14
86IowaC-13
87F-565
87T-487

Gumpert, Randy
49B-87
50B-184
51B-59
52B-106
52T-247

Gundelfinger, Matt
81Redwd-14
83Sprin/LF-18

Gunderson, Eric
87Everett-13
88CalLgAS-5
88SanJose/Cal-131
88SanJose/Pro-114
89Shreve/Pro-1833

Gunderson, Greg
89Batav/Pro-1938

Gunn, Clay
86Cram/PCL-126
87Wausa-10
88SnBer/Best-18
88SnBer/Cal-32

Gunnarson, Bob
86Chatt-10
87Chatt/Best-13

Gunning, Thomas
N172
N690

Gunson, Joseph
N172

Gunter, Chet
76Shrev

Gura, Larry
71OPC-203
71T-203
73OPC-501
73T-501
74OPC-616
74T-616
74T/Tr-616T
75OPC-557
75T-557
75T/M-557
76OPC-319
76T-319
77T-193
78T-441
79T-19
80OPC-154
80T-295
81Coke
81D-461
81F-38
81F/St-102
81K-59
81OPC-130
81T-130
81T/SO-51
81T/St-88
82D-338
82F-410
82F/St-205
82OPC-147
82T-790
82T-96TL
82T/St-195
83D-160
83F-113
83K-42
83OPC-340
83OPC-395AS
83T-340
83T-395
83T/St-77
84D-100
84F-347
84Nes/792-625
84Nes/792-96TL
84OPC-264
84T-625
84T/St-285
85D-217
85F-202
85T-595
85T/St-278

Gurchiek, Chris
88AppFx/Pro-156
88Boise/Pro-1609

Gurtcheff, Jeff
86Watertn-8

Gust, Chris
88Madis-12

Gustafson, Edward
89Everett/Star-9

Gustave, Michael
78Wisco

Gustavson, Duane
82FtMyr-10
83CharR-25
85FtMyr-26
86FtMyr-13MG
87Memph-21
87Memph/Best-2C
88Orlan/Best-3

Gustine, Frank
47TipTop
48L-88
49B-99
49Eureka-57
Exh47

Guthrie, Mark
88Visal/Cal-167
89Orlan/Best-14
89Orlan/Pro-1335
89SLAS-19
90D-622
90T-317
90UD-436

Gutierrez, Cesar
69OPC-16R
69T-16R
70OPC-269
70T-269
71MLB/St-392
71OPC-154
71T-154
72T-743

Gutierrez, Dimas
85PrWill-8
86Nashua-10
87Harrisbg-22
88EastLAS/Pro-15
88Harris/Pro-841
89Mia/Star/25-8

Gutierrez, Felipe
85VeroB-7

Gutierrez, Israel
78Ashev
79Wausa-7

Gutierrez, Jackie
84F/X-47
84T/X-46
85D-335
85F-160
85T-89
85T/St-216
85T/St-373YS
86D-335
86F-350
86F/Up-U47
86OPC-73
86T-633
87D-601
87F-471
87T-276
89Pawtu/CMC-19
89Pawtu/Dunkin-21
89Pawtu/Pro-694
89UD-430

Gutierrez, Joaquin
79Elmir-7

Gutierrez, Julian
78StPet
80ArkTr-16
82ArkTr-15

Gutierrez, Ricky
89Freder/Star-8

Gutierrez, Robert
(Bob)
84Newar-21
85Newar-15

Gutrirrez, Willie
79Knoxv/TCMA-13

Gutteridge, Don
60T-458C
70OPC-123
70T-123

Guzik, Rob
89Kingspt/Star-11

Guzman, Correa
88Knoxv/Best-18

Guzman, Doinini
89Medford/Best-10

Guzman, Hector
83VeroB-18

Guzman, Jose
83BurlR-4
83BurlR/LF-7
84Tulsa-29
85OKCty-11
86D-30
86D/Rook-24
86F-559
86Rangers-23
86T/Tr-43T
87D-101
87F-124
87Leaf-50
87Moth/Rang-23
87Smok/R-3
87T-363
88D-136
88D/Best-88
88F-467
88Leaf-55
88Moth/R-23
88OPC-98
88Score-322
88Smok/R-20
88T-563
89Bimbo/Discs-11
89Brist/Star-10
89D-284
89F-520
89Moth/R-25
89OPC-209
89Panini/St-445
89Score-143
89Score/YS/II-11
89Smok/R-11
89T-462
89T/St-241
89UD-73
90T-308
90UD-617

Guzman, Juan
86VeroB-8
87Bakers-5
89Syrac/CMC-9
89Syrac/Pro-797

Guzman, Luis
79Knoxv/TCMA-3
80Utica-17

Guzman, Ruben
83Water-18
86GlenF-8
87GlenF-1

Guzman, Santiago
70T-716R
72OPC-316R
72T-316

Gwinn, Tony
87PrWill-27

Gwosdz, Doug
81Hawai
82T-731R
84D-383
84Moth/Padres-16
84Nes/792-753
84Smok/Padres-11
84T-753
85Moth/Giants-22
86Jacks/TCMA-11
87Calgary-23
88Nashvl/CMC-16
88Nashvl/Pro-480
89Nashvl-7
89Nashvl/CMC-11
89Nashvl/Pro-1277

Gwynn, Anthony
(Tony)
81Hawai-10
82Hawai-10
83D-598
83F-360
83OPC-143
83T-482
84D-324
84F-301
84FunFood/Pin-28
84Moth/Padres-9
84Nes/792-251
84Smok/Padres-12
84T-251
84T/St-160
85D-25
85D-63
85D/AAS-19
85D/DKsuper-25
85Drake-14
85F-34
85F/LimEd-11
85F/St-8
85Leaf-25DK
85Moth/Padres-2
85OPC-383
85Seven-11W
85T-660
85T-717AS
85T/3D-13
85T/Gloss22-6
85T/Gloss40-29
85T/St-146
85T/St-170
85T/St-174
85T/Super-5
86D-112
86D/AAS-1
86D/PopUp-1
86F-323
86F/LimEd-22
86F/Mini-69
86F/Slug-15
86F/St-50
86KayBee-17
86Leaf-41
86OPC-10
86Quaker-7
86S-13
86S-135M
86S-181M
86T-10
86T/Gloss22-17
86T/Gloss60-57
86T/Mini-65
86T/St-105
86T/St-146
86T/Super-29
86Woolwth-13
87Bohem-19
87Class-26
87D-64
87D/AAS-16
87D/HL-12
87D/OD-146
87D/PopUp-16
87Drake-11
87F-416
87F/AwardWin-19
87F/Lim-20
87F/McCror-19
87F/Mini-50
87F/Slug-17
87F/St-52

87Ho/St-16
87KayBee-15
87Kraft-44
87Leaf-235
87MnM's-23
87MSA/Discs-16
87OPC-198
87RedFoley/St-113
87S-117M
87S-197M
87S-31
87T-530
87T-599AS
87T/Coins-34
87T/Gloss22-6
87T/Gloss60-2
87T/HL-16
87T/Mini-35
87T/St-106
87T/St-155
87Woolwth-16
88Woolwth-12
88Bz-9
88ChefBoy-6
88Class/Blue-220
88Coke/Padres-19
88D-164
88D-BC6
88D/AS-51
88D/Best-154
88F-585
88F-631M
88F-634M
88F/AwardWin-16
88F/BB/AS-13
88F/BB/MVP-17
88F/Excit-17
88F/Hottest-15
88F/LL-16
88F/Mini-112
88F/RecSet-17
88F/Slug-17
88F/St-123
88F/TL-11
88FanSam-18
88KayBee-13
88KingB/Disc-5
88KMart-12
88Leaf-90
88Nestle-40
88OPC-360
88OPC-F
88Panini/St-410
88Panini/St-437
88SanDiegoSt-7M
88SanDiegoSt-8
88Score-385
88Sf-16
88Smok/Padres-10
88T-360
88T-402
88T/Big-161
88T/Coins-36
88T/Gloss60-38
88T/Mini-74
88T/Revco-1
88T/RiteAid-11
88T/St-115
88T/St/Backs-16
88T/UK-29
88T/WaxBox-F
89B-461
89Bz-13
89Cadaco-27
89Class-30
89Crunch-5
89D-128
89D-6DK
89D/Best-42
89D/DKsuper-6DK
89D/MVP-BC20
89F-305
89F/BBAS-19
89F/BBMVP's-17
89F/Excit-20
89F/Heroes-20
89F/LL-19
89F/Superstar-21
89F/WaxBox-C12
89Holsum/Discs-6
89KayBee-17
89KingB/Discs-21
89KMart/DT-29
89KMart/Lead-2
89OPC-51
89Panini/St-203
89Panini/St-222
89RedFoley/St-54
89Score-90
89Score/HotSt-40
89Score/Mast-37
89Sf-160
89T-570
89T/Big-58
89T/Coins-4
89T/Gloss60-58
89T/HeadsUp-1
89T/Hills-16
89T/Mini-38
89T/St-109
89T/St/Backs-50
89T/UK-36
89UD-384
89UD-683TC
90Class-17
90Class-87
90D-705AS
90D-86
90D/Bon/MVP-BC4
90D/Preview-6
90F-157
90F/WaxBox-C12
90Score-255
90Score-685DT
90Score/100St-3
90Sf-98
90T-403AS
90T-730
90UD-344

Gwynn, Chris
87Albuq/Pol-27
88AAA/Pro-2
88Albuq/CMC-12
88Albuq/Pro-259
88F-647
88SanDiegoSt-6
88SanDiegoSt-7M
88Score-640
89Albuq/CMC-15
89Albuq/Pro-64
89F-59
89Score/HotRk-21
89UD-607
90Class-111
90T-456
90UD-526

Gyarmati, Jeff
83Beloi/LF-4
89Boise/Pro-1985

Gyselman, Dick
43Centen-11
44Centen-10

Haas, Berthold
49Eureka-105
Exh47

Haas, Bill
63T-544R
64T-398R

Haas, Bryan
(Moose)
75BurlB
78T-649
79T-448
80T-181
81D-85
81F-516
81OPC-327
81T-327
81T/St-98
82D-206
82F-143
82F/St-139
82OPC-12
82Pol/Brew
82Pol/Brew-30
82T-12
83D-204
83F-35
83Gard-9
83OPC-317
83Pol/Brew-30
83T-503
84D-368
84F-202
84F/St-61
84Gard-8
84Nes/792-271
84Nes/792-726TL
84OPC-271
84Pol/Brew-30
84T-271
84T-726TL
84T/St-292
85D-473
85F-583
85Gard-8
85OPC-151
85Pol/Brew-30
85T-151
85T/St-293
86D-237
86F-489
86F/Up-U48
86Moth/A's-16
86OPC-9
86T-759
86T/St-201
86T/Tr-44T
87D-528
87F-393
87Leaf-54
87OPC-369
87Smok/A's-5
87T-413
88Score-177
88T-606

Haas, Dave
87Anchora-16
89Lakel/Star-7

Haas, G. Edwin
(Eddie)
59T-126
79Savan-16
81Richm-21
82Richm-27
83Richm-23
84Richm-27
85Ho/Braves-1MG
85Pol/Atl-22MG
85T/Tr-44T

Haas, George W.
(Mule)
29Exh/4-27
31Exh/4-28
32Orbit/num-19
32Orbit/un-25
33G-219
35BU-170
35G-8B
35G-9B
40PB-184
61F-109
PR1-15
R305
R310
R312/M
R314
R315-A14
R315-B14
V355-68
W517-32
WG8-26

Haas, Randy
75Clint

Haberle, Dave
83Cedar-18
83Cedar/LF-11
84Cedar-28

Habyan, John
85CharO-21
86D-45
86RochR-5
87Class-95
87D-494
87RochR-24
87RochR/TCMA-4
88D-354
88F-562
88RochR-10
88RochR-9
88RochR/CMC-6
88RochR/Gov-9
88RochR/Pro-215
88Score-353
88T-153

Hack, Stan
34DS-107
34DS-34
35BU-137
40Wheat-12
41DP-2
41Wheat-21
47TipTop
52Mother-60
53Mother-49
54Wilson
55T-6
55T/DH-24
61F-110
80Cram/Leg-83
R302
R312/M
R313
V355-105
WG8-27

Hacker, Warren
51B-318
52Dix
52StarCal/L-80G
52T-324
53B/Col-144
53Dix
53NB
53RM-NL23
54B-125
55B-8
56T-282
57Kahn
57T-370
58T-251

Hackett, John
86Erie-11

Haddix, Harvey
53Hunter
53T-273
54Hunter
54T-9
55Armour-8
55Hunter
55T-43
55T/DH-42
56T-77
56T/Hocus-A6
56T/Hocus-B8
56T/Pin-47P
57T-265
58Kahn
58T-118
59T-184
60Kahn
60NuCard-9
60T-340
61Kahn
61NuCard-478
61P-134
61T-100
61T-410M
61T/RO-33
62J-180
62Kahn
62P-180
62P/Can-180
62T-67
63Kahn
63T-239
64T-439
65OPC-67
65T-67
76Laugh/Jub-31
76SSPC-623
79TCMA-39
82D-651
88Pac/Leg-11
89Swell-13

Haddock, George
N172
N300/unif

Hadley, Irving
(Bump)
32Orbit/num-24
32Orbit/un-26
33G-140
34Exh/4-15
35G-1C
35G-275
35G-2C
35G-6C
35G-7C
38G-251
38ONG/Pin-14
61F-111
R305
R316
V354-15

Hadley, Kent
59T-127
60L-135
60T-102
61Union

Haeberle, Kevin
89Idaho/Pro-2037

Haefner, Mickey
49B-144
50B-183

Hafey, Charles J.
(Chick)
29Exh/4-16
31Exh/4-16
32Orbit/un-27
33DL-19
33Exh/4-4
34DS-18
34Exh/4-4
34G-34
35BU-16
35Exh/4-4
61F-39
80Cram/Leg-116
80SSPC/HOF
87Conlon/2-14
88Conlon/NatAS-10
89HOF/St-34
R300
R305
R308-207
R310
R316
R328-8
R332-5
V354-78

V355-94
W517-29

Hafey, Daniel A.
(Bud)
35BU-163

Hafey, Tom
46Remar-12
47Remar-11
47Signal
47Smith-18
48Smith-12

Hafey, Will
47Remar-16
47Smith-19
48Signal
48Smith-3

Hagan, Kevin
81Louvl-6
84Louvl-11
84Nes/792-337
85Louvl-7
88Tucso-12
88Tucso/CMC-5
88Tucso/Pro-180

Hageman, Kurt
T207

Hagemann, Tim
80Clint-9

Hagen, Kevin
81ArkTr-16
82ArkTr-2
84T-337
86Maine-10
87Portl-13
87Tucso-17

Hagen, Walter
33SK-8

Hagermann, Ken
79Elmir-3

Haggerty, Roger
86Elmir-7
87WinHav-26
88WinHav/Star-9

Hagman, Keith
81Durhm-9
82Durhm-2

Hague, Joe
69T-559R
70OPC-362
70T-362
71MLB/St-274
71OPC-96
71T-96
71T/Coins-139
72T-546
73OPC-447
73T-447

Hahn, Don
71MLB/St-129
71OPC-94
71T-94
72OPC-269
72T-269
74OPC-291
74T-291
75OPC-182
75T-182
75T/M-182
77Phoen

Hahn, Ed
E254
E90/3
M116
T206

Hahn, Eric
87Savan-5

Hahn, Frank
E107

Hahn, Willie
N172

Hailey, Fred
87Oneon-15
88FtLaud/Star-11
89FtLaud/Star-8

Hailey, Roger
88Pulas/Pro-1766
89Pulas/Pro-1907

Hain, Bill
60HenryH-6
60Union-7

Haines, Allan
(Abner)
80GlenF/B-27tr
80GlenF/C-22tr

Haines, Dennis
77SnJos-11
79Ogden/TCMA-8

Haines, Jesse
21Exh-66
32Orbit/un-28
33G-73
40PB-227
61F-40
80SSPC/HOF
89Pac/Leg-208
E120
E121/120
E210-30
R305
R316
V100
V354-44
V355-93
V61-103
W501-76
W513
W573
W575

Haines, Michael
86Jamestn-11

Hainline, Jeff
88Butte-25

Hairston, Jerry
74OPC-96
74T-96
75OPC-327
75T-327
75T/M-327
76OPC-391
76SSPC-153
76T-391
83D-616
83F-236
83T-487
84D-86
84F-60
84Nes/792-177
84T-177
84TrueVal/WS-15
85Coke/WS-17
85D-135
85F-515
85T-596
86Coke/WS-17
86D-424
86F-207
86T-778
87Coke/WS-11
87D-285
87F-498
87OPC-299
87T-685
88D-285
88T-281

Hairston, Sam Sr.
87BirmB/Bst-2C
89BirmB/Best-29
89BirmB/Pro-112

Halama, Scott
87Erie-22
88Hamil/Pro-1720

Halberg, Eric
83Clint/LF-2

Hale, A. Odell
36Wheat-8
37OPC-128
38Exh/4-11
R313
R314
V300

Hale, Bob
56T-231
57T-406
59T-507
60T-309
61T-532
79TCMA-129

Hale, Chip
88Orlan/Best-18
89Portl/CMC-24
89Portl/Pro-208
90D-690
90Score-588
90Score/100Ris-98
90Sf-223
90T-704
90UD-475

Hale, Dan
86Greens-10
87Greens-20

Hale, DeMarlo
86NewBrit-12
88Huntsvl/BK-5
88Madis-13

Hale, Diane
81ArkTr-23M

Hale, John
76OPC-228
76T-228
77T-523
78T-584
79OPC-23
79T-56
80Indianap-6
81RochR-6

Hale, Samuel
25Exh-108
29Exh/4-28
W517-44

Haley, Bart
86Elmir-8
87WinHav-6
88Lynch/Star-8
89Lynch/Star-10

Haley, Bill
78Green

Haley, Mark
85Anchora-13CO

Haley, Sam
83Wausa/LF-23
86WPalm-19

Halicki, Ed
75OPC-467
75T-467
75T/M-467
76OPC-423
76T-423
77T-343
78Ho-12
78T-107
79OPC-354
79Pol/Giants-28
79T-672
80OPC-115
80Pol/Giants-28
80T-217
81D-53
81T-69

Halicki, Kevin
82Redwd-4

Hall, Albert
82Richm-19
83Richm-18
85F-326
85Ho/Braves-10
85Pol/Atl-2
85T-676
86Richm-8
87F/U-U39
87Smok/Atl-25
87T/Tr-41T
88D-290
88D/Best-253
88F-541
88OPC-213
88Panini/St-249
88Score-148
88T-213
88T/St-39
89F-593
89OPC-153
89Score-74
89T-433
89T/Big-104
89T/St-30
89UD-93

Hall, Andy
86Cram/PCL-198
86Macon-11
88CLAS/Star-8
88Salem/Star-7
89BuffB/CMC-10
89BuffB/Pro-1672
89Harris/Star-8

Hall, Bob
49Eureka-10

Hall, Charles Louis
E90/1
M116
T207

Hall, Chris
89Brist/Star-11

Hall, Darren
87Myrtle-4
88Duned/Star-8
89Duned/Star-6

Hall, Dave
63MilSau-1

Hall, Dave
81Cedar-26
82Cedar-19
83Tampa-14

Hall, Dean
78Newar

Hall, Drew
86Pittsf-8
87D-594
87IowaC-2
88D/Cubs/Bk-NEW
88T-262
89B-221
89D-522
89F-643M
89OkCty/Pro-1517
89Smok/R-12
89T-593
89UD-324
90F-299
90Score-516
90T-463
90UD-631

Hall, Gardner C.
87BirmB/Best-14

Hall, Grady
88Vanco/CMC-8
88Vanco/Pro-761
89BirmB/Best-11
89BirmB/Pro-108
89F-650M

Hall, Greg
85Spoka/Cram-6
87CharRa-5
88River/Cal-219
88River/Pro-1415
89River/Best-26
89River/Cal-6
89River/Pro-1397
89Spoka/SP-8

Hall, Jeff
80Elmir-11

Hall, Jimmie
64T-73
64T/Coins-16
64T/St-3
65T-580
66OPC-190
66T-190
66T/RO-51
67T-432
68OPC-121
68T-121
69MB-99
69OPC-61
69T-61
70T-649

Hall, Joe
88Hamil/Pro-1747
89StPet/Star-15

Hall, Kevin
88Poca/Pro-2093
89Everett/Star-10

Hall, Lamar
88Idaho/Pro-1840
89Sumter/Pro-1106

Hall, Marty
86Madis-10
86Madis/Pol-10
87Ashvl-10

Hall, Matthew
86Chatt-11
87Chatt/Best-21

Hall, Mel
82IowaC-4
83D-126
83T/X-39
83Thorn-27
84D-411
84F-493
84F/St-106
84Nes/792-508
84OPC-4
84T-508
84T/St-380YS
84T/X-47
84Wheat/Ind-34
85D-338
85F-449
85OPC-263
85Polar/Ind-27
85T-263
85T/St-254
86D-276
86F-587
86OhHenry-27
86OPC-138
86T-647
87D-473
87F-252
87F/Excit-21
87F/St-53
87Gator-27
87OPC-51
87S-180
87T-51
87T/St-206
88D-342
88D/Best-173
88F-610
88Gator-27
88Leaf-109
88OPC-318
88Panini/St-79
88Score-441
88Sf-189
88T-318
88T/Big-114
88T/St-205
89D-73
89D/Tr-36

89F-406
89F/Up-49
89OPC-173
89Panini/St-328
89RedFoley/St-55
89Score-17
89Score/NWest-20
89Score/Tr-54
89Sf-144
89T-173
89T/Big-13
89T/Tr-44T
89UD-538
89UD/Ext-729
90D-598
90F-444
90Score-383
90T-436
90UD-458

Hall, Richard W.
55T-126
55T/DH-57
56T-331
57T-308
60T-308
61T-197
61T/St-160
62T-189
63T-526
67T-508
68OPC-17
68T-17
70OPC-182
70T-182
71MLB/St-297
71OPC-417
71T-417

Hall, Robert L.
55B-113

Hall, Robert P.
T206

Hall, Rocky
78Newar
79BurlB-6
79Holyo-24

Hall, Roy
85Greens-15

Hall, Todd
87Penin-24
88Tampa/Star-10
89Saraso/Star-9

Hall, Tom E.
69T-658R
70OPC-169
70T-169
71MLB/St-462
71OPC-313
71T-313
72MB-124
72OPC-417
72T-417
73OPC-8
73T-8
74OPC-248
74T-248
75OPC-108
75T-108
75T/M-108
76OPC-621
76SSPC-556
76T-621

Hall, William
59T-49

Halla, John
E254
E270/1

Hallahan, Bill
31Exh/4-16
32Orbit/num-72
32Orbit/un-29
33Exh/4-8
33G-200
34DS-23
34Exh/4-8
34G-82
35BU-121
35BU-40
87Conlon/2-15
R305
R313
R314
V355-70
WG8-28

Hallas, Bob
83Madis/LF-16
84Albany-13

Hallberg, Lance
78Wisco
80OrlTw-8
82OrlTw/A-11

Halle, Andrew
88BurlR/Pro-1797

Haller, Tom
62T-356
63J-108
63P-108
63T-85
64T-485
65T-465
65T/trans-16
66T-308
67OPC-65
67T-65
68OPC-185
68T-185
69MB-100
69MLB/St-148
69OPC/DE-10
69T-310
69T/DE-23
69T/decal
69T/S-47
69T/St-45
70K-25
70MB-9
70MLB/St-51
70T-685
71MLB/St-105
71OPC-639
71T-639
72MB-125
72OPC-175
72OPC-176IA
72T-175
72T-176A
73OPC-454
73T-454
79Pol/Giants-5
84Moth/Giants-5
87Smok/Dodg-11
89Smok/Dodg-74

Hallgren, Robert
76Dubuq
77Cocoa
78Ashev

Hallgren, Tim
86Salem-11C

Hallinan, Ed
T207

Hallion, Tom
88Umpire-57
89Umpires-55

Hallman, William W.
E107
N172
N300/SC
T206

Hallstrom, Charles
N172

Hally
E254

Ham, Michael
87Everett-17
88Clint/Pro-709
89Phoen/Pro-1478
89SanJose/Best-26
89SanJose/Cal-220
89SanJose/Pro-461
89SanJose/Star-12

Hamblin, Bob
88Eugene/Best-1

Hambright, Roger
72OPC-124R
72T-124R

Hamelin, Bob
89Memph/Best-1
89Memph/Pro-1201
89Memph/Star-12
89SLAS-9
89Star/Wax-42
90UD-45

Hamilton, Billy
61F-112
80SSPC/HOF
89HOF/St-43
BF2-40
N172
N300/SC

Hamilton, Bob
85VeroB-1
87SnAnt-18

Hamilton, Carl
86Pittsf-9
87IowaC-1
88Peoria/Ko-13

Hamilton, Darryl
85Anchora-14
87Stockton-8
88Denver/CMC-24
88Denver/Pro-1274
88F/U-U38
88Score/Tr-72T
89Denver/CMC-13
89Denver/Pro-39
89F-187
89Score/HotRk-44
89T-88
89UD-301
90F-325

Hamilton, Dave
73T-214
74OPC-633
74T-633
75OPC-428
75T-428
75T/M-428
76OPC-237
76T-237
77OPC-224
77T-367
78T-288
79T-147
80T-86
81Tacom-8

Hamilton, Earl
15CJ-171
D328-68
D329-75
D350/2-74
E120
E135-68
M101/4-75
M101/5-74
T207
T222
V61-68
W573

Hamilton, Jack
62T-593R
63T-132
65T-288
66T-262
67OPC-2
67T-2
68OPC-193
68T-193
69T-629

Hamilton, Jamie
80ElPas-23

Hamilton, Jeff
86Albuq-10
87Albuq/Pol-19
87D-464
87Pol/Dodg-16
87T-266
88D-525
88F-515
88Moth/Dodg-19
88Panini/St-312
88Pol/Dodg-33
88T-62
89D-550
89D/Best-290
89F-60
89Moth/Dodg-19
89Pol/Dodg-3
89Score-570
89T-736
89UD-615
90D-321
90F-396
90Score-132
90T-426
90UD-296

Hamilton, Mike
88Butte-1

Hamilton, Robert
80Water-13

Hamilton, Scott W.
86Erie-12
87Sprin/Best-17
88StPet/Star-8

Hamilton, Steve
63T-171
64T-206
65T-309
66T-503
67T-567
68T-496
69MB-101
69MLB/St-75
69OPC-69
69T-69
70MLB/St-246
70OPC-349
70T-349
71OPC-627
71T-627
72MB-126
72T-766
73OPC-214
WG10-9
WG9-11

Hamilton, Z.B.
89Princet/Star-8

Hamlin, Ken
60T-542
61P-89
61T-263
62Salada-34A
62Salada-34B
62Shirriff-34
62T-296
66OPC-69
66T-69

Hamlin, Luke
39PB-13
40PB-70
41PB-53

Hamm, Pete
71OPC-74R
71T-74R
72OPC-501
72T-501

Hamm, Tim
81Hawai-18
82Hawai-18

Hammagren, Tucker
88CapeCod/Sum-166

Hammaker, Atlee
81Omaha-6
82T-471R
83D-298
83F-261
83Moth/Giants-13
83T-342
83T/St-324
84D-236
84F-373
84F/St-65
84Moth/Giants-9
84Nes/792-137LL
84Nes/792-576TL
84Nes/792-85
84OPC-85
84Seven-15W
84T-137
84T-85
84T/Gloss40-7
84T/St-165
84T/St-175
85D-509
85F-608
85Moth/Giants-6
85OPC-351
85T-674
85T/St-165
86D-445
86F-544
86Leaf-220
86Moth/Giants-6
86T-223
87F/U-U40
87OPC-358
87Phoen-24
87T-781
88D-450
88F-83
88Moth/Giants-19
88Score-528
88T-157
88T/Big-259
89D-414
89F-329
89Moth/Giants-19
89OPC-2
89Score-422
89T-572
89T/Big-21
89UD-544
90D-532
90F-57
90Score-231
90T-447
90UD-620

Hammer, James
(Pete)
77Wausa
79Jacks-12

Hammett, Ann
81ArkTr-23M

Hammon, Randy
78Cr/PCL-85
79Phoen

Hammond, Arthur S.
81VeroB-6

Hammond, Chris
87Tampa-15
88BBAmer-17
88Chatt/Best-2
88SLAS-36
89Nashvl-8
89Nashvl/Pro-1279
90F-421
90Score-629
90UD-52

Hammond, Steve
78Green
80Richm-6

81Richm-16
83F-114
83Omaha-18
84Omaha-10
86IowaC-14

Hammonds, Reggie
86Nashua-11

Hamner, Granny
49Eureka-135
49Lummis
50B-204
51B-148
51BR-B7
51T/BB-29
52B-35
52NTea
52RM-NL7
52T-221
52TipTop
53B/Col-60
53RM-NL18
53T-146
54B-47
54T-24
55B-112
55RFG-18
55RM-NL15
56T-197
57T-335
58Hires-20
58T-268
59T-436
79TCMA-309
PM10/Sm-66
Rawl

Hamner, Ralph
49B-212

Hampton, Anthony
86Osceola-10

Hampton, Isaac
76SSPC-601
78T-503

Hampton, Ray
82Evans-21

Hamric, Odbert
55T-199
58T-336

Hamric, Rusty
80Penin/B-18
80Penin/C-24
82OkCty-10
84Cram/PCL-216

Hamrick, Ray
47Remar-17
47Smith-6
48Signal
48Smith-7
49Remar
50Remar

Hamrick, Stephen
78SnJos-15

Hamza, Tony
86Geneva-8
86Peoria-10

Hance, Bill
83TriCit-13
84Tulsa-28

Hancock, Andy
80Ashev-5

Hancock, Chris
89Clint/Pro-890
89Everett/Star-11

Hancock, Garry
79T-702R
81F-229
82Coke/BOS
82D-608
82F-295
82T-322
84F-445
84Moth/A's-16
84Nes/792-197
84T-197

Hancock, Jeff
89Watertn/Star-9

Hancock, Lee
89SnBer/Best-16
89SnBer/Cal-71

Hand, James
82Tucso-23

Hand, Rich
71MLB/St-369
71OPC-24
71T-24
71T/tatt-8
72OPC-317
72T-317
73OPC-398
73T-398
74OPC-571
74T-571

Handford, Charles
C46-21

Handler, Marve
80Elmir-34

Handley, Gene
40Hughes-9
49B/PCL-34
52Mother-7
53Mother-21

Handley, Jim
76AppFx

Handley, Lee E.
40PB-221
41DP-33
49B/PCL-28

Hands, Bill
66T-392R
67T-16
68T-279
69T-115
70T-405
71T-670
72T-335
73T-555
74T-271
75T-412
75T/M-412
76SSPC-253
76T-509

Hands, Bill
67OPC-16
69MLB/St-120
69OPC-115
69T/St-13
70MLB/St-16
70OPC-405
71MLB/St-31
71OPC-670
72MB-127
72OPC-335
73OPC-555
74OPC-271
75OPC-412
76OPC-509

Hanebrink, Harry
58T-454
59T-322

Haney, Fred G.
26Exh-66
27Exh-34
29Exh/4-16
47Signal
52Mother-13
54T-75
58T-475AS
59T-551AS
87Conlon/2-16

Haney, Joe
86Beloi-9

Haney, Larry
68OPC-42
69OPC-209
73OPC-563
75OPC-626
76OPC-446

Haney, Todd
88Wausa/Feder-14
88Wausa/GS-14
89SnBer/Best-25
89SnBer/Cal-81
89Wmspt/Star-8

Haney, W. Larry
67T-507R
68T-42
69T-209
70T-648
73T-563
75T-626
75T/M-626
76SSPC-502
76T-446
77T-12
78T-391
78TCMA-228
83Pol/Brew-12C
86Pol/Brew-12C

Hanford, Charles
E254
E270/2
T205

Hanggie, Dan
84Chatt-4
85Orlan-6

Hanker, Fred
88Madis-14

Hankinson, Frank
E223
N172
N172/ST
N284
N690/2

Hanks, Chris
89Elmir/Puc-4
89WinHav/Star-9

Hanley, John
79Knoxv/TCMA-15
81AppFx-17

Hanlon, Edward J.
(Ned)
75F/Pion-9
E107
N172
N284
Scrapps
WG1-22
WG3-20

Hanna, Dave
83Idaho-5

Hanna, Preston
79T-296
80T-489
81D-523
81F-264
81Pol/Atl-49
81T-594
82BK/Lids-9
82F-435
82Pol/Atl-49
83T-127

Hannah, Joe
61BeeHive-7

Hannah, Mike
75OkCty
75SnAnt
76Wmspt

Hannah, Truck
28Exh/PCL-9

Hannahs, Gerry
79Albuq-9
80Albuq-25
81Toled-5

Hannahs, Mitch
88CapeCod/Sum-45

Hannan, Jim
63T-121
64T-261
65T-394
66T-479
67T-291
69OPC-106
69T-106
69T/St-236
70T-697
71OPC-229
71T-229
72MB-128

Hanneman, Mike
89Panini/St-333

Hannifan, John J.
T206

Hannon, John
76BurlB
77Holyo

Hannon, Phil
87WinSal-6
88Peoria/Ko-12
89WinSal/Star-9

Hanrahan, William
N172

Hansel, Damon
87Macon-18

Hanselman, Carl
88Poca/Pro-2099
89Clint/Pro-903
89Everett/Star-12

Hansen, Andy
49Eureka-106
52T-74
53B/BW-64

Hansen, Bob
75OPC-508
75T-508
75T/M-508

Hansen, Darel
83Idaho-6
84Madis/Pol-15
85Madis-15
85Madis/Pol-12
86Modesto-10

Hansen, Dave
87Bakers-21
88FSLAS/Star-7
88VeroB/Star-9
89SnAnt/Best-17
90F-642M

Hansen, Guy
83Butte-31
89Memph/Best-26
89Memph/Pro-1192

Hansen, Jon
82ElPas-11

Hansen, Mike
87Lakel-16
88FSLAS/Star-39
88Lakel/Star-13
89London/Pro-1376

Hansen, Ray
86Greens-11
87Greens-17

Hansen, Roger
81CharR-6
82CharR-2
84Memph-18
86Omaha-9
86Omaha/TCMA-5
87Chatt/Best-14
88Calg/CMC-21
88Calg/Pro-790
89Calg/CMC-15
89Calg/Pro-530

Hansen, Ron Jr.
83TriCit-17

Hansen, Ron
59T-444
60T-127
61P-72
61T-240
61T/St-102
62J-30
62P-30
62P/Can-30
62Salada-89
62Shirriff-89
62T-245
62T/St-6
63F-2
63J-60
63P-60
63T-88
64T-384
64T/Coins-41
65MacGregor-4
65OPC-146
65T-146
66T-261
67OPC-9
67T-9
68T-411
69MB-102
69T-566
70MLB/St-184
70OPC-217
70T-217
71MLB/St-489
71OPC-419
71T-419
72MB-129
72T-763
78TCMA-142
83Pol/Brew-18C
86Provigo-28CO

Hansen, Terrel
87Jamestn-10

Hansen, Todd
86Macon-12
88Charl/Pro-1206
89River/Best-6
89River/Cal-22
89River/Pro-1413

Hanson, Erik
87Chatt/Best-10
88Calg/Pro-786
89B-206
89Class-145
89D-32RR
89D/Best-320
89D/Rook-49
89F-549
89Moth/Sea-16
89T/Tr-45T
89UD/Ext-766
90D-345
90F-514
90Score-530
90Score/100Ris-85
90T-118
90UD-235

Hanyuda, Tad
88SanJose/Cal-119
88SanJose/Pro-128

Haraguchi, Ted
87SanJose-10

Hardamon, Derrick
86Geneva-9

Harden, Curry
88CapeCod/Sum-67

Harden, Ty
85BurlR-21
86DayBe-10

Harder, Mel
32Orbit/num-29
32Orbit/un-30
34G-66
35BU-134
35Exh/4-11
35G-8I
35G-9I
36Exh/4-11
41DP-134

55Gol/Ind-10
55Salem
60T-460C
62Sugar-15
63Sugar-15
88Conlon/AmAS-14
89Pac/Leg-205
89Swell-41
R305
R311/Gloss
R311/Leath
R312
R313
R314
WG8-29

Hardgrave, Eric
86Beaum-13
87ElPas-7
88GlenF/Pro-915

Hardgrove, Tom
88CapeCod/Sum-132
89Martins/Star-14

Hardin, Jim
68T-222
69MB-103
69T-532M
69T-610
69T/St-124
70T-656
71MLB/St-298
71OPC-491
71T-491
72MB-130
72OPC-287
72T-287
73OPC-124
73T-124

Harding, Greg
88StCath/Pro-2029
89Myrtle/Pro-1468

Hardwick, Anthony
86Bakers-12

Hardwick, Willie
82Amari-19
83Beaum-18
84ArkTr-15

Hardy, Alex
C46-78

Hardy, Carroll
58T-446
59T-168
60T-341
61T-257
62Salada-220
62Shirriff-220
62T-101
63Pep
63T-468

Hardy, Howard L.
(Larry)
75OPC-112
75T-112
75T/M-112
76SSPC-120
78Charl
79Charl-15
80Utica-1
82Knoxv-21
84Syrac-2
86Knoxv-9MG
87Phoen-11

Hardy, Jack
87Hawai-3
88Vanco/CMC-10
88Vanco/Pro-755
89Vanco/CMC-5
89Vanco/Pro-586

Hardy, John Graydon
87BirmB/Best-18

Hardy, Mark
86Jamestn-12

Hare, Shawn
89Lakel/Star-8

Harer, Wayne
80Colum-4
81Colum-19
82Colum-3
82Colum/Pol-22

Hargan, Steve
66T-508
67Kahn
67T-233LL
67T-440
68Kahn
68OPC-35
68T-35
68T/G-15
69T-348
70OPC-136
70T-136
71MLB/St-370
71OPC-375
71T-375
71T/Coins-110
72MB-131
72T-615
75OPC-362
75T-362
75T/M-362
76K-1
76OPC-463
76SSPC-254
76T-463
77OPC-247
77T-37

Hargesheimer, Al
81F-457
81Phoen-13
81T-502R
82Phoen
83IowaC-4
84Omaha-4
85Omaha-26
86Omaha/TCMA-21
87Omaha-13
88Omaha/CMC-6
88Omaha/Pro-1517

Hargis, Gary
76Shrev
78Colum
79Portl-13
80Port-15
81Buffa-15

Hargrave, Eugene F.
(Bubbles)
28Exh-14
28Yueng-33
E120
V61-60
W501-33
W572
W573
WG7-21

Hargrave, Wm.
26Exh-113
27Exh-57
33G-172

Hargraves, Charles R.
28Exh-7
29Exh/4-14

Hargrove, Dudley M.
(Mike)
75Ho-106
75OPC-106
75T-106
75T/M-106
76Ho-88
76K-51
76OPC-485
76SSPC-263
76T-485
77Ho-18
77K-30
77OPC-35
77Pep-5
77T-275
77T/CS-20
78BK/R-11
78Ho-41
78K-56
78OPC-176
78T-172
79Ho-148
79OPC-311
79T-591
80OPC-162
80T-308
81D-78
81F-387
81K-66
81MSA/Disc-15
81OPC-74
81T-74
81T/SO-32
81T/St-68
82D-389
82Drake-16
82F-368
82F/St-198
82OPC-310
82T-310
82T-559TL
82T/St-180
82Wheat/Ind
83D-450
83F-409
83OPC-37
83T-660
83T/St-56
83Wheat/Ind-16
84D-495
84F-543
84FunFood/Pin-101
84Nes/792-546TL
84Nes/792-764
84OPC-79
84Seven-10C
84T-764
84T/St-260
84Wheat/Ind-21
85D-398
85F-450
85GenMills-18
85OPC-252
85Polar/Ind-21
85T-425
85T/St-248
86D-590
86F-588
86Leaf-228
86T-136
88EastLAS/Pro-52
88Wmspt/Pro-1306
89ColrSp/CMC-10
89ColSp/Pro-246

Harigen, Charlie
81Tacom-29M

Harkey, Mike
88BBAmer-2
88EastLAS/Pro-26
88Peoria/Ko-35M
88Pittsf/Pro-1377
89B-286
89D-43RR
89F-427
89IowaC/CMC-5
89IowaC/Pro-1704
89Panini/St-48
89Score-624
89Score/HotRk-48
89Score/YS/II-31
89Sf-132
89T-742FS
89UD-14
90D-522
90F-33
90UD-107

Harkins, John
N172

Harkness, Don
77Cocoa
78DaytB

Harkness, Thomas W.
(Tim)
61Union
62T-404
63T-436
64T-57

Harlan, Dan
88BBCity/Star-13

Harley, Richard
E107

Harlow, Larry
76SSPC-397
78T-543
79T-314
80T-68
81F-289
81T-121
82F-462
82T-257

Harmon, Charles
(Chuck)
54T-182
55T-82
55T/DH-55
56T-308
57T-299
58T-48

Harmon, Kevin
86Sumter-8TR
87Sumter-12

Harmon, Mark
89SnBer/Best-28M

Harmon, Robert
10Domino-52
11Helmar-169
12Sweet/Pin-147
D329-76
E286
E300
M101/4-76
M116
T202
T205
T207

Harmon, Terry
69T-624R
70OPC-486
70T-486
71MLB/St-179
71OPC-682
71T-682
72OPC-377
72T-377
72T/Cloth-16
73OPC-166
73T-166
74OPC-642
74T-642
75OPC-399
75T-399
75T/M-399
76OPC-247
76T-247
77T-388
78T-118

Harmon, Tommy
83MidldC-2

Harmon, Wayne
83Cedar-28
83Cedar/LF-6TR

Harms, Tom
88Hagers/Star-8
89Freder/Star-9

Harnisch, Pete
88BBAmer-11
88CharlK-18
88CharlK/Pep-18
88RochR-10
88RochR/Gov-10
88SLAS-32
89B-4
89D-44RR
89French-42
89RochR/Pro-1649
89Score/Tr-110
89UD/Ext-744
90Class-44
90D-596
90F-177
90Score-355
90Score/100Ris-76
90T-324
90UD-623

Haro, Sam
84PrWill-22
85Nashua-11
86Hawai-11
87Vanco-10

Harper, Brian
80ElPas-9
81SLCty-15
84D-142
84Nes/792-144
84T-144
85D-566
85F-466
85T-332
86D-547
86F-36
86KAS/Disc-8
86Nashv-10
86T-656
88F/U-U42
88Martins/Star-16
88Portl/CMC-11
88Portl/Pro-651
89B-155
89D-641
89F-114
89Score-408
89T-472
89UD-379
90D-355
90F-377
90Score-189
90Sf-121
90T-47
90UD-391

Harper, Charles W.
E107

Harper, David
77Tucso
78Cr/PCL-28

Harper, George W.
21Exh-68
25Exh-41
26Exh-43
27Exh-18
29Exh/4-2
E121/120
W501-107
W513-85

Harper, Greg
88Idaho/Pro-1847
88Sumter/Pro-401
89Sumter/Pro-1117

Harper, Harry C.
D327
D328-69
E135-69
W575

Harper, Jon
77Cedar

Harper, Marshal
76AppFx
77AppFx

Harper, Milt
86Water-12
87Kinston-22
88Wmspt/Pro-1327
Harper, Terry Joe
(Terry)
79Richm-14
80Richm-17
81Pol/Atl-19
81T-192R
82BK/Lids-10
82Richm-24
82T-507
83D-607
83F-137
83Pol/Atl-19
83T-339
84F-180
84Nes/792-624
84Pol/Atl-19
84T-624
85F-327
85Pol/Atl-19
85T/Tr-45T
86D-627
86F-516
86Leaf-246
86OPC-247
86Pol/Atl-19
86T-247
86T/St-41
87D/OD-217
87F-517
87F/Excit-22
87T-49
87T/Tr-42T
88F-331
Harper, Terry
82Redwd-22
83Redwd-12
Harper, Tommy
63FrBauer-7
63T-158R
64Kahn
64T-330
64T/Coins-40
64T/St-43
65Kahn
65OPC-47
65T-47
66Kahn
66T-214
67Kahn
67T-392
68T-590
69MB-104
69MLB/St-95
69OPC-42
69Sunoco/Pin-10
69T-42
69T/St-225
70K-74
70McDon-5
70MLB/St-270
70OPC-370
70T-370
70T/CB
70T/S-9
71Bz
71Bz/Test-30
71K-47
71MD
71MLB/St-437
71OPC-260
71T-260
71T/Coins-140
71T/GM-42
71T/S-63
71T/tatt-2
72MB-132
72OPC-455
72T-455
73OPC-620
73T-620
74OPC-204LL
74OPC-325
74T-204LL
74T-325
74T/St-134
75OPC-537
75T-537
75T/M-537
76OPC-274
76T-274
77T-414
Harrah, Toby
72OPC-104
72T-104
73OPC-216
73T-216
74OPC-511
74T-511
74T/St-235
75Ho/Twink-14
75OPC-131
75T-131
75T/M-131
76Ho-14
76Ho-48
76Ho/Twink-48
76OPC-412
76SSPC-264
76T-412
77Ho-37
77OPC-208
77T-301
78BK/R-13
78Ho-123
78OPC-74
78T-44
79Ho-150
79OPC-119
79T-234
80OPC-333
80T-636
81D-318
81F-389
81OPC-67
81T-721
81T/SO-46
81T/St-65
82D-72
82F-369
82F/St-193
82OPC-16
82T-532
82T/St-177
82Wheat/Ind
83D-13DK
83D-337
83D/AAS-39
83F-410
83F-635M
83K-44
83OPC-356
83T-141TL
83T-480
83T/Gloss-13
83T/Gloss40-13
83T/St-58
83Wheat/Ind-17
84D-251
84F-544
84F/X-48
84Nes/792-348
84OPC-348
84T-348
84T/St-251
84T/X-48
85F-130
85F/Up-U49
85Rang-11
85T-94
85T/Tr-46T
86D-159
86F-560
86Leaf-86
86OPC-72
86Rang-11
86T-535
86T/Mini-32
86T/St-238
87D-408
87F-125
87OKCty-12
87T-152
88AAA/Pro-51
88OkCty/CMC-25
88OkCty/Pro-46
89Smok/R-13
Harrell, Bill
58T-443
59T-433
61T-354
63MilSau-2
Harrell, Greg
87PortChar-13
88Tulsa-27TR
89Tulsa/GS-4
Harrell, John
70OPC-401R
70T-401R
Harrelson, Bill
69T-224R
Harrelson, Derrel M.
(Bud)
67T-306
68OPC-132
68T-132
69MB-105
69MLB/St-166
69MLBPA/Pin-45
69T-456
69T/St-64
70K-68
70MLB/St-77
70T-634
70Trans/M-25
71K-66
71MD
71MLB/St-155
71OPC-355
71T-355
71T/Coins-67
71T/GM-55
71T/tatt-13
72MB-133
72OPC-496KP
72OPC-53
72OPC-54IA
72T-496BP
72T-53
72T-54A
72T/Post-22
73OPC-223
73T-223
73T/Lids-20
74OPC-380
74T-380
74T/St-63
75Ho-45
75OPC-395
75T-395
75T/M-395
76Ho-52
76Ho/Twink-52
76OPC-337
76SSPC-545
76T-337
77OPC-172
77T-44
78T-403
79T-118
80OPC-294
80T-566
81T-694
84LitFalls-13
88Kahn/Mets-3CO
89Kahn/Mets-3CO
Harrelson, Ken
64T-419
65T-479
66OPC-55
66T-55
66T/RO-107
67OPC-188
67T-188
68T-566
69MB-106
69MLB/St-13
69MLBPA/Pin-8
69OPC-3LL
69OPC-5LL
69OPC/DE-8
69T-240
69T-3LL
69T-417AS
69T-5LL
69T/DE-3
69T/S-4
69T/St-134
70K-68
70MLB/St-198
70OPC-545
70T-545
70T/PI-6
71Bz/Test-15
71MLB/St-371
71OPC-510
71T-510
71T/Coins-134
72MB-134
78TCMA-247
86Coke/WS-xx
88Pac/Leg-14
Harridge, Will
56T-1
57T-100M
58T-300M
80SSPC/HOF
Harring, Ken Jr.
89Idaho/Pro-2014
Harrington, Jody
89Elizab/Star-10
Harrington, John
86Miami-8
87Miami-20
Harris, Alonzo
(Candy)
67T-564R
68OPC-128R
68T-128R
Harris, Anthony S.
(Spence)
E120
E220
Harris, B. Gail
56T-91
57T-281
58T-309
59T-378
60T-152
79TCMA-275
Harris, Carry
83Knoxv-10
Harris, Craig
80WHave-11
Harris, David Stanley
25Exh-7
33G-9
R337-412
V353-9
Harris, Donald
89Butte/SP-4
90Score-661DC
90T-314FDP
Harris, Doyle
81Louvl-29
84Louvl-7
Harris, Frank
77Evansvl/TCMA-14
80Ogden-12
82Madis-18
89Clmbia/Best-26
Harris, Franklyn
89Medford/Best-3
Harris, Gene
86Jamestn-13
87WPalm-26
88Jaxvl/Best-5
88Jaxvl/Pro-980
89D/Best-325
89F/Up-58
89T/Tr-46T
90D-247
90F-515
90Score-548
90Score/100Ris-54
90T-738
90UD-565
Harris, Glenn
84Savan-18
Harris, Greg (LHP)
87Wichi-11
88Wichi-19
89Wich/Roc-19
Harris, Greg A.
79Jacks-21
80Tidew-11
81Tidew-23
82Coke/Reds
82Indianap-13
82T-783
82T/Tr-41T
83D-295
83F-590
83Indianap-6
83T-296
84Stuart-22
85F-35
85Rang-27
85T-242
85T/Tr-47T
86D-465
86F-561
86OPC-128
86Rang-27
86T-586
86T/St-245
87D-382
87F-126
87F/St-54
87Leaf-82
87Moth/Rang-11
87OPC-44
87S-126
87Smok/R-2
87T-44
87T/St-238
88D-427
88F-468
88Score-179
88T-369
89D-548
89F-570
89Score-476
89T-627
Harris, Greg W.
85Spoka/Cram-7
86Cram/PCL-161
87TexLgAS-23
88AAA/Pro-23
88F/U-U109
88LasVeg/CMC-3
88LasVeg/Pro-227
89D-34
89D/Rook-46
89F-306
89Score/Tr-87
89T-194

89UD/Ext-724
90D-582
90D-65
90F-158
90Score-257
90Score/100Ris-24
90T-529
90T-572
90UD-622

Harris, Gregg S.
86CharRa-10
87CharRa-3

Harris, James William
(Billy)
69T-569
70OPC-512
70T-512

Harris, James
89Kingspt/Star-12

Harris, Joe
28Yueng-51
E120
W502-51
W513-81
W572

Harris, John
77QuadC
79SLCty-16
80SLCty-12
81T-214R
82D-444
82F-463
82Spoka-16
82T-313
83Indianap-29
84Evans-15

Harris, Keith
89Utica/Puc-10

Harris, Larry
81Wisco-5

Harris, Lenny
84Cedar-25
86Vermont-9
87Nashv-9
88Nashvl/CMC-12
88Nashvl/Pro-489
89F-645M
89K/Reds-7
89UD/Ext-781
90D-434
90F-397
90Score-23
90Score/100Ris-83
90T-277
90UD-423

Harris, Luman
60T-455C
65OPC-274MG
65T-274
66OPC-147MG
66T-147
68T-439
69OPC-196MG
69T-196
70OPC-86MG
70T-86
71OPC-346MG
71T-346
72OPC-484MG
72T-484

Harris, Mark
79WHave-26

Harris, Maurice
(Mickey)
47TipTop
48L-27
49B-151
50B-160
51B-311
52B-135
52T-207

Harris, Mike
82Sprin-19
83ArkTr-13
84ArkTr-26

Harris, Rafael
80Utica-6

Harris, Ray
88SoOreg/Pro-1713

Harris, Reggie
87Elmir/Red-30
88Lynch/Star-9
89WinHav/Star-10

Harris, Robert A.
W753

Harris, Robert
87Watertn-3
88Aug/Pro-386

Harris, Rusty
87AubAs-2
88Osceola/Star-12
89Osceola/Star-7

Harris, Sam
21Exh-69

Harris, Stanley
(Bucky)
25Exh-124
26Exh-124
28Exh-62
28Yueng-41
34DS-91
36G
40PB-129
51B-275
52B-158
53B/BW-46
80SSPC/HOF
86Conlon/1-25
E120
E210-41
E220
R310
R312/M
R313
R314
V100
V117-21
V355-130
W502-14
W517-9
W572

Harris, Steve
85Bend/Cram-10

Harris, Tracy
81LynnS-5
82SLCty-10
83Chatt-17

Harris, Twayne
83Idaho-21
86Modesto-11

Harris, Vic
73OPC-594
73T-594
74OPC-157
74T-157
74T/St-13
75OPC-658
75T-658
75T/M-658
76SSPC-321
77Phoen
78T-436
79T-338
79Vanco-2
80Vanco-21
84Louvl-18

Harris, Vince
88Utica/Puc-6
89CharRa/Pro-976

Harris, Walt
88Hagers/Star-9
89RochR/CMC-19
89RochR/Pro-1651

Harris, Walter
(Buddy)
71OPC-404R
71T-404R

Harris, William
60DF-18
60T-128

Harris, William
V100

Harrison, Brett
87StPet-7
88ArkTr/GS-13
88TexLgAS/GS-13

Harrison, Brian Lee
86Cram/PCL-164
87CharRa-8
88River/Cal-210
88River/Pro-1428
89River/Best-7
89River/Cal-17
89River/Pro-1410

Harrison, Charles
66T-244R
67OPC-8
67T-8
69OPC-116
69T-116

Harrison, Doug
78Clint
80Albuq-9

Harrison, Keith
86Cram/PCL-173
86Elmir-9
87CharRa-22
88Charl/Pro-1207

Harrison, Mack
79Ogden/TCMA-7

Harrison, Mathew
86FSLAS-20
86FtLaud-11
87Albany-13
88Colum/CMC-5
88Colum/Pol-3
88Colum/Pro-317

Harrison, Phil
86Geneva-10
87Peoria-23
88CLAS/Star-28
88WinSal/Star-5
89CharlK-21

Harrison, R.J.
80LynnS-19
81LynnS-6
82Wausa-17
83Wausa/LF-30MG
86Chatt-12MG

Harrison, Robert Lee
79TCMA-76

Harrison, Robert
77StPet

Harrison, Ron
82Madis-21
83Albany-18
87Beloi-16
87Denver-8

Harrison, Roric E.
72OPC-474R
72T-474R
73OPC-229
73T-229
74OPC-298
74T-298
74T/St-5
75OPC-287
75T-287
75T/M-287
76OPC-547
76SSPC-507
76T-547
77Evansvl/TCMA-15
78T-536

Harrison, Wayne
85Durhm-25
86Durhm-13

Harriss, Bryan"Slim"
28Exh-34
E126-46
V61-38

Harriss, William
(Slim)
21Exh-70
E120
W573

Harrist, Earl
50Remar
52T-402
53T-65

Harry, Whitney
82BurlR-22
83BurlR-18
83BurlR/LF-15
84Tulsa-20

Harryman, Jeff
77Newar
78BurlB

Harsh, Nick
82FtMyr-7

Harshman, Jack
54T-173
55RM-AL6
55T-104
55T/DH-66
56T-29
56T/Pin-33
57T-152
58T-217
59T-475
60T-112
79TCMA-33

Hart, Darrin
89Watlo/Star-10
89Watlo/Star-29

Hart, James Henry
T206
T213/brown

Hart, James M.
81RochR-7
83Colum-24

Hart, Jeff
89CharRa/Pro-987
89Watlo/Pro-1781

Hart, Jim Ray
64T-452R
65OPC-4LL
65T-395
65T-4
65T/E-4
66T-295
66T/RO-28
67T-220
68Coke
68OPC-73
68T-73
69MB-107
69MLB/St-199
69MLBPA/Pin-46
69T-555
69T/St-104
70MLB/St-124
70OPC-176
70T-176
71MLB/St-249
71OPC-461
71T-461
72MB-135
72T-733
73OPC-538
73T-538
74OPC-159
74T-159
78TCMA-269
84Moth/Giants-20
PM10/Sm-67

Hart, John
85CharO-14
86RochR-6MG
87RochR-3
87RochR/TCMA-24
88French-47CO
90T-141MG

Hart, Kim
82IowaC-31
83IowaC-28

Hart, Mike
79Tucso-17
80Charl-10
80LynnS-7
81Spoka-7
82SLCty-11
83Toled-20
85IntLgAS-30
85Toled-21
86RochR-7
87RochR-10
87RochR/TCMA-18
88CLAS/Star-2
88T-69
89Readg/Pro-658

Hart, William F.
N172
N284
N526
T206
T213/brown

Hart, William W.
46Remar-6
47Smith-15

Hartenstein, Chuck
68OPC-13
68T-13
69T-596
70OPC-216
70T-216
77OPC-157
77T-416
80Hawai-11
81Hawai-24
82Hawai-24
84Cram/PCL-134CO
86Penin-11CO

Harter, Andy
88Ashvl/Pro-1052

Hartgraves, Dean
87AubAs-24
88Ashvl/Pro-1072
89Ashvl/Pro-960

Hartley, Grover
11Helmar-128
D328-70
E135-70
T207
W753

Hartley, Michael
83StPet-7
85Sprin-13
87Bakers-1
88Albuq/CMC-9
88Albuq/Pro-263
89Albuq/CMC-4
89Albuq/Pro-67
90F-651M
90Score-641

Hartley, Todd
86Cram/PCL-63

Hartley, Tom
86AppFx-10

Hartman, Albert
82BurlR-23

Hartman, Ed
87Watertn-16
88Aug/Pro-366
89Salem/Star-10
89Star/Wax-94

Hartman, Harry
W711/1

W711/2
Hartman, J.C.
61T/St-161
63Pep
63T-442
Hartman, Jeff
86VeroB-9
88VeroB/Star-10
Hartman, Ralph
(Doc)
81Redwd-26
82Redwd-27
Hartman, Robert
59T-128
60T-129
Hartmann, Reid
89Kingspt/Star-13
Hartnett, Charles
(Gabby)
21Exh-67
25Exh-22
26Exh-22
27Exh-11
28Exh-10
28Yueng-5
29Exh/4-5
30CEA/Pin-5
31Exh/4-5
32Orbit/un-31
33CJ/Pin-13
33G-202
35BU-136
35Exh/4-3
36Exh/4-3
36Wheat
37Dix
37Exh/4-3
38Dix
38Exh/4-3
38ONG/Pin-15
39Exh
50Callahan
60F-29
61F-41
61GP-11
80Cram/Leg-72
80SSPC/HOF
86S/Dec-13
87Conlon/2-17
E120
E210-5
PM10/Sm-68
PR1-16
R305
R306
R308-200
R311/Leath
R312/M
R314
R332-38
V355-57
W502-5
WG8-30
Hartnett, Dave
86Cram/PCL-101
87Wausa-22
Hartsel, Tully
(Topsy)
10Domino-53
12Sweet/Pin-45
E101
E106
E107
E254
E90/1
E92
E97
S74-31
T205
T206
T208
T213/brown
T215/blue
T215/brown
T216
W555
Hartsfield, Bob
75Cedar
76Clint
82AubAs-2MG
Hartsfield, Roy
51B-277
52B-28
52T-264
73OPC-237CO
73T-237C
77OPC-238MG
77T-113MG
78OPC-218MG
78T-444
79OPC-262MG
79T-282MG
79TCMA-123
83Indianap-3MG
Hartshorn, Kyle
85Lynch-12
86Jacks/TCMA-5
88Jacks/GS-6
Hartsock, Brian
82Danvi-24
83Peoria/LF-24
86MidldA-9
87SnBer-13
89Reno/Cal-249
Hartsock, Jeff
88GreatF-21
89Bakers/Cal-183
Hartung, Clint
47TipTop
48B-37
49B-154
49Eureka-107
50B-118
50Drake-2
51B-234
52BR
52T-141
R346-47
Hartwig, Dan
77Cedar
Hartzell, Paul
75QuadC
77T-179
78T-529
79OPC-212
79T-402
80OPC-366
80T-721
84ElPas-20
Hartzell, Roy
D303
D329-77
D350/2-76
E126
E254
E270/1
E90/1
E91
M101/4-77
M101/5-76
M116
T201
T204
T216
Harvell, Rod
89GreatF-26
Harvey, Bryan
86PalmSp-16
86PalmSp/Smok-12
87MidldA-25
88D/Rook-53
88Edmon/CMC-5
88F/U-U14
88Score/Tr-87T
88Smok/Angels-21
88T/Tr-45T
89B-40
89D-525
89D/Best-317
89F-479
89F/BBMVP's-18
89F/Heroes-21
89OPC-287
89Panini/St-284
89Score-185
89Score/HotRk-92
89Score/YS/I-30
89Sf-130
89T-632
89T/St-180
89ToysRUs-13
89UD-594
90D-372
90F-134
90Score-8
90Sf-31
90T-272
90UD-686
Harvey, Craig
77Watlo
Harvey, Don
88Pac/8Men-16
Harvey, Greg
88Eugene/Best-3
89AppFx/Pro-853
Harvey, Harold
(Doug)
84Smok/SDP-13ump
88Umpire-1
89Umpires-1
Harvey, Ken
87SnAnt-23
Harvey, Randy
82BirmB-12
86QuadC-14
Harvey, Steve
82Readg-20
Harvick, Brad
87Erie-19
88Savan/Pro-345
89Savan/Pro-365
Harwell, David
88Kinston/Star-10
Harwell, Ernie
88Domino-6
89Pac/Leg-172
Harwell, Jim
61Union
Haryd, Mark
87BurlEx-20
Haselman, Bill
88CharlR/Star-9
89Tulsa/GS-11
Hasler, Curt
89Saraso/Star-10
Haslerig, Bill
78Green
79Savan-4
Hasley, Mike
75Dubuq
76Dubuq
Haslin, Mickey
35BU-104
Haslock, Chris
88Spoka/Pro-1945
89CharRa/Pro-981
Hassamaer, William L.
N172
Hassett, John
(Buddy)
39Exh
39PB-57
40PB-62
41DP-121
R303/A
Hassey, Ron
79Tacom-1
80T-222
81D-80
81F-405
81OPC-187
81T-564
81T/St-71
82D-463
82F-370
82OPC-54
82T-54
82Wheat/Ind
83D-159
83F-411
83F-642M
83T-689
83T/St-62
83Wheat/Ind-18
84D-460
84F-545
84F/X-49
84Nes/792-308
84OPC-308
84SevenUp-15
84T-308
84T/St-262
84T/X-49
85F/Up-U50
85T-742
85T/Tr-48T
86D-370
86F-107
86OPC-157
86T-157
87Coke/WS-15
87D-532
87F-499
87OPC-61
87T-667
87T/St-285
88D-580
88D/A's/Bk-NEW
88D/Best-302
88F-399
88Moth/A's-16
88Score/Tr-33T
88T-458
88T/Tr-46T
89B-194
89D-361
89F-9
89Moth/A's-15
89OPC-272
89Score-334
89T-272
89T/Big-171
89T/St-173
89UD-564
90D-450
90F-8
90Score-168
90T-527
90UD-195
Hassler, Andy
75OPC-261
75T-261
75T/M-261
76OPC-207
76SSPC-186
76T-207
77T-602
78T-73
79T-696
80T-353
81D-581
81F-290
81T-454
81T/St-55
82D-519
82F-464
82T-94
83D-290
83F-92
83T-573
84ArkTr-25
84D-255
84F-519
84Nes/792-719
84T-719
85Louvl-6
Hasty, Robert
E120
V100
Hatcher, Billy
83MidldC-13
84IowaC-24
85D-41RR
85F-649
85IowaC-10
85SevenUp-22
86D-433
86F-371
86F/Up-U49
86Pol/Ast-23
86T-46
86T/Tr-45T
87D-481
87D/OD-18
87F-59
87F/RecSet-15
87Moth/Ast-26
87Pol/Ast-6
87T-578
88D-23DK
88D-261
88D/Best-150
88D/DKsuper-23DK
88F-449
88Leaf-110
88Leaf-23DK
88Moth/Ast-6
88OPC-306
88Panini/St-300
88Pol/Ast-11
88RedFoley/St-30
88Score-505
88Sf-63
88T-306
88T/Big-3
88T/Mini-49
88T/St-28
88T/UK-30
89D-187
89D/Best-150
89F-359
89Lennox/Ast-1
89Moth/Ast-5
89OPC-252
89Panini/St-92
89Score-61
89Sf-174
89T-252
89T/Big-118
89T/St-19
89UD-344
90D-616
90F-467
90Score-562
90T-119
90UD-598
Hatcher, Hal
81CharR-5
82FtMyr-2
84Memph-20
Hatcher, Johnny
83Durhm-5
84Durhm-5
85Durhm-26
87Greenv/Bst-25
Hatcher, Mickey
79Albuq-11
80Pol/Dodg-44
80T-679R

81D-526
81F-135
81Pol/Dodg-44A
81T-289
81T/Tr-768
82D-480
82F-467
82OPC-291
82T/St-212
83D-615
83F-614
83T-121
84D-147
84F-566
84Nes/792-746
84T-746
85D-194
85F-279
85Leaf-224
85Seven/Minn-3
85T-18
85T/St-304
86D-269
86F-396
86Leaf-143
86OPC-356
86T-356
86T-786M
87D-491
87F-542
87F/U-U41
87Moth/Dodg-25
87OPC-341
87T-504
87T/St-276
87T/Tr-43T
88D-299
88F-516
88Leaf-122
88Moth/Dodg-25
88OPC-339
88Pol/Dodg-9
88Score-298
88T-607
88T/St-71
89B-347
89D-346
89F/WS-1
89Moth/Dodg-25
89OPC-254
89OPC-390
89Panini/St-105
89Panini/St-23
89Pol/Dodg-6
89Score-332
89T-483
89T/Big-63
89UD/Ext-709
89Woolwth-31
90D-439
90F-398
90Score-359
90T-226
90UD-283

Hatcher, Rick
82Durhm-18

Hatfield, Fred
52B-153
52T-354
53B/Col-125
53Glen
53T-163
54B-119
55B-187
56T-318
57T-278
58T-339
59DF
80Richm-5MG
86Miami-9MG

Hatfield, Gilbert
N172
N338/2

Hatfield, Rob
86Macon-13
87Salem-4

Hathaway, Shawn
88Sprin/Best-6
89Star/Wax-50
89StPet/Star-16

Hattaway, Wayne
85Orlan-23
88Orlan/Best-26
89Orlan/Best-27
89Orlan/Pro-1336

Hatten, Joe
47TipTop
49B-116
49Eureka-36
50B-166
51B-190
52B-144
52T-194
D305

Hatton, Grady
49B-62
49Eureka-85
50B-26
51B-47
51T/RB-34
52T-6
53T-45
54T-208
55T-131
55T/DH-72
56T-26
56T/Pin-23
66T-504
67T-347
68T-392
73OPC-624CO
73T-624C
74OPC-31CO
74T-31C
Exh47
PM10/Sm-69

Haugen, Troy
89Helena/SP-7

Haugstad, Phil
52T-198

Haurado, Yanko
87PrWill-2

Hauser, Arnold
10Domino-54
11Helmar-170
12Sweet/Pin-148
14Piedmont/St-27
S74-119
T201
T202
T205

Hauser, Jeff
88Rockford-16
89Rockford-16

Hauser, Joe
26Exh-108
28Exh-55
61F-113
88MinorLg/Leg-10
E120
V61-53
W572

Hausladen, Bob
83BurlR-19
83BurlR/LF-1

Hausman, George
49Eureka-109

Hausman, Thomas
74Sacra
76OPC-452
76T-452
77Spoka
77T-99
78Tidew
79OPC-339
79T-643
80T-151
81D-396
81F-333
81T-359
82D-301
82F-526
82T-524
83T-417

Hausmann, Clem
V362-13

Hausterman, David
86DayBe-11TR

Havens, Brad
82D-382
82OrlTw/A-16
82T-92
83D-480
83F-615
83T-751
84Nes/792-509
84T-509
84Toled-8
85IntLgAS-40
85RochR-16
86D-599
87F-472
87RochR-17
87RochR/TCMA-5
87T-398
87T/Tr-44T
88F-517
88Moth/Dodg-22
88Pol/Dodg-41
88T-698
89F-407
89T-204

Hawarny, Dave
82BirmB-16
83BirmB-6

Hawes, Roy Lee
55B-268

Hawkins, Andy
81Hawai-14
82Hawai-14
84F-302
84Moth/Padres-18
84Nes/792-778
84T-778
85D-528
85D/HL-14
85D/HL-15
85F-36
85Moth/Padres-13
85T-299
86D-284
86F-324
86F/Mini-70
86F/St-51
86Leaf-158
86OPC-5
86S-191
86T-478
86T/St-108
87Bohem-40
87D-264
87F-417
87T-183
88F-586
88Score-347
88Smok/Padres-11
88T-9
88T/Big-257
89B-166
89D-583
89D/Best-52
89D/Tr-52
89F-307
89F/Up-50
89Panini/St-194
89Score-118
89Score/NWest-19
89Score/Tr-14
89Sf-84
89T-533
89T/St-111
89T/Tr-47T
89UD-495
89UD/Ext-708
90Class-135
90D-159
90F-445
90T-335
90UD-339

Hawkins, Cedric
86LitFalls-13

Hawkins, Chris
87AubAs-11

Hawkins, Hersey
88Peoria/Ko-14

Hawkins, John
84Nashvl-9
85Albany-32
86FSLAS-21
86FtLaud-12

Hawkins, Todd
87Everett-18
88Fresno/Cal-9
88Fresno/Pro-1242

Hawkins, Walter
87Idaho-11

Hawkins, Wynn
60T-536
61T-34
63T-334

Hawks, Nelson
25Exh-42
W575

Hawley, Billy
83Cedar/LF-10
86Vermont-10
87Tampa-26

Haydel, Hal
71OPC-692R
71T-692R
72OPC-28R
72T-28R

Hayden, Alan
86Columbia-12
87Lynch-11
88Jacks/GS-25
89Chatt/Best-25
89Chatt/GS-23
89Jacks/GS-30
89Nashvl-9

Hayden, John F.
T206

Hayden, Paris
89Freder/Star-10

Hayden, Richard
84Butte-12

Hayes, Ben
82Indianap-21
83F-591
84F-470
84Nes/792-448
84T-448
85Louvl-25

Hayes, Bill
80Wichi-5
82IowaC-5
83IowaC-12
84IowaC-15
85IowaC-2
86Omaha-10
86Omaha/TCMA-1
87IowaC-14
88Geneva/Pro-1654

Hayes, Brian
78LodiD
79LodiD-19

Hayes, Charlie
86Shrev-11
87Shrev-17
87TexLgAS-27
88Phoen/CMC-15
88Phoen/Pro-57
89F-330
89F/Up-106
89Phoen/CMC-13
89Phoen/Pro-1487
89Score-628
89Score/HotRk-39
89UD/Ext-707
90Class-98
90D-548
90F-558
90Score-507
90Score/100Ris-12
90Sf-36
90T-577
90UD-437

Hayes, Chris
87Modesto-13

Hayes, Damon
47Remar-21
47Smith-21
48Smith-13

Hayes, Dan
84Newar-13

Hayes, Frank
(Blimp)
39PB-108
40PB-24
41DP-47
41G-13
41PB-41
47TipTop

Hayes, Jimmy
88Brist/Pro-1874

Hayes, Minter
(Jackie)
29Exh/4-32
34G-63
35BU-111M
35G-8B
35G-9B
37OPC-102
V300

Hayes, Terry
82Wausa-29

Hayes, Todd
87SnBer-22
88SnBer/Best-25
88SnBer/Cal-51

Hayes, Tom
81Durhm-7
84Richm-6

Hayes, Von
80Watlo
81Charl-15
82D-237
82F-371
82T-141
82T/Tr-42T
82Wheat/Ind
83D-324
83F-412
83OPC-325
83T-325
83T/St-311
83T/X-40
84D-477
84F-33
84Nes/792-587
84OPC-259
84T-587
84T/St-124
85CIGNA-2
85D-326
85D/HL-16
85F-253
85Leaf-93
85OPC-68
85T-68

85T/St-115
86CIGNA-3
86D-305
86F-443
86F/Mini-92
86F/St-52
86Keller-2
86Leaf-176
86OPC-146
86T-420
86T/St-120
87BK-8
87Class-63
87D-113
87D-12DK
87D/DKsuper-12
87D/OD-152
87Drake-3
87F-175
87F/Excit-23
87F/GameWin-19
87F/Mini-51
87F/St-55
87Kraft-24
87Leaf-12DK
87Leaf-130
87OPC-389
87RedFoley/St-72
87S-193
87T-666
87T/Coins-35
87T/Mini-28
87T/St-121
88D-207
88D/Best-128
88F-304
88F/Excit-18
88F/Mini-99
88F/St-108
88Leaf-197
88OPC-215
88Panini/St-356
88Score-515
88Sf-62
88T-215
88T/Big-139
88T/St-117
89B-406
89D-160
89D/Best-47
89F-571
89KingB/Discs-18
89OPC-385
89Panini/St-151
89RedFoley/St-56
89Score-38
89Sf-181
89T-385
89T/Big-302
89T/St-115
89UD-246
90Class-113
90D-278
90D/Bon/MVP-BC25
90F-559
90Score-36
90Score/100St-62
90Sf-147
90T-710
90UD-453
90UD-7TC

Hayford, Don
79Elmir-10

Haynes, Joe
49B-191
51B-240
52B-103
52T-145
54T-223

Haynes, Marvin
87Vermont-26

Haynes, Rick
75Dubuq

Hays, Darrin
89Butte/SP-23

Hayward, Jeff
86Tampa-6

Hayward, Ray
83Beaum-19
84Cram/PCL-219
85Cram/PCL-104
86LasVegas-6
87D-632
87LasVegas-12
88F/U-U63
88Moth/R-16
88OkCty/CMC-7
88OkCty/Pro-49
88Score/Tr-67T
88T/Tr-47T
89D-521
89F-521
89Score-514

Haywood, Albert
78Laugh/Black-20

Hayworth, Ray
34DS-90
35BU-165
39PB-140
40PB-155
R300
R314
V355-50
WG8-31

Hazewood, Drungo L.
81RochR-8
83RochR-20

Hazle, Robert S.
(Hurricane)
58T-83

Headley, Kent
88Virgini/Star-9

Heakins, Craig
86Watertn-9
87Macon-19

Healey, John
N172
N284

Healy, Bob
77QuadC

Healy, Fran
72T-663
73OPC-361
73T-361
74OPC-238
74T-238
74T/St-182
75OPC-120
75OPC-251
75T-251
75T/M-251
76OPC-394
76SSPC-184
76T-394
77BK/Y-3
77T-148
78T-582

Heard, Jehosie
54Esskay
54T-226

Hearn, Ed
83Lynch-22
84Jacks-xx
85IntLgAS-10
85Tidew-21
86D/Rook-54
86Tidew-13
87D-446
87D/OD-201
87F-10
87T-433
87ToysRUs-11
88Score-569
88T-56
89AAA/Pro-4
89D-297
89Omaha/CMC-12
89Omaha/Pro-1732
89T-348
89UD-42

Hearn, Jim
49B-190
49Eureka-184
50B-208
51B-61
52B-49
52BR
52RM-NL8
52T-337
52TipTop
53B/Col-76
53NB
53T-38
54NYJour
55B-220
55Gol/Giants-12
56T-202
57T-348
58T-298
59T-63
R423-44

Hearn, Tommy
86Miami-10

Hearron, Jeff
86Tor/Fire-16
87D-490
87Knoxv-21
87OPC-274
87Syrac/TCMA-3
87T-274
87Tor/Fire-13
87Tor/Fire-13
89LasVeg/CMC-17
89LasVeg/Pro-11

Heath, Al
82AppFx-28
83AppFx/LF-29
84Madis/Pol-8
86Kinston-9
87PalmSp-2

Heath, Dave
83Peoria/LF-6
85MidldA-6
86MidldA-10
87Edmon-3

Heath, John Jeffrey
39Exh
47TipTop
49B-169
49Eureka-11
79TCMA-97
R303/A
R303/B

Heath, Kelly
81Omaha-17
83Omaha-16
84Colum-2
84Colum/Pol-11
85Colum-16
85Colum/Pol-12
85IntLgAS-31
86Richm-9
87Richm/TCMA-18
88Syrac/CMC-20
88Syrac/Pro-811
89Syrac/CMC-17
89Syrac/Pro-800

Heath, Lee
89Pulas/Pro-1911

Heath, Mickey
28Exh/PCL-10

Heath, Mike
76FtLaud
77WHave
79T-710R
80T-687
81D-120
81F-583
81T-437
82D-413
82F-91
82Granny-3
82OPC-318
82T-318
83D-517
83F-518
83Granny-2
83T-23
83T/St-104
84D-223
84F-446
84Moth/A's-9
84Nes/792-567
84T-567
84T/St-337
85D-298
85F-422
85F-424
85Moth/A's-4
85OPC-396
85T-662
85T/St-326
86D-253
86F-418
86F/Up-U50
86OPC-148
86Schnucks-7
86T-148
86T/St-174
86T/Tr-46T
87Cain's-3
87Coke/Tigers-8
87D-496
87D/OD-214
87F/U-U42
87T-492
88D-338
88D/Best-69
88F-56
88Pep/T-8
88RedFoley/St-31
88Score-156
88T-237
89D-271
89D/Best-147
89F-132
89Mara/Tigers-8
89Score-131
89T-609TL
89T-743
89UD-654
90D-209
90F-603
90Score-172
90T-366
90UD-306

Heath, Thomas
52Mother-46
53Mother-43
R314/Can

Heath, William
66T-539R
67OPC-172
67T-172
70OPC-541
70T-541

Heathcock, Jeff
83ColumAst-14
84Cram/PCL-65
86D-182
86F-302
86Tucso-6
87Tucso-18
88F-450
88Moth/Ast-18
88Pol/Ast-12
89Tucso/CMC-7
89Tucso/Pro-196

Heathcote, Clifton E.
21Exh-71
26Exh-23
27Exh-12
33G-115
E120
E210-35
V354-9

Heaton, Neal
82Charl-5
83Wheat/Ind-19
84D-373
84F-546
84F/St-113
84Wheat/Ind-44
85D-373
85F-451
85Polar/Ind-44
86D-338
86F-589
86Leaf-203
86OhHenry-44
87D-615
87F-543
87F/U-U43
87T/Tr-45T
88D-134
88D/Best-124
88F-185
88F/Mini-89
88Ho/Disc-10
88OPC-354
88Panini/St-319
88RedFoley/St-32
88Score-430
88Sf-81
88T-765
88T/Big-33
88T/St-80
88T/St/Backs-29
89D-224
89F-377
89F/Up-113
89OPC-197
89Score-253
89T-197
89UD-99
90D-658
90F-468
90T-539
90UD-86

Heaverlo, Dave
76OPC-213
76SSPC-95
76T-213
77Phoen
77T-97
78T-338
79T-432
80T-177
81D-407
81F-594
81Tacom-26
82Tacom-3
83Tacom-21

Hebner, Rich
69OPC-82R
69T-82R
70MLB/St-101
70OPC-264
70T-264
71MLB/St-203
71OPC-212
71T-212
72MB-136
72T-630
73OPC-2
73T-2
74/DE-35
74OPC-450
74T-450

74T/St-84
75Ho-57
75K-57
75OPC-492
75T-492
75T/M-492
76OPC-376
76SSPC-579
76T-376
77OPC-168
77T-167
78OPC-194
78T-26
79OPC-293
79T-567
80OPC-175
80T-331
81Coke
81D-125
81F-474
81OPC-217
81T-217
82D-328
82F-268
82OPC-96
82T-603
83F-307
83T-778
84F-251
84F/X-50
84Nes/792-433
84SevenUp-18
84T-433
84T/X-50
85D-564
85F-59
85SevenUp-18
85T-124
86T-19
88Myrtle/Pro-1188
88SALAS/GS-1MG

Hebrard, Mike
82Amari-24

Hecht, Steve
89SanJose/Best-24
89SanJose/Cal-221
89SanJose/Pro-457
89SanJose/Star-13

Hecker, Guy
N172

Heckman, Tom
82Madis-8

Hedfelt, Pancho
85Utica-10

Hedge, Pat
89Erie/Star-5

Hedlund, Mike
65T-546R
69T-591
70OPC-187
70T-187
71OPC-662
71T-662
72MB-137
72OPC-81
72T-81
73OPC-591
73T-591

Hedrick, Craig
78Cedar

Heep, Danny
80Tucso-1
81F-72
81T-82R
82F-217
82T-441
83D-443
83F-449
83T-538
83T/X-41
84D-434
84F-586
84Nes/792-29
84T-29
85D-556
85F-84
85OPC-339
85T-339
86D-556
86F-83
86T-619
87D-649
87F-11
87T-241
88Moth/Dodg-20
88Pol/Dodg-12
88Score-417
88T-753
89D-368
89F-61
89Score-343
89Score/Tr-57
89T-198
90D-358
90F-278
90Score-113
90T-573

Heffernan, Bert
89Beloi/Star-9

Heffner, Don
39PB-44
40PB-51
41DP-147
41G-11
60T-462C
66T-269
W753

Heffner, Robert
64T-79
65OPC-199
65T-199
66T-432

Hegan, J. Mike
67T-553R
68T-402
69Sunoco/Pin-11
69T-577
70McDon-3
70MLB/St-271
70OPC-111
70T-111
70T/SO
71MLB/St-438
71OPC-415
71T-415
71T/Coins-116
72T-632
73OPC-382
73T-382
74OPC-517
74T-517
75OPC-99
75T-99
75T/M-99
76A&P/Milw
76Laugh/Jub-21
76OPC-377
76OPC-69FS
76OPC-69FS
76SSPC-235
76T-377
76T-69M
77T-507

Hegan, Jim
48L-28
50B-7
50NumNum
51B-79
51T/RB-12
52B-187
52NumNum-2
52RM-AL11
52StarCal/L-74D
52T-17
53B/Col-102
53T-80
54DanDee
54RH
54T-29
55Gol/Ind-11
55RFG-5
55RM-AL7
55Salem
55T-7
55T/DH-67
56T-48
56T/Pin-8C
57T-136
58T-345
59T-372
73OPC-116CO
73T-116C
76OPC-69FS
76T-69M
79TCMA-139
Exh47
PM10/Sm-70

Hegman, Bob
81CharR-10
84Memph-13
85Omaha-30
86Omaha-11
86Omaha/TCMA-8

Heidemann, Jack
71MLB/St-372
71OPC-87
71T-87
72OPC-374
72T-374
73OPC-644
73T-644
75OPC-649
75T-649
75T/M-649
76SSPC-544
77T-553
79Spoka-15

Heiden, Shawn
89Bluef/Star-11

Heidenreich, Curt
82Cedar-3
83Water-3

Heiderscheit, Pat
89James/Pro-2143

Heidrick, John
E107

Heifferon, Mike
86Albany/TCMA-11
87PrWill-14
88Albany/Pro-1354
89AAA/Pro-3
89Colum/Pol-24M

Height, Ron
88LitFalls/Puc-5

Heilmann, Harry E.
21Exh-72
25Exh-92
26Exh-93
27Exh-48
29Exh/4-24
31Exh/4-7
50Callahan
60F-65
61F-42
63Bz/ATG-2
80Laugh/3/4/5-28
80SSPC/HOF
86Conlon/1-42
D327
D328-71
E120
E121/120
E122
E135-71
E210-22
E220
R423-46
V100
V61-27
W501-6
W502-22
W515-18
W517-14
W573
W575

Heimer, Todd
79Tacom-8
80Tacom-18
81Chatt-10

Heimueller, Gorman
81WHave-20
82Tacom-5
83Tacom-4
84Cram/PCL-95
84D-131
85Orlan-25
86Toled-12
87Visal-24
88Visal/Cal-174
88Visal/Pro-105
89Visal/Cal-119CO
89Visal/Pro-1420

Heinen, Joe
75Cedar

Heinkel, Don
83BirmB-9
84Evans-19
86Nashv-11
87Toled-7
87Toled/TCMA-2
88F/U-U27
88Score/Tr-79T
89B-427
89F-133
89Louvl-21
89Score-168
89T-499

Heinle, Dana
87Kenosha-15
88Visal/Cal-168
88Visal/Pro-82
89VeroB/Star-11

Heins, Jim
89NiagFls/Puc-10

Heintzelman, Ken
49B-108
49Eureka-136
50B-85
51B-147
51BR-C10
52B-148
52T-362
53T-136
79TCMA-78
R423-42

Heintzelman, Tom
74OPC-607R
74T-607R
75Phoen-17
76Phoen
79Phoen

Heise, Benjamin
75OkCty

Heise, Larry Wayne
84Newar-19
87Greenv/Bst-22

Heise, Robert
70OPC-478
70T-478
71MLB/St-250
71OPC-691
71T-691
72OPC-402
72T-402
73OPC-547
73T-547
74/Tr-51T
74OPC-51
74T-51
75OPC-441
75T-441
75T/M-441

Heist, Al
58Union
61T-302
62Salada-195
62Shirriff-195
62T-373
62T/St-126
89Smok/Ast-24

Heitmuller, William
(Heinie)
E90/1
M116

Held, Matt
83Idaho-16

Held, Woodie
58T-202
59Kahn
59T-226
60Kahn
60L-2
60T-178
61Bz-33
61Kahn
61NuCard-405
61T-60
61T/St-136
62Bz
62J-44
62Kahn
62P-44
62P/Can-44
62Salada-5
62Shirriff-5
62Sugar-12
62T-215
62T/bucks
62T/St-35
63J-69
63P-69
63Sugar-12
63T-435
64Kahn
64T-105
64T/Coins-29
64T/St-29S3
64T/SU
64T/tatt
65T-336
66OPC-136
66T-136
67T-251
68T-289
69MB-108
69T-636
78TCMA-284
79TCMA-174

Heller, John
83Lynch-17

Heller, Mark
86Albuq-11

Hellman, Anthony
N172

Hellman, Jeff
87FtLaud-25

Helm, J. Ross
T206

Helmick, Tony
89GreatF-6

Helmquist, Doug
84BuffB-25

Helms, Tommy
65OPC-243R
65T-243R
66T-311R
67Kahn
67T-505
68T-405
69MB-109

69MLB/St-129
69MLBPA/Pin-47
69OPC-70
69OPC/DE-9
69T-418AS
69T-70
69T/DE-20
69T/decal
69T/S-40
69T/St-24
70MLB/St-28
70OPC-159
70T-159
71MLB/St-61
71OPC-272
71T-272
72MB-138
72OPC-204
72T-204
73OPC-495
73T-495
74OPC-67
74T-67
74T/St-32
75OPC-119
75T-119
75T/M-119
76OPC-583
76SSPC-56
76T-583
76T/Tr-583T
77T-402
78T-618
86TexGold-CO
88Kahn/Reds-CO
90T-110MG

Helsom, Bob
83StPet-21
84ArkTr-7

Helton, Keith
88CalLgAS-29
88SnBer/Best-19
88SnBer/Cal-44
89Wmspt/Pro-645
89Wmspt/Star-9

Heman, Russell
59T-283

Hemmerly, John
89Erie/Star-6

Hemond, Scott
87Madis-3
88Huntsvl/BK-6
89Huntsvl/Best-1
90F-646
90Score-598

Hempen, Hal
88Savan/Pro-342

Hempfield, Keith
83CharR-7

Hemphill, Charles
12Sweet/Pin-35
E107
E97
S74-22
T204
T205
T206
W555

Hemsley, Ralston
34Exh/4-15
35BU-71
35Exh/4-15
35G-8C
35G-9C
36Exh/4-15
36G
36Wheat
37Exh/4-15
40PB-205
41DP-133
41PB-34
44Yank/St-14
47Centen-8
54T-143
PR1-17
R312/M
R314
WG8-32

Hemus, Solly
52B-212
52T-196
53B/Col-85
53Hunter
53T-231
54B-94
54Hunter
54T-117
55B-107
55Hunter
57T-231
58T-207
59T-527
60T-218
61T-139
79TCMA-93

Henderson, Bill
88Fay/Pro-1102
89Lakel/Star-9

Henderson, Brad
86FSLAS-22TR
86StPet-10TR
87ArkTr-24
88ArkTr/GS-2

Henderson, Craig
82Wisco-26
83Visal/LF-20
85Orlan-26

Henderson, Dave
80Spoka-16
82T-711R
83F-481
83T-732
84D-557
84F-611
84Moth/Mar-3
84Nes/792-154
84OPC-154
84T-154
84T/St-343
85F-489
85Moth/Mar-4
85OPC-344
85T-344
85T/St-338
86D-318
86F-465
86Leaf-187
86Moth/Mar-4
86OPC-221
86T-221
86T-546M
86T/St-222
87D-622
87D/OD-189
87F-36
87F/Hottest-19
87F/WS-10M
87Leaf-103
87T-452
87T/HL-22
87T/St-23WS
87Woolwth-22
88D/A's/Bk-NEW
88F-84
88F/U-U53
88Moth/A's-14
88Score-228
88Score/Tr-49T
88T-628
88T/Big-131
88T/Tr-48T
89AubAs/Pro-2185
89B-200
89D-20DK
89D-450
89D/Best-190
89D/DKsuper-20DK
89F-10
89Moth/A's-13
89OPC-327
89Panini/St-423
89Score-533
89Sf-127
89T-527
89T/Big-326
89T/St-164
89T/St/Backs-17
89UD-174
90D-243
90F-9
90Score-325
90T-68
90UD-206

Henderson, Frank
88AppFx/Pro-154
88Eugene/Best-23
89AppFx/Pro-857

Henderson, Harry IV
89Bill/Pro-2059

Henderson, James H.
(Hardie)
N172
N184

Henderson, Joe
76Indianap-5
77Indianap-3
77T-487R
81Clint-22
82Beloi-2
83ElPas-3
84MidldC-1

Henderson, John
77QuadC

Henderson, Ken
65T-497R
66OPC-39
66T-39
67T-383
68T-309
70OPC-298
70T-298
71MLB/St-251
71OPC-155
71T-155
71T/Coins-97
71T/tatt-2
72OPC-443
72OPC-444IA
72T-443
72T-444A
73OPC-101
73T-101
74OPC-394
74T-394
74T/St-154
75Ho-136
75Ho/Twink-136
75OPC-59
75T-59
75T/M-59
76OPC-464
76SSPC-147
76T-464
76T/Tr-464T
77T-242
78Ho-126
78T-212
79T-73
80T-523

Henderson, Matt
79Wisco-8

Henderson, Mike
78Holyo
79Holyo-17
80Vanco-17

Henderson, Ramon
86Readg-9
87Readg-15
88Maine/CMC-19
88Maine/Pro-295
89Readg/Best-13
89Readg/Pro-653
89Readg/Star-13

Henderson, Rickey
77Modesto
79Ogden/TCMA-9
80T-482
81D-119
81F-351
81F-574
81F/St-54
81K-33
81OPC-261
81Sqt-28
81T-261
81T-4LL
81T/SO-39
81T/St-115
81T/St-15
82D-113
82F-643
82F-92
82F/St-123
82Granny-4
82K-4
82OPC-268
82T-156TL
82T-164LL
82T-610
82T/St-221
82T/St-8
83D-11DK
83D-35
83D/AAS-22
83F-519
83F-639
83F-646
83Granny-35
83K-8
83OPC-180
83OPC-391AS
83T-180
83T-2M
83T-391
83T-531
83T-704
83T/Gloss-33
83T/Gloss40-33
83T/St-103
83T/St-159
83T/St-197
83T/St-198
83T/St-199
83T/St-200
83T/St-201
83T/St-202
83T/St-21
83T/St/Box-8
84D-54
84D/AAS-9
84F-447
84F/St-53
84F/St-92
84FunFood/Pin-17
84MiltBrad-13
84Moth/A's-2
84Nes/792-134LL
84Nes/792-156TL
84Nes/792-230
84Nes/792-2HL
84OPC-230
84Ralston-15
84Seven-21W
84T-134
84T-2
84T-230
84T/Cereal-15
84T/Gloss40-6
84T/St-202
84T/St-3
84T/St-327
84T/St-4
84T/Super-19
84T/Super-19
85D-176
85D/HL-17
85D/HL-42
85F-425
85F-629IA
85F/St-54
85F/Up-U51
85Leaf-208
85OPC-115
85Seven-12W
85T-115
85T-706AS
85T/3D-10
85T/St-283
85T/St-321
85T/Super-14
85T/Tr-49T
85Woolwth-17
86D-51
86D/AAS-10
86D/PopUp-10
86Dorman-7
86Drake-5
86F-108
86F/AS-7
86F/LimEd-23
86F/Mini-23
86F/St-53
86Leaf-37
86OPC-243
86Quaker-25
86S-184M
86S-6
86S/Dec-69
86T-500
86T-716
86T/3D-11
86T/Gloss22-7
86T/Gloss60-5
86T/Mini-27
86T/St-155
86T/St-297
86T/Super-30
87BK-9
87Class-12
87D-228
87D/AAS-6
87D/OD-248
87D/PopUp-6
87Drake-12
87F-101
87F/Excit-24
87F/HL-4
87F/Hottest-20
87F/Mini-52
87F/Slug-18
87F/St-56
87Jiffy-14
87KayBee-16
87KMart-27
87Kraft-31
87Leaf-191
87Moth/A's-20
87MSA/Discs-18
87OPC-7
87OPC-E
87RedFoley/St-80
87S-157M
87S-159M
87S-198M
87S-4
87Seven-E3
87T-311TBC
87T-735
87T-E

87T/Board-8
87T/Coins-12
87T/Gloss22-18
87T/Gloss60-21
87T/HL-3
87T/Mini-64
87T/St-147
87T/St-296
87Woolwth-3
88ChefBoy-20
88Class/Blue-234
88D-277
88D/AS-4
88D/Best-76
88D/PopUp-4
88D/Y/Bk-277
88F-209
88F/Hottest-16
88F/Mini-40
88F/Slug-C2
88F/SS-C2
88F/St-S4
88KMart-13
88Leaf-145
88OPC-60
88OPC-M
88Panini/St-158
88Panini/St-231M
88Panini/St-434
88Score-13
88Score/WaxBox-7
88Sf-11
88Sf/Gamewin-8
88T-60
88T/Big-165
88T/Gloss22-7
88T/Gloss60-25
88T/Mini-26
88T/St-155
88T/St-297
88T/St/Backs-51
88T/UK-31
88T/WaxBox-M
89Ames-16
89B-181
89Bz-14
89Cadaco-28
89Class-50
89D-245
89D/AS-4
89D/Best-78
89D/PopUp-4
89F-254
89F/BBAS-20
89F/Excit-21
89F/Superstar-22
89F/Up-54
89KayBee-18
89KMart/Lead-15
89Modesto/Ch-33
89OPC-282
89Panini/St-239AS
89Panini/St-408
89Score-657
89Score-70
89Score/HotSt-45
89Score/Tr-50
89Sf-145
89T-380
89T/Big-271
89T/Gloss22-7
89T/Gloss60-35
89T/Mini-66
89T/St-145
89T/St-312
89T/St/Backs-18
89T/Tr-48T
89T/UK-37
89T/WaxBox-F
89UD-210
90Class-37
90D-304
90F-10
90Score-360
90Score-686DT
90Score-698M
90Score/100St-90
90Sf-208
90T-450
90T-7RB
90UD-334

Henderson, Steve
77Indianap-14
78OPC-53
78T-134
79OPC-232
79T-445
80OPC-156
80T-299
81Coke
81D-157
81F-321
81K-25
81OPC-44
81T-619
81T/SO-79
81T/St-193
81T/Tr-769
82D-183
82F-597
82F/St-98
82OPC-89
82RedLob
82T-89
82T/St-30
83D-252
83F-496
83T-335
83T/X-42
84D-389
84F-612
84Moth/Mar-21
84Nes/792-501
84OPC-274
84T-501
84T/St-341
85D-145
85F-490
85F/Up-U52
85Moth/A's-26
85OPC-38
85T-640
85T/Tr-50T
86D-375
86F-419
86Moth/A's-20
86T-748
87Tacom-13
88Moth/Ast-12
88Pol/Ast-13
88Score-547
88T-527
89AAA/Pro-22
89BuffB/CMC-14
89BuffB/Pro-1676

Henderson, Ted
81Tacom-29M

Henderson, Valentine
89Well/Puc-13

Henderson, Wendell
82QuadC-15

Hendley, C. Bob
61T-372
62T-361
63T-62
64T-189
64T/Coins-94
65T-444
66OPC-82
66T-82
67T-256
68T-345
69OPC-144
69T-144

Hendrick, George
72OPC-406
72T-406
73OPC-13
73OPC-201ALCS
73T-13
74OPC-303
74T-303
74T/St-167
75Ho-140
75K-46
75OPC-109
75T-109
75T/M-109
76OPC-570
76SSPC-527
76T-570
77Ho-123
77OPC-218
77Pep-40
77T-330
78Ho-82
78OPC-178
78T-30
79Ho-66
79OPC-82
79T-175
80OPC-184
80T-350
81Coke
81D-430
81Drake-22
81F-542
81K-35
81OPC-230
81T-230
81T/SO-85
81T/St-22
81T/St-220
81T/St-256
82D-40
82D-9DK
82Drake-17
82F-113
82F/St-25
82OPC-295
82Sqt-16
82T-420
82T/St-91
83D-404
83Drake-10
83F-7
83K-25
83OPC-148
83T-650
83T/St-153
83T/St-154
83T/St-285
84D-475
84D/AAS-32
84Drake-12
84F-324
84F/St-9
84FunFood/Pin-52
84Nes/792-386AS
84Nes/792-540
84OPC-163
84OPC-386AS
84T-386
84T-540
84T/Gloss40-23
84T/St-139
84T/St-185
84T/St/Box-11
85D-181
85F-225
85F/St-27
85F/Up-U53
85Leaf-259
85OPC-60
85T-60
85T/St-134
85T/Tr-51T
86F-158
86OPC-190
86Smok/Cal-14
86T-190
87D/OD-3
87F-82
87OPC-248
87Smok/Cal-22
87T-725
88D-479
88Score-308
88Smok/Angels-24
88T-304

Hendrick, Harvey
29Exh/4-3
34DS-41
R315-C2
R316
W513-63

Hendrick, Pete
86ElPas-14

Hendricks, Elrod
(Ellie)
69MB-110
69T-277
70OPC-528
70T-528
71MLB/St-299
71OPC-219
71T-219
72MB-139
72OPC-508
72T-508
75OPC-609
75T-609
75T/M-609
76OPC-371
76SSPC-384
76T-371
88French-44CO
89French-44
89Swell-64

Hendricks, Steve
87Spoka-22
88River/Cal-221
88River/Pro-1409
89AubAs/Pro-7
89Watlo/Pro-1772
89Watlo/Star-11

Hendrickson, Craig
77QuadC

Hendrickson, Dan
89Everett/Star-13

Hendrix, Claude
14CJ-76
15CJ-76
BF2-64
D328-72
D329-78
D350/2-77
E135-72
E220
M101/4-78
M101/5-77
W514-9
WG4-9

Hendrix, James
87CharWh-2
88Virgini/Star-10

Hendry, Ted
88Umpire-35
89Umpires-33

Henerson, Rob
78Cedar

Hengel, Dave
86Calgary-11
87Calgary-9
88Calg/CMC-18
88Calg/Pro-1550
88D-629
88F-375
89ColrSp/CMC-18
89ColSp/Pro-243
89T-531

Hengle, Emory
N172

Henika, Ron
84Cedar-27
86Vermont-11
87Nashv-10

Henion, Scott
87Columbia-17
88Salem/Star-8
89WPalm/Star-12

Henke, Rick
83Watlo/LF-26TR
86Water-13TR
87Wmspt-15

Henke, Tom
82Tulsa-1
83OKCty-9
84D-134
84OKCty-10
85D-403
85IntLgAS-41
85Syrac-8
85Tor/Fire-14
86Ault-50
86D-437
86F-60
86F/St-54
86Leaf-206
86OPC-333
86T-333
86T/St-189
86Tor/Fire-17
87D-197
87F-228
87F/Excit-25
87F/Slug-19
87F/St-57
87Leaf-73
87OPC-277
87Smok/AL-14
87T-510
87T/Mini-76
87T/St-185
87Tor/Fire-12
87Tor/Fire-12
88D-490
88D/AS-28
88D/Best-104
88F-112
88F/AS-2
88F/AwardWin-18
88F/Excit-19
88F/LL-17
88F/Mini-62
88F/St-73
88F/TL-12
88Ho/Disc-23
88OPC-220
88Panini/St-213
88RedFoley/St-33
88Score-57
88Sf-65
88T-220
88T-396
88T/Big-41
88T/Gloss60-35
88T/Mini-38
88T/Revco-31
88T/St-186
88T/St/Backs-64
88T/UK-32
88Tor/Fire-50
89B-246
89D-385
89D/Best-301
89F-235
89F/Excit-22
89OPC-75
89Panini/St-461

89Score-318
89Score/HotSt-63
89Sf-126
89T-75
89T/St-195
89Tor/Fire-50
89UD-264
90D-349
90F-84
90Score-157
90Sf-42
90T-695
90UD-282

Henkemeyer, Dick
82Wisco-17

Henley, Dan
85Anchora-15
88Bakers/Cal-235
89SnAnt/Best-12

Henley, Mike
83AppFx/LF-11

Henley, Weldon
E107
E254

Henline, Noah
C46-64

Henline, Walter
(Butch)
25Exh-43
26Exh-44
27Exh-8
87Conlon/2-18
E120
E126-31
E220
V100
V61-59
W572

Henneman, Mike
86Nashv-12
87D/Rook-32
87F/U-U44
87S/Rook-29
87T/Tr-46T
87Toled-16
87Toled/TCMA-13
88Class/Blue-241
88D-420
88D/Best-91
88F-57
88F/St-25
88OPC-3
88Pep/T-39
88Score-520
88Score/YS/I-15
88Sf-129
88T-582
88T/Big-256
88T/Gloss60-10
88T/JumboR-7
88ToysRUs-13
89B-98
89Class-94
89D-327
89D/Best-237
89F-134
89F/Excit-23
89Mara/Tigers-39
89OPC-365
89Pol/Tigers-39
89Score-293
89Score/HotSt-59
89Sf-56
89T-365
89T/Big-252
89T/St-273
89UD-373
90D-296
90F-604
90Score-184
90Sf-144
90T-177
90UD-537

Hennessy, Brendan
83BurlR-20
83BurlR/LF-18
83TriCit-24

Hennessy, Mike
82Cedar-9
86Sumter-9

Hennigan, Phil
71MLB/St-373
71OPC-211
71T-211
72T-748
73OPC-107
73T-107

Henninger, Rai
88Idaho/Pro-1852

Henninger, Rich
74OPC-602R
74T-602R
75OkCty

Hennis, Randall
87AubAs-10
88FSLAS/Star-8
88Osceola/Star-13
89ColMud/Best-9
89ColMud/Pro-137
89ColMud/Star-12

Henrich, Bobby
58T-131

Henrich, Tom
39PB-52
40PB-4
41DP-111
41PB-39
47TipTop
48B-19
48L-55
49B-69
49Royal-12
50B-10
50Drake-23
51B-291
51BR-B3
53Exh/Can-27
79TCMA-35
Exh47
PM10/Sm-71
PM10/Sm-72
R302
R303/A
R346-42
R423-47

Henriksen, Olaf
D328-73
D329-79
D350/2-78
E135-73
M101/4-79
M101/5-78
T207

Henry, Bill F.
68T-384R

Henry, Bill R.
55B-264
59T-46
60Kahn
60T-524
61T-66
62Kahn
62T-562
63FrBauer-8
63T-378
64T-49
65T-456
66OPC-115
66T-115
67T-579
68T-239

Henry, Butch
88Cedar/Pro-1159
88MidwLAS/GS-12
89Chatt/Best-9
89Chatt/GS-11

Henry, Carlos
88Ashvl/Pro-1074
89Ashvl/Pro-965

Henry, Chris
80Wausa-17

Henry, Dan
77Clint
77LodiD

Henry, Doug
86Beloi-10
87Beloi-12
88Stock/Cal-177
88Stock/Pro-747
89ElPas/GS-8

Henry, Dwayne
82BurlR-24
83Tulsa-11
84Tulsa-36
85Tulsa-29
86D-603
86F-562
86S-179M
87D-637
87OKCty-18
88OkCty/CMC-2
88OkCty/Pro-33
88T-178
89Richm/CMC-4
89Richm/Ko-38
89Richm/Pro-844
89T-496
89UD-51

Henry, John M.
N172

Henry, John Park
D327
D328-74
D329-80
D350/2-79
E135-74
M101/4-80
M101/5-79
T222

Henry, Kevin
88Idaho/Pro-1846

Henry, Mark
86Penin-12
87DayBe-10

Henry, Michael
87Savan-10
88Sprin/Best-4

Henry, Tim
82BurlR-1
82Tulsa-6
83Tulsa-10

Hensich, Phil
R314/Can
V355-123

Hensley, Chuck
82WHave-6
83Tacom-5
84Cram/PCL-86
86Phoen-9
87Richm/TCMA-6
88Albuq/CMC-10
88Albuq/Pro-273
89Calg/CMC-2
89Calg/Pro-531

Hensley, Mike
89Savan/Pro-364

Hentgen, Pat
87Myrtle-10
88Duned/Star-9
89Duned/Star-7

Hepler, William
66T-574R
67OPC-144
67T-144

Herbel, Ron
61Union
63T-208R
64T-47R
65OPC-84
65T-84
66T-331
67OPC-156
67T-156
68T-333
69T-251
70OPC-526
70T-526
71MLB/St-11
71OPC-387
71T-387
72MB-140
72OPC-469
72T-469

Herberholz, Craig
81BurlB-7

Herbert, Ray
53Glen
54T-190
55Rodeo
55T-138
55T/DH-106
58T-379
59T-154
60T-252
60T/tatt
60T/tatt-21
61P-87
61T-498
61T/St-162
62Salada-6
62Shirriff-6
62T-8
62T/St-25
63Bz-29
63Exh
63F-9
63J-45
63P-45
63Salada-42
63T-560
63T-8LL
63T/SO
64T-215
65T-399
66OPC-121
66T-121
Exh47

Heredia, Geysi
86Osceola-11

Heredia, Gilbert
87Everett-2
88CalLgAS-2
88SanJose/Cal-132
88SanJose/Pro-130

Heredia, Hector
87Albuq/Pol-10
88Albuq/CMC-11
88Albuq/Pro-274
89Albuq/CMC-5
89Albuq/Pro-66

Heredia, Ubaldo
77LodiD
78LodiD
87Indianap-11

Herman, Billy
28Yueng-22
32Orbit/num-67
32Orbit/un-33
33G-227
35BU-138
36Exh/4-3
36Wheat
37Exh/4-3
37Wheat-10
38Exh/4-3
38Wheat
40Wheat-10
41DP-3
50Remar
52T-394
54T-86
55Gol/Dodg-11
55T-19
55T/DH-53
60T-456C
65OPC-251MG
65T-251
66OPC-37MG
66T-37
80Cram/Leg-23
80SSPC/HOF
89Kahn/Coop-6
89Smok/Dodg-9
R303/A
R303/B
R305
R312/M
V355-16
WG8-33

Herman, Floyd C.
(Babe)
29Exh/4-4
31Exh/4-4
32Orbit/un-32
33G-5
35G-8K
35G-9K
36Exh/4-4
61F-114
88Conlon/5-16
R305
R306
R308-195
R312/M
R314
R315-A15
R315-B15
R316
R337-418
V353-5
W513-84

Herman, Greg
77AppFx

Herman, Ty
80Elmir-8

Hermann, Jeff
86GlenF-9
87GlenF-18
88Wichi-27

Hermann, LeRoy
R314/Can

Hermanski, Gene
47TipTop
48L-102
49B-20
49Eureka-37
50B-113
51B-55
51T/RB-11
52B-136
52T-16
52TipTop
53T-179
54T-228
79TCMA-165
89Rini/Dodg-36
Exh47

Hermoso, Angel
70OPC-147
70T-147

Hernaiz, Jesus R.
76OkCty
83Colum-12
88SoOreg/Pro-1718

Hernandez, Carlos
85BurlR-19
87Bakers-25
88Bakers/Cal-243
89SnAnt/Best-13

Hernandez, Cesar
86BurlEx-8
87WPalm-14
88Rockford-17
89Rockford-17
Hernandez, Chuck
86PalmS-17C
86PalmS/Smk-3C
87MidldA-18
88Edmon/Pro-563
89Edmon/CMC-24
89Edmon/Pro-562
Hernandez, Enrique
89Oneon/Pro-2100
Hernandez, Enzo
71MLB/St-229
71OPC-529R
71T-529R
72OPC-7
72T-7
73OPC-438
73T-438
74McDon
74OPC-572
74T-572
75OPC-84
75T-84
75T/M-84
76OPC-289
76SSPC-125
76T-289
77T-522
78Cr/PCL-84
Hernandez, Jackie
68T-352
69T-258
69T/St-185
70MLB/St-221
70T-686
71MLB/St-204
71OPC-144
71T-144
72MB-141
72OPC-502
72T-502
73OPC-363
73T-363
74OPC-566
74T-566
Hernandez, Jeremy
87Erie-26
88Sprin/Best-3
89StPet/Star-17
Hernandez, Jose
89Gasto/Pro-1018
89Gasto/Star-8
Hernandez, Keith
75OPC-623R
75T-623R
75T/M-623R
76OPC-542
76T-542
77Ho-115
77OPC-150
77T-95
78Ho-22
78OPC-109
78T-143
79Ho-108
79OPC-371
79T-695
80BK/PHR-16
80K-43
80OPC-170
80T-201LL
80T-321
80T/S-26
81Coke
81D-67
81F-545
81K-31
81MSA/Disc-16
81OPC-195
81T-420
81T/SO-67
81T/St-18
81T/St-219
82D-278
82F-114
82F/St-23
82K-23
82KMart-36
82OPC-210
82T-186TL
82T-210
82T/St-92
83D-152
83D-20DK
83D/AAS-20
83F-8
83K-49
83OPC-262
83T-700
83T/Gloss-4
83T/Gloss40-4
83T/St-188
83T/St-290
83T/X-43
84D-238
84D/AAS-23
84D/Champs-46
84Drake-13
84F-587
84F/St-49
84FunFood/Pin-104
84Nes/792-120
84OPC-120
84Ralston-32
84Seven-24E
84T-120
84T/Cereal-32
84T/Mets/Fan-4
84T/St-107
84T/St/Box-6
84T/Super-26
84T/Super-26
85D-68
85D/AAS-41
85D/HL-21M
85D/HL-27
85Drake-15
85F-85
85F/LimEd-12
85F/St-25
85Leaf-62
85OPC-80
85Seven-10E
85T-712AS
85T-80
85T/3D-11
85T/Gloss40-13
85T/Mets/Fan-6
85T/St-98
85T/Super-36
86D-190
86Dorman-9
86Drake-10
86F-84
86F/Mini-20
86F/St-55
86Leaf-124
86OPC-252
86S-127M
86S-15
86S-181M
86S-62M
86T-203
86T-520
86T-701
86T/3D-10
86T/Gloss60-7
86T/Mets/Fan-5
86T/Mini-53
86T/St-99
86T/Super-31
86Woolwth-14
87BK-10
87Class-4
87D-76
87D/AAS-11
87D/OD-124
87D/PopUp-11
87Drake-10
87F-12
87F-629M
87F-637M
87F-C6
87F/HL-5
87F/Hottest-21
87F/McCror-20
87F/Mini-53
87F/St-58
87F/WaxBox-C6
87F/WS-2M
87Jiffy-4
87KayBee-17
87Leaf-233
87MSA/Discs-4
87OPC-350
87RedFoley/St-32
87S-133
87S-195M
87Seven-E10
87Seven-ME13
87T-350
87T-595AS
87T/Board-12
87T/Coins-36
87T/Gloss22-2
87T/Gloss60-26
87T/HL-31
87T/Mini-24
87T/St-102
87T/St-157
87Woolwth-31
88ChefBoy-12
88D-316
88D/AS-49
88D/Best-152
88D/Mets/Bk-316
88F-136
88F-639M
88F/Hottest-17
88F/LL-18
88F/Mini-93
88F/St-103
88Jiffy-9
88Kahn/Mets-17
88KMart-14
88Leaf-117
88Nestle-42
88OPC-68
88Panini/St-339
88Score-400
88Sf-31
88Sf/Gamewin-11
88T-610
88T/Big-59
88T/Gloss60-32
88T/Mets/Fan-17
88T/St-97
88T/St/Backs-3
88T/UK-33
89B-385
89Class-59
89D-117
89D/Best-208
89D/GrandSlam-8
89F-37
89Kahn/Mets-17
89KMart/Lead-8
89OPC-63
89Panini/St-137
89RedFoley/St-57
89Score-41
89Score/HotSt-23
89Sf-60
89T-291TL
89T-480
89T/Big-185
89T/St-93
89T/WaxBox-G
89UD-612
90D-388
90F-205
90Score-193
90Score/100St-29
90Sf-106
90T-230
90UD-222
Hernandez, Leo
83T/X-44
84Nes/792-71
84RochR-15
84T-71
85RochR-5
86Colum-11
86Colum/Pol-10
Hernandez, Leonardo
78Clint
Hernandez, Manny
82DayBe-5
83DayBe-6
84Cram/PCL-59
85Cram/PCL-56
86Tucso-7
87Tucso-7
88D-481
88Tucso-13
88Tucso/CMC-1
88Tucso/Pro-169
89Portl/CMC-2
89Portl/Pro-221
Hernandez, Marino
88Poca/Pro-2085
89Clint/Pro-884
Hernandez, Martin
86Nashua-12
87Salem-11
Hernandez, Nick
78Newar
79BurlB-8
Hernandez, Pedro J.
81Syrac-15
82Syrac-21
85Cram/PCL-71
Hernandez, Pete
78DaytB
Hernandez, Ramon
67T-576R
68T-382
73OPC-117
73T-117
74OPC-222
74T-222
75OPC-224
75T-224
75T/M-224
76OPC-647
76SSPC-567
76T-647
77T-468
Hernandez, Robert
(Bobby)
86LitFalls-14
87Columbia-15
Hernandez, Robert
86Cram/PCL-100
87Kenosha-2
87QuadC-8
Hernandez, Roberto
88QuadC/GS-20
89MidldA/GS-18
Hernandez, Rudy
61T-229
Hernandez, Rudy
89StLucie/Star-9
Hernandez, Toby
80Utica-18
83Syrac-14
84Syrac-15
85Toled-13
Hernandez, Willie
(Guillermo)
76OkCty
78T-99
79T-614
80T-472
81D-589
81F-310
81T-238
82RedLob
82T-23
83D-174
83F-497
83T-568
83T/X-45
84D-163
84F-34
84F/X-51
84FunFood/Pin-79
84Nes/792-199
84OPC-199
84T-199
84T/X-51
85Cain's-10
85D-212
85Drake-37
85F-10
85F/St-101
85Leaf-235
85OPC-333
85Seven-10D
85Seven-1G
85Seven-7C
85T-333
85T/St-257
85T/Super-2
85Wendy-11
86Cain's-8
86D-227
86D/AAS-43
86D/WaxBox-PC5
86F-228
86F/LL-18
86F/St-56
86Leaf-102
86OPC-341
86S-65M
86S-85
86T-670
86T/St-275
87Cain's-13
87Coke/Tigers-15
87D-522
87D/AAS-43
87F-153
87F/Excit-26
87F/GameWin-20
87F/Mini-54
87F/St-59
87OPC-339
87S-105
87Seven-DT4
87T-515
87T/Mini-54
87T/St-272
87Toled-27
88D-398
88D/Best-125
88F-58
88Panini/St-84
88Pep/T-21
88Score-507
88T-713
88T/Big-206
89Bimbo/Discs-9
89D-62
89F-135

89Mara/Tigers-21
89OPC-43
89Pol/Tigers-21
89Score-275
89T-43
89UD-279
90D-610
90F-605
90Score-267
90UD-518

Hernandez, Xavier
88Myrtle/Pro-1178
88SALAS/GS-21
89Knoxv/Best-9
89Knoxv/Pro-1144
90D-682
90UD-26

Herndon, Larry
75Phoen-20
76Phoen
77Ho-47
77OPC-169
77T-397
78T-512
79OPC-328
79Pol/Giants-31
79T-624
80Pol/Giants-31
80T-257
81D-196
81F-451
81OPC-108
81T-409
81T/St-236
82D-172
82F-390
82OPC-182
82T-182
82T/St-109
82T/Tr-43T
83D-585
83D/AAS-5
83F-330
83OPC-13
83T-13
83T-261TL
83T/St-68
84D-349
84F-82
84Nes/792-333
84OPC-333
84T-334
84T/St-264
85Cain's-11
85D-150
85F-11
85Leaf-249
85OPC-9
85Seven-4D
85T-591
85T/St-266
85Wendy-12
86Cain's-9
86D-593
86F-229
86Leaf-230
86OPC-61
86T-688
86T/St-271
87Cain's-11
87Coke/Tigers-2
87D/OD-211
87F-154
87Seven-DT5
87T-298
88D-353
88F-59
88OPC-146
88Pep/T-31
88Pol/T-6
88RedFoley/St-34
88Score-138
88T-743
88T/Big-56
89Score-279
89UD-49

Herr, Edward
N172

Herr, Thomas
77StPet
80T-684R
81Coke
81D-68
81F-550
81T-266
82D-530
82F-115
82F/St-30
82T-27
83D-217
83F-9
83OPC-97
83T-489
83T/St-286
84D-596
84F-325
84Nes/792-649
84OPC-117
84T-649
84T/St-142
85D-425
85D/AAS-43
85F-226
85OPC-113
85T-113
85T/St-142
86D-83
86D/AAS-2
86D/PopUp-2
86Drake-21
86F-37
86F/AS-2
86F/Mini-8
86F/St-57
86KAS/Disc-15
86Leaf-79
86OPC-94
86S-113
86Schnucks-8
86T-550
86T-702
86T/Gloss22-14
86T/Gloss60-32
86T/Mini-62
86T/St-147
86T/St-49
86T/Super-32
87D-140
87D/OD-61
87F-296
87F/LL-22
87Leaf-121
87OPC-181
87RedFoley/St-60
87Smok/Cards-20
87T-721
87T/St-49
88D-208
88D/Best-326
88F-35
88F/Hottest-18
88F/U-U43
88F/WS-10
88F/WS-7M
88Leaf-201
88OPC-310
88Panini/St-391
88Score-84
88Score/Tr-8T
88Sf-141
88T-310
88T/Big-31
88T/St-50
88T/St/Backs-4
88T/Tr-49T
89B-403
89Class/Up/2-166
89D-301
89D/Best-72
89D/Tr-4
89F-115
89F/Up-107
89Score-191
89Score/Tr-9
89T-709
89T/Big-283
89T/Tr-49T
89UD-558
89UD/Ext-720
90D-21DK
90D-75
90F-560
90Score-171
90Score/100St-77
90Sf-63
90T-297
90UD-488

Herrera, Hector
87AubAs-20

Herrera, Jose
69T-378

Herrera, Juan
(Poncho)
58T-433
59T-129
60L-5
60T-130
61Bz-27
61P-121
61T-569AS
61T/RO-36
61T/St-56
62J-192
62P-192
62Salada-122
62Shirriff-122

Herrera, Ramon
26Exh-67

Herrick, Neal
81Miami-16

Herring, Paul
80Water-5
81Indianap-27
82Water-16

Herrmann, Ed
69T-439R
70OPC-368
70T-368
71OPC-169
71T-169
72OPC-452
72T-452
73OPC-73
73T-73
74OPC-438
74T-438
74T/St-155
75Ho-86
75OPC-219
75T-219
75T/M-219
76OPC-406
76SSPC-440
76T-406
77T-143
78BK/A-3
78T-677
79OPC-194
79T-374

Herrmann, Tim
89NiagFls/Puc-11

Herrnstein, John
63T-553R
64T-243R
65T-534
66T-304
78TCMA-124

Herron, Tony
84Pawtu-11A
84Pawtu-11B
85Pawtu-16

Hersh, Dave
77BurlB

Hersh, Earl
61BeeHive-8

Hershberger, N. Mike
62T-341
63T-254
64T-465
65OPC-89
65T-89
66T-236
67T-323
68OPC-18
68T-18
69MB-111
69MLB/St-86
69T-655
70McDon-3
70MLB/St-272
70T-596
71OPC-149
71T-149
72MB-142
78TCMA-287

Hershberger, Willard
39PB-119
40PB-77
W711/1
W711/2

Hershiser, Gordon
88VeroB/Star-11
89SnAnt/Best-7

Hershiser, Orel
82Albuq-4
83Albuq-3
84FunFood/Pin-83
84Pol/Dodg-55
85D-581
85F-371
85F/St-96
85Leaf-38
85OPC-273
85T-493
85T/St-74
86D-18
86D-226
86D/DKsuper-18
86Drake-31
86F-131
86F/LimEd-24
86F/Slug-16
86F/St-58
86Leaf-18DK
86OPC-159
86Pol/Dodg-55
86S-9
86T-159
86T/3D-12
86T/Gloss60-24
86T/Mini-45
86T/St-73
86T/Super-33
87Class-92
87D-106
87D/HL-13
87D/OD-79
87F-441
87F/RecSet-16
87Leaf-246
87Moth/Dodg-6
87OPC-385
87Pol/Dodg-28
87RedFoley/St-5
87S-43
87Seven-W6
87Smok/Dodg-12
87T-385
87T/Mini-14
88D-94
88D/AS-56
88D/Best-148
88F-518
88F-632M
88F/AwardWin-17
88F/BB/AS-14
88F/Excit-20
88F/Hottest-19
88F/LL-19
88F/Mini-84
88F/RecSet-18
88F/Slug-18
88F/SS-15
88F/St-92
88F/TL-13
88Leaf-62
88Moth/Dodg-6
88OPC-40
88Panini/St-303
88Pol/Dodg-55
88Score-470
88Sf-160
88T-40
88T/Big-91
88T/Mini-53
88T/Revco-12
88T/St-68
88T/UK-34
89B-341
89Bz-15
89Cadaco-29
89Class-1
89Class-105
89Class/Up/2-173
89Crunch-3
89D-197
89D-648M
89D/AS-50
89D/Best-225
89D/MVP-BC4
89F-62
89F/AS-7
89F/BBAS-21
89F/BBMVP's-19
89F/Excit-24
89F/Heroes-22
89F/LL-20
89F/Superstar-23
89F/WaxBox-C14
89F/WS-11
89F/WS-6
89Holsum/Discs-18
89KayBee-19
89KingB/Discs-12
89Moth/Dodg-6
89Nissen-18
89OPC-380
89OPC-41
89Panini/St-13LCS
89Panini/St-18
89Panini/St-19
89Panini/St-225
89Panini/St-25
89Panini/St-474
89Panini/St-9
89Panini/St-97
89Pol/Dodg-29
89Ralston-5
89RedFoley/St-58
89Score-370
89Score-582M
89Score-653HL
89Score/HotSt-35
89Score/Mast-21
89Sf-222M
89Sf-36
89Smok/Dodg-100
89T-394AS
89T-550
89T-5RB

89T-669TL
89T/Big-1
89T/Coins-2
89T/DH-21
89T/Gloss60-48
89T/Hills-17
89T/Mini-18
89T/St-12
89T/St-65
89T/St/Backs-60
89T/UK-38
89Tetley/Discs-10
89UD-130
89UD-661CY
89UD-665M
89UD-667M
89Woolwth-21
89Woolwth-25
89Woolwth-33
89Woolwth-4
90Class-81
90D-197
90D/Bon/MVP-BC5
90F-399
90F/WaxBox-C14
90Score-50
90Score/100St-94
90Sf-197
90T-780
90UD-10TC
90UD-256

Hershmann, William
87StPet-21
88Savan/Pro-340
89Savan/Pro-366

Hertel, Rick
78Duned

Hertz, Steve
64T-544R

Hertzler, Paul
85Indianap-18
86Jacks/TCMA-15

Herz, Steve
80Toled-13
81Toled-12
82Spoka-11
82Vanco-11
84Cram/PCL-142
85Cram/PCL-244

Herzig, Lynn
(Spike)
77Holyo
78Holyo

Herzog, Charles
(Buck)
11Helmar-129
12Sweet/Pin-114
12Sweet/Pin-67
14CJ-85
15CJ-85
40PB-229
75F/Pion-27
BF2-71
D304
D327
D328-75
D329-81
D350/2-80
E135-75
E96
M101/4-81
M101/5-80
M116
S74-44
T201
T205
T206
T207
T213/blue
T215/blue
T3-45
W514-104

Herzog, Hans
84Savan-8
86StPet-11
87StPet-16

Herzog, Whitey
57T-29
58T-438
59T-392
60L-71
60T-92
61P-88
61T-106
61T/St-163
62T-513
63T-302
73OPC-549MG
73T-549MG
76SSPC-185
76T-236MG
77T-371MG
78T-299
79T-451MG
81T-684MG
82D-190
83D-530
83T-186
84Nes/792-561MG
84T-561
84T/Gloss22-12MG
85T-683MG
86T-441
87D/AAS-20MG
87D/PopUp-20MG
87Smok/Cards-25
87T-243MG
87T/Gloss22-1MG
88Smok/Card-1MG
88T-744
89D/AS-42MG
89D/PopUp-42MG
89Smok/Cards-8
89T-654MG
89T/Gloss22-12MG
90T-261MG
Exh47

Hesketh, Joe
83Memph-19
84Indianap-6
85D-157
85F-652
85T/Tr-52T
86D-341
86F-250
86Leaf-150
86OPC-42
86Provigo-21
86S-177M
86T-472
86T/Gloss60-19
87D-134
87F-320
87Leaf-62
87OPC-189
87T-189
88D-504
88Indi/Pro-512
88OPC-371
88T-371
89D-460
89F-378
89OPC-74
89Score-498
89T-614
89UD-60
90D-511
90F-349
90Score-483
90T-24
90UD-512

Heslet, Harry
V362-27

Hester, Steve
88Greens/Pro-1570
89Cedar/Best-29
89Cedar/Pro-919
89Cedar/Star-27
89Cedar/Star-8

Hetki, John
53T-235
54T-161
55T/DH-62

Hetrick, Kent
88Beloi/GS-13
89Stock/Best-9
89Stock/Cal-161
89Stock/Pro-376
89Stock/Star-10

Hetzel, Eric
85Greens-18
87WinHav-22
88Pawtu/CMC-8
88Pawtu/Pro-449
89D-660
89Pawtu/CMC-3
89Pawtu/Dunkin-31
89Pawtu/Pro-703
90D-539
90F-279
90Score-543
90Score/100Ris-23
90T-629
90UD-673

Heuer, Mark
87SnAnt-24

Heving, Joe A.
29Exh/4-17
35BU-43
39PB-20
40PB-35
41DP-136

Hewatt, B.
88Poca/Pro-2090

Hewes, Pat
87Savan-9
88StPet/Star-9
89Penin/Star-7

Hiatt, Jack
65T-497R
66T-373R
67T-368
68Coke
68T-419
69MB-112
69OPC-204
69T-204
70OPC-13
70T-13
71MLB/St-83
71OPC-371
71T-371
72MB-143
72T-633
73OPC-402
73T-402
80Wichi-8
82Holyo-23
83ColumAst-22
88Poca/Pro-2101

Hibbard, Greg
86Cram/PCL-43
87AppFx-27
87FtMyr-6
88Vanco/CMC-11
88Vanco/Pro-770
89Vanco/CMC-3
89Vanco/Pro-584
90D-384
90F-534
90Score-369
90Score/100Ris-77
90T-769
90UD-543

Hibbett, Wendell
78Charl

Hibbs, Al
85Utica-11
86Cram/PCL-132

Hibbs, Loren
84Evrt/Cram-15

Hibner, Dave
78Ashev
80Ashev-8

Hice, Bob
84CharO-1
85CharO-27
87CharO/WBTV-xx

Hickerson, Brian
87Clint-28

Hickerson, Bryan
89SanJose/Best-15
89SanJose/Cal-212
89SanJose/Pro-443
89SanJose/Star-14

Hickey, Bob
75SnAnt

Hickey, James Joseph
85BuffB-20
87BirmB/Best-16
89ColMud/Best-19

Hickey, Kevin
79AppFx-6
80GlenF/B-10
80GlenF/C-7
82D-631
82F-344
82OPC-362
82T-778
83D-445
83F-237
83T-278
84D-135
84F-61
84Nes/792-459
84T-459
86Portl-8
87Hawai-18
88RochR-11
88RochR/Gov-11
89F/Up-4
89French-23
90D-583
90F-178
90Score-214
90T-546
90UD-299

Hickman, Charles
E107
T201
T213/brown
WG2-23

Hickman, Gordon J.
T206

Hickman, Jim
61Union
62T-598R
63T-107
64T-514
64T/Coins-92
65OPC-114
65T-114
66T-402
67T-346
69MB-113
69OPC-63
69Sunoco/Pin-3
69T-63
70T-612
71K-11
71MD
71MLB/St-32
71OPC-175
71T-175
71T/Coins-27
72T-534

73OPC-565
73T-565

Hickox, Tom
88CapeCod/Sum-86

Hicks, Aman
89Erie/Star-7

Hicks, Clay
77AppFx

Hicks, Ed
76Wausa

Hicks, Jim
67T-532
69T-559R
70OPC-173
70T-173

Hicks, Mike
77Ashev

Hicks, Rob
86Portl-9
87Readg-26
88ElPas/Best-27

Hicks, Robert
82Sprin-7

Hicks, William J.
(Joe)
60L-74
61T-386
62T-428
79QuadC-11
83IowaC-14
84IowaC-9
86IowaC-15
87PrWill-26

Higbe, Kirby
39Exh
41DP-24
41PB-52
47TipTop
48L-129
49B-215
49Eureka-108
50B-200
89Smok/Dodg-50
Exh47

Higgins, Bob
T207

Higgins, Dennis
66T-529R
67OPC-52
67T-52
68T-509
69T-441
69T/St-237
70OPC-257
70T-257
71MLB/St-374
71OPC-479
71T-479
72MB-144
72OPC-278
72T-278

Higgins, Frank
36Exh/4-14
WG8-34

Higgins, Kevin
89Spoka/SP-19

Higgins, Mark
80BurlB-23
81BurlB-23
86Watlo-11
87Wmspt-9
88ColSp/CMC-13
88ColSp/Pro-1544
89ColrSp/CMC-15
89ColSp/Pro-255

Higgins, Mike
(Pinky)
34G-78
35BU-171
35G-1B
35G-2B
35G-6B

35G-7B
36B
40PB-199
41DP-55
41PB-35
55T-150
61T-221
62T-559
72F/FFeat-30
72Laugh/GF-11
88Conlon/AmAS-15
PM10/Sm-73
R303/A
R303/B
R313
R314
W501-26

Higgins, Ted
86FSLAS-23
86FtLaud-13
87Albany-8

Higgs, Darrel
87Orlan-24

High, Andrew
21Exh-73
26Exh-2
27Exh-3
33G-182
88Conlon/3-13
R316

High, Hugh
D328-76
D329-82
D350/2-81
E135-76
M101/4-82
M101/5-81

Hightower, Barry
86Columbia-13
87Columbia-1
88Spoka/Pro-1942

Higson, Chuck
86Cram/PCL-185
88Fresno/Cal-22
88Fresno/Pro-1225

Higuera, Ted
84ElPas-15
85F/Up-U54
85Pol/Brew-49
85T/Tr-53T
86D-351
86F-490
86F/St-59
86Jay's-10
86Leaf-157
86Pol/Brew-49
86S-114
86T-347
87Class/Up-147
87D-16DK
87D-49
87D/AAS-57
87D/DKsuper-16
87D/OD-56
87F-346
87F/Excit-27
87F/GameWin-21
87F/Hottest-22
87F/LL-23
87F/McCror-21
87F/Mini-55
87F/Slug-20
87F/St-60
87Leaf-16DK
87Leaf-95
87OPC-250
87RedFoley/St-74
87S-11
87S-111M
87T-250
87T-615AS
87T/Gloss22-22
87T/Mini-60
87T/St-199
88D-90
88D/Best-127
88F-166
88F/AS-3
88F/AwardWin-19
88F/BB/AS-15
88F/BB/MVP-18
88F/Excit-21
88F/Hottest-20
88F/LL-20
88F/Mini-30
88F/RecSet-19
88F/Slug-19
88F/SS-16
88F/St-37
88F/TL-15
88Leaf-53
88OPC-110
88Panini/St-116
88Pol/Brew-49
88Score-280
88Sf-20
88T-110
88T/Big-87
88T/Mini-18
88T/St-196
88T/UK-35
89B-129
89Class-136
89D-175
89D/Best-183
89ElPas/GS-16
89F-188
89F/BBMVP's-20
89F/Heroes-23
89F/Superstar-24
89Gard-7
89OPC-292
89Panini/St-366
89Pol/Brew-49
89RedFoley/St-59
89Score-132
89Score/HotSt-49
89Sf-47
89T-595
89T/Mini-57
89T/St-198
89T/St/Backs-28
89T/UK-39
89UD-424
90D-339
90F-326
90Score-305
90Sf-44
90T-15
90UD-627

Hilbert, Adam
88Poca/Pro-2081

Hildebrand, Oral
34G-38
35BU-123
35G-1L
35G-2E
35G-6E
35G-7E
36G
37Exh/4-15
40PB-123
R308-163
R313
R314

Hildebrand, Tom
86Penin-13

Hildebrand, Umpire
21Exh-74

Hildreth, Brad
89Erie/Star-8

Hilgenberg, Scot
86Cedar/TCMA-17
87Tampa-24

Hilgendorf, Tom
63Pep/Tul
70OPC-482
70T-482
74OPC-13
74T-13
75OPC-377
75T-377
75T/M-377
76OPC-168
76T-168

Hill, A.J.
77AppFx
80GlenF/B-21
80GlenF/C-20M
80GlenF/C-30
81AppFx-18
83MidldC-26
84Chatt-20

Hill, Brad
85BurlR-4
86Salem-12

Hill, Chris
88LitFalls/Puc-17
89Clmbia/Best-13
89Clmbia/GS-9

Hill, Clay
85Cram/PCL-100
86Calgary-12
88Mia/Star-9

Hill, Darryl
78Duned

Hill, Don
(Clay)
83Chatt-15
84Chatt-27

Hill, Donnie
82WHave-14
83Tacom-11
84D-96
84F-448
84Moth/A's-13
84Nes/792-265
84T-265
85D-375
85F-426
85Moth/A's-12
85T/Tr-54T
86D-340
86F-420
86Leaf-148
86Moth/A's-12
86OPC-310
86T-484
87Coke/WS-9
87D-405
87D/OD-237
87F-394
87T-339
87T/Tr-47T
88Coke/WS-10
88D-87
88F-400
88OPC-132
88Score-572
88T-132
88T/Big-137
88T/St-286
89Score-583
89T-512
89Tacom/CMC-18
89Tacom/Pro-1562
89UD-527

Hill, Elmore
(Moe)
78Wisco

Hill, Garry
70OPC-172R
70T-172R

Hill, Glenallen
85Kingst-19
86Knoxv-10
86SLAS-16
87D-561
87Syrac-23
87Syrac/TCMA-20
88Syrac/CMC-15
88Syrac/Pro-812
89AAA/Pro-31
89Syrac/CMC-15
89Syrac/Pro-804
90Class-88
90D-627
90Score-601
90T-194

Hill, H.A.
79Knoxv/TCMA-22

Hill, Herman
70OPC-267R
70T-267R

Hill, Jim
47Centen-9

Hill, Ken
87ArkTr-19
89D-536
89D/Best-304
89D/Rook-31
89F-652M
89F/Up-119
89Louvl-22
89Louvl/Pro-1268
89Score/Tr-98
89Smok/Cards-9
89T/Tr-50T
90D-397
90F-251
90Score-233
90Score/100Ris-34
90T-233
90UD-336

Hill, Lew
87Oneon-1
89Oneon/Pro-2111

Hill, Marc
75OPC-620R
75T-620R
75T/M-620R
76OPC-577
76SSPC-100
76T-577
77T-57
78T-359
79Pol/Giants-2
79T-11
80OPC-125
80Pol/Giants-2
80T-236
81T-486
81T/Tr-770
82T-748
83D-230
83T-124
84D-330
84F-62
84Nes/792-698
84T-698
84TrueVal/WS-16
85Coke/WS-7
85D-160
85F-516
85T-312
86Coke/WS-7
86T-552

Hill, Milton
88Cedar/Pro-1163
89Chatt/Best-6
89Chatt/GS-10

Hill, Nate
85Spoka/Cram-8

Hill, Orsino
83Cedar-23
83Cedar/LF-23
88Jaxvl/Best-12
88Jaxvl/Pro-965
89CharlK-24

Hill, Perry W.
86DayBe-12C

Hill, Pete
74Laugh/Black-10

Hill, Quency
76OkCty
78Knoxv
82QuadC-27

Hill, Roger
88Watlo/Pro-685

Hill, Ron
80Elmir-9

Hill, Sandy
78Salem

Hill, Stephen F.
85Anchora-16
86StPet-12
87Peoria-7
87Sprin/Best-12
88StPet/Star-10
88WinSal/Star-6
89ArkTr/GS-7
89SnBer/Best-15
89SnBer/Cal-84

Hill, Tony
86Elmir-10
87Greens-14

Hillegas, Shawn
87Albuq/Pol-11
87S/Rook-30
88Albuq/CMC-1
88Albuq/Pro-265
88D-35
88F-519
88Leaf-35RR
88Pol/Dodg-57M
88Score-612
88T-455
89B-58
89Coke/WS-11
89D-503
89F-498
89Panini/St-301
89Score-488
89Score/YS/II-29
89T-247
89UD-478
90D-619
90F-535
90Score-329
90T-93
90UD-541

Hillemann, Charlie
87Spoka-9
88Charl/Pro-1197
89AubAs/Pro-4
89Wich/Roc-18
89Wich/Roc/Up-6

Hiller, Chuck
61T-538
62Salada-106
62Shirriff-106
62T-188
63J-102
63P-102
63T-185
64T-313
65T-531
66OPC-154
66T-154
67T-198
68T-461
73OPC-549CO
73T-549C

Hiller, Frank
52B-114
52T-156
R346-37

Hiller, John
66T-209R
68T-307

69MB-114
69T-642
70OPC-12
70T-12
71MLB/St-393
71OPC-629
71T-629
72MB-146
73OPC-448
73T-448
74/DE-17
74OPC-208LL
74OPC-24
74T-208LL
74T-24
74T/St-175
75K-19
75OPC-415
75T-415
75T/M-415
76OPC-37
76SSPC-353
76T-37
77Ho-28
77OPC-257
77T-595
78BK/T-9
78T-258
79OPC-71
79T-151
80OPC-229
80T-614
86GlenF-10CO
87Toled-25
88Domino-7

Hillman, Dave
57T-351
58T-41
59T-319
60T-68
61T-326
62T-282

Hillman, Eric
88Clmbia/GS-5
89Clmbia/Best-11
89Clmbia/GS-10

Hillman, Joe
88SoOreg/Pro-1716
89Modesto/Cal-275
89Modesto/Ch-29

Hillman, Trey
86Watlo-12
87Kinston-19

Hilpert, Adam
89Clint/Pro-883

Hilton, Dave
73T-615R
74OPC-148
74T-148
75OPC-509
75T-509
75T/M-509
77OPC-139
77T-163
81Portl-11
89SnJos/Cal-238C

Hilton, Howard
86StPet-13
87Sprin/Best-13
88ArkTr/GS-12
89Louvl-23
89Louvl/CMC-6
89Louvl/Pro-1251

Hilton, John
84Visal-10

Hilton, Stan
88Wmspt/Pro-1316
89ColSp/Pro-244

Hina, Fred
88Clmbia/GS-18

Hinchman, Harry
E254
E270/1
T201
T206

Hinchman, William
E97
T206
W555

Hinde, Michael
88CapeCod/Sum-62
89Elizab/Star-11

Hindman, Randy
86Cedar/TCMA-18

Hinds, Kevin
81Cedar-11

Hinds, Sam
77Spoka
78T-303
79Holyo-29
79Vanco-19

Hines, Ben
87Albuq/Pol-2CO

Hines, Henry
N172

Hines, Paul
N172
N284
WG1-33

Hines, Tim
89StLucie/Star-10

Hinkel, John
78Wausa

Hinkle, Mike
87Erie-28
88Savan/Pro-331
89ArkTr/GS-8

Hinnrichs, Dave
84Evrt/Cram-16
86Fresn/Smok-13

Hinrichs, Phil
81Phoen-17
83Phoen/BHN-11

Hinshaw, George
82Amari-1
84Cram/PCL-234
85Cram/PCL-113
87Albuq/Pol-28
88Albuq/CMC-13
88Albuq/Pro-268

Hinsley, Jerry
64T-576R
65T-449R

Hinson, Bo
82AubAs-10

Hinson, Gary
82BirmB-14

Hinton, Chuck
62T-347
62T/St-96
63Bz-25
63Exh
63J-93
63P-93
63T-2LL
63T-330
63T/SO
64Bz-25
64T-52
64T/Coins-162AS
64T/Coins-38
64T/S-20
64T/St-47
64T/SU
65Bz-3
65Kahn
65OldLond-26
65OPC-235
65T-235
65T/E-60
65T/trans-48
66T-391
67OPC-189
67T-189
68T-531
69MB-115
69MLB/St-22
69T-644
70MLB/St-199
70OPC-27
70T-27
71MLB/St-375
71OPC-429
71T-429
72MB-147
78TCMA-252
78TCMA-265
89Swell-93
Exh47

Hinton, Rich
72T-724R
73OPC-321
73T-321
76Indianap-20
76OPC-607
76SSPC-158
76T-607

Hinzo, Thomas
87Kinston-21
88ColSp/CMC-14
88ColSp/Pro-1527
88D-526
88F-611
88OPC-294
88Panini/St-73
88Score-567
88T-576
89ColrSp/CMC-16
89ColSp/Pro-256
89UD-34

Hippauf, Herb
66T-518R
87Idaho-18
88Idaho/Pro-1860

Hirose, Sam
87SanJose-1
88SanJose/Cal-142
88SanJose/Pro-123

Hirsch, Jeff
86Peoria-11
87WinSal-23
88IowaC/CMC-6
88IowaC/Pro-532
89CharlK-18

Hirschbeck, John
88Umpire-50
89Umpires-48

Hirschbeck, Mark
89Umpires-59

Hirtensteiner, Rick
88CapeCod/Sum-25

Hiser, Gene
72OPC-61R
72T-61R
74OPC-452
74T-452
76SSPC-314

Hisey, Steve
88SnBer/Best-20
88SnBer/Cal-39

Hisle, Larry
68T-579R
69OPC-206R
69T-206R
70K-45
70MLB/St-89
70OPC-288
70T-288
71MLB/St-180
71OPC-616
71T-616
72MB-148
72OPC-398
72T-398
73OPC-622
73T-622
74OPC-366
74T-366
75Ho-128
75OPC-526
75T-526
75T/M-526
76Ho-73
76OPC-59
76SSPC-220
76T-59
77OPC-33
77T-375
78Ho-13
78OPC-3LL
78PapaG/Disc-38
78T-203LL
78T-520
78Wiffle/Discs-29
79Ho-95
79OPC-87
79T-180
79T/Comics-10
80K-22
80OPC-222
80T-430
81D-87
81F-509
81F/St-94
81OPC-215
81T-215
82D-358
82F-144
82Pol/Brew-9
82T-93
83T-770

Hiss, William
75SnAnt
77Watlo

Hitchcock, Billy
51B-191
52B-89
52T-182
53Glen
53T-17
60T-461C
62T-121
63T-213MG
67T-199MG

Hithe, Victor
87Ashvl-19
88Osceola/Star-14
89Hagers/Best-5
89Hagers/Pro-272
89Hagers/Star-11

Hitt, Danny
89Savan/Pro-369

Hitta, Chief Powa
78Richm

Hittle, Floyd
(Red)
48Smith-21
53Mother-42

Hivizda, Jim
88Butte-2

Hixon, Alan
86Miami-11

Hoag, Myril
34G-95
39PB-109
40PB-52
R312/M
R313
R314

Hoak, Don
52Park-57
53Exh/Can-33
53T-176
54T-211
55B-21
55Gol/Dodg-13
55T-40
55T/DH-26
56T-335
57Kahn
57T-274
58Kahn
58T-160
59Kahn
59T-25
60Kahn
60T-373
61Kahn
61P-130
61T-230
61T/St-65
62Exh
62J-171
62Kahn
62P-171
62P/Can-171
62Salada-107
62Shirriff-107
62Sugar-C
62T-95
62T/bucks
62T/St-178
63Exh
63J-140
63P-140
63T-305
64T-254
79TCMA-273
Exh47

Hoban, John
81Watlo-9
82Beloi-7

Hobaugh, Brian
83Wisco/LF-17
84Visal-12

Hobaugh, Ed
60T-131
61T-129
62T-79
63T-423

Hobbie, Glen
58T-467
59T-334
60Bz-32
60L-20
60T-182
60T/tatt
60T/tatt-22
61P-197
61T-264
61T-393M
62Salada-145
62Shirriff-145
62T-585
62T/St-108
63F-31
63T-212
64T-578

Hobbs, Jack
82Orlan/B-5
82OrlTw/A-17
83Orlan-16

Hobbs, Jon
88Fresno/Cal-4
88Fresno/Pro-1237

Hobbs, Rodney
80LynnS-3
81LynnS-22
82WHave-22
84Albany-4
86Nashv-13

Hoblitzell, Richard
10Domino-55
11Helmar-116
12Sweet/Pin-102
14CJ-55
15CJ-55
D328-77
D329-83
D350/2-82

E135-77
E270/2
M101/4-83
M101/5-82
M116
PM1-6
S74-77
T202
T204
T206
T213/blue
T215/blue
T215/brown
T3-97
WG5-19
WG6-18

Hobson, Butch
77T-89
78Ho-1
78OPC-187
78PapaG/Disc-4
78T-155
79Ho-129
79OPC-136
79T-270
80OPC-216
80T-420
81D-542
81F-227
81OPC-7
81T-595
81T/HT
81T/St-54
81T/Tr-771
82D-577
82F-465
82F/St-213
82OPC-357
82T-357
82T/St-164
83Colum-21
83T-652
84Colum-16
84Colum/Pol-12
85Colum-17
85Colum/Pol-13
87Columbia-10
88Clmbia/GS-1
89NewBrit/Pro-617
89NewBrit/Star-23

Hockenbury, Bill
52Park-81

Hocking, David
89Everett/Star-14

Hocutt, Mike
86Indianap-22
88Louvl-22

Hodapp, Urban J.
(Johnny)
33DH-22
88Conlon/AmAS-16
R316

Hodde, Rodney
82BurlR-2

Hoderlein, Mel
53Briggs
54B-120

Hodge, Clarence
E120
E121/120
W501-42
W573

Hodge, Eddie
80OrlTw-5
82Orlan-24
83Toled-4
84F/X-52
85F-280
85T-639
85Toled-8

Hodge, Gomer
81Watlo-1
82Watlo/B-26MG
82Watlo/C-2MG
83Watlo/LF-28
86Beloi-11MG
87Beloi-18
88Beloi/GS-1
89Jaxvl/Best-20

Hodge, Kevin
88BuffB/Pro-1482

Hodge, Pat
83Durhm-6
84Durhm-4

Hodge, Tim
88StCath/Pro-2016
89Myrtle/Pro-1457

Hodges, Gil
49B-100
49Eureka-38
50B-112
50Drake-11
51B-7
51FB
51T/RB-31
52B-80
52BR
52Coke
52StarCal/L-79A
52T-36
52TipTop
53B/Col-92
53Briggs
53Exh/Can-13
53SM
54B-138
54DanDee
54NYJour
54RM-NL22
54SM
54T-102
54Wilson
55B-158
55Gol/Dodg-12
55RM-NL3
55SM
55T-187
56T-145
56T/Pin-50
56YellBase/Pin-15
57T-400M
57T-80
58BB
58T-162
59HRDerby-7
59Morrell
59T-270
60Bz-23
60Morrell
60NuCard-41
60T-295
61BB-14
61NuCard-441
61P-168
61T-460
62Bz
62J-101
62P-101
62P/Can-101
62Salada-146A
62Salada-146B
62Shirriff-146
62T-85
62T/bucks
62T/St-155
63J-193
63P-193
63T-245
63T-68M
64T-547
65OPC-99
65T-99
66T-386
67T-228
68OPC-27MG
68T-27
69T-564
70OPC-394
70T-394
71OPC-183
71T-183
72OPC-465
72T-465
79TCMA-43
79TCMA-71
80Cram/Leg-63
85CircK-29
85West/2-30
86S/Dec-38M
88Pac/Leg-87
89B-I4
89Rini/Dodg-31
89Smok/Dodg-54
89Swell-33
89T-664TBC
D305
Exh47
PM10/Sm-74A
PM10/Sm-74B
PM10/Sm-75
PM10/Sm-76

Hodges, Ronald W.
(Ron)
74OPC-448
74T-448
75Cedar
75OPC-134
75T-134
75T/M-134
76Cedar
77T-329
78T-653
79T-46
80T-172
81T-537
82F-527
82T-234
83D-476
83F-445
83T-713
84D-603
84F-588
84Nes/792-418
84T-418
85T-363

Hodgin, Elmer Ralph
47TipTop
49B/PCL-3

Hodgson, Gordon
79QuadC-18

Hodgson, Paul
82Knoxv-13
83Knoxv-18

Hodo, Doug
86Cram/PCL-134

Hoeft, Billy
52T-370
53B/BW-18
53Glen
53T-165
54B-167
54Dix
56T-152
57T-60
58T-13
59T-343
60L-90
60T-369
61T-256
62T-134
63T-346
64T-551
65T-471
66T-409
79TCMA-37

Hoeksema, Dave
83Memph-9
85Indianap-23

Hoeme, Steve
88Eugene/Best-2
89AppFx/Pro-852

Hoenstine, Dave
80Cedar-3
81Cedar-12

Hoerner, Joe
64T-544R
66T-544R
67OPC-41
67T-41
68T-227
69T-522
70MLB/St-90
70OPC-511
70T-511
71MLB/St-181
71OPC-166
71T-166
72OPC-482
72T-482
73OPC-653
73T-653
74OPC-493
74T-493
75OPC-629
75T-629
75T/M-629
77T-256

Hofer, John
89AppFx/Pro-878

Hoff, Chester
(Red)
T207

Hoff, Jim
83Tampa-28
88Bill/Pro-1827

Hoff, Michael
86VeroB-11

Hoffinger, Glenn
86Cram/PCL-61

Hoffman, Danny
14CJ-9
15CJ-9
E300
E90/3
E91
E95
M116
T205
T206
T213/brown
W575

Hoffman, Dennis
88Martins/Star-17

Hoffman, Frank J.
N172

Hoffman, Fred
28Exh-35
W753

Hoffman, Glenn
81D-95
81F-237
81OPC-349
81T-349
81T/HT
82Coke/BOS
82D-460
82F-296
82F/St-168
82T-189
83D-282
83F-185
83OPC-108
83T-108
84D-606
84F-399
84Nes/792-523
84OPC-141
84T-523
84T/St-223
85T-633
86D-457
86F-351
86OPC-38
86T-38
87Pawtu-13
87T-374
88Pawtu/CMC-13
88Pawtu/Pro-465
88T-202
90D-407

Hoffman, Guy
80T-664R
82Edmon-6
86F/Up-U51
86Gator-50
86IowaC-16
87F-566
87F/U-U45
87Kahn-30
87T/Tr-48T
88D-452
88F-235
88Score-609
88T-496

Hoffman, Harry C.
T206

Hoffman, Hunter
89Wausa/GS-18

Hoffman, Jeff
88Oneon/Pro-2057

Hoffman, John
88Wausa/Feder-9
88Wausa/GS-9
89SnBer/Cal-77

Hoffman, Rich
89StPet/Star-18

Hoffman, Trevor
89Bill/Pro-2068

Hoffmann, Greg
85IowaC-24

Hoffner, William
N172

Hofman, Arthur
(Solly)
10Domino-56
11Helmar-96
12Sweet/Pin-52
E254
M116
T201
T206
T213/blue
T215/blue
T215/brown
T3-98

Hofman, Robert G.
(Bobby)
49B-223
50Remar
52T-371
53T-182
54NYJour
54T-99
55Gol/Giants-13
55T-17
55T/DH-96
56T-28
56T/Pin-40
78TCMA-59

Hogan, Ben
51BR-A16
52Wheat

Hogan, J. Francis
(Shanty)
28Exh-18
29Exh/4-10
31Exh/4-9
33DH-23
33G-30

34DS-20
34Exh/4-1
34G-20
35Exh/4-1
35G-2E
35G-4E
35G-7E
87Conlon/2-42
R310
R316
V353-30
V354-66

Hogan, Mike
82AubAs-8
83DayBe-8
86Modesto-12
88Phoen/CMC-6
88Phoen/Pro-73

Hogan, Robert
N172

Hogan, William
(Happy)
E270/2
T207

Hogg, David
82Edmon-16

Hogue, Bobby
49Eureka-12
52T-9

Hogue, Cal
53T-238
54T-134

Hohn, Eric
86Erie-13

Holles, Chris
87GlenF-2
88Toled/CMC-19
88Toled/Pro-597
89RochR/Pro-1640

Hoke, Leon
81Miami-17
83SanJose-23

Holbert, Ray
89Watlo/Pro-1791
89Watlo/Star-12

Holbert, William
N172
N172/ST

Holcomb, Scott
87Modesto-24
88Huntsvl/BK-7
89Huntsvl/Best-16

Holcomb, Ted
86Bakers-13
87Bakers-18
88Durhm/Star-7

Holcombe, Ken
49B/PCL-19
51B-267
52T-95

Holden, Gary
81Batav-21

Holder, Brooks
46Remar
47Remar-3
47Signal
47Smith-4
48Signal
48Smith-2
49Sommer

Holdridge, Dave
88QuadC/GS-11
89Clearw/Star-11

Holdsworth, Fred
74OPC-596R
74T-596R
75OPC-323
75T-323
75T/M-323
77T-466
80Vanco-18
81Tacom-21

Holifield, Rick
89StCath/Pro-2096

Holke, Walter
21Exh-75
21Exh-76
25Exh-44
D327
D328-78
E120
E121/120
E121/80
E122
E135-78
V100
W501-91
W575

Hollacher, Charlie
V61-110

Holland, Al
77Shrev
78Colum
79Portl-1
80Pol/Giants-19
81F-445
81T-213
82D-377
82F-391
82T-406
83D-146
83F-262
83T-58
83T/St-306
83T/X-46
84D-204
84F-35
84F/St-68
84FunFood/Pin-87
84Nes/792-138LL
84Nes/792-564
84Nestle/DT-22
84OPC-206
84T-138
84T-564
84T/St-125
84T/St-289
84T/Super-10
84T/Super-10
85D-427
85F-254
85F-637IA
85F/St-107
85F/Up-U55
85Leaf-151
85OPC-185
85T-185
85T/St-113
85T/Tr-55T
86Colum-12
86Colum/Pol-11
86D-573
86F-159
86OPC-369
86T-369
87Colum-26
87Colum/Pol-12
87Colum/TCMA-6

Holland, Bill
78Laugh/Black-21

Holland, Donny
82Wausa-20

Holland, John
81Buffa-2
82Buffa-12

Holland, Mike
74Cedar

Holland, Monty
80Batav-9

Holland, Randy
86Knoxv-11TR
87Knoxv-22
88AAA/Pro-53
88Syrac/CMC-2
88Syrac/Pro-829
89Syrac/CMC-13
89Syrac/Pro-795

Holland, Tim
89Watlo/Pro-1779
89Watlo/Star-13

Holle, Gary
77Holyo
78Holyo

Hollenback, Dave
88Modesto-3tr
88Modesto/Cal-83tr
89Modesto/Cal-290
89Modesto/Ch-3tr

Holley, Bobby
88Eugene/Best-22

Holley, Ed
34G-55
R310

Holley, Kenny
88Wythe/Pro-1994

Holliday, James
N172

Hollifield, David
76QuadC
77QuadC

Hollingsworth, Al
W711/1

Hollins, Dave
87Spoka-8
88CalLgAS-44
88River/Cal-222
88River/Pro-1418
89AubAs/Pro-12
89Wich/Roc-7
89Wich/Roc/HL-11

Hollins, Paul
86Chatt-13

Hollinshed, Joe
86Erie-14

Hollis, Jack
52Mother-62

Hollis, Jack
78Duned

Hollmig, Stan
49Eureka-137

Hollocher, Charles J.
21Exh-77
E120
E121/120
E121/80
E122
E220
V100
W501-57
W514-53
W515-59
W572
W573
W575

Holloway, Crush
78Laugh/Black-24

Holloway, K.
29Exh/4-22

Holloway, Rick
81WHave-13

Hollowell, Chuck
80Batav-12

Holly, Jeff
78OrlTw
79T-371

Holm, Dave
75Clint

Holm, Mike
85Newar-8

Holm, Roscoe
33G-173

Holman, Brian
86Jaxvl/TCMA-23
86SLAS-21
87Jaxvl-24
88F/U-U100
88Indi/CMC-9
88Indi/Pro-504
89B-357
89D-511
89F-379
89T/Tr-51T
89UD-356
90Class-66
90D-143
90F-516
90Score-387
90T-616
90UD-362

Holman, Dale
82Albuq-20
84Syrac-28
85Syrac-5
86Syrac-12
87Richm/TCMA-23

Holman, Gary
69T-361

Holman, Nat
33SK-3

Holman, R. Scott
77Wausa
79Tidew-17
82Tidew-18
83D-224
84F-589
84Nes/792-13
84T-13
84Tidew-1
85IowaC-15

Holman, Shawn
84PrWill-4
85PrWill-16
86Nashua-13
87Harrisbg-1
88EastLAS/Pro-7
88GlenF/Pro-929
89Toled/CMC-5
89Toled/Pro-781
90F-606
90Score-620

Holman, Steve
78Cedar

Holmberg, Dennis
75BurlB
76BurlB
77Newar
78Duned
85Syrac-28
87Duned-7C

Holmes, Bill
89Princet/Star-9

Holmes, Bob
C46-79

Holmes, Carl
86Cram/PCL-158

Holmes, Chris
88Reno/Cal-282

Holmes, Darren
86VeroB-10
87VeroB-5
89SnAnt/Best-4

Holmes, Ducky
C46-60

Holmes, Stan
83Visal/LF-10
85Toled-22
86Orlan-8
87MidldA-17
88Edmon/CMC-14
88Edmon/Pro-571
89Edmon/CMC-11
89Edmon/Pro-555

Holmes, Tim
88Watertn/Puc-6

Holmes, Tommy
39Exh
48L-133
49B-72
49Eureka-13
50B-110
51T/RB-52
52T-289
53Exh/Can-18
D305

Holmes, William
WG2-24

Holmquist, Doug
83Nashvl-8MG
85Colum-25

Holsman, Rich
87Spoka-6
88River/Cal-211
88River/Pro-1427
89AubAs/Pro-20
89Wich/Roc-17
89Wich/Roc/Up-20

Holt, Dave
79Elmir-14
86FSLAS-24MG
86WinHav-10
87NewBrit-18

Holt, Gene
44Centen-11

Holt, Goldie
49Eureka-162

Holt, Jim
71MLB/St-463
71OPC-7
71T-7
72T-588
73OPC-259
73T-259
74OPC-122
74T-122
74T/St-207
75OPC-607
75T-607
75T/M-607
76OPC-603
76SSPC-498
76T-603
76Tucso-37
77T-349

Holt, Mike
78Clint

Holt, Roger
79Colum-18
80Colum-7

Holton, Brian
81Albuq/TCMA-10
82Albuq-5
83Albuq-4
84Cram/PCL-168
85Cram/PCL-164
86Albuq-12
87D-598
87D/Rook-54
87Moth/Dodg-26
87Pol/Dodg-27
87T/Tr-49T
88D-402
88Moth/Dodg-26
88Pol/Dodg-51
88RedFoley/St-35
88Score-208
88T-338
89B-2
89D-439
89D/Tr-20
89F-63
89F/Up-5
89French-37
89Score-507
89Score/Tr-59
89T-368
89T/Tr-52T
89UD-72
90D-635
90F-179
90Score-177

90T-179
90UD-175
Holton, Mark
80Utica-19
Holtz, Ed
76AppFx
84Chatt-6
88Sumter/Pro-420
89Sumter/Pro-1088
Holtz, Fred
75AppFx
76AppFx
Holtz, Gerald
87CharO/WBTV-17
88CharlK-19
88CharlK/Pep-19
88RochR-12
88RochR/Gov-12
89Readg/Star-14
Holtzman, Ken
67OPC-185
67T-185
68Bz-4
68OPC-60
68T-380AS
68T-60
69MB-116
69T-288
70MLB/St-18
70OPC-505
70T-505
71MD
71MLB/St-33
71OPC-410
71T-410
72MB-149
72T-670
73OPC-60
73T-60
74K-31
74OPC-180
74T-180
74T/St-224
75Ho-16
75Ho/Twink-16
75OPC-145
75T-145
75T/M-145
76OPC-115
76SSPC-482
76T-115
77BK/Y-8
77T-625
78T-387
79T-522
80T-298
87Moth/A's-11
89Pac/Leg-138
89Swell-129
Holub, Edward
88Boise/Pro-1612
Holyfield, Vince
85Bend/Cram-11
87Spart-20
88Readg/Pro-883
89Readg/Best-14
89Readg/Pro-661
89Readg/Star-15
Holzemer, Mark
89QuadC/Best-9
89QuadC/GS-21
Homstedt, Vic
78Watlo
Honeycutt, Rick
79T-612
80T-307
81D-46
81OPC-33
81T-33
81T/Tr-772
82D-494
82F-318
82T-751
83D-415
83F-568
83Rang-40
83T-557
84D-494
84F-101
84F/St-66
84Nes/792-137LL
84Nes/792-222
84Nes/792-37TL
84OPC-222
84Pol/Dodg-40
84T-137
84T-222
84T/St-176
84T/St-84
85D-215
85F-372
85Leaf-156
85OPC-174
85T-174
85T/St-78
86D-372
86F-132
86Pol/Dodg-40
86T-439
87Class-93
87D-402
87F-442
87F/Excit-28
87Moth/Dodg-16
87OPC-167
87Pol/Dodg-20
87T-753
87T/St-71
88D-590
88D/A's/Bk-590
88D/Best-211
88F-281
88Moth/A's-23
88Score-87
88T-641
89B-187
89D-328
89D/Best-313
89F-11
89Moth/A's-25
89Score-416
89T-328
89UD-278
89Woolwth-28
90D-386
90F-11
90Score-317
90T-582
90UD-151
Honochick, Jim
55B-267ump
Hood, Dennis
86Sumter-10
87Durhm-27
88Greenv/Best-5
89Greenv/Pro-1169
89Greenv/Star-8
89Greenvl/Best-1
Hood, Don
74OPC-436
74T-436
75OPC-516
75T-516
75T/M-516
76OPC-132
76SSPC-508
76T-132
77T-296
78T-398
79T-667
80T-89
81Omaha-8
82Omaha-5
83D-390
83F-115
83T-443
84F-348
84Nes/792-743
84T-743
Hood, Mike
80Wausa-16
Hood, Scott
82Durhm-3
83Durhm-7
84Durhm-17
Hood, Wally
28Exh/PCL-11
Hoog, James
88CapeCod/Sum-178
Hook, Jay
60Kahn
60T-187
61Kahn
61T-162
62T-94
62T/St-156
63T-469
64T-361
Hook, Mike
88Ashvl/Pro-1073
89FtLaud/Star-9
Hooker, W.E.
(Buck)
T206
Hooks, Alex
R314
Hooper, Ed
W516-27
Hooper, Harry
12Sweet/Pin-4
14CJ-35
15CJ-35
25Exh-75
40PB-226
80SSPC/HOF
87Conlon/2-35
89HOF/St-52
BF2-4
D327
D328-79
D329-84
D350/2-83
E120
E121/120
E121/80
E135-79
E220
E224
E254
E270/1
E91
M101/4-84
M101/5-83
M116
T207
V100
V61-13
W501-47
W514-64
W572
W573
W575
Hooper, Jeff
88Wausa/Feder-16
88Wausa/GS-16
89Wmspt/Pro-639
89Wmspt/Star-10
Hooper, Robert
51B-33
52B-10
52T-340
53T-84
54B-4
55B-271
55Salem
Hooten, Leon
75Tucso-10
76Tucso-16
77OPC-67
77T-478R
Hooton, Burt
72OPC-61R
72T-61R
73OPC-367
73T-367
74OPC-378
74T-378
74T/St-14
75Ho-11
75Ho/Twink-11
75OPC-176
75T-176
75T/M-176
76OPC-280
76SSPC-67
76T-280
77T-284
78K-42
78T-41
79Ho-49
79OPC-370
79T-694
80OPC-96
80Pol/Dodg-46
80T-170
81D-541
81F-113
81F/St-61
81OPC-53
81Pol/Dodg-46
81T-565
81T/HT
81T/St-180
82D-32
82F-8
82F/St-5
82K-15
82OPC-315
82Pol/Dodg
82Pol/Dodg-46
82T-311TL
82T-315
82T/St-53
83D-32
83F-208
83OPC-82
83Pol/Dodg-46
83T-775
84D-459
84F-102
84Nes/792-15
84OPC-15
84Pol/Dodg-46
84T-15
85D-104
85F-373
85F/Up-U56
85OPC-201
85Rang-46
85T-201
85T/Tr-56T
86D-300
86F-563
86OPC-36
86T-454
86T/St-242
87Smok/Dodg-13
88Smok/Dodg-19
89Pac/Leg-219
89Smok/Dodg-95
Hoover, Charles
N172
Hoover, John
85CharO-22
85T-397
87CharO/WBTV-20
88Jaxvl/Best-4
88Jaxvl/Pro-989
Hoover, William
N172
Hope, John
89LittleSun-18
Hopke, Fred
60L-91
Hopkins, Dave
83BurlR-5
83BurlR/LF-23
Hopkins, Don
76Tucso-11
77SnJos-13
Hopkins, Gail
70OPC-483
70T-483
71MLB/St-416
71OPC-269
71T-269
72T-728
73OPC-441
73T-441
74OPC-652
74T-652
Hopkins, Randy
75Shreve/TCMA-5
76Shrev
78Colum
Hopkins, Rick
86WinSal-9
87Pittsf-20
Hopp, John
48L-139
49B-207
49Eureka-163
50B-122
51B-146
52T-214
54T-193
89Pac/Leg-139
Exh47
W754
Hoppe, Willie
33SK-36
Hopper, Brad
88Eugene/Best-9
Hopper, Clay
52Mother-55
53Mother-51
Hopper, Jim
47Centen-10
Hoppert, Dave
88Stock/Pro-740
Horan, Dave
89Salin/Cal-128
89Salin/Pro-1800
Horlen, Joel
62T-479
63T-332
64T-584
65OPC-7LL
65T-480
66T-560
66T/RO-5
67OPC-107
67T-107
67T-233LL
68Bz-11
68Kahn
68OPC-125
68OPC-8LL
68T-125
68T-377AS
68T-8LL
69Kahn
69Kelly/Pin-7
69MB-117
69MLB/St-30
69MLBPA/Pin-9
69T-328
69T/S-12
69T/St-154

70K-23
70MLB/St-185
70OPC-35
70T-35
70T/PI-1
70T/S-20
71OPC-345
71T-345
71T/Coins-120
72MB-150
72T-685
88Clmbia/GS-28CO
89Pac/Leg-217

Horn, Sam
86NewBrit-13
87Pawtu-2
87Pawtu/TCMA-14
87S/Rook-38
88Class/Blue-204
88D-498
88D/RedSox/Bk-498
88F-355
88F/Mini-8
88Leaf-237
88OPC-377
88Score-201
88Score/YS/I-3
88Sf-114
88T-377
88T/Big-252
88T/St-246
88ToysRUs-14

Horn, Walt
82WHave-29
86Tacom-8TR
89Tacom/Pro-1543

Hornacek, Jay
86Bakers-14
87VeroB-20
88Bakers/Cal-245
89SoBend/GS-29

Horne, Jeffrey
82AlexD-5
84Greens-5

Horner, Bob
79Ho-98
79T-586
79T/Comics-18
80OPC-59
80T-108
80T/S-27
81D-99
81Drake-17
81F-244
81F/St-99
81K-61
81MSA/Disc-17
81OPC-355
81Pol/Atl-5
81T-355
81T/SO-61
81T/St-145
81T/St-20
82BK/Lids-11
82D-173
82Drake-18
82F-436
82F/St-69
82K-13
82OPC-145
82Pol/Atl-5
82T-145
82T/St-18
83D-58
83D/AAS-46
83Drake-11
83F-138
83K-54
83OPC-50
83Pol/Atl-5
83T-50
83T/Gloss-12
83T/Gloss40-12
83T/St-214
84D-14
84D-535
84D/AAS-10
84Drake-14
84F-181
84FunFood/Pin-122
84Nes/792-760
84OPC-239
84Pol/Atl-5
84Seven-10W
84T-760
84T/Gloss40-13
84T/St-30
85D-77
85F-328
85Ho/Braves-11
85Leaf-240
85OPC-262
85Pol/Atl-11
85T-276FDP
85T-410
85T/St-24
86D-188
86D/HL-22
86F-517
86F-635M
86F/LL-19
86F/Mini-104
86F/St-60
86Leaf-121
86OPC-220
86Pol/Atl-11
86S-115
86S-66M
86T-220
86T/Gloss60-44
86T/St-34
87Class-38
87D-389
87F-518
87F-632M
87F/Hottest-23
87F/LL-24
87F/St-61
87F/St-S7
87Leaf-136
87OPC-116
87RedFoley/St-21
87S-196M
87S-73
87T-660
87T/Board-23
87T/Mini-1
87T/St-41
88F/Mini-107
88F/U-U120
88Smok/Card-14
88T/Big-245
88T/Tr-50T
89F-452
89OPC-255
89Score-68
89T-510
89T/St-35
89UD-125

Horner, William F.
N172

Hornsby, Dave
84Evrt/Cram-11
86Clint-10

Hornsby, Rogers
21Exh-78
25Exh-61
26Exh-60
27Exh-19
28Exh-2
28Yueng-13
29Exh/4-5
30CEA/Pin-6
31Exh/4-5
32Orbit/un-34
33G-119
33G-188
34DS-44
35BU-35
37OPC-140
48Exh/HOF
50Callahan
61F-43
61GP-7
61T-404M
63Bz/ATG-32
69Bz/Sm
72F/FFeat-2
72K/ATG-2
72K/ATG-2
72Laugh/GF-15
76OPC-342AS
76T-342M
79T-414M
80Cram/Leg-20
80Laugh/3/4/5-17
80Laugh/FFeat-39
80SSPC/HOF
84D/Champs-20
85Woolwth-18
86Conlon/1-44
87Nestle/DT-2
88Conlon/3-14
89Pac/Leg-148
89Swell-20
D327
D328-80
E120
E121/120
E121/80
E122
E135-80
E210-13
E220
R305
R310
R311/Leath
R312
R312/M
R313
R315-A16
R315-B16
R316
R328-11
R332-7
R423-48
V100
V300
V354-1
V61-81
W501-114
W512-9
W514-56
W515-55
W516-7
W517-38
W572
W573
W575

Hornung, Michael
N172
N284
WG1-3

Horowitz, Ed
88CapeCod/Sum-140
89Erie/Star-9

Horsley, Clint
88Savan/Pro-343

Horsman, Vince
87Myrtle-6
88Duned/Star-10
89Duned/Star-8

Horta, Nedar
86Ashvl-13
87Ashvl-15
88Ashvl/Pro-1057
88AubAs/Pro-1965

Horton, David
86Erie-15
87StPet-12

Horton, Ricky
81Louvl-23
82ArkTr-3
82Louvl-11
84F/X-53
84T/X-52
85D-83
85F-227
85Leaf-253
85OPC-321
85T-321
86D-138
86F-38
86Schnucks-9
86T-783
87D-234
87F-297
87OPC-238
87Smok/Cards-5
87T-542
88Coke/WS-11
88D-430
88F-36
88F/U-U17
88OPC-34
88Score-412
88Score/Tr-24T
88T-34
88T/St-48
88T/Tr-51T
89B-338
89D-582
89Moth/Dodg-20
89Pol/Dodg-18
89Score-145
89T-232
89UD-629
90D-666
90T-133

Horton, Tony
68Kahn
69Kahn
69MB-118
69MLB/St-41
69MLBPA/Pin-10
69NTF
70MLB/St-200
71K-69
71MLB/St-376
72MB-151
78TCMA-128

Horton, Willie
64T-512R
65OPC-206
65T-206
66Bz-2
66OPC-20
66T-20
66T-218LL
66T-220LL
66T/RO-62
67T-465
68Bz-8
68Kahn
68T-360
69Citgo-6
69MB-119
69MLB/St-48
69MLBPA/Pin-11
69OPC-180
69OPC-5LL
69OPC/DE-11
69T-180
69T-429AS
69T-5LL
69T/DE-9
69T/decal
69T/S-16
69T/St-173
69Trans-2
70MLB/St-207
70OPC-520
70T-520
71MLB/St-394
71MLB/St-560
71OPC-120
71T-120
71T/Coins-130
72MB-152
72OPC-494KP
72T-494BP
72T-750
73OPC-433
73T-433
74K-23
74OPC-115
74T-115
74T/DE-72
74T/St-176
75Ho-36
75Ho/Twink-36
75OPC-66
75T-66
75T/M-66
76Crane-19
76Ho-26
76Ho/Twink-26
76MSA/Disc
76OPC-320
76SSPC-360
76T-320
77Pepsi-31
77T-660
78T-290
79OPC-252
79T-239
80OPC-277
80T-532
81Portl-12
82Portl-14
88Domino-8

Hoscheidt, John
77DaytB

Hoscheit, Vern
73OPC-179CO
73T-179C

Hosey, Dwayne
89Madis/Star-11

Hosey, Steve
89Everett/Star-15
90Score-666DC

Hoskins, Dave
54T-81
55Salem
55T-133
55T/DH-7

Hoskinson, Keith
86Lakel-7

Hosley, Tim
72OPC-257R
72T-257R
76OPC-482
76SSPC-313
76T-482
77SnJos-10
78T-261
79Ogden/TCMA-2
80Ogden-1
82Tacom-12

Hostetler, Dave
79Memph
83D-89
83F-569
83OPC-339
83Rang-12
83T-584
83T/St-312
84D-159
84F-418
84Nes/792-62

84OPC-62
84T-62
85Indianap-17
85IowaC-23

Hostetler, Tom
87Everett-16
88Clint/Pro-697
88MidwLAS/GS-7
89SanJose/Best-19
89SanJose/Cal-213
89SanJose/Pro-444
89SanJose/Star-15

Hotaling, Pete
E223
N172

Hotchkiss, John
83Tacom-12
84Cram/PCL-93
86MidldA-11
87MidldA-11

Houck, Byron Simon
T222

Hough, Charlie
72OPC-198R
72T-198R
73OPC-610R
73T-610R
74OPC-408
74T-408
75OPC-71
75T-71
75T/M-71
76OPC-174
76SSPC-68
76T-174
77K-47
77T-298
78T-22
79OPC-266
79T-508
80Pol/Dodg-49
80T-644
81T-371
82D-447
82F-319
82T-718
83D-69
83F-570
83OPC-343
83Rang-49
83T-412TL
83T-479
83T/St-125
83T/St-312
84D-638
84F-419
84FunFood/Pin-114
84Nes/792-118
84OPC-118
84Rang-49
84T-118
84T/St-356
85D-422
85F-558
85Leaf-108
85OPC-276
85Rang-49
85SpokAT/Cram-8
85T-571
85T/St-345
86D-342
86F-564
86F/St-61
86Leaf-152
86OPC-275
86Rang-49
86T-275
86T-666M
86T/Mini-33
86T/St-241
87D-470
87D-7DK
87D/AAS-49
87D/DKsuper-7
87D/OD-178
87F-127
87F-641M
87F/Lim-21
87F/Mini-56
87F/St-62
87Leaf-7DK
87Moth/Rang-3
87OPC-70
87RedFoley/St-26
87Smok/AL-12
87Smok/R-1
87T-70
87T/St-240
88D-99
88D/Best-256
88F-469
88F/AwardWin-20
88F/BB/AS-16
88F/BB/MVP-19
88F/Mini-55
88F/St-64
88Leaf-89
88Moth/R-3
88OPC-121
88Panini/St-197
88Score-140
88Sf-87
88Smok/R-13
88T-680
88T/Big-47
88T/Coins-15
88T/Mini-36
88T/Revco-32
88T/St-236
88T/UK-36
89B-224
89D-165
89F-522
89Moth/R-4
89OPC-345
89Panini/St-446
89RedFoley/St-60
89Score-295
89Sf-92
89Smok/R-14
89T-345
89T/St-245
89T/UK-40
89UD-437
90D-411
90F-300
90Score-202
90T-735
90UD-314

Hough, Stan
79Jacks-22
79Tidew-16
83DayBe-2
85Cram/PCL-62
86Osceola-12C
88Tulsa-11CO
89OkCty/CMC-24
89OkCty/Pro-1521

Houk, Ralph
52T-200
60T-465C
61T-133
62T-88
63T-382
67T-468
68OPC-47MG
68T-47
69T-447
70OPC-273MG
70T-273
71OPC-146MG
71T-146
72T-533
73OPC-116MG
73T-116MG
74OPC-578MG
74T-578MG
75OPC-18MG
75T-18MG
75T/M-18MG
76SSPC-352
76T-361MG
77T-621MG
78BK/T-1
78T-684
81T-662MG
82D-282
83T-786
84Nes/792-381MG
84T-381
85T-11MG
89Swell-42

House, Brian
86WinSal-10
87Pittsf-7
88EastLAS/Pro-27
88Pittsf/Pro-1361
89IowaC/CMC-17
89IowaC/Pro-1700

House, Gary
77Newar

House, H. Frank
52T-146
54T-163
55T-87
55T/DH-14
56T-32
56T/Pin-37
57T-223
58T-318
59T-313
60T-372
79TCMA-214

House, Mike
89Elizab/Star-12

House, Thomas R.
69T-331R
72OPC-351R
72T-351R
74OPC-164
74T-164
75OPC-525
75T-525
75T/M-525
76OPC-231
76SSPC-2
76T-231
76T/Tr-231T
77T-358
78T-643
79T-31
82Amari-25C
84Cram/PCL-232C
87Smok/R-20CO
89Smok/R-15CO

Householder, Brian
87CharO/WBTV-21
88CharlK-1
88CharlK/Pep-1
88SLAS-33

Householder, Paul
79Nashvl
80Indianap-15
81D-303
81F-217
81Indianap-4
81T-606R
82Coke/Reds
82D-314
82F-68
82T-351
83D-566
83F-592
83T-34
84F-471
84Nes/792-214
84T-214
84T/St-61
85Pol/Brew-7
86D-414
86F-491
86Pol/Brew-7
86T-554

Houser, Ben
T207

Houser, Brett
78StPet

Houser, Chris
87Erie-24
88Hamil/Pro-1719

Housey, Joe
81QuadC-20
84MidldC-7
86Geneva-12
87Peoria-11
89WinSal/Star-20

Housie, Wayne
87Lakel-1
88GlenF/Pro-913
89London/Pro-1382

Houston, Barry
82Wisco-16

Houston, K.R.
(Ken)
81Evans-21
82Evans-24
83Wausa/LF-1tr
86Osceola-13tr
87Osceola-24

Houston, Kevin
78DaytB
82Buffa-10

Houston, Mel
86WPalm-20
87WPalm-19
88Indi/CMC-23
88Indi/Pro-507
89Jaxvl/Best-3
89Jaxvl/Pro-170

Houston, Pete
88Reno/Cal-289

Houston, Tyler
89Idaho/Pro-2021
89LittleSun-5
90Score-677DC
90T-564

Houtteman, Art
50B-42
51B-45
52T-238
53B/Col-4
53Glen
54B-20
54DanDee
55B-144
55Gol/Ind-12
55Salem
56T-281
57T-385
79TCMA-242

Hovley, Steve
70McDon-2
70MLB/St-273
70OPC-514
70T-514
71MLB/St-515
71OPC-109
71T-109
72T-683
73OPC-282
73T-282

Howard, Bruce
64T-107R
65OPC-41R
65T-41R
66T-281
67OPC-159
67T-159
68T-293
69T-226

Howard, Chris
87PrWill-11
88CLAS/Star-9
88PrWill/Star-12
89FtLaud/Star-10
89Star/Wax-78
89Wausa/GS-27

Howard, Dave
87FtMyr-32
88AppFx/Pro-145
89BBCity/Star-9
89Princet/Star-10

Howard, Dennis
80Utica-20
82Knoxv-4
83Syrac-8
84Syrac-4
85Syrac-9
86Syrac-13

Howard, Doug
77OPC-112
88SLCty-19

Howard, Elston
55B-68
56T-208
57T-82
58T-275
59T-395
60T-65
61P-2
61T-495
61T/St-194
62J-8
62P-8
62P/Can-8
62Salada-95
62Shirriff-95
62T-400
62T-473AS
62T-51LL
62T/bucks
62T/St-86
63J-18
63Kahn
63P-18
63Salada-45
63T-306M
63T-60
64Bz-29
64T-100
64T/Coins-135AS
64T/Coins-23
64T/S-21
64T/St-72
64T/SU
64Wheat/St-21
65Bz-29
65OPC-1LL
65T-1LL
65T-450
65T/trans
66T-405
67OPC-25
67T-25
68OPC-167
68T-167
73OPC-116CO
73T-116C
75OPC-201M
75T-201MV
75T/M-201MV
76SSPC-619
78TCMA-236
79TCMA-271
82KMart-3
86S/Dec-49M
88Pac/Leg-19
Exh47
PM10/L-17
PM10/Sm-77

WG10-10
WG9-12
Howard, Ernest E.
T206
Howard, Frank
60DF-17
60T-132
61Morrell
61T-280
61T/RO-34
61T/St-27
62BB-25
62Bz
62T-175
62T/bucks
62T/St-135
63Exh
63T-123
64T-371
64T/Coins-61
64T/S-24
64T/St-83
64T/SU
64T/tatt
65OPC-40
65T-40
65T/trans-49
66Bz-3
66T-515
66T/RO-33
67Bz-3
67OPC/PI-7
67T-255
67T/PI-7
67T/Test/SU-15
68Bz-7
68OPC-6LL
68T-320
68T-6LL
68T/G-21
68T/Post-3
69Citgo-10
69MB-120
69MLB/St-105
69MLBPA/Pin-12
69OPC-170
69OPC-3LL
69OPC-5LL
69OPC/DE-12
69T-170
69T-3LL
69T-5LL
69T/DE-16
69T/decal
69T/S-30
69T/St-238
69Trans-29
70K-6
70MB-10
70MLB/St-283
70OPC-66LL
70T-550
70T-66LL
70T/PI-22
70T/S-16
70Trans-12
71Bz
71Bz/Test-20
71K-14
71MD
71MLB/St-542
71MLB/St-561
71OPC-620
71OPC-65LL
71T-620
71T-63LL
71T-65LL
71T/Coins-22
71T/GM-48
71T/S-17
71T/tatt-8
71T/tatt-8a
72MB-153
72OPC-350
72T-350
72T/Cloth-17
73OPC-560
73T-560
78TCMA-220
81T-685MG
83MLBPA/Pin-9
83T/X-47
84Nes/792-621MG
84T-621
85CircK-23
85Woolwth-19
86Pol/Brew-33C
88Pac/Leg-17
88Smok/Dodg-3
Exh47
Howard, Fred
77AppFx
78Knoxv
80T-72
Howard, George Elmer
(Del)
E254
T204
T206
T215/brown
WG3-21
Howard, Ivan Chester
D328-81
D329-85
D350/2-84
E135-81
M101/4-85
M101/5-84
Howard, Jim
86Knoxv-12
87Albany-12
Howard, Larry
71OPC-102R
71T-102R
Howard, Mathew
88CapeCod/Sum-120
89GreatF-23
Howard, Mike
75QuadC
79Jacks-14
81Pawtu-2
81Tidew-12
82Tidew-5
83Tidew-18
84Cram/PCL-135
Howard, Ron
88Brist/Pro-1870
89Fay/Pro-1592
Howard, Steve
83Idaho-27
86Modesto-13
88Huntsvl/BK-8
88SLAS-3
89Tacom/CMC-21
89Tacom/Pro-1552
Howard, Thomas
86Cram/PCL-171
87TexLgAS-18
87Wichi-13
88LasVeg/CMC-11
88LasVeg/Pro-239
89LasVeg/CMC-15
89LasVeg/Pro-8
89UD/Ext-726
Howard, Wilbur
74OPC-606R
74T-606R
75OPC-563
75T-563
75T/M-563
76OPC-97
76SSPC-65
76T-97
77T-248
78BK/A-20
78T-534
79Charl-17
79T-642
Howarth, Jim
73OPC-459
73T-459
74OPC-404
74T-404
Howe, Art
76SSPC-585
78BK/A-16
78T-13
79OPC-165
79T-327
80OPC-287
80T-554
81Coke
81D-258
81F-51
81OPC-129
81T-129
81T/HT
81T/SO-99
81T/St-170
82D-92
82F-218
82K-34
82OPC-248
82T-453
82T-66TL
82T/St-43
82T/Tr-48T
83D-396
83F-450
83OPC-372
83T-639
83T/St-236
84F-227
84F/X-54
84Nes/792-679
84T-679
84T/X-53
85F-228
85T-204
87Smok/R-25CO
89Lennox/Ast-25
89Moth/Ast-1MG
89T/Tr-53MG
90T-579MG
Howe, Greg
83Visal/LF-21
85Toled-23
Howe, Steve
81D-511
81F-136
81OPC-159
81Pol/Dodg-57
81T-693
81T/HT
82D-158
82F-9
82OPC-14
82Pol/Dodg
82Pol/Dodg-57
82T-14
83D-630
83F-209
83OPC-170
83Pol/Dodg-57
83T-170
84F-103
84Nes/792-425
84OPC-196
84T-425
86SanJose-10
87Smok/Dodg-14
88D-593
88Score-543
89London/Pro-1357
89Smok/Dodg-98
Howell, David
89Oneon/Pro-2113
Howell, Harry
E107
E90
E92
M116
T204
T206
T213/brown
WG2-25
Howell, Homer
(Dixie)
48Sommer-19
49Eureka-86
51B-252
52B-222
52T-135
53T-255
Howell, Jack
85Cram/PCL-24
86D-524
86Edmon-15
86OPC-127
86T-127
87D-305
87F-83
87OPC-2
87Smok/Cal-16
87T-422
88D-333
88D/Best-59
88F-491
88OPC-114
88Panini/St-44
88Score-124
88Smok/Angels-3
88T-631
88T/Big-121
88T/St-175
89B-48
89D-288
89D/Best-307
89F-480
89OPC-216
89Panini/St-293
89RedFoley/St-61
89Score-261
89T-216
89T/Big-228
89T/St-181
89UD-138
90D-254
90F-135
90Score-206
90T-547
90UD-19
Howell, Jay
79Indianap-24
80Indianap-11
82IowaC-16
82T-51R
83D-587
84F-128
84Nes/792-239
84T-239
85D-103
85D/HL-18
85F-131
85F/Up-U57
85Leaf-244
85Moth/A's-18
85T-559
85T/Tr-57T
86D-223
86D/AAS-57
86F-421
86F/Mini-89
86F/St-62
86Leaf-100
86Moth/A's-18
86OPC-115
86S-192
86T-115
86T/St-175
86T/Super-34
87D-503
87F-395
87F/St-63
87Moth/A's-25
87OPC-391
87RedFoley/St-89
87Smok/A's-6
87T-391
88D-55
88D/AS-11
88F-282
88F/U-U95
88Moth/Dodg-16
88OPC-91
88Pol/Dodg-50
88Score-522
88Score/Tr-35T
88Sf-86
88T-690
88T/St-166
88T/Tr-52T
89B-335
89D-610
89D/Best-36
89F-64
89Moth/Dodg-16
89OPC-212
89Panini/St-22
89Panini/St-98
89Pol/Dodg-26
89Score-378
89Smok/Dodg-89
89T-425
89T/Big-79
89T/St-61
89UD-610
89Woolwth-30
90D-203
90F-400
90Score-227
90Sf-78
90T-40
90UD-508
Howell, Ken
84Cram/PCL-165
85D-592
85F-374
85T/Tr-58T
86D-275
86F-133
86OPC-349
86Pol/Dodg-43
86T-654
86T/St-69
87D-229
87F-443
87Moth/Dodg-19
87OPC-187
87Pol/Dodg-22
87T-477
88D-130
88F-520
88Moth/Dodg-24
88OPC-149
88Pol/Dodg-43
88Score-406
88T-149
89B-394
89D/Best-184
89F/Up-108
89T-93
89T/Tr-54T
90D-430
90F-561
90T-756
90UD-559
Howell, Millard
(Dixie)

56T-149
57T-221
58T-421
Howell, Roy Lee
74Spoka
76OPC-279
76SSPC-265
76T-279
77T-608
78Ho-84
78OPC-31
78T-394
79Ho-137
79K-54
79OPC-45
79T-101
80OPC-254
80T-488
81D-392
81F-417
81OPC-40
81T-581
81T/Tr-773
82D-204
82F-145
82Pol/Brew-13
82T-68
83D-358
83F-36
83Pol/Brew-13
83T-218
84Gard-9
84Nes/792-687
84Pol/Brew-13
85D-577
85T-372
Howerton, Bill
50B-239
51B-229
52B-119
52T-167
53Mother-16
Howerton, Rick
77Watlo
Howerton, Troy
84Newar-3
Howes, Jeff
84LitFalls-12
Howes, John
87BurlEx-22
88WPalm/Star-11
Howes, William
N172
Howey, Todd
87Clearw-26
88Clearw/Star-14
Howie, Mark
85Madis-16
85Madis/Pol-13
86Madis-11
86Madis/Pol-11
88EastLAS/Pro-39
88Wmspt/Pro-1322
89MidldA/GS-19
Howitt, Dann
86Cram/PCL-67
87Modesto-20
88Modesto-27
88Modesto/Cal-67
89Huntsvl/Best-7
90F-644M
Howley, Dan
33G-175
Howser, Dick
61T-416
62Bz-10
62J-94
62P-94
62P/Can-94
62Salada-31
62Shirriff-31
62T-13
62T/bucks
62T/St-53
63F-15
63T-124
64T-478
65Kahn
65OPC-92
65T-92
66T-567
67T-411
68T-467
69MB-121
73OPC-116CO
73T-116C
78TCMA-233
81F-84
83D-590
83T-96
84Nes/792-471MG
84T-471MG
85T-334MG
86NatPhoto-10MG
86T-199MG
87D/AAS-10MG
87D/PopUp-10MG
87T-18MG
87T/Gloss22-12MG
90T-661TBC
Hoy, Pete
89Elmir/Puc-5
Hoy, William
(Dummy)
73F/Wild-8
N172
WG1-65
Hoyer, Brad
88Spoka/Pro-1937
89Watlo/Pro-1794
89Watlo/Star-14
Hoyt, Dave
82Wisco-5
83Sprin/LF-16
Hoyt, LaMarr
78AppFx
81D-160
81T-164
82D-117
82F-345
82F/St-190
82T-428
83D-632
83F-238
83OPC-226
83T-591TL
83T-618
83T-705LL
83T/St-16
83T/St-53
84D-488
84F-63
84FunFood/Pin-91
84Nes/792-135LL
84Nes/792-405AS
84Nes/792-97
84Nestle/DT-9
84OPC-177AS
84OPC-97
84Seven-23C
84T-135
84T-405
84T-97
84T/Gloss40-32
84T/St-11LCS
84T/St-178
84T/St-192
84T/St-240
84T/Super-3
84T/Super-3
84TrueVal/WS-17
85D-86
85D/HL-23
85F-517
85F/Up-U58
85Leaf-37
85Moth/Padres-17
85OPC-312
85T-520
85T/Tr-59T
86D-139
86D/AAS-9
86D/PopUp-9
86F-325
86F/LimEd-25
86F/St-63
86Leaf-61
86OPC-380
86S-193
86S-57M
86T-380
86T/Gloss22-21
86T/St-113
86T/St-154
87D-434
87F-418
87T-275
Hoyt, Waite
28Yueng-30
29Exh/4-25
31Exh/4-24
33G-60
35G-1E
35G-3C
35G-4C
35G-5C
40PB-118
60F-69
61F-44
80SSPC/HOF
86Conlon/1-26
89HOF/St-71
89Smok/Dodg-10
E120
E220
R310
R313
R314
R316
V100
V117-7
V353-60
V355-39
V61-44
W501-32
W502-30
W513-62
W515-8
W572
W573
W575
Hrabcsak, Edward
52Park-87
Hrabosky, Al
71OPC-594R
71T-594R
73OPC-153
73T-153
74OPC-108
74T-108
75OPC-122
75T-122
75T/M-122
76Crane-20
76Ho-50
76Ho/Twink-50
76K-23
76MSA/Disc
76OPC-205LL
76OPC-315
76SSPC-291
76T-205LL
76T-315
77Pep-37
77T-495
78T-230
78Wiffle/Discs-30
79Ho-25
79OPC-19
79T-45
80OPC-306
80T-585
81D-550
81F-262
81OPC-354
81Pol/Atl-39
81T-636
82BK/Lids-12
82D-97
82F-438
82OPC-393
82Pol/Atl-39
82T-393
83D-475
89Pac/Leg-115
Hrbek, Kent
80Wisco
82D-557
82T-766R
82T/Tr-44T
83D-179
83D-19DK
83D/AAS-49
83F-616
83F-633
83K-53
83OPC-251
83T-690
83T-771
83T/Gloss-35
83T/Gloss40-35
83T/St-313
83T/St-88
84D-70
84D/AAS-37
84F-567
84FunFood/Pin-111
84Nes/792-11TL
84Nes/792-345
84OPC-345
84Seven-11C
84T-345
84T/St-305
85D-70
85D/AAS-40
85Drake-16
85F-281
85F/LimEd-13
85Leaf-200
85OPC-308
85Seven-11C
85Seven/Minn-4
85T-510
85T/St-296
85T/Super-41
86D-70
86D/HL-19
86Dorman-6
86F-397
86F/LL-20
86F/Mini-84
86F/Slug-17
86F/St-64
86Leaf-67
86OPC-63
86S-36
86T-430
86T/St-277
86TrueVal-24
87Class-53
87D-73
87D/OD-228
87F-544
87F/Excit-29
87F/McCror-22
87F/Mini-57
87F/St-64
87Kraft-25
87Leaf-99
87OPC-161
87RedFoley/St-49
87S-15
87T-679
87T/Board-28
87T/Coins-13
87T/Gloss60-25
87T/St-281
88Woolwth-30WS6
88Class/Red-192
88D-320
88D/Best-102
88F-13
88F/BB/AS-17
88F/LL-21
88F/Mini-35
88F/SS-17
88F/St-44
88F/TL-14
88F/WS-9
88Jiffy-10
88Leaf-139
88Master/Disc-10
88OPC-45
88Panini/St-136
88Score-43
88Sf-95
88Smok/Minn-3
88T-45
88T/Big-84
88T/Gloss60-8
88T/Mini-22
88T/St-24
88T/St-274
88T/UK-37
89B-157
89Cadaco-30
89Class-55
89D-199
89D/Best-18
89F-116
89KMart/Lead-16
89OPC-265
89Panini/St-387
89RedFoley/St-62
89Score-382
89Score/HotSt-14
89Sf-188
89T-265
89T/Big-209
89T/Coins-42
89T/Gloss60-7
89T/St-287
89T/UK-41
89UD-213
90D-81
90F-378
90Score-381
90Sf-203
90T-125
90UD-452
Hriniak, Walt
69T-611R
70OPC-392
70T-392
Hrovat, Dale
76Watlo
77Holyo
Hrynko, Larry
81Watlo-4
82Charl-6
83Charl-3
Hubbard, Cal
55B-315ump
80SSPC/HOF
89HOF/St-99
Hubbard, Don
78Watlo
Hubbard, Glenn
78Richm
79T-715R

80Richm-15
81D-459
81F-260
81OPC-247
81Pol/Atl-17
81T-247
81T/St-149
82BK/Lids-13
82D-436
82F-437
82Pol/Atl-17
82T-482
82T/St-23
83D-184
83F-139
83OPC-322
83Pol/Atl-17
83T-624
83T/St-215
84D-432
84F-182
84Nes/792-25
84OPC-25
84Pol/Atl-17
84T-25
84T/St-29
85D-199
85F-329
85Ho/Braves-12
85Leaf-242
85OPC-195
85Pol/Atl-17
85T-195
85T/St-33
86D-141
86F-518
86Leaf-71
86OPC-112
86Pol/Atl-17
86T-539
86T/St-36
87D-634
87D/OD-48
87F-519
87OPC-68
87Smok/Atl-21
87T-745
88D-22DK
88D-314
88D/A's/Bk-NEW
88D/DKsuper-22DK
88F-542
88Leaf-22DK
88Moth/A's-18
88OPC-325
88Panini/St-243
88RedFoley/St-36
88Score-111
88Score/Tr-58T
88T-325
88T/Big-200
88T/Tr-53T
89B-199
89D-568
89F-12
89Moth/A's-19
89Score-34
89T-237
89T/Big-232
89UD-395

Hubbard, Trent
86AubAs-12
87Ashvl-2
88Osceola/Star-15
89ColMud/Pro-132
89ColMud/Star-13

Hubbard, Ty III
83Tampa-15

Hubbell, Carl
33G-230
33G-234
33SK-42
33SK-42
34DS-39
34Exh/4-5
34G-12
35BU-5
35Exh/4-5
35Wheat
36Exh/4-5
36Wheat
37Dix
37Exh/4-5
37Wheat-6
38Dix
38Exh/4-5
38ONG/Pin-16
38Wheat
39Exh
39PB-53
40PB-87
41DP-140
41G-20
41G-20
41PB-6
48Exh/HOF
48Swell-8
50Callahan
60F-4
60NuCard-11
61F-45
61GP-6
61NuCard-479
72Laugh/GF-36
74Laugh/ASG-34
80Cram/Leg-89
80SSPC/HOF
83D/HOF-33
84D/Champs-55
85West/2-32
86Conlon/1-15
86S/Dec-6
87Nestle/DT-10
88Conlon/3-15
88Conlon/NatAS-11
89HOF/St-75
PM10/Sm-78A
PM10/Sm-78B
R302
R314
R315-A17
R315-B17
R332-22
V354-71
WG8-35

Hubbell, Wilbert
21Exh-79
25Exh-45
E120
E220
V61-96
W572

Hubbs, Ken
62T-461
63Bz-27
63Exh
63J-174
63P-174
63T-15
63T/SO
64T-550
Exh47

Huber, Clarence
26Exh-45

Hudek, John
89Saraso/Star-11
89Star/Wax-59

Hudgens, Dave
83Tacom-16
84Cram/PCL-74

Hudler, Rex
82Nashv-14
84Colum-8
84Colum/Pol-13
85Colum-18
85Colum/Pol-14
85D-469
86RochR-8
87RochR/TCMA-28
88F/U-U101
88Indi/CMC-10
88Indi/Pro-513
89B-364
89D-452
89F-380
89OPC-346
89Score-470
89T-346
89T/Big-248
89UD-405
90D-366
90Score-287
90T-647
90UD-411

Hudlin, Willis
33G-96
34DS-79
35BU-103
35BU-48
35G-1K
35G-3B
35G-5B
35G-6B
R313
R316
V353-72

Hudson, Charles
83Portl-19
84D-448
84F-36
84Nes/792-432
84T-432
84T/St-17
85CIGNA-16
85D-355
85F-255
85OPC-379
85T-379
85T/St-120
86CIGNA-13
86D-622
86F-444
86Leaf-239
86T-792
87D-630
87F-176
87F/U-U46
87T-191
87T/Tr-50T
88D-374
88D/Y/Bk-374
88F-210
88T-636
88T/Big-212
89D-514
89D/Tr-50
89Mara/Tigers-27
89OPC-236
89Score-415
89T-236
89T/Big-88
89UD-586
90UD-520

Hudson, David
(Hap)
86Louisvl-3tr
87Louvl-29
88Louvl-51
88Louvl/Pro-434
89AAA/Pro-12
89Louvl-38
89Louvl/CMC-5
89Louvl/Pro-1253

Hudson, Jack
76Watlo

Hudson, Jesse James
70OPC-348R
70T-348R

Hudson, Jim
89BBCity/Star-10

Hudson, John
39PB-154
40PB-147

Hudson, Kevin
89Bill/Pro-2039

Hudson, Lance
86Miami-12
88Lakel/Star-14

Hudson, Nathaniel
N172
N172/BC
N370
Scrapps

Hudson, Robert
81Wausa-3
83Chatt-14

Hudson, Sid
41PB-46
48L-84
50B-17
51B-169
51T/RB-44
52B-123
52T-60
53B/BW-29
53T-251
54B-194
54T-93
55B-318

Hudson, Teressa
81ArkTr-23M

Hudson, Tony
80Tulsa-3
81Tulsa-21
82BurlR-3
85Tulsa-20
86Knoxv-13
87Syrac-12

Huebner, John
88GreatF-18
89Bakers/Cal-196

Huey, John
83Madis/LF-26
84MidldC-5

Huff, Brad
88Wythe/Pro-1979

Huff, Matt
88Mia/Star-10

Huff, Mike
87SnAnt-16
88SnAnt/Best-19
88TexLgAS/GS-33
89AAA/Pro-48
89Albuq/CMC-24
89Albuq/Pro-79
90F-649
90Score-597

Huffman, Kris
88Savan/Pro-351
89Sprin/Best-9

Huffman, Phil
80OPC-79
80Syrac-9
80T-142
81OPC-2
81Syrac-5
81T-506
82Omaha-6
85RochR-17
86RochR-9
87RochR-1
87RochR/TCMA-6

Hufford, Scott
87Spart-26
88Lakel/Star-15

Huffstickler, Danny
79Elmir-4

Hufft, Fuzzy
28Exh/PCL-12

Huggins, Miller
10Domino-57
11Helmar-171
12Sweet/Pin-149A
12Sweet/Pin-149B
14CJ-75
14Piedmont/St-28
15CJ-75
61F-46
80SSPC/HOF
86Conlon/1-16
BF2-93
D329-86
D350/2-85
E121/120
E121/80
E270/2
E300
M101/4-86
M101/5-85
M116
S74-120
T201
T202
T204
T205
T206
T207
T213/blue
T213/brown
T215/blue
T215/brown
T222
V100
W514-34
W515-36
W575
WG3-22
WG5-20
WG6-19

Hughes, Butch
82Readg-3
83Phoen/BHN-18
86Modesto-14
87Modesto-9

Hughes, Gregory
80Water-22
81Tulsa-23

Hughes, Jim
52Park-56
53T-216
54NYJour
54T-169
55B-156
55Gol/Dodg-14
55T-51
55T/DH-20
79TCMA-268

Hughes, Jim
76Ho/Twink-53
76OPC-11
76SSPC-211
76T-11
77T-304
78Cr/PCL-62
78T-395

Hughes, John
83Clint/LF-16

Hughes, Keith
85Albany-35
86Albany/TCMA-7
87Colum-21
87Colum/Pol-13
87Colum/TCMA-21
88D-643
88F-305
88RochR-11
88RochR-13
88RochR/CMC-15
88RochR/Gov-13

88RochR/Pro-213
88Score-635
88T-781
89AAA/Pro-23
89RochR/CMC-13
89RochR/Pro-1659
Hughes, Leo
(Doc)
48Sommer-29
49Sommer-23
Hughes, Michael
N172
Hughes, Richard
62Kahn/Atl
62Pep/Tul
67T-384R
68T-253
69OPC-39
69T-39
Hughes, Sammy
78Laugh/Black-15
Hughes, Steve
80Cedar-8
Hughes, Terry W.
73OPC-603R
73T-603R
74OPC-604R
74T-604R
75OPC-612
75T-612
75T/M-612
Hughes, Thomas
11Helmar-71
C46-66
E254
E91
M116
Hughes, Tim
75Cedar
Hughson, Cecil
(Tex)
47TipTop
49B-199
Exh47
Huismann, Mark
81CharR-18
82FtMyr-16
84D-339
85D-583
85F-203
85Omaha-15
85T-644
86NatPhoto-38
87F-586
87Moth/Sea-16
87T-187
88AAA/Pro-42
88Toled/CMC-11
88Toled/Pro-588
89RochR/CMC-10
89RochR/Pro-1650
Hulett, Tim
81GlenF-12
84TrueVal/WS-18
85Coke/WS-32
85D-645
85F/Up-U59
85T/Tr-60T
86Coke/WS-32
86D-404
86F-208
86OPC-87
86T-724
86T/St-295
87Coke/WS-18
87D-260
87D/OD-231
87F-500
87OPC-286
87T-566
87T/St-289
88Indi/CMC-17
88Indi/Pro-522
88T-158
89RochR/CMC-16
89RochR/Pro-1653
Hull, Jeff
85FtMyr-8
86FtMyr-14
88EastLAS/Pro-35
88Vermont/Pro-961
89Calg/CMC-8
89Calg/Pro-526
Hulse, Jeff
88Eugene/Best-14
89AppFx/Pro-866
Hulstrom, Bruce
87Penin-14
Hulswitt, Rudy
E254
E270/1
E270/2
M116
T206
Humber, Frank
89GreatF-21
Hume, Thomas
76Indianap-9
77Indianap-5
78T-701R
79T-301
80T-149
81F-211
81OPC-292
81T-419
81T-8LL
81T/HT
81T/St-166
81T/St-31M
82Coke/Reds
82D-229
82F-69
82OPC-79
82T-763
83D-229
83F-593
83OPC-86
83T-86
84D-550
84F-472
84Nes/792-607
84OPC-186
84T-607
84T/St-59
85D-408
85F-538
85OPC-223
85T-223
86D-365
86F-179
86F/Up-U52
86T-573
86T/Tr-47T
87F-177
87OPC-251
87T-719
88F-236
88Score-494
Hummel, Dean
86Shrev-10
Hummel, John E.
10Domino-58
11Helmar-87
12Sweet/Pin-74
14CJ-50
14Piedmont/St-29
15CJ-50
E254
E270/2
E300
M116
S74-53
T202
T204
T205
T206
T213/blue
T215/blue
T215/brown
Humphrey, Daryl
83Greens-10
Humphrey, Sly
83Idaho-28
Humphrey, Terry
72OPC-489R
72T-489R
73OPC-106
73T-106
76OPC-552
76SSPC-373
76T-552
77T-369
78T-71
79T-503
Humphreys, Mike
88Spoka/Pro-1926
89River/Best-8
89River/Cal-5
89River/Pro-1400
Humphreys, Robert W.
(Bob)
65OPC-154
65T-154
66T-342
67T-478
68T-268
69OPC-84
69T-84
70OPC-538
70T-538
71MLB/St-439
71OPC-236
71T-236
72MB-154
81Syrac-23MG
83Syrac-26
Humphries, Joe
87Myrtle-25
88SnAnt/Best-20
Humphry, Brandt
80ElPas-1
81Holyo-22
Hund, John
75QuadC
Hundhammer, Paul
84Pawtu-10A
84Pawtu-10B
85Pawtu-5
Hundley, Randy
66T-392R
67OPC-106
67T-106
68OPC-136
68T-136
69MB-122
69MLB/St-121
69Sunoco/Pin-4
69T-347
69T/St-14
70Dunkin-3
70K-31
70MLB/St-17
70OPC-265
70T-265
71Bz
71Bz/Test-46
71MD
71MLB/St-34
71OPC-592
71T-592
71T/Coins-51
71T/tatt-3
72MB-155
72OPC-258
72T-258
73OPC-21
73T-21
74OPC-319
74T-319
74T/St-15
74T/Tr-319T
76OPC-351
76SSPC-121
76T-351
77T-502
89Pac/Leg-207
Hundley, Todd
88LitFalls/Puc-6
89Clmbia/Best-1
89Clmbia/GS-11
Hunger, Chris
81Wausa-9
83Chatt-3
Hungler
N172
Hungling, Bernard
E120
Hunnefield, William
26Exh-76
27Exh-38
30CEA/Pin-15
31Exh/4-21
Hunsacker, Frank
77StPet
80ArkTr-15
Hunsinger, Alan
82Sprin-17
83ArkTr-18
Hunt, Ben
75Clint
Hunt, Ken L.
60L-33
60T-522
61T-156
62J-79
62P-79
62P/Can-79
62Salada-76A
62Salada-76B
62Shirriff-76
62T-68
62T/bucks
62T/St-65
63T-207
64Bz-26
64T-294
64T/Coins-89
65Bz-26
Hunt, Ken R.
61T-556
62J-129
62Kahn
62P-129
62P/Can-129
62T-364
Hunt, Randy
82Sprin-20
83ArkTr-11
85Louvl-11
86Indianap-6
86T-218
87D-625
88Memph/Best-15
Hunt, Ronald K.
(Ron)
61T/St-172
63T-558R
64T-235
64T/Coins-164AS
64T/S-6
64T/St-93
64T/SU
65OldLond-12
65T-285
65T/E-35
65T/trans-50
66T-360
67OPC/PI-31
67T-525
67T/PI-31
68Coke
68OPC-15
68T-15
69MB-123
69MLB/St-200
69T-664
69T/St-105
70MLB/St-125
70OPC-276
70T-276
71MLB/St-130
71OPC-161
71T-578
72MB-156
72OPC-110
72T-110
73OPC-149
73T-149
74K-25
74OPC-275
74T-275
74T/St-55
74Weston-33
75OPC-610
75T-610
75T/M-610
78TCMA-212
Hunt, Ronald
81Redwd-15
82Holyo-15
82Redwd-21
Hunt, Tom
80LynnS-16
81Wausa-28
82Wausa-30
83Chatt-23
84Chatt-10
86Chatt-14tr
87Chatt/Bst-26tr
Hunter, Bert
86Ashvl-14
86AubAs-13
87Ashvl-16
88Osceola/Star-16
89ColMud/Pro-148
89ColMud/Star-14
Hunter, Bob
88Oneon/Pro-2056
Hunter, Brian
88MidwLAS/GS-18
89Greenv/Pro-1158
89Greenv/Star-9
89Greenvl/Best-2
89Star/Wax-35
Hunter, George
E254
M116
T206
T213/brown
Hunter, Gordon
(Billy)
53T-166
54B-5
54T-48
55B-69
57T-207
58T-98
59T-11
73OPC-136CO
73T-136C
74OPC-306CO
74T-306C
78T-548
79TCMA-118
Hunter, James
88ElPas/Best-28
Hunter, Jeff
80Elmir-21
Hunter, Jim
(Catfish)

65T-526R
66OPC-36
66T-36
67T-369
67T/Test/SU-23
68Bz-2
68T-385
68T/Post-5
69MB-124
69MLB/St-87
69T-235
69T/St-216
70MLB/St-259
70T-565
71Bz
71Bz/Test-48
71MD
71MLB/St-516
71OPC-45
71T-45
71T/Coins-80
71T/tatt-9
72K-22
72MB-157
72OPC-330
72T-330
73K-20
73OPC-235
73OPC-344KP
73T-235
73T-344BP
73T/Lids-21
74K-44
74OPC-196
74OPC-339AS
74T-339M
74T-7
74T/DE-6
74T/St-225
75Ho-148
75K-44
75OPC-230
75OPC-310LL
75OPC-311LL
75T-230
75T-310LL
75T-311LL
75T/M-230
75T/M-310LL
75T/M-311LL
76Crane-21
76Ho-141
76K-5
76Laugh/Jub-7
76MSA/Disc
76OPC-100
76OPC-200LL
76OPC-202LL
76SSPC-425
76T-100
76T-200LL
76T-202LL
77BK/Y-4
77Ho-79
77OPC-10
77T-280
77T/CS-21
78BK/R-1
78BK/Y-7
78OPC-69
78T-460
78Wiffle/Discs-31
79BK/Y-6
79OPC-352
79T-670
83MLBPA/Pin-10
86S/Dec-63M
87D/HL-19
87Moth/A's-6
88Pac/Leg-16
88T/Gloss22-11
89ElPas/GS-9
89HOF/St-82
89Pac/Leg-193
89Swell-10

Hunter, Jim
86BurlEx-9
87Stockton-19

Hunter, Marion
81Redwd-16

Huntz, Steve
69OPC-136R
69T-136R
70OPC-282
70T-282
71MLB/St-252
71OPC-486
71T-486
72OPC-73
72T-73
76SSPC-126

Hunziker, Kent
76Clint
77AppFx

Huppert, David B.
81RochR-9
83RochR-11
84Cram/PCL-37
86ElPas-13
88CalLgAS-19
88Stock/Cal-202
89Stock/Best-29
89Stock/Cal-176MG
89Stock/Pro-386
89Stock/Star-22

Hurd, Thomas
55T-116
55T/DH-120
56T-256

Hurdle, Clint
76Watlo
78T-705R
79T-547
80OPC-273
80T-525
81D-224
81F-45
81OPC-98
81Pol/Royals-4
81T-98
81T/St-85
82Coke/Reds
82D-516
82F-411
82T-297
83Tidew-4
84Tidew-28
86D-434
86Schnucks-10
86T-438
87F-298
87OPC-317
87T-317
87Tidew-1
87Tidew/TCMA-22
89StLucie/Star-6
89Tidew/CANDL-12

Hurdle, Mike
80Utica-29

Hurley, Battling
T3/Box-71

Hurley, Edwin
55B-260ump

Hurni, Rick
88SLCty-12

Hursey, Darren
87Fayette-13
88Lakel/Star-16
89London/Pro-1370

Hurst, Bruce
81Pawtu-3
81T-689R
82F-297
82T-381
83D-134
83F-186
83T-82
84D-213
84F-400
84Nes/792-213
84OPC-213
84T-213
84T/St-226
85D-493
85F-161
85Leaf-73
85OPC-134
85T-451
85T/St-211
86D-517
86D/HL-47
86F-352
86OPC-193
86T-581
86T/Mini-6
87Class-83
87D-174
87F-37
87F/Lim-22
87F/St-65
87F/WS-1
87Leaf-253
87OPC-31
87S-38
87T-705
87T/HL-19
87T/HL-28
87T/Mini-43
87T/St-19WS
87Woolwth-19
87Woolwth-28
88D-252
88D/AS-14
88D/Best-233
88D/RedSox/Bk-252
88F-356
88F/BB/AS-18
88F/St-10
88Leaf-179
88OPC-125
88Panini/St-22
88RedFoley/St-37
88Score-380
88Sf-197
88T-125
88T/St-253
88T/St/Backs-62
89B-451
89Class/Up/2-194
89D-423
89D/Best-77
89D/Tr-45
89F-91
89F/Up-124
89Panini/St-271
89Score-325
89Score/HotSt-79
89Score/Tr-19
89Sf-175
89T-675
89T/Gloss60-28
89T/Mini-49
89T/St/Backs-29
89T/Tr-55T
89T/UK-42
89UD-387
89UD/Ext-792
90Class-102
90D-183
90F-159
90Score-270
90Score/100St-18
90Sf-47
90T-315
90UD-433

Hurst, Charles
89Martins/Star-15

Hurst, Frank O.
(Don)
29Exh/4-11
31Exh/4-12
33Exh/4-6
34Exh/4-6
34G-33
R316
V354-80

Hurst, Jody
88CapeCod/Sum-110
89NiagFls/Puc-12

Hurst, Jonathan
88CharlR/Star-10

Hurt, Mike
89Readg/Best-26

Hurta, Bob
88Spart/Pro-1026
88Spart/Star-24
88Spart/Star-8

Hurtado, Jose
85Bend/Cram-12

Husband, Perry
85Visal-3

Huseby, Ken
87Tampa-4
88Greens/Pro-1564
89Aug/Pro-503

Huson, Jeff
86BurlEx-10
87WPalm-23
88Jaxvl/Best-18
88Jaxvl/Pro-966
88SLAS-18
89AAA/Pro-11
89Indi/CMC-18
89Indi/Pro-1233
89Score/HotRk-69
90D-693
90F-350
90Score-615
90Score/100Ris-14
90Sf-176
90T-72
90UD-434

Hutcheson, Todd
83Miami-28
84Beaum-23
85Beaum-23
86LasVegas-7
87LasVegas-13
88LasVeg/Pro-226
89LasVeg/Pro-28

Hutchings, John R.
W711/2

Hutchingson, Chris
86Osceola-14

Hutchins, Lance
88SanJose/Cal-144
88SanJose/Pro-124

Hutchinson, Don
88CapeCod/Sum-68

Hutchinson, Fred
47TipTop
48L-163
49B-196
50B-151
51B-141
52B-3
52StarCal/L-72E
52T-126
53B/Col-132
53NB
53T-72
60T-219
61T-135
62T-172
63FrBauer-9
63T-422
64T-207
79TCMA-138
80Cram/Leg-25
Exh47
R303/A

Hutchinson, Ira
39PB-142
W754

Hutchinson, Ray
(Harpo)
76Dubuq

Hutchinson, Sean
89Pulas/Pro-1909

Hutchinson, William
N172

Huth, Ken
84Savan-7

Hutson, Scott
89StCath/Pro-2074

Hutto, Jim
75IntAS/TCMA-11
75IntAS/TCMA-17
76SSPC-385
84Newar-23
84RochR-4

Hutton, Mark
89Oneon/Pro-2118

Hutton, Tom
67T-428R
69T-266R
72T-741R
73OPC-271
73T-271
74OPC-443
74T-443
75OPC-477
75T-477
75T/M-477
76OPC-91
76SSPC-472
76T-91
77T-264
78Ho-103
78T-568
79OPC-355
79T-673
80OPC-219
80T-427
81D-93
81F-164
81OPC-374
81T-374
85SpokAT/Cram-9

Huyke, Woody
78Charl

Huyler, Mike
88Watertn/Puc-19
89Aug/Pro-509

Hvizda, Jim
89Gasto/Pro-1019
89Gasto/Star-9

Hyatt, Robert Ham
D322
E104
E286
E90/2
M116
T207

Hyde, Dick
57T-403
58T-156
59T-498
60T-193

Hyde, Mickey
89Batav/Pro-1931

Hyman, Don
81QuadC-2
83MidldC-17
84MidldC-3

Hyman, Pat
89Clmbia/Best-24

Hypes, Kyle
75Lafay

76Phoen
77Phoen
78Cr/PCL-22
79Phoen
Hyson, Cole
89AubAs/Pro-2170
Iadarola, George
80WHave-18
Iannini, Steve
87Modesto-15
Iasparro, Donnie
86Visal-11
Iaverone, Greg
87Peoria-9
Ibarguen, Ricky
89Brist/Star-12
Ibarguen, Steve
82Jacks-5
Ibarra, Carlos
82Edmon-1
Ibarra, Luis
85Tigres-28
Ickes, Mike
87WinHav-25
Iglesias, Luis
87Spart-18
88Clearw/Star-15
Ignasiak, Mike
89Stock/Best-3
89Stock/Cal-157
89Stock/Pro-400
89Stock/Star-5
Ilsley, Blaise
86Ashvl-15
87ColAst/Pro-8
87ColumAst-8
88ColAst/Best-17
89Osceola/Star-8
Imes, Rod
87Oneon-25
88FtLaud/Star-12
89Albany/Best-21
89Albany/Pro-314
89Albany/Star-8
Impagliazzo, Joe
86Albany/TCMA-27
Inagaki, Shuji
87Miami-13
88Mia/Star-12
Incaviglia, Pete
86D/Rook-23
86F/Up-U53
86Rang-29
86S/Rook-3
86T/Tr-48T
87Class-16
87Class/Up-131
87D-224
87D/OD-175
87F-128
87F-625M
87F/Hottest-24
87F/LL-25
87F/Mini-58
87F/Slug-21
87F/St-66
87Kraft-39
87Leaf-185
87Moth/Rang-2
87OPC-384
87RedFoley/St-130
87S-37
87Smok/R-15
87T-550
87T/Coins-14
87T/Gloss60-29
87T/GlossRk-6
87T/St-236
87T/St-308
87ToysRUs-12
88Class/Red-177
88D-304
88D/Best-55
88F-470
88F/Mini-56
88F/Slug-20
88F/SS-C1
88F/St-65
88Leaf-147
88Moth/R-2
88Nestle-20
88OPC-280
88Panini/St-207
88Score-485
88Score/YS/I-32
88Sf-169
88Smok/R-4
88T-280
88T/Big-73
88T/St-239
89B-238
89D-3DK
89D-56
89D/Best-144
89D/DKsuper-3DK
89F-523
89F/LL-21
89KingB/Discs-24
89Moth/R-10
89OPC-42
89Panini/St-455
89RedFoley/St-63
89Score-201
89Sf-112
89Smok/R-16
89T-706
89T/Big-127
89T/St-249
89UD-484
90D-48
90F-301
90Score-93
90T-430
90UD-333
Incavigua, Tony
81Buffa-20
Infante, Alexis
85Syrac-14
86Syrac-14
87Syrac-8
87Syrac/TCMA-15
88Syrac/CMC-21
88Syrac/Pro-813
89D/Rook-30
Infante, Kennedy
(Ken)
86StPet-14
87ArkTr-5
88ArkTr/GS-11
89Cedar/Best-15
89Cedar/Star-28
Infante, Tom
89Hamil/Star-19
Ingle, Mike
86Kinston-10
Ingle, Randy
83Ander-4
84Durhm-29
87Greenvl/Best-4
89Greenv/Pro-1177
89Greenvl/Best-21
Ingram, Gerald
88Eugene/Best-26
Ingram, Jeff
89Utica/Puc-11
Ingram, Linty
89Fay/Pro-1572
Ingram, Riccardo
89Lakel/Star-10
Innis, Brian
83VeroB-5
Innis, Jeff
84Jacks-6
85Lynch-4
86Jacks/TCMA-6
87Tidew-8
87Tidew/TCMA-5
88D/Mets/Bk-NEW
88F/U-U105
88T/Tr-54T
88Tidew/CANDL-21
88Tidew/CMC-3
88Tidew/Pro-1582
89Tidew/CMC-3
89Tidew/Pro-1950
90D-408
90F-206
90T-557
90UD-562
Intorcia, Trent
87Wausa-21
88Mia/Star-13
Iorg, Dane
76OkCty
80T-139
81D-311
81F-543
81T-334
82D-166
82F-116
82T-86
83D-469
83F-10
83T-788
83T/St-189
83T/St-190
84D-571
84F-326
84F/X-55
84Nes/792-416
84T-416
84T/X-54
85D-252
85F-204
85T-671
86F-9
86F/Up-U54
86Kitty/Disc-9
86S-186M
86T-269
86T/St-18WS
86T/Tr-49T
87OPC-151
87T-690
Iorg, Garth
75FtLaud
78T-704R
79Syrac-12
80Syrac-1
81F-423
81OPC-78
81OPC/Post-16
81T-444
82D-353
82F-616
82OPC-83
82T-518
83D-306
83F-430
83OPC-326
83T-326
84D-561
84F-157
84Nes/792-39
84OPC-39
84T-39
84Tor/Fire-17
85D-363
85F-107
85OPC-168
85T-168
85Tor/Fire-15
86Ault-16
86D-640
86F-61
86Leaf-252
86OPC-277
86T-694
86Tor/Fire-18
87D-394
87F-229
87OPC-59
87T-751
87Tor/Fire-14
87Tor/Fire-14
88D-444
88F-113
88OPC-273
88Panini/St-220
88Score-204
88T-273
Ireland, Billy
83Miami-13
Ireland, Tim
77Jaxvl
81Omaha-18
81T-66R
89Salin/Cal-146MG
89Salin/Pro-1822
Irvin, Kyle
88Eugene/Best-7
Irvin, Monte
51B-198
51T/RB-50
52B-162
52BR
52Dix
52RM-NL9
52StarCal/L-78F
52T-26
53B/Col-51
53Briggs
53Dix
53Exh/Can-6
53NB
53SM
53T-62
54DanDee
54Dix
54NYJour
54RM-NL5
54SM
54T-3
55Gol/Giants-14
55SM
55T-100
55T/DH-3
56T-194
79TCMA-168
80SSPC/HOF
83D/HOF-15
88Pac/Leg-79
89HOF/St-32
Exh47
PM10/Sm-79
PM10/Sm-80
PM10/Sm-81
Irvine, Daryl
85Greens-17
86WinHav-11
87NewBrit-14
88NewBrit/Pro-890
89NewBrit/Pro-611
89NewBrit/Star-7
Irvine, Ed
81ElPas-1
82Vanco-8
84Cram/PCL-44
Irwin, Arthur
N172
N284
N690
WG1-52
WG1-66
Irwin, Charles
E90/1
Irwin, Dennis
78Cr/PCL-9
Irwin, John
N172
Isa, Kelsey
87Penin-21
Isaac, Joe Keith
78Wisco
Isaac, Luis
76Wmspt
81Batav-28
88Gator-7CO
Isaacson, Christopher
88Kinston/Star-11
Isales, Orlando
79OkCty
80OkCty
81OkCty/TCMA-8
82Indianap-10
83Indianap-18
Isbell, Frank
WG2-26
Isbell, William
E107
E90/1
T206
Ishmael, Michael
(Mike)
87BurlEx-19
87Jamestn-3
Issac, Richard
86AppFx-11
Ithier, Pete
76Wmspt
78SnJos-10
Iverson, Tom
89Greens/Pro-430
Ivie, Lonnie
81Miami-15
Ivie, Mike
72OPC-457R
72T-457R
73OPC-613R
73T-613R
76Ho-103
76OPC-134
76SSPC-127
76T-134
77OPC-241
77T-325
78T-445
79Pol/Giants-15
79T-538
80OPC-34
80Pol/Giants-15
80T-62
81D-312
81F-435
81OPC-236
81T-236
81T/Tr-744
82D-396
82T-734
82T/Tr-45T
83D-485
83F-331
83OPC-117
83T-613
Jabalera, Francisco
83ColumAst-12
Jablonowski, Pete
33G-83
V354-34
Jablonski, Ray
53Hunter
53T-189
54Hunter
54T-26
54Wilson
55RM-NL21
55T-56
55T/DH-51
56Kahn
56T-86

57Kahn
57T-218
58Hires-35
58SFCall
58T-362
59T-342
61Union-H1

Jacas, Andre
86Madis-12
86Madis/Pol-12

Jacas, Dave
87Kenosha-12
88Keno/Pro-1389
89Visal/Cal-109
89Visal/Pro-1447

Jaccar, Mike
77Ashev

Jack, Stanley
41DP-97

Jacklitsch, Fred
C46-62
D303
E101
E104
E105
E106
E107
E92
M116
T205
T206
T216

Jackowski, Bill
55B-284ump

Jackson, Alvin
62T-464
63Bz-19
63F-48
63T-111
63T/SO
64T-494
64T/Coins-17
64T/St-85
64T/SU
64T/tatt
65T-381
65T/trans-17
66T-206
67OPC-195
67T-195
68T-503
69MB-125
69T-649
70OPC-443
70T-443
83Tidew-24C
84Tidew-22
88LitFalls/Puc-27
89French-31

Jackson, Bo
86D/HL-43
86D/Rook-38
86S/Rook-40
86SLAS-13
86T/Tr-50T
87Class-15
87Class/Up-109
87D-35RR
87D/OD-205
87D/Rook-14
87F-369
87F/Slug-M4
87F/St-132M
87Leaf-35RR
87S-190
87T-170
87ToysRUs-13
88Class/Blue-208
88D-220
88D/Best-119
88F-260
88Leaf-187
88OPC-8
88Panini/St-110
88RedFoley/St-38
88Score-180
88Sf-148
88Smok/Royals-5
88T-750
88T/Big-49
88T/St-258
89Ames-17
89B-126
89Class-122
89Class/Up/2-157
89D-208
89D/Best-169
89F-285
89KingB/Discs-11
89OPC-84
89Panini/St-358
89RedFoley/St-64
89Score-330
89Score/Mast-1
89Score/YS/I-5
89Sf-70
89T-540
89T-789TL
89T/Big-238
89T/HeadsUp-8
89T/St-265
89T/UK-43
89Tastee/Discs-6
89UD-221
90Class-2
90Class-59
90D-1DK
90D-61
90D-650AS
90D/Bon/MVP-BC1
90D/Preview-1
90F-110
90F-635M
90F-635M
90F/WaxBox-C15
90Score-280
90Score-566AS
90Score-687DT
90Score-697M
90Score/100St-40
90Sf-200
90T-300
90UD-105
90UD-32TC
90UD-75M

Jackson, Bubba
88Tulsa-17

Jackson, Chuck
85Cram/PCL-67
86Tucso-8
87D/Rook-55
87F/U-U47
88Moth/Ast-25
88Pol/Ast-14
88Score-222
88T-94
89Score-584
89Tucso/CMC-20
89Tucso/Pro-205
89UD-323

Jackson, Danny
82CharR-6
83Omaha-6
84D-461
85D-374
85F-205
86D-95
86F-10
86Kitty/Disc-16
86Leaf-30
86NatPhoto-25
86S-186M
87D-157
87D/OD-203
87F-370
87T/Tr-51T
88D-132
88D/Best-166
88F-261
88F/Slug-21
88F/U-U84
88Kahn/Reds-20
88OPC-324
88Score-398
88Score/Tr-2T
88T-324
88T/Tr-55T
89B-304
89Cadaco-31
89Class-123
89D-124
89D/AS-52
89D/Best-54
89F-163
89F-636M
89F/BBAS-22
89F/BBMVP's-21
89F/Excit-25
89F/Heroes-24
89F/LL-22
89F/WaxBox-C15
89K/Reds-20
89KingB/Discs-23
89OPC-319
89Panini/St-225
89Panini/St-67
89Richm/Ko-CO
89Score-555
89Score/HotSt-75
89Score/YS/II-41
89Sf-80
89T-395AS
89T-730
89T/DH-22
89T/Gloss60-57
89T/Hills-18
89T/Mini-10
89T/St-143
89T/St/Backs-62
89UD-640
90D-80
90F-422
90Score-289
90Sf-89
90T-445
90UD-120

Jackson, Darrell
78OrlTw
79T-246
79Toled-18
80T-386
81D-547
81F-567
81OPC-89
81T-89
82D-179
82F-555
82T-193

Jackson, Darrin
82QuadC-22
84MidldC-16
86Pittsf-10
87IowaC-25
88Berg/Cubs-30
88D/Cubs/Bk-NEW
88D/Rook-45
88F-641
88F/U-U78
88Score/Tr-109T
88T/Tr-56T
89F-428
89Score-360
89T-286
89T/JumboR-12
89ToysRUs-14
89UD-214
90D-641
90F-160
90Score-541
90T-624
90UD-414

Jackson, Doug
78DaytB

Jackson, Gayron
86AubAs-14

Jackson, Grant
66T-591R
67T-402R
68T-512
69OPC-174
69T-174
70MLB/St-91
70OPC-6
70T-6
71Bz
71MLB/St-300
71OPC-392
71T-392
72MB-158
72OPC-212
72T-212
73JP
73OPC-396
73T-396
74OPC-68
74T-68
74T/St-126
75OPC-303
75T-303
75T/M-303
76OPC-233
76SSPC-378
76T-233
77T-49
78T-661
79T-117
80OPC-218
80T-426
81D-15
81F-378
81OPC-232
81T-519
82D-518
82F-191
82OPC-104
82T-779
82T/Tr-46T
88EastLAS/Pro-48
89CharlK-2

Jackson, Greg
86Cram/PCL-85
87QuadC-30

Jackson, James B.
T206

Jackson, Jason
88NewBrit/Pro-912

Jackson, Jeff
89Martins/Star-16
90Score-678DC
90T-74

Jackson, Joe
(Shoeless)
14CJ-103
15CJ-103
40PB-225
80Cram/Leg-107
80Laugh/3/4/5-13
80Laugh/FFeat-24
88Pac/8Men-110
88Pac/8Men-13
88Pac/8Men-31
88Pac/8Men-32
88Pac/8Men-36
88Pac/8Men-37
88Pac/8Men-55M
88Pac/8Men-62
88Pac/8Men-69
88Pac/8Men-77
89Pac/Leg-220
D327
D328-82
D329-87
D350/2-86
E135-82
E224
E90/1
M101/4-87
M101/5-86
W514-15

Jackson, Joe
76Clint

Jackson, Ken
86Readg-10
87Maine-7
87Maine/TCMA-11
88Maine/Pro-287
89ScrWB/CMC-17
89ScrWB/Pro-729

Jackson, Kenny
86Cram/PCL-37
87AppFx-28
88BBCity/Star-14
88Maine/CMC-17

Jackson, Larry
81Cedar-1

Jackson, LaVerne
85Greens-26
86WinHav-12
87WinHav-8
89NewBrit/Pro-615
89NewBrit/Star-2

Jackson, Lawrence C.
(Larry)
55Hunters-1
56T-119
57T-196
58T-97
59T-399
60L-15
60T-492
61P-174
61T-535
61T-75M
61T/St-88
62J-165
62P-165
62P/Can-165
62T-306M
62T-83
62T/bucks
62T/St-184
63T-95
64T-444
64T/Coins-114
64T/St-13
64T/tatt
64Wheat/St-22
65Bz-2
65OPC-10LL
65T-10LL
65T-420
66T-595
67T-229
68OPC-81
68T-81
69MB-126
78TCMA-222
78TCMA-286

Jackson, Lloyd
86Clint-11

Jackson, Lou
59T-130
61BeeHive-9
64T-511
78TCMA-115

Jackson, Mark
86Cedar/TCMA-20
87Tampa-18

Jackson, Michael
86Readg-11

87D/Rook-36
87F/U-U48
87S/Rook-33
88D-139
88F-306
88F/U-U60
88Moth/Sea-19
88RedFoley/St-39
88Score-144
88Score/Tr-62T
88T-651
89B-207
89D-652
89F-550
89F/BBMVP's-22
89Moth/Sea-19
89OPC-169
89Score-398
89Score/YS/I-14
89T-169
89UD-142
90F-517
90Score-546
90T-761
90UD-494

Jackson, Mikki

83Madis/LF-20

Jackson, Randy

52B-175
52StarCal/L-80C
52T-322
53B/BW-12
54B-189
55B-87
56T-223
57T-190
58T-301
59T-394

Jackson, Reginald M.

(Reggie)
69MB-127
69T-260
69T/decal
69T/S-28
70K-32
70MB-11
70MLB/St-260
70OPC-140
70OPC-459AS
70OPC-64LL
70OPC-66LL
70T-140
70T-459AS
70T-64LL
70T-66LL
70T/CB
70T/S-28
70Trans-11
71Bz/Test-18
71MLB/St-517
71MLB/St-562
71OPC-20
71T-20
71T/Coins-108
71T/GM-47
71T/S-38
71T/tatt-3
72K-20
72MB-159
72OPC-435
72OPC-436IA
72OPC-90LL
72T-435
72T-436A
72T-90LL
73K-22
73OPC-255
73T-255
73T/Comics-8
73T/Lids-22
73T/PinUps-8
74K-20
74Laugh/ASG-71
74OPC-130
74OPC-202LL
74OPC-203LL
74OPC-338AS
74OPC-470ALCS
74OPC-477WS
74T-130
74T-202LL
74T-203LL
74T-338AS
74T-470ALCS
74T-477WS
74T/DE-61
74T/Puzzles-6
74T/St-226
75Ho-88
75K-54
75OPC-211M
75OPC-300
75OPC-461WS
75T-211MV
75T-300
75T-461WS
75T/M-211MV
75T/M-300
75T/M-461WS
76Crane-22
76Ho-146
76K-8
76MSA/Disc
76OPC-194LL
76OPC-500
76SSPC-494
76T-194LL
76T-500
77BK/Y-17
77Ho-3
77OPC-200
77Pep-34
77T-10
77T/CS-22
78BK/Y-21
78Ho-47
78OPC-110
78OPC-242RB
78PapaG/Disc-26
78T-200
78T-7M
78T-413WS
78Wiffle/Discs-32
79BK/Y-21
79K-46
79OPC-374
79T-700
79T/Comics-12
80BK/PHR-17
80K-26
80OPC-314
80T-600
80T/S-6
81D-228
81D-348
81D-468
81Drake-10
81F-650M
81F-79
81F/St-115
81F/St-CLI
81K-3
81MSA/Disc-18
81OPC-370
81Sqt-5
81T-2LL
81T-400
81T/HT
81T/Nat/Super-8
81T/S
81T/SO-3
81T/St-107
81T/St-11M
81T/St-245
82D-535
82D-575M
82Drake-19
82F-39
82F/St-110M
82F/St-112
82K-14
82KMart-23
82OPC-300
82OPC-301IA
82OPC-377AS
82Sqt-5
82T-300
82T-301A
82T-551
82T/St-216
82T/Tr-47T
83D-115
83D-3DK
83D/AAS-3
83Drake-12
83F-640M
83F-645M
83F-93
83K-3
83OPC-219SV
83OPC-390AS
83OPC-56
83Seven-5
83T-390
83T-500
83T-501A
83T-702
83T/Gloss-39
83T/Gloss40-39
83T/St-163
83T/St-17M
83T/St-41
83T/St-5
83T/St/Box-4
84D-57
84D/AAS-36
84D/Champs-9
84Drake-15
84F-520
84FunFood/Pin-16
84MiltBrad-14
84Nes/792-100
84Nes/792-711LL
84Nes/792-712LL
84Nes/792-713LL
84OPC-100
84Ralston-19
84Seven-12W
84Smok/Cal-11
84T-100
84T-711
84T-712
84T-713
84T/Cereal-19
84T/St-102B
84T/St-231
84T/Super-21
84T/Super-21
85CircK-13
85D-57
85D/AAS-39
85Drake-17
85F-303
85F-639IA
85F/LimEd-14
85GenMills-19
85Leaf-170
85OPC-200
85Seven-12C
85Seven-13W
85Smok/Cal-2
85T-200
85T/3D-14
85T/Gloss22-19
85T/Gloss40-15
85T/St-187
85T/St-220
85T/Super-29
86BK/AP-12
86D-377
86D/HL-10
86Dorman-11
86Drake-3
86F-160
86F/HOF-6
86F/LimEd-26
86F/Mini-32
86F/Slug-18
86F/St-65
86Jiffy-8
86Leaf-173
86Meadow/Blank-7
86Meadow/Stat-6
86OPC-394
86OPC-I
86Quaker-26
86S-145M
86S-147M
86S-37
86S-59M
86S-61M
86S-71M
86S/Dec-53
86Smok/Cal-2
86T-700
86T/3D-13
86T/Gloss60-2
86T/St-177
86T/Super-35
86T/WaxBox-I
86TrueVal-13
86Woolwth-15
87Class-24
87D-210
87D/OD-22
87F-84
87F/U-U49
87KMart-16
87Leaf-201
87Moth/A's-27M
87Moth/A's-5
87OPC-300
87RedFoley/St-108
87S-44
87Smok/A's-7
87T-300
87T-312TBC
87T/Coins-15
87T/Gloss60-54
87T/HL-4
87T/Tr-52T
87Woolwth-4
88F-283
88Panini/St-175
88Score-500--504
88Sf-120
89Pac/Leg-111
89Smok/Angels-15

Jackson, Reggie

83Lynch-1
84Jacks-5

Jackson, Roland

(Sonny)
65OPC-16R
65T-16R
66T-244R
67T-415
68Coke
68OPC-187
68T-187
69MB-128
69OPC-53
69T-53
69T/St-5
70OPC-413
70T-413
71MLB/St-12
71OPC-587
71T-587
72MB-160
72OPC-318
72T-318
73OPC-403
73T-403
74OPC-591
74T-591
79Savan-8C
80Ander-8
83Pol/Atl-36
84Durhm-30
85Richm-25
87Greenvl/Bst-3
89Richm/CMC-24CO
89Richm/Pro-832

Jackson, Ron H.

55Armour-9
55T-66
55T/DH-49
56T-186
58T-26
59T-73
60L-29
60T-426

Jackson, Ron

85Louvl-30
86Bakers-15
87Gasto-20
88Vanco/Pro-768
89BirmB/Best-26
89BirmB/Pro-113

Jackson, Ronnie D.

75SLCty
77T-153
78T-718
79K-59
79OPC-173
79T-339
80OPC-5
80T-18
81D-489
81F-557
81OPC-271
81T-631
81T/St-103
82D-602
82F-269
82OPC-359
82Spoka-21
82T-488
82T/Tr-48T
83D-639
83F-94
83T-262
84D-133
84F-521
84Nes/792-548
84Smok/Cal-12
84T-548

Jackson, Roy Lee

78Tidew
79Tidew-1
80Tidew-19
81D-36
81T-223
81T/Tr-775
82D-541
82OPC-71
82OPC/Post-7
82T-71
83D-479
83F-431
83OPC-194
83T-427
84D-195
84F-158
84Nes/792-339
84OPC-339
84T-339
84Tor/Fire-18
85D-606

85F-108
85Leaf-106
85OPC-37
85T-516
85T/St-364
86F-326
86T-634
87F-545
87T-138
Jackson, Travis C.
(Stonewall)
25Exh-35
29Exh/4-10
31Exh/4-9
33CJ/Pin-14
33G-102
34DS-63
35BU-180
35G-1K
35G-3B
35G-4B
35G-5B
35Wheat
40PB-158
61F-115
80Cram/Leg-87
R315-A18
R315-B18
V354-24
W517-12
WG4-10
WG5-21
WG6-20
Jacob, Mark
83SanJose-12
Jacobo, Ed
85VeroB-10
86VeroB-12
Jacobs, Anthony R.
55T-183
Jacobs, Elmer
WG7-22
Jacobs, Forrest
(Spook)
52Park-54
53Exh/Can-46
54T-129
55Rodeo
55T-61
55T/DH-47
56T-151
56T/Hocus-A17
PM10/Sm-82
Jacobs, Jake
89Eugene/Best-4
Jacobs, Ron
77Holyo
78Holyo
79Vanco-3
Jacobsen, Nels
87BurlEx-3
88FSLAS/Star-9
88WPalm/Star-12
Jacobsen, Robert
85VeroB-16
86VeroB-13
Jacobson, Albert
WG2-27
Jacobson, Jeff
82AubAs-3
85CharO-3
Jacobson, Kevin
82Redwd-23
Jacobson, William
(Baby Doll)
21Exh-80
25Exh-114
26Exh-114
87Conlon/2-43
88Conlon/4-14
D327
E120
E121/120
E121/80
E122
E126-45
E220
V100
V117-18
W514-61
W572
W573
W575
Jacoby, Brook
80Ander-27
82Richm-13
83Richm-13
84D-542
84F/X-56
84T/X-55
84Wheat/Ind-26
85D-154
85F-452
85OPC-327
85Polar/Ind-26
85T-327
85T/St-251
85T/St-370YS
86D-154
86F-590
86F/Mini-116
86Leaf-82
86OhHenry-26
86OPC-116
86T-116
86T/St-207
87Class-40
87D-104
87D-8DK
87D/AAS-37
87D/DKsuper-8
87D/OD-112
87F-253
87Gator-26
87Ho/St-22
87Leaf-134
87Leaf-8DK
87OPC-98
87RedFoley/St-53
87S-109
87T-405
87T/St-212
88D-131
88D/Best-229
88F-612
88F/Excit-22
88F/St-20
88Gator-26
88Leaf-51
88OPC-248
88Panini/St-76
88Score-39
88Sf-72
88T-555
88T/Big-17
88T/St-211
88T/UK-38
89B-86
89D-114
89D/Best-61
89F-408
89OPC-1
89Panini/St-326
89RedFoley/St-65
89Score-19
89Sf-192
89T-141TL
89T-739
89T/Big-195
89T/St-212
89UD-198
90D-83
90F-493
90Score-56
90Sf-155
90T-208
90UD-459
Jaeckel, Paul
65T-386R
Jaffee, Irving
33SK-34
Jagnow, Jim
85BurlR-17
Jaha, John
86Cram/PCL-195
87Beloi-3
88Stock/Cal-193
88Stock/Pro-743
89Stock/Best-16
89Stock/Cal-165
89Stock/Pro-380
89Stock/Star-3
Jaime, Ismael
85Tigres-16
Jaime, Jorge
89LittleSun-17
Jakubowski, John
81Batav-30
Jakubowski, Stan
77Ashev
79Tucso-6
Jakucki, Jack
47Signal
Jakucki, Sigmund
47Centen-11
James, Art
79RochR-6
James, Artie
77Evansvl/TCMA-16
James, Bob
82Hygrade
84D-87
84F-277
84Nes/792-579
84OPC-336
84Stuart-10
84T-579
85Coke/WS-43
85D-279
85F-400
85F/Up-U60
85OPC-114
85T-114
85T/Tr-61T
86Coke/WS-43
86D-379
86F-209
86F/St-66
86OPC-284
86S-158
86T-467
86T/St-290
86T/Super-36
87Coke/WS-24
87D-493
87F-501
87F/St-67
87OPC-342
87RedFoley/St-15
87T-342
88D-507
88F-401
88OPC-232
88Panini/St-54
88T-232
88T/St-289
James, Calvin
86Osceola-15
87Osceola-7
88ColAst/Best-26
James, Charles
60T-517
61T-561
62T-412
63J-163
63P-163
63T-83
64T-357
65OPC-141
65T-141
78TCMA-292
James, Chris
85Cram/PCL-29
86F/Up-U55
86Portl-10
87D-42RR
87F/U-U50
87Leaf-42RR
87T/Tr-53T
88D-453
88D/Best-159
88F-307
88OPC-1
88Panini/St-362
88Score-409
88Score/YS/I-14
88T-572
88T/St-122
89B-404
89D-312
89D/Best-266
89F-572
89OPC-298
89Panini/St-156
89RedFoley/St-66
89Score-202
89Score/Tr-46
89T-298
89T/St-119
89T/Tr-56T
89UD-513
90D-323
90F-161
90Score-498
90T-178
90UD-435
James, Cleo
72OPC-117
72T-117
James, Darin
84Evrt/Cram-6B
James, Dewey
82Beloi-11
83Beloi/LF-3
James, Dion
82ElPas-2
84D-31
84F/X-57
84Pol/Brew-14
85D-211
85F-584
85Gard-9
85Leaf-162
85Pol/Brew-14
85T-228
86D-89
86T-76
86Vanco-13
87Class/Up-144
87D/OD-44
87F/U-U51
87Smok/Atl-24
87T/Tr-54T
88D-190
88D/Best-29
88F-543
88F/Mini-64
88F/St-76
88OPC-82
88Panini/St-250
88Score-395
88Score/YS/I-7
88Sf-36
88T-408
88T/Big-220
88T/Coins-44
88T/Mini-40
88T/St-42
88T/UK-39
89B-277
89D-340
89D/Best-253
89F-594
89Panini/St-44
89Score-163
89Score/Tr-51
89T-678
89T/Big-223
89T/St-24
89UD-587
90D-428
90F-494
90Score-514
90T-319
90UD-591
James, Duane
85Tulsa-29
86Salem-13
James, Jeff
69T-477
70OPC-302
70T-302
James, Joey
89Watertn/Star-10
James, John
60T-499
61T-457
James, Mike
88GreatF-23
89Bakers/Cal-186
James, Paul
86DayBe-13
James, Richard
83StPet-22
James, Robert Byrne
33G-208
James, Skip
75Phoen-14
76Phoen
77Phoen
79Vanco-1
James, Sonny
84Savan-1
James, Todd
89PalmSp/Cal-56
James, Troy
86Columbia-14
87Lynch-23
88Visal/Cal-164
• 88Visal/Pro-88
James, William
15CJ-153
88Conlon/5-17
BF2-52
D328-84
D329-88
D350/2-87
E135-84
M101/4-88
M101/5-87
Jamieson, Charles
21Exh-81
25Exh-82
28Exh-41
33G-171
D328-85
E120
E126-21
E135-85
R316
V100
W572
Jamison, Bob
87Nashv-25M
Janeski, Gerry
71MLB/St-543
71OPC-673
71T-673
Janikowski, Randy
88Boise/Pro-1619

Janney, Barry
77Spart
Janowicz, Vic
53T-222
54B-203
54T-16
55B-114
72T/Test-8
Jansen, Larry
48B-23
48L-56
49B-202
49Eureka-110
50B-66
51B-162
51FB
51T/RB-21
52B-90
52BR
52RM-NL10
52StarCal/L-78D
52T-5
52TipTop
53B/BW-40
54B-169
54NYJour
54T-200
73OPC-81CO
73T-81C
79TCMA-255
D305
R346-6
Jantzen, A.C.
N172
Janus, Ed
82Madis-33
83Madis/LF-1GM
Janvrin, Harold
15CJ-149
D327
D328-83
D329-89
D350/2-88
E135-83
M101/4-89
M101/5-88
Jarlett, Al
46Sunbeam
Jarquin, Gersan
(Skeeter)
78RochR
79Holyo-13
Jarrell, Joe
87CharO/WBTV-13
88CharlK-9
88CharlK/Pep-9
Jarrett, Mark
82Madis-12
Jarvis, LeRoy
47TipTop
49Sommer-9
Jarvis, Ray
70OPC-361
70T-361
71OPC-526
71T-526
Jarvis, Robert Pat
(Pat)
67OPC-57
67T-57
68Coke
68OPC-134
68T-134
69MB-129
69MLB/St-114
69T-282
69T/St-6
70MLB/St-7
70OPC-438
70T-438
71MLB/St-13
71OPC-623
71T-623
71T/Coins-85
72MB-161
72T-675
73OPC-192
73T-192
78TCMA-264
Jaster, Larry
66Pep/Tul
67T-356
68OPC-117
68T-117
69T-496
69T/St-56
70OPC-124
70T-124
71MLB/St-14
72MB-162
86Durhm-14CO
87Sumter-21
88Sumter/Pro-415
89Durhm/Star-27
Jaster, Scott
86Columbia-15
87Lynch-21
88Clmbia/GS-25
89StLucie/Star-11
Jata, Paul
72OPC-257R
72T-257R
Javier, Alfredo
73Cedar
75Iowa/TCMA-9
Javier, Ignacio
80Wichi-10
Javier, M. Julian
60T-133
61T-148
61T/St-89
62T-118
62T/St-185
63J-159
63P-159
63T-226
64T-446
64Wheat/St-23
65T-447
66T-436
67T-226
68Bz-5
68OPC-25
68T-25
69MB-130
69MLB/St-212
69T-497
69T/St-116
70MLB/St-140
70OPC-415
70T-415
71MLB/St-275
71OPC-185
71T-185
71T/Coins-39
72MB-163
72T-745
78TCMA-288
Javier, Stan
83Greens-24
84Nashvl-10
85Huntsvl/BK-20
86D-584
86F/Up-U56
86Tacom-9
87D-590
87F/U-U52
87T-263
88D/A's/Bk-NEW
88D/Best-155
88Moth/A's-15
88Score-367
89D-185
89F-13
89Moth/A's-21
89OPC-248
89Score-322
89T-622
89T/Big-277
89UD-581
90D-568
90F-12
90Score-394
90T-102
90UD-209
Javier, Vincente
88Bill/Pro-1824
89Greens/Pro-422
Jay, Joe
54JC-47
54T-141
55Gol/Braves-13
55JC-47
55T-134
58T-472
59T-273
60L-23
60Lake
60T-266
61Kahn
61T-233
61T/St-43
62Bz-13
62J-124
62Kahn
62P-124
62P/Can-124
62Salada-126
62Shirriff-126
62T-263M
62T-440
62T-58LL
62T/bucks
62T/St-116
63Exh
63FrBauer-10
63J-133
63Kahn
63P-133
63T-225
63T-7LL
64Kahn
64T-346
65Kahn
65OPC-174
65T-174
66T-406
78TCMA-216
Exh47
Jeannette, Joe
T3/Box-68
Jeansonne, Kevin
77Watlo
Jeffcoat, Hal
49Eureka-58
51B-211
52B-104
52T-341
53B/BW-37
53T-29
54B-205
55B-223
56T-289
57Kahn
57T-93
58Kahn
58T-294
59T-81
Jeffcoat, Mike
81Watlo-10
82Watlo-4
83Charl-2
84D-43
84F/X-58
84T/X-56
84Wheat/Ind-46
85D-251
85F-453
85T-303
86F-545
86Phoen-10
86T-571
87OKCty-10
89F-524
89OkCty/CMC-4
89OkCty/Pro-1520
90D-521
90F-302
90Score-158
90T-778
Jefferies, Greg
86Columbia-16
87TexLgAS-11
88AAA/Pro-40
88Class/Blue-243
88D-657
88D/Mets/Bk-657
88F-137
88F/Mini-94
88Leaf-259
88Score-645
88Tidew/CANDL-9
88Tidew/CMC-15
88Tidew/Pro-1600
89B-381
89Bz-16
89Class-6
89Class/Up/2-154
89D-35RR
89D/Best-152
89D/Rook-2
89F-38
89F/Excit-26
89F/LL-23
89F/Superstar-25
89Holsum/Discs-11
89Kahn/Mets-9
89KMart/DT-11
89Nissen-11
89OPC-233
89Panini/St-128
89Score-600
89Score/HotRk-1
89Score/Mast-39
89Score/YS/I-1
89Sf-223M
89Sf-90
89T-233FS
89T/Big-253
89T/HeadsUp-10
89T/JumboR-13
89T/Mets/Fan-9
89T/UK-44
89ToysRUs-15
89UD-9
89Woolwth-22
90D-270
90F-207
90Score-468
90Score/100Ris-10
90Sf-14
90T-457
90UD-166
Jeffers, Steve
87Erie-6
88Sprin/Best-20
Jefferson, Jesse
73OPC-604R
73T-604R
74OPC-509
74T-509
75OPC-539
75T-539
75T/M-539
76OPC-47
76T-47
77OPC-184
77T-326
78BK/R-8
78OPC-22
78T-144
79OPC-112
79T-221
80OPC-244
80T-467
81F-419
82F-466
82F/St-173
82RedLob
82T-682
82T/Tr-49T
Jefferson, Jim
86FSLAS-25
86Tampa-7
87Vermont-2
88Chatt/Best-19
Jefferson, Reggie
87Cedar-14
88Cedar/Pro-1146
89Chatt/Best-1
89Chatt/GS-12
Jefferson, Stan
86Tidew-14
87Bohem-22
87D-642
87D/Rook-43
87F/U-U53
87S/Rook-9
87T/Tr-55T
88Coke/Padres-22
88D-187
88F-587
88OPC-223
88Panini/St-411
88Score-114
88Score/YS/I-11
88Smok/Padres-12
88T-223
88T/Big-86
88T/St-109
89B-180
89Colum/CMC-28
89Score-519
89T-689
89T/Big-165
Jeffery, Scott
88Greens/Pro-1553
89Cedar/Best-3
89Cedar/Pro-913
89Cedar/Star-9
Jeffries, James
82BurlR-4
Jeffries, James
T3/Box-55
Jefts, Chris
86Penin-14
87DayBe-16
Jelic, Chris
86FtMyr-15
87Lynch-4
88Jacks/GS-8
89Jacks/GS-5
Jelks, Greg
86Portl-11
87Maine-9
87Maine/TCMA-12
88F-648
88Maine/CMC-18
88Maine/Pro-298
89Louvl-24
89Louvl/CMC-19
89Louvl/Pro-1258
Jelks, Pat
85Greens-22
86NewBrit-14
88River/Cal-228
88River/Pro-1411
88Wichi-28
Jeltz, Steve
82Readg-15

83Portl-6
84Cram/PCL-205
85CIGNA-10
85D-44
85F-653
85T/Tr-62T
86CIGNA-9
86T-453
87D-359
87D/OD-157
87F-178
87T-294
88D-576
88F-308
88OPC-126
88Panini/St-361
88Score-435
88T-126
89D-431
89D/Best-271
89F-573
89Score-355
89T-707
89T/Big-52
89T/St-114
89UD-219
90D-133
90F-562
90Score-421
90T-607
90UD-495
Jemison, Greg
77Ashev
79WHave-15
83BurlR-27
83BurlR/LF-26CO
84Tulsa-14CO
Jendra, Rick
80Cedar-11
Jenkins, Bernie
88AubAs/Pro-1959
89Osceola/Star-9
Jenkins, Fats
74Laugh/Black-28
Jenkins, Fergie
66T-254R
67T-333
68Bz-10
68Kahn
68OPC-11LL
68OPC-9LL
68T-11LL
68T-410
68T-9LL
69MB-131
69MLB/St-122
69OPC-10LL
69OPC-12LL
69Sunoco/Pin-5
69T-10LL
69T-12LL
69T-640
69T/decal
69T/S-37
69T/St-15
70MLB/St-19
70OPC-240
70OPC-69LL
70OPC-71LL
70T-240
70T-69LL
70T-71LL
71Bz/Test-13
71MD
71MLB/St-35
71MLB/St-563
71OPC-280
71OPC-70LL
71OPC-72LL
71T-280
71T-70LL
71T-72LL
71T/Coins-7
71T/S-42
71T/tatt-10
71T/tatt-10a
72K-8
72MB-164
72OPC-410
72OPC-93LL
72OPC-95LL
72T-410
72T-93LL
72T-95LL
72T/Post-10
73K-28
73OPC-180
73T-180
73T/Lids-23
74Laugh/ASG-67
74OPC-87
74T-87
74T/DE-59
74T/St-236
75Ho-116
75K-22
75OPC-310LL
75OPC-60
75T-310LL
75T-60
75T/M-310LL
75T/M-60
76Ho-138
76OPC-250
76SSPC-255
76T-250
76T/Tr-250T
77K-3
77OPC-187
77T-430
78T-420
79T-544
80K-47
80OPC-203
80T-390
81D-146
81F-622
81F/St-84
81T-158
82D-643
82F-320
82OPC-137
82T-624
83D-300
83F-498
83OPC-230
83OPC-231SV
83T-230
83T-231A
83T-51
83T/St-224
83Thorn-31
84D-189
84D/Champs-33
84F-494
84Nes/792-456TL
84Nes/792-483
84Nes/792-706LL
84OPC-343
84Seven-20C
84T-483
84T-706
84T/St-48
85West/2-46
88OkCty/CMC-6
88OkCty/Pro-50
88Pac/Leg-43
89OkCty/CMC-25
89OkCty/Pro-1513
Jenkins, Garrett
89Elmir/Puc-6
Jenkins, Jack
70OPC-286R
70T-286R
Jenkins, Jerry
77Newar
78BurlB
82ElPas-13
Jenkins, Mack
88Greens/Pro-1566
Jennings, Doug
86PalmSp-18
86PalmSp/Smok-26
87MidldA-16
87TexLgAS-4
88D/A's/Bk-NEW
88D/Rook-13
88F/Slug-22
88F/U-U54
88Moth/A's-24
89D-505
89F-14
89Score-459
89T-166
89Tacom/CMC-19
89Tacom/Pro-1541
89UD-585
Jennings, Hugh
09Buster/Pin-6
10Domino-59
11Helmar-32
12Sweet/Pin-25A
12Sweet/Pin-25B
14CJ-77
15CJ-77
40PB-223
48Exh/HOF
50Callahan
60F-67
61F-47
72Laugh/GF-23
80SSPC/HOF
89HOF/St-16
89Smok/Dodg-11
D303
D327
D328-86
D329-90
D350/2-89
E101
E103
E104
E105
E106
E121/80
E135-86
E254
E270/2
E90/1
E92
E93
E94
E96
E98
L1-128
M101/4-90
M101/5-89
M116
S81-103
T201
T202
T205
T206
T213/blue
T215/blue
T215/brown
T216
T222
T3-18
W514-206
W515-34
W555
W575
WG4-11
WG5-22
WG6-21
Jennings, William
52Park-5
Jenny, Shane
88Keno/Pro-1401
Jensen, Dave
85Lynch-8
Jensen, Forrest
(Woody)
R313
R314
Jensen, Jackie
49Remar
51B-254
52B-161
52Dix-53
52T-122
53B/Col-24
53Briggs
53Dix
53NB
53RM-AL6
53T-265
54B-2
54Dix
54T-80
55Armour-10
55RM-AL19
55T-200
56T-115
56T/Pin-24OF
57Swift-15
57T-220
58Hires-56
58T-130
58T-489AS
59Armour-10
59Bz
59HRDerby-8
59T-400
60Bz-21
60T/tatt
60T/tatt-23
60T/tatt-90
61T-173M
61T-476MV
61T-540
61T/St-112
62J-62
62P-62
62P/Can-62
62Salada-73
62Shirriff-73
75OPC-196M
75T-196MV
75T/M-196MV
79TCMA-229
Exh47
PM10/Sm-83
PM10/Sm-84
PM10/Sm-85
Jensen, John
(Swede)
49B/PCL-13
Jensen, John
89WinSal/Star-10
Jernigan, Pete
63MilSau-3
63T-253R
Jessup, Steve
88Utica/Puc-28
Jestadt, Garry
70OPC-109R
70T-109R
71OPC-576R
71T-576R
72OPC-143
72T-143
77Phoen
Jester, Billy
86Clearw-10
Jeter, John
70OPC-141R
70T-141R
71MLB/St-205
71OPC-47
71T-47
72OPC-288
72T-288
73OPC-423
73T-423
74OPC-615
74T-615
Jeter, Shawn
87Duned-21
88Duned/Star-12
89Knoxv/Best-10
89Knoxv/Pro-1130
89Knoxv/Star-8
Jethroe, Sam
50B-248
51B-242
51BR-D10
51T/BB-12
52B-84
52T-27
53B/Col-3
53Exh/Can-10
79TCMA-44
89Pac/Leg-206
89Swell-62
Jevne, Frederick
N172
Jewell, Jim
43Centen-12
Jewett, Earl
89Pulas/Pro-1897
Jewett, Trent
89Salem/Star-11
Jewtraw, C.
33SK-11
Jimaki, Jim
88CapeCod/Sum-84
Jimenez, Alex
88Clmbia/GS-15
89Clmbia/Best-29
89Clmbia/GS-12
Jimenez, Cesar
86Durhm-15
87Durhm-1
88Durhm/Star-8
88F/U-U72
Jimenez, Felix
(Elvio)
65OPC-226R
65T-226R
69T-567R
Jimenez, German
88F/U-U72
89Greenv/Pro-1153
89Greenv/Star-10
89Greenvl/Best-23
89T-569
89UD-113
Jimenez, Houston
83Toled-15
84Nes/792-411
84T-411
85D-269
85F-282
85T-562
85Toled-16
87Vanco-12
Jimenez, Juan
86BurlEx-11C
Jimenez, Manuel
62T-598R
63J-87
63P-87
63T-195
64T-574
66T-458
67T-586
68T-538
69MB-132

Jimenez, Manuel
75QuadC
Jimenez, Ray
83Peoria/LF-1
Jiminez, Alex
86LitFalls-15
87Columbia-28
Jiminez, Luis
78Charl
Jirschele, Mike
78Ashev
79Wausa-21
80Ashev-28
80Tulsa-15
81Tulsa-29
82Tulsa-19
83OKCty-10
84OKCty-9
85OKCty-4
89Omaha/CMC-17
Job, Ryan
86ColumAst-15
Jockish, Mike
88StCath/Pro-2031
89StCath/Pro-2078
Jodo, Daijiro
88SanJose/Cal-120
Johdo, Joe
88SanJose/Pro-136
John, Oliver
E270/2
John, Tommy
64T-146R
65OPC-208
65T-208
66T-486
67T-609
68OPC-72
68T-72
69MB-133
69MLB/St-31
69NTF
69T-465
69T/St-155
69Trans-22
70MLB/St-186
70OPC-180
70T-180
71K-74
71MD
71OPC-520
71T-520
71T/Coins-56
72MB-165
72OPC-264
72T-264
73OPC-258
73T-258
74OPC-451
74T-451
75OPC-47
75T-47
75T/M-47
76OPC-416
76SSPC-69
76T-416
77T-128
78Ho-7
78K-36
78T-375
79BK/Y-9
79OPC-129
79T-255
80OPC-348
80T-690
81D-107
81F-81
81F/St-121
81K-52
81OPC-96
81T-550
81T/HT
81T/SO-52
81T/St-114
81T/St-250
81T/St-2M
82D-409
82D-558M
82F-40
82F/St-115
82OPC-75
82T-486TL
82T-75
82T/St-214
83D-570
83F-95
83OPC-144SV
83OPC-196
83Seven-9
83T-735
83T-736A
84D-301
84D/Champs-36
84F-522
84FunFood/Pin-92
84Nes/792-415
84Nes/792-715LL
84OPC-284
84Smok/Cal-13
84T-415
84T-715
84T/St-232
85D-423
85F-304
85OPC-179
85Smok/Cal-23
85T-179
85T/St-229
86F-422
86F/Up-U57
86T-240
87F-102
87OPC-236
87Smok/Dodg-15
87T-236
88D-17DK
88D-401
88D/Best-220
88D/DKsuper-17DK
88D/Y/Bk-401
88F-211
88Leaf-17DK
88Leaf-230
88Panini/St-148
88Score-240
88Sf-122
88T-611
89Class-40
89F-255
89Score-477
89Smok/Dodg-91
89T-359
89T/St-310
89UD-230
Johnigan, Steve
87Watlo-4
Johns, Ronald M.
86FSLAS-26
86StPet-15
87Sprin/Best-6
88Harris/Pro-849
Johnson, Abner
78Wisco
81CharR-19
Johnson, Alex
65T-352
66OPC-104
66Pep/Tul
66T-104
67OPC-108
67T-108
68T-441
69Kahn
69T-280
69T/St-25
70MLB/St-173
70OPC-115
70T-115
71JB
71K-54
71MD
71MLB/St-346
71MLB/St-564
71OPC-590
71OPC-61LL
71T-590
71T-61LL
71T/Coins-84
71T/GM-17
71T/S-8
71T/tatt-15
72MB-166
72OPC-215
72T-215
73OPC-425
73T-425
74OPC-107
74T-107
74T/St-237
75OPC-534
75T-534
75T/M-534
77T-637
Johnson, Anthony
80Memph-3
83D-629
83Syrac-22
84Syrac-7
Johnson, Ban
50Callahan
61F-48
63Bz/ATG-16
69Bz-Sm
80SSPC/HOF
88Pac/8Men-78
89HOF/St-96
WG1-4
WG2-28
Johnson, Ben
60T-528
Johnson, Bert
82CharR-9
Johnson, Bill
83Readg-7
84IowaC-29
85IowaC-16
Johnson, Billy
87Louvl-30
89Spoka/SP-12
Johnson, Bob
79Wausa-12
Johnson, Bobby E.
78Ashev
80Tulsa-21
82T-418R
83D-494
83Rang-8
83T/X-48
84D-500
84F-420
84Nes/792-608
84T-608
Johnson, Brian
88BurlR/Pro-1798
89Kinston/Star-10
Johnson, C. Barth
70T-669R
71OPC-156
71T-156
72OPC-126
72T-126
73OPC-506
73T-506
74OPC-147
74T-147
75OPC-446
75T-446
75T/M-446
76OPC-513
76T-513
77T-177
Johnson, Carl
88VeroB/Star-12
89Keno/Pro-1065
89Keno/Star-9
Johnson, Charles
81GlenF-4
87Savan-2
88Sprin/Best-12
89StPet/Star-19
Johnson, Chet
45Centen-12
Johnson, Chris
88Beloi/GS-25
89Beloi/Star-10
Johnson, Cliff
75OPC-143
75T-143
75T/M-143
76OPC-249
76SSPC-51
76T-249
77T-514
78BK/Y-3
78T-309
79BK/Y-3
79OPC-50
79T-114
80OPC-321
80T-612
81D-484
81F-303
81OPC-17
81T-17
81T/Tr-776
82F-93
82Granny-5
82OPC-333
82T-422
82T/St-226
83D-601
83F-520
83T-762
83T/X-49
84D-512
84F-159
84Nes/792-221
84OPC-221
84T-221
84T/St-366
84Tor/Fire-19
85D-512
85F-109
85F/Up-U61
85Leaf-115
85OPC-7
85Rang-44
85T-4RB
85T-568
85T/St-367
85T/Tr-63T
85Woolwth-20
86Ault-44
86D-639
86F-62
86Leaf-250
86OPC-348
86T-348
86Tor/Fire-19
87D-645
87F-230
87OPC-118
87T-663
Johnson, Clifford
(Connie)
56T-326
57T-43
58T-266
59T-21
Johnson, Clint
81Brist-20
Johnson, Curtis
88StCath/Pro-2022
89Myrtle/Pro-1470
Johnson, Dana
87Duned-8
Johnson, Dante
88Bill/Pro-1812
89Greens/Pro-417
Johnson, Daron
89Well/Puc-14
Johnson, Darrell
54Esskay
57T-306
58T-61
59T-533
60T-263
62T-16
74OPC-403MG
74T-403MG
75OPC-172MG
75T-172MG
75T/M-172MG
76SSPC-417
76T-118MG
77T-597MG
78T-79
79T-659MG
83T-37
Johnson, Dave (P)
84PrWill-30
85Nashua-12
86Hawai-12
86QuadC-15
87Vanco-9
88BuffB/CMC-4
88BuffB/Polar-2
88BuffB/Pro-1476
89RochR/CMC-11
89RochR/Pro-1656
90D-702
90Score-528
90Score/100Ris-43
90T-416
90UD-425
Johnson, David A.
(Davey)
65T-473R
66T-579R
67T-363
68Coke
68T-273
69MB-135
69MLB/St-4
69OPC-203
69T-203
69T/St-125
70MLB/St-150
70OPC-45
70T-45
71MD
71MLB/St-301
71OPC-595
71T-595
71T/Coins-2
71T/tatt-4
72K-43
72MB-168
72OPC-224WS 72T-680
73OPC-550
73T-550
74K-50
74OPC-45
74T-45
74T/St-6
75OPC-57
75T-57
75T/M-57
78T-317
83Tidew-23

84Jacks/Smk-6MG
84T/Mets/Fan-1MG
84T/X-57
85T-492
86T-501MG
87T-543MG
88D/AS-42MG
88D/PopUp-20MG
88Kahn/Mets-5MG
88T-164
88T/Gloss22-12MG
89Kahn/Mets-5MG
89T-684MG
90T-291MG

Johnson, David C.
77T-478R
78T-627

Johnson, David M.
77SnJos-24
78StPet
79ArkTr-21
80ArkTr-14

Johnson, David
83AlexD-20
87PalmSp-3

Johnson, Dean
85LitFalls-25

Johnson, Deron Jr.
86Cram/PCL-105
87Wausa-18
88Albany/Pro-1351
88Watertn/Puc-20

Johnson, Deron
59T-131
60T-134
61T-68
62T-82
64T-449
65Kahn
65MacGregor-5
65OPC-75
65T-75
66Kahn
66T-219LL
66T-440
67Kahn
67OPC-135
67T-135
68Kahn
68T-323
69MB-136
69T-297
70OPC-125
70T-125
70T/CB
71MLB/St-182
71OPC-490
71T-490
71T/Coins-79
71T/S-58
72MB-169
72OPC-167
72OPC-168IA
72T-167
72T-168A
73OPC-590
73T-590
74OPC-312
74T-312
74T/St-227
76OPC-529
76T-529
78Cr/PCL-10
78TCMA-213

Johnson, Dodd
86Sumter-11
87Durhm-28
88Durhm/Star-9
89Penin/Star-8

Johnson, Dominick
89Clint/Pro-904

Johnson, Don
47TipTop
52T-190
53B/BW-55
54T-146
55B-101
55Esskay
55T-165

Johnson, Earl
47TipTop
49B-231
50B-188
51B-321
52Mother-14

Johnson, Erik
88Clint/Pro-708
88MidwLAS/GS-3
89Shreve/Pro-1845

Johnson, Ernest R.
21Exh-82
E120
E220
V100
W573

Johnson, Ernest T.
53JC-7
54B-144
54JC-32
55B-157
55Gol/Braves-14
55JC-32
56T-294
57T-333
58T-78
59T-279
60T-228

Johnson, Frank
69T-227
71MLB/St-253
71OPC-128
71T-128
75Phoen-23

Johnson, George
78Laugh/Black-25

Johnson, Greg
77QuadC
79Savan-10

Johnson, Greg
87AubAs-18
88Ashvl/Pro-1051
89Ashvl/Pro-959

Johnson, Hank
33G-14
R314/Can
R337-409
V353-14

Johnson, HomeRun
74Laugh/Black-22

Johnson, Howard
81BirmB
83D-328
83F-332
85D-247
85F-12
85F/Up-U62
85OPC-192
85T-192
85T/St-262
85T/Tr-64T
86D-312
86F-85
86OPC-304
86T-751
86T/Mets/Fan-6
86T/St-101
87D-646
87D/HL-43
87D/OD-132
87F-13
87OPC-267
87T-267
88D-569
88D/Best-97
88D/Mets/Bk-569
88F-138
88F/Mini-95
88F/RecSet-20
88F/St-104
88Kahn/Mets-20
88KayBee-14
88Leaf-238
88OPC-85
88OPC-K
88Panini/St-343
88Panini/St-439
88RedFoley/St-40
88Score-69
88Sf-138
88Sf/Gamewin-17
88T-85
88T/Big-129
88T/Gloss60-52
88T/Mets/Fan-20
88T/Mini-61
88T/St-99
88T/WaxBox-K
89Ames-18
89D-235
89D/Best-126
89F-39
89Kahn/Mets-20
89OPC-383
89Score-136
89T-383
89T/Big-208
89T/Gloss60-22
89T/St-91
89T/St/Backs-41
89UD-582
90Class-144
90D-18DK
90D-654AS
90D-99
90D/Bon/MVP-BC2
90D/Preview-8
90F-208
90F-639M
90F/WaxBox-C16
90Score-124
90Score/100St-83
90Sf-109
90T-399AS
90T-680
90UD-263

Johnson, Jack
T3/Box-76

Johnson, James H.
21Exh-83

Johnson, James
81Clint-19

Johnson, Jay
87Sumter-30

Johnson, Jeff
88Oneon/Pro-2069
89PrWill/Star-9

Johnson, Jerry
69T-253
70OPC-162
70T-162
71MLB/St-254
71OPC-412
71T-412
72OPC-35
72OPC-36IA
72T-35
72T-36A
73OPC-248
73T-248
75OPC-218
75T-218
75T/M-218
76OPC-658
76T-658
78OPC-184
78T-169
84Louvl-26

Johnson, Jerry
81ArkTr-11
81Hawai-5
82Hawai-5
83ArkTr-9
84Beaum-19
85RochR-18

Johnson, Jim
(Jimmy)
80Tucso-9
81Tucso-12
82Tucso-24MG
85Cram/PCL-53MG

Johnson, Jim
88GreatF-26

Johnson, Joe
84Richm-21
85IntLgAS-17
86D-624
86F-519
86Pol/Atl-38
86Syrac-15
87D-650
87F-231
87Leaf-91
87T/Tr-56T
87Tor/Fire-15
87Tor/Fire-15
88Edmon/CMC-7
88Edmon/Pro-560
88OPC-347
88T-347

Johnson, John Henry
75Cedar
76Cedar
79Ho-39
79K-6
79OPC-361
79T-681
80OPC-97
80T-173
81T-216
82D-550
82F-321
82T-527
84D-91
84F-401
84Nes/792-419
84T-419
85Cram/PCL-246
85F-162
85T-734
86Vanco-14
87F-347
87T-377

Johnson, John Ralph
N172

Johnson, John
87FtLaud-23

Johnson, Judd
89Sumter/Pro-1102

Johnson, Karl
89Elizab/Star-13

Johnson, Ken T.
60T-135
61BeeHive-10
61T-24
62T-278
63Pepsi
63T-352
64T-158
64T/S-2
64T/St-70
64T/SU
64T/tatt
65OldLond-13
65T-359
66T-466
66T/RO-96
67Kahn
67OPC-101
67T-101
68Coke
68T-342
69T-238
78TCMA-232
89Smok/Ast-5

Johnson, Ken
49Eureka-185
51B-293
D301

Johnson, Kevin
80Clint-12

Johnson, Lamar
76OPC-596R
76T-596R
77T-443
78Ho-59
78T-693
79Ho-43
79OPC-192
79T-372
80T-242
81Coke
81D-38
81F-350
81OPC-366
81T-589
81T/HT
81T/SO-26
81T/St-58
82D-269
82F-346
82T-13
82T/Tr-50T
83D-142
83F-571
83T-453

Johnson, Lance
86ArkTr-8
87Louvl-16
88Coke/WS-12
88D-31
88F-37
88Leaf-31RR
88T/Big-251
89AAA/Pro-30
89D-606
89F-499
89Panini/St-312
89RedFoley/St-67
89Score/HotRk-33
89T-122
89Vanco/CMC-18
89Vanco/Pro-576
90D-573
90F-536
90Score-570
90T-587
90UD-90

Johnson, Larry D.
80RochR-20
81Evans-12

Johnson, Lindsey
86Kinston-11
89Mia/Star/22-7
89Mia/Star/25-9

Johnson, Lloyd
34G-86

Johnson, Lou
60T-476
61BeeHive-11
63T-238
66OPC-13
66T-13
67T-410
68OPC-184
68T-184
69JB
69MB-137
69T-367

Johnson, Luther
88Martins/Star-18
89AubAs/Pro-2176
Johnson, Mark
88CapeCod-2
88CapeCod/Sum-1
88Umpire-51
89Umpires-49
Johnson, Mike
79AppFx-10
82Wausa-18
84Chatt-14
Johnson, Mitch
80Elmir-18
85Pawtu-19
86Pawtu-11
87Pawtu-8
87Pawtu/TCMA-7
88Pawtu/CMC-3
88Pawtu/Pro-455
89Tucso/CMC-2
89Tucso/Pro-187
Johnson, Otis
T201
Johnson, Owen
66T-356R
Johnson, Perry
83Idaho-7
Johnson, Randall G.
81Richm-22
82BK/Lids-14
82Pol/Atl-6
83Pol/Atl-6
83T-596
84D-321
84F-183
84Nes/792-289
84Pol/Atl-6
84T-289
85D-531
85F-330
85Richm-14
85T-458
86Phoen-11
89Everett/Star-16
Johnson, Randall S.
(Randy)
80GlenF/B-18
80GlenF/C-4
81GlenF-18
82T/Tr-51T
83D-305
83F-617
83T-354
83Toled-21
85BuffB-14
Johnson, Randy
86WPalm-21
87Jaxvl-23
87SLAS-16
88Indi/CMC-1
88Indi/Pro-510
89Class-95
89D-42RR
89D/Best-80
89D/Rook-43
89F-381
89F/Up-59
89OPC-186
89Panini/St-111
89Score-645
89Score/HotRk-63
89Score/Tr-77
89Score/YS/II-32
89Sf-224M
89T-647
89T/Big-287
89T/Tr-57T
89UD-25
89Woolwth-13
90D-379
90F-518
90Score-415
90Score/100Ris-52
90Sf-64
90T-431
90UD-563
Johnson, Rich
86Ashvl-16
87ColAst/Pro-23
87ColumAst-23
88ColAst/Best-14
Johnson, Robert D.
70T-702R
71T-365
71T-71LL
72T-27
73T-657
74T-269
74T/Tr-269T
Johnson, Robert L.
(Indian Bob)
34G-68
35BU-20
35Exh/4-14
35G-8J
35G-9J
36Exh/4-14
37Exh/4-14
37OPC-123
38Exh/4-14
38Wheat-6
39Exh
39PB-97
40PB-25
41DP-49
41PB-22
47Centen-12
47Signal
R314
V100
Johnson, Robert W.
62T-519
62T/St-97
63J-96
63P-96
63T-504
64T-304
65T-363
66OPC-148
66T-148
67OPC-38
67T-38
68T-338
69MB-134
69T-261
70T-693
71OPC-365
71OPC-71LL
72MB-167
72OPC-27
73OPC-657
74OPC-269
78TCMA-79
Johnson, Roger
86Kinston-12
Johnson, Rondin
81Omaha-19
82Omaha-17
84Indianap-24
84Omaha-25
85Omaha-21
86Omaha-12
86Omaha/TCMA-2
87FtMyr-34
87Omaha-11
88Omaha/CMC-10
88Omaha/Pro-1515
Johnson, Roy
32Orbit/un-35
33G-8
34Exh/4-9
35BU-63
38Exh/4-1
44Centen-12
82Wichi-6
82Wichi-7M
88Conlon/AmAS-17
88Tacom/CMC-15
88Tacom/Pro-621
R305
R316
R337
V353-8
Johnson, Roy
83D-492
84Indianap-7
85Indianap-5
87Tacom-15
Johnson, Scott
81Miami-21
87Watlo-9
88Kinston/Star-12
89SoBend/GS-6
Johnson, Sean
88SLCty-30M
Johnson, Silas
33DH-24
35BU-54
47TipTop
R332-34
Johnson, Stan
61Union
Johnson, Steve
83Beaum-3
84Beaum-20
86Watlo-13
Johnson, Sylvester
39PB-28
40PB-99
43Centen-13
44Centen-13
45Centen-13
E120
V117-13
V61-24
W572
W573
Johnson, Terence
(T.J.)
84LitFalls-14
85LitFalls-19
Johnson, Terry
83BurlR-6
83BurlR/LF-10
83Tulsa-24
84Tulsa-34
85Tulsa-30
Johnson, Tim
74OPC-554
74T-554
75OPC-556
75T-556
75T/M-556
76A&P/Milw
76OPC-613
76T-613
77T-406
78T-542
79OPC-89
79T-182
80OPC-155
80T-297
89Bak/Cal-206MG
Johnson, Tom R.
75OPC-618R
75T-618R
75T/M-618R
76OPC-448
76T-556
77T-202
78K-9
78T-54
79OPC-77
79T-162
80GlenF/B-3
80GlenF/C-28
81QuadC-13
88Virgini/Star-11
89BBCity/Star-11
Johnson, Tom
83MidldC-23
86BurlEx-12
87FtMyr-19
Johnson, Wallace
(Wally)
82F-192
82Wichi-8
83F-285
85Indianap-21
86Indianap-19
87F-321
87OPC-234
87T-588
88F-186
88OPC-228
88Score-433
88T-228
89D-484
89F-382
89OPC-138
89Panini/St-120
89Score-196
89T-138
89UD-124
90D-570
90F-351
90Score-479
90T-318
Johnson, Walter P.
10Domino-60
11Helmar-72
12Sweet/Pin-60A
12Sweet/Pin-60B
14CJ-57
15CJ-57
21Exh-84
25Exh-125
26Exh-125
27Exh-62
40PB-120
48Exh/HOF
48Swell-4
49Leaf/Prem-4
50Callahan
51T/CM
60Exh/HOF-13
60F-6
60NuCard-40
61F-49
61GP-29
61NuCard-440
61T-409M
63Bz/ATG-12
69Bz-6
69Bz-Sm
72F/FFeat-8
72K/ATG-1
72K/ATG-1
72Laugh/GF-2
73OPC-476LL
73OPC-478LL
73T-476LL
73T-478LL
76OPC-349AS
76T-349AS
79T-417M
79T-418M
80Cram/Leg-45
80Laugh/3/4/5-3
80Laugh/FFeat-25
80SSPC/HOF
83D/HOF-2
84D/Champs-37
85Woolwth-21
86Conlon/1-4
87Conlon/2-6
87Nestle/DT-9
89Pac/Leg-192
89Swell-3
BF2-45
D327
D328-87
D329-91
D350/2-90
E120
E121/120
E121/80
E122
E126-28
E135-87
E210-45
E224
E300
E91
L1-135
M101/4-91
M101/5-90
M116
PM1-7
PM10/Sm-86
R310
R423-54
S74-39
S81-110
T201
T202
T204
T205
T206
T207
T213/blue
T215/blue
T215/brown
T222
T3-99
V100
V117-30
V61-47
W501-17
W514-94
W515-38
W516-8
W573
W575
WG5-23
WG6-22
WG7-23
Johnson, Wayne
82Watlo/B-5
82Watlo/C-25
83BuffB-2
85Water-10
Johnson, William
44Yank/St-15
48B-33
48L-14
49B-129
50B-102
51B-74
51BR-A5
51T/BB-21
52B-122
52T-83
53Hunter
53T-21
79TCMA-230
Exh47
R346-1
Johnson, William
(Judy)
74Laugh/Black-36
78Laugh/Black-29
88Conlon/NegAS-6
Johnson, Willy
88Sumter/Pro-417
89Sumter/Pro-1092
Johnson, Ching
33SK-30

Johnston, Chris
83Knoxv-11
Johnston, Craig
88Martins/Star-19
89Kingspt/Star-14
Johnston, Dan
88Geneva/Pro-1644
Johnston, Greg
78Cr/PCL-47
79Phoen
79T-726R
80T-686R
81T-328R
Johnston, James H.
25Exh-13
D327
D328-88
E120
E121/80
E122
E135-88
E220
V100
W515-41
W572
W575
Johnston, Jody
82Jacks-6
82Lynch-22
Johnston, Joel
88Eugene/Best-11
89BBCity/Star-12
Johnston, Mark
79WHave-1
82ElPas-10
83Beloi/LF-10
Johnston, Richard
E223
N172
N284
N526
Johnston, Ryan
88Savan/Pro-352
Johnston, Stan
86Bakers-16TR
87Bakers-14TR
88Bakers/Cal-264
89Albuq/Pro-74
Johnston, Wheeler
(Doc)
15CJ-150
E120
W573
Johnstone, Jay
67T-213
68T-389
69JB
69MB-138
69OPC-59
69T-59
70MLB/St-174
70OPC-485
70T-485
70T/CB
71OPC-292
71T-292
72MB-170
72OPC-233
72T-233
75OPC-242
75T-242
75T/M-242
76OPC-114
76SSPC-463
76T-114
77K-35
77OPC-226
77Pep-71
77T-415
78T-675
79OPC-287
79T-558
80OPC-15
80Pol/Dodg-21
80T-31
81BK/Y-5
81D-300
81F-128
81OPC-372
81Pol/Dodg-21
81T-372
82D-262
82F-10
82Pol/Dodg
82Pol/Dodg-21
82RedLob
82T-774
82T/Tr-52T
83D-561
83F-499
83OPC-152
83T-152
83T/St-220
83Thorn-21
84D-540
84F-495
84Nes/792-249
84SevenUp-21
84T-249
84T/St-50
86T-496
Joiner, Dave
88Clmbia/GS-16
89Clmbia/Best-8
89Clmbia/GS-13
Joiner, Roy
(Pop)
40PB-211
Jok, Stan
52Park-93
54T-196
55B-251
Jolley, Smead
28Exh/PCL-13
30CEA/Pin-16
31Exh/4-20
32Orbit/num-25
32Orbit/un-36
87Conlon/2-23
88MinorLg/Leg-8
R305
R315-C3
R315-D3
V355-98
Jolly, Dave
53JC-8
54JC-17
54T-188
55B-71
55Gol/Braves-15
55JC-16
55T-35
55T/DH-95
57T-389
58T-183
Jonas, Pete
43Centen-14
47Centen-13
47Signal
Jones, Al
82AppFx-7
83AppFx/LF-20
85D-404
85T-437
86BuffB-13
86T-227
87Denver-26
Jones, Barry
85PrWill-3
86Hawai-13
86Sumter-12
87D-602
87Durhm-2
87F-611
87T-494
88F/U-U114
88Greenv/Best-8
88SLAS-14
88T-168
89Coke/WS-12
89D-647
89F-500
89Richm/CMC-20
89Richm/Ko-18
89Richm/Pro-846
89Score-333
89T-539
89UD-457
90Score-152
90T-243
Jones, Bill
86StPet-16
Jones, Bobby
(Ducky)
28Exh/PCL-14
Jones, Bobby
33SK-38
Jones, Brian
85PrWill-31
86PrWill-13
87Harrisbg-17
Jones, Bryan
76Watlo
Jones, Calvin
87Chatt/Best-6
88Vermont/Pro-962
89SnBer/Cal-64
89Wmspt/Star-11
Jones, Carl
87Sumter-14
Jones, Charles
E107
T204
Jones, Charlie
83VeroB-6
Jones, Chris L.
88CapeCod/Sum-164
Jones, Chris
78Wausa
82Tucso-2
83Tucso-19
84Cram/PCL-52
85Cram/PCL-51
86Cedar/TCMA-21
86Phoen-12
87Duned-17
87Phoen-1
87Vermont-22
88Chatt/Best-6
88Idaho/Pro-1843
88Knoxv/Best-16
88SanDiegoSt-9
89Knoxv/Best-11
89Knoxv/Pro-1134
89Knoxv/Star-9
89Nashvl/CMC-20
89Nashvl/Pro-1290
Jones, Clarence W.
68T-506
Jones, Clarence
86Sumter-13
87Sumter-6
Jones, Clarence
88Richm/CMC-25
88Richm/Pro-17
Jones, Cleon
65T-308R
66T-67R
67Kahn
67T-165
67T/PI-13
68T-254
69T-512
69T/S-50
70K-3
70T-575
70T-61LL
70T/CB
70Trans-1
70Trans/M-24
71T-527
71T/tatt-1
72T-31
72T-32A
73T-540
74T-245
75Ho-123
75K-21
75T-43
75T/M-43
Jones, Cleon
66OPC-67R
67OPC-165
67OPC/PI-13
69MB-139
69MLB/St-167
69T/St-65
70MLB/St-78
70OPC-61LL
71MLB/St-156
71OPC-527
71T/Coins-103
72MB-171
72OPC-31
72OPC-32IA
73OPC-540
74OPC-245
74OPC-476WS
74T/St-64
75OPC-43
Jones, Craig
84Richm-13
Jones, D.J.
87Durhm-23
Jones, Dan
83Miami-15
Jones, Darryl
78Cr/PCL-24
79Colum-28
80T-670R
Jones, David
11Helmar-33
E103
E104
E107
E254
E270/1
E93
M116
S74-15
T202
T205
T3-100
W555
Jones, David
85Durhm-7
86Sumter-14
Jones, Dennis
87Myrtle-13
88BBAmer-19
88Knoxv/Best-19
89Knoxv/Best-12
89Knoxv/Pro-1136
89Knoxv/Star-10
Jones, DeWayne
88SoOreg/Pro-1698
Jones, Donny
77QuadC
80ElPas-18
Jones, Doug
78Newar
79BurlB-12
81ElPas-11
82Pol/Brew
82Pol/Brew-45
82Vanco-13
84Cram/PCL-39
84ElPas-7
85Water-12
86Maine-11
87Gator-46
88D-588
88D/Best-325
88F-613
88Gator-11
88Score-594
88T-293
89B-78
89Class-89
89D-438
89D/AS-20
89D/Best-173
89F-409
89F/BBAS-23
89F/BBMVP's-23
89OPC-312
89Panini/St-319
89Panini/St-5
89Score-387
89Score-656HL
89Score/HotSt-41
89Sf-38
89T-690
89T-6RB
89T/Mini-51
89T/St-215
89T/St-3
89T/St/Backs-32
89UD-540
89Woolwth-14
90Class-114
90D-320
90F-495
90Score-130
90Sf-96
90T-75
90UD-632
Jones, Earl
(Lefty)
48Signal
49Remar
Jones, Elijah
C46-52
Jones, Eric
81Batav-22
Jones, Eugene
89Greens/Pro-416
Jones, Fielder
87Conlon/2-44
BF2-41
D328-89
D329-92
D350/2-91
E135-89
M101/4-92
M101/5-91
T206
W514-50
WG2-29
Jones, Gary
71OPC-559R
71T-559R
Jones, Gary
83QuadC-21
86Fresno/Smok-4
87Tacom-5
88SanJose/Cal-121
88SanJose/Pro-112
88Tacom/CMC-23
88Tacom/Pro-612
89Huntsvl/Best-17
Jones, Geary
86Columbia-17
87Lynch-17
88Jacks/GS-3
Jones, George
85Evrt/Cram-6A
85Evrt/Cram-6B
Jones, Glenn
82Clint-21

Jones, Gordon
55Hunter
55T-78
55T/DH-6
59T-458
60L-73
60T-98
61T-442

Jones, Gordon
82Redwd-5

Jones, Grover
(Deacon)
63T-253R

Jones, Gus
86Cram/PCL-47
87FtMyr-14

Jones, Hank
77LodiD
78LodiD
79LodiD-20

Jones, Harold
62T-49

Jones, J. Dalton
64T-459R
65OPC-178
65T-178
66T-317
67OPC-139
67T-139
67T/Test/RSox-8
68Coke
68OPC-106
68T-106
69MB-140
69T-457
70T-682
71MLB/St-395
71OPC-367
71T-367
72MB-172
72OPC-83
72T-83
73OPC-512
73T-512

Jones, James
88CapeCod/Sum-70
88CapeCod-3

Jones, Jeffrey A.
79Ogden/TCMA-23
81T-687
82D-213
82F-94
82F/St-130
82T-139
82Tacom-24
83D-651
83T-259
83Tacom-28
84Cram/PCL-82
84Nes/792-464
84T-464
85T-319

Jones, Jeffrey R.
80Cedar-19
81Cedar-16
82Cedar-24
84D-262
84MidldC-20
87GlenF-4
88GlenF/Pro-936
89Fay/Pro-1570

Jones, Jim
84Madis/Pol-14
86Modesto-15
87SLAS-12
88Tacom/Pro-618
89Denver/Pro-40
89SanJose/Best-23
89SanJose/Cal-222
89SanJose/Pro-460
89SanJose/Star-16

Jones, Jimmy
84Beaum-1
85Beaum-8
86Cram/PCL-25
86LasVegas-8
87D-557
87F-650M
87F/U-U54
87LasVegas-17
87S/Rook-35
88Coke/Padres-45PAN
88D-141
88D/Best-189
88F-588
88Huntsvl/BK-9
88Score-246
88Smok/Padres-13
88T-63
88Tacom/CMC-21
89B-169
89Colum/CMC-9
89Colum/Pol-10
89Colum/Pro-752
89D-247
89D/Best-217
89Denver/CMC-17
89F-308
89Score-294
89Score/NWest-26
89T-748
89T/Tr-58T
89UD-286
90T-359

Jones, Joe
77Spart

Jones, Keith
(Kiki)
89GreatF-18
90Score-676DC

Jones, Keith
82BurlR-5
84Tulsa-6

Jones, Ken
78Wausa
81Water-4
82Water-4
83Water-4
87Madis-14

Jones, Kevin
89Everett/Star-17

Jones, Kirk
80Batav-6

Jones, Lance
88CapeCod/Sum-133

Jones, Larry K.
80RochR-7
81RochR-19
82IowaC-17
82WHave-17
83IowaC-5

Jones, Lee
83Redwd-13

Jones, Lynn
78Indianap-20
80T-123
81T-337
82D-542
82F-270
82T-64
83F-333
83T-483
84Nes/792-731
84T-731
84T/X-58
85T-513
86D-466
86F-11
86NatPhoto-35
86T-671

Jones, Mack
62T-186
63T-137
65OPC-241
65T-241
66Kahn
66T-446
67T-435
68Kahn
68T-353
69Fud's-5
69MLB/St-159
69T-625
69T/St-57
70MLB/St-66
70OPC-38
70T-38
70T/SO
71MLB/St-131
71OPC-142
71T-142
71T/Coins-135
72MB-173
76Laugh/Jub-20

Jones, Mark
88Visal/Cal-173

Jones, Michael C.
(Mike)
81Omaha-9
81T-66R
82Clint-7
82F-412
82T-471
84Omaha-20
84Shrev/FB-9
85D-640
85T-244
86D-419
86F-12
86Richm-10
86Shrev-12
86T-514
86Ventura-9
87Duned-4

Jones, Mike
74Cedar
88Brist/Pro-1889
88Knoxv/Best-4
88Nashvl/CMC-6
88Nashvl/Pro-485
89Lakel/Star-11
89RochR/CMC-1
89RochR/Pro-1657
89Star/Wax-31

Jones, Norm
89Denver/Pro-56

Jones, Odell
78Colum
78T-407
80Port-17
80T-342
81Portl-13
82Portl-4
83Rang-21
83T/X-50
84D-256
84F-421
84Nes/792-734
84OPC-382
84Rang-21
84T-734
85D-525
85F-560
85RochR-19
85T-29
86RochR-10
87D-582
87Syrac/TCMA-5
88Pol/Brew-28
89F-189
89Score-579
89UD-608

Jones, Percy
E120
E126-18
R316

Jones, Randy
74McDon
74OPC-173SD
74T-173
74T/St-94
75OPC-248
75T-248
75T/M-248
76Crane-23
76Ho-143
76K-4
76MSA/Disc
76OPC-199LL
76OPC-201LL
76OPC-310
76SSPC-118
76T-199LL
76T-201LL
76T-310
77Ho-26
77K-17
77OPC-113
77OPC-5LL
77T-550
77T-5LL
78Ho-121
78OPC-101
78T-56
78Wiffle/Discs-33
79Ho-99
79OPC-95
79T-194
80OPC-160
80T-305
81Coke
81D-122
81F-487
81OPC-148
81T-458
81T/Tr-777
82F-528
82OPC-274
82T-626
83F-546
83OPC-29
83T-29

Jones, Rex
83ColumAst-24
84Cram/PCL-56
85Cram/PCL-74TR
86Tucso-9TR
88Tucso/Pro-192

Jones, Rick
88Portl/CMC-14
88Portl/Pro-656
89Spart/Pro-1032

Jones, Ricky
83RochR-16
85CharO-23
85RochR-6
86RochR-11
87CharO/WBTV-7

Jones, Robert O.
(Bobby)
77T-16
78Cr/PCL-79
83OKCty-11
83Rang-6
84Nes/792-451
84Rang-6
84T-451
85D-134
85F-559
85Rang-6
85T-648
86OKCty-8
86T-142
87Beloi-8

Jones, Robert Walter
E120
V100

Jones, Robert
(Bobby)
88CalLgAS-13
88Stock/Cal-190
88Stock/Pro-732
89Stock/Best-24
89Stock/Cal-166
89Stock/Pro-383
89Stock/Star-15

Jones, Ron
85Bend/Cram-13
86Clearw-11
86FSLAS-27
87Maine-23
87Maine/TCMA-17
88Maine/CMC-14
88Maine/Pro-280
89B-407
89Class-96
89D-40RR
89D/Rook-42
89F-574
89Panini/St-143
89Score-639
89Score/HotRk-25
89Score/YS/II-3
89Sf-178
89Sf-225M
89T-349
89ToysRUs-16
89UD-11
90D-487
90F-563
90Score-364
90Score/100Ris-31
90T-129
90UD-94

Jones, Ronnie
81BurlB-25

Jones, Ross
82Albuq-17
83Albuq-16
84Tidew-18
85BurlR-26
85Tidew-22
85Utica-2
86Chatt-15
86DayBe-14
87Gasto-17
88F-262
88Score-598
88T-169
88WPalm/Star-13
89WPalm/Star-13

Jones, Ruppert
77T-488R
78OPC-20
78T-141
79OPC-218
79T-422
80OPC-43
80T-78
81D-349
81F-101
81OPC-225
81T-225
81T/HT
81T/Tr-778
82D-346
82F-573
82F/St-102
82OPC-217
82T-511
82T/St-99
83D-373
83F-361
83OPC-287
83T-695
83T/Gloss-38
83T/Gloss40-38
83T/St-295
84D-261

84F-303
84F/X-59
84Nes/792-327
84OPC-327
84T-327
84T/St-158
84T/X-59
85D-612
85F-13
85F/Up-U63
85Smok/Cal-19
85T-126
85T/Tr-65T
86D-423
86F-161
86OPC-186
86Smok/Cal-19
86T-464
86T/St-184
87D-428
87F-85
87Smok/Cal-21
87T-53
88F-492
88Panini/St-47
88Score-333

Jones, Sam P.
21Exh-85
28Exh-63
28Yueng
29Exh/4-32
33G-81
E120
R316
V100
V354-31
V61-43
W502-38
W514-8
W515-43
W573

Jones, Sam
75BurlB
76BurlB
77DaytB

Jones, Samuel
(Sad Sam)
52NumNum-19
52T-382
53T-6
56T-259
57T-287
58T-287
59T-75
60L-14
60T-410
60T/tatt
60T/tatt-24
61P-143
61T-49LL
61T-555
61T/RO-31
62J-138
62P-138
62P/Can-138
62Salada-162
62Shirriff-162
62T-92
62T/St-127
84Moth/Giants-15

Jones, Scott
83Cedar-2
83Cedar/LF-18

Jones, Shannon
89Geneva/Pro-1881

Jones, Sheldon
(Available)
48B-34
49B-68
49Eureka-111
50B-83
50Drake-7
51B-199
52B-215
52BR
52NTea
52T-130
D305

Jones, Sherman
61T-161

Jones, Stacy
89Freder/Star-11

Jones, Steve
69OPC-49R
69T-49R

Jones, Terry R.
76OkCty

Jones, Terry
87FtMyr-21

Jones, Thomas F.
(Rick)
77T-118
79Portl-23
82RochR-13

Jones, Thomas
09Buster/Pin-7
12Sweet/Pin-26
E254
E270/1
M116
T205
T206

Jones, Tim
75Shreve/TCMA-6
87ArkTr-14
87Louvl-17
88Louvl-23
88Louvl/CMC-13
88Louvl/Pro-433
89B-439
89D-555
89D/Rook-28
89F-453
89Score-649
89Score/HotRk-28
89Smok/Cards-10
89UD-348
90D-686
90Score-579
90Score/100Ris-62
90T-533
90UD-501

Jones, Tim
77Clint
78Clint
78T-703R

Jones, Tommy
80Clint-27
81Phoen-16
83Butte-30
87Albany-19
88Albany/Pro-1352
89Wausa/GS-2

Jones, Tracy
83Tampa-26
86D/Rook-2
86F/Up-U58
86TexGold-29
87D-413
87F-651M
87F/U-U55
87Kahn-29
87T-146
88Class/Red-185
88D-310
88D/Best-174
88F-237
88Kahn/Reds-29
88Leaf-107
88OPC-101
88Panini/St-283
88Score-326
88Score/YS/I-38
88Sf-38
88T-553
89B-479
89D-574
89F-383
89F/Up-31
89Moth/Giants-14
89OPC-373
89Panini/St-124
89Score-510
89Score/Tr-43
89T-373
89UD-96
89UD/Ext-798
90D-636
90F-607
90Score-291
90T-767
90UD-309

Jones, Vernal
(Nippy)
49Eureka-186
50B-238
52T-213
58Union
R302-111
R423-51

Jones, Willie
49B-92
49Eureka-138
49Lummis
50B-67
51B-112
51BR-B8
51FB
51T/BB-43
52B-20
52RM-NL11
52T-47
52TipTop
53B/Col-133
53T-88
54B-143
54T-41
55B-172
56T-127
57T-174
58Hires-60
58T-181
59T-208
60L-98
60T-289
61T-497
79TCMA-29
PM10/Sm-87

Jongewaard, Steve
87Erie-8

Jonnard, Clarence
35G-1E
35G-3C
35G-5C
35G-6C

Jonson, Greg
81CharR-1
82FtMyr-6

Joost, Eddie
39PB-67
40PB-151
41DP-117
48B-15
48L-62
49B-55
50B-103
51B-119
51FB
51T/BB-15
52B-26
52RM-AL12
52T-45
52TipTop
53B/Col-105
53RM-AL7
54B-35
55B-263
61F-116
D305
R302-115
R423-50
W711/1
W711/2

Jordan
N172

Jordan, Adolph
(Dutch)
E254
E270/1
T206
T213/brown

Jordan, Baxter
(Buck)
34DS-49
34G-31
38Wheat
R314
V354-75

Jordan, Harry K.
75Phoen-24
76Phoen
77Phoen
78Cr/PCL-117
79Phoen
80Phoen-26
81Phoen-2
82Phoen

Jordan, Jim
78BurlB

Jordan, Jim
R310

Jordan, Milton
53Glen

Jordan, Ricky
86Readg-12
87Readg-16
88F/U-U110
88Maine/CMC-11
88Maine/Pro-286
88Score/Tr-68T
89B-401
89Bz-17
89Class-129
89D-624
89D/Best-103
89F-575
89F/BBAS-24
89F/Excit-27
89F/Heroes-25
89Panini/St-144
89Score-548
89Score/HotRk-88
89Score/YS/I-15
89Sf-44
89T-358
89T/Big-246
89T/Coins-17
89T/HeadsUp-4
89T/JumboR-14
89T/UK-45
89ToysRUs-17
89UD-35
90Class-32
90D-76
90F-564
90Score-16
90Sf-153
90T-216
90UD-576

Jordan, Scott
86Watlo-14
87Kinston-12
88EastLAS/Pro-40
88Wmspt/Pro-1326
89D-609

Jordan, Steve
81BurlB-16

Jordan, Tim
77Newar
78Newar

Jordan, Tim
C46-87
E103
E254
E90/1
M116
T206
T213/blue
T3-20

Jordan, Tony
80Wausa-4

Jorgens, Arndt
34G-72
39PB-42
40PB-2

Jorgensen, Mike
70OPC-348R
70T-348R
71OPC-596
71T-596
72OPC-16
72T-16
73OPC-281
73T-281
74OPC-549
74T-549
74T/St-56
74Weston-16
75Ho-105
75OPC-286
75T-286
75T/M-286
76Ho-144
76OPC-117
76SSPC-327
76T-117
77OPC-9
77T-368
78T-406
79T-22
80T-213
81D-274
81F-324
81T-698
82D-224
82F-529
82T-566
83F-547
83T-107
83T/X-51
84Nes/792-313
84Pol/Atl-11
84T-313
84T/X-60
85F-229
85T-783
86T-422
87Louvl-1MG
88Louvl-1MG
88Louvl/CMC-25
88Louvl/Pro-441
89Louvl-6MG
89Louvl/CMC-25MG
89Louvl/Pro-1256

Jorgenson, John
(Spider)
47TipTop
49Eureka-39
53Mother-55

Jorgenson, Terry
88Orlan/Best-15
89Orlan/Best-15
89Orlan/Pro-1352
89SLAS-12
90Score-655

Jorn, David A.
78StPet
80ArkTr-25
81ArkTr-12

Jose, Domingo
85Madis-17
Jose, Elio
88CharWh/Best-23
Jose, Felix
85Madis/Pol-14
86Modesto-16
88Tacom/CMC-24
88Tacom/Pro-614
89D-38RR
89F-15
89Moth/A's-22
89Score-629
89Score/HotRk-22
89Tacom/CMC-14
89Tacom/Pro-1542
89UD-22
90D-564
90F-13
90Score-321
90T-238
90UD-228
Jose, Manny
85Greens-4
86WinHav-13
87WinHav-17
88NewBrit/Pro-897
89London/Pro-1385
Joseph, Ricardo
68T-434
69T-329
70OPC-186
70T-186
72MB-174
Joseph, Sam
86QuadC-16tr
Josephson, Duane
67T-373R
68T-329
69MB-141
69MLB/St-32
69T-222
69T/St-156
70MLB/St-187
70OPC-263
70T-263
71OPC-56
71T-56
71T/Coins-92
72MB-175
72T-543
Josephson, Paul
83Albany-5
84Durhm-21
Joshua, Von
71OPC-57
71T-57
73OPC-544
73T-544
74OPC-551
74T-551
75OPC-547
75T-547
75T/M-547
76A&P/Milw
76K-39
76OPC-82
76SSPC-109
76T-82
77T-651
78T-108
80T-209
85SpokAT/Crm-10
88Albuq/Pro-254
89Albuq/Pro-73
Joslin, Chris
83BurlR-7
83BurlR/LF-16
Joslyn, John
88Virgini/Star-12
Joss, Adrian
(Addie)
61F-117
80Cram/Leg-114
80SSPC/HOF
E107
E254
E90/1
E93
M116
T205
T206
T3-19
W555
WG2-30
Joyce, Kevin
78Clint
Joyce, Michael
63T-66
64T-477
Joyce, Robert Emmett
48Sommer-6
Joyce, Tom
76AppFx
Joyce, William
N300/unif
Joyner, Wally
85Cram/PCL-2
86D/HL-23
86D/Rook-1
86F/Slug-19
86F/Up-U59
86S/Rook-7
86Smok/Cal-22
86T/Tr-51T
87BK-11
87Class-6
87Class/Up-108
87D-135
87D-1DK
87D/AAS-1
87D/DKsuper-1
87D/HL-35
87D/OD-7
87D/PopUp-1
87Drake-2
87F-628M
87F-86
87F-C7
87F/Excit-30
87F/GameWin-22
87F/Hottest-25
87F/Lim-23
87F/LL-26
87F/McCror-23
87F/Mini-59
87F/RecSet-17
87F/Slug-22
87F/St-68
87F/WaxBox-C7
87Ho/St-20
87KayBee-18
87Kraft-9
87Leaf-1DK
87Leaf-252
87MnM's-1
87MSA/Discs-10
87OPC-80
87RedFoley/St-82
87S-26
87S-75M
87Seven-W3
87Smok/Cal-12
87T-80
87T/Coins-16
87T/Gloss22-13
87T/Gloss60-39
87T/GlossRk-7
87T/Mini-45
87T/St-150
87T/St-174
87T/St-313
87ToysRUs-14
88Bz-10
88Class/Blue-206
88D-110
88D-BC13
88D/Best-115
88F-493
88F-622M
88F-C4
88F/AwardWin-21
88F/BB/AS-19
88F/BB/MVP-20
88F/Excit-23
88F/Hottest-21
88F/LL-22
88F/Mini-11
88F/RecSet-21
88F/SS-18
88F/St-12
88F/TL-16
88F/WaxBox-C4
88FanSam-4
88Jiffy-11
88KayBee-15
88KingB/Disc-9
88Leaf-50
88Nestle-44
88OPC-168
88Panini/St-40
88RedFoley/St-41
88Score-7
88Score/YS/I-27
88Sf-75
88Smok/Angels-17
88T-420
88T/Big-52
88T/Coins-16
88T/Gloss60-48
88T/Mini-6
88T/RiteAid-15
88T/St-179
88T/St/Backs-34
88T/UK-40
89B-47
89Class-29
89D-52
89D/Best-139
89D/MVP-BC21
89F-481
89F/Excit-28
89F/Superstar-26
89F/WaxBox-C16
89Holsum/Discs-1
89Master/Discs-7
89Nissen-1
89OPC-270
89Panini/St-291
89RedFoley/St-68
89Score-65
89Score/HotSt-73
89Sf-2
89Smok/Angels-18
89T-270
89T/Big-201
89T/St-183
89T/UK-46
89UD-573
89UD-668TC
90D-94
90F-136
90Score-120
90Score/100St-81
90Sf-49
90T-525
90UD-693
Juarbe, Ken
89Oneon/Pro-2114
Judd, Oscar
40Hughes-10
Juden, Jeff
90T-164
Judge, Joe
21Exh-86
25Exh-126
26Exh-126
28Yueng-35
29Exh/4-31
31Exh/4-32
33DH-25
33Exh/4-16
33G-155
61F-118
88Conlon/3-16
BF2-46
D327
D328-90
D329-93
E120
E121/80
E122
E126-26
E135-90
E220
M101/4-93
R316
V100
V353-88
W501-13
W502-35
W517-53
W572
W575
Judnich, Walt
41PB-67
47TipTop
49Sommer-28
52Mother-8
Exh47
W753
Judson, Howard
50B-185
51B-123
52B-149
52NTea
52T-169
53B/BW-42
53T-12
55B-193
Juenke, Dan
86FSLAS-28
86Miami-13
Jundy, Lorin
85LitFalls-6
86LitFalls-16
89BBCity/Star-13
Junker, Lance
81Clint-27
83Redwd-14
Jurak, Ed
81Brist-12
84D-127
84F-402
84Nes/792-628
84T-628
85D-579
85T-233
86T-749
87TexLgAS-9
88AAA/Pro-6
88D/A's/Bk-NEW
88Tacom/CMC-13
88Tacom/Pro-615
89Moth/Giants-20
Jurgens, Scott
89Boise/Pro-1980
Jurges, Bill
32Orbit/num-33A
32Orbit/num-33B
32Orbit/un-37
33G-225
35BU-139
39PB-35
40PB-89
41PB-59
60T-220MG
R305
R312/M
V355-97
WG8-36
Jury, Frank
88Boise/Pro-1630
Justice, Dave
86Sumter-15
87Greenvl/Best-9
88Richm-18
88Richm/CMC-17
88Richm/Pro-24
89Richm/CMC-15
89Richm/Ko-20
89Richm/Pro-838
89Score/HotRk-26
90D-704
90F-586
90Score-650
Justis, Walter
C46-42
Jutze, Alfred Henry
(Skip)
73OPC-613R
73T-613R
74OPC-328
74T-328
76OPC-489
76SSPC-52
76T-489
78T-532
Kaage, George
77Clint
78LodiD
Kaaihue, Kala
87Hawai-20
Kaat, Jim
60T-136
61Clover-9
61Peters-7
61T-63
61T/St-180
62T-21
63F-22
63J-10
63P-10
63Salada-40
63T-10LL
63T-165
64T-567
65OPC-62
65T-62
66T-224LL
66T-445
67Bz-18
67T-235LL
67T-237LL
67T-300
68Coke
68OPC-67CL
68T-450
69MB-142
69MLB/St-67
69T-290
69T/St-194
70MLB/St-233
70OPC-75
70T-75
71MLB/St-464
71OPC-245
71T-245
71T/GM-7
72MB-176
72T-709
72T-710A
73OPC-530
73T-530
74OPC-440
74T-440
75Ho/Twink-110
75OPC-243
75T-243
75T/M-243

76Crane-24
76Ho-110
76K-25
76MSA/Disc
76OPC-80
76SSPC-136
76T-80
76T/Tr-80T
77T-638
78T-715
79T-136
80T-250
81D-536
81F-536
81T-563
82D-217
82F-117
82F/St-240M
82T-367
83D-343
83F-11
83OPC-211
83OPC-383SV
83T-672
83T-673SV
83T/St-135
83T/St-136
88Pac/Leg-88
89Swell-88

Kable, David
81ArkTr-9
81Louvl-28
82Louvl-12
84Louvl-29
85Louvl-9
86ArkTr-9

Kaczmarski, Randy
82Amari-21
83Beaum-4

Kahanamoku, Duke
33SK-20

Kahmann, Jim
86WPalm-22TR
87Jaxvl-28
88Jaxvl/Pro-974
89Orlan/Best-6
89Orlan/Pro-1349

Kahoe, Michael
E107
T204

Kain, Marty
82Amari-20
84Cram/PCL-100
85Cram/PCL-11

Kainer, Don W.
79Tucso-11

Kainer, Ronald
76Watlo

Kairis, Bob
88BurlR/Pro-1794

Kaiser, Bart
86Clearw-12
87Clearw-25

Kaiser, C. Don
56T-124
57T-134

Kaiser, Jeff
85Moth/A's-25
86Tacom-10
87BuffB-16
88ColSp/CMC-4
88ColSp/Pro-1531
88Gator-47
89ColrSp/CMC-3
89F-410
89Salin/Cal-142
89Salin/Pro-1805

Kaiser, Keith
88Greens/Pro-1573
89Chatt/Best-2
89Chatt/GS-13

Kaiser, Ken
88Umpire-31
89Umpires-29

Kaiserling, George
15CJ-157

Kajima, Ken
89Salin/Cal-148CO

Kaler
T207

Kalin, Frank
53Mother-44

Kaline, Al
54T-201
55B-23
55T-4
55T/DH-45
56T-20
56T/Pin-38OF
56YellBase/Pin-16
57T-125
58T-304M
58T-70
59HRDerby-9
59T-360
59T-463M
59T-562AS
60Armour-12
60Bz-18
60NuCard-65
60P
60T-50
60T-561AS
60T/tatt
60T/tatt-25
61Bz-20
61NuCard-465
61P-35
61T-429
61T-580AS
61T/Dice-6
61T/St-152A
61T/St-152B
62Bz-12
62Exh
62J-20
62P-20
62P/Can-20
62Salada-67
62Shirriff-67
62T-150
62T-470AS
62T-51LL
62T/bucks
62T/St-47
63Bz-34
63Exh
63J-51
63P-51
63Salada-63
63T-25
63T/SO
64Bz-34
64Det/Lids-7
64T-12LL
64T-250
64T-331M
64T-8LL
64T/Coins-100
64T/Coins-129AS
64T/S-12
64T/St-95
64T/SU
64T/tatt
64Wheat/St-24
65Bz-34
65OldLond-27
65OPC-130
65T-130
65T/E-13
65T/trans
65T/trans-51
66Bz-46
66T-410
66T/RO-66
67Bz-46
67OPC-30
67OPC/PI-21
67T-216M
67T-239LL
67T-30
67T/PI-21
67T/Test/SU-10
68Bz-1
68OPC-2LL
68T-240
68T-2LL
68T/G-13
68T/Post-9
69Kelly/Pin-8
69MB-143
69MLB/St-49
69MLBPA/Pin-13
69NTF
69OPC-166WS
69T-410
69T/St-174
69Trans-6
70K-52
70MLB/St-208
70T-640
70T/SO
70Trans-14
71Bz/Test-14
71K-44
71MLB/St-396
71MLB/St-565
71OPC-180
71T-180
71T/Coins-62
71T/GM-19
71T/S-54
71T/tatt-5
71T/tatt-5a
72MB-177
72T-600
73K-52
73OPC-280
73T-280
73T/Lids-24
74Laugh/ASG-57
74OPC-215
74T-215
74T/St-177
75OPC-4RB
75T-4M
75T/M-4M
78TCMA-40
79TCMA-184
80Cram/Leg-65
80SSPC/HOF
82CJ-12
83D/HOF-18
83MLBPA/Pin-11
84West/1-12
85CircK-21
86S/Dec-51M
88Domino-9
88Pac/Leg-104
89Swell-40
Exh47
Rawl
WG10-30
WG9-31

Kallevig, Greg
86Peoria-12
87WinSal-2
88MidwLAS/GS-28
88Peoria/Ko-18
89CharlK-16

Kallio, Rudy
28Exh/PCL-15

Kamanaka, Masaaki
89VeroB/Star-12

Kamei, Kat
87SanJose-8

Kamieniecki, Scott
87PrWill-6
88FtLaud/Star-13
89Albany/Best-25
89Albany/Pro-316

Kamm, Willie
21Exh-87
25Exh-76
26Exh-77
27Exh-39
28Yueng-40
29Exh/4-19
30CEA/Pin-17
31Exh/4-19
32Orbit/num-10
32Orbit/un-38
33G-75
34Exh/4-11
34G-14
35BU-39
35Exh/4-11
35G-1J
35G-1L
35G-2E
35G-3A
35G-5A
35G-6A
35G-6E
35G-7E
R305
R308-164
R316
V353-68
V354-60
W502-40
W515-42
W517-13

Kammeyer, Bob
78Cr/PCL-34
79Colum-23
80Colum-10

Kammeyer, Tim
82Redwd-6
83Redwd-15

Kampouris, Alex
35G-8D
35G-9D
36Exh/4-4
41DP-13
R314
W711/1

Kampsen, Doug
85Cedar-9

Kane, John
M116

Kane, Kevin
81Brist-3
85Pawtu-18

Kane, Tom
86Greens-12
87Greens-1

Kanehl, Rod
62T-597R
63F-49
63J-199
63P-19
63T-371
64T-582

Kaney, Joe
47Centen-14

Kannenberg, Scott
86QuadC-17
87QuadC-9
88PalmSp/Cal-88
88PalmSp/Pro-1444

Kanter, John
85Madis-18
85Madis/Pol-15
86Modesto-17

Kanwisher, Gary
85Beloi-20
86Stockton-11
87Stockton-25

Kappell, Henry
N172

Kappesser, Bob
89Helena/SP-19

Karasinski, Dave
89BurlB/Pro-1611
89BurlB/Star-11

Karcher, Kevin
86Cram/PCL-41

Karchner, Matt
89Eugene/Best-6

Karczewski, Ray
88SLCty-7
89SLCty-7SS

Karger, Edwin
10Domino-61
12Sweet/Pin-5
E90/1
E91
E96
M116
T204
T205
T206

Karkovice, Ron
83AppFx/LF-22
86SLAS-5
87Coke/WS-3
87D-334
87D/OD-234
87F-645M
87Seven-C11
87T-491
88Score-374
88T-86
88Vanco/CMC-15
88Vanco/Pro-773
89Coke/WS-13
89T-308
89UD-183
90D-413
90Score-22
90T-717
90UD-69

Karmeris, Joe
85VeroB-14

Karpuk, Greg
86Watlo-15
87Wmspt-26

Karr, Benjamin
E120
E126-20
W573

Karr, Jeff
84LitFalls-7

Karros, Eric
88GreatF-2
89Bakers/Cal-201

Kaseda, Yuki
89Salin/Cal-130
89Salin/Pro-1808

Kasko, Eddie
57T-363
58T-8
59T-232
60Kahn
60L-9
60T-61
61Kahn
61P-185
61T-534
61T/St-18
62J-119
62Kahn
62P-119
62P/Can-119
62Salada-147
62Shirriff-147

62T-193
62T/St-117
63FrBauer-11
63J-128
63Kahn
63P-128
63T-498
70OPC-489MG
70T-489
71OPC-578
71T-31
72OPC-218MG
72T-218
73OPC-131MG
73T-131MG
78TCMA-249
Kasper, Kevin
89Everett/Star-18
Kaspryzak, Dennis
77Jaxvl
Kastelic, Bruce
82Lynch-5
Kasunick, Joe
83Butte-29
Kating, Jim
87Bakers-11
88SnAnt/Best-9
89Huntsvl/Best-6
Kats, Bill
43Centen-15
45Centen-14
Katt, Ray
54B-121
54NYJour
55B-183
55Gol/Giants-15
57T-331
58Hires-57
58T-284
60T-468C
61Union
62Sugar-17
79TCMA-235
Katzaroff, Robbie
88CapeCod/Sum-163
Katzler, Jerry
89BirmB/Best-15
Kaub, Keith
88James/Pro-1911
89Mia/Star/25-21
Kauff, Benjamin
15CJ-160
BF2-76
D327
D328-92
D329-94
D350/2-92
E135-92
M101/4-94
M101/5-92
PM1-9
W514-100
W516-16
Kaufman, Al
T3/Box-73
Kaufman, Curt
82Colum-5
82Colum/Pol-24
83Colum-11
84Smok/Cal-14
85Cram/PCL-20
85D-524
85F-305
85T-61
Kaufman, Ron
82QuadC-9
Kaufman, Tony
21Exh-88
Kaufmann, Anthony
47TipTop
Kaull, Kurt
83Erie-25
84Savan-5
Kautz, Scott
88Harris/Pro-862
Kautzer, Bill
75AppFx
76AppFx
Kavanagh, Mike
75Shreve/TCMA-7
Kavanaugh, Tim
83Erie-19
Kawabata, Yasuhiro
89VeroB/Star-13
Kaye, Jeff
86Clearw-13
87Clearw-8
88Readg/Pro-872
Kayser, Tom
77Holyo
79Holyo-30
80Holyo-10
81Holyo-3
Kazak, Edward
49Eureka-187
50B-36
51B-85
52T-165
53T-194
79TCMA-16
Kazanski, Ted
54T-78
55T-46
55T/DH-5
57T-27
58T-36
59T-99
Kazmierczak, William
87Peoria-28
88WinSal/Star-7
Kealey, Steve
69T-224R
71OPC-43
71T-43
72OPC-146
72T-146
73OPC-581
73T-581
Keane, Johnny
60T-468C
62T-198
63T-166
64T-413
65OPC-131MG
65T-131
66T-296
Kearney, Robert
78Cedar
80Phoen-15
81Tacom-5
82Tacom-27
83D-539
83T/X-52
84D-462
84F-449
84F/X-60
84Moth/Mar-4
84Nes/792-326
84T-326
84T/St-381YS
84T/X-61
85D-362
85F-491
85Moth/Mar-13
85OPC-386
85T-679
85T/St-335
86D-74
86F-466
86Moth/Mar-23
86OPC-13
86T-13
87D-445
87F-587
87Moth/Sea-12
87OPC-73
87T-498
Kearns, John
83Wisco/LF-10
Kearse, Edward
47Remar-7
47Smith-14
Keas
N172
Keathley, Robin
83TriCit-8
85BurlR-22
Keating, Dave
89NiagFls/Puc-5B
Keating, Dennis
79AppFx-2
Keating, Ray
14CJ-95
15CJ-95
28Exh/PCL-32
T222
Keatley, Greg
81Omaha-14
82Omaha-11
Keckler, Mike
85FtMyr-23
Keedy, Pat
81Holyo-16
82Holyo-16
84Cram/PCL-118
85Cram/PCL-1
86Edmon-16
87Hawai-27
88T-486
88Tucso-14
88Tucso/CMC-22
88Tucso/Pro-175
Keefe, George
N172
Keefe, Kevin
78Cr/PCL-104
79Albuq-8
80Albuq-17
81Albuq/TCMA-11
Keefe, Timothy
80SSPC/HOF
E223
N162
N172
N28
N284
N403
WG1-41
Keefer, Pal
89Well/Puc-15
Keegan, Ed
61T-248
62T-249
Keegan, Robert
53T-196
54T-100
55T-10
55T/DH-52
56T-54
57T-99
58T-200
59T-86
60T-291
77T-436M
Keehn, Mike
83TriCit-18
Keeler, Jay
(Devo)
83Watlo/LF-9
Keeler, Willie
40PB-237
48Exh/HOF
50Callahan
63Bz/ATG-31
69Bz/Sm
72F/FFeat-40
72Laugh/GF-31
80Cram/Leg-99
80SSPC/HOF
89HOF/St-51
89Smok/Dodg-12
E107
E254
E270/2
E90/1
E97
T204
T206
T3-101
W555
WG2-31
Keeley, Robert
54JC-35
54T-176
55JC-35
Keenan, James
N172
V100
Keenan, Kerry
77Ashev
79Wausa-4
80Ashev-15
Keenan, Kevin
80Elmir-10
Keener, Jeff
81Louvl-10
82ArkTr-4
84Louvl-22
85Louvl-8
Keenum, Larry
76Baton
Keeton, Garry
83AppFx/LF-26
Keeton, Rickey
(Buster)
79Vanco-10
82D-618
82F-146
82T-268
82Tucso-13
83Tucso-3
84Omaha-6
85Omaha-28
Keim, Chris
89Bill/Pro-2062
Keitges, Jeff
89Wausa/GS-24
Kekich, Mike
65T-561R
69T-262
70OPC-536
70T-536
71MLB/St-490
71OPC-703
71T-703
72OPC-138
72T-138
73OPC-371
73T-371
74OPC-199
74T-199
76OPC-582
76T-582
78SnJos-24
Kelbe, Frank
89Watertn/Star-27
Keliipuleole, Carl
88Kinston/Star-13
89Canton/Best-18
89Canton/Pro-1300
89Canton/Star-9
Kell, Everett
(Skeeter)
52B-242
Kell, George
47TipTop
48L-120
49B-26
49Royal-3
50B-8
51B-46
51FB
51T/CAS
52B-75
52BR
52RM-AL13
52Royal
52StarCal/L-72A
52T-246
52TipTop
53B/Col-61
53RM-AL8
53T-138
54B-50
54RH
54RM-AL4
55B-213
56T-195
57T-230
58T-40
79TCMA-86
80Cram/Leg-118
86S/Dec-24M
88Pac/Leg-69
89HOF/St-24
Exh47
R423-57
Kelleher, Frank
47Signal
49B/PCL-27
53Mother-37
Kelleher, John
E120
V61-87
Kelleher, Mick
76SSPC-605
77T-657
78T-564
79T-53
80T-323
81D-513
81T-429
81T/Tr-779
82D-601
82T-184
82T/Tr-53T
83T-79
Kellelmark, Joe
87VeroB-19
Keller, Carlton
(Buzz)
77ArkTr
Keller, Charlie
39Exh
39PB-88
40PB-9
41DP-64
41DP-84
41PB-21
44Yank/St-16
47TipTop
49B-209
50B-211
51B-177
89Pac/Leg-194
D305
Exh47
R346-48
Keller, Dave
86Tampa-8C
88Bill/Pro-1802
89Bill/Pro-2048
Keller, Jerry
79Richm-19
80Richm-12
81Richm-3
82Richm-10
83Portl-7
84Syrac-10
85Syrac-18

Keller, Steve
89Spart/Pro-1055
89Spart/Star-10
Kellert, Frank
55Gol/Dodg-15
56T-291
Kelley, Anthony
86ColumAst-16
87Tucso-21
88Tucso-15
88Tucso/CMC-2
88Tucso/Pro-186
89Tucso/CMC-3
Kelley, Dean
87Oneon-29
88CLAS/Star-10
Kelley, Harry
37Exh/4-14
37OPC-121
38Exh/4-14
V300
Kelley, Jack
C46-15
Kelley, Joe
80SSPC/HOF
89HOF/St-35
89Smok/Dodg-13
C46-27
E107
T206
WG3-23
Kelley, M.
W516-26
Kelley, Richard
64T-476R
66OPC-84R
66T-84R
67OPC-138
67T-138
68T-203
69MLB/St-193
69T-359
70MLB/St-114
70OPC-474
70T-474
72MB-178
72OPC-412
72T-412
Kelley, Steve
75QuadC
Kelley, Thomas
64T-552R
66OPC-44R
66T-44R
67T-214
71OPC-463
71T-463
72OPC-97
72T-97
Kellman, Howard
88Indi/Pro-525M
89Indi/Pro-1216
Kellner, Alex
49B-222
50B-14
51B-57
51FB
52B-226
52T-201
53B/Col-107
53Exh/Can-64
54B-51
55B-53
55Rodeo
56T-176
57T-280
58T-3
59T-101
79TCMA-55
Exh47
Kelly, Anthony
86SLAS-22
89Tucso/Pro-186
Kelly, Bill
47Signal
Kelly, Bill
80Indianap-23
81Indianap-22
82Omaha-7
Kelly, Brian
75Clint
Kelly, Bryan
83Evans-4
86Nashv-14
87Toled-29
Kelly, Charles H.
N172
Kelly, Dean
88PrWill/Star-13
89FtLaud/Star-11
Kelly, Eliqio
78Newar
Kelly, George L.
21Exh-89
28Yueng-20
29Exh/4-7
40PB-141
49Remar
50Remar
80Cram/Leg-62
80SSPC/HOF
87Conlon/2-45
89HOF/St-8
89Smok/Dodg-14
E120
E121/120
E121/80
E122
E126-60
E210-20
E220
V100
V61-119
W501-72
W502-20
W515-32
W517-11
W572
W575
Kelly, H. Pat
69T-619R
70MLB/St-222
70OPC-57
70T-57
71OPC-413
71T-413
72MB-179
72OPC-326
72T-326
73OPC-261
73T-261
74K-47
74OPC-46
74T-46
74T/St-156
75OPC-82
75T-82
75T/M-82
76OPC-212
76SSPC-152
76T-212
77T-469
78T-616
79T-188
80T-543
81D-600
82T-417
Kelly, Hal
79Tulsa-22
Kelly, Jimy
88Knoxv/Best-5
89Duned/Star-9
Kelly, John O.
N172
Kelly, Joseph
88CapeCod/Sum-173
Kelly, Kevin
89BurlB/Pro-1623
89BurlB/Star-12
Kelly, Leonard
87BurlEx-1
Kelly, Michael
88CapeCod/Sum-10
88WinHav/Star-10
Kelly, Michael
(King)
50Callahan
75F/Pion-8
80SSPC/HOF
E223
N162
N172
N172
N28
N284
N403
N526
N690/2
WG1-5
Kelly, Mike
87Elmir-15
87Elmir/Red-15
89Lynch/Star-11
Kelly, Pat
75QuadC
78Syrac
79T-714R
80OPC-329R
80Syrac-15
80T-674R
82F-372
83GlenF-11
86CharRa-11MG
88Oneon/Pro-2043
88Wichi-40MG
89AubAs/Pro-15
89PrWill/Star-10
89Star/Wax-89
89Wich/Roc-6MG
89Wich/Roc/Up-2
Kelly, Rafael
75QuadC
76QuadC
Kelly, Robert Edward
52T-348
Kelly, Roberto
83Greens-19
84Greens-4
86Albany/TCMA-2
87Colum-18
87Colum/Pol-14
87Colum/TCMA-22
88D-635
88D/Rook-16
88D/Y/Bk-635
88F-212
88Score-634
88T/Tr-57T
89B-183
89Class/Up/2-167
89D-433
89D/Best-273
89F-256
89Panini/St-395
89Score-487
89Score/HotRk-90
89Score/NWest-18
89Score/YS/II-25
89T-691
89T/Big-152
89ToysRUs-18
89UD-590
90D-192
90F-446
90Score-100
90Score/100St-57
90Sf-184
90T-109
90UD-193
Kelly, Tim
86Bakers-17CO
87PalmSp-18
88MidldA/GS-3
Kelly, Tom
82Orlan/B-13MG
82OrlTw/A-12MG
87T-618MG
88T-194
89D/AS-10MG
89D/PopUp-10MG
89T-14MG
89T/Gloss22-1MG
90T-429MG
Kelly, William J.
D304
E254
E270/2
E97
T207
T213/blue
T215/blue
Kelso, Bill
65OPC-194R
65T-194R
67T-367R
68T-511
Keltner, Ken
39Exh
41DP-79
48L-45
49B-125
50B-186
89Pac/Leg-143
89Swell-87
D305
Exh47
R303/A
R303/B
R311/Gloss
Kemmerer, Russ
55B-222
55T-18
55T/DH-4
58T-137
59T-191
60T-362
61T-56
61T/St-121
62T-576
63T-338
Kemmler, Rudolph
N172
N172/BC
N370
Scrapps
Kemnitz, Brent
85Anchora-17CO
87Anchora-17CO
Kemp, Hugh
84Cedar-7
87Nashv-11
88AAA/Pro-27
88Nashvl/CMC-7
88Nashvl/Pro-479
89Nashvl-10
89Nashvl/CMC-5
89Nashvl/Pro-1294
Kemp, Joe
88SnBer/Best-21
88SnBer/Cal-35
89Modesto/Cal-280
Kemp, Rod
79LodiD-1
Kemp, Steve
77T-492R
78BK/T-18
78Ho-55
78OPC-167
78T-21
79Ho-15
79OPC-97
79T-196
80K-33
80OPC-166
80T-315
80T/S-29
81Coke
81D-249
81Drake-27
81F-459
81F/St-7
81MSA/Disc-19
81OPC-152
81Sqt-27SP
81T-593
81T/SO-11
81T/St-74
82D-594
82F-271
82F/St-160
82K-39
82OPC-296
82T-666TL
82T-670
82T/St-185
82T/Tr-54T
83D-269
83Drake-13
83F-239
83OPC-260
83RoyRog/Disc-5
83T-260
83T/St-50
83T/X-53
84D-469
84Drake-16
84F-129
84FunFood/Pin-58
84Nes/792-440
84OPC-301
84T-440
85D-225
85F-132
85F/Up-U64
85Leaf-100
85OPC-120
85T-120
85T/Tr-66T
86D-200
86F-610
86LasVegas-9
86T-387
87OKCty-11
88Moth/R-8
Kemper, Robbie
89Clint/Pro-896
Kenaga, Jeff
82Evans-22
83Evans-20
84CharO-8
Kendall, Fred
72T-532
73OPC-221
73T-221
74McDon
74OPC-53SD
74T-53
74T/St-95
75OPC-332
75T-332
75T/M-332
76OPC-639
76SSPC-122
76T-639
77OPC-213
77T-576
78PapaG/Disc-13
78T-426
79T-83
80T-598

Kendrick, Pete
83Madis/LF-23
84Albany-14
87ElPas-4
88Denver/Pro-1269
Kenins, John N.
N172
Kennedy, Bo
87Penin-23
89Saraso/Star-12
Kennedy, Dan
89WinSal/Star-11
Kennedy, Dave
89Elmir/Puc-23
Kennedy, John E.
64T-203
65OPC-119
65T-119
66T-407
67OPC-111
67T-111
69T-631
70McDon-2
70OPC-53
70T-53
71MLB/St-319
71OPC-498
71T-498
72T-674
73OPC-437
73T-437
86Alban/TCM-24C
Kennedy, Junior
76Indianap-13
77Phoen
79T-501
80T-377
81D-424
81F-203
81T-447
82D-188
82F-70
82RedLob
82T-723
82T/Tr-55T
83D-529
83F-500
83T-204
Kennedy, Kevin
78RochR
79RochR-3
80RochR-11
81RochR-10
87Bakers-15
88SnAnt/Best-23
88TexLgAS/GS-22
89Albuq/Pro-72
Kennedy, Lloyd Vernon
37Exh/4-10
37OPC-135
38G-256
38G-280
V300
WG8-37
Kennedy, Monte
47TipTop
49B-237
49Eureka-112
50B-175
51B-163
52B-213
52BR
52T-124
Kennedy, Robert D.
47TipTop
51B-296
51T/RB-29
52NumNum-16
52T-77
53T-33
54Esskay
54T-155
55Esskay
55T-48
55T/DH-87
56T-38
56T/Pin-34
57T-149
64T-486
65T-457
68OPC-183MG
68T-183
85T-135FS
Kennedy, Terry
78ArkTr
79T-724R
80T-569
81D-428
81F-541
81OPC-353
81T-353
81T/Tr-780
82D-121
82Drake-20
82F-574
82F/St-105
82OPC-65
82T-65
82T/St-100
83D-220
83D-26
83D/AAS-11
83F-362
83OPC-274
83T-274
83T-742
83T/Gloss-6
83T/Gloss40-6
83T/St-293
84D-112
84D/AAS-8
84F-304
84FunFood/Pin-47
84Moth/Pad-5
84Nes/792-366TL
84Nes/792-455
84OPC-166
84Seven-17W
84Smok/Pad-14
84T-455
84T/St-154
85D-429
85F-37
85Leaf-33
85Moth/Pad-10
85OPC-194
85T-135FS
85T-635
85T/St-148
86D-356
86D/AAS-7
86D/PopUp-7
86F-327
86OPC-230
86T-230
86T-306M
86T/Gloss22-20
86T/St-111
86T/St-152
87D-205
87D/OD-142
87F-419
87F/U-U56
87OPC-303
87T-540
87T/St-108
87T/Tr-57T
88D-150
88D/AS-9
88D/Best-30
88D/PopUp-9
88F-563
88French-15
88Leaf-99
88OPC-180
88Panini/St-227M
88Panini/St-7
88Score-123
88Score/WaxBox-1
88Sf-94
88T-180
88T/Gloss22-9
88T/St-161
88T/St-225
88T/St/Backs-55
89B-470
89D-141
89F-610
89F/Up-128
89Moth/Giants-8
89OPC-309
89Panini/St-256
89Score-123
89Score/Tr-30
89T-705
89T/Big-180
89T/St-235
89T/Tr-59T
89UD-469
90D-602
90F-58
90Score-7
90T-372
90UD-397
Kennedy, Theodore A.
N172
Kennedy, William G.
(Bill)
49B-105
52T-102
53T-94
60HenryH-25
Kennedy, William
N284
N300/unif
Kennelley, Steve
87Columbia-11
Kennemur, Paul
76Baton
Kenner, Jeff
86ArkTr-10
Kenney, Jerry
69T-519
70OPC-219
70T-219
71MLB/St-491
71OPC-572
71T-572
72MB-180
72OPC-158
72T-158
73OPC-514
73T-514
Kenny, Terry
75Cedar
Kent, Bernard
85Beloi-12
Kent, Dave
89Oneon/Pro-2119
Kent, Jeff
88CapeCod/Sum-169
89StCath/Pro-2091
Kent, John
(Bo)
86Cram/PCL-73
87Modesto-1
88Huntsvl/BK-10
Kent, Lewis
87Kinston-7
88Kinston/Star-14
Kent, Matt
86Stockton-12
Kent, Troy
88Martins/Star-20
89Spart/Pro-1033
89Spart/Star-11
Kent, Wes
81AppFx-26
82AppFx-13
83GlenF-3
Kenworthy, Dick
68OPC-63
68T-63
Kenworthy, William
(Duke)
WG7-24
Kenyon, J.J.
N172
Kenyon, Robert
81VeroB-7
82VeroB-7
Keough, Joseph
69T-603
70T-589
71MLB/St-417
71OPC-451
71T-451
72OPC-133
72T-133
Keough, Matt
78T-709R
79Ho-59
79OPC-284
79T-554
80OPC-74
80T-134
81D-358
81F-588
81OPC-301
81T-301
82D-71
82F-95
82F/St-129
82Granny-6
82OPC-87
82T-87
82T/St-225
83D-239
83F-521
83Granny-27
83T-413
83T/St-109
83T/X-54
84D-627
84F-130
84Nes/792-203
84OPC-203
84T-203
85Louvl-16
87Moth/A's-18
Keough, R. Marty
58T-371
59T-303
60T-71
61T-146
62J-69
62P-69
62P/Can-69
62Salada-79
62Shirriff-79
62T-258
63FrBauer-12
63J-135
63P-135
63T-21
64T-166
65OPC-263
65T-263
66T-334
Kepshire, Kurt
81Cedar-2
82Cedar-5
83ArkTr-4
84Louvl-17
85D-382
85F-230
85T-474
86D-504
86F-39
86KAS/Disc-13
86Louisvl-14
86Schnucks-11
86T-256
88Indi/CMC-2
88Indi/Pro-506
89Portl/CMC-3
89Portl/Pro-215
Kerfeld, Charlie
85Cram/PCL-73
86D/Rook-6
86F-303
86Pol/Ast-10
86S/Rook-23
86T/Tr-52T
87D-209
87F-60
87F/Excit-31
87Leaf-195
87Moth/Ast-12
87OPC-145
87S-146
87T-145
87T/St-28
87ToysRUs-15
88ColAst/Best-1
88OPC-392
88Score-479
88T-608
89Tucso/CMC-8
89Tucso/Pro-188
Keriazakos, Const.
(Gus)
55B-14
Kerkes, Kevin
89Wausa/GS-22
Kern, Jim
75OkCty
75OPC-621R
75T-621R
75T/M-621R
76SSPC-509
77Pep-7
77T-41
78OPC-165
78T-253
79OPC-297
79T-573
80OPC-192
80T-369
81D-27
81F-618
81F/St-18
81OPC-197
81T-197
82Coke/Reds
82D-89
82F-322
82OPC-59
82T-463
82T/Tr-56T
83D-355
83F-240
83T-772
86OhHenry-46
Kern, Lloyd D.
77WHave
79WHave-28
79WHave-29M
80LynnS-22
81LynnS-26
Kernek, George B.
66Pep/Tul
66T-544
Kerns, Russ
V362-38
Kerr, John Francis
33G-214
49Remar
Kerr, John J.
(Buddy)

48B-20
49B-186
49Eureka-113
50B-55
50Drake-15
51B-171
79TCMA-113
D305
R302-102

Kerr, John L.
28Exh/PCL-16
29Exh/4-19

Kerr, Richard
(Dickie)
21Exh-90
88Pac/8Men-47
88Pac/8Men-56
88Pac/8Men-97
E121/120
E121/80
E122
E220
W501-37
W514-23
W575

Kerr, Zack
89Erie/Star-10

Kerrigan, Joe
77OPC-171
77T-341
78OPC-108
78T-549
79RochR-2
79T-37
81Indianap-24
82OkCty-13
84Stuart-33
86Provigo-14CO
87Jaxvl-26
88Indi/Pro-499M

Kerrigan, Rob
87Jamestn-21
88James/Pro-1898
88Rockford-18
89Rockford-18

Kershaw, Scott
86AppFx-12

Keshock, Christopher
87CharWh-22

Kesler, Mike
87QuadC-13

Kesselmark, Joe
88SnAnt/Best-11
89SnAnt/Best-9

Kesses, Steve
76Wausa

Kessinger, Don
66OPC-24
66T-24
67T-419
68OPC-159
68T-159
69Kelly/Pin-9
69MB-144
69MLB/St-123
69MLBPA/Pin-48
69Sunoco/Pin-6
69T-225
69T-422AS
69T/S-18
69T/St-16
70Dunkin-4
70MLB/St-20
70OPC-456AS
70OPC-80
70T-456AS
70T-80
71K-9
71MD
71MLB/St-36
71OPC-455
71T-455
71T/Coins-119
71T/tatt-15
72MB-181
72OPC-145
72T-145
73OPC-285
73T-285
74OPC-38
74T-38
74T/DE-52
74T/St-16
75Ho-77
75Ho/Twink-77
75OPC-315
75T-315
75T/M-315
76Crane-25
76Ho-134
76MSA/Disc
76OPC-574
76SSPC-315
76T-574
77T-229
78T-672
79T-404MG
79T-467
89Swell-112

Kessinger, Keith
89Bluef/Star-12

Kester, Rick
70T-621R
71OPC-494R
71T-494
72OPC-351R
72T-351

Ketchel, Stanley
T3/Box-67

Ketleers, Cotuit
88CapeCod-24

Key, Greg
83Redwd-16
85MidldA-3

Key, Jimmy
84F/X-61
84T/X-62
84Tor/Fire-20
85D-559
85F-110
85OPC-193
85T-193
85Tor/Fire-16
86Ault-22
86D-561
86D/AAS-53
86F-63
86F-642M
86KayBee-18
86Leaf-219
86OPC-291
86T-545
86T/Mini-35
86T/St-191
86Tor/Fire-20
87D-244
87D/OD-37
87F-232
87Leaf-187
87OPC-29
87T-29
87T/St-192
87Tor/Fire-16
87Tor/Fire-16
88Class/Blue-249
88D-72
88D/Best-143
88F-114
88F/AwardWin-22
88F/Excit-24
88F/Hottest-22
88F/LL-23
88F/Mini-63
88F/RecSet-22
88F/SS-19
88F/St-74
88F/TL-17
88Ho/Disc-24
88Leaf-67
88OPC-47
88Panini/St-214
88RedFoley/St-42
88Score-216
88Sf-116
88T-395
88T-682
88T/Coins-17
88T/Mini-39
88T/Revco-27
88T/St-190
88Tor/Fire-22
89B-243
89D-188
89D/Best-87
89F-236
89OPC-229
89Panini/St-462
89Score-480
89Sf-167
89T-229
89T/St-186
89Tor/Fire-22
89UD-291
90D-231
90F-85
90Score-407
90T-371
90UD-462

Keyes, Stewart
88CapeCod/Sum-148

Keyser, Brian
89Utica/Puc-12

Khalifa, Sammy
83AlexD-2
85Cram/PCL-227
86D-308
86F-611
86Leaf-178
86T-316
86T/St-127
87T-164
87Vanco-11
89BuffB/CMC-15
89BuffB/Pro-1667

Khoury, Mike
86Watertn-10

Khoury, Scott
86Hagers-8
87Hagers-26
88Watlo/Pro-672
89Canton/Best-19
89Canton/Pro-1310
89Canton/Star-10

Kibbe, Jay
81Redwd-4
84Cram/PCL-119

Kibler, John
88Umpire-4
89Umpires-2

Kibler, Russell
85Madis-19
85Madis/Pol-16
86Madis-13
86Madis/Pol-13

Kida, Masao
88Mia/Star-14

Kiecker, Dana
86NewBrit-15
87NewBrit-17
88Pawtu/CMC-10
88Pawtu/Pro-461
89Pawtu/CMC-4
89Pawtu/Dunkin-19
89Pawtu/Pro-701

Kiefer, Mark
89Beloi/Star-11

Kiefer, Steve
82Madis-3
83Albany-12
84Cram/PCL-78
85Cram/PCL-139
85D-35
85F-647
85Leaf-27
86D-420
86Vanco-15
87Denver-18
88D-542
88F-167
88Pol/Brew-30
88Score-630
88T-187
89Colum/CMC-15
89Colum/Pol-11
89Colum/Pro-740

Kiely, John
89Lakel/Star-12

Kiely, Leo
52T-54
54T-171
55T-36
55T/DH-43
58T-204
59T-199
60T-94

Kiernan, J.F.
T206

Kierst, Kevin
87Knoxv-24

Kies, Norman
V355-120

Kiess, Paul
80Penin/B-17
80Penin/C-23

Kilduff, Pete
D327
E121/120
E121/80
E122
E220
V100
W501-93
W575

Kile, Darryl
89ColMud/Best-4
89ColMud/Pro-133
89ColMud/Star-15

Kiley, Craig
84LitFalls-15

Kilgo, Rusty
89James/Pro-2156

Kilgus, Paul
86Tulsa-20
87OKCty-1
88D-469
88D/Best-111
88F-471
88Moth/R-19
88Score-536
88T-427
89B-285
89D-283
89D/Best-149
89D/Tr-42
89F-525
89F/Up-76
89Mara/Cubs-39
89OPC-276
89Score-271
89T-276
89T/Tr-60T
89UD-335
89UD/Ext-797
90D-276
90F-34
90Score-196
90T-86
90UD-155

Kilkenny, Mike
69T-544
70MLB/St-209
70OPC-424
70T-424
71MLB/St-397
71OPC-86
71T-86
72OPC-337
72T-337
73OPC-551
73T-551

Killebrew, Cameron
79Wausa-22

Killebrew, Harmon
55T-124
55T/DH-111
56T-164
58T-288
59HRDerby-10
59T-515
60Bz-20
60NuCard-49
60P
60T-210
60T/tatt
60T/tatt-26
60T/tatt-91
61Clover-10
61NuCard-449
61P-92
61Peters-18
61T-80
61T/St-181
62Bz
62Exh
62J-85
62P-85
62P/Can-85
62Salada-36
62Shirriff-36
62T-316M
62T-53LL
62T-70
62T/bucks
62T/St-76
63Bz-7
63Exh
63J-5
63P-5
63T-4LL
63T-500
63T/SO
64Bz-7
64T-10LL
64T-12LL
64T-177
64T-81M
64T/Coins-112
64T/Coins-133AS
64T/S-38
64T/St-34
64T/SU
64T/tatt
64Wheat/St-25
65Bz-7
65OldLond-28
65OPC-3LL
65OPC-5LL
65T-3LL
65T-400
65T-5LL
65T/E-56
65T/trans-52
66Bz-11
66OPC-120
66T-120
66T/RO-50
67Bz-11
67OPC/PI-23
67T-241LL
67T-243LL

67T-334M
67T-460
67T/Pl-23
67T/Test/SU-6
68Bz-8
68Coke
68OPC-4LL
68OPC-6LL
68T-220
68T-361AS
68T-490M
68T-4LL
68T-6LL
68T/G-5
68T/Post-10
69Citgo-4
69MB-145
69MLB/St-68
69MLBPA/Pin-14
69T-375
69T/decal
69T/S-19
69T/St-195
69Trans-11
70K-61
70MB-12
70MLB/St-234
70OPC-150
70OPC-64LL
70OPC-66LL
70T-150
70T-64LL
70T-66LL
70T/S-4
70T/SO
70Trans-15
71Bz
71Bz/Test-17
71K-55
71MD
71MLB/St-465
71MLB/St-566
71OPC-550
71OPC-65LL
71T-550
71T-65LL
71T/Coins-100
71T/GM-8
71T/S-60
71T/tatt-6
71T/tatt-6a
72MB-182
72OPC-51
72OPC-52IA
72OPC-88LL
72T-51
72T-52A
72T-88LL
72T/Post-20
73OPC-170
73T-170
73T/Comics-9
73T/Lids-25
73T/PinUps-9
74OPC-400
74T-400
74T/St-208
75OPC-207M
75OPC-640
75T-207MV
75T-640
75T/M-207MV
75T/M-640
76Laugh/Jub-13
76SSPC-168
78TCMA-90
80Cram/Leg-69
80Laugh/3/4/5-14
82CJ-15
82KMart-15
84West/1-23
85CircK-5
86BLChew-5
86S/Dec-48M
87KMart-4
87Nestle/DT-22
88Pac/Leg-86
89Kahn/Coop-7
89Pac/Leg-163
89Swell-70
Exh47
PM10/Sm-88
Rawl

Killian, Ed
12Sweet/Pin-27
E254
T201
T205
T206
T213/brown

Killifer, William
09Buster/Pin-8
14CJ-135
14Piedmont/St-30
15CJ-135
21Exh-91
BF2-86
D327
D328-93
D329-95
D350/2-93
E121/120
E121/80
E122
E135-93
E254
E286
M101/4-95
M101/5-93
M116
V100
W501-56
W514-87

Killingsworth, Kirk
83Tulsa-12
85Tulsa-32
86Tulsa-3
87OKCty-9

Killingsworth, Sam
75BurlB

Kilner, John Steven
86Durhm-16
87Greenv/Bst-14
88Greenv/Best-20
89Greenv/Star-11
89Richm/Ko-30

Kilroy, Mathew
N172
N284

Kim, Wendell
75Lafay
77Phoen
78Cr/PCL-98
81Clint-2
82Clint-2
86Shrev-13
86Shrev-14
87Phoen-23
88Phoen/CMC-24
88Phoen/Pro-65

Kimball, Rick
88CapeCod/Sum-142

Kimberlin, Keigh
89NiagFls/Puc-13

Kimm, Bruce
77T-554
81F-355
81T-272
83Cedar-1
83Cedar/LF-22
86TexGold-CO
88Kahn/Reds-CO

Kin, Clinton
82Clint-32

Kindall, Jerry
58T-221
59T-274
60T-444
61P-199
61T-27
62AmTract-51A
62AmTract-51B
62J-191
62P-191
62P/Can-191
62Sugar-13
62T-292
63F-13
63J-68
63P-68
63Sugar-13
63T-36
78TCMA-218
78TCMA-271

Kinder, Ellis
50B-152
51B-128
52T-78
53T-44
54B-98
54T-47
55T-115
55T/DH-130
56T-336
57T-352
79TCMA-115
Exh47
R423-55

Kindred, Curt
83Visal/LF-22
84Visal-2
86Cedar/TCMA-6
87Cedar-4

Kindred, Vincent L.
87Sprin/Best-23
89Savan/Pro-355

Kiner, Ralph
47TipTop
48B-3
48L-91
49B-29
49Eureka-164
50B-33
51BR-C1
51T/CAS
51T/RB-15
52B-11
52BR
52Dix-53
52RM-NL12
52StarCal/L-77B
52Wheat
53B/Col-80
53Exh/Can-22
53RM-NL15
53T-191
54B-45
54Dix
54RH
55B-197
55Gol/Ind-13
55Salem
60F-79
61F-50
74Laugh/ASG-51
77T-437M
79TCMA-13
80Cram/Leg-81
80SSPC/HOF
82CJ-16
83D/HOF-38
85CircK-30
85West/2-36
86S/Dec-35
88Pac/Leg-9
D305
Exh47
PM10/Sm-89
R302-110
R346-7
R423-58

King, Bryan
88SnBer/Best-22
88SnBer/Cal-28
89SnBer/Best-20
89SnBer/Cal-80

King, Charles F.
(Silver)
N172

King, Charles G.
(Chick)
55B-133
59T-538

King, Clyde
51B-299
52B-56
52T-205
69T-274
70T-624
75OPC-589MG
75T-589MG
75T/M-589MG
83T-486
89Rini/Dodg-12
V362-26

King, Edward Lee
E120
W572

King, Eric
86D/Rook-27
86S/Rook-42
86T/Tr-53T
87Cain's-19
87D-250
87F-155
87T-36
87T/GlossRk-8
87ToysRUs-16
88D-50
88F-60
88OPC-108
88Pep/T-25
88Score-471
88T-499
88T/St-271
88Toled/CMC-5
88Toled/Pro-592
89Coke/WS-14
89D-535
89D/Best-235
89D/Tr-37
89F-136
89F/Up-19
89Score-471
89Score/Tr-26
89Score/YS/II-7
89T-238
89T/Tr-61T
89UD-493
90D-337
90F-537
90Score-28
90T-786
90UD-651

King, Frank J.
T206

King, Hal
R314/Can
V355-121

King, Harold
69MB-146
70OPC-327
70T-327
71MLB/St-15
71OPC-88
71T-88
72T-598
74OPC-362
74T-362

King, James H.
56T-74
57T-186
58T-332
61T-351
62T-42
63T-176
64T-217
65OPC-38
65T-38
65T/E-54
65T/trans-53
66T-369
67T-509
78TCMA-207

King, Jeff
87Salem-24
88EastLAS/Pro-16
88F-653M
88Harris/Pro-859
89BuffB/CMC-16
89BuffB/Pro-1671
89F/Up-114
90D-480
90F-469
90Score-549
90Score/100Ris-71
90T-454
90UD-557

King, Jerome
83Tacom-6

King, Jerry
81Brist-13

King, Joe
82Danvi-22
83Peoria/LF-2

King, Kenny
87Miami-1
88Bakers/Cal-254

King, Kevin
80Wausa-20
81Wausa-27
83Chatt-18
84Chatt-2
86MidldA-12
87Edmon-8
88CapeCod/Sum-99
88Edmon/CMC-25
88Edmon/Pro-573

King, Lee
V100
V61-92

King, Lynn
40Hughes-11
43Centen-16

King, Michael J.
87CharRa-4
88Charl/Pro-1202
89Watlo/Pro-1787
89Watlo/Star-15

King, Mike
81QuadC-17
84Nashvl-11

King, Nelson
55T-112
57T-349
79TCMA-247

King, Randy
85Newar-2

King, Ron
86Salem-14

King, Steve
86Jamestn-14
89Boise/Pro-2002

King, Tom
75AppFx
76Clint

Kingery, Mike
82CharR-12
84Memph-7
85Omaha-23

86Omaha-13
86Omaha/TCMA-4
86S/Rook-37
87D-424
87D/OD-119
87F-371
87F/U-U57
87Moth/Sea-17
87T-203
87T/Tr-58T
88D-322
88F-376
88Leaf-104
88Moth/Sea-17
88OPC-119
88Panini/St-193
88Score-178
88T-532
88T/Big-160
89Calg/CMC-20
89Calg/Pro-545
89T-413
90D-601

Kingman, Brian
77SnJos-19
79Ogden/TCMA-13
80T-671R
81D-360
81F-529
81T-284
82D-87
82F-96
82OPC-231
82T-476
82Tacom-25
83F-522
83T-312
84Cram/PCL-15

Kingman, Dave
72OPC-147
72T-147
73K-44
73OPC-23
73T-23
74OPC-610
74T-610
74T/St-106
75Ho-85
75OPC-156
75T-156
75T/M-156
76Crane-26
76Ho-15
76Ho/Twink-15
76MSA/Disc
76OPC-193LL
76OPC-40
76SSPC-542
76T-193LL
76T-40
77Ho-60
77K-35
77OPC-98
77Pep-69
77T-500
77T/CS-24
78Ho-26
78T-570
78Wiffle/Discs-34
79Ho-146
79OPC-191
79T-370
79T/Comics-20
80K-6
80OPC-127
80T-240
80T/S-16
81Coke
81D-553
81Drake-19
81F-291
81F/St-111
81OPC-361
81Sqt-14
81T-450
81T/HT
81T/St-151
81T/St-69
81T/Tr-781
82D-17DK
82D-182
82Drake-21
82F-530
82F/St-85
82K-19
82OPC-276
82T-690
82T/St-72
83D-301
83Drake-14
83F-548
83OPC-160
83OPC-161SV
83T-160
83T-161A
83T-702
83T/St-11
83T/St-207
83T/St-259
84D-360
84D/Champs-3
84F-590
84F/X-62
84FunFood/Pin-36
84Moth/A's-15
84Nes/792-573
84Nes/792-703LL
84OPC-172
84T-573
84T-703
84T/X-63
85CircK-26
85D-54
85D/AAS-32
85F-427
85F/LimEd-15
85F/St-14
85F/St-29
85F/St-48
85Leaf-182
85Moth/A's-2
85OPC-123
85T-730
85T/3D-12
85T/Gloss40-5
85T/St-320
85T/Super-59
86D-54
86F-423
86F/St-67
86Moth/A's-2
86OPC-322
86S-116
86S-145M
86S-68M
86T-410
86T/St-167
86Woolwth-16
87D-425
87F-396
87F/LL-27
87OPC-266
87RedFoley/St-115
87S-178
87T-709
87T/Mini-69
87T/St-173
89Pac/Leg-175

Kingman, Eamon
88CapeCod/Sum-17

Kingsolver, Kurt
80BurlB-19
82ElPas-4

Kingwood, Tyrone
88WPalm/Star-14

Kinnard, Kenneth Joe
(Ken)
86Ventura-10
87Greenv/Bst-27

Kinney, Brad
84Butte-13

Kinney, Dennis
75SnAnt
79Hawai-18
81D-363
81Evans-22
81F-505
81T-599
82Tacom-6

Kinnunen, Mike
81Toled-6
83Memph-24
85Omaha-18
86RochR-12
88AAA/Pro-10
88Colum/CMC-9
88Colum/Pol-4
88Colum/Pro-316
89Denver/CMC-4
89Denver/Pro-33

Kinsel, David
83AppFx/LF-23

Kinslow, Thomas
N300/unif

Kinyoun, Tavis
89Brist/Star-13

Kinzer, Matt
85Sprin-14
86StPet-17
88ArkTr/GS-14
88Louvl-24
89Louvl-25
89Louvl/CMC-7
89Louvl/Pro-1255
90F-652
90Score-628

Kipfer, Greg
82Wisco-2

Kipp, Fred
59T-258
60T-202

Kipper, Bob
83Peoria/LF-25
83TriCit-3
86D-44
86D/Rook-46
86F-648M
86T/Tr-54T
87D-572
87F-612
87T-289
88D-115
88F-332
88T-723
88T/Big-141
89B-414
89D-409
89F-211
89Score-354
89T-114
89UD-520
90D-362
90F-470
90T-441
90UD-560

Kipper, Thornton
54T-108
55T-62
55T/DH-10

Kirby, Butch
81BurlB-18
82Beloi-15
83Beloi/LF-1

Kirby, Chris
78Wausa

Kirby, Clay
69T-637R
70MLB/St-115
70OPC-79
70T-79
71MLB/St-230
71OPC-333
71T-333
72OPC-173
72OPC-174IA
72T-173
72T-174A
73OPC-655
73T-655
73T/Lids-26
74OPC-287
74T-287
74T/St-96
75OPC-423
75T-423
75T/M-423
76OPC-579
76SSPC-28
76T-579
76T/Tr-579T

Kirby, Wayne
76Tucso-15
85VeroB-8
86VeroB-14
87Bakers-23
88Bakers/Cal-249
88SnAnt/Best-8
89SnAnt/Best-8

Kirchenwitz, Arno
78StPet
79ArkTr-1

Kirk, Thomas
52Park-79

Kirk, Tim
86Watertn-11
87Salem-8
88CLAS/Star-11
88Salem/Star-9

Kirk, Tom
89Penin/Star-9

Kirke, Judson
T207

Kirkland, Willie
58SFCall
58T-128
59T-484
60T-172
61Kahn
61P-146
61T-15
62J-41
62Kahn
62P-41
62P/Can-41
62Salada-61
62Shirriff-61
62Sugar-11
62T-447
63J-72
63P-72
63Sugar-11
63T-187
64T-17
65OPC-148
65T-148
66T-434

Kirkpatrick, Bill
75IntAS/TCMA-14

Kirkpatrick, Ed
63T-386R
64T-296
65T-393
66OPC-102
66T-102
67T-293
68T-552
69MB-147
69MLB/St-59
69T-529
70MLB/St-223
70OPC-165
70T-165
70T/PI-19
71MLB/St-418
71OPC-299
71T-299
72MB-183
72T-569
72T-570A
73OPC-233
73T-233
74OPC-262
74T-262
74T/St-183
74T/Tr-262T
75OPC-171
75T-171
75T/M-171
76OPC-294
76SSPC-580
76T-294
77T-582
78T-77

Kirkpatrick, Stephen
88Clearw/Star-16
88Spart/Star-9
88Spart/Star-9
89Clearw/Star-12

Kirkwood, Don
76OPC-108
76T-108
77T-519
78T-251
79OPC-334
79T-632

Kirsch, Paul
82Cedar-14
84Cedar-5
85Cedar-26
86Cedar/TCMA-24
87Cedar-24

Kiser, Bob
88CapeCod-10
88CapeCod/Sum-74

Kiser, Dan
89Modesto/Ch-4

Kiser, Garland
86Cram/PCL-154
89Watertn/Star-12

Kiser, Larry G.
76OkCty

Kish, Bobby
82Sprin-14
83StPet-8
84Savan-12

Kisinger, Charles S.
(Rube)
T206

Kison, Bruce
72OPC-72
72T-72
73OPC-141
73T-141
75OPC-598
75T-598
75T/M-598
76OPC-161
76SSPC-568
76T-161
77T-563
78T-223
79T-661
80T-28
81F-284
81T-340
82D-66
82F-467
82T-442
83D-267

83F-96
83T-712
84D-499
84F-523
84Nes/792-201
84OPC-201
84Smok/Cal-15
84T-201
84T/St-235
85D-377
85F-306
85F/Up-U65
85T-544
85T/Tr-67T
86D-616
86F-353
86T-117
Kissell, George
73OPC-497CO
73T-497C
74OPC-236CO
74T-236C
Kissinger, John
C46-72
Kisten, Dale
88Hamil/Pro-1728
89Sprin/Best-20
Kite, Dan
88Elmir-6
Kitson, Frank R.
E107
Kittle, Hub
73OPC-624CO
73T-624C
74OPC-31CO
74T-31C
77StPet
Kittle, Ron
77Clint
79Knoxv/TCMA-12
81GlenF-19
82Edmon-13
83F-241
83T/X-55
84D-18
84D-244
84Drake-17
84F-64
84F/St-109
84F/St-22
84FunFood/Pin-53
84MiltBrad-15
84Nes/792-480
84OPC-373
84Seven-17C
84T-480
84T/St-382YS
84T/Super-11
84T/Super-11
84TrueVal/WS-19
85Coke/WS-40
85D-180
85D/AAS-13
85D/WaxBox-PC3
85F-518
85F/LimEd-16
85Leaf-210
85OPC-105
85T-105
85T/St-232
86Coke/WS-42
86D-526
86F-210
86F/Mini-45
86F/St-68
86Jay's-11
86Leaf-257
86OPC-288
86S-67M
86S-86
86T-574
86T/St-289
87D-351
87F-103
87T-584
88D-422
88F-213
88Gator-33
88Leaf-251
88Score-449
88Score/Tr-44T
88T-259
88T/Tr-58T
89B-69
89Coke/WS-15
89D-428
89D/Best-249
89D/Tr-51
89F/Up-20
89OPC-268
89Score-96
89T-771
89T/Tr-62T
89UD-228
89UD/Ext-711
90D-148
90F-538
90Score-529
90T-79
Kittredge, Malachi
E107
Kizer, Craig
82AubAs-14
Kizer, Hal
(Bubba)
79QuadC-15
Kizziah, Daren
89StCath/Pro-2076
Klages, Fred
67T-373R
68T-229
69MB-148
Klancnik, Joe
88James/Pro-1919
89James/Pro-2155
Klaus, Robert
61T/St-203
64T-524R
65OPC-227
65T-227
66OPC-108
66T-108
69T-387
Klaus, William
55B-150
56T-217
57T-292
58T-89
59T-299
60T-406
61P-79
61T-187
62J-67
62P-67
62P/Can-67
62Salada-10
62Shirriff-10
62T-571
63T-551
78TCMA-19
79TCMA-251
Exh47
Klawitter, Tom
84Toled-14
Klebba, Rob
80WHave-6
Kleean, Tom
86Beloi-12
Klein, Bob
75AppFx
Klein, Bruce
89Aug/Pro-513
Klein, Chuck
31Exh/4-11
33DH-26
33DL-22
33Exh/4-6
33G-128
34Exh/4-3
34G-10
35BU-185
35Exh/4-3
35G-1F
35G-3D
35G-4D
35G-5D
35Wheat
36G
38Exh/4-6
39PB-82
40PB-102
41PB-60
49Exh
60F-30
61F-51
72F/FFeat-36
80Cram/Leg-112
80Laugh/FFeat-6
80SSPC/HOF
88Conlon/NatAS-12
89HOF/St-48
PR1-18
R300
R306
R308-157
R314
R315-A19
R315-B19
R316
R328-21
R332-17
V354-56
V355-13
W517-10
WG8-38
Klein, Gary
83Butte-6
Klein, Larry
85BurlR-3
86Tulsa-24
88OkCty/CMC-17
88OkCty/Pro-32
Klein, Lou
49Eureka-188
60T-457C
Kleinke, Norbert
40Hughes-12
Kleinow, John
(Red)
E101
E102
E105
E92
E94
E97
T204
T205
T206
T216
T3-21
W555
Klem, Bill
21Exh-92
50Callahan
72F/FFeat-31
80SSPC/HOF
86Conlon/1-5
88Conlon/4-15
89Umpires-63
R332-6
Klenoshek, Bill Jr.
88CapeCod/Sum-50
Klesko, Ryan
89LittleSun-20
Kleven, Mark
88Charl/Pro-1205
Klimas, Phil
77Cocoa
80Tulsa-13
81Tulsa-3
Klimchock, Lou
60L-116
60T-137
61T-462
62T-259
63T-542
65T-542
66T-589
70OPC-247
70T-247
Klimkowski, Ron
70T-702R
71MLB/St-492
71OPC-28
71T-28
72OPC-363
72T-363
72T/Cloth-18
Kline, Bob
84Newar-24
Kline, Doug
88Visal/Cal-169
88Visal/Pro-107
89WPalm/Star-14
Kline, Greg
75Clint
76Clint
Kline, John Robert
55T-173
Kline, Kris
83Peoria/LF-7
Kline, Ron
53T-175
56T-94
57Kahn
57T-256
58Hires-31
58Kahn
58T-82
59Kahn
59T-265
59T-428M
60Kahn
60L-105
60T-197
61T-127
61T/St-90
62T-216
63T-84
64T-358
65OPC-56
65T-56
65T/trans-54
66T-453
67OPC-133
67T-133
68KDKA-27
68T-446
69MB-149
69T-243
69T/St-86
78TCMA-251
Kline, Steve
71MLB/St-493
71OPC-51
71T-51
72OPC-467
72T-467
73K-50
73OPC-172
73T-172
74OPC-324
74T-324
75OPC-639
75T-639
75T/M-639
76SSPC-532
Klinefelter, David
88AubAs/Pro-1972
Kling, John
11Helmar-79
61F-52
E254
E300
E91
E96
E98
M116
S74-63
T201
T202
T205
T206
T207
T3-102
WG3-24
Klingbell, Scott
85Visal-23
Klinger, Robert
39PB-90
40PB-165
41DP-35
41DP-98
48Smith-25
Klink, Joe
85Lynch-13
86Orlan-9
89Huntsvl/Best-27
Klippstein, John
51B-248
52T-148
53T-46
54B-29
54T-31
55B-152
56Kahn
56T-249
57Kahn
57T-296
58T-242
59T-152
60BB-12
60T-191
61T-539
61T/St-204
62T-151
63T-571
64T-533
65T-384
66T-493
67T-588
79TCMA-62
Klipstein, Dave
84ElPas-18
86Vanco-16
87Denver-12
88Nashvl/CMC-20
88Nashvl/Pro-474
Kloff, August
N172
Klonoski, Jason
88CapeCod/Sum-127
Klopp, Frank
85PrWill-26
Klump, Ken
83Wisco/LF-21
85Orlan-17
Klusman, William F.
N172
Kluszewski, Ted
48L-38
49Eureka-87
50B-62
51B-143
51FB
51T/RB-39
52Dix-53
52T-29
53B/Col-62

53NB
53RM-NL6
53T-162
54Dix
54RH
54RM-NL6
54T-7
55Armour-11
55Kahn
55RFG-10
55RM-NL16
55T-120
55T/DH-121
56Kahn
56T-25
56T/Hocus-A12
56T/Hocus-B14
56T/Pin-56
56YellBase/Pin-17
57Kahn
57T-165
58Hires-67
58Kahn
58T-178
58T-321M
59Kahn
59T-17M
59T-35
60Kahn
60MacGregor-10
60NuCard-57
60T-505
61Bz-18
61NuCard-457
61P-31
61T-65
61T/St-173
62P-82
73OPC-296CO
73T-296C
74OPC-326CO
74T-326C
76SSPC-618
79TCMA-12
85West/2-48
86S/Dec-38M
88Pac/Leg-72
Exh47
PM10/Sm-90

Klutts, Gene
(Mickey)
77T-490R
78T-707R
80T-717
81D-110
81F-584
81T-232
82F-97
82T-148
83D-465
83T-571
83T/X-56

Kluttz, Clyde
52T-132
V362-41

Kmak, Joe
85Evrt/Cram-7
86Fresno/Smok-6
88Shreve/Pro-1280
89Reno/Cal-252

Knabe, Franz Otto
11Helmar-144
14CJ-1
15CJ-1
D303
E101
E102
E104
E105
E106
E254
E270/2
E92
M116
T206
T207
T213/blue
T213/brown
T216

Knabenshue, Chris
85Spoka/Cram-9
86CharRa-12
87Wichi-7
88TexLgAS/GS-34
88Wichi-14
89LasVeg/CMC-23
89LasVeg/Pro-19

Knackert, Brent
88FSLAS/Star-40
88Tampa/Star-11
89Saraso/Star-13

Knapp, John
87CharWh-12
88Bakers/Cal-236
89VeroB/Star-14

Knapp, Michael
86Cram/PCL-87
87QuadC-27
88MidldA/GS-13
88TexLgAS/GS-36
89MidldA/GS-20

Knapp, Rick
86Tulsa-9B
88Gasto/Pro-1000

Knapp, Robert C.
(Chris)
77T-247
78T-361
79T-453
80T-658
81D-173
81SLCty-7
81T-557
82IowaC-18

Knecht, Bobby
88AppFx/Pro-161
88MidwLAS/GS-41

Knell, Phillip
N172

Knepper, Bob
75Phoen-10
76Phoen
77Phoen
78T-589
79Ho-52
79K-35
79OPC-255
79Pol/Giants-39
79T-486
80OPC-61
80Pol/Giants-39
80T-111
81D-194
81F-447
81OPC-279
81T-279
81T/Tr-782
82D-41
82F-219
82F/St-49
82K-31
82OPC-389
82T-672
82T/St-45
83D-92
83F-451
83T-382
84D-572
84Moth/Ast-16
84Nes/792-93
84OPC-93
84T-93
85D-476
85F-352
85Leaf-61
85Moth/Ast-20
85OPC-289
85T-455
85T-721AS
85T/St-62
86D-161
86F-304
86Leaf-90
86Moth/Ast-22
86OPC-231
86Pol/Ast-15
86T-590
87D-112
87F-61
87F/AwardWin-20
87F/GameWin-23
87F/Mini-60
87Leaf-249
87Moth/Ast-5
87OPC-129
87Pol/Ast-20
87RedFoley/St-17
87S-29
87T-722
87T/Gloss60-13
87T/Mini-10
87T/St-32
88D-138
88D/Best-176
88F-451
88Moth/Ast-5
88Pol/Ast-15
88Score-344
88T-151
89D-123
89D/AS-54
89F-360
89F/BBAS-25
89Lennox/Ast-10
89Moth/Ast-7
89OPC-280
89Panini/St-82
89Score-273
89Score/HotSt-38
89T-280
89T/St-22
89T/St/Backs-63
89UD-422
90D-485
90T-104
90UD-599

Knetzer, Elmer
14CJ-84
15CJ-84
T207

Kneuer, Frank
83Nashvl-9

Knicely, Alan
75Dubuq
76Dubuq
80T-678R
80Tucso-14
81T-82R
81Tucso-4
83D-620
83F-452
83T-117
83T/X-57
84F-473
84Nes/792-323
84T-323
85T/Tr-68T
86Louisvl-15
86OPC-316
86T-418
87OKCty-22

Knickerbocker, Wm.
35BU-58
35G-8I
35G-9I
40PB-182
R313
R314

Kniffen, Chuck
88Wausa/Feder-2
88Wausa/GS-2
89SnBer/Best-10
89SnBer/Cal-89CO

Knight, Brock
85Elmir-9

Knight, C. Ray
(Ray)
76Indianap-3
78T-674
79OPC-211
79T-401
80OPC-98
80T-174
81Coke
81D-61
81F-198
81OPC-325
81T-325
81T/HT
82D-374
82F-71
82F/St-18
82OPC-319
82T-525
82T/St-39
82T/St-39
82T/Tr-57T
83D-522
83F-453
83OPC-275
83T-275
83T-441
83T/Gloss-18
83T/Gloss40-18
83T/St-238
84D-12
84D-232
84F-229
84F/St-10
84Moth/Ast-6
84Nes/792-660
84OPC-321
84T-660
84T/St-68
84T/St/Box-9
85D-617
85F-86
85Indianap-28
85OPC-274
85T-590
86D-597
86F-86
86Moth/Ast-24
86OPC-27
86T-27
87D-586
87D/OD-137
87F-14
87F/AwardWin-21
87F/RecSet-18
87F/U-U58
87F/WS-11M
87F/WS-12
87Leaf-166
87OPC-275
87S-88
87T-488
87T/HL-30
87T/HL-33
87T/St-24WS
87T/Tr-59T
87Woolwth-30
87Woolwth-33
88D-108
88F-564
88F/U-U28
88OPC-124
88Panini/St-12
88Pep/T-22
88RedFoley/St-43
88Score-96
88Score/Tr-17T
88Sf-115
88T-124
88T/St-229
88T/Tr-59T
89Score-135
89UD-259

Knight, Dennis
83TriCit-5

Knight, John
10Domino-62A
10Domino-62B
11Helmar-73
12Sweet/Pin-36B
12Sweet/Pin-36A
14Piedmont/St-31
E101
E105
E254
E90/1
E92
M116
S74-23
T202
T204
T205
T206
T216

Knight, Tim
82Nashv-15
83Nashvl-10
84Nashvl-12
85Albany-33
85Colum-20
85Colum/Pol-15
86Portl-12

Knoblauch, Chuck
88CapeCod-15
88CapeCod/Sum-94
90Score-672DC

Knoblaugh, Jay
88Oneon/Pro-2067
89Penin/Star-10

Knoop, Bobby
64T-502R
65OPC-26
65T-26
65T/trans-18
66T-280
66T/RO-81
67OPC-175
67OPC/PI-17
67T-175
67T/PI-17
68Bz-3
68T-271
69MB-150
69MLB/St-23
69T-445
69T/St-145
69Trans-17
70MLB/St-188
70T-695
71OPC-506
71T-506
72MB-184
72T-664
75QuadC
78TCMA-234
89Smok/Angels-4

Knorr, Randy
87Myrtle-12
88Myrtle/Pro-1182
89Duned/Star-10

Knott, Jack
39PB-91
40PB-13
41PB-68

Knout, Edward
(Fred)
N172
Knowles, Darold
64T-418R
65T-577R
66OPC-27R
66T-27R
67T-362
68T-483
70OPC-106
70T-106
71MLB/St-544
71OPC-261
71T-261
72T-583
73OPC-274
73T-274
74OPC-472WS
74OPC-57
74T-57
75OPC-352
75T-352
75T/M-352
76OPC-617
76SSPC-307
76T-617
77T-169
78T-414
79OPC-303
79T-581
80T-286
88Louvl-3
Knox, Jeff
86Clearw-14
87Albany-17
Knox, John
74OPC-604R
74T-604R
75OPC-546
75T-546
75T/M-546
76Indianap-21
76OPC-218
76SSPC-361
76T-218
Knox, Kerry
89Spoka/SP-14
Knox, Mike
83Cedar-4
83Cedar/LF-9
83Durhm-8
84Durhm-15
Knox, Scott
85PrWill-29
Knudsen, Kurt
89Lakel/Star-13
Knudson, Mark
83DayBe-7
85Cram/PCL-60
86Tucso-10
87Denver-20
88D-495
88Denver/CMC-1
88Denver/Pro-1275
88T-61
89Pol/Brew-41
90D-575
90F-327
90Score-539
90T-566
Knudtson, Jim
87Cedar-27
Kobel, Kevin
74OPC-605R
74T-605R
75OPC-337
75T-337
75T/M-337
76OPC-588
76T-588
77Spoka
79OPC-6
79T-21
80OPC-106
80T-189
Kobernus, Jeff
82Madis-25
Kobza, Greg
89Utica/Puc-13
Koch, Donn
82AppFx-18
Koch, Ken
87Orlan-8
Kochanski, Mark
82Idaho-9
Kocher, Bradley
C46-82
Koegel, Pete
71OPC-633R
71T-633R
72OPC-14R
72T-14R
77Jaxvl
Koehnke, Odie
75AppFx
76AppFx
Koenecke, Leonard
34Exh/4-2
Koenig, Fred
83Thorn-26CO
88Pulas/Pro-1749
89Pulas/Pro-1900
Koenig, Mark
29Exh/4-26
31Exh/4-24
32Orbit/num-30
32Orbit/un-39
33G-39
34G-56
35E-8A
35G-9A
87Conlon/2-41
88Conlon/4-16
R305
R315-A20
R315-B20
R316
V353-39
W513-83
Koenigsfeld, Ron
82ElPas-3
84Cram/PCL-25
Koh, Joe
87Idaho-20
Kohlogi, Acey
(Asst.)
89Visal/Cal-121
Kokos, Dick
49B-31
50B-50
51B-68
51T/RB-19
53T-232
54B-37
54Esskay
54T-106
Kolarek, Frank
79Ogden/TCMA-19
Kolb, Gary
62Pep/Tul
63Pep/Tul
64T-119
65T-287
68KDKA-10
68T-407
69MB-151
69T-307
78TCMA-268
78TCMA-283
Kolb, Pete
86ElPas-15TR
87ElPas-9
88Denver/Pro-1252
89Denver/Pro-50
Kolbe, Brian
82Jacks-7
Koller, Mark
87Watertn-25
88Watertn/Puc-7
Koller, Mike
88Brist/Pro-1880
89Fay/Pro-1576
Kolloway, Don
49B-28
50B-133
51B-105
52B-91
52T-104
53T-97
Exh47
Kolodny, Mike
80Batav-5
Kolotka, Chuck
82Madis-6
83Miami-8
84Beaum-22
Kolp, Ray
33G-150
V100
V353-82
Kolstad, Harold
62T-276
63T-574
Komadina, Tony
75AppFx
Komazaki, Yukiichi
83SanJose-9
Komminsk, Brad
80Ander-28
81Durhm-10
83Richm-19
84D-36
84F/X-63
84Richm-10M
84Richm-11
85D-321
85F-331
85Ho/Braves-13
85Pol/Atl-36
85T-292
86F-520
86OPC-210
86Richm-11
86T-698
87Denver-6
88D-583
88Denver/CMC-21
88Denver/Pro-1263
89F/Up-28
90D-350
90F-496
90Score-496
90T-476
90UD-428
Konderla, Mike
83Cedar-7
83Cedar/LF-14
84Cedar-9
87Nashv-12
88Denver/CMC-2
88Denver/Pro-1276
Konetchy, Ed
10Domino-63
11Helmar-172
12Sweet/Pin-150
14CJ-118
15CJ-118
21Exh-93
D328-94
D329-96
D350/2-94
E135-94
E254
E270/2
E96
M101/4-96
M101/5-94
M116
PM1-8
S74-121
T202
T204
T205
T206
T207
T213/blue
T215/blue
T3-103
W514-93
WG5-24
WG6-23
Konieczny, Doug
75OPC-624R
75T-624R
75T/M-624R
76OPC-602
76SSPC-49
76T-602
Konopa, Bob
82Orlan/B-6
82OrlTw-18/A
84CharO-15
Konstanty, Jim
49Eureka-139
50B-226
51B-27
51BR-D6
51FB
51T/CAS
52T-108
53B/BW-58
55B-231
56T-321
61T-479MV
79TCMA-53
Exh47
PM10/Sm-91
R423-56
Rawl
Kooman, Chris
87Everett-14
Koonce, Cal
63T-31
65OPC-34
65T-34
66T-278
67OPC-171
67T-171
68T-486
69T-303
70OPC-521
70T-521
71MLB/St-320
71OPC-254
71T-254
72MB-185
Koontz, Jim
81ElPas-10
82ElPas-20
84Cram/PCL-45
Koopman, Bob
86PrWill-14
87Salem-20
Koosman, Jerry
68OPC-177R
68T-177R
69Citgo-12
69MLB/St-168
69MLBPA/Pin-49
69OPC-90
69T-434AS
69T-90
69T/DE-25
69T/decal
69T/S-51
69T/St-66
69Trans-46
70MLB/St-79
70OPC-309WS
70OPC-468AS
70T-468AS
70T-610
70Trans-5
70Trans/M-22
71MLB/St-157
71OPC-335
71T-335
71T/Coins-23
71T/tatt-3
72MB-186
72T-697
72T-698A
73OPC-184
73T-184
74OPC-356
74T-356
74T/St-65
75OPC-19
75T-19
75T/M-19
76Crane-27
76Laugh/Jub-22
76MSA/Disc
76OPC-64
76SSPC-609
76T-64
77Ho-77
77K-29
77OPC-26
77T-300
78Ho-80
78T-565
78Wiffle/Discs-35
79Ho-149
79OPC-345
79T-655
80BK/PHR-5
80OPC-144
80T-275
80T/S-38
81D-531
81F-552
81F/St-19
81OPC-298
81T-476
81T/St-104
82D-603
82F-347
82OPC-63
82T-714
83D-39
83F-242
83OPC-153
83T-153
84D-501
84F-65
84F/X-64
84Nes/792-311
84Nes/792-716LL
84OPC-311
84T-311
84T-716
84T/X-64
85CIGNA-7
85D-233
85F-256
85Leaf-178
85OPC-15
85T-15
85T/St-117
86D-23
86D/DKsuper-23
86Leaf-23DK
86OPC-343
86S-64M
86T-505
88Pac/Leg-66
89Swell-109

Kopacz, George
71OPC-204R
71T-204R
Koperda, Mike
80Ander-21
Kopetsky, Brian
86Bakers-18
Kopf, Dave
86Pittsf-11
87IowaC-10
88Pittsf/Pro-1373
Kopf, William
88Pac/8Men-91
E120
E220
W514-118
W572
Koplitz, Howard
62T-114
63T-406
64T-372
66OPC-46
66T-46
78TCMA-221
Koppe, Joe
59T-517
60T-319
61T-179
62Salada-209
62Shirriff-209
62T-39
63J-26
63P-26
63T-396
64T-279
Kopyta, Jeff
58T-403
59T-284
60L-79
60T-56
86Cram/PCL-66
87Madis-18
88Modesto-12
88Modesto/Cal-63
89Modesto/Cal-272
Korczyk, Steve
82Toled-3
83Toled-5
Kordish, Steve
83TriCit-2
84Tulsa-30
86Salem-15
Korince, George
67OPC-72R
67T-526R
67T-72R
68T-447R
Kornfeld, Craig
79QuadC-16
Kortright, Jim
88Idaho/Pro-1858
89Idaho/Pro-2031
Kosc, Greg
89Umpires-23
Kosco, Andrew
87Wausa-14
88Wausa/Feder-26
88Wausa/GS-26
89Wmspt/Pro-626
Kosco, Andy
66T-264R
67T-366
68T-524
69MB-152
69OPC-139
69T-139
69T/St-204
70OPC-535
70T-535
71MLB/St-440
71OPC-746
71T-746
72MB-187
72OPC-376
72T-376
74OPC-34
74T-34
Kosco, Bryn
88James/Pro-1896
Kose, Greg
88Umpire-25
Kosenski, John
88CapeCod/Sum-108
Koshorek, Clem
52T-380
53B/Col-147
53T-8
Koslo, George B.
(Dave)
47TipTop
48B-48
49B-34
49Eureka-114
50B-65
51B-90
52B-182
52BR
52T-336
54Esskay
55Gol/Braves-16
55JC-20
79TCMA-231
Koslofski, Kevin
86FtMyr-16
87FtMyr-24
88BBCity/Star-15
89BBCity/Star-14
Kostickhka, Steve
87Beloi-6
Kostlich, Billy
89LittleSun-15
Kostro, Frank
63T-407R
65T-459
68OPC-44
68T-44
69T-242
Kotchman, Randy
89Mia/Star/22-8
Kotchman, Tom
86PalmSp-19MG
86PalmSp/Smok-2
87Edmon-12
88Edmon/CMC-22
88Edmon/Pro-580
89AAA/Pro-28
89Edmon/CMC-25
89Edmon/Pro-549
Kouba, Curtis
82Wausa-5
Koufax, Sandy
55Gol/Dodg-16
55T-123
56T-79
57T-302
58BB
58T-187
59Morrell
59T-163
60BB-9
60Morrell
60T-343
61BB-32
61Morrell
61T-207M
61T-344
61T-49LL
62BB-32
62Bz
62Exh
62J-109
62P-109
62P/Can-109
62Salada-109
62Shirriff-109
62T-5
62T-60M
62T/bucks
62T/St-136
63Exh
63F-42
63J-121
63P-121
63Salada-4
63T-210
63T-412M
63T-5LL
63T-9LL
63T/SO
64Bz-32
64T-1LL
64T-200
64T-3LL
64T-5LL
64T/Coins-106
64T/Coins-159AS
64T/S-3
64T/St-91
64T/SU
64T/tatt
65Bz-32
65OPC-8LL
65T-300
65T-8LL
65T/E-8
65T/trans-55
66Bz-1
66OPC-100
66T-100
66T-221LL
66T-223LL
66T-225LL
66T/RO-14
67T-234LL
67T-236LL
67T-238LL
72Laugh/GF-4
75OPC-201M
75T-201MV
75T/M-201MV
76Laugh/Jub-4
78TCMA-130
79TCMA-49
80Cram/Leg-10
80SSPC/HOF
81Albuq/TCMA-23B
82KMart-4
83MLBPA/Pin-24
87Smok/Dodg-16
88Smok/Dodg-4
88Smok/Dodg-6M
89HOF/St-79
89Smok/Dodg-15
90T-665TBC
Exh47
Kounas, Tony
88CapeCod/Sum-144
Kovach, Ty
89Watertn/Star-13
Koy, Ernest
41DP-118
Koza, Dave
81Pawtu-16
83Pawtu-17
Kozar, Al
49B-16
50B-15
R302
Kracl, Darin
89Medford/Best-13
Kraeger, Don
79AppFx-23
Kraemer, Joe
86Peoria-13
87IowaC-9
88IowaC/CMC-7
88IowaC/Pro-549
89IowaC/CMC-3
89IowaC/Pro-1715
Kraft, Ken
86Clearw-15
Krafve, Keith
86Cram/PCL-24
Krakauskas, Joe
40PB-188
41DP-77
47Signal
Kralick, Jack
61Clover-11
61Peters-6
61T-36
62T-346
62T/St-77
63J-11
63P-11
63Sugar-28
63T-448
64Kahn
64T-338
65Kahn
65T-535
65T/E-72
66OPC-129
66T-129
67T-316
78TCMA-134
Kraly, Steve
54NYJour
55T-139
Kramer, Jack
52Wheat
Kramer, Joe
85Madis-20
85Madis/Pol-17
86Modesto-18
Kramer, John
(Jack)
41G-14
47TipTop
49B-53
50B-199
51B-200
79TCMA-107
W753
Kramer, Mark
85BurlR-18
86DayBe-15
87PortChar-19
88CharlR/Star-11
89Mia/Star/22-9
Kramer, Randy
83BurlR-8
83BurlR/LF-5
86Kinston-13
86Tulsa-23
87Vanco-16
88BuffB/CMC-5
88BuffB/Pro-1464
89D-480
89D/Best-213
89D/Rook-48
89F-647M
89F/Up-115
89Panini/St-159
89Score/HotRk-57
89T-522
90D-409
90F-471
90Score/100Ris-41
90T-126
90UD-519
Kramer, Tommy
88MidwLAS/GS-22
88Watlo/Pro-689
89Kinston/Star-11
89Star/Wax-76
Kranepool, Ed
63T-228R
64T-393M
64T-566
65OPC-144
65T-144
65T/E-6
65T/trans-56
66Bz-9
66T-212
66T/RO-20
67Kahn
67OPC-186M
67T-186M
67T-452
68OPC-92
68T-92
69MB-153
69MLB/St-169
69T-381
69T/St-67
70K-1
70MLB/St-80
70T-557
70Trans/M-21
71MLB/St-158
71OPC-573
71T-573
72MB-188
72OPC-181
72OPC-182IA
72T-181
72T-182A
73OPC-329
73T-329
74OPC-561
74T-561
75OPC-324
75T-324
75T/M-324
76OPC-314
76SSPC-533
76T-314
77OPC-60
77T-201
78OPC-205
78T-49
78Wiffle/Discs-36
79OPC-265
79T-505
80OPC-336
80T-641
89Pac/Leg-114
89Swell-28
Exh47
PM10/Sm-92
Kranitz, Rick
80Holyo-1
81ElPas-17
82Vanco-19
86WinSal-11C
88Peoria/Ko-19
89Peoria/Ko-31
Krattli, Tom
77DaytB
Kraus, Jeff
77Spart
Kraus, Ralph
87PrWill-5
88FtLaud/Star-14
89FtLaud/Star-12
Krause, Andrew
85Madis-21
85Madis/Pol-18
Krause, Harry
10Domino-64
11Helmar-56
12Sweet/Pin-46
28Exh/PCL-17
E104
E90/1
E91
E95
M116

S74-32
T202
T205
T206
T207
T208
T213/blue
T215/blue
T215/brown
T3-22
WG7-25

Krauss, Ron
82CharR-15

Krauss, Timothy
81Redwd-17
82Holyo-17
84Cram/PCL-98
85Cram/PCL-17
86BuffB-14
87Hawai-23

Krausse, Lew
63T-104
64T-334
65T-462
66T-256
67T-565
68T-458
69MB-154
69OPC-23
69Sunoco/Pin-12
69T-23
69T/St-217
70McDon-4
70OPC-233
70T-233
71MLB/St-441
71OPC-372
71T-372
71T/Coins-20
72T-592
73OPC-566
73T-566
75OPC-603
75T-603
75T/M-603
75Tucso-20

Krauza, Ron
89BuffB/CMC-19

Kravec, Ken
77T-389
78T-439
79OPC-141
79T-283
80OPC-299
80T-575
81T-67
81T/Tr-783
82D-378
82IowaC-19
82RedLob
82T-639
87FtMyr-28
88Memph/Best-14

Kravitz, Dan
57T-267
58T-444
59T-536
60T-238
61T-166

Krawczyk, Ray
82AlexD-4
84Cram/PCL-129
85Cram/PCL-245
86Hawai-14
87Hawai-17
89Denver/CMC-7
89Denver/Pro-32

Krebs, Dave
87Savan-3
88Savan/Pro-338

Kreevich, Mike
38Exh/4-10
39Exh
R303/A
R303/B
R312/M
WG8-39

Krehmeyer, Charles
N172/PCL

Kremer, Ken
89Beloi/Star-12

Kremer, Remy
(Ray)
25Exh-53
26Exh-53
27Exh-26
28Exh-25
29Exh/4-14
31Exh/4-14
33G-54
R306
V354-38
WG7-26

Kremers, Jimmy
89Greenv/Pro-1163
89Greenv/Star-12
89Greenvl/Best-24
89SLAS-8

Krenchicki, Wayne
78RochR
80RochR-16
80T-661R
82Coke/Reds
82F-168
82T-107
82T/Tr-58T
83D-314
83F-594
83T-374
84D-334
84F-83
84F/X-65
84Nes/792-223
84T-223
84T/X-65
85D-140
85F-539
85T-468
86D-140
86F-180
86F/Up-U60
86OPC-81
86Provigo-20
86T-777
86T/Tr-55T
87D-406
87F-322
87OPC-81
87T-774
87Tacom-6
88Louvl-25
88Tacom/CMC-14
88Tacom/Pro-635

Kress, Ralph
(Red)
29Exh/4-29
31Exh/4-30
33G-33
35BU-169
35G-2C
35G-4C
35G-7C
39PB-115
40PB-45
54T-160
54T-219
55Gol/Ind-14
55Salem
55T-151
60T-460C
PR1-19
R316
V353-33

Kretlow, Lou
52B-221
52T-42
53B/Col-50
54B-197
54Esskay
55B-108
55Esskay
57T-139

Kreuter, Chad
86Salem-16
87PortChar-25
88TexLgAS/GS-3
88Tulsa-19
89Class-27
89D-579
89F-526
89Panini/St-444
89Score-638
89Score/HotRk-51
89Score/YS/II-40
89Sf-43
89Smok/R-17
89T-432
89UD-312
90D-520
90F-303
90Score-406
90Score/100Ris-51
90T-562
90UD-609

Kreutzer, Frank
64T-107R
65T-371
66T-211
78TCMA-116

Krichell, Paul
E270/2

Krieg, William
N172
N284

Kripner, Mike
80Cedar-23
82Water-12

Krippner, Curt
88Beloi/GS-16

Krist, Howie
W754

Kristan, Kevin
85Cram/PCL-124
87WPalm-22

Krizmanich, Mike
75IntAS/TCMA-23
75IntAS/TCMA-3

Krock, August
E223
N172
N403

Kroener, Chris
86Visal-12

Kroh, Floyd
(Rube)
12Sweet/Pin-83
E254
E97
M116
T205
T206

Krol, David
88CapeCod/Sum-180

Krol, Jack
88Charl/Pro-1219
89CharRa/Pro-991

Kroll, Gary
65T-449R
66T-548
66T/RO-2
78TCMA-27

Kroll, Jack
84Smok/SDP-15C
87LasVegas-3MG

Kroll, Todd
87Bakers-8
88Bakers/Cal-255

Kromy, Ted
79Wisco-19
82Orlan/B-19
82OrlTw/A-19
83Orlan-17

Krsnich, Mike
62T-289

Krsnich, Rocco
53T-229

Krueger, Arthur T.
E286
M116
T206

Krueger, Bill
82WHave-7
84Cram/PCL-84
84F-450
84Nes/792-178
84OPC-178
84T-178
85D-467
85F-428
85Moth/A's-21
85T-528
86D-298
86F-424
86Moth/A's-21
86T-58
87T-238
88Albuq/CMC-3
88Albuq/Pro-271
90F-328
90Score-366
90T-518

Krueger, Kirby
81Wisco-6
83Orlan-18

Krueger, Steve
81LynnS-7
82LynnS-5

Krug, Everett B.
(Chris)
62Pep/Tul
63Pep/Tul
66OPC-166
66T-166

Krug, Martin
E120

Kruk, John
83Beaum-11
84Cram/PCL-228
84Cram/PCL-250
85Cram/PCL-103
86D/Rook-42
86F/Up-U61
86S/Rook-1
86T/Tr-56T
87Bohem-8
87D-328
87F-420
87Leaf-217
87S-61
87T-123
87T/St-113
87ToysRUs-17
88Class/Blue-203
88Class/Red-162
88Coke/Padres-8
88D-205
88D/Best-245
88F-589
88F/Mini-113
88F/SS-20
88F/St-124
88Leaf-176
88OPC-32
88OPC-G
88Panini/St-403
88RedFoley/St-44
88Score-36
88Score/YS/I-17
88Sf-64
88Smok/Padres-14
88T-596
88T/Big-60
88T/Coins-45
88T/Mini-75
88T/St-110
88T/UK-41
88T/WaxBox-G
89B-460
89D-86
89D/Best-240
89F-309
89F/Up-109
89OPC-235
89Panini/St-200
89RedFoley/St-69
89Score-148
89Score/Tr-70
89Sf-184
89T-235
89T/Big-216
89T/St-102
89T/Tr-63T
89UD-280
90D-160
90F-565
90Score-467
90Sf-124
90T-469
90UD-668

Krukow, Mike
77T-493R
78T-17
79T-592
80OPC-223
80T-431
81Coke
81F-312
81OPC-176
81T-176
81T/HT
82D-351
82F-598
82F/St-92
82OPC-215
82T-215
82T/St-31
82T/Tr-59T
83D-119
83F-163
83Moth/Giants-12
83OPC-331
83T-331
83T/X-58
84D-509
84F-374
84Nes/792-633
84OPC-37
84T-633
85D-630
85F-609
85Moth/Giants-11
85OPC-74
85T-74
85T/St-163
86D-143
86D/HL-49
86F-546
86Moth/Giants-11
86OPC-126
86T-752
86T/St-93
87BK-12
87Class-67
87D-609
87D/AAS-58
87D/AS/Wax-PC15
87D/OD-98
87F-275

87F-630M
87F/GameWin-24
87F/McCror-24
87F/Mini-61
87F/St-69
87Ho/St-17
87Leaf-86
87Moth/SFG-6
87OPC-241
87S-62
87Smok/NL-12
87T-580
87T/Mini-36
87T/St-92
88D-116
88D/Best-50
88F-85
88Moth/Giants-6
88OPC-393
88Panini/St-417
88RedFoley/St-45
88Score-185
88T-445
89Class-114
89D-258
89D/Best-135
89F-331
89Moth/Giants-6
89OPC-125
89Score-190
89T-125
89T/St-83
89UD-46
90Score-215
90T-241
90UD-639

Krum, Sandy
89Chatt/Best-24
89Chatt/GS-3

Krumback, Mark
88Boise/Pro-1625
89Greens/Pro-425

Krume, Sandy
88Cedar/Pro-1140

Krusinski, Clar
89Peoria/Ko-33ow

Kryhoski, Dick
49B-218
49Remar
50B-242
52B-133
52T-149
53B/Col-127
54B-117
54Esskay
54T-150
79TCMA-241

Kryka, Mark
77Clint
78Clint

Kryzanowski, Rusty
86AubAs-15
87Kenosha-9
88Keno/Pro-1383
89Keno/Pro-1077
89Keno/Star-10

Kuahn, Bill
89Well/Puc-33

Kubala, Brian
86SanJose-11

Kubek, Tony
57T-312
58T-393
59T-505
60T-83
61P-9
61T-265
61T/Dice-7
61T/St-195
62J-4
62P-4
62P/Can-4
62Salada-18
62Shirriff-18
62T-311M
62T-430
62T/St-87
63Kahn
63T-20
64T-415
65OPC-65
65T-65
65T/E-71
79TCMA-244
88Pac/Leg-29
89Swell-68
Exh47
WG10-11
WG9-13

Kubiak, Ted
68OPC-79
68T-79
69Sunoco/Pin-13
69T-281
70McDon-1
70T-688
71MLB/St-442
71OPC-516
71T-516
72MB-189
72OPC-23
72T-23
73OPC-652
73T-652
74OPC-228
74T-228
75OPC-329
75T-329
75T/M-329
76OPC-578
76SSPC-129
76T-578
77T-158
89Modesto/Ch-1

Kubit, Joe
83Visal/LF-17

Kubski, Gil
78Cr/PCL-35
79SLCty-16
80SLCty-21
81Syrac-18
81Vanco-9
82Indianap-28

Kucab, John
52T-358

Kucek, Jack
75OPC-614R
75T-614R
75T/M-614R
76OPC-597R
76T-597R
77T-623
79OkCty
80Syrac-11
81Syrac-6

Kucharski, Joe
84RochR-18
85RochR-20
87CharO/WBTV-37
87RochR/TCMA-27

Kucks, John
56T-88
57T-185
58T-87
59T-289
60L-96
60T-177
61T-94
62Kahn/Atl
62T-241

Kuder, Jeff
89Aug/Pro-491
89Well/Puc-16

Kuecker, Mark
77Cedar
79Phoen

Kuehl, John
88Spoka/Pro-1934
89CharRa/Pro-986

Kuehl, Karl
75IntAS/TCMA-25
76SSPC-611
76T-216MG

Kuehne, William
N172
WG1-60

Kuenn, Harvey
53Glen
54B-23
54RH
54T-25
55Armour-12A
55Armour-12B
55B-132
56T-155
57T-88
58T-304M
58T-434
59Armour-11
59Bz
59T-70
60Bz-34
60Kahn
60NuCard-59
60T-330
60T-429M
60T/tatt-27
61Bz-15
61NuCard-459
61P-57
61T-500
61T/St-77
62J-135
62P-135
62P/Can-135
62Salada-121
62Shirriff-121
62T-480
62T/bucks
62T/St-197
63Exh
63J-105
63P-105
63T-30
64T-242
65OPC-103
65T-103
66T-372
73OPC-646CO
73T-646C
74T-99C
78Newar
79TCMA-104
80Cram/Leg-66
82D-578
83D-608
83Gard-1MG
83Pol/Brew-32MG
83T-726
84Nes/792-321MG
84T-321
84T/Gloss22-1MG
88Pac/Leg-56
89Swell-9
Exh47

Kuhaulua, Fred
77SLCty
79Hawai-20
80Hawai-25
81Hawai-17
82Hawai-17
82T-731R

Kuhel, Joe
33G-108
34DS-78
34Exh/4-16
34G-16
35BU-128
35BU-80
35G-8H
35G-9H
37Exh/4-16
37OPC-127
38G-243
38G-267
40PB-185
41PB-31
47TipTop
49Exh
61F-119
88Conlon/5-18
88Conlon/AmAS-18
R310
R313
R314
V300
V354-52
V355-63

Kuhlman, Eric
88Idaho/Pro-1851
89Idaho/Pro-2028

Kuhlmann, Hank
62Pep/Tul

Kuhn, Chad
88Spoka/Pro-1935
89Watlo/Pro-1797
89Watlo/Star-16

Kuhn, Ken
55Salem
57T-266

Kuhn, Walter
(Red)
T207

Kuilan, Jorge
88WinHav/Star-11

Kuiper, Duane
76OPC-508
76SSPC-522
76T-508
77OPC-233
77Pep-19
77T-85
78Ho-34
78OPC-39
78T-332
79Ho-13
79OPC-67
79T-146
80OPC-221
80T-429
81D-319
81OPC-226
81T-612
82D-198
82F-373
82OPC-233
82T-233
82T/Tr-60T
83F-263
83Moth/Giants-11
83T-767
84D-553
84F-375
84Nes/792-542
84OPC-338
84T-542
84T/St-169
85F-610
85T-22

Kuiper, Glen
85Spoka/Cram-10
86Erie-16

Kuld, Pete
88Watlo/Pro-682
89Mia/Star/25-22

Kume, Mike
52Park-100

Kunkel, Jeff
84Rang-20
85D-587
85F-561
85OKCty-3
85OPC-288
85T-136FS
85T-288
85T/St-350
86OKCty-9
87Moth/Rang-24
88OkCty/CMC-18
88OkCty/Pro-30
88Score-407
89B-231
89D-496
89F-527
89Moth/R-19
89Score-484
89Smok/R-18
89T-92
89UD-463
90D-496
90F-304
90Score-431
90T-174
90UD-394

Kunkel, Jim
85T-136FS

Kunkel, Kevin
86Cram/PCL-70
87Madis-19

Kunkel, William
61T-322
62T-147
63T-523

Kuntz, Lee
86Watlo-16tr
88Wmspt/Pro-1303

Kuntz, Rusty
78Knoxv
81D-282
81T-112R
82Edmon-20
82F-348
82T-237
84F-568
84F/X-66
84Nes/792-598
84T-598
84T/X-66
85D-516
85F-14
85T-73
85Wendy-13

Kuoda, Masa
89Salin/Cal-134
89Salin/Pro-1804

Kupsey, John
89Pulas/Pro-1913

Kurczewski, Tommy
88Watlo/Pro-665
89BurlB/Pro-1603

Kurosaki, Ryan
77ArkTr
80ArkTr-13

Kurowski, George
(Whitey)
47TipTop
48L-81
62Pep/Tul
Exh47

Kurpiel, Ed
78Tidew

Kush, Emil
47TipTop
49Eureka-59

Kusick, Craig
75OPC-297
75T-297
75T/M-297
77T-38

78T-137
79T-472
80Hawai-7
80OPC-374
80T-693
81Evans-16

Kusnyer, Art
72OPC-213R
72T-213R
77Spoka

Kutcher, Randy
80Clint-14
83Phoen/BHN-15
84Cram/PCL-18
85Cram/PCL-177
86Phoen-13
87D-547
87F-276
87Phoen-12
88Pawtu/CMC-11
88Pawtu/Pro-464
89T/Tr-64T
90Score-551
90T-676

Kutina, Joe
T207

Kutner, Mike
82Miami-20

Kutsukos, Pete
84Beaum-2
85Beaum-7

Kutyna, Marty
60T-516
61T-546
62T-566

Kutzler, Jerry
88Tampa/Star-12
89BirmB/Pro-117
89SLAS-15
90D-503

Kuykendall, Kevin
87Watlo-12

Kuzava, Robert
50B-5
51B-97
51T/BB-22
52B-233
52BR
52T-85
53B/BW-33
54Esskay
54NYJour
54T-230
55B-215
55Esskay

Kuzma, Greg
88Butte-3

Kuzniar, Paul
87Watlo-19
88Wmspt/Pro-1321
89Canton/Best-20
89Canton/Pro-1305
89Canton/Star-11

Kvansnicka, Jay
89Keno/Pro-1063
89Keno/Star-11

Kwolek, Joe
86Osceola-16

Kyles, Stan
81QuadC-19
83MidldC-19
84Albany-15
85Cram/PCL-138
87Tacom-3
88Albuq/CMC-2
88Albuq/Pro-275

Laabs, Chester
40PB-206
V362-31
W753

LaBare, Jay
80Elmir-39

Labay, Steve
86Readg-13

Labine, Clem
52T-342
53T-14
54B-106
54NYJour
54T-121
55Gol/Dodg-17
55T-180
56T-295
57T-53
58Hires-34
58T-305
59Morrell
59T-262M
59T-403
60BB-6
60L-60
60T-29
61T-22
79TCMA-31
89Rini/Dodg-19
89Smok/Dodg-61

Labossiere, Dave
80Tucso-12
81Tucso-14
82Tucso-27
83Tucso-25

Laboy, Carlos
87AubAs-14
88Ashvl/Pro-1056
89Osceola/Star-10

Laboy, Jose A.
(Coco)
66Pep/Tul
69Fud's-6
69T-524R
70K-66
70MLB/St-67
70OPC-238
70T-238
71LaPizza-5
71MLB/St-132
71OPC-132
71T-132
72MB-190
72T-727
73OPC-642
73T-642
87FtLaud-20
88PrWill/Star-14

Labozzetta, Al
86GlenF-11

LaCasse, Michael
79Newar-10

Lacer, Mike
86Pittsf-12tr

LaCerra, Tony
88Reno/Cal-270

Lacey, Robert
76Tucso-19
77SnJos-14
78T-29
79T-647
80OPC-167
80T-316
81D-240
81F-578
81T-481
81T/Tr-784
82T-103
85Cram/PCL-191
85F-611

LaChance, George
(Candy)
E107

Lachemann, Bill
83Clint/LF-29
86QuadC-18MG
87PalmSp-17
88CalLgAS-35
88PalmSp/Cal-112
88PalmSp/Pro-1436
89PalmSp/Cal-63MG
89PalmSp/Pro-489

Lachemann, Marcel
71MLB/St-518
71OPC-84
71T-84
82Danvi-14

Lachemann, Rene
65T-526R
66OPC-157
66T-157
67T-471
68T-422
77SnJos-2
78SnJos-2
79Spoka-16
80Spoka-18
81Spoka-13
82D-600
83T-336
84Gard-1MG
84Pol/Brew-9MG
84T/X-67
85T-628

Lachowetz, Anthony J.
81VeroB-8
82VeroB-23

Lachowicz, Al
82Tulsa-7
84OKCty-1
85Tulsa-36

Lackey, John
83LynnP-4

Lacko, Rich
87Lakel-14
88GlenF/Pro-920

Lacks, Charles K.
55Gol/Braves-17

LaCock, R. Pete
75OPC-494
75T-494
75T/M-494
76OPC-101
76SSPC-317
76T-101
77T-561
78T-157
79T-248
80OPC-202
80T-389
81D-344
81F-47
81T-9

LaCorte, Frank
76OPC-597R
76SSPC-612
76T-597R
78Richm
80T-411
81D-143
81F-55
81OPC-348
81T-513
82D-270
82F-220
82T-248
83D-218
83F-454
83T-14
84D-283
84F-230
84F/X-67
84Nes/792-301
84Smok/Cal-16
84T-301
84T/X-68
85OPC-153
85T-153

LaCoss, Mike
77Indianap-11
78Indianap-4
79T-717R
80OPC-111
80T-199
81D-183
81OPC-134
81T-474
82D-440
82F-72
82T-294
82T/Tr-61T
83D-344
83F-455
83T-97
84D-206
84F-231
84Moth/Ast-24
84Nes/792-507
84T-507
85D-405
85F-353
85F/Up-U66
85T-666
85T/Tr-69T
86F/Up-U62
86Moth/Giants-17
86T-359
86T/Tr-57T
87D-636
87F-277
87Moth/SFG-21
87T-151
88D-436
88F-86
88Moth/Giants-21
88Panini/St-418
88Score-465
88T-754
89D-602
89F/Up-129
89Moth/Giants-21
89RedFoley/St-70
89Score-500
89T-417
89UD-48
90D-652
90F-59
90Score-253
90T-53
90UD-140

Lacy, Lee
73OPC-391
73T-391
74OPC-658
74T-658
75OPC-631
75T-631
75T/M-631
76OPC-99
76SSPC-78
76T-99
76T/Tr-99T
77T-272
78T-104
79OPC-229
79T-441
80T-536
81D-376
81F-374
81T-332
82D-276
82F-483
82F/St-80
82T-752
83D-276
83F-308
83OPC-69
83T-69
84D-479
84F-252
84Nes/792-462
84OPC-229
84T-462
84T/St-138
85D-508
85F-467
85F/St-9
85F/Up-U67
85Leaf-40
85T-669
85T/St-126
85T/Tr-70T
86D-228
86F-277
86Leaf-104
86OPC-226
86S-87
86T-226
86T/St-229
87D-336
87F-473
87OPC-182
87S-86
87T-182
87T/St-231
88F-565
88Score-173
88T-598

Lacy, Steve
76Watlo
77DaytB

Ladd, Pete
80T-678R
81Tucso-19
82Vanco-17
83F-37
83Pol/Brew-27
84D-124
84F-204
84F/St-77
84Gard-10
84Nes/792-243
84Pol/Brew-27
84T-243
85D-271
85F-585
85Gard-10
85Pol/Brew-27
85T-471
86F-492
86F/Up-U63
86Moth/Mar-17
86T-163
86T/Tr-58T
87Albuq/Pol-12
87D-660
87F-588
87T-572

Lade, Doyle
49B-168
49Eureka-60
50B-196
51B-139

Ladnier, Deric
86FtMyr-17
87AppFx-8
89Memph/Best-11
89Memph/Pro-1189
89Memph/Star-13
89Star/Wax-43

Ladrum, Ced
89CharlK-4

Lafata, Joe
49Eureka-115

LaFever, Greg
86Watlo-17
87Wmspt-17
88SnAnt/Best-4

Lafitte, Edward
(Doc)
E254
E270/2

Lafitte, James A.
T206

LaFountain, James
77Visal
LaFrancois, Roger
81Pawtu-23
83D-534
83Pawtu-12
83T-344
84Richm-14
85Durhm-27
88James/Pro-1894
89SoBend/GS-4
Laga, Mike
82Evans-16
83Evans-15
84D-491
84Evans-16
86D-578
86T/Tr-59T
87D-293
87Louvl-23
87Smok/Cards-15
87T-321
88Louvl-26
89Phoen/CMC-17
89Phoen/Pro-1493
89Score-536
LaGrow, Lerrin
710PC-39R
71T-39R
730PC-369
73T-369
740PC-433
74T-433
750PC-116
75T-116
75T/M-116
760PC-138
76SSPC-356
76T-138
780PC-152
78T-14
79T-527
80T-624
LaHonta, Ken
76Dubuq
Lahoud, Joe
690PC-189R
69T-189R
700PC-78
70T-78
71MLB/St-321
710PC-622
71T-622
72MB-191
720PC-321
72T-321
72T/Cloth-19
730PC-212
73T-212
740PC-512
74T-512
75Ho-10
75Ho/Twink-10
750PC-317
75T-317
75T/M-317
760PC-612
76SSPC-20
76T-612
78T-382
Lahrman, Tom
86Penin-15
87Penin-22
88Tampa/Star-13
Lahti, Jeffrey Allen
80Water-2
81Indianap-16
82Louisvl-13
83F-12
83T-284
84D-327
84F-327
84Nes/792-593
84T-593
85F-231
85T-447
86D-475
86F-40
86KAS/Disc-18
86Leaf-233
86Schnucks-12
86T-33
87D-577
87F-299
87T-367
Lain, Marty
83Beaum-9
Laird, Tony
85Nashua-13
86Nashua-14
Lajeskie, Dick
48Sommer-22
49B/PCL-16
49Sommer-12
Lajoie, Napoleon
10Domino-65
11Helmar-24
12Sweet/Pin-18
14CJ-66
15CJ-66
33G-106
40PB-173
48Exh/HDF
50Callahan
60F-1
61F-120
61GP-31
63Bz/ATG-8
69Bz/Sm
72F/FFeat-28
73F/Wild-35M
75F/Pion-18
80Cram/Leg-74
80Laugh/3/4/5-9
80SSPC/HOF
89HOF/St-10
BF2-35
D303
D304
D329-97
E101
E102
E103
E105
E106
E107
E254
E270/2
E300
E90/1
E92
E93
E94
E96
E98
L1-121
M101/4-97
M116
PM1-10
S81-96
T201
T206
T213/blue
T215/blue
T215/brown
T216
T3-23
W514-62
W555
WG2-32
WG4-12
WG5-25
WG6-24
Lajszky, Werner
80Wausa-21
Lake, Dan
85Anchora-18
Lake, Edward
47TipTop
49B-107
50B-240
51B-140
Exh47
Lake, Fred
M116
Lake, Joe
11Helmar-61
E94
M116
T201
T206
T215/blue
W555
Lake, Ken
89James/Pro-2148
89Mia/Star/25-10
Lake, Mike
77LodiD
78LodiD
Lake, Steve
80Holyo-17
81Vanco-25
82Tucso-5
83Thorn-16
84D-198
84Nes/792-691
84T-691
85SevenUp-16
85T-98
86Gator-29
86T-588
87D-604
87F-300
87Smok/Cards-10
87T-84
88D-510
88F-38
88Score-596
88Smok/Card-11
88T-208
89B-399
89F-454
89Score-363
89Score/Tr-12
89T-463
89T/Tr-65T
90D-431
90F-566
90Score-435
90T-183
90UD-491
Lakeman, Al
49Eureka-14
Laker, Tim
88James/Pro-1904
89James/Pro-2137
Lamabe, Jack
62T-593R
63T-251
64T-305
650PC-88
65T-88
66T-577
67T-208
68T-311
85Beaum-24C
Lamanno, Ray
49B-113
LaMar, Danny
82Cedar-12
83Tampa-16
84Cedar-18
LaMarche, Michel
87Spart-10
Lamb, Randy
77Cocoa
78Wausa
Lamb, Ray
700PC-131R
70T-131R
71MLB/St-377
710PC-727
71T-727
720PC-422
72T-422
730PC-496
73T-496
85SpokAT/Crm-11
Lamb, Todd
84Durhm-19
86Durhm-17
Lambert, Gene
82Clint-17
83Clint/LF-10
Lambert, Ken
87VeroB-10
Lambert, Reese
87Madis-23
88Tacom/CMC-4
88Tacom/Pro-631
89Tacom/CMC-3
89Tacom/Pro-1548
Lambert, Reggie
86PalmSp-20
86PalmSp/Smok-27
87PalmSp-5
88PalmSp/Cal-113
88PalmSp/Pro-1461
Lambert, Rob
87PrWill-25
88Colum/CMC-14
88Colum/Pro-319
Lambert, Tim
82Idaho-10
84Albany-17
85Cram/PCL-140
86Tacom-11
87Memph-13
87Memph/Best-16
Lamle, Adam
88CharlR/Star-12
88FSLAS/Star-41
89Mia/Star/22-10
89Tulsa/GS-12
Lamonde, Larry
82AlexD-3
84Cram/PCL-124
85Nashua-14
Lamont, Gene
710PC-39R
71T-39R
750PC-593
75T-593
75T/M-593
840maha-2
850maha-22MG
LaMotta, Jake
D305
Lamp, Dennis
78T-711R
79T-153
800PC-129
80T-54
81D-573
81F-305
81T-331
81T/Tr-785
82D-619
82F-349
82T-216TL
82T-622
83D-165
83F-243
830PC-26
83T-434
84D-526
84F-66
84F/X-68
84Nes/792-541
84T-541
84T/St-239
84T/X-69
84Tor/Fire-21
85D-119
85F-111
850PC-83
85T-774
85Tor/Fire-17
86Ault-53
86D-626
86F-64
86Leaf-244
860PC-219
86T-219
86T/St-193
86Tor/Fire-21
87F-233
870PC-336
87T-768
88D/RedSox/Bk-NEW
88F-284
88Score-616
88Score/Tr-6T
89D-633
89F-92
89Score-508
89T-188
89T/Big-169
89UD-503
90D-423
90F-280
90Score-471
90T-338
Lampard, C. Keith
700PC-492R
70T-492R
710PC-728R
71T-728R
720PC-489R
72T-489R
Lampe, Ed
88Hamil/Pro-1742
Lampert, Ken
86VeroB-15
Lamphere, Larry
88AubAs/Pro-1947
89Ashvl/Pro-967
Lampkin, Tom
87Watlo-23
88BBAmer-7
88EastLAS/Pro-41
88Wmspt/Pro-1304
89AAA/Pro-35
89ColSp/Pro-254
89D-639
90T-172
Lamson, Chuck
78Ashev
80Tulsa-20
Lancaster, Lester
86WinSal-12
87D/Rook-10
88Berg/Cubs-50
88D-561
88D/Best-172
88D/Cubs/Bk-561
88F-421
88Score-602
88T-112
89D-341
89F-429
89IowaC/CMC-8
89IowaC/Pro-1689
89Mara/Cubs-50
89Score-60
89T-694
89UD-84
90D-628

90F-35
90Score-413
90T-437
90UD-584
Lance, Gary
79Spoka-11
83Idaho-32
84Madis/Pol-2
85Huntsvl/BK-24
87CharRa-9
88Charl/Pro-1212
89AubAs/Pro-28
89Wich/Roc-38CO
Lance, Mark
83Durhm-19
84Durhm-2
Lancellotti, Rick
78Salem
80Port-20
81Hawai-11
82Hawai-11
84Cram/PCL-230
85Tidew-1
86Phoen-14
89Pawtu/Dunkin-29
Landers, Hank
83Beloi/LF-7
Landestoy, Rafael
75Water
78Cr/PCL-6
79T-14
80T-268
81Coke
81D-19
81F-70
81OPC-326
81T-597
81T/St-168
81T/Tr-786
82Coke/Reds
82F-73
82T-361
83F-595
83T-684
83T/X-59
84Nes/792-477
84Pol/Dodg-17
84T-477
85Albany-17
85Cram/PCL-61
Landford, Ray
89ArkTr/GS-9
Landis, Craig
78Cedar
80Phoen-14
81Richm-5
Landis, Jim
57T-375
58T-108
59T-493
60MacGregor-11
60T-550
61P-27
61T-271
61T/St-122
62Bz
62Exh
62P-50
62P/Can-50
62Salada-49
62Shirriff-49
62T-50
62T-540
62T/bucks
62T/St-26
63Exh
63F-10
63J-40
63P-40
63Salada-60
63T-485
64T-264
65T-376
66OPC-128
66T-128
67T-483
Exh47
Landis, Kenesaw M.
(Judge)
50Callahan
60F-64
61F-53
63Bz-30
80SSPC/HOF
88Pac/8Men-66
88Pac/8Men-67
88Pac/8Men-79
89HOF/St-95
Landis, William
68OPC-189
68T-189
69T-264
72MB-192
Landmark, Neil
85Visal-20
Landreaux, Ken
79T-619
80OPC-49
80T-88
81D-565
81F-553
81F/St-46
81K-30
81OPC-219
81Pol/Dodg-44B
81T-219
81T/SO-41
81T/St-101
81T/Tr-787
82D-388
82F-11
82OPC-114
82Pol/Dodg
82Pol/Dodg-44
82T-114
82T/St-49
83D-236
83F-210
83Pol/Dodg-44
83T-376
83T/St-246
84D-470
84F-104
84F/St-2
84Nes/792-533
84OPC-216
84Pol/Dodg-44
84Smok/Dodg-1
84T-533
84T/St-76
85D-494
85F-375
85T-418
85T/St-75
86D-470
86F-134
86OPC-2
86Pol/Dodg-44
86T-782
87D-352
87D/OD-81
87F-444
87Moth/Dodg-24
87OPC-123
87Pol/Dodg-23
87T-699
88RochR-14
88RochR/Gov-14
88Score-247
88T-23
Landreth, Harry
83Chatt-25
84Chatt-15
Landreth, Larry
78T-701R
Landrith, Dave
83Butte-13
Landrith, Hobie
54B-220
55B-50
56T-314
57T-182
58T-24
59T-422
60T-42
61P-150
61T-114
61T/St-78
62Salada-181
62Shirriff-181
62T-279
62T/St-157
63T-209
Landrum
46Sunbeam
Landrum, Bill
82Water-1
83Water-5
87Kahn-43
88F-238
88IowaC/CMC-8
88IowaC/Pro-541
88T-42
89BuffB/CMC-2
89BuffB/Pro-1674
89F/Up-116
90D-668
90F-472
90Score-456
90T-425
90UD-442
Landrum, Cedric
86Geneva-13CO
87WinSal-4
88Pittsf/Pro-1370
Landrum, Darryl
86Ventura-11
87Duned-11
88Wmspt/Pro-1319
Landrum, Don
58T-291
61P-175
61T-338
62T-323
63T-113
64T-286
65T-596
66OPC-43
66T-43
66T/RO-99
Landrum, Terry
(Tito)
76ArkTr
77ArkTr
78StPet
79ArkTr-4
81F-539
81Louvl-12
81T-244R
82D-292
82F-118
82T-658
83D-498
83F-13
83T-357
84F/X-69
84T/St-14LCS
85D-168
85F-232
85OPC-33
85T-33
86D-425
86F-41
86KAS/Disc-3
86OPC-171
86Schnucks-13
86T-498
86T/St-19WS
87D-386
87D/OD-66
87F-301
87OPC-288
87Smok/Cards-23
87T-288
88Pol/Dodg-21M
88RochR/CMC-22
88T-581
89Nashvl-11
Landry, Greg
89Beloi/Star-13
89Helena/SP-10
Landry, Howard
89WinHav/Star-11
Landuyt, Doug
78Cedar
81Shrev-14
83Phoen/BHN-25tr
Landy, Brian
88Bill/Pro-1820
89Greens/Pro-412
Lane, Brian
88Greens/Pro-1555
88SALAS/GS-7
89Chatt/Best-4
89Chatt/GS-14
Lane, Gene
82Durhm-24
Lane, Heath
89Beloi/Star-14
Lane, Ira
82DayBe-14
Lane, Jerald H.
(Jerry)
54T-97
Lane, Jerry
81ElPas-7
Lane, Marvin
77Evansvl/TCMA-17
Lane, Nolan
88CapeCod/Sum-46
Lane, Scott
88Rockford-19AGM
89Rockford-19AGM
Lane, William C.
52Park-50
Lanfair, Dave
75Water
Lang, Perry
88Pac/8Men-15
Lang, Robert
(Chip)
77OPC-216
77T-132
Langdon, Ted
83Tampa-17
84Cedar-2
86Tampa-9
87Vermont-3
Lange, Clark
87Visal-26
Lange, Frank H.
E254
T205
T207
Lange, Fred
N172
Lange, Richard
74OPC-429
74T-429
75OPC-114
75T-114
75T/M-114
76OPC-176
76T-176
77SLCty
Langfield, Paul
80Utica-28
Langford, Rick
75Shrev
75Shreve/TCMA-8
78Ho-120
78OPC-33
78T-327
79T-29
80OPC-284
80T-546
81D-238
81F-572
81F/St-27
81K-55
81OPC-154
81T-154
81T/St-121
82D-161
82F-98
82F/St-126
82Granny-7
82OPC-43
82T-454
83D-365
83F-523
83Granny-22
83T-286
83T-531
83T/St-106
84F-451
84Nes/792-629
84OPC-304
84T-629
85T-347
86F-425
86Moth/A's-14
86T-766
88Colum/CMC-10
88Colum/Pol-5
88Colum/Pro-308
Langford, Sam
T3/Box-65
Langiotti, Fred
89Sprin/Best-24
Langley, Lee
87VeroB-28
88Bakers/Cal-256
89Clearw/Star-13
Langston, Keith
88CapeCod/Sum-109
89NiagFls/Puc-14
Langston, Mark
83Chatt-11
84F/X-70
84FunFood/Pin-18
84Moth/Mar-13
84T/X-70
85D-557
85Drake-38
85F-492
85F/LimEd-17
85F/St-109
85Leaf-56
85Moth/Mar-3
85OPC-259
85T-625
85T/3D-22
85T/St-281
85T/St-337
85T/St-371M
85T/Super-20
86D-118
86F-467
86Moth/Mar-3
86OPC-198
86T-495
86T/St-225
87Class-89
87D-568
87D/HL-34
87D/OD-116
87F-589
87F/AwardWin-22

87F/Hottest-26
87F/Mini-62
87F/St-70
87Leaf-55
87Moth/Sea-5
87OPC-215
87RedFoley/St-45
87S-102
87T-215
87T/Mini-71
87T/St-219
88Class/Blue-250
88D-20DK
88D-317
88D/AS-26
88D/Best-136
88D/DKsuper-20DK
88F-377
88F/BB/AS-20
88F/BB/MVP-21
88F/Hottest-23
88F/LL-24
88F/Mini-52
88F/Slug-23
88F/St-60
88F/TL-18
88Leaf-123
88Leaf-20DK
88Moth/Sea-5
88OPC-80
88Panini/St-181
88RedFoley/St-46
88Score-30
88Sf-46
88T-80
88T/Big-176
88T/Coins-18
88T/Mini-34
88T/Revco-33
88T/St-214
88T/St/Backs-63
88T/UK-42
89B-205
89D-227
89D/Best-68
89F-551
89F/Excit-29
89F/Superstar-27
89F/Up-97
89KMart/DT-21
89Moth/Sea-5
89OPC-355
89Panini/St-430
89RedFoley/St-71
89Score-161
89Score/HotSt-67
89Score/Mast-13
89Score/Tr-25
89Sf-159
89T-355
89T/Hills-19
89T/Mini-73
89T/St-221
89T/Tr-66T
89T/UK-47
89UD-526
90Class-72
90D-338
90F-352
90Score-401
90Score-688DT
90Score/100St-96
90Sf-110
90T-530
90UD-647

Laniauskas, Vitas
89Ashvl/Pro-941

Lanier, H. Max
50B-207
51B-230
52B-110
52T-101
W754

Lanier, Hal
65OPC-118
65T-118
66OPC-156M
66T-156M
66T-271
67OPC-4
67T-4
68T-436
69MB-155
69MLB/St-201
69T-316
69T/St-106
70MLB/St-126
70T-583
71MLB/St-255
71OPC-181
71T-181
72MB-193
72T-589
73OPC-479
73T-479
74OPC-588
74T-588
78StPet
86Pol/Ast-6MG
86T/Tr-60T
87Moth/Ast-1
87Pol/Ast-7MG
87T-343MG
88Moth/Ast-1MG
88Pol/Ast-25MG
88T-684
89T-164MG
PM10/Sm-93

Lankard, Steve
86Salem-17
87PortChar-3
88Tulsa-20
89Tulsa/GS-13

Lankford, Ray
88MidwLAS/GS-26
88Sprin/Best-14

Lanning, David P.
81VeroB-9

Lanok, Dale
85BurlR-7

Lanoux, Marty
86Kenosha-11
87Visal-23
88CalLgAS-39
88Visal/Cal-153
88Visal/Pro-104
89Orlan/Best-26
89Orlan/Pro-1328

Lansford, Carney
76QuadC
79T-212
80OPC-177
80T-337
81Coke
81D-409
81F-270
81F/St-12
81OPC-245
81T-639
81T/HT
81T/SO-25
81T/St-43
81T/Tr-788
82Coke/BOS
82D-82
82F-298
82F/St-164
82K-41
82OPC-91
82T-161LL
82T-786TL
82T-91
82T/St-156
82T/St-2
83D-408
83F-187
83Granny-4
83OPC-318
83T-523
83T/St-32
83T/X-60
84D-176
84D/AAS-39
84F-452
84FunFood/Pin-55
84Moth/A's-7
84Nes/792-767
84OPC-59
84T-767
84T/St-328
85D-345
85D-8
85D/DKsuper-8
85F-429
85Leaf-8DK
85Moth/A's-8
85OPC-347
85T-422
85T/St-330
86D-131
86F-426
86Leaf-55
86Moth/A's-8
86OPC-134
86S-75M
86T-134
86T/St-169
86Woolwth-17
87D-158
87D/OD-20
87F-397
87F/Lim-24
87F/Mini-63
87F/St-71
87OPC-69
87RedFoley/St-37
87S-138
87Smok/A's-8
87T-678
87T/St-171
88D-178
88D/A's/Bk-178
88D/Best-246
88F-285
88F/Slug-C3
88F/St-55
88Leaf-195
88Moth/A's-6
88OPC-292
88Panini/St-169
88Score-253
88Sf-202
88T-292
88T/Big-221
88T/St-167
89B-198
89D-243
89D/AS-17
89D/Best-22
89F-16
89F-633M
89KMart/Lead-20
89Moth/A's-5
89OPC-47
89Panini/St-421
89RedFoley/St-72
89Score-179
89Score/HotSt-12
89Sf-53
89T-47
89T/Big-57
89T/St-170
89UD-562
90Class-12
90D-95
90F-14
90Score-296
90Score/100St-20
90Sf-84
90T-316
90UD-253

Lansford, Joe
81Hawai-6
82Hawai-6
84Cram/PCL-220
85Cram/PCL-146
87LasVegas-4

Lantigua, Manny
75SnAnt
79Portl-16

Lantz, Tom
75Clint

LaPalme, Paul
52T-166
53B/BW-19
53T-201
54B-107
54DanDee
54T-107
55B-61
55Hunter
57T-344

Lapchick, Joe
33SK-32

Lapenta, Jerry
86Geneva-14
87Peoria-6
88Peoria/Ko-20
88Pittsf/Pro-1366

LaPoint, Dave
77Newar
78BurlB
80Vanco-7
83D-544
83F-14
83T-438
84D-290
84F-328
84Nes/792-627
84T-627
84T/St-146
85D-138
85F-233
85F/Up-U68
85Moth/Giants-16
85OPC-229
85T-229
85T/St-143
85T/Tr-71T
86Cain's-10
86D-387
86F-547
86F/Up-U64
86OPC-162
86T-551
86T/Tr-61T
87D-607
87F-421
87OPC-319
87T-754
88Coke/WS-13
88D-552
88D/Best-123
88F-402
88F/BB/AS-21
88F/Slug-24
88Score-589
88T-334
89B-165
89D-488
89D/Best-244
89D/Tr-27
89F-212
89OPC-89
89Score-384
89Score/NWest-15
89Score/Tr-4
89T-89
89T/Tr-67T
89UD-600
89UD/Ext-706
90D-72
90Score-357
90T-186
90UD-507

LaPoint, J. Anthony
(Tony)
86Geneva-15
87CharWh-19

LaPorte, Frank
10Domino-66
11Helmar-62
12Sweet/Pin-53B
12Sweet/Pin-53A
14CJ-98
14Piedmont/St-48
15CJ-98
E254
M116
T201
T202
T205
T206
T213/brown

Lapp, John
BF2-13
D329-98
D350/2-96
E104
E300
M101/4-98
M101/5-96
M116
T201
T207
T208
T222

Lapple, Bob
80Cedar-10

Lara, Crucito
87StPet-20
88StPet/Star-11
89StLucie/Star-12

Larcom, Mark
82Wisco-22
83Wisco/LF-12

Lardner, Ring
88Pac/8Men-30
88Pac/8Men-35M
88Pac/8Men-42M

Laribee, Russ
81Pawtu-20

Larios, John
86Cram/PCL-35
87AppFx-3

Lariviere, Chris 42
88Rockford-20
89Rockford-20

Larker, Norm
53Exh/Can-37
59Morrell
59T-107
60BB-1
60T-394
61BB-5
61Bz-34
61Morrell
61P-156
61T-130
61T-41LL
61T/St-28
62Bz
62J-113
62P-118
62P/Can-118
62Salada-194
62Shirriff-194
62T-23
62T/bucks
63J-188

63P-188
63T-536
89Smok/Ast-14
89Smok/Dodg-67

Larkin, Barry
86S/Rook-34
87Class-18
87Class/Up-133
87D-492
87D/OD-191
87F-204
87Kahn-15
87T-648
87ToysRUs-18
88D-492
88D/Best-222
88F-239
88Kahn/Reds-11
88Leaf-226
88OPC-102
88Panini/St-280
88Score-72
88Score/YS/II-34
88T-102
88T/Big-74
88T/St-140
89B-311
89Cadaco-32
89Class-70
89Class/Up/2-165
89D-257
89D/AS-47
89D/Best-110
89F-164
89F/BBAS-26
89K/Reds-11
89OPC-363
89Panini/St-74
89RedFoley/St-73
89Score-31
89Score/HotSt-52
89Score/Mast-24
89Sf-136
89T-515
89T/Big-199
89T/Mini-11
89T/St-137
89T/St/Backs-44
89UD-270
90Class-48
90D-71
90F-423
90Score-155
90Score-689DT
90Sf-160
90T-10
90UD-167
90UD-99TC

Larkin, Gene
85Visal-14
86Orlan-10
87D/Rook-23
87F/U-U59
87Portl-19
87S/Rook-34
87T/Tr-60T
88D-564
88D/Best-158
88F-14
88OPC-384
88Panini/St-145
88RedFoley/St-47
88Score-276
88Sf-107
88Smok/Minn-5
88T-746
88T/Big-264
88T/St-279
89B-160
89D-355
89F-117
89Panini/St-388
89Score-280
89Score/YS/II-6
89T-318
89T/Big-226
89T/St-294
89UD-580
90D-436
90F-379
90Score-276
90T-556
90UD-471

Larkin, Henry
(Ted)
N172
N690

Larkin, Pat
84Evans-5

Larkin, Steve
34G-92

LaRoche, Dave
71OPC-174
71T-174
72OPC-352
72T-352
73OPC-426
73T-426
74OPC-502
74T-502
75OPC-258
75T-258
75T/M-258
76OPC-21
76SSPC-510
76T-21
77OPC-61
77Pep-15
77T-385
78T-454
79OPC-317
79T-601
80T-263
81F-285
81T-529
81T/Tr-789
82D-564
82T-142
83F-384
83OPC-333
83OPC-334SV
83T-333
83T-334A
85Albany-24
86Colum-13CO
87Syrac-19
87Syrac/TCMA-24

LaRocque, Gary
76BurlB
77Holyo
88Bakers/Cal-262

LaRosa, Bill
78Ashev

Larosa, John
88Spart/Pro-1031
88Spart/Star-10
88Spart/Star-10
89Spart/Pro-1054
89Spart/Star-12

LaRosa, Mark
88CapeCod/Sum-77

Larose, Steve
88Clmbia/GS-6
89StLucie/Star-13

LaRose, Vic
69T-404

Larsen, Bill
88Rockford-21
89Rockford-21AGM

Larsen, Dan
81OkCty/TCMA-7
86Kinston-14

Larsen, Don
54B-101
54Esskay
55B-67
56T-332
57T-175
58T-161
59T-205
60NuCard-18
60T-353
61NuCard-418
61T-177
61T-402M
62T-33
63T-163
64T-513
65T-389
69T-383M
72Laugh/GF-45
76Laugh/Jub-17
78TCMA-211
78TCMA-266
79TCMA-272
88Pac/Leg-42
Exh47

Larsen, Jim
86Cram/PCL-36

Larson, Dan
77T-641
79OkCty
83IowaC-6
84Butte-14
84OKCty-6
86Wausa-12
87BurlEx-26

Larson, Duane
82Syrac-27

Larson, Jamie
85Anchora-36bb

Larson, Michael
88Boise/Pro-1620
89Boise/Pro-2003

LaRussa, Tony
64T-244
68T-571
72OPC-451
72T-451
78Knoxv
78TCMA-229
81D-402
81F-344
82D-319
83D-571
83T-216
84F/St-126MG
84Nes/792-591MG
84T-591
84TruVl/WS-20MG
85Coke/WS-10
85T-466
86Coke/WS-MG
86T-531
87T-68MG
88Moth/A's-1MG
88T-344
89Moth/A's-1MG
89Pac/Leg-140
89T-224MG
90T-639MG

Lary, Frank
55B-154
56T-191
57T-168
58T-245
59T-393
60L-3
60T-85
60T/tatt
60T/tatt-28
61P-38
61T-243
61T-48LL
61T-50LL
61T/St-153
62J-22
62P-22
62P/Can-22
62Salada-58
62Shirriff-58
62T-474AS
62T-57LL
62T/bucks
62T/St-48
63F-14
63J-55
63P-55
63T-140
63T-218M
64Det/Lids-8
64T-197
65OPC-127
65T-127
78TCMA-253
79TCMA-183

Lary, Lynford H.
28Exh/PCL-18
31Exh/4-26
33G-193
35G-1C
35G-2C
35G-6C
35G-7C
R314

Lasek, Jim
77Spart

Laseke, Eric
85Elmir-10
86WinHav-14
87WinHav-7
89WinHav/Star-12

Laseter, Tom
76Watlo

Lasher, Fred
68T-447R
69T-373
70OPC-356
70T-356
71MLB/St-347
71OPC-707
71T-707
72MB-194
88Domino-10

Lashley, Mickey
77Clint
78LodiD

Laskey, Bill
81Omaha-10
83D-424
83F-264
83Moth/Giants-15
83OPC-218
83T-171TL
83T-518
83T/St-325
84D-358
84F-376
84Nes/792-129
84OPC-129
84T-129
84T/St-172
85D-387
85F-612
85Moth/Giants-9
85OPC-331
85T-331
86D-585
86F-251
86Moth/Giants-24
86OPC-281
86T-603
87Toled-21
87Toled/TCMA-4
88Gator-17

Lasky, Larry
86Ashvl-17TR
87ColAst/Pro-21
87ColumAst-21
88ColAst/Best-15
89Tucso/Pro-182

Lasorda, Tom
52Park-58
53Exh/Can-50
54T-132
55Gol/Dodg-18
73OPC-569CO
73T-569C
74OPC-144CO
74T-144C
77T-504MG
78T-189
79T-526MG
81D-420
81F-116
81Pol/Dodg-2
81T-679MG
82D-110
82F/St-111M
82Pol/Dodg
82Pol/Dodg-2
83D-136
83Pol/Dodg-2
83T-306
84F/St-124MG
84Nes/792-681MG
84Pol/Dodg-2
84T-681
85SpokAT/Crm-12
85T-601
86Pol/Dodg-2
86T-291
87Moth/Dodg-1
87Pol/Dodg-1
87Smok/Dodg-17
87T-493MG
88Moth/Dodg-1MG
88Pol/Dodg-2MG
88Pol/Dodg-MG
88Smok/Dodg-23
88T-74
89Moth/Dodg-1MG
89Pol/Dodg-2MG
89Rini/Dodg-13
89T-254MG
89T/WaxBox-H
90T-669MG
V362-45

Lassard, Paul
87FtLaud-14

Lata, Tim
88CapeCod/Sum-129
89Hamil/Star-20

Latham, Bill
83Lynch-3
84Tidew-6
85Tidew-10
87Portl-18
87Tidew-22
87Tidew/TCMA-28

Latham, John
89Well/Puc-17

Latham, W. Arlie
12Sweet/Pin-115
N172
N172/BC
N284
N300/unif
N338/2
N370
Scrapps
T202
T205
T206
T207
T215/brown

Lathers, Charles
M116

Latman, Barry
59T-477

60T-41
61T-560
61T/St-137
62Kahn
62Sugar-1
62T-145
62T-37M
62T/St-36
63Sugar-1
63T-426
64T-227
65T-307
66T-451
67OPC-28
67T-28

Latmore, Bob
86Miami-14
87Miami-10
88Hagers/Star-10
89Hagers/Best-4
89Hagers/Pro-271
89Hagers/Star-12

Latta, Greg
85BuffB-3
86BuffB-15TR
87Hawai-25
89Vanco/Pro-574

Latter, Dave
89Medford/Best-12

Lattimore, William
T206

Lau, Charley
58T-448
60T-312
61T-261
62T-533
63T-41
64T-229
65OPC-94
65T-94
66T-368
67T-329
73OPC-593CO
73T-593C
74T-166C

Lau, David
88Clmbia/GS-13
89StLucie/Star-14

Lauck, Jeff
84Savan-2

Laudner, Tim
80OrlTw-12
82D-549
82OrlTw/A-8
82T-766R
83D-177
83F-618
83T-529
83T/St-314
83T/St-93
84F-569
84Nes/792-363
84T-363
85D-652
85F-283
85Seven/Minn-12
85T-71
86D-391
86F-398
86T-184
87D-320
87F-546
87OPC-392
87T-478
88D-631
88F-15
88Master/Disc-5
88OPC-78
88Panini/St-135
88Score-153
88Smok/Minn-7
88T-671
88T/Big-243
88T/St-278
89B-154
89D-615
89D/AS-19
89F-118
89OPC-239
89Panini/St-384
89Score-134
89Sf-152
89T-239
89T/St-290
89UD-62
90D-419
90F-380
90Score-318
90T-777
90UD-419

Lauer, John Charles
N172

Laureano, Francisco
86BurlEx-13
87AppFx-7
88Virgini/Star-13
89BBCity/Star-15

Lauzerique, George
69T-358R
70McDon-6
70OPC-41
70T-41
75Dubuq
76Dubuq

Lav, David
87Columbia-5

Lavagetto, Harry
(Cookie)
35BU-51
39PB-74
40PB-69
41DP-17
47TipTop
48Signal
49Remar
50Remar
52T-365
59T-74M
60T-221
61Peters-10
61T-226
89Rini/Dodg-10
89Rini/Dodg-35
89Smok/Dodg-40
R313
R314

LaValliere, Mike
83Readg-12
85Louvl-22
86D/Rook-35
86F/Up-U65
86Schnucks-14
87D-331
87F-302
87F/U-U60
87T-162
87T/Tr-61T
87ToysRUs-19
88D-312
88D/Best-129
88F-333
88F/Slug-25
88Leaf-112
88OPC-57
88Panini/St-369
88Score-421
88Sf-193
88T-539
88T/Big-61
88T/St-131
89B-417
89D-244
89D/Best-201
89F-213
89OPC-218
89Panini/St-168
89RedFoley/St-74
89Score-33
89Sf-98
89T-218
89T/Big-306
89T/St-128
89T/St/Backs-56
89UD-417
90Class-42
90D-211
90F-473
90Score-116
90Sf-157
90T-478
90UD-578

Lavan, John
(Doc)
21Exh-94
BF2-42
D327
D328-95
D329-99
D350/2-97
E120
E121/120
E121/80
E122
E135-95
M101/4-99
M101/5-97
V100
V61-102
W501-108
W514-4
W575

Lavelle, Gary
75OPC-624R
75T-624R
75T/M-624R
76OPC-105
76SSPC-96
76T-105
77T-423
78Ho-32
78T-671
79Pol/Giants-46
79T-311
80Pol/Giants-46
80T-84
81D-314
81F-448
81OPC-62
81T-588
82D-60
82F-392
82OPC-209
82T-209
83D-60
83F-265
83Moth/Giants-14
83OPC-376
83T-791
84D-573
84D/AAS-1
84F-377
84Moth/Giants-10
84Nes/792-145
84OPC-145
84T-145
84T/St-164
85D-265
85F-613
85F/Up-U69
85Leaf-114
85OPC-2
85OPC/Post-24
85T-462
85T/St-159
85T/Tr-72T
85Tor/Fire-18
86Ault-46
86D-621
86F-65
86OPC-22
86T-622
86Tor/Fire-22
87Tor/Fire-17
87Tor/Fire-17

Lavender, Bob
88Gasto/Pro-996

Lavender, James
14CJ-105
15CJ-105
BF2-65
D328-96
D329-100
D350/2-98
E135-96
M101/4-100
M101/5-98
T206
WG4-13

LaVigne, Randy
82IowaC-6
83MidldC-24

Lavrusky, Chuck
87Idaho-7
88Boise/Pro-1621

Law, Joe
83Idaho-14
85Huntsvl/BK-40
87Modesto-19
89Tacom/CMC-6
89Tacom/Pro-1550

Law, Rudy
77LodiD
78Cr/PCL-56
79Albuq-19
79T-719R
81Albuq/TCMA-20
81D-180
81F-139
81Pol/Dodg-3
81T-127
82D-582
83D-521
83F-244
83T-514
84D-257
84F-67
84F/St-93
84Nes/792-47
84OPC-47
84T-47
84T/St-245
84TrueVal/WS-21
85Coke/WS-23
85D-244
85F-519
85Leaf-117
85OPC-286
85T-286
85T/St-241
86D-632
86F-211
86F/Up-U66
86OPC-6
86T-637
86T/St-291
86T/Tr-62T
87D-343
87F-372
87T-382

Law, Travis
88Butte-23

Law, Vance
79Portl-5
80Port-9
81Portl-14
81T-551R
82D-582
82F-484
82T-291
83D-117
83F-245
83OPC-98
83T-98
84D-546
84F-68
84Nes/792-667
84T-667
84T/St-249
84TrueVal/WS-22
85D-122
85F-520
85F/Up-U70
85Leaf-183
85OPC-81
85T-137FS
85T-413
85T/St-242
85T/Tr-73T
86D-132
86F-252
86Leaf-57
86OPC-99
86Provigo-23
86T-787
86T/St-81
87D-212
87D/OD-94
87F-323
87OPC-127
87T-127
88Berg/Cubs-2
88D-212
88D/Best-60
88D/Cubs/Bk-NEW
88F-187
88F/U-U79
88OPC-346
88Panini/St-324
88Score-85
88Score/Tr-16T
88Sf-41
88T-346
88T/Tr-60T
89B-293
89D-276
89D/AS-49
89F-430
89F/BBAS-27
89Mara/Cubs-2
89OPC-338
89Panini/St-57
89Score-102
89Sf-162
89T-501
89T/Big-143
89T/St-46
89T/St/Backs-42
89UD-473
90D-629
90F-36
90Score-73
90T-287
90UD-380

Law, Vern
51B-203
52B-71
52T-81
54B-187
54T-235
55B-199
56T-252
57T-199
58Hires/T
58Kahn
58T-132
59Kahn
59T-12
59T-428M
60Kahn
60T-453

60T/tatt
60T/tatt-29
61Kahn
61NuCard-406
61P-126
61T-250M
61T-400
61T-47LL
61T/St-66
62J-179
62P-179
62P/Can-179
62T-295
63F-58
63T-184
64T-472
65T-515
66Bz-18
66EH-32
66OPC-15
66T-15
66T-221LL
66T/RO-48
67T-351
67T/Test/PP-11
78TCMA-239
79TCMA-42
85T-137FS

Lawless, Thomas
80Water-18
81Water-14
82Indianap-15
83D-400
83Indianap-12
83T-423
86Schnucks-15
86T-228
87Smok/Cards-19
87T-647
88Woolwth-25WS4
88Smok/Card-15
88T-183
88T/St-22
89B-255
89T-312
89Tor/Fire-18
90D-681
90T-49

Lawless
N172

Lawrence, Andy
85Lynch-22
86Jacks/TCMA-16
87Jaxvl-7
88Jaxvl/Best-19
88Jaxvl/Pro-972

Lawrence, Bill
43Centen-17

Lawrence, Brooks
55B-75
55Hunter
55RM-NL4
56Kahn
56T-305
57Kahn
57T-66
58Kahn
58T-374
59T-67
60Kahn
60L-36
60T-434
79TCMA-217

Lawrence, Scott
86Erie-17
87Savan-25
88StPet/Star-12
89Sprin/Best-13

Lawrenson, Scott
87Lynch-27

Lawson, Alfred
38Wheat

Lawson, Jim
88SoOreg/Pro-1712
89Madis/Star-12

Lawson, Rex
V355-104

Lawson, Steve
73OPC-612R
73T-612R

Lawton, Marcus
86Lynch-14
87TexLgAS-24
88Tidew/Pro-1591
89Tidew/CMC-23
89Tidew/Pro-1967
90T-302

Laxton, William
76SSPC-615
77T-394

Laya, Jesus
88Poca/Pro-2096
89Everett/Star-19

Layana, Tim
87Albany-11
88Albany/Pro-1333
89Albany/Best-5
89Albany/Pro-329
89Albany/Star-9

Layne, Hillis
47Centen-15
47Signal

Layton, Tom
87IowaC-8

Lazar, John Dan
69T-439R
70T-669R
72MB-195

Lazor, Joe
87Cedar-5
88Chatt/Best-4
88SLAS-35
89Chatt/Best-5
89Chatt/GS-15

Lazor, John Paul
49B/PCL-30

Lazorko, Jack
80Tulsa-6
81Tulsa-19
83ElPas-23
84Cram/PCL-48
85Cram/PCL-176
85T-317
86D-628
86Nashv-15
87Edmon-2
87F/U-U61
87T/Tr-62T
88D-160
88Edmon/CMC-3
88Edmon/Pro-556
88F-494
88Score-437
88T-601
89Edmon/CMC-1
89F-482
89T-362

Lazzeri, Anthony
26Exh-100
27Exh-50
28Yueng-29
29Exh/4-25
31Exh/4-25
32Orbit/num-107
33CJ/Pin-15
33Exh/4-13
33G-31
34DS-74
35BU-45
35Exh/4-13
35G-2D
35G-4D
35G-7D
36Exh/4-13
37Exh/4-13
37OPC-117
40PB-238
60Exh/HOF-14
60F-31
61F-54
69Bz-3
80Laugh/FFeat-26
88Conlon/3-17
88Conlon/AmAS-19
PR1-20
R311/Leath
R315-A21
R315-B21
R328-18
V300
V353-31
W502-29
W513-79
W517-27

Lea, Charles
79Memph
80Memph-2
81F-165
81OPC-293
81T-293
82D-320
82F-193
82Hygrade
82OPC-38
82T-38
83D-414
83F-286
83OPC-253
83Stuart-23
83T-629
84D-376
84F-278
84Nes/792-421
84Nes/792-516TL
84OPC-142
84OPC-332TL
84Stuart-8
84T-421
84T/St-98
85D-177
85D-21
85D/DKsuper-21
85F-401
85Leaf-21DK
85OPC-345
85OPC/Post-10
85T-345
85T/Gloss22-10
85T/Gloss40-30
85T/St-182
85T/St-84
86D-376
86F-253
86Leaf-172
86OPC-376
86T-526
87WPalm-17
88F/U-U44
89D-473
89F-119
89Score-501
89UD-81

Leach, Chris
89WinHav/Star-13

Leach, Don
80Elmir-19

Leach, Fred
28Exh-21
33G-179
R315-A22
R315-B22
R316

Leach, Martin
82Tulsa-3
85Water-13

Leach, Rick
80Evans-24
82D-583
82F-272
82T-266
83D-81
83F-334
83T-147
84F-84
84F/X-71
84Nes/792-427
84Syrac-6
84T-427
84T/X-71
84Tor/Fire-22
85F-112
85IntLgAS-29
85OPC-52
85Syrac-11
85T-593
86T/Tr-63T
86Tor/Fire-23
87D-567
87F-234
87F/U-U63
87OPC-5
87T-716
87Tor/Fire-18
87Tor/Fire-18
88D-518
88F-115
88Leaf-247
88OPC-323
88Score-258
88T-323
88Tor/Fire-9
89B-234
89D-638
89F-237
89Moth/R-16
89OPC-284
89Score-540
89Smok/R-19
89T-682
89T/Tr-68T
89UD-554
90D-613
90F-305
90Score-426
90T-27
90UD-640

Leach, Terry
76Baton
79Savan-19
81Tidew-29
82T-623R
82Tidew-14
83D-634
83T-187
83Tidew-5
84Richm-19
84Tidew-26
85Tidew-2
86F-87
86T-774
86Tidew-15
87F/U-U62
87T/Tr-63T
88D-603
88D/Mets/Bk-603
88F-139
88Kahn/Mets-26
88OPC-391
88Score-203
88Sf-139
88T-457
89D-502
89F-40
89Score-431
89Score/Tr-24
89T-207
89T/Big-96
89T/Tr-69T
89UD-288
90D-534
90F-111
90Score-502
90T-508
90UD-642

Leach, Thomas
10Domino-67
11Helmar-161
12Sweet/Pin-138
12Sweet/Pin-138
14CJ-41
15CJ-41
D322
E103
E107
E254
E286
E90
E90/2
E91
E93
E94
E95
M116
S74-111
T201
T202
T205
T206
T207
T213/blue
T215
T222
T3-3
W555
WG3-25

Leader, Ramon
77Cocoa
78DaytB

Leaks, Charles
54JC
55JC

Leal, Carlos
80Utica-27

Leal, Luis
81OPC-238R
81T-577R
82D-255
82F-617
82OPC-368
82OPC/Post-9
82T-412
83D-129
83F-432
83OPC-109
83T-109
84D-485
84F-160
84Nes/792-783
84OPC-207
84T-783
84T/St-371
84Tor/Fire-23
85D-317
85F-113
85Leaf-29
85OPC-31
85T-622
85T/St-361
85Tor/Fire-19
86D-315
86OPC-365
86Syrac-16
86T-459
88Syrac/Pro-806

Leary, Rob
87WPalm-1
88Rockford-22
89Rockford-22
89WPalm/Star-15

Leary, Timothy
82T-623R
83Tidew-9
84Jacks/Smok-7
85Cram/PCL-203
86D-577
86Pol/Brew-39
86T/Tr-64T
87D-232
87F-348
87Moth/Dodg-21
87Pol/Dodg-11
87T-32
87T/Tr-64T
88F-521
88Moth/Dodg-21
88Pol/Dodg-54
88Score-224
88T-367
89B-339
89D-552
89D/Best-309
89F-65
89F/Excit-30
89Moth/Dodg-21
89OPC-249
89Panini/St-99
89Pol/Dodg-28
89Score-429
89Score/HotSt-9
89Score/Tr-52
89Sf-81
89T-249
89T/Big-17
89T/St-62
89UD-94
90D-670
90F-424
90Score-504
90T-516
90UD-662
Leatherwood, Del
78DaytB
81Tucso-2
LeBlanc, Michael
88CapeCod/Sum-61
LeBlanc, Richie Jr.
88BBCity/Star-16
88FSLAS/Star-42
Lebo, Mike
78Duned
LeBoeuf, Alan
85Cram/PCL-32
86Portl-13
87Maine-22
87Maine/TCMA-13
88Readg/Pro-864
Lebron, David
78Newar
LeBron, Jose
89Watlo/Pro-1775
89Watlo/Star-17
Leclair, Keith
88Idaho/Pro-1850
LeClaire, George
(Frenchy)
C46-3
Ledbetter, Gary
77Cedar
Ledbetter, Jeff
86ArkTr-11
Ledduke, Dan
79WHave-9
Ledezma, Carlos
81Buffa-8
82Portl-26
84Cram/PCL-143
86Hawai-15TR
87Vanco-4
88AAA/Pro-48
88BuffB/Pro-1481
89BuffB/CMC-3
89BuffB/Pro-1678
Leduc, Jean
78Charl
Lee, Ben
87AppFx-13
Lee, Bob
85Visal-15
86Kenosha-12
87Visal-6
88Keno/Pro-1403
89Keno/Pro-1058
Lee, Chris
88Ashvl/Pro-1059
Lee, Derek
88Utica/Puc-7
89SoBend/GS-27
Lee, Don
57T-379
59T-132
60T-503
61Clover-12
61Peters-9
61T-153
62T-166
63F-18
63T-372
64T-493
65T-595
Lee, Dudley
21Exh-95
28Exh/PCL-19
Lee, Eddie
79Elmir-11
Lee, Greg
88Poca/Pro-2086
89Salin/Cal-141
89Salin/Pro-1806
Lee, Hal
R310
Lee, Harvey
86FtLaud-14
87SanJose-5
Lee, John
76Dubuq
Lee, Leron
70OPC-96R
70T-96R
71MLB/St-276
71OPC-521
71T-521
72OPC-238
72T-238
73OPC-83
73T-83
74OPC-651
74T-651
75OPC-506
75T-506
75T/M-506
76OPC-487
76T-487
Lee, Manny
85F/Up-U71
85Tor/Fire-20
86Knoxv-14
86OPC-23
86Syrac-17
86T-23
87D-518
87OPC-289
87Syrac-14
87Syrac/TCMA-16
87T-574
88D-650
88F-116
88OPC-303
88Score-561
88T-722
88Tor/Fire-4
89D-504
89F-238
89OPC-371
89Panini/St-468
89Score-326
89T-371
89T/Big-70
89Tor/Fire-4
89UD-271
90D-620
90F-86
90Score-482
90T-113
90UD-285
Lee, Mark
79T-138
80Hawai-17
80T-557
81Portl-15
82Evans-4
86Lakel-8
87GlenF-15
87Lakel-17
88Lakel/Star-17
89Memph/Best-4
89Memph/Pro-1190
89Memph/Star-14
Lee, Michael
60T-521
Lee, Robert D.
64T-502R
65OPC-46
65T-46
66T-481
67T-313
68Kahn
68T-543
Lee, Ronnie
53Exh/Can-51
V362-25
Lee, Terry
75Cedar
80Holyo-21
81Vanco-14
83Cedar-19
83Cedar/LF-13
89Chatt/Best-10
89Chatt/GS-16
Lee, Thornton
35BU-109
47TipTop
89Pac/Leg-158
R313
Lee, Wiley
88MidwLAS/GS-24
88QuadC/GS-4
89PalmSp/Cal-39
89PalmSp/Pro-485
Lee, William C.
35BU-140
37Exh/4-3
39Exh
39Wheat-4
41DP-103
47TipTop
PM10/Sm-94
V355-109
Lee, William F.
70OPC-279
70T-279
71MLB/St-322
71OPC-58
71T-58
72T-636
73OPC-224
73T-224
74OPC-118
74T-118
74T/St-135
75Ho-66
75OPC-128
75T-128
75T/M-128
76K-29
76OPC-396
76SSPC-421
76T-396
77T-503
78PapaG/Disc-9
78T-295
79OPC-237
79T-455
80OPC-53
80T-97
81D-211
81F-157
81OPC-371
81T-633
82D-194
82F-194
82OPC-323
82T-323
WG8-40
Lee, Wyatt
(Watty)
C46-71
E107
E270/2
T205
Leech, Skip
77Charl
Leek, Eugene
61T-527
62Salada-82A
62Salada-82B
62Shirriff-82
Leeper, Dave
83Omaha-22
84Omaha-22
85Omaha-24
86D-461
86Hawai-16
87Vanco-14
Leever, Sam
10Domino-68
12Sweet/Pin-139
D322
E104
E107
E90/1
E90/2
E91
M116
T205
LeFebvre, Jim
65T-561R
66T-57
67T-260
68Bz-2
68T-457
69T-140
69Trans-47
70T-553
71T-459
72T-369
78TCMA-263
80Pol/Giants-5
85Cram/PCL-187
86Phoen-15MG
Lefebvre, Jim
66OPC-57
69MB-156
69MLB/St-149
69OPC-140
69T/St-46
70MLB/St-52
71MLB/St-106
71OPC-459
72MB-196
72OPC-369
72T/Cloth-20
87Smok/Dodg-18
89Moth/Sea-1
89Smok/Dodg-71
89T/Tr-70TMG
90T-459MG
Lefebvre, Joe
77FtLaud
79WHave-25
80Colum-26
81D-571
81F-103
81OPC-88
81T-88R
81T/Tr-790
82D-373
82F-575
82T-434
83D-523
83F-363
83T-644
83T/X-61
84D-82
84F-37
84Nes/792-148
84T-148
85D-285
85F-257
85T-531
87Readg-3
88Maine/CMC-25
88Maine/Pro-301
89ScrWB/CMC-18
89ScrWB/Pro-722
Lefebvre, Tip
84Cram/PCL-14
Lefferts, Craig
82IowaC-20
83Thorn-32
84D-388
84F-496
84F/X-72
84Moth/Padres-19
84Nes/792-99
84T-99
84T/X-72
85D-261
85F-38
85Moth/Padres-15
85OPC-76
85T-608
86D-307
86F-328
86OPC-244
86T-244
87Bohem-37
87D-387
87F-422
87F/RecSet-19
87F/U-U64
87OPC-287
87T-501
88D-515
88D/Best-330
88F-87
88Moth/Giants-24
88Score-553
88T-734
89B-464
89D-59
89F-332
89Moth/Giants-24
89Score-178
89T-372
89UD-541
90Class-109
90D-376
90F-60
90Score-209
90Sf-130
90T-158
90UD-399
LeFlore, Ron
75OPC-628
75T-628
75T/M-628
76Ho-69
76K-17

76OPC-61
76SSPC-363
76T-61
77Ho-50
77K-25
77OPC-167
77Pep-28
77T-240
78BK/T-19
78Ho-95
78OPC-88
78T-480
78Wiffle/Discs-37
79Ho-34
79OPC-348
79T-4LL
79T-660
79T/Comics-8
80BK/PHR-27
80OPC-45
80T-80
81Coke
81D-576
81F-154
81F/St-2
81MSA/Disc-20
81OPC-104
81Sqt-26
81T-204M
81T-4LL
81T-710
81T/HT
81T/St-23
81T/Tr-791
82D-165
82F-350
82F/St-182
82OPC-140
82T-140
82T/St-172
83D-543
83F-246
83OPC-297
83T-560

Leger, Frank
83LynnP-24

Legg, Greg
83Readg-14
85Cram/PCL-48
87Maine-4
87Maine/TCMA-14
88Readg/Pro-882
89ScrWB/CMC-19
89ScrWB/Pro-708

Leggatt, Rich
82Buffa-1
83Durhm-20
84Durhm-18
86Toled-13

Legumina, Gary
83SanJose-15
85VeroB-9

Lehman, Bill
76AppFx

Lehman, Ken
55B-310
57T-366
58Hires-52
58T-141
59T-31
79TCMA-258

Lehman, Mike
89Freder/Star-12

Lehner, Paul
47TipTop
49B-131
50B-158
51B-8

Lehnerz, Daniel
88Idaho/Pro-1857

Lehnerz, Mike
89Kingspt/Star-15

Leiber, Hank
38Exh/4-5

Leibold, Harry
(Nemo)
88Pac/8Men-101
D327
D328-97
D329-101
D350/2-99
E120
E121/80
E135-97
E220
M101/4-101
M101/5-99
T222
V100
W575

Leibrandt, Charles
79Indianap-7
81D-421
81F-208
81Indianap-5
81OPC-126
81T-126
82Coke/Reds
82F-74
82T-169
83D-421
83F-596
83Indianap-4
83T-607
84Omaha-1
85D-399
85D/HL-4
85D/HL-46
85F-206
85Indianap-33
85T-459
86D-297
86F-13
86F/LL-21
86F/Slug-20
86F/St-69
86Kitty/Disc-10
86Leaf-171
86NatPhoto-37
86OPC-77
86S-159
86S-186M
86T-77
86T/Mini-19
86T/St-262
86T/Super-37
87D-220
87F-373
87OPC-223
87T-223
87T/St-258
88D-157
88D/Best-151
88F-263
88F/St-31
88Leaf-76
88OPC-218
88Panini/St-100
88Score-61
88Sf-21
88Smok/Royals-13
88T-569
88T/St-260
89B-116
89Class-82
89D-89
89D/Best-231
89F-286
89OPC-301
89Panini/St-351
89Score-133
89T-301
89Tastee/Discs-10
89UD-637
90D-208
90F-112
90Score-82
90T-776
90UD-658

Leifield, Albert
(Lefty)
10Domino-69
11Helmar-162
12Sweet/Pin-140
D322
M116
S74-112
T201
T202
T205
T206
T207
T215/blue
T215/brown

Leighton, John
N172

Lein, Chris
82Nashv-16
83AlexD-14
85PrWill-13
87Salem-28
89Harris/Pro-301

Leinan, Pat
88CapeCod/Sum-102
89Erie/Star-11

Leiper, Dave
82Idaho-11
83Madis/LF-27
86Tacom-12
87D-472
87F-398
87T-441
88D-557
88F/U-U123
88Score-348
88Smok/Padres-15
89D-465
89F-310
89Score-515
89T-82
89UD-363
90Score-212
90T-773

Leiper, Tim
86FSLAS-29
86Lakel-9
87GlenF-9
88GlenF/Pro-938
88Toled/CMC-21
88Toled/Pro-603
89London/Pro-1373

Leister, John
86Pawtu-12
87Pawtu-5
87Pawtu/TCMA-26
88Pawtu/CMC-4
88Pawtu/Pro-470
89Pawtu/CMC-5
89Pawtu/Dunkin-22
89Pawtu/Pro-681

Leiter, Al
87Colum-30
87Colum/Pol-15
88Class/Blue-238
88D-43
88D/Best-132
88D/Rook-27
88D/Y/Bk-43
88F/U-U49
88Leaf-43RR
88Score/Tr-97T
88T-18
89B-170
89Class-112
89D-315
89F-257
89F/Up-70
89Panini/St-396
89Score-580
89Score/HotRk-80
89Score/YS/I-17
89T-659
89T/Big-125
89T/JumboR-15
89T/Tr-71T
89ToysRUs-19
89UD-588
89UD/Ext-705
90D-543
90T-138

Leiter, Kurt
83SanJose-24
84CharO-23
86Miami-15

Leiter, Mark
89Colum/CMC-29
89FtLaud/Star-13

Leius, Scott
87Kenosha-21
88Visal/Cal-154
88Visal/Pro-102
89Orlan/Best-16
89Orlan/Pro-1332
89SLAS-6
90F-647M

Leiva, Jose
86Readg-14
87Readg-22
88Readg/Pro-884
89Canton/Best-22
89Canton/Pro-1312
89Canton/Star-24

Leix, Tom
81Wisco-2

Leja, Frank
54NYJour
54T-175
55T-99
60L-121

LeJohn, Don
(Ducky)
66OPC-41
66T-41
75Water
77Clint
78Clint
86Bakers-19MG

Lekang, Anton
33SK-10

Leland, Stan
78DaytB
81Tucso-15

Lelivelt, William
E254
E270/1
T222

Lemanczyk, Dave
75OPC-571
75T-571
75T/M-571
76OPC-409
76SSPC-355
76T-409
77OPC-229
77T-611
78OPC-85
78T-33
79OPC-102
79T-207
80OPC-68
80T-124
81D-292
81T-391

LeMaster, Denny
63T-74
64T-152
65Kahn
65T-441
66Kahn
66T-252
67T-288
68Coke
68T-491
69MB-157
69OPC-96
69T-96
69T/St-34
70MLB/St-42
70OPC-178
70T-178
71MLB/St-84
71OPC-636
71T-636
72MB-197
72OPC-371
72T-371
78TCMA-17

LeMaster, Johnnie
75Phoen-12
76OPC-596R
76Phoen
76T-596R
77T-151
78T-538
79Pol/Giants-10
79T-284
80OPC-224
80Pol/Giants-10
80T-434
81D-432
81F-450
81OPC-84
81T-84
82D-524
82F-393
82T-304
82T/St-108
83D-125
83F-266
83Moth/Giants-4
83OPC-154
83T-154
83T/St-304
84D-649
84F-378
84Nes/792-663
84OPC-107
84T-663
84T/St-168
85D-114
85F-614
85Moth/Giants-14
85OPC-302
85T-772
85T/St-164
85T/Tr-74T
86OPC-289
86T-289

LeMasters, Jim
87Sumter-20
88MidwLAS/GS-20
89Greenv/Pro-1176
89Greenv/Star-13
89Greenvl/Best-10
89Star/Wax-36

Lemay, Richard
62T-71
63T-459
66Pep/Tul

Lembo, Steve
53Exh/Can-36
V362-7

Lemke, Mark
86Sumter-16
87Durhm-26
88BBAmer-16
88Greenv/Best-10
88SLAS-15
89AAA/Pro-55
89Class-52

89D-523
89Richm/CMC-19
89Richm/Ko-16
89Richm/Pro-830
89T-327
89UD-19
90D-624
90F-587
90Score-593
90T-451
90UD-665

Lemle, Rob
88Clmbia/GS-21
89Clmbia/Best-4
89Clmbia/GS-14

Lemon, Chet
75Tucso-3
76OPC-590R
76T-590R
77OPC-195
77T-58
78BK/Y-1
78Ho-124
78OPC-224
78T-127
79Ho-40
79OPC-169
79T-333
79T/Comics-5
80K-45
80OPC-309
80T-589
80T/S-57
81Coke
81D-281
81F-354
81K-19
81OPC-242
81Sqt-33
81T-242
81T/HT
81T/SO-34
81T/St-57
82D-291
82F-351
82F/St-191
82K-54
82OPC-13
82T-216TL
82T-493
82T/St-168
82T/Tr-62T
83D-511
83F-335
83OPC-53
83T-727
84D-171
84F-85
84FunFood/Pin-97
84Nes/792-611
84OPC-86
84T-611
84T/St-271
85Cain's-12
85D-90
85F-15
85Leaf-77
85OPC-20
85Seven-11D
85Seven-9G
85T-20
85T/Gloss22-18
85T/St-190
85T/St-21WS
85T/St-260
85Wendy-14
86Cain's-11
86D-90
86F-230
86Leaf-85
86OPC-160
86T-160
86T/St-274
87Cain's-10
87Coke/Tigers-10
87D-353
87D/OD-213
87F-156
87Leaf-227
87OPC-206
87Seven-DT6
87T-739
87T/St-268
88D-215
88D/Best-147
88F-61
88Leaf-166
88OPC-366
88Panini/St-96
88Pep/T-34
88Pol/T-7
88Score-119
88T-366
88T/Big-147
89D-209
89D/Best-69
89F-137
89Mara/Tigers-34
89OPC-328
89Panini/St-344
89Pol/Tigers-34
89Score-44
89Sf-171
89T-514
89T/Big-202
89T/St-283
89UD-128
90D-60
90F-608
90Score-106
90T-271
90UD-348

Lemon, Don
89Idaho/Pro-2033

Lemon, Jim
54T-103
55B-262
57T-57
58T-15
59HRDerby-11
59T-215
59T-74M
60T-440
61Bz-12
61Clover-13
61P-93
61Peters-17
61T-44LL
61T-450
61T/St-182
62J-89
62P-89
62P/Can-89
62Salada-9A
62Salada-9B
62Shirriff-9
62T-510
63T-369
68T-341
69T-294
79TCMA-180
PM10/Sm-97

Lemon, Leo
81Redwd-19

Lemon, Robert
49B-238
50B-40
50NumNum
51B-53
51BR-A2
51FB
51T/CAS
52B-23
52BR
52Dix
52NumNum-4
52StarCal/L-74C
52T-268
52Wheat
53B/BW-27
53Dix
53Exh/Can-31
53NB
53RM-AL17
54B-196
54DanDee
54RH
54RM-AL21
55B-191
55Gol/Ind-15
55RM-AL8
55Salem
56T-255
57T-120
58T-2
60T-460C
71OPC-91MG
71T-91
72OPC-449MG
72T-449
77T-418MG
78T-574
79T-626MG
79TCMA-19
80Cram/Leg-120
80SSPC/HOF
82D-635
83D/HOF-30
85West/2-45
86S/Dec-39M
88Pac/Leg-32
89HOF/St-68
Exh47
PM10/Sm-95
PM10/Sm-96
R302-119
R423-59

Lemonds, Dave
71OPC-458R
71T-458R
72OPC-413R
72T-413R
73OPC-534
73T-534

Lemongello, Mark
77T-478R
78BK/A-9
78T-358
79T-187
80Wichi-22

Lemons, Tim
86BurlEx-14
87Sprin/Best-7

Lemperle, John
86Alban/TCM-19bb

Lemuth, Steve
89Medford/Best-19

Lenderman, Dave
86Pittsf-13

Lenhardt, Don
51T/BB-33
52T-4
53B/Col-20
54B-53
54Esskay
54T-157
73OPC-131CO
73T-131C

Lennon, Patrick
86Cram/PCL-128
87Wausa-7
88Vermont/Pro-947
89Wmspt/Pro-632
89Wmspt/Star-12

Lennon, Robert
55T-119
56T-104
57T-371

Lennox, James E.
11Helmar-97
M116
T202
T205
T206
T207
T213/blue
T213/brown
T3-104

Lenti, Mike
81Clint-23

Lentine, James
81Charl-17
81D-250
81F-476

Lentz, Harry
(Sentz, sic)
T206
T213/brown

Leon, Danilo
87Jamestn-23
88James/Pro-1913
88WPalm/Star-15
89Jaxvl/Best-21
89Jaxvl/Pro-169

Leon, Eduardo
70OPC-292
70T-292
71MLB/St-378
71OPC-252
71T-252
72T-721
73OPC-287
73T-287
74OPC-501
74T-501
75OPC-528
75T-528
75T/M-528

Leon, Jose
89Elizab/Star-14

Leon, Maximino
75OPC-442
75T-442
75T/M-442
76OPC-576
76SSPC-3
76T-576
77T-213

Leon, Mike
87AppFx-22
88AppFx/Pro-163
89Memph/Best-27
89Memph/Pro-1191

Leon, Ron
85Sprin-15
87Erie-5

Leonard, Andy
86BurlEx-15

Leonard, Bernardo
78Holyo

Leonard, Buck
74Laugh/Black-11
88Conlon/NegAS-7

Leonard, Dennis
75OPC-615R
75T-615R
75T/M-615R
76A&P/KC
76OPC-334
76SSPC-164
76T-334
77Ho-72
77OPC-91
77T-75
78Ho-88
78OPC-41
78OPC-5LL
78T-205LL
78T-665
79Ho-109
79OPC-109
79T-218
80OPC-293
80T-565
81Coke
81D-102
81F-42
81OPC-185
81Pol/Royals-5
81T-185
81T/St-87
82D-264
82F-413
82F/St-208
82OPC-369
82Sqt-10
82T-495
82T/St-191
83D-412
83F-116
83OPC-87
83Pol/Royals-3
83T-785
84F-349
84Nes/792-375
84OPC-375
84T-375
86F/Up-U67
86NatPhoto-22
86T/Tr-65T
87F-374
87OPC-38
87RedFoley/St-33
87T-38

Leonard, Emil
(Dutch)
39PB-21
40PB-23
41PB-24
48B-24
48L-113
49B-115
49Eureka-61
50B-170
51B-102
52B-159
52StarCal/L-80B
52T-110
52TipTop
53B/BW-50
53T-155
55B-247
61F-121

Leonard, Hubert
(Dutch)
72F/FFeat-17
72Laugh/GF-34
79T-418M
85Woolwth-22
BF2-5
D327
D328-98
D329-102
D350/2-100
E135-98
E220
M101/4-102
M101/5-100

Leonard, Jeffrey
80T-106
81D-264
81F-67
81T-469
82D-438
82T-47
83D-474
83Moth/Giants-8
83T-309
84D-567
84F-379

84Nes/792-576TL
84Nes/792-748
84T-748
84T/St-166
85D-358
85F-615
85F/LimEd-18
85GenMills-4
85Leaf-92
85Moth/Giants-4
85OPC-132
85Seven-14W
85T-619
85T-718AS
85T/St-161
86D-79
86F-548
86Leaf-74
86Moth/Giants-4
86OPC-381
86T-490
86T/St-84
87Class-64
87D-391
87D/OD-103
87F-278
87F/GameWin-25
87F/Slug-23
87Moth/SFG-8
87OPC-280
87RedFoley/St-102
87T-280
87T/St-90
88Woolwth-17
88Class/Red-175
88D-327
88D/AS-54
88F-88
88F/Mini-117
88F/RecSet-23
88F/SS-21
88F/St-128
88F/U-U39
88Leaf-118
88Moth/Giants-8
88OPC-152
88Panini/St-427
88Panini/St-446
88RedFoley/St-48
88Score-580
88Sf-82
88T-570
88T/Coins-46
88T/RiteAid-32
88T/St-16
88T/St-86
88T/St/Backs-17
88T/Tr-61T
88T/UK-43
89Ames-19
89B-218
89D-457
89D/Best-107
89D/Tr-1
89F-190
89F/Up-60
89Moth/Sea-8
89OPC-160
89Score-557
89Score/Tr-7
89T-160
89T/St-199
89T/Tr-72T
89UD-263
89UD/Ext-789
90Class-93
90D-93
90F-519
90Score-98
90Score/100St-91
90Sf-20
90T-455
90UD-331

Leonard, Kathy
81Redwd-24

Leonard, Mark
86Cram/PCL-182
87Clint-14
88CalLgAS-3
88SanJose/Cal-122
88SanJose/Pro-134
89Phoen/CMC-5
89Phoen/Pro-1498

Leonard, Mathew
88Geneva/Pro-1645
88Wythe/Pro-1996
89CharWh/Best-9
89CharWh/Pro-1758

Leonard, Tom
81Redwd-23

Leonard, Wilfred
48Sommer-20

Leonardo, Juan
75AppFx

Leonette, Mark
83Idaho-8
85Madis-22
85Madis/Pol-19
87Pittsf-16
88Pittsf/Pro-1371

Leonhard, Dave
68OPC-56R
68T-56R
69MB-158
69T-228
70T-674
71MLB/St-302
71OPC-716
71T-716
72MB-198
72T-527

Leopold, Jim
83Beaum-6
84Beaum-14
85Cram/PCL-119
86Nashua-15
88Louvl-27
88Louvl/CMC-10
88Louvl/Pro-437

Lepcio, Ted
52T-335
53T-18
54B-162
54T-66
55T-128
55T/DH-126
57T-288
58T-29
59T-348
60T-97
61T-234

Lepley, John
88Hamil/Pro-1737
89ArkTr/GS-10

Leppert, Don
62T-36
63T-243
64T-463
64Wheat/St-26
73OPC-517CO
73T-517C
74OPC-489CO
74T-489C
77T-113C
78TCMA-101
78TCMA-110
86Kenosha-13MG
87Kenosha-27
88Keno/Pro-1399
89Keno/Pro-1070

Lepson, Mark
79BurlB-11
80BurlB-4
81BurlB-9

Lerch, Randy
76OkCty
76OPC-595R
76T-595R
77T-489R
78T-271
79BK/P-8
79T-52
80BK/P-18
80OPC-181
80T-344
81D-574
81F-25
81T-584
81T/Tr-792
82D-595
82F-147
82Pol/Brew
82Pol/Brew-35
82T-466
83F-287
83OPC-22
83Stuart-28
83T-686
84F-380
85D-309
85F-616
85T-103
86Portl-14

Lersch, Barry
69OPC-206R
69T-206R
71MLB/St-183
71OPC-739
71T-739
72OPC-453
72T-453
73OPC-559
73T-559
74OPC-313
74T-313
74T/Tr-313T
75OkCty

Leshnock, Don
75Shreve/TCMA-9

Lesley, Brad
81Cedar-3
82Indianap-5
83D-547
83Indianap-26
85Cram/PCL-202
85T-597

Leslie, Roy Reid
E120

Leslie, Sam
34DS-68
34Exh/4-2
34G-49
35BU-46
35G-1G
35G-3E
35G-4E
35G-5E
37Exh/4-5
R314
V355-4

Lesslie, Bob
75Water

Lester, Jimmy
88Wichi-22
89CharRa/Pro-989

Letendre, Mark
79Colum-11
80Colum-18
81Colum-25

Lett, Jim
80Cedar-22
82Water-23
83Water-19
84Cedar-12
86TexGold-CO
88Kahn/Reds-CO

Letterio, Shane
88Greens/Pro-1556
89Mia/Star/22-11
89Mia/Star/25-11

LeVasseur, Tom
86Cram/PCL-169
88River/Cal-223
88River/Pro-1417
89AubAs/Pro-26
89Wich/Roc-21SS
89Wich/Roc/HL-13

Leverette, Gorham
(Dixie)
E120
W573

Levey, James
32Orbit/num-52
32Orbit/un-40
R305

Levi, Stan
80BurlB-27
83ElPas-11

Levinson, Davis
81Redwd-25

Levinson, Steve
81Redwd-30

Levis, Jesse
88CapeCod-13
88CapeCod/Sum-116

Levritz, Jim
87FtLaud-24

Lewallyn, Dennis
78Cr/PCL-110
79Albuq-7
80Albuq-8
82T-356
82Wheat/Ind
83VeroB-29
85VeroB-25

Lewis, Alan
88Bakers/Cal-237
89VeroB/Star-15

Lewis, Craig
88Watertn/Puc-8

Lewis, Curt
78OrlTw

Lewis, Dan
87AubAs-8
88Ashvl/Pro-1061
89Osceola/Star-11

Lewis, Darren
89Modesto/Cal-278
89Modesto/Ch-30

Lewis, George
(Duffy)
55JC
87Conlon/2-36
88Conlon/4-17
BF2-6
D327
D328-99
D329-103
D350/2-101
E121/80
E122
E135-99
E254
E270/2
M101/4-103
M101/5-101
T207
W575

Lewis, Harry
T3/Box-63

Lewis, Herman
80Utica-26

Lewis, Irving
T207

Lewis, James
88River/Cal-212

Lewis, Jay
83Peoria/LF-18

Lewis, Jerry
78Newar

Lewis, Jim M.
79Spoka-13
80Colum-16
81Colum-6
82Colum-22
82Colum/Pol-21
83Toled-6
84Cram/PCL-180
85Cram/PCL-77
86CharRa-13

Lewis, Jim
88River/Pro-1423
89AubAs/Pro-14
89Wich/Roc-20RHP

Lewis, Joe
89Gasto/Pro-1007
89Gasto/Star-10

Lewis, John K.
(Buddy)
37OPC-101
37Wheat-7
38ONG/Pin-17
39PB-47
40PB-20
41PB-47
89Pac/Leg-119
Exh47
V300

Lewis, John
86Peoria-14
87WinSal-16
88WinSal/Star-8

Lewis, Johnny
62Kahn/Atl
62Pep/Tul
64T-479R
65OPC-277
65T-277
66T-282
66T/RO-24
67OPC-91
67T-91
74OPC-236CO
74T-236C

Lewis, Ken
89Brist/Star-14

Lewis, Mark
88BurlR/Pro-1800
89B-87
89Kinston/Star-12
89T-222FDP

Lewis, Mica
88AubAs/Pro-1974
89Ashvl/Pro-966
89AubAs/Pro-2186

Lewis, Richie
88Jaxvl/Best-10
88Jaxvl/Pro-992

Lewis, Scott
89MidldA/GS-21

Lewis, Steve
83AlexD-25
84PrWill-19
85PrWill-9

Lewis, T.R.
89Bluef/Star-13

Lewis, Timothy
77WHave
79WHave-18

Lewis, Tony
87Spoka-3
88Charl/Pro-1214
89River/Best-9
89River/Cal-24
89River/Pro-1395

Lewis, Willie
T3/Box-74

Lexa, Michael
87Kenosha-10
88Keno/Pro-1395

Ley, Terry
72OPC-506R
72T-506R

Leyland, Jim
75Clint
80Evans-17
81Evans-1
86T/Tr-66T
87T-93MG
88T-624
89T-284MG
90T-699MG

Leyritz, Jim
88Albany/Pro-1344
89Albany/Best-2
89Albany/Pro-325
89Albany/Star-10

Leyva, Nick
77ArkTr
83ArkTr-23
89T-74MG
90T-489MG

Lezcano, Carlos
81D-521
81F-307
81T-381R
82F-51
83IowaC-23
84Cram/PCL-79

Lezcano, Sixto
74Sacra
76A&P/Milw
76OPC-353
76SSPC-241
76T-353
77Ho-12
77K-27
77OPC-71
77T-185
78Ho-35
78OPC-102
78T-595
78Wiffle/Discs-38
79Ho-136
79OPC-364
79T-685
80OPC-114
80T-215
80T/S-31
81Coke
81D-207
81F-513
81OPC-25
81T-25
81T/SO-45
81T/St-218
81T/Tr-793
82D-64
82F-119
82OPC-271
82T-727
82T/St-95
82T/Tr-63T
83D-499
83F-364
83OPC-244
83T-455
83T/St-298
84F-38
84Nes/792-185
84OPC-185
84T-185
85D-529
85F-258
85F/Up-U72
85OPC-89
85T-556
85T/Tr-75T
86T-278

Libke, Al
44Centen-14
47Signal

Liburdi, John
84Albany-10
85Albany-34
86Albany/TCMA-13

Lich, Rod
84Cedar-23
85Cedar-29
86Tampa-10TR
87Vermont-27

Lickert, John
83Pawtu-13
85Richm-11

Liddell, Dave
86Peoria-15
87Columbia-13
88Reno/Cal-287
89Jacks/GS-25
89Tidew/CMC-18

Liddle, Don
53JC-9
54NYJour
54T-225
55B-146
55Gol/Giants-16
56T-325

Liddle, Steve
82Redwd-7
83Nashua-10
84Cram/PCL-105
85Cram/PCL-13
86Edmon-17
87Portl-10
88Portl/CMC-12
88Portl/Pro-655
89Keno/Pro-1084
89Keno/Star-25

Liebert, Al
86Lakel-10
87Fayette-15
88CLAS/Star-29
88Kinston/Star-15
89Canton/Best-21
89Canton/Pro-1314
89Canton/Star-12

Liebhardt, Glenn
T206

Liebold, Harry
21Exh-96
21Exh-97

Lien, Al
48Sommer-7
49Sommer-5
52Mother-47

Lienhard, Steve
88Clint/Pro-694
89SanJose/Best-20
89SanJose/Cal-214
89SanJose/Pro-456
89SanJose/Star-17

Lieppman, Keith
76Tucso-6
79Ogden/TCMA-26
82Idaho-30
82WHave-27
84Albany-7
85Cram/PCL-126MG
86Tacom-13MG
87Tacom-14

Lifgren, Kelly
88Spoka/Pro-1925
89River/Best-10
89River/Cal-16
89River/Pro-1392

Lillard, Robert E.
37Wheat
46Sunbeam
47Remar-22
47Signal
47Smith-6
48Signal
48Smith-8

Lilliquist, Derek
88Richm-24
88Richm/CMC-2
88Richm/Pro-21
89B-264
89Class/Up/2-172
89D-653
89D/Best-226
89D/Rook-54
89F/Up-73
89Score-631
89Score/HotRk-23
89T/Tr-73T
89UD/Ext-753
90D-286
90F-588
90Score-243
90Score/100Ris-19
90Sf-24
90T-282
90UD-234

Lillis, Bob
59DF
59T-133
60T-3
61BB-11
61T-38
62Salada-108A
62Salada-108B
62Shirriff-108
62T-74
63J-191
63P-191
63Pep
63T-119
64T-321
74OPC-31CO
74T-31C
78TCMA-42
83T-66
84D-84
84Moth/Ast-15MG
84Nes/792-441MG
84T-441
85Moth/Ast-1MG
85T-186
86T-561
89Smok/Ast-17

Limbach, Chris
86Cram/PCL-147
88Clearw/Star-17
88FSLAS/Star-10

Limmer, Lou
52Park-86
54T-232
55B-80
55T-54
55T/DH-16

Limoncelli, Bill
79Elmir-23
80Elmir-34
87Elmir-2
87Elmir/Red-2
88Elmir-27MG

Linares, Antonio
88Martins/Star-22
89Spart/Pro-1046
89Spart/Star-13
89Star/Wax-55

Linares, Rufino
79Savan
81Pol/Atl-25
82BK/Lids-15
82D-310
82F-439
82Pol/Atl-25
82T-244
83D-275
83F-140
83T-467
84Richm-2
85T-167
86Edmon-18

Lincoln, Lance
86Beloi-13
87Beloi-14

Lind, Carl
29Exh/4-21

Lind, Jack
83Redwd-30
87Nashv-13MG
88Nashvl/CMC-23
88Nashvl/Pro-486

Lind, Jose
85PrWill-17
86Nashua-16
87Vanco-19
88Class/Red-195
88D-38
88D/Best-145
88F-334
88Leaf-38RR
88Panini/St-371
88Score-597
88Score/YS/II-4
88T-767
88T/Big-106
88T/St-127
89B-421
89Bimbo/Discs-7
89Class-20
89D-290
89D/Best-101
89F-214
89OPC-273
89Panini/St-170
89RedFoley/St-75
89Score-87
89Sf-62
89T-273
89T/Big-25
89T/St-126
89UD-334
90D-172
90F-474
90Score-83
90Sf-58
90T-168
90UD-424

Lind, Orlando
85PrWill-1
86Nashua-17
87Harrisbg-14
88Harris/Pro-847
89Harris/Pro-300
89Harris/Star-9

Lind, Randy
87Everett-11

Lindaman, Vivian
T206

Lindblad, Paul
66T-568R
67T-227
68OPC-127
68T-127
69T-449
70OPC-408
70T-408
71MLB/St-519
71OPC-658
71T-658
72OPC-396
72T-396
73OPC-406
73T-406
74OPC-369
74T-369
75OPC-278
75T-278
75T/M-278
76K-52
76OPC-9
76SSPC-479
76T-9
77T-583
78T-314
79T-634
87ElPas-20C
88ElPas/Best-10
89ElPas/GS-2

Lindell, John
44Yank/St-17
47TipTop
48B-11
48L-82
48Swell-17
49B-197
50B-209
52Mother-1
53T-230
54B-159
54T-51
D305
Exh47
R346-5

Lindeman, Ernest
E254
T204

Lindeman, Jim
86Louisvl-16
87Class/Up-111
87D-37RR
87D/OD-59
87D/Rook-41
87F/Mini-64
87F/U-U65
87Leaf-37RR
87S/Rook-43
87Smok/Cards-14
87T/Tr-65T
88D-540
88F-39
88Louvl-28
88OPC-16
88Score-302
88T-562
89Louvl-26
89Smok/Cards-11
89T-791

Linden, Mark
89Geneva/Pro-1878

Lindquist, Dan
83TriCit-11
84Visal-25

Lindsay, Chuck
80LynnS-5

Lindsey, Darrell
88Martins/Star-21
89Spart/Pro-1040
89Spart/Star-14

Lindsey, Don
89Eugene/Best-5

Lindsey, Doug
82Danvi-12
88Spart/Pro-1042
88Spart/Star-11
88Spart/Star-11

Lindsey, Elmer
(Bee)
62Pep/Tul
63Pep/Tul

Lindsey, Jon
82Readg-16

Lindsey, William D.
(Bill)
85Albany-12
86Albany/TCMA-22
87BirmB/Best-26
88F-403
88Vanco/CMC-16
88Vanco/Pro-758

Lindstrom, Fred
26Exh-36
27Exh-20
28Exh-19
29Exh/4-10

31Exh/4-9
33DL-11
33Exh/4-5
33G-133
35BU-122
36Exh/4-2
80Cram/Leg-100
80SSPC/HOF
88Conlon/NatAS-13
89Smok/Dodg-103
R306
R312/M
R314
R315-A23
R315-B23
R316
V354-17
V355-65
W517-24

Lines, Richard
61Union
67T-273
68T-291

Lingerman, Nemo
78Wisco

Link, Dave
83StPet-30

Link, Robert
86Water-14
87Wmspt-7
88GlenF/Pro-937
89Toled/CMC-6
89Toled/Pro-778

Linke, Fred
M116

Linnert, Tom
75SnAnt
76Wmspt

Lino, Rivera Ortiz
87Gasto-9

Linskey, Mike
89Freder/Star-13

Lint, Royce
54Hunter
55B-62

Linton, Dave
85Utica-3
86DayBe-16

Linton, Doug
87Myrtle-5
88Knoxv/Best-15

Lintz, Larry
74OPC-121
74T-121
75OPC-416
75T-416
75T/M-416
76OPC-109
76SSPC-286
76T-109
77T-323

Lintz, Ricky
81Watlo-11
82Watlo/B-6
82Watlo/C-5

Linz, Phil
62T-596R
63T-264
64T-344
65T-369
66T-522
67OPC-14
67T-14
68T-594
78TCMA-97
Exh47
WG10-12
WG9-14

Linzy, Frank
65T-589R
66OPC-78
66T-78
67T-279
68Coke
68OPC-147
68T-147
69MLB/St-202
69T-345
70MLB/St-127
70OPC-77
70T-77
71MLB/St-277
71OPC-551
71T-551
72MB-199
72OPC-243
72T-243
73OPC-286
73T-286

Lipe, Perry H.
T206

Lipon, John
51B-285
52B-163
52T-89
53B/Col-123
53T-40
54T-19
61BeeHive-12
76Shrev
78Colum
79Portl-9
81Buffa-1
82AlexD-21
83AlexD-11
84PrWill-29
85Nashua-27
87Fayette-17
88FSLAS/Star-28

Lipski, Robert
63T-558R

Lipson, Stefan
83Butte-7

Liranzo, Rafael
78RochR

Liriano, Felix
88Fay/Pro-1093

Liriano, Julio
88Watlo/Pro-675

Liriano, Nelson
85Kingst-13
86Knoxv-15
87Syrac-2
87Syrac/TCMA-17
88D-32
88F-117
88Leaf-32RR
88OPC-205
88Score-621
88Score/YS/I-13
88T-205
88T/Big-155
88Tor/Fire-2
89Class/Up/2-196
89D-627
89D/Best-160
89F-239
89OPC-76
89Score-577
89T-776
89T/Big-207
89Tor/Fire-2
89UD-109
90D-267
90F-87
90Score-77
90T-543
90UD-134

Lis, Joe
70OPC-56R
70T-56R
71OPC-138R
71T-138R
74OPC-659
74T-659
75OkCty
75OPC-86
75T-86
75T/M-86
76SSPC-523
77Ho-125
77T-269

Liscio, Joe
59DF

Lisenbee, Horace
33G-68
V354-45

Lisi, Rick
79Tulsa-14
80Charl-9
82RochR-14
83RochR-21
84Richm-7

Liska, Ad
R316

Listach, Pat
89Stock/Best-22
89Stock/Cal-173
89Stock/Pro-379
89Stock/Star-4

Littell, Mark
74OPC-596R
74T-596R
76OPC-593R
76SSPC-181
76T-593R
77T-141
78T-331
79T-466
80T-631
81D-580
81F-544
81T-255
82D-442
82F-120
82T-56
89Watlo/Pro-1784
89Watlo/Star-27

Little, Bryan
83Stuart-24
83T/X-62
84D-157
84F-279
84Nes/792-188
84OPC-188
84Stuart-30
84T-188
85BuffB-9
85F-402
85OPC-257
85T-257
86D-452
86F-212
86T-346
87Colum-14
87Colum/Pol-16
87Colum/TCMA-14
88BuffB/CMC-16
88BuffB/Polar-3
88BuffB/Pro-1491
89AubAs/Pro-27
89Wich/Roc-4CO

Little, Doug
87DayBe-8
88BirmB/Best-26
89BirmB/Best-22
89BirmB/Pro-93

Little, Grady
84CharO-10
85Kingst-24
89Durhm/Star-26

Little, Jeff
75Lafay
78Cr/PCL-37
79Phoen
82Toled-4
83F-619
83T-499
83Toled-7

Little, Martin
80Wausa-5

Little, Randy
86Cram/PCL-119

Little, Richard
82Wichi-9

Little, Ronald
82Water-21
83Indianap-20

Little, Scott
84LitFalls-4
85Lynch-27
86Jacks/TCMA-21
88Harris/Pro-838
89BuffB/CMC-20
89BuffB/Pro-1681

Little, Thomas
86Cram/PCL-109

Littlefield, John
77StPet
79ArkTr-6
81D-309
81F-535
81T-489
81T/Tr-794
82D-145
82F-576
82Syrac-5
82T-278

Littlefield, Richard
52B-209
54B-213
54Esskay
55B-200
57T-346
58T-241
79TCMA-14

Littlejohn, Dennis
78Cr/PCL-61
79Phoen
80Phoen-16
80T-686R
81D-313
81F-455
81Phoen-18
81T-561

Littleton, Larry
79Portl-19
80Tacom-3
82Charl-20

Litton, Greg
84Evrt/Cram-1
86Shrev-15
87Shrev-8
89F/Up-130
89Score/Tr-86
90D-453
90F-61
90Score-497
90Score/100Ris-91
90T-66
90UD-677

Littrell, Jack Jr.
78Clint
79Wausa-15

Littrell, Jack Sr.
55Rodeo

Litwhiler, Dan
41DP-100
41DP-45
47TipTop
49B-97
49Eureka-88
50B-198
51B-179

Litzinger, Jeff
88CapeCod-8
88CapeCod/Sum-185

Livchak, Robert
87StPet-27
88StPet/Star-13

Lively, Everett
49Eureka-89

Lively, Henry
T207

Livengood, Wes
W711/1

Livernois, Derek
85Elmir-11
86Greens-13
87WinHav-23
89Lynch/Star-12

Livesay, Jeff
87Anchora-19
88Oneon/Pro-2052
89PrWill/Star-11

Livin, Jeff
86Osceola-17
87ColAst/Pro-20
87ColumAst-20

Livingston, Dennis
86Albuq-13
87Albuq/Pol-13

Livingston, Paddy
10Domino-70
11Helmar-25
12Sweet/Pin-47
E104
M116
T205
T206
T207
T208

Livingston, T.
(Mickey)
47TipTop

Livingstone, Scott
89London/Pro-1381

Llanes, Pedro
86Miami-16
87Savan-13

Llano, Jorge
82Miami-11

Llanos, Aurelio
88Martins/Star-23
89Martins/Star-17

Llenas, Winston
71OPC-152R
71T-152R
74OPC-467
74T-467
75OPC-597
75T-597
75T/M-597
76SSPC-195
83Nashua-20
85Cram/PCL-14MG
86Edmon-19MG
88Tor/Fire-57CO

Llewellyn, Paul
83Ander-28

Llodrat, Fernando
76Watlo

Lloyd, Graeme
88Myrtle/Pro-1167

Lloyd, John Henry
74Laugh/Black-33
88Conlon/NegAS-8

Lloyd, Mike
89Elizab/Star-15

Lobe, Bill
55Gol/Ind-16
55Salem

Lobert, John
(Hans)
10Domino-71
11Helmar-145
12Sweet/Pin-127
14Piedmont/St-32
15CJ-70

40PB-160
BF2-77
D303
D329-104
D350/2-102
E101
E102
E105
E106
E90/1
E92
E94
M101/4-104
M101/5-102
M116
S74-101
T201
T202
T204
T205
T206
T216
T222
T3-105
Lobozzetta, Al
87Cedar-1
Lochner, Dave
83Cedar-3
83Cedar/LF-8
Lock, Don
63T-47
64T-114
64T/Coins-53
64T/St-24
64T/SU
64T/tatt
65OldLond-29
65T-445
66OPC-165
66T-165
66T/RO-34
67T-376
68OPC-59
68T-59
69MB-159
69T-229
69T/St-76
78TCMA-34
Exh47
WG10-31
Locke, Bobby
60T-44
61T-537
62T-359
65T-324
68OPC-24
68T-24
Locke, Roger Dale
88Ashvl/Pro-1064
Locke, Ron
64T-556R
65T-511
Locke, William H.
D322
Lockenmeyer, Mark
84Jacks-3
Locker, John
89Elmir/Puc-29
Locker, Robert
65T-541R
66T-374
67T-338
68OPC-51
68T-51
69T-548
70McDon-5
70MLB/St-274
70OPC-249
70T-249
71MLB/St-520
71OPC-356
71T-356
72T-537
73OPC-645
73T-645
74OPC-62
74T-62
74T/Tr-62T
75OPC-434
75T-434
75T/M-434
Lockhart, Bruce
85Greens-6
86WinHav-15
87WinHav-13
Lockhart, Keith
87Cedar-13
88Chatt/Best-9
88SLAS-5
89Nashvl-12
89Nashvl/CMC-16
89Nashvl/Pro-1278
Lockie, Randy
83QuadC-13
Locklear, Gene
75OPC-13
75T-13
75T/M-13
76OPC-447
76T-447
Lockley, Blain
86Watertn-12
87Macon-12
Lockman, Carroll
(Whitey)
47TipTop
48B-30
49B-2
49Eureka-116
50B-82
50Drake-8
51B-37
51T/RB-41
52B-38
52BR
52RM-NL13
52StarCal/L-78G
52TipTop
53B/Col-128
53Briggs
53RM-NL7
53SM
54B-153
54NYJour
54SM
55B-219
55Gol/Giants-17
55SM
56T-205
57T-232
58Hires-62
58SFCall
58T-195
59T-411
60T-535
73OPC-81MG
73T-81MG
74OPC-354MG
74T-354MG
79TCMA-26
D305
Exh47
PM10/Sm-98
R423-60
Lockwood, Claude
(Skip)
65T-526R
70OPC-499
70T-499
71MLB/St-443
71OPC-433
71T-433
72OPC-118
72T-118
73OPC-308
73T-308
74OPC-532
74T-532
75OPC-417
75T-417
75T/M-417
75Tucso-23
76OPC-166
76SSPC-549
76T-166
77T-65
78T-379
79OPC-250
79T-481
80OPC-295
80T-567
81D-217
81T-233
Lockwood, Rick
85CharO-4
86Jacks/TCMA-18
88Louvl-29
Lodbell, Dick
87Anchora-38
Lodigiani, Dario
41G-15
47Remar-19
47Signal
48Signal
48Smith-15
49Remar
Loehr, Ted
75AppFx
Loera, Javier
89GreatF-7
Loes, Billy
52B-240
52T-20
53B/Col-14
53T-174
54B-42
54NYJour
55B-240
55Gol/Dodg-19
56T-270
57T-244
58Hires-48
58T-359
59T-336
60T-181
61T-237
79TCMA-50
PM10/L-18
Lofton, Kenny
88AubAs/Pro-1953
89AubAs/Pro-2166
Lofton, Rodney
89Freder/Star-14
Loftus, Thomas
N172
Logan, H. Dan
80RochR-4
81RochR-11
82RochR-15
83RochR-17
Logan, Joe Jr.
88CapeCod/Sum-19
89James/Pro-2158
Logan, Johnny
53JC-20
53T-158
54B-80
54JC-23
54RM-NL20
54T-122
55B-180
55Gol/Braves-18
55JC-23
55RM-NL5
56T-136
56YellBase/Pin-18
57Swift-12
57T-4
58T-110
59T-225
60Lake
60T-205
61P-105
61T-524
62T-573
63T-259
79TCMA-158
Exh47
Logan, Robert Dean
(Lefty Bob)
86Indianap-18
Loggins, Mike
86FtMyr-18
87Memph-4
87Memph/Best-18
88Omaha/CMC-13
88Omaha/Pro-1504
89Omaha/CMC-20
89Omaha/Pro-1738
LoGrande, Angelo
78Watlo
81Charl-14
82Charl-15
83Charl-10
Logue, Matt
89NiagFls/Puc-15
Lohbeck
N172
Lohrke, Jack
47TipTop
48B-16
49B-59
49Eureka-117
51B-235
52B-251
53B/BW-47
Lohrman, Bill
40PB-210
Lohuis, Mark
81Shrev-21
Lois, Alberto
76Shrev
78Colum
79Portl-14
80T-683R
Lolich, Mickey
64T-128
65T-335
65T/E-55
66T-226LL
66T-455
66T/RO-65
67OPC-88
67T-88
68T-414
69Kelly/Pin-10
69MB-160
69MLB/St-50
69MLBPA/Pin-15
69OPC-168WS
69T-270
69T/St-175
70K-65
70MB-13
70MLB/St-210
70OPC-72LL
70T-715
70T-72LL
71MLB/St-398
71OPC-133
71OPC-71LL
71T-133
71T-71LL
71T/Coins-106
71T/GM-23
71T/tatt-13
72K-38
72MB-200
72OPC-450
72OPC-94LL
72OPC-96LL
72T-450
72T-94LL
72T-96LL
72T/Post-5
73K-3
73OPC-390
73T-390
73T/Comics-10
73T/Lids-27
73T/PinUps-10
74OPC-166
74T-9
74T/St-178
75Ho-6
75Ho/Twink-6
75OPC-245
75T-245
75T/M-245
76Crane-28
76Laugh/Jub-3
76MSA/Disc
76OPC-385
76OPC-3RB
76SSPC-354
76T-385
76T-3M
76T/Tr-385T
77T-565
79T-164
80T-459
88Domino-11
88Pac/Leg-39
89Swell-97
Lolich, Ron
71OPC-458R
71T-458R
Lollar, Sherm
50B-142
51B-100
51T/BB-24
52B-237
52Hawth/Pin-5
52NTea
52T-117
53B/Col-157
53T-53
54B-182
54RH
54RM-AL5
54T-39
55B-174
55T-201
56T-243
57T-23
58T-267
58T-491AS
59T-385
60T-495
60T-567AS
61P-28
61T-285
61T-514
61T/St-123
62J-53
62P-53
62P/Can-53
62Salada-55
62Shirriff-55
62T-514
63J-42
63P-42
63T-118
79TCMA-73
Lollar, Tim
79WHave-20
80Colum-1
81F-108
81T-424R
82T-587

83D-61
83D/AAS-37
83F-365
83OPC-185
83T-185
83T-742TL
83T/St-296
84D-284
84F-305
84Moth/Padres-3
84Nes/792-644
84OPC-267
84Smok/Padres-16
84T-644
85Coke/WS-46
85D-324
85F-39
85F/Up-U73
85Leaf-111
85OPC-13
85T-13
85T/St-153
85T/Tr-76T
86D-620
86F-354
86T-297
87F-38
87T-396

Loman, Doug
78BurlB
80Holyo-15
81ElPas-8
82Vanco-10
84Cram/PCL-28
85D-46
85Pol/Brew-5

Lomastro, Jerry
83Orlan-12
85Toled-24
86Toled-14
87Hagers-7
87RochR/TCMA-26

Lombardi, Al
89Penin/Star-11

Lombardi, Ernie
32Orbit/num-58
32Orbit/un-41
34DS-105
34DS-36
34Exh/4-4
34G-35
35BU-129
35Exh/4-4
36Exh/4-4
37Exh/4-4
37Wheat
38Exh/4-4
38G-246
38G-270
38Wheat
39Exh
39Wheat-1
41DP-12
47TipTop
48Signal
60F-17
61F-55
80Cram/Leg-11
86D/HL-33
86S/Dec-23
89HOF/St-58
89Smok/Dodg-102
R303/A
R303/B
R305
R312
R314
V354-82
W711/1
W711/2

Lombardi, Phil
83Greens-15
85Albany-13
86Colum-14
86Colum/Pol-12
87Colum-16
87Colum/Pol-17
87Colum/TCMA-15
87D-401
87F-648M
87S-118M
88T-283
88Tidew/CANDL-10
88Tidew/CMC-12
88Tidew/Pro-1578
89Tidew/CMC-12
89Tidew/Pro-1975

Lombardi, Vic
47TipTop
49Eureka-165
51B-204
52Park-7

Lombardo, Chris
78StPet

Lombardozzi, Chris
87PrWill-13
89Cedar/Best-28
89Cedar/Pro-935
89Chatt/Best-17
89Chatt/GS-25

Lombardozzi, Steve
83Orlan-6
84Toled-1
85Toled-17
86D-598
86D/Rook-18
86F/Up-U68
86S-178M
86S/Rook-17
87D-318
87D/OD-227
87F-547
87T/Tr-66T
88D-196
88F-16
88Master/Disc-6
88Panini/St-137
88Score-174
88T-697
89D-554
89F-120
89OPC-376
89Score-421
89T-376
89Tucso/CMC-23
89Tucso/Pro-181
89UD-179
90D-688

Lombarski, Tom
82OkCty-14
83MidldC-14
84IowaC-17
85IowaC-4
86Peoria-16
87Tidew-17
87Tidew/TCMA-14

Lomeli, Michael
87Idaho-14
88Boise/Pro-1622
89Boise/Pro-2004

Lonborg, Jim
65T-573R
66OPC-93
66T-93
67T-371
67T/Test/RSox-9
67T/Test/SU-4
68Bz-11
68Coke
68OPC-10LL
68OPC-12LL
68OPC-155WS
68T-10LL
68T-12LL
68T-460
68T/3D
68T/G-14
68T/Post-11
69Citgo-3
69MB-161
69MLB/St-14
69MLBPA/Pin-16
69NTF
69OPC-109
69T-109
69T/St-135
70K-49
70MLB/St-159
70T-665
71MLB/St-323
71OPC-577
71T-577
72MB-201
72OPC-255
72T-255
73OPC-3
73T-3
74JP
74OPC-342
74T-342
74T/St-75
75OPC-94
75T-94
75T/M-94
76OPC-271
76SSPC-462
76T-271
77K-41
77T-569
78T-52
79OPC-233
79T-446
88Pac/Leg-80
89Swell-48

Lond, Joel
86FSLAS-30

Londos, Jim
33SK-14

Long, Bruce
86Readg-15
87Readg-10

Long, Dale
55T-127
55T/DH-115
56T-56
56T/Pin-43
56YellBase/Pin-19
57Kahn
57Swift-3
57T-3
58T-7
59T-147M
59T-414
60T-375
61T-117
61T/St-205
62J-65
62P-65
62P/Can-65
62Salada-35
62Shirriff-35
62T-228
63T-484
72Laugh/GF-48
78TCMA-223
79TCMA-41
Exh47

Long, Danny
N172/PCL

Long, Dennis
81Tulsa-14
82Tulsa-4
83Tulsa-8

Long, Don
87QuadC-19
89PalmSp/Cal-60CO
89PalmSp/Pro-476

Long, Herman
(Germany)
E107
N172
N300/unif

Long, James V.
88PalmSp/Cal-89
88PalmSp/Pro-1460

Long, Jeoff
62Pep/Tul
64T-497

Long, Kevin
88CapeCod/Sum-98
89Eugene/Best-14

Long, Rich
89Utica/Puc-14

Long, Robert E.
(Bob)
78Salem
80Port-21
81Portl-16
82Portl-5
82T-291R
84Cram/PCL-179
85Cram/PCL-95
86F-468
86Richm-12
87CharO/WBTV-14

Long, Thomas
D328-100
D329-105
D350/2-103
E135-100
M101/4-105
M101/5-103

Long, Tony
86Lakel-11

Long, William
(Bill)
82Amari-18
84Beaum-11
85BuffB-21
86BuffB-16
87D/Rook-48
87F/U-U66
87Hawai-16
87T/Tr-67T
88Coke/WS-14
88D-306
88F-404
88OPC-309
88RedFoley/St-49
88Score-539
88T-309
89B-56
89Coke/WS-16
89D-573
89F-501
89OPC-133
89Score-351
89T-133
89UD-499
90Score-526
90T-499

Longenecker, Jere
83Butte-18
87Memph-9
87Memph/Best-19

Longmire, Tony
87Macon-8
88Salem/Star-10

Longull, Rich
87Sumter-15
88Durhm/Star-10
89BurlB/Pro-1624
89BurlB/Star-14

Lonigro, Greg
87Cedar-15
88Cedar/Pro-1152
88MidwLAS/GS-9
89Chatt/Best-16
89Chatt/GS-17

Lonnett, Joe
57T-241
58T-64
73OPC-356CO
73T-356C
74OPC-221CO
74T-221C

Lono, Joel
86Tampa-11
87Cedar-6

Look, Bruce
69T-317

Looper, Eddie
87Savan-18
88Savan/Pro-350
89Sprin/Best-23

Lopat, Ed
47TipTop
49B-229
50B-215
51B-218
51BR-C6
51T/BB-39
52B-17
52BR
52Coke
52StarCal/L-70B
52T-57
52TipTop
53Exh/Can-15
53T-87
54NYJour
54T-5
55T-109
55T/DH-41
56T/Hocus-A2
60T-465C
61Peters-2
63T-23
64T-348
79TCMA-91
Exh47
PM10/L-19
R346-40
R423-61

Lopata, Stan
49B-177
49Eureka-140
50B-206
51B-76
51BR-B9
54B-207
55B-18
56T-183
57T-119
58Hires-29
58Hires/T
58T-353
59T-412
60T-515
79TCMA-151
PM10/Sm-99

Lopes, Dave
73OPC-609R
73T-609R
74OPC-112
74T-112
74T/St-46
75Ho-67
75Ho/Twink-67
75OPC-93
75T-93
75T/M-93
76Ho-105
76OPC-197LL
76OPC-4RB
76OPC-660
76SSPC-79
76T-197LL
76T-4M
76T-660

77Ho-14
77OPC-4LL
77OPC-96
77T-180
77T-4LL
78Ho-112
78OPC-222
78Wiffle/Discs-39
79Ho-114
79K-52
79OPC-144
79T-290
80BK/PHR-28
80K-29
80OPC-291
80Pol/Dodg-15
80T-560
80T/S-60
81D-416
81F-114
81F/St-67
81K-29
81OPC-50
81Pol/Dodg-15
81T-50
81T/HT
81T/SO-92
81T/St-175
82D-327
82F-12
82F/St-10
82Granny-8
82OPC-218
82OPC-338AS
82OPC-85IA
82T-338
82T-740
82T-741A
82T/Tr-64T
83D-339
83F-524
83Granny-15
83OPC-365
83T-365
83T/St-105
84D-400
84F-453
84Moth/A's-21
84Nes/792-669
84Nes/792-714LL
84OPC-17
84T-669
84T-714
84T/St-331
85D-604
85F-60
85OPC-12
85SevenUp-15
85SpokAT/Crm-13
85T-12
86D-388
86D-9
86D/DKsuper-9
86F-372
86Gator-15
86Leaf-9DK
86OPC-125
86S-144M
86S-194
86T-125
87D-455
87F-62
87Moth/Ast-16
87OPC-311
87Pol/Ast-8
87Smok/Dodg-19
87T-445
87T-4RB
87T/St-7
88Score-489
88Smok/Dodg-15M
88Smok/Dodg-18
88T-226
89Smok/Dodg-96
89Smok/R-20

Lopez, Al
33DH-27
33Exh/4-2
34DS-28
34DS-97
34Exh/4-2
35BU-3
35Exh/4-2
37Exh/4-1
38G-257
38G-281
51B-295
52NumNum-20
53B/Col-143
54DanDee
55B-308
55Gol/Ind-17
55Salem
60MacGregor-12
60T-222
61T-132
61T-337M
62T-286
63T-458
64T-232
65T-414
69T-527
80Cram/Leg-98
80SSPC/HOF
86Indianap-21MG
89Pac/Leg-197
89Smok/Dodg-38
89Swell-90
R312/M
R314
V355-131

Lopez, Antonio
79Wisco-1

Lopez, Art
65T-566R

Lopez, Aurelio
78Sprin
79T-444
80T-101
81Coke
81F-483
81OPC-291
81T-291
82D-359
82F-273
82T-278
83T/X-63
84D-516
84F-86
84FunFood/Pin-98
84Nes/792-95
84OPC-95
84T-95
84T/St-268
85Cain's-13
85D-349
85F-16
85Leaf-160
85Seven-9D
85T-539
85T/St-265
85Wendy-15
86D-293
86F-231
86F/Up-U69
86T-367
87D-629
87F-63
87Moth/Ast-18
87Pol/Ast-13
87T-659

Lopez, Carlos
77T-492R
78OPC-219
78T-166
79RochR-8
79T-568

Lopez, Fred
89Idaho/Pro-2016

Lopez, Hector
55Rodeo
56Rodeo
56T-16
56T/Pin-13
57T-6
58T-155
59T-402
60T-163
61P-12
61T-28
62T-502
63T-92
64T-325
65T-532
66OPC-177
66T-177
78TCMA-272
79TCMA-195
PM10/L-20
WG9-15

Lopez, Javier
78Cedar
89Pulas/Pro-1892

Lopez, Juan
77Spoka
79Vanco-12
80Evans-23
81Evans-17
82Evans-17
83Evans-16
83Watlo/LF-6
84Evans-1
87Fayette-18
87Osceola-2
88ColAst/Best-10
89NiagFls/Puc-26

Lopez, Luis
85VeroB-21
86FSLAS-31
86VeroB-16
87Bakers-10
88SnAnt/Best-26
88Spoka/Pro-1930
88TexLgAS/GS-37
89CharRa/Pro-984
89SnAnt/Best-15

Lopez, Marcelino
63T-549R
65T-537R
66OPC-155
66T-155
67T-513
70OPC-344
70T-344
71MLB/St-303
71OPC-137
71T-137
72T-652

Lopez, Marcos
89Peoria/Ko-4

Lopez, Marcus
88CharWh/Best-16

Lopez, Pancho
73Cedar

Lopez, Pedro
89Watlo/Pro-1790
89Watlo/Star-18

Lopez, Rob
86FSLAS-32
86Tampa-12
87Vermont-9
88Nashvl/CMC-8
88Nashvl/Pro-487
89Nashvl-13
89Nashvl/CMC-6
89Nashvl/Pro-1295

Lopez, Steve
88Idaho/Pro-1859
89Sumter/Pro-1096

Lora, Ramon Antonio
80OkCty
81Syrac-10
82Syrac-12

Lord, Bristol
10Domino-72
11Helmar-11
12Sweet/Pin-11A
12Sweet/Pin-11B
14Piedmont/St-33
E104
E224
E254
E270/1
M116
T205
T207
T208

Lord, Harry
14CJ-48
E103
E254
E270/1
E270/2
E91
E94
E95
M116
T201
T202
T204
T205
T206
T207
T215
T3-106

Lorenz, Joe
82Durhm-4

Lorenzo, Gary
79AppFx-9

Losa, Bill
88Butte-13
88Gasto/Pro-1013

Losauro, Carmelo
86DayBe-17
88Virgini/Star-14

Loscalzo, Bob
82Idaho-24
83Madis/LF-15
84Madis/Pol-13

Loseke, Scott
84Cedar-22

Lott, Bill
89LittleSun-4

Lotzar, Greg
85Elmir-12
86FSLAS-33
86WinHav-16
87NewBrit-6

Loubier, Stephen
88River/Cal-213
88River/Pro-1432
89AubAs/Pro-24
89River/Best-11
89River/Cal-20
89River/Pro-1389

Loubier, Steve
89Wich/Roc/Up-14

Loucks, Scott
78DaytB
81Tucso-11
83Tucso-22
85Cram/PCL-228

Louden, William
D328-101
E135-101

Louis, Joe
D305

Loun, Don
65OPC-181R
65T-181R

Lovdal, Stewart
89Martins/Star-18

Love, John
87Macon-6
88Salem/Star-11

Love, William
(Will)
89Madis/Star-13
89Star/Wax-66

Lovelace, Vance
82QuadC-10
83VeroB-7
86MidldA-13
87MidldA-24
88Edmon/CMC-4
88Edmon/Pro-557
89Edmon/Pro-559
89F-651M

Lovell, Don
86Water-15
87BuffB-1
88ColSp/CMC-15
88ColSp/Pro-1523

Lovell, Jim
88Greenv/Best-11
89Greenv/Pro-1167
89Greenvl/Best-22

Lovett, Thomas
N172
N300/unif

Loviglio, John
(Jay)
80OkCty
81T-526R
82Edmon-8
82T-599R
83IowaC-15
86Geneva-16MG
87WinSal-13
89WinSal/Star-19

Lovins, Steve
(Sarge)
80Memph-1

Lovitto, Joe
73OPC-276
73T-276
74OPC-639
74T-639
75OPC-36
75T-36
75T/M-36
76OPC-604
76SSPC-271
76T-604

Lovrich, Pete
63T-549R
64T-212

Lovullo, Torey
88EastLAS/Pro-8
88GlenF/Pro-923
89D/Rook-17
89F-648M
89Mara/Tigers-23
89Panini/St-332
89Score/HotRk-17
89UD/Ext-782
90UD-332

Lowdermilk, Grover
T207

Lowe, Chris
88Martins/Star-24
89Martins/Star-19

Lowe, Donald
79Wausa-17

Lowe, Jamie
89Orlan/Best-29

Lowe, Q.V.
82Oneon-6
83Greens-29

86Jaxvl/TCMA-10
87Jamestn-29
88James/Pro-2039
89James/Pro-2152

Lowe, Robert
N172
N300/unif

Lowe, Steve
(Doc)
76Wausa
78Wausa

Lowenstein, John
71OPC-231R
71T-231R
72OPC-486
72T-486
73OPC-327
73T-327
74OPC-176
74T-176
75OPC-424
75T-424
75T/M-424
76OPC-646
76SSPC-528
76T-646
77OPC-175
77T-393
78BK/R-21
78T-87
79T-173
80T-287
81D-235
81F-186
81OPC-199
81T-591
82D-599
82F-169
82T-747
82T/St-102
83D-153
83F-63
83OPC-337
83T-473
83T/St-24
84D-228
84D/AAS-26
84F-10
84F/St-116
84Nes/792-604
84T-604
84T/St-209
84T/St-20WS
85D-245
85F-180
85OPC-316
85T-316
85T/St-206

Lowery, Josh
89Batav/Pro-1942

Lowman, Mel
77DaytB

Lown, Omar
(Turk)
52B-16
52T-330
53B/Col-154
53T-130
54B-157
57T-247
58T-261
59T-277
60T-313
60T-57M
61P-32
61T-424
61T/RO-35
62T-528
V362-14

Lowrey, Harry
(Peanuts)
47TipTop
48L-33
49B-22
49Eureka-62
50B-172
51B-194
52B-102
52T-111
53Exh/Can-29
53Hunter
53T-16
54Hunter
54T-158
72T/Test-2
Exh47

Lowrey, Steve
82Cedar-4

Lowry, Dwight
83BirmB-4
87Cain's-5
87Coke/Tigers-11
87D-338
87F-157
87Seven-DT7
87T-483
87Toled/TCMA-25

Lowry, Mike
78Wausa

Loy, Darren
86Readg-16
87Maine-21
87Maine/TCMA-9
88CharlR/Star-13
89OkCty/CMC-20
89OkCty/Pro-1526

Loynd, Mike
86Rang-46
86Tulsa-8
87D-506
87F/U-U67
87Moth/Rang-21
87Smok/R-27
87T-126
88D-550
88F-472
88Score-491
88T-319
88Tucso/CMC-3
88Tucso/Pro-185
89ColMud/Pro-147
89ColMud/Star-16

Lozado, Willie
79BurlB-7
81ElPas-2
82Vanco-5
83Indianap-10
85D-595
85F-644
85Louvl-19
86OKCty-10

Lozinski, Tony
89Batav/Pro-1916

Lubert, Dennis
83Durhm-21

Lubratich, Steve
80SLCty-14
81SLCty-19
82Spoka-17
84Cram/PCL-112
84Cram/PCL-249
84D-377
84F-524
84Nes/792-266
84T-266
85Cram/PCL-106
86Beaum-14CO
86LasVegas-10
87Spoka-10
88LasVeg/Pro-243
88Spoka/Pro-1928
89River/Best-22
89River/Cal-25MG
89River/Pro-1411

Luby, Hugh
48Sommer-23

Lucadello, John
W753

Lucarelli, Vito
79AppFx-3

Lucas, Brian
78Charl

Lucas, C. Fred
(Red)
29Exh/4-8
31Exh/4-8
32Orbit/num-40
32Orbit/un-42
33DH-28
33DH-29
33Exh/4-4
33G-137
34DS-106
34DS-46
35G-2B
35G-7B
R305
R313
R316
R332-43
V354-7

Lucas, Charles S.
R314/Can

Lucas, Gary
79Hawai-9
81D-243
81F-502
81OPC-259
81T-436
82D-296
82F-577
82OPC-120
82T-120
83D-187
83F-366
83OPC-364
83T-761
84D-307
84F-306
84F/X-73
84Nes/792-7
84OPC-7
84Stuart-12
84T-7
84T/St-161
84T/X-73
85D-498
85F-403
85OPC-297
85T-297
86D-453
86F-254
86OPC-351
86T-601
87D-618
87F-87
87OPC-382
87Smok/Cal-4
87T-696
88D-579
88F-495
88T-524

Lucchesi, Frank
70T-662
71OPC-119MG
71T-119
72OPC-188MG
72T-188
74OPC-379CO
74T-379C
76SSPC-272
76T-172MG
77T-428MG
88T-564
89Nashvl-27
89Nashvl/CMC-25
89Nashvl/Pro-1284

Lucero, Robert
88Clint/Pro-714

Lucia, Danny
78Green
81Durhm-20

Luciani, Randy
88Fay/Pro-1098

Luderus, Fred
11Helmar-146
14CJ-45
15CJ-45
BF2-87
D328-102
D329-106
D350/2-104
E135-102
M101/4-106
M101/5-104

Ludwick, Bob
53Exh/Can-38

Ludwig, Jeff
89Geneva/Pro-1869

Ludwig, William
E254

Ludy, John
85Beloi-19
86Stockton-13
87Stockton-16

Luebber, Steve
72T-678
77T-457
79Syrac-20
80RochR-15
81RochR-12
83Evans-5
86Beaum-15CO
87Wichi-23
88Wichi-42
89LasVeg/Pro-26

Luecken, Rick
84Chatt-19
85Cram/PCL-98
86Chatt-16
87Memph-18
87Memph/Best-22
88Memph/Best-20
89AAA/Pro-38
89Omaha/CMC-7
89Omaha/Pro-1734
90D-562
90F-113
90T-87
90UD-621

Lugo, Angel
89Elizab/Star-16

Lugo, Rafael
82Danvi-26
83Peoria/LF-20
85Cram/PCL-9

Lugo, Urbano
85F/Up-U74
86D-329
86F-162
86T-373
87Smok/Cal-9
87T-92
88AAA/Pro-15
88Edmon/CMC-6
88Edmon/Pro-581
89Indi/Pro-1232

Lujack, Johnny
51Wheat
52Wheat

Lukachyk, Rob
88Utica/Puc-1
89SoBend/GS-22

Lukevics, Mitch
76AppFx
78Knoxv
79Knoxv/TCMA-11

Lukish, Tom
80Utica-25
82Knoxv-5
83Syrac-9
84Syrac-20

Lum, Mike
68T-579R
69MB-162
69T-514
70OPC-367
70T-367
71MLB/St-16
71OPC-194
71T-194
72T-641
73OPC-266
73T-266
74OPC-227
74T-227
74T/St-7
75Ho-33
75Ho/Twink-33
75OPC-154
75T-154
75T/M-154
76OPC-208
76SSPC-11
76T-208
76T/Tr-208T
77T-601
78T-326
79OPC-286
79T-556
80T-7
81F-258
81T-457
81T/Tr-795
82D-300
82F-599
82T-732

Luman, Charley
83Butte-8

Lumenti, Ralph
58T-369
59T-316
60L-130
61T-469

Lumley, Harry G.
E90/1
T204
T206
WG3-26

Lumley, Mike
89Lakel/Star-14

Lumpe, Jerry
58T-193
59T-272
60L-47
60T-290
61P-81
61T-119M
61T-365
61T/St-164
62J-93
62P-93
62P/Can-93
62Salada-25
62Shirriff-25
62T-127M
62T-305
62T/bucks
62T/St-54
63F-16
63J-86
63P-86
63T-256
63T/SO
64Det/Lids-9
64T-165
64T/Coins-124AS
64T/Coins-28
64T/St-86S9

64T/SU
65T-353
66OPC-161
66T-161
67T-247
78TCMA-55

Luna, Guillermo (Memo)
52Mother-26
54B-222
54Hunter

Lunar, Luis
76Wausa
77Wausa
79Jacks-13

Lund, Don
53Glen
53T-277
54B-87
54T-167

Lund, Gordon
70T-642R
75AppFx
79Knoxv/TCMA-4

Lund, Greg
89Everett/Star-27

Lundahl, Rich
86LitFalls-17
87Columbia-7

Lundblade, Rick
87Readg-13
88Maine/CMC-15
88Maine/Pro-291
89Tidew/CMC-19
89Tidew/Pro-1968

Lundeen, Larry
88Boise/Pro-1615

Lundgren, Carl
T206
WG3-27

Lundgren, Kurt
86Jacks/TCMA-7

Lundstedt, Thomas
74OPC-603R
74T-603R

Lundy, Dick
78Laugh/Black-6

Lundy, Gordy
82Edmon-22

Lung, Rod
88QuadC/GS-16

Lupien, Ulysses (Tony)
47Signal
49B-141

Luplow, Al
62T-598R
63J-73
63P-73
63Sugar-19
63T-351
64T-184
66OPC-188
66T-188
67T-433

Luque, Adolpho
21Exh-98
28Exh-15
28Yueng-18
33G-209
40PB-231
61F-56
87Conlon/2-46
88Conlon/5-19
88Pac/8Men-90
E120
E210-18
V61-72
W502-18
W513-71
W514-17

Lusader, Scott
86GlenF-12
87Toled-3
87Toled/TCMA-8
88D-615
88F-62
88Toled/CMC-13
88Toled/Pro-594
89Score/HotRk-15
89T-487
90D-696
90Score-575
90Score/100Ris-42
90T-632

Lush, John Charles
C46-33
E270/2
M116
T201
T204
T205

Lush, William L.
E107

Lusted, Chuck
84Shrev/FB-10

Luther, Brad
83StPet-18
85Sprin-16

Lutticken, Bob
86Cram/PCL-156
87Spoka-18
88Charl/Pro-1217
89River/Best-1
89River/Cal-11
89River/Pro-1403

Luttrell, Lyle
57T-386

Luttrull, Bruce
85Bend/Cram-14

Lutz, Chris
88Geneva/Pro-1653
89CharWh/Pro-1760

Lutz, Rollin Joseph
52Park-74
73OPC-449CO
73T-449C

Lutzke, Walter
25Exh-83
26Exh-82
27Exh-42

Luzinski, Greg
71OPC-439R
71T-439R
72OPC-112
72T-112
73OPC-189
73T-189
73T/Lids-28
74JP
74K-9
74OPC-360
74T-360
74T/DE-24
74T/St-76
75Ho-27
75Ho/Twink-27
75OPC-630
75T-630
75T/M-630
76Crane-29
76Ho-125
76K-18
76MSA/Disc
76OPC-193LL
76OPC-195LL
76OPC-610
76SSPC-467
76T-193LL
76T-195LL
76T-610
77Ho-25
77K-12
77OPC-118
77Pep-72
77T-30
78Ho-8
78K-33
78OPC-42
78T-420
78Wiffle/Discs-40
79BK/P-19
79Ho-30
79OPC-278
79T-540
80BK/P-11
80OPC-66
80T-120
81Coke
81D-175
81F-10
81F/St-75
81OPC-270
81T-270
81T/HT
81T/SO-74
81T/Tr-796
82D-193
82Drake-22
82F-352
82F/St-187
82OPC-152
82OPC-69IA
82T-720
82T-721A
82T/St-165
83D-395
83D/AAS-4
83F-247
83K-50
83OPC-310
83T-310
83T-591
83T/St-51
84D-122
84D/AAS-41
84D/Champs-13
84Drake-18
84F-69
84F/St-47
84FunFood/Pin-34
84Nes/792-20
84Nes/792-712LL
84OPC-20
84Ralston-5
84T-20
84T-712
84T/Cereal-5
84T/St-244
84T/St-7
84T/St-8
84TrueVal/WS-23
85D-546
85F-521
85Leaf-75
85OPC-328
85T-650
85T/St-238
89Swell-24

Luzon, Bob
82Durhm-5
83Durhm-9

Lychak, Perry
85Kingst-6
86Kinston-15

Lyden, Mitch
87Colum-9
87Colum/Pol-18
87Colum/TCMA-11
89Albany/Best-14
89Albany/Pro-320
89Albany/Star-11
89Star/Wax-98

Lydy, Scott
89Medford/Best-8

Lyle, Don
79Indianap-15
80Indianap-24

Lyle, Sparky
69MB-163
69T-311
70MLB/St-160
70OPC-116
70T-116
71MLB/St-324
71OPC-649
71T-649
72MB-202
72OPC-259
72T-259
73K-15
73OPC-394
73OPC-68LL
73T-394
73T-68LL
74K-41
74OPC-66
74T-66
74T/St-212
75Ho-134
75K-47
75OPC-485
75T-485
75T/M-485
76OPC-545
76SSPC-429
76T-545
77BK/Y-10
77OPC-89
77T-598
78BK/Y-9
78Ho-68
78K-43
78OPC-214
78OPC-237RB
78T-2M
78T-35
79Ho-143
79OPC-188
79T-365
80OPC-62
80T-115
81D-284
81F-17
81F/St-91
81OPC-337
81T-719
82D-189
82F-247
82OPC-285
82T-285
83OPC-208
83OPC-92SV
83T-693
83T-694A

Lyman, Billy
44Centen-15
45Centen-15

Lynch, Charlie
80Elmir-40

Lynch, David
89Tulsa/GS-14

Lynch, Ed
78Ashev
78Charl
79Tucso-20
80Tidew-21
81Tidew-16
82D-641
82F-531
82T-121
83D-308
83F-549
83T-601
84D-75
84F-591
84Nes/792-293
84T-293
85D-623
85F-87
85T-467
86D-631
86F-88
86OPC-68
86T-68
87Berg/Cubs-37
87D-516
87F-567
87OPC-16
87T-697
88D-77
88F-422
88Score-506
88T-336

Lynch, Jerry
54T-234
55T-142
55T/DH-73
56T-97
57T-358
58T-103
59Kahn
59T-97
60Kahn
60L-45
60T-198
60T-352M
61Kahn
61P-187
61T-97
61T/St-19
62J-127
62Kahn
62P-127
62P/Can-127
62Salada-198
62Shirriff-198
62T-487
63J-129
63Kahn
63P-129
63T-37
64Kahn
64T-193
65Kahn
65T-291
66EH-24
66OPC-182
66T-182
72Laugh/GF-22

Lynch, Joe
85Spoka/Cram-11
87TexLgAS-3
87Wichi-10
88LasVeg/CMC-9
88LasVeg/Pro-223
89LasVeg/CMC-3
89LasVeg/Pro-22

Lynch, John H.
N172
N172/SP
N690

Lynch, Rich
80WHave-21
81WHave-22

Lynes, Mike
83Albany-6

Lynn, Chuck
86Lynch-15

Lynn, Fred
75OPC-622R
75T-622R
75T/M-622R
76Crane-30
76Ho-1
76Ho/Twink-1
76K-31
76MSA/Disc
76OPC-192LL

76OPC-196LL
76OPC-50
76SSPC-402
76T-192LL
76T-196LL
76T-50
77Ho-51
77OPC-163
77Pep-21
77T-210
78OPC-62
78PapaG/Disc-19
78T-320
78Wiffle/Discs-41
79K-30
79OPC-249
79T-480
80BK/PHR-18
80K-40
80OPC-60
80T-110
80T/S-10
81D-218
81Drake-9
81F-223
81F/St-98
81K-40
81MSA/Disc-21
81OPC-313
81Sqt-25
81T-720
81T/HT
81T/SO-5
81T/St-42
81T/Tr-797
82D-367
82F-468
82F/St-214
82KMart-27
82OPC-251
82OPC-252IA
82T-251
82T-252A
82T/St-161
83D-241
83D/AAS-59
83F-97
83K-51
83OPC-182
83OPC-392AS
83Seven-3
83T-392
83T-520
83T/St-158
83T/St-44
84D-108
84D-17
84D/AAS-27
84D/Champs-59
84Drake-19
84F-525
84F-626
84FunFood/Pin-54
84Nes/792-680
84OPC-247
84Ralston-29
84Seven-16W
84Smok/Cal-18
84T-680
84T/Cereal-29
84T/Gloss22-7
84T/St-230
84T/St-5
84T/St-6
84T/Super-23
84T/Super-23
85D-133
85F-307
85F/Up-U75
85Leaf-198
85OPC-220
85Seven-9S
85T-220
85T/St-225
85T/Tr-77T
86D-245
86F-278
86F/St-70
86Leaf-120
86OPC-55
86S-137M
86S-145M
86S-38
86S-63M
86S-71M
86S-73M
86S/Rook-46M
86T-55
86T/St-228
86Woolwth-18
87Class-23
87D-108
87D-9DK
87D/DKsuper-9
87D/OD-135
87F-474
87F/Excit-32
87F/Lim-25
87F/St-72
87Leaf-83
87Leaf-9DK
87OPC-370
87S-198M
87S-49
87T-370
87T/St-226
88D-248
88D/Best-297
88F-566
88French-19
88Leaf-163
88Panini/St-15
88RedFoley/St-50
88Score-42
88Sf-23
88T-707
88T/Big-169
89D-563
89F-138
89Mara/Tigers-9
89OPC-27
89Pol/Tigers-9
89RedFoley/St-76
89Score-126
89Sf-68
89Smok/Angels-14
89T-416
89UD/Ext-761
90F-609
90Score-131
90T-107
90T-663TBC
90UD-247

Lynn, Greg
83Clint/LF-6tr

Lynn, Japhet
(Red)
47Signal
53Mother-58

Lynn, Ken
83Ander-11

Lynn, Thomas
83LynnP-26

Lyons, Albert
52Mother-42

Lyons, Barry
86Tidew-16
87T/Tr-68T
88D-619
88D/Mets/Bk-619
88F-140
88Kahn/Mets-33
88Score-387
88T-633
89D-572
89F/Up-101
89Kahn/Mets-33
89Score-456
89T-412
89UD-176
90D-526
90F-209
90Score-29
90T-258
90UD-473

Lyons, Bobby
83AlexD-1

Lyons, Dennis
N172
N690

Lyons, Harry P.
N172

Lyons, Jimmie
74Laugh/Black-14

Lyons, Steve
84Pawtu-18
85D-29
85F/Up-U76
86D-579
86F-355
86T-233
86T/Tr-67T
87Coke/WS-6
87D-409
87F-502
87T-511
88Coke/WS-15
88D-532
88D/Best-291
88F-405
88Panini/St-60
88T-108
89B-63
89Coke/WS-17
89D-253
89F-502
89OPC-334
89Panini/St-308
89Score-388
89T-334
89T/Big-105
89T/St-298
89UD-224
90D-651
90F-539
90Score-88
90T-751
90UD-390

Lyons, Ted
28Exh-39
31Exh/4-19
32Orbit/un-43
33CJ/Pin-16
33DH-30
33Exh/4-10
33G-7
34DS-43
35BU-111M
35BU-119
35BU-36
35Exh/4-10
35G-8B
35G-9B
36Exh/4-10
38Exh/4-10
50Callahan
61F-122
63Bz-38
80Cram/Leg-77
80SSPC/HOF
PR1-21
R305
R306
R308-172
R332-33
V353-7
W517-45

Lyons, William Allen
81Louvl-27
82Louisvl-14
82Sprin-4
84Louvl-14
85Louvl-17
86Louisvl-17
87Louvl-24
88Louvl-30
88Louvl/CMC-12
88Louvl/Pro-432

Lysander, Richard
76Tucso-28
79Ogden/TCMA-11
80Ogden-6
81Tacom-23
82Tucso-16
84D-560
84F-570
84Nes/792-639
84T-639
84Toled-23
85D-560
85F-284
85T-383
86F-399
86T-482

Lysgaard, Jim
77WHave
78Cr/PCL-59

Lytle, Wade
89Princet/Star-11

Lyttle, Jim
70OPC-516R
70T-516R
71OPC-234
71T-234
72T-648
74OPC-437
74T-437
76SSPC-337

Maack, Mike
83Wisco/LF-18

Maas, Duane
(Duke)
56T-57
57T-405
58T-228
59T-167
60T-421
61T-387
61T/RO-28
79TCMA-117

Maas, Jason
86FtLaud-15
87PrWill-24
88Albany/Pro-1346
89Albany/Best-24
89Albany/Pro-334
89Albany/Star-12

Maas, Kevin
87FtLaud-19
88EastLAS/Pro-2
88PrWill/Star-15
89AAA/Pro-18
89Colum/CMC-17
89Colum/Pol-12
89Colum/Pro-737
90F-641M
90Score-606
90Score/100Ris-27
90UD-70

Maasberg, Gary
88Spart/Pro-1041

Mabe, Robert
59T-356
60T-288

Mabe, Todd
85FtMyr-2

Mabee, Vic
77Ashev
79Wausa-6

Macaluso, Nick
88Martins/Star-25

Macauley, Drew
80Buffa-6
81Buffa-7

Macavage, Joe
87Watertn-26
88Aug/Pro-372

MacCormack, Franc
78SnJos-4

MacDonald, Bill
51B-239
52T-138

MacDonald, Jim
81Tucso-23
82Tucso-12

MacDonald, Kevin
79Newar-11

MacDonald, Rob
88Myrtle/Pro-1191
89Knoxv/Best-13
89Knoxv/Pro-1139
89Knoxv/Star-11

MacDonald, Ronald
79Jacks-23
80Tidew-9
81Tidew-3
82Tidew-10

Mace, Jeff
83BurlR-21
83BurlR/LF-24
85Tulsa-24
88Boise/Pro-1616
89Boise/Pro-1977

Macfarlane, Mike
87Omaha-24
88D/Rook-55
88F/U-U31
88Score/Tr-76T
88Smok/Royals-17
88T/Tr-62T
89B-118
89D-416
89F-287
89Score-319
89Score/HotRk-97
89Score/YS/I-13
89T-479
89T/Big-86
89UD-546
90D-498
90F-114
90T-202
90UD-307

MacFayden, Dan
31Exh/4-18
33Exh/4-9
33G-156
35G-2F
35G-4F
35G-7F
36Exh/4-1
37Exh/4-1
38Exh/4-1
R314
V353-87

Macha, Ken
78Colum
78T-483
81D-540
81F-167
82F-618
82OPC-282
82T-282
86Provigo-28CO

Macha, Mike
78Richm

Machado, Julian
89Penin/Star-12

Machado, Julio
87Clearw-21

89Jacks/GS-11
90D-47
90T-684
90UD-93

Machalec, Mark
84Butte-15

Machemer, Dave
77SLCty
78Cr/PCL-25
80Evans-16
81Toled-13
82Toled-14
85Beloi-26
86Stockton-14MG
87Stockton-3
88ElPas/Best-6
89Denver/CMC-25
89Denver/Pro-37

Machuca, Freddy
82Danvi-19

Macias, Bob
82Amari-6

Macias, Henry
77Cedar
78Cedar

Mack, Connie
14CJ-12
15CJ-12
32Orbit/un-44
40PB-132
48Exh/HOF
50Callahan
51T/CM
60F-14
61F-123
63Bz/ATG-18
69Bz/Sm
80Laugh/FFeat-37
80SSPC/HOF
85West/2-39
86Conlon/1-18
89HOF/St-85
BF2-36
D329-107
D350/2-105
E104
E223
E96
E98
M101/4-107
M101/5-105
M116
N172
R305
R308-188
R311/Leath
R312/M
R423-67
T208
V100
V355-110
WG1-67
WG2-33
WG5-26
WG6-25

Mack, Henry
77Spart

Mack, Jerry
86Kenosha-14

Mack, Joseph
N172

Mack, Quinn
88WPalm/Star-16
89Jaxvl/Best-14
89Jaxvl/Pro-153

Mack, Shane
85Beaum-4
85T-398
86Beaum-16
87D/Rook-42
87LasVegas-18
87S/Rook-31
87T/Tr-69T
88D-411
88F-590
88LasVeg/CMC-10
88LasVeg/Pro-233
88OPC-283
88Score-414
88Score/YS/II-36
88Smok/Padres-16
88T-548
89D-538
89Score-270
89UD-182

Mack, Tony Lynn
(Toby)
83Redwd-17
85Cram/PCL-6
86Edmon-20
87MidldA-19
88SnAnt/Best-5
89Mia/Star/22-12

MacKanin, Pete
74OPC-597R
74T-597R
76OPC-287
76SSPC-324
76T-287
77OPC-260
77T-156
78T-399
79BK/P-17
81F-565
81T-509
82D-354
82F-556
82T-438
83OKCty-12
84lowaC-12
86Peoria-17MG
88lowaC/CMC-24
88lowaC/Pro-543
88Peoria/Ko-35M
89AAA/Pro-43
89lowaC/CMC-25
89lowaC/Pro-1707

MacKay, Bill
83Ander-1

MacKay, Joey
83Greens-25
84Greens-8

MacKenzie, Gordon
77Jaxvl
83Evans-22
84Evans-4
89Phoen/CMC-25
89Phoen/Pro-1504

MacKenzie, Ken
60T-534
61T-496
62T-421
63T-393
64T-297

MacKenzie, Shaun
86Cram/PCL-20
87Everett-20

Mackey, Biz
74Laugh/Black-27

Mackie, Bart
81Batav-9
82Wausa-6

Mackie, Scott
89Mia/Star/25-12

MacKiewicz, Felix
48Sommer-16

MacKinnon, Tim
88Boise/Pro-1629

Macko, Steve
80T-676R
80Wichi-18
81D-535
81T-381R

MacLeod, Kevin
88SoOreg/Pro-1709
89Modesto/Cal-273

Maclin, Lonnie
88StPet/Star-14
89Sprin/Best-25

MacMillan, Darrell
89Boise/Pro-1986

MacNeil, Tim
88Butte-4
89Gasto/Pro-1024
89Gasto/Star-11

MacPhail, Larry
89Rini/Dodg-20

MacPherson, Bruce
78OrlTw
80Toled-4
81Toled-7
82RochR-3

Macullar, James
N172

MacWhorter, Keith
81Pawtu-4
81T-689R
83Pawtu-8
84Maine-21

Macy, Frank
82lowaC-30

Madden, Bob
76AppFx
77AppFx
79QuadC-17

Madden, Michael
(Kid)
N172
N526

Madden, Mike
81ElPas-14
82Vanco-14
83T/X-64
84D-161
84F-232
84Moth/Ast-25
84Nes/792-127
84T-127
85T-479
86Pol/Ast-18
86T-691

Madden, Morris
83VeroB-8
86GlenF-13
87Toled-18
87Toled/TCMA-15
88BuffB/CMC-6
88BuffB/Polar-8
88BuffB/Pro-1466
89Score/HotRk-32

Madden, Scott
86Clearw-16
88Reno/Cal-273

Madden, Thomas
E254
E270/2
M116

Maddern, Clarence
49B-152
52Mother-44
53Mother-34

Maddon, Joe
76QuadC
85MidldA-10
86MidldA-14MG

Maddox, Elliott
71MLB/St-545
71OPC-11
71T-11
72OPC-277
72T-277
72T/Cloth-21
73OPC-658
73T-658
74OPC-401
74T-401
75Ho-90
75K-9
75OPC-113
75T-113
75T/M-113
76OPC-503
76SSPC-451
76T-503
77T-332
78Ho-133
78T-442
79OPC-28
79T-69
80OPC-357
80T-707
81D-397
81F-326
81OPC-299
81T-299

Maddox, Garry
73OPC-322
73T-322
74OPC-178
74T-178
74T/St-107
75Ho-43
75Ho/Twink-43
75K-37
75OPC-240
75T-240
75T/M-240
76OPC-38
76T-38
77K-37
77OPC-42
77T-520
78Ho-40
78K-28
78OPC-93
78T-610
78Wiffle/Discs-42
79BK/P-20
79K-16
79OPC-245
79T-470
80BK/P-10
80OPC-198
80T-380
81Coke
81D-55
81F-19
81F/St-70
81OPC-160
81T-160
81T/HT
81T/St-204
82D-315
82F-248
82F/St-57
82OPC-20
82T-20
82T/St-73
83D-63
83F-164
83OPC-41
83T-615
84D-305
84F-39
84F/St-122
84Nes/792-755
84OPC-187
84T-755
84T/St-123
85CIGNA-11
85D-137
85F-259
85OPC-235
85T-235
85T/St-121
86D-407
86F-445
86OPC-362
86T-585
86T/St-117

Maddox, Jerry
78Richm
79Richm-6

Maddox, Leland
87Madis-13

Maddox, Nicholas
10Domino-73
12Sweet/Pin-141
D322
E104
E254
E270/2
E90/1
E95
M116
T205
T206

Maddux, Greg
86Pittsf-14
87Berg/Cubs-31
87D-36RR
87D/Rook-52
87F/U-U68
87Leaf-36RR
87T/Tr-70T
88Berg/Cubs-31
88D-539
88D/Best-82
88D/Cubs/Bk-539
88F-423
88OPC-361
88Peoria/Ko-21
88Peoria/Ko-34M
88T-361
88T/St-59
89B-284
89Cadaco-33
89Class-121
89D-373
89D/AS-56
89D/Best-37
89F-431
89F/BBMVP's-24
89F/Rec-5
89F/Superstar-28
89Mara/Cubs-31
89OPC-240
89Panini/St-49
89RedFoley/St-77
89Score-119
89Score/HotSt-48
89Score/YS/I-39
89Sf-108
89T-240
89T/Mini-4
89T/St-48
89UD-241
90D-158
90F-37
90Score-403
90Sf-211
90T-715
90UD-213

Maddux, Mike
85Cram/PCL-38
86Portl-15
87D-535
87F-179
87Maine/TCMA-5
87T-553
88F-309
88T-756
89B-391
89D-487
89F-576
89OPC-39
89Score-393
89T-39
89T/Big-74
89UD-338

90D-312
90T-154

Madison, Dave
52T-366
53Glen
53T-99

Madison, Helene
33SK-37

Madison, Scott
83Albuq-12
86Nashv-16
87Omaha-17
88Smok/Royals-18
88T/Tr-63T
89AAA/Pro-2
89Nashvl-14
89Nashvl/CMC-21
89Nashvl/Pro-1271

Madlock, Bill
74OPC-600R
74T-600R
75Ho-125
75Ho/Twink-125
75OPC-104
75T-104
75T/M-104
76Crane-31
76Ho-100
76K-20
76MSA/Disc
76OPC-191LL
76OPC-640
76SSPC-309
76T-191LL
77Ho-118
77K-43
77OPC-1LL
77OPC-56
77T-1LL
77T-250
77T/CS-25
78Ho-117
78OPC-89
78T-410
79Ho-138
79OPC-96
79Pol/Giants-18
79T-195
80OPC-30
80T-55
81Coke
81D-252
81F-381
81OPC-137
81T-715
81T/St-213
82D-653
82Drake-23
82F-485
82F/St-77
82K-55
82OPC-365
82T-161LL
82T-365
82T-696TL
82T/St-1
82T/St-83
83D-311
83D/AAS-30
83Drake-15
83F-309
83K-18
83OPC-335
83T-291
83T-645
83T/Gloss-26
83T/Gloss40-26
83T/St-275
84D-113
84D-20
84D/AAS-33
84D/Champs-22
84Drake-20
84F-253
84F/St-6
84FunFood/Pin-31
84MiltBrad-16
84Nes/792-131LL
84Nes/792-250
84Nes/792-696TL
84Nes/792-701LL
84OPC-250
84Ralston-26
84Seven-11E
84T-131
84T-250
84T-701
84T/Cereal-26
84T/Gloss40-19
84T/St-131
84T/St-99
84T/St/Box-12
84T/Super-8
84T/Super-8
85D-200
85F-468
85F/LimEd-19
85Leaf-185
85OPC-157
85Seven-11E
85T-560
85T/St-122
86D-617
86F-135
86F/Mini-29
86Leaf-238
86OPC-47
86Pol/Dodg-12
86S-131M
86S-181M
86S-58M
86S-88
86T-470
86T/St-12NLCS 86T/St-70
86TrueVal-23
86Woolwth-19
87D-155
87D/OD-78
87F-445
87F/Mini-65
87F/St-73
87F/U-U69
87Leaf-120
87Moth/Dodg-8
87OPC-276
87Pol/Dodg-5
87RedFoley/St-109
87S-130
87T-734
87T/St-67
87T/Tr-71T
88D-496
88F-63
88Leaf-232
88OPC-145
88Score-445
88Sf-123
88T-145
88T/St-266

Madrid, Alex
85Beloi-18
87Denver-10
88Denver/CMC-3
88Denver/Pro-1251
89D-604
89Score/HotRk-58
89ScrWB/CMC-5
89ScrWB/Pro-720

Madril, Mike
83Redwd-18
85Cram/PCL-3
86MidldA-15

Madsen, Erik
89GreatF-24

Madsen, Lance
89AubAs/Pro-2164

Maebe, Art
80Clint-11

Maeda, Koji
88SanJose/Cal-133
88SanJose/Pro-108

Mag, Rick
88Brist/Pro-1862

Magadan, Dave
86Tidew-17
87Class-19
87D-575
87D/Rook-34
87F-648M
87F/U-U70
87S/Rook-10
87Sf/Rook-3
87T-512
87T/GlossRk-9
88Class/Blue-230
88D-323
88D/Mets/Bk-323
88F-141
88Kahn/Mets-29
88Leaf-108
88MSA/Disc-13
88OPC-58
88RedFoley/St-51
88Score-41
88Score/YS/I-23
88Sf-83
88T-58
88T/St-104
89B-384
89D-408
89D/Best-264
89F-41
89Kahn/Mets-29
89OPC-81
89Score-312
89T-655
89T/Big-71
89UD-388
90D-383
90F-210
90Score-46
90Sf-173
90T-135
90UD-243

Magallanes, Everado
88Kinston/Star-16
89Canton/Best-23
89Canton/Pro-1309
89Canton/Star-13

Magallanes, William
86AppFx-13
88BirmB/Best-25

Magee, Lee
15CJ-147
D328-103
D329-108
D350/2-106
E135-103
M101/4-108
M101/5-106

Magee, Sherry
11Helmar-147
12Sweet/Pin-128
14CJ-108
14Piedmont/St-34
15CJ-108
BF2-53
D328-104
D329-109
E101
E102
E135-104
E300
E92
E94
L1-123
M101/4-109
M116
S81-98
T202
T205
T206
T213/blue
T215/brown
T216
T222
T3-31

Magee, Warren
87Clearw-14
88EastLAS/Pro-33
88Readg/Pro-871
89Readg/Best-2
89Readg/Pro-674
89Readg/Star-16

Maggio, Aggie
79WHave-29M
80WHave-22

Magistri, Greg
85Elmir-13

Maglie, Sal
51B-127
52B-66
52BR
52RM-NL14
52StarCal/L-78C
52TipTop
53B/Col-96
53RM-NL8
54B-105
54NYJour
55B-95
55Gol/Giants-18
55RM-NL6
57T-5
58T-43
59T-309
60NuCard-70
60T-456C
61NuCard-470
67T/Test/RSox-17CO
79TCMA-256
88Pac/Leg-85
89NiagFls/Puc-29
89Rini/Dodg-11
89Swell-99
Exh47
PM10/Sm-100

Magnante, Michael
89Memph/Best-21
89Memph/Pro-1198
89Memph/Star-15

Magnante, Rick
89NiagFls/Puc-25

Magner, Rich
75Water
79Albuq-17

Magnuson, Jim
72T-597

Magnusson, Brett
88GreatF-3
89Star/Wax-30
89VeroB/Star-16

Magrane, Joe
86ArkTr-12
87Class/Up-117
87D/Rook-40
87F/Slug-24
87F/U-U71
87Louvl-25
87S/Rook-11
87T/Tr-72T
88Class/Blue-240
88D-140
88D/Best-100
88F-40
88Louvl-31
88OPC-380
88Panini/St-385
88RedFoley/St-52
88Score-94
88Score/YS/I-9
88Sf-128
88Smok/Card-6
88T-380
88T/Gloss60-40
88T/JumboR-20
88T/St-51
88ToysRUs-15
89B-432
89Class-148
89D-201
89D/Best-131
89F-455
89F/LL-24
89OPC-264
89Panini/St-178
89Score-460
89Smok/Cards-12
89T-657
89T/Big-203
89T/Mini-35
89UD-103
90Class-145
90D-13DK
90D-163
90F-252
90Score-17
90Sf-151
90T-406AS
90T-578
90UD-242

Magrann, Tom
86Hagers-8
87Miami-24
89Canton/Best-10
89Canton/Pro-1313
89Canton/Star-14
90D-374

Magria, Javier
89Well/Puc-18

Magrini, Pete
66T-558R

Maguire, Fred
29Exh/4-2
31Exh/4-2
33Exh/4-1
R316

Mahaffey, Art
60T-138
61Bz-1
61T-433
61T/St-57
62Bz
62Exh
62J-199
62P-199
62P/Can-199
62Salada-112
62Shirriff-112
62T-550
62T/bucks
62T/St-171
63Bz-35
63Exh
63F-54
63J-183
63P-183
63Salada-10
63T-385
63T-7LL
63T/SO
64T-104
65T-446
66T-570
Exh47
WG10-32
WG9-32

Mahaffey, Leroy
33G-196
34DS-10

35BU-15
35Exh/4-14
35G-1B
35G-2B
35G-6B
35G-7B
R308-175
Mahan, George
76Wmspt
Mahaney, Dan
N172
Mahar, Eddie
87Syrac/TCMA-32
Mahlberg, Greg
77Tucso
78Cr/PCL-3
79Tucso-15
80Charl-6
80T-673R
81Indianap-12
88CharWh/Best-3
89CharWh/Best-25
89CharWh/Pro-1755
Mahler, Mickey
78T-703R
79T-331
80Port-10
81SLCty-8
82Spoka-4
84Louvl-28
85F/Up-U77
85Indianap-16
86F/Up-U70
86T/Tr-68T
87Louvl-18
Mahler, Rick
78Richm
80Richm-11
81Pol/Atl-42
82BK/Lids-16
82D-349
82F-440
82Pol/Atl-42
82T-126TL
82T-579
83D-527
83F-141
83OPC-76
83T-76
84Pol/Atl-42
85D-385
85F-332
85Ho/Braves-14
85OPC-79
85Pol/Atl-42
85T-79
85T/St-26
86D-21
86D-77
86D/DKsuper-21
86F-521
86Leaf-21DK
86OPC-39
86Pol/Atl-42
86T-437
86T/St-43
87D-190
87D/OD-41
87F-520
87OPC-242
87Smok/Atl-5
87T-242
87T/St-43
88D-389
88D/Best-114
88OPC-171
88Panini/St-239
88Score-319
88T-706
89B-302
89D-222
89D/Best-286
89D/Tr-24
89F-595
89F/Up-85
89K/Reds-42
89OPC-393
89Panini/St-35
89Score-229
89Score/Tr-79
89T-621
89T/St-29
89T/Tr-74T
89UD-74
89UD/Ext-760
90D-375
90F-425
90Score-87
90T-151
90UD-220
Mahomes, Pat
89Keno/Pro-1067
89Keno/Star-12
Mahoney, Jim
73OPC-356CO
73T-356C
74OPC-221CO
74T-221C
77Charl/MG
78Salem
80Port-6MG
81GlenF-22
88Portl/CMC-24
88Portl/Pro-650
Mahoney, Robert
52T-58
Maietta, Bub
89LittleSun-7
Maietta, Ron
89Brist/Star-15
Mails, John
E120
E121/120
E220
V100
W501-23
Mails, Walter
(Duster)
21Exh-99
28Exh/PCL-20
WG7-27
Main, Forrest
52T-397
53T-198
Main, Kevin
87CharWh-16
Mains, Willard
N172
Maisel, George
15CJ-158
21Exh-100
T222
WG4-14
Maitland, Mike
79AppFx-20
81GlenF-5
83GlenF-14
Majeski, Henry
41DP-120
48L-149
49B-127
50B-92
51B-12
51T/BB-2
52B-58
52T-112
55B-127
55Gol/Ind-18
55Salem
Exh47
R346-23
Majia, Alfredo
79LodiD-4
Majtyka, Roy
63Pep/Tul
77Indianap-2
78Indianap-2
79Indianap-2
82Evans-25MG
83BirmB-25
85IntLgAS-22
85Richm-26
86Richm-13
87Richm/TCMA-21
Makarewicz, Scott
89AubAs/Pro-2163
Makemson, Jay
87Oneon-18
88Oneon/Pro-2063
89Penin/Star-13
Maki, Timothy
82BurlR-6
83BurlR-9
83BurlR/LF-19
Maksudian, Michael
88MidwLAS/GS-48
89Mia/Star/22-15
Malarcher, Dave
74Laugh/Black-20
88Conlon/NegAS-9
Malarkey, William
C46-73
T206
Malave, Benito
86Wausa-13
87StPet-22
88ArkTr/GS-17
Malave, Omar
85Kingst-17
86Ventura-12
87Knoxv-4
88Myrtle/Pro-1181
89Knoxv/Best-14
89Knoxv/Pro-1127
89Knoxv/Star-13
Malchesky, Tom
88Hamil/Pro-1741
89Sprin/Best-19
Malden, Chris
79LodiD-18
Maldonado, Candy
79Clint
81Albuq/TCMA-21
82Albuq-21
83Albuq-14
83D-262
83F-212
83Pol/Dodg-20
84D-93
84Nes/792-244
84Pol/Dodg-20
84T-244
85D-250
85F-376
85T-523
85T/St-81
86F-136
86F/Up-U71
86Moth/Giants-9
86T-87
86T/Tr-69T
87D-327
87D/OD-102
87F-279
87F/AwardWin-23
87Leaf-216
87Moth/SFG-7
87OPC-335
87S-78
87T-335
87T/Mini-37
87T/St-94
88D-391
88D/Best-247
88F-89
88F/BB/AS-22
88F/Mini-118
88F/St-129
88KingB/Disc-16
88Leaf-239
88Moth/Giants-7
88OPC-190
88Panini/St-428
88Score-54
88Sf-126
88T-190
88T/Big-35
88T/St-95
88T/UK-44
89B-478
89Bimbo/Discs-2
89D-177
89F-333
89Moth/Giants-7
89OPC-269
89Panini/St-221
89RedFoley/St-78
89Score-47
89T-495
89T/Big-197
89T/St-89
89UD-502
90D-611
90F-62
90Score-138
90T-628
90UD-136
Maldonado, Carlos
88Brist/Pro-1863
Maldonado, Felix
87Elmir-30
Maldonado, Jerry
(Asst.) 89Reno/Cal-264
Maldonado, Johnny
89Sumter/Pro-1105
Maldonado, Pete
87Spart-2
88Clearw/Star-18
Maldonado, Phil
87Idaho-3
88Durhm/Star-11
89Durhm/Star-13
Maler, James
80Spoka-14
81Spoka-22
83SLCty-17
83T-54
84Nes/792-461
84T-461
85OKCty-20
86OKCty-11
Malespin, Gus
79Elmir-19
82Sprin-10
83Sprin/LF-25
Maley, Dennis
83Miami-27
Malinak, Mike
88Cedar/Pro-1164
89Cedar/Pro-911
89Cedar/Star-29
Malkin, John
81Watlo-19
82Watlo/B-12
82Watlo/C-20
83BuffB-10
84Cram/PCL-145
85Cram/PCL-247
Malkmus, Robert
58T-356
59T-151
60T-251
61T-530
Mallea, Luis
88AppFx/Pro-138
Mallette, Malcolm
52Park-60
Malley, Mike
89Greens/Pro-424
Mallicoat, Rob
86ColumAst-17
86Tucso-11
87ColAst/Pro-22
87ColumAst-22
87SLAS-15
88F-452
88Score/YS/II-10
89ColMud/Pro-131
89ColMud/Star-17
Mallinak, Mel
87Hagers-24
Mallory, Sheldon
78Syrac
79Tacom-21
Malloy, Bob
87Gasto-11
88Tulsa-22
89Tulsa/GS-15
Malmberg, Harry
60HenryH-2
61Union
Malone, Charles
(Chuck)
86Cram/PCL-136
87Clearw-4
88BBAmer-6
88EastLAS/Pro-34
88Readg/Pro-869
89Readg/Best-3
89Readg/Pro-656
89Readg/Star-17
Malone, Earl
88Boise/Pro-1617
Malone, Ed
47Signal
49B/PCL-31
50Remar
53Mother-20
Malone, Eddie
82Idaho-25
Malone, Jack
89Boise/Pro-1990
Malone, Kevin
80Batav-19
88James/Pro-1893
Malone, Perce
(Pat)
32Orbit/num-13
32Orbit/un-45
33G-55
35G-2D
35G-4D
35G-7D
R305
R308-192
R316
V354-30
Malone, Rubio
79Wisco-18
Malone, Todd
89Oneon/Pro-2122
Maloney, Chris
85Lynch-17
88Sprin/Best-25
89ArkTr/GS-2
Maloney, Jim
61Kahn
61T-436
62Kahn
63FrBauer-13
63Kahn
63T-444
64Bz-19
64Kahn
64T-3LL
64T-420
64T-5LL
64T/Coins-158AS
64T/Coins-60

64T/S-34
64T/St-32
64T/SU
65Kahn
65T-530
65T/E-68
65T/trans-19
66Bz-45
66Kahn
66OPC-140
66T-140
66T/RO-93
67Bz-45
67Kahn
67OPC-80
67T-80
68Kahn
68T-425
68T/3D
69Kahn
69MB-164
69MLB/St-130
69MLBPA/Pin-50
69T-362
69T/St-26
70K-10
70MLB/St-29
70OPC-320
70T-320
71MLB/St-348
71OPC-645
71T-645
72MB-203
72T-645
78TCMA-10

Maloney, Kevin
89Clmbia/Best-28
89Clmbia/GS-5

Maloney, Mark
88Kinston/Star-17

Maloney, Rich
87Sumter-18
88Durhm/Star-12
89Durhm/Star-14

Maloney, William A.
T206
WG3-28

Maloof, Jack
77Indianap-24
83Beaum-21
85Spok/Crm-12MG

Malpeso, Dave
84Pawtu-17
85Pawtu-7

Malseed, James
88Fresno/Cal-12
88Fresno/Pro-1232
89SanJose/Best-22
89SanJose/Cal-223
89SanJose/Pro-437
89SanJose/Star-18

Maltzberger, Gordon
49B/PCL-12

Malzone, Frank
55B-302
56T-304
57T-355
58T-260
58T-481AS
59Armour-12
59T-220
59T-519M
59T-558AS
60Armour-13A
60Armour-13B
60Bz-12
60T-310
60T-557AS
60T/tatt
60T/tatt-30
61Bz-9
61P-48
61T-173M
61T-445
61T/St-113
62Exh
62J-58
62P-58
62P/Can-58
62Salada-14
62Shirriff-14
62T-225
62T/bucks
62T/St-14
63Exh
63J-79
63P-79
63T-232
64T-60
64T/Coins-126AS
64T/Coins-7
64T/St-6
64T/SU
64T/tatt
64Wheat/St-27
65T-315
65T/E-37
66OPC-152
66T-152
78TCMA-177
80Elmir-37C
87Elmir-31
Exh47
PM10/Sm-101
PM10/Sm-102
WG10-33
WG9-33

Mamaux, Al
BF2-91
D327
D328-105
D329-110
D350/2-107
E120
E121/80
E122
E135-105
M101/4-110
M101/5-107
W514-19
W515-2
W575

Manabe, Bullet
88Fresno/Cal-21
88Fresno/Pro-1235

Manahan, Austin
89B-420

Mancini, Joe
88Boise/Pro-1626
88Fresno/Cal-3
88Fresno/Pro-1247
89Boise/Pro-1991

Mancini, Pete
85Newar-21

Mancuso, August
(Gus)
33G-237
33G-41
35BU-67
35G-1K
35G-2A
35G-3B
35G-4A
35G-4B
35G-5B
35G-7A
35Wheat
36Exh/4-5
37Exh/4-5
38ONG/Pin-18
40PB-207
41DP-38
R303/A
R303/B
R310
R332-24
V353-41
V355-9
W754

Mancuso, Frank
84Omaha-28
85Omaha-4

Mancuso, Paul
83Wisco/LF-22
84Visal-18
85Orlan-18
86Beaum-17

Manderfield, Steve
77Newar
78Newar
79BurlB-25
80BurlB-8
82ElPas-15

Mandeville, Bob
86Peoria-18

Mandl, Steve
89James/Pro-2151

Manering, Mark
87FtLaud-27

Manfre, Mike
83Cedar-20
83Cedar/LF-20
84Cedar-21
86Vermont-12
87Nashv-14

Mangham, Eric
87Bakers-19
88VeroB/Star-13
89SnAnt/Best-3

Mangiardi, Paul
83Erie-1

Mangrum, Lloyd
52Wheat

Mangual, Angel
70T-654R
71OPC-317R
71T-317R
72OPC-62
72T-62
73OPC-625
73T-625
75OPC-452
75T-452
75T/M-452
76SSPC-503
76Tucso-8

Mangual, Jose
(Pepe)
75OPC-616R
75T-616R
75T/M-616R
76OPC-164
76SSPC-335
76T-164
77T-552
78Tidew
79SLCty-22
80SLCty-22
81SLCty-22
82Spoka-22

Mangum, Leo
33G-162
V353-92

Mangum, Wade
83Idaho-9

Manion, Clyde
33G-80
V354-35

Manion, George A.
T206

Mankowski, Phil
77T-477R
78BK/T-17
78T-559
79T-93
80T-216
81Tidew-6
82Tidew-9

Mann, Bill
88Jaxvl/Best-15

Mann, Dave
61Union

Mann, Fred
N172
N690

Mann, Garth
(Red)
46Sunbeam
47Signal
47Sunbeam

Mann, Kelly
86Geneva-17
87Peoria-25
88CLAS/Star-30
88WinSal/Star-9
89CharlK-9
89SLAS-4
90D-46
90F-642
90Score-627
90Score/100Ris-56
90T-744
90UD-33

Mann, Les
D328-106
D329-111
D350/2-108
E135-106
M101/4-111
M101/5-108
W514-49

Mann, Scott
86WPalm-23
87Jaxvl-8
88Jaxvl/Pro-964

Mann, Skip
79LodiD-5
81VeroB-10

Manning, Dick
83GlenF-24

Manning, Henry
88CapeCod/Sum-150

Manning, James
N172
N284

Manning, Melvin
(Al)
77BurlB
78BurlB
81ElPas-3

Manning, Rick
76Ho-12
76Ho/Twink-12
76OPC-275
76SSPC-529
76T-275
77Ho-53
77K-15
77OPC-190
77Pep-12
77T-115
78Ho-91
78OPC-151
78T-11
79OPC-220
79T-425
80OPC-292
80T-564
80T/S-44
81D-202
81F-403
81OPC-308
81T-308
81T/SO-19
81T/St-69
82D-85
82F-374
82F/St-195
82OPC-202
82T-202
82T/St-179
82Wheat/Ind
83D-198
83F-413
83OPC-147
83T-757
83T/St-60
83T/X-65
83Wheat/Ind-20
84D-170
84F-205
84Gard-11
84Nes/792-128
84OPC-128
84Pol/Brew-28
84T-128
84T/St-299
85D-237
85F-586
85Gard-11
85OPC-389
85Pol/Brew-28
85T-603
85T/St-291
86D-368
86F-493
86OPC-49
86Pol/Brew-28
86T-49
87D-521
87F-349
87OPC-196
87T-706
88D-486
88F-168
88Score-593
88T-441

Manning, Rube
T204
T206
T3-107

Manning, Tony
75SnAnt

Manning, Vida
81ArkTr-23M

Manon, Ramon
87PrWill-23
89FtLaud/Star-14

Manos, Pete Charles
79OkCty

Manrique, Fred
82Syrac-18
83Syrac-17
84Syrac-12
85Indianap-12
86Louisvl-18
87Coke/WS-5
87F/U-U72
88Coke/WS-17
88D-493
88F-406
88Panini/St-57
88Score-139
88T-437
88T/JumboR-6
88ToysRUs-16
89B-66
89D-489
89F-503
89OPC-108
89Score-457
89T-108
89T/Big-84
89T/St-300
89UD-628
90D-165
90F-306
90Score-166
90T-242
90UD-392

Mansalino, Doug
85Crm/PCL-192C
Manser
C46-59
E254
Manship, Ray
78Newar
Mansolino, Doug
89Vanco/Pro-575
Manti, Sam
89Penin/Star-14
Mantick, Dennis
78OrlTw
79Toled-21
Mantilla, Felix
57T-188
58T-17
59T-157
60Lake
60T-19
61T-164
61T/St-44
62Salada-183
62Shirriff-183
62T-436
62T/bucks
62T/St-158
63J-198
63P-198
63T-447
64T-228
65OPC-29
65T-29
66T-557
66T/RO-112
67T-524
Mantle, Mickey
51B-253
52B-101
52BR
52StarCal/L-70G
52T-311
52TipTop
53B/Col-44M
53B/Col-59
53Briggs
53SM
53T-82
54B-65
54DanDee
54NYJour
54RH
54SM
55Armour-13A
55Armour-13B
55B-202
55SM
56T-135
56YellBase/Pin-20
57T-407M
57T-95
58T-150
58T-418M
58T-487AS
59Bz
59HRDerby-12
59T-10
59T-461M
59T-564AS
60Armour-14
60Bz-31
60NuCard-22
60NuCard-50
60P
60T-160M
60T-350
60T-563AS
60T/tatt-31
60T/tatt-92
61Bz-2
61NuCard-422
61NuCard-450
61P-4
61T-300
61T-406M
61T-44LL
61T-475MV
61T-578AS
61T/Dice-8
61T/St-196
62Bz
62Exh
62J-5
62P-5
62P/Can-5
62Salada-41
62Shirriff-41
62T-18M
62T-200
62T-318M
62T-471AS
62T-53LL
62T/bucks
62T/St-88
63Bz-1
63Exh
63J-15
63P-15
63Salada-56
63T-173M
63T-200
63T-2LL
63T/SO
64Bz-1
64T-331M
64T-50
64T/Coins-120
64T/Coins-131AS
64T/S-25
64T/St-53
64T/SU
64T/tatt
65Bz-1
65OldLond-30
65OPC-134WS 65OPC-3LL
65OPC-5LL
65T-350
65T-3LL
65T-5LL
65T/E-11
65T/trans-57
66Bz-7
66OPC-50
66T-50
66T/RO-57
67Bz-7
67OPC-103CL 67OPC-150
67OPC/PI-6
67T-150
67T/PI-6
67T/Test/SU-8
68Bz-11
68T-280
68T-490M
68T/G-2
68T/Post-18
69T-500
69T/decal
69T/S-24
69T/St-205
69Trans-30
72Laugh/GF-33
75OPC-194M
75OPC-195M
75OPC-200M
75T-194MV
75T-195MV
75T-200MV
75T/M-194MV
75T/M-195MV
75T/M-200MV
78TCMA-262
79TCMA-7
80Cram/Leg-6
80Laugh/3/4/5-18
80SSPC/HOF
82CJ-5
82KMart-1
83D/HOF-43pz
83D/HOF-7
83MLBPA/Pin-12
84D/Champs-50
84West/1-4
85CircK-6
85D/HOF-6
85Woolwth-23
86BLChew-6
86S/Dec-26
87KMart-5
87Nestle/DT-17
88Pac/Leg-7
89B-I5
89B-I6
89HOF/St-40
Exh47
PM10/L-21
PM10/Sm-103
PM10/Sm-104
PM10/Sm-105
PM10/Sm-106
PM10/Sm-107
PM10/Sm-108
PM10/Sm-109
WG10-13
WG9-16
Manto, Jeff
86QuadC-19
87PalmSp-4
88BBAmer-29
88MidldA/GS-21
88TexLgAS/GS-39
89Edmon/CMC-20
89Edmon/Pro-570
89F/Up-13
90F-137
Mantrana, Manny
87Fayette-12
88Clmbia/GS-19
Manuel, Barry
88CharlR/Star-14
89Tulsa/GS-16
Manuel, Charles
(Charlie)
70OPC-194
70T-194
71MLB/St-466
71OPC-744
71T-744
76SSPC-86
83Wisco/LF-27
85Orlan-22
86Toled-15MG
87Portl-22
88Gator-9CO
Manuel, Jerry
76OPC-596R
76T-596R
77Evansvl/TCMA-18
82F-195
83lowaC-17
87Indianap-5
Manuel, Jose
88SnAnt/Best-18
Manush, Heine
29Exh/4-29
31Exh/4-31
33Exh/4-16
33G-107
33G-187
33G-47
34DS-30
34Exh/4-16
34G-18
35BU-77
35Exh/4-16
35G-1C
35G-2C
35G-6C
35G-7C
37Wheat-8
39PB-94
40PB-176
54T-187
60F-18
61F-57
80Cram/Leg-2
80SSPC/HOF
86Conlon/1-19
88Conlon/AmAS-20
89HOF/St-36
89Smok/Dodg-16
R308-178
R310
R314
R316
R337-416
V353-47
V354-68
V355-73
W517-28
Manwaring, Kirt
87Shrev-10
87TexLgAS-22
88D-39
88F-651
88F/Mini-119
88Leaf-39RR 88Phoen/CMC-12
88Phoen/Pro-61
88Score-627
88T/Tr-64T
89B-469
89D-494
89D/Best-330
89F-334
89Moth/Giants-23
89Panini/St-208
89Score-619
89Score/HotRk-46
89Score/YS/I-22
89T-506
89UD-500
90D-59
90F-63
90Score-146
90T-678
90UD-457
Manzanillo, Josias
85Elmir-14
87NewBrit-21
89NewBrit/Pro-606
89NewBrit/Star-8
Manzanillo, Ravelo
83AlexD-27
85Nashua-15
88FSLAS/Star-43
88Tampa/Star-14
89BirmB/Best-13
Manzon, Howard
86Kenosha-15
Mapel, Steve
79Wisco-9
80OrlTw-6
80Toled-1
82OrlTw/B-20
Mapes, Cliff
50B-218
51B-289
51BR-D1
52B-13
52T-103
R346-33
R423-64
Maples, Tim
81Miami-18
Marabell, Scott
89Bakers/Cal-195
Marak, Paul
87Sumter-9
88Durhm/Star-13
89Greenv/Pro-1174
89Greenv/Star-14
89Greenvl/Best-17
Maranda, Georges
60T-479
61Clover-15
61Union
Maranville, Walter
(Rabbit)
14CJ-136
15CJ-136
21Exh-101
25Exh-23
26Exh-15
31Exh/4-1
33CJ/Pin-17
33DL-13
33G-117
34DS-3
35BU-37
35G-1J
35G-3A
35G-4A
35G-5A
50Callahan
60Exh/HOF-15
60F-21
61F-124
63Bz-14
69Bz/Sm
80Cram/Leg-3
80SSPC/HOF
87Conlon/2-47
89HOF/St-17
89Smok/Dodg-18
BF2-54
D327
D328-107
D329-112
D350/2-109
E120
E121/120
E121/80
E122
E135-107
E220
M101/4-112
M101/5-109
R300
R316
R328-10
V100
V354-4
V355-129
V61-90
W501-83
W515-50
W572
W573
W575
WG4-15
WG7-28
Marberry, Fred
(Firpo)
31Exh/4-31
33DH-31
33Exh/4-16
33G-104
34Exh/4-12
35BU-66
35G-1H
35G-3F
35G-5F
35G-6F
61F-125
R310
R315-A24
R315-B24
R332-47
V354-8
V355-10

Marcelle, Oliver
74Laugh/Black-3
Marcero, Doug
89NiagFls/Puc-16
Marchese, John
89QuadC/Best-18
89QuadC/GS-10
Marchese, Joseph
86Elmir-11
87Greens-11
88CLAS/Star-12
88Lynch/Star-10
89NewBrit/Pro-616
89NewBrit/Star-9
Marcheskie, Lee
82AlexD-2
83LynnP-5
85Nashua-16
Marchildon, Phil
49B-187
Marchio, Frank
53Exh/Can-53
Marchok, Chris
87Jamestn-28
88Rockford-23
89Jaxvl/Best-4
89Jaxvl/Pro-166
89Rockford-23
Marcuci
46Sunbeam
Marcum, John
34G-69
35G-8J
35G-9J
R314
V355-58
Mardsen, Steve
84BuffB-17
Marett, John
89Bluef/Star-14
Margoneri, Joe
57T-191
Marguardt, Chuck
88Gasto/Pro-1023
Maria, Esteban
75BurlB
Mariano, Bob
84CharO-12
85CharO-18
89Albany/Best-28
89Albany/Pro-324
Marichal, Juan
61T-417
61T/St-79
62J-140
62P-140
62P/Can-140
62T-505
62T/St-198
63J-109
63P-109
63Salada-5
63T-440
64T-280
64T-3LL
64T/Coins-157AS
64T/Coins-36
64T/S-37
64T/St-39S4 64T/SU
64Wheat/St-28
65Bz-24
65OPC-10LL
65OPC-50
65T-10LL
65T-50
65T/trans-20
66Bz-10
66T-221LL
66T-420
66T/RO-29
67Bz-10
67OPC/PI-28
67T-234LL
67T-236LL
67T-500
67T/PI-28
68Bz-5
68Coke
68OPC-107CL 68T-205
69Kelly/Pin-11
69MB-165
69MLB/St-203
69MLBPA/Pin-51
69NTF
69OPC-10LL
69OPC/DE-15
69T-10LL
69T-370
69T-572M
69T/DE-32
69T/S-64
69T/St-107
69Trans-32
70K-13
70MB-14
70MLB/St-128
70OPC-210
70OPC-466AS
70OPC-67LL
70OPC-69LL
70T-210
70T-466AS
70T-67LL
70T-69LL
70T/SO
70Trans-3
71Bz/Test-19
71MLB/St-256
71OPC-325
71T-325
71T/Coins-125
71T/tatt-1
72K-47
72MB-204
72T-567
72T-568A
73OPC-480
73T-480
74OPC-330
74T-330
74T/Tr-330T
78TCMA-2
83MLBPA/Pin-25
84Moth/Giants-3
86S/Dec-46
87KMart-6
88Pac/Leg-54
89Smok/Dodg-17
PM10/Sm-110
WG10-34
WG9-34
Marichal, Victor
75BurlB
Marietta, Lou
78Cedar
82WHave-8
Marigny, Ron
87GlenF-11
87Lakel-9
89Lakel/Star-15
Marina, Juan
87Columbia-18
88Clmbia/GS-7
89StLucie/Star-15
Marino, Mark
86QuadC-20
87PalmSp-30
88Stock/Pro-752
89Stock/Best-31M
89Stock/Pro-402M
89Stock/Star-28M
Marion, Marty
39Exh
47TipTop
48B-40
48L-97
49B-54
49Eureka-189
50B-88
51B-34
52B-85
53B/Col-52
60F-19
61F-58
61NuCard-473
79TCMA-99
Exh47
PM10/Sm-111
R346-3
W754
Maris, Roger
58T-47
59T-202
60T-377
60T-565AS
60T/tatt
60T/tatt-32
61Bz-5
61NuCard-416
61T-2
61T-44LL
61T-478MV
61T-576AS
61T/St-197
62Bz-14
62Exh
62J-6
62P-6
62P/Can-6
62Salada-23
62Shirriff-23
62T-1
62T-313M
62T-401M
62T-53LL
62T/bucks
62T/St-89
63Exh
63J-16
63P-16
63Salada-57
63T-120
63T-4LL
64T-225
64T-331M
65OldLond-31
65OPC-155
65T-155
66T-365
67OPC-45
67T-45
68T-330
72Laugh/GF-50
75OPC-198M
75OPC-199M
75T-198MV
75T-199MV
75T/M-198MV
75T/M-199MV
76Laugh/Jub-30
78TCMA-11
79T-413M
79TCMA-161
80Cram/Leg-101
85Woolwth-24
86T-405M
87KMart-7
88Pac/Leg-89
Exh47
PM10/L-22
PM10/L-23
PM10/Sm-112
PM10/Sm-113
PM10/Sm-114
WG10-14
WG9-17
Markell, Duke
52Park-19
Markert, Jim
86Penin-16
88BirmB/Best-5
Markham, Bobby
80WHave-12
Markland, Gene
V362-37
Markle, Cliff
E120
Markley, Scot
86Ashvl-18
87Osceola-23
Marks, John
82Clint-28
83Wisco/LF-26GM
Marlowe, Richard
53Glen
55B-91
Marone, Lou
70T-703
71MLB/St-206
Maropis, Pete
76AppFx
Marquard, Richard
(Rube)
10Domino-75
11Helmar-130
12Sweet/Pin-116
72Laugh/GF-14
80SSPC/HOF
86Conlon/1-27
89HOF/St-66
89Smok/Dodg-19
BF2-58
D303
D304
D328-108
D329-113
D350/2-110
E106
E120
E135-108
E224
E254
E90/1
E96
L1-111
M101/4-113
M101/5-110
S74-87
S81-86
T202
T205
T206
T207
T213/blue
T213/brown
T215/blue
T215/brown
T215/brown
T216
T222
T227
V100
W572
WG4-16
WG5-27
WG6-26
Marquardt, Chuck
89Gasto/Pro-1010
Marquardt, John
84Madis/Pol-12
85Huntsvl/BK-18
86Orlan-11
Marquess, Mark
88T/Tr-65T
Marquez, Edgar
88Myrtle/Pro-1170
88StCath/Pro-2025
Marquez, Edwin
86QuadC-21
87MidldA-12
88Edmon/CMC-19
88Edmon/Pro-575
89Edmon/CMC-13
89Edmon/Pro-552
Marquez, Gonzalo
73OPC-605R
73T-605R
74OPC-422
74T-422
Marquez, Isidrio
89SnAnt/Best-16
Marr, Alan
83Clint/LF-18
85Evrt/Cram-8CO
Marr, Charles
N172
Marrero, Conrado
51B-206
52T-317
53Briggs
53T-13
54B-200
Marrero, Oreste
89Beloi/Star-15
89Star/Wax-5
Marrero, Roger
89AubAs/Pro-2181
Marrero, Vilato
89Beloi/Star-16
Marrett, Scott
86PalmSp-21
86PalmSp/Smok-13
87SnBer-15
Marris, Mark
87Oneon-26
88PrWill/Star-16
89PrWill/Star-12
Marrs, Terry
87Elmir-10
87Elmir/Red-10
88Elmir-22
89WinHav/Star-14
Marsans, Armando
14CJ-134
15CJ-134
D328-109
D350/2-111
E135-109
E224
M101/5-111
T207
Marsh, Fred
52T-8
53T-240
54T-218
55Esskay
55T-13
55T/DH-39
56T-23
Marsh, Quinn
88Greens/Pro-1552
89Cedar/Best-4
89Cedar/Pro-929
89Cedar/Star-10
Marsh, Randy
88Umpire-43
89Umpires-41
Marsh, Tom
88Batav/Pro-1676
89Spart/Pro-1047
89Spart/Star-15
Marsh, Trent
89Stock/Star-26M
Marshall, Bret
89SoBend/GS-13
Marshall, Charlie
V362-35
Marshall, Clarence
43Centen-18

52NTea
52T-174
Marshall, Dave
69T-464
70OPC-58
70T-58
71MLB/St-159
71OPC-259
71T-259
72MB-205
72T-673
73OPC-513
73T-513
Marshall, Jim
74OPC-354CO
75OPC-638MG
Marshall, John
88Martins/Star-26
89Spart/Pro-1045
89Spart/Star-16
89Star/Wax-56
Marshall, Keith
76Indianap-19
Marshall, Max
40Hughes-13
47Smith-22
Marshall, Mike A.
79LodiD-6
81Albuq/TCMA-16
82Albuq-22
82D-562
82F-13
82T-681R
83D-362
83F-211
83OPC-324
83Pol/Dodg-5
83T-324
84D-348
84F-105
84FunFood/Pin-64
84Nes/792-634
84OPC-52
84Pol/Dodg-5
84T-634
84T/St-85
85D-12
85D-296
85D/AAS-22
85D/DKsuper-12
85F-377
85Leaf-12DK
85OPC-85
85T-85
85T/St-72
86D-52
86Drake-8
86F-137
86F/Mini-30
86F/St-71
86Leaf-40
86OPC-26
86Pol/Dodg-5
86S-89
86T-728
86T/St-71
87D-176
87D/OD-77
87F-446
87F/McCror-25
87Moth/Dodg-5
87OPC-186
87Pol/Dodg-3
87RedFoley/St-31
87S-82
87Seven-W8
87Smok/Dodg-20
87Smok/Dodg-21
87T-664
87T/St-66
88D-229
88D/Best-178
88F-522
88Moth/Dodg-5
88OPC-249
88Panini/St-315
88Pol/Dodg-5
88Score-135
88Sf-220
88Smok/Dodg-16
88Smok/Dodg-29
88T-249
88T/Big-133
88T/St-69
89B-350
89D-110
89D/Best-204
89D/GrandSlam-2
89F-66
89F/BBMVP's-25
89F/WS-7
89Moth/Dodg-5
89OPC-323
89Panini/St-108
89Pol/Dodg-4
89Score-186
89Sf-54
89Smok/Dodg-101
89Smok/Dodg-84
89T-582
89T/Big-48
89T/Coins-18
89T/St-67
89T/UK-48
89UD-70
89Woolwth-26
90D-84
90F-401
90Score-384
90T-198
90UD-262
Marshall, Mike G.
68T-201
69OPC-17
69T-17
71MLB/St-133
71OPC-713
71T-713
72OPC-505
72T-505
73OPC-355
73T-355
73T/Lids-30
74OPC-208LL
74OPC-73
74T-208LL
74T-73
74T/St-57
74T/Tr-73T
75K-36
75OPC-313LL
75OPC-330
75OPC-6RB
75T-313LL
75T-330
75T-6M
75T/M-313LL
75T/M-330
75T/M-6M
76OPC-465
76T-465
77T-263
82F-532
Marshall, R. James
(Jim)
52Mother-9
58T-441
59T-153
60T-267
61T-188
62T-337
74T-354C
75T-638MG
75T/M-638MG
76SSPC-308
76T-277MG
84Nashvl-13MG
86BuffB-17MG
Marshall, Randy
89Butte/SP-20
89Fay/Pro-1581
Marshall, Willard
47TipTop
48B-13
49B-48
49Eureka-118
49Royal-17
50B-73
50Drake-17
51B-98
52B-97
52T-96
53B/Col-58
53T-95
54B-70
55B-131
79TCMA-124
D305
Exh47
R423-65
Marshall, William R.
(Doc)
T206
T213/brown
Marte, Alexis
84Visal-4
85Orlan-7
86Toled-16
87Portl-17
Marte, Roberto
86Erie-18
87Erie-10
88Savan/Pro-341
89Sprin/Best-21
Marte, Vic
78Charl
Martel, Ed
87Oneon-30
88Oneon/Pro-2040
89FtLaud/Star-15
Martel, Jay
87Savan-7
Marten, Tom
88Keno/Pro-1405
Marteniz, Ivan
88Wythe/Pro-1995
Martes, Sixto
84Evrt/Cram-14
Martig, Rich
86Modesto-19
Martin, Al
86Sumter-17
87Sumter-24
88MidwLAS/GS-19
89Durhm/Star-15
Martin, Alfred
(Billy)
48Signal
48Smith-17
49Remar
52BR
52T-175
53B/Col-118
53B/Col-93M
53T-86
54B-145
54RH
54T-13
56T-181
57T-62
58T-271
59Kahn
59T-295
60Kahn
60T-173
61T-89
61T/RO-26
61T/St-20
62J-84
62P-84
62P/Can-84
62Salada-43
62Shirriff-43
62T-208
69T-547
71OPC-208MG
71T-208
72OPC-33
72OPC-34IA
72T-33
72T-34IA
73OPC-323MG
73T-323MG
74OPC-379MG
74T-379MG
75OPC-511MG
75T-511MG
75T/M-511MG
76SSPC-453
76T-17MG
77T-387MG
78BK/Y-1
78T-721
79TCMA-143
81D-479
81F-581
81T-671MG
82D-491
82Granny-9
82T/St-115
83D-575
83T-156
83T/X-66
84Nes/792-81MG
84T-81
85T/Tr-78T
86T-651
87Moth/A's-23
PM10/L-24
Martin, Boris
(Babe)
49B-167
Martin, Chris
88Keno/Pro-1397
Martin, Darryl
87Fayette-10
89Fay/Pro-1585
Martin, Derrell
61Union
Martin, Elwood
(Speed)
E121/120
W501-55
Martin, Fred
79TCMA-121
Martin, Gregg
89StCath/Pro-2070
Martin, Herschel
39PB-12
40PB-100
46Remar
47Remar-12
47Signal
Martin, Jake
56T-129
Martin, Jared
80Wichi-16
82IowaC-7
Martin, Jerry
76SSPC-475
77T-596
78T-222
79T-382
80OPC-256
80T-493
81D-555
81F-295
81OPC-103
81T-103
81T/SO-98
81T/Tr-798
82D-298
82F-394
82T-722
82T/Tr-65T
83D-138
83F-117
83OPC-309
83T-626
84F/X-74
84Nes/792-74
84T-74
84T/X-74
85T-517
Martin, Joey
75Lafay
77Phoen
Martin, John
77AppFx
80Evans-14
82D-343
82F-121
82Louvl-15
82T-236
83D-617
83StPet-9
83T-721
84ArkTr-17
84Nes/792-24
84T-24
86ArkTr-13
87Louvl-19
88Louvl-32
88Louvl/CMC-3
88Louvl/Pro-423
89ScrWB/CMC-3
89ScrWB/Pro-719
Martin, John
(Pepper)
32Orbit/num-21
32Orbit/un-46
33DL-17
33G-62
34DS-26
34Exh/4-8
35BU-125
35BU-7
35Exh/4-8
35G-2F
35G-4F
35G-7F
35Wheat
36G
36Wheat
37Wheat
38Wheat
62Pep/Tul
63Pep/Tul
80Cram/Leg-106
86Conlon/1-22
88Conlon/3-18
88Conlon/NatAS-14
R305
R306
R308-159
R310
R311/Gloss
R312
R313
R314
R332-36
V353-62
Martin, Joseph C.
(J.C.)
60L-92
60T-346
61T-124
61T/St-124
62T-91
62T/St-27

63T-499
64T-148
65T-382
66OPC-47
66T-47
67T-538
68T-211
69MB-166
69OPC-112
69T-112
70OPC-308WS 70OPC-488
70T-488
71MLB/St-37
71OPC-704
71T-704
72MB-206
72T-639
73OPC-552
73T-552
74OPC-354CO
74T-354C

Martin, Justin
89QuadC/Best-11

Martin, Lefty
49Eureka-40

Martin, Mark
87Idaho-4
88Oneon/Pro-2068

Martin, Mike
82Amari-9
83Beaum-1
84Cram/PCL-227
85Cram/PCL-217
86Pittsf-15

Martin, Morris
52T-131
53B/BW-53
53T-227
54B-179
54T-168
58T-53
59T-38

Martin, Norberto
87CharWh-25
88Tampa/Star-15

Martin, R. Hollis
81VeroB-11

Martin, Renie
80T-667R
81D-103
81F-39
81OPC-266
81T-452
82D-238
82F-414
82T-594
82T/Tr-66T
83D-272
83F-267
83T-263
84D-445
84F-381
84Nes/792-603
84T-603
85Omaha-14
86Omaha-14

Martin, Russ
87Jamestn-1

Martin, Sam
81Batav-17
82Watlo/B-17
82Watlo/C-21
83Sprin/LF-4

Martin, Steve
82VeroB-8
85Cram/PCL-172
89Spoka/SP-18

Martin, Stuart
37Exh/4-8
38Exh/4-8

Martin, T. Eugene
70T-599R

Martin, Tom
89Bluef/Star-15

Martin, Tony
77LodiD

Martin, Vic
83Chatt-7
86Calgary-13

Martina, Mario
89PalmSp/Cal-37

Martindale, Denzel
77StPet

Martineau, Paul Peter
86Jamestn-15

Martinez, Alfredo
(Fred)
79Jacks-24
81D-172
81F-288
81SLCty-9
81T-227
82Spoka-5
82T-659

Martinez, Angel
88Modesto-24
88VeroB/Star-14
89Madis/Star-14

Martinez, Art
84Memph-4

Martinez, Bert
83TriCit-20

Martinez, Carlos
86Albany/TCMA-9
87Hawai-21
88BirmB/Best-16
89D/Rook-14
89Score/Tr-103
89Vanco/CMC-17
89Vanco/Pro-579
90D-531
90F-540
90Score-314
90Score/100Ris-70
90Sf-213
90T-461
90UD-347

Martinez, Carmelo
83IowaC-16
84D-623
84F-497
84F/X-75
84Moth/Padres-20
84Nes/792-267
84T-267
84T/St-383
84T/X-75
85D-478
85F-40
85Moth/Padres-24
85OPC-365
85T-558
85T/St-157
85T/St-375
86D-324
86F-329
86OPC-67
86T-67
86T/St-109
87Bohem-14
87D/OD-151
87F-423
87OPC-348
87T-348
88Coke/Padres-14
88D-287
88F-591
88Leaf-142
88OPC-148
88Panini/St-412
88Score-181
88Smok/Padres-17
88T-148
88T/Big-238
88T/Coins-47
88T/St-106
89B-459
89Bimbo/Discs-1
89D-601
89F-311
89OPC-332
89Panini/St-204
89Score-517
89T-449
89T/Big-11
89UD-365
90Class-56
90D-482
90F-162
90Score-114
90T-686
90UD-592

Martinez, Chito
85FtMyr-16
87Omaha-7
88Memph/Best-21
89Memph/Best-12
89Memph/Pro-1200
89Memph/Star-16

Martinez, Christian
83StPet-10

Martinez, Dave
83QuadC-26
86IowaC-17
87Berg/Cubs-1
87D-488
87T/Tr-73T
88D-438
88D/Best-149
88D/Cubs/Bk-438
88F-424
88Panini/St-266
88Score-223
88T-439
89B-370
89D-102
89F-384
89OPC-395
89Score-77
89T-763
89UD-444
90D-452
90F-353
90Score-27
90T-228
90UD-470

Martinez, David
86PalmSp-22
87MidldA-2
88MidldA/GS-20
89MidldA/GS-22

Martinez, Domingo
86Ventura-13
87Duned-23
88Knoxv/Best-6
88SLAS-25
89Knoxv/Best-15
89Knoxv/Pro-1148
89Knoxv/Star-12

Martinez, Edgar
86Chatt-17
87Calgary-1
88Calg/CMC-16
88Calg/Pro-782
88D/Rook-36UER 88F-378
89B-216
89D-645
89D/Rook-15
89F-552
89Moth/Sea-11
89Panini/St-428
89Score-637
89Score/HotRk-40
89UD/Ext-768
90F-520
90Score-324
90T-148
90UD-532

Martinez, Felix
(Tippy)
76OPC-41
76T-41
77OPC-254
77T-238
78T-393
79T-491
80T-706
81D-354
81F-179
81OPC-119
81T-119
82D-205
82F-171
82T-583
83D-357
83F-65
83OPC-263
83T-621
84D-472
84F-12
84F-635IA
84Nes/792-215
84OPC-215
84T-215
84T/St-208
85D-210
85F-182
85OPC-247
85T-445
85T/St-200
86D-514
86F-280
86OPC-82
86T-82
87OPC-269
87RedFoley/St-14
87T-728

Martinez, Fred
85Louvl-20
86Louisvl-19

Martinez, Gabriel
(Tony)
63T-466R
64T-404
66T-581

Martinez, Gil
87Greens-15
88Lynch/Star-11
89Lynch/Star-13

Martinez, J. Dennis
77T-491R
78T-119
79OPC-105
79T-211
80OPC-2
80T-10
81D-533
81F-180
81OPC-367
81T-367
82D-79
82F-170
82OPC-135
82T-165LL
82T-712
82T/St-10LL
83D-231
83F-64
83OPC-167
83T-553
84D-633
84F-11
84Nes/792-631
84T-631
85D-514
85F-181
85T-199
86D-454
86F-279
86T-416
87F-324
87Indianap-31
87OPC-252
87T-252
88D-549
88D/Best-146
88F-188
88Leaf-262
88OPC-76
88Score-601
88T-76
88T/St-84
89B-359
89Class-45
89D-106
89D/Best-90
89F-385
89OPC-313
89Panini/St-114
89Score-114
89Score/HotSt-13
89Sf-106
89T-313
89T/St-74
89UD-377
90D-156
90F-354
90Score-47
90Sf-53
90T-763
90UD-413

Martinez, John
(Buck)
70T-609
71OPC-163
71T-163
72OPC-332
72T-332
75OPC-314
75T-314
75T/M-314
76A&P/KC
76OPC-616
76SSPC-165
76T-616
77T-46
78T-571
79Ho-32
79T-243
80T-477
81D-444
81F-526
81T-56
81T/Tr-799
82D-561
82OPC-314
82T-314
83D-178
83F-433
83OPC-308
83T-733
84D-612
84F-161
84Nes/792-179
84OPC-179
84T-179
84Tor/Fire-24
85F-114
85OPC-119
85OPC/Post-13
85T-673
85Tor/Fire-21
86Ault-13
86F-66
86OPC-363
86T-518
86Tor/Fire-24
87F-235

Martinez, Jose
70OPC-8

70T-8
71MLB/St-207
71OPC-712
71T-712
77DaytB/MG
79OkCty
80OkCty
88Berg/Cubs-CO
88StCath/Pro-2024

Martinez, Julian
87Savan-19
88StPet/Star-15
89ArkTr/GS-11

Martinez, Louis
89SnAnt/Best-14

Martinez, Luis
86Cram/PCL-57
87Madis-8
88FSLAS/Star-11
88Modesto/Cal-74
89Savan/Pro-350

Martinez, Nicio
88Batav/Pro-1667

Martinez, Orlando
(Marty)
67T-504
68T-578
69MB-167
69T-337
70OPC-126
70T-126
71MLB/St-85
71OPC-602
71T-602
72MB-207
72OPC-336
72T-336
72T/Cloth-22
80Wausa-23
81Spoka-32MG

Martinez, Orlando
61Clover-16

Martinez, Pedro
89CharRa/Pro-992

Martinez, Porfi
86Lakel-12

Martinez, Rafael
88StCath/Pro-2026
89Myrtle/Pro-1467

Martinez, Ramon
86Bakers-20
87VeroB-7
88BBAmer-21
88SnAnt/Best-1
88TexLgAS/GS-28
89AAA/Pro-47
89Albuq/CMC-7
89Albuq/Pro-69
89Class-130
89D-464
89D/Rook-45
89F-67
89Pol/Dodg-24
89Princet/Star-12
89Score-635
89Score/HotRk-55
89Score/YS/I-40
89Sf-224M
89T-225
89UD-18
90Class-76
90D-685
90F-402
90Score-461
90Score/100Ris-59
90Sf-68
90T-62
90UD-675

Martinez, Randy
83Sprin/LF-19

Martinez, Ray
81Batav-13
83Watlo/LF-19

Martinez, Rey
85Lynch-23

Martinez, Roman
89PalmSp/Cal-38
89PalmSp/Pro-467

Martinez, Silvio
76Shrev
79T-609
80OPC-258
80T-496
81D-429
81F-546
81T-586
82Charl-7
82D-469
82F-122
82T-181

Martinez, Ted
71OPC-648R
71T-648R
72T-544
73OPC-161
73T-161
74OPC-487
74T-487
75OPC-637
75T-637
75T/M-637
76OPC-356
76SSPC-499
76T-356
78T-546
79OPC-59
79T-128
80Albuq-14
80Pol/Dodg-23
80T-191

Martinez, Thomas
83AlexD-17

Martinez, Tino
88T/Tr-66TOLY 89B-211
89T/Big-93
89Wmspt/Pro-635
89Wmspt/Star-13
90Score-596
90UD-37

Martinez, Wilfredo
83Erie-5

Marting, Tim
71OPC-423R
71T-423R

Martinson, Evon
78Clint
79LodiD-21

Martinson, Mike
75QuadC
76QuadC

Marto, Johnny
T3/Box-61

Marty, Joe
40PB-216
41PB-28
46Sunbeam
47Signal
47Sunbeam
49B/PCL-26
52Mother-20

Martyn, Bob
58T-39
59T-41
79TCMA-254

Martz, Randy
80Wichi-7
81F-300
81T-381R
82D-126
82F-600
82RedLob
82T-188
82T-456TL
83D-151
83F-501
83T-22
84Richm-18
85Cram/PCL-66

Marx, Bill
86CharRa-14
88River/Cal-214
88River/Pro-1424
89River/Cal-14
89River/Pro-1416

Marx, Jerry
62Pep/Tul
63Pep/Tul

Marzan, Jose
88Visal/Cal-155
88Visal/Pro-89
89Visal/Cal-111
89Visal/Pro-1443

Marzano, John
85T-399
86NewBrit-16
87Pawtu-1
87Pawtu/TCMA-11
87S/Rook-49
88Class/Red-189
88D-421
88D/RedSox/Bk-421
88F-357
88Leaf-245
88Score-584
88T-757
88ToysRUs-17
89Pawtu/CMC-17
89Pawtu/Dunkin-20
89Pawtu/Pro-687

Mashore, Clyde
71OPC-376R
71T-376R
73OPC-401
73T-401

Masi, Phil
49B-153
49Eureka-15
50B-128
51B-160
51T/RB-19
52T-283
R346-12

Maskery, Sam
N172

Maskovich, George
52Park-97

Mason, Don
66T-524R
69T-584
71MLB/St-231
71OPC-548
71T-548
72T-739

Mason, Henry
60L-80
60T-331

Mason, Jim
72OPC-334R
72T-334R
73OPC-458
73T-458
74OPC-618
74T-618
74T/Tr-618T
75OPC-136
75T-136
75T/M-136
76SSPC-448
77OPC-211
77T-212
78T-588
79T-67
80OPC-259
80T-497

Mason, Martin
82Sprin-16
83Sprin/LF-7
84ArkTr-19
86StPet-18CO
87StPet-19
88Savan/Pro-336

Mason, Mike
82Tulsa-5
83OKCty-20
84F/X-76
84Rang-16
84T/X-76
85D-281
85F-562
85OPC-144
85Rang-16
85T-464
85T/St-354
86D-422
86F-565
86OPC-189
86Rang-16
86T-189
87D-284
87F-129
87F/U-U73
87OPC-208
87Smok/R-4
87T-646
88T-87

Mason, Rob
88WPalm/Star-17

Mason, Roger
83BirmB-24
84Evans-21
85Cram/PCL-190
86D-633
86F/Up-U72
86Moth/Giants-23
86T/Tr-70T
87D-204
87F-280
87Moth/SFG-23
87T-526
88Phoen/CMC-4
88Phoen/Pro-62
89Tucso/CMC-4
89Tucso/Pro-195

Masone, Tony
80Cedar-9

Massarelli, John
87AubAs-1
88AubAs/Pro-1961
89Ashvl/Pro-945

Masse, Bill
88T/Tr-67T
89PrWill/Star-13
89Star/Wax-90
89T/Big-179

Massey, Jim
86Cram/PCL-17
87Everett-21

Massicotte, Jeff
88Peoria/Ko-15
89Peoria/Ko-5

Massie, Bret
88Spart/Star-24
88Spart/Star-8

Masters, Burke
88CapeCod/Sum-101

Masters, Dave
86WinSal-13
87Pittsf-14
88IowaC/CMC-9
88IowaC/Pro-533
89IowaC/CMC-6
89IowaC/Pro-1698

Masters, Frank
86GlenF-14
88Madis-15
89Madis/Star-15

Masterson, Walt
49B-157
50B-153
51B-307
52B-205
52T-186
53B/BW-9
53Briggs

Masuyama, Daryl
86Shrev-16TR

Mata, Vic
83Nashvl-11
84Colum-10
84Colum/Pol-14
85Colum-1
85D-629
85F-644
86Colum-15
86Colum/Pol-13
88RochR-12
88RochR-15
88RochR/CMC-23
88RochR/Gov-15
88RochR/Pro-197

Matas, Jim
86Geneva-18
87WinSal-26
88WinSal/Star-10

Matchett, Steve
89Brist/Star-16

Matchick, J. Tom
67OPC-72R
67T-72R
68OPC-113R
68T-113R
69MB-168
69T-344
70T-647
71MLB/St-419
71OPC-321
71T-321
72MB-208
73OPC-631
73T-631
88Domino-12

Mateo, Luis
89Madis/Star-16

Matheson, Bill
43Centen-19
44Centen-16
45Centen-16

Mathews, Chuck
86ColumAst-18

Mathews, Eddie
52T-407
53B/Col-97
53JC-21
53T-37
54B-64
54JC-41
54RM-NL23
54T-30
55B-103
55Gol/Braves-19
55JC-41
55T-155
56T-107
56T/Hocus-B21
56T/Pin-18
56YellBase/Pin-21
57T-250
58T-351M
58T-440
58T-480AS
59HRDerby-13
59T-212M
59T-450
60Armour-15
60P
60T-420
60T-558AS
60T/tatt
60T/tatt-33
61Bz-11

61NuCard-412
61P-106
61T-120
61T-43LL
61T/St-45
62Bz
62Exh
62J-147
62P-147
62P/Can-147
62Salada-111
62Shirriff-111
62T-30
62T/bucks
62T/St-148
63Exh
63J-151
63P-151
63T-275
64T-35
64T/Coins-33
64T/St-97
64T/SU
64T/tatt
65salada-28
65T-500
65T/E-26
66T-200
66T/RO-118
67OPC-166
67T-166
68OPC-58
68T-58
69MB-169
73OPC-237MG
73T-237MG
74OPC-634MG
74T-634MG
79TCMA-157
80Laugh/3/4/5-25
80SSPC/HOF
82CJ-2
83MLBPA/Pin-26
84West/1-17
85CircK-11
86BLChew-10
86S/Dec-34
86Sumter-18
87Durhm-16
87Nestle/DT-25
88Domino-13
88Greenv/Best-22
89HOF/St-25
89Kahn/Coop-8
89Pac/Leg-116
89Richm/CMC-10
89Richm/Ko-26
89Richm/Pro-845
Exh47
WG10-35
WG9-35

Mathews, Greg
86D/Rook-26
86F/Up-U73
86S/Rook-41
87D-208
87F-303
87Smok/Cards-8
87T-567
87T/Gloss60-60
87ToysRUs-20
88D-84
88D/Best-324
88F-41
88Louvl-33
88Score-226
88Smok/Card-7
88T-133
88T/Big-177
89D-281
89F-456
89Score-286
89T-97
89UD-531
90Score-537
90T-209
90UD-678

Mathews, Jim
78Ashev

Mathews, Nelson
63T-54R
64T-366
65OPC-87
65T-87

Mathews, Rick
81CharR-26
82FtMyr-22
84Memph-1

Mathews, Robert
N172
N690

Mathews, Terry
88CharlR/Star-15
89Tulsa/GS-17

Mathews, Tom
86Fresno/Smok-22

Mathewson, Christy
10Domino-76
11Helmar-131
12Sweet/Pin-117A
12Sweet/Pin-117B
14CJ-88
15CJ-88
40PB-175
48Exh/HOF
49Leaf/Prem-5
50Callahan
51T/CM
60Exh/HOF-16
60F-2
60NuCard-8
61F-59
61GP-24
61NuCard-477
61T-408M
63Bz/ATG-4
69Bz/Sm
72F/FFeat-3
72Laugh/GF-25
73F/Wild-22
80Cram/Leg-34
80Laugh/3/4/5-5
80Laugh/FFeat-22
80SSPC/HOF
83D/HOF-3
85Woolwth-25
86Conlon/1-23
86Conlon/1-32
86Conlon/1-46
87Conlon/2-3
89HOF/St-65
D303
D304
E101
E102
E103
E105
E106
E107
E224
E286
E90/1
E91
E93
E95
E98
L1-133
M116
PM1-11
R332-10
R423-68
S74-88
S81-108
T201
T202
T205
T206
T213/blue
T213/brown
T215/brown
T215blue
T216
T3-27
W514-72
W516-24
W555
WG4-17
WG5-28
WG6-27

Mathias, Carl
60T-139
61BeeHive-13

Mathiot, Mike
89Keno/Pro-1059
89Keno/Star-13

Mathis, Ron
83Tucso-4
84Cram/PCL-72
85F/Up-U78
85Moth/Ast-26
85T/Tr-79T
86F-305
86T-476
86Tucso-12
87Tucso-14
88ColSp/CMC-5
88ColSp/Pro-1548

Mathison, Chuck
84Greens-15

Matias, John
70OPC-444R
70T-444R
71OPC-546
71T-546

Matilla, Pedro
88Elmir-14
89WinHav/Star-15

Matlack, Jon
71OPC-648R
71T-648R
72OPC-141R
72T-141R
73K-12
73OPC-55
73T-55
74OPC-153
74OPC-471NLCS
74T-153
74T/DE-44
74T/St-66
75K-10
75OPC-290
75T-290
75T/M-290
76Ho-97
76K-49
76OPC-190
76SSPC-554
76T-190
77Ho-114
77OPC-132
77Pep-68
77T-440
78BK/R-5
78OPC-98
78T-25
78Wiffle/Discs-43
79Ho-122
79K-58
79OPC-159
79T-315
80OPC-312
80T-592
81D-266
81F-621
81F/St-51
81OPC-339
81T-656
81T/HT
81T/St-135
82D-215
82F-323
82F/St-176
82OPC-239
82T-239
83D-195
83F-572
83Rang-32
83T-749
84D-378
84F-422
84Nes/792-149
84T-149
89Pac/Leg-214
89River/Best-23
89River/Cal-26CO
89River/Pro-1408
89Tidew/CANDL-3

Matlock, Leroy
78Laugh/Black-32

Matos, Carlos
82Danvi-11

Matos, Francisco
89Modesto/Cal-283
89Modesto/Ch-24

Matos, Rafael
84Butte-16

Matrisciano, Ron
80Clint-7

Matsuo, Hideharu
87Miami-22

Mattern, Al
10Domino-77
11Helmar-80
12Sweet/Pin-68B
12Sweet/Pin-68A
E254
M116
S74-45
T201
T205
T206

Matthews
E254

Matthews, Gary
73OPC-606R
73T-606R
74OPC-386
74T-386
75Ho-31
75Ho/Twink-31
75OPC-79
75T-79
75T/M-79
76Ho-142
76OPC-133
76SSPC-110
76T-133
77Ho-142
77T-194
78Ho-19
78OPC-209
78T-475
78Wiffle/Discs-44
79Ho-42
79OPC-35
79T-85
80K-48
80OPC-186
80T-355
81D-306
81F-251
81OPC-186
81T-228
81T/SO-76
81T/St-144
81T/Tr-800
82D-441
82F-249
82F/St-58
82OPC-151
82T-680
82T/St-79
83D-420
83Drake-16
83F-165
83OPC-64
83T-780
83T/St-269
84D-233
84Drake-21
84F-40
84F/St-121
84F/X-77
84FunFood/Pin-70
84Nes/792-637TL
84Nes/792-70
84OPC-70
84Seven-23E
84SevenUp-36
84T-70
84T/St-118
84T/St-18LCS
84T/X-77
85D-239
85Drake-18
85F-61
85F/St-24
85Leaf-220
85OPC-210
85Seven-10S
85SevenUp-36
85T-210
85T/St-44
85T/Super-19
86D-76
86F-373
86Gator-36
86OPC-292
86S-66M
86T-485
86T/St-59
87Berg/Cubs-36
87F-568
87OPC-390
87Seven-C10
87T-390
87T/St-62
88OPC-156
88Score-599
88T-156
88T/St-223
89Swell-118

Matthews, Greg
88Score/YS/II-35

Matthews, Jeff
78Green

Matthews, Jeremy
89Wausa/GS-15

Matthews, W.C. (Wid)
21Exh-102

Mattick, Robert
80T-577MG
81D-570
81F-431
81T-674MG
82T-606MG

Mattimore, Michael
N172

Mattingly, Don
81Nashvl
82Colum-21
82Colum/Pol-19
84D-248
84F-131
84FunFood/Pin-77
84Nes/792-8
84OPC-8
84T-8
84T/St-325

85D-295
85D-651
85D-7
85D/AAS-48
85D/DKsuper-7
85D/HL-36
85D/HL-44
85D/HL-45
85Drake-19
85F-133
85F/LimEd-20
85F/St-37
85F/St-4
85Leaf-140M
85Leaf-7DK
85OPC-324
85Seven-12E
85T-665
85T/3D-8
85T/Gloss40-27
85T/St-171
85T/St-310
85T/Super-4
86BK/AP-19
86D-173
86D/AAS-50
86D/HL-48
86D/HL-53
86Dorman-13
86Drake-7
86F-109
86F-627M
86F-639M
86F/AS-1
86F/LimEd-27
86F/LL-22
86F/Mini-24
86F/Slug-21
86F/St-72
86Jiffy-6
86KayBee-19
86Leaf-103
86Meadow/Blank-8
86Meadow/Milk-5
86Meadow/Stat-5
86OPC-180
86OPC-J
86Quaker-18
86S-176M
86S-179M
86S-180M
86S-183M
86S-184M
86S-2
86S-54M
86S-75M
86S/Dec-65
86T-180
86T-712
86T/3D-15
86T/Gloss60-31
86T/Mini-28
86T/St-296
86T/Super-1
86T/WaxBox-J
86TrueVal-5
86Woolwth-20
87BK-13
87Class-10
87Class/Up-104
87D-52
87D/AAS-33
87D/HL-17
87D/HL-23
87D/HL-48
87D/OD-241
87Drake-8
87F-104
87F-638M
87F/AS-1
87F/AwardWin-24
87F/Excit-33
87F/GameWin-26
87F/Hottest-27
87F/Lim-26
87F/LL-28
87F/McCror-26
87F/Mini-66
87F/RecSet-20
87F/Slug-25
87F/St-131M
87F/St-74
87F/St-S8
87Ho/St-27
87Jiffy-6
87KayBee-19
87KMart-28
87Kraft-29
87Leaf-150
87MnM's-11
87MSA/Discs-6
87OPC-229
87Ralston-5
87RedFoley/St-106
87S-1
87S-159M
87S-75M
87Seven-E12
87T-500
87T-606AS
87T/Board-32
87T/Coins-17
87T/Gloss60-1
87T/HL-15
87T/Mini-65
87T/St-294
87Woolwth-15
88Woolwth-4
88Bz-11
88ChefBoy-16
88Class/Blue-211
88Class/Blue-247M
88Class/Red-151M
88Class/Red-152
88CMC/Kit-1
88CMC/Kit-20
88D-217
88D-BC21
88D/AS-1
88D/Best-1
88D/PopUp-1
88D/Y/Bk-217
88F-214
88F/AwardWin-23
88F/BB/AS-23
88F/BB/MVP-22
88F/Excit-25
88F/Head-1
88F/Hottest-24
88F/LL-25
88F/Mini-41
88F/RecSet-24
88F/Slug-26
88F/SS-22
88F/St-48
88F/TL-19
88FanSam-9
88KayBee-16
88KingB/Disc-15
88KMart-15
88Leaf-177
88MSA/Disc-3
88Nestle-15
88OPC-300
88Panini/St-152
88Panini/St-227M
88Panini/St-430
88RedFoley/St-53
88Score-1
88Score-650M
88Score-658HL
88Score/WaxBox-2
88Sf-1
88Sf-222
88Sf/Gamewin-1
88T-2RB
88T-300
88T-386
88T/Big-229
88T/Coins-19
88T/Gloss22-2
88T/Gloss60-11
88T/Mini-27
88T/RiteAid-22
88T/St-156
88T/St-299
88T/St-3
88T/St/Backs-35
88T/UK-45
89B-176
89Cadaco-34
89Class-106
89Class-5
89Crunch-8
89D-26DK
89D-74
89D/AS-21
89D/Best-1
89D/DKsuper-26DK
89F-258
89F/BBAS-28
89F/BBMVP's-26
89F/Excit-31
89F/Heroes-26
89F/LL-25
89F/Rec-6
89F/Superstar-29
89Holsum/Discs-15
89Holsum/Discs-4
89KayBee-20
89KMart/DT-12
89KMart/Lead-3
89Master/Discs-6
89Nissen-4
89OPC-26
89Panini/St-404
89Ralston-11
89RedFoley/St-79
89Score-100
89Score/HotSt-10
89Score/Mast-6
89Score/NWest-1
89Sf-50
89T-397AS
89T-700
89T/Big-50
89T/Coins-43
89T/DH-1
89T/Gloss60-51
89T/HeadsUp-19
89T/St-314
89T/St/Backs-2
89T/UK-49
89Tetley/Discs-1
89UD-200
89UD-693TC
90Class-16
90D-190
90F-447
90F-626
90F-638M
90F/WaxBox-C19
90Score-1
90Score/100St-10
90Sf-150
90T-200
90UD-191

Mattingly, Steve
89Boise/Pro-1989

Mattocks, Rich
84Greens-24

Mattox, Frank
85Beloi-11
86Stockton-18
87ElPas-8
88ElPas/Best-29
88TexLgAS/GS-38
89ElPas/GS-23

Mattson, Kurt
83Clint/LF-22
84Shrev/FB-11

Mattson, Ronnie
77Spart

Matula, Rick
80T-596
81D-317
81F-263
81T-611
82Evans-5

Matuszak, Len
80OkCty
81OkCty/TCMA-10
82OkCty-8
83Portl-8
83T-357
84D-549
84F-41
84Nes/792-275
84OPC-275
84T-275
85D-259
85F-260
85F/Up-U79
85OPC-226
85T-688
85T/Tr-80T
85Tor/Fire-22
86D-494
86F-138
86Pol/Dodg-17
86T-109
87D-423
87F-447
87Moth/Dodg-20
87Pol/Dodg-8
87T-457
88Pol/Dodg-17M
88Score-424
88T-92

Matzen, Mark
82Cedar-13

Mauch, Gene
49Eureka-63
51B-312
57T-342
61T-219
62T-374
63T-318
64T-157
65T-489
66T-411
67T-248
68OPC-122MG
68T-122
69T-606
70OPC-442MG
70T-442
71LaPizza-6
71OPC-59MG
71T-59
72OPC-276MG
72T-276
73OPC-377MG
73T-377MG
74OPC-531MG
74T-531MG
75OPC-101MG
75T-101MG
75T/M-101MG
76SSPC-597
77T-228MG
78T-601
79T-41MG
82D-141
83T-276
85Smok/Cal-24
85T/Tr-81T
86Smok/Cal-24
86T-81MG
87T-518MG
88T-774

Mauch, Thomas
87StPet-17
88StPet/Star-16

Maul, Al
N172
N690
WG1-61

Mauldin, Weldon
(Hunky)
62Pep/Tul
63Pep/Tul

Mauney, Terry
84CharO-2
85CharO-28
87CharO/WBTV-xx

Maurer, Rob
88Butte-15
89Star/Wax-7

Mauro, Carmen
52Park-71
53Exh/Can-47
79TCMA-109

Mauser, Tim
88Spart/Star-12
88Spart/Star-12
89Clearw/Star-14
89Star/Wax-13

Max, Bill
82Beloi-21
83ElPas-13
84Jacks-12
89River/Best-12

Maxey, Kevin
88StPet/Star-17

Maxie, Larry
64T-94R
78TCMA-59

Maxson, Dan
78Newar

Maxvill, Dal
62Pep/Tul
63T-49
64T-563
65OPC-78
65T-78
66T-338
67T-421
68OPC-141
68T-141
69MB-174
69MLB/St-213
69T-320
69T/St-117
70MLB/St-141
70OPC-503
70T-503
71MLB/St-278
71OPC-476
71T-476
72MB-214
72OPC-206
72T-206
73OPC-483
73T-483
74OPC-358
74T-358
78TCMA-241
82Pol/Atl-53CO
83Pol/Atl-53
84Pol/Atl-53

Maxwell, Charlie
52T-180
55B-162
55Esskay
57T-205
58T-380
59T-34M
59T-481
60L-48

60T-443
61P-37
61T-37
61T/RO-22
61T/St-154
62J-25
62P-25
62P/Can-25
62T-506
63J-41
63P-41
63T-86
64T-401

Maxwell, Jim
80Ashev-16

Maxwell, Marty
78OrlTw

May, Carlos
69T-654R
70K-16
70OPC-18
70T-18
71K-45
71OPC-243
71T-243
71T/Coins-144
72MB-209
72OPC-525
72T-525
73K-45
73OPC-105
73T-105
74OPC-195
74T-195
74T/St-157
75Ho-44
75OPC-480
75T-480
75T/M-480
76Crane-32
76Ho-34
76Ho/Twink-34
76MSA/Disc
76OPC-110
76SSPC-148
76T-110
77BK/Y-22
77T-568
77T-633M

May, Dave
68OPC-56R
68T-56R
69OPC-113
69T-113
70OPC-81
70T-81
71MLB/St-444
71OPC-493
71T-493
72T-549
73OPC-152
73T-152
74K-13
74OPC-12
74T-12
74T/DE-58
74T/St-196
75OPC-650
75T-650
75T/M-650
76Ho-148
76OPC-281
76SSPC-19
76T-281
78T-362
83Ander-5C

May, Davis
79Syrac-16

May, Derrick
87Peoria-12
88Peoria/Ko-35M
88WinSal/Star-11
89CharlK-5
90F-645M

May, Frank
E122

May, Jackie
E126-56

May, Jerry
65OPC-143R
65T-143R
66EH-12
66OPC-123R
66T-123R
67T-379
67T/Test/PP-13
68KDKA-12
68T-598
69MB-170
69MLB/St-186
69T-263
69T/St-87
70MLB/St-102
70OPC-423
70T-423
71MLB/St-420
71OPC-719
71T-719
72MB-210
72OPC-109
72T-109
73OPC-558
73T-558

May, Larry
82Orlan-20

May, Lee
66T-424R
67Kahn
67T-222R
68Kahn
68T-487
69Kahn
69MB-171
69MLB/St-131
69T-405
69T/St-27
69Trans-52
70MLB/St-30
70OPC-225
70OPC-65LL
70T-225
70T-65LL
71MLB/St-62
71OPC-40
71T-40
71T/Coins-29
71T/tatt-5
72K-37
72MB-211
72OPC-480
72OPC-89LL
72T-480
72T-89LL
73OPC-135
73T-135
73T/Lids-31
74OPC-500
74T-500
74T/St-33
75Ho-142
75OPC-25
75T-25
75T/M-25
76Ho-98
76OPC-210
76SSPC-389
76T-210
77Ho-55
77OPC-125
77OPC-3LL
77T-380
77T-3LL
77T-633M
78Ho-53
78OPC-47
78T-640
78Wiffle/Discs-45
79OPC-1
79T-10
80OPC-255
80T-490
81F-183
82D-570
82F-415
82T-132
83D-538
83F-118
83OPC-377
83OPC-378SV
83T-377
83T-378A
83T/St-9
85CircK-34
86Moth/Ast-12
88Kahn/Reds-CO
88LitFalls/Puc-1
89Clmbia/Best-10
89Clmbia/GS-15

May, Merrill
(Pinky)
39Exh
39PB-45
40PB-98
41DP-46
41PB-9

May, Milt
71OPC-343R
71T-343R
72OPC-247
72T-247
73OPC-529
73T-529
74OPC-293
74T-293
75Ho-35
75Ho/Twink-35
75OPC-279
75T-279
75T/M-279
76OPC-532
76SSPC-53
76T-532
76T/Tr-532T
77OPC-14
77T-98
78BK/T-2
78OPC-115
78T-176
79T-316
80OPC-340
80Pol/Giants-7
80T-647
81D-193
81OPC-273
81T-463
81T/St-237
82D-503
82F-395
82F/St-62
82OPC-242
82T-242
82T-576TL
82T/St-110
83D-312
83F-268
83T-84
83T/St-301
84D-386
84F-254
84Nes/792-788
84T-788
85D-410
85T-509

May, Rudy
65T-537R
69JB
70MLB/St-175
70OPC-203
70T-203
71JB
71MLB/St-349
71OPC-318
71T-318
72T-656
73OPC-102
73T-102
74OPC-302
74T-302
75OPC-321
75T-321
75T/M-321
76OPC-481
76SSPC-427
76T-481
77T-56
78Ho-115
78T-262
79OPC-318
79T-603
80OPC-281
80T-539
81F-90
81OPC-179
81T-179
81T-7LL
81T/HT
81T/St-3
82D-325
82F-41
82OPC-128
82T-735
83D-135
83F-385
83T-408
84D-626
84Nes/792-652
84T-652

May, Scott
86Albuq-14
87SnAnt-11
88OkCty/CMC-3
88OkCty/Pro-27
89D-636
89OkCty/CMC-5
89OkCty/Pro-1523

May, Ted
79QuadC-7

Mayberry, Greg
85VeroB-20
88VeroB/Star-15
89SnAnt/Best-19

Mayberry, John
70OPC-227R
70T-227R
71MLB/St-86
71OPC-148
71T-148
72OPC-373
72T-373
73OPC-118
73T-118
73T/Lids-32
74K-29
74OPC-150
74T-150
74T/DE-51
74T/St-184
75Ho-92
75OPC-95
75T-95
75T/M-95
76A&P/KC
76Crane-33
76Ho-91
76K-46
76MSA/Disc
76OPC-194LL
76OPC-196LL
76OPC-440
76SSPC-169
76T-194LL
76T-196LL
76T-440
77Ho-56
77OPC-16
77T-244
77T/CS-27
78OPC-168
78PapaG/Disc-40
78T-550
78Wiffle/Discs-46
79Ho-82
79OPC-199
79T-380
79T/Comics-17
80OPC-338
80T-643
81D-29
81Drake-31
81F-416
81OPC-169
81OPC/Post-13
81T-169
81T/SO-15
81T/St-139
82D-25DK
82D-306
82Drake-24
82F-619
82F/St-235
82OPC-382
82OPC-53TL
82OPC/Post-1
82T-470
82T-606TL
82T/St-248
82T/Tr-677
83F-386
83OPC-45
83T-45
85Syrac-20

Maye, A. Lee
60Lake
60T-246
61T-84
62J-156
62P-156
62P/Can-156
62Salada-216
62Shirriff-216
62T-518
63T-109
64T-416
65Kahn
65T-407
65T/E-62
65T/trans-21
66OPC-162
66T-162
67T-258
68OPC-94
68T-94
69MB-172
69T-595
69T/St-165
70OPC-439
70T-439
71OPC-733
71T-733
72MB-212
78TCMA-107
78TCMA-51

Maye, Stephen
86WinSal-14
88Modesto-13
88Modesto/Cal-66
89Huntsvl/Best-10

Mayer, Ed
58T-461

Mayer, James Erskine
15CJ-172
D328-110
D329-114
D350/2-112
E135-110
M101/4-114
M101/5-112
Maynard, Elerton
89Wausa/GS-7
Mayne, Brent
90Score-664DC
Mayo, Edward
47TipTop
49B-75
54T-247
Exh47
Mayo, John
(Jackie)
49B-228
49Eureka-141
V362-36
Mayo, Todd
88CapeCod/Sum-119
89James/Pro-2146
Mays, Al
N172/ST
N690
N690/2
Mays, Carl W.
21Exh-103
28Yueng-17
87Conlon/2-48
88Conlon/4-18
E120
E121/120
E121/80
E210-17
R332-8
V100
V61-7
W501-29
W502-17
W514-103
W515-20
W573
W575
Mays, Henry
77StPet
Mays, Jeff
86Salem-18
87PortChar-11
88CharlR/Star-16
Mays, Willie
51B-305
52B-218
52BR
52Coke
52RM-NL15
52StarCal/L-78E
52T-261
53Briggs
53T-244
54B-89
54NYJour
54RM-NL25
54SM
54T-90
55B-184
55Gol/Giants-20
55RFG-1
55RM-NL7
55T-194
56T-130
56T/Pin-41OF
57T-10
58Hires-25
58Hires/T
58SFCall
58T-436M
58T-486AS
58T-5
59Bz
59HRDerby-14
59T-317M
59T-464M
59T-50
59T-563AS
60Armour-16
60Bz-13
60MacGregor-13
60NuCard-27
60T-200
60T-564AS
60T-7M
60T/tatt
60T/tatt-34
60T/tatt-93
61Bz-23
61NuCard-404
61NuCard-427
61P-145
61T-150
61T-41LL
61T-482MV
61T-579AS
61T/Dice-9
61T/St-80
62Bz
62Exh
62J-142
62P-142
62P/Can-142
62Salada-149
62Shirriff-149
62T-18M
62T-300
62T-395AS
62T-54LL
62T/bucks
62T/St-199
63Bz-12
63Exh
63F-5
63J-106
63P-106
63Salada-22
63T-300
63T-3LL
63T/SO
64Bz-12
64T-150
64T-306M
64T-423M
64T-9LL
64T/Coins-151AS
64T/Coins-80
64T/S-51
64T/St-20S2
64T/SU
64T/tatt
64Wheat/St-29
65Bz-12
65MacGregor-6
65OldLond-14
65OPC-250
65OPC-4LL
65OPC-6LL
65T-250
65T-4LL
65T-6LL
65T/E-27
65T/trans-58
66Bz-16
66OPC-1
66T-1
66T-215LL
66T-217LL
66T-219LL
66T/RO-27
67Bz-16
67OPC-191CL
67OPC/PI-12
67T-200
67T-244LL
67T-423M
67T/PI-12
67T/Test/SU-19
68Bz-14
68Coke
68OPC-50
68T-490M
68T-50
68T/G-8
68T/Post-20
69Kelly/Pin-12
69MB-173
69MLB/St-204
69MLBPA/Pin-52
69NTF
69OPC-190
69OPC/DE-16
69T-190
69T/DE-33
69T/decal
69T/S-65
69T/St-108
69Trans-34
70K-12
70MB-15
70MLB/St-129
70T-600
70T/CB
70T/S-18
70Trans-1
71Bz
71Bz/Test-47
71K-10
71MD
71MLB/St-257
71MLB/St-567
71OPC-600
71T-600
71T/Coins-153
71T/GM-41
71T/S-56
71T/tatt-16
71T/tatt-16a
72K-54
72MB-213
72OPC-49
72OPC-50IA
72T-49
72T-50
72T/Post-17
73OPC-1M
73OPC-305
73T-1M
73T-305
73T/Lids-33
74Laugh/ASG-60
74OPC-473WS
75OPC-192M
75OPC-203M
75T-192MV
75T-203MV
75T/M-192MV
75T/M-203MV
76Laugh/Jub-18
76SSPC-616
78TCMA-280
79TCMA-6
80Cram/Leg-48
80Laugh/3/4/5-10
80SSPC/HOF
82CJ-4
82KMart-8
83MLBPA/Pin-27
83T/St-3F
84Moth/Giants-1
84West/1-13
85CircK-3
85Woolwth-26
86BLChew-3
86S/Dec-50
86S/Rook-46M
86T-403M
87KMart-8
87Nestle/DT-28
88Pac/Leg-24
89B-I7
Exh47
PM10/L-25
PM10/L-26
PM10/Sm-115
PM10/Sm-116
PM10/Sm-117
PM10/Sm-118
PM10/Sm-119
PM10/Sm-120
PM10/Sm-121
Maysey, Matt
85Spoka/Cram-13
86CharRa-15
87CharRa-14
88Wichi-43
89LasVeg/CMC-6
89LasVeg/Pro-5
Mazeroski, Bill
57Kahn
57T-24
58Hires-36
58Kahn
58T-238
59Bz
59Kahn
59T-415
59T-555AS
60Kahn
60MacGregor-14
60T-55
61Bz-24
61Kahn
61NuCard-403
61P-128
61T-430
61T-571AS
61T/Dice-10
61T/St-67
62J-170
62Kahn
62P-170
62P/Can-170
62Salada-131
62Shirriff-131
62T-353
62T-391AS
62T/St-179
63Bz-6
63Exh
63F-59
63J-138
63Kahn
63P-138
63Salada-14
63T-323
63T/SO
64Kahn
64T-570
64T/Coins-143AS
64T/Coins-27
64T/St-40S4
64T/SU
64T/tatt
65Kahn
65OldLond-15
65OPC-95
65T-95
65T/E-23
65T/trans-59
66EH-9
66Kahn
66T-210
66T/RO-45
67Kahn
67T-510
67T/Test/PP-14
68Bz-7
68Coke
68Kahn
68KDKA-9
68T-390
69Kahn
69MB-175
69MLB/St-187
69T-335
69T/St-88
69Trans-60
70MLB/St-103
70OPC-440
70T-440
71Bz/Test-3
71MLB/St-208
71OPC-110
71T-110
71T/Coins-15
71T/tatt-11
72MB-215
72T-760
73OPC-517CO
73T-517C
74OPC-489CO
74T-489C
76Laugh/Jub-6
78TCMA-62
88Pac/Leg-60
89Swell-67
Exh47
WG10-36
WG9-36
Mazey, Randy
88BurlR/Pro-1776
89Mia/Star/25-13
Mazur, Bob
77Salem
Mazzilli, Lee
77T-488R
78OPC-26
78T-147
79Ho-7
79K-42
79OPC-183
79T-355
80K-38
80OPC-11
80T-25
80T/S-8
81Coke
81D-34
81Drake-33
81F-316
81F/St-42
81K-46
81MSA/Disc-22
81OPC-167
81Sqt-21
81T-510
81T/HT
81T/SO-75
81T/St-191
82D-49
82F-533
82F/St-90
82OPC-243
82T-465
82T/St-67
82T/Tr-68T
83D-638
83F-387
83OPC-306
83T-685
83T/X-67
84D-166
84F-255
84Jacks/Smok-8
84Nes/792-225
84OPC-225
84T-225
85D-386
85F-469

85OPC-323
85T-748
86D-288
86F-612
86OPC-373
86T-578
87D-562
87F-15
87T-198
88D-614
88D/Best-209
88D/Mets/Bk-614
88Kahn/Mets-13
88Leaf-223
88OPC-308
88Score-158
88T-308
89Kahn/Mets-13
89Score-217
89T-58
89UD-657
90D-584
90F-88
90Score-459
90T-721

Mazzone, Leo
75Tucso-18
79Savan-17
83Durhm-29
84Durhm-9
85Pol/Atl-52C
86Sumter-19CO
87Greenv/Bst-2C
87SLAS-25
88Richm/CMC-24
88Richm/Pro-16
89Richm/CMC-24CO
89Richm/Ko-CO
89Richm/Pro-833

McAbee, Monte
82Madis-15
82WHave-15
83GlenF-4

McAfee, Brett
82Wausa-13

McAleer, James
M116
N172
T204
WG2-34

McAleese, John
T206

McAllister, Lewis
C46-57
E107
E270/2
T205

McAllister, Steve
83DayBe-21
85Nashua-17
86Nashua-18

McAlpin, Mike
88StCath/Pro-2015
89StCath/Pro-2093

McAnally, Ernie
71OPC-376R
71T-376R
72OPC-58
72T-58
73OPC-484
73T-484
74OPC-322
74T-322
74Weston-21
75OPC-318
75T-318
75T/M-318

McAnany, Jim
88PalmSp/Cal-104
88PalmSp/Pro-1452

McAnarney, James
88Clmbia/GS-8

McAndrew, James
69T-321
70OPC-246
70T-246
71MLB/St-160
71OPC-428
71T-428
72T-781
73OPC-436
73T-436

McAndrew, Jamie
89GreatF-5

McAuliffe, David
89Greens/Pro-411

McAuliffe, Dick
62T-527
63J-48
63P-48
63T-64
64Det/Lids-10
64T-363
65OPC-53
65T-53
66T-495
66T/RO-64
67OPC-170
67T-170
68Kahn
68T-285
69MB-176
69MLB/St-51
69T-305
69T/St-176
70MLB/St-211
70OPC-475
70T-475
71MLB/St-399
71OPC-3
71T-3
71T/Coins-10
71T/tatt-9
72MB-216
72T-725
73OPC-349
73T-349
74OPC-495
74T-495
78TCMA-94
88Domino-14
89Swell-14

McAvoy, Thomas
60L-108

McBean, Alvin
62T-424
63J-146
63P-146
63T-387
64Kahn
64T-525
64T/Coins-66
64T/St-17 65Kahn
65OPC-25
65T-25
65T/E-14
66EH-34
66T-353
67T-203
67T/Test/PP-12
68KDKA-34
68T-514
69MB-177
69OPC-14
69T-14
69T/St-96
70T-641
72MB-217

McBride, Bake
74OPC-601R
74T-601R
75Ho-41
75K-13
75OPC-174
75T-174
75T/M-174
76Crane-34
76Ho-93
76MSA/Disc
76OPC-135
76SSPC-277
76T-135
77Ho-97
77K-34
77T-516
78OPC-156
78T-340
78Wiffle/Discs-47
79BK/P-21
79OPC-332
79T-630
80BK/P-9
80OPC-257
80T-495
81Coke
81D-404
81F-9
81F/St-31
81OPC-90
81T-90
81T/HT
81T/SO-58
81T/St-202
82D-497
82F-250
82OPC-92
82T-745
82T/Tr-69T
82Wheat/Ind
83F-414
83OPC-248
83T-248
83Wheat/Ind-21
84F-547
84Nes/792-569
84OPC-81
84T-569
84T/St-256

McBride, George
10Domino-78
11Helmar-74
12Sweet/Pin-61
14Piedmont/St-35
BF2-47
D327
D328-111
D329-115
D350/2-113
E135-111
E254
E270/1
E91
M101/4-115
M101/5-113
M116
T201
T202
T205
T206
T207
T213
T222
T3-110
V100

McBride, Ivan
88Watlo/Pro-677

McBride, Ken
60T-276
61P-33
61T-209
62Bz
62Salada-91A
62Salada-91B
62Shirriff-91
62T-268
62T/bucks
62T/St-66
63Exh
63Salada-41
63T-510
64Bz-4
64T-405
64T/Coins-52
64T/St-89
64T/SU
64T/tatt
64Wheat/St-30
65OPC-268
65T-268
65T/E-30
Exh47
WG10-37
WG9-37

McBride, Loy
89Visal/Cal-107
89Visal/Pro-1449

McBride, Thomas
49B-74

McCabe, James
T201

McCabe, Joseph
64T-564R
65OPC-181R
65T-181R

McCahan, Bill
48B-31
49B-80

McCain, Mike
82Orlan-10
83Orlan-7
83Toled-27

McCall, John
(Windy)
55Gol/Giants-21
55T-42
55T/DH-88
56T-44
57T-291
79TCMA-200

McCall, Larry
78Cr/PCL-44
79Tucso-23
80Tacom-8

McCall, Robert
(Dutch)
47Signal
48L-57

McCall, Trey
85Bend/Cram-15
87Spart-14
88Clearw/Star-19
89Clearw/Star-15

McCallum, Thomas
N172

McCament, Randy
86Fresno/Smok-11
87Shrev-16
88Phoen/CMC-9
88Phoen/Pro-71
89Shreve/Pro-1853
90F-64
90Score-580
90T-361
90UD-657

McCann, Brian
82AlexD-19
83LynnP-25
86Wausa-14TR
87Pittsf-6
88EastLAS/Pro-49
88Pittsf/Pro-1364
89CharlK-23

McCann, Frank
77Jaxvl
82BirmB-19

McCann, Joe
79Newar-12

McCarter, Edward
86SanJose-12

McCarthy, Alex
E254
E270/2
T207

McCarthy, Danny
79WHave-22M

McCarthy, Dave
77Ashev

McCarthy, Greg
88Spart/Pro-1028
88Spart/Star-13
88Spart/Star-13
89Spart/Pro-1034
89Spart/Star-17

McCarthy, Joe
30CEA/Pin-7
38ONG/Pin-19
44Yank/St-18MG
80Cram/Leg-58
80Laugh/FFeat-33
80SSPC/HOF
86Conlon/1-28
89HOF/St-87
R314/M

McCarthy, John A.
E107
N300/unif

McCarthy, John J.
40PB-215
49B-220
V355-53

McCarthy, Shawn
76BurlB

McCarthy, Steve
88Bill/Pro-1817
89Cedar/Best-10
89Cedar/Pro-914
89Cedar/Star-11

McCarthy, Thomas F.
50Callahan
75F/Pion-13
80SSPC/HOF
89Smok/Dodg-20
N172

McCarthy, Tom
79Elmir-8
80Elmir-17
85Pawtu-17
86Tidew-19
87Tidew-13
87Tidew/TCMA-6
88Tidew/CANDL-22
88Tidew/CMC-7
88Tidew/Pro-1599
89T/Tr-75T
89Vanco/CMC-4
89Vanco/Pro-593
90F-541
90Score/100Ris-57
90T-326

McCarty, G. Lewis
D328-112
E135-112
W514-37

McCarty, John
N172

McCarty, Tom
C46-89
T201

McCarver, Tim
62Kahn/Atl
62T-167
62T/St-186
63T-394
64T-429
64T/Coins-156AS
65T-294
65T/E-7
66T-275
66T/RO-40

67T-485
67T/Test/SU-14
68Bz-3
68T-275
68T-376AS
68T/G-18
68T/Post-19
69Kelly/Pin-13
69MB-178
69MLB/St-214
69MLBPA/Pin-53
69OPC-164WS 69T-475
69T/decal
69T/S-61
69T/St-118
70K-34
70MLB/St-92
70OPC-90
70T-90
70T/S-61
70T/SO
71Bz/Test-1
71MLB/St-184
71OPC-465
71T-465
71T/Coins-107
71T/GM-25
71T/S-34
72MB-218
72OPC-139
72T-139
73OPC-269
73T-269
74OPC-520
74T-520
74T/St-115
75OPC-586
75T-586
75T/M-586
76OPC-502
76T-502
77T-357
78T-235
79BK/P-3
79T-675
80T-178
81F-27
WG10-38

McCaskell, Kirk
83Redwd-19
85Cram/PCL-7
86D-474
86F-163
86Smok/Cal-5
86T-628
87D-381
87F-88
87F/GameWin-27
87F/Hottest-29
87F/Mini-67
87F/St-75
87Leaf-223
87OPC-194
87S-127
87Seven-W5
87Smok/Cal-5
87T-194
87T/St-181
88D-381
88D/Best-83
88F-496
88Panini/St-36
88Score-552
88Sf-78
88Smok/Angels-12
88T-16
88T/Big-168
89B-38
89D-136
89D/Best-83
89F-483
89OPC-348
89Panini/St-285
89Score-181
89Sf-214
89T-421
89T/Big-149
89T/St-184
89UD-223
90D-170
90F-138
90Score-217
90Score/100St-38
90Sf-169
90T-215
90UD-506

McCatty, Steve
78T-701R
80T-231
81D-478
81F-589
81OPC-59
81T-503
82D-35
82F-99
82F/St-131
82Granny-10
82OPC-113
82T-113
82T-156TL
82T-165LL
82T-167LL
82T/St-10LL
82T/St-14
82T/St-228
83D-491
83D/AAS-14
83F-525
83Granny-54
83T-493
84D-420
84F-454
84Moth/A's-8
84Nes/792-369
84OPC-369
84T-369
85D-497
85F-430
85Moth/A's-20
85T-63
85T/St-324
86BuffB-18
86F-427
86T-624
87SanJose-26

McCauley
T206

McCauley, Drew
82Buffa-4

McCawley, Bill
52Mother-11

McCawley, James
N172

McCerod, George
86Pawtu-13

McClain, Joe Jr.
79QuadC-8

McClain, Joe Sr.
61T-488
62Salada-54
62Shirriff-54
62T-324
62T/St-98
63T-311

McClain, Michael
83Miami-2
85Beaum-12
86Beaum-18

McClain, Ron
76Indianap-25TR
77Indianap-26
78Indianap-26
79Indianap-30

McClear, Michael
86FtLaud-16

McClellan, Bobby
75AppFx

McClellan, Dan
74Laugh/Black-32

McClellan, Harvey
E120
V100
W573

McClellan, Paul
86Cram/PCL-2
87Clint-21
88Shreve/Pro-1290
89Shreve/Pro-1850

McClellan, William
N172
N284

McClelland, Tim
88Umpire-46
89Umpires-44

McClendon, Lloyd
82Lynch-16
83Water-9
87F/U-U74
87Kahn-23
88Kahn/Reds-30
88T-172
89B-287
89D-595
89D/Best-228
89F/Up-77
89IowaC/CMC-12
89IowaC/Pro-1695
89Mara/Cubs-10
89Score-521
89T-644
89T/Tr-76T
89UD-446
90D-341
90F-38
90Score-176
90T-337
90UD-398

McClinton, Tim
89Kingspt/Star-16

McClure, Jack
44Centen-17

McClure, Jack
65T-553R

McClure, Rich
79QuadC-9

McClure, Robert
76OPC-599R
76SSPC-182
76T-599R
77T-472R
78T-243
79T-623
80T-357
81D-510
81F-520
81OPC-156
81T-156
82Pol/Brew-10
82T-487
83D-582
83F-38
83Gard-10
83Pol/Brew-10
83T-62
84D-359
84F-206
84Gard-12
84Nes/792-582
84Pol/Brew-10
84T-582
85D-536
85F-587
85Gard-12
85Pol/Brew-10
85T-203
86F-494
86Pol/Brew-10
86T-684
86T/Tr-71T
87F-325
87OPC-133
87T-707
88D-529
88F-189
88OPC-313
88Score-381
88T-313
89B-43
89F-42
89F/Up-14
89Score-572
89Score/Tr-58
89T-182
90D-470
90F-139
90Score-117
90T-458
90UD-81

McClure, Todd
87Ashvl-21
87AubAs-3
88FSLAS/Star-12
88Osceola/Star-17
89Keno/Star-14
89Star/Wax-52
89Visal/Pro-1436

McCollom, Jim
87QuadC-21
88MidldA/GS-22
88TexLgAS/GS-27

McCollum, Greg
87Elmir-23
87Elmir/Red-23
88Lynch/Star-12

McCollum, Lou
47Sunbeam

McConachie, Dale
89Albany/Best-26

McConnell, Ambrose
11Helmar-12
E254
E91
E97
M116
S74-6
T202
T204
T205
T3-29
W555

McConnell, Walt
86FSLAS-34
86VeroB-17
87SnAnt-14
88SnAnt/Best-16
89Albuq/CMC-21
89Albuq/Pro-83

McCool, Bill
64T-356R
65Kahn
65OPC-18
65T-18
66Kahn
66T-459
67Kahn
67T-353
68Kahn
68T-597
69MB-179
69MLB/St-194
69OPC-129
69T-129
70MLB/St-116
70OPC-314
70T-314
72MB-219

McCorkle, Dave
86Wausa-15
88Vermont/Pro-963

McCormack, Brian
88AppFx/Pro-152
89BBCity/Star-16

McCormack, Don R.
79OkCty
80OkCty
81OkCty/TCMA-9
82Evans-12
88Batav/Pro-1664

McCormack, John
N172

McCormack, Mark
83Nashua-23

McCormack, Ron
83CharR-21

McCormack, Tim
86Jaxvl/TCM-26tr
87Indianap-32
88Indi/Pro-498
89Indi/CMC-9
89Indi/Pro-1226

McCormick, Frank A.
(Buck)
39Exh
39PB-36
40PB-75
41DP-9
41PB-5
41Wheat-18
49B-239
W711/1
W711/2

McCormick, Harry
(Moose)
E254
T204
T206

McCormick, Jim
N172
N284

McCormick, John
89AppFx/Pro-873

McCormick, Mike F.
49Eureka-41
58SFCall
58T-37
59T-148
60MacGregor-15
60T-530
61P-141
61T-305
61T-383M
61T-45LL
61T/St-81
62J-139
62P-139
62P/Can-139
62Salada-134
62Shirriff-134
62T-107
62T-319M
62T-56LL
62T/bucks
62T/St-200
63T-563
64T-487
65T-343
66OPC-118
66T-118
67OPC-86
67T-86
68Bz-12
68Coke
68OPC-9LL
68T-400
68T-9LL
68T/G-17
69MB-180
69MLB/St-205

69T-517
70MLB/St-130
70OPC-337
70T-337
71MLB/St-494
71OPC-438
71T-438
72MB-220
72T-682
79TCMA-245
84Moth/Giants-16
88Pac/Leg-67

McCormick, Mike
79ArkTr-14tr
80ArkTr-24tr

McCormick, Myron
(Mike)
41DP-116
49B-146
52Mother-57
W711/2

McCormick, William J.
E107

McCoskey, W. Barney
40PB-201
41DP-53
41PB-36
41Wheat-20
48B-25
48L-63
49B-203
51B-84
52T-300
Exh47

McCovey, Willie
60NuCard-67
60T-316
60T-554AS
61P-147
61T-517
61T/St-82
62J-131
62P-131
62P/Can-131
62Salada-142
62Shirriff-142
62T-544
63J-112
63P-112
63T-490
64Bz-21
64T-350
64T-41M
64T-9
64T/Coins-22
64T/St-94
64T/SU
64Wheat/St-31
65OPC-176
65T-176
66Bz-14
66T-217LL
66T-550
66T/RO-26
67Bz-14
67OPC/PI-32
67T-423M
67T-480
67T/PI-32
68Bz-13
68OPC-5LL
68T-290
68T-5LL
69Citgo-19
69MB-181
69MLB/St-206
69MLBPA/Pin-54
69OPC-4LL
69OPC-6LL
69OPC/DE-13
69T-416AS
69T-440
69T-4LL
69T-572M
69T-6LL
69T/DE-31
69T/decal
69T/S-66
69T/St-109
69Trans-36
70K-4
70MB-16
70MLB/St-131
70OPC-250
70OPC-450AS
70OPC-63LL
70OPC-65LL
70T-250
70T-450AS
70T-63LL
70T-65LL
70T/PI-7
70T/S-13
70Trans-2
71Bz
71Bz/Test-4
71K-33
71MD
71MLB/St-258
71OPC-50
71T-50
71T/Coins-57
71T/GM-52
71T/S-46
71T/tatt-13
71T/tatt-13a
72K-7
72MB-221
72OPC-280
72T-280
72T/Cloth-23
72T/Post-24
73OPC-410
73T-410
73T/Comics-11
73T/Lids-29
73T/PinUps-11
74Laugh/ASG-69
74McDon
74OPC-250
74T-250
74T/DE-28
74T/St-97
75Ho-19
75Ho/Twink-19
75OPC-207M
75OPC-450
75T-207MV
75T-450
75T/M-207MV
75T/M-450
76Ho-124
76OPC-520
78Ho-73
78K-23
78OPC-185
78OPC-238RB
78T-34
78T-3M
79K-17
79OPC-107
79Pol/Giants-44
79T-215
80Laugh/3/4/5-30
80OPC-176
80Pol/Giants-44
80T-335
81F-434
82KMart-16
83MLBPA/Pin-28
84Moth/Giants-2
85CircK-8
85T/Gloss22-11
86D/HL-34
86S/Dec-48M
89HOF/St-4
PM10/Sm-122
WG10-39
WG9-38

McCoy, Benjamin
41DP-130

McCoy, Brent
88Pulas/Pro-1762
89Pulas/Pro-1894

McCoy, Kevin
80BurlB-2
81BurlB-3
83ElPas-20

McCoy, Larry
88Umpire-10
89Umpires-8

McCoy, Tim
86Cram/PCL-13
88Shreve/Pro-1300
89PalmSp/Cal-57
89PalmSp/Pro-468

McCoy, Trey
88Butte-18
89Gasto/Pro-1012
89Gasto/Star-12

McCrae, Brian
88BBCity/Star-17

McCrary, Arnold
77Ashev
78Ashev
79Wausa-23
80Wausa-22

McCrary, Sam
86Jacks/TCM-23tr
88Tidew/CANDL-1TR
88Tidew/Pro-1580
89Tidew/CMC-28

McCraw, Tom
64T-283
65T-586
66OPC-141
66T-141
67OPC-29
67T-29
68T-413
69MB-182
69MLB/St-33
69T-388
70MLB/St-189
70T-561
71OPC-373
71T-373
72MB-222
72T-767
73OPC-86
73T-86
74OPC-449
74T-449
75OPC-482
75T-482
75T/M-482
82BK/Ind-5CO
82BK/Ind-6
82BK/Ind-7
82BK/Indians-5
82BK/Indians-6
82BK/Indians-7
82Wheat/Ind
89French-40

McCray, Eric
89Gasto/Pro-1008
89Gasto/Star-13

McCray, Rod
86CharRa-16
89Saraso/Star-14

McCreadie, Brant
89LittleSun-16

McCreary, Bob
88CapeCod/Sum-82
89Elizab/Star-17

McCue, Deron
86Shrev-17
87Shrev-19
88Phoen/CMC-23
88Phoen/Pro-58

McCulla, Harry
82Sprin-22
83Sprin/LF-17
84Savan-16
85Sprin-17
86ArkTr-14

McCullers, Lance
85Cram/PCL-109
86D-41
86F-330
86S/Rook-8
86T-44
87Bohem-41
87Class-80
87D-237
87F-424
87F/Mini-68
87F/St-76
87OPC-71
87T-559
87T/St-111
88Coke/Padres-41
88D-451
88D/Best-210
88F-592
88F/Mini-114
88OPC-197
88Panini/St-399
88Score-150
88Sf-85
88Smok/Padres-18
88T-197
88T/Big-38
88T/St-114
89B-168
89D-129
89D/Best-220
89D/Tr-13
89F-312
89OPC-307
89Score-158
89Score/NWest-14
89Score/Tr-63
89Score/YS/II-19
89Sf-76
89T-307
89T/St-108
89T/Tr-77T
89UD-382
89UD/Ext-710
90D-433
90F-448
90Score-186
90T-259
90UD-615

McCullock, Alec
84BuffB-10

McCullough, Clyde
47TipTop
49B-163
49Eureka-166
50B-124
51B-94
52B-99
52T-218
55B-280
61Peters-21
72T/Test-8

McCune, Gary
83Knoxv-22
89Knoxv/Pro-1121

McCurdy, Harry
28Exh-40
31Exh/4-12
33G-170

McCure, Gary
88Knoxv/Best-21

McCutcheon, Greg
88StCath/Pro-2020
89StCath/Pro-2094

McCutcheon, James
87Gasto-21
88Gasto/Pro-1004
89Gasto/Pro-1011
89Gasto/Star-14

McDaniel, Jim
59T-134

McDaniel, Lindy
57T-79
58T-180
59T-479
60T-195
61P-175
61T-266
61T-75
61T/St-91
62J-163
62P-163
62P/Can-163
62Salada-144
62Shirriff-144
62T-306M
62T-522
62T/St-187
63J-167
63P-167
63T-329
64T-510
65OPC-244
65T-244
66T-496
67OPC-46
67T-46
68T-545
69MB-183
69OPC-191
69T-191
70OPC-493
70T-493
71MLB/St-495
71OPC-303
71T-303
72MB-223
72OPC-513
72T-513
73OPC-46
73T-46
74OPC-182
74T-182
74T/Tr-182T
75OPC-652
75T-652
75T/M-652
79TCMA-280
Exh47

McDaniel, M. Von
58T-65
89Smok/Ast-21

McDaniel, Terry
88Clmbia/GS-22
89StLucie/Star-16

McDermott, Maurice
(Mickey)
50B-97
50Drake-31
51B-16
51T/RB-43
52B-25
52T-119
53B/Col-35
53Briggs
53NB
53T-55
54B-56
55B-165
56T-340
57T-318
79TCMA-207

McDevitt, Danny
58T-357
59T-364
60BB-3
60L-50
60T-333
61T-349
62T-493
McDevitt, Terry
86Cram/PCL-170
87CharRa-12
88River/Cal-224
88River/Pro-1430
89Watlo/Star-31
McDonald, Ben
87Anchora-20
90Class-130
90D-32
90D/Preview-2
90F-180
90Score-680DC
90Score/100Ris-93
90T-774
90UD-54
McDonald, Dave
70OPC-189R
70T-189R
McDonald, Ed
T207
McDonald, George
45Centen-17
McDonald, James
86Jamestn-16
McDonald, Jeff
84Chatt-28
86Chatt-18
McDonald, Jerry
77Salem
80Port-4
McDonald, Jim
55B-77
55Esskay
McDonald, Jim
78DaytB
79WHave-10
80Colum-11
83ColumAst-15
McDonald, Kirk
86Madis-14
86Madis/Pol-14
88Huntsvl/BK-11
89Modesto/Cal-274
89Modesto/Ch-13
McDonald, Manny
81OkCty/TCMA-12
McDonald, Mark
(Mac)
82Madis-29
McDonald, Michael
86Cram/PCL-103
87Wausa-20
88MidwLAS/GS-55
88Wausa/Feder-11
88Wausa/GS-11
89Everett/Star-20
89SnBer/Best-22
89SnBer/Cal-87
McDonald, Rod
82Watlo/B-7
82Watlo/C-8
83BuffB-5
McDonald, Russ
83Tacom-7
McDonald, Rusty
78Clint
McDonald, Shelby
88Spart/Star-14
88Spart/Pro-1030
89Clearw/Star-16
McDonald, T.J.
84Evrt/Cram-22B
86Fresno/Smok-24
87Shrev-18
88Shreve/Pro-1302
89SanJose/Best-25
89SanJose/Cal-224
89SanJose/Pro-436
89SanJose/Star-19
McDonald, Tony
82OkCty-15
82Readg-21
McDonald, Webster
78Laugh/Black-10
McDonough, Brian
82Miami-4
83SanJose-5
McDougal, Julius
86WinSal-15
87Portl-12
88EastLAS/Pro-9
88GlenF/Pro-919
89Canton/Best-2
89Canton/Pro-1321
89Canton/Star-15
McDougald, Gil
52B-33
52BR
52Coke
52RM-AL14
52T-372
52TipTop
53B/Col-63
53Briggs
53RM-AL23
53SM
53T-43
54B-97
54Dix
54NYJour
54RH
54RM-AL25
54SM
55B-9
55SM
56T-225
57Swift-9
57T-200
58T-20
59T-237M
59T-345
60MacGregor-16
60T-247
61P-10
79TCMA-155
Exh47
PM10/L-27
PM10/Sm-123
McDowell, Jack
88Coke/WS-16
88D-47
88D/Rook-40
88F-407
88F/Hottest-25
88F/Mini-16
88Leaf-47RR
88Score/Tr-85T
88T/Tr-68T
89B-61
89D-531
89F-504
89OPC-143
89Panini/St-302
89Score-289
89T-486
89T/St-302
89ToysRUs-20
89UD-530
89Vanco/Pro-577
90UD-625
McDowell, Mike
89AubAs/Pro-2173
McDowell, Oddibe
85D/HL-24
85F/Up-U80
85OKCty-18
85Rang-0
85T-400
85T/Tr-82T
86D-56
86F-566
86F/LimEd-28
86F/LL-23
86F/Mini-111
86F/St-73
86KayBee-20
86Leaf-46
86OPC-192
86OPC-K
86Rang-0
86S-160
86T-480
86T/Gloss60-1
86T/St-237
86T/St-307
86T/WaxBox-K
87Class/Up-115
87D-161
87D/OD-177
87F-130
87F/McCror-27
87F/St-77
87Leaf-51
87Moth/Rang-4
87OPC-95
87RedFoley/St-78
87S-131
87Smok/R-16
87T-95
87T/St-243
88D-382
88F-473
88F/St-66
88Leaf-154
88Moth/R-4
88OPC-234
88Panini/St-208
88Score-215
88Score/YS/II-27
88Sf-175
88Smok/R-5
88T-617
88T/Big-198
88T/St-237
89B-90
89D-378
89D/Tr-49
89F-528
89OPC-183
89Panini/St-456
89Score-59
89Score/Tr-72
89T-183
89T/Big-245
89T/Tr-78T
89UD-333
89UD/Ext-796
90D-340
90F-589
90Score-476
90Sf-207
90T-329
90UD-145
McDowell, Roger
85F/Up-U81
85T/Tr-83T
86D-629
86F-89
86KayBee-21
86Leaf-248
86OPC-139
86S-161
86T-547
86T/Gloss60-39
86T/Mets/Fan-7
86T/St-103
86T/St-312
87Class-76
87D-241
87F-16
87F/AwardWin-25
87Leaf-49
87OPC-185
87S-160
87Smok/NL-6
87T-185
87T/Gloss60-8
87T/Mets/Fan-4
87T/St-104
88D-651
88D/Best-126
88D/Mets/Bk-651
88F-142
88F/BB/AS-24
88F/Mini-96
88F/St-105
88Kahn/Mets-42
88Leaf-243
88OPC-355
88Score-188
88Sf-42
88T-355
88T/Big-101
88T/Mets/Fan-42
88T/Mini-62
88T/St-100
89D-265
89D/Best-16
89F-43
89F/Up-110
89OPC-296
89Panini/St-132
89Score-281
89Score/Tr-53
89Sf-79
89T-735
89T/Mets/Fan-42
89T/St-92
89T/Tr-79T
89UD-296
90D-251
90F-567
90Score-445
90Sf-75
90T-625
90UD-416
McDowell, Sam
62T-591R
63Sugar-26
63T-317
64T-391
65Kahn
65OPC-76
65T-76
66Bz-17
66Kahn
66T-222LL
66T-226LL
66T-470
67Bz-17
67Kahn
67OPC/PI-8
67T-237LL
67T-295
67T-463M
67T/PI-8
68Kahn
68OPC-115
68OPC-12LL
68T-115
68T-12LL
69Kahn
69MB-184
69MLB/St-42
69MLBPA/Pin-17
69OPC-11LL
69OPC-7LL
69T-11LL
69T-220
69T-435AS
69T-7LL
69T/decal
69T/S-14
69T/St-166
70K-50
70MB-17
70MLB/St-201
70OPC-469AS
70OPC-72LL
70T-469AS
70T-650
70T-72LL
70T/S-10
70Trans-14
71Bz
71Bz/Test-11
71K-37
71MD
71MLB/St-379
71MLB/St-568
71OPC-150
71OPC-71LL
71T-150
71T-71LL
71T/Coins-86
71T/GM-50
71T/S-16
71T/tatt-4
71T/tatt-4a
72K-33
72MB-224
72T-720
73OPC-342KP 73OPC-511
73T-342BP
73T-511
74OPC-550
74T-550
78TCMA-103
89Pac/Leg-155
89Swell-71
McElroy, Charles
87Spart-5
88Readg/Pro-875
89Readg/Best-1
89Readg/Pro-669
89Readg/Star-18
90F-650
McElroy, Glen
86Penin-17
87DayBe-26
89BirmB/Pro-116
McElveen, Pryor
M116
T205
T206
T213brown
McEnaney, Will
75OPC-481
75T-481
75T/M-481
76Icee
76OPC-362
76T-362
77OPC-50
77T-160
78OPC-81
78T-603
80T-563
McFadden, Leon
69OPC-156R
69T-156R
70T-672
72MB-225
McFarland, Dustin
85Anchora-19
87Anchora-21
McFarland, Ed
E107
McFarland, Herm
E107

McFarland, Kelly
85Anchora-43
McFarland, Packey
T3/Box-58
McFarland, Steve
85Anchora-20MG
87Anchora-22MG
McFarlane, Hemmy
85Newar-6
McFarlane, Orlando
62T-229
64T-509R
66T-569
67T-496
69MB-185
McFarlin, Jason
89Everett/Star-28
McGaffigan, Andy
79WHave-14
80Nashvl
81Colum-8
82Phoen
82T-83R
83Moth/Giants-20
83T/X-68
84D-309
84F-382
84F/X-78
84Nes/792-31
84Stuart-34
84T-31
84T/X-78
85D-646
85F-540
85T-323
86F-181
86F/Up-U74
86Provigo-4
86T-133
86T/Tr-72T
87D-380
87F-326
87Leaf-220
87OPC-351
87T-742
88D-380
88F-190
88OPC-56
88Score-366
88T-488
89B-356
89D-338
89F-386
89OPC-278
89Score-138
89T-278
89T/Big-315
89T/St-75
89UD-359
90D-574
90F-355
90Score-224
90T-559
90UD-597
McGaha, Mel
62Sugar-18
62T-242
65T-391
McGann, Dennis
E254
T206
WG3-29
McGann, Don
83Greens-30
84Nashvl-14TR
86Nashv-17TR 87Toled-23
88Toled/Pro-606
89Edmon/Pro-560
McGannon, Paul
81Omaha-3
82Omaha-27
83Omaha-26

McGarr, James
N172
McGeachy, John
(Jack)
N172
N284
McGee
10Domino-74
W555
McGee, Ron
80Spoka-6
McGee, Tim
86WinHav-17
87Greens-16
88Lynch/Star-13
88NewBrit/Pro-901
McGee, Tony
89Spoka/SP-5
McGee, Willie D.
79WHave-13
82Louvl-16
83D-190
83F-15
83OPC-49
83T-49
83T/St-147
83T/St-326
84D-353
84D-625
84D/AAS-2
84F-329
84FunFood/Pin-33
84Nes/792-310
84OPC-310
84Seven-9C
84T-310
84T/St-141
84T/St/Box-8
85D-475
85D/HL-29M
85D/HL-38
85D/HL-52
85F-234
85Leaf-125
85OPC-57
85T-757
85T/St-141
86BK/AP-16
86D-109
86D-3
86D-651M
86D/AAS-36
86D/DKsuper-3
86Dorman-15
86Drake-23
86F-42
86F-636M
86F/LimEd-29
86F/LL-24
86F/Mini-9
86F/Slug-22
86F/St-74
86Jiffy-15
86KAS/Disc-20
86Leaf-225M
86Leaf-3DK
86Meadow/Blank-9
86Meadow/Milk-6
86Meadow/Stat-10
86OPC-117
86OPC-L
86Quaker-1
86S-176M
86S-183M
86S-184M
86S-19
86Schnucks-16
86T-580
86T-707
86T/3D-14
86T/Gloss60-9
86T/Mini-63

86T/St-144
86T/St-45
86T/Super-2
86T/WaxBox-L
86Woolwth-21
87Class-31
87D-84
87Drake-9
87F-304
87F/Hottest-30
87F/Lim-27
87F/LL-29
87Leaf-113
87OPC-357
87RedFoley/St-86
87S-74
87Smok/Cards-22
87T-440
87T/St-48
88Woolwth-26WS4 88Bz-12
88Class/Red-173
88D-307
88D/AS-44
88D/Best-131
88F-42
88F/Mini-108
88F/St-118
88F/TL-20
88KayBee-17
88Leaf-103
88OPC-160
88Panini/St-396
88Score-40
88Sf-91
88Smok/Card-21
88T-160
88T/Big-79
88T/Gloss60-36
88T/Mini-71
88T/St-55
88T/UK-46
89B-442
89Class-98
89D-161
89D/AS-51
89F-457
89KMart/Lead-12
89Louvl-27
89OPC-225
89Panini/St-189
89Score-88
89Score/HotSt-93
89Sf-206
89Smok/Cards-13
89T-640
89T/Big-183
89T/St-36
89UD-621
90D-632
90F-253
90Score-374
90T-285
90UD-505
McGeehee, Connor
82Buffa-3
83LynnP-21
McGhee, Warren E.
53T-195
54T-215
55T-32
55T/DH-78
McGilberry, Randy
77Jaxvl
79T-707R
80Tidew-25
McGinley, James
C46-2
E254
E270/1
T206
McGinn, Dan
69Fud's-7

69T-646R
70OPC-364
70T-364
71MLB/St-134
71OPC-21
71T-21
72MB-226
72OPC-473
72T-473
73OPC-527
73T-527
McGinnis
N284
McGinnis, Russ
86Beloi-14
87Beloi-13
89Tacom/CMC-16
89Tacom/Pro-1556
McGinnity, Joe
(Iron Man)
50Callahan
61F-126
72F/FFeat-1
72Laugh/GF-6
80SSPC/HOF
89Smok/Dodg-21
C46-77
E107
E254
E270
E91
T201
T206
WG3-30
McGlone, John
N172
McGlothen, Lynn
73OPC-114
73T-114
75K-20
75OPC-272
75T-272
75T/M-272
76OPC-478
76SSPC-297
77T-47
78T-478
78T-581
79T-323
80T-716
81D-562
81F-302
81T-609
82T-85
McGlothlin, Ezra
(Pat)
52Park-53
V362-10
McGlothlin, Jim
66T-417R
67OPC-19
67T-19
68Bz-8
68T-493
69JB
69MB-186
69MLB/St-24
69T-386
69T/St-146
70MLB/St-31
70OPC-132
70T-132
71MLB/St-63
71OPC-556
71T-556
71T/Coins-9
72K-36
72MB-227
72OPC-236
72T-236
73OPC-318
73T-318

74OPC-557
74T-557
McGlynn, Ulysses
T201
T206
McGorkle, Robbie
82DayBe-18
McGough, Tom
75OkCty
76Wmspt
McGovern, Phil
T3/Box-70
McGowan, Donnie
85Elmir-15
86Greens-14
87WinHav-5
88WinHav/Star-12
McGrath
T222
McGrath, Charles
83Erie-15
84Savan-6
85Sprin-20
86StPet-19
87ArkTr-3
89ArkTr/GS-12
89Louvl-28
McGraw, Frank E.
(Tug)
65T-533R
66OPC-124
66T-124
67T-348
68T-236
69T-601
70OPC-26
70T-26
70Trans/M-24
71MLB/St-161
71OPC-618
71T-618
72MB-228
72OPC-163
72OPC-164IA
72T-163
72T-164A
73K-21
73OPC-30
73T-30
74OPC-265
74T-265
74T/St-67
75Ho-149
75OPC-67
75T-67
75T/M-67
76OPC-565
76SSPC-457
76T-565
77OPC-142
77T-164
78T-446
78Wiffle/Discs-48
79BK/P-10
79OPC-176
79T-345
80BK/P-20
80OPC-346
80T-655
81Coke
81D-273
81F-657
81F-7
81F/St-83
81K-37
81T-40
81T/HT
81T/St-205
81T/St-262
82D-420
82F-251
82F/St-55

820PC-250
82T-250
83D-371
83F-166
830PC-166
830PC-187SV 83T-510
83T-511A
84D-547
84D/Champs-53
84F-42
84Nes/792-709LL
84Nes/792-728
840PC-161
84T-709
84T-728
85F-261
85T-157
88Pac/Leg-96
89Swell-96

McGraw, Gary
82Idaho-26

McGraw, John J.
10Domino-79
11Helmar-132
12Sweet/Pin-118A
12Sweet/Pin-118B
14CJ-69
14Piedmont/St-36
15CJ-69
21Exh-104
28Yueng-42
40PB-235
48Exh/HOF
49Leaf/Prem-6
60Exh/HOF-17
60F-66
61F-60
61GP-23
63Bz/ATG-20
69Bz/Sm
72K/ATG-3
72K/ATG-3
75F/Pion-15
80Cram/Leg-43
80SSPC/HOF
83D/HOF-35
86Conlon/1-29
88Conlon/5-20
89HOF/St-89
BF2-78
D303
D327
D328-113
D329-116
D350/2-114
E101
E104
E105
E106
E107
E121/120
E121/80
E122
E135-113
E210-42
E224
E286
E91
E92
E93
E94
E98
L1-116
M101/4-116
M101/5-114
M116
R332-41
S74-89
S81-91
T202
T205
T206
T207
T213/blue
T216
T3-26
V100
W501-103
W501-73
W502-42
W514-52
W515-45
W555
W575
WG3-31
WG4-18
WG5-29
WG6-28

McGreachery
N172

McGregor, Scott
750PC-618R
75T-618R
75T/M-618R
77T-475R
78T-491
790PC-206
79T-393
80T-237
81D-114
81F-174
81F/St-10
810PC-65
81T-65
81T/St-37
82D-331
82F-172
82F/St-149
820PC-246AS
820PC-316
82T-555AS
82T-617
82T/St-143
83D-483
83F-66
830PC-216
83T-745
84D-594
84F-13
84F-646IA
84F/St-64
84FunFood/Pin-102
84Nes/792-260
840PC-260
84T-260
84T/St-207
85D-413
85F-183
85Leaf-72
850PC-228
85T-550
85T/St-198
86D-291
86F-281
86F/St-75
86Leaf-165
860PC-110
86T-110
86T/St-230
87D-520
87F-475
87Leaf-243
870PC-347
87T-708
880PC-254
88Score-315
88T-419
89Swell-56

McGrew, Charley
86Beloi-15
87Stockton-12
88Beloi/GS-7
89Modesto/Cal-284

McGriff, Fred
85Syrac-2
85Syrac-25M
86D-28
86Leaf-28RR
86Syrac-18
87D-621
87D/HL-39
87D/OD-38
87D/Rook-31
87F/U-U75
87S/Rook-12
87T/Tr-74T
87Tor/Fire-20
87Tor/Fire-20
88D-195
88D/Best-160
88F-118
88Ho/Disc-15
880PC-395
88RedFoley/St-54
88Score-107
88Score/YS/II-28
88Sf-168
88T-463
88Tor/Fire-19
88ToysRUs-18
89B-253
89Cadaco-35
89Class-116
89D-16DK
89D-70
89D/Best-104
89D/DKsuper-16DK
89D/MVP-BC19
89F-240
89F/BBMVP's-27
89F/Heroes-27
89F/LL-26
89F/Superstar-30
89F/WaxBox-C19
890PC-258
89Panini/St-467
89Score-6
89Score/HotSt-65
89Sf-14
89T-745
89T/Big-15
89T/Coins-44
89T/Hills-20
89T/Mini-77
89T/St-185
89T/UK-50
89Tor/Fire-19
89UD-572
89UD-671TC
90Class-19
90D-188
90F-89
90Score-271
90Score/100St-45
90Sf-13
90T-295
90T-385AS
90UD-108

McGriff, Terrence
(Terry)
83Tampa-18
87D-512
88D-556
88F-240
88Kahn/Reds-8
88Score-281
88T-644
89Nashvl-15
89T-151

McGuire, Bill
87Chatt/Best-15
88BBAmer-10
88Vermont/Pro-943
89Calg/CMC-21
89Calg/Pro-533
89F-553

McGuire, James
(Deacon)
E107
E286
M116
N172
N690
WG2-35

McGuire, Mike
88Wausa/Feder-20
88Wausa/GS-20
89Wausa/GS-1

McGuire, Steve
86QuadC-22
87MidldA-26
88MidldA/GS-12
89PalmSp/Cal-54
89QuadC/Best-14
89QuadC/GS-17

McGunnigle, William
N172

McGwire, Mark
85T-401
86SLAS-3
87Class/Up-121
87Class/Up-150M
87D-46
87D/HL-27
87D/HL-40M
87D/HL-46
87D/HL-54
87D/Rook-1
87F/Slug-26
87F/U-U76
87Leaf-46RR
87S/Rook-13
87T-366
88Woolw-15
88Bz-13
88ChefBoy-1
88Class/Blue-212
88Class/Blue-247M
88Class/Red-151M
88Class/Red-153
88Class/Red-197M
88D-1DK
88D-256
88D-BC23
88D/A's/Bk-256
88D/AS-19
88D/Best-169
88D/DKsuper-1DK
88F-286
88F-624M
88F-629M
88F-633M
88F/AwardWin-24
88F/BB/AS-25
88F/BB/MVP-23
88F/Excit-26
88F/Head-2
88F/Hottest-26
88F/LL-26
88F/Mini-46
88F/RecSet-25
88F/Slug-27
88F/SS-23
88F/St-56
88F/St-S6M
88F/TL-21
88FanSam-3
88KayBee-18
88KingB/Disc-6
88KMart-16
88Leaf-194
88Leaf-1DK
88Moth/A's-2
88Moth/McGwire-1
88Moth/McGwire-2
88Moth/McGwire-3
88Moth/McGwire-4
88MSA/Disc-4
88Nestle-10
880PC-394
88Panini/St-167
88Panini/St-438
88RedFoley/St-55
88Score-5
88Score-648M
88Score-659HL
88Score/YS/I-1
88Sf-100
88Sf-221
88Sf/Gamewin-2
88T-3RB
88T-580
88T/Big-179
88T/Coins-3
88T/Gloss60-39
88T/JumboR-13
88T/Mini-31
88T/Revco-17
88T/RiteAid-23
88T/St-1
88T/St-164
88T/St-309
88T/St/Backs-36
88T/UK-47
88ToysRUs-19
89B-197
89Cadaco-36
89Class-104
89Class-4
89Class/Up/2-190
89Crunch-22
89D-95
89D/AS-1
89D/Best-43
89D/GrandSlam-7
89D/PopUp-1
89F-17
89F-634M
89F/BBAS-29
89F/BBMVP's-28
89F/Excit-32
89F/Heroes-28
89F/LL-27
89F/Superstar-31
89F/WS-8
89Holsum/Discs-14
89KayBee-21
89KingB/Discs-4
89Modesto/Ch-35
89Moth/A's-2
89Moth/ROY's-2
89Moth/ROY's-4M
89Moth/McGwire-1
89Moth/McGwire-2
89Moth/McGwire-3
89Moth/McGwire-4
89Nissen-14
890PC-174
890PC-70
89Panini/St-20
89Panini/St-244AS
89Panini/St-420
89RedFoley/St-80
89Score-3
89Score/HotSt-25
89Score/Mast-32
89Sf-200
89T-70
89T/Big-34
89T/Coins-45
89T/DH-12
89T/Gloss22-2
89T/Gloss60-41
89T/HeadsUp-14
89T/Mini-70
89T/St-151
89T/St-172
89T/St/Backs-3
89T/UK-51

89Tacom/Pro-1537
89Tetley/Discs-3
89UD-300
89Woolwth-27
90Class-59
90D-185
90D-697AS
90F-15
90F-638M
90F/WaxBox-C20
90Score-385
90Score/100St-25
90Sf-141
90T-690
90UD-171
90UD-36TC

McHenry, Austin
E120
V100

McHenry, Vance
80Spoka-9
81Spoka-20
82SLCty-12
85Syrac-23

McHugh, Chip
86Lakel-13
87GlenF-25

McHugh, Mike
88GreatF-6

McHugh, Scott
87Jamestn-4

McHugh, Tom
82CharR-4

McIlwain, W. Stover
60L-114

McInerney, Steve
86GlenF-15TR
87GlenF-7
89Toled/CMC-24
89Toled/Pro-762

McInerny, Dan
83SanJose-7

McInnis, Bill
86NewBrit-17
87NewBrit-8
88Pawtu/CMC-12
88Pawtu/Pro-456

McInnis, John
(Stuffy)
14CJ-10
15CJ-10
21Exh-105
21Exh-106
25Exh-29
27Exh-22
28Yueng-60
80Laugh/FFeat-29
88Conlon/5-21
BF2-37
D328-114
D329-117
D350/2-115
E120
E121/120
E121/80
E122
E126-41
E135-114
E210-60
E90/1
M101/4-117
M101/5-115
M116
T222
V100
W501-18
W502-60
W514-20
W575
WG4-19
WG7-29

McIntire, Harry
11Helmar-98
12Sweet/Pin-84
S74-64
WG3-32

McIntire, John Reed
10Domino-81
M116
T202
T205
T206
T207
T3-28

McIntosh, Joe
76OPC-497
76T-497
76T/Tr-497T

McIntosh, Tim
87Beloi-26
88CalLgAS-12
88Stock/Cal-189
88Stock/Pro-733
89ElPas/GS-18
90F-329

McIntyre, James J.
80ArkTr-12

McIntyre, Matthew
09Buster/Pin-9
10Domino-82
11Helmar-13
12Sweet/Pin-12B
12Sweet/Pin-12A
E104
E254
E90/1
E95
E97
M116
T202
T204
T205
T206
T207
T213/brown
T3-25

McIver, Jeryl
76Wausa

McIver, Larry
82AubAs-9

McKay, Alan
85Kingst-7
86Pittsf-16

McKay, Dave
76OPC-592R
76T-592R
77Ho-130
77OPC-40
77T-377
79OPC-322
79T-608
81D-350
81F-592
81T-461
82D-391
82F-100
82T-534
83D-213
83F-526
83T-47
83Tacom-29B

McKay, Karl
80BurlB-28
81BurlB-26

McKay, Troy
86Jaxvl/TCMA-16

McKean, Edward
N172

McKean, Jim
88Umpire-20
89Umpires-16

McKechnie, Bill
40PB-153
80Cram/Leg-86
80SSPC/HOF
89HOF/St-88
T207
V117-25
V355-108
W711/1
W711/2

McKee, Matt
89Ashvl/Pro-940

McKee, Ron
80Ashev-9GM
88Ashvl/Pro-1077
89Ashvl/Pro-942

McKelvey, Mitch
84PrWill-24
85Nashua-18
86FtMyr-19

McKelvie, Ron
83Visal/LF-12tr

McKenzie, Don
81Wausa-10

McKenzie, Doug
83Peoria/LF-8
85MidldA-7

McKeon, Jack
73OPC-593MG
73T-593MG
74T-166MG
75OPC-72MG
75T-72MG
75T/M-72MG
77T-74MG
78T-328
84Smok/Padres-17
88Coke/Pad-15MG
88T/Tr-69MG
89T-624MG
90T-231MG

McKeon, Joel
83AppFx/LF-5
85BuffB-22
86D/Rook-55
86F/Up-U75
87Coke/WS-25
87F-503
88LasVeg/CMC-4
88LasVeg/Pro-225
88T-409
89Indi/Pro-1212

McKeon, Kasey
89Brist/Star-17

McKeown, Dan
85Anchora-37bb

McKercher, Tim
88SLCty-24

McKinght, Jeff
89Tidew/CMC-13

McKinley, Pat
88Virgini/Star-15

McKinley, Tim
88Salem/Star-12
89Harris/Pro-312
89Harris/Star-11

McKinley, W.F.
55B-226ump

McKinney, C. Rich
71OPC-37
71T-37
72T-619
73OPC-587
73T-587
75Tucso-14
76SSPC-587
76Tucso-22

McKinney, Charlie
80Cedar-12

McKinney, Greg
81Cedar-25

McKinney, John
85Bend/Cram-16

McKinney, Lynn
79Hawai-2

McKinnis, Tim
88QuadC/GS-26

McKinnon, Alex
N172

McKinzie, Phil
87AppFx-29

McKnight, Jack
83Knoxv-5
86Phoen-16
87Phoen-14

McKnight, James
62Salada-199
62Shirriff-199
62T-597R

McKnight, Jeff
86Jacks/TCMA-17
87Tidew-4
87Tidew/TCMA-15
88Tidew/CANDL-16
88Tidew/CMC-19
88Tidew/Pro-1587
89Tidew/Pro-1953
90UD-162

McKnight, Jim
82DayBe-21

McKown, Steven
76Cedar

McKune, Jerry
81ArkTr-22
81Louvl-3
82Louvl-17
84Louvl-3
85Louvl-4

McLain, Dennis
65OPC-236
65T-236
66T-226LL
66T-540
67Bz-24
67OPC/PI-20
67T-235LL
67T-420
67T/PI-20
68OPC-40
68T-40
69Citgo-1
69Kelly/Pin-14
69MB-187
69MLB/St-52
69MLBPA/Pin-18
69OPC-11LL
69OPC-150
69OPC-57CL
69OPC-9LL
69OPC/DE-14
69T-11LL
69T-150
69T-433AS
69T-9LL
69T/DE-8
69T/decal
69T/S-17
69T/St-177
69Trans-4
70K-73
70MLB/St-212
70OPC-400
70OPC-467AS
70OPC-70LL
70T-400
70T-467AS
70T-70LL
70T/PI-24
70T/S-17
70Trans-11
71MLB/St-546
71MLB/St-569
71OPC-750
71T-750
71T/GM-20
72MB-229
72OPC-210
72T-210
72T-753TR
73OPC-630
73T-630
75OPC-206M
75T-206MV
75T/M-206MV
78TCMA-210
82KMart-13
85West/2-43
88Domino-15

McLain, Tim
86Wausa-16
88SnBer/Cal-46

McLane, Larry
82BurlR-7
83Tulsa-6

McLaren, John
75Dubuq
83Knoxv-19
86Tor/Fire-25CO
87Tor/Fire-21
87Tor/Fire-21CO
88Maine/CMC-6
88Maine/Pro-281
88Tor/Fire-7CO
89Tor/Fire-7

McLarnan, John
87Readg-23

McLauchlin, Dick
81Albuq/TCMA-26

McLaughlin, Burke
52Park-12

McLaughlin, Byron
78SnJos-17
79T-712R
80T-197
81D-287
81T-344
84Nes/792-442
84T-442

McLaughlin, Colin
82Knoxv-6
83Syrac-10
85Syrac-15
86Knoxv-16
87Syrac/TCMA-6
88Syrac/CMC-3
88Syrac/Pro-823
89Calg/CMC-3
89Calg/Pro-532

McLaughlin, Dave
83AppFx/LF-3

McLaughlin, Dick
(Mac)
77Clint
78Clint
82Albuq-26
83Albuq-25
84Cram/PCL-169CO
85Cram/PCL-160
86Albuq-15CO

McLaughlin, Joey
78Richm
79Richm-1
80T-384
81D-271
81F-420
81OPC-248
81T-248
82D-507
82F-620
82OPC-376
82OPC/Post-8
82T-739
83D-255
83F-434
83OPC-9
83T-9
84D-617

84F-162
84F/X-79
84Nes/792-556
84OPC-11
84Rang-53
84T-556
85T-678
86Tacom-14
87Hawai-19

McLaughlin, Michael
(Bo)
77T-184
78Charl
78T-437
80Richm-23
80T-326
82T-217

McLaughlin, Steve
86AppFx-14tr

McLaughlin, Thomas
N172/ST

McLaughlin, Tom
81Clint-24

McLaughlin, Wm.
40Hughes-14

McLaurine, Bill
77Spoka

McLean, John R.
(Larry)
10Domino-80
11Helmar-117
12Sweet/Pin-103B
12Sweet/Pin-103A
14Piedmont/St-37
E101
E103
E105
E254
E270/2
E300
E90/1
E92
E98
M116
T201
T202
T204
T205
T206
T207
T213/blue
T216
T222
WG5-30

McLean, Bobby
33SK-12

McLemore, Mark
83Peoria/LF-9
85MidldA-17
86D-35
86F-650M
86MidldA-16
87Class/Up-119
87D-479
87D/OD-8
87D/Rook-7
87F/U-U77
87S/Rook-14
87Smok/Cal-13
87T/Tr-75T
88D-181
88D/Best-251
88F-497
88Leaf-159
88OPC-162
88Panini/St-41
88Score-152
88Score/YS/II-29
88Smok/Angels-22
88T-162
89D-94
89F-484
89Score-208
89T-51TL
89T-547
89T/Big-30
89UD-245

McLeod, Bill
63MilSau-4

McLish, Cal
49Eureka-64
57T-364
58T-208
59T-445
60Kahn
60T-110
60T/tatt
60T/tatt-35
61T-157
62T-453
63T-512
64T-365
69Fud's-8
73OPC-377CO
73T-377C
74OPC-531CO
74T-531C
79TCMA-221

McLish, Tom
78Newar

McLoughlin, Tim
86Salem-19

McMahon, Don
58T-147
59T-3
60Lake
60T-189
61T-278
62T-483
63Pep
63T-395
64T-122
65Kahn
65T-317
66OPC-133
66T-133
67OPC-7
67T-7
67T/Test/RSox-10
68T-464
69T-616
70OPC-519
70T-519
71MLB/St-259
71OPC-354
71T-354
72OPC-509
72T-509
73OPC-252CO
73T-252C
74OPC-78CO
74T-78C
80Pol/SFG-47C
83Wheat/Ind-22
85Polar/Ind-xx
88Domino-16

McMahon, Jack
83Visal/LF-9

McManaman, Steve
80OrlTw-17

McManus, Jim
61Union

McManus, Jim
87Richm/TCMA-24

McManus, Martin
25Exh-115
26Exh-115
29Exh/4-23
31Exh/4-23
32Orbit/num-7
32Orbit/un-47
33DL-1
33G-48
34G-80
35G-1J
35G-3A
35G-4A
35G-5A
E120
E210-48
R305
V353-48
V61-41
W572
W573
WG7-30

McMath, Shelton
80Ashev-27

McMichael, Chuck
81CharR-14

McMichael, Gregory
88BurlR/Pro-1796
89Canton/Best-24
89Canton/Pro-1315
89Canton/Star-16

McMillan, Roy
52B-238
52T-137
53B/Col-26
53T-259
54B-12
54RH
54T-120
54Wilson
55Kahn
55T-181
56Kahn
56T-123
56T/Pin-57SS
57Kahn
57T-69
58Kahn
58T-360
59Bz
59Kahn
59T-405
60Bz-33
60Kahn
60T-45
61P-183
61T-465
61T/St-46
62J-148
62P-148
62P/Can-148
62Salada-159
62Shirriff-159
62T-211M
62T-393AS
62T/St-149
63J-150
63P-150
63T-156
64T-238
64T/Coins-148AS
64T/S-8
65OPC-45
65T-45
65T/E-44
66Bz-13
66T-421
70McDon-4
73OPC-257CO
73T-257C
74OPC-179CO
74T-179C
77Visal
79TCMA-154
80OrlTw-22MG

McMillan, Thomas E.
75OkCty
77T-490R
78SnJos-18

McMillan, Thomas Law
M116

McMillan, Tim
86PrWill-15
87CharWh-17
88Salem/Star-13

McMorris, Mark
86WinSal-16
87WinSal-1

McMuirray, Brock
88GreatF-16

McMullen, Ken
63T-537R
64T-214
65T-319
66T-401
66T/RO-35
67OPC-47
67T-47
68OPC-116
68T-116
69MB-188
69MLB/St-106
69T-319
69T/St-239
70MLB/St-284
70OPC-420
70T-420
71MLB/St-350
71OPC-485
71T-485
72MB-230
72T-756
73OPC-196
73T-196
74OPC-434
74T-434
75OPC-473
75T-473
75T/M-473
76OPC-566
76SSPC-80
76T-566
77T-181

McMullen, Rick
82Jacks-15

McMullin, Fred
88Pac/8Men-105
88Pac/8Men-15

McMurtrie, Dan
86LitFalls-18
87Columbia-24

McMurtry, Craig
82Richm-6
83Pol/Atl-29
83T/X-69
84D-599
84F-184
84F/St-105
84Nes/792-126TL
84Nes/792-543
84OPC-219
84Pol/Atl-29
84T-543
84T/St-384
85D-188
85F-333
85Ho/Braves-15
85Leaf-45
85OPC-362
85Pol/Atl-29
85T-362
85T/St-28
86Pol/Atl-29
86T-194
87T-461
87Tor/Fire-22
87Tor/Fire-22
88OkCty/CMC-4
88OkCty/Pro-44
89D-520
89Moth/R-20
89Smok/R-21
89T-779
90T-294

McNabb, Glenn
89Aug/Pro-508

McNair, Bob
80Utica-24

McNair, Donald Eric
35BU-61
39PB-105
40PB-14
R303/A
R314

McNally, Bob
86Sumter-20
87Sumter-5

McNally, Dave
63T-562R
64T-161
65OPC-249
65T-249
66OPC-193
66T-193
67T-382
68Coke
68T-478
69Citgo-2
69MB-189
69MLB/St-5
69OPC-7LL
69OPC-9LL
69T-340
69T-532M
69T-7LL
69T-9LL
69T/decal
69T/S-1
69T/St-126
69Trans-15
70K-14
70MLB/St-151
70OPC-20
70OPC-70LL
70T-20
70T-70LL
71Bz
71Bz/Test-27
71K-59
71MD
71MLB/St-304
71OPC-196ALCS
71OPC-320
71OPC-69LL
71T-320
71T-69LL
71T/Coins-26
71T/S
71T/tatt-12
72K-29
72MB-231
72OPC-223WS
72OPC-344KP
72OPC-490
72T-344BP
72T-490
72T/Post-1
73OPC-600
73T-600
74OPC-235
74T-235
74T/St-127
75Ho-150
75OPC-26
75T-26
75T/M-26
78TCMA-270
88Pac/Leg-38

McNally, Mike
E120
E121/120
E121/80
W501-33
W575

McNamara, James
86Cram/PCL-10
87Clint-9
88SanJose/Cal-123
88SanJose/Pro-133
89Salin/Cal-145
89Salin/Pro-1811

McNamara, John
70T-706
73OPC-252CO
73T-252C
74McDon
74OPC-78CO
74T-78C
75OPC-146MG
75T-146MG
75T/M-146MG
76SSPC-123
76T-331MG
77T-134MG
81T-677MG
82D-526
83T/X-70
84Nes/792-651MG
84Smok/Cal-19MG
84T-651
85T-732MG
85T/Tr-84T
86T-771MG
87T-368MG
88D/AS-10MG
88D/PopUp-10MG
88T-414
88T/Gloss22-1MG

McNamara, Mike
88CapeCod/Sum-85

McNamara, Reggie
33SK-15

McNamee, Bill
62Pep/Tul

McNaney, Scott
89Watlo/Star-32

McNary, Mike
88CapeCod/Sum-32

McNeal, Paul
86Hagers-10CO
87Hagers-2

McNealy, Derwin
83Nashvl-12
85Syrac-29
86Colum-16
86Colum/Pol-14

McNealy, Rusty
82WHave-23
83Tacom-17
86Chatt-19
87SanJose-27

McNeely, Earl
25Exh-127
26Exh-127

McNeely, Jeff
89Elmir/Puc-30

McNees, Kevin
87Idaho-8
88Hagers/Star-11

McNeil, Johnny
86Columbia-18

McNertney, Gerald
(Jerry)
64T-564R
68OPC-14
68T-14
69MB-190
69T-534
69T/St-226
70McDon-4
70MLB/St-275
70OPC-158
70T-158
71MLB/St-279
71OPC-286
71T-286
71T/Coins-68
72MB-232
72T-584
79Colum-9
80Colum-22
81Colum-28
82Colum-24M
87Albany-10
87Colum-5

McNulty, Bill
73OPC-603R
73T-603R

McNutt, Larry
83Lynch-2

McPhail, Marlin
86Tidew-18
87BirmB/Best-5
88Vanco/CMC-25
88Vanco/Pro-777
89Vanco/CMC-15
89Vanco/Pro-596

McPhee, John
(Bid)
N172

McPheeters, Kourtney
87Anchora-35bb

McPherson, Barry
84Savan-3

McQuade, John H.
N172/ump

McQuaide, James H.
N172

McQueen, Mike
70T-621R
71OPC-8
71T-8
72OPC-214
72T-214

McQuillan, George
15CJ-152
D303
E103
E106
E120
E90/1
E96
M116
T206
T213/blue
T216

McQuillan, Hugh
26Exh-37
W515-33

McQuinn, George
39Exh
39PB-122
40PB-53
41G-5
41PB-23
49B-232

McRae, Brian
86Cram/PCL-28
87FtMyr-26
89Memph/Best-13
89Memph/Pro-1205
89Memph/Star-17
89Star/Wax-44

McRae, Hal
68T-384R
70T-683R
71MLB/St-64
71OPC-177
71T-177
72OPC-291
72OPC-292IA
72T-291
72T-292A
72T/Cloth-24
73OPC-28
73T-28
74OPC-563
74T-563
75Ho-104
75K-53
75OPC-268
75T-268
75T/M-268
76A&P/KC
76Ho-135
76OPC-72
76SSPC-176
76T-72
77Ho-17
77K-10
77OPC-215
77T-340
78Ho-6
78K-20
78T-465
78Wiffle/Discs-49
79Ho-90
79OPC-306
79T-585
80OPC-104
80T-185
81Coke
81D-463
81F-41
81F-653M
81OPC-295
81Pol/Royals-6
81T-295
81T/St-86
82D-196
82F-416
82F/St-210
82OPC-384
82T-625
83D-238
83D/AAS-16
83Drake-17
83F-110
83K-5
83OPC-25
83Pol/Royals-4
83T-25
83T-703
83T/St-19
83T/St-75
84D-11
84D-297
84D/AAS-25
84D/Champs-17
84F-350
84F/St-44
84FunFood/Pin-63
84Nes/792-340
84Nes/792-96TL
84OPC-340
84T-340
84T/St-278
84T/St/Box-3
85D-588
85F-207
85Leaf-34
85OPC-284
85T-773
85T/St-270
86D-521
86F-14
86Kitty/Disc-4
86Leaf-251
86NatPhoto-11
86OPC-278
86T-415
86T-606M
86Woolwth-22
87D-471
87F-375
87OPC-246
87RedFoley/St-59
87T-573
88Class/Blue-235

McRae, Norm
70OPC-207R
70T-207R
71OPC-93R
71T-93R

McReynolds, Kevin
84D-34
84F-307
84Moth/SDP-13
84Smok/SDP-18
85D-139
85F-41
85Leaf-43
85Moth/SDP-3
86D-80
86F-331
86Leaf-76
87Class/Up-126
87D-14DK
87D-451
87D/DKsuper-14
87D/OD-125
87F-425
87F/GameWin-28
87F/U-U78
87Leaf-14DK
87Leaf-214
87RedFoley/St-35
87S-135
87S-155M
87T/Mets/Fan-5
87T/Tr-76T
88D-617
88D/Best-153
88D/Mets/Bk-617
88F-143
88F/SS-24
88Kahn/Mets-22
88Leaf-228
88OPC-37
88Panini/St-346
88RedFoley/St-56
88Score-21
88Sf-56
88Sf/Gamewin-22
88T-735
88T/Big-158
88T/St-102
89Ames-20
89B-388
89Class-24
89D-99
89D/Best-70
89D/GrandSlam-4
89F-44
89F/BBMVP's-29
89F/Heroes-29
89Kahn/Mets-22
89OPC-85
89Panini/St-139
89Score-93
89Score/HotSt-96
89Sf-97
89T-291TL
89T-7RB
89T-85
89T/Big-116
89T/Gloss60-26
89T/Mets/Fan-22
89T/Mini-27
89T/St-10
89T/St-95
89T/St/Backs-51
89T/UK-52
89UD-367
89Woolwth-15
90D-218
90F-211
90Score-5
90Sf-127
90T-545
90UD-265

McSherry, John
88Umpire-12
89Umpires-10

McSparron, Greg
81Clint-25

McTammy, James
N172

McVey, George
N172

McWane, Rick
88LitFalls/Puc-28
89Visal/Cal-122TR
89Visal/Pro-1431

McWeeney, Douglas
26Exh-13
R316
V100

McWhirter, Kevin
78OrlTw
80OrlTw-20

McWilliam, Tim
89River/Best-13
89River/Cal-2
89River/Pro-1401

McWilliams, Larry
79T-504
80T-309
81F-267
81Richm-14
81T-44
82BK/Lids-17
82D-527
82Pol/Atl-27
82T-733
83D-45
83F-310
83T-253
84D-566
84F-256
84F/St-58
84F/St-80
84Nes/792-668
84OPC-341
84T-668
84T/St-133
85D-78
85F-470
85Leaf-247
85OPC-183
85T-183
85T/St-132
86D-264
86F-613
86Leaf-136
86OPC-204
86T-425
87F-613
87OPC-14
87T-564
88Score/Tr-23T
88Smok/Card-22
88T/Big-261
88T/Tr-70T
89B-397
89D-516
89F-458
89Score-259
89T-259
89T/Tr-80T
89UD-143
90D-709

Meacham, Bobby
83Colum-20
84D-336
84Nes/792-204
84T-204
85D-126
85F-134
85Leaf-147
85OPC-16
85T-16
85T/St-315

86D-638
86F-110
86OPC-379
86T-379
86T/St-304
87Colum-10
87Colum/Pol-19
87Colum/TCMA-16
87F-105
87T-62
88D-616
88D/Y/Bk-616
88F-215
88SanDiegoSt-10
88SanDiegoSt-11
88Score-137
88T-659
89BuffB/CMC-17
89BuffB/Pro-1663
89Score-509
89T-436
89UD-77

Meacham, Rusty
88Brist/Pro-1868
89Fay/Pro-1575

Mead, Timber
86Clint-12
87Tampa-16
88Chatt/Best-1
89Chatt/Best-13
89Chatt/GS-24

Meadows, Chuck
83AlexD-3

Meadows, Henry
D328-115
E120
E135-115
E220
W515-23
W572
W573

Meadows, Jeff
82AubAs-7

Meadows, Jim
86DayBe-18
86FSLAS-35

Meadows, Lee
21Exh-107
88Conlon/3-19
E126-4

Meadows, Louie
83DayBe-26
86Tucso-13
87Tucso-9
88F/U-U92
88Tucso/CMC-20
88Tucso/Pro-177
89F-361
89T-643
89Tucso/CMC-14
89Tucso/Pro-191
89UD-401
90T-534
90UD-160

Meadows, Scott
89Freder/Star-15
89Watlo/Pro-1773
89Watlo/Star-20

Meads, Dave
86Ashvl-19
87D/Rook-46
87F/U-U79
87Moth/Ast-17
87Pol/Ast-9
87T/Tr-77T
88D-455
88F-453
88RedFoley/St-57
88Score-243
88T-199
88Tucso-16
88Tucso/CMC-4
88Tucso/Pro-183
89D-424
89F-362
89Moth/Ast-26
89Score-593
89T-589
89Tucso/CMC-5
89Tucso/Pro-180

Meagher, Adrian
86Albuq-16
88ElPas/Best-24

Meagher, Brad
77BurlB

Meagher, Tom
85Spoka/Cram-14
86CharRa-17
88SanJose/Cal-134
88SanJose/Pro-120

Mealy, Tony
87Macon-5
88Greens/Pro-1563
89Cedar/Best-21
89Cedar/Pro-926
89Cedar/Star-12

Meamber, Tim
87Erie-14
88Savan/Pro-344
89Sprin/Best-22

Mears, Ronnie
78Wisco

Mecerod, George
80Elmir-16

Meche, Carl
75QuadC

Meckes, Tim
83ColumAst-16
84Tulsa-24

Medich, George
(Doc)
73OPC-608R
73T-608R
74OPC-445
74T-445
74T/St-213
75Ho-78
75OPC-426
75T-426
75T/M-426
76Crane-35
76MSA/Disc
76OPC-146
76SSPC-430
76T-146
76T/Tr-146T
77OPC-222
77T-29
78BK/R-7
78Ho-86
78T-583
79OPC-347
79T-657
80T-336
81D-386
81F-627
81T-702
82D-142
82F-324
82T-36TL
82T-78
83F-39
89Swell-18

Medina, Facanel
89Martins/Star-20

Medina, Luis
86Watlo-18
87Wmspt-24
88AAA/Pro-8
88ColSp/CMC-21
88ColSp/Pro-1543
89Class-67
89D-36RR
89D/Rook-20
89F-411
89Panini/St-315
89Score-633
89Score/HotRk-5
89Score/YS/II-26
89T-528
89UD-2
90Class-103

Medina, Pedro
82Oneon-17
83Greens-20
84Greens-23

Medina, Val
82DayBe-22

Medina, Victor
89Bluef/Star-16

Medlinger, Irving
52Park-11
V362-33

Medvin, Scott
86Shrev-18
87Shrev-7
88BuffB/CMC-10
88BuffB/Pro-1484
89BuffB/CMC-6
89BuffB/Pro-1680
89D-597
89Panini/St-160
89Score/HotRk-38
89T-756

Medwick, Joe
(Ducky)
34DS-66
35BU-145
35Wheat
36Exh/4-8
36Wheat
37Dix
37Exh/4-8
37Wheat
38Exh/4-8
38G-262
38G-286
38ONG/Pin-20
38Wheat
39Exh
39Wheat
40Wheat
41DP-22
60F-22
61F-61
74Laugh/ASG-37
80Laugh/FFeat-19
80SSPC/HOF
86S/Dec-15M
88Conlon/NatAS-15
89Pac/Leg-160
89Smok/Dodg-22
PR1-22
R302
R313
R314
R326-11A
R326-11B
R342-11
R423-69
V355-75
WG8-41

Mee, Jimmy
88Greens/Pro-1571

Mee, Tommy
78Green

Meek, Rich
89Erie/Star-12

Meeks, Tim
85Cram/PCL-169
86Albuq-17
87Albuq/Pol-14
88Tacom/CMC-5
88Tacom/Pro-633

Mehl, Steve
87CharWh-9
88Utica/Puc-8
89SoBend/GS-18

Mehrtans, Pat
88Tampa/Star-16
88Utica/Puc-21
89Utica/Puc-15

Meier, Brian
80Batav-14

Meier, Dave
82Orlan-9
83Toled-22
85D-147
85F-285
85T-356
86F-400
87OKCty-6
88IowaC/CMC-20
88IowaC/Pro-536

Meier, Jeff
89Sumter/Pro-1118

Meier, Kevin
88SanJose/Cal-135
88SanJose/Pro-132
89SanJose/Best-18
89SanJose/Cal-215
89SanJose/Pro-447
89SanJose/Star-20

Meier, Randy
82Wausa-8
83Wausa/LF-15

Meier, Scott
81AppFx-19
82AppFx-9
83GlenF-5

Meine, Heine
33G-205
R332-50

Meister, Ralph
88Sumter/Pro-418

Meizosa, Gus
87Gasto-12
89Jacks/GS-9

Mejia, Cesar
88EastLAS/Pro-10
88GlenF/Pro-924
89RochR/CMC-4
89RochR/Pro-1635

Mejia, Oscar
82Tulsa-16
84Tulsa-7
85Tulsa-7
86Water-16
87Wmspt-4

Mejia, Secar
87Myrtle-14

Mejias, Marcos
75BurlB

Mejias, Roman
57T-362
58T-452
59T-218
60T-2
62T-354
63J-186
63P-186
63T-432
64T-186

Mejias, Sam
77T-479R
78OPC-99
78T-576
79OPC-42
79T-97
81F-219
81T-521
82D-295
82F-75
82T-228

Mejias, Simeon
87Peoria-21

Mele, Albert
(Dutch)
Exh47
V362-48

Mele, Sabath
(Sam)
49B-118
50B-52
51B-168
51T/BB-25
52B-15
52StarCal/L-73H
52T-94
54B-22
54Esskay
54RM-AL6
54T-240
55B-147
55Salem
60T-470C
61Peters-16
62T-482
63T-531
64T-54
65T-506
66OPC-3
66T-3
67T-418
80Elmir-36C
Exh47

Melendez, Diego
77Cocoa
78DaytB

Melendez, Francisco
83Readg-15
84Cram/PCL-199
85Cram/PCL-43
86Portl-16
87Phoen-25
88Phoen/Pro-64
89D-611
89French-43
89RochR/CMC-3
89RochR/Pro-1654

Melendez, Jose
85PrWill-4
86PrWill-16
87Harrisbg-5
88Harris/Pro-848
89Wmspt/Pro-633
89Wmspt/Star-14

Melendez, Luis A.
71OPC-216R
71T-216R
72T-606
73OPC-47
73T-47
74OPC-307
74T-307
75OPC-353
75T-353
75T/M-353
76OPC-399
76SSPC-282
76T-399
78Syrac
87Fayette-22
88Fay/Pro-1083
88Hamil/Pro-1733

Melendez, Steve
86Geneva-19tr
88Peoria/Ko-16
89WinSal/Star-21

Melendez, William
73Cedar
76Dubuq

Meleski, Mark
86NewBrit-18
87Pawtu-25
87Pawtu/TCMA-28
88Pawtu/CMC-25
88Pawtu/Pro-454
89Pawtu/CMC-24CO
89Pawtu/Dunkin-5

89Pawtu/Pro-696
Melillo, Oscar
26Exh-116
29Exh/4-30
31Exh/4-29
33DH-32
33DL-3
33Exh/4-15
34DS-53
34Exh/4-15
34G-45
35BU-151
35Exh/4-15
35G-1F
35G-3D
35G-5D
35G-6D
55Rodeo
61F-127
R300
R309/2
R310
R313
R316
R332-39
V354-94
Melito, Chuck
80Batav-17
Mello, John
88MidwLAS/GS-43
88Rockford-24
89Rockford-24
89WPalm/Star-16
Mellody, Honey
T3/Box-72
Meloan, Paul
M116
Melrose, Jeff
86DayBe-19
86Tulsa-21
88Gasto/Pro-1012
Melson, Gary
79Tacom-9
80Richm-8
Melton, Cliff
39PB-125
40PB-83
41DP-26
41DP-94
48Sommer-8
49Sommer-6
PM10/Sm-124
Melton, David
58T-391
Melton, Larry
86PrWill-17
87Salem-3
88EastLAS/Pro-17
88Harris/Pro-857
89BuffB/CMC-8
89BuffB/Pro-1673
Melton, Reuben
47TipTop
Melton, Sam
87Elmir-11
87Elmir/Red-11
Melton, William
69T-481
70MLB/St-190
70OPC-518
70T-518
71Bz
71Bz/Test-21
71MD
71OPC-80
71T-80
71T/Coins-76
71T/GM-33
71T/S-47
71T/tatt-14
72K-12
72MB-233
72OPC-183
72OPC-184IA
72OPC-495KP
72OPC-90LL
72T-183
72T-184A
72T-495BP
72T-90LL
72T/Post-3
73OPC-455
73T-455
74OPC-170
74T-170
74T/DE-68
74T/St-158
75Ho-8
75Ho/Twink-8
75OPC-11
75T-11
75T/M-11
76OPC-309
76SSPC-155
76T-309
76T/Tr-309T
77T-107
Melvin, Bob
82BirmB-7
83BirmB-12
84Evans-11
86D-456
86Moth/Giants-12
86T-479
87D-239
87F-281
87Moth/SFG-12
87T-549
88D-638
88F-90
88Moth/Giants-12
88OPC-41
88Score-477
88T-41
89B-8
89F-335
89French-36
89OPC-329
89Score-617
89Score/Tr-61
89T-329
89T-351TL
89UD-227
90D-451
90F-181
90Score-453
90T-626
90UD-644
Melvin, Doug
77WHav
Melvin, Ken
75Shreve/TCMA-10
Melvin, Scott
86Kinston-16
87Sprin/Best-24
88StPet/Star-18
89StPet/Star-20
Melvin, William
87CharWh-1
88Peoria/Ko-17
Mena, Andres
87SnAnt-2
Menard, Dyrryl
86Osceola-18
Mendazona, Mike
89Gasto/Pro-1026
89Gasto/Star-15
Mendek, William
87Chatt/Best-24
88Vermont/Pro-958
Mendenhall, Shannon
88Lynch/Star-14
Mendez, Eddie
89Myrtle/Pro-1453
Mendez, Jesus
86StPet-20
87StPet-3
88ArkTr/GS-15
Mendez, Jose
74Laugh/Black-9
Mendez, Julio
89Savan/Pro-361
Mendez, Raul
86Cram/PCL-124
Mendez, Roberto
85Tigres-2
Mendon, Kevin
80Memph-14
Mendonca, Robert
89Batav/Pro-1918
Mendoza, Dave
76Cedar
Mendoza, Jesus
88Sumter/Pro-398
89BurlB/Pro-1605
89BurlB/Star-13
Mendoza, Mario
75OPC-457
75T-457
75T/M-457
76SSPC-606
78T-383
79T-509
80OPC-344
80T-652
81D-45
81F-613
81OPC-76
81T-76
81T/Tr-801
82D-394
82F-325
82OPC-212
82T-212
Mendoza, Mike
75Dubuq
76Dubuq
79Charl-19
80Tucso-21
81Tidew-19
Mendoza, Minnie
81Miami-6
88French-40CO
Menees, Gene
80Indianap-21
81Indianap-18
82Water-5
Menefee, John
E107
Menendez, Antonio G.
87BirmB/Best-10
88BirmB/Best-20
89BirmB/Best-3
89BirmB/Pro-103
Menendez, William
86WinSal-17
Mengwasser, Brad
82Tulsa-2
Menke, Denis
62T-597R
63T-433
64T-53
64T/Coins-90
65Kahn
65T-327
66Kahn
66OPC-184
66T-184
66T/RO-119
67Kahn
67T-396M
67T-518
68Coke
68T-232
69MB-191
69MLB/St-140
69T-487
69T/St-35
70MB-18
70MLB/St-43
70OPC-155
70T-155
70T/CB
71K-8
71MLB/St-87
71OPC-130
71T-130
71T/Coins-89
72MB-234
72T-586
73OPC-52
73T-52
74OPC-134
74T-134
77BurlB
78Duned
78TCMA-58
82Tucso-26
86Moth/Ast-9
Menosky, Mike
E120
V100
V61-46
W572
W573
Mentzer, Troy
89Everett/Star-21
Meoli, Rudy
74OPC-188
74T-188
75OPC-533
75T-533
75T/M-533
76Indianap-10
76OPC-254
76SSPC-196
76T-254
77Indianap-18
78T-489
Mercado, Candy
75AppFx
76AppFx
77AppFx
Mercado, Manny
86Watlo-19
87Watlo-2
Mercado, Orlando
80LynnS-9
81Spoka-5
82SLCty-13
83T/X-71
84D-318
84F-613
84Moth/Mar-14
84Nes/792-314
84T-314
85OKCty-1
85T-58
86OKCty-12
87Albuq/Pol-16
87D/OD-209
87T-514
88Tacom/CMC-22
88Tacom/Pro-624
89Portl/CMC-12
89Portl/Pro-209
89UD-624
Merced, Orlando
86Macon-15
88Aug/Pro-364
89Harris/Pro-299
89Harris/Star-10
Mercedes, Guillermo
86Macon-14
Mercedes, Hector
89StCath/Pro-2080
Mercedes, Henry
89Modesto/Ch-20
Mercedes, Luis
89Freder/Star-16
Mercedes, Manuel
76QuadC
Mercer, Mark
78Ashev
79Tulsa-10
80Charl-11
83OKCty-13
Mercerod, George
85Pawtu-21
Merchant, James A.
(Andy)
76OPC-594R
76T-594R
Merchant, John
81Batav-18
Merchant, Mark
88Aug/Pro-1576
89Aug/Pro-496
89SnBer/Best-27
89SnBer/Cal-93
Mercker, Kent
87Durhm-12
88CLAS/Star-31
88Durhm/Star-14
89AAA/Pro-5
89Richm/CMC-5
89Richm/Ko-24
89Richm/Pro-835
90Class-15
90D-31
90F-590
90UD-63
Mercurio, Tony
88Tidew/CANDL-30
Merejo, Domingo
87Watertn-13
88Watertn/Puc-21
89Salem/Star-12
Merejo, Jesus
88Utica/Puc-9
89Utica/Puc-16
Merejo, Luis
86Cram/PCL-92
87QuadC-11
88PalmSp/Cal-90
88PalmSp/Pro-1437
89MidldA/GS-23
Meridith, Ron
81Hawai-16
81Tucso-16
82Hawai-16
83Tucso-5
84IowaC-27
85IowaC-17
86D-533
86F-374
86IowaC-18
87Moth/Rang-16
87OKCty-13
88Louvl-34
Merigliano, Frank
88Utica/Puc-22
89SoBend/GS-8
Merkle, Cliff
E120
W573
Merkle, Fred
10Domino-83
11Helmar-133
12Sweet/Pin-119
14CJ-78
14CJ-78
60NuCard-17
61NuCard-417
86Conlon/1-49
88Conlon/4-19
BF2-79
D304
D328-116
D329-118

D350/2-116
E135-116
E254
E270/2
E300
E95
M101/4-118
M101/5-116
M116
S74-90
T201
T202
T204
T205
T206
T213/blue
T215/brown
T3-108
W514-74

Merrifield, Bill
85MidldA-19
86MidldA-17
87Edmon-14
88OkCty/CMC-15
88OkCty/Pro-36

Merrifield, Doug
81Spoka-12
82SLCty-1
83SLCty-26
86Calgary-14TR
88Calg/CMC-22
88Calg/Pro-787

Merrill, Carl
(Stump)
77WHave
79WHave-8
84Colum-23
84Colum/Pol-15MG
85Colum/Pol-16MG

Merrill, Durwood
88Umpire-30
89Umpires-28

Merrill, Mike
86Durhm-18
87Durhm-17tr

Merriman, Brett
88BurlR/Pro-1795
89Mia/Star/25-14
89Watertn/Star-14

Merriman, Lloyd
49Eureka-90
50B-173
51B-72
52B-78
55B-135

Merritt, George
E254
T205
T206

Merritt, Jim
66OPC-97
66T-97
67T-523
68OPC-64
68T-64
69MLB/St-132
69T-661
70MLB/St-32
70T-616
71Bz
71Bz/Test-7
71K-25
71MD
71MLB/St-65
71OPC-420
71T-420
71T/Coins-129
71T/tatt-15
72T-738
74OPC-318
74T-318
75OPC-83
75T-83
75T/M-83

Merritt, Lloyd
58T-231
84Savan-21MG
85Sprin-10

Mersh, Neil
78Cr/PCL-19
79WHave-30

Merson, John
52T-375

Mertens, Warren
78OrlTw

Mertes, Sam
E107

Merullo, Matt
87DayBe-14
88BirmB/Best-22
88SLAS-7
89D/Rook-50
89F/Up-21
90F-542
90Score-605
90UD-67

Mesa, Ivan
79AppFx-12
81GlenF-13
82Toled-15

Mesa, Jose
85Kingst-8
86Ventura-14
87Knoxv-1
88D-601
88RochR-13
88RochR/CMC-3
88RochR/Pro-206
89Hagers/Best-3
89RochR/Pro-1636

Mesh, Mike
85Pawtu-8
86Pawtu-14
87Pawtu-18
87Pawtu/TCMA-15
88Pawtu/CMC-18
88Pawtu/Pro-463
89Omaha/CMC-16
89Omaha/Pro-1730

Mesner, Steve
46Sunbeam
47Signal
47Sunbeam
W754

Messaros, Mike
80Cedar-20

Messer, Doug
89Salin/Cal-125
89Salin/Pro-1817

Messerly, Mike
88SoOreg/Pro-1704
89Madis/Star-7

Messersmith, John
(Andy)
69JB
69T-296
70MLB/St-176
70OPC-430
70OPC-72LL
70T-430
70T-72LL
70T/PI-9
70T/S-25
71JB
71MD
71MLB/St-351
71OPC-15
71T-15
71T/Coins-112
72K-42
72MB-235
72OPC-160
72T-160
72T/Post-18
73OPC-515
73T-515
74OPC-267
74T-267
74T/St-47
75Ho-79
75Ho/Twink-79
75K-30
75OPC-310LL
75OPC-440
75T-310LL
75T-440
75T/M-310LL
75T/M-440
76Crane-36
76MSA/Disc
76OPC-199LL
76OPC-201LL
76OPC-203LL
76OPC-305
76SSPC-70
76T-199LL
76T-201LL
76T-203LL
76T-305
77Ho-150
77K-54
77OPC-155
77T-80
77T/CS-28
78OPC-79
78T-156
78Wiffle/Discs-50
79OPC-139
79T-278
87Smok/Dodg-22
89Smok/Dodg-85

Messier, Tom
84Evrt/Cram-30A
86Fresno/Smok-10

Messitt, John
N172

Mestek, Barney
75Water

Metcalf, Thomas
64T-281R
WG10-15
WG9-18

Metheny, Bud
44Yank/St-19

Methven, Marlin
81Watlo-23
82Chatt-12
82Watlo/C-18

Metil, Bill
82Cedar-18

Metkovich, George
48Signal
49B/PCL-2
49Remar
50Remar
51B-274
52B-108
52T-310
53T-58
54JC-27
55Gol/Braves-20

Metkovich, John
52Park-89

Metoyer, Tony
86Ashvl-20
87Osceola-12
89Mia/Star/22-13

Metro, Charles
46Remar-11
66Pep/Tul
70OPC-16MG
70T-16

Mettler, Bradley
85Greens-27

Metts, Carey
89Erie/Star-13

Metzger, Clarence E.
(Butch)
75Hawai
76OPC-593R
76T-593
77Ho-99
77T-215
78T-431
80Richm-13

Metzger, Curt
86ArkTr-15tr

Metzger, Roger
71OPC-404R
71T-404
72OPC-217
72T-217
73OPC-395
73T-395
74OPC-224
74T-224
74T/St-34
75Ho-115
75OPC-541
75T-541
75T/M-541
76Ho-67
76OPC-297
76SSPC-57
76T-297
77Ho-20
77OPC-44
77T-481
78BK/A-15
78Ho-85
78T-697
79Pol/Giants-16
79T-167
80OPC-164
80Pol/Giants-16
80T-311

Metzler, Alex
29Exh/4-20

Meulens, Hensley
87PrWill-1
88Albany/Pro-1349
88BBAmer-1
88EastLAS/Pro-3
89Albany/Best-17
89Albany/Pro-337
89Albany/Star-13
89Class-110
89D-547
89F/Up-51
89Score/HotRk-12
89Star/Wax-99
89UD/Ext-746
90Class-133
90F-449
90Score-636
90Score/100Ris-53
90T-83
90UD-546

Meusel, Robert W.
21Exh-114
25Exh-98
26Exh-101
27Exh-51
28Yueng-7
86Conlon/1-34
87Conlon/2-21
88Conlon/5-22
E121/120
E121/80
E126-39
E210-7
E220
V100
W501-35
W502-7
W515-21
W517-49
W572
W575
WG7-31

Meusel, Emil
(Irish)
25Exh-36
26Exh-38
87Conlon/2-22
E120
E121/120
E121/80
E126-34
E220
V100
V117-17
V61-55
W501-113
W501-36
W515-21
W572
W573
W575

Meyer, Alfred
77StPet

Meyer, Basil
88Keno/Pro-1404
89Visal/Cal-94
89Visal/Pro-1445

Meyer, Bob B.
64T-488R
65OPC-219
65T-219
70McDon-2
70T-667
71MLB/St-445
71OPC-456
71T-456

Meyer, Brad
88Gasto/Pro-1015

Meyer, Brian
86AubAs-16
87Osceola-13
88ColAst/Best-5
88SLAS-31
89B-319
89D-640
89Tucso/CMC-9
89Tucso/Pro-189
90D-648
90F-232
90T-766
90UD-22

Meyer, Dan
75OPC-620R
75T-620R
75T/M-620R
76Ho-132
76OPC-242
76SSPC-365
76T-242
77Ho-135
77OPC-186
77T-527
78Ho-97
78K-12
78OPC-55
78T-57
79OPC-363
79T-683
80OPC-207
80T-396
81D-43
81F-603
81OPC-143
81Pol/Mariners-5
81T-143
81T/SO-40
81T/St-125
82D-176
82F-512
82T-413
82T/Tr-70T
83D-413

83F-527
83T-208
83T/St-110
84Cram/PCL-96
84F-455
84Nes/792-609
84T-609
85Moth/A's-23

Meyer, Jack
56T-269
57T-162
58T-186
59T-269
60L-137
60T-64
61T-111

Meyer, Joey
86Vanco-17
87D-460
87Denver-5
88D-36
88D/Best-239
88D/Rook-38
88F-645
88F/U-U40
88Leaf-36RR
88Pol/Brew-23
88Score/Tr-75T
88T-312
89B-138
89Class-10
89D-339
89F-191
89Gard-13
89OPC-136
89Panini/St-363
89Pol/Brew-23
89Score-374
89Score/HotRk-93
89Score/YS/I-33
89Sf-135
89T-136
89T/Big-153
89UD-403
90Score-532
90T-673

Meyer, Lambert
(Dutch)
No Cards.

Meyer, Lee
E254

Meyer, Randy
81CharR-20

Meyer, Rick
89Martins/Star-21

Meyer, Russ
49Lummis
51B-75
51BR-D7
52B-220
52T-339
53B/Col-129
54B-186
54NYJour
55B-196
55Gol/Dodg-20
56T-227
59T-482
79TCMA-194
88FSLAS/Star-29
89Albany/Best-27
89Albany/Pro-322

Meyer, Scott
80WHave-9
81WHave-21

Meyer, Stephen W.
86Erie-19
87Sprin/Best-4
88Sprin/Best-18

Meyer, William
49Eureka-167
51B-272
52B-155
52T-387
PM10/Sm-125

Meyers
WG1-34
WG1-68

Meyers, Benny
C46-28

Meyers, Brian
88AppFx/Pro-139

Meyers, Glenn
86QuadC-23

Meyers, Henry W.
V100

Meyers, John
(Chief)
10Domino-84
11Helmar-134
12Sweet/Pin-120
14Piedmont/St-38
BF2-59
D304
D328-117
D329-119
D350/2-117
E135-117
E224
E254
E270/1
E286
E91
E96
E97
E98
M101/4-119
M101/5-117
S74-91
T201
T202
T205
T206
T213
T215/brown
T3-50
W501-94
W555
WG4-20
WG5-31
WG6-29

Meyers, Paul
87Shrev-2
88Shreve/Pro-1288
89Phoen/CMC-22
89Phoen/Pro-1490

Meyett, Don
89Beloi/Star-17

Micelotta, Bob
54T-212

Michael, Bill
75Clint

Michael, Gene
66EH-45
67T-428R
68T-299
69T-626
70OPC-114
70T-114
71MLB/St-496
71OPC-483
71T-483
72T-713
72T-714A
73OPC-265
73T-265
74OPC-299
74T-299
74T/St-214
75OPC-608
75T-608
75T/M-608
76SSPC-369
79Colum-7
81D-500
81T-670MG
86Gator-4MG
86T/Tr-73T
87Berg/Cubs-4
87T-43MG

Michael, Steve
82ElPas-12
84ElPas-4
87Elmir-19
87Elmir/Red-19
88Elmir-3
89Elmir/Puc-7

Michaels, Cass
47TipTop
48L-13
49B-12
50B-91
51B-132
51FB
52B-36
52T-178
53B/Col-130
54B-150
55B-85

Michalak, Tony
87Everett-15
88Clint/Pro-710

Micheal, Matt
89Penin/Star-15

Michel, Domingo
86VeroB-18
87SnAnt-7
88SnAnt/Best-6
89Albuq/CMC-22
89Albuq/Pro-81

Michel, John
82Idaho-19
83Madis/LF-19

Micheu, Buddy
89Butte/SP-25

Michno, Tim
88WinSal/Star-12

Michno, Tom
89CharlK-15

Mickan, Dan
84Newar-5

Middlekauff, Craig
89NiagFls/Puc-17

Middleton, Damon
77Clint

Mielke, Gary
88OkCty/CMC-5
88OkCty/Pro-35
89OkCty/CMC-6
89OkCty/Pro-1528
90D-679
90Score-574
90T-221
90UD-612

Mielke, Greg
75AppFx
76AppFx

Miggins, Larry
53B/Col-142
53Hunter
79TCMA-285

Miggins, Mark
77Cocoa
79Charl-10
81Tucso-9
82Tucso-17
83Miami-26

Miglio, John
81QuadC-21
82Watlo/B-8
82Watlo/C-16
83Watlo/LF-11
85Water-8
87ElPas-12
87TexLgAS-20
88Denver/CMC-4
88Denver/Pro-1260
89ElPas/GS-10

Mijares, Willie
85Evrt/Cram-9
87Clint-6
88SanJose/Cal-124
88SanJose/Pro-110

Mikan, George
51Wheat
52Wheat

Mikesell, Larry James
82Wisco-12

Mikkelsen, Pete
64T-488R
65OPC-177
65T-177
66EH-19
66T-248
67T-425
67T/Test/PP-15
68T-516
71MLB/St-107
WG10-16

Miksis, Eddie
47TipTop
49Eureka-42
51B-117
52B-32
52StarCal/L-80A
52T-172
53T-39
54B-61
55B-181
56T-285
57T-350
58T-121
59T-58
89Rini/Dodg-24

Mikulik, Joe
86ColumAst-19
87ColAst/Pro-15
87ColumAst-15
88Tucso-17
88Tucso/CMC-18
88Tucso/Pro-176

Milacki, Bob
86Hagers-11
87CharO/WBTV-30
88AAA/Pro-35
88RochR-16
88RochR/Gov-16
89Class-92
89D-651
89D/Best-254
89D/Rook-22
89F-649M
89F/Up-6
89French-18
89Panini/St-251
89Score-651
89Sf-224M
89T-324
89UD/Ext-735
90D-333
90F-182
90Score-239
90Score/100Ris-68
90T-73
90UD-635

Milan, J. Clyde
10Domino-85
11Helmar-75
12Sweet/Pin-62
14CJ-56
15CJ-56
21Exh-108
40PB-130
BF2-48
D327
D328-118
D329-120
D350/2-118
E120
E121/120
E121/80
E122
E135-118
E220
E254
E91
M101/4-120
M101/5-118
M116
T202
T204
T205
T206
T207
V100
W501-15
W516-25
W573
W575
WG5-32
WG6-30

Milbourne, Larry
75OPC-512
75T-512
75T/M-512
76SSPC-58
78T-366
79OPC-100
79T-199
80T-422
81D-486
81F-611
81T-583
81T/Tr-802
82D-614
82F-42
82T-669
82T/Tr-71T
83D-411
83F-415
83T-91
83T/X-72
84Moth/Mar-10
84Nes/792-281
84T-281
84T/X-79
85F-493
85T-754

Milchin, Mike
89Hamil/Star-21

Milene, Jeff
89Elizab/Star-18

Miles, Eddie
82AppFx-20
83GlenF-6

Miles, James
69T-658R
70OPC-154R
70T-154R

Miles, Wilson
(Dee)
40PB-195

Mileur, Jerome
83Nashua-25
85Nashua-29

Miley, Dave
81Cedar-9
83Water-10
87Vermont-17
89Cedar/Best-22
89Cedar/Pro-927
89Cedar/Star-22

Miley, Michael
76OPC-387
76T-387
77T-257

Milholland, Eric
86AppFx-15
87DayBe-3
88Tampa/Star-17

Miljus, John
V100
W513-65
Millan, Felix
67OPC-89
67T-89
68T-241
69MB-192
69MLB/St-115
69OPC-210
69T-210
69T/St-7
70MLB/St-8
70OPC-452AS
70T-452AS
70T-710
71MD
71MLB/St-17
71OPC-81
71T-81
71T/Coins-5
71T/S-33
71T/tatt-12
72MB-236
72T-540
73OPC-407
73T-407
74K-53
74OPC-132
74T-132
74T/DE-26
74T/St-68
75Ho-111
75OPC-445
75T-445
75T/M-445
76Ho-120
76K-9
76OPC-245
76SSPC-536
76T-245
77Ho-96
77OPC-249
77T-605
78T-505
78TCMA-31
Millay, Gar
87PortChar-23
88OkCty/CMC-13
88OkCty/Pro-40
88Tulsa-21
89Tulsa/GS-18
Miller, Bill
89GreatF-31
89Idaho/Pro-2020
Miller, C. Bruce
75OPC-606
75T-606
75T/M-606
76OPC-367
76Phoen
76SSPC-102
76T-367
82Sprin-3
Miller, Charles B.
(Molly)
T206
Miller, Danny
75QuadC
Miller, Darrell
81Holyo-17
82Holyo-22
84Cram/PCL-107
85D-644
86Smok/Cal-18
86T-524
87Smok/Cal-11
87T-337
88D-551
88Edmon/CMC-12
88Edmon/Pro-579
88F-498
88Score-463
88T-679
89Colum/CMC-19
89Colum/Pol-13
89Colum/Pro-733
89Score-499
89T-68
89UD-462
Miller, Dave
87Durhm-11
88Greenv/Best-14
88Richm-20
89Freder/Star-17
89OkCty/CMC-7
89OkCty/Pro-1522
Miller, Don (Killer)
88Stock/Cal-204
88Stock/Pro-750
89Stock/Best-27
89Stock/Cal-175GM
89Stock/Pro-397
89Stock/Star-24
Miller, Dyar
75IntAS/TCMA-2
75OPC-614R
75T-614R
75T/M-614R
76OPC-555
76SSPC-379
76T-555
77T-77
78T-239
79T-313
80Tidew-10
81Louvl-4
81T-472
82F-534
82Louvl-18
82T-178
84Louvl-4
86Louisvl-2
Miller, Edmund
(Bing)
21Exh-109
25Exh-109
26Exh-109
31Exh/4-27
33G-59
40PB-137
60F-39
61F-62
E120
R315-A25
R315-B25
R316
V353-59
V61-23
W517-31
W573
Miller, Edward Lee
78Richm
79Richm-24
80Richm-22
80T-675R
81Pol/Atl-45
82D-425
82F-441
82T-451
83Portl-20
85Beaum-13
Miller, Edward R.
39PB-49
40PB-56
41PB-1
48L-68
Miller, Edward S.
R314/Can
Miller, Elmer
E120
E121/120
E121/80
V100
W573
W575
Miller, George
E223
N172
N284
N29
N403
N43
Miller, Gerry
81BurlB-24
82Beloi-3
Miller, Jeff
89Wausa/GS-23
Miller, Jerry
86Miami-17C
Miller, Jim
77Charl
Miller, John Allen
69T-641R
Miller, John B.
(Dots)
14CJ-49
14Piedmont/St-39
15CJ-49
D303
D322
D329-121
E102
E104
E105
E106
E254
E270/2
E90/1
E90/2
E91
E92
M101/4-121
M116
T205
T206
T207
T213/blue
Miller, John E.
63T-208R
65OPC-49R
65T-49R
66T-427
67OPC-141
67T-141
Miller, Joseph
N172
Miller, Keith
85Lynch-18
86Jacks/TCMA-27
86Portl-17
86Readg-17
87Maine-8
87Maine/TCMA-15
87S/Rook-50
87Tidew-10
87Tidew/TCMA-16
88D-562
88D/Mets/Bk-562
88F-144
88Maine/CMC-20
88Maine/Pro-290
88Score-639
88Sf-225
88T-382
88Tidew/CANDL-11
88Tidew/CMC-20
88Tidew/Pro-1604
89AAA/Pro-24
89B-380
89Class-16
89D-623
89F-45
89Score-464
89Score/HotRk-62
89Score/YS/I-23
89ScrWB/CMC-13
89ScrWB/Pro-716
89T-268
89T-557
89T/Mets/Fan-25
89Tidew/CMC-14
89Tidew/Pro-1948
89UD/Ext-739
90D-507
90Score-559
90T-58
90UD-190
Miller, Kenny
86Cram/PCL-142
87Spart-9
Miller, Larry Don
65T-349
69T-323
Miller, Larry
59DF
Miller, Lawrence H.
(Hack)
21Exh-110
E120
V61-86
W573
WG7-32
Miller, Lemmie
83Albuq-22
84Cram/PCL-150
85Cram/PCL-165
Miller, Lowell Otto
14CJ-53
15CJ-53
BF2-60
D121/80
D327
D328-119
D329-122
D350/2-119
E121/120
E122
E135-119
M101/4-122
M101/5-119
T207
V100
W501-95
W575
Miller, Mark
80Cedar-16
80ElPas-8
80Indianap-18
Miller, Michael
83Butte-19
86Clearw-17
86Omaha-15
87Memph/Best-15
87Pittsf-9
87Readg-25
87WinSal-20
88Clmbia/GS-9
88Memph/Best-22
88SALAS/GS-14
89StLucie/Star-17
Miller, Mickey
76Baton
Miller, Mike
79Savan-25
Miller, Norm
67T-412R
68OPC-161
68T-161
69OPC-76
69T-76
70T-619
71MLB/St-88
71OPC-18
71T-18
72MB-237
72OPC-466
72T-466
73OPC-637
73T-637
74OPC-439
74T-439
Miller, Orlando
89Oneon/Pro-2124
Miller, Paul
89Salem/Star-13
Miller, Ralph Jr.
77StPet
78StPet
83StPet-27GM
Miller, Randall
80OPC-351R
80T-680R
Miller, Ray
86T-381MG
Miller, Richard A.
(Rick)
72T-741R
74OPC-247
74T-247
74T/St-136
75OPC-103
75T-103
75T/M-103
76OPC-302
76SSPC-416
76T-302
77T-566
78T-482
79T-654
80OPC-27
80T-48
81D-294
81F-279
81OPC-239
81T-239
83OPC-188
84D-493
84F-403
84Nes/792-344
84T-344
85D-517
85F-163
85T-502
86T-424
Miller, Richard
(Rich)
76Dubuq
78Tidew
79Jacks-18
86LitFalls-19MG
88Tidew/CANDL-4C
88Tidew/CMC-26
88Tidew/Pro-1585
89Tidew/CMC-25
Miller, Robert G.
(Bob)
54T-241
55T-9
56T-263
62T-572
Miller, Robert J.
(Bob)
50B-227
51B-220
52T-187
55B-110
55T-157
55T/DH-60
56T-334
57T-46
58T-326
59T-379
79TCMA-289
Miller, Robert L.
(Bob)
60T-101
61T-314
62Salada-185
62Shirriff-185

62T-293
62T/St-159
63T-261
64T-394
65OPC-98
65T-98
66T-208
67T-461
68T-534
69T-403
70OPC-47
70T-47
71MLB/St-38
71OPC-542
71T-542
72OPC-414
72T-414
73OPC-277
73T-277
74OPC-624
74T-624
77T-113C

Miller, Roger
77Spoka

Miller, Roger
88CapeCod/Sum-184

Miller, Roscoe
E107

Miller, Roy
(Doc)
10Domino-86
11Helmar-163
12Sweet/Pin-142
D303
E286
S74-113
T201
T202
T207
T215/blue
T216

Miller, Scott
82QuadC-23
88CapeCod/Sum-87

Miller, Steve
86Shrev-19
87Phoen-26

Miller, Stu
53B/BW-16
53Hunter
53T-183
54B-158
54Hunter
54T-164
56T-293
58SFCall
58T-111
59T-183
60T-378
61T-72
62J-143
62P-143
62P/Can-143
62Salada-205
62Shirriff-205
62T-155
62T/bucks
62T/St-201
63T-286
64T-565
65T-499
66T-265
67T-345
78TCMA-254
84Moth/Giants-18

Miller, Ted
86Kenosha-16

Miller, Todd
85Evrt/Cram-10
86Clint-13
88Clint/Pro-706

Miller, Tom
82Lynch-11

Miller, Ward
14CJ-5
15CJ-5
T207

Miller, Warren
M116

Miller, William Paul
52T-403
53B/BW-54
53T-100
54NYJour
55B-245
55Esskay
79TCMA-209
PM10/L-28

Miller-Jones, Garry
85Pawtu-9
86Pawtu-15
87Pawtu-19
87Pawtu/TCMA-16

Miller-Jones, Gary
88Pawtu/CMC-19
88Pawtu/Pro-459
89Pawtu/CMC-12
89Pawtu/Dunkin-11
89Pawtu/Pro-689

Milles, Rhadames G.
81ArkTr-6

Millette, Joe
89Batav/Pro-1922

Millies, Walter
40PB-218

Milligan, John
N172
N690

Milligan, Randy
82Lynch-15
83Lynch-7
84Jacks-25
86Jacks/TCMA-26
86Tidew-20
87Tidew-28
87Tidew/TCMA-17
88D/Rook-32
88F/U-U115
88Score-623
89B-10
89F/Up-7
89French-15
89T/Tr-81T
89Tidew/CANDL-13
89UD-559
89UD/Ext-740
90D-519
90F-183
90Score-252
90T-153
90UD-663

Milligan, William J.
T206

Milliken, Bob
53Exh/Can-44
53T-221
54T-177
55T-111
55T/DH-118
62Kahn/Atl
79TCMA-234

Millner, Tim
83MidldC-9

Mills, Alan
86Cram/PCL-81
87PrWill-7
88PrWill/Star-17
89FtLaud/Star-16

Mills, Art
47TipTop

Mills, Brad
80Memph-15
82F-196
82Hygrade
82OPC-118R
82T-118R
83D-366
83F-288
83OPC-199
83Stuart-30
83T-744
84Indianap-9
85Cram/PCL-75
86IowaC-19
88CharWh/Best-2
89Peoria/Ko-30MG

Mills, Colonel
(Buster)
54T-227

Mills, Craig
86GlenF-16
87Lakel-3

Mills, E.L.
N172

Mills, Gil
52Park-59
53Exh/Can-55

Mills, Gotay
82Louvl-19
83ArkTr-21
84ArkTr-21

Mills, Jim
76Wausa

Mills, Ken
83Clint/LF-19

Mills, Michael
85Beaum-17
86Beaum-19
88Wichi-31
89Duned/Star-11
89Knoxv/Best-16
89Knoxv/Pro-1141
89Knoxv/Star-23

Mills, Richard Allen
71OPC-512R
71T-512R

Milnar, Al
40PB-202
41PB-33

Milne, Bill
49Eureka-119

Milne, William
(Pete)
53Mother-28

Milner, Brian
81OPC-238R
81T-577R
82Knoxv-10
82OPC-203R
82T-203

Milner, Eddie
79Indianap-10
80Indianap-10
81Indianap-9
82T/Tr-72T
83D-169
83F-597
83OPC-363
83T-449
84Borden-20
84D-365
84F-474
84Nes/792-34
84OPC-34
84T-34
84T/St-60
85D-428
85F-541
85OPC-198
85T-198
85T/St-53
86D-325
86F-182
86T-544
86TexGold-20
87D-433
87F-205
87Moth/SFG-15
87OPC-253
87T-253
87T/St-144
87T/Tr-78T
88F-91
88Kahn/Reds-9
88Score-548
88T-677

Milner, John
72T-741R
73OPC-4
73T-4
74OPC-234
74T-234
74T/St-69
75Ho-15
75Ho/Twink-15
75OPC-264
75T-264
75T/M-264
76OPC-517
76SSPC-547
76T-517
77T-172
78T-304
79T-523
80OPC-38
80T-71
81D-377
81F-386
81T-618
82D-266
82F-197
82Hygrade
82OPC-331
82T-638
83F-311

Milner, Ted
84Savan-9
86SanJose-13

Miloszewski, Frank
78Salem

Milstein, David
86Elmir-12
87WinHav-14
88WinHav/Star-13
89NewBrit/Pro-621
89NewBrit/Star-10

Mims, Fred
73Cedar
74Cedar

Mims, Larry
87Miami-23
88Hagers/Star-12
89AubAs/Pro-6
89Hagers/Pro-264
89Wich/Roc/Up-13

Minarcin, John
78Wisco
79Wisco-10

Minarcin, Rudy
55T-174
56T-36

Minaya, Omar
81Wausa-22

Minaya, Robert
88Pulas/Pro-1767
89Sumter/Pro-1111

Minch, John
87Modesto-7
88Huntsvl/BK-12

Mincher, Don
60T-548
61Clover-17
61Peters-5
61T-336
62T-386
63T-269
64T-542
65OPC-108
65T-108
66T-388
67T-312
68Bz-12
68OPC-75
68T-75
69MB-193
69MLB/St-96
69T-285
69T/decal
69T/S-33
69T/St-227
70K-75
70MB-19
70MLB/St-261
70OPC-185
70T-185
70T/PI-17
71K-27
71MLB/St-521
71OPC-680
71T-680
72MB-238
72OPC-242
72T-242
78TCMA-54
89Smok/Angels-5

Minchey, Nate
88OPC-6
88Rockford-25
89Rockford-25

Miner, J.R.
86BurlEx-16MG
87BurlEx-24

Miner, James
82CharR-1
84Memph-16
85Cram/PCL-72
86Tucso-14
87Tucso-13

Minetto, Craig
80Ogden-3
80T-494
81T-316
82RochR-4
83RochR-5
84Cram/PCL-69

Mingori, Steve
69T-339R
71OPC-612R
71T-612R
72OPC-261
72T-261
73OPC-532
73T-532
74OPC-537
74T-537
75OPC-544
75T-544
75T/M-544
76OPC-541
76SSPC-161
76T-541
77T-314
78T-696
79T-72
80T-219
86Syrac-19CO
87Duned-13

Minick, Jeff
86Lakel-14

Minier, Pablo
77Spart

Minissale, Frank
88LitFalls/Puc-29

Minium, Matt
80Batav-24

Minker, Al
80WHave-1

Minnehan
N172

Minnema, Dave
86Lakel-15
Minner, Paul
49Eureka-43
52B-211
52T-127
53B/Col-71
53T-92
54B-13
54T-28
56T-182
79TCMA-163
Minnick, Don
80LynnS-8
Minnifield, Wallace
89Kingspt/Star-17
Minor, Blas
89Salem/Star-14
Minoso, Minnie
52B-5
52BR
52RM-AL15
52StarCal/L-73E
52T-195
53B/Col-36
53NB
53T-66
54B-38
54Dix
54RH
54RM-AL7
55B-25
55RM-AL24
56T-125
56YellBase/Pin-22
57T-138
58T-295
59Kahn
59T-166M
59T-80
60T-365
61Bz-7
61P-25
61T-380
61T-42LL
61T/St-125
62J-51
62P-51
62P/Can-51
62Salada-39A
62Salada-39B
62Shirriff-39
62T-28
62T/bucks
62T/St-188
63T-190
64T-538
77AppFx
77OPC-262RB
77T-232M
79TCMA-286
80Cram/Leg-96
84TrueVal/WS-24
86Coke/WS-CO
87Coke/WS-29
88Coke/WS-18
88Pac/Leg-51
89Coke/WS-30
89Swell-59
Exh47
PM10/Sm-126
Minton, Greg
75Phoen-8
77Phoen
77T-489R
78Cr/PCL-102
78T-312
79T-84
80Pol/Giants-38
80T-588
81D-579
81F-449
81OPC-111
81T-111
81T/St-238
82D-348
82F-396
82OPC-144
82T-687
82T/St-107
83D-186
83D/AAS-10
83F-269
83K-46
83Moth/Giants-5
83OPC-107
83T-3M
83T-470
83T/St-137
83T/St-138
83T/St-249
84D-187
84F-383
84F/St-69
84Moth/Giants-8
84Nes/792-205
84OPC-205
84T-205
85D-143
85F-617
85Moth/Giants-8
85OPC-45
85T-45
85T/St-167
86D-480
86F-549
86Moth/Giants-8
86T-310
86T-516M
87F-282
87F/U-U80
87Moth/SFG-9
87OPC-333
87T-724
87T/Tr-79T
88D-505
88F-499
88OPC-129
88Score-176
88Smok/Angels-11
88T-129
88T/St-176
89D-490
89D/Best-283
89F-485
89OPC-306
89Score-543
89T-576
89UD-635
90D-116
90F-140
90Score-48
90T-421
90UD-83
Minton, Jesse
87Sumter-17
Mintz, Alan
80Elmir-41
Minutelli, Gino
86Cedar/TCMA-7
87Tampa-20
88Chatt/Best-16
Mirabella, Paul
78Cr/PCL-48
79Colum-26
81D-151
81OPC-11
81T-382
82D-629
82OPC-163
82T-499
83D-541
83F-573
83T-12
84Moth/Mar-17
85Cram/PCL-89
85F-494
85T-766
86Moth/Mar-13
87Denver-9
88Denver/CMC-5
88Denver/Pro-1258
89D-654
89F-192
89Pol/Brew-27
89Score-569
89T-192
89UD-322
Mirabito, Tim
86Tampa-13
87Vermont-8
Miranda, Angel
88Stock/Cal-180
88Stock/Pro-749
Miranda, Willie
53T-278
54T-56
55B-79
55Esskay
55T-154
56T-103
56T/Pin-2SS
57T-151
58Hires-32
58T-179
59T-540
Miscik, Bob
82Buffa-2
84Cram/PCL-136
85Cram/PCL-239
86Hawai-17
87Edmon-4
88Edmon/CMC-15
88Edmon/Pro-577
Miscik, Dennis
77Cocoa
80Tucso-13
81OkCty/TCMA-11
Misuraca, Mike
89Elizab/Star-19
89Keno/Pro-1071
89Keno/Star-15
Mitchell, Albert
(Roy)
E270/2
Mitchell, Charlie
84Pawtu-1
85D-40
85IntLgAS-18
85Pawtu-20
86Toled-17
89Nashvl-16
89Nashvl/CMC-1
89Nashvl/Pro-1273
Mitchell, Clarence
10Domino-87
11Helmar-118
12Sweet/Pin-104
28Yueng-15
D328-120
E120
E135-120
E210-15
L1-118
S81-93
W502-15
W573
Mitchell, Craig
75Tucso-15
76OPC-591R
76T-591R
76Tucso-32
77SnJos-15
77T-491R
78T-711
79Ogden/TCMA-21
79Ogden/TCMA-5
Mitchell, Fred F.
C46-47
E107
E270/2
E90/1
M116
T206
V100
W514-96
Mitchell, Glenn
88Idaho/Pro-1837
88Sumter/Pro-408
89Sumter/Pro-1116
Mitchell, Howie
78Cr/PCL-116
Mitchell, J.W.
79QuadC-10
Mitchell, Joe
77Newar
Mitchell, John
83Beloi/LF-5
86Tidew-21
87D/Rook-37
87F/U-U81
87Idaho-24
87T/Tr-80T
87Tidew-20
87Tidew/TCMA-7
88F-145
88Score-249
88T-207
88Tidew/CANDL-23
88Tidew/CMC-8
88Tidew/Pro-1577
89Tidew/CMC-4
89Tidew/Pro-1970
Mitchell, John
W575
Mitchell, Jorge
87Jamestn-11
88James/Pro-1916
Mitchell, Joseph
85Beloi-3
86Stockton-15
87ElPas-2
88ElPas/Best-25
89Denver/CMC-20
89Denver/Pro-43
Mitchell, Keith
88Sumter/Pro-390
89BurlB/Pro-1609
89BurlB/Star-15
Mitchell, Kevin
82Lynch-6
84Tidew-23
85IntLgAS-4
85Tidew-18
86D/Rook-17
86F/Up-U76
86S/Rook-49
86T/Tr-74T
87Bohem-7
87D-599
87D/OD-145
87F-17
87F/RecSet-21
87F/U-U82
87Leaf-170
87OPC-307
87S-144
87T-653
87T/Gloss60-50
87T/Tr-81T
87ToysRUs-21
88D-66
88F-92
88F/Hottest-27
88F/St-S5
88Leaf-87
88Moth/Giants-3
88OPC-387
88Panini/St-424
88Panini/St-448IA
88Score-481
88T-497
88T/Big-57
88T/St-88
88T/UK-48
89B-474
89Class-31
89Class/Up/2-198
89D-485
89D/Best-281
89F-336
89Moth/Giants-3
89OPC-189
89Panini/St-216
89Score-39
89Score/Mast-12
89Score/YS/II-38
89Sf-142
89T-189
89T/Big-129
89T/St-84
89UD-163
90Class-150
90Class-64
90D-11DK
90D-715AS
90D-98
90D/Bon/MVP-BC11
90D/Preview-4
90F-637M
90F-65
90F/WaxBox-C21
90Score-343
90Score/100St-50
90Sf-1
90T-401AS
90T-500
90UD-117
90UD-40TC
Mitchell, L. Dale
48L-165
49B-43
50B-130
50NumNum
51B-5
51T/RB-13
52B-239
52NumNum-15
52StarCal/L-74F
52T-92
52TipTop
53B/Col-119
53RM-AL9
53T-26
54B-148
54DanDee
55B-314
55Gol/Ind-19
55Salem
56T-268
79TCMA-140
Exh47
Mitchell, Mark
87Oneon-22
88FtLaud/Star-15
Mitchell, Michael F.
14Piedmont/St-40
15CJ-62
E254
E270/2
E90/1
M116
S74-78
T202
T204
T205
T206
T207
T213/blue
T213/brown

T215/blue
T3-24
Mitchell, Paul
76OPC-393
76T-393
77SnJos-25
77T-53
78T-558
79OPC-118
79T-233
80T-131
81D-205
81T-449
Mitchell, Robert V.
(Bobby Van)
79Albuq-18
80Albuq-20
81Albuq/TCMA-22
82F-14
82Toled-28
83F-620
83T-647
83T/St-91
84Cram/PCL-202
84F-571
84Nes/792-307
84T-307
84Toled-10
Mitchell, Robert V.
(Bobby Vance)
71OPC-111R
71T-111R
74OPC-497
74T-497
75OPC-468
75T-468
75T/M-468
76OPC-479
76SSPC-242
76T-479
79Hawai-1
80Hawai-10
81Portl-18
82Portl-15
Mitchell, Ron
75Shreve/TCMA-11
76Shrev
78Colum
79Portl-8
80Buffa-2
Mitchell, Scot
82Madis-11
Mitchell, William
D329-123
D350/2-120
M101/4-123
M101/5-120
T207
Mitchener, Mike
89SoBend/GS-14
Mitta, Chris
88Pulas/Pro-1763
Mitterwald, George
68T-301R
69T-491R
70OPC-118
70T-118
71MLB/St-467
71OPC-189
71T-189
72OPC-301
72OPC-302IA
72T-301
72T-302A
74OPC-249
74T-249
74T/St-209
74T/Tr-249T
75OPC-411
75T-411
75T/M-411
76OPC-506
76SSPC-318
76T-506
77T-124
78SnJos-20
78T-688
86Orlan-12MG
87Orlan-9
Miyauchi, Hector
88Fresno/Cal-15
88Fresno/Pro-1233
Mize, John
38Exh/4-8
39Exh
40Wheat-6
41DP-39
41DP-99
48B-4
48L-46
49B-85
49Eureka-120
50B-139
51B-50
51BR-A7
51FB
51T/BB-50
52B-145
52BR
52T-129
53B/BW-15
53NB
53RM-AL18
53T-77
60F-38
61F-63
72Laugh/GF-17
72T/Test-3
74Laugh/ASG-47
80Cram/Leg-49
83D/HOF-10
85CircK-32
85D/HOF-4
85West/2-44
86S/Dec-24M
88Pac/Leg-63
89HOF/St-3
89Pac/Leg-180
89Swell-55
D305
R302
R312
R346-30
R423-70
W754
Mize, Paul
80WHave-8
81Tacom-16
82Tacom-15
82WHave-16
Mizell, Wilmer
52T-334
53B/BW-23
53Hunters
53T-128
54T-249
56T-193
57T-113
58T-385
61Kahn
61P-140
Mizerock, John
84D-380
85Cram/PCL-68
86D-502
86Tucso-15
87D-653
87Richm/TCMA-10
87T-408
88Richm-25
88Richm/CMC-21
88Richm/Pro-19
89Richm/CMC-12
89Richm/Ko-25
89Richm/Pro-827
Mmahat, Kevin
88FSLAS/Star-44
88FtLaud/Star-16
89Albany/Best-23
89Albany/Pro-341
89Albany/Star-14
90D-481
90Score-643
Moates, Dave
76OPC-327
76T-327
77T-588
77Tucso
Mobley, Anton
89StCath/Pro-2084
Moccia, Mario
89NiagFls/Puc-18
Moeller, Daniel
C46-76
T206
Moeller, Dennis
86Cram/PCL-50
87AppFx-26
88AppFx/Pro-160
89BBCity/Star-17
Moeller, Joe
63T-53
64T-549
65OPC-238
65T-238
66T-449
67OPC-149
67T-149
68T-359
69T-444
70OPC-97
70T-97
71MLB/St-108
71OPC-288
71T-288
85SpokAT/Crm-14
Moeller, Ron
61T-466
63T-541
Moesche, Carl
84Butte-7
Moffet, Samuel
N172
Moffitt, G. Scott
76QuadC
77QuadC
80SLCty-4
81SLCty-23
Moffitt, Randy
73OPC-43
73T-43
74OPC-156
74T-156
75OPC-132
75T-132
75T/M-132
76OPC-553
76T-553
77T-464
78T-284
78Wiffle/Discs-51
79Pol/Giants-17
79T-62
80Pol/Giants-17
80T-359
81D-195
81F-446
81T-622
83D-545
83F-456
83T-723
83T/X-73
84D-390
84F-163
84Nes/792-108
84OPC-108
84T-108
Moford, Herb
59T-91
Mogridge, George
E120
T207
V100
W572
W573
Moharter, Dave
77Tucso
78Cr/PCL-13
79Tucso-16
80Charl-7
87Macon-25
88Aug/Pro-383
Mohorcic, Dale
81Portl-17
83LynnP-6
85OKCty-26
86OKCty-13
86Rang-34
87D-531
87F-131
87Moth/Rang-15
87Smok/R-5
87T-497
88D-470
88D/Best-144
88F-474
88Moth/R-15
88OPC-163
88Score-452
88Smok/R-6
88T-163
88T/St-242
89D-630
89F-259
89Score-420
89Score/NWest-16
89T-26
89UD/Ext-727
90F-450
90Score-191
90UD-530
Mohr, Ed
79QuadC-2
Mohr, Tommy
83Butte-25
85FtMyr-19
Moisan, William
52Mother-64
Mokan, John
25Exh-46
26Exh-46
27Exh-23
E120
Moldes, Orestes
80Batav-11
Molero, Juan
87Greens-13
88Lynch/Star-15
89Lynch/Star-14
Molesworth, Carlton
E270/2
T206
T213/brown
Molina, Albert
89Salem/Star-15
Molina, Mario
88QuadC/GS-18
89PalmSp/Pro-477
Molinaro, Bob
77Evansvl/TCMA-19
79T-88
81Coke
81F-340
81T-466
81T/HT
81T/St-61
82D-417
82F-353
82RedLob
82T-363
83D-596
83F-167
83T-664
85RochR-12
86Hagers-12MG
87RochR-27
89Canton/Best-17
89Canton/Pro-1319
Moline, Stan
76Cedar
Molitor, Paul
78T-707R
79K-20
79OPC-8
79T-24
80OPC-211
80T-406
81D-203
81F-515
81F/St-82
81K-53
81OPC-300
81T-300
81T/SO-35
81T/St-91
82D-78
82F-148
82F/St-136
82OPC-195
82Pol/Brew-4
82T-195
82T/St-200
83D-484
83F-40
83Gard-11
83OPC-371
83Pol/Brew-4
83T-630
83T/St-139
83T/St-140
83T/St-156
83T/St-83
84D-107
84D/AAS-35
84D/Champs-54
84F-207
84FunFood/Pin-105
84Gard-13
84Nes/792-60
84OPC-60
84Pol/Brew-4
84Seven-18C
84T-60
84T/St-294
85D-359
85F-588
85Gard-13
85OPC-395
85Pol/Brew-4
85T-522
86D-124
86D/AAS-39
86F-495
86F/LimEd-30
86F/Mini-101
86F/St-76
86Jay's-12
86Leaf-70
86OPC-267
86Pol/Brew-4
86S-128M
86S-39
86T-267
86T/St-203
87Class-45
87D-117
87D/HL-29
87D/OD-54
87F-350
87F/St-78

87Leaf-71
87OPC-184
87RedFoley/St-22
87S-54
87T-741
87T/St-200
88Class/Blue-232
88D-249
88D-7DK
88D-BC3
88D/Best-165
88D/DKsuper-7DK
88F-169
88F/AS-12
88F/AwardWin-25
88F/LL-27
88F/Mini-31
88F/St-38
88F/TL-22
88FanSam-5
88Jiffy-12
88KayBee-19
88KingB/Disc-23
88KMart-17
88Leaf-168
88Leaf-7DK
88OPC-231
88Panini/St-125
88Panini/St-432
88Pol/Brew-4
88Score-340
88Score-660HL
88Sf-221
88Sf-79
88T-465
88T/Big-1
88T/Coins-20
88T/Gloss60-57
88T/Mini-19
88T/Revco-20
88T/RiteAid-20
88T/St-194
88T/St/Backs-42
88T/UK-49
89B-140
89Cadaco-37
89Class-12
89D-291
89D/AS-3
89D/Best-15
89D/MVP-BC9
89D/PopUp-3
89F-193
89F/AS-8
89F/BBAS-30
89Gard-1
89KMart/Lead-10
89Master/Discs-8
89OPC-110
89Panini/St-243AS
89Panini/St-373
89Pol/Brew-4
89RedFoley/St-81
89Score-565
89Score/HotSt-57
89Sf-209
89T-110
89T/Big-330
89T/Coins-46
89T/Gloss22-3
89T/Gloss60-43
89T/Mini-58
89T/St-146
89T/St-204
89T/St/Backs-9
89T/UK-53
89UD-525
89UD-673TC
90D-103
90D/Bon/MVP-BC15
90F-330
90Score-460
90Score/100St-98
90Sf-183
90T-360
90UD-254

Mollwitz, Fred
D329-124
D350/2-121
M101/4-124
M101/5-121

Moloney, Bill
81Brist-2
83Pawtu-9

Moloney, Richard
71OPC-13R
71T-13R

Monasterio, Juan
76Wausa

Monbouquette, Bill
59T-173
60T-544
61T-562
61T/St-114
62Salada-99
62Shirriff-99
62T-580
62T/St-15
63Bz-21
63F-7
63Salada-35
63T-480
63T/SO
64T-25
64T/Coins-47
64T/St-19
64T/tatt
65OPC-142
65T-142
66T-429
66T/RO-114
67T-482
68T-234
69OPC-64
69T-64
76Wausa
78TCMA-111
86Albany/TCMA-8
89Myrtle/Pro-1466
PM10/Sm-127

Moncerratt, Pablo
84Butte-17
86Wausa-17

Monchak, Al
73OPC-356CO
73T-356C
74OPC-221CO
74T-221C
86Pol/Atl-52C

Moncrief, Homer
82BirmB-4
83GlenF-15

Moncrief, Tony
83Idaho-29

Monda, Greg
85Cedar-17
86Vermont-13
88Nashvl/CMC-13
88Nashvl/Pro-491

Monday, Rick
67T-542R
68Bz-10
68T-282
68T/G-26
69MB-194
69MLB/St-88
69MLBPA/Pin-19
69NTF
69OPC-105
69T-105
69T/DE-14
69T/decal
69T/S-27
69T/St-218
69Trans-10
70MLB/St-262
70T-547
71K-73
71MLB/St-522
71OPC-135
71T-135
71T/Coins-40
71T/tatt-15
72MB-239
72T-730
73OPC-44
73T-44
74K-2
74OPC-295
74T-295
74T/St-17
75Ho-113
75Ho/Twink-113
75OPC-129
75T-129
75T/M-129
76Crane-37
76Ho-80
76MSA/Disc
76OPC-251
76SSPC-311
76T-251
77Ho-30
77OPC-230
77T-360
78T-145
79K-57
79OPC-320DP
79T-605
80OPC-243
80Pol/Dodg-16
80T-465
81F-122
81K-53
81OPC-177
81Pol/Dodg-16
81T-726
81T/HT
82D-514
82F-15
82F/St-2
82OPC-6
82Pol/Dodg
82Pol/Dodg-16
82T-577
83D-643
83F-213
83OPC-63
83Pol/Dodg-16
83Seven-10
83T-63
84F-106
84Nes/792-274
84Pol/Dodg-16
84T-274
84T/St-83
87Moth/A's-2
87Smok/Dodg-23
89Smok/Dodg-90

Mondile, Steve
89Freder/Star-18

Monegro, David
88Elmir-15

Monegro, Miguel
87Elmir-4
87Elmir/Red-4
88WinHav/Star-14

Monell, Johnny
85LitFalls-26
87Columbia-9
89Jacks/GS-16

Money, Don
69T-454R
70T-645
71MLB/St-185
71OPC-49
71T-49
71T/Coins-31
71T/tatt-7
72MB-240
72T-635
73OPC-386
73T-386
74OPC-413
74T-413
74T/St-197
75Ho-112
75Ho/Twink-112
75OPC-175
75T-175
75T/M-175
76A&P/Milw
76Ho-136
76OPC-402
76SSPC-236
76T-402
77T-79
78T-24
79OPC-133
79T-265
80OPC-313
80T-595
81D-443
81F-524
81OPC-106
81T-106
82D-384
82F-149
82OPC-294
82Pol/Brew-7
82T-709
83D-132
83F-41
83Gard-12
83OPC-259
83Pol/Brew-7
83T-608
84F-208
84Nes/792-374
84T-374

Money, Kyle
82Readg-4
83Portl-4
86Portl-18

Monge, Sid
75SLCty
76OPC-595R
76T-595R
77T-282
78T-101
79T-459
80OPC-39
80T-74
81D-81
81F-395
81OPC-333
81T-333
82D-620
82F-375
82T-601
82T/Tr-73T
83D-245
83F-168
83T-564
83T/St-274
83T/X-74
84D-139
84F-308
84Moth/Padres-21
84Nes/792-224
84Smok/Padres-19
84T-224
84T/X-80
85F-17
85T-408

Monheimer, Len
88Aug/Pro-389

Monico, Mario
86Stockton-16
87Stockton-7
88ElPas/Best-26
88TexLgAS/GS-24
89ElPas/GS-30

Monita, Greg
87Vermont-21

Monroe, Bill
74Laugh/Black-31

Monroe, Gary
81QuadC-14

Monroe, Larry
75AppFx
78Knoxv
79Knoxv/TCMA-14

Monroe, Zack
59T-108
60T-329
79TCMA-219

Mons, Jeffrey
88VeroB/Star-17

Monson, Steve
87Beloi-5
88Stock/Cal-175
88Stock/Pro-722
89ElPas/GS-11
89Stock/Best-4
89Stock/Cal-160
89Stock/Pro-384

Montague, Ed
88Umpire-27
89Umpires-25

Montague, John
75OPC-405
75T-405
75T/M-405
76OkCty
78T-117
79OPC-172
79T-337
80T-253
81T-652

Montalvo, Rafael
83VeroB-9
85Cram/PCL-173
86Tucso-16
87Tucso-5
88Tucso-18
88Tucso/CMC-6
88Tucso/Pro-170

Montalvo, Robert
88StCath/Pro-2021

Montanari, Dave
86PalmSp-23
86PalmSp/Smok-21

Montanez, Willie
71OPC-138R
71T-138R
72T-690
73OPC-97
73T-97
74JP
74OPC-515
74T-515
74T/St-77
75Ho-137
75K-31
75OPC-162
75T-162
75T/M-162
76OPC-181
76SSPC-103
76T-181
77Ho-19
77K-31
77OPC-79
77T-410
77T/CS-29
78Ho-143
78OPC-43
78T-38

78T/Zest-4
79Ho-100
79OPC-153
79T-305
80OPC-119
80T-224
81F-506
81OPC-63
81OPC/Post-1
81T-559
82F-486
82T-458

Montano, Francisco
85Tigres-8

Montano, Martin
85Beloi-22
86Stockton-17
87Stockton-13
88Fresno/Pro-1245

Monteagudo, Aurelio
64T-466R
65T-286R
66T-532
67T-453
71MLB/St-421
71OPC-129
71T-129
72OPC-458
72T-458
74OPC-139
74T-139
74T/Tr-139T
85MidldA-20
86MidldA-18
87Knoxv-5

Monteau, Sam
75BurlB
76BurlB

Montefusco, John
76Crane-38
76Ho-41
76Ho/Twink-41
76MSA/Disc
76OPC-203LL
76OPC-30
76SSPC-97
76T-203LL
76T-30
77Ho-31
77K-5
77OPC-232
77Pep-42
77T-370
77T/CS-30
78OPC-59
78T-142
79OPC-288
79Pol/Giants-26
79T-560
80OPC-109
80Pol/Giants-26
80T-195
81D-434
81F-439
81Pol/Atl-24
81T-438
81T/Tr-804
82F-442
82T-697
82T/Tr-74T
83D-313
83F-367
83OPC-223
83T-223
83T/St-297
84D-126
84F-132
84Moth/Giants-24
84Nes/792-761
84OPC-265
84T-761
85D-580
85F-135
85OPC-301
85T-301
85T/St-319

Monteiro, Dave
88Idaho/Pro-1841

Montejo, Steve
88Watertn/Puc-22

Monteleone, Rich
86Calgary-15
87Calgary-24
87Moth/Sea-24
88Calg/CMC-3
88Calg/Pro-797
89Edmon/CMC-2
89Edmon/Pro-564
89Score/Tr-92
90D-462
90F-648
90Score-565
90T-99

Montero, Sixto
89Martins/Star-22

Montes, Dan
89Everett/Star-22

Montgomery, Al
80Utica-23

Montgomery, Dan
87Bakers-2
88Bakers/Cal-238
89VeroB/Star-17

Montgomery, Jeff
87Nashv-15
88F-642
88F/U-U32
88Omaha/CMC-7
88Omaha/Pro-1501
88Score-497
88Score/Tr-71T
88T-447
89B-113
89D-440
89D/Best-319
89F-288
89Score-367
89T-116
89UD-618
90D-380
90F-115
90Score-365
90T-638
90UD-698

Montgomery, Larry
77BurlB
78BurlB
81ElPas-12
85Cram/PCL-58

Montgomery, Monty
72OPC-372R
72T-372R
73OPC-164
73T-164

Montgomery, Reggie
85MidldA-24
86Edmon-21
88RochR/Pro-207

Montgomery, Robert
71OPC-176R
71T-176R
72OPC-411
72T-411
73OPC-491
73T-491
74OPC-301
74T-301
75OPC-559
75T-559
75T/M-559
76OPC-523
76SSPC-414
76T-523
77T-288
78PapaG/Disc-10
78T-83
79OPC-219
79T-423
80T-618

Montoya, Charlie
88CalLgAS-16
88Stock/Cal-199
88Stock/Pro-737
89Stock/Best-14
89Stock/Cal-172
89Stock/Pro-381
89Stock/Star-12

Monzant, Ray
56T-264
58SFCall
58T-447
59T-332
60T-338
79TCMA79-199

Monzon, Dan
73OPC-469
73T-469
74OPC-613
74T-613
78Wausa
82Lynch-1

Monzon, Jose
89Myrtle/Pro-1459

Moody, James
89Oneon/Pro-2105

Moon, Glen
80Clint-19

Moon, Wally
54T-137
55Hunter
55T-67
55T/DH-37
56T-55
56T/Pin-48OF
57T-65
58T-210
59T-530
60Bz-3
60Morrell
60T-5
60T/tatt
60T/tatt-36
61BB-9
61P-159
61T-325
61T/St-29
62BB-9
62Exh
62Salada-124
62Shirriff-124
62T-190
62T-52LL
62T/bucks
62T/St-137
63Exh
63T-279
64T-353
65OPC-247
65T-247
79TCMA-137
88Pac/Leg-81
89Smok/Dodg-65
89Swell-81
Exh47

Mooney, James
34G-83

Mooney, Troy
89Princet/Star-13

Mooneyham, Bill
81Holyo-23
82Holyo-6
83Nashua-5
84Cram/PCL-110
85Huntsvl/BK-21
86D/Rook-50
86F/Up-U77
87D-302
87F-399
87T-548
87Tacom-18
88Denver/Pro-1254
88ElPas/Best-9

Moore, Alvin
(Junior)
78Green
78T-421
79T-275
80T-186
81Durhm-13

Moore, Archie
64T-581R

Moore, Balor
71OPC-747R
71T-747R
73OPC-211
73T-211
74OPC-453
74T-453
75OPC-592
75T-592
75T/M-592
78T-368
79OPC-122
79T-238
80OPC-6
80T-19
81Vanco-10

Moore, Bart
89Elmir/Puc-9

Moore, Billy
86Indianap-35
87Indianap-18
88Indi/CMC-13
88Indi/Pro-497
89Indi/CMC-13
89Indi/Pro-1211
89RochR/Pro-1647

Moore, Bobby
88BBCity/Star-18
89BBCity/Star-18

Moore, Brad
86Cram/PCL-144
87Clearw-2
88Readg/Pro-866
89OPC-202
89ScrWB/CMC-8
89ScrWB/Pro-709
89T-202

Moore, Calvin
75Cedar

Moore, Cary
89Erie/Star-14

Moore, Charlie
74OPC-603R
74T-603R
75OPC-636
75T-636
75T/M-636
76A&P/Milw
76OPC-116
76SSPC-231
76T-116
77T-382
78T-51
79T-408
80OPC-302
80T-579
81D-324
81F-521
81OPC-237
81T-237
82D-280
82F-150
82OPC-308
82Pol/Brew-22
82T-308
83D-206
83F-42
83Gard-13
83Pol/Brew-22
83T-659
83T/St-157
84D-292
84F-209
84Gard-14
84Nes/792-751
84OPC-138
84Pol/Brew-22
84T-751
84T/St-301
85D-351
85F-589
85Gard-14
85Pol/Brew-22
85T-83
86D-246
86F-496
86F/St-77
86OPC-137
86Pol/Brew-22
86T-137
86T-426M
86T/St-204
87D-372
87F-351
87OPC-93
87SanJose-6
87T-676
87T/Tr-82T
88Score-444

Moore, Dave
78Indianap-11
79Indianap-4
81Albuq/TCMA-1
82Albuq-6

Moore, Don
81ArkTr-3
82ArkTr-17

Moore, Donnie
78T-523
79T-17
82Richm-7
84F-185
84Nes/792-207
84Pol/Atl-31
84T-207
85D-650
85F-334
85F/Up-U82
85OPC-61
85Smok/Cal-21
85T-699
85T/Tr-85T
86D-255
86D/AAS-46
86F-164
86Leaf-130
86OPC-345
86Smok/Cal-21
86T-345
86T/St-182
87D-110
87F-89
87F/LL-30
87OPC-115
87RedFoley/St-56
87Smok/Cal-8
87T-115
87T/Mini-46
87T/St-177
88D-621
88F-500
88OPC-204
88Score-195
88Smok/Angels-20
88T-471
89Score-535

Moore, Earl A.
11Helmar-148
14CJ-124

15CJ-124
E104
E107
E224
E94
E97
M116
T201
T207
W555
WG2-36

Moore, Ed
79QuadC-3

Moore, Eugene
39PB-160
40PB-143
41DP-122
41DP-37
41PB-25
R314

Moore, Graham E.
33G-180

Moore, Greg
86Knoxv-17

Moore, J.B.
85PrWill-27

Moore, Jackie S.
65T-593R
70McDon-6
730PC-549CO
73T-549C
740PC-379CO
74T-379C
77T-113C
84T/X-81
85Moth/A's-1MG
85T-38
86Moth/A's-1
86T-591

Moore, Jim
85FtMyr-25

Moore, Joe G.
(Jo-Jo)
33G-126
33G-231
37Wheat
38ONG/Pin-21
41DP-30
V355-8

Moore, John F.
(Johnny)
30CEA/Pin-18
36Exh/4-6
37Exh/4-2
37Exh/4-6
38Wheat
R310

Moore, Kelvin
80Ogden-20
81Tacom-18
82D-534
82T-531R
82Tacom-31
83D-87
83Tacom-32
84Cram/PCL-31
84ElPas-13
85BuffB-10

Moore, Kerwin
89Eugene/Best-17

Moore, Lloyd
(Whitey)
39PB-162
40PB-150
W711/1
W711/2

Moore, Mark
80Cedar-1

Moore, Meredith
89WinHav/Star-16

Moore, Michael
88Boise/Pro-1608

Moore, Mike
80LynnS-1
83D-428
83F-482
83SLCty-7
83T-209
84D-634
84F-614
84Moth/Mar-5
84Nes/792-547
84T-547
85D-440
85F-495
85Moth/Mar-8
85T-279FDP
85T-373
86D-240
86F-469
86Leaf-114
86Moth/Mar-21
86Penin-18
86S-162
86T-646
86T/Mini-30
86T/St-221
87D-70
87F-590
87Moth/Sea-3
870PC-102
87Smok/AL-11
87T-727
87T/St-215
88D-75
88D/Best-192
88F-379
88Moth/Sea-3
88Score-464
88T-432
88T/Big-241
89B-189
89D-448
89D/Best-246
89D/Tr-21
89F-554
89F/Up-55
89Moth/A's-12
890PC-28
89Panini/St-431
89Score-274
89Score/Tr-5
89Sf-77
89T-28
89T/St-220
89T/Tr-82T
89UD-123
89UD/Ext-758
90Class-104
90D-214
90F-16
90Score-190
90Score/100St-42
90Sf-185
90T-175
90UD-275

Moore, Pat
87Erie-27

Moore, R. Barry
670PC-11
67T-11
68T-462
69T-639
700PC-366
70T-366
72MB-241

Moore, Randolph
31Exh/4-1
33G-69
35G-2E
35G-4E
35G-7E
R308-171
R314
V354-26

Moore, Randy
88Beloi/GS-21

Moore, Ray
55Esskay
55T-208
56T-43
57T-106
58T-249
59T-293
60T-447
61Clover-18
61Peters-13
61T-289
61T/RO-20
62T-437
63T-26

Moore, Rick
86Chatt-20

Moore, Robert
(Bobby)
83GlenF-16
84Shrev/FB-12
86Phoen-17

Moore, Ronald
86Cram/PCL-159

Moore, Roy Daniel
E120

Moore, Sam
86Fresno/Smok-8
87Clint-23

Moore, Steve
82Tulsa-13

Moore, Terry
49B-174
R314
R423-71
W754

Moore, William Wilcey
W513-77

Moorhead, Bob
62T-593R

Moose, Bob
68KDKA-38
680PC-36R
68T-36R
69T-409
70MLB/St-104
700PC-110
70T-110
70T/Cb
71MLB/St-209
710PC-690
71T-690
71T/Coins-147
72MB-242
72T-647
730PC-499
73T-499
740PC-382
74T-382
750PC-536
75T-536
75T/M-536
760PC-476
76SSPC-570
76T-476

Mooty, J.T.
(Jake)
49B/PCL-23
R314/Can

Mora, Andres
77T-646
78T-517
79T-287

Morales, Edwin
87PortChar-8

Morales, Joe Edwin
82Beloi-16
84ElPas-21

Morales, Jose
760PC-418
76SSPC-323
76T-418
770PC-263RB 770PC-90
77T-102
77T-233RB
780PC-63
78T-374
79T-552
800PC-116
80T-218
81D-495
81F-571
81T-43
81T/Tr-806
82D-203
82F-173
82T-648
82T/Tr-75T
83Pol/Dodg-43
83T/X-75
84D-275
84F-107
84F-498
84Nes/792-143
84Pol/Dodg-43
84T-143
89Swell-38

Morales, Julio
(Jerry)
700PC-262R
70T-262R
710PC-696
71T-696
730PC-268
73T-268
740PC-258
74T-258
74T/St-98
750PC-282
75T-282
75T/M-282
76Crane-39
76Ho-140
76MSA/Disc
760PC-79
76SSPC-312
76T-79
77Ho-49
77T-639
780PC-23
78T-175
790PC-235
79T-452
80T-572
81F-338
81T-377
81T/Tr-805
82D-309
82F-601
82F/St-93
82RedLob
82T-33
83F-502
83T-729
83Thorn-24

Morales, Manuel
85Tigres-20

Morales, Rich
69T-654R
700PC-91
70T-91
710PC-267
71T-267
72T-593
730PC-494
73T-494
740PC-387SD
74T-387
81QuadC-30
88Vermont/Pro-954
89Calg/CMC-24
89Calg/Pro-538

Morales, William
87PrWill-29
88PrWill/Star-18

Moralez, Paul
86Kinston-17
87Bakers-24

Moran, Bill
(Bugs)
78Knoxv

Moran, Dino
86Watertn-13

Moran, Frank
88Hamil/Pro-1746

Moran, Jim
53Mother-12

Moran, Joseph Herbert
D350/2-122
M101/5-122
T206

Moran, Opie
87Erie-2
89ArkTr/GS-13

Moran, Owen
T3/Box-60

Moran, Pat J.
10Domino-88A
10Domino-88B
11Helmar-149
12Sweet/Pin-129
14Piedmont/St-41
15CJ-111
88Pac/8Men-89
BF2-88
D329-125
D350/2-123
E270/2
M101/4-125
M101/5-123
M116
S74-102
T202
T204
T205
T206
T207
T3-109
W514-12
WG7-33

Moran, Richard Alan
63T-558R
64T-288

Moran, Steve
86AppFx-16

Moran, William
(Billy)
58T-388
59T-196
61BeeHive-14
62T-539
63J-25
63P-25
63Salada-48
63T-57
64T-333
64T/St-67
65T-562

Morandini, Mickey
88T/Tr-71TOLY
89Spart/Pro-1030
89Spart/Star-18
89Star/Wax-57
89T/Big-162

Morando, Dean
78Wisco

Moraw, Carl
86Beloi-16
87Stockton-21
88Stock/Cal-184
88Stock/Pro-746
89ElPas/GS-12
89Stock/Best-5
89Stock/Cal-156

89Stock/Pro-378

Mordecai, Mike
88CapeCod-17
88CapeCod/Sum-42

Moreau, Guy
R314/Can

Morehead, Dave
63T-299R
64T-376
65T-434
66OPC-135
66T-135
67T-297
67T/Test/RSox-11
68Coke
68T-212
69MLB/St-60
69OPC-29
69T-29
70MLB/St-224
70OPC-495
70T-495
71MLB/St-422
71OPC-221
71T-221
72MB-243

Morehead, Seth
59T-253
60L-87
60T-504
61T-107

Morehouse, Richard
86QuadC-24
87PalmSp-28
88PalmSp/Cal-91
88PalmSp/Pro-1449
89MidldA/GS-24

Morehouse, Scott
88CapeCod/Sum-162

Moreland, Keith
79OkCty
80BK/P-3
81D-382
81F-13
81T-131
82D-119
82F-252
82RedLob
82T-384
82T/Tr-76T
83D-309
83F-503
83OPC-58
83OPC-85
83T-619
83T/St-222
83Thorn-6
84D-483
84F-499
84Nes/792-23
84Nes/792-456TL
84OPC-23
84SevenUp-6
84T-23
84T/St-39
85D-117
85F-62
85Leaf-197
85OPC-197
85SevenUp-6
85T-538
85T/St-39
86D-167
86Drake-9
86F-375
86F/LL-25
86F/Mini-79
86F/St-78
86Gator-6
86Jay's-13
86Leaf-94
86OPC-266
86S-90
86T-266
86T/Mini-38
86T/St-54
87Berg/Cubs-6
87D-169
87D-24DK
87D/DKsuper-24
87D/OD-71
87Drake-7
87F-569
87F/LL-31
87F/Mini-69
87F/St-79
87Leaf-24DK
87Leaf-77
87OPC-177
87S-122
87Seven-C12
87Seven-ME7
87T-177
87T/St-65
88Coke/Padres-7
88D-201
88D/Best-266
88F-425
88F/U-U124
88Leaf-160
88OPC-31
88Panini/St-263
88RedFoley/St-58
88Score-71
88Score/Tr-9T
88Sf-164
88Smok/Padres-19
88T-416
88T/Big-207
88T/St-58
88T/Tr-72T
89B-109
89D-111
89D/Best-203
89F-313
89Mara/Tigers-10
89OPC-293
89Score-42
89Score/Tr-29
89Sf-141
89T-773
89T/St-105
89T/Tr-83T
89UD-361
90Score-444
90Sf-139
90UD-401

Moreland, Owen III
84LitFalls-11

Morelli, Frank
89Elmir/Puc-10

Morelock, Charlie
83Ander-12
86Durhm-19

Moren, Lew
E104
M116

Morena, Jamie
87CharRa-18

Moreno, Angel
82F-469
84Cram/PCL-99

Moreno, Armando
86Jaxvl/TCMA-4
87Jaxvl-12
88Jaxvl/Best-27
88Jaxvl/Pro-983
88SLAS-21
89Indi/CMC-19
89Indi/Pro-1222

Moreno, Carlos
82Miami-5

Moreno, Chris
89Stock/Best-26M

Moreno, Douglas
86Macon-16
86Watertn-14

Moreno, Jaime
86CharRa-18
88Charl/Pro-1218
89Watlo/Pro-1785
89Watlo/Star-26

Moreno, Jorge
73Cedar
74Cedar
75Dubuq

Moreno, Jose
79Tidew-3
80Tidew-2

Moreno, Michael
83Wisco/LF-24
85Orlan-8

Moreno, Omar
77T-104
78T-283
79Ho-12
79OPC-321
79T-4LL
79T-607
80BK/PHR-29
80OPC-372
80T-165
81Coke
81D-17
81F-361
81F/St-100
81OPC-213
81T-535
81T/SO-100
81T/St-211
81T/St-24
82D-347
82F-487
82F/St-79
82OPC-395
82T-395
82T/St-81
83D-347
83F-312
83OPC-332
83T-485
83T/St-278
83T/X-76
84D-637
84F-133
84Nes/792-16
84Nes/792-714LL
84OPC-16
84T-16
84T-714
84T/St-322
85D-591
85F-136
85T-738
86F-15
86F/Up-U78
86Pol/Atl-18
86T/Tr-75T
87F-521
87T-214
87T/St-44

Moreno, Ric
87Duned-14

Morenz, Howie
33SK-24

Moret, Rogelio
(Roger)
71OPC-692R
71T-692R
72OPC-113
72T-113
73OPC-291
73T-291
74OPC-590
74T-590
74T/St-137
75OPC-8
75T-8
75T/M-8
76OPC-632
76SSPC-420
76T-632
76T/Tr-632T
77T-292
78T-462

Moreta, Manuel
76Watlo

Morfin, Arvid
84Butte-18
86Cram/PCL-116

Morgan, Bill
79QuadC-5

Morgan, Bob M.
50B-222
52T-355
53B/Col-135
53T-85
55B-81
56T-337
58T-144
79TCMA-193

Morgan, Chris
86FSLAS-36
86Lakel-16
87GlenF-17

Morgan, Curt
86Miami-18

Morgan, Eddie
31Exh/4-21
33Exh/4-11
33G-116
35BU-60
V354-2

Morgan, Gene
87Memph-16
87Memph/Best-17

Morgan, Harry
(Cy)
BF2-49
E104
E95
M116
T204
T207
T208
T222

Morgan, Joe L.
65OPC-16R
65T-16R
66OPC-195
66T-195
66T/RO-9
67OPC/PI-25
67T-337
67T/PI-25
68Coke
68OPC-144
68T-144
68T-364AS
69MB-195
69MLB/St-141
69OPC-35
69T-35
69T/St-36
70K-72
70MLB/St-44
70OPC-537
70T-537
71MLB/St-89
71OPC-264
71T-264
71T/Coins-117
71T/GM-34
72MB-244
72OPC-132
72T-132
72T-752TR
73K-34
73OPC-230
73T-230
74K-36
74OPC-333AS
74OPC-85
74T-333M
74T-85
74T/St-28
75Ho-5
75Ho/Twink-5
75K-27
75OPC-180
75T-180
75T/M-180
76Crane-40
76Ho-2
76Ho/Twink-2
76Icee
76K-27
76MSA/Disc
76OPC-197LL
76OPC-420
76SSPC-38
76T-197LL
76T-420
77Ho-2
77OPC-220
77Pep-46
77T-100
77T/CS-31
78Ho-87
78OPC-160
78T-300
78Wiffle/Discs-52
79Ho-61
79OPC-5DP
79T-20
80BK/PHR-30
80OPC-342
80T-650
81D-18
81F-78
81F/St-109
81K-22
81T-560
81T/Tr-807
82D-312
82F-397
82F/St-63
82KMart-28
82KMart-30
82OPC-146IA
82OPC-208
82T-754
82T-755A
83D-24DK
83D-438
83D-648M
83F-270
83OPC-264SV
83OPC-81
83T-171
83T-603
83T-604A
83T/St-303
83T/X-77
84D-355
84D/Champs-44
84F-43
84F-636IA
84F/St-100
84F/St-120
84F/X-80
84FunFood/Pin-74
84Moth/A's-3
84Nes/792-210
84Nes/792-705LL
84OPC-210
84T-210
84T-705
84T/St-116
84T/X-82

85D-584
85F-431
85Leaf-28
85OPC-352
85T-352
85T-5RB
85T/St-325
85T/St-5
85T/St-6
86Moth/Ast-3
86S/Dec-56

Morgan, Joe M.
60T-229
61T-511
62Kahn/Atl
81Pawtu-12
89T-714MG
90T-321MG

Morgan, Ken
87Visal-3
88Visal/Cal-146
88Visal/Pro-90
89Orlan/Best-17
89Orlan/Pro-1341

Morgan, Michael
79Ogden/TCMA-3
80T-671R
83D-108
83F-388
83T-203
83T/X-78
84Nes/792-423
84OPC-6
84Syrac-22
84T-423
85Moth/Mar-25
86Moth/Mar-25
86T-152
87D-366
87F-591
87Moth/Sea-8
87T-546
88D-120
88D/Best-86
88F-380
88French-12
88Score-295
88T-32
88T/Big-98
88T/Tr-73T
89D-164
89D/Best-122
89F/Up-91
89Moth/Dodg-13
89Pol/Dodg-23
89T-788
89T/Tr-84T
89UD-653
90D-132
90F-403
90Score-342
90T-367
90UD-317

Morgan, Ray
D327
D328-121
D329-126
D350/2-124
E135-121
M101/4-126
M101/5-124
T207

Morgan, Tom S.
52B-109
52BR
52T-331
53T-132
54NYJour
55B-100
57T-239
58T-365
59T-545
60L-97
60T-33
61T-272
62T-11
63T-421
73OPC-421CO
73T-421C
74OPC-276CO
74T-276C
PM10/L-29

Morgan, Vern
73OPC-49CO
73T-49C
74OPC-447CO
74T-447C

Morhardt, Greg
85Orlan-9
86Orlan-13
87Portl-20

Morhardt, Moe
62T-309

Mori, Dan
87SanJose-12

Moriarty, Edward
R314

Moriarty, George
09Buster/Pin-10
11Helmar-34
14CJ-114
15CJ-114
D329-127
D350/2-125
E104
E254
E270/1
M101/4-127
M101/5-125
M116
S74-16
T202
T205
T206
T207

Moriarty, Todd
84Evrt/Cram-26

Moriarty, Umpire
21Exh-111

Moritz, Chris
85Greens-7
86WinHav-18
87NewBrit-23
88NewBrit/Pro-907
89NewBrit/Pro-603
89NewBrit/Star-11

Morlan, John
75OPC-651
75T-651
75T/M-651

Morlock, Allen
83Sprin/LF-24
84ArkTr-8
86ArkTr-16
87Edmon-9

Morman, Russ
86BuffB-19
86S/Rook-33
87Coke/WS-8
87D-306
87F-645M
87Hawai-22
87T-233
88Vanco/CMC-17
88Vanco/Pro-760
89Vanco/CMC-16
89Vanco/Pro-590

Morogiello, Dan
79Richm-18
80Richm-1
82Louvl-20
83RochR-6
84Nes/792-682
84T-682
85Richm-5

Moronko, Jeff
80Batav-28
81Chatt-12
82Chatt-21
83BuffB-17
84BuffB-1
85Maine-19
85Tulsa-22
86OKCty-14
87Colum-15
87Colum/TCMA-17
88Colum/CMC-18
88Colum/Pol-20
88Colum/Pro-328

Morrill, John
E223
N172
N28
N284
N43
WG1-6

Morris, Angel
81BurlB-14
82Beloi-26
85FtMyr-7
87FtMyr-30
88Virgini/Star-16
89Memph/Best-14
89Memph/Pro-1203
89Memph/Star-18

Morris, Danny W.
69OPC-99R
69T-99R

Morris, Dave
81BurlB-1
83Ander-29
85Durhm-8
86Clint-14

Morris, Don
80WHave-4
81WHave-16

Morris, Edward
N172

Morris, Fred
78DaytB

Morris, Hal
87Albany-21
88Colum/CMC-20
88Colum/Pol-21
88Colum/Pro-327
89AAA/Pro-20
89Class-28
89Colum/CMC-16
89Colum/Pol-14
89Colum/Pro-743
89D-545
89F-260
89Score/HotRk-8
89Score/NWest-29
90D-514
90Score-602
90Score/100Ris-87
90T-236
90UD-31

Morris, Jack
77Evans
77Evansvl/TCMA-20
78BK/T-8
78T-703R
79T-251
80T-371
81Coke
81D-127
81F-475
81OPC-284
81T-572
81T/St-80
82D-107
82F-274
82F/St-159
82K-5
82OPC-108
82OPC-47AS
82T-165LL
82T-450
82T-556AS
82T/St-10LL
82T/St-139
82T/St-183
83D-107
83D-5DK
83F-336
83K-35
83OPC-65
83T-65
83T/St-69
84D-415
84F-87
84F/St-83
84FunFood/Pin-59
84Nes/792-136LL
84Nes/792-195
84Nes/792-666TL
84OPC-195
84T-136
84T-195
84T/Gloss40-10
84T/St-263
85Cain's-14
85D-415
85F-18
85F/LimEd-21
85F/St-82
85Leaf-142
85OPC-382
85Seven-12D
85T-610
85T/3D-28
85T/Gloss40-26
85T/St-15WS
85T/St-256
85T/St-9ALCS
85T/Super-43
85Wendy-16
86Cain's-12
86D-105
86D/AAS-18
86D/HL-27
86D/PopUp-18
86Dorman-2
86F-232
86F/Mini-48
86F/Slug-23
86F/St-79
86Leaf-38
86OPC-270
86S-117
86S-141M
86T-270
86T/3D-17
86T/Gloss22-10
86T/Mini-14
86T/St-163FOIL
86T/St-268
86T/Super-38
87Cain's-14
87Class-90
87Coke/Tigers-7
87D-13DK
87D-173
87D/DKsuper-13
87D/OD-212
87Drake-27
87F-158
87F/Lim-28
87F/McCror-28
87F/Mini-70
87F/Slug-27
87F/St-80
87Jiffy-3
87KayBee-20
87Leaf-135
87Leaf-13DK
87MnM's-6
87OPC-376
87RedFoley/St-114
87S-111M
87S-87
87Seven-DT8
87Smok/AL-6
87T-778
87T/Coins-18
87T/Gloss60-47
87T/Mini-55
87T/St-266
88ChefBoy-3
88Class/Red-174
88Clint/Pro-717
88D-127
88D/AS-24
88D/Best-181
88F-626M
88F-64
88F/AwardWin-26
88F/BB/AS-26
88F/BB/MVP-24
88F/Excit-27
88F/Head-3
88F/Hottest-28
88F/LL-28
88F/Mini-22
88F/RecSet-26
88F/St-26
88F/TL-23
88Leaf-85
88OPC-340
88Panini/St-85
88Pep/T-47
88Pol/T-8
88Score-545
88Sf-176
88T-340
88T/Big-170
88T/Coins-21
88T/Gloss60-17
88T/Mini-11
88T/RiteAid-27
88T/St-268
88T/St/Backs-59
88T/UK-50
89B-93
89Clint/Pro-901
89D-234
89F-139
89F/BBMVP's-30
89Mara/Tigers-47
89OPC-266
89Panini/St-334
89Pol/Tigers-47
89RedFoley/St-82
89Score-250
89Score/Mast-8
89Sf-5
89T-645
89T/Big-61
89T/St-277
89T/UK-54
89UD-352
90D-639
90F-610
90Score-203
90T-555
90UD-573

Morris, Jeff
83Tucso-6
87Everett-26

Morris, Jim
87Stockton-23
89Saraso/Star-15

Morris, John W.
69OPC-111
69T-111
70McDon-1
71MLB/St-446
71OPC-721

71T-721
75OPC-577
75T-577
75T/M-577

Morris, John
84Omaha-8
85D-32RR
85Louvl-23
85Omaha-19
86Louisvl-20
87D-480
87F/U-U83
87Louvl-20
87S/Rook-42
87T-211
87T/GlossRk-10
88D-480
88F-43
88Louvl-35
88Score-346
88T-536
89Smok/Cards-14
89T-578
90D-516
90F-254
90Score-134
90T-383

Morris, Ken
88AubAs/Pro-1957

Morris, Rick
87Durhm-20
88CLAS/Star-32
88Durhm/Star-15
89Greenv/Pro-1172
89Greenv/Star-15
89Greenvl/Best-5
89Star/Wax-37

Morris, Rod
88Butte-19
89Star/Wax-8

Morris, Steve
89Elizab/Star-20
89Keno/Pro-1060
89Keno/Star-16
89Star/Wax-53

Morrisette, James
89Clmbia/Best-15
89Clmbia/GS-16

Morrisey
N172
N284

Morrison, Anthony
87Oneon-2

Morrison, Brian
87SnBer-17
88FSLAS/Star-13
88Mia/Star-15
89Knoxv/Best-17
89Knoxv/Pro-1146

Morrison, Bruce
83Lynch-9

Morrison, Dan
88Umpire-47
89Umpires-45

Morrison, Jim
76OkCty
79OkCty
79T-722R
80OPC-272
80T-522
81Coke
81D-158
81F-357
81T-323
81T/HT
81T/St-60
82D-395
82F-354
82OPC-154
82T-654
82T/Tr-77T
83D-150
83F-313
83T-173
84D-322
84F-257
84Nes/792-44
84T-44
85D-532
85F-471
85T-433
86D-386
86Elmir-13
86F-614
86OPC-56
86T-553
86T/St-133
87D-484
87D/OD-169
87F-614
87F/GameWin-29
87F/Mini-71
87F/St-81
87Greens-22
87Leaf-215
87OPC-237
87T-237
87T/St-133
88D-543
88F-65
88OPC-288
88Score-272
88T-751
88T/Big-237
88T/St-272
89Elmir/Puc-8
89UD-568

Morrison, John
21Exh-112
E120
V100
V61-115
W572
W573

Morrison, Perry
80ElPas-19
81Holyo-24
82Holyo-7

Morrison, Red
89FtLaud/Star-17

Morrison, Tony
88FSLAS/Star-45
88FtLaud/Star-17

Morrissey, Joe
33G-97
R310

Morrow, Ben
87Salem-9

Morrow, Chris
88GreatF-5
89Bakers/Cal-204

Morrow, David
86Jamestn-17
87BurlEx-17

Morrow, Red
88CalLgAS-50

Morrow, Steve
82FtMyr-23
84Memph-22
87Memph-26TR
87Memph/Best-27
88Memph/Best-4
89Omaha/CMC-24
89Omaha/Pro-1723

Morrow, Timmie
89Butte/SP-26

Morse, Mike
81AppFx-20
83GlenF-7

Morse, Randy
84Shrev/FB-13

Morse, Scott
87PortChar-4

Mortillaro, John
83Ander-13
84Durhm-24

Mortimer, Bob
86Salem-20

Morton, Carl
69Fud's-9
69T-646R
70OPC-109R
70T-109R
71K-23
71MLB/St-135
71OPC-515
71T-515
71T/Coins-35
71T/GM-4
71T/S-28
71T/tatt-16
72OPC-134
72T-134
73OPC-331
73T-331
74OPC-244
74T-244
74T/St-8
75OPC-237
75T-237
75T/M-237
76Ho-43
76Ho/Twink-43
76OPC-328
76SSPC-4
76T-328
77T-24

Morton, Guy
BF2-23
D327
D328-122
D329-128
D350/2-126
E121/80
E122
E135-122
M101/4-128
M101/5-126
W575
WG7-34

Morton, Kevin
88CapeCod-12
88CapeCod/Sum-139
89Elmir/Puc-27

Morton, Lew
52Park-13

Morton, Maurice
85Spoka/Cram-15

Morton, Ron
88Spoka/Pro-1946
89Watlo/Pro-1782
89Watlo/Star-21

Morton, Stan
80Clint-22

Morton, Wycliffe
(Bubba)
62T-554
63T-164
67OPC-79
67T-79
68T-216
69MB-196
69T-342

Moryn, Walt
52Park-72
53Exh/Can-39
55B-261
57T-16
58T-122
59T-147
59T-488
60L-17
60T-74
60T/tatt
60T/tatt-37
61T-91
61T/RO-32
79TCMA-141

Mosby, Linvel
78Ashev
80Ashev-20

Moscaret, Jeff
84MidldC-11

Moscat, Frank
85Lynch-20

Moschitto, Ross
65T-566R

Moscrey, Mike
88Cedar/Pro-1139
89Chatt/Best-19
89Chatt/GS-18

Moseby, Lloyd
80Syrac-16
81F-421
81OPC-52
81OPC/Post-24
81T-643
82D-129
82F-621
82OPC-223
82OPC/Post-4
82T-223
82T/St-246
83D-556
83F-435
83OPC-124
83T-452
83T/St-130
84D-363
84F-164
84FunFood/Pin-132
84Nes/792-403AS
84Nes/792-606TL
84Nes/792-92
84Nestle/DT-7
84OPC-289
84OPC-3AS
84OPC-92
84T-403
84T-92
84T/St-191
84T/St-365
84T/St/Box-4
84Tor/Fire-25
85D-437
85D/AAS-5
85F-115
85F-636IA
85Leaf-143
85OPC-77
85OPC/Post-19
85T-545
85T/St-359
85T/Super-39
85Tor/Fire-23
86Ault-15
86D-73
86F-67
86F/LL-26
86Leaf-72
86OPC-360
86T-360
86T/St-195
86Tor/Fire-26
87D-21DK
87D-74
87D/AAS-59
87D/DKsuper-21
87D/OD-36
87F-236
87F/McCror-29
87F/Mini-72
87F/RecSet-22
87Leaf-105
87Leaf-21DK
87OPC-210
87RedFoley/St-55
87S-96
87T-210
87T/St-190
87Tor/Fire-23
87Tor/Fire-23
88D-367
88D/Best-199
88F-119
88F/St-75
88Ho/Disc-20
88Leaf-140
88OPC-272
88Panini/St-225
88Score-109
88Sf-74
88T-565
88T/Big-113
88T/St-189
88T/UK-51
88Tor/Fire-15
89D-231
89F-241
89OPC-113
89Panini/St-473
89RedFoley/St-83
89Score-12
89T-113
89T/Big-262
89T/St-188
89Tor/Fire-15
89UD-381
90D-504
90F-90
90Score-404
90T-779
90UD-421

Moser, Larry
83Ander-30

Moser, Steve
86Watertn-15
87Salem-13

Moses, Gerald
(Gerry)
65T-573R
69T-476R
70OPC-104
70T-104
71MLB/St-352
71OPC-205
71T-205
71T/Coins-6
72OPC-356
72T-356
73OPC-431
73T-431
74OPC-19
74T-19
75OPC-271
75T-271
75T/M-271

Moses, John
81Wausa-25
83AppFx/LF-24
83SLCty-19
84Chatt-24
84D-74
84Nes/792-517
84T-517
85Cram/PCL-83
86Calgary-16
87D-393
87F-592
87Moth/Sea-18
87T-284
88D-440
88F-381
88F/U-U45
88Portl/CMC-22
88Portl/Pro-643
88Score-309
88T-712
89D-626

89F-121
89Score-432
89T-72
89UD-242
90D-590
90F-381
90Score-391
90T-653
90UD-240
Moses, Mark
80Ander-13
Moses, Steve
85Cram/PCL-30
86Readg-18
87Wmspt-6
Moses, Wallace
35BU-98
37Dix
37Exh/4-14
37OPC-109
38Exh/4-14
38Wheat
39PB-64
40PB-26
41DP-126
41PB-42
51B-261
53B/Col-95
55B-294
60T-459C
R313
R314
R326-5A
R326-5B
R342-5
V300
Mosher, Peyton
82VeroB-9
Moskau, Paul
77Indianap-9
78Indianap-3
78OPC-181
78T-126
79OPC-197
79T-377
80T-258
81F-207
81OPC-358
81T-546
82D-355
82F-76
82T-97
Mosley, Reggie
83TriCit-15
Mosley, Tony
87Elmir-17
87Elmir/Red-17
88WinHav/Star-15
89Elmir/Puc-11
Moss, Barry
77Indianap-23
88SLCty-18
89SLCty-15
Moss, Darren
87Anchora-36BB
Moss, J. Lester
47TipTop
50B-251
51B-210
52T-143
54B-181
54Esskay
55Esskay
57T-213
58T-153
59T-453
77Evansvl/TCMA-21
79T-66MG
Mossi, Don
55B-259
55Gol/Ind-20
55Salem
55T-85
55T/DH-84
56T-39
56T/Pin-9P
57T-8
58T-35
59T-302
60T-418
60T/tatt
60T/tatt-38
61P-42
61T-14
62J-23
62P-23
62P/Can-23
62T-105
62T-55LL
62T/St-49
63J-56
63P-56
63T-218M
63T-530
64T-335
66OPC-74
66T-74
79TCMA-215
Mostil, Johnny A.
21Exh-113
28Yueng-24
61F-64
E120
E121/120
E210-24
V100
V61-45
W501-40
W502-24
W572
W573
WG7-35
Mota, Andres
(Andy) 87AubAs-7
88AubAs/Pro-1966
89Osceola/Star-12
89Star/Wax-16
Mota, Carlos
88BurlR/Pro-1783
89Watertn/Star-15
Mota, Jose
77Cocoa
78DaytB
80Cedar-13
86Tulsa-27
89Huntsvl/Best-26
89Wich/Roc/HL-15
89Wich/Roc/Up-11
Mota, Manny
63T-141
64T-246
65T-463
66EH-15
66OPC-112
66T-112
67OPC-66
67T-66
67T/Test/PP-16
68KDKA-15
68T-325
69Fud's-10
69MB-197
69MLB/St-160
69T-236
69T/St-58
70MLB/St-53
70OPC-157
70T-157
71MLB/St-109
71OPC-112
71T-112
72MB-245
72T-596
73OPC-412
73T-412
74K-49
74OPC-368
74T-368
75OPC-414
75T-414
75T/M-414
76OPC-548
76SSPC-87
76T-548
77T-386
78T-228
78T/Zest-5
79T-644
80T-3M
81D-299
81F-141
87Smok/Dodg-24
88Smok/Dodg-5
89Smok/Dodg-80
Mota, Miguel
87Bakers-4
Mota, Willie
89Elizab/Star-21
Motley, Darryl
81Omaha-22
82D-390
82F-417
82Omaha-19
82T-471R
83Evans-21
84D-344
84F/X-81
85D-461
85F-208
85Leaf-69
85T-561
85T/St-276
86D-217
86F-16
86Kitty/Disc-14
86Leaf-95
86NatPhoto-24
86S-186M
86T-332
86T/St-22WS
87OPC-99
87Richm/TCMA-19
87T-99
89Indi/CMC-22
89Indi/Pro-1238
Motton, Curt
68T-549R
69OPC-37
69T-37
70OPC-261
70T-261
71MLB/St-305
71OPC-684
71T-684
72MB-246
72OPC-393
72T-393
86RochR-13C
87RochR-13
87RochR/TCMA-23
88RochR-14
88RochR-29
88RochR/CMC-25
88RochR/Gov-29
88RochR/Pro-218
Moulder, Glen
49B-159
Moulton, Brian
77Cedar
Mount, Chuck
86Cram/PCL-42
87AppFx-1
88BirmB/Best-27
89BirmB/Best-18
89BirmB/Pro-92
Moure, Brian
88CapeCod/Sum-12
Moushon, Dan
89Sprin/Best-28
Mowrey, Harry
(Mike)
11Helmar-173
D328-123
D329-129
E135-123
E224
E300
E96
M101/4-129
M116
T213/blue
T213/brown
W555
Mowry, Joe
34G-59
R310
Moyer, Greg
81Shrev-22
Moyer, Jamie
86Gator-49
86Pittsf-17
87Berg/Cubs-49
87D-315
87F-570
87T-227
88Berg/Cubs-49
88D-169
88D/Best-228
88D/Cubs/Bk-169
88F-426
88OPC-36
88Panini/St-255
88Score-573
88T-36
88T/St-62
89B-223
89D-157
89D/Tr-39
89F-432
89F/Up-65
89Moth/R-17
89OPC-171
89Score-263
89Smok/R-22
89T-549TL
89T-717
89T/St-53
89T/Tr-85T
89UD-63
89UD/Ext-791
90D-378
90F-307
90Score-107
90T-412
90UD-619
Moyer, Jim
71MLB/St-260
72OPC-506R
72T-506R
Mraz, Don
76QuadC
Mrozinski, Ron
55B-287
Mueller, Clarence F.
25Exh-62
26Exh-61
V100
Mueller, Don
49Eureka-121
50B-221
51B-268
52B-18
52BR
52Coke
52Dix
52NTea
52T-52
52TipTop
53B/Col-74
53Brigg
53Dix
53SM
54B-73
54NYJour
54RM-NL7
54SM
54T-42
55Armour-14
55Gol/Giants-22
55RFG-9
55RM-NL8
55SM
56T-241
57T-148
58T-253
59T-368
79TCMA-149
Exh47
PM10/Sm-128
Mueller, Emmett
(Heinie)
39PB-63
40PB-96
Mueller, Pete
86Osceola-19
Mueller, Ray
49Eureka-122
51B-313
61F-128
Mueller, Willard
75BurlB
76BurlB
76Clint
77BurlB
78Holyo
79Vanco-23
80T-668R
80Vanco-2
81Vanco-15
82Wichi-10
Muffett, Billy
58T-143
59T-241
61T-16
62T-336
76SSPC-614
88Pep/T-CO
89Mara/Tigers-CO
Muh, Steve
89Keno/Pro-1079
89Keno/Star-17
Muhammad, Bob
89Beloi/Star-18
Muir, Joseph
52T-154
Mulcahy, Hugh
39PB-145
40PB-95
41G-1
49Exh
Mulden, Chris
78Clint
Mulholland, Terry
84Evrt/Cram-20
86Phoen-18
87D-515
87Phoen-5
87T-536
88Phoen/CMC-10
88Phoen/Pro-77
89F/Up-111
89Phoen/CMC-4
89Phoen/Pro-1480
89Score-474
89T-41
90Class-127
90D-515
90F-568
90Score-542

90T-657
90UD-474

Mull, Jack
75Phoen-2
76Phoen
77Cedar
78Cedar
81Shrev-1
83Phoen/BHN-24
84Cram/PCL-24
86Clint-15MG
87Shrev-25
87TexLgAS-6
88Shrev/Pro-1279
88TexLgAS/GS-1MG
89Phoen/CMC-21
89Phoen/Pro-1503

Mullane, Anthony
(Count)
N172

Mullaney, Dominic
T206

Mulleavy, Greg
60T-463C

Mullen, Charles
14CJ-24
15CJ-24
E286

Mullen, Ford
43Centen-20

Mullen, Tom
81AppFx-5
81GlenF-6
83GlenF-17
85BuffB-23
86Omaha-16
86Omaha/TCMA-22
87Omaha-26
88Omaha/CMC-8
88Omaha/Pro-1507

Muller, Fred
37Wheat

Muller, Mike
87Memph-22

Mulligan, Bill
86FtMyr-20
87FtMyr-1

Mulligan, Bob
82Orlan/A-21
83Toled-8
84Toled-9
85Orlan-19

Mulligan, Edward
E121/120
W501-45
W575

Mullin, George
09Buster/Pin-11
10Domino-89
11Helmar-35
12Sweet/Pin-28A
12Sweet/Pin-28B
E104
E254
E270/1
E90/1
E96
E97
E98
M116
S74-17
T202
T205
T206
T207
T213/blue
T215/blue
T215/brown
T3-30
W555
WG2-37

Mullin, Pat
47TipTop
49B-56
50B-135
51B-106
52B-183
52T-275
53B/BW-4
53Glen
54B-151

Mulliniks, S. Rance
77SLCty
78T-579
79SLCty-11
81D-504
81F-48
81T-433
82D-630
82F-418
82T-104
82T/Tr-78T
83D-432
83F-436
83OPC-277
83T-277
84D-584
84F-165
84Nes/792-762
84OPC-19
84T-762
84T/St-374
84Tor/Fire-26
85D-485
85F-116
85Leaf-153
85OPC-336
85OPC/Post-17
85T-336
85Tor/Fire-24
86Ault-5
86D-606
86F-68
86OPC-74
86T-74
86Tor/Fire-27
87D-319
87D/OD-32
87F-237
87OPC-91
87T-537
87Tor/Fire-24
87Tor/Fire-24
88D-197
88D/Best-328
88F-120
88Ho/Disc-14
88Leaf-204
88OPC-167
88Score-235
88T-167
88Tor/Fire-5
89B-250
89D-87
89F-242
89OPC-111
89Score-385
89T-618
89T/St-192
89Tor/Fire-5
89UD-43
90D-607
90F-91
90Score-204
90T-466
90UD-132

Mulliniks, Steve
75QuadC

Mullino, Ray
87Peoria-1
88CharWh/Best-25
89WinSal/Star-12

Mullins, Fran
80GlenF/B-23
80GlenF/C-12
81T-112R
82Edmon-9
85Cram/PCL-180
85T-283
86OhHenry-22

Mullins, Ron
87Cedar-8
88Greens/Pro-1561
88SALAS/GS-9
89Mia/Star/22-14

Mulvaney, Michael
88Bill/Pro-1808
89Greens/Pro-410

Mulvey, Joseph
N172
N28
N284
N690
WG1-53

Mulville, Duane
88Bill/Pro-1805
89Cedar/Best-11
89Cedar/Pro-924
89Cedar/Star-13

Mumaw, Steve
86Ventura-15
87Duned-10
88Duned/Star-11
89ArkTr/GS-14

Mumphrey, Jerry
76SSPC-289
77T-136
78T-452
79T-32
80OPC-196
80T-378
81D-124
81Drake-26
81F-494
81OPC-196
81Sqt-23
81T-556
81T/SO-97
81T/St-227
81T/Tr-808
82D-261
82F-43
82OPC-175
82T-175
82T-486TL
82T/St-220
83D-360
83F-389
83OPC-246
83RoyRog/Disc-6
83T-670
83T-81
83T/St-97
84D-426
84F-233
84Moth/Ast-9
84Nes/792-45
84OPC-45
84T-45
84T/St-70
85D-206
85F-354
85Leaf-124
85Moth/Ast-15
85OPC-186
85T-736
85T/St-60
86D-84
86F-306
86F/Up-U79
86Gator-22
86Moth/Ast-27
86OPC-282
86T-282
86T/Tr-76T
87Berg/Cubs-22
87D-324
87F-571
87F/Mini-73
87F/St-82
87T-372
87T/St-58
88Berg/Cubs-22
88D-447
88D/Cubs/Bk-447
88F-427
88F/Mini-69
88OPC-63
88Panini/St-267
88Score-467
88T-466
88T/Big-70
89Score-288

Muncrief, Bob
41G-8
47TipTop
49B-221
W753

Mundy, Rick
88Geneva/Pro-1640
89Geneva/Pro-1883
89Peoria/Ko-12C

Munez, Jose
88Syrac/CMC-4

Munger, George
(Red)
47TipTop
49B-40
49Eureka-190
50B-89
51B-11
51T/BB-14
52B-243
52T-115

Mungin, Mike
88SoOreg/Pro-1710

Mungo, Van Lingle
34DS-102
34DS-19
35BU-131
35BU-26
35Exh/4-2
36Exh/4-2
36Wheat
37Exh/4-2
37Wheat
38Exh/4-2
38G-254
38G-278
38Wheat
39PB-111
40PB-64
89Smok/Dodg-45
PR1-23
R303/A
R311/Leath
R312
R313
R326-6A
R326-6B
R342-6
WG8-42

Munley, John
83TriCit-7

Munninghoff, Scott
80OkCty
81OkCty/TCMA-13
82Chatt-2

Munoz, Jose
88Bakers/Cal-239
89VeroB/Star-18

Munoz, Lou
88Elmir-16
89Elmir/Puc-12

Munoz, Luis
88WinHav/Star-16

Munoz, Michael
87Bakers-27
88BBAmer-26
88SnAnt/Best-7
88TexLgAS/GS-30
89Albuq/CMC-8
89Albuq/Pro-62
90Score-653

Munoz, Omer
87WPalm-18
88WPalm/Star-18

Munoz, Pedro
87Duned-26
88Duned/Star-13
89Knoxv/Best-18
89Knoxv/Pro-1126
89Knoxv/Star-14

Munson, Jay
83Cedar-25
83Cedar/LF-7

Munson, Joseph M.
26Exh-24

Munson, Thurman
70OPC-189R
70T-189R
71MD
71MLB/St-497
71OPC-5
71T-5
71T/Coins-118
71T/GM-1
71T/tatt-10
72OPC-441
72OPC-442IA 72T-441
72T-442A
73OPC-142
73T-142
73T/Lids-34
74OPC-340
74T-340
74T/DE-7
74T/St-215
75Ho-138
75OPC-20
75T-20
75T/M-20
76Crane-41
76Ho-16
76Ho/Twink-16
76K-53
76MSA/Disc
76OPC-192LL
76OPC-650
76SSPC-433
76T-192LL
76T-650
77BK/Y-2
77Ho-5
77K-23
77OPC-30
77Pep-36
77T-170
77T/CS-32
78BK/Y-2
78Ho-150
78K-30
78OPC-200
78PapaG/Disc-27
78T-60
78Wiffle/Discs-53
79BK/Y-2
79Ho-26
79OPC-157
79T-310
80Laugh/FFeat-13
82KMart-29
84West/1-15
86S/Dec-62M
88Pac/Leg-34
89Score/NWest-32

Mura, Steve
79T-725R

80T-491
81D-362
81F-496
81T-134
82D-523
82F-578
82T-641
82T/Tr-79T
83D-293
83F-16
83OPC-24
83T-24
84Cram/PCL-196
85Cram/PCL-147
86T-281

Murakami, Masanori
65OPC-282R
65T-282R
78TCMA-182

Muratti, Rafael
86Macon-17
87Salem-17
88Mia/Star-16

Murcer, Bobby
66T-469R
67OPC-93R
67T-93R
69T-657
70K-60
70MLB/St-247
70OPC-333
70T-333
70T/CB
71Bz
71Bz/Test-9
71MLB/St-498
71OPC-635
71T-635
71T/Coins-54
71T/GM-46
72K-16
72MB-247
72OPC-86LL
72T-699
72T-700IA
72T-86LL
73K-19
73OPC-240
73OPC-343KP
73T-240
73T-343M
73T/Comics-12
73T/Lids-35
73T/PinUps-12
74K-22
74OPC-336AS
74OPC-90
74T-336AS
74T-90
74T/DE-63
74T/Puzzles-7
74T/St-216
75Ho-141
75OPC-350
75T-350
75T/M-350
76Crane-42
76Ho-123
76K-38
76MSA/Disc
76OPC-470
76SSPC-111
76T-470
77Ho-29
77OPC-83
77T-40
77T/CS-33
78Ho-90
78OPC-95
78T-590
79Ho-6
79OPC-63
79T-135
80OPC-190
80T-365
81D-111
81F-94
81OPC-253
81T-602
82D-486
82F-44
82T-208
83D-261
83F-390
83OPC-122
83OPC-304SV
83T-782
83T-783A
84Moth/Giants-23
89Pac/Leg-196
PM10/Sm-129

Murch, Simeon
E254

Murdock, Joe
89CharRa/Pro-982

Murdock, Kevin
88Tampa/Star-18

Murelli, Don
81Miami-5

Murff, John
(Red)
57T-321

Murillo, Javier
89Mia/Star/25-15

Murillo, Ray
79Knoxv/TCMA-19

Murnane, Tim
T204

Murphy, C.R.
N566-134

Murphy, Dale
77T-476R
78T-708R
79Ho-121
79OPC-15
79T-39
80OPC-143
80T-274
81D-437
81F-243
81F/St-119
81OPC-118
81Pol/Atl-3
81T-504
81T/SO-72
81T/St-146
82BK/Lids-18
82D-299
82F-443
82OPC-391
82Pol/Atl-3
82T-668
82T/St-19
83D-12DK
83D-47
83D/AAS-45
83Drake-18
83F-142
83K-52
83OPC-21AS
83OPC-23
83Pol/Atl-3
83T-401
83T-502
83T-703
83T-760
83T/Gloss-16
83T/Gloss40-16
83T/St-160
83T/St-206M
83T/St-211
84D-66
84D/AAS-40
84D/Champs-49
84Drake-22
84F-186
84F/St-17
84F/St-32
84F/St-50
84FunFood/Pin-103
84MiltBrad-17
84Nes/792-126TL
84Nes/792-133LL
84Nes/792-150
84Nes/792-391AS
84Nestle/DT-18
84OPC-150
84OPC-391AS
84Pol/Atl-3
84Ralston-12
84Seven-3C
84Seven-3E
84Seven-3W
84T-126TL
84T-133LL
84T-150
84T-391
84T/Cereal-12
84T/Gloss22-19
84T/Gloss40-31
84T/St-180FOIL
84T/St-199
84T/St-27
84T/Super-2
84T/Super-2
85D-66
85D/AAS-25
85D/HL-5
85Drake-20
85F-335
85F/LimEd-22
85F/St-18
85F/St-33
85GenMills-5
85Ho/Braves-16
85Leaf-222
85OPC-320
85Pol/Atl-3
85Seven-1S
85Seven-3W
85T-320
85T-716AS
85T/3D-3
85T/Gloss22-7
85T/Gloss40-1
85T/St-177
85T/St-22
85T/St-96
85T/Super-11
86BK/AP-11
86D-66
86D/AAS-4
86D/HL-41
86D/PopUp-4
86Dorman-10
86Drake-12
86F-522
86F-635M
86F-640M
86F/LimEd-31
86F/LL-27
86F/Mini-105
86F/Slug-24
86F/St-132CL
86F/St-80
86F/WaxBox-C4
86Jiffy-16
86Leaf-60
86Meadow/Blank-10
86Meadow/Milk-7
86Meadow/Stat-4
86OPC-M
86Pol/Atl-3
86Quaker-8
86S-183M
86S-5
86S-62M
86S/Dec-67
86T-456M
86T-600
86T-705
86T/3D-16
86T/Gloss22-18
86T/Gloss60-37
86T/Mini-37
86T/St-145
86T/St-149
86T/St-35
86T/Super-39
86T/WaxBox-M
86TrueVal-10
86Woolwth-23
87Class-37
87Class/Up-106
87D-3
87D-78
87D-PC10
87D/AAS-14
87D/DKsuper-3
87D/OD-40
87D/PopUp-14
87D/WaxBox-PC10
87Drake-13
87F-522
87F-C8
87F/AwardWin-26
87F/GameWin-30
87F/Hottest-28
87F/Lim-29
87F/McCror-30
87F/Mini-74
87F/RecSet-23
87F/Slug-28
87F/St-83
87F/WaxBox-C8
87Ho/St-7
87Jiffy-2
87KayBee-21
87KMart-29
87Kraft-2
87Leaf-141
87Leaf-3DK 87MnM's-9
87MSA/Discs-15
87OPC-359
87RedFoley/St-47
87S-155M
87S-159M
87S-3
87Smok/Atl-14
87Smok/NL-2
87T-490
87T/Board-3
87T/Coins-37
87T/Gloss22-7
87T/Gloss60-6
87T/Mini-2
87T/St-161
87T/St-36
88ChefBoy-17
88Class/Blue-201M
88Class/Blue-215
88Class/Red-156
88D-78
88D-BC14
88D/AS-46
88D/Best-113
88F-544
88F-639M
88F-C6
88F/AwardWin-27
88F/BB/AS-27
88F/BB/MVP-25
88F/Excit-28
88F/Hottest-29
88F/LL-29
88F/Mini-65
88F/RecSet-27
88F/Slug-28
88F/SS-25
88F/St-77
88F/TL-24
88F/WaxBox-C6
88FanSam-13
88KayBee-20
88KingB/Disc-2
88KMart-18
88Leaf-83
88MSA/Disc-14
88Nestle-2
88OPC-90
88Panini/St-251
88RedFoley/St-59
88Score-450
88Sf-170
88T-90
88T-549TL
88T/Big-14
88T/Coins-48
88T/Gloss60-26
88T/Mini-41
88T/RiteAid-1
88T/St-45
88T/St/Backs-18
88T/UK-52
89Ames-21
89B-276
89Class-124
89Crunch-11
89D-104
89D/Best-29
89F-596
89F/Excit-33
89F/LL-28
89KayBee-22
89OPC-210
89Panini/St-45
89RedFoley/St-84
89Score-30
89Score/HotSt-66
89Score/Mast-15
89Sf-110
89T-210
89T/Big-172
89T/Coins-19
89T/HeadsUp-23
89T/Hills-21
89T/Mini-1
89T/St-32
89T/UK-55
89Tetley/Discs-20
89UD-357
89UD-672TC
90D-168
90F-591
90F-623
90Score-66
90Score/100St-64
90Sf-189
90T-750
90UD-533

Murphy, Daniel F.
(Danny)
10Domino-90
11Helmar-57
12Sweet/Pin-48
14CJ-140
14Piedmont/St-42
15CJ-140
BF2-14
D303
E101
E102
E105
E106
E107
E254
E270
E91
E92
M116

S74-33
T202
T205
T206
T208
T213/blue
T213/brown
T215/blue
Murphy, Daniel F.
61T-214
62T-119
63T-272
70OPC-146
70T-146
Murphy, Daniel Jr.
82Tulsa-17
83Tulsa-21
84OKCty-23
84Tulsa-16
85MidldA-9
86ElPas-16
87ElPas-22
89LasVeg/CMC-7
89LasVeg/Pro-2
90T-649
Murphy, Dwayne
79T-711R
80T-461
81D-359
81F-590
81OPC-341
81T-341
81T/St-119
82D-239
82F-101
82F/St-122
82Granny-11
82K-57
82OPC-29
82T-29
82T/St-227
83D-161
83F-528
83Granny-21
83OPC-184
83T-598
83T/St-107
84D-101
84D-3
84F-456
84FunFood/Pin-93
84Moth/A's-4
84Nes/792-103
84OPC-103
84T-103
84T/St-332
85D-420
85F-432
85F/St-30
85GenMills-20
85Leaf-74
85Moth/A's-6
85T-231
85T/St-323
86D-176
86F-428
86F/Mini-90
86Moth/A's-6
86OPC-8
86T-216M
86T-8
86T/St-171
86TrueVal-27
87D-379
87D/OD-27
87F-400
87OPC-121
87Smok/A's-9
87T-743
87T/St-170
88D-405
88F-287
88OPC-334
88Panini/St-176
88Score-455
88T-424
89Ames-22
89Score-545
89T-667
90F-569
Murphy, Eddie
48Smith-24
Murphy, Gary
86Ashvl-21
89QuadC/Best-16
89QuadC/GS-19
Murphy, James
88Geneva/Pro-1638
89CharWh/Best-10
89CharWh/Pro-1745
89Fay/Pro-1586
Murphy, John Edward
15CJ-165
D327
D329-130
D350/2-127
E121/80
E122
M101/4-130
M101/5-127
W575
Murphy, John J.
80ArkTr-21
Murphy, John Joseph
35BU-154
41DP-110
44Yank/St-20
88Conlon/3-20
Murphy, John V.
87Louvl-21
88Louvl-36
88Louvl/CMC-16
88Louvl/Pro-429
88Sprin/Best-22
Murphy, John
87StPet-13
Murphy, Kent
86Water-17
87BuffB-2
88Wmspt/Pro-1305
Murphy, Micah
89Geneva/Pro-1880
Murphy, Michael
86Water-18
87BuffB-17
Murphy, Miguel
87Kenosha-25
88Fay/Pro-1100
Murphy, Mike
77ArkTr
Murphy, Morgan
N300/unif
Murphy, P.L.
N172
Murphy, Patrick J.
N172
N338/2
Murphy, Pete
87Macon-11
87Watertn-24
88Salem/Star-14
89Harris/Pro-308
89Harris/Star-12
Murphy, Red
WG7-36
Murphy, Rob
82Cedar-2
83Cedar-13
83Cedar/LF-24
87Class-70
87D-452
87F-206
87Kahn-46
87T-82
88D-82
88D/Best-230
88F-241
88Kahn/Reds-46
88Score-559
88T-603
89B-22
89Class/Up/2-183
89D-139
89D/Best-196
89D/Tr-15
89F-165
89F/Up-10
89OPC-182
89Score-141
89Score/Tr-8
89T-446
89T/Tr-86T
89UD-372
89UD/Ext-759
90D-186
90F-281
90Score-181
90T-268
90UD-461
90UD-464
Murphy, Tim
74Gasto
Murphy, Tom A.
69JB
69T-474
70OPC-351
70T-351
71OPC-401
71T-401
71T/tatt-5
72MB-248
72OPC-354
72T-354
73OPC-539
73T-539
74OPC-496
74T-496
74T/Tr-496T
75OPC-28
75T-28
75T/M-28
76OPC-219
76SSPC-227
76T-219
77T-396
78OPC-193
78T-103
79OPC-308
79T-588
Murphy, Tommy
T3/Box-59
Murphy, Wayne
87WinHav-18
Murphy, William E.
66T-574R
Murray, Bill
88SLCty-2
88SLCty-29
89SLCty-29OWN
Murray, Brian
88SLCty-2
Murray, Dale
75OPC-568
75T-568
75T/M-568
76OPC-18
76SSPC-350
76T-18
77T-252
78Ho-31
78T-149
79Ho-115
79OPC-198
79T-379
80OPC-274
80T-559
81Syrac-7
83D-381
83F-437
83OPC-42
83T-42
83T/X-79
84D-577
84F-134
84Nes/792-697
84OPC-281
84T-697
85F-137
85OKCty-27
85T-481
86OPC-197
Murray, Dave
86Salem-21
Murray, Eddie
78K-25
78OPC-154
78T-36
79OPC-338
79T-640
79T/Comics-1
80K-24
80OPC-88
80T-160
80T/S-28
81D-112
81Drake-6
81F-184
81F/St-117
81K-18
81MSA/Disc-23
81OPC-39
81Sqt-15SP
81T-490
81T/SO-9
81T/St-34
82D-483
82Drake-25
82F-174
82F/St-151
82K-64
82OPC-390
82T-162LL
82T-163LL
82T-390
82T-426TL
82T/St-145
82T/St-4LL
82T/St-6
83D-405
83D/AAS-1
83Drake-19
83F-67
83K-11
83OPC-141
83T-21
83T-530
83T/Gloss-37
83T/Gloss40-37
83T/St-29
84D-22
84D-47
84D/AAS-50
84D/Champs-19
84Drake-23
84F-14
84F/St-23
84F/St-38
84FunFood/Pin-119
84Nes/792-240
84Nes/792-397AS
84Nestle/DT-1
84OPC-240
84OPC-291AS 84Ralston-1
84Seven-6C
84Seven-6E
84Seven-6W
84T-240
84T-397
84T/Cereal-1
84T/Gloss40-4
84T/St-195FOIL
84T/St-203
84T/St-26WS
84T/St/Box-12
84T/Super-25
84T/Super-25
85D-47
85D/AAS-9
85D/HL-34
85Drake-21
85F-184
85F/LimEd-23
85F/St-20
85F/St-62SA
85F/St-63
85F/St-64
85F/St-65
85F/St-66
85F/St-67
85GenMills-21
85Leaf-203
85OPC-221
85Seven-1E
85Seven-4G
85Seven-4W
85T-700
85T-701AS
85T/3D-2
85T/Gloss40-28
85T/St-196
85T/Super-18
86BK/AP-14
86D-88
86D/AAS-13
86D/PopUp-13
86Dorman-12
86Drake-25
86F-282
86F/LimEd-32
86F/Mini-58
86F/Slug-25
86F/St-81
86Jiffy-10
86Leaf-83
86OPC-30
86Quaker-27
86S-140M
86S-4
86S-73M
86S/Dec-70
86S/Rook-48M
86T-30
86T/3D-19
86T/Gloss22-2
86T/Gloss60-33
86T/Mini-1
86T/St-158
86T/St-227
86T/Super-40
86TrueVal-3
86Woolwth-24
87Class-51
87D-48
87D/AAS-31
87D/HL-37
87D/OD-136
87Drake-24
87F-476
87F-636M
87F/LL-32
87F/McCror-31
87F/Mini-75
87F/RecSet-24
87F/St-84
87Ho/St-18
87KayBee-22
87KMart-30
87Kraft-1
87Leaf-110
87OPC-120

87Ralston-8
87RedFoley/St-66
87S-159M
87S-6
87S-75M
87Seven-ME12
87T-120
87T/Board-2
87T/Coins-19
87T/Gloss60-12
87T/Mini-39
87T/St-224
88Woolwth-5
88D-231
88D/Best-142
88F-567
88F/BB/AS-28
88F/Mini-1
88F/St-2
88French-33
88Jiffy-13
88Leaf-172
88OPC-4
88Panini/St-442
88Panini/St-8
88Score-18
88Sf-59
88T-495
88T-4RB
88T/Big-215
88T/Coins-22
88T/St-11
88T/St-233
88T/UK-53
89B-346
89Class/Up/2-160
89Crunch-15
89D-96
89D/Best-92
89D/Tr-12
89F-611
89F/Up-92
89KayBee-23
89KingB/Discs-2
89KMart/Lead-11
89Moth/Dodg-2
89OPC-148
89Panini/St-260
89Pol/Dodg-21
89RedFoley/St-85
89Score-94
89Score/HotSt-83
89Score/Tr-31
89Sf-147
89T-625
89T/Big-319
89T/Coins-20
89T/Hills-22
89T/Mini-44
89T/St-238
89T/Tr-87T
89T/UK-56
89UD-275
89UD/Ext-763
90D-77
90F-404
90Score-80
90T-305
90UD-277

Murray, George
R314/Can

Murray, Jack
14Piedmont/St-43

Murray, James
C46-5

Murray, Jed
81LynnS-8
82LynnS-6
83SLCty-9
84Cram/PCL-177
86Calgary-17
87Toled-13
87Toled/TCMA-18

Murray, Jeremiah
N172

Murray, Jim
75Clint

Murray, John Joseph
10Domino-91
11Helmar-135
12Sweet/Pin-121
D350/2-128
E104
E254
E270/2
E91
E94
E96
E97
M101/5-128
M116
S74-92
T202
T205
T205
T206
T213/blue
T215/blue
T215/brown
T222
T3-48
W555
WG4-21

Murray, Joseph
52Park-99

Murray, Larry
76SSPC-449
80T-284

Murray, Mike
87Myrtle-8
88Myrtle/Pro-1179
89Kingspt/Star-28

Murray, Ray
50NumNum
52B-118
52T-299
53B/BW-6
53T-234
54B-83
54Esskay
54T-49

Murray, Rich
76Cedar
77Cedar
78Cr/PCL-32
79Phoen
80Phoen-19
81F-452
81Phoen-24
81T-195
82Charl-16
83Phoen/BHN-6
84Cram/PCL-6
85Omaha-8

Murray, Richard
82Wichi-11

Murray, Scott
86StPet-21
88SanJose/Cal-125
88SanJose/Pro-113

Murray, Steve
84Beaum-7
88SnBer/Cal-29
89Wausa/GS-20

Murray, Venice
78Cedar

Murrell, Ivan
68T-569
69T-333
70OPC-179
70T-179
71MLB/St-232
71OPC-569
71T-569
72MB-249
72T-677
73OPC-409
73T-409
74OPC-628
74T-628
87Wmspt-11

Murrell, Rodney
86LitFalls-20
87Columbia-22
88Clmbia/GS-17
89Penin/Star-16

Murtaugh, Danny
48L-142
49B-124
49Eureka-168
50B-203
51B-273
52NTea
59T-17
60T-223
61T-138
61T-567AS
62T-503
63T-559
64T-141
64T-268
70OPC-532MG
70T-532
71OPC-437MG
71T-437
74OPC-489MG
74T-489MG
75OPC-304MG 75T-304MG
75T/M-304MG
76SSPC-586
76T-504
PM10/Sm-130

Murtaugh, Tim
75Shreve/TCMA-12
76Shrev

Murtha, Brian
82Clint-20

Muscat, Scott
89Helena/SP-24

Muser, Tony
73OPC-238
73T-238
74OPC-286
74T-286
75OPC-348
75T-348
75T/M-348
76OPC-537
76SSPC-390
76T-537
77T-251
78T-418
81ElPas-23
82ElPas-23
84Cram/PCL-27
86Pol/Brew-35C

Musial, Stan
48B-36
48L-4
49B-24
49Eureka-191
49Royal-1
51BR-B1
51Wheat
52B-196
52BR
52RM-NL16
52Royal
52StarCal/L-81E
52StarCal/L-81F
52Wheat
53B/Col-32
53Exh/Can-57
53Hunter
53RM-NL26
54Hunter
54RH
55Hunter
55Rawl-1
55Rawl-1A
55Rawl-2
55Rawl-2A
55Rawl-3
55Rawl-4
56YellBase/Pin-23
58T-476AS
59T-150
59T-470M
60NuCard-21
60T-250
60T/tatt-39
60T/tatt-94
61NuCard-421
61T-290
61T/Dice-11
61T/St-92
62Exh
62T-1LL
62T-317M
62T-50
62T/bucks
62T/St-189
63Bz-23
63Exh
63T-138M
63T-250
63T/SO
72Laugh/GF-24
74Laugh/ASG-55
79TCMA-9
80Cram/Leg-8
80SSPC/HOF
83D/HOF-32
83MLBPA/Pin-29
85CircK-15
85D/HOF-5
85Woolwth-27
86S/Dec-30
87Nestle/DT-23
88D-641PUZ
88Leaf-263PUZ
88Pac/Leg-6
88T-665TBC
89HOF/St-30
D305
Exh47
PM10/Sm-131
PM10/Sm-132
PM10/Sm-133
R423-72

Musolino, Mike
88PalmSp/Cal-105
88QuadC/GS-30
89QuadC/Best-20
89QuadC/GS-15

Musselman, Jeff
86Ventura-16
87D-591
87D/Rook-53
87F/U-U84
87S/Rook-15
87T/Tr-83T
87Tor/Fire-25
87Tor/Fire-25
88D-630
88F-121
88Leaf-234
88OPC-229
88Score-478
88Score/YS/II-30
88T-229
88T/Big-69
88T/JumboR-22
88T/St-308
88Tor/Fire-13
88ToysRUs-20
89B-240
89D-656
89F-243
89OPC-362
89Score-558
89T-591
89Tor/Fire-13
89UD-41
90D-623
90F-212
90Score-525
90T-382
90UD-585

Musselman, Ron
80LynnS-23
81Spoka-17
82SLCty-14
83OKCty-14
85F/Up-U83
85Tor/Fire-25
86Syrac-20
87Portl-21

Mustad, Eric
80Hawai-5
81Tacom-4
82Tacom-7
84Indianap-11

Mustari, Frank
88VeroB/Star-16

Mute, Frank
89QuadC/Best-13

Muth, Bill
77Wausa

Mutis, Jeff
88BurlR/Pro-1792
89Kinston/Star-13

Mutrie, James
E223
N172
N338/2

Mutz, Frank
88QuadC/GS-12
88Reno/Cal-276
89QuadC/GS-22

Mutz, Tommy
77Indianap-16
78Indianap-10
79Indianap-8

Myaer, Jeff
86Cram/PCL-153

Myatt, George
60Lake
60T-464C
V353-10
V355-26

Myatt, Glenn
25Exh-84
26Exh-83
27Exh-43
28Exh-42
33G-10
34DS-58
35G-1K
35G-3B
35G-5B
35G-6B
R314/Can
R337-417

Myer, Charles M.
(Buddy)
29Exh/4-32
31Exh/4-32
33G-153
34DS-4
35BU-133
35BU-19
35Exh/4-16
35G-8H
35G-9H
36Exh/4-16
37Exh/4-16
37OPC-114
38Exh/4-16
39PB-100

40PB-17
41DP-73
R313
R314
V300
V353-78
V355-132

Myerchin, Mike
82Beloi-12

Myers, Al
N172
N284

Myers, Brad
88CapeCod/Sum-135

Myers, Chris
88Hagers/Star-13
89Freder/Star-19

Myers, Dave
77Cedar
83Wausa/LF-12
86Chatt-21
87Chatt/Best-20
87SLAS-11
88Vermont/Pro-952

Myers, Ed
84Albany-18
86Vanco-18

Myers, Elmer
D328-124
E120
E135-124
W573

Myers, George
N172
N284

Myers, Glen
87Visal-2

Myers, Greg
86Ventura-17
87Syrac-4
87Syrac/TCMA-10
88D-624
88F-644
88Syrac/CMC-18
88Syrac/Pro-821
89Tor/Fire-16
90D-706
90T-438

Myers, Henry
(Hy)
21Exh-115
D327
D328-125
D329-131
D350/2-129
E120
E121/120
E121/80
E135-125
E300
M101/4-131
M101/5-129
M116
T206
T213/brown

Myers, Jim
88Poca/Pro-2076
89Clint/Pro-886

Myers, Linwood
39PB-133

Myers, Michael S.
88CapeCod/Sum-158

Myers, Michael
88Charl/Pro-1199
89Cedar/Best-5
89Cedar/Pro-918
89Cedar/Star-14

Myers, Mike
87Spoka-24

Myers, Randy
86Tidew-22
87D-29RR
87F/U-U85
87Leaf-29
87T-213
88D-620
88D/Best-265
88D/Mets/Bk-620
88F-146
88Kahn/Mets-48
88Score-336
88T-412
88T/JumboR-12
88T/Mets/Fan-48
88ToysRUs-21
89B-374
89Class/Up/2-197
89D-336
89D/Best-153
89F-46
89Kahn/Mets-48
89OPC-104
89Panini/St-135
89Score-306
89Score/YS/I-41
89T-610
89T/St-97
89T/St/Backs-66
89UD-634
90Class-107
90D-336
90F-213
90Score-351
90T-105
90UD-581

Myers, Richard
52Mother-58
53Mother-15

Myers, William
35G-8D
35G-9D
39PB-38
40PB-80
W711/1
W711/2

Myles, Rick
81Cedar-4
82Lynch-17
84Jacks-2

Myllykangas, Lauri
R314/Can
V355-82

Myrick, Robert
77T-627
78T-676
78Tidew
79Tucso-21

Nabekawa, Tom
87SanJose-13

Naber, Bob
83Clint/LF-13

Naccarato, Stan
81Tacom-30
82Tacom-22
83Tacom-19
88Tacom/Pro-620
89Tacom/Pro-1566

Naehring, Mark
78Knoxv

Naehring, Tim
88Elmir-17
89Lynch/Star-15

Nagel, William T.
(Bill)
41DP-50

Nagelson, Russell C.
(Rusty)
70OPC-7R
70T-7R
71OPC-708
71T-708

Nagle, Thomas E.
(Tom)
N172

Nago, Garrett
83ElPas-12
84ElPas-25
85Cram/PCL-223
86ElPas-17
87ElPas-5
88Indi/CMC-22
88Indi/Pro-515
89ColMud/Best-3
89ColMud/Pro-146
89ColMud/Star-18

Nagy, Charles
88T/Tr-74T
89B-73
89Kinston/Star-14
89Star/Wax-77
89T/Big-217
90Score-611

Nagy, Mike
70OPC-39
70T-39
71MLB/St-325
71OPC-363
71T-363
72OPC-488
72T-488

Nagy, Steve
49Sommer-7

Nahem, Sam
W754

Nahorodny, William G.
(Bill)
76OkCty
78T-702R
79T-169
80OPC-286
80T-552
81F-254
81Pol/Atl-15
81T-295
82Charl-11
83F-416
83T-616
84Cram/PCL-181
85Cram/PCL-39

Naihing, Mark
79Knoxv/TCMA-1

Nail, Charlie
82BirmB-21
83Evans-6

Nakamura, Hector
87SanJose-2

Nakashima, Yoshi
86SanJose-14

Nalley, Jerry
81Batav-14
82Watlo/B-21
82Watlo/C-6

Nalls, Gary
86QuadC-25
87PalmSp-32
88PalmSp/Cal-106
88PalmSp/Pro-1454
89Reno/Cal-250

Namar, Robert
79WHave-29M

Nandin, Bob
83Syrac-18
84Syrac-13
86ElPas-18

Nanni, Tito
81LynnS-23
82LynnS-15
83SLCty-13
84Cram/PCL-174
85MidldA-1

Napier, Jim
61Union
76AppFx
79QuadC-22
82IowaC-25MG
83IowaC-26
84IowaC-11
86Maine-12MG

Napoleon, Daniel
(Danny)
65T-533R
66OPC-87
66T-87

Napoleon, Ed
78Cr/PCL-109
79WHave-2
82Nashv-28CO
83Wheat/Ind-23CO
85Polar/Ind-xx

Napp, Larry
55B-250ump

Naragon, Harold R.
(Hal)
55B-129
55Gol/Ind-21
55Salem
56T-311
57T-347
58T-22
59T-376
60T-231
61Clover-19
61Peters-8
61T-92
62T-164

Narcisse, Ron
85LitFalls-14
86LitFalls-21

Narleski, Bill
88Watlo/Pro-674

Narleski, Ray
55B-96
55Gol/Ind-22
55Salem
55T-160
56T-133
57T-144
58Hires-22
58T-439
59T-442
60T-161

Narleski, Steve
77Watlo
81Chatt-5
82Chatt-19

Narron, Jerry A.
(Jerry)
77WHave
78Cr/PCL-54
80T-16
81D-405
81OPC-249
81Pol/Sea-12
81T-637
82D-433
82F-513
82Spoka-12
82T-719
84Smok/Cal-20
85D-643
85Smok/Cal-10
85T-234
86D-451
86Smok/Cal-10
86T-543
87Calgary-21
87D-603
87T-474
88RochR-15
88RochR-17
88RochR/CMC-14
88RochR/Gov-17
88RochR/Pro-216
89Freder/Star-25

Narron, Johnny
75AppFx

Narron, Sam
49Eureka-44
60T-467C

Narum, L.F.
(Buster)
64T-418R
65OPC-86
65T-86
66T-274
78TCMA-44

Nash, Charles F.
(Cotton)
71OPC-391R
71T-391R

Nash, Dave
86Cram/PCL-184
88Fresno/Cal-13
88Fresno/Pro-1228

Nash, Jim
67OPC-90
67T-90
68T-324
69MB-198
69MLB/St-89
69T-546
69T/St-219
70MLB/St-9
70OPC-171
70T-171
71MLB/St-18
71OPC-306
71T-306
72MB-250
72OPC-401
72T-401
73OPC-509
73T-509

Nash, William M.
(Billy)
N142
N172
N300/unif
N403
WG1-7

Nastu, Phil
77Cedar
78Cr/PCL-27
79Phoen
80Phoen-7
80T-686R

Natal, Bob
(Rob) 87Jamestn-18
88FSLAS/Star-14
88WPalm/Star-19
89Jaxvl/Best-17
89Jaxvl/Pro-176

Natera, Luis
85LitFalls-20
86LitFalls-22
87Columbia-14

Nattile, Sam
85Pawtu-10
86NewBrit-19

Nattress, William W.
(Natty)
C46-8
E254
T206

Natupsky, Hal
79Elmir-20

Naughton, Danny
87Columbia-19
88Clmbia/GS-23
89StLucie/Star-18

Naumann, Rick
81AppFx-6

Navarro, Jaime
88Stock/Cal-182
88Stock/Pro-736
89ElPas/GS-13
89F/Up-39
90D-640
90F-331
90Score-569

90UD-646

Navarro, Julio
60T-140
63T-169R
64T-489
65T-563
66T-527

Naveda, Edgar
86Kenosha-17
87Kenosha-5
88Visal/Cal-156
88Visal/Pro-103
89Orlan/Best-18
89Orlan/Pro-1347

Navilliat, James
86Cram/PCL-157
87CharRa-11

Naworski, Andy
86Bakers-21
86Cram/PCL-187
87FtMyr-9

Naylor, Roleine C.
21Exh-116
E120
W573

Nazabal, Robert
85Bend/Cram-17

Neagle, Dennis
88CapeCod/Sum-53
89Elizab/Star-22

Neal, Bob
80Penin/B-25GM
80Penin/C-9GM
88AubAs/Pro-1964
89AubAs/Pro-2178

Neal, Bryan
82Durhm-6
83Durhm-10

Neal, Charles Lenard
(Charlie)
55B-278
56T-299
57T-242
58Hires-54
58T-16
59Morrell
59T-427
60Morrell
60T-155
60T-556AS
60T/tatt
60T/tatt-40
61BB-43
61P-157
61T-423
61T/St-30
62J-102
62P-102
62P/Can-102
62Salada-102A
62Salada-102B
62Shirriff-102
62T-365
63Exh
63J-195
63P-195
63T-511
64T-436
89Smok/Dodg-66
Exh47

Neal, Dave
89PalmSp/Cal-49
89PalmSp/Pro-474

Neal, Earl A.
21Exh-117

Neal, Scott
85PrWill-2
86Hawai-18
87Harrisbg-9

Neal, Willie
81CharR-25
82CharR-22

Neale, Alfred Earle
(Greasy)
88Conlon/4-20
88Pac/8Men-88
D327
D328-126
E120
E121/120
E135-126
E220
V100
W501-51
W514-6
W575

Nealeigh, Rod
83Memph-13

Nedin, Tim
89Elizab/Star-23

Nee, John
T205

Needham, Thomas J.
(Tom)
10Domino-92
11Helmar-99
12Sweet/Pin-85
14Piedmont/St-44
E286
M116
S74-65
T202
T205
T206
T207
T213/blue

Neel, Troy
88MidwLAS/GS-21
88Watlo/Pro-681
89Canton/Best-25
89Canton/Pro-1324
89Canton/Star-17

Neely, Jeff
89Aug/Pro-495

Neeman, Calvin A.
(Cal)
57T-353
58T-33
59T-367
60T-337
79TCMA-142

Negray, Ron
56T-7
56T/Pin-20
57T-254
61BeeHive-15

Negron, Miguel
80LynnS-10
83Chatt-10

Nehf, Art
21Exh-118
25Exh-37
28Yueng-43
61F-65
75F/Pion-28
D327
D328-127
E120
E121/120
E121/80
E126-59
E135-127
E220
V61-93
W502-43
W515-22
W516-17
W572
W575

Neibauer, Gary
69T-611R
70OPC-384
70T-384
71OPC-668
71T-668
72OPC-149
72T-149

Neidinger, Joe
89Brist/Star-18

Neidlinger, Jim
85PrWill-10
86Nashua-19
87Harrisbg-20
88Harris/Pro-842
89Albuq/CMC-9
89Albuq/Pro-71

Neiger, Al
61T-202

Neilson, Jerry
89Star/Wax-91

Neis, Bernard E.
(Bernie)
26Exh-6
27Exh-44
E220

Nelloms, Skip
88Oneon/Pro-2048
89FtLaud/Star-18

Nelson, Albert
(Red)
E254
T207

Nelson, Battling
T3/Box-57

Nelson, Chester
77Newar

Nelson, Darren
87Erie-25
88StPet/Star-19

Nelson, David Earl
(Dave)
69MB-199
69T-579
70OPC-112
70T-112
71MLB/St-547
71OPC-241
71T-241
72T-529
73OPC-111
73T-111
74OPC-355
74T-355
74T/DE-4
74T/St-238
75OPC-435
75Shreve/TCMA-13
75T-435
75T/M-435
76OPC-535
76Shrev
76SSPC-273
76T-535

Nelson, Doug
75Shreve/TCMA-14
76Shrev
88AppFx/Pro-141
89BBCity/Star-19

Nelson, Eric
89Well/Puc-19

Nelson, Frank
47Sunbeam
49Remar
50Remar

Nelson, Gene
81T/Tr-809
82D-513
82F-45
82T-373
82T/Tr-80T
83D-55
83T-106
85Coke/WS-30
85D-615
85F-522
85T/Tr-86T
86Coke/WS-30
86D-501
86F-213
86Leaf-245
86T-493
87D-580
87F-504
87F/U-U86
87T-273
87T/Tr-84T
88D-133
88D/A's/Bk-133
88F-288
88Moth/A's-25
88Score-588
88T-621
89B-185
89D-540
89F-18
89Moth/A's-26
89OPC-318
89Score-434
89T-581
89UD-643
89Woolwth-16
90D-540
90F-17
90Score-441
90T-726
90UD-80

Nelson, Glenn Richard
(Rocky)
52Park-61
52T-390
53Exh/Can-49
54T-199
59T-446
60L-127
60T-157
61Kahn
61P-137
61T-304
61T/St-68

Nelson, Jackson
N172/SP
N284
N690

Nelson, James Lorin
71T-298

Nelson, Jamie
83SLCty-16
84Cram/PCL-43
84Nes/792-166
84T-166
85Cram/PCL-221
87Memph-8
87Memph/Best-26
88Colum/CMC-12
88Colum/Pol-23
88Colum/Pro-305
89Edmon/CMC-19
89Edmon/Pro-569

Nelson, Jeff
86Bakers-22
88SnBer/Best-23
88SnBer/Cal-48
89Wmspt/Pro-637
89Wmspt/Star-15

Nelson, Jerome
86Modesto-20
87Modesto-5
88Huntsvl/BK-13
89Chatt/Best-23
89Chatt/GS-19

Nelson, Jim
71OPC-298

Nelson, Jim
81LynnS-13
82LynnS-9

Nelson, Kim
79Wisco-11

Nelson, Lynn B.
(Lynn)
34G-60
39PB-118
40PB-135

Nelson, Mel
60DF-11
61Union
63T-522R
64T-273
65T-564
66T-367
69OPC-181
69T-181

Nelson, Pat
78Ashev

Nelson, Rick
84D-636
84F-615
84Nes/792-672
84T-672
84T/St-347
85Cram/PCL-91
85Evrt/Cram-11A
85Evrt/Cram-11B
85T-296
86Calgary-18
86Clint-16
87Tidew-16
88Shreve/Pro-1294

Nelson, Rob
83Idaho-22
84Madis/Pol-11
85Huntsvl/BK-41
86Tacom-15
87D-595
87D/OD-25
87F-653M
88D-574
88LasVeg/CMC-16
88LasVeg/Pro-237
89LasVeg/CMC-16
89LasVeg/Pro-24
90UD-51

Nelson, Robert S.
(Bob)
56T-169

Nelson, Roger
68T-549R
69MLB/St-61
69T-279
69T/S-23
69T/St-186
70MLB/St-225
70T-633
71OPC-581
71T-581
73OPC-251
73T-251
74OPC-491
74T-491
75OPC-572
75T-572
75T/M-572
75Tucso-25
78Colum

Nelson, Ron
87Spart-12

Nelson, Scott
88Clint/Pro-698
89Salin/Cal-127
89Salin/Pro-1824

Nelson, Spike
49Eureka-192

Nelson, Thomas C.
(Tom)
47Sunbeam

Nemeth, Carey
86Erie-20
87Savan-16

Nemeth, Joe
79Wausa-9

80Ashev-12
81Tulsa-11
82Readg-17
82Tulsa-24
83Tulsa-19

Nen, Richard LeRoy
(Dick)
64T-14R
65T-466R
66OPC-149
66T-149
67T-403
68T-591
69MB-200

Nen, Robb
88Butte-5
88Gasto/Pro-1003
89Gasto/Pro-1003
89Gasto/Star-16

Nenad, David
82Clint-9

Nerone, Phil
75AppFx
76AppFx

Nettles, Graig
69OPC-99R
69T-99R
70OPC-491
70T-491
71MLB/St-380
71OPC-324
71T-324
72T-590
73OPC-498
73T-498
74OPC-251
74T-251
74T/St-217
75Ho-24
75Ho/Twink-24
75OPC-160
75T-160
75T/M-160
76Ho-81
76OPC-169
76SSPC-437
76T-169
77BK/Y-15
77Ho-116
77OPC-217
77OPC-2LL
77T-20
77T-2LL
78BK/Y-14
78Ho-132
78OPC-10
78T-250
78Wiffle/Discs-54
79BK/Y-15
79Ho-110
79OPC-240
79T-460
80K-18
80OPC-359
80T-710
81D-105
81F-87
81F/St-72
81OPC-365
81T-365
81T/HT
82D-335
82Drake-26
82F-46
82F/St-119
82F/St-238M
82HB/LS
82OPC-21IA
82OPC-62
82T-505
82T-506A
82T/St-215
83D-83
83F-391
83OPC-207SV
83OPC-293
83RoyRog/Disc-7
83T-635
83T-636A
83T/St-13
84D-518
84D/Champs-12
84F-135
84F/X-82
84FunFood/Pin-66
84Moth/Padres-22
84Nes/792-175
84Nes/792-712LL
84Nes/792-713LL
84OPC-175
84T-175
84T-712
84T-713
84T/St-326
84T/X-83
85D-234
85F-42
85Leaf-177
85Moth/Padres-4
85OPC-35
85T-35
85T/St-155
86D-478
86D/AAS-6
86D/PopUp-6
86F-332
86OPC-151
86S-91
86T-450
86T/Gloss22-15
86T/St-106
86T/St-151
87F-426
87OPC-205
87RedFoley/St-87
87Smok/Atl-15
87T-205
87T/Tr-85T
88SanDiegoSt-12
88Score-440
88Score/Tr-25T
88T-574
89Score-277

Nettles, James W.
(Jim)
71OPC-74R
71T-74R
72OPC-131
72T-131
73OPC-358
73T-358
75OPC-497
75T-497
75T/M-497
80Colum-12
81Tacom-12
82Tacom-17
83Idaho-30
83Tacom-20
85Madis-23
85Madis/Pol-20
86Madis-15
86Madis/Pol-24
87Madis-4
88Madis-16
89Madis/Star-17

Nettles, Morris Jr.
75OPC-632
75T-632
75T/M-632
76OPC-434
76SSPC-202
76T-434
76T/Tr-434T

Nettles, Robert
86Erie-21

Neuendorff, Tony
83Durhm-11
84Durhm-16

Neuenschwander, Doug
80Water-4
81Water-5

Neufang, Gerry
82Tulsa-20
83Tulsa-23

Neuzil, Jeff
84Memph-10

Neville, Dan
65T-398R

Newberg, Tom
88Vermont/Pro-955

Newcomb, Joe Dean
89Knoxv/Best-19
89Knoxv/Pro-1135
89Knoxv/Star-15

Newcombe, Donald
(Don)
49Eureka-45
50B-23
51B-6
52B-128
52BR
52StarCal/L-79D
53Briggs
53Exh/Can-16
54B-154
54NYJour
54SM
55B-143
55Gol/Dodg-21
55RFG-21
55SM
56T-235
56YellBase/Pin-24
57T-130
58Hires-13
58T-340
59T-312
60Kahn
60L-19
60T-345
60T/tatt
60T/tatt-41
61T-483MV
75OPC-194M
75T-194MV
75T/M-194MV
79TCMA-182
86S/Dec-39M
88Pac/Leg-33
89Rini/Dodg-3
89Smok/Dodg-55
89Swell-122
Exh47
PM10/L-30
PM10/Sm-134
PM10/Sm-135
PM10/Sm-136
R423-74
Rawl

Newell, Tom
86Clearw-18
87Maine-20
87Maine/TCMA-6
88D-604
88F-648
88Maine/CMC-8
88Maine/Pro-293

Newhauser, Don
74OPC-33
74T-33

Newhouser, Hal
39Exh
48L-98
52StarCal/L-72B
53Exh/Can-12
53T-228
55Salem
55T-24
55T/DH-109
60F-68
61F-66
61NuCard-446
72T/Test-7
86S/Dec-19
Exh47
R423-73

Newman, Al
84Beaum-4
85Indianap-14
86D/Rook-9
86F/Up-U80
86Provigo-18
87D-426
87F-327
87OPC-323
87T-323
87T/Tr-86T
88D-645
88F-17
88SanDiegoSt-13
88SanDiegoSt-14
88Score-252
88Smok/Minn-11
88T-648
89B-156
89D-436
89F-122
89Score-493
89T-503
89UD-197
90D-506
90F-382
90Score-128
90T-19
90UD-199

Newman, Danny
88Ashvl/Pro-1071

Newman, Fred
63T-496R
64T-569
65OPC-101
65T-101
66T-213
66T/RO-82
67T-451
69T-543

Newman, Jeff
76Tucso-12
77T-204
78T-458
79OPC-319
79T-604
80K-7
80OPC-18
80T-34
81D-477
81F-577
81T-587
81T/St-120
82D-517
82F-102
82Granny-12
82T-187
83D-635
83F-529
83T-784
83T/X-80
84D-249
84F-404
84Nes/792-296
84T-296
85T-376
87Moth/A's-19
88Modesto-1MG
88Modesto/Cal-81
89Huntsvl/Best-20
89SLAS-25

Newman, Mark
82FtMyr-20

Newman, Randy
83Wausa/LF-25
86Calgary-19

Newman, Ray
72T-667
73OPC-568
73T-568

Newman, Todd
87AubAs-17

Newman, Tom
89Idaho/Pro-2036

Newsom, Gary
83VeroB-19
85VeroB-4
86Albuq-18
87Durhm-9

Newsom, Norman
(Bobo)
35Exh/4-15
36Exh/4-16
36G
36Wheat
37Exh/4-16
37OPC-139
38Exh/4-15
39Exh
41DP-51
53T-15
54Esskay
55Esskay
60F-70
61F-67
R313
R314
V300

Newsome, Lamar A.
(Skeeter)
39PB-84
R313

Newson, Warren
86Cram/PCL-174
88CalLgAS-45
88River/Cal-225
88River/Pro-1416
89AubAs/Pro-2
89Wich/Roc-24
89Wich/Roc/HL-10
89Wich/Roc/Up-7

Newton, Eustace
(Doc)
T204

Newton, Marty
86Cram/PCL-15

Newton, Steve
88LitFalls/Puc-18
89Clmbia/Best-18
89Clmbia/GS-17

Newton, Warren
(Newt)
87CharRa-16

Nezelek, Andy
88Greenv/Best-19
89D-616
89Richm/CMC-6
89Richm/Ko-34
89Richm/Pro-839
90D-523

Niarhos, Constantine
(Gus)
49B-181
50B-154
51B-124
52B-129
52T-121
53T-63
R346-25

Nicastro, Steve
79Newar-2

Nice, Bill
80Ander-14

Nicely, Roy M.
48Sommer-24
49Sommer-13
Nicely, Tony
78Charl
Nicholas, Franci
R314/Can
Nicholls, Simon B.
E104
E91
T204
T206
W555
Nichols, Brian
88Bill/Pro-1819
89Bill/Pro-2043
Nichols, Carl
83SanJose-20
85CharO-9
87RochR-11
87RochR/TCMA-10
88D-477
88D/Rook-39
88RochR-18
88RochR/Gov-18
89AAA/Pro-45
89F-612
89Tucso/CMC-15
89Tucso/Pro-185
Nichols, Charles A.
(Kid)
50Callahan
61F-129
80SSPC/HOF
E97
N172
N300/unif
WG3-33
Nichols, Chet
52B-120
52T-288
54JC-16
55B-72
55Gol/Braves-22
55JC-17
56T-278
61T-301
62T-403
63T-307
Nichols, Dolan
59T-362
Nichols, Fred
74Gasto
Nichols, Gary
88Sprin/Best-23
Nichols, Howard Jr.
86Readg-19
87Readg-14
88Readg/Pro-879
89IowaC/CMC-18
89IowaC/Pro-1712
Nichols, Lance
82RochR-20
83RochR-1
Nichols, Rod
86Watlo-20
87Kinston-24
89D-649
89T-443
90D-546
90F-497
90T-108
90UD-572
Nichols, Samuel
N172
Nichols, Scott
87Savan-6
89StPet/Star-21
Nichols, Thomas Reid
(Reid)
81T-689R
82Coke/BOS
82D-632
82F-300
82T-124
83D-460
83F-189
83T-446
84D-614
84F-405
84Nes/792-238
84T-238
85D-636
85F-164
85T-37
86Coke/WS-20
86D-574
86F-214
86Leaf-224
86T-364
87D/OD-87
87F/U-U89
87T-539
87T/Tr-87T
88F-191
88OPC-261
88T-748
Nichols, Ty
85Newar-3
86Hagers-13
88CharlK-22
88CharlK/Pep-22
89Hagers/Best-28
89Hagers/Pro-279
89Hagers/Star-13
Nicholson, Carl
78Watlo
79Tacom-18
Nicholson, David L.
(Dave)
61T-182
62T-577
63T-234
64T-31
64T/Coins-32
64T/St-26
64T/tatt
65OPC-183
65T-183
66T-576
67OPC-113
67T-113
69T-298
78TCMA-99
Nicholson, J.W.
N172
Nicholson, Keith
87Lakel-2
88Fay/Pro-1079
Nicholson, Larry
80Buffa-14
Nicholson, Rick
77Newar
78Holyo
Nicholson, Thomas
N172
Nicholson, William B.
(Bill)
49B-76
49Eureka-142
49Lummis
50B-228
51B-113
52T-185
53B/BW-14
R346-11
Nichting, Chris
88FSLAS/Star-15
88VeroB/Star-18
89SnAnt/Best-22
Nickerson, Drew
74Gasto
77Cedar
Nickerson, Jim
77Spart
Nicol, Hugh N.
(Hugh)
E223
N172
N172/BC
N284
N370
Scrapps
Nicolosi, Chris
59DF
60DF-1
Nicolosi, Sal
85Visal-5
86Visal-13
Nicometi, Tony
86Jaxvl/TCMA-1
Nicosia, Steven R.
(Steve)
75Shrev
75Shreve/TCMA-15
78Colum
80T-519
81D-373
81F-371
81OPC-212
81T-212
82D-45
82F-488
82T-652
83D-528
83F-314
83T-462
84Nes/792-98
84T-98
85F-618
85T-191
85T/Tr-87T
89Erie/Star-15
Nied, Dave
88Sumter/Pro-413
89Durhm/Star-16
Niedenfuer, Tom
82Albuq-7
82F-16
82Pol/Dodg
82Pol/Dodg-49
83D-536
83F-214
83Pol/Dodg-49
83T-477
84D-128
84F-108
84Nes/792-112
84Pol/Dodg-49
84Smok/Dodg-2
84T-112
85D-153
85F-378
85OPC-281
85T-782
85T/St-80
86D-397
86F-139
86Leaf-186
86Pol/Dodg-49
86T-56
87D-218
87F-448
87Leaf-204
87Moth/Dodg-14
87OPC-43
87Pol/Dodg-26
87T-538
87T/Tr-88T
88D-294
88D/Best-321
88F-568
88French-49
88OPC-242
88Score-261
88T-242
88T/St-232
89B-204
89D-282
89D/Tr-54
89F-613
89Moth/Sea-12
89OPC-14
89Panini/St-254
89Score-252
89T-651
89T/St-236
89UD-488
90T-306
Niehoff, John Albert
(Bert)
14CJ-125
15CJ-125
D328-128
D329-132
D350/2-130
E135-128
M101/4-132
M101/5-130
Niekro, Joe
67T-536R
68T-475
69OPC-43
69T-43
70OPC-508
70T-508
71MLB/St-400
71OPC-695
71T-695
72MB-251
72OPC-216
72T-216
73OPC-585
73T-585
74OPC-504
74T-504
75Iowa/TCMA-12
75OPC-595
75T-595
75T/M-595
76OPC-273
76SSPC-50
76T-273
77BK/A-5
77T-116
78T-306
80BK/PHR-6
80OPC-226
80T-436
81Coke
81D-380
81F-54
81OPC-102
81T-722
81T/St-174
81T/St-26
82D-167
82F-221
82F/St-45
82OPC-74
82T-611
83D-10DK
83D-470
83D-613
83D/AAS-51
83F-457
83OPC-221
83T-221
83T-441
83T/St-240
84D-110
84F-234
84FunFood/Pin-128
84Moth/Ast-2
84Nes/792-586
84OPC-384
84T-586
84T/St-69
85D-182
85F-355
85F/St-88
85Leaf-189
85Moth/Ast-6
85OPC-295
85T-295
85T/St-69
86D-601
86D-645M
86Leaf-243M
86Moth/Ast-17
86OPC-135
86T-135
87Class/Up-120M
87D-217
87F-106
87F/U-U87
87T-344
87T/Tr-89T
88F-18
88OPC-233
88Score-237
88T-473
88T-5RB
Niekro, Phil
64T-541R
65T-461R
66OPC-28
66T-28
67T-456
68Coke
68OPC-7LL
68T-257
68T-7
69MB-201
69MLB/St-116
69T-355
70MB-20
70MLB/St-10
70OPC-160
70OPC-69LL
70T-160
70T-69
70T/PI-2
70T/S-15
71MLB/St-19
71OPC-30
71T-30
71T/Coins-37
72MB-252
72T-620
73K-29
73OPC-503
73T-503
74OPC-29
74T-29
74T/St-9
75Ho-99
75OPC-130
75OPC-310LL
75T-130
75T-310LL
75T/M-130
75T/M-310LL
76Ho-3
76Ho/Twink-3
76OPC-435
76SSPC-5
76T-435
77Ho-111
77OPC-43
77T-615
78Ho-122
78OPC-155
78OPC-6LL
78T-10
79Ho-62
79K-28
79OPC-313
79T-595

79T/Comics-19
80K-51
80OPC-130
80T-245
81D-328
81F-242
81F/St-23
81K-12
81OPC-201
81Pol/Atl-35
81T-387
81T/St-148
82BK/Lids-19
82D-10DK
82D-475
82F-444
82F/St-68
82K-36
82OPC-185
82Pol/Atl-35
82T-185
82T/St-20
83D-613
83D-97
83D/AAS-12
83F-143
83OPC-316SV
83OPC-94
83Pol/Atl-35
83T-410
83T-411A
83T-502
83T/St-218
84D-188
84D/Champs-34
84F-187
84F/X-83
84FunFood/Pin-115
84Nes/792-650
84OPC-29
84T-650
84T/St-31
84T/X-84
85D-458
85D/AAS-49
85D/HL-50
85F-138
85F/St-93
85Leaf-138
85OPC-40
85Seven-11S
85T-40
85T/Gloss40-32
85T/St-309
86D-580
86D-645M
86F-112
86F-630M
86F/LL-28
86F/St-82
86F/Up-U81
86Leaf-243M
86OhHenry-35
86OPC-246
86Quaker-28
86S-130M
86S-163
86S-182M
86S-53M
86T-204
86T-790
86T/St-7
86T/Tr-77T
87D-465
87F-254
87F-626M
87F/RecSet-25
87Gator-35
87Leaf-181
87OPC-6
87S-147
87T-694
88Class/Red-198
88Class/Red-199
88Class/Red-200
88Score-555
88T-5RB
89Pac/Leg-212
89Swell-22

Niell, Scott
89Watertn/Star-16

Nielsen, Dan
88Watertn/Puc-9

Nielsen, Gerald
88Oneon/Pro-2062
89PrWill/Star-14

Nielsen, Scott
84Nashvl-15
85Albany-9
87D-597
87Hawai-15
87T-57
88AAA/Pro-11
88Colum/CMC-3
88Colum/Pol-6
88Colum/Pro-310
89Colum/CMC-2
89Colum/Pol-15
89Colum/Pro-754
89F-261

Nielsen, Steve
78Ashev
79Tulsa-9
80Tulsa-19
81Tulsa-9
82BurlR-26C
83Tulsa-18
85BurlR-11

Nieman, Robert C.
(Bob)
53Glen
55B-145
56T-267
57T-14
58Hires-26
58T-165
59T-375
60T-149
61T-178
62Sugar-10
62T-182
79TCMA-211

Niemann, Art
82AppFx-23

Niemann, Randy
80T-469
81F-77
81T-148
82D-473
82Portl-6
83T-329
85Tidew-7
86F/Up-U82
86T/Tr-78T
87F-18
87Portl-3
87T-147
88Tidew/CANDL-24
88Tidew/CMC-10

Niemann, Tom
83Butte-14
85FtMyr-6

Nieporte, Jay
85Spoka/Cram-16

Niethammer, Darren
88CharlR/Star-17

Nieto, Andy
87DayBe-23

Nieto, Thomas Andrew
(Tom)
81Louvl-9
82ArkTr-12
84Louvl-8
85D-596
85F-235
85OPC-294
85T-294
86D-327
86F-43
86Indianap-30
86KAS/Disc-12
86T-88
87D/OD-220
87F/U-U88
87OPC-124
87T-416
87T/Tr-90T
88D-612
88T-317

Nieva, Wilfredo
88James/Pro-1895

Nieves, Adelberto
81Batav-10
81Watlo-30

Nieves, Juan
86D-40
86D/Rook-12
86F/Up-U83
86Pol/Brew-20
86S/Rook-5
86T/Tr-79T
87Class/Up-136
87D-90
87D/HL-1
87F-352
87OPC-79
87T-79
87T/GlossRk-11
88D-126
88F-170
88OPC-104
88Panini/St-117
88Panini/St-431
88Pol/Brew-20
88RedFoley/St-60
88Score-513
88Score-655HL
88Score/YS/II-33
88Sf-180
88Sf-211
88T-515
88T/Big-190
89B-131
89Bimbo/Discs-10
89D-575
89Gard-10
89Pol/Brew-20
89Score-410
89T-287
89UD-646
90T-467
90UD-648

Nieves, Melvin
89Pulas/Pro-1893

Nieves, Raul
76Dubuq

Niggling, John
W753

Niles, Harry Clyde
(Harry)
E91
M116
T204
T206
T3-111

Nilsson, Dave
88Beloi/GS-19
89Stock/Best-1
89Stock/Cal-162
89Stock/Pro-374
89Stock/Star-21

Nipp, Mark
80Albuq-21

Nipper, Al
85D-614
85F-165
85T-424
86D-538
86F-356
86T-181
87D-297
87F-39
87OPC-64
87T-617
88Berg/Cubs-45
88D-523
88D/Best-250
88D/Cubs/Bk-NEW
88F-358
88Score-527
88T-326
88T/Tr-75T
89D-394
89F-433
89Score-532
89T-86
89UD-494

Nipper, Mike
85Durhm-28
86Durhm-20

Nipper, Ronald
87Greenvl/Best-6

Nischwitz, Ron
62T-591R
63T-152
66OPC-38
66T-38

Nishimura, Hioetsugu
88VeroB/Star-19

Nitschke, David
75Tucso-5

Nittoli, Mike
86SanJose-15

Nivens, Toby
87Orlan-12
88Orlan/Best-6
89Jacks/GS-6

Nix, Dave
81AppFx-21
82AppFx-15
83GlenF-8
86Madis-16
86Madis/Pol-15

Nix, John
75Cedar

Nixon, Donell
81Wausa-17
82Wausa-9
84Chatt-11
87Calgary-19
87D/OD-114
87Moth/Sea-19
88Calg/CMC-11
88F-382
88F/U-U129
88Score-436
88T-146
89B-477
89F-337
89Moth/Giants-25
89Score-481
89T-447
89T/Big-214
90D-571
90F-66
90Score-538
90T-658

Nixon, Otis
83Colum-25
85Polar/Ind-20
86F-591
86OhHenry-20
86T/Tr-80T
87F-255
87Gator-20
87T-486
88Indi/CMC-14
88Indi/Pro-518
89B-366
89F-387
89OPC-54
89Score-451
89T-674
89T/Big-234
89T/Mini-23
89UD-480
90D-456
90F-356
90Score-241
90T-252
90UD-379

Nixon, Russell E.
(Russ)
58T-133
59Kahn
59T-344
60Kahn
60MacGregor-17
60T-36
61P-52
61T-53
61T/St-115
62T-523
62T/St-16
63T-168
64T-329
65OPC-162
65T-162
66T-227
67T-446
68Coke
68T-515
69T-363
83T-756
84Nes/792-351MG
84Stuart-5CO
84T-351MG
86Pol/Atl-2C
88T/Tr-76MG
89T-564MG
90T-171MG

Nixon, Willard
51B-270
52T-269
53B/BW-2
53T-30
54B-114
55B-177
56T-122
57T-189
58Hires-47
58T-395
59T-361

Noble, Rafael Miguel
(Ray)
50Remar
51B-269
52BR

Noble, Ray
85Utica-20
86Tucso-17

Nobles, Jim
79LodiD-10

Noboa, Milicades A.
(Junior)
81Batav-15
82Watlo/B-18
82Watlo/C-28
83Watlo/LF-8
84BuffB-4
85Maine-20
86Maine-13
87BuffB-8
87Gator-17
88Edmon/Pro-564
88T-503
89AAA/Pro-8
89Indi/CMC-20
89Indi/Pro-1235

Nocas, Luke
87AppFx-25
89AppFx/Pro-877
Nocciolo, Mark
80SLCty-5
81Holyo-18
Noce, Paul
83Miami-17
84MidldC-21
85IowaC-5
86IowaC-20
87D/Rook-51
87IowaC-11
88D-315
88D/Cubs/Bk-315
88F-428
88IowaC/CMC-16
88IowaC/Pro-538
88RedFoley/St-61
88Score-329
88T-542
89Calg/CMC-16
89Calg/Pro-539
Noch, Douglas
88VeroB/Star-20
89VeroB/Star-19
Nodell, Ray
83Miami-12
Noelke, Michael
88LitFalls/Puc-7
89Clmbia/Best-9
89Clmbia/GS-18
Nokes, Matt
82Clint-4
84Shrev/FB-14
86Nashv-18
87Class/Up-129
87D/Rook-12
87F/U-U90
87S/Rook-16
87T/Tr-91T
88Class/Blue-207
88Class/Red-166
88D-152
88D/AS-16
88D/Best-237
88F-638M
88F-66
88F/AS-1
88F/BB/AS-29
88F/Excit-29
88F/Mini-23
88F/SS-26
88F/St-27
88Leaf-60
88MSA/Disc-5
88Nestle-41
88OPC-266
88Panini/St-88
88Pep/T-33
88Pol/T-9
88RedFoley/St-62
88Score-15
88Score-648
88Score/YS/I-5
88Sf-6
88Sf/Gamewin-18
88T-393
88T-645
88T/Big-185
88T/Gloss60-59
88T/JumboR-8
88T/St-269
88T/St-311
88T/St/Backs-56
88T/UK-54
88ToysRUs-22
89B-101
89Class-113
89D-116
89D/Best-181
89F-140
89Holsum/Discs-13
89Mara/Tigers-33
89Nissen-13
89OPC-116
89Panini/St-339
89Pol/Tigers-33
89RedFoley/St-86
89Score-23
89Sf-203
89T-445
89T/Big-303
89T/St-280
89UD-150
90Class-141
90D-178
90F-611
90Score-55
90T-131
90UD-226
Nolan, Bob
75Phoen-4
77SLCty
Nolan, Gary
68OPC-196
68T-196
69MLB/St-133
69T-581
70K-53
70MLB/St-33
70OPC-484
70T-484
71K-36
71MLB/St-66
71OPC-75
71T-75
71T/tatt-4
72MB-253
72OPC-475
72T-475
73K-30
73OPC-260
73T-260
73T/Lids-36
74OPC-277
74T-277
75OPC-562
75T-562
75T/M-562
76Icee
76OPC-444
76SSPC-29
77Ho-113
77OPC-70
77Pep-51
Nolan, Joseph W. Jr.
(Joe)
78T-617
79T-464
80T-64
81D-302
81F-212
81OPC-149
81T-149
81T/HT
82D-62
82F-77
82T-327
82T/Tr-81T
83D-79
83F-68
83T-242
84D-489
84F-15
84Nes/792-553
84T-553
85D-594
85F-185
85T-652
86T-781
Noland, James
89Watlo/Pro-1778
89Watlo/Star-22
Nold, Dick
68OPC-96R
68T-96R
Noles, Dickie
79OkCty
80T-682R
81D-568
81F-12
81OkCty/TCMA-14
81T-406
82F-253
82RedLob
82T-530
82T/Tr-82T
83D-426
83F-504
83OPC-99
83T-99
83Thorn-48
84D-266
84F-500
84Nes/792-618
84Rang-36
84T-618
85OPC-149
85Rang-36
85T-149
86D-587
86F-567
86OhHenry-48
86T-388
87Berg/Cubs-47
87F-256
87F/U-U91
87T-244
87T/Tr-92T
88RochR-16
88RochR-19
88RochR/CMC-8
88RochR/Gov-19
88RochR/Pro-219
88T-768
89Colum/CMC-3
89Colum/Pol-16
89Colum/Pro-749
Nolte, Eric
85Spoka/Cram-17
86CharRa-19
87Wichi-12
88D-534
88F-593
88Score-568
88Smok/Padres-20
88T-694
89LasVeg/CMC-8
89LasVeg/Pro-12
Nonnenkamp, Leo W.
(Red)
40PB-196
Noonan, Jim
78Wausa
Noore, Daryl
89Bluef/Star-27
Norbert, Ted
45Centen-18
Nordbrook, Timothy C.
(Tim)
76OPC-252
76SSPC-391
76T-252
78OPC-139
78T-369
79Vanco-6
80Vanco-10
83Beloi/LF-16
Nordhagen, Wayne O.
76OkCty
78T-231
79K-4
79T-351
80OPC-253
80T-487
81Coke
81D-401
81F-348
81T-186
81T/HT
81T/St-59
82D-67
82F-355
82OPC-139
82T-597
83F-438
83OPC-47
83T-714
Nordstrom, Carl
88Bill/Pro-1831
88Cedar/Pro-1158
89Greens/Pro-429
Nored, Mike
76AppFx
Noren, Irving Arnold
(Irv)
50B-247
51B-241
51FB
51T/BB-38
52B-63
52T-40
53B/BW-45
53T-35
54NYJour
55B-63
55RM-AL9
56T-253
57T-298
58T-114
59T-59
60L-101
60T-433
73OPC-179CO
73T-179C
PM10/L-31
Norko, Tom
80Utica-7
Norman, Bull
83Tampa-30
Norman, Daniel E.
(Dan)
77Indianap-10
78Tidew
79T-721R
79Tidew-11
80T-681R
81F-337
81Tidew-28
82Hygrade
83F-289
83OPC-237
83T-237
84MidldC-17
89Kingspt/Star-27
Norman, Fred
64T-469R
65T-386R
70OPC-427
70T-427
71MLB/St-280
71OPC-348
71T-348
72OPC-194
72T-194
73OPC-32
73T-32
74OPC-581
74T-581
75OPC-396
75T-396
75T/M-396
76OPC-609
76SSPC-30
76T-609
77K-8
77OPC-181
77Pep-56
77T-139
78T-273
79OPC-20
79T-47
80OPC-362
80T-714
81D-92
81F-158
81OPC-183
81T-497
Norman, Greg
83BirmB-13
Norman, H. Willis
53T-245
Norman, Nelson A.
78Cr/PCL-95
80Charl-4
80OPC-270
80T-518
81D-509
82Portl-16
83LynnP-15
84Cram/PCL-133
85RochR-7
86Jaxvl/TCMA-22
87Indianap-29
88Indi/Pro-517
Norman, Scott
83Clint/LF-3
87Sprin/Best-28
Norman, Terry
80Batav-2
Normand, Guy
85Anchora-21
86AubAs-17
87Ashvl-13
88Osceola/Star-18
89Osceola/Star-13
Norrid, Tim
76Wmspt
79T-705R
79Tacom-22
80Tacom-2
81Charl-9
82Charl-12
83Charl-14
Norris, Allen
59DF
60DF-23
Norris, James Frances
(Jim)
75OkCty
78T-484
79T-611
80T-333
81D-388
81F-634
81T-264
Norris, Mike
76OPC-653
76SSPC-487
76T-653
77T-284
78T-434
79T-191
80T-599
81D-118
81F-573
81F/St-6
81MSA/Disc-24
81OPC-55
81T-55
81T/SO-53
81T/St-122
81T/St-2M
81T/St-4
81T/St-6
82D-197
82D-19DK
82F-103
82F/St-125

82Granny-13
82K-59
82OPC-370
82T-370
82T/St-222
83D-139
83F-530
83Granny-17
83OPC-276
83T-620
84F-457
84Nes/792-493
84OPC-49
84T-493
85T-246
87Moth/A's-22

North, Jay
85Sprin-21
86StPet-22
87StPet-25
88StPet/Star-20
89Savan/Pro-343

North, Mark
88Peoria/Ko-22
89Keno/Pro-1061
89Keno/Star-18

North, Roy
80Ander-18
81Durhm-21

North, William Alex
(Billy)
73OPC-234
73T-234
74OPC-345
74T-345
74T/St-228
75K-23
75OPC-121
75OPC-309LL
75T-121
75T-309LL
75T/M-121
75T/M-309LL
76OPC-33
76SSPC-491
76T-33
77Ho-33
77K-22
77OPC-106
77OPC-4LL
77T-4LL
77T-551
78Ho-76
78T-163
79OPC-351
79Pol/Giants-36
79T-668
80BK/PHR-31
80OPC-213
80Pol/Giants-36
80T-408
81D-76
81F-441
81OPC-47
81T-713

Northern, Hubbard
T207

Northey, Ronald J.
(Ron)
49B-79
50B-81
51B-70
52T-204
57T-31
Exh47

Northey, Scott R.
(Scott)
70OPC-241R
70T-241R
71OPC-633R
71T-633R

Northrup, George
E270/1

Northrup, James T.
(Jim)
65OPC-259R
65T-259R
66T-554
67T-408
68OPC-78
68T-78
69MB-202
69MLB/St-53
69OPC-167
69OPC-3LL
69T-3LL
69T-580
69T/St-178
70MLB/St-213
70OPC-177
70T-177
71K-63
71MLB/St-401
71OPC-265
71T-265
71T/Coins-82
71T/GM-21
71T/S-55
72MB-254
72OPC-408
72T-408
73OPC-168
73T-168
74OPC-266
74T-266
75OPC-641
75T-641
75T/M-641
76SSPC-399
88Domino-17

Norton, Doug
83Beloi/LF-11
86Stockton-19

Norwood, Aaron
89Bluef/Star-19

Norwood, Steve
78Newar
79BurlB-24
80BurlB-15
81BurlB-4

Norwood, Willie
78T-705R
79T-274
80T-432
80Toled-10
81D-516

Nosek, Randy
88Lakel/Star-18
89London/Pro-1377
90Score-607
90UD-2

Nossek, Joseph R.
(Joe)
64T-532R
65T-597R
66OPC-22
66T-22
67T-209
69OPC-143
69T-143
73OPC-646CO
73T-646C
74T-99C

Nottebart, Don
60T-351
61T-29
62T-541
63T-204
64T-434
64T/Coins-119
65T-469
66OPC-21
66T-21
67T-269
68OPC-171
68T-171
69T-593
78TCMA-72

Nottle, Ed
74Gasto
77Tucso
80WHave-20
81Tacom-6
82Tacom-19
84Cram/PCL-90
86Pawtu-16MG
87Pawtu-22
87Pawtu/TCMA-21
88AAA/Pro-52
88Pawtu/CMC-24
88Pawtu/Pro-469
89Pawtu/CMC-25
89Pawtu/Dunk-17
89Pawtu/Pro-678

Novak, Tom
87Tampa-11

Novick, Walter
52Park-77

Novikoff, Lou
43MP-18
47Centen-16
47Signal
88MinorLg/Leg-4

Novoa, Rafael
88CapeCod/Sum-36

Novotney, Rube
49Eureka-65

Nowak, Matt
88Hagers/Star-14

Nowlan, Bill
81BurlB-28
82Beloi-25
83Beloi/LF-13

Nowlin, James
87Sumter-25

Noworyta, Steve
83AppFx/LF-9

Nozling, Paul
88Brist/Pro-1890
89Fay/Pro-1591

Nugent, Barney
86Readg-20TR
87Maine-10
88Maine/CMC-3
88Maine/Pro-299
89ScrWB/CMC-2
89ScrWB/Pro-712

Nulsmer, Jack
81Chatt-7
82Charl-8

Nunamaker, Leslie G.
(Les)
14CJ-132
15CJ-132
D350/2-131
E120
E121/120
M101/5-131
T207
W501-115
W514-7
W573

Nunez, Bernardino
88Myrtle/Pro-1169
89Duned/Star-12

Nunez, Dario
86PalmSp-24
86PalmSp/Smok-25
87PalmSp-22
88PalmSp/Pro-1448

Nunez, Edwin
80Wausa-6
81Wausa-4
83SLCty-1
84Cram/PCL-183
84D-435
85D-484
85F-496
85Moth/Mar-24
85T-34
86D-145
86F-470
86Leaf-66
86Moth/Mar-24
86OPC-364
86T-511
86T/St-223
87D-243
87F/U-U92
87Moth/Sea-11
87T-427
88D-445
88D/Rook-36
88F-383
88Moth/Sea-11
88OPC-258
88Panini/St-182
88T-258
88T/St-216
89Toled/Pro-773
90D-563
90T-586

Nunez, Jose
85FtMyr-13
87F/U-U93
87Tor/Fire-26
87Tor/Fire-26
88D-611
88F-122
88OPC-28
88Score-312
88Syrac/Pro-820
88T-28
89Syrac/CMC-2
89Syrac/Pro-806
89Tor/Fire-45
90D-467

Nunez, Mauricio
86StPet-23
87StPet-6
88ArkTr/GS-10
89Savan/Pro-357

Nunley, Angelo
85Sprin-22
86Tampa-14
87Vermont-13
88Chatt/Best-25

Nunn, Howard
59T-549
61T-346
62T-524

Nunn, Wally
77Spart

Nuxhall, Joe
52T-406
53B/Col-90
53T-105
54B-76
55B-194
55Kahn
56Kahn
56T-218
57Kahn
57T-103
58Kahn
58T-63
59Kahn
59T-389
60Kahn
60T-282
61T-444
63FrBauer-14
63Kahn
63T-194
64Kahn
64T-106
65Kahn
65T-312
66T-485
67OPC-44
67T-44
78TCMA-65
89Pac/Leg-161
89Swell-53
Rawl

Nyce, Frederick
N172

Nye, Rich
67T-608R
68T-339
69MB-203
69OPC-88
69T-88
70OPC-139
70T-139
71LaPizza-7
72MB-255
78TCMA-281

Nyman, Christopher C.
(Chris)
78Knoxv
82Edmon-5
84Nes/792-382
84T-382
86BuffB-20
86Nashv-19

Nyman, Gerald
69OPC-173R
69T-173R
70T-644
71MLB/St-233
71OPC-656
71T-656
89Salin/Cal-147CO
89Salin/Pro-1820

Nyman, Nyls W.
(Nyls)
75OPC-619R
75T-619R
75T/M-619R
76OPC-258
76SSPC-149
76T-258

Nyquist, Mike
89SLCty-5

Nyssen, Dan
87AubAs-13
88Osceola/Star-19
89Osceola/Star-14

O'Berry, Preston M.
(Mike)
80T-662R
82Coke/Reds
82D-538
82F-78
82T-562
84Colum-20
84Colum/Pol-16
84Nes/792-184
84T-184
84T/X-86
85Colum-12

O'Bradovich, James T.
(Jim)
78Charl

O'Brien, Charlie
83Albany-10
86Vanco-19
87Denver-24
88Denver/CMC-15
88Denver/Pro-1268
88Pol/Brew-11
88T-566
89F-194
89Pol/Brew-22
89Score-606
89T-214
90D-410
90F-332

90T-106
90UD-650
O'Brien, Dan
77StPet
80Richm-10
80T-684R
81Richm-18
O'Brien, Edward J.
(Eddie)
53T-249
54T-139M
56T-116
57T-259
O'Brien, John Joseph
(Jack)
T3/Box-75
O'Brien, John K.
(Jack)
N172
WG1-69
O'Brien, John Thomas
(Johnny)
53T-223
54T-139M
55T-135
56T-65
56T/Pin-44
58T-426
59T-499
60HenryH-4
O'Brien, Peter James
(Pete)
T206
O'Brien, Peter M.
(Pete)
80Ashev-13
81Tulsa-16
83Rang-9
83T/X-81
84D-281
84F-423
84Nes/792-534
84OPC-71
84Rang-9
84T-534
84T/St-357
85D-178
85F-563
85Leaf-201
85OPC-196
85Rang-9
85T-196
85T/St-344
86D-99
86F-568
86F/Mini-112
86OPC-328
86Rang-9
86T-328
86T/St-236
87Class/Up-138
87D-259
87D/OD-174
87F-132
87F/GameWin-31
87F/Mini-76
87Ho/St-30
87Leaf-186
87Moth/Rang-9
87OPC-17
87S-52
87Smok/R-12
87T-17
87T/Mini-72
87T/St-239
88D-284
88D/Best-167
88F-475
88F/St-67
88Leaf-132
88Moth/R-9
88OPC-381
88Panini/St-200
88RedFoley/St-63
88Score-29
88Sf-145
88Smok/R-2
88T-721
88T/Big-227
88T/St-240
89B-84
89Class/Up/2-184
89D-107
89D/Best-5
89D/Tr-16
89F-529
89F/Up-29
89OPC-314
89Panini/St-452
89RedFoley/St-87
89Score-22
89Score/Tr-6
89Sf-8
89T-629
89T/Big-115
89T/St-248
89T/Tr-88T
89T/UK-57
89UD-54
89UD/Ext-800
90D-202
90D-24DK
90F-498
90Score-175
90Sf-92
90T-265
90UD-110
O'Brien, Robert
72OPC-198R
72T-198R
O'Brien, Sydney L.
(Sid)
59T-628R
70OPC-163
70T-163
71MLB/St-353
71OPC-561
71T-561
72OPC-289
72T-289
72T/Cloth-25
O'Brien, Thomas
T207
O'Brien, William D.
N172
O'Brien, William S.
(Billy)
R314/Can
O'Brien, William S.
N172
N284
O'Connell, Daniel F.
(Danny)
51B-93
53T-107
54B-160
54Dix
54JC-4
55B-44
55Gol/Braves-23
55JC-4
56T-272
57T-271
58Hires-19
58SFCall
58T-166
59T-87
60T-192
61T-318
62Salada-221
62Shirriff-221
62T-411
62T/St-99
PM10/Sm-137
O'Connell, James J.
W515-13
O'Connell, Jimmy
WG7-37
O'Connell, Mark
81Clint-11
O'Connell, P.J.
N172
O'Conner, Tim
86Kenosha-18
87Visal-17
O'Conner, Tom
88Orlan/Best-2
O'Connor, Bill
84Shrev/FB-15
85Visal-4
86Visal-14
O'Connor, Bob
82Clint-25
O'Connor, Jack
82D-539
82F-557
82T-353
82Toled-5
83D-51
83F-621
83T-33
83Toled-29
84Nes/792-268
84T-268
84Toled-15
85Indianap-22
86Calgary-20
87RochR-20
87RochR/TCMA-7
88Score-434
88Syrac/CMC-10
88Syrac/Pro-805
89Syrac/CMC-3
89Syrac/Pro-812
O'Connor, John J.
(Jack)
E107
M116
N172
O'Connor, Patrick F.
(Paddy)
D322
E90/1
M116
O'Day, Henry Francis
(Hank)
N172
O'Dea, James Kenneth
(Ken)
40PB-214
WG8-43
O'Dell, Bill
55T-57
55T/DH-8
57T-316
58T-84
59T-250
60T-303
61P-155
61T-383
61T-96
61T/St-83
62T-429
63Exh
63F-66
63J-111
63P-111
63T-235
63T-7
63T-9
64T-18
64T/Coins-115
65T-476
66T-237
67OPC-162
67T-162
67T/Test/PP-17
Exh47
O'Dell, James Wesley
86ColumAst-20
87BirmB/Best-4
88CharlK-7
88CharlK/Pep-7
O'Donnell, George
60DF-15
O'Donnell, Glen
86Elmir-14
O'Donnell, Stephen P.
88CapeCod-18
88CapeCod/Sum-41
89GreatF-25
O'Donoghue, John
64T-388R
65OPC-71
65T-71
66T-501
66T/RO-105
67OPC-127
67T-127
68T-456
70McDon-1
70OPC-441
70T-441
71LaPizza-8
71MLB/St-136
71OPC-743
71T-743
72MB-257
O'Dougherty, Pat
44Yank/St-21
O'Doul, Francis J.
(Lefty)
29Exh/4-11
31Exh/4-3
32Orbit/num-31A
32Orbit/num-31B
32Orbit/un-48
33DH-33
33DL-10
33Exh/4-2
33G-232
33G-58
48Sommer-1
49Sommer-1
53Mother-9
60F-37
61F-130
72F/FFeat-34
80Cram/Leg-29
80Laugh/FFeat-31
88Conlon/5-23
R300
R305
R315-A26
R315-B26
R316
R328-24
R423-75
V353-58
O'Dowd,Tom
80Utica-22
O'Farrell, Robert A.
(Bob)
26Exh-62
27Exh-31
31Exh/4-10
33Exh/4-5
33G-34
35G-2F
35G-4F
35G-7F
61F-131
E120
E210-12
E220
R306
R310
R315-A27
R315-B27
V100
V353-34
V355-115
V61-76
W502-12
W572
W573
O'Halloran, Greg
89StCath/Pro-2079
O'Hara, Duane
88CapeCod/Sum-73
O'Hara, Pat
82Madis-27
O'Hara, William A.
C46-1
E101
E106
E92
M116
T204
T206
T216
O'Hearn, Bob
85BurlR-16
86Salem-22
O'Keeffe, Richard
76BurlB
80Water-11
81Water-6
82Syrac-27
O'Leary, Bill
84Butte-20
O'Leary, Charles T.
(Charley)
12Sweet/Pin-29
E104
E90/1
M116
T202
T202
T204
T205
T206
T215/blue
T215/brown
W575
O'Leary, Troy
89Beloi/Star-19
89Helena/SP-11
89Star/Wax-6
O'Malley, Mike
81VeroB-12
O'Malley, Thomas P.
(Tom)
81Shrev-4
82Phoen
83D-96
83F-271
83Moth/Giants-10
83T-663
84Cram/PCL-11
84D-601
84F-384
84Nes/792-469
84T-469
84T/St-170
86RochR-14
87F-477
87OKCty-20
87T-154
88AAA/Pro-28
88OkCty/CMC-19
88OkCty/Pro-48
88Score-534
88Smok/R-1
88T-77
89AAA/Pro-13
89Tidew/CMC-15
89Tidew/Pro-1965
90T-504

O'Malley, Walter
89Rini/Dodg-22
O'Mara, Oliver E.
(Ollie)
D329-134
D350/2-133
M101/4-134
M101/5-133
O'Neal, Kelley
89Brist/Star-19
O'Neal, Randy
82BirmB-8
83Evans-7
84Evans-17
85F-645
86Cain's-13
86D-394
86F-233
86T-73
87D-584
87F-159
87Smok/Atl-3
87T-196
88Louvl-37
88Louvl/CMC-4
88Louvl/Pro-430
89ScrWB/Pro-726
O'Neil, George M.
(Mickey)
21Exh-121
25Exh-8
26Exh-14
E120
V100
W573
WG3-34
O'Neil, Johnny
47Centen-17
O'Neil, Randy
89ScrWB/CMC-10
O'Neil, William John
T206
O'Neill, Dan
87Fayette-3
88Lakel/Star-19
89Lakel/Star-16
O'Neill, J.F.
21Exh-123
O'Neill, James E.
(Tip)
E223
N172/BC
N184
N284
N370
Scrapps
O'Neill, John J.
(John)
47Signal
O'Neill, Paul
80Indianap-12
82Cedar-21
83Tampa-19
86D-37
86F-646M
87F/U-U94
87Kahn-21
87S/Rook-17
88D-433
88F/U-U85
88Kahn/Reds-21
88RedFoley/St-64
88Score-304
88T-204
89B-313
89D-360
89D/Best-230
89F-166
89K/Reds-21
89OPC-187
89Panini/St-77
89Score-206
89Score/YS/II-5
89T-604
89T/Big-39
89UD-428
90Class-117
90D-198
90F-427
90Score-295
90Score/100St-17
90Sf-4
90T-332
90UD-161
O'Neill, Steve F.
15CJ-48
21Exh-122
35BU-160
51B-202
54T-127
88Conlon/3-21
D327
D328-129
D329-135
D350/2-134
E120
E121/120
E135-129
E220
M101/4-135
M101/5-134
R311/Leath
R312
R313
V100
V355-67
V61-22
W501-116
W514-26
W572
W573
W575
WG7-39
O'Neill, Ted
76Wausa
O'Quinn, Steven
87CharWh-21
O'Rear, John
78Cr/PCL-90
79Albuq-12
80Albuq-7
O'Regan, Dan
82Oneon-5
O'Reilly, Jim
89CharWh/Best-26
89CharWh/Pro-1746
O'Riley, Don
70T-552R
71OPC-679
71T-679
O'Rourke, Francis J.
(Frank)
25Exh-93
26Exh-94
29Exh/4-30
31Exh/4-29
33G-87
E254
V354-43
O'Rourke, James
50Callahan
73F/Wild-24
80SSPC/HOF
E223
N172
N284
N403
N690
WG1-42
O'Rourke, Thomas J.
(Tom)
N172
O'Toole, Dennis
73OPC-604R
73T-604R
O'Toole, Jack
85Anchora-24
87Anchora-23CO
O'Toole, Jim
59T-136
60Kahn
60T-32
60T-325
61Kahn
61P-189
61T-328
61T/St-21
62J-126
62Kahn
62P-126
62P/Can-126
62T-450
62T-56
62T-58
62T-60
62T/bucks
62T/St-118
63FrBauer-16
63J-136
63Kahn
63P-136
63T-70
64T-185
64T/Coins-85
64T/St-55
64T/SU
64Wheat/St-32
65Bz-6
65Kahn
65OPC-60
65T-60
65T/trans-22
66T-389
67T-467
78TCMA-92
89Pac/Leg-147
WG10-40
WG9-39
O'Toole, Martin J.
11Helmar-164
14CJ-54
15CJ-54
D304
E300
L1-112
S81-87
T207
WG5-33
WG6-31
Oakes, Ennis T.
(Rebel)
10Domino-93
11Helmar-174
12Sweet/Pin-151B
12Sweet/Pin-151A
14CJ-139
14Piedmont/St-45
15CJ-139
D303
E106
E254
E90/1
M116
S74-122
T202
T205
T206
T207
T213/blue
T213/brown
T215/blue
T216
Oakes, Todd
87Clint-18
88SanJose/Cal-143
88SanJose/Pro-122
89SanJose/Best-29
89SanJose/Cal-236
89SanJose/Pro-455
Oates, Johnny Lane
(Johnny)
72OPC-474R
72T-474R
73OPC-9
73T-9
74OPC-183
74T-183
74T/St-10
75OPC-319
75T-319
75T/M-319
76OPC-62
76SSPC-468
76T-62
77T-619
78T-508
79T-104
80Pol/Dodg-5
80T-228
81F-99
81T-303
82D-404
82F-47
82Nashv-28MG
83Colum-1
88RochR-17
88RochR-30
88RochR/CMC-24
88RochR/Gov-30
88RochR/Pro-211
89French-46
Obal, Dave
76Baton
Obando, Sherman
89Oneon/Pro-2102
Oberdank, Jeff
89QuadC/Best-5
89QuadC/GS-20
Oberkfell, Kenneth R.
(Ken)
76ArkTr
80T-701R
81Coke
81D-583
81F-532
81OPC-32
81T-32
81T/St-222
82F-123
82F/St-21
82OPC-121
82T-474
82T/St-89
83D-246
83F-17
83OPC-206
83T-206
83T/St-287
84D-504
84F-330
84F/X-84
84Nes/792-102
84OPC-102
84T-102
84T/St-148
84T/St/Box-2
84T/X-85
85D-432
85F-336
85Ho/Braves-17
85Leaf-141
85OPC-307
85Pol/Atl-24
85T-569
85T/St-32
86D-531
86F-523
86OPC-334
86Pol/Atl-24
86T-334
86T/St-38
87D-437
87D/OD-46
87F-523
87Leaf-171
87OPC-1
87RedFoley/St-99
87Smok/Atl-16
87T-627
87T/St-38
88D-67
88D/Best-226
88F-545
88OPC-67
88Panini/St-244
88Score-245
88Sf-165
88T-67
88T/St-37
89B-418
89D-506
89OPC-97
89Score-139
89T-751
89UD-313
90D-494
90F-67
90Score-422
90T-488
90UD-360
Oberlander, Hartman
N172
Oberlin, Frank
T206
Obregon, Francisco
60HenryH-3
60Union-4
Ocasio, Javier
89Saraso/Star-16
Oceak, Frank
60T-467C
Ochs, Kevin
84Butte-19
Oddo, Ron
80Elmir-23
Odekirk, Rick
88OkCty/CMC-10
88OkCty/Pro-29
Odierno, Scott
88CapeCod/Sum-60
Odle, Page
86PrWill-18
Odom, Joe
84Madis/Pol-6
Odom, John
(Blue Moon)
65T-526R
67T-282
68T-501
69MB-204
69MLB/St-90
69OPC-195
69T-195
69T/St-220
69Trans-8
70K-38
70MLB/St-263
70OPC-55
70T-55
70Trans-15
71MLB/St-523
71OPC-523
71T-523
72MB-256
72T-557
72T-558
73OPC-207WS
73OPC-315
73T-315
74OPC-461

74T-461
75OPC-69
75T-69
75T/M-69
76OPC-651
76T-651
77SnJos-3
78TCMA-68
87Moth/A's-3

Odom, Tim
87FtMyr-10
88AppFx/Pro-150
89Aug/Pro-493

Odor, Rouglas
88BurlR/Pro-1780
89Kinston/Star-15
89Watertn/Star-17

Odwell, Frederick W.
(Fred)
E254
T201

Oedewaldt, Larry
89Stock/Best-15
89Stock/Cal-167
89Stock/Pro-375
89Stock/Star-2

Oelkers, Bryan
83Toled-28
84D-486
86Maine-14
87BuffB-18
87D-596
87F-257
87T-77
89Louvl-29
89Louvl/Pro-1244

Oertli, Chuck
86Geneva-20

Oeschger, Joe
21Exh-119
61T-403M
72F/FFeat-19M
72Laugh/GF-37M
E120
E121/120
E220
V100
V61-98
W501-92
W572
W575
WG7-38

Oester, Ronald John
(Ron)
77Indianap-6
78Indianap-6
79Indianap-3
79T-717R
81Coke
81D-423
81F-218
81OPC-21
81T-21
81T/HT
82Coke/Reds
82D-500
82F-79
82F/St-20
82T-427
82T/St-34
82T/St-34
83D-526
83F-598
83OPC-269
83T-269
83T/St-230
84Borden-16
84D-62
84D/AAS-46
84F-475
84Nes/792-526
84Nes/792-756TL
84OPC-99
84T-526
84T/St-53
85D-81
85F-542
85Indianap-30
85OPC-314
85T-314
85T/St-54
86D-81
86F-183
86Leaf-78
86OPC-264
86T-627
86T/St-138
86TexGold-16
87D-206
87D/OD-195
87F-207
87Kahn-16
87OPC-172
87T-172
87T/St-141
88D-246
88F-242
88OPC-17
88Score-183
88T-17
88T/St-144
89B-310
89D-553
89K/Reds-16
89Score-615
89T-772
89T/Big-229
89UD-287
90D-317
90Score-59
90T-492
90UD-118

Offerman, Jose
88GreatF-22
89Bakers/Cal-194
89SnAnt/Best-27
90Class-45
90UD-46

Office, Rowland J.
75OPC-262
75T-262
75T/M-262
76OPC-256
76SSPC-20
76T-256
77T-524
78T-632
79OPC-62
79T-132
80T-39
81D-213
81F-147
81OPC-319
81T-319
82F-198
82OkCty-2
82OPC-165
82T-479
83Colum-27

Officer, Jim
76QuadC

Ogawa, Kuni
79Vanco-15
80Holyo-8

Ogden, Charles
88CLAS/Star-33
88Kinston/Star-18
89Canton/Best-27

Ogden, John M.
33G-176

Ogden, Todd
89Canton/Pro-1322
89Canton/Star-18

Ogden, Warren
(Curly)
28Exh-58
33G-174

Ogier, Moe
68T-589R

Ogiwara, Mitsuru
88Mia/Star-17

Oglesbee, Mike
85Anchora-22
86Cram/PCL-29
87Ashvl-22

Oglesby, Ron
88River/Cal-232
88River/Pro-1407
89CharRa/Pro-978

Ogliaruso, Mike
89Myrtle/Pro-1463

Oglivie, Benjamin A.
72T-761R
73OPC-388
73T-388
75OPC-344
75T-344
75T/M-344
76OPC-659
76SSPC-359
76T-659
77OPC-236
77T-122
78T-286
79T-519
80T-53
81D-446
81F-508
81F/St-14
81K-20
81OPC-340
81Sqt-3
81T-2LL
81T-415
81T/SO-7
81T/St-11M
81T/St-14m
81T/St-92
82D-484
82F-151
82F/St-138
82OPC-280
82Pol/Brew
82Pol/Brew-24
82T-280
82T/St-197
83D-384
83Drake-20
83F-43
83F-640
83Gard-14
83OPC-91
83Pol/Brew-24
83T-750
83T/St-82
84D-229
84D/Champs-6
84F-210
84FunFood/Pin-67
84Gard-15
84Nes/792-190
84OPC-190
84Pol/Brew-24
84T-190
84T/St-296
85D-333
85F-590
85Gard-15
85Leaf-123
85OPC-332
85Pol/Brew-24
85T-681
85T/St-292
86D-333
86F-497
86Leaf-199
86OPC-372
86Pol/Brew-24
86T-372
86T/St-200
86Woolwth-25
87D-419
87F-353
87F/RecSet-26
87F/St-85
87RedFoley/St-100
87T-586

Ogrodowski, Bruce
40Hughes-15
48Sommer-21

Ohlms, Mark
89PrWill/Star-15
89Star/Wax-92

Ohman, Ed
89Star/Wax-9

Ohnoutka, Brian
86Shrev-20
87Shrev-12
88Phoen/CMC-7
88Phoen/Pro-79

Ojea, Alex
87Sprin/Best-3
88Sprin/Best-17

Ojeda, Bob
81Pawtu-5
82Coke/BOS
82D-540
82F-301
82T-274
83D-260
83F-190
83T-654
84D-538
84F-406
84Nes/792-162
84Nes/792-786TL
84OPC-162
84T-162
85D-371
85F-166
85OPC-329
85T-477
86D-636
86F-357
86F/Up-U84
86OPC-11
86T-11
86T/Tr-81T
87Class-73
87D-364
87D/OD-127
87F-19
87F/GameWin-32
87F/Lim-30
87F/Mini-77
87F/St-86
87Leaf-94
87OPC-83
87S-36
87T-746
87T/Gloss60-36
87T/HL-24
87T/Mets/Fan-6
87T/Mini-25
87T/St-99
87Woolwth-24
88D-632
88D/Best-238
88D/Mets/Bk-632
88F-147
88Kahn/Mets-19
88Score-563
88T-558
88T/Big-234
89B-371
89D-218
89D/Best-209
89F-47
89Kahn/Mets-19
89OPC-333
89Score-116
89T-333
89UD-386
90D-117
90F-214
90Score-53
90T-207
90UD-204

Ojeda, Luis
82ArkTr-16
83ArkTr-16
86Miami-19
87Miami-26

Ojeda, Ray
86Beloi-17
87Beloi-22

Okerlund, Ron
85Anchora-39GM

Okubo, Dave
86SanJose-16

Olah, Bob
89Clmbia/Best-7
89Clmbia/GS-19

Olander, Jim
85Cram/PCL-36
86Readg-21
87Maine-1
87Maine/TCMA-18
88Maine/CMC-21
88Maine/Pro-277
89ScrWB/CMC-15
89ScrWB/Pro-723

Olden, Paul
82Spoka-6

Oldham, J.C.
V100

Oldis, Robert Carl
(Bob)
53Briggs
53T-262
54T-91
55T-169
60T-361
61T-149
62T-269
63T-404

Oldring, Reuben Henry
(Rube)
10Domino-94
11Helmar-58
12Sweet/Pin-49
14CJ-8
15CJ-8
BF2-38
D329-133
D350/2-132
E104
E286
E300
E91
M101/4-133
M101/5-132
M116
S74-34
T201
T202
T205
T206
T207
T208
T215/blue
T222

Oleksak, Mike
79Newar-8

Olerud, John
90Class-35
90D-711
90Score-589
90Score/100Ris-39

90UD-56
Olin, Steve
88MidwLAS/GS-30
88Watlo/Pro-688
89AAA/Pro-34
89ColSp/Pro-252
90D-438
90F-499
90Score-590
90Sf-178
90T-433
90UD-553
Oliva, Antonio Pedro
(Tony)
63T-228R
64T-116R
64T/S-44
65Bz-4
65MacGregor-7
65OPC-1LL
65T-1LL
65T-340
65T/trans-60
66Bz-41
66T-216LL
66T-220LL
66T-450
66T/RO-52
67Bz-41
67OPC-50
67OPC/PI-18
67T-239LL
67T-50
67T/PI-18
68Bz-9
68Coke
68OPC-165
68T-165
68T-371AS
68T-480
69MB-205
69MLB/St-69
69MLBPA/Pin-20
69NTF
69OPC-1LL
69T-1LL
69T-427AS
69T-600
69T/decal
69T/S-20
69T/St-196
69Trans-7
70K-63
70MLB/St-235
70OPC-510
70OPC-62LL
70T-510
70T-62LL
70T/CB
70T/S-26
70Trans-13
71Bz/Test-36
71K-12
71MD
71MLB/St-468
71OPC-290
71OPC-61LL
71T-290
71T-61LL
71T/Coins-128
71T/GM-11
71T/S-11
71T/tatt-16
72K-25
72MB-258
72OPC-400
72OPC-86LL
72T-400
72T-86LL
72T/Post-7
73K-4
73OPC-80
73T-80
74OPC-190
74T-190
74T/DE-62
74T/St-210
75Ho-20
75Ho/Twink-20
75OPC-325
75T-325
75T/M-325
76Ho-10
76Ho/Twink-10
76OPC-35
76SSPC-217
76T-35
78TCMA-71
82CJ-7
83MLBPA/Pin-13
85West/2-41
86S/Dec-51M
88Pac/Leg-59
89Swell-12
89T-665TBC
Oliva, Jose
89Butte/SP-12
Oliva, Steve
77QuadC
Olivares, Edward B.
(Ed)
62T-598R
Olivares, Jose
89Myrtle/Pro-1472
Olivares, Omar
87CharRa-13
88Charl/Pro-1210
88SALAS/GS-10
89AubAs/Pro-11
89Wich/Roc-26
89Wich/Roc/HL-4
89Wich/Roc/Up-4
Oliver, Albert
(Al)
69OPC-82R
69T-82R
70MLB/St-105
70OPC-166
70T-166
71MLB/St-210
71OPC-388
71T-388
72T-575
73OPC-225
73T-225
74OPC-52
74T-52
74T/St-85
75Ho-81
75K-15
75OPC-555
75T-555
75T/M-555
76Crane-43
76Ho-112
76MSA/Disc
76OPC-620
76SSPC-576
76T-620
77Ho-45
77K-46
77OPC-203
77T-130
77T/CS-34
78BK/R-17
78OPC-97
78T-430
78Wiffle/Discs-55
79Ho-80
79OPC-204
79T-391
79T/Comics-16
80OPC-136
80T-260
81D-387
81Drake-24
81F-626
81F/St-64
81K-4
81OPC-70
81Sqt-22
81T-70
81T/HT
81T/SO-4
81T/St-131
81T/St-246
82D-116
82F-326
82F/St-178
82Hygrade
82K-61
82OPC-22IA
82OPC-326
82T-36TL
82T-590
82T-591A
82T/St-239
82T/Tr-83T
83D-140
83D/AAS-6
83Drake-21
83F-290
83OPC-111TL
83OPC-311
83OPC-5SV
83Stuart-6
83T-111
83T-420
83T-421A
83T-701
83T-703
83T/Gloss40-30
83T/St-174
83T/St-205
83T/St-206M
83T/St-251
84D-177
84D-9
84D/Champs-30
84Drake-24
84F-280
84F-632IA
84F/St-27
84F/X-85
84MiltBrad-18
84Nes/792-516TL
84Nes/792-620
84Nes/792-704LL
84OPC-307
84OPC-332TL
84T-620
84T-704
84T/Gloss22-13
84T/Gloss40-21
84T/St-87
84T/St/Box-1
84T/X-87
85D-598
85F-262
85F/Up-U84
85Leaf-67
85OPC-130
85T-130
85T/St-118
85T/Tr-88T
86D-485
86F-69
86OPC-114
86S-126M
86S-135M
86S-164
86T-775
86T/St-14ALCS
86Woolwth-26
Oliver, Bruce
81Clint-5
Oliver, Darren
89Gasto/Pro-1021
89Gasto/Star-17
Oliver, David Jacob
(Dave)
78T-704R
79T-705R
79Tacom-12
80Tacom-15
81Batav-27
83TriCit-26
85OKCty-15
86OKCty-15MG
87Smok/R-30
89Smok/R-23
Oliver, Eugene George
(Gene)
59T-135
60T-307
61T-487
62T-561
63F-62
63J-164
63P-164
63T-172
64T-316
65Kahn
65OPC-106
65T-106
66T-541
67OPC-18
67T-18
68T-449
69MB-206
69T-247
81QuadC-31C
Oliver, Harry
82Redwd-19
Oliver, Joe
84Cedar-14
87Vermont-19
88Nashvl/CMC-17
88Nashvl/Pro-483
89Nashvl-17
89Nashvl/CMC-12
89Nashvl/Pro-1283
89Score/Tr-104
90D-586
90F-426
90Score-576
90Score/100Ris-26
90Sf-71
90T-668
90UD-568
Oliver, Nathaniel
(Nate)
63T-466R
65OPC-59
65T-59
66T-364
68OPC-124
68T-124
69T-354
70OPC-223
70T-223
88Reno/Cal-291
89MidldA/GS-2
Oliver, Rick
76Wmspt
80SLCty-10
Oliver, Robert Lee
(Bob)
69T-662R
69T/St-187
70MLB/St-226
70T-567
71MLB/St-423
71OPC-470
71T-470
71T/Coins-48
71T/tatt-11
72MB-259
72OPC-57
72T-57
73OPC-289
73T-289
74OPC-243
74T-243
74T/St-143
75OPC-657
75T-657
75T/M-657
76OkCty
79QuadC-26
Oliver, Scott
82Danvi-16
83Redwd-20
85Cram/PCL-5
Oliver, Thomas
54Esskay
54T-207
R314/Can
V355-119
Oliver, Warren
82FtMyr-5
Oliveras, David
88BurlR/Pro-1789
89Kinston/Star-16
Oliveras, Francisco
81Miami-10
85CharO-15
87CharO/WBTV-12
88Orlan/Best-24
89D/Rook-9
89Portl/CMC-9
89Portl/Pro-229
Oliveras, Herbie
84CharO-27
Oliveras, Max
75Shreve/TCMA-16
86FSLAS-37CO
87MidldA-15
88MidldA/GS-1MG
89MidldA/GS-1
Oliveras, Ossie
77Salem
78Colum
79Portl-2
Oliverio, Steve
85Cedar-10
86Vermont-14
87Vermont-14
88Nashvl/CMC-9
88Nashvl/Pro-482
89Calg/CMC-4
89Calg/Pro-543
89ColMud/Best-24
Olivo, Frederico
(Chi-Chi)
66T-578
Olivo, Mike
70OPC-381R
70T-381R
Olker, Joe
84Evrt/Cram-4
86Fresno/Smok-12
88Shreve/Pro-1282
88TexLgAS/GS-8
89Phoen/CMC-8
89Phoen/Pro-1497
Ollar, Rick
78Clint
Oller, Jeff
86Jamestn-18
87BurlEx-8
88WPalm/Star-20
Ollom, James
67OPC-137R
67T-137R
68OPC-91
68T-91
Ollom, Mike
87Penin-9
88Tampa/Star-19

89BirmB/Best-2
89BirmB/Pro-95
Olmeda, Jose
89Idaho/Pro-2015
Olmstead, Fred
T205
Olmstead, Reed
87Erie-4
87Savan-17
88Savan/Pro-346
89Spart/Pro-1048
89Spart/Star-19
Olmsted, Alan
80ArkTr-11
81T-244R
82Louvl-21
Olsen, Al
86Ventura-18tr
87MidldA-9
88Edmon/Pro-584tr
89PalmSp/Cal-61tr
89PalmSp/Pro-480
Olsen, Lefty
52Mother-23
Olsen, Lew
77Jaxvl
Olsen, Rick
78Newar
79Holyo-9
80Vanco-22
81Vanco-13
82Vanco-15
Olson, Dan
89Boise/Pro-1995
Olson, Dean
77Visal
Olson, Greg
83Lynch-8
84Jacks-xx
86Jacks/TCMA-12
87Tidew-19
87Tidew/TCMA-11
88Tidew/CANDL-6
88Tidew/CMC-13
88Tidew/Pro-1597
89Portl/CMC-13
89Portl/Pro-225
Olson, Gregg
89B-6
89Class-132
89D-46RR
89D/Best-322
89D/Rook-35
89French-30
89Score/Tr-96
89T-161FDP
89T/Tr-89T
89UD/Ext-723
90Class-3
90D-377
90F-184
90Score-63
90Score/100Ris-32
90Sf-215
90T-655
90UD-604
Olson, Ivan M.
(Ollie)
21Exh-120
E120
E220
T207
V100
W514-70
Olson, James Vincent
87BurlEx-2
Olson, Jimmy
86AubAs-18
87Ashvl-9
Olson, Karl Arthur
(Karl)
52T-72
54T-186
55T-72
55T/DH-35
56T-322
57T-153
Olson, Kurt
88CapeCod/Sum-47
Olson, Mike
81CharR-4
Olson, Warren
86Beloi-18
88WinHav/Star-17
Olsson, Dan
86Tulsa-19
Olszta, Ed
75AppFx
77AppFx
Olwine, Ed
83Nashvl-13
84Tidew-11
85Tidew-12
86Richm-14
87D-560
87F-524
87Smok/Atl-6
87T-159
88Score-379
88T-353
89Omaha/CMC-8
89Omaha/Pro-1725
89UD-435
Omachi, George
88Fresno/Pro-1246
Omo, Bob
78Cedar
Ongarato, Mike
81Pawtu-21
Ontiveros, Steve
(Steve)
83Albany-7
84Cram/PCL-83
86D-589
86F-429
86Moth/A's-22
86T-507
87D-221
87D/HL-15
87F-401
87T-161
88D-467
88D/A's/Bk-467
88F-289
88Moth/A's-13
88Score-511
88T-272
89D-596
89D/Tr-11
89Score-337
89T-692
89T/Tr-90T
Ontiveros, Steven R.
(Steve)
74OPC-598R
74T-598R
75OPC-483
75T-483
75T/M-483
76OPC-284
76SSPC-104
76T-284
78K-44
78T-76
79OPC-150
79T-299
80OPC-268
80T-514
Opdyke, Paul
88Idaho/Pro-1854
Opie, James
83AlexD-6
85Cram/PCL-226
86Nashua-20
87Jaxvl-13
Oppenheimer, Jose
77BurlB
Oppenheimer, Juan
78Cedar
Opperman, Dan
88GreatF-10
89VeroB/Star-20
Oquendo, Ismael
84RochR-8
Oquendo, Jorge
82Idaho-27
Oquendo, Jose Manuel
(Jose)
82Tidew-15
83Tidew-29
84D-643
84F-592
84Nes/792-208
84OPC-208
84T-208
84T/St-112
85F-88
85Louvl-15
85T-598
86Schnucks-17
86T/Tr-82T
87D-510
87F-305
87Smok/Cards-18
87T-133
88D-234
88D/Best-313
88F-44
88Score-248
88Smok/Card-16
88T-83
88T/St-18
89B-438
89Bimbo/Discs-5
89D-319
89D/Best-100
89F-459
89OPC-69
89Panini/St-184
89Score-529
89Score/YS/II-16
89Smok/Cards-15
89T-442
89T/Big-77
89T/St-45
89Tetley/Discs-19
89UD-514
90D-161
90F-255
90Score-68
90Sf-85
90T-645
90UD-319
Oquist, Mike
89Erie/Star-16
Oravetz, Ernest E.
(Ernie)
56T-51
57T-179
Orengo, Joseph C.
(Joe)
41DP-29
47Sunbeam
Orensky, Herb
80Penin/B-23
80Penin/C-15
82OkCty-20
Orhan, Hugh
47Sunbeam
Oropeza, Clemente
82Idaho-20
Orosco, Jesse
79Tidew-23
80T-681R
81Tidew-20
82D-646
83D-434
83F-550
83T-369
84D-197
84F-593
84F/St-60
84Jacks/Smok-9
84Nes/792-396AS
84Nes/792-54
84OPC-396AS
84OPC-54
84T-396
84T-54
84T/Gloss40-33
84T/Mets/Fan-5
84T/St-104
85D-22
85D-75
85D/DKsuper-22
85F-89
85F/St-106
85Leaf-22DK
85OPC-250
85T-250
85T/Gloss40-2
85T/St-101
85T/Super-54
86D-646
86F-90
86OPC-182
86T-465
87Class-75
87D-439
87F-20
87F/Mini-78
87F/RecSet-27
87F/St-87
87Leaf-175
87OPC-148
87RedFoley/St-84
87S-76
87T-704
88D-192
88D/Best-234
88F-148
88F/U-U96
88Moth/Dodg-13
88Pol/Dodg-47
88Score-495
88Score/Tr-64T
88Sf-89
88T-105
88T/Tr-77T
89B-81
89D-228
89D/Tr-26
89F-68
89Score-356
89T-513
89T/Tr-91T
89UD-87
90D-154
90F-500
90Score-353
90T-636
90UD-588
Oroz, Felix Andres
81VeroB-13
84Cram/PCL-233
Orphal, John
47Centen-18
Orr, David L.
N172
N172/SP
N284
N338/2
N690
Orr, William
T222
Orsag, Jim
86Greens-15
87WinHav-28
88CLAS/Star-13
88Lynch/Star-16
89NewBrit/Pro-610
89NewBrit/Star-12
Orsatti, Ernesto R.
(Ernie)
33G-201
35G-1A
35G-2A
35G-6A
35G-7A
Orsino, John Joseph
(Johnny)
61Union
62T-377
63T-418
64T-63
64T/Coins-3
65T-303
65T/E-51
66OPC-77
66T-77
66T/RO-09
67T-207
Orsulak, Joe
82AlexD-22
85F/Up-U85
85T/Tr-89T
86D-444
86F-615
86F/LL-29
86F/Mini-118
86F/St-83
86Leaf-218
86S-177M
86T-102
86T/St-132
87D-291
87F-615
87F/RecSet-28
87T-414
87T/St-132
88D/Best-310
88F/U-U2
88French-6
88Score/Tr-41T
88T/Tr-78T
89D-287
89D/Best-310
89F-614
89French-6
89Panini/St-263
89Score-247
89T-727
89T/Big-181
89UD-429
90D-287
90F-185
90Score-41
90Sf-38
90T-212
90UD-270
Orta, Jorge Nunez
(Jorge)
73OPC-194
73T-194
74OPC-376
74T-376
74T/St-159
75Ho-122
75Ho/Twink-122
75K-14
75OPC-184
75T-184
75T/M-184
76Ho-57
76Ho/Twink-57
76K-45
76OPC-560
76SSPC-144
76T-560
77T-109

78Ho-105
78OPC-77
78T-42
78Wiffle/Discs-56
79Ho-126
79OPC-333
79T-631
80T-442
81D-439
81F-388
81OPC-222
81T-222
82D-211
82F-376
82OPC-26
82Pol/Dodg
82Pol/Dodg-31
82T-26
82T/St-175
82T/Tr-84T
83D-388
83F-215
83T-722
83T/X-82
84D-317
84F-166
84F/X-86
84Nes/792-312
84OPC-312
84T-312
84T/X-88
85D-130
85F-209
85Leaf-226
85T-164
85T/St-273
86D-339
86F-17
86Kitty/Disc-6
86Leaf-205
86NatPhoto-3
86OPC-44
86T-541
87D-348
87F-376
87OPC-63
87T-738

Ortega, Dan
81AppFx-7

Ortega, Eduardo
89Batav/Pro-1939

Ortega, Kirk
81Clint-16

Ortega, Phil
59DF
62T-69
63T-467
64T-291
65OPC-152
65T-152
66T-416
66T/RO-32
67T-493
68T-595
69MB-207
69T-406

Ortegon, Ronnie
89PalmSp/Cal-35
89PalmSp/Pro-478

Orteig, Ray
48Sommer-25
52Mother-50
53Mother-31

Orth, Albert Lewis
(Al)
E107
E254
T206

Ortiz, Adalberto Jr.
(Junior)
77Charl
78Charl
80Buffa
81Portl-19
82Portl-11
84D-319
84F-594
84Nes/792-161
84T-161
84T/St-114
85T-439
86D-508
86T-682
87D-449
87D/OD-164
87F-616
87T-583
88D-168
88F-335
88Score-404
88T-274
89AAA/Pro-46
89D-387
89D/Best-269
89F-215
89Score-402
89T-769
89T/Big-66
89UD-86
90F-475
90Score-143
90T-322
90UD-389

Ortiz, Alfredo
86Ventura-19C

Ortiz, Andy
83Watlo/LF-5
84BuffB-15

Ortiz, Angel
88Watlo/Pro-667
89Kinston/Star-17

Ortiz, Darrell
80Tulsa-23

Ortiz, Hector
89VeroB/Star-21

Ortiz, Javier
84Tulsa-31
85Tulsa-31
86Tulsa-17
87OKCty-15
88SnAnt/Best-22
89Albuq/CMC-25
89Albuq/Pro-84

Ortiz, Joe
88Ashvl/Pro-1066
88CalLgAS-22
88Reno/Cal-285
89Beloi/Star-20
89Osceola/Star-15

Ortiz, Jorge
81Wisco-7

Ortiz, Lou
55T-114
55T/DH-91
D301

Ortiz, Miguel
80Utica-21

Ortman, Doug
87Madis-9

Orton, John
85Anchora-23
88PalmSp/Cal-107
88PalmSp/Pro-1433
89MidldA/GS-25
90F-647
90Score-582
90Score/100Ris-64
90Sf-132
90UD-672

Oruna, Roland
82CharR-17
83CharR-11

Osaka, Rocky
87SanJose-7

Osborn, Dan
76OPC-282
76SSPC-135
76T-282

Osborn, Don
47Signal
74OPC-489CO
74T-489CO

Osborn, Pat
No Cards.

Osborn, Wilfred
E254

Osborne, Jeff
89Aug/Pro-494

Osborne, Lawrence S.
(Bobo)
59T-524
60T-201
61T-208
62T-583
63T-514

Osinski, Dan
63T-114
64T-537
65OPC-223
65T-223
66OPC-168
66T-168
67T-594
68T-331
69T-622

Osmon, Scott
89Idaho/Pro-2032

Osofsky, Alvin
75Dubuq

Osowski, Tom
83Butte-33
84Butte-6
85Evrt/Cram-12
86PalmS/Smk-1GM

Osteen, Claude
59T-224
60T-206
62T-501
63J-100
63P-100
63T-374
64T-28
64T/Coins-13
64T/St-74
64T/SU
64T/tatt
65MacGregor-8
65T-570
66T-270
67T-330
68OPC-9LL
68T-440
68T-9LL
68T/G-12
69MB-208
69MLB/St-150
69T-528
69T/St-47
70MLB/St-54
70OPC-260
70T-260
70T/S-1
70T/SO
71Bz
71Bz/Test-39
71K-70
71MD
71MLB/St-110
71OPC-10
71T-10
71T/Coins-45
71T/S-27
72K-34
72MB-260
72OPC-297
72OPC-298IA
72T-297
72T-298A
73K-49
73OPC-490
73T-490
74OPC-42
74T-42
74T/DE-38
74T/St-48
74T/Tr-42T
75OPC-453
75T-453
75T/M-453
76OPC-488
76T-488
78TCMA-273
87Smok/Dodg-25
89Pac/Leg-132
89Smok/Dodg-73
89SnAnt/Best-26
89Swell-17

Osteen, Dave
87StPet-1
88ArkTr/GS-23
89ArkTr/GS-15

Osteen, Gavin
89Medford/Best-29

Osteen, M. Darrell
66T-424R
67T-222R
68T-199R

Oster, Dave
88Geneva/Pro-1659

Oster, Paul
89Oneon/Pro-2127

Ostermueller, Fred
(Fritz) 34DS-73
34G-93
35G-8G
35G-9G
39PB-22
40PB-33
41G-12
47TipTop
49B-227
R314
W753

Ostopowicz, Rich
89Kingspt/Star-18

Ostrosser, Brian L.
(Brian)
75OkCty

Ostrowski, Joe P.
49Royal-20
52BR
52Mother-2
52T-206

Ostrowski, John T.
(John)
47Signal

Osuna, Al
87AubAs-22
88Osceola/Star-20
89Osceola/Star-16

Otero, Regino J.
(Reggie)
47Signal
60T-459C
63FrBauer-15

Otey, William
T206

Otis, Amos Joseph
(Amos)
69OPC-31R
69T-31R
70OPC-354
70T-354
71Bz
71Bz/Test-42
71K-38
71MLB/St-424
71OPC-610
71T/Coins-96
71T/S-45
71T/tatt-4
72K-2
72OPC-10
72T-10
72T/Post-6
73K-1
73OPC-510
73T-510
73T/Lids-37
74K-17
74OPC-337AS
74OPC-65
74T-337AS
74T-65
74T/DE-1
74T/St-185
75Ho-50
75OPC-520
75T-520
75T/M-520
76A&P/KC
76Ho-51
76Ho/Twink-51
76OPC-198LL
76OPC-510
76SSPC-177
76T-198
76T-510
77Ho-92
77OPC-141
77Pep-33
77T-290
78OPC-16
78T-490
79Ho-132
79OPC-185
79T-360
7IT-610
80OPC-72
80T-135
80T/S-50
81Coke
81D-104
81F-32
81F/St-28
81OPC-288
81Pol/Royals-7
81T-585
82D-70
82F-419
82F/St-211
82OPC-162
82OPC-350IA
82T-725
82T-726A
82T/St-194
83D-364
83F-120
83OPC-75
83Pol/Royals-5
83T-75
83T/St-72
84F-351
84F/X-87
84Nes/792-655
84OPC-53
84T-655
84T/X-89
88Smok/Padres-21
89Tidew/CANDL-4

Otis, David
86Madis-17

Ott, Melvin Thomas
(Mel)
29Exh/4-9
31Exh/4-10
33G-127
33G-207
34DS-50
34Exh/4-5

35BU-27
35Exh/4-5
35G-2A
35G-7A
35Wheat
36Exh/4-5
36Wheat
37Exh/4-5
38Exh/4-5
38ONG/Pin-22
39Exh
39PB-51
39Wheat
40PB-88
40Wheat
41DP-31
41DP-89
41G-33
41G-33
41PB-8
43MP-19
50Callahan
52Mother-53
60Exh/HOF-18
60F-36
60NuCard-58
61F-68
61GP-1
61NuCard-458
63Bz-36
69Bz/Sm
72F/FFeat-25
73F/Wild-17
80Cram/Leg-35
80Laugh/3/4/5-12
80Laugh/FFeat-14
80SSPC/HOF
83D/HOF-40
85CircK-12
86BLChew-11
86Conlon/1-36
86S/Dec-8
88Conlon/4-21
89HOF/St-49
89Pac/Leg-189
R300
R302
R309/2
R310
R316
R326-3A
R326-3B
R342-3
R346-18
WG8-44

Ott, Nathan Edward
(Ed)
76OPC-594R
76T-594
77T-197
78OPC-161
78T-28
79Ho-31
79OPC-289
79T-561
80OPC-200
80T-383
81Coke
81D-133
81F-365
81OPC-246
81T-246
81T/St-214
81T/Tr-810
82D-192
82F-470
82OPC-225
82T-469
83F-98
83T-131
84Cram/PCL-120CO
85PrWill-23
86Watertn-16MG

Ott, William
65T-354R

Otten, Brian
86Geneva-21
87Peoria-15
88WinSal/Star-13

Otten, Jim
75OPC-624R
75T-624R
75T/M-624R
77T-493

Otto, Dave
86Madis/Pol-16
88F-652
89Score/HotRk-60
89T-131
89Tacom/CMC-10
89Tacom/Pro-1547
89UD-4

Otto, Steve
88Eugene/Best-4
89AppFx/Pro-876

Ouellette, Phil
82Clint-5
84Cram/PCL-1
85Cram/PCL-182
86Phoen-19
88AAA/Pro-7
88Calg/CMC-12
88Calg/Pro-801

Outlaw, James Paulus
(Jimmy)
39PB-155
47TipTop

Overall, Orval
12Sweet/Pin-86
E254
E90/1
E90/3
E91
M116
S74-66
T202
T205
T206
T3-32
WG3-35

Overeem, Steve
88James/Pro-1914

Overmire, Frank
(Stubby)
47TipTop
48L-17
51B-280
52T-155

Overton, Jeff
82AppFx-2

Overton, Mike
79Newar-5

Overy, Mike
77SLCty
77T-489R
78Cr/PCL-108
79SLCty-9
80SLCty-26

Owchinko, Bob
78T-164
79OPC-257
79T-488
80OPC-44
80T-79
81D-563
81T-536
81T/Tr-811
82D-287
82F-104
82T-243
83D-265
83F-531
83T-338
84F/X-88
85Cram/PCL-144
85D-506
85F-543
85T-752
86Indianap-9

Owen, Arnold Malcolm
(Mickey)
38G-263
38G-287
39PB-135
40PB-111
41DP-15
50B-78
51B-174
60NuCard-15
61NuCard-475
89Rini/Dodg-32
89Smok/Dodg-44

Owen, Billy
WG2-38

Owen, Dave
83IowaC-18
84IowaC-18
84SevenUp-19
85D-483
85IowaC-6
85T-642
86OKCty-16
87OKCty-3
88Omaha/CMC-16
88Omaha/Pro-1510
89IowaC/CMC-19
89IowaC/Pro-1694
89Lynch/Star-16

Owen, Frank Malcomb
T206

Owen, Lawrence T.
(Larry)
79Richm-5
82Richm-11
82T-502R
83Pol/Atl-24
84Richm-8
85IntLgAS-9
85Richm-12
86Richm-15
88Omaha/CMC-18
88Omaha/Pro-1516
88Score-230
89T-87
89UD-528

Owen, Marvin James
(Marv)
34DS-67
35BU-168
R314
V355-69

Owen, Spike D.
83SLCty-23
84D-313
84F-616
84Moth/Mar-6
84Nes/792-413
84T-413
84T/St-349
85D-435
85D/AAS-4
85F-497
85Leaf-167
85Moth/Mar-7
85T-84
85T/St-339
86D-362
86F-471
86Moth/Mar-20
86OPC-248
86T-248
86T/St-224
87D-633
87D/OD-185
87F-40
87Leaf-87
87T-591
88D-544
88D/RedSox/Bk-544
88F-359
88OPC-188
88Panini/St-30
88Score-372
88T-733
89B-363
89D-593
89D/Best-236
89D/Tr-14
89F-93
89F/Up-98
89Score-218
89Score/Tr-13
89T-123
89T/Big-221
89T/Tr-92T
89UD-161
89UD/Ext-717
90D-102
90F-357
90Score-247
90T-674
90UD-291

Owen, Tim
85BurlR-14
86DayBe-20

Owens, Frank Walter
(Frank)
14CJ-74
15CJ-74
E254

Owens, Jim
55T-202
55T/DH-122
56T-114
59T-503
60L-39
60T-185
61P-116
61T-341
62T-212
63FrBauer-17
63T-483
64T-241
65T-451
66T-297
67T-582
73OPC-624CO
73T-624C

Owens, Larry
88CapeCod/Sum-52

Owens, Mark
87Everett-30
88Clint/Pro-704
88MidwLAS/GS-1

Owens, Markus
89Shreve/Pro-1849

Owens, Marty
88Geneva/Pro-1658

Owens, Michael
88Batav/Pro-1675
89Batav/Pro-1930

Owens, Paul
84F-643IA
84F/St-123MG
84Nes/792-229MG
84T-229MG
85T-92
85T/Gloss22-1MG

Owens, Steve
88CharWh/Best-8

Owens, Tom
79Wausa-25
81Watlo-12
82Chatt-9
83BuffB-6

Ownbey, Rick
82Tidew-1
83F-551
83T-739
84Louvl-23
85Louvl-26
86F/Up-U85
86Schnucks-18

Oxner, Stan
83Butte-15

Oyler, Raymond F.
(Ray)
65OPC-259R
65T-259R
66OPC-81
66T-81
67T-352
68T-399
69MB-209
69MLB/St-97
69OPC-178
69T-178
69T/St-228
70MLB/St-264
70T-603
72MB-261
88Domino-18

Oyster, Jeff
87ArkTr-18
88ArkTr/GS-24
88Louvl-38
89ArkTr/GS-16

Ozark, Danny
73OPC-486MG
73T-486MG
74OPC-119MG
74T-119MG
75OPC-46MG
75T-46MG
75T/M-46MG
76SSPC-476
76T-384
77T-467
78BK/P-1MG
78T-631
79T-112
85T-365

Ozawa, Kouichi
89Visal/Cal-114
89Visal/Pro-1422

Ozuna, Gabriel
89Savan/Pro-345

Ozuna, Mateo
89Savan/Pro-359

Pace, Jim
88Reno/Cal-288

Pace, Tubby
85Cedar-23

Pacella, John
78Tidew
79Tidew-2
81Colum-22
81T-414
82Colum-1
82Colum/Pol-17
83D-130
83F-622
83T-166
87Toled-8
87Toled/TCMA-14

Pacheco, Tony
74OPC-521CO
74T-521C

Pacho, Juan
81Watlo-24
83Charl-11
89Greenv/Pro-1155
89Greenv/Star-16
89Greenvl/Best-8

Pacholec, Joe
87Watertn-23
88Aug/Pro-373
89Salem/Star-16

Pacillo, Pat
85T-402

53T-220
72T/Test-1
74Laugh/Black-15
80Cram/Leg-60
80SSPC/HOF
83D/HOF-11
83MLBPA/Pin-14
85West/2-37
88Conlon/NegAS-10
89B-I8
Exh47
PM10/Sm-140
Rawl

Paine, Phil
54JC-11
55JC-11
58T-442
59DF

Painton, Tim
80Clint-15

Paixao, Paulino
85Utica-4

Palacios, Rey
86GlenF-17
87Toled-15
87Toled/TCMA-1
88AAA/Pro-43
88Toled/CMC-18
88Toled/Pro-605
89F-648M
89UD-21

Palacios, Vicente
87Vanco-22
88Class/Red-191
88D-45
88F-336
88Leaf-45
88Score-643
88Sf-224
88T-322
89F-216
89Score/HotRk-2

Palafox, Juan
85Tigres-12

Palermo, Pete
86Hagers-14
87Hagers-17
88Hagers/Star-16

Palermo, Steve
88Umpire-29
89Umpires-27

Palica, Alex
45Centen-19

Palica, Ambrose
46Remar-22
47Remar-10
47Smith-12

Palica, Erv
51B-189
52T-273
54NYJour
55B-195
56T-206
60HenryH-21
61Union
79TCMA-233

Palica, John
81Wisco-22
83Orlan-8

Pall, Donn Steven
86AppFx-17
87BirmB/Best-15
88AAA/Pro-45
88Vanco/CMC-9
88Vanco/Pro-759
89Coke/WS-18
89D/Rook-7
89F-505
89Score/Tr-102
89T-458
90D-606
90F-543
90Score-304
90Score/100Ris-7
90T-219
90UD-386

Pallas, Ted
82Beloi-27

Pallone, Dave
88Umpire-37
89Umpires-35

Palma, Brian
89Reno/Cal-258

Palma, Jay
83Ander-22

Palmeiro, Rafael
86Pittsf-18
87D-43RR
87D/Rook-47
87IowaC-24
87Leaf-43
87S-158M
87S/Rook-32
87Sf/Rook-2
87T-634
87T/GlossRk-12
88Berg/Cubs-25
88D-324
88D/Best-93
88D/Cubs/Bk-324
88F-429
88F/Slug-C4
88OPC-186
88Panini/St-268
88Peoria/Ko-23
88Peoria/Ko-34M
88Score-186
88T-186
89B-237
89Class/Up/2-163
89D-49
89D/AS-53
89D/Best-88
89D/Tr-6
89F-434
89F-631M
89F/Up-66
89Moth/R-5
89OPC-310
89Panini/St-60
89RedFoley/St-88
89Score-199
89Score/HotSt-56
89Score/Tr-1
89Score/YS/I-35
89Sf-30
89Smok/R-24
89T-310
89T/Big-257
89T/Coins-47
89T/Mini-5
89T/St-47
89T/St/Backs-52
89T/Tr-93T
89T/UK-58
89UD-235
89UD/Ext-772
90Class-74
90D-225
90F-308
90Score-405
90Score/100St-58
90Sf-9
90T-755
90UD-335

Palmer, Bob
75AppFx
82Holyo-11

Palmer, David
80OPC-21
80T-42
81D-451
81F-160
81OPC-243
81T-607
82F-199
82OPC-292
82T-292
83D-68
83F-291
83OPC-164
83T-164
84Stuart-23
85D-341
85F-404
85Leaf-105
85OPC-211
85OPC/Post-3
85T-526
86D-254
86F-255
86F/Up-U87
86OPC-143
86Pol/Atl-46
86T-421
86T/Tr-84T
87D-325
87F-525
87Smok/Atl-4
87T-324
87T/St-45
88D-266
88F-546
88F/U-U111
88Score-457
88T-732
88T/Tr-79T
89D-133
89F-577
89OPC-67
89Score-544
89T-67
89Toled/CMC-4
89Toled/Pro-789
89UD-515

Palmer, Dean
87Gasto-8
88CharlR/Star-18
88FSLAS/Star-47
89Tulsa/GS-19
90D-529
90Score-594
90Score/100Ris-38
90Sf-225
90UD-74

Palmer, Denzil
76Clint

Palmer, Donald
87BuffB-28

Palmer, Doug
85Visal-2
86Orlan-15
87Orlan-17
88NewBrit/Pro-892

Palmer, Jim
66OPC-126
66T-126
67OPC-152WS
67T-475
68T-575
69T-573
70OPC-449
70OPC-68LL
70T-449
70T-68LL
71K-60
71MD
71MLB/St-306
71OPC-197ALCS
71OPC-570
71OPC-67LL
71T-570
71T-67LL
71T/Coins-90
71T/tatt-3
72K-13
72MB-263
72OPC-270
72OPC-92LL
72T-270
72T-92LL
73JP
73K-17
73OPC-160
73OPC-341KP
73T-160
73T-341BP
73T/Comics-13
73T/Lids-38
73T/PinUps-13
74K-6
74OPC-206LL
74OPC-40
74T-206LL
74T-40
74T/DE-45
74T/Puzzles-8
74T/St-128
75Ho-126
75OPC-335
75T-335
75T/M-335
76Crane-44
76Ho-56
76Ho/Twink-56
76K-37
76MSA/Disc
76OPC-200LL
76OPC-202LL
76OPC-450
76SSPC-380
76T-200LL
76T-202LL
76T-450
77Ho-1
77OPC-5LL
77OPC-80
77Pep-20
77T-5LL
77T-600
77T/CS-36
78Ho-116
78OPC-179
78OPC-5LL
78PapaG/Disc-31
78T-160
78T-205LL
78Wiffle/Discs-57
79Ho-11
79K-5
79OPC-174
79T-340
80BK/PHR-7
80K-15
80OPC-310
80T-4M
80T-590
81D-353
81D-473
81F-169
81F/St-124
81K-2
81OPC-210
81T-210
81T/Nat/Super-9
81T/S
81T/SO-50
81T/St-39
82D-231
82F-175
82F/St-143
82K-42
82OPC-80
82OPC-81SA
82T-80
82T-81A
82T/St-146
83D-4DK
83D-77
83F-69
83K-39
83OPC-299
83OPC-328SV
83T-21
83T-490
83T-491A
83T/Gloss-19
83T/Gloss40-19
83T/St-175
83T/St-23
83T/St/Box-5
84D-576
84D/Champs-35
84F-16
84F/St-102
84Nes/792-715LL
84Nes/792-717LL
84Nes/792-750
84OPC-194
84Ralston-23
84T-715
84T-717
84T-750
84T/Cereal-23
84T/St-21
84T/St-211
86S/Dec-58
87KMart-17
89Swell-105

Palmer, Ken
76Baton

Palmer, Lowell
70OPC-252
70T-252
71OPC-554
71T-554
72T-746

Palmer, Mickey
82FtMyr-8

Palmer, Mike
81QuadC-33tr

Palmieri, John
82Readg-5

Palmquist, Ed
60DF-7

Palyan, Vince
89Everett/Star-23

Palys, Stanley F.
(Stan)
58T-126

Pancoski, Tracey
88Fresno/Cal-7
88Fresno/Pro-1240

Panetta, Mario
83QuadC-4

Panick, Frank
77SLCty

Pankovits, James F.
(Jim)
77Cocoa
80Tucso-19
81Tucso-17
82Hawai-4
83Tucso-16
84Cram/PCL-61
85D-502
85Moth/Ast-25
86D-450
86F-307
86Pol/Ast-1
86T-618
87D-605
87F-64
87Moth/Ast-22
87Pol/Ast-25
87T-249
88Moth/Ast-22
88Pol/Ast-16
88T-487
88T/Big-109

89BuffB/CMC-18
89BuffB/Pro-1664
89F-363
89Score-192
89T-153
89UD-100

Papageorge, Greg
88Virgini/Star-17
89Penin/Star-17

Papai, Al
50B-245

Paparella, J.A.
55B-235ump

Pape, Kenneth Wayne
(Ken)
77Tucso
78Syrac
79Spoka-8
81Spoka-21

Pape, Lawrence
E270/1

Papi, Stanley Gerard
(Stan)
79OPC-344
79T-652
81D-246
81F-480
81T-273
82D-333
82F-280
82T-423

Papke, William
T3/Box-64

Pappageorgas, Bob
77Wausa

Pappas, Erik
86PalmSp-25
86PalmSp/Smok-6
87PalmSp-23
88MidldA/GS-14
89CharlK-12

Pappas, Milt
58T-457
59T-391
60Bz-5
60L-57
60T-12
60T-399M
60T/tatt
60T/tatt-42
61P-71
61T-295
61T-48LL
61T/St-103
62Bz
62Exh
62J-34
62P-34
62P/Can-34
62Salada-98
62Shirriff-98
62T-55LL
62T-75
62T/St-7
63Exh
63F-3
63J-65
63P-65
63Salada-43
63T-358
64T-45
64T/Coins-70
64T/S-5
64T/St-4
64T/tatt
65OPC-270
65T-270
65T/E-20
65T/trans-61
66Bz-29
66Kahn
66OPC-105
66T-105
66T/RO-88
67T-254
68OPC-74
68T-74
69MB-212
69MLB/St-117
69OPC-79
69T-79
69T/St-8
70MLB/St-11
70T-576
71MD
71MLB/St-39
71OPC-441
71T-441
72MB-264
72OPC-208
72T-208
73OPC-70
73T-70
74OPC-640
74T-640
78TCMA-56
89Pac/Leg-204
89Swell-113
Exh47
WG10-41
WG9-40

Paquette, Craig
89Medford/Best-22

Paquette, Darryl
78Wausa

Parachke, Greg
89Utica/Puc-17

Parascand, Steve
87Fayette-4
88Fay/Pro-1088

Pardo, Al
81Miami-2
83RochR-12
84CharO-7
85RochR-2
86D-489
86RochR-15
86T-279
88Tidew/Pro-1594
89ScrWB/CMC-21
89ScrWB/Pro-711

Pardo, Bed
89Eugene/Best-8

Pardo, Larry
86DayBe-21
87QuadC-6
88QuadC/GS-6
89QuadC/Best-12
89QuadC/GS-24

Paredes, Jesus
87Jamestn-6
88Rockford-26
89Rockford-26

Paredes, Johnny
86Jaxvl/TCMA-2
87Indianap-20
88D/Rook-29
88Indi/CMC-11
88Indi/Pro-516
89D-570
89F-388
89OPC-367
89Score/HotRk-27
89T-367
89UD-477

Parent, Eric
82Wausa-11
83Wausa/LF-10
84Greens-16

Parent, Frederick A.
(Freddy)
10Domino-95
11Helmar-14
12Sweet/Pin-13
14Piedmont/St-46
C46-44
E107
E254
M116
S74-7
T205
T206
WG2-39

Parent, Mark
82Amari-10
83Beaum-13
84Beaum-8
85Cram/PCL-105
86LasVegas-11
88Coke/Padres-27
88D/Rook-8
88F/U-U125
88Smok/Padres-22
88T/Tr-80T
89D-420
89F/Up-125
89Score-576
89T-617
89UD-492
90D-229
90F-164
90Score-119
90T-749
90UD-569

Parese, Billy
89StCath/Pro-2082

Parfrey, Brian
82Redwd-26

Parham, Bill
89Bakers/Cal-191

Paris, Juan
85Spoka/Cram-18
86CharRa-20
87Greens-12
88WinHav/Star-19
89Lynch/Star-17

Paris, Kelly Jay
(Kelly)
77StPet
78StPet
80ArkTr-22
82Louvl-22
84Cram/PCL-123
84D-384
84F-476
84Nes/792-113
84T-113
85IntLgAS-28
85RochR-8
86RochR-16
88Vanco/CMC-12
89F-506
89UD-192
89Vanco/CMC-11
89Vanco/Pro-594

Paris, Zacarias
82Tucso-14
83ColumAst-17
86Ventura-20

Parish, Jack
76Clint

Parisotto, Barry
89GreatF-20

Parke, Jim
77Charl

Parker, Bob
86ColumAst-21

Parker, Carrol
86Erie-22
87Savan-14

Parker, Clay
86Wausa-18
88Colum/CMC-2
88Colum/Pol-7
88Colum/Pro-309
88F-649
89Colum/CMC-4
89Colum/Pol-17
89Colum/Pro-751
89D/Best-164
89D/Rook-52
89Score/NWest-30
89Score/Tr-94
89T/Tr-94T
90D-363
90F-451
90Score-316
90Score/100Ris-17
90T-511

Parker, Darrell
76Watlo
77Jaxvl

Parker, David Gene
(Dave)
74OPC-252
74T-252
74T/St-86
75OPC-29
75T-29
75T/M-29
76Crane-45
76Ho-133
76K-15
76MSA/Disc
76OPC-185
76SSPC-572
76T-185
77K-19
77OPC-242
77T-270
78Ho-135
78K-52
78OPC-1LL
78OPC-60
78T-201
78T-560
78Wiffle/Discs-58
79Ho-53
79K-21
79OPC-223
79T-1LL
79T-430
79T/Comics-29
80BK/PHR-19
80K-23
80OPC-163
80T-310
80T/S-17
81Coke
81D-136
81Drake-4
81F-360
81F/St-26
81K-13
81MSA/Disc-25
81OPC-178
81Sqt-10
81T-640
81T/Nat/Super-10
81T/S
81T/SO-59
81T/St-210
81T/St-257
82D-12DK
82D-95
82F-489
82F/St-241M
82F/St-71
82K-48
82KMart-34
82OPC-343AS
82OPC-40
82OPC-41IA
82T-343
82T-40
82T-41A
82T/St-87
82T/St-127
83D-473
83F-315
83OPC-205
83T-205
83T/St-280
84Borden-39
84D-288
84D/Champs-57
84F-258
84F/X-89
84FunFood/Pin-80
84Nes/792-701LL
84Nes/792-775
84OPC-31
84T-701
84T-775
84T/St-130
84T/X-90
85D-62
85D/AAS-35
85D/HL-13
85Drake-22
85F-544
85Leaf-169
85OPC-175
85T-175
85T/St-47
85T/Super-42
86D-203
86D/AAS-24
86Drake-4
86F-184
86F-640M
86F/AS-6
86F/LimEd-33
86F/LL-30
86F/Mini-39
86F/St-84
86Leaf-135
86OPC-287
86Quaker-9
86S-181M
86S-183M
86S-23
86S-58M
86T-595
86T/3D-18
86T/Gloss60-13
86T/Mini-41
86T/St-135
86T/Super-41
86TexGold-39
86Woolwth-27
87Class-33
87D-388
87D/AAS-34
87D/OD-198
87Drake-18
87F-208
87F-639M
87F-C10
87F/AwardWin-27
87F/Mini-80
87F/Slug-29
87F/St-88
87F/WaxBox-C10
87Kahn-39
87KayBee-23
87Leaf-79
87OPC-352
87Ralston-7
87RedFoley/St-90
87S-117M
87S-35
87T-600AS
87T-691
87T/Board-20
87T/Coins-38
87T/Gloss60-17
87T/Gloss60-17
87T/Mini-6
87T/St-145

88D-388
88D/A's/Bk-NEW
88D/Best-190
88F-243
88F/Mini-47
88F/U-U55
88KayBee-21
88Moth/A's-5
88OPC-315
88Panini/St-284
88Score-17
88Score/Tr-50T
88Sf-101
88T-315
88T/Big-242
88T/Gloss60-34
88T/Mini-48
88T/St-136
88T/St/Backs-19
88T/Tr-81T
88T/UK-55
89Ames-23
89B-202
89D-150
89D/Best-336
89F-19
89KMart/Lead-13
89Moth/A's-4
89OPC-199
89Panini/St-424
89Score-108
89Sf-49
89T-475
89T/Big-144
89T/St-169
89UD-605
90Class-95
90D-328
90F-18
90Score-135
90T-45
90UD-192

Parker, Francis James
(Salty)
60T-469C
62Sugar-16
73OPC-421CO
73T-421C
74OPC-276CO
74T-276C
76Cedar

Parker, Harry
74OPC-106
74T-106
75OPC-214
75T-214
75T/M-214

Parker, James
87Chatt/Best-4

Parker, Jarrod
89Pulas/Pro-1906

Parker, Joel
81BurlB-27

Parker, Mark
80Wichi-4
82IowaC-21

Parker, Maurice W.
(Wes)
64T-456R
65T-344
66OPC-134
66T-134
67T-218
68T-533
69MB-213
69MLB/St-151
69T-493
70MLB/St-55
70OPC-5
70T-5
71MLB/St-111
71OPC-430
71T-430
71T/Coins-121
71T/GM-30
71T/S-14
71T/tatt-8
72K-17
72MB-265
72OPC-265
72T-265
73OPC-151
73T-151
88Smok/Dodg-10

Parker, Mike
89Idaho/Pro-2035

Parker, Olen
87Clearw-5

Parker, Rich
85Bend/Cram-18
87Clearw-1
88Readg/Pro-878
89Readg/Best-9
89Readg/Pro-660
89Readg/Star-19

Parker, Rob
87ColAst/Pro-10
87ColumAst-10

Parker, Stacy
89Butte/SP-1

Parker, Steve
87Peoria-24
88Pittsf/Pro-1369
89WinSal/Star-13

Parker, William David
(Billy)
72OPC-213R
72T-213R
73OPC-354
73T-354

Parkins, Rob
86WinHav-19

Parkinson, Eric
89Princet/Star-14

Parkinson, Frank J.
E120
V100

Parks, Danny
81Pawtu-6

Parks, Derek
87Kenosha-19
88BBAmer-12
88Orlan/Best-1
88SLAS-12
89Orlan/Best-19
89Orlan/Pro-1350

Parks, Jack
55T-23
55T/DH-68

Parks, Jeff
85Spoka/Cram-19

Parmalee, LeRoy
33G-239
35BU-94
R312
V355-20

Parmenter, Gary
86IowaC-21
87IowaC-7
88Pittsf/Pro-1378

Parnell, Mark
89AppFx/Pro-875

Parnell, Mel
50B-1
51FB
51T/RB-10
52B-241
52BR
52Dix
52StarCal/L-71A
52T-30
53B/Col-66
53Dix
53NB
53RM-AL25
53T-19
54Dix
54RM-AL8
54T-40
55RFG-28
55T-140
55T/DH-119
56T/Hocus-A18
57T-313
63MilSau-5
79TCMA-58
PM10/Sm-141
R423-77

Parrett, Jeff
86F/Up-U88
86Provigo-25
88D-406
88F/U-U102
88OPC-144
88T-588
89B-390
89D-334
89D/Best-296
89D/Tr-55
89F-389
89F/Up-112
89OPC-176
89Score-377
89Score/Tr-33
89Score/YS/I-18
89T-176
89T/St-73
89T/Tr-95T
89UD-398
89UD/Ext-741
90D-369
90F-570
90T-439
90UD-92

Parrill, Marty
78RochR

Parris, Steve
88CapeCod/Sum-43
89Batav/Pro-1923

Parrish, Lance M.
77Evansvl/TCMA-22
78T-708R
79T-469
80K-54
80OPC-110
80T-196
81Coke
81D-366
81F-467
81OPC-8
81T-15
81T-392
81T/SO-14
81T/St-73
82D-281
82F-276
82F/St-152
82OPC-214
82T-535
82T/St-188
83D-407
83D/AAS-50
83F-337
83K-40
83OPC-285
83T-285
83T-4M
83T/Gloss-27
83T/Gloss40-27
83T/St-193
83T/St-194
83T/St-63
84D-15
84D-49
84D/AAS-34
84F-637IA
84F-88
84FunFood/Pin-2
84Nes/792-640
84Nestle/DT-8
84OPC-158
84T-640
84T/Gloss40-2
84T/St-265
85Cain's-15
85D-49
85D/AAS-53
85Drake-23
85F-19
85F/St-31
85Leaf-41
85OPC-160
85Seven-13C
85Seven-14D
85T-160
85T-708AS
85T/Gloss22-20
85T/St-189
85T/St-259
85T/Super-55
85Wendy-17
86Cain's-14
86D-334
86F-234
86F/LL-31
86F/Mini-49
86F/St-85
86Jiffy-3
86Leaf-201
86OPC-147
86S-92
86S/Dec-72M
86T-36M
86T-740
86T/Gloss60-8
86T/Mini-15
86T/St-273
87D-91
87D/AAS-9
87D/OD-153
87D/PopUp-9
87F-160
87F/AwardWin-28
87F/U-U96
87Jiffy-13
87Leaf-107
87MSA/Discs-19
87OPC-374
87RedFoley/St-36
87S-101
87S-154M
87T-613AS
87T-791
87T/Board-19
87T/Gloss22-20
87T/Gloss60-58
87T/St-149
87T/St-269
87T/Tr-94T
88D-359
88D/Best-184
88F-310
88KayBee-22
88Leaf-130
88OPC-95
88Panini/St-355
88RedFoley/St-65
88Score-131
88Sf-143
88T-95
88T/Big-45
88T/St-123
89B-45
89D-278
89D/AS-55
89D/Best-59
89F-578
89F/Up-15
89OPC-114
89Score-95
89Score/Tr-36
89Sf-59
89T-470
89T/Big-250
89T/Tr-96T
89UD-240
89UD/Ext-775
90D-213
90F-141
90Score-35
90T-575
90UD-674

Parrish, Larry A.
76Ho-126
76OPC-141
76SSPC-326
76T-141
77OPC-72
77T-526
78OPC-153
78T-294
79OPC-357
79T-677
80OPC-182
80T-345
80T/S-53
81D-89
81F-146
81F/St-69
81OPC-15
81OPC/Post-4
81T/SO-89
81T/St-183
82D-466
82F-200
82F/St-34
82OPC-353
82OPC/Post-15
82T-445
82T/St-64
82T/Tr-86T
83D-467
83F-574
83OPC-2
83Rang-15
83T-776
83T/St-120
84D-21
84D-422
84D/AAS-42
84F-424
84Nes/792-169
84OPC-169
84Rang-15
84T-169
84T/St-354
85D-300
85D/AAS-29
85F-564
85F/St-38
85Leaf-96
85OPC-203
85Rang-15
85T-548
85T/St-346
86D-178
86F-569
86F/St-86
86Leaf-110
86OPC-238
86Rang-15
86T-238
86T/St-240
87Class-25
87Class-50
87D-469
87D/HL-10
87D/OD-173
87F-134
87F/GameWin-33

87F/LL-34
87F/Mini-81
87F/RecSet-29
87F/St-89
87Leaf-209
87Moth/Rang-5
87RedFoley/St-104
87S-174
87Smok/R-18
87T-629
87T/St-234
88ChefBoy-9
88D-347
88D/AS-21
88D/Best-334
88F-476
88F/Mini-57
88F/RecSet-28
88F/St-68
88F/TL-25
88F/U-U7
88KingB/Disc-21
88Leaf-119
88Moth/R-5
88OPC-226
88Panini/St-205
88RedFoley/St-66
88Score-191
88Score/Tr-65T
88Sf-49
88Smok/R-14
88T-490
88T/St-243
88T/UK-56
89F-94
89Score-495
89T-354
89UD-36

Parrot, Steve
82ElPas-19
83ElPas-16

Parrott, Mike
79OPC-300
79T-576
80T-443
81Pol/Mar-10
81T-187
82D-226
82T-358
83Omaha-7
84Omaha-11
85OKCty-12
86OKCty-17
88Rockford-27
89Rockford-27CO

Parrotte, Brian
89Bill/Pro-2050

Parry, Bob
88Madis-17
89Modesto/Cal-286
89Modesto/Ch-31

Parry, Dave
82Tucso-28M

Parsons, Bill
59DF

Parsons, Bill
72K-5
72OPC-281
72T-281
73OPC-231
73T-231
74OPC-574
74T-574
75OPC-613
75T-613
75T/M-613

Parsons, Bob
78Salem

Parsons, Casey R.
(Casey)
78Cr/PCL-42
79Phoen
80Phoen-13
81Spoka-26
82F-515
82SLCty-15
85Louvl-27
86Louisvl-22
87BuffB-9
88Memph/Best-9

Parsons, Charles
N172

Parsons, Scott
87LasVegas-5

Parsons, Thomas
62T-326
65T-308R

Partee, Roy Robert
(Roy)
47TipTop
49B-149

Partin, Billy
89Sumter/Pro-1089

Partley, Calvin
74Cedar

Partrick, Dave
89QuadC/Best-24

Partridge, Glenn
77BurlB

Pascarella, Andy
79Newar-24

Paschall, Bill
77Jaxvl
80T-667R
81Omaha-11

Pascual, Camilo Jr.
83Idaho-10

Pascual, Camilo
55T-84
55T/DH-104
56T-98
57T-211
58T-219
59T-291
59T-413
60Bz-14
60L-4
60T-483
60T-569AS
60T/tatt
60T/tatt-43
61Clover-20
61NuCard-411
61P-99
61Peters-23
61T-235
61T/Dice-12
61T/St-183
62J-91
62P-91
62P/Can-91
62Salada-78
62Shirriff-78
62T-230
62T-59
62T/bucks
62T/St-78
63Bz-13
63Exh
63J-9
63P-9
63Salada-36
63T-10LL
63T-220
63T-8LL
64Bz-13
64T-2LL
64T-4LL
64T-500
64T/Coins-137AS
64T/Coins-76
64T/S-32
64T/St-92
64T/SU
64T/tatt
65OPC-11LL
65OPC-255
65T-11LL
65T-255
65T/trans-23
66T-305
67OPC-71
67T-71
68T-395
69MB-214
69MLB/St-107
69T-513
69T/decal
69T/S-31
69T/St-240
69Trans-27
70OPC-254
70T-254
78TCMA-32
Exh47

Pashnick, Larry
81Evans-5
83D-233
83Evans-8
83F-338
84D-394

Pasillas, Andy
77AppFx
78Knoxv
79Knoxv/TCMA-20
80GlenF/B-15
80GlenF/C-6
81GlenF-10

Paskert, George H.
(Dode)
10Domino-96
11Helmar-150
12Sweet/Pin-130A
12Sweet/Pin-130B
14Piedmont/St-47
BF2-89
D327
D328-130
D329-136
D350/2-135
E135-130
E254
E270
M101/4-136
M101/5-135
M116
S74-103
T202
T204
T205
T206
T207
T213/blue
T213/brown
T215/blue
T215/brown
T3-112
V100
W514-55

Pasley, Kevin P.
(Kevin)
77T-476R
78T-702R
80Syrac-3
81Syrac-8
82BirmB-17

Pasqua, Dan
84Nashvl-16
85Colum-21
85Colum/Pol-17
85D-637
85F/Up-U86
86Colum-17
86Colum/Pol-15
86D-417
86F-114
86KayBee-22
86Leaf-195
86T-259
86T/Gloss60-20
87Class-13
87D-474
87D/OD-244
87F-108
87F/Mini-79
87OPC-74
87S-143
87T-74
87T/St-297
88Coke/WS-19
88D-463
88D/Best-137
88F-217
88F/U-U18
88OPC-207
88Panini/St-159
88Score-196
88Score/Tr-56T
88T-691
88T/Big-164
88T/Tr-82T
89B-67
89Coke/WS-19
89D-294
89D/Best-123
89F-507
89OPC-31
89Panini/St-313
89Score-338
89T-558
89T/Big-44
89T/St-301
89UD-204
90D-176
90F-544
90Score-306
90T-446
90UD-286

Pasquali, Jeff
83Erie-13

Passalacqua, Ricky
76Watlo

Passeau, Claude
39Exh

Passero, Joe
45Centen-20

Passmore, Jay
76BurlB
77BurlB

Pastore, Frank
78Indianap-23
80T-677R
81F-204
81OPC-1
81T-499
82Coke/Reds
82D-122
82F-80
82F/St-13
82T-128
83D-62
83F-599
83OPC-119
83T-658
84D-164
84F-477
84Nes/792-87
84OPC-87
84T-87
85D-550
85F-545
85OPC-292
85T-727
86F-185
86T-314
86T/Tr-85T
87OKCty-4
87T-576

Pastorius, James
E103
E90/1
E93
T206
W555

Pastornicky, Cliff
81CharR-16
82CharR-21
83Omaha-17
84Omaha-21
86Water-19

Pastors, Greg
82Buffa-5
83LynnP-16

Pastrovich, Steve
80GlenF/B-1
80GlenF/C-16
81AppFx-8
82AppFx-11
83GlenF-18

Patchett, Hal
45Centen-21

Patchin, Steve
75Water
80Evans-22

Pate, Robert Wayne
(Bobby)
81D-545
81OPC-136R
81T-479R
83Tucso-21
87BurlEx-23

Patek, Freddie Joe
69T-219
70OPC-94
70T-94
71MLB/St-425
71OPC-626
71T-626
72MB-266
72T-531
73OPC-334
73T-334
74OPC-88
74T-88
74T/St-186
75Ho-32
75Ho/Twink-32
75OPC-48
75T-48
75T/M-48
76A&P/KC
76OPC-167
76SSPC-170
76T-167
77Ho-109
77K-36
77OPC-244
77T-422
78Ho-48
78OPC-4LL
78OPC-91
78T-204
78T-274
79Ho-46
79K-36
79OPC-273
79T-525
80OPC-356
80T-705
81D-170
81F-283
81T-311
82D-241
82F-471
82T-602

Patrick, Bronswell
89Madis/Star-18

Patrick, Dave
89QuadC/GS-9

Patrick, Hisel
59DF
Patrick, Ron
77Ashev
Pattee, Harry Ernest
(Harry)
T206
Patten, Case
WG2-40
Patterson, Bob
83Beaum-7
84Cram/PCL-221
85Cram/PCL-117
86Hawai-19
87D/OD-166
88BuffB/CMC-7
88BuffB/Pro-1467
88F-337
88T-522
89BuffB/Pro-1684
Patterson, Daryl
68OPC-113R
68T-113R
69OPC-101
69T-101
70T-592
71MLB/St-402
71OPC-481
71T-481
88Domino-19
Patterson, Dave
77LodiD
79Albuq-6
80Albuq-10
80T-679R
81Albuq/TCMA-2
82Tacom-8
86Cram/PCL-12
87Clint-3
88CalLgAS-1
88SanJose/Cal-126
88SanJose/Pro-111
89Shreve/Pro-1843
Patterson, Gil
77T-472R
Patterson, Glenn
87Gasto-2
88Gasto/Pro-1021
Patterson, Greg
88WinSal/Star-14
89Geneva/Pro-1882
Patterson, Jeff
89Martins/Star-23
Patterson, Jimmy
52Wheat
Patterson, Joe
62Pep/Tul
63Pep/Tul
Patterson, Ken
82CharR-16
86FtLaud-17
87FtLaud-30
88Vanco/CMC-6
88Vanco/Pro-757
89Coke/WS-20
89D/Rook-37
89F-508
89Score/HotRk-61
89Score/Tr-97
89T-434
90D-371
90F-545
90Score-207
90Score/100Ris-89
90T-156
Patterson, Larry
80LynnS-2
81Spoka-23
82Holyo-12
83Nashua-11
Patterson, Michael L.
79Ogden/TCMA-24
80WHave-15
82Colum-20
82Colum/Pol-14
83Colum-22
Patterson, Pat
78Laugh/Black-18
Patterson, Reggie
80GlenF/B-9
80GlenF/C-18
82Edmon-15
82T-599R
83IowaC-7
84IowaC-31
86F-376
Patterson, Rick
77Wausa
Patterson, Rick
88Utica/Puc-26
89SoBend/GS-2
Patterson, Roy
E107
Patterson, Scott
80Ander-9
81Durhm-22
82Colum-19
82Colum/Pol-11
83Nashvl-15
84Colum-14
84Colum/Pol-18
85Albany-10
86Colum-18
86Colum/Pol-16
Pattin, Marty
69Sunoco/Pin-14
69T-563
70McDon-6
70OPC-31
70T-31
71MLB/St-447
71OPC-579
71T-579
72OPC-144
72T-144
73OPC-415
73T-415
74OPC-583
74T-583
74T/St-187
75OPC-413
75T-413
75T/M-413
76OPC-492
76SSPC-162
76T-492
77T-658
78T-218
79T-129
80T-26
81D-343
81F-37
81T-389
Pattison, James
R314/Can
Patton, Eric
89Helena/SP-20
Patton, Jack
88Bakers/Cal-266
89Reno/Cal-263GM
Patton, Jeff
84PrWill-17
Patton, Owen
N172
Paul, Mike
69T-537
70T-582
71MLB/St-381
71OPC-454
71T-454
72MB-267
72T-577
73OPC-58
73T-58
74OPC-399
74T-399
85Cram/PCL-208
86Vanco-21CO
Paula, Carlos C.
(Carlos)
55T-97
56T-4
56T/Pin-58
58Union
79TCMA-205
Paulesic, David
66Pep/Tul
Paulino, Elvin
87Peoria-17
88Peoria/Ko-24
89Peoria/Ko-24
Paulino, Luis
87Hagers-14
88Hagers/Star-15
89Freder/Star-20
Paulino, Victor
84Savan-19
Paulis, George
89Watlo/Star-28
Pautt, Juan
83Pawtu-23
84Pawtu-12
Pavlas, Dave
86WinSal-18
87Pittsf-15
88TexLgAS/GS-21
88Tulsa-23
89OkCty/CMC-8
89OkCty/Pro-1529
Pavletich, Donald S.
(Don)
59T-494
62T-594R
63FrBauer-18
65T-472
66OPC-196
66T-196
67Kahn
67T-292
68OPC-108
68T-108
69MB-215
69OPC-179
69T-179
70OPC-504
70T-504
71MLB/St-326
71OPC-409
71T-409
72OPC-359
72T-359
Pavlick, Greg
78Tidew
79Tidew-20
84Jacks-10
88Kahn/Mets-52
89Kahn/Mets-52
Pavlik, John
84PrWill-9
Pavlik, Roger
87Gasto-15
88Gasto/Pro-1020
Pawling, Eric
86Clint-17
86Cram/PCL-193
Pawlowski, John
86Penin-19
87BirmB/Best-17
88Coke/WS-20
88D-457
89Vanco/CMC-7
89Vanco/Pro-595
90Score-617
Paxton, Mike
78T-216
79OPC-54
79T-122
80T-388
80Tacom-27
81Charl-5
81F-401
Payne, Frederick T.
(Fred)
E90/3
M116
S74-8
T201
T202
T205
T206
Payne, Jim
79Wausa-24
81Wisco-17
Payne, Joe
V362-15
Payne, Larry
76Indianap-2
77Indianap-7
78Indianap-13
Payne, Mike
80Ander-15
81Durhm-23
82Durhm-19
85Richm-6
87Jaxvl-16
Paynter, Billy
88Wythe/Pro-1983
89Peoria/Ko-13
Payton, Dave
87Erie-21
88Sprin/Best-15
89Sprin/Best-15
Payton, Ray
88MidwLAS/GS-49
89Saraso/Star-17
Pazik, Mike
76OPC-597R
76T-597
77T-643
80GlenF/B-24MG
80GlenF/C-21MG
82AppFx-30
88CharlK-14
88CharlK/Pep-14
Peacock, John Gaston
(Johnny)
39PB-16
40PB-34
Pearce, Jim
55T-170
Pearce, Steve
77Cedar
Pearn, Joe
87PortChar-27
88Gasto/Pro-1006
Pearse, Steve
88Rockford-30
89Rockford-28
Pearsey, Les
81Holyo-19
82Spoka-18
Pearson, Albert G.
(Albie)
58T-317
59T-4
60T-241
61T-288
62J-78
62P-78
62P/Can-78
62Salada-63A
62Salada-63B
62Shirriff-63
62T-343
62T/St-67
63F-19
63J-29
63P-29
63T-182
64T-110
64T/Coins-111
64T/Coins-132AS
64T/S-23
64T/St-42
64T/SU
64T/tatt
64Wheat/St-33
65T-358
66OPC-83
66T-83
78TCMA-16
Exh47
Pearson, Darren
85Evrt/Cram-13A
85Evrt/Cram-13B
86Clint-18
Pearson, Don
77Wausa
78Wausa
Pearson, Ike
47Centen-19
Pearson, Kevin
87Tampa-6
88Greens/Pro-1560
89Chatt/Best-18
89Chatt/GS-20
89Nashvl-18
Pearson, Monte
37OPC-131
39PB-71
40PB-5
R310
V300
V355-114
Pearson, Steve
88SLCty-16M
Pechek, Wayne
76Cedar
81Phoen-19
Peck, Hal
49B-182
Peckinpaugh, Roger
14CJ-91
15CJ-91
21Exh-125
21Exh-126
61F-132
86Conlon/1-37
D327
D328-131
D329-137
D350/2-136
E120
E121/120
E121/80
E122
E135-131
E210
E220
M101/4-137
M101/5-136
V100
V117-23
W502-56
W514-44
W516-20
W575
WG7-40
Pecota, Bill
82FtMyr-21
84Memph-24
85Omaha-29
86Omaha-17
86Omaha/TCMA-12
87F/U-U97
88D-466
88F-264
88Score-377
88Smok/Royals-22
88T-433

89F-289
89Omaha/CMC-15
89Score-339
89T-148
89T/Big-292
89UD-507
Peden, Les
53T-256
Pedersen, Mark
81Wausa-6
Pederson, Don
89NiagFls/Puc-1
Pederson, Stu
82VeroB-24
85Cram/PCL-167
86Albuq-19
87Albuq/Pol-29
89Syrac/CMC-16
89Syrac/Pro-798
Pedraza, Nelson
83Watlo/LF-7
85Water-1
Pedre, Jorge
88AppFx/Pro-137
88MidwLAS/GS-37
89BBCity/Star-20
Pedrique, Alfredo
82Jacks-16
84Jacks-23
85IntLgAS-14
85Tidew-24
86Tidew-24
88D-361
88F-338
88Panini/St-375
88Score-301
88T-294
88T/JumboR-17
88T/St-128
88T/St-304
88ToysRUs-23
89B-104
89Mara/Tigers-17
89Score-614
89T-566
89T-699TL
Peek, Timothy
88Spart/Pro-1027
88Spart/Star-15
88Spart/Star-15
Peel, Homer
34G-88
Peel, Jack
87CharWh-24
88Tampa/Star-20
89Saraso/Star-18
Peguero, Jerry
87Modesto-17
88Huntsvl/BK-14
Peguero, Jose
89Beloi/Star-21
Peguero, Julio
87Macon-16
88CLAS/Star-14
88Salem/Star-15
89Harris/Pro-294
89Harris/Star-13
Peguero, Pablo
77LodiD
78Cr/PCL-114
79Albuq-1
80Albuq-3
Pegues, Steve
88Fay/Pro-1081
89Fay/Pro-1594
Peitz, Henry
E107
E254
Pellagrini, Ed
49B-172
51B-292
52T-405
53T-28
Pellant, Gary
80LynnS-14
82Wausa-23
83Wausa/LF-3
Pellegrino, Tony
86Cram/PCL-172
88Charl/Pro-1194
89AubAs/Pro-3
89Wich/Roc-12
Pells, Harry
76QuadC
77QuadC
Peltier, Dan
89Butte/SP-27
Pelty, Barney
10Domino-97
11Helmar-63
12Sweet/Pin-54
E286
M116
S74-35
T202
T204
T205
T206
T207
T215/blue
T215/brown
Peltz, Peter
81GlenF-14
Pemberton, Jose
87Elmir-26
87Elmir/Red-26
Pemberton, Rudy
89Brist/Star-20
Pena, Abelino
75BurlB
76BurlB
Pena, Adriano
81Wisco-8
Pena, Alejandro
79Clint
81Albuq/TCMA-4
82Pol/Dodg
82Pol/Dodg-26
83Pol/Dodg-26
83T/X-83
84D-250
84F-109
84Nes/792-324
84Pol/Dodg-26
84T-324
84T/St-82
85D-337
85F-379
85F/St-94
85Leaf-64
85OPC-110
85Seven-15W
85T-110
85T/Gloss40-33
85T/St-73
85T/Super-17
86F-140
86Pol/Dodg-26
86T-665
87F-449
87Moth/Dodg-18
87OPC-363
87Pol/Dodg-13
87T-787
88D-598
88F/U-U97
88Moth/Dodg-18
88Pol/Dodg-26
88T-277
89D-557
89F-69
89Moth/Dodg-18
89Pol/Dodg-16
89Score-389
89T-57
89UD-137
90D-664
90F-405
90Score-39
90T-483
90UD-279
Pena, Bert
81Tucso-7
82Tucso-1
83Tucso-17
84Cram/PCL-67
86Tucso-18
87Moth/Ast-24
87Tucso-16
88Colum/CMC-13
88Colum/Pol-16
88Colum/Pro-322
Pena, Dan
87VeroB-4
88Bakers/Cal-257
Pena, George
73OPC-601R
73T-601R
75Iowa/TCMA-13
Pena, Geronimo
87Savan-4
88FSLAS/Star-16
88StPet/Star-21
Pena, Hipolito
86Nashua-21
87Vanco-18
88Colum/CMC-7
88Colum/Pol-8
88Colum/Pro-315
89Colum/CMC-5
89Colum/Pol-18
89Colum/Pro-744
89D-598
89F-263
89T-109
Pena, Jaime
89Erie/Star-17
Pena, James
86Cram/PCL-14
87Clint-19
89SanJose/Best-16
89SanJose/Cal-216
89SanJose/Pro-445
89SanJose/Star-21
Pena, Jose
69T-339R
70OPC-523
70T-523
71MLB/St-112
71OPC-693
71T-693
72OPC-322
72T-322
86Clint-19
88Shreve/Pro-1292
88Utica/Puc-23
89Shreve/Pro-1848
Pena, Luis
86Macon-18
Pena, Manny
83Orlan-13
Pena, Orlando
59T-271
63T-214
64T-124
65T-311
66T-239
67T-449
68T-471
69T/St-97
73JP
74OPC-393
74T-393
75OPC-573
75T-573
75T/M-573
75Tucso-12
Pena, Pedro
89Medford/Best-11
Pena, R. Roberto
65T-549R
66T-559
69OPC-184
69T-184
70OPC-44
70T-44
71MLB/St-448
71OPC-334
71T-334
Pena, Ramon
86GlenF-18
87GlenF-20
88Toled/CMC-6
88Toled/Pro-610
89Mara/Tigers-18
89Toled/CMC-2
89Toled/Pro-779
Pena, Tony
77Salem
80Port-24
81T-551R
82D-124
82F-490
82F/St-72
82T-138
83D-59
83D/AAS-35
83F-316
83OPC-133
83T-590
83T/St-281
84D-186
84D/AAS-3
84F-259
84FunFood/Pin-88
84Nes/792-645
84Nestle/DT-19
84OPC-152
84Seven-18E
84T-645
84T/St-129
85D-24
85D-64
85D/AAS-10
85D/DKsuper-24
85F-472
85F/LimEd-24
85Leaf-24DK
85OPC-358
85T-358
85T/St-124
86BK/AP-1
86D-64
86D/AAS-22
86F-616
86F/LimEd-34
86F/Mini-119
86F/St-87
86Leaf-58
86OPC-260
86S-165
86S/Dec-72M
86T-260
86T/St-125
87BK-15
87Class-34
87D-115
87D/AAS-46
87D/OD-64
87F-617
87F/Lim-31
87F/LL-35
87F/McCror-32
87F/St-90
87F/U-U98
87Ho/St-14
87Kraft-12
87Leaf-256
87MnM's-2
87MSA/Discs-5
87OPC-60
87RedFoley/St-25
87S-151M
87S-93
87Smok/Cards-11
87T-60
87T/Coins-39
87T/St-129
87T/Tr-95T
88D-170
88D/Best-156
88F-45
88F/WS-5M
88Leaf-95
88OPC-117
88Panini/St-387
88Panini/St-447IA
88Panini/St-449IA
88RedFoley/St-67
88Score-48
88Sf-142
88Smok/Card-13
88T-410
88T/St-52
89B-435
89Cadaco-38
89D-163
89D/Best-299
89F-460
89KMart/DT-30
89OPC-94
89Panini/St-180
89Score-36
89Smok/Cards-17
89T-715
89T/St-38
89UD-330
90D-181
90F-256
90Score-122
90T-115
90UD-276
Penafeather, Pat
88AubAs/Pro-1952
Pendergast, Steve
W514-117
Pendleton, Jim
52Park-69
53JC-25
53T-185
54JC-3
54T-165
55Gol/Braves-25
55JC-2
55T-15
55T/DH-33
57T-327
58T-104
59T-174
62T-432
89Smok/Ast-25
Pendleton, Terry
83ArkTr-15
84Louvl-15
85D-534
85F-236
85OPC-346
85T-346
86D-205
86F-44
86KAS/Disc-14
86KayBee-23
86Leaf-137
86OPC-321
86Schnucks-19
86T-528
86T/St-53
87D-183
87D/OD-62
87F-306

87Leaf-124
87OPC-8
87Smok/Cards-16
87T-8
87T/St-54
88D-454
88D/Best-187
88F-46
88F/AwardWin-28
88F/SS-27
88F/St-119
88Leaf-246
88OPC-105
88Panini/St-392
88RedFoley/St-68
88Score-190
88Sf-159
88Smok/Card-17
88T-635
88T/Big-53
88T/St-49
88T/St/Backs-7
89B-437
89D-230
89D/Best-156
89F-461
89OPC-375
89Panini/St-185
89Score-137
89Sf-99
89Smok/Cards-18
89T-375
89T/Big-151
89T/St-42
89UD-131
90D-299
90F-257
90Score-208
90Sf-174
90T-725
90UD-469

Penigar, C.L.
86Clint-20
88MidldA/GS-17
89BirmB/Best-23
89BirmB/Pro-115

Penland, Ken
88Butte-6

Penn, Trevor
88Rockford-28
89Rockford-29
89WPalm/Star-21

Penniall, David
77StPet
80ArkTr-10

Pennington, Brad
89Bluef/Star-18

Pennington, Ken
87Sumter-23
88Durhm/Star-16
89Durhm/Star-17
89Star/Wax-72

Pennock, Herb
28Yueng-8
31Exh/4-25
33Exh/4-13
33G-138
50Callahan
60Exh/HOF-19
60F-35
61F-133
63Bz/Sm
80Cram/Leg-111
80Laugh/FFeat-2
80SSPC/HOF
86Conlon/1-51
89HOF/St-67
E120
E210-8
E220
R315-A28
R315-B28
R316
R423-84
V100
V117-27
V354-16
W502-8
W513-68

Pennye, Darwin
88Watertn/Puc-23
89Aug/Pro-504

Pennyfeather, William
89Well/Puc-1

Penrod, Jack
88Poca/Pro-2102

Penson, Paul
54T-236

Penton, Jack
28Exh/PCL-6

Pentz, Gene
77T-308
78BK/A-11
78T-64
79Portl-12
80Port-25
81Phoen-20

Penvose, Randy
86Geneva-22

Peoples, James
N172
N284

Pepitone, Joe
62T-596R
63T-183
64T-360
64T/Coins-121AS
64T/St-22
64Wheat/St-34
65OPC-245
65T-245
66OPC-79
66T-79
67OPC/PI-22
67T-340
67T/PI-22
68Bz-5
68OPC-195
68T-195
69MB-216
69MLB/St-76
69MLBPA/Pin-21
69Sunoco/Pin-7
69T-589
69T/St-206
70K-59
70MLB/St-45
70T-598
70T-90
71MLB/St-40
71OPC-90
71T/GM-53
72MB-268
72OPC-303
72OPC-304IA
72T-303
72T-304
73OPC-580
73T-580
78TCMA-6
PM10/Sm-142
WG10-17
WG9-19

Pepper, Hugh
(Laurin)
55T-147
56T-108

Pepper, Tony
75Phoen-18

Pequignot, Jon
86VeroB-19
87SnAnt-19

Peralta, Amado
85Tigres-21

Peralta, Martin
88SLCty-22

Peraza, Luis
86AppFx-18

Peraza, Oswald
86Knoxv-18
87Knoxv-18
88French-23
88Score/Tr-77T
89B-1
89D-524
89F-615
89Score-571
89T-297
89T/Big-219
89UD-651

Perconte, Jack
77LodiD
79Albuq-13
80Albuq-16
81Albuq/TCMA-17
81T-302R
82T/Tr-87T
82Wheat/Ind
83Charl-13
83D-463
83F-417
83T-569
84F/X-90
84Moth/Mar-15
85D-74
85F-498
85Leaf-221
85Moth/Mar-11
85T-172
85T/St-341
86F-472
86T-146
87Albuq/Pol-20

Perdomo, Felix
83Greens-21
86Columbia-19
87Lynch-12
88Jacks/GS-24

Perdue, Alphie
77Salem

Perdue, Doran
81Shrev-15

Perdue, Hubbard
14CJ-121
15CJ-121
T206
T207
T213/brown
T222

Pereira, Ray
84LitFalls-8

Perez, Alex
88Keno/Pro-1385

Perez, Beban
89QuadC/Best-28
89QuadC/GS-23

Perez, Benny
78Duned

Perez, Carlos
75QuadC
78Cr/PCL-99
79SLCty-18
80SLCty-13
81SLCty-10

Perez, David
89Butte/SP-2

Perez, Dick
85D/DKsuper-28

Perez, Eduardo
89Sumter/Pro-1112

Perez, Eulogio
88Martins/Star-27
89Martins/Star-24

Perez, Francisco
86Erie-23
89Ashvl/Pro-963
89AubAs/Pro-2174

Perez, Fred
85Utica-21

Perez, Gorky
87Ashvl-26
87AubAs-15
88Ashvl/Pro-1062
89Osceola/Star-17

Perez, Hector
82Madis-32
83Madis/LF-29TR
84LitFalls-17
86Lynch-16
87Lynch-10
89Penin/Star-18

Perez, Joel
77AppFx
79Knoxv/TCMA-16

Perez, Julio
80GlenF-16
83Readg-16
86Macon-19
87Macon-14
88Mia/Star-18
89Harris/Pro-307
89Harris/Star-14

Perez, Leo
88Beloi/GS-18
89Stock/Best-13
89Stock/Cal-158
89Stock/Pro-373

Perez, Manuel R.
48Sommer-17
49Sommer-8

Perez, Mario
85Bend/Cram-19

Perez, Marty
71OPC-529R
71T-529R
72OPC-119
72T-119
73OPC-144
73T-144
74OPC-374
74T-374
75OPC-499
75T-499
75T/M-499
76Dubuq
76Ho-65
76K-26
76OPC-177
76T-177
77OPC-183
77T-438
78Ho-4
78T-613
78Tidew

Perez, Melido
86BurlEx-17
88Coke/WS-21
88D-589
88D/Best-179
88D/Rook-21
88F-265
88F/U-U19
88Score/Tr-108T
88T/Tr-83T
89B-59
89Class-88
89Coke/WS-21
89D-58
89D/Best-179
89F-509
89OPC-88
89Panini/St-300
89RedFoley/St-89
89Score-386
89Score/HotRk-79
89Score/YS/I-7
89Sf-118
89T-786
89T/Big-235
89T/JumboR-16
89T/St-296
89ToysRUs-21
89UD-243
90D-101
90F-546
90Score-311
90T-621
90UD-525

Perez, Michael I.
87Sprin/Best-15
88ArkTr/GS-21
89ArkTr/GS-17

Perez, Paco
79Jacks-1

Perez, Pascual
77Charl
79Portl-20
80Port-7
81Portl-20
81T-551R
82Portl-7
82F-491
82T-383
83D-557
83F-144
83Pol/Atl-27
83T/X-84
84D-507
84F-188
84F/St-59
84Nes/792-675
84OPC-1
84Pol/Atl-27
84T-675
84T/St-36
85D-507
85D/AAS-18
85F-337
85Ho/Braves-18
85Leaf-55
85OPC-106
85Pol/Atl-27
85T-106
86F-524
86T-491
87D/HL-50
87Indianap-26
88D-591
88D/Best-236
88F-192
88Leaf-248
88OPC-237
88Score-459
88T-647
88T/Big-196
89B-354
89Class-85
89D-248
89D/Best-302
89F-390
89OPC-73
89Panini/St-115
89Score-299
89T-73
89T/St-71
89UD-498
90D-342
90F-358
90Score-486
90T-278
90UD-487

Perez, Ramon
73Cedar
74Cedar
75Iowa/TCMA-14
78Charl
79Charl-9

Perez, Segio
86Clearw-19

Perez, Tony
65T-581R
66OPC-72
66T-72
67Kahn
67T-476
68Bz-12
68Kahn
68OPC-130
68T-130
68T/3D
69Kahn
69MB-217
69MLB/St-134
69T-295
69T/St-28
70MLB/St-34
70OPC-380
70OPC-63LL
70T-380
70T-63
70T/SO
71K-58
71MD
71MLB/St-67
71OPC-580
71OPC-64LL
71OPC-66LL
71T-580
71T-64
71T-66
71T/Coins-105
71T/GM-14
71T/S-6
71T/tatt-9
72MB-269
72OPC-80
72T-80
73OPC-275
73T-275
74OPC-230
74T-230
74T/DE-54
74T/St-29
75Ho-127
75OPC-560
75T-560
75T/M-560
76Crane-46
76Ho-86
76Icee
76MSA/Disc
76OPC-195LL
76OPC-325
76SSPC-39
76T-195
76T-325
77OPC-135
77T-655
77T/CS-37
78OPC-90
78T-15
78Wiffle/Discs-59
79OPC-261
79T-495
80OPC-69
80T-125
81Coke
81D-334
81F-241
81F/St-66
81K-17
81OPC-231
81T-275
81T/HT
81T/SO-8
81T/St-44
82Coke/BOS
82D-408
82F-302
82F/St-170
82OPC-255
82OPC-256IA
82T-255
82T-256A
82T/St-152
83D-578
83F-191
83OPC-355
83OPC-74SV
83T-715
83T-716A
83T/St-8
83T/X-85
84Borden-24
84D-503
84D/Champs-29
84F-44
84F-636IA
84F/X-91
84FunFood/Pin-99
84Nes/792-385
84Nes/792-702LL
84Nes/792-703LL
84Nes/792-704LL
84OPC-385
84T-385
84T-702
84T-703
84T-704
84T/St-126
84T/X-91
85CircK-28
85D/HL-9
85F-546
85OPC-212
85T-675
86D-15
86D-428
86D/DKsuper-15
86F-186
86Leaf-15DK
86OPC-85
86S-138M
86T-205RB
86T-85
86T/St-143
86T/St-8
86TexGold-24
87F-209
88Kahn/Reds-CO

Perez, Vladimir
87Spart-23
88LitFalls/Puc-19
89Clmbia/Best-2
89Clmbia/GS-20

Perez, William
89Modesto/Ch-14

Perez, Yorkis
86Kenosha-19
87WPalm-16
88Jaxvl/Best-11
88Jaxvl/Pro-973
89WPalm/Star-17

Perezchica, Tony
84Evrt/Cram-30B
86Fresn/Smok-20
87Shrev-6
88AAA/Pro-32
88Phoen/CMC-16
88Phoen/Pro-75
89F-338
89Phoen/CMC-14
89Phoen/Pro-1502
89Score/HotRk-50

Perkins, Broderick
79T-725R
80Hawai-22
81D-525
81F-498
81T-393
81T/St-226
82D-397
82F-579
82F/St-103
82OPC-192
82T-192
82T/St-98
83D-121
83F-368
83T-593
83T/St-292
83T/X-86
83Wheat/Ind-24
84D-276
84F-548
84Nes/792-212
84T-212
84Wheat/Ind-15
85T-609

Perkins, Harold
82VeroB-19
83VeroB-20
89RochR/CMC-18
89RochR/Pro-1643

Perkins, Ralph
(Cy)
21Exh-127
25Exh-110
26Exh-110
E120
E210-29
E220
V100
V355-24
V61-11
W572
W573

Perkins, Ray
82AubAs-5
86FSLAS-38
86Miami-20

Perkins, Tom
75Clint

Perkowski, Harry
52B-202
52T-142
53B/Col-87
53T-236
54B-44
54T-125
55T-184

Perlman, Jon
83IowaC-8
84IowaC-6
85IowaC-19
86Phoen-20
87Phoen-13
88ColSp/CMC-6
88ColSp/Pro-1542
88F-93
88F/U-U22
89Score-591
89T-476

Perlozzo, Sam
78T-704R
79Hawai-11
79T-709R
81Tidew-22
83Lynch-11
84Jacks-16
86Tidew-23MG
88Kahn/Mets-34CO
89Kahn/Mets-34CO

Perno, Donn
87Everett-23

Pernoll, H. Hub
M116

Perodin, Ron
80Clint-21

Perozo, Danny
88Bill/Pro-1813
89Bill/Pro-2058
89Greens/Pro-409

Perozo, Ender
89Elmir/Puc-13

Perranoski, Ron
61T-525
62BB-16
62T-297
63T-403
64T-30
64T/Coins-64
64T/St-46
64T/tatt
64Wheat/St-35
65T-484
66T-555
67T-197
68T-435
68T-435
69OPC-77
69T-77
69T/St-197
70MLB/St-237
70OPC-226
70T-226
71MLB/St-469
71OPC-475
71T-475
71T/Coins-104
72OPC-367
72T-367
WG10-42
WG9-41

Perrier, Hip
N172/PCL

Perring, George
14CJ-119
15CJ-119
M116
T206

Perritt, William D.
(Pol)
D327
D328-132
E135-132

Perry, Alonzo
49Remar

Perry, Bob
86Kenosha-20

Perry, David
89Boise/Pro-1981

Perry, Eric
88CharWh/Best-7
88Geneva/Pro-1633
89Peoria/Ko-19

Perry, Gaylord
61Union
62T-199
62T/bucks
63T-169R
64T-468
65OPC-193
65T-193
66T-598
67T-236LL
67T-320
68Coke
68OPC-11LL
68OPC-85
68T-11LL
68T-85
69MB-218
69MLB/St-207
69T-485
69T/St-110
70K-20
70MLB/St-132
70T-560
71K-6
71MD
71MLB/St-261
71OPC-140
71OPC-70LL
71T-140
71T-70LL
71T/Coins-73
71T/S-2
72MB-270
72OPC-285
72T-285
73K-38
73OPC-346KP
73OPC-400
73OPC-66LL
73T-346BP
73T-400
73T-66LL
73T/Comics-14
73T/Lids-39
73T/PinUps-14
74OPC-35
74T-35
74T/St-168
75Ho-84
75K-45
75OPC-530
75T-530
75T/M-530
76Ho-4
76Ho/Twink-4
76OPC-204LL
76OPC-55
76T-204LL
76T-55
77Ho-73
77OPC-149
77T-152
78Ho-139
78T-686
78Wiffle/Discs-60
79Ho-83
79K-49
79OPC-161
79T-321
79T-5LL
80OPC-148
80T-280
81D-471
81F-91
81Pol/Atl-46
81T-582
81T/Tr-812
82D-543
82F-445
82F/St-67
82OPC-115
82T-115
82T/St-24
82T/Tr-88T
83D-307
83D/AAS-28
83F-483
83F-630M
83Nalley-1
83OPC-159SV
83OPC-96
83T-463
83T-464A
83T/St-114
84D-LLA
84D/Champs-32
84F-352
84F-638IA
84F-641
84F/St-98
84Moth/Giants-4
84Nes/792-4HL
84Nes/792-6HL
84T-4
84T-6
89Pac/Leg-152
PM10/Sm-143

Perry, Gerald
82ArkTr-6
82Richm-14
83Richm-14
84D-263
84F/X-92

84Pol/Atl-28
84T/X-92
85D-443
85F-338
85Ho/Braves-19
85Pol/Atl-28
85T-219
86D-165
86F-525
86Richm-16
86T-557
87Smok/Atl-17
87T-639
88D-437
88D/Best-58
88F-547
88Leaf-216
88Panini/St-242
88Score-136
88T-39
88T/Big-40
89B-273
89Cadaco-39
89Class-118
89D-22DK
89D-239
89D/AS-57
89D/Best-291
89D/DKsuper-22DK
89D/MVP-BC24
89F-597
89F-638M
89F/BBAS-31
89F/BBMVP's-31
89F/Heroes-30
89OPC-130
89Panini/St-40
89RedFoley/St-90
89Score-101
89Score/HotSt-20
89Sf-164
89T-130
89T/Big-279
89T/Coins-21
89T/Mini-2
89T/St-33
89T/UK-59
89UD-431
90D-153
90F-592
90Score-249
90T-792
90UD-101

Perry, Herbert Scott
E220
E270/1

Perry, Jeff
84Savan-14
87Visal-7

Perry, Jim
59Kahn
59T-542
60Kahn
60L-49
60T-324
61Bz-22
61Kahn
61P-59
61T-385
61T-48LL
61T-584AS
61T/St-138
62J-43
62Kahn
62P-43
62P/Can-43
62Salada-32
62Shirriff-32
62Sugar-5
62T-37M
62T-405
62T/St-37
63Sugar-5
63T-535
64T-34
65T-351
66T-283
67T-246
68T-393
69MB-219
69OPC-146
69T-146
70K-64
70MLB/St-236
70OPC-70LL
70T-620
70T-70LL
71K-3
71MD
71MLB/St-470
71OPC-500
71OPC-69LL
71T-500
71T-69LL
71T/Coins-12
71T/GM-10
71T/S-24
71T/tatt-14
72MB-271
72OPC-220
72OPC-497KP
72T-220
72T-497BP
73OPC-385
73T-385
74OPC-316
74T-316
75OPC-263
75T-263
75T/M-263
78TCMA-105
81Tacom-31
88Pac/Leg-18
89Swell-37

Perry, Melvin
(Bob)
64T-48

Perry, Parnell
86Geneva-23
87Peoria-22

Perry, Pat
83ColumAst-18
84ArkTr-18
85Louvl-18
86D-596
86F/Up-U89
86Schnucks-20
87D-430
87F-307
87Smok/Cards-4
87T-417
88Berg/Cubs-37
88D-626
88F-244
88Score-557
88T-282
89D-404
89F-435
89Score-364
89T-186
89T/Big-329
89UD-345
90Score-436
90T-541

Perry, Ron
80GlenF/B-17
80GlenF/C-1
81GlenF-15

Perry, Shawn
83Tacom-33

Perry, Steve
79LodiD-8
81VeroB-14
83Albuq-9
84Cram/PCL-154

Person, Carl
75QuadC

Persons, Archie
T206
T213/brown

Pertica, William
E120

Perzanowski, Stan
76OPC-388
76T-388
77SLCty

Pesavento, Mike
85VeroB-22

Pesky, Johnny
47TipTop
48L-121
49B-86
50B-137
50Drake-32
51B-15
51T/BB-5
52B-45
52T-15
53B/Col-134
53Glen
54B-135
54T-63
55B-241
61Union
63T-343
64T-248
67T/Test/PP-20CO
76SSPC-625
D305
Exh47
PM10/Sm-144
R302

Pesut, Nick
47Sunbeam

Peterek, Jeff
86Stockton-20
87ElPas-23
88ElPas/Best-21
89Denver/CMC-8
89Denver/Pro-46
90D-530
90F-333

Peters, Dan
88Beloi/GS-20

Peters, Frank
68T-409R

Peters, Gary
60T-407
61T-303
63T-522R
64Bz-27
64T-130
64T-2LL
64T/Coins-140AS
64T/Coins-71
64T/S-1
64T/St-56
64T/SU
64T/tatt
65Bz-27
65OldLond-32
65OPC-9LL
65T-430
65T-9LL
65T/E-18
65T/trans-62
66OPC-111
66T-111
67Bz-9
67T-233LL
67T-310
67T/Test/SU-2
68Bz-14
68Kahn
68OPC-8LL
68T-210
68T-379AS
68T-8LL
68T/G-13
68T/Post-13
69Kahn
69MB-220
69MLB/St-34
69OPC-34
69T-34
69T/St-157
70MLB/St-161
70OPC-540
70T-540
71MLB/St-327
71OPC-225
71T-225
71T/tatt-10
72MB-272
72OPC-503
72T-503
78TCMA-125
89Pac/Leg-159
Exh47

Peters, Jay
79SLCty-20
80SLCty-11

Peters, John
(Jack)
E120
V61-63

Peters, Oscar
T207

Peters, Ray
No Cards.

Peters, Reed
88PalmSp/Cal-108
88PalmSp/Pro-1439
89MidldA/GS-26

Peters, Richard D.
(Ricky)
81D-10
81F-470
81T-177
81T/St-77
82D-155
82F-277
82OPC-269
82T-504
83Tacom-29A
84F-458
84Nes/792-436
84T-436
85Cram/PCL-130
86Moth/A's-24

Peters, Steve
87ArkTr-9
87TexLgAS-19
88D/Rook-22
88Louvl-39
88Smok/Card-23
88T/Tr-84T
89F-462
89Louvl-30
89Louvl/CMC-9
89Louvl/Pro-1247
89T-482
89UD/Ext-771

Peters, Tim
88MidwLAS/GS-47
89Jaxvl/Best-13
89Jaxvl/Pro-154

Peterson, Adam C.
86Penin-20
87BirmB/Best-13
87SLAS-20
88F-646
88Vanco/CMC-7
88Vanco/Pro-776
89D-619
89Vanco/CMC-2
89Vanco/Pro-589
90T-299

Peterson, Carl
(Buddy)
52Mother-29
53Mother-8

Peterson, Charles
(Cap)
64T-568R
65T-512
66T-349
67T-387
68OPC-188
68T-188
69T-571

Peterson, D. Scott
77Ashev
78Ashev

Peterson, Dave
85Greens-19
86NewBrit-20

Peterson, Eric
(Ricky)
77Charl
82Buffa-17C

Peterson, Erik
82Nashv-17
83Nashvl-16
84Nashvl-17

Peterson, Fritz
66T-584R
67T-495
68T-246
69MLB/St-77
69OPC-46
69T-46
70MLB/St-248
70OPC-142
70T-142
71MD
71MLB/St-499
71OPC-460
71T-460
71T/Coins-138
71T/GM-44
71T/S-13
72T-573
72T-574A
73OPC-82
73T-82
74OPC-229
74T-229
75OPC-62
75T-62
75T/M-62
76Ho-32
76Ho/Twink-32
76OPC-255
76SSPC-511
76T-255

Peterson, Geoff
86FtMyr-21

Peterson, Harding
58T-322

Peterson, Jerry
76Watlo

Peterson, Jim
77Clint

Peterson, Kent
48L-42
49Eureka-92
51B-215

Peterson, Rick
88ColSp/Pro-1530
89BirmB/Best-28
89BirmB/Pro-99

Peterson, Rob
89Well/Puc-20

Peterson, Robert A.
E254

Peterson, Tim
76Cedar

Petestio, Doug
84MidldC-12

Petitt, Steven
86StPet-24
Petkovsek, Mark
88CharlR/Star-19
89Tulsa/GS-20
Petralli, Eugene J.
(Geno)
81Syrac-9
82Syrac-13
83D-623
83F-439
83Syrac-15
85Maine-16
85OKCty-5
86Rang-12
86T-296
87D-619
87F-135
87Moth/Rang-20
87Smok/R-8
87T-388
88D-506
88F-477
88Leaf-241
88Moth/R-20
88Score-373
88Smok/R-3
88T-589
89D-343
89D/Best-312
89F-530
89Moth/R-11
89OPC-137
89Panini/St-451
89Score-526
89Smok/R-25
89T-137
89T/Big-12
89T/St/Backs-24
89UD-482
90D-56
90F-309
90Score-153
90T-706
90UD-633
Petrizzo, Tom
86DayBe-22CHM
Petrocelli, Rico
65OPC-74R
65T-74R
66T-298
67T-528
67T/Test/RSox-13
68Bz-5
68Coke
68OPC-156
68T-430
69Citgo-8
69MB-221
69MLB/St-15
69OPC-215
69T-215
69T/St-136
69Trans-21
70K-54
70MB-21
70MLB/St-162
70OPC-457AS
70T-457AS
70T-680
70T/CB
70T/S-14
70Trans-15
71Bz
71Bz/Test-10
71MD
71MLB/St-328
71OPC-340
71T-340
71T/Coins-30
71T/GM-39
71T/S-19
71T/tatt-11
72MB-273
72OPC-30
72T-30
73OPC-365
73T-365
74OPC-609
74T-609
75Ho-132
75OPC-356
75T-356
75T/M-356
76OPC-445
76SSPC-413
76T-445
77T-111
87BirmB/Best-1
87SLAS-23
88BirmB/Best-8
88SLAS-38
89Swell-123
PM10/Sm-145
Petry, Dan
80T-373
81D-128
81F-468
81T-59
82D-133
82F-278
82T-211
82T-666TL
83D-359
83F-339
83OPC-79
83T-261TL
83T-638
83T/St-70
84D-105
84F-89
84FunFood/Pin-60
84Nes/792-147
84OPC-147
84T-147
84T/St-269
85Cain's-16
85D-334
85F-20
85F/St-83
85Leaf-188
85OPC-392
85Seven-7D
85T-435
85T/Gloss40-25
85T/St-264
85Wendy-18
86Cain's-15
86D-212
86D/AAS-42
86F-235
86Leaf-144
86OPC-216
86T-540
86T/St-270
87Cain's-15
87Coke/Tigers-12
87D-373
87F-161
87Leaf-228
87OPC-27
87Seven-DT9
87T-752
88D-476
88D/Best-139
88F-67
88Score-461
88Score/Tr-26T
88Smok/Angels-8
88T-78
88T/Tr-85T
89D-344
89F-486
89Score-122
89T/Big-178
89UD-552
90F-142
90Score-211
90T-363
90UD-690
Pettaway, Ike
78Green
83Durhm-22
Pettee, Patrick E.
N172
Pettengill, Tim
89Savan/Pro-352
Pettibone, Jay
80Ashev-17
82Orlan/B-22
83Orlan-14
84Toled-24
Pettibone, Jim
82Cedar-10
83Water-6
84Cedar-3
85Cedar-11
Pettini, Joe
80Phoen-20
81F-453
81Phoen-21
81T-62
82F-398
82T-568
83T-143
84Cram/PCL-13
84Nes/792-449
84T-449
85Louvl-12
86Louisvl-23
87Louvl-2CO
88Louvl-2CO
88Louvl/CMC-24
88Louvl/Pro-435
89Hamil/Star-27
Pettis, Gary
81Holyo-20
82Spoka-23
84D-647
84F-526
84Smok/Cal-21
84T/X-93
85D-499
85F-308
85F/St-57
85OPC-39
85Smok/Cal-9
85T-497
85T/St-226
86D-158
86F-165
86F/Mini-33
86F/St-88
86Leaf-84
86OPC-323
86Smok/Cal-9
86T-604
86T/Mini-7
87Class/Up-134
87D-160
87D/OD-10
87F-90
87F/AwardWin-29
87Leaf-152
87OPC-278
87S-157M
87Seven-W7
87Smok/Cal-20
87T-278
87T/Mini-47
87T/St-16
87T/St-175
88D-210
88D/Best-203
88F/U-U29
88OPC-71
88Panini/St-48
88Pep/T-24
88Score-255
88Score/Tr-38T
88T-71
88T/St-178
88T/Tr-86T
89B-108
89D-60
89F-141
89Mara/Tigers-24
89OPC-146
89Panini/St-345
89Score-26
89T-146
89T/Mini-53
89T/St-279
89UD-117
90D-661
90F-612
90Score-136
90Sf-202
90T-512
90UD-385
Pettis, Stacey
84PrWill-34
86PalmSp-26
Pettit
N172
WG1-13
Pettit, Bob
60P
Pettit, Paul
60HenryH-15
Petty, Brian
85Evrt/Cram-14
Petty, Jesse
33G-90
V354-42
Petway, Bruce
78Laugh/Black-7
Pevey, Marty
86Louisvl-24
89Indi/CMC-15
89Indi/Pro-1217
90T-137
90UD-628
Peyton, Byron
82Cedar-17
Peyton, Eric
82ElPas-1
83ElPas-2
84Cram/PCL-41
Peyton, Mickey
88Aug/Pro-362
Pfaff, Bob
86Sumter-21
87Durhm-4
89BurlB/Pro-1606
89BurlB/Star-16
Pfaff, Rich
89Beloi/Star-22
Pfeffer, Edward
(Jeff)
D327
D328-133
D350/2-137
E121/80
E122
E135-133
E220
M101/5-137
V100
W575
Pfeffer, Francis
(Big Jeff)
M116
T206
W514-58
WG3-36
Pfeffer, Nathaniel F.
E223
N172
N284
N300/Unif
WG1-14
Pfeil, Bobby
66Pep/Tul
70OPC-99
70T-99
72T-681
Pfiester, John
12Sweet/Pin-87
E254
E96
M116
T204
T205
T206
T3-33
Pfister, Dan
62T-592R
63T-521
64T-302
Phelan, Art
C46-35
M116
T206
T222
Phelan, James D.
N172
Phelan, James F.
T205
T206
Phelan, John
89Spoka/SP-6
Phelps, Edward
10Domino-98
11Helmar-175
12Sweet/Pin-152
C46-36
E90/1
M116
T205
T206
Phelps, Ernest Gordon
(Babe)
37Exh/4-2
38Exh/4-2
39PB-96
40PB-66
89Smok/Dodg-41
R313
Phelps, Ken
76Watlo
77DaytB
77Jaxvl
82F-420
82Wichi-12
82Wichi-7M
85D-318
85F-499
85Leaf-129
85Moth/Mar-18
85OPC-322
85T-582
86Moth/Mar-18
86T-34
87D-317
87D/OD-118
87F-593
87F/GameWin-34
87F/Slug-30
87Moth/Sea-7
87T-333
87T/St-222
88D-489
88D/Best-248
88F-384
88F/Slug-29
88F/St-61
88Moth/Sea-7
88OPC-182
88RedFoley/St-69

88Score-256
88T-182
88T/Big-189
89B-177
89D-363
89D/Best-276
89F-264
89Score-242
89Score/NWest-10
89T-741
89T/Big-293
89UD-167
90D-675
90T-411
Philley, Dave
48L-85
49B-44
50B-127
51B-297
52NTea
52T-226
53T-64
54B-163
54RM-AL9
54T-159
55Gol/Ind-23
55Salem
56T-222
57T-124
58Hires-12
58T-116
59T-92
60T-52
61T-369
62T-542
72Laugh/GF-46
79TCMA-192
Exh47
R423-80
Phillip, Jim
86WinSal-19
Phillippe, Charles
(Deacon)
10Domino-99
12Sweet/Pin-143
72F/FFeat-37
D322
E104
E107
E254
E90/1
E91
E93
M116
S74-114
T202
T205
T206
W555
WG3-37
Phillips, Adolfo
66OPC-32
66T-32
67OPC-148
67T-148
68T-202
69MB-222
69T-372
69T/St-17
70T-666
71LaPizza-9
71MLB/St-137
71OPC-418
71T-418
Phillips, Bill
83CharR-8
86Peoria-19
Phillips, Charlie
77LodiD
80ElPas-24
80SLCty-8
Phillips, Chris
83Knoxv-6
Phillips, Dave
88Umpire-9
89Umpires-7
Phillips, J.R.
89QuadC/Best-22
89QuadC/GS-7
Phillips, Jack
52T-240
53Mother-57
57T-307
D301
Phillips, Jim
87Pittsf-12
89Martins/Star-25
Phillips, John
(Bubba)
55B-228
57T-395
58T-212
59T-187
60T-243
61Kahn
61T-101
61T/St-140
62J-39
62Kahn
62P-39
62P/Can-39
62Salada-74
62Shirriff-74
62Sugar-14
62T-511
62T/St-38
63J-70
63P-70
63T-177
64Det/Lids-11
64T-143
65T-306
78TCMA-192
Phillips, Lanny
77Holyo
Phillips, Lefty
70OPC-376MG
70T-376
71JB
71OPC-279MG
71T-279
Phillips, Lonnie
87Everett-5
88Clint/Pro-720
89SanJose/Best-5
89SanJose/Cal-217
89SanJose/Pro-452
Phillips, Mike
74OPC-533
74T-533
75OPC-642
75T-642
75T/M-642
76OPC-93
76SSPC-540
76T-93
77T-532
78T-88
79T-258
80T-439
81D-188
81F-538
81T-113
82F-201
82OPC-263
82T-762
Phillips, Montie
88CalLgAS-8
89SanJose/Best-12
89SanJose/Pro-433
89SanJose/Star-22
Phillips, Richard E.
(Dick)
61Union
63T-544R
64T-559
78TCMA-179
79Hawai-6
Phillips, Robbie
84Cedar-1
Phillips, Steve
85Lynch-16
86Lynch-17
Phillips, Thomas G.
E120
W573
Phillips, Tony
80Memph-16
81WHave-14
82Tacom-32
83T/X-87
84D-278
84F-459
84Moth/A's-23
84Nes/792-309
84T-309
85D-101
85F-433
85T-444
85T/St-329
86D-542
86F-430
86Moth/A's-19
86T-29
87D-103
87D/OD-26
87F-402
87Smok/A's-10
87T-188
88D-221
88D/A's/Bk-221
88F-290
88Moth/A's-12
88OPC-12
88Panini/St-168
88Score-294
88T-673
88T/St-165
89D/Best-211
89F/Up-56
89Moth/A's-11
89Score-156
89T-248
89UD-267
90D-91
90F-19
90Score-84
90T-702
90UD-154
Phillips, Vince
89PrWill/Star-16
Phillips, W. Taylor
57T-343
58T-159
59T-113
60T-211
Phillips, Wade
87Fayette-9
87Lakel-15
88Lakel/Star-20
Phillips, William
N172
N284
Philyaw, Thad
75Water
Phipps, Ron
83Peor/LF-26tr
Phoebus, Tom
67T-204R
68Coke
68OPC-97
68T-97
69MB-223
69MLB/St-6
69OPC-185
69T-185
69T-532M
69T/St-127
70MLB/St-152
70T-717
71MLB/St-234
71OPC-611
71T-611
72MB-274
72OPC-477
72T-477
Piatt, Bruce
83Butte-32
Piatt, Doug
88BurlR/Pro-1790
89Kinston/Star-18
89Watertn/Star-18
Piatt, Wiley
E107
Piazza, Anthony
87Everett-4
Picciolo, Dustin
87Spoka-25
Picciolo, Rob
76Tucso-9
78T-528
79T-378
80T-158
81D-357
81F-582
81T-604
81T/Tr-813
82D-465
82F-106
82Granny-14
82T-293
82T/Tr-89T
83D-456
83Pol/Brew-8
83T-476
84D-455
84Nes/792-88
84Smok/Cal-22
84T-88
84T/X-94
85Moth/A's-13
85T-756
85T/Tr-90T
86Cram/PCL-177
86D-497
86OPC-3
86T-672
87LasVegas-26
87Spoka-26
Pichardo, Nelson
77WHave
Piche, Ron
61T-61
62T-582
63T-179
65T-464
66Pep/Tul
Picinich, Val J.
21Exh-128
21Exh-129
25Exh-67
29Exh/4-7
33G-118
E120
E220
V354-3
W573
Pickens, Kevin
89BBCity/Star-21
Pickering, Oliver
E107
E254
T206
Pickett, Antoine
88Modesto-28
Pickett, John
N172
Pickett, Rich
83Lynch-21
84Tidew-12
Pickett, Tony
87AppFx-23
Pico, Jeff
86WinSal-20
87Pittsf-19
88Berg/Cubs-41
88F/U-U80
88IowaC/CMC-3
88IowaC/Pro-546
88Peoria/Ko-25
88Score/Tr-94T
88T/Tr-87T
89D-513
89F-436
89Mara/Cubs-41
89Panini/St-50
89Score-13
89T-262
89ToysRUs-22
89UD-491
90D-585
90F-39
90Score-428
90T-613
Picota, Lenin
87Savan-23
88StPet/Star-22
89ArkTr/GS-18
Piechowski, Tim
88James/Pro-1902
Piela, D.
88Pulas/Pro-1765
Pierce, Ben
89AppFx/Pro-874
Pierce, Billy
51B-196
51T/BB-45
52B-54
52Hawth/Pin-6
52RM-AL16
52StarCal/L-73B
52T-98
53B/Col-73
53RM-AL16
53T-143
54B-102
54RH
54RM-AL10
55B-214
55RFG-27
56T-160
57Swift-4
57T-160
58T-334M
58T-50
59Bz
59T-156M
59T-410
59T-466M
59T-572AS
60T-150
60T-571AS
60T/tatt
60T/tatt-44
60T/tatt-95
61P-21
61T-205
61T/St-126
62J-54
62P-54
62P/Can-54
62Salada-2
62Shirriff-2
62T-260
63T-331M
63T-50
64T-222
79TCMA-16
88Coke/WS-22

89Pac/Leg-134
89Swell-57
Exh47

Pierce, Chris
86PrWill-19

Pierce, Dominic
88Butte-16
89Gasto/Pro-1001
89Gasto/Star-18
89Star/Wax-38

Pierce, Don Diego
82Wausa-24

Pierce, Ed
89Eugene/Best-9

Pierce, G.
C46-68
D350/2-138
M101/5-138

Pierce, L. Jack
76OPC-162
76SSPC-386
76T-162
78SnJos-23
79Spoka-7

Pierce, Tony
67T-542R
68OPC-38
68T-38

Pierce, Walter
83ArkTr-5
84ArkTr-24

Piercy, Bill
21Exh-130
21Exh-131

Pieretti, Marino
(Chick)
49B-217
50B-181
50NumNum
52Mother-12
53Mother-35

Pierorazio, Wes
83Watlo/LF-23
85Visal-19
86Visal-15
87Orlan-22

Piersall, Jim
51B-306
52B-189
53B/BW-36
54B-210
54B-66B
54RM-AL11
55B-16
55RM-AL21
56T-143
57T-75
58T-280
59T-355
60T-159
61T-345
61T/St-139
62Bz
62Salada-88A
62Salada-88B
62Shirriff-88
62T-51LL
62T-90
62T/bucks
62T/St-100
63Exh
63F-29
63T-443
64T-586
65OPC-172
65T-172
66T-565
67T-584
79TCMA-188
89Pac/Leg-182
89Swell-83
Exh47
PM10/Sm-146

Pierson, Larry
88StPet/Star-23
89StPet/Star-22

Piet, Tony
33G-228
34DS-72
34Exh/4-4
34G-8
35BU-142
35BU-70
35G-1H
35G-3F
35G-4F
35G-5F
88Conlon/NatAS-16
R314
V354-63
V355-95

Pietroburgo, Rob
79Spoka-18
80Tacom
81Charl-23
82Charl-9

Pifer, Gary
87CharWh-10
88Lakel/Star-21

Piggot, Rusty
81QuadC-4

Pignatano, Joe
58T-373
59T-16
60BB-10
60L-126
60T-292M
60T-442
61T-74
62J-97
62P-97
62P/Can-97
62Salada-45
62Shirriff-45
62T-247
73OPC-257CO
73T-257C
74OPC-179CO
74T-179C
79TCMA-204
82Pol/Atl-52C
83Pol/Atl-52C
84Pol/Atl-52C

Pike, Mark
87Watlo-6
88Watlo/Pro-683
89Kinston/Star-19

Pilarcik, Al
57T-311
58Hires-76
58Hires/T
58T-259
59T-7
60T-498
61T-62
79TCMA-212

Pilkington, Eric
86Clint-21
88SanJose/Cal-136
88SanJose/Pro-127

Pilkinton, Lem
86Elmir-15
87Greens-23
89Penin/Star-19

Pill, Mike
78Charl

Pilla, Tony
82Orlan-11
83Orlan-2

Pillette, Duane
51B-316
52T-82
53B/BW-59
53T-269
54B-133
54Esskay
54T-107
55B-244
55Esskay
55T-168
79TCMA-191

Pillette, Herman
21Exh-132
46Sunbeam
E120
V61-19
W572
W573

Pimentel, Rafael D.
81ArkTr-13
82ArkTr-5
86MidldA-19

Pina, Horacio
71MLB/St-548
71OPC-497
71T-497
72T-654
73OPC-138
73T-138
74OPC-516
74T-516
74T/Tr-516T
75OPC-139
75T-139
75T/M-139

Pina, Mickey
87Elmir/Red-33
88Lynch/Star-17
89NewBrit/Pro-619
89NewBrit/Star-14

Pinchny, George
N172

Pinder, Chris
88Hagers/Star-17
89Hagers/Best-27
89Hagers/Pro-268

Pineda, Rafael
87QuadC-15

Pinelli, Ralph
(Babe)
55B-307ump
87Conlon/2-20
88Conlon/4-22
E120
V61-78
W572
W573
WG7-41

Pinelli, Willie
87Bakers-29

Piniella, Lou
64T-167R
68OPC-16R
68T-16R
69T-394R
70MLB/St-227
70OPC-321
70T-321
70T/S-32
70T/SO
71MLB/St-426
71OPC-35
71T-35
71T/Coins-152
71T/GM-38
71T/S-62
71T/tatt-9
72MB-275
72OPC-491KP
72T-491BP
72T-580
73K-24
73OPC-140
73T-140
73T/Comics-15
73T/Lids-40
73T/PinUps-15
74OPC-390
74T-390
74T/St-188
74T/Tr-390T
75K-34
75OPC-217
75T-217
75T/M-217
76OPC-453
76SSPC-445
76T-453
77BK/Y-23
77K-48
77T-96
78BK/Y-18
78OPC-82
78T-159
79BK/Y-18
79Ho-69
79OPC-342
79T-648
80OPC-120
80T-225
81D-109
81F-85
81F/St-45
81OPC-306
81T-724
82D-135
82F-48
82F/St-114
82OPC-236
82T-538
83D-335
83F-392
83OPC-307
83RoyRog/Disc-8
83T-307
84D-274
84F-136
84Nes/792-408
84OPC-351
84T-408
86T/Tr-86T
87T-168MG
88T-44

Pinkerton, Wayne
77Tucso
78Cr/PCL-33
79Tucso-12
80Charl-3

Pinkham, Bill
83Knoxv-8

Pinkus, Jeff
77Salem

Pino, Rolando
83AppFx/LF-12
87BirmB/Best-19
89Keno/Pro-1082
89Keno/Star-19

Pinol, Juan
87Tampa-7

Pinson, Vada
58T-420
59Kahn
59T-448
60Armour-17
60Kahn
60T-176
60T-32M
61Kahn
61P-181
61T-110
61T-25M
61T/St-22
62Bz
62Exh
62J-121
62Kahn
62P-121
62P/Can-121
62Salada-118
62Shirriff-118
62T-52LL
62T-80
62T/bucks
62T/St-119
63Exh
63F-34
63FrBauer-19
63J-130
63Kahn
63P-130
63T-265
64Kahn
64T-162M
64T-80
64T/Coins-152AS
64T/Coins-45
64T/S-56
64T/St-2
64T/SU
65Kahn
65OldLond-16
65T-355
65T/E-42
65T/trans-24
66Kahn
66OPC-180
66T-180
67Kahn
67T-550
68Bz-9
68Kahn
68OPC-90
68T-90
69Kahn
69MB-224
69OPC-160
69T-160
69T/St-119
70MLB/St-202
70OPC-445
70T-445
70T/CB
70T/S-31
71MLB/St-382
71OPC-275
71T-275
71T/Coins-18
71T/GM-12
71T/tatt-5
72MB-276
72OPC-135
72T-135
73OPC-75
73T-75
74OPC-490
74T-490
74T/St-144
75OPC-295
75T-295
75T/M-295
76OPC-415
76SSPC-178
76T-415
77T-597C
78TCMA-146
82D-445
88Pep/T-CO
89Mara/Tigers-CO
Exh47

Pinto, Gustavo
89NiagFls/Puc-19

Pipgras, George
33DH-34
33G-12
61F-134
R315-A29
R315-B29
R337-404

Piphus, Ben
83Watlo/LF-3

Pipik, Gary
89James/Pro-2138
Pipp, Wally
21Exh-133
25Exh-99
26Exh-29
27Exh-14
BF2-34
D328-134
D329-138
D350/2-139
E120
E121/120
E121/80
E122
E135-134
E220
M101/4-138
M101/5-139
V100
V61-48
W514-84
W515-39
W572
W573
W575
WG7-42
Pippen, Henry
(Cotton)
39PB-8
40PB-136
46Remar
47Remar
47Signal
47Smith-9
Pippin, Craig
83LynnP-7
86Maine-15
87Omaha-15
Pirruccello, Mark
83CharR-1
84Memph-23
Pirtle, Jerry
79RochR-12
79T-720R
Pisacreta, Mike
89Pulas/Pro-1890
Pisarkiewicz, Mike
77StPet
78StPet
Piscetta, Rob
89Bakers/Cal-187
Pisel, Ron
78Cedar
83Phoen/BHN-19
Pisker, Don
76Dubuq
78Charl
79Syrac-8
79T-718R
80Syrac-23
81SLCty-24
Piskol, Pete
84PrWill-8
Piskor, Steve
88LitFalls/Puc-9
Pisoni, Jim
57T-402
59T-259
Pitcher, Scott
89Wausa/GS-8
Pitler, Jake
49Eureka-46
52T-395
55Gol/Dodg-22
79TCMA-187
Pitlock, Lee
(Skip)
71OPC-19
71T-19
75OPC-579
75T-579
75T/M-579
76Tucso-44
Pittaro, Chris
85F/Up-U87
85T/Tr-91T
86D-150
86T-393
87Portl-6
88Portl/CMC-19
88Portl/Pro-653
Pittenger, Clark A.
29Exh/4-8
E120
V61-42
W573
Pittinger, Charley
WG3-38
Pittman, Doug
87Salem-27
88Keno/Pro-1388
Pittman, James
88Orlan/Best-8
Pittman, Joe
76Dubuq
80Tucso-3
81Tucso-3
82D-218
82F-222
82T-119
82T/Tr-90T
83D-247
83F-369
83T-346
Pittman, Mike
82Sprin-5
83Sprin/LF-20
Pittman, Park
87Visal-11
89Orlan/Best-20
89Orlan/Pro-1334
Pitts, Gaylen
75Tucso-16
76Tucso-42
81ArkTr-21
81Louvl-2
82ArkTr-22MG
82Louvl-23
84Louvl-2
87Sprin/Best-1
89ArkTr/GS-1
Pitz, Michael
87Bakers-28
88SnAnt/Best-3
89SnAnt/Best-23
Pivnick, Phil
85Albany-31
Pizarro, Juan
57T-383
59T-188
60L-51
60Lake
60T-59
61P-112
61T-227
62T-255
62T-59LL
62T/bucks
62T/St-28
63J-44
63P-44
63T-10LL
63T-160
64T-2LL
64T-430
64T/Coins-14
64T/S-53
64T/St-31
64T/SU
64Wheat/St-36
65OPC-125
65OPC-9LL
65T-125
65T-9LL
65T/trans-25
66T-335
67T-602
67T/Test/PP-5
68KDKA-29
68OPC-19
68T-19
69T-498
71MLB/St-41
71OPC-647
71T-647
72OPC-18
72T-18
78TCMA-79
Pizarro, Miguel
78Ashev
Placeres, Benigno
88StCath/Pro-2009
Pladson, Gordy
75Dubuq
76Dubuq
77Cocoa
79Charl-13
80Tucso-18
81T-491
81Tucso-18
82Tucso-21
83Tucso-7
Plainte, Brandon
80Elmir-15
Planco, Radhames
89Clmbia/GS-21
Plank, Ed
76Phoen
77Phoen
78Cr/PCL-66
79Phoen
80Phoen-6
Plank, Edward A.
14CJ-6
15CJ-6
48Exh/HOF
50Callahan
60F-46
61F-135
63Bz/ATG-9
69Bz/Sm
72F/FFeat-26
80Laugh/3/4/5-22
80SSPC/HOF
87Conlon/2-49
88Conlon/3-22
89HOF/St-78
D303
E104
E106
E107
E224
E90/1
E91
E93
E95
M116
T204
T206
T208
T216
W555
WG2-41
WG4-22
Plante, Bill
85Elmir-16
86Greens-16
Plantier, Phil
87Elmir/Red-34
88WinHav/Star-20
89Lynch/Star-18
Plants, Dan
84ElPas-17
Plaskett, Elmo
63T-549R
Platel, Mark
79AppFx-22
80GlenF/B-5
80GlenF/C-9
81AppFx-9
Platt, Mizell
48L-159
49B-89
Platts, Jim
87Spart-1
88Spart/Pro-1048
Plautz, Rick
82FtMyr-9
Plaza, Ron
62Kahn/Atl
Pleasac, Joe
86CharRa-21
Pledger, Kinnis
89SoBend/GS-19
Pleicones, Johnnie
86FtLaud-18
Pleis, Scott
83Erie-14
Pleis, William
62T-124
63T-293
64T-484
65OPC-122
65T-122
78TCMA-135
Plemel, Lee
88Hamil/Pro-1726
89Sprin/Best-11
Plemmons, Ron
89Utica/Puc-18
Plesac, Dan
86D/Rook-14
86F/Up-U90
86Pol/Brew-37
86S/Rook-10
86T/Tr-87T
87D-214
87F-354
87T-279
87T/St-201
87ToysRUs-22
88D-109
88D/AS-18
88D/Best-221
88F-171
88F-625M
88F/Mini-32
88F/St-39
88OPC-317
88Panini/St-118
88Pol/Brew-37
88RedFoley/St-70
88Score-77
88Score/YS/II-32
88Sf-191
88T-670
88T/Mini-20
88T/St-203
88T/St/Backs-65
89B-133
89Cadaco-40
89D-382
89D/AS-22
89D/Best-165
89F-195
89F/LL-29
89F/Superstar-32
89Gard-8
89OPC-167
89Panini/St-367
89Pol/Brew-37
89Score-320
89Score/HotSt-32
89Sf-128
89T-740
89T/St-197
89UD-630
90D-175
90F-334
90Score-86
90Score/100St-86
90Sf-102
90T-490
90UD-477
Pless, Rance
56T-339
79TCMA-176
Plews, Herb
57T-169
58T-109
59T-373
61BeeHive-16
Ploucher, George
77Cocoa
Plumb, Dave
87Sumter-13
88CLAS/Star-34
88Durhm/Star-17
89Greenv/Pro-1164
89Greenv/Star-17
89Greenvl/Best-25
Plummer, Bill
73OPC-177
73T-177
74OPC-524
74T-524
75OPC-656
75T-656
75T/M-656
76OPC-627
76SSPC-32
76T-627
77T-239
78SnJos-19
78T-106
79OPC-208
79Spoka-10
79T-396
81Wausa-29
84Chatt-9
86Calgary-21MG
87Calgary-4
88AAA/Pro-49
88Calg/CMC-24
88Calg/Pro-800
Plummer, Dale
88LitFalls/Puc-20
89Jacks/GS-28
89Star/Wax-23
89StLucie/Star-19
Plunk, Eric
85Huntsvl/BK-33
86D/Rook-40
86F-649M
86Tacom-16
87D-178
87F-403
87T-587
88D-503
88D/A's/Bk-503
88D/Best-267
88F-291
88Moth/A's-20
88Score-614
88T-173
89B-191
89D-125
89D/Best-49
89F-20
89Moth/A's-16
89OPC-141
89Score-392
89T-448
89UD-353
90D-196
90F-452
90T-9
90UD-630

Plympton, Jeff
88Lynch/Star-18
89NewBrit/Pro-622
89NewBrit/Star-16
Poat, Ray
48B-42
Pocekay, Walter
53Mother-10
Poche, Gerry
76Baton
Pocoroba, Biff
76OPC-103
76SSPC-15
76T-103
77T-594
78Ho-99
78T-296
79OPC-285
79T-555
80OPC-73
80T-132
81F-257
81Pol/Atl-4
81T-326
82BK/Lids-20
82F-446
82Pol/Atl-4
82T-88
83D-436
83F-145
83OPC-367
83Pol/Atl-4
83T-676
84D-77
84F-189
84Nes/792-438
84T-438
Podbielan, Clarence
(Bud)
52T-188
53B/BW-21
53T-237
54T-69
55T-153
56T-224
V362-12
Podres, Johnny
52Park-76
53T-263
54T-166
55B-97
55Gol/Dodg-23
55T-25
55T/DH-112
56T-173
57Swift-1
57T-277
58BB
58Hires-42
58T-120
59Armour-13
59Morrell
59T-262M
59T-49560T-425
60BB-19
60Morrell
60NuCard-2
61BB-22
61NuCard-474
61P-169
61T-109
61T-207M
61T/St-31
62BB-22
62J-108
62P-108
62P/Can-108
62Salada-172
62Shirriff-172
62T-280
62T/bucks
62T/St-138
63Salada-9
63T-150
63T-412M
64T-580
65T-387
66T-468
67T-284
69T-659
73OPC-12CO
73T-12C
78TCMA-156
79TCMA-239
79TCMA-267
82D-566
87Smok/Dodg-26
88Pac/Leg-105
89Rini/Dodg-6
89Smok/Dodg-63
PM10/L-32
PM10/Sm-147
WG10-43
WG9-42
Poe, Rick
82Jacks-13
Poehl, Michael
86Watlo-21
87Kinston-9
88EastLAS/Pro-42
88Wmspt/Pro-1325
Poff, John William
79OkCty
80OkCty
Pohle, Rich
88Idaho/Pro-1861
Pohle, Walt
85Beloi-2
86Stockton-21
87ElPas-19
Poholsky, Tom
52T-242
54Hunter
54T-142
55B-76
55Hunter
56T-196
57T-235
Poindexter, Mike
81Batav-5
83Watlo/LF-24
Pointer, Aaron
67T-564R
Poissant, Rod
86Lakel-17
87GlenF-16
89SnBer/Cal-75
Polanco, Nicolas
89Kingspt/Star-19
Polanco, Radhames
88LitFalls/Puc-10
89Clmbia/Best-21
Polanco, Roger
75Dubuq
Poland, Philip
T206
Poldberg, Brian
82Nashv-18
83Omaha-11
84Omaha-23
85Omaha-31
87AppFx-17
88AppFx/Pro-162
89AppFx/Pro-872
Pole, Dick
74OPC-596R
74T-596R
74T/Tr-596T
75OPC-513
75T-513
75T/M-513
76OPC-326
76T-326
77T-187
78T-233
80Port-11
83QuadC-3
86Pittsf-19CO
87IowaC-21CO
88Berg/Cubs-CO
Poles, Spot
74Laugh/Black-21
Polese, Joe
77Newar
Polhemus, Mark
N284
Poli, Crip
R314/Can
V355-84
Polidor, Gus
81Holyo-21
82Holyo-18
83Nashua-14
85Cram/PCL-12
86Edmon-22
86F-650M
87D-579
87Smok/Cal-18
88D-356
88F-501
88Score-341
88Smok/Angels-6
88T-708
89Pol/Brew-14
90D-412
90T-313
90UD-480
Poling, Mark
88Clint/Pro-699
Polinski, Bob
78Cr/PCL-82
79Colum-15
Polk, Riley
87Watlo-24
Polka, Fritz
86LitFalls-23
87Columbia-21
88FSLAS/Star-17
Pollack, Chris
87Jamestn-30
88Rockford-29
89Rockford-30
Pollack, Rick
88BirmB/Best-15
Pollard, Jim
52Wheat
Pollet, Howard
39Exh
49B-95
49Eureka-193
50B-72
51B-263
51T/RB-7
52B-83
52T-63
53NB
53T-83
54T-89
55T-76
55T/DH-31
56T-262
60T-468C
R423-83
Polley, Dale
88Greenv/Best-12
89Greenv/Pro-1160
89Greenv/Star-18
89Greenvl/Best-15
Poloni, John
77Tucso
83Wausa/LF-2CO
87Myrtle-17
88Knoxv/Best-23
89Knoxv/Best-29
89Knoxv/Pro-1147
89Knoxv/Star-25
Polonia, Luis
84Madis/Pol-7
85Huntsvl/BK-11
86Tacom-17
87D/Rook-25
87F/U-U99
87S/Rook-18
87T/Tr-96T
88D-425
88D/A's/Bk-425
88F-292
88Leaf-256
88OPC-238
88Panini/St-177
88RedFoley/St-71
88Score-64
88Score/YS/I-22
88Sf-71
88T-238
88T/Big-65
88T/JumboR-14
88T/St-172
88Tacom/CMC-16
88Tacom/Pro-638
88ToysRUs-24
89D-386
89F-21
89Moth/A's-17
89OPC-386
89Panini/St-425
89Score-380
89Score/NWest-4
89Score/Tr-38
89Sf-133
89T-424
89UD-162
90D-547
90Score-442
90T-634
90UD-316
Polverini, Steve
87AubAs-9
Pomeranz, Mike
89Keno/Pro-1081
89Keno/Star-20
Pomorski, John
V355-92
Ponce, Carlos
81BurlB-22
83ElPas-19
84Cram/PCL-34
85Cram/PCL-224
86D-595
Ponder, Charles Elmer
V100
WG7-43
Ponder, Kevin
88Clmbia/GS-10
89Mia/Star/22-16
89Mia/Star/25-16
Pone, Vince
78Newar
79BurlB-22
80BurlB-11
81BurlB-2
Pontiff, Wally
74Gasto
Pool, Harlin
R314/Can
Poole, Ed
E107
Poole, James
88T/Tr-88T
89T/Big-263
89VeroB/Star-22
Poole, Mark
85Syrac-17
86Syrac-21
86Tulsa-1
Poole, Stine
82Evans-13
83Toled-12
Poorman, Thomas
N172
Pope, Dave
55B-198
55Gol/Ind-24
55Salem
56T-154
57T-249
61BeeHive-17
Pope, Greg
81Watlo-13
Pope, Mike
78StPet
Popham, Art
80Tacom-22
81Tacom-3
82Tacom-21
83Tacom-23
Popovich, Nick
77Spart
Popovich, Paul
67T-536R
68T-266
69OPC-47
69T-47
69T/St-48
70OPC-258
70T-258
71MLB/St-42
71OPC-726
71T-726
72OPC-512
72T-512
73OPC-309
73T-309
74OPC-14
74T-14
75OPC-359
75T-359
75T/M-359
Popowski, Eddie
73OPC-131CO
73T-131C
74OPC-403CO
74T-403C
87Elmir-32
Popplewell, Tom
87Oneon-9
88PrWill/Star-19
89FtLaud/Star-19
Poquette, Tom
75OPC-622R
75T-622R
75T/M-622R
76A&P/KC
77K-24
77OPC-66
77T-93
78OPC-197
78T-357
79T-476
80T-597
81T-153
82T-657
88Omaha/Pro-1495
89Omaha/Pro-1741
Porte, Carlos
80Cedar-6
83Water-12
85Cedar-18
Porter, Bob
78Green
79Savan-22
81Richm-7
82Richm-21
83Richm-20
85Durhm-16
Porter, Brad
84Evrt/Cram-22A
Porter, Brian
89AubAs/Pro-2169

Porter, Chuck
76QuadC
78Cr/PCL-65
79SLCty-19
81Vanco-2
82T-333R
82Vanco-21
84D-333
84F-211
84Nes/792-452
84Pol/Brew-43
84T-452
85D-115
85F-591
85Gard-16
85T-32
86T-292
86Vanco-22
Porter, Darrell
72OPC-162R
72T-162R
73OPC-582
73T-582
74OPC-194
74T-194
74T/St-198
75Ho-62
75OPC-52
75T-52
75T/M-52
76A&P/Milw
76Ho-117
76OPC-645
76SSPC-232
76T-645
77OPC-116
77T-214
78Ho-130
78OPC-66
78T-19
79Ho-4
79K-25
79OPC-295
79T-571
80K-12
80OPC-188
80T-360
80T-39
81Coke
81D-505
81F-36
81T-610
81T/St-224
81T/Tr-814
82D-498
82F-124
82F/St-29
82OPC-348IA
82OPC-98
82T-447
82T-448A
82T/St-93
83D-278
83F-18
83OPC-103
83T-103
83T/St-148
83T/St-149
83T/St-182
83T/St-183
84D-303
84F-331
84MiltBrad-19
84Nes/792-285
84OPC-285
84T-285
84T/St-143
85D-353
85F-237
85Leaf-258
85OPC-246
85T-525
85T/St-140
86D-290
86F-45
86F/Up-U91
86KAS/Disc-16
86OPC-84
86Rang-17
86S-148M
86T-757
86T/Tr-88T
87D-593
87F-136
87Moth/Rang-10
87OPC-213
87RedFoley/St-52
87Smok/R-10
87T-689
88Score-537
Porter, Dick
32Orbit/num-36
32Orbit/un-49
34G-43
R305
V354-88
Porter, Eric
82Wisco-20
Porter, Henry
E223
N172
N284
Porter, J.W.
53T-211
55T-49
55T/DH-9
58T-32
59T-246
Porter, Jeff
83Memph-22
84Indianap-31TR
Porterfield, Erwin
(Bob)
49B-3
50B-216
52B-194
52RM-AL17
52T-301
52TipTop
53B/Col-22
53Briggs
53RM-AL19
53T-108
54B-24
54RM-AL10
54RM-AL18
55B-104
55RFG-7
56T-248
56YellBase/Pin-25
57T-118
58T-344
59T-181
79TCMA-284
Exh47
R423-81
Porterfield, Ron
88AubAs/Pro-1954
Portocarrero, Arnold
54T-214
55Rodeo
55T-77
55T/DH-12
56T-63
58T-465
59T-98
60T-254
79TCMA-196
Portugal, Mark
82Wisco-14
83Visal/LF-24
85Toled-10
86D/Rook-44
87D-566
87F-548
87T-419
88Portl/CMC-5
88Portl/Pro-658
89B-318
89F-123
89Score-482
89T-46
89UD-358
90Class-121
90D-542
90Score-552
90T-253
90UD-502
Posada, Leo
61T-39
62J-96
62P-96
62P/Can-96
62Salada-62
62Shirriff-62
62T-168
62T/St-55
73Cedar
74Cedar
78DaytB/MG
Pose, Scott
89Bill/Pro-2063
Posedel, Bill
39PB-121
40PB-58
41G-19
41G-19
47Centen-20
49Eureka-169
52T-361
54Hunter
55Hunter
60T-469C
Posey, Bob
85Durhm-29
86Durhm-21
Posey, John
87Hagers-13
88CharlK-11
88CharlK/Pep-11
89Hagers/Best-26
89Hagers/Star-14
89RochR/CMC-12
Post, John
88Elmir-28TR
Post, Wally
52T-151
55B-32
55Kahn
56Kahn
56T-158
57Kahn
57T-157
58Hires-14
58Kahn
58T-387
59HRDerby-15
59T-398
60T-13
61Kahn
61T-378
61T/St-23
62J-128
62Kahn
62P-128
62P/Can-128
62T-148
63T-462
64T-253
79TCMA-90
Postier, Paul
87Gasto-16
88Tulsa-24
89Tulsa/GS-21
Poston, Mark
85Beaum-16
86Beaum-20
87LasVegas-10
Potestio, Doug
86IowaC-22
87IowaC-6
Potestio, Frank
87DayBe-17
88Sprin/Best-10
89ArkTr/GS-19
89Louvl-31
Pott, Larry
85Tulsa-17
Potter, Mike
79Spoka-3
Potter, Nelson
41DP-129
47TipTop
49Eureka-16
Potthoff, Michael
89GreatF-4
Pottinger, Mark
86Clearw-20
87Lakel-20
Potts, Dave
86AubAs-19
87Osceola-16
88Osceola/Star-21
89Osceola/Star-18
Poulin, Jim
88Beloi/GS-3
89Stock/Best-25
89Stock/Cal-178TR
89Stock/Pro-387
89Stock/Star-27
Pounders, Brad
87TexLgAS-5
87Wichi-8
88LasVeg/CMC-15
88LasVeg/Pro-247
89F-642M
Powell, Alonzo
83Clint/LF-14
86SLAS-15
86WPalm-24
87D/OD-93
87Indianap-33
87Sf/Rook-8
88Indi/CMC-15
88Indi/Pro-520
89Indi/Pro-1210
89WPalm/Star-18
Powell, Alvin Jacob
38ONG/Pin-23
39PB-1
40PB-11
Powell, Charlie
78Charl
Powell, Dennis
85Cram/PCL-154
86D-250
86Pol/Dodg-48
87Calgary-6
87D-499
87F-450
87T-47
88Calg/CMC-4
88Calg/Pro-796
88T-453
89F/Up-61
89T/Tr-97T
90F-521
90Score-308
90UD-229
Powell, Grover
64T-113
Powell, Hosken
79OPC-346
79T-656
80T-471
81D-567
81F-559
81T-137
82D-228
82F-558
82T-584
83D-644
83F-440
83OPC-77
83T-77
84Cram/PCL-38
Powell, James E.
N172
Powell, John J.
11Helmar-64
E107
M116
T204
T206
Powell, John
(Boog)
62T-99
63J-62
63P-62
63T-398
64T-89
64T/Coins-104
64T/St-36
64T/SU
64T/tatt
65Bz-11
65OldLond-33
65OPC-3LL
65T-3LL
65T-560
65T/E-29
65T/trans-63
66OPC-167
66T-167
67OPC/Pl-1
67T-230
67T-241LL
67T-243LL
67T-521M
67T/Pl-1
68Coke
68T-381
68T/3D
69MB-225
69MLB/St-7
69MLBPA/Pin-22
69OPC-15
69OPC/DE-17
69T-15
69T/DE-2
69T/St-128
70K-19
70MB-22
70MLB/St-153
70OPC-200ALCS
70OPC-410
70OPC-451AS
70OPC-64LL
70T-410
70T-451AS
70T-64LL
70T/S-38
70T/SO
71K-20
71MD
71MLB/St-307
71MLB/St-570
71OPC-195ALCS
71OPC-327WS
71OPC-63LL
71OPC-700
71T-63LL
71T-700
71T/Coins-74
71T/S-5
71T/tatt-7
71T/tatt-7a
72MB-277
72OPC-250
72T-250

73JP
730PC-325
73T-325
740PC-460
74T-460
750PC-208M
750PC-625
75T-208MV
75T-625
75T/M-208MV
75T/M-625
76Ho-75
76K-50
760PC-45
76SSPC-524
76T-45
77T-206
78TCMA-80
82KMart-17
Exh47

Powell, Paul Ray
76SSPC-82

Powell, Ray
21Exh-134
21Exh-135
E120
V100
V61-95
W572

Powell, Robert LeRoy
56T-144

Powell, Ross
89Cedar/Star-30

Power, John
86Watlo-22

Power, Ted
80Albuq-22
81Albuq/TCMA-5
82F-17
84D-447
84F-478
84Nes/792-554
84T-554
85D-286
85F-547
85T-342
85T/St-50
86D-408
86F-187
860PC-108
86S-166
86T-108
86T/St-140
86TexGold-48
87D-536
87F-210
87Kahn-48
87T-437
88D-142
88F-245
88F/U-U33
880PC-236
88Panini/St-272
88Score-242
88Smok/Royals-14
88T-236
88T/Tr-89T
89D-153
89F-142
89Louvl-32
89Louvl/Pro-1249
890PC-331
89Score-348
89T-777
90D-653
90F-258
90T-59
90UD-340

Power, Vic
54T-52
55Rodeo
55T-30
55T/DH-29
56T-67
56T/Pin-14
57T-167
58T-406
59Kahn
59T-229
60Bz-16
60Kahn
60L-65
60T-75
61Clover-21
61Kahn
61P-63
61T-255
61T/St-141
62J-37
62Kahn
62P-37
62P/Can-37
62Salada-44
62Shirriff-44
62T-445
62T/bucks
62T/St-39
63F-23
63J-1
63P-1
63T-40
64T-355
65T-442
660PC-192
66T-192
78TCMA-196
79TCMA-147

Powers, John
58Kahn
58T-432
59T-489
60T-422

Powers, Larry
79LodiD-11

Powers, Michael
E107
T206

Powers, Scott
87Elmir-12
87Elmir/Red-12
88Lynch/Star-19
89Lynch/Star-19

Powers, Steve
75QuadC
77Salem

Powers, Tad
89Penin/Star-20

Powers, Ted
89Louvl/CMC-10

Powers, Thomas
N172/PCL

Prager, Howard
88CapeCod/Sum-175
89AubAs/Pro-2175

Pramesa, John
51B-324
52B-247
52T-105
PM10/Sm-148

Prather, Billy Ray
76Cedar

Pratt, Crestwell
(Cressy)
82Water-22
83Tampa-20

Pratt, Derrill
(Del)
14CJ-93
15CJ-93
21Exh-136
21Exh-137
D327
D328-135
D329-139
D350/2-140
E120
E121
E135-135
E220
M101/4-139
M101/5-140
V100
W501-11

Pratt, Louis A.
79Savan-21
81ArkTr-20

Pratt, Steve
89Clint/Pro-908

Pratt, Todd
85Elmir-17
86Greens-17
87WinHav-29
88EastLAS/Pro-22
88NewBrit/Pro-906
89NewBrit/Pro-624
89NewBrit/Star-15

Pratts, Alberto
88Elmir-2

Pratts, Alfredo
89WinHav/Star-17

Prendergast, Jim
V362-39

Prescott, George
61Union

Presko, Joe
52B-62
52T-220
53Hunter
54B-190
54Hunter
54T-135
79TCMA-178

Presley, Jim
80Wausa-13
81Wausa-20
82LynnS-13
84Cram/PCL-184
85D-240
85F-500
85Moth/Mar-20
85T/Tr-92T
86D-313
86D-506
86F-473
86F/Mini-98
86F/St-89
86KayBee-24
86Leaf-183
86Moth/Mar-7
860PC-228
86S-40
86T-598
86T/St-219
87Class-48
87D-120
87D-23DK
87D/AAS-29
87D/DKsuper-23
87D/OD-123
87F-594
87F/McCror-33
87F/Mini-82
87F/St-91
87Leaf-154
87Leaf-23DK
87Moth/Sea-4
870PC-45
87RedFoley/St-19
87S-179
87T-45
87T/St-214
88D-366
88D/Best-219
88F-385
88Moth/Sea-4
880PC-285
88Panini/St-189
88Score-46
88Sf-54
88T-285
88T/Big-90
88T/St-217
89B-214
89D-379
89D/Best-331
89F-555
89Moth/Sea-4
890PC-112
89Panini/St-437
89Score-73
89Sf-7
89T-112
89T/Big-75
89T/St-223
89UD-642
90D-497
90F-522
90Score-34
90T-346
90UD-315

Pressnell, Forest
(Tot)
39PB-134
40PB-146

Preston, Dayton
88ColAst/Best-24

Preston, Steve
88Eugene/Best-20
89AppFx/Pro-861

Prevost, Eric
78Wisco

Prewitt, Larry
80Phoen-5

Price, Al
81ElPas-24
82ElPas-24
83ElPas-18
85Crm/PCL-225tr
87Denver-3

Price, Bill
81Wisco-18

Price, Bryan
85MidldA-2
86PalmSp-27
86PalmSp/Smk-15
88Vermont/Pro-940
89Calg/CMC-9
89Calg/Pro-540
89Wmspt/Star-16

Price, Harris
75AppFx
76AppFx

Price, Jimmie
670PC-123R
67T-123R
68T-226
69T-472
700PC-129
70T-129
71MLB/St-403
710PC-444
71T-444
72MB-278
88Domino-20

Price, Joe
79Nashvl
80Indianap-5
81F-210
81T-258
82Coke/Reds
82D-481
82F-81
82T-492
83D-481
83F-600
83T-191
84D-506
84F-479
84Nes/792-686
840PC-159
84T-686
84T/St-58
85D-627
85F-548
850PC-82
85T-82
85T/St-56
86F-188
86T-523
86TexGold-49
87F-211
87Phoen-17
87T-332
88D-655
88Moth/Giants-26
88T-786
89D-376
89F-339
89Moth/Giants-26
89Score-444
89T-217
89UD-505
90F-282
90T-473

Price, John Thomas
46Remar-16

Price, Kevin
82Danvi-9
83Redwd-21
86Jaxvl/TCMA-14
86SLAS-25
87Jaxvl-20
87SLAS-17
88CharlK-4
88CharlK/Pep-4

Price, Phil
87Spart-25
88Virgini/Star-18

Priddy, Gerald
41DP-109
48L-111
49B-4
50B-212
51B-71
51T/BB-46
52B-139
52Dix
52NTea
52T-28
53Dix
53Glen
53NB
53T-113
79TCMA-213
R423-79

Priddy, Robert
64T-74R
65T-482
66T-572
670PC-26
67T-26
68T-391
69T-248
70T-687
71MLB/St-20
710PC-147
71T-147

Pries, Jeff
86Albany/TCMA-15
86Colum-19
86Colum/Pol-17
87Albany-18

Priessman, Kraig
83SanJose-17

Prieto, Arnie
88Mia/Star-19
89Mia/Star/25-23

Prieto, Pedro
(Pete)
76Dubuq

77Cocoa
Prim, Ray
47Signal
Prince, Ray
77DaytB
Prince, Tom
86PrWill-20
87Harrisbg-3
88AAA/Pro-5
88BuffB/CMC-19
88BuffB/Pro-1488
88D-538
89D-527
89F-217
89Score-626
89Score/HotRk-45
89T-453
89UD-311
Prioleau, Laney
86Lakel-18
Prior, Dan
82Readg-6
Pritchard, Harold
(Buddy)
58T-151
Pritikin, James
86Cram/PCL-113
88Wausa/Feder-12
88Wausa/GS-12
89SnBer/Best-14
89SnBer/Cal-86
Procopio, Jim
87Idaho-16
88Idaho/Pro-1853
Procter, Craig
88Spoka/Pro-1944
Proctor, Dave
88LitFalls/Puc-21
89B-378
89StLucie/Star-20
Proctor, Jim
60T-141
Proffitt, Steve
89LittleSun-9
Prohaska, Tim
89NiagFls/Puc-28
Proly, Michael
76Tulsa
79T-514
80T-399
81D-596
81F-358
81T-83
81T/Tr-815
82D-345
82F-254
82IowaC-22
82RedLob
82T-183
82T/Tr-92T
83D-225
83F-505
83T-597
83Thorn-36
84D-320
84F-501
84Nes/792-437
84Syrac-16
84T-437
Provence, Todd
86Ventura-21
87Knoxv-11
88Myrtle/Pro-1192
89Myrtle/Pro-1455
Pruett, Hubert (Hub)
87Conlon/2-50
88Conlon/5-24
Pruitt, Darrell Ray
86Penin-21
87BirmB/Best-21
88Chatt/Best-11
88SLAS-6
89Greenv/Pro-1171
89Greenv/Star-19
89Greenvl/Best-3
Pruitt, Ed
86Jacks/TCMA-8
Pruitt, Ron
77T-654
78T-198
79T-226
80T-13
81T-442
82Phoen
83Portl-21
Pruitt, Russell
79Elmir-12
Prusia, Greg
89AppFx/Pro-858
Prybylinski, Bruce
88Oneon/Pro-2061
89PrWill/Star-17
Pryce, Ken
81QuadC-22
83MidldC-11
84IowaC-1
85IowaC-20
86IowaC-23
Pryor, Buddy
83Cedar-14
83Cedar/LF-2
86Vermont-15
87Nashv-17
89Tacom/CMC-15
89Tacom/Pro-1558
Pryor, Greg
79T-559
80OPC-91
80T-164
81D-278
81F-359
81T-608
82D-521
82F-356
82T-76
82T/Tr-93T
83D-264
83F-121
83T-418
84D-374
84F-353
84Nes/792-317
84T-317
85D-277
85F-210
85T-188
86D-344
86NatPhoto-4
86T-773
87D-378
87OPC-268
87T-761
Pryor, Jim
76Cedar
77Cedar
Pryor, Randy
88CapeCod/Sum-107
Psaltis, Spiro
82CharR-20
85MidldA-16
Puccinelli, George
36Exh/4-14
38Exh/4-1
V355-127
Puckett, Kirby
83Visal/LF-6
84F/X-93
85D-438
85F-286
85F/St-122
85Leaf-107
85OPC-10
85Seven/Minn-1
85T-536
85T/St-307
85T/St-376YS
86D-72
86D/HL-7
86F-401
86F/LL-32
86F/Mini-85
86F/Slug-M5
86F/St-90
86KayBee-25
86Leaf-69
86OPC-329
86S-93
86T-329
86T/St-285
87Class-55
87Class/Up-112
87D-149
87D-19DK
87D/AAS-4
87D/DKsuper-19
87D/HL-30
87D/OD-221
87D/PopUp-4
87Drake-19
87F-549
87F-633M
87F-C11
87F/AS-5
87F/AwardWin-30
87F/Lim-32
87F/LL-36
87F/Mini-83
87F/Slug-31
87F/St-92
87F/WaxBox-C11
87Ho/St-26
87KayBee-24
87Kraft-27
87Leaf-19DK
87Leaf-56
87MnM's-15
87OPC-82
87RedFoley/St-23
87S-198M
87S-7
87Smok/AL-8
87T-450
87T-611AS
87T/Coins-20
87T/Gloss22-19
87T/Gloss60-57
87T/Mini-63
87T/St-146
87T/St-274
88Woolwth-31
88Bz-14
88ChefBoy-13
88Class/Red-164
88D-368
88D-BC15
88D/AS-15
88D/Best-186
88F-19
88F-638M
88F-C7
88F/AwardWin-29
88F/BB/AS-30
88F/BB/MVP-26
88F/Excit-30
88F/Hottest-30
88F/LL-30
88F/Mini-36
88F/RecSet-29
88F/Slug-30
88F/SS-28
88F/St-45
88F/TL-26
88F/WaxBox-C7
88F/WS-8
88FanSam-1
88KayBee-23
88KingB/Disc-3
88Leaf-144
88Master/Disc-8
88MSA/Disc-6
88Nestle-39
88OPC-120
88Panini/St-144
88Panini/St-444
88RedFoley/St-72
88Score-24
88Score-653HL
88Sf-180
88Sf-8
88Smok/Minn-12
88T-120
88T-391
88T/Big-36
88T/Coins-23
88T/Gloss60-27
88T/Mini-23
88T/Revco-21
88T/RiteAid-21
88T/St-283
88T/St/Backs-52
88T/UK-57
89Ames-24
89B-162
89Cadaco-41
89Class-15
89Class/Up/2-176
89Crunch-20
89D-182
89D/AS-23
89D/Best-130
89D/MVP-BC1
89F-124
89F-639M
89F/BBAS-32
89F/BBMVP's-32
89F/Excit-34
89F/Heroes-31
89F/LL-30
89F/Superstar-33
89F/WaxBox-C20
89Holsum/Discs-8
89KayBee-24
89KMart/DT-16
89KMart/Lead-4
89Master/Discs-2
89Nissen-8
89OPC-132
89Panini/St-247
89Panini/St-393
89Ralston-8
89Score-20
89Score/HotSt-11
89Score/Mast-19
89Sf-156
89T-403AS
89T-650
89T/Big-167
89T/Coins-48
89T/DH-7
89T/Gloss60-1
89T/HeadsUp-20
89T/Hills-23
89T/Mini-62
89T/St-293
89T/St/Backs-19
89T/UK-60
89Tetley/Discs-12
89UD-376
90Class-28
90D-269
90D-683AS
90D/Bon/MVP-BC8
90D/Preview-10
90F-383
90F-635M
90F-635M
90F/WaxBox-C22
90Score-400
90Score-690DT
90Score/100St-1
90Sf-11
90T-391AS
90T-700
90UD-236
90UD-48TC
Pugh, Tim
89Bill/Pro-2064
Puhl, Terry
75Dubuq
78BK/A-19
78T-553
79K-33
79T-617
80OPC-82
80T-147
81Coke
81D-24
81F-24
81K-42
81OPC-64
81T-411
81T/HT
81T/SO-88
81T/St-171
82D-370
82F-223
82F/St-44
82OPC-277
82T-277
82T/St-42
83D-167
83F-458
83OPC-39
83T-39
83T/S-239
84D-476
84F-235
84Moth/Ast-10
84Nes/792-383
84OPC-383
84T-383
84T/St-67
85D-426
85F-356
85GenMills-6
85Leaf-80
85Moth/Ast-7
85OPC-283
85Seven-14C
85T-613
85T/St-67
86D-206
86F-308
86Leaf-138
86Moth/Ast-16
86OPC-161
86Pol/Ast-21
86T-763
87D-431
87F-65
87Moth/Ast-7
87OPC-227
87Pol/Ast-15
87T-693
88D-533
88F/U-U90
88Moth/Ast-7
88Pol/Ast-17
88Score-282
88T-587
89D-472
89D/Best-294
89F-364
89Lennox/Ast-22
89Moth/Ast-6
89Score-567
89T-119
90D-354
90F-233
90Score-473

90T-494
90UD-201

Puig, Ed
87Stockton-27
88ElPas/Best-22
88TexLgAS/GS-31
89ElPas/GS-14

Pulkunas, Ed
86Shrev-21
87Shrev-15
88Phoen/CMC-11
88Phoen/Pro-74
88Shreve/Pro-1301
89Phoen/CMC-2
89Phoen/Pro-1492

Pujols, Luis
73Cedar
74Cedar
75Dubuq
78Charl
79Charl-14
79T-139
81D-379
81F-68
81T-313
82D-576
82F-224
82T-582
83D-642
83F-459
83OPC-112
83T-752
83Tucso-13
84Cram/PCL-71
84F-236
84Nes/792-446
84T-446
85Rang-8
86OKCty-18
87Indianap-6

Pujols, Ruben
88Virgini/Star-19
89BBCity/Star-22

Pulchinski, Thomas
77Watlo
78Watlo

Puleo, Charles
80Knoxv
81Tidew-13
82T/Tr-94T
83D-128
83F-552
83OPC-358
83T-549
83T/X-88
84D-530
84F-480
84Nes/792-273
84T-273
86Richm-17
87Smok/Atl-2
88D-537
88F-548
88Score-454
88T-179
89B-263
89D-286
89F-598
89Score-448
89T-728
89UD-589

Pulford, Don
47Centen-21

Pulido, Alfonso
84Cram/PCL-121
85Colum-8
85Colum/Pol-18
85D-34
86Colum-20
86Colum/Pol-18
87Colum-24
87Colum/Pol-20
87Colum/TCMA-7
87T-642

Pulido, Phil
77DaytB

Pulli, Frank
88Umpire-14
89Umpires-12

Pulliam, Harry C.
WG3-39

Pulliam, Harvey Jr.
88BBCity/Star-19
89Memph/Best-15
89Memph/Pro-1204
89Memph/Star-19
89SLAS-1

Pullins, Jimmie
89Idaho/Pro-2011

Purcell, William
N172
N284

Purcey, Walter
R314/Can

Purdin, John
65T-331R
68T-336
69OPC-161
69T-161
71OPC-748
71T-748
85SpokAT/Crm-16

Purdy, E.V.
29Exh/4-8

Purkey, Bob
54T-202
55T-118
55T/DH-114
57T-368
58Kahn
58T-311
59Kahn
59T-506
60Kahn
60L-67
60T-4
61Kahn
61P-184
61T-9
62J-123
62Kahn
62P-123
62P/Can-123
62Salada-153
62Shirriff-153
62T-120
62T-263M
62T/bucks
62T/St-120
63Bz-26
63F-35
63FrBauer-20
63J-134
63Kahn
63P-134
63Salada-6
63T-350
63T-5LL
63T-7LL
63T/SO
64Kahn
64T-480
65OPC-214
65T-214
66T-551
79TCMA-260
88Pac/Leg-77

Purpura, Dan
82Amari-8
83Beaum-10

Purpura, Joe
78Clint

Purtell, William
C46-30
E254
E90/3
M116
T206
T213/blue
T215/blue

Purvis, Glenn
77Visal

Puryear, Nate
77Watlo
79Tacom-17
81Charl-22
82Chatt-1

Pust, John
87Visal-21

Putman, Ed
80Evans-7
80T-59
81RochR-13

Putnam, Pat
77Tucso
78Cr/PCL-91
78T-706R
79T-713R
80OPC-8
80T-22
81D-265
81F-630
81OPC-302
81T-498
82D-520
82F-327
82F/St-180
82OPC-149
82T-149
82T/St-241
83T/X-89
84D-145
84F-617
84Moth/Mar-16
84Nes/792-336TL
84Nes/792-636
84OPC-226
84T-636
84T/St-339
85F-287
85Omaha-9
85T-535

Puttman, Ambrose
T206

Puzey, James W.
86StPet-25
87Sprin/Best-5
88ArkTr/GS-22
88Louvl-40
89Louvl-33
89Louvl/CMC-12
89Louvl/Pro-1243

Pyburn, James
57T-276

Pyburn, Jeff
81Hawai-12
82Hawai-12

Pye, Eddie
88GreatF-9
89Bakers/Cal-198

Pyfrom, Joel
82Miami-6

Pyle, Scott
81WHave-23
82WHave-28
83Tacom-26

Pytlak, Frank A.
34Exh/4-11
37Exh/4-11
38G-245
38G-269
41DP-107
R308-180
R314

Pyznarski, Tim
83Albany-13
84Cram/PCL-87
85Cram/PCL-122
86LasVegas-12
87D-654
87Denver-2
87S-158M
87T-429
88AAA/Pro-13
88Denver/CMC-11
88Denver/Pro-1273
88RochR-21
88RochR/Gov-21
89Omaha/Pro-1726

Quade, Mike
82AlexD-10
83AlexD-28
86Macon-20MG
87Jaxvl-27

Qualls, Jim
69T-602R
70OPC-192
70T-192
71OPC-731
71T-731
88Boise/Pro-1610

Qualters, Tom
54T-174
55T-33
55T/DH-108
58T-453
59T-341

Quantrill, Paul
89Elmir/Puc-31

Quealey, Steve
82BirmB-20

Queen, Mel D.
64T-33R
66T-556
67T-374
68T-283
69OPC-81
69T-81
71MLB/St-354
71OPC-736
71T-736
72OPC-196
72T-196
80Tacom-7
81Charl-21
82BK/Ind-8CO
82BK/Ind-9
82BK/Indians-8
82BK/Indians-9
82Wheat/Ind
87Syrac/TCMA-28

Queen, Mel J.
47TipTop
51B-309
52B-171

Quesada, Ed
89Everett/Star-24

Quezada, Rafael
80Ander-29

Quezada, Silvano
75Lafay
76Phoen

Quick, Gene
76Clint

Quick, Jim
88Umpire-26
89Umpires-24

Quick, Ron
81Shrev-17

Quigley, Jerry
76QuadC

Quilici, Frank
66T-207
68T-557
69MB-226
69T-356
70T-572
71MLB/St-471
71OPC-141MG
71T-141
72MB-279
73OPC-49MG
73T-49MG
74OPC-447MG
74T-447MG
75OPC-443MG
75T-443MG
75T/M-443MG

Quillin, Lee
T206

Quinlan, Tom
87Myrtle-11
88Knoxv/Best-25
89Knoxv/Best-20
89Knoxv/Pro-1123
89Knoxv/Star-16

Quinn, Frank W.
51B-276

Quinn, Jack
25Exh-68
26Exh-68
31Exh/4-4
87Conlon/2-51
88Conlon/3-23
E126-14

Quinn, James
77Newar

Quinn, John P.
10Domino-100
11Helmar-45
12Sweet/Pin-37
33G-78
E120
E121/80
S74-24
T202
T205
T206
T207
T213/blue
T215/brown
V353-53
W517-17
W572
W575

Quinn, Joseph J.
N172
N526

Quinn, Thomas G.
N172

Quinones, Hector
83Beloi/LF-26
86Fresno/Smok-18

Quinones, Luis
83Albany-14
84Maine-20
85Maine-21
86F/Up-U92
86Phoen-21
87IowaC-20
87T-362
88D-365
88Nashvl/CMC-14
88Nashvl/Pro-490
88T-667
89Nashvl/CMC-17
89Nashvl/Pro-1272
90Class-132
90D-595
90F-428
90Score-499
90T-176
90UD-593

Quinones, Rene
(Rey)
77BurlB
79Holyo-1
80Vanco-16
81Vanco-18
83BuffB-18

83ElPas-8
84BuffB-5
86D/Rook-48
86F/Up-U93
86Pawtu-17
86T/Tr-89T
87D-638
87D/OD-121
87F-595
87Moth/Sea-20
87T-561
88D-198
88D/Best-275
88F-386
88Moth/Sea-20
88OPC-358
88Panini/St-190
88Score-192
88T-358
88T/St-215
89B-213
89Bimbo/Discs-4
89D-330
89D/Best-185
89F-556
89OPC-246
89Panini/St-438
89Score-361
89T-246
89T/St-224
89T/Tr-98T
89UD-508
89UD/Ext-750

Quintana, Al
86Watertn-17

Quintana, Carlos
85Elmir-18
86Greens-18
87NewBrit-12
88Pawtu/CMC-20
88Pawtu/Pro-453
89Class-133
89D-37
89F-95
89Pawtu/CMC-13
89Pawtu/Dunkin-18
89Pawtu/Pro-688
89Score-623
89Score/HotRk-13
89T-704
89T/Big-142
89UD-26
90D-517
90F-283
90Score-658
90Score/100Ris-49
90T-18
90UD-465

Quintana, Luis
77SLCty
82Wichi-13

Quintero, Frank
77Visal
78OrlTw

Quinzer, Paul
86Cram/PCL-165
88Wichi-23
89Wich/Roc-27
89Wich/Roc/Up-16

Quirk, Art
62T-591R
63T-522R

Quirk, Jamie
76OPC-598R
76T-598R
77T-463
78T-95
79T-26
80T-248
81D-341
81F-50
81T-507
82D-212
82F-421
82T-173
83T-264
83T/X-90
84F-332
84Nes/792-671
84T-671
85Omaha-16
87F-377
87T-354
88D-404
88F-266
88Panini/St-103
88Score-577
88Smok/Royals-19
88T-477
89B-173
89F-290
89Score-461
89T-702
89UD-620

Quiros, Gus
79Vanco-11
80Vanco-4
81Vanco-11

Quisenberry, Dan
75Watlo
76Watlo
77Jaxvl
80T-667R
81Coke
81D-222
81F-31
81F/St-24
81OPC-206
81T-493
81T-8LL
81T/St-7
82D-112
82D-212
82F-422
82F/St-204
82T-264
83D-70
83F-122
83K-32
83OPC-155
83OPC-396AS
83Pol/Roy-6
83T-155
83T-396
83T-708
83T/St-165
83T/St-22
83T/St-74
84D-583
84D/AAS-56
84F-354
84F-635IA
84F/St-73
84FunFood/Pin-25
84Nes/792-138LL
84Nes/792-3HL
84Nes/792-407AS
84Nes/792-570
84Nes/792-718LL
84Nestle/DT-11
84OPC-273
84OPC-69AS
84Ralston-25
84Seven-24C
84T-138
84T-3
84T-407
84T-570
84T-718
84T/Cereal-25
84T/Gloss40-38
84T/St-10
84T/St-279
84T/St-290
84T/St-9
84T/Super-9
84T/Super-9
85D-6
85D-95
85D/AAS-8
85D/DKsuper-6
85Drake-39
85F-211
85F/LimEd-25
85F/St-99
85Leaf-6DK
85OPC-270
85Seven-15C
85T-270
85T-711AS
85T/3D-24
85T/Gloss40-35
85T/St-173
85T/St-269
85T/Super-8
85Woolwth-28
86D-541
86F-18
86F/AS-9
86F/Mini-2
86F/St-91
86Kitty/Disc-8
86Leaf-208
86NatPhoto-29
86OPC-50
86Quaker-29
86S-118
86S-186M
86S-55M
86T-50
86T-722
86T/3D-21
86T/Gloss60-35
86T/St-257
86T/Super-5
87D-177
87F-378
87F/Lim-33
87F/Mini-84
87F/St-93
87OPC-15
87RedFoley/St-7
87S-167
87T-714
87T/St-257
88D-471
88F-267
88OPC-195
88Panini/St-101
88Score-290
88Score/Tr-18T
88Sf-76
88Smok/Royals-15
88T-195
88T/St-256
89F/Up-120
89OPC-13
89Score-520
89Smok/Cards-19
89T-612
89UD-533
90D-437
90F-259
90Score-475
90T-312
90UD-659

Rabb, John
81Shrev-2
82Phoen
83Phoen/BHN-1
84D-143
84Nes/792-228
84T-228
85Cram/PCL-183
85D-236
85IntLgAS-12
85Richm-22
85T-696
86Richm-18
87Richm/TCMA-20

Rabe, Charles
58Kahn
58T-376

Rabouin, Andre
88AppFx/Pro-159
89AppFx/Pro-871

Rackley, Marv
47TipTop

Raczka, Mike
87CharO/WBTV-10
88RochR-22
88RochR/Gov-22
89RochR/CMC-5
89RochR/Pro-1648

Radatz, Dick
62T-591R
63T-363
64T-170
64T/Coins-30
64T/S-40
64T/St-41
64Wheat/St-37
65Bz-10
65OldLond-34
65T-295
65T/E-48
65T/trans-64
66T-475
66T/RO-111
67OPC-174
67T-174
69T-663
74Laugh/ASG-63
78TCMA-76
89Pac/Leg-122
89Swell-46
PM10/Sm-149
WG10-44
WG9-43

Radbourn, Charles
(Hoss)
50Callahan
75F/Pion-5
80SSPC/HOF
N172
N284
N403

Radcliff, Ray
(Rip)
37OPC-125
37Wheat
38G-261
38G-285
PR1-24
R314
V300
WG8-45

Radcliffe, Ernest Jr.
87Erie-9
88Virgini/Star-20

Radcliffe, Ted
78Laugh/Black-36

Rader, Dave
72OPC-232R
72T-232R
73OPC-121
73T-121
74OPC-213
74T-213
74T/St-108
75OPC-31
75T-31
75T/M-31
76Ho-21
76Ho/Twink-21
76OPC-54
76T-54
77T-427
78T-563
79OPC-369
79T-693
80T-296
81D-512
81OPC-359
81T-378

Rader, Doug
67T-412R
68T-332
69MB-227
69MLB/St-142
69OPC-119
69T-119
69T/St-37
70MLB/St-46
70OPC-355
70T-355
71MLB/St-90
71OPC-425
71T-425
71T/Coins-17
72K-14
72MB-280
72T-536
73OPC-76
73T-76
74OPC-395
74T-395
74T/DE-14
74T/St-35
75Ho-89
75OPC-165
75T-165
75T/M-165
76OPC-44
76SSPC-59
76T-44
76T/Tr-44T
77T-9
78OPC-166
78T-651
80Hawai-2
81Hawai-23
82Hawai-23
83Rang-11MG
83T/X-91
84Nes/792-412MG
84Rang-11
84T-412
85T-519MG
89T/Tr-99TMG
90T-51MG

Radford, Paul
N172

Radinsky, Scott
87Penin-12
89SoBend/GS-7

Radison, Dan
88Hamil/Pro-1732
89Sprin/Best-29

Radloff, Scott
83Cedar-15
83Cedar/LF-21

Radovich, Robert
66Pep/Tul

Raeside, John
82Lynch-23

Raether, Richard
86Tulsa-22
87PortChar-9
88Tulsa-26

Raffensberger, Ken
49B-176
49Eureka-93
51B-48
52B-55
52T-118
52TipTop
53B/Col-10
53T-276
54B-92

54T-46
Raffo, Thomas
88CapeCod-9
88CapeCod/Sum-79
Ragan, Don
D329-140
M101/4-140
T207
Ragland, Tom
72OPC-334R
72T-334R
74OPC-441
74T-441
Ragni, John
52Mother-34
Ragsdale, Jerry
83Ander-27
Raich, Eric
76OPC-484
76T-484
77T-62
Raimondi, Bill
46Remar
47Remar-1
47Signal
47Smith-2
48Signal
48Smith-1
49B/PCL-18
49Remar
53Mother-36
Raimondo, Pasquale
81VeroB-15
Rainbolt, Ray
74Gasto
79Tulsa-8
Rainer, Rick
85Tidew-28
86Tidew-25TR
87Tidew-30
87Tidew/TCMA-25
Raines, Larry
58T-243
Raines, Mike
81Cedar-5
Raines, Tim
79Memph
81D-538
81OPC-136R
81T-479R
82D-214
82F-202
82F/St-31
82Hygrade
82K-53
82OPC-70
82OPC/Post-17
82T-164LL
82T-3M
82T-70
82T/St-116
82T/St-62
82T/St-7
82Zeller-3
83D-540
83F-292
83OPC-227
83OPC-352AS
83Stuart-9
83T-403
83T-595
83T-704
83T/St-210
83T/St-253
84D-299
84F-281
84F-631
84F/St-51
84F/St-88
84FunFood/Pin-41
84Nes/792-134LL
84Nes/792-370
84Nes/792-390AS
84Nestle/DT-17
84OPC-370
84OPC-390AS
84Seven-20E
84Stuart-20
84Stuart-36AS
84Stuart-37M
84T-134
84T-370
84T-390
84T/Gloss22-17
84T/Gloss40-37
84T/St-179
84T/St-201
84T/St-91
84T/St/Box-4
85D-299
85D/AAS-1
85Drake-24
85F-405
85F/LimEd-26
85F/St-42
85F/St-58
85Leaf-218
85Leaf-252CG
85OPC-277
85OPC/Post-7
85Seven-12S
85T-630
85T/3D-17
85T/St-282
85T/St-82
85T/Super-15
86D-177
86D/AAS-20
86Drake-15
86F-256
86F-632M
86F/LL-33
86F/Mini-54
86F/St-92
86Leaf-108
86OPC-280
86Provigo-7
86Quaker-10
86S-11
86S-127M
86S-144M
86S/Dec-74M
86T-280
86T/Gloss60-15
86T/Mini-49
86T/St-75
86T/Super-42
87Class-29
87D-56
87D/AAS-36
87D/HL-16
87D/HL-7
87F-328
87F-642M
87F/AS-12
87F/Excit-34
87F/Lim-34
87F/Mini-85
87F/RecSet-30
87F/Slug-32
87F/St-94
87KayBee-25
87Leaf-149
87OPC-30
87RedFoley/St-39
87S-152M
87S-197M
87S-199M
87S-34
87T-30
87T/Board-24
87T/Gloss60-48
87T/HL-11
87T/Mini-17
87T/St-85
87Woolwth-11
88Bz-15
88Class/Red-168
88D-2DK
88D-345
88D-BC18
88D/AS-57
88D/AS-62
88D/Best-180
88D/DKsuper-2DK
88F-193
88F-631M
88F/AwardWin-30
88F/BB/AS-31
88F/BB/MVP-27
88F/Excit-31
88F/Head-6
88F/Hottest-31
88F/LL-31
88F/Mini-90
88F/RecSet-30
88F/SS-29
88F/St-97
88F/TL-27
88FanSam-16
88Ho/Disc-11
88Jiffy-14
88KayBee-24
88KMart-19
88Leaf-114
88Leaf-211MVP
88Leaf-2DK
88Nestle-31
88OPC-243
88Panini/St-330
88Score-3
88Score-649
88Sf-2
88T-403
88T-720
88T/Big-116
88T/Coins-49
88T/Gloss60-12
88T/Mini-57
88T/Revco-5
88T/RiteAid-6
88T/St-76
88T/St/Backs-20
88T/UK-58
89B-369
89Class-42
89D-97
89D/Best-258
89F-391
89KayBee-25
89KMart/DT-27
89KMart/Lead-7
89OPC-87
89Panini/St-125
89Ralston-6
89RedFoley/St-91
89Score-40
89Score/HotSt-95
89Sf-150
89T-560
89T-81TL
89T/Big-73
89T/Coins-22
89T/Gloss60-53
89T/St-77
89T/UK-61
89UD-402
90Class-118
90D-216
90D/Bon/MVP-BC7
90F-359
90Score-409
90Score/100St-75
90Sf-69
90T-180
90UD-177
90UD-29TC
Rainey, Chuck
80T-662R
81T-199
82Coke/BOS
82F-303
82T-522
83D-334
83F-192
83T-56
83T/X-92
83Thorn-30
84D-76
84F-502
84Nes/792-334
84OPC-334
84T/St-47
85D-618
Rainey, Scott
83Clint/LF-9
87Wichi-16
Raisanen, Keith
87Watertn-8
88Salem/Star-16
89Aug/Pro-506
Rajsich, Dave
78Cr/PCL-73
79T-710R
80T-548
81D-267
83OKCty-15
85RochR-21
86Louisvl-25
88Louvl-41
88Louvl/CMC-9
88Louvl/Pro-443
Rajsich, Gary
77Cocoa
80Tucso-16
81Tidew-9
83D-599
83F-553
83T-317
83Tidew-8
84Louvl-6
85Moth/Giants-24
Rakow, Ed
60T-551
61T-147
62T-342
63J-90
63P-90
63T-82
64Det/Lids-12
64T-491
65T-454
Raley, Dan
89Lakel/Star-17
Raley, Tim
88Beloi/GS-5
89Stock/Best-20
89Stock/Cal-169
89Stock/Pro-401
89Stock/Star-9
Ralston, Bobby
85Orlan-10
86Toled-18
87Orlan-6
88Portl/CMC-21
88Portl/Pro-657
89Portl/CMC-15
89Portl/Pro-232
Ramazzotti, Bob
49Eureka-67
51B-247
52T-184
53B/BW-41
Rambo, Matt
88Spart/Pro-1025
88Spart/Star-16
88Spart/Star-16
89Clearw/Star-17
Rameriez, Nick
88CharWh/Best-26
Rametta, Steve
75SnAnt
Ramie, Vern
82Knoxv-17
83Syrac-23
Ramirez, Alex
80OrlTw-18
Ramirez, D. Allan
(Allan)
82RochR-5
83RochR-7
84D-332
84Nes/792-347
84RochR-16
84T-347
85CharO-25
Ramirez, Fausto
86Cram/PCL-125
88Wausa/Feder-3
88Wausa/GS-3
Ramirez, Frank
87Idaho-23
Ramirez, J.D.
89SLCty-11
Ramirez, Jack
79Tulsa-12
Ramirez, Luis
78Newar
Ramirez, Mario
76Wausa
78Tidew
79Tidew-12
84F-309
84Moth/Padres-23
84Nes/792-94
84T-94
85Moth/Padres-16
85T-427
86D-568
86T-262
86Toled-19
Ramirez, Milt
71MLB/St-281
71OPC-702
71T-702
77SnJos-5
80Ogden-14
Ramirez, Nick
88Geneva/Pro-1634
Ramirez, Orlando
76SSPC-197
77T-131
Ramirez, Rafael
78Green
79Savan-23
80Richm-2
81F-266
81Pol/Atl-16
81T-192R
82BK/Lids-21
82D-546
82F-447
82Pol/Atl-16
82T-536
83D-310
83F-146
83Pol/Atl-16
83T-439
84D-589
84F-190
84F/St-26
84Nes/792-234
84OPC-234
84Pol/Atl-16
84T-234
84T/St-33
85D-141
85F-339
85Ho/Braves-20
85Leaf-86

85OPC-232
85Pol/Atl-16
85T-647
85T/St-27
86D-263
86F-526
86OPC-107
86Pol/Atl-16
86T-107
86T/St-42
87D-202
87F-526
87Smok/Atl-18
87T-76
87T/St-42
88D-448
88F/U-U91
88Moth/Ast-17
88OPC-379
88Panini/St-247
88Pol/Ast-18
88Score-426
88Score/Tr-12T
88T-379
88T/Tr-90T
89B-330
89D-509
89D/Best-64
89F-365
89Lennox/Ast-16
89Moth/Ast-16
89OPC-261
89Panini/St-90
89Score-113
89T-749
89T/Big-268
89T/St-17
89UD-341
90D-241
90F-234
90Score-42
90T-558
90UD-144

Ramirez, Randy
84Chatt-21

Ramirez, Ray
86Orlan-16TR
87OKCty-24
88OkCty/Pro-51
89OkCty/Pro-1533

Ramirez, Richard
87Gasto-23

Ramirez, Russell
78Newar
79BurlB-2

Ramon, Julio
87Oneon-16

Ramon, Ray
86Readg-22

Ramos, Domingo
77WHave
78Cr/PCL-78
79Syrac-6
80Syrac-22
82SLCty-16
84D-440
84Nes/792-194
84T-194
85Moth/Mar-12
85T-349
86Moth/Mar-12
86T-462
87Moth/Sea-21
87T-641
88ColSp/CMC-16
88ColSp/Pro-1534
88D-622
88F/U-U23
88Score-362
88T-206
89Mara/Cubs-15
90D-491
90Score-489
90T-37
90UD-150

Ramos, George
78Green

Ramos, John
87PrWill-28
88CLAS/Star-15
88PrWill/Star-20
89Albany/Best-13
89Albany/Pro-336
89Albany/Star-15
89Star/Wax-100

Ramos, Jose
87Fayette-2
88Fay/Pro-1086
89London/Pro-1387

Ramos, Pedro
56T-49
57T-326
58T-331
59T-291M
59T-78
60L-21
60T-175
61Clover-22
61P-98
61Peters-3
61T-50LL
61T-528
61T/St-184
62Sugar-19
62T-485
62T/bucks
62T/St-79
63Sugar-19
63T-14
64Kahn
64T-562
65OPC-13
65T-13
66T-439
67OPC-187
67T-187
WG10-18

Ramos, Richard
82Wichi-14

Ramos, Roberto
(Bobby)
79SLCty
81F-162
81OPC-136R
81T-479R
82Colum-18
82Colum/Pol-31
82F-203
82OPC-354
82T-354
83Stuart-20
83T/X-93
84D-209
84F-282
84Nes/792-32
84OPC-32
84Stuart-9
84T-32
85Cram/PCL-15
85OPC-269
85T-407
86IowaC-24
87Omaha-21
88Phoen/CMC-13
88Phoen/Pro-69
89ColMud/Best-20
89ColMud/Pro-121

Ramos, Wolf
80Elmir-24

Ramppen, Frank
83Visal/LF-7

Ramsdell, J. Willard
47Signal
47Sunbeam
51B-251
52B-22
52T-114
53Mother-3
79TCMA-279

Ramsey, Fernando
88CharWh/Best-22
89Peoria/Ko-25

Ramsey, Michael J.
(Mike)
76ArkTr
77ArkTr
81F-549
81T-366
82D-316
82F-125
82T-574
83D-568
83F-19
83T-128
84D-382
84F-333
84Nes/792-467
84T-467
85F-406
85OPC-62
85T-62
86Tampa-15
87Albuq/Pol-30
87D/OD-80
87Edmon-6
87Moth/Dodg-11
88Albuq/CMC-14
88Albuq/Pro-267
88Score-267
89Edmon/CMC-16
89Edmon/Pro-561

Ramsey, Thomas
N172

Ramstack, Curt
76AppFx

Rand, Dick
54Hunter
58T-218

Rand, Kevin
85Albany-27
87Colum-2

Randahl, Rick
81Tacom-2

Randall, Bob
77T-578
78T-363
79T-58
80OPC-90
80T-162
80Toled-2

Randall, James
(Sap)
82Redwd-8
83Nashua-18
84Cram/PCL-101
85Cram/PCL-10
86MidldA-20
87Edmon-16
88AAA/Pro-46
88Vanco/CMC-20
88Vanco/Pro-765

Randall, Mark
89Martins/Star-26

Randall, Newton
T206

Randle, Carl
88Butte-7
89Gasto/Pro-1005
89Gasto/Star-19

Randle, Len
72T-737
73OPC-378
73T-378
74OPC-446
74T-446
75OPC-259
75T-259
75T/M-259
76OPC-31
76SSPC-266
76T-31
77T-196
78Ho-102
78K-22
78OPC-132
78T-544
79OPC-236
79T-454
81D-485
81F-301
81Pol/Mariners-9
81T-692
81T/TR-817
82D-307
82F-516
82OPC-312
82T-312
82T/ST-230
87Watlo-27

Randle, Michael
87Kenosha-3
88CalLgAS-37
88Visal/Cal-147
88Visal/Pro-85
89Orlan/Best-21
89Orlan/Pro-1339

Randle, Randy
86Osceola-20
87Osceola-5
88Modesto/Cal-77
89NewBrit/Pro-618
89NewBrit/Star-17

Randolph, Bob
81LynnS-26
83Chatt-13

Randolph, Willie
76OPC-592R
76SSPC-584
76T-592R
76T/Tr-592T
77BK/Y-13
77OPC-110
77T-359
78BK/Y-13
78Ho-89
78OPC-228
78T-620
79BK/Y-13
79OPC-125
79T-250
80OPC-239
80T-460
81D-345
81F-109
81F/St-107
81OPC-60
81T-60
81T/HT
81T/So-36
81T/St-108
81T/St-242
82D-461
82F-49
82F/St-121
82OPC-159IA
82OPC-213AS
82OPC-37
82T-548
82T-569
82T-570A
82T/St-219
83D-283
83F-393
83OPC-140
83RoyRog/Disc-9
83T-140
83T/St-95
84D-417
84F-137
84FunFood/Pin-20
84Nes/792-360
84OPC-360
84T-360
84T/St-324
85D-92
85F-140
85Leaf-83
85OPC-8
85T-765
85T/St-312
86D-16
86D-92
86D/DKsuper-16
86F-115
86Leaf-16DK
86OPC-332
86T-276M
86T-455
86T/St-305
87D-154
87D/OD-246
87F-109
87F/Lim-35
87Leaf-58
87OPC-377
87RedFoley/St-2
87T-701
87T/St-302
88D-228
88D/AS-3
88D/Best-108
88D/PopUp-3
88D/Y/Bk-228
88F-218
88F/BB/AS-32
88F/BB/MVP-28
88F/Mini-42
88F/St-50
88Leaf-162
88Nestle-22
88OPC-210
88Panini/St-153
88Panini/St-228M
88Score-266
88Score/WaxBox-3
88Sf-47
88Sf/Gamewin-6
88T-210
88T-387
88T/Big-76
88T/Gloss22-3
88T/Gloss60-42
88T/Mini-28
88T/St-162
88T/St-294
88T/St/Backs-37
88T/UK-59
89B-344
89D-395
89D/Best-148
89D/Tr-8
89F-265
89F/Up-93
89Moth/Dodg-10
89OPC-244
89Panini/St-405
89Pol/Dodg-8
89RedFoley/St-92
89Score-45
89Score/Tr-41
89Smok/Dodg-57
89T-519TL
89T-635
89T/Big-244
89T/St-309
89T/Tr-100T
89UD-237
89UD/Ext-777
90Class-122
90D-19DK

90D-250
90F-406
90Score-395
90Score/100St-4
90Sf-175
90T-25
90UD-183

Ranew, Merritt
62T-156
64T-78
66OPC-62
66T-62
89Smok/Ast-11

Rannow, John
86Cram/PCL-19
87Clint-10

Ransom, Gene
82Madis-9
83Madis/LF-18

Ransom, Jeff
81Phoen-22
83Phoen/BHN-5
87Toled-24
87Toled/TCMA-11

Rantz, Mike
83Idaho-24

Raper, Ron
88CapeCod/Sum-37

Rapp, Earl
49Remar
50Remar
53Mother-30

Rapp, Joe
(Goldie)
21Exh-138
E120
E220
V100
V61-104
W573

Rapp, Vern
77T-183MG
78T-324
83Stuart-3CO
84T/X-95

Rariden, Bill
14CJ-137
15CJ-137
88Pac/8Men-86
D327
D328-136
D329-141
D350/2-141
E135-136
E270
M101/4-141
M101/5-141

Raschi, Vic
49B-35
50B-100
51B-25
51BR-C4
52B-37
52BR
52StarCal/L-70D
53B/Col-27
53Exh/Can-5
54B-33
54Hunter
55B-185
55Hunter
55Rodeo
74Laugh/ASG-48
79TCMA-186
88Pac/Leg-70
Exh47
PM10/Sm-150
R346-32

Rasmus, Tony
86Cram/PCL-191

Rasmussen
T207

Rasmussen, Dennis
81Holyo-25
83Colum-8
84Colum-25
84Colum/Pol-19
84D-446
85D-518
85F-141
85Leaf-48
85T-691
86D-336
86T-301
87Class-87
87D-175
87D/OD-247
87F-110
87F/Excit-35
87F/GameWin-35
87F/Mini-86
87F/St-95
87Leaf-260
87OPC-364
87S-71
87T-555
87T/Mini-66
87T/St-303
88D-575
88F-246
88F/U-U126
88Score-560
88T-135
88T/St-145
88T/Tr-91T
89B-450
89Class-86
89D-559
89F-314
89OPC-32
89Panini/St-195
89Score-562
89Sf-212
89T-32
89UD-645
90D-420
90F-165
90Score-129
90T-449
90UD-594

Rasmussen, Harold
(Eric)
76OPC-182
76SSPC-296
76T-182
77T-404
78T-281
79T-57
80T-531
81D-123
81F-497
81T-342
83T-594
84Cram/PCL-49
84Nes/792-724
84OPC-377
84T-724
86Miami-21
86RochR-17
87RochR-8
87RochR/TCMA-8
88Watlo/Pro-686
89Canton/Best-11
89Canton/Pro-1308

Rasmussen, Jim
81OkCty/TCMA-25
82OkCty-18
82Readg-7
84Nashvl-18
87Hawai-11

Rasmussen, Neil
73Cedar
75BurlB
77Holyo
78Holyo

Rasp, Ronnie
88Wythe/Pro-2001
89CharWh/Best-17
89CharWh/Pro-1764

Rath, Maurice
88Pac/8Men-85
E270
W514-57

Rather, Dody
86FSLAS-39
86Osceola-21
87ColAst/Pro-17
87ColumAst-17

Rathjen, Dennis
80Clint-2

Ratliff, Danny
86Stockton-22

Ratliff, Darryl
89Princet/Star-15

Ratliff, Kelly Eugene
65T-553R

Ratliff, Paul
63T-549R
70OPC-267R
70T-267R
71OPC-607
71T-607

Ratzer, Steve
82Tidew-21

Rau, Doug
73OPC-602R
73T-602R
74OPC-64
74T-64
75OPC-269
75T-269
75T/M-269
76OPC-124
76SSPC-71
76T-124
77K-11
77OPC-128
77T-421
78OPC-24
78T-641
79K-56
79OPC-178
79T-347
80Pol/Dodg-31
80T-527
81F-133
81Redwd-9
81T-174
81T/Tr-819

Raubolt, Art
86Lakel-19

Rauch, Al
(Rocky)
78Watlo

Rauth, Chris
85LitFalls-8
86Columbia-20
87Lynch-15
89Jacks/GS-24

Rautzhan, Clarence G.
(Lance)
75Water
78T-709R
79Holyo-25
79OPC-193
79T-373
80Vanco-9

Rawdon, Chris
86Elmir-16

Rawley, Billy
83Cedar-6

Rawley, Shane
75WPalm
79OPC-30
79T-74
80OPC-368
80T-723
81D-167
81OPC-51
81Pol/Mar-16
81T-423
81T/St-129
82D-352
82F-517
82T-197
82T/Tr-95T
83D-513
83F-394
83T-592
84D-295
84F-138
84F/X-94
84Nes/792-254
84OPC-254
84T-254
85CIGNA-15
85D-599
85D/HL-39
85F-263
85Leaf-31
85OPC-169
85T-636
86CIGNA-6
86D-233
86F-446
86Leaf-109
86OPC-361
86T-361
86T/St-123
87D-83
87D/AAS-56
87D/OD-159
87F-180
87F/RecSet-31
87F/St-96
87Leaf-139
87OPC-239
87RedFoley/St-124
87S-181
87T-771
87T/St-120
88D-13DK
88D-83
88D/Best-240
88D/DKsuper-13DK
88F-311
88F-C8
88F/Hottest-32
88F/Mini-100
88F/SS-C4
88F/St-109
88F/WaxBox-C8
88Leaf-13DK
88Leaf-92
88OPC-66
88Panini/St-352
88Score-375
88Sf-51
88T-406
88T-66
88T/Gloss60-45
88T/Mini-65
88T/St-121
89B-151
89D-251
89F-579
89F/Up-44
89OPC-24
89Score-170
89T-494
89T/St-118
89T/Tr-101T
89UD-427
89UD/Ext-786
90D-537
90F-384
90Score-71
90T-101
90UD-438

Rawlings, John
E120
E121/120
E121/80
V100
W501-61
W573
W575

Ray
M116

Ray, Art
83AlexD-9

Ray, Bregg
84Butte-21

Ray, Glenn
81CharR-7

Ray, Jay
86Bakers-23
88VeroB/Star-21

Ray, Jim F.
68T-539R
69T-257
70OPC-113
70T-113
71MLB/St-91
71OPC-242
71T-242
72T-603
73OPC-313
73T-313
74OPC-458
74T-458
74T/Tr-458T
75Cedar
75OPC-89
75T-89
75T/M-89

Ray, Johnny
80Colum
81Tucso-10
82D-528
82F-492
82T-291R
82T/Tr-96T
83D-437
83F-317
83K-24
83OPC-149
83T-149
83T/St-327
84D-308
84F-260
84FunFood/Pin-69
84Nes/792-387AS
84Nes/792-537
84Nestle/DT-13
84OPC-323
84OPC-387AS
84T-387
84T-537
84T/Gloss40-5
84T/St-134
84T/St-186
84T/St/Box-7
85D-186
85D/AAS-50
85F-473
85F/St-43
85GenMills-7
85Leaf-212
85OPC-96
85T-96
85T/St-130
86D-186
86D-19
86D/DKsuper-19
86D/HL-9
86F-617
86F/St-93
86Leaf-19DK
86OPC-37

86T-615
86T/St-124
87D-144
87D/OD-162
87F-618
87F/AwardWin-31
87F/Excit-36
87F/Mini-87
87F/St-97
87Kraft-14
87Leaf-147
87OPC-291
87RedFoley/St-51
87S-116M
87S-121
87Smok/NL-8
87T-747
87T/Gloss60-55
87T/St-135
88D-428
88D/Best-171
88F-502
88F/Slug-31
88Leaf-260
88OPC-115
88Score-254
88Sf-186
88Smok/Angels-2
88T-115
88T/Big-97
89B-49
89Cadaco-42
89D-12DK
89D-331
89D/AS-25
89D/Best-195
89D/DKsuper-12DK
89F-487
89F/BBAS-33
89F/Heroes-32
89KMart/Lead-18
89OPC-109
89Panini/St-292
89RedFoley/St-93
89Score-14
89Score/HotSt-99
89Sf-195
89Smok/Angels-20
89T-455
89T/Big-7
89T/Coins-49
89T/Hills-24
89T/Mini-50
89T/St-182
89T/UK-62
89UD-481
90D-234
90F-143
90Score-293
90Sf-82
90T-334
90UD-509
Ray, Larry
82Tucso-10
83Tucso-20
84Cram/PCL-70
86ColumAst-22
86SLAS-11
87Vanco-20
Ray, Rick
89Utica/Puc-31
Ray, Steve
83Greens-11
Raybon, Shannon
86Visal-16TR
87Visal-27
88Orlan/Best-25
Raydon, Curt
59T-305
60T-49
Rayford, Floyd
79SLCty-20
80RochR-18
81RochR-14
81T-399R
83RochR-13
83T-192
84F-334
84F/X-95
84Nes/792-514
84T-514
84T/X-96
85D-576
85F-186
85T-341
86D-332
86F-283
86Leaf-197
86T-623
87T-426
88Score-359
88T-296
89ScrWB/CMC-22
89ScrWB/Pro-727
Raymer, Greg
83Miami-9
86Jaxvl/TCMA-12
Raymond, Arthur
(Bugs)
E254
M116
S74-93
T202
T204
T205
T206
T3-113
Raymond, Claude
63T-519
64T-504
65OPC-48
65T-48
66T-586
67T-364
68OPC-166
68T-166
69T-446
70MLB/St-68
70OPC-268
70T-268
71MLB/St-138
71OPC-202
71OPC-536
71T-536
78TCMA-46
86Moth/Ast-4
Raziano, Michael S.
87Sprin/Best-19
88Sprin/Best-16
Razook, Mark
87Anchora-24
89Wmspt/Star-17
Read, James
88Pac/8Men-11
Reade, Bill
80Utica-30
Reade, Curtis
81VeroB-16
Ready, Randy
81BurlB-17
82ElPas-7
84Pol/Brew-2
84T/X-97
85F-592
85Pol/Brew-2
86D-481
86F-498
86Pol/Brew-2
86T-209
87Bohem-5
87F/U-U100
87T/Tr-97T
88Coke/Padres-5
88D-264
88F-594
88OPC-151
88Panini/St-407
88Score-512
88Smok/Padres-23
88T-426
88T/Big-102
89D-365
89D/Best-215
89F-315
89OPC-82
89Panini/St-201
89Score-426
89Score/Tr-60
89T-551
89T/St-106
89T/Tr-102T
89UD-474
90D-396
90F-571
90Score-376
90T-356
90UD-404
Reagan, Edward
T206
T213/brown
Reagan, Kyle
89Bill/Pro-2047
Reagans, Javan
88James/Pro-1917
Reardon, Jeff
79Tidew-5
81D-156
81F-335
81OPC-79
81T-456
81T/Tr-819
82D-547
82F-204
82F/St-37
82Hygrade
82OPC-123
82OPC/Post-23
82T-667
83D-194
83F-293
83OPC-290
83Stuart-5
83T-290
83T/St-254
84D-279
84F-283
84F/St-71
84Jacks/Smok-10
84Nes/792-595
84OPC-116
84Stuart-13
84T-595
84T/St-89
85D-331
85F-407
85Leaf-126
85OPC-375
85OPC/Post-12
85T-375
85T/St-85
86D-209
86D/AAS-33
86D/HL-14
86F-257
86F/LimEd-35
86F/Slug-26
86F/St-94
86Leaf-214
86OPC-35
86Provigo-13
86S-119
86T-35
86T-711
86T/3D-20
86T/Gloss60-55
86T/St-76
86T/Super-6
87Class-94
87D-PC11
87D/AAS-52
87D/WaxBox-PC11
87F-329
87F/McCror-34
87F/Mini-88
87F/Slug-33
87F/St-98
87F/U-U101
87Kraft-40
87Leaf-143
87OPC-165
87RedFoley/St-65
87S-77M
87T-165
87T/Gloss60-15
87T/Mini-18
87T/St-81
87T/Tr-98T
88D-122
88D/Best-242
88F-20
88F/AwardWin-31
88F/BB/AS-33
88F/Mini-37
88F/Slug-32
88F/St-46
88F/TL-28
88Master/Disc-4
88Nestle-27
88OPC-99
88Panini/St-133
88RedFoley/St-73
88Score-91
88Sf-53
88Smok/Minn-4
88T-425
88T/Big-10
88T/Mini-24
88T/RiteAid-28
88T/St-14
88T/St-280
89B-148
89Cadaco-43
89D-155
89D/AS-24
89D/Best-242
89F-125
89F/Superstar-34
89OPC-86
89Panini/St-382
89RedFoley/St-94
89Score-305
89Score/HotSt-24
89Sf-168
89T-775
89T/Gloss60-54
89T/Mini-63
89T/St-284
89T/St-8
89T/St/Backs-33
89UD-596
89Woolwth-17
90Class-101
90D-119
90F-385
90Score-522
90Sf-37
90T-235
90UD-417
Reaves, Scott
88Clearw/Star-20
88Spart/Star-1
88Spart/Star-17
89Clearw/Star-18
Reberger, Frank
69T-637R
70MLB/St-117
70OPC-103
70T-103
71MLB/St-262
71OPC-251
71T-251
72T-548
83Nashua-21
84Cram/PCL-242
85Cram/PCL-23
86Edmon-23CO
87Edmon-17
Reboulet, James
83Erie-4
84Savan-10
86FSLAS-40
86StPet-26
87ArkTr-23
88BuffB/CMC-17
88BuffB/Polar-7
88BuffB/Pro-1470
Reboulet, Jeff
87Orlan-15
88Orlan/Best-19
89Orlan/Pro-1345
Rech, Ed
82Lynch-8
Redd, Rick R.
88Harris/Pro-840
Redding, Dick
(Cannonball)
74Laugh/Black-25
Redding, Mike
86Kenosha-21
87Visal-16
88Visal/Cal-160
88Visal/Pro-93
89Orlan/Best-22
89Orlan/Pro-1333
Reddish, Mike
83Nashvl-17
85CharO-10
86RochR-18
Redfern, Pete
77T-249
78T-81
79T-113
80T-403
81D-548
81F-560
81T-714
82D-51
82F-559
82T-309
83D-256
83F-623
83T-559
Redfield, Joe
87MidldA-13
87TexLgAS-12
88Edmon/CMC-20
88Edmon/Pro-555
89ScrWB/CMC-20
89ScrWB/Pro-731
Redick, Kevin
86Cram/PCL-6
87Clint-13
Redington, Thomas
88Sumter/Pro-412
89BurlB/Pro-1610
89BurlB/Star-17
Redman, Tim
87Erie-29
88Hamil/Pro-1729
89Hamil/Star-22
Redmon, Glen
75Phoen-13
76Wmspt
Redmond, Andre
89Princet/Star-16
Redmond, Dan
87Watlo-28
89Canton/Best-9
Redmond, H. Wayne
71OPC-728R

71T-728R
Redus, Gary
81Water-15
82Indianap-17
83T/X-94
84Borden-2
84D-184
84D/AAS-16
84F-481
84Nes/792-475
84OPC-231
84T-475
84T/St-52
85D-306
85F-549
85Indianap-34
85Leaf-47
85OPC-146
85T-146
85T/St-49
86CIGNA-12
86D-306
86F-189
86F/Up-U94
86Keller-3
86OPC-342
86T-342
86T/Tr-90T
87Coke/WS-13
87D-288
87D/OD-229
87F-181
87F/U-U102
87OPC-42
87T-42
87T/St-119
87T/Tr-99T
88Coke/WS-24
88D-370
88F-408
88OPC-332
88Panini/St-64
88Score-443
88T-657
88T/Mini-9
89B-425
89D-605
89F-218
89OPC-281
89Score-177
89T-281
89T/Big-131
89UD-419
90D-597
90F-476
90Score-14
90T-507
90UD-248
Reece, Jeff
86Stockton-23
87Wichi-14
Reece, Thad
83Madis/LF-9
84Albany-5
85Cram/PCL-135
86Tacom-18
87Tacom-10
88Memph/Best-24
Reed, Billy
89LittleSun-23CO
89Watlo/Pro-1788
89Watlo/Star-23
Reed, Bob E.
70OPC-207R
70T-207R
71MLB/St-404
71OPC-732
71T-732
Reed, Curt
82AppFx-12
83GlenF-9
Reed, Darren
86Albany/TCMA-23
87Albany-16
88Tidew/CANDL-17
88Tidew/CMC-16
88Tidew/Pro-1603
89Tidew/CMC-17
89Tidew/Pro-1957
Reed, Dennis
87Anchora-25
Reed, Howard
60L-84
61Union
65T-544
66T-387
70T-548
71LaPizza-10
71OPC-398
71T-398
Reed, Jamie
84CharO-14
85RochR-28
87RochR-22
88RochR-31
88RochR/Gov-31
88RochR/Pro-214
Reed, Jeff
81Wisco-14
83Orlan-5
84Toled-2
85D-30
85IntLgAS-38
85Toled-14
86F/Up-U95
87D/OD-92
87F-550
87T-247
87T/Tr-100T
88D-88
88F-194
88OPC-176
88Score-408
88T-176
89D-469
89F-167
89K/Reds-34
89Score-99
89T-626
89T/Big-158
89UD-276
90D-351
90F-429
90Score-147
90T-772
90UD-165
Reed, Jerry M.
80OkCty
82OkCty-9
83Charl-4
84Maine-2
85Maine-8
85Polar/Ind-35
86Calgary-22
86F-592
86T-172
87Moth/Sea-22
87T-619
88D-517
88F-387
88Moth/Sea-22
88Score-488
88T-332
89D-657
89F-557
89Moth/Sea-22
89Score-427
89T-441
89UD-529
90D-614
90F-523
90Score-492
90T-247
90UD-210
Reed, Jody
86NewBrit-21
87Pawtu-6
87Pawtu/TCMA-17
88D-41
88D/Best-196
88D/RedSox/Bk-41
88D/Rook-44
88F-360
88Leaf-41
88Score-625
88Sf-225
88T-152
88T/Big-202
89B-30
89D-305
89D/Best-289
89F-96
89OPC-232
89Panini/St-268
89RedFoley/St-95
89Score-486
89Score/HotRk-85
89Score/YS/I-2
89Sf-210
89T-321TL
89T-734
89T/Big-97
89T/Gloss60-60
89ToysRUs-23
89UD-370
90D-398
90F-284
90Score-11
90T-96
90UD-321
Reed, Ken
87DayBe-7
Reed, Marty
86Kinston-18
87MidldA-27
87TexLgAS-15
88Edmon/CMC-9
88Edmon/Pro-562
Reed, Richard
(Rick)
87Macon-10
88Salem/Star-17
88Umpire-48
89BuffB/CMC-9
89BuffB/Pro-1675
89Umpires-46
90D-527
90F-477
90Score-544
90Score/100Ris-8
Reed, Ron
68OPC-76R
68T-76R
69OPC-177
69T-177
69T/St-9
70MLB/St-12
70OPC-546
70T-546
71MLB/St-21
71OPC-359
71T-359
72MB-281
72T-787
73OPC-72
73T-72
74OPC-346
74T-346
75OPC-81
75T-81
75T/M-81
76OPC-58
76T-58
76T/Tr-58T
77T-243
78T-472
79BK/P-7
79OPC-84
79T-177
80BK/P-21
80OPC-318
80T-609
81D-44
81F-11
81T-376
82D-399
82F-255
82T-581
83D-567
83F-169
83T-728
84D-529
84F-45
84F/X-96
84Nes/792-43
84T-43
84T/X-98
84TrueVal/WS-26
85D-282
85F-524
85T-221
Reed, Sean
88Wythe/Pro-1981
89CharWh/Best-16
89CharWh/Pro-1762
Reed, Steve
78BurlB
80Holyo-18
Reed, Steve
88Poca/Pro-2082
89Clint/Pro-906
Reed, Tom
84Visal-13
Reed, Toncie
89AubAs/Pro-2167
Reeder, Bill E.
49Eureka-194
52Mother-48
Reeder, Mike
88CharWh/Best-5
Reedy, Jerry
78Cr/PCL-101
Reelhorn, John
81OkCty/TCMA-15
82OkCty-19
Reese, Andrew
29Exh/4-9
R315-A30
R315-B30
Reese, Chip
83Ander-10
89Boise/Pro-1979
Reese, Harold H.
(Pee Wee)
41DP-23
41PB-54
41Wheat-18
43MP-20
48Swell-18
49B-36
49Eureka-47
49MP-106
49Royal-2
50B-21
50Drake-19
51B-80
52B-8
52BR
52Coke
52RM-NL17
52Royal
52StarCal/L-79B
52T-333
53B/Col-33
53Exh/Can-21
53RM-NL10
53T-76
54B-58
54NYJour
54RM-NL15
55Armour-15
55B-37
55Gol/Dodg-24
55RM-NL17
56T-260
56YellBase/Pin-26
57T-30
58BB
58Hires-23
58T-375
60NuCard-37
61NuCard-437
79TCMA-84
80Cram/Leg-52
85West/2-34
86S/Dec-21
88Pac/Leg-21
89Rini/Dodg-5
89Smok/Dodg-23
D305
Exh47
PM10/Sm-151
PM10/Sm-152
PM10/Sm-153
PM10/Sm-154
R302-106
R423-86
Reese, Jimmie
28Exh/PCL-21
31Exh/4-26
73OPC-421CO
73T-421C
74OPC-276CO
74T-276C
76SSPC-630
Reese, Kyle
86Erie-24
87FtMyr-27
88Virgini/Star-21
89Memph/Best-16
89Memph/Pro-1206
89Memph/Star-20
Reese, Rich
65T-597R
67T-486R
68OPC-111
68T-111
69MB-228
69OPC-56
69T-56
70MLB/St-238
70OPC-404
70T-404
71MLB/St-472
71OPC-349
71T-349
71T/Coins-72
72MB-282
72T-611
89Pac/Leg-112
Reeve, Bob
85Anchora-41
Reeves, Jim
78StPet
Reeves, Matt
82VeroB-10
Reeves, Mel
47Smith-24
Reeves, Robert E.
29Exh/4-17
31Exh/4-17
31Exh/4-17
Regalado, Rudy
55B-142
60HenryH-14
Regalado, Uvaldo
82DayBe-6
83DayBe-9

Regan, Michael J.
E254
Regan, Phil
61T-439
62J-24
62P-24
62P/Can-24
62T-366
63T-494
64Det/Lids-13
64T-535
65OPC-191
65T-191
66T-347
67Bz-29
67OPC-130
67T-130
68OPC-88
68T-88
69MB-229
69MLB/St-124
69T-535
69T/St-18
70MLB/St-21
70OPC-334
70T-334
71MLB/St-43
71OPC-634
71T-634
72MB-283
72OPC-485
72T-485
87Smok/Dodg-27
88Smok/Dodg-9
89Smok/Dodg-72
Regan, William W.
29Exh/4-18
R316
Regira, Gary
89James/Pro-2154
Rehbaum, Chris
80Batav-27
81Batav-23
82Watlo/B-22
82Watlo/C-17
Rehm, Vic
60L-61
Rehse
N172
Rehwinkel, Pat
89Helena/SP-4
Reiber, Frank
V355-111
Reich, Andy
89Clmbia/Best-19
89Clmbia/GS-22
Reich, Herman
49Eureka-68
Reichard, Clyde
(Bud)
78Wisco
85Tulsa-37
89Penin/Star-21
Reichardt, Rick
65OPC-194R
65T-194R
66T-321
67Bz-1
67OPC-40
67T-40
68T-570
69JB
69MB-230
69MLB/St-25
69MLBPA/Pin-23
69OPC-205
69T-205
69T/decal
69T/S-8
69T/St-147
69Trans-18
70K-18
70MLB/St-177
70T-720
70Trans-12
71OPC-643
71T-643
71T/Coins-102
72MB-284
Reichel, Tom
87Penin-19
Reichle, Darrin
87Spoka-2
88Charl/Pro-1208
88SALAS/GS-11
89River/Best-14
89River/Cal-15
89River/Pro-1393
Reid, Jessie
84Shrev/FB-16
86Phoen-22
87Phoen-16
88F-643
89Tacom/CMC-17
89Tacom/Pro-1549
Reid, Scott D.
70OPC-56R
70T-56R
71OPC-439R
71T-439R
Reilley, John
88Sumter/Pro-394
89Wausa/GS-5
Reilly, Charles T.
N172
Reilly, Ed
83DayBe-10
Reilly, John G.
N172
Reilly, Mike
88Umpire-33
89Umpires-31
Reilly, Neil
85BurlR-6
Reilly, Thomas H.
E254
T204
Reimer, Kevin
86Salem-23
87PortChar-26
88Tulsa-25
89F-641M
89OkCty/CMC-19
89OkCty/Pro-1527
89Score/HotRk-59
90F-310
Rein, Fred
77Charl
Reinbach, Mike
75IntAS/TCMA-5
Reinebold, Jim
89SoBend/GS-3
Reinke, Jeff
75Clint
Reis, Dave
88Pulas/Pro-1757
89BurlB/Pro-1619
89BurlB/Star-18
Reis, Paul
88Pulas/Pro-1759
89Sumter/Pro-1090
Reis, Robert
R314
Reis, Tom
47Centen-22
Reiser, James
86Cram/PCL-52
87Madis-10
88Madis-18
Reiser, Pete
39Exh
41DP-18
43MP-21
48B-7
48L-146
48Swell-2
49B-185
49Eureka-17
50B-193
51B-238
52T-189
60T-463C
73OPC-81CO
73T-81C
80Cram/Leg-88
89Smok/Dodg-47
PM10/Sm-155
Reish, Steve
84Memph-17
Reisling, Frank
(Doc)
M116
Reiter, Gary
81Durhm-24
82Durhm-20
83Richm-8
84Richm-15
85Richm-7
Reitz, Ken
73OPC-603R
73T-603R
74OPC-372
74T-372
75OPC-27
75T-27
75T/M-27
76OPC-158
76SSPC-280
76T-158
76T-158TR
77K-38
77T-297
78Ho-106
78T-692
79Ho-23
79OPC-307
79T-587
80OPC-103
80T-182
81Coke
81D-307
81F-530
81OPC-316
81T-441
81T/HT
81T/So-101
81T/St-158
81T/Tr-820
82D-277
82F-602
82F/St-91
82OPC-245
82T-245
82T/St-26
85Tulsa-0
86SanJose-17
87SanJose-3
Relaford, Winnie
88Sumter/Pro-400
89Sumter/Pro-1103
Relmink, Bob
89NiagFls/Puc-20
Rembielak, Rick
82Miami-16
Remlinger, Mike
87Everett-31
88Shreve/Pro-1296
89Shreve/Pro-1832
Remmerswaal, Win
81D-98
81Pawtu-7
81T-38
Remo, Jeff
82QuadC-16
Remy, Jerry
76OPC-229
76SSPC-198
76T-229
77K-44
77T-342
78Ho-66
78PapaG/Disc-2
79OPC-325
79T-618
80OPC-85
80T-155
81D-215
81F-238
81OPC-131
81T-549
82Coke/Bos
82D-156
82F-304
82F/St-171
82OPC-25
82Sqt-2
82T-25
82T/St-132
82T/St-149
83D-74
83F-193
83OPC-295
83T-295
83T/St-33
84D-172
84F-407
84Nes/792-445
84OPC-58
84T-445
84T/St-215
85F-167
85OPC-173
85T-761
85T/St-218
Rende, Sal
79Tacom-11
80Tacom-14
81Chatt-17
82Chatt-11
83BuffB-13
87Chatt/Best-1MG
88Memph/Best-26
89AAA/Pro-37
89Omaha/CMC-23
89Omaha/Pro-1740
Rendina, Mike
88Brist/Pro-1877
89Brist/Star-21
89Fay/Pro-1584
Renfroe, Cohen
(Laddy)
86WinSal-21
87Pittsf-8
88IowaC/CMC-4
88IowaC/Pro-551
89CharlK-1
Renfroe, Marshall
60L-99
Renick, Rick
68T-301R
69MB-231
70OPC-93
70T-93
71MLB/St-473
71OPC-694
71T-694
72MB-285
72OPC-459
72T-459
83Memph-23
86Provigo-28CO
Reniff, Hal
62T-139
62T-159
63T-546
64T-36
65T-413
66OPC-68
66T-68
67T-201
78TCMA-106
WG10-19
WG9-20
Renko, Steve
70OPC-87
70T-87
71MLB/St-139
71OPC-209
71T-209
72OPC-307
72OPC-308IA
72T-307
72T-308A
73OPC-623
73T-623
74OPC-49
74T-49
74T/St-58
74Weston-18
75Ho-69
75OPC-34
75T-34
75T/M-34
76OPC-264
76T-264
77T-586
78T-493
79T-352
80T-184
81D-337
81F-231
81T-63
81T/Tr-821
82D-38
82F-472
82T-702
83D-393
83F-99
83OPC-236
83T-236
83T/X-95
84F-355
84Nes/792-444
84T-444
Renna, Bill
54T-112
55Rodeo
55T-121
55T/DH-99
56T-82
58T-473
59T-72
Renneau, Charlie
77Visal
Rennert, Dutch
88Umpire-18
89Umpires-18
Rennicke, Dean
83Albuq-5
84Cram/PCL-160
85Cram/PCL-151
Renninger, Bob
74Cedar
Renteria, Edison
87AubAs-23
88Ashvl/Pro-1058
89Osceola/Star-19
Renteria, Rich
82AlexD-27
83LynnP-17
85Tigres-22
86Hawai-20
87Moth/Sea-23
88Moth/Sea-23
89B-212
89Moth/Sea-20
89Score-142
89T/Big-109
89UD-547

Rentschuler, Tom
83Peoria/LF-16
83Redwd-22
Renz, Kevin
86Penin-22
87Penin-2
88BirmB/Best-28
Replogle, Andy
77ArkTr
79T-427
79Vanco-8
81Vanco-16
Repoz, Craig
85LitFalls-21
86Columbia-21
87Lynch-1
89Jacks/GS-4
Repoz, Roger
66OPC-138
66T-138
67T-416
68T-587
69MB-232
69MLB/St-26
69OPC-103
69T-103
69T/St-148
70MLB/St-178
70OPC-397
70T-397
71MLB/St-355
71OPC-508
71T-508
72MB-286
72T-541
Repulski, Rip
53T-172
54B-46
54Hunter
54RM-NL17
54T-115
55B-205
55Hunter
55T-55
55T/DH-125
56T-201
57T-245
58Hires-15
58T-14
59T-195
60BB-5
60L-86
60T-265
61T-128
Rescigno, Xavier
47Signal
49B/PCL-5
Resetar, Gary
89Keno/Pro-1075
89Keno/Star-21
Resinger, Grover
63Pep/Tul
Resnikoff, Bob
89Saraso/Star-19
Restilli, Dino
48Sommer-12
49Sommer-17
50B-123
Restin, Eric
76BurlB
77BurlB
Retes, Lorenzo
85Tigres-10
Rettenmund, Merv
69OPC-66R
69T-66R
70T-629
71MLB/St-308
71OPC-393
71T-393
72K-11
72MB-287
72OPC-235
72OPC-86LL
72T-235
72T-86LL
73JP
73OPC-56
73T-56
74OPC-585
74T-585
74T/Tr-585T
75OPC-369
75T-369
75T/M-369
76OPC-283
76SSPC-46
76T-283
77T-659
78T-566
79T-48
80T-402
Retzer, Ed
83Madis/LF-10
83Tacom-31
Retzer, Ken
62T-594R
63J-94
63P-94
63T-471
64T-277
65OPC-278
65T-278
Reulbach, Ed
10Domino-101
11Helmar-100
12Sweet/Pin-88
14CJ-80
15CJ-80
69Bz-12
72F/FFeat-29
E254
E286
E91
E95
M116
S74-67
T202
T204
T205
T206
T207
T213/blue
T215/blue
T215/brown
T222
WG3-40
Reuschel, Paul
77T-333
77T-634M
78T-663
79T-511
Reuschel, Rick
73OPC-482
73T-482
74OPC-136
74T-136
74T/St-18
75Ho-51
75OPC-153
75T-153
75T/M-153
76Ho-17
76Ho/Twink-17
76OPC-359
76SSPC-301
76T-359
77Ho-103
77OPC-214
77T-530
77T-634M
78Ho-131
78K-45
78OPC-56
78T-50
79Ho-67
79K-47
79OPC-123
79T-240
80OPC-99
80T-175
81Coke
81D-561
81F-293
81F/St-93
81OPC-205
81T-645
81T/HT
81T/St-157
81T/Tr-822
82D-157
82F-50
82OPC-204
82T-405
84SevenUp-47
85Cram/PCL-230
85F-63
85F/Up-U88
85OPC-306
85T-306
85T/Tr-93T
86D-532
86F-618
86F/Slug-27
86F/St-95
86Leaf-207
86T-779
86T/Mini-57
86T/St-126
87D-188
87F-619
87OPC-154
87RedFoley/St-129
87T-521
87T/St-128
88D-613
88D/AS-52
88D/Best-218
88F-94
88F/LL-32
88F/St-130
88Leaf-219
88Moth/Giants-15
88OPC-278
88Score-519
88Sf-136
88T-660
88T/Big-188
88T/Mini-76
88T/Revco-13
88T/RiteAid-30
89B-466
89D-11DK
89D-335
89D/Best-162
89D/DKsuper-11DK
89F-340
89Moth/Giants-15
89OPC-65
89Panini/St-210
89Score-5
89Score/HotSt-22
89Sf-72
89T-65
89T/Mini-42
89T/St-79
89T/UK-63
89UD-194
90D-112
90D-663AS
90F-68
90Score-465
90Score/100St-7
90Sf-161
90T-190
90UD-696
Reuss, Jerry
70OPC-96R
70T-96R
71OPC-158
71T-158
72T-775
73OPC-446
73T-446
74OPC-116
74T-116
74T/St-38
75OPC-124
75T-124
75T/M-124
76Crane-47
76Ho-29
76Ho/Twink-29
76K-43
76MSA/Disc
76OPC-60
76SSPC-562
76T-60
77Ho-119
77OPC-97
77Pep-65
77T-645
78T-255
79T-536
80Pol/Dodg-41
80T-318
81D-417
81F-118
81OPC-153
81Pol/Dodg-41
81T-440
81T/HT
81T/So-103
81T/St-181
82D-284
82F-18
82F/St-7
82OPC-278
82Pol/Dodg
82Pol/Dodg-41
82T-710
82T/St-56
83D-158
83F-216
83OPC-90
83Pol/Dodg-41
83T-90
83T/St-247
84D-418
84F-110
84Nes/792-170
84OPC-170
84Pol/Dodg-41
84T-170
84T/St-81
85D-226
85F-380
85OPC-66
85T-680
86D-104
86F-141
86OPC-236
86Pol/Dodg-41
86S-53M
86T-577
86T/St-66
87F-451
87OPC-373
87Pol/Dodg-21
87Smok/Dodg-28
87T-682
88Coke/WS-23
88Score-270
88Score/Tr-61T
88Smok/Dodg-6M
88T-216
89B-57
89Coke/WS-22
89D-413
89D/Best-305
89F-510
89Score-489
89T-357
89UD-151
90D-528
90F-335
90T-424
90UD-96
Reuteman, R.C.
(AGM)
88Tidew/CANDL-26
Revak, Ray
86Greens-19
Revelle, R.H.
(Dutch)
T206
Revering, Dave
76Indianap-7
77Indianap-4
78T-706R
79Ho-139
79OPC-113
80OPC-227
80T-438
80T/S-58
81D-117
81F-576
81F/St-4
81OPC-57
81T-568
81T/So-22
81T/St-117
81T/Tr-823
82D-234
82F-51
82OPC-109
82T-109
82T/Tr-97T
83F-484
83OPC-291
83T-677
85Indianap-29
Rex, Mike
76Cedar
79Phoen
80Phoen-18
81Phoen-11
82Phoen
Rey, Everett
81Chatt-9
82Chatt-3
83BuffB-12
Reyes, Carlos
86Ashvl-22
Reyes, Gilberto
85Cram/PCL-170
86Albuq-20
86D-581
87Albuq/Pol-17
87Pol/Dodg-7
88Albuq/CMC-21
88Albuq/Pro-257
89Indi/CMC-11
89Indi/Pro-1240
Reyes, Giovanny
86Cram/PCL-77
86QuadC-26
87QuadC-5
88PalmSp/Cal-109
Reyes, Jesus
73Cedar
74Cedar
Reyes, Jose
77Clint
80OrlTw-7
82OrlTw/A-22
Reyes, Joselito
84Memph-21
85Kingst-18
86Omaha-18

Reyes, Juan
86Beloi-19
89Brist/Star-22
Reyes, Pablo
85Kingst-9
86Ventura-22
Reyes, Steve
88Bill/Pro-1810
Reyes, Wascar
78Charl
Reyna, Dion
88Madis-19
Reyna, Luis
86Ventura-23
87Knoxv-9
88Syrac/CMC-12
88Syrac/Pro-810
Reynolds, Allie
47TipTop
48B-14
49B-114
50B-138
50Drake-28
51B-109
51BR-C3
51T/RB-6
52BR
52Dix
52StarCal/L-70A
52T-67
52TipTop
53B/Col-68
53Dix
53NB
53T-141
54B-113
54NYJour
55Armour-16
55B-201
61F-69
79TCMA-185
88Pac/Leg-41
89Swell-101
PM10/L-33
R346-21
R423-89
Reynolds, Archie
71MLB/St-356
71OPC-664R
71T-664R
72T-672
Reynolds, Carl
29Exh/4-20
30CEA/Pin-19
31Exh/4-20
32Orbit/num-2
32Orbit/un-50
33CJ/Pin-18
33G-120
35BU-49
35BU-95
35G-1G
35G-3E
35G-5E
35G-6E
R300
R305
R310
R315-C4
V354-12
Reynolds, Charles
N172
Reynolds, Craig
76OPC-596R
76SSPC-582
76T-596R
77T-474R
78T-199
79K-51
79OPC-251
80OPC-71
80T-129
81D-378
81F-74
81OPC-12
81T-617
81T/St-46
82D-344
82F-225
82OPC-57
82T-57
83D-317
83F-460
83T-328
84D-405
84F-237
84Moth/Ast-26
84Nes/792-776
84T-776
85D-328
85F-357
85Moth/Ast-14
85OPC-156
85T-156
85T/St-65
86D-232
86F-309
86Leaf-107
86Moth/Ast-18
86OPC-298
86Pol/Ast-13
86T-298
87D-384
87D/OD-19
87F-66
87Moth/Ast-19
87OPC-298
87Pol/Ast-10
87T-779
88D-209
88F-454
88Leaf-205
88Moth/Ast-19
88OPC-18
88Panini/St-297
88Pol/Ast-19
88Score-207
88T-557
88T/Big-219
89B-328
89D-477
89F-366
89Lennox/Ast-15
89Moth/Ast-18
89Score-468
89T-428
89T/Big-312
89UD-284
90T-637
Reynolds, Dave
86AppFx-19
87Penin-11
88Tampa/Star-21
89Saraso/Star-20
Reynolds, Don
79Hawai-13
79T-292
80Hawai-23
88SnBer/Best-28
88SnBer/Cal-55
Reynolds, Doug
89Erie/Star-18
Reynolds, Harold
81Wausa-18
82LynnS-17
83SLCty-22
84Cram/PCL-185
85Moth/Mar-23
86Calgary-23
86D-484
86T-769
87D-489
87D/OD-117
87F-596
87Moth/Sea-10
87T-91
87T/St-216
88D-563
88D/AS-13
88D/Best-304
88F-388
88F/AwardWin-32
88F/Mini-53
88F/RecSet-31
88F/St-62
88Leaf-227
88Moth/Sea-10
88OPC-7
88Panini/St-188
88Score-277
88Sf-127
88T-485
88T/Big-142
88T/Mini-35
88T/Revco-19
88T/St-221
88T/UK-60
89B-210
89Class-147
89D-21DK
89D-93
89D/AS-27
89D/Best-51
89D/DKsuper-21DK
89F-558
89F/BBAS-34
89F/Heroes-33
89F/LL-31
89KMart/DT-13
89Moth/Sea-10
89OPC-208
89Panini/St-436
89RedFoley/St-96
89Score-310
89Score/HotSt-82
89Sf-165
89T-580
89T/Big-2
89T/Mini-74
89T/St-226
89T/St/Backs-5
89UD-249
90Class-128
90D-227
90F-524
90Score-167
90Score/100St-43
90Sf-119
90T-161
90UD-179
Reynolds, Jeff
83Syrac-19
86Jaxvl/TCMA-21
87Indianap-16
88Toled/CMC-15
88Toled/Pro-585
89Nashvl-19
Reynolds, Ken
71OPC-664R
71T-664R
72OPC-252
72T-252
73OPC-638
73T-638
76SSPC-292
78Syrac
79Syrac-19
89Geneva/Pro-1885
Reynolds, Larry
80Tulsa-9
81Tulsa-7
82ArkTr-21
83ArkTr-22
84ArkTr-9
Reynolds, Mike
79Richm-2
82Richm-18
84Richm-1
85Durhm-30
86Durhm-22
Reynolds, Robert J.
(R.J.)
81VeroB-17
84Cram/PCL-148
84F/X-97
85D-128
85F-381
85T-369
86D-552
86F-619
86F/Mini-120
86Leaf-212
86OPC-306
86T-417
87D-65
87F-620
87OPC-109
87RedFoley/St-77
87T-109
87T/St-134
88D-65
88D/Best-201
88F-339
88OPC-27
88Panini/St-379
88Score-34
88T-27
89D-134
89D/Best-257
89F-219
89Score-91
89T-658
89UD-315
90D-447
90F-478
90Score-469
90T-592
90UD-540
Reynolds, Robert
71OPC-664R
71T-664R
72OPC-162R
72T-162R
73JP
73OPC-612R
73T-612R
74OPC-259
74T-259
75OPC-142
75T-142
75T/M-142
82IowaC-28GM
Reynolds, Ronn
82Jacks-11
84Tidew-25
86F-92
86Portl-19
86T-649
87T-471
87Tucso-20
88Denver/CMC-16
88Denver/Pro-1262
Reynolds, Shane
89AubAs/Pro-2161
Reynolds, Thomas D.
(Tommie)
64T-528R
65T-333
67T-487
69T-467
70OPC-259
70T-259
71OPC-676
71T-676
77Spoka
86Modesto-21MG
87Modesto-23
88Huntsvl/BK-15
Reynolds, Tim
83Cedar-9
83Cedar/LF-1
Reynolds, William
86Cram/PCL-56
Rhem, Charles Flint
33DH-35
33G-136
35G-8L
35G-9L
87Conlon/2-52
88Conlon/4-23
V354-5
Rhiel, William
R314
R314/Can
V355-81
Rhoades, James
88Aug/Pro-387
Rhoads, Robert
T206
T213/brown
T3-114
Rhodas, Kevin
83Miami-10
Rhoden, Rick
75OPC-618R
75T-618R
75T/M-618R
76OPC-439
76SSPC-72
76T-439
77OPC-57
77T-245
78OPC-159
78T-605
79OPC-66
79T-145
80Port-27
80T-92
81F-377
81OPC-312
81T-312
82D-423
82F-493
82T-513
82T/St-82
83D-250
83F-318
83OPC-181
83T-781
84D-552
84F-261
84Nes/792-485
84Nes/792-696TL
84OPC-46
84T-485
85D-552
85F-474
85F/St-97
85Leaf-63
85OPC-53
85T-695
85T/St-127
86D-166
86D/HL-20
86F-620
86OPC-232
86T-232
86T-756M
86T/St-130
87D-10DK
87D-435
87D/AAS-24
87D/DKsuper-10
87F-621
87F/U-U103
87Leaf-10DK
87OPC-365
87RedFoley/St-103
87S-129
87Smok/Dodg-29

87T-365
87T/Mini-31
87T/St-130
87T/Tr-101T
88D-128
88D/Best-161
88D/Y/Bk-128
88F-219
88F/SS-30
88F/St-51
88Leaf-98
88OPC-185
88Panini/St-149
88RedFoley/St-74
88Score-74
88Sf-104
88Sf/Gamewin-16
88T-185
88T/Big-108
88T/St-298
89B-323
89D-429
89D/Tr-40
89F-266
89F/Up-89
89Lennox/Ast-3
89Moth/Ast-24
89OPC-18
89Panini/St-399
89Score-317
89Smok/Dodg-87
89T-18
89T/Big-237
89UD-56
90F-235
90T-588
90UD-504

Rhodes, Art
89Erie/Star-19

Rhodes, Charles
T206

Rhodes, Dusty
28Exh/PCL-22

Rhodes, Dusty
89Helena/SP-27

Rhodes, James L.
(Dusty)
54NYJour
54T-170
55Gol/Giants-24
55RM-NL22
55SM
55T-1
55T/DH-27
56T-50
56T/Hocus-A4
56T/Hocus-B6
57T-61
61Union
79TCMA-190

Rhodes, Jeff
83Cedar-24
83Cedar/LF-15

Rhodes, Karl
87Ashvl-1
88FSLAS/Star-18
88Osceola/Star-22
89ColMud/Best-22
89ColMud/Pro-142
89ColMud/Star-19

Rhodes, Mike
83ArkTr-1
86ArkTr-17
89FtLaud/Star-20
89Star/Wax-79

Rhodes, Ricky
89Oneon/Pro-2123

Rhomberg, Kevin
78Watlo
80Tacom-20
81Chatt-23
82Charl-17
83Charl-17
85Cram/PCL-193

Rhown, Bobby
52Park-4

Rhyne, Hal
28Exh/PCL-23
29Exh/4-18
31Exh/4-18
33Exh/4-9

Ribant, Dennis
65OPC-73
65T-73
66T-241
67Kahn
67T-527
67T/Test/PP-3
68T-326
69T-463

Ribbie
85Coke/WS
86Coke/WS
87Coke/WS-30M

Ricanelli, John
76QuadC
78Cr/PCL-69

Riccelli, Frank
74OPC-599R
74T-599R
75Lafay
76Phoen
77Phoen
80T-247
81Buffa-24
82Syrac-6

Ricci, Chuck
89Watlo/Pro-1783
89Watlo/Star-24

Ricci, Frank
82Nashv-19
83Beaum-17

Ricciardi, J.P.
88SoOreg/Pro-1714

Rice, Del
47TipTop
49Eureka-195
50B-125
51B-156
52B-107
52T-100
53B/Col-53
53Hunter
53T-68
54B-30
54Hunter
54RM-NL9
55B-106
55Hunter
57T-193
58T-51
59T-104
60T-248
61T-448
72T-718
Exh47
R302-112
R423-87

Rice, Edgar
(Sam)
21Exh-140
29Exh/4-32
31Exh/4-32
33DH-36
33G-134
34DS-32
60F-34
61F-70
80SSPC/HOF
D327
D328-137
E120
E121/120
E121/80
E122
E126-29
E135-137
E210-3
E220
R316
V100
V354-18
W501-14
W502-36
W514-79
W572
W575
WG7-44

Rice, Hal
51B-300
52T-398
53T-93
54B-219
54T-95
55B-52

Rice, Harry F.
29Exh/4-23
R316

Rice, Jim
75OPC-616R
75T-616R
75T/M-616R
76Ho-127
76K-10
76OPC-340
76SSPC-405
76T-340
77OPC-62
77T-60
78Ho-45
78K-49
78OPC-163
78OPC-2LL
78PapaG/Disc-14
78T-202LL
78T-670
78Wiffle/Discs-61
79Ho-2
79K-15
79OPC-210
79T-2LL
79T-3LL
79T-400
79T/Comics-2
80BK/PHR-20
80K-46
80OPC-112
80T-200
80T/S-5
81Coke
81D-338
81Drake-8
81F-222
81F/St-53
81K-9
81OPC-68
81Sqt-7
81T-500
81T/HT
81T/Nat/Super-11
81T/S
81T/So-13
81T/St-41
82Coke/Bos
82D-200
82Drake-27
82F-305
82F/St-163
82KMart
82OPC-366
82T-750
82T/St-150
83D-208
83Drake-22
83F-194
83K-13
83OPC-30
83T-30
83T-381
83T/St-37
84D-50
84D/AAS-52
84D/Champs-4
84Drake-25
84F-408
84F/St-20
84F/St-37
84FunFood/Pin-5
84Nes/792-132LL
84Nes/792-133LL
84Nes/792-401AS
84Nes/792-550
84Nestle/DT-5
84OPC-184AS
84OPC-364
84Ralston-9
84Seven-15E
84T-132
84T-133
84T-401
84T-550
84T/Cereal-9
84T/Gloss22-6
84T/Gloss40-22
84T/St-102A
84T/St-189
84T/St-200B
84T/St-217
84T/Super-5
84T/Super-5
85D-15
85D-50
85D/AAS-27
85D/DKsuper-15
85Drake-25
85F-168
85F/LimEd-27
85F/St-13
85F/St-23
85GenMills-22
85Leaf-15
85OPC-150
85Seven-2W
85Seven-4E
85T-150
85T/3D-6
85T/Gloss40-6
85T/St-208
85T/Super-50
86BK/AP-8
86D-213
86D/AAS-16
86D/PopUp-16
86Dorman-20
86Drake-13
86F-358
86F/Mini-76
86F/St-96
86Jiffy-1
86Leaf-146
86Meadow/Stat-14
86OPC-320
86Quaker-30
86S-139M
86S-146M
86S-17
86S-52M
86S-61M
86S/Dec-57
86T-320
86T/3D-23
86T/Gloss22-6
86T/Gloss60-36
86T/St-161
86T/St-246
86T/Super-43
86TrueVal-7
86Woolwth-28
87BK-16
87Class-59
87D-92
87D/AAS-45
87D/OD-182
87Drake-15
87F-41
87F-633M
87F/Excit-37
87F/HL-6
87F/McCror-35
87F/Mini-89
87F/St-99
87Jiffy-19
87KayBee-26
87KMart-18
87Kraft-5
87Leaf-247
87OPC-146
87OPC-F
87RedFoley/St-44
87S-80M
87S-97
87Seven-E14
87Seven-ME14
87T-480
87T-610AS
87T-F
87T/Board-5
87T/Coins-21
87T/Gloss60-42
87T/HL-27
87T/HL-5
87T/Mini-44
87T/St-17
87T/St-248
87Woolwth-27
87Woolwth-5
88ChefBoy-21
88D-399
88D/Best-28
88D/RedSox/Bk-399
88F-361
88Leaf-215
88OPC-61
88Panini/St-33
88Score-14
88Sf-158
88T-662TBC
88T-675
88T/Big-181
88T/St-247
89B-33
89D-122
89F-97
89KMart/Lead-9
89OPC-245
89Panini/St-281
89Score-85
89Sf-173
89T-245
89T/Big-18
89T/St-256
89T/WaxBox-I
89UD-413
90T-785
90UD-373

Rice, Lance
88GreatF-7
89Bakers/Cal-192

Rice, Pat
87Wausa-24
88SnBer/Best-6
88SnBer/Cal-43
89Wmspt/Pro-646
89Wmspt/Star-18

Rice, Pete
83AlexD-8
85Nashua-19
86Nashua-22
87Salem-7
88Toled/CMC-23

88Toled/Pro-598
Rice, Tim
86WinSal-22
87Pittsf-24
88BBCity/Star-20
Rice, Woolsey
83Beloi/LF-2
Rich, Woody
R303/A
Richard, J.R.
72OPC-101R
72T-101R
74OPC-522
74T-522
74T/St-36
75OPC-73
75T-73
75T/M-73
76Ho-110
76OPC-625
76T-625
77Ho-112
77OPC-227
77T-260
78BK/A-4
78Ho-92
78OPC-149
78T-470
79Ho-29
79K-10
79OPC-310
79T-203M
79T-590
79T-6LL
79T/Comics-23
80BK/PHR-8
80K-57
80OPC-28
80T-50
80T/S-25
81Coke
81D-140
81F-56
81F/St-44
81K-16
81MSA/Disc-26
81OPC-350
81T-350
82F-226
82OPC-190
82T-190
86Moth/Ast-21
Richard, Lee
(Bee Bee)
72OPC-476
72T-476
75OPC-653
75T-653
75T/M-653
76OPC-533
76SSPC-145
76T-533
Richardi, Rick
87Miami-8
88Mia/Star-20
Richards, Dave
78LodiD
81Albuq/TCMA-8
81Hawai-2
82Hawai-2
88Fay/Pro-1095
89Lakel/Star-18
Richards, Eugene
(Gene)
76Hawai
77T-473R
78T-292
79T-364
80OPC-323
80T-616
81D-4
81F-486
81F/St-17
81OPC-171
81T-171
81T/So-86
81T/St-225
82D-499
82F-580
82F/St-104
82OPC-253
82T-708
82T/St-103
83D-271
83F-370
83OPC-7
83T-7
83T/St-294
84D-429
84F-310
84F/X-98
84Nes/792-594
84T-594
84T/X-99
85F-619
85T-434
Richards, Fred
(Fuzzy)
53Mother-50
Richards, Kevin
81Tulsa-22
82Tulsa-8
Richards, Nicky
83CharR-2
Richards, Paul
33G-142
51B-195
52B-93
52T-305
53B/Col-39
54Wilson
55B-225
60L-112
60T-224
61T-131
61T-566AS
88Conlon/5-25
Richards, Rusty
87Sumter-8
89Richm/CMC-7
89Richm/Ko-40
89Richm/Pro-829
Richards, Todd
80Batav-4
81Batav-6
Richards, Vincent
33SK-23
Richardson, A.H.
(Hardy)
N172
N284
N526
Scrapps
WG1-23
WG1-43
Richardson, A.J.
88Visal/Cal-157
88Visal/Pro-87
89Orlan/Best-23
89Orlan/Pro-1346
Richardson, Bobby
57T-286
58T-101
59T-237M
59T-76
60T-405
61NuCard-415
61P-8
61T-180
61T/Dice-13
62AmTract-43A
62AmTract-43B
62AmTract-43C
62AmTract-43D
62J-2
62P-2
62P/Can-2
62Salada-64
62Shirriff-64
62T-65
62T/St-90
63F-25
63J-13
63Kahn
63P-13
63Salada-52
63T-173M
63T-420
63T/SO
64T-190
64T/Coins-123AS
64T/Coins-72
64T/St-12
64T/SU
64Wheat/St-38
65MacGregor-9
65OPC-115
65T-115
65T/E-65
65T/trans-26
66T-490
66T/RO-56
78TCMA-112
88Pac/Leg-74
89Swell-49
Exh47
WG10-20
WG9-21
Richardson, C.N.
29Exh/4-24
Richardson, Daniel
E223
N172
N284
N338/2
N690
Richardson, David
89Sprin/Best-16
Richardson, Don
86WinSal-23
Richardson, Gordon
62Pep/Tul
63Pep/Tul
66OPC-51
66T-51
Richardson, James
88Kinston/Star-19
89Kinston/Star-20
Richardson, Jeff
85LitFalls-9
86Lynch-18
87Lynch-24
87Tampa-12
88Chatt/Best-22
88PalmSp/Cal-92
88PalmSp/Pro-1463
89Nashvl-20
89Nashvl/CMC-18
89Nashvl/Pro-1291
89PalmSp/Cal-51
89PalmSp/Pro-469
Richardson, Jim
87Watlo-3
Richardson, Jon
78Richm
79Richm-7
Richardson, Keith
88Watertn/Puc-1
89Salem/Star-17
89Star/Wax-95
Richardson, Kenny
78Newar
Richardson, Kerry
87Kinston-23
88Wmspt/Pro-1328
Richardson, Lenny
88CapeCod/Sum-5
Richardson, Mike
89Erie/Star-20
Richardson, Milt
88Eugene/Best-27
89Eugene/Best-18
Richardson, Ron
83MidldC-18
Richardson, Ronnie
87Elmir-27
87Elmir/Red-27
88Lynch/Star-20
Richardson, Tim
86Hagers-15
87Hagers-19
Richardt, Mike
80Charl-8
83D-368
83F-575
83Rang-2
83T-371
84Nes/792-641
84T-641
Richartz, Scott
75AppFx
76AppFx
Richbourg, Lance
29Exh/4-2
31Exh/4-2
33Exh/4-1
R316
Richert, Pete
62T-131
63T-383
64T-51
65OPC-252
65T-252
66Bz-43
66OPC-95
66T-95
66T/RO-36
67Bz-43
67T-590
68T-354
69MLBPA/Pin-24
69OPC-86
69T-86
70T-601
71MLB/St-311
71OPC-273
71T-273
72T-649
73OPC-239
73T-239
74OPC-348
74T-348
74T/Tr-348T
88Modesto-2CO
88Modesto/Cal-82
89Modesto/Cal-287
89Modesto/Ch-2
Richey, Rodney
88Idaho/Pro-1838
89Sumter/Pro-1104
Richie, Bennie
83Visal/LF-19
84Visal-1
Richie, Lewis
10Domino-102
11Helmar-101
12Sweet/Pin-89
E90/1
M116
T202
T204
T205
Richie, Rob
88BBAmer-3
88EastLAS/Pro-11
88GlenF/Pro-925
89Toled/Pro-765
90T-146
90UD-76
Richmond, Bob
87Clint-25
Richmond, Don
51B-264
V362-43
Richter
11Helmar-102
Rick, Dean
78Salem
Ricker, Drew
86Cram/PCL-9
87Clint-22
Ricker, Troy
85Utica-22
86Jamestn-19
87Jamestn-13
88Rockford-31
89Rockford-31
89WPalm/Star-19
Rickert, Marv
47TipTop
52T-50
Rickert, Rick
49Eureka-18
Ricketts, Dave
65T-581R
66Pep/Tul
67T-589
68OPC-46
68T-46
69MB-233
69T-232
70T-626
72MB-288
73OPC-517CO
73T-517C
Ricketts, Dick
59T-137
60T-236
Rickey, W. Branch
14CJ-133
15CJ-133
60F-55
80SSPC/HOF
89HOF/St-91
V100
W754
Rickman, Andy
88Greens/Pro-1568
89Cedar/Best-13
89Cedar/Pro-932
89Cedar/Star-15
Ricks, Ed
89Madis/Star-19
Rico, Alfredo
70T-552R
Riddle, David
89Erie/Star-21
Riddle, Elmer
49Eureka-170
W711/2
Riddle, John L.
(Johnny)
53T-274
54Hunter
54T-147
55Hunter
55T-98
75Cedar
Riddleberger, Dennis
71OPC-93R
71T-93R
72T-642
73OPC-157
73T-157
Riddoch, Greg
88Smok/Padres-24
Ridenour, Dana
87FtLaud-9
88Albany/Pro-1342

88EastLAS/Pro-4
89Wmspt/Pro-647

Ridzik, Steve
53B/BW-48
54B-223
55B-111
57T-123
60T-489
61BeeHive-18
64T-92
65OPC-211
65T-211
66T-294

Riel, Franich
40Hughes-16

Riemer, Robin
86Cram/PCL-183

Riemer, Tim
89Watertn/Star-19

Riesgo, Nikco
88Spoka/Pro-1936
89CharRa/Pro-995

Riewerts, Tom
82AubAs-15

Rigby, Kevin
81Durhm-3

Riggar, Butch
79Holyo-18

Riggins, Mark A.
81ArkTr-14
82ArkTr-7
83StPet-11
86ArkTr-18CO
87Sprin/Best-2C
89Louvl/CMC-24
89Louvl/Pro-1254

Riggleman, James D.
75Water
77ArkTr
79ArkTr-5
80ArkTr-4
81ArkTr-19
83StPet-29
86ArkTr-19MG
87ArkTr-7
88ArkTr/GS-4

Riggs, Jim
82Oneon-2
83Greens-22
85Albany-18
86Albany/TCMA-1

Riggs, Lew
34DS-96
37Exh/4-4
38Exh/4-4
39PB-77
40PB-78
41DP-141
R314
W711/1
W711/2

Righetti, Dave
79WHave-21
80Colum-17
81Colum-9
82D-73
82F-52
82T-439
83D-199
83F-395
83OPC-176
83T-176
83T-81
84D-10
84D-103
84D/AAS-59
84F-139
84F-639IA
84F/St-86
84FunFood/Pin-116
84Nes/792-5HL
84Nes/792-635
84OPC-277
84T-5
84T-635
84T/Gloss40-28
84T/St-287B
84T/St-315
85D-336
85D/HL-37
85Drake-40
85F-142
85F/St-102
85Leaf-219
85OPC-260
85Seven-13E
85T-260
85T/St-314
85T/Super-58
86D-214
86D/HL-52
86F-116
86F/Mini-25
86F/St-97
86Leaf-89
86OPC-34
86S-141M
86S-41
86S-72M
86S/Rook-48M
86T-560
86T/St-303
86T/Super-44
87Class-86
87D-128
87D/AAS-55
87F-111
87F-627M
87F-C12
87F/AwardWin-32
87F/Hottest-31
87F/Mini-90
87F/RecSet-32
87F/Slug-34
87F/St-100
87F/WaxBox-C12
87KayBee-27
87Leaf-53
87MSA/Discs-20
87OPC-40
87S-119M
87S-194M
87S-57
87Seven-E9
87T-40
87T-5RB
87T-616AS
87T/Coins-22
87T/Gloss60-24
87T/HL-14
87T/Mini-67
87T/St-299
87T/St-8
87T/St-9
87Woolwth-14
88Woolwth-16
88Bz-16
88D-93
88D/AS-29
88D/Best-164
88D/Y/Bk-93
88F-220
88F-625M
88F/AwardWin-33
88F/Mini-43
88F/RecSet-32
88F/Slug-33
88F/St-52
88F/TL-29
88KMart-20
88Leaf-57
88Nestle-28
88OPC-155
88Panini/St-150
88RedFoley/St-75
88Score-351
88Sf-135
88Sf/Gamewin-19
88T-790
88T/Mini-29
88T/St-300
88T/St/Backs-66
89B-167
89D-78
89D/Best-76
89F-267
89OPC-335
89Panini/St-400
89RedFoley/St-97
89Score-225
89Score/HotSt-37
89Score/NWest-6
89Sf-158
89T-335
89T/St-307
89UD-59
90Class-41
90D-311
90F-453
90Score-194
90Score/100St-39
90Sf-88
90T-160
90UD-479

Righetti, Steve
78Ashev

Rightnowar, Ron
87Fayette-24
88Lakel/Star-22
89London/Pro-1369

Riginos, Tom
88CapeCod/Sum-58

Rigler, Umpire
21Exh-141

Rigney, Emory E.
21Exh-142
25Exh-94
26Exh-69
E120
E210-38
V61-17
W573

Rigney, John D.
41DP-72
47TipTop

Rigney, William J.
(Bill)
48B-32
49B-170
49Eureka-123
50B-117
51B-125
52BR
52NTea
52T-125
53B/BW-3
58SFCall
60MacGregor-18
60T-225
60T-7M
61T-225
62T-549
63T-294
64T-383
65OPC-66MG
65T-66
66T-249
67T-494
68T-416
69OPC-182MG
69T-182
70OPC-426MG
70T-426
71OPC-532MG
71T-532
72OPC-389MG
72T-389
89Smok/Angels-1
PM10/Sm-156

Rigoli, Joe
79Newar-3
83Erie-2
85Louvl-2
86Erie-25MG
87Erie-3

Rigos, John
83Erie-3
85Sprin-1
86StPet-27
87Salem-14
88Harris/Pro-834

Rigsby, Rickey
88Pulas/Pro-1761
89Idaho/Pro-2013

Rijo, Jose
84F/X-99
84T/X-100
85Cram/PCL-133
85D-492
85F-143
85T-238
86D-522
86D/HL-2
86F-431
86Moth/A's-13
86T-536
87D-55
87F-404
87Leaf-119
87T-34
88D-548
88F/U-U86
88Kahn/Reds-27
88Score-392
88Score/Tr-27T
88T-316
88T/Tr-92T
89B-300
89Class-141
89D-375
89D/Best-278
89F-168
89K/Reds-27
89OPC-135
89Panini/St-68
89Score-552
89Score/YS/I-31
89T-135
89T/Mini-12
89T/St-140
89UD-619
90D-115
90F-430
90Score-511
90T-627
90UD-216

Riles, Earnest
83ElPas-21
84Cram/PCL-35
85Cram/PCL-207
85F/Up-U89
86D-359
86F-499
86F/LL-34
86F/Mini-102
86F/St-98
86Jay's-14
86KayBee-26
86Leaf-161
86Pol/Brew-1
86S-16
86T-398
86T/Gloss60-40
86T/St-310
87D-151
87F-355
87F/GameWin-36
87F/Mini-91
87Leaf-66
87OPC-318
87T-523
87T/St-203
88D-478
88F-172
88F/U-U130
88Pol/Brew-1
88Score-349
88Score/Tr-57T
88T-88
88T/Tr-93T
89B-475
89Class-87
89D-625
89D/Best-50
89F-341
89Gard-14
89Moth/Giants-16
89Score-458
89T-676
89UD-497
90D-131
90F-69
90Score-447
90T-732
90UD-378

Riley, Darren
85Cedar-24
86FSLAS-41
86Tampa-16
87Vermont-25
88Chatt/Best-24

Riley, Ed
89Elmir/Puc-14

Riley, George
80Wichi-20
81D-588
81T-514
83Readg-8
84Cram/PCL-206

Riley, Mike
79Wisco-3
82Cedar-6

Riley, P.J.
89AubAs/Pro-2180

Riley, Randy
84Newar-1

Riley, Tim
77DaytB

Riley, Tom
74Cedar
75Dubuq
83Cedar-16
83Cedar/LF-5
84Cedar-15
85Cedar-31

Rincon, Andrew
80ArkTr-9
81Louvl-17
81T-244R
82Louvl-24
82T-135
89ArkTr/GS-20

Rincones, Hector
81Water-16
83Water-13
85Cram/PCL-157

Rineer, Jeff
78RochR
79RochR-16
80RochR-8

Rinehart, Robert Jr.
86Columbia-22

Ring, James J.
21Exh-143
26Exh-39
28Exh-22
88Pac/8Men-87
E120
E126-24
E220

V100
V61-120
W516-11
Ringler, Tim
88Knoxv/Best-22
89Knoxv/Best-30
89Knoxv/Pro-1122
Rings, Frank
N172
Rios, Carlos Rafael
77AppFx
78Charl
81Buffa-19
82Knoxv-15
85IntLgAS-5
85Richm-15
87Greenvl/Best-5
88Richm-6
88Richm/CMC-18
88Richm/Pro-8
89Richm/CMC-13
89Richm/Ko-6
89Richm/Pro-842
Rios, Enrique
87Kenosha-29
88CLAS/Star-16
88Lynch/Star-21
Rios, Jesus
85Tigres-1
Rios, Juan
69T-619R
70OPC-89
70T-89
72MB-289
Ripken, Bill
86SLAS-1
87D/Rook-16
87RochR-12
87RochR/TCMA-13
87S/Rook-28
88Class/Red-163
88D-336
88D-625M
88D/Best-254
88F-569
88F-640M
88French-7
88Leaf-134
88MSA/Disc-7
88OPC-352
88Panini/St-9
88Score-200
88Score/YS/I-20
88Sf-216
88T-352
88T/JumboR-1
88T/St-227
88ToysRUs-25
89B-12
89D-259
89D/Best-318
89F-616
89French-3
89OPC-22
89Panini/St-261
89RedFoley/St-98
89Score-18
89T-571
89T/Big-27
89UD-283
90D-164
90F-186
90Score-174
90T-468
90UD-184
Ripken, Cal Jr.
81RochR-15
82D-405
82F-176
82T-21R
82T/Tr-98T
83D-279
83D/AAS-52
83Drake-23
83F-70
83OPC-163
83T-163
83T/St-26
83T/St-315
84D-106
84D/AAS-20
84D/Champs-48
84Drake-26
84F-17
84F/St-15
84F/St-29
84FunFood/Pin-118
84MiltBrad-20
84Nes/792-400AS
84Nes/792-426TL
84Nes/792-490
84Nestle/DT-4
84OPC-2AS
84OPC-363
84Seven-14E
84T-400
84T-490
84T/St-197
84T/St-204
84T/St-24
84T/St/Box-13
84T/Super-1
84T/Super-1
85D-14
85D-169
85D/AAS-7
85D/DKsuper-14
85Drake-26
85F-187
85F-626IA
85F/LimEd-28
85F/St-41
85Leaf-14DK
85OPC-30
85Seven-14E
85T-30
85T-704AS
85T/3D-16
85T/Gloss22-16
85T/Gloss40-24
85T/St-185
85T/St-197
85T/Super-48
86BK/AP-15
86D-210
86D/AAS-14
86D/PopUp-14
86Dorman-4
86Drake-11
86F-284
86F-633M
86F/AS-5
86F/LimEd-36
86F/LL-35
86F/Mini-59
86F/Slug-28
86F/St-99
86Jiffy-9
86Leaf-142
86Meadow/Blank-11
86Meadow/Milk-8
86Meadow/Stat-11
86OPC-340
86Quaker-31
86S-128M
86S-54M
86S-59M
86S-69M
86S-73M
86S-8
86S/Dec-73M
86S/Rook-48M
86T-340
86T-715
86T/Gloss22-5
86T/Gloss60-14
86T/Mini-2
86T/St-159
86T/St-226
86T/Super-45
86TrueVal-22
87Class-52
87D-89
87D/AAS-5
87D/HL-38
87D/OD-133
87D/PopUp-5
87Drake-6
87F-478
87F/AwardWin-33
87F/GameWin-37
87F/Lim-36
87F/Mini-92
87F/Slug-35
87F/St-101
87Jiffy-8
87Kraft-3
87Leaf-98
87MnM's-13
87MSA/Discs-14
87OPC-312
87Ralston-12
87RedFoley/St-118
87S-113M
87S-9
87Seven-ME16
87T-609AS
87T-784
87T/Board-22
87T/Coins-23
87T/Gloss22-16
87T/Gloss60-37
87T/Mini-40
87T/St-151
87T/St-233
88Bz-17
88ChefBoy-7
88Class/Red-176
88D-171
88D-26DK
88D-625M
88D-BC1
88D/AS-5
88D/Best-198
88D/DKsuper-26DK
88D/PopUp-5
88F-570
88F-635M
88F-640M
88F/RecSet-33
88F/Slug-34
88F/SS-31
88F/St-3
88F/TL-30
88French-8
88KayBee-25
88KingB/Disc-24
88KMart-21
88Leaf-100
88Leaf-26DK
88OPC-74
88Panini/St-13
88Panini/St-230M
88RedFoley/St-76
88Score-550
88Score-651
88Score/WaxBox-5
88Sf-152
88T-650
88T/Big-62
88T/Coins-24
88T/Gloss22-5
88T/Gloss60-6
88T/RiteAid-13
88T/St-160
88T/St-228
88T/St/Backs-44
88T/UK-61
89B-260FS
89B-9
89Cadaco-44
89Class-56
89Crunch-6
89D-51
89D/AS-5
89D/Best-142
89D/MVP-BC15
89D/PopUp-5
89F-617
89F/BBAS-35
89F/Heroes-34
89F/LL-32
89French-8
89KMart/DT-15
89Master/Discs-12
89OPC-250
89Panini/St-241AS
89Panini/St-262
89RedFoley/St-99
89Score-15
89Score/HotSt-77
89Score/Mast-3
89Sf-66
89T-250
89T/Big-286
89T/Coins-50
89T/Gloss22-5
89T/Gloss60-47
89T/St-150
89T/St-237
89T/St/Backs-11
89T/UK-64
89T/WaxBox-J
89Tetley/Discs-16
89UD-467
89UD-682TC
90Class-24
90D-676AS
90D-96
90D/Bon/MVP-BC18
90F-187
90F-624
90Score-2
90Score/100St-66
90Sf-100
90T-388AS
90T-570
90T-8RB
90UD-266
Ripken, Cal Sr.
82D-579
87T/Tr-102T
88D-625M
88F-635M
88T-444
89B-260FS
89French-7
90F-634M
Ripley, Allen
78PapaG/Disc-1
79T-702R
80T-413
81F-454
81T-144
82D-125
82F-399
82RedLob
82T-529
82T/Tr-99T
83D-57
83F-506
83T-73
Rippelmeyer, Ray
60HenryH-28
60Union-10
61T-276
62T-271
73OPC-486CO
73T-486C
74OPC-119CO
74T-119C
89Nashvl/CMC-24
89Nashvl/Pro-1280
Ripple, Charles
47Centen-23
47Signal
Ripple, Jimmy
38Exh/4-5
38ONG/Pin-24
39PB-66
41DP-11
41DP-95
44Centen-18
V355-28
Rippley, Steve
88Umpire-49
89Umpires-47
Ripslager, Charles
N172/SP
Risberg, Charles
(Swede)
88Pac/8Men-103
88Pac/8Men-16
88Pac/8Men-26
88Pac/8Men-70
W514-105
Riscen, Fred
88SLCty-21
Risley, Bill
88Greens/Pro-1551
89Cedar/Best-6
89Cedar/Pro-912
89Cedar/Star-16
Ritch, Harry
85VeroB-13
Ritchey, Claude
E107
E254
T206
WG3-41
Ritchey, Larry
86Cram/PCL-60
Ritchie, Dave
89Eugene/Best-11
Ritchie, Gregg
86Cram/PCL-5
87Clint-4
88SanJose/Cal-127
88SanJose/Pro-131
89Shreve/Pro-1841
Ritchie, Jay
65T-494
Ritchie, Lewis
14Piedmont/St-49
Ritchie, Wally
86Clearw-21
87F/U-U104
87Maine-17
87T/Tr-103T
88D-555
88F-312
88OPC-322
88Score-526
88T-494
89ScrWB/CMC-9
89ScrWB/Pro-715
Ritter, Chris
86PrWill-21
87Harrisbg-25
88Harris/Pro-845
Ritter, Darren
89Pulas/Pro-1905
Ritter, Ken
89Medford/Best-15
Ritter, Louis
E254
T206
Ritter, Reggie
83Watlo/LF-15
85Water-11

86Maine-16
86OhHenry-53
87BuffB-19
88ColSp/CMC-7
88ColSp/Pro-1540
Ritter, William
D328-138
E135-138
Rittwage, James
65T-501R
Rittweger, Bill
82Jacks-18
Ritz, Kevin
87GlenF-6
88GlenF/Pro-926
89Toled/CMC-7
89Toled/Pro-786
90Class-131
90D-415
90F-613
90Score-572
90Score/100Ris-11
90Sf-29
90T-237
90UD-98
Rivard, John
89Mia/Star/25-17
Rivas, Martin
77Charl
Rivas, Rafael
80Utica-31
Rivell, Robert
88CapeCod/Sum-72
Rivera, Angel
88James/Pro-1900
Rivera, Ben
88Sumter/Pro-410
89Durhm/Star-18
Rivera, Carlos
87Fayette-14
88Elmir-11
88WinHav/Star-21
89Elmir/Puc-15
Rivera, Dave
77Ashev
82Charl-22
Rivera, Elvin
86QuadC-27
87QuadC-16
88Reno/Cal-269
Rivera, German
78Clint
83Albuq-17
84Pol/Dodg-25
85Cram/PCL-162
85D-638
85F-382
85T-626
86Nashv-20
87Toled-4
87Toled/TCMA-3
88AAA/Pro-14
88Denver/CMC-12
88Denver/Pro-1253
Rivera, Hector
89WPalm/Star-20
Rivera, Jesus
(Bombo)
77OPC-54
77T-178
78T-657
79T-449
80OPC-22
80T-43
81D-593
81F-556
81Omaha-23
81T-256
82Omaha-20
83Omaha-19
Rivera, Jim
83Ander-14
84Durhm-26
Rivera, Jose
83Greens-23
83QuadC-23
87Memph-23
87Memph/Best-4
88Memph/Best-25
Rivera, Lino
88CharlR/Star-20
89Fay/Pro-1573
Rivera, Luis
83VeroB-13
86Indianap-28
87F-330
87Indianap-27
88T/Big-223
88T/Tr-94T
89B-29
89D-578
89F-392
89OPC-257
89Pawtu/CMC-20
89Pawtu/Dunkin-14
89Pawtu/Pro-697
89Score-169
89T-431
89T/St-68
89UD-423
90D-421
90F-285
90T-601
90UD-482
Rivera, Manuel J.
(Jim)
53T-156
54T-34
55T-58
55T/DH-90
56T-70
56T/Hocus-A11
56T/Hocus-B13
56T/Pin-35
57T-107
58T-11
59T-213
60L-55
60T-116
61P-33
61T-367
Rivera, Pablo
89CharlK-25
Rivera, Ricardo
82AubAs-17
83DayBe-22
Rivero, Marty
88Peoria/Ko-26
89WinSal/Star-14
Rivers, Ken
87Duned-27
88Knoxv/Best-14
89Knoxv/Best-21
89Knoxv/Pro-1132
89Knoxv/Star-17
Rivers, Mickey Jr.
88Elmir-23
89WinHav/Star-18
Rivers, Mickey Sr.
72OPC-272
72T-272
73OPC-597
73T-597
74OPC-76
74T-76
75Ho-22
75Ho/Twink-22
75OPC-164
75T-164
75T/M-164
76Ho-102
76K-41
76OPC-198LL
76OPC-85
76SSPC-203
76T-198LL
76T-85
76T/Tr-85T
77BK/Y-18
77K-51
77OPC-69
77T-305
78BK/Y-20
78Ho-110
78K-17
78OPC-182
78T-690
79BK/Y-20
79OPC-24
79T-60
80OPC-251
80T-485
81D-496
81F-617
81F/St-32
81OPC-145
81T-145
81T/HT
81T/So-31
81T/St-132
82D-242
82F-328
82F/St-174
82OPC-356
82OPC-51IA
82T-704
82T-705
82T/St-243
83D-394
83F-576
83OPC-224
83Rang-17
83T-224
84D-465
84F-425
84Nes/792-504
84OPC-269
84Rang-17
84T-504
84T/St-361
85D-465
85F-565
85Leaf-35
85OPC-371
85T-371
85T/St-355
Rixey, Eppa
21Exh-144
25Exh-30
26Exh-30
27Exh-15
28Yueng-16
33G-74
61F-71
80SSPC/HOF
89HOF/St-69
D327
D328-139
D329-142
D350/2-142
E120
E121/120
E121/80
E122
E135-139
E210
M101/4-142
M101/5-142
V100
V354-32
W501-54
W502-16
W572
W575
Rizza, Jerry
88SoOreg/Pro-1715
Rizzo, Johnny
39Exh
39PB-11
40PB-108
41DP-124
47Signal
47Sunbeam
Rizzo, Mike
83Peoria/LF-14
Rizzo, Rick
81CharR-23
82FtMyr-1
84Memph-3
Rizzo, Tom
88Pulas/Pro-1754
89Sumter/Pro-1087
Rizzuto, Phil
41DP-62
47TipTop
48B-8
48L-11
49B-98
49Royal-11
50B-11
50Drake-25
51B-26
51BR-A3
51T/CAS
51T/RB-5
52B-52
52BR
52Royal
52StarCal/L-70F
52T-11
52TipTop
52Wheat
53B/Col-9
53B/Col-93M
53Briggs
53Exh/Can-25
53RM-AL10
53SM
53T-114
54B-1
54DanDee
54NYJour
54RM-AL17
54SM
54T-17
55B-10
55SM
55T-189
56T-113
56T/Pin-29
60NuCard-45
61NuCard-445
61T-471MV
79TCMA-144
80Cram/Leg-82
83MLBPA/Pin-15
86S/Dec-22
88Pac/Leg-10
89Swell-111
D305
Exh47
PM10/L-34
PM10/Sm-157
Roach, Brett
88Brist/Pro-1884
89Fay/Pro-1589
Roach, John
N172
Roach, Mel
54T-181
55Gol/Braves-26
55T-117
59T-54
60Lake
60T-491
61P-163
61T-217
62T-581
Roadcap, Steve
83QuadC-16
86Pittsf-20
88Wythe/Pro-1991
Roarke, Mike
61T-376
62T-87
63T-224
64T-292
83Pawtu-26
Roarke, Tom
82AubAs-1
Robarge, Dennis
88Elmir-29ASST
89Elmir/Puc-26
Robbe, Fletcher
53Mother-5
Robbins, Bruce
80Evans-18
80T-666R
81D-129
81F-477
81T-79
82Evans-6
83BirmB-10
Robbins, Doug
88T/Tr-95T
89T/Big-49
Robbins, Leroy
80WHave-3
Roberge, Al
V362-46
Roberge, Bert
77Cocoa
80T-329
80Tucso-23
81Tucso-21
82Tucso-15
83D-496
83F-461
83T-611
83Tucso-8
85F-525
85T-388
85T/Tr-94T
86D-575
86F-258
86OPC-154
86Provigo-16
86T-154
Roberson, Kevin
88Wythe/Pro-1978
89CharWh/Best-7
89CharWh/Pro-1747
Roberts, Bill
76Dubuq
Roberts, Brent
88BurlR/Pro-1772
Roberts, Cliff
77DaytB
Roberts, Curt
54DanDee
54T-242
55T-107
55T/DH-11
56T-306
60DF-6
61Union
Roberts, Dave A.
69T-536R
70OPC-151
70T-151
71MLB/St-235
71OPC-448
71T-448
72K-15
72OPC-360
72OPC-91LL
72T-360
72T-91LL
73OPC-133
73OPC-39

73T-39
74McDon
74OPC-177
74OPC-309
74T-177
74T/St-37
74T/St-99
75OPC-301
75OPC-558
75T-301
75T/M-301
76OPC-107
76OPC-649
76T-107
77Ho-10
77OPC-193
77OPC-38
77T-363
78T-501
79Pol/Giants-25
79T-473
80T-212
81D-490
81F-636
81T-431
82Phoen

Roberts, Dave L.
63T-158R
66T-571

Roberts, Dave W.
73T-133
74T-309
75T-558
75T/M-558
76T-649
76T/Tr-649T
77T-537
78T-501
79T-342
80T-93
81D-501
81F-607
81T-57
81T/Tr-824
82D-625
82F-227
82T-218
83D-273
83T-148

Roberts, Drex
85Kingst-20

Roberts, Jay
83Ander-31

Roberts, Jeff
86Wausa-19

Roberts, John
86Greens-20
87Greens-8
88EastLAS/Pro-23
88NewBrit/Pro-894
89Pawtu/CMC-21
89Pawtu/Dunkin-24
89Pawtu/Pro-693

Roberts, Leon K.
(Leon)
75OPC-620R
75T-620R
75T/M-620R
76OPC-292
76SSPC-362
76T-292
76T/Tr-292T
77T-456
79Ho-37
79OPC-81
79T-166
79T/Comics-15
80OPC-266
80T-507
81D-48
81F-608
81T-368
81T/Tr-825
82D-415
82F-329
82OPC-186
82T-688
83OPC-89
83T-89
83T/X-96
84D-399
84F-356
84Nes/792-784
84T-784
85T-217
86Nashv-21MG
87Toled-20
87Toled/TCMA-21
88Fay/Pro-1104

Roberts, Leon
(Bip)
84PrWill-1
85Nashua-20
86D/Rook-33
86F/Up-U96
86T/Tr-91T
87D-114
87F-427
87LasVegas-23
87T-637
88LasVeg/CMC-14
88LasVeg/Pro-245
89F/Up-126
89T/Tr-103T
90D-347
90F-166
90Score-51
90Sf-116
90T-307
90UD-303

Roberts, Mel
88SALAS/GS-2
88Spart/Pro-1033
88Spart/Star-22
88Spart/Star-6
89Spart/Pro-1050

Roberts, Mike
80Tulsa-5
81Tulsa-17

Roberts, Norman
86Hagers-16

Roberts, Pete
88LasVeg/CMC-5
88LasVeg/Pro-228
89LasVeg/CMC-9
89LasVeg/Pro-13

Roberts, Robin
49B-46
49Eureka-143
49Lummis
50B-32
51B-3
51BR-D8
51T/CAS
52B-4
52BR
52NTea
52RM-NL18
52T-59
52TipTop
53B/Col-65
53RM-NL11
54B-95
54RM-NL18
55B-171
56T-180
56YellBase/Pin-27
57T-15
58T-90
59T-156M
59T-352
60Bz-26
60MacGregor-19
60NuCard-44
60T-264
60T/tatt
60T/tatt-45
61NuCard-444
61P-117
61T-20
61T/St-58
62J-198
62P-198
62P/Can-198
62T-243
63J-66
63P-66
63T-125
63T-6LL
64T-285
65OPC-15
65T-15
66T-530
79TCMA-4
80Cram/Leg-56
82CJ-9
83D/HOF-41
83MLBPA/Pin-30
86S/Dec-39M
88Pac/Leg-15
Exh47
PM10/Sm-158
PM10/Sm-159

Roberts, Scott
84Cram/PCL-42
85Cram/PCL-218
86Maine-17
87BuffB-20

Robertson, Alfred J.
(Jim)
54B-211
54T-149
55B-5
55Rodeo
55T-177

Robertson, Andre
81Colum-3
82Colum-17
82Colum/Pol-2
82T-83
83D-387
83F-396
83RoyRog/Disc-10
83T-281
83T/St-316
84Colum-9
84Colum/Pol-20
84D-347
84F-140
84Nes/792-592
84OPC-282
84T-592
84T/St-323
85F-144
85T-354
86Colum-21
86Colum/Pol-19
86D-469
86F-117
86T-738
87Chatt/Best-25
88Huntsvl/BK-16
88Tacom/CMC-19
88Tacom/Pro-634
89OkCty/CMC-14
89OkCty/Pro-1514

Robertson, Bob E.
68OPC-36R
68T-36R
69T-468R
70T-664
71K-4
71MLB/St-212
71OPC-255
71T-255
72K-45
72OPC-429
72OPC-430IA
72T-429
72T-430A
73OPC-422
73T-422
74OPC-540
74T-540
75OPC-409
75T-409
75T/M-409
76OPC-449
76SSPC-578
76T-449
77T-176
79OPC-158
79T-312
89Swell-107

Robertson, Bryant
85LitFalls-27

Robertson, Charles
21Exh-145
E120
V61-10
W573

Robertson, Dale
81Pawtu-13
84Pawtu-4

Robertson, Daryl
62Pep/Tul

Robertson, David A.
D327
D328-140
D329-143
D350/2-143
E135-140
M101/4-143
M101/5-143
V100

Robertson, Doug
86Clint-22
87Clint-1
88CalLgAS-6
88SanJose/Cal-137
88SanJose/Pro-115
89Shreve/Pro-1851

Robertson, Jason
89LittleSun-14

Robertson, Jay
78Duned
80Syrac-6

Robertson, Jerry L.
69T-284R
70T-661
71OPC-651
71T-651

Robertson, Michael
86Jamestn-20
87StPet-5
88ArkTr/GS-20
89ArkTr/GS-21

Robertson, Richard P.
69OPC-16R
69T-16R
70OPC-229
70T-229
71MLB/St-263
71OPC-443
71T-443
72T-618

Robertson, Rod
86Cram/PCL-130
88Spart/Pro-1034
88Spart/Star-18
88Spart/Star-2
89Clearw/Star-19

Robertson, Sherry
50B-161
51B-95
52T-245

Robicheaux, Randy
86Watertn-18

Robidoux, Billy Jo
83Beloi/LF-21
86D-515
86F-652M
86F/Up-U97
86Pol/Brew-13
86S-178M
86S/Rook-28
86T/Tr-92T
87D-240
87D/OD-51
87F-356
87T-401
87T/GlossRk-13
87T/St-202
88Denver/CMC-13
88Denver/Pro-1267
88Score-334
89Coke/WS-23

Robinette, Gary
81AppFx-22

Robinson, Aaron
47TipTop
49B-133
50B-95
51B-142
53Mother-6
D305

Robinson, Bill H.
67T-442R
68T-337
68T/3D
69MB-234
69MLB/St-78
69T-313
69T/St-207
70MLB/St-249
70OPC-23
70T-23
72MB-290
73OPC-37
73T-37
74OPC-174
74T-174
74T/M-501
74T/St-78
75OPC-501
75T-501
75T/M-501
76OPC-137
76SSPC-577
76T-137
77T-335
78OPC-128
78T-455
79OPC-336
79T-637
80OPC-138
80T-264
81D-137
81F-373
81T-51
82D-402
82F-494
82T-543
82T/Tr-100T
83F-170
83T-754
88Kahn/Mets-28CO
88QuadC/GS-8
89Kahn/Mets-28

Robinson, Brad
88Greens/Pro-1557

Robinson, Brett
88Peoria/Ko-27
89Peoria/Ko-7P

Robinson, Brian
85Cedar-19
86Vermont-16
87Cedar-17

Robinson, Brooks
57T-328

58T-307
59T-439
60L-27
60T-28
61P-75
61T-10
61T-572AS
61T/Dice-14
61T/St-104
62J-29
62P-29
62P/Can-29
62Salada-40
62Shirriff-40
62T-45
62T-468AS
62T/bucks
62T/St-8
63Bz-30
63Exh
63F-4
63J-59
63P-59
63Salada-53
63T-345
63T/SO
64Bz-30
64T-230
64T/Coins-125AS
64T/Coins-18
64T/S-50
64T/St-21
64T/SU
64Wheat/St-39
65Bz-30
65OldLond-35
65OPC-150
65OPC-1LL
65OPC-5LL
65T-150
65T-1LL
65T-5LL
65T/trans
65T/trans-65
66Bz-34
66T-390
66T/RO-90
67Bz-34
67OPC-1M
67OPC/PI-3
67T-1M
67T-600
67T/PI-3
68Bz-8
68Coke
68OPC-20
68T-20
68T-365AS
68T-530M
68T/G-9
69MB-235
69MLB/St-8
69MLBPA/Pin-25
69NTF
69OPC/DE-18
69T-421AS
69T-550
69T/DE-1
69T/S-3
69T/St-129
69Trans-13
70K-21
70MLB/St-154
70OPC-230
70OPC-455AS
70T-230
70T-455AS
71Bz
71Bz/Test-22
71MD
71MLB/St-309
71MLB/St-571
71OPC-300
71OPC-331WS
71T-300
71T/Coins-114
71T/GM-9
71T/S
71T/tatt-1
71T/tatt-1a
72MB-291
72OPC-222ALCS
72OPC-498KP
72T-498BP
72T-550
73JP
73OPC-90
73T-90
73T/Comics-16
73T/Lids-41
73T/PinUps-16
74Laugh/ASG-66
74OPC-160
74OPC-334AS
74T-160
74T-334M
74T/DE-25
74T/St-129
75Ho-144
75K-18
75OPC-202M
75OPC-50
75T-202MV
75T-50
75T/M-202MV
75T/M-50
76Crane-48
76Ho-36
76Ho/Twink-36
76Laugh/Jub-11
76MSA/Disc
76OPC-95
76SSPC-392
76T-95
77T-285
78OPC-239RB
78T-4M
78TCMA-190
80Cram/Leg-54
82CJ-13
82KMart-5
83MLBPA/Pin-16
84West/1-7
86S/Dec-45
87KMart-9
87Nestle/DT-14
88Pac/Leg-3
89Kahn/Coop-9
89Pac/Leg-129
89Swell-134
Exh47

Robinson, Bruce

79Colum-16
79T-711R
80Colum-15
81T-424R
84Cram/PCL-73

Robinson, Clyde

E254
W501-96

Robinson, Craig

74OPC-23
74T-23
74T/Tr-23T
75OPC-367
75T-367
75T/M-367
76SSPC-12
81Richm-23
82Richm-29
83Richm-24

Robinson, Darryl

88AppFx/Pro-144
88MidwLAS/GS-38
89AppFx/Pro-860

Robinson, David T.

71OPC-262R
71T-262R
88SanDiegoSt-15

Robinson, Dewey

80T-664R
81T-487
82T-176
87Penin-7

Robinson, Don

79T-264
80T-719
81D-375
81F-366
81OPC-168
81T-168
82F-495
82OPC-332
82T-332
83D-171
83F-319
83OPC-44
83T-44
83T/St-277
84D-532
84F-262
84Nes/792-616
84OPC-22
84T-616
85D-264
85F-475
85OPC-129
85T-537
86D-357
86F-621
86Leaf-159
86T-731
87D-608
87F-622
87OPC-387
87T-712
88D-573
88F-95
88F/Mini-120
88F/St-131
88F/TL-31
88Moth/Giants-22
88Score-619
88Sf-90
88T-52
88T/St-94
89B-463
89D-571
89D/Best-191
89F-342
89F/BBAS-36
89Moth/Giants-22
89Panini/St-211
89Score-440
89T-473
89T/St-86
89UD-523
90D-258
90F-70
90Score-112
90T-217
90UD-616

Robinson, Earl

60DF-20
61T-343
62T-272
78TCMA-81

Robinson, Emmett

86Kinston-19

Robinson, Floyd

62Salada-214
62Shirriff-214
62T-454
62T/bucks
62T/St-29
63Bz-24
63J-39
63P-39
63T-2LL
63T-405
63T/SO
64Bz-24
64T-195
64T/Coins-39
64T/St-18
64T/SU
65T-345
66OPC-8
66T-199M
66T-8
66T/RO-94
67OPC-120
67T-120
68T-404
71T/tatt-11
Exh47

Robinson, Frank

56Kahn
57Kahn
57Swift-16
57T-35
58Kahn
58T-285
58T-386M
58T-484AS
59Armour-14
59HRDerby-16
59Kahn
59T-435
60Bz-29
60Kahn
60MacGregor-20
60T-352M
60T-490
60T/tatt
60T/tatt-46
61Bz-31
61Kahn
61P-182
61T-25M
61T-360
61T-581AS
61T/Dice-15
61T/St-24
62Bz
62J-122
62Kahn
62P-122
62P/Can-122
62Salada-165
62Shirriff-165
62T-350
62T-396AS
62T-54LL
62T/bucks
62T/St-121
63Bz-31
63Exh
63FrBauer-22
63J-131
63Kahn
63P-131
63Salada-29
63T-1LL
63T-3LL
63T-400
63T/SO
64Bz-31
64Kahn
64T-260
64T/Coins-154AS
64T/Coins-37
64T/S-29
64T/St-15
64T/SU
64T/tatt
65Bz-31
65Kahn
65OldLond-17
65OPC-120
65T-120
65T/E-22
65T/trans
65T/trans-66
66Bz-32
66T-219LL
66T-310
66T/RO-3
67Bz-32
67OPC-100
67OPC-1M
67OPC-62CL
67OPC/PI-19
67T-100
67T-1M
67T-239LL
67T-241LL
67T-243LL
67T/PI-19
67T/Test/SU-3
68Bz-3
68Coke
68OPC-2LL
68OPC-4LL
68T-2LL
68T-373AS
68T-4LL
68T-500
68T-530M
68T/G-7
68T/Post-24
69MB-236
69MLB/St-9
69MLBPA/Pin-26
69NTF
69T-250
69T/decal
69T/S
69T/St-130
69Trans-16
70K-15
70MB-23
70MLB/St-155
70OPC-463AS
70T-463AS
70T-700
70T/PI-12
70T/S-37
70Trans-12
71Bz/Test-2
71K-15
71MD
71MLB/St-310
71MLB/St-572
71OPC-329WS
71OPC-63LL
71OPC-640
71T-640
71T/Coins-50WS
72MB-292
72OPC-100
72OPC-228WS
72OPC-88LL
72T-100
72T-754TR
72T-88LL
73OPC-175
73T-175
73T/Lids-42
74Laugh/ASG-59
74OPC-55
74T-55
74T/DE-66
74T/St-145
75OPC-199M
75OPC-204M
75OPC-331MG
75OPC-580
75T-199MV
75T-204MV

75T-331MG
75T-580
75T/M-199MV
75T/M-204MV
75T/M-331MG
75T/M-580
76Crane-49
76Laugh/Jub-5
76MSA/Disc
76SSPC-525
76T-477MG
77T-18MG
78RochR
78TCMA-140
80Cram/Leg-123
80Laugh/3/4/5-23
82D-424
82KMart-9
83D-564
83D-648M
83D/HOF-19
83Moth/Giants-1
83T-576
83T/St-4
84D/Champs-43
84Nes/792-171MG
84T-171
85CircK-4
85D/HOF-8
85Woolwth-29
86BLChew-4
86S/Dec-41
86T-404M
87KMart-10
87Nestle/DT-16
88French-20MG
88T/Tr-96MG
89French-20
89Smok/Angels-8
89Smok/Dodg-24
89T-774MG
90T-381MG
Exh47

Robinson, Henry
86FtMyr-22

Robinson, Humberto
55T-182
59T-366
60L-70
60T-416

Robinson, Jackie R.
47Bond/JR-1--13
48L-79
48Swell-3
49B-50
49Eureka-48
50B-22
52BR
52StarCal/L-79G
52T-312
53Exh/Can-19
53T-1
54NYJour
54T-10
55Gol/Dodg-25
55T-50
55T/DH-25
56T-30
56T/Hocus-A14
56T/Pin-51
60NuCard-53
61NuCard-428
72T/Test-4
74Laugh/ASG-49
76Laugh/Jub-26
79TCMA-291
80Cram/Leg-15
80Laugh/FFeat-18
80SSPC/HOF
83D/HOF-6
83MLBPA/Pin-31
84West/1-1
86S/Dec-28
87Nestle/DT-24
88Pac/Leg-40
89B-I9
89HOF/St-12
89Rini/Dodg-18
89Rini/Dodg-27
89Smok/Dodg-25
D302-Set
D305
Exh47
PM10/Sm-160--166
R346-36
Rawl

Robinson, Jeff
88D/Best-241
88OPC-244
88Pep/T-44
88Pol/T-10
88T/Big-123
88T/St-133
89B-410
89B-97
89Class-93
89D-18DK
89D-370PP
89D-470
89D/Best-129
89D/DKsuper-18DK
89F-143
89F-220
89F/LL-33
89OPC-267
89OPC-351
89Panini/St-164
89Panini/St-335
89Score-284
89Score-309
89Score/HotSt-34
89Score/YS/II-8
89Sf-193
89T-267
89T-681
89T/Big-274
89T/Big-45
89T/St-129
89UD-332
89UD-472
90D-134
90D-417
90F-479
90F-614
90Score-333
90T-42
90T-723
90UD-403
90UD-552

Robinson, Jeffrey D.
(Jeff)
84F/X-100
84T/X-101
85D-201
85F-620
85OPC-5
85T-592
86Moth/Giants-15
86T/Tr-93T
87D-559
87F-283
87Moth/SFG-25
87T-389
88D-558
88Score-439
88T-244

Robinson, Jeffrey M.
(Jeff)
85Cram/PCL-184
86Nashv-22
87D/Rook-13
87F/U-U105
87S/Rook-47
87T/Tr-104T
88D-296
88F-68
88Score-549
88T-449
89Mara/Tigers-44
89Pol/Tigers-44

Robinson, Jerry
63T-466R

Robinson, Jim
78Newar
79BurlB-4

Robinson, Kevin
87Erie-20
88Hamil/Pro-1730

Robinson, M.C.
N172

Robinson, Marteese
88Madis-20
89Modesto/Cal-285

Robinson, Mike
83Erie-24
85Sprin-25
86ArkTr-20
87ArkTr-2
88ArkTr/GS-19
88Louvl-42

Robinson, Randall
87CharWh-27

Robinson, Randy
83Butte-9

Robinson, Ron
81Cedar-6
82Water-9
85D-649
85F-650
86D-121
86F-190
86T-442
86TexGold-33
87D-310
87F-212
87F/GameWin-38
87F/Mini-93
87Kahn-33
87T-119
88D-166
88D/Best-308
88F-247
88F/Mini-75
88Kahn/Reds-33
88OPC-342
88Score-476
88T-517
89B-303
89D-308
89F-169
89K/Reds-33
89OPC-16
89Score-559
89T-16
89T/Big-132
89UD-187
90D-553
90F-431
90Score-495
90T-604

Robinson, Wilbert
50Callahan
60F-33
63Bz-27
72F/FFeat-10
72Laugh/GF-30
80SSPC/HOF
89HOF/St-86
89Smok/Dodg-104
D329-144
D350/2-144
E121/120
E210-43
M101/4-144
M101/5-144
N142
N172/BC
N300/SC
N690
W515-53
W575

Robinson, William E.
(Eddie)
49Royal-22
50B-18
51B-88
51T/RB-51
52B-77
52BR
52Hawth/Pin-7
52NTea
52RM-AL18
52Royal
52StarCal/L-73C
52T-32
53B/BW-20
53Mother-59
53RM-AL11
53T-73
54B-193
54NYJour
54T-62
55B-153
56T-302
57T-238
60T-455C
79TCMA-283
Exh47

Robinson, William H.
N172
N284
N370
Scrapps

Robitaille, Martin
88James/Pro-1921

Robles, Gabriel
(Gabby)
86Kinston-20
87WinSal-18

Robles, Greg
82Idaho-21
83Madis/LF-22
84Albany-25

Robles, Jorge
89Wausa/GS-19

Robles, Rafael
69T-592R
70T-573R
71OPC-408
71T-408

Robles, Ruben
83Tucso-26
84Cram/PCL-66

Robles, Sergio
73OPC-601R
73T-601R
74OPC-603R
74T-603R

Robles, Silvano
75AppFx
76AppFx

Robson, Gary
88Beloi/GS-2
89Beloi/Star-26M

Robson, Tom
79Wausa-16
80Ashev-2
87Smok/R-21CO
89Smok/R-26CO

Roby, Ellis
86Sumter-22
87Durhm-10
88Durhm/Star-18
89Greenv/Pro-1159
89Greenv/Star-20
89Greenvl/Best-9

Roca, Gilbert
86Macon-21
87Salem-16
88Harris/Pro-851
89Jacks/GS-17

Rocco, Michael
(Mickey)
47Centen-24
48Sommer-26
49Sommer-14

Roche, Rod
86VeroB-20
87Bakers-17

Roche, Steve
80Wausa-7
81Chatt-8
82Chatt-15
82Watlo/C-10

Roche, Tim
77Clint
78LodiD

Roche, Titi
88LitFalls/Puc-11
89Star/Wax-24
89StLucie/Star-21

Rochford, Mike
84Pawtu-21
86Pawtu-18
87Pawtu-9
87Pawtu/TCMA-9
88Pawtu/CMC-2
88Pawtu/Pro-447
89F-650M
89Pawtu/CMC-6
89Pawtu/Dunkin-26
89Pawtu/Pro-700
90UD-694

Rock, Bob
77Charl
78Salem
80Buffa-12
81Buffa-10

Rock, Royal
C46-10
E254

Rockenfeld, Isaac B.
T206
T213/brown

Rockett, Pat
78T-502
79Richm-20
80Syrac-5

Rockey, Jim
86Durhm-23

Rockman, Marv
88Gasto/Pro-995
89Tulsa/GS-22

Rockne, Knute
33SK-35

Rockweiler, Dean
86Jamestn-21

Rodas, Richard
(Rick)
82Albuq-9
83Albuq-6
84Cram/PCL-147
84Pol/Dodg-56
85Cram/PCL-174

Roddy, Phil
77Ashev

Rode, Don
48Sommer-30M

Rodgers, Andre
57T-377
59T-216
60L-42
60T-431
61P-153
61T-183
62J-185
62P-185
62P/Can-185
62Salada-155A
62Salada-155B

62Shirriff-155
62T-477
63J-173
63P-173
63T-193
64T-336
65T-536
66EH-16
66T-592
67T-554
78TCMA-51

Rodgers, Darrell
86Fresno/Smok-15
88MidwLAS/GS-13
89Chatt/Best-15
89Chatt/GS-21

Rodgers, Dirk
79WHave-22M

Rodgers, Kevin
88Poca/Pro-2091

Rodgers, Paul
87Myrtle-30
88Duned/Star-14
89Duned/Star-13

Rodgers, Robert L.
(Buck)
62T-431
62T/St-68
63Bz-2
63F-20
63J-31
63P-31
63T-280
63T/SO
64T-426
64T-61M
65T-342
65T/trans-27
66T-462
67T-281
68T-433
69MB-237
69MLB/St-27
69OPC-157
69T-157
69T/St-149
73OPC-49CO
73T-49C
74OPC-447CO
74T-447C
78TCMA-63
81D-327
81T-668MG
82D-232
82Pol/Brew-37MG
84Indianap-2MG
85Indianap-36MG
85T/Tr-95T
86OPC-141MG
86Provigo-3MG
86T-171
87OPC-293MG
87T-293MG
88OPC-134MG
88T-504
89OPC-193
89T-474MG
90T-81MG
Exh47

Rodgers, Tim
84Syrac-17
86Tulsa-7
87OKCty-17

Rodiles, Jose
85FtMyr-30
87ColumAst-18

Rodiles, Jose
87ColAst/Pro-18

Rodiles, Steve
85IowaC-36

Rodrigues, Roman
89Princet/Star-18

Rodriguez, A.
86Ashvl-23

Rodriguez, Ahmed
89Savan/Pro-353

Rodriguez, Alex
75BurlB

Rodriguez, Andy
75SnAnt

Rodriguez, Angel
85Beloi-10
87Stockton-10
88ElPas/Best-23
88Stock/Cal-198
88Stock/Pro-742

Rodriguez, Antonio H.
(Hector)
52Hawth/Pin-8
53B/Col-98

Rodriguez, Aurelio
69JB
69T-653
70MLB/St-179
70OPC-228
70T-228
71MLB/St-405
71OPC-464
71T-464
71T/Coins-124
72MB-293
72OPC-319
72T-319
72T/Cloth-27
73OPC-218
73T-218
74OPC-72
74T-72
74T/St-179
75OPC-221
75T-221
75T/M-221
76OPC-267
76SSPC-366
76T-267
77Ho-120
77OPC-136
77T-574
78BK/T-14
78OPC-64
78T-342
79OPC-83
79T-176
80OPC-245
80T-468
81F-105
81T-34
82F-53
82OPC/Post-10
82T-334
82T/Tr-101T
83D-369
83F-249
83T-758
83T/X-97
84Nes/792-269
84T-269
88ColSp/CMC-25
88ColSp/Pro-1536

Rodriguez, Buena
89James/Pro-2131

Rodriguez, Carlos
88FtLaud/Star-18
89FtLaud/Star-21

Rodriguez, Dave
83Tacom-30B

Rodriguez, Ed
84Cram/PCL-240
85Cram/PCL-108
89PalmSp/Cal-41

Rodriguez, Eddie
83Peor/LF-28C
86QuadC-28
87QuadC-18
88QuadC/GS-1MG
89Brist/Star-23
89QuadC/Best-2
89QuadC/GS-1

Rodriguez, Edgar
87QuadC-3
88QuadC/GS-7
89PalmSp/Pro-465

Rodriguez, Eduardo
71MLB/St-449
74OPC-171
74T-171
75OPC-582
75T-582
75T/M-582
76OPC-92
76SSPC-228
76T-92
77T-361
78T-623
79T-108
80T-273
81Holyo-1

Rodriguez, Edwin
83Colum-18
86LasVegas-13
87LasVegas-19

Rodriguez, Eligio
88Geneva/Pro-1646

Rodriguez, Eliseo
(Ellie)
69OPC-49R
69T-49R
70OPC-402
70T-402
71OPC-344
71T-344
72MB-294
72OPC-421
72T-421
73K-2
73OPC-45
73T-45
73T/Lids-43
74OPC-405
74T-405
74T/St-146
75Ho-34
75Ho/Twink-34
75OPC-285
75T-285
75T/M-285
76OPC-512
76SSPC-193
76T-512
77T-448

Rodriguez, Ernie
85Bend/Cram-20
88Butte-28
89Butte/SP-28

Rodriguez, F. Boi
87Jamestn-7
88WPalm/Star-21
89Jaxvl/Best-16
89Jaxvl/Pro-177

Rodriguez, Gabriel
88FtLaud/Star-19
88Peoria/Ko-28
89FtLaud/Star-22
89Star/Wax-80

Rodriguez, Henry
89VeroB/Star-23

Rodriguez, Iggy
86WPalm-25

Rodriguez, Ivan
78BurlB
80Holyo-6
81Vanco-8
89Gasto/Pro-1006
89Gasto/Star-20

Rodriguez, Jonis
84Greens-20

Rodriguez, Jose
79Wisco-21
81Buffa-13
82Jacks-8
82Portl-21
83LynnP-22
83StPet-23
86ArkTr-21
86BurlEx-18
87AppFx-20
89Brist/Star-24
89Princet/Star-17

Rodriguez, Juan
77DaytB

Rodriguez, Luis E.
80OkCty
81OkCty/TCMA-16
82OkCty-16

Rodriguez, Miguel
80Utica-32

Rodriguez, Mike
79Ogden/TCMA-4

Rodriguez, Ramon
85Spoka/Cram-20
86CharRa-22

Rodriguez, Rich
84LitFalls-25
86Lynch-19
87Lynch-19
88Jacks/GS-13
89AubAs/Pro-19
89Wich/Roc-29LHP

Rodriguez, Richard
77Charl

Rodriguez, Rick
86Tacom-19
88ColSp/CMC-8
88ColSp/Pro-1549
88F-293
88F/U-U24
88T-166
89Vanco/CMC-8
89Vanco/Pro-580

Rodriguez, Rigo
85Beaum-10

Rodriguez, Roberto
68T-199R
69T-358R
71MLB/St-44
71OPC-424
71T-424

Rodriguez, Rosario
88Greens/Pro-1567

Rodriguez, Ruben
83AlexD-26
85Nashua-21
86Nashua-23
87Vanco-23
89Boise/Pro-1992
89Denver/CMC-18
89Denver/Pro-34

Rodriguez, Tomas
88Bill/Pro-1816
89Bill/Pro-2044

Rodriguez, Victor
82RochR-16
85Cram/PCL-101
85D-535
87Louvl-26
88Portl/CMC-20
88Portl/Pro-649
89AAA/Pro-40
89Portl/CMC-17
89Portl/Pro-210

Roe, Preacher
47TipTop
49B-162
50B-167
50Drake-1
51B-118
51T/RB-16
52B-168
52BR
52Dix
52NTea
52StarCal/L-79F
52T-66
52Wheat
53B/BW-26
53Dix
53Exh/Can-1
53NB
53T-254
54B-218
54Dix
54NYJour
54T-14
55B-216
79TCMA-145
79TCMA-239
89Rini/Dodg-33
89Smok/Dodg-56
Exh47
PM10/Sm-167

Roe, Rocky
88Umpire-42
89Umpires-40

Roebuck, Ed
52Park-75
53Exh/Can-41
55Gol/Dodg-26
55T-195
56T-58
58T-435
60BB-13
60T-519
61BB-37
61P-70
61T-6
61T/St-32
62BB-37
62T-535
63T-295
64T-187
64T/Coins-20
64T/St-35
64T/SU
65OPC-52
65T-52
78TCMA-165

Roebuck, Joe
89Helena/SP-13

Roebuck, Ron
86Ashvl-24
86AubAs-20

Roebuck, Scott
83Wausa/LF-20

Roeder, Jack
82Wausa-3

Roenicke, Gary
76SSPC-338
80T-568
81D-116
81F-187
81OPC-37
81T-37
82D-509
82F-177
82T-204
83D-27
83F-71
83OPC-382
83T-605
84D-392
84F-18
84Nes/792-372
84OPC-372
84T-372
84T/St-205
85D-123
85F-188
85OPC-109
85T-109
86D-472

86F-285
86F/Up-U98
86OPC-183
86T-494
86T/Tr-94T
87D/OD-47
87OPC-283
87Smok/Atl-23
87T-683
87T/Tr-105T
88Panini/St-252
88Score-482
88T-523

Roenicke, Ron
78LodiD
80Albuq-6
81Albuq/TCMA-9
82F-19
82Pol/Dodg
82Pol/Dodg-40
82T-681R
83D-327
83F-217
83Pol/Dodg-40
83T-113
84Cram/PCL-237
84D-484
84F-618
84Nes/792-647
84T-647
86F/Up-U99
86T-63
87D-412
87F-182
87T-136
87T-329
88Nashvl/CMC-21
88Nashvl/Pro-475
88Score-566
88T-783
89OkCty/CMC-16
89OkCty/Pro-1519

Roesch, John
77Newar
78Newar

Roesler, Mike
86Cedar/TCMA-8
87Tampa-5
88Nashvl/CMC-11
88Nashvl/Pro-492
89Nashvl-21
89Nashvl/CMC-7
89Nashvl/Pro-1282
90F-645
90Score-648
90T-203

Roetter, Randy
82QuadC-28
88Wausa/Feder-28
88Wausa/GS-28
89Wmspt/Pro-634

Roettger, W.
31Exh/4-8

Rogalski, Wayne
86Ashvl-25

Rogan, Pat
65T-486R

Rogell, William
33G-11
34DS-76
35BU-177
35G-1D
35G-2D
35G-6D
35G-7D
R313
R314
V353-11
V355-52

Rogers, Brad
88Batav/Pro-1691

Rogers, Danny
87Sumter-22

Rogers, Darrell
88Cedar/Pro-1162

Rogers, Dennis
86Nashua-24MG
87Macon-24

Rogers, Doug
89Idaho/Pro-2027

Rogers, Dusty
86Tampa-17
87Cedar-11

Rogers, Jimmy
88Myrtle/Pro-1190
88SALAS/GS-22
89Knoxv/Best-22
89Knoxv/Pro-1133
89Knoxv/Star-18

Rogers, Kenny
88Tulsa-28
89D/Best-315
89D/Rook-13
89Moth/R-21
89Score/Tr-107
89Smok/R-27
89T/Tr-104T
90D-283
90F-311
90Score-301
90Score/100Ris-46
90Sf-216
90T-683
90UD-606

Rogers, Kevin
89Clint/Pro-891

Rogers, Mac
85Durhm-9
86Durhm-24

Rogers, Marte
85Elmir-19

Rogers, Randy
78Tidew
83Ander-15

Rogers, Robbie
88Reno/Cal-283

Rogers, Steve
74OPC-169
74T-169
74T/DE-65
74T/St-59
75OPC-173
75T-173
75T/M-173
76Crane-50
76MSA/Disc
76OPC-71
76SSPC-349
76T-71
77Ho-22
77OPC-153
77T-316
78OPC-9DP
78T-425
78Wiffle/Discs-62
79OPC-120
79T-235
80K-8
80OPC-271
80T-520
81D-330
81F-143
81F/St-57
81OPC-344
81OPC/Post-9
81T-725
81T/So-106
81T/St-190
82D-36
82F-205
82F/St-36
82Hygrade
82OPC-52
82OPC/Post-20
82T-605
82T/St-59
82Zeller-2
83D-18DK
83D-320
83F-294
83OPC-106AS
83OPC-111TL
83OPC-320
83Stuart-10
83T-111TL
83T-320
83T-405AS
83T-707LL
83T/St-208
83T/St-256
84D-219
84D/AAS-48
84F-284
84Nes/792-394AS
84Nes/792-708LL
84Nes/792-80
84OPC-394AS
84OPC-80
84Seven-20W
84Stuart-19
84Stuart-36AS
84T-394
84T-708
84T-80
84T/Gloss40-3
84T/St-182FOIL
84T/St-88
85D-219
85F-408
85Leaf-192
85OPC-205
85OPC/Post-11
85T-205
85T/St-89

Rogers, Stu
85BurlR-23

Rogers, Thomas
E121/120
W501-28
W575

Roggenburk, Garry
63T-386R
64T-258
66T-582
67T-429
68T-581

Rogodzinski, Mike
74OPC-492
74T-492
76SSPC-607

Rogon, Bullet
74Laugh/Black-19

Rogovin, Saul
52B-165
52RM-AL19
52T-159
52TipTop
53B/Col-75
54B-140
57T-129
PM10/Sm-168

Rogozenski, Karl
83StPet-28

Rohan, Tony
85Newar-7
87Miami-9
88Mia/Star-22

Rohde, Brad
86Cram/PCL-112
86Wausa-20

Rohde, Dave
86AubAs-21
87Osceola-29
88ColAst/Best-11
89ColMud/Best-21
89ColMud/Pro-123
89ColMud/Star-20
89Star/Wax-2

Rohde, Dr. Richard
63FrBauer-21

Rohlfing, Wayne
79QuadC-6

Rohlof, Scott
86Visal-17

Rohm, Dave
78Duned

Rohn, Andy
87Everett-7

Rohn, Dan
80Wichi-6
82IowaC-8
83IowaC-19
84IowaC-8
85IntLgAS-36
85Maine-22
86OhHenry-15
87Tacom-16
88OkCty/CMC-20
88OkCty/Pro-31
89OkCty/CMC-15
89OkCty/Pro-1530

Rohr, Les
68T-569R

Rohr, William
67T-547R
68T-314R

Rohrmeier, Dan
88FSLAS/Star-48
88Tampa/Star-22
89Saraso/Star-21

Roig, Tony
59DF
60DF-16
61Union

Rois, Luis
80GlenF/B-6
80GlenF/C-17
81GlenF-20

Rojas, Cookie
63T-221
64T-448
65T-474
66OPC-170
66T-170
66T/RO-77
67T-595
68OPC-39
68T-39
69MB-238
69MLB/St-176
69T-507
69T/S-55
69T/St-77
69Trans-55
70MLB/St-142
70T-569
71MLB/St-427
71OPC-118
71T-118
72K-39
72MB-295
72OPC-415
72T-415
73OPC-188
73T-188
74K-42
74OPC-278
74T-278
74T/St-189
75Ho-2
75Ho/Twink-2
75OPC-169
75T-169
75T/M-169
76A&P/KC
76OPC-311
76SSPC-171
76T-311
77T-509
88Smok/Angels-1MG
88T/Tr-97MG

Rojas, Francisco
78Cedar

Rojas, Homar
85Tigres-17
87SnAnt-21
88FSLAS/Star-19
88VeroB/Star-22
89SnAnt/Best-21

Rojas, Jeff
85Visal-18

Rojas, Luis
82WHave-24

Rojas, Melquiades
(Mel)
87BurlEx-27
89Jaxvl/Best-28
89Jaxvl/Pro-156
89SLAS-20

Rojas, Mike
83Idaho-17

Rojas, Minnie
67OPC-104
67T-104
68T-305
69T-502

Rojas, Ricardo
89Wmspt/Star-19

Rojas, Ricky
86FtMyr-23
87FtMyr-20
88EastLAS/Pro-36
88Vermont/Pro-959

Rojek, Stan
49B-135
49Eureka-171
49Royal-15
50B-86
51B-166
52B-137
52NTea
52T-163
PM10/Sm-169

Rokosz, Keith
77AppFx

Roland, James
63T-522R
64T-341
65OPC-171
65T-171
68T-276
69T-336
70T-719
71MLB/St-524
71OPC-642
71T-642
72OPC-464
72T-464

Roldan, Sal
88Mia/Star-21
88SLCty-27

Rolfe, Robert
(Red)
34DS-104
34DS-29
34G-94
35BU-181
35BU-22
35G-8E
35G-9E
41DP-65
51B-319
52T-296
72F/FFeat-22
R314
V355-38

Rolland, Dave
86DayBe-23
87SanJose-15

Rollin, Rondal
82BirmB-13
84Evans-3
87BirmB/Best-7
87SLAS-2

Rollings, Bill
79Tulsa-23ow

Rollings, William R.
(Red)
33G-88
V354-40

Rollins, Rich
61Clover-23
62T-596R
63F-24
63J-4
63P-4
63Salada-49
63T-110
64Bz-10
64T-270
64T-8LL
64T/Coins-51
64T/St-52
64T/SU
65OPC-90
65T-90
66T-473
67OPC-98
67T-98
68Coke
68T-243
69MB-239
69MLB/St-98
69T-451
69T/St-229
70McDon-4
70MLB/St-276
70T-652
72MB-296
78TCMA-119
89Pac/Leg-169
Exh47
WG10-45
WG9-44

Rolls, David
88Eugene/Best-12

Romagna, Randy
85Kingst-14
86Kinston-21

Roman, Bob
77Spart

Roman, Dan
87Oneon-7
88FtLaud/Star-20
89FtLaud/Star-23

Roman, Jose
81Batav-3
82Watlo/C-24
83Watlo/LF-12
84BuffB-8
85F-646
85Maine-13
86Maine-18
87BuffB-21
87Tidew-23
87Tidew/TCMA-29
88Tidew/CANDL-25
88Tidew/CMC-9
88Tidew/Pro-1601

Roman, Junior
77Watlo
78Wausa

Roman, Miguel
81Batav-26
83Watlo/LF-13
86Water-20
87Wmspt-13
88Jacks/GS-17

Roman, Ray
87Readg-11
88Readg/Pro-885

Roman, William A.
65T-493R

Romanick, Ron
81Redwd-5
82Holyo-8
83Nashua-6
84F/X-101
84Smok/Cal-23
84T/X-102
85D-451
85F-309
85OPC-280
85Smok/Cal-11
85T-579
85T/St-231
86D-85
86F-166
86F/Mini-34
86F/St-100
86Leaf-81
86OPC-76
86Smok/Cal-11
86T-733
86T/St-180
87Colum-27
87Colum/Pol-21
87Colum/TCMA-8
87OPC-136
88Stock/Cal-176
88Stock/Pro-731

Romano, James
52Park-73

Romano, John
59T-138
60T-323
61Kahn
61T-5
61T/RO-19
61T/St-142
62Bz
62J-42
62Kahn
62P-42
62P/Can-42
62Salada-94
62Shirriff-94
62Sugar-7
62T-330
62T/bucks
62T/St-40
63Bz-18
63J-76
63P-76
63Salada-46
63Sugar-7
63T-392M
63T-72
63T/SO
64Kahn
64T-515
64T/Coins-9
64T/S-59
64T/St-48
64T/SU
64T/tatt
65OPC-17
65T-17
65T/E-10
66T-199M
66T-413
67OPC-196
67T-196

Romano, Thomas
82Madis-28
83Albany-19
84Cram/PCL-77
85Cram/PCL-131
86Indianap-7
87Indianap-14
88BuffB/CMC-13
88BuffB/Polar-4
88BuffB/Pro-1485
89BuffB/CMC-21
89BuffB/Pro-1670

Romanovsky, Mike
86PalmSp-28
86PalmSp/Smok-10
87MidldA-22

Romero, Al
83Nashua-19
85Cram/PCL-25
86Edmon-24

Romero, Brian
89Butte/SP-6

Romero, Charlie
88QuadC/GS-24
89PalmSp/Cal-36
89PalmSp/Pro-470

Romero, Ed
76BurlB
77Holyo
79T-708R
79Vanco-17
80Vanco-13
81T-659R
82D-536
82Pol/Brew-11
82T-408
83D-584
83F-44
83Gard-15
83Pol/Brew-11
83T-271
84D-89
84F-212
84Gard-16
84Nes/792-146
84Pol/Brew-11
84T-146
85D-515
85F-593
85Gard-17
85Pol/Brew-11
85T-498
86D-455
86F-500
86OPC-317
86T-317
86T/Tr-95T
87D-606
87F-42
87OPC-158
87T-675
88D-623
88D/RedSox/Bk-623
88F-362
88Score-259
88T-37
89T/Tr-105T
89UD-40

Romero, Elbi
87Spart-19

Romero, Elvis
86Cram/PCL-140
87Kenosha-23

Romero, Esmyel
82Redwd-9

Romero, Mandy
89Aug/Pro-498

Romero, Ramon
78Watlo
79Wausa-14
81AppFx-23
81Watlo-14
82AppFx-6
82Watlo-9
83BuffB-9
83GlenF-10
84BuffB-16
84Maine-1
85BuffB-11
85Polar/Ind-50
86D-495
86T-208
86Toled-20

Romero, Ronaldo
89Gasto/Pro-1016
89Gasto/Star-21

Romero, Tony
87Elmir-21
87Elmir/Red-21

Romine, Kevin
84Pawtu-13
85Pawtu-11
86Pawtu-19
87Pawtu-4
87Pawtu/TCMA-18
87T-121
88D/RedSox/Bk-NEW
88F-363
88Score-644
89F-98
89Pawtu/CMC-18
89Pawtu/Dunkin-16
89Pawtu/Pro-682
89Score-541
89UD-524
90D-476
90F-286
90Score-458
90UD-441

Rommel, Ed
21Exh-146
25Exh-111
26Exh-111
28Yueng-55
55B-239ump
87Conlon/2-19
E120
E210-55
R306
R316
V100
V61-9
W501-1
W501-102
W502-55
W515-5
W572
W573
W575
WG7-45

Rommell, Rick
80ElPas-6
81Holyo-26

Romo, Enrique
78OPC-186
78T-278
79OPC-281
79T-548
80T-332
81D-255
81F-385
81OPC-28
81T-28
82D-59
82F-496
82T-106
83F-320
83T-226

Romo, Robert
87AubAs-16

Romo, Vicente
69T-267
70MLB/St-163
70OPC-191
70T-191
71MLB/St-329
71OPC-723
71T-723
72MB-297
72OPC-499
72T-499
73OPC-381
73T-381
74OPC-197SD
74T-197
75OPC-274
75T-274
75T/M-274
83F-218
83T-633

Romonosky, John
59T-267
60T-87

Ronan, Kernan
82Clint-16
83Phoen/BHN-10
84Shrev/FB-17
89PalmSp/Cal-62CO
89PalmSp/Pro-481

Rondon, Alberto
76Dubuq

Rondon, Isidro
86Tampa-18

Ronk, Jeff
82Amari-7
83Beaum-14
84Beaum-25

Ronning, Al
52Park-49
53Exh/Can-56

Ronson, Tod
86Cram/PCL-21
87Clint-8
88SanJose/Cal-128
88SanJose/Pro-126
89Salin/Cal-143
89Salin/Pro-1821

Roobarb
85Coke/WS
86Coke/WS
87Coke/WS-30M

Rood, Nelson
86Tucso-19
87Tucso-15
88Tucso-19
88Tucso/CMC-13
88Tucso/Pro-191

Roof, Eugene L.
(Gene)
78StPet
79ArkTr-22
81Louvl-5
82D-615
82Louisvl-25
82T-561R
83F-20
84Louvl-5
85Richm-20
86Nashv-23
87Toled-22
87Toled/TCMA-22
88Toled/Pro-599
89Fay/Pro-1577

Roof, Phil
63T-324R
64T-541R
65T-537R
66T-382
67OPC-129
67T-129
68T-484
69MB-240
69Sunoco/Pin-15
69T-334
70McDon-5
70OPC-359
70T-359
71MLB/St-450
71OPC-22
71T-22
72MB-298
72OPC-201
72T-201
73OPC-598
73T-598
74OPC-388

74T-388
75OPC-576
75T-576
75T/M-576
76OPC-424
76SSPC-224
76T-424
77OPC-121
77T-392
83Orlan-1

Rooker, Dave
83Butte-26
86PrWill-22
87Harrisbg-4

Rooker, Jim
69T-376R
70OPC-222
70T-222
71MLB/St-428
71OPC-730
71T-730
71T/Coins-32
72T-742
74OPC-402
74T-402
75OPC-148
75T-148
75T/M-148
76OPC-243
76SSPC-566
76T-243
77OPC-161
77T-82
78T-308
79T-584
80T-694
81F-368

Rooker, Michael
88Pac/8Men-9

Rooks, George
N172
N284

Roomes, Rolando
82QuadC-24
83QuadC-27
86WinSal-24
87Pittsf-25
89D-577
89F-644M
89F/Up-86
89K/Reds-36
89Nashvl/CMC-22
89Nashvl/Pro-1286
89Score/HotRk-37
89Score/Tr-109
89UD-6
90Class-38
90D-360
90F-432
90Score-417
90Score/100Ris-92
90T-364
90UD-170

Rooney, Jim
84Newar-16

Rooney, Pat
80Memph-17
82Wichi-15
84Colum-3
84Colum/Pol-21
85Syrac-16

Root, Charley H.
28Exh-11
29Exh/4-6
30CEA/Pin-8
31Exh/4-6
32Orbit/un-51
33Exh/4-3
33G-226
60T-457C
88Conlon/3-24
R303/A
R305
R306
R308-190
R316
R332-44

Roper, Brian
89Butte/SP-3

Roque, Jorge
72OPC-316R
72T-316R
73OPC-606R
73T-606R

Rosa, Julio
88Brist/Pro-1869
89Fay/Pro-1587

Rosado, Ed
88Martins/Star-28
89Batav/Pro-1944
89Spart/Pro-1029
89Spart/Star-20

Rosado, Luis
(Papo)
78Tidew
79Syrac-18
80Tidew-22
84RochR-12
85RochR-3

Rosar, Warren
(Buddy)
41G-4
48B-10
48L-128
49B-138
50B-136
51B-236
R346-19

Rosario, Alfonso
78Cedar

Rosario, Angel
(Jimmy)
72OPC-366
72T-366

Rosario, David
87Peoria-16
88WinSal/Star-15
89CharlK-13

Rosario, Francisco
88Savan/Pro-358

Rosario, Jose
78Duned

Rosario, Jossy
89CharWh/Best-8
89CharWh/Pro-1750

Rosario, Julio
86Elmir-17
87Elmir-8
87Elmir/Red-8
88Elmir-18
88WinHav/Star-22
89Elmir/Puc-16

Rosario, Maximo
83Ander-16

Rosario, Mel
86Kinston-22
87FtLaud-26
88Albany/Pro-1343
89FtLaud/Star-24

Rosario, Sal
75BurlB

Rosario, Simon
76Dubuq
77Cocoa
78DaytB
81Tucso-8
84Durhm-1

Rosario, Victor
85Elmir-20
86Greens-21
87Greens-19
88Martins/Star-29
89Readg/Star-20
89ScrWB/CMC-23
89ScrWB/Pro-710

Roscoe, Greg
88Watlo/Pro-691
89Kinston/Star-21
89Watertn/Star-20

Rose
53Exh/Can-42

Rose, Carl
86Watertn-19

Rose, Don
73OPC-178
73T-178
75Phoen-7

Rose, Kevin
79Newar-20

Rose, Pete Jr.
82F-640M
89Erie/Star-22
89Freder/Star-27
90Class-75

Rose, Pete
63FrBauer-23
63T-537R
64Kahn
64T-125
64T/Coins-82
65Kahn
65OPC-207
65T-207
66Bz-38
66Kahn
66OPC-30
66T-30
66T/RO-95
67Bz-38
67Kahn
67T-430
67T/Test/SU-1
68Bz-15
68Bz-6
68T-230
68T/G-30
68T/Post-23
69Citgo-14
69Kelly/Pin-15
69MB-241
69MLB/St-135
69MLBPA/Pin-55
69NTF
69OPC-120
69OPC-2LL
69OPC-424AS
69T-2LL
69T-120
69T-424AS
69T/DE-21
69T/decal
69T/S-41
69T/St-29
69Trans-54
70K-2
70MB-24
70MLB/St-35
70OPC-458AS
70OPC-61LL
70T-458AS
70T-580
70T-61LL
70T/CB
70Trans-1
71Bz
71Bz/Test-32
71K-65
71MD
71MLB/St-573
71MLB/St-68
71OPC-100
71T-100
71T/Coins-101
71T/GM-15
71T/S-20
71T/tatt-14
72K-6
72MB-299
72T-559
72T-560A
72T/Post-11
73K-6
73OPC-130
73T-130
73T/Lids-44
74K-38
74OPC-201LL
74OPC-300
74OPC-336AS
74T-201LL
74T-300
74T-336M
74T/DE-16
74T/St-30
75Ho-29
75Ho/Twink-29
75K-11
75OPC-211M
75OPC-320
75T-211MV
75T-320
75T/M-211MV
75T/M-320
76Crane-51
76Ho-66
76Icee
76K-55
76MSA/Disc
76OPC-240
76SSPC-41
76T-240
77Ho-8
77K-20
77OPC-240
77Pep-43
77T-450
77T/CS-38
78Ho-128
78OPC-100DP
78OPC-240RB
78T-20
78T-5M
78Wiffle/Discs-63
79BK/P-13
79Ho-144
79K-22
79OPC-343
79T-204M
79T-650
79T/Comics-28
80BK/P-4
80BK/PHR-21
80K-35
80OPC-282
80T-4RB
80T-540
80T/S-19
81Coke
81D-131
81D-251
81D-371
81Drake-3
81F-1
81F-645M
81F/St-43M
81F/St-74
81K-63
81MSA/Disc-27
81OPC-180
81Sqt-11
81T-180
81T-205M
81T/HT
81T/Nat/Super-12
81T/S
81T/So-62
81T/St-200
82D-168
82D-1DK
82D-585M
82Drake-28
82F-256
82F-640M
82F/St-107M
82F/St-109M
82F/St-51
82K-18
82KMart-24
82KMart-44
82OPC-24IA
82OPC-337AS
82OPC-361
82Sqt-12
82T-337AS
82T-4M
82T-636TL
82T-780
82T-781A
82T/St-117
82T/St-121
82T/St-78
83D-42
83D/AAS-31
83Drake-24
83F-171
83F-634M
83K-6
83OPC-100
83OPC-101SV
83OPC-373AS
83T-100
83T-101A
83T-397AS
83T/Gloss-14
83T/Gloss40-14
83T/St-272
83T/St/Box-7
84D-61
84D/AAS-54
84D/Champs-27
84Drake-27
84F-46
84F-636IA
84F/St-119
84F/St-99
84F/X-102
84FunFood/Pin-4
84MiltBrad-21
84Nes/792-300
84Nes/792-701LL
84Nes/792-702LL
84OPC-300
84Ralston-4
84Seven-22C
84Stuart-17
84T-300
84T-701
84T-702
84T/Cereal-4
84T/Gloss40-1
84T/St-115
84T/X-103
85D-254
85D-641
85D/HL-10
85D/HL-40
85F-550
85F-640IA
85F/LimEd-29
85F/St-1
85F/St-2
85F/St-3
85Leaf-144
85OPC-116
85Seven-10G
85T-547
85T-600
85T-6RB
85T/3D-15
85T/Gloss40-10

85T/St-57
85T/Super-32
85Woolwth-30
86BK/AP-4
86D-62
86D-644M
86D-653M
86D/AAS-34
86D/DKsuper-27
86Drake-22
86F-191
86F-628M
86F-638M
86F/HOF-1
86F/LimEd-37
86F/LL-36
86F/Mini-40
86F/Slug-29
86F/St-101
86Jiffy-11
86Leaf-209M
86Leaf-260M
86Leaf-53
86Meadow/Blank-12
86Meadow/Milk-9
86Meadow/Stat-8
86OPC-1
86OPC-N
86Quaker-11
86S-138M
86S-150M
86S-181M
86S-182M
86S-50
86S-51M
86S-58M
86S-60M
86S-69M
86S/Dec-60
86S/Rook-46M
86T-1
86T-206RB
86T-2M
86T-3M
86T-4M
86T-5M
86T-6M
86T-741
86T-7M
86T/3D-22
86T/Gloss60-51
86T/Rose-1
86T/Rose-120
86T/St-134
86T/St-1FOIL
86T/St-2
86T/Super-46
86T/WaxBox-N
86TexGold-14A
86TexGold-14B
86TexGold-14C
86TrueVal-4
86Woolwth-29
87Class-1
87Class/Up-103
87D-186
87F-213
87F/Excit-38
87F/Hottest-32
87F/Lim-37
87F/LL-37
87F/McCror-36
87F/RecSet-33
87F/St-102
87KMart-19
87Kraft-34
87Leaf-129
87OPC-200
87RedFoley/St-64
87S-25
87T-200
87T-393MG
87T/Gloss60-41
87T/St-139
88Class/Blue-226
88Kahn/Reds-14
88KMart-22
88T-475
89Class-71
89K/Reds-14MG
89T-505MG

Rose, Robert
(Bob)
86QuadC-29
88MidwLAS/GS-23
88QuadC/GS-14
89MidldA/GS-27
90F-651
90Score-604
90UD-77

Roseboro, Jaime
86LitFalls-24
87Columbia-6
88Clmbia/GS-24
89StLucie/Star-22

Roseboro, John
58T-42
59Morrell
59T-441
60BB-7
60MacGregor-21
60Morrell
60T-292M
60T-88
61P-166
61T-363
61T/St-33
62BB-8
62J-107
62P-107
62P/Can-107
62Salada-133
62Shirriff-133
62T-32
62T-397AS
62T/St-139
63J-120
63Salada-12
63T-120
63T-487
64T-88
65T-405
65T/trans-28
66OPC-189
66T-189
66T/RO-15
67T-365
68Bz-7
68Coke
68OPC-65
68T-65
69MB-242
69MLB/St-70
69OPC-218
69T-218
69T/St-198
70MLB/St-285
70T-655
72MB-300
73OPC-421CO
73T-421C
74OPC-276CO
74T-276C
78TCMA-185
87Smok/Dodg-30
88Smok/Dodg-2
89Smok/Dodg-64

Roselli, Bob
56T-131
61T-529
62T-363

Rosello, Dave
74OPC-607R
74T-607R
76OPC-546
76T-546
77T-92
78T-423
80T-122
81D-79
82Charl-18
82D-617
82F-377
82T-724

Roseman, James
E223
N172/ST
N284
N690
N690/2

Rosen, Al
50B-232
50NumNum
51B-187
51BR-A1
51T/RB-35
52B-151
52NTea
52NumNum-10
52StarCal/L-74B
52T-10
53B/Col-8
53NB
53RM-AL24
53T-135
54DanDee
54RH
54RM-AL12
54T-15
55Armour-17
55Gol/Ind-25
55RM-AL11
55Salem
55T-70
55T/DH-1
56T-35
56T/Hocus-A8
56T/Pin-10
61T-474MV
72T/Test-6
74Laugh/ASG-54
75OPC-191M
75T-191MV
75T/M-191MV
79TCMA-175
PM10/Sm-170
R423-85

Rosen, Goodwin
39PB-76

Rosenberg, Steve
87Albany-1
88Vanco/CMC-3
88Vanco/Pro-754
89Coke/WS-24
89D-219
89F/Up-22
89T-616
89UD/Ext-715
90D-253
90F-547
90Score-523
90T-379
90UD-522

Rosenfield, Dave
88Tidew/CANDL-5GM

Rosenthal, Wayne
87Gasto-18
88CharlR/Star-21

Rosfelder, Chris
89Elmir/Puc-17

Rosinski, Brian
80Wichi-17

Roskom, Bryan
89Keno/Pro-1069
89Keno/Star-22

Roslund, John
75QuadC

Roso, Jimmy
89Bluef/Star-17

Ross, Chester
41G-31

Ross, Chuck
76BurlB
77BurlB
78Holyo

Ross, Dan
89London/Pro-1361

Ross, David
89Martins/Star-27

Ross, Don
49B/PCL-20

Ross, Floyd
52T-298
54T-189

Ross, Gary
69T-404R
70T-694
71MLB/St-236
71OPC-153
71T-153
73OPC-112
73T-112
77T-544
78T-291

Ross, Joe
89Oneon/Pro-2125

Ross, Mark
82Tucso-3
84Cram/PCL-68
85Cram/PCL-54
86Tucso-20
87Vanco-5
88Syrac/CMC-5
88Syrac/Pro-824
89Syrac/CMC-4
89Syrac/Pro-814

Ross, Michael
88Hamil/Pro-1727
89Sprin/Best-10

Ross, Ron
89NiagFls/Puc-27

Ross, Sean
87Sumter-27
89Durhm/Star-19

Rosser, Rex
75OkCty

Rossi, Joe
52T-379
53T-74

Rossi, Tom
83Erie-21

Rossman, Claude
09Buster/Pin-12
E96
E97
T206
T213/brown

Rossum, Floyd
85Bend/Cram-21

Rossy, Elem
86Miami-22

Rossy, Rico
85Newar-14
87CharO/WBTV-5
88BuffB/CMC-18
88BuffB/Pro-1471
89Harris/Pro-289
89Harris/Star-15

Rostel, Bud
87Anchora-26

Rotblatt, Marv
51B-303

Roth, Bob F.
D327
D328-141
D329-145
D350/2-145
E121/80
E135-141
M101/145
M101/5-145
W514-47
W575

Roth, Greg
89SoBend/GS-26

Roth, Kris
86Peoria-20
87WinSal-22
88Pittsf/Pro-1376

Rothermal, Russ
75Iowa/TCMA-15
79Charl-3

Rothey, Mark
81Cedar-7
82Cedar-1
83Water-7

Rothford, Jim
81Shrev-19

Rothrock, John
29Exh/4-17
31Exh/4-17
34Exh/4-8

Rothschild, Larry
77Indianap-17
79Indianap-9
80Indianap-14
81Evans-6
82Evans-7
85IowaC-21
89Cedar/Best-26
89Cedar/Pro-933

Rothstein, Arnold
88Pac/8Men-28M

Rountree, Brian
89Brist/Star-25

Rountree, Mike
86Watlo-23
88Reno/Cal-284

Rouse, Chuck
77Charl

Rouse, Randy
76Dubuq
77Cocoa
78DaytB

Rousey, Steve
87WPalm-25

Roush, Ed
15CJ-161
25Exh-31
26Exh-31
28Exh-20
61F-72
80Cram/Leg-70
80SSPC/HOF
87Conlon/2-54
88Pac/8Men-84
89Pac/Leg-216
89Swell-35
D327
D328-142
D329-146
D350/2-146
E120
E121/120
E121/80
E135-142
E210-53
E220
M101/4-146
M101/5-146
R316
V100
V117-28
V61-79
W501-53
W502-53
W513-61
W514-85
W515-57

W572
W575
W711/1
Rovasio, Dom
89Keno/Pro-1066
89Keno/Star-23
Rover, Vince
83Cedar-21
83Cedar/LF-19
Rowan, John Albert
10Domino-103
11Helmar-103
12Sweet/Pin-131
14Piedmont/St-50
E154
E286
M116
S74-104
T202
T205
Rowdon, Wade
82AppFx-5
83Water-14
85D-642
87IowaC-19
87T-569
88F-430
88RochR-23
88RochR/Gov-23
Rowe, Davis E.
N172
WG1-24
Rowe, Don
63T-562R
83Redwd-28
84Cram/PCL-243
87Hawai-10
Rowe, Harold
(Butch)
78Wisco
Rowe, Jim
85Beloi-4
86Beloi-20TR
87Beloi-11
88ElPas/Best-11
Rowe, John Charles
N172
Scrapps
Rowe, Ken
63T-562R
65T-518
82RochR-22C
87Colum-4
89Colum/Pol-24CO
Rowe, Lynwood
(Schoolboy)
34DS-33
34DS-98
34Ward's/Pin-7
35BU-184
35Exh/4-12
35G-8F
35G-9F
36Exh/4-12
36Wheat
37Exh/4-12
37OPC-134
49B-216
49Eureka-144
49Lummis
54T-197
61F-73
80Laugh/FFeat-17
PR1-25
R309/2
R311/Gloss
R312/M
R313
R314
V300
V355-44
Rowe, Matt
86Sumter-23
Rowe, Pete
78Duned
82AlexD-14
83LynnP-13
Rowe, Ralph
73OPC-49CO
73T-49C
74OPC-447CO
74T-447C
76SSPC-603
89Sumter/Pro-1091
Rowe, Tom A.
80RochR-9
81RochR-16
85IntLgAS-42
85Maine-9
86Maine-19
Rowell, Carvel
41DP-44
47TipTop
Rowen, Rob
87SnAnt-6
88Fresno/Cal-19
88Fresno/Pro-1244
Rowland, Clarence
BF2-15
D328-143
D329-147
D350/2-147
E135-143
M101/4-147
M101/5-147
Rowland, Donnie
86FSLAS-42
86Lakel-20
87Lakel-6
88Toled/CMC-22
88Toled/Pro-589
89London/Pro-1363
Rowland, Mike
78Cr/PCL-17
79Phoen
80Phoen-4
81Phoen-10
81T-502R
82Phoen
Rowland, Rich
88Brist/Pro-1872
89Fay/Pro-1578
Rowley, Bill
87Indianap-36
Rowley, Steve
89Butte/SP-10
Roy, Jean-Pierre
52Park-90
Roy, Kevin
83Wausa/LF-13
Roy, Norman
51B-278
Roy, Pat
76Cedar
Royalty, Doug
87AubAs-26
88Ashvl/Pro-1065
Royer, Stan
88SoOreg/Pro-1701
89B-195
89Modesto/Cal-276
89Modesto/Ch-25
Royster, Jerry
74Albuq
76OPC-592R
76T-592R
77Ho-38
77OPC-251
77T-549
78T-187
79T-344
80OPC-241
80T-463
81D-339
81F-250
81Pol/Atl-1
81T-268
82BK/Lids-22
82D-555
82F-448
82Pol/Atl-1
82T-608
83D-425
83F-147
83Pol/Atl-1
83T-26
84D-531
84F-191
84Nes/792-572
84Pol/Atl-1
84T-572
84T/St-37
85F-340
85F/Up-U90
85Moth/Padres-18
85T-776
85T/Tr-96T
86D-446
86F-333
86OPC-118
86T-118
87Coke/WS-1
87D-534
87F-428
87OPC-324
87T-403
87T/Tr-106T
88D-660
88F-221
88T-257
89UD-433
Royster, Willie
79RochR-5
82RochR-11
83Evans-12
Rozek, Richard
52NumNum-11
52T-363
Rozema, Dave
75Clint
78BK/T-5
78Ho-36
78K-21
78OPC-38
78T-124
79OPC-12
79T-33
80OPC-151
80T-288
81D-9
81F-464
81T-614
82D-259
82F-279
82F/St-153
82T-319
83D-133
83F-340
83T-562
84D-272
84F-90
84Nes/792-457
84OPC-133
84T-457
85D-125
85F-21
85F/Up-U91
85Rang-30
85Seven-5D
85T-47
85T/Tr-97T
86D-343
86F-570
86Leaf-154
86OPC-208
86T-739
Rozman, Richard
88SoOreg/Pro-1694
Roznovsky, Ron
75Iowa/TCMA-16
Roznovsky, Vic
65T-334
66T-467
67OPC-163
67T-163
68T-428
69T-368
Rozook, Mark
89Wausa/GS-12
Rub, Jerry
88PrWill/Star-21
89Albany/Best-12
89Albany/Pro-328
89Albany/Star-16
Rub, Ron
87FtLaud-15
Rubel, John
83Butte-27
Rubel, Mike
82Tulsa-28
83Tulsa-15
84OKCty-14
85OKCty-22
87Phoen-27
Rubeling, Albert
52Park-82
Ruberto, John E.
(Sonny)
76Indianap-11
80ArkTr-5
Ruby, J. Gary
87QuadC-20
88CalLgAS-36
88PalmSp/Cal-114
88PalmSp/Pro-1435
89MidldA/GS-3
Rucker, Dave
80Evans-9
82Evans-8
82T-261R
83D-641
83Evans-9
83F-341
83T-304
84D-260
84Nes/792-699
84T-699
85Cram/PCL-26
85D-260
85F-238
85F/Up-U92
85T-421
85T/Tr-98T
86D-448
86F-447
86T-39
87OKCty-27
88BuffB/CMC-8
88BuffB/Pro-1472
89BuffB/CMC-5
89BuffB/Pro-1662
89UD-436
Rucker, George
(Nap)
10Domino-104
11Helmar-88
12Sweet/Pin-75
12Sweet/Pin-75A
14CJ-51
15CJ-51
BF2-61
D304
D329-148
D350/2-148
E103
E254
E300
E96
L1-117
M101/4-148
M101/5-148
M116
S74-54
S81-92
T201
T202
T204
T205
T206
T207
T213/blue
T215/blue
T215/brown
T3-34
WG4-23
WG5-34
WG6-32
Rucker, Johnny
40PB-213
41DP-137
47Centen-25
49B/PCL-7
Ruckman, Scott
86Cram/PCL-133
88Spart/Pro-1037
88Spart/Star-19
88Spart/Star-3
Rudi, Joe
69T-587
70OPC-102
70T-102
71MLB/St-525
71OPC-407
71T-407
72OPC-209
72T-209
73K-36
73OPC-360
73T-360
74OPC-264
74T-264
74T/St-229
75Ho-40
75Ho/Twink-40
75K-28
75OPC-45
75OPC-465WS
75T-45
75T/M-45
76K-7
76OPC-475
76SSPC-490
76T-475
77Ho-146
77OPC-206
77T-155
77T/CS-39
78Ho-114
78OPC-28
78T-635
78Wiffle/Discs-64
79Ho-84
79OPC-134
79T-267
80OPC-289
80T-556
81D-174
81F-272
81F/St-113
81OPC-362
81T-701
81T/Tr-826
82D-586
82F-306
82OPC-388
82T-388
82T/Tr-102T
83D-287
83F-532

83T-87
87Moth/A's-9
Rudolph, Blaine
88Brist/Pro-1879
89Fay/Pro-1579
Rudolph, F. Don
58T-347
59T-179
60HenryH-33
60Union-17
62T-224
63T-291
64T-427
Rudolph, Ken
70OPC-46
70T-46
71MLB/St-45
71OPC-472
71T-472
72OPC-271
72T-271
73OPC-414
73T-414
74OPC-584
74T-584
75OPC-289
75T-289
75T/M-289
76OPC-601
76SSPC-287
76T-601
Rudolph, Richard
15CJ-154
BF2-55
C46-22
D328-144
D329-149
D350/2-149
E135-144
E254
M101/4-149
M101/5-149
T206
T213/blue
W514-13
W516-15
Ruel, Harold
(Muddy)
21Exh-147
25Exh-128
26Exh-128
27Exh-63
28Exh-64
29Exh/4-31
33DH-37
33Exh/4-12
33G-18
35G-1J
35G-3A
35G-5A
35G-6A
40PB-127
E120
E121/120
E126-25
R306
R316
V100
V117-24
V353-18
W501-10
W573
W575
Ruether, Walter
(Dutch)
21Exh-139
28Yueng-2
88Pac/8Men-83
E120
E121/120
E210-2
V61-64
W501-98
W502-2
W514-108
W515-40
W573
Ruffin, Bruce
86Readg-23
86S/Rook-29
87D-555
87F-183
87F/Hottest-33
87Leaf-168
87T-499
87T/GlossRk-14
87T/St-123
87T/St-312
87ToysRUs-23
88D-165
88F-313
88OPC-268
88Panini/St-353
88Score-492
88T-268
88T/St-119
89B-393
89D-515
89F-580
89OPC-222
89Panini/St-148
89Score-328
89ScrWB/Pro-728
89T-518
89T/St-122
89UD-319
90F-572
90T-22
90UD-580
Ruffin, Johnny
89Utica/Puc-19
Ruffing, Charles H.
(Red)
25Exh-69
26Exh-70
29Exh/4-17
33CJ/Pin-19
33G-56
34DS-60
35G-2D
35G-4D
35G-7D
36Exh/4-13
37OPC-136
37Wheat
38ONG/Pin-25
39PB-3
40PB-10
40Wheat
41DP-68
41DP-86
43MP-22
60F-63
61F-74
80Cram/Leg-109
80SSPC/HOF
83D/HOF-31
86S/Dec-14M
89HOF/St-83
PM10/Sm-171
R300
R310
R311/Leath
R312
R316
R328-20
V300
V354-48
V355-102
Ruffner, Mark
89Readg/Best-24
Rugg, Rusty
89Helena/SP-6
Ruhle, Vern
75OPC-614R
75T-614R
75T/M-614R
76Ho-46
76Ho/Twink-46
76OPC-89
76T-89
77OPC-212
77T-311
78Charl
78T-456
79T-49
80T-234
81D-261
81F-53
81T-642
82D-293
82F-228
82T-539
83D-627
83F-462
83T-172
84D-564
84F-238
84Moth/Ast-23
84Nes/792-328
84T-328
85D-380
85F-358
85F/Up-U93
85Polar/Ind-48
85T-426
85T/Tr-99T
86F-593
86T-768
87F-91
87T-221
Ruiz, Augie
79LodiD-2
82Evans-9
83Richm-9
Ruiz, Benny
86GlenF-19
87GlenF-14
88Toled/CMC-16
88Toled/Pro-602
Ruiz, Hiraldo S.
(Chico)
63T-407R
64T-356R
65T-554
66OPC-159
66T-159
67T-339
68Kahn
68T-213
69MB-243
69T-469
70T-606
71MLB/St-357
71OPC-686
71T-686
72MB-301
78TCMA-35
Ruiz, Manuel
(Chico)
78Richm
79Richm-13
81Richm-9
82Richm-15
83Richm-15
Ruiz, Nelson
80Batav-29
Ruling, Steve
77Spoka
Rumler, William G.
D328-145
E135-145
Runge, Ed
55B-277ump
Runge, Paul
81Richm-10
82Richm-16
83Richm-16
84Richm-24
85Pol/Atl-12
85T/Tr-100T
86Richm-19
86T-409
87Richm/TCMA-14
88F/U-U71
89LasVeg/CMC-21
89T-38
89T/Big-23
89UD-55
Runge, Paul
88Umpire-17
89Umpires-17
Runge, Scott
86Watertn-20
87Watertn-5
88Aug/Pro-376
89SnBer/Best-19
89Wmspt/Pro-638
Runnells, Tom
81Phoen-23
82Phoen
83Phoen/BHN-9
86D-569
87Vermont-16
88Chatt/Best-14
89Indi/CMC-25
89Indi/Pro-1220
Runnels, James E.
(Pete)
52T-2
53B/Col-139
53Briggs
53T-219
54T-6
55B-255
55RM-AL20
56T-234
57T-64
58Hires-38
58T-265
59T-370
59T-519M
60T-15
60T/tatt
60T/tatt-47
61Bz-32
61NuCard-407
61P-47
61T-210
61T-42LL
61T/St-116
62J-57
62P-57
62Salada-47A
62Salada-47B
62Shirriff-47
62T-3
62T/bucks
62T/St-17
63Exh
63J-77
63P-77
63Pep
63Salada-61
63T-230
63T-2LL
64T-121
Exh47
Rupe, Brian
83Visal/LF-25
Rupp, Mark
89Erie/Star-23
Rupp, Terry
89Spoka/SP-9
Rush, Andy
89Elmir/Puc-18
Rush, Bob
49Eureka-69
50B-61
51B-212
52NTea
52StarCal/L-80D
52T-153
53B/Col-110
54B-77
55B-182
55RFG-13
56T-214
57T-137
58T-313
59T-396
60Lake
60T-404
79TCMA-164
Rush, Eddie
88Cedar/Pro-1155
89Greens/Pro-418
Rush, Larry
79Holyo-20
80Vanco-1
81Vanco-12
82Vanco-7
Rush, Rod
84Evrt/Cram-13B
Rusie, Amos
75F/Pion-12
80SSPC/HOF
86Indianap-8
87Conlon/2-53
N172
N300/unif
N566-175
Ruskin, Scott
87Macon-22
88Salem/Star-18
89Salem/Star-18
Russ, Kevin
86Madis-18
Russell, Bill E.
70MLB/St-56
70OPC-304
70T-304
71MLB/St-113
71OPC-226
71T-226
72T-736
73OPC-108
73T-108
74OPC-239
74T-239
74T/DE-40
74T/St-49
75Ho-91
75OPC-23
75T-23
75T/M-23
76OPC-22
76T-22
77T-322
78T-128
79T-546
80OPC-40
80Pol/Dodg-18
80T-75
81D-57
81F-117
81F/St-68
81OPC-20
81Pol/Dodg-18
81T-465
81T/HT
81T/St-179
82D-453
82F-20
82F/St-8
82Pol/Dodg
82Pol/Dodg-18
82T-279

83D-210
83F-219
83OPC-123
83Pol/Dodg-18
83T-661
83T/St-249
84D-587
84F-111
84Nes/792-792
84OPC-14
84Pol/Dodg-18
84T-792
84T/St-77
85D-93
85F-383
85Leaf-232
85OPC-343
85SpokAT/Cram-17
85T-343
85T/St-76
86D-153
86F-142
86Pol/Dodg-18
86T-506
86T-696M
87F-452
87Smok/Dodg-31
87T-116
88Smok/Dodg-13
88Smok/Dodg-15M
89Smok/Dodg-81

Russell, Dan
88Modesto-25

Russell, Dave
80WHave-18

Russell, Ewell A.
(Reb)
14CJ-15
15CJ-15
BF2-16
D328-146
D329-150
D350/2-150
E135-146
M101/4-150
M101/5-150
V100
WG4-24

Russell, Fred
88Eugene/Best-15
89Eugene/Best-19

Russell, Glen David
39Exh
47TipTop

Russell, Jack Erwin
33G-123
33G-167
R316

Russell, James W.
47TipTop
49B-235
49Eureka-20
50B-223
52Mother-52
52T-51

Russell, Jeff
82Water-8
83Indianap-14
84Borden-46
84D-569
84Nes/792-270
84T-270
85D-487
85F-551
85T-651
86OKCty-19
86Rang-40
87D-550
87F-137
87Moth/Rang-26
87Smok/R-32
87T-444
88D-531
88F-478
88Moth/R-26
88Score-514
88Smok/R-17
88T-114
89B-226
89D-403
89D/AS-26
89D/Best-200
89F-531
89Moth/R-6
89OPC-166
89Panini/St-447
89Score-438
89Smok/R-28
89T-565
89T/Big-309
89T/St-243
89UD-461
90D-284
90F-312
90F-633M
90Score-263
90Score/100St-23
90Sf-192
90T-395AS
90T-80
90UD-638

Russell, Joe
79Tulsa-2
81Tulsa-27

Russell, John
83Portl-17
84Cram/PCL-208
85D-648
85F-653
86CIGNA-14
86D-82
86F-448
86T-392
87D-207
87F-184
87T-379
88Maine/CMC-12
88Maine/Pro-285
88T-188
89UD-532
90D-458

Russell, Larry
88CapeCod/Sum-28

Russell, Rob
85PrWill-7
86PrWill-23
87Harrisbg-12
88Harris/Pro-858
89Harris/Pro-303
89Harris/Star-16

Russell, Ron
86DayBe-24

Russell, Tony
83Greens-26
85Albany-21
86Albany/TCMA-10
87Albany-2

Russo, Marius
41DP-112
44Yank/St-22

Russo, Tony
87Erie-16
88Savan/Pro-333
89StPet/Star-23

Ruth, George Herman
(Babe)
21Exh-148
21Exh-149
25Exh-100
26Exh-102
27Exh-52
28Exh-51
28FrJoy-Set
28Yueng-6
29Exh/4-26
31Exh/4-26
33Exh/4-13
33G-144
33G-149
33G-181
33G-53
33SK-2
33SK-2
34Exh/4-13
35Exh/4-1
35G-1J
35G-3A
35G-4A
35G-5A
48BRS-Set
48Exh/HOF
48L-3
48Swell-12
49Leaf/Prem-7
50Callahan
51T/CM
56T/Hocus-B1
60Exh/HOF-20
60F-3
60NuCard-1
60NuCard-16
60NuCard-47
61F-75
61GP-3
61NuCard-447
61NuCard-455
61T-401M
62T-135M
62T-136M
62T-137M
62T-138M
62T-139M
62T-140M
62T-141M
62T-142M
62T-143M
62T-144M
63Bz-17
69Bz-10
69Bz-11
69Bz-9
69Bz/Sm
72F/FFeat-20
72K/ATG-14
72K/ATG-14
72K/ATG-6
72K/ATG-6
72Laugh/GF-32
73F/Wild-34M
73OPC-1M
73OPC-474LL
73T-1LL
73T-474LL
74Laugh/ASG-33
76Laugh/Jub-32
76OPC-345AS
76T-345M
80Cram/Leg-1
80Laugh/3/4/5-2
80Laugh/FFeat-16
80SSPC/HOF
83T/St-2F
84D/Champs-1
85CircK-2
85D/HOF-1
85West/2-47
85Woolwth-31
86BLChew-2
86Conlon/1-13
86Conlon/1-20
86Conlon/1-48
86Conlon/1-50
86Conlon/1-54
86S/Dec-1
87Nestle/DT-5
88Conlon/3-25
88Conlon/AmAS-21
89Cadaco-45
89HOF/St-47
89Pac/Leg-176
89Smok/Dodg-26
89Swell-1
D327
D328-146
D329-151
D350/2-151
E120
E121/120
E121/80
E126-38
E135-146
E210-6
E220
M101/4-151
M101/5-151
PM10/Sm-172
R309/1
R310
R315-A31
R315-B31
R316
R328-32
R332-26
R332-42
R337-402
R423-92
Rawl
V100
V117-8
V353-80
V353-93
V354-28
V61-37
W501-49
W502-6
W512-6
W514-2
W515-3
W515-47
W516-1
W517-20
W517-4
W573
W575

Rutherford, John
52T-320
53T-137

Ruthven, Dick
74OPC-47
74T-47
75OPC-267
75T-267
75T/M-267
76OPC-431
76SSPC-477
76T-431
77Ho-74
77T-575
78T-75
79BK/P-6
79T-419
80BK/P-19
80T-136
81D-153
81F-16
81OPC-285
81T-691
81T/HT
82D-525
82F-257
82F/St-52
82OPC-317
82T-317
83D-497
83F-172
83OPC-313
83T-484
83T/X-98
83Thorn-44
84D-510
84F-503
84Nes/792-736
84OPC-156
84SevenUp-44
84T-736
84T/St-49
85F-64
85OPC-268
85SevenUp-44
85T-563
86D-564
86F-377
86T-98

Rutledge, Jeff
82QuadC-19
86Pittsf-21

Ruzek, Don
77LodiD
78LodiD
83AppFx/LF-27

Ryal, Mark
82Omaha-21
83Omaha-20
84Omaha-24
85BuffB-15
86Edmon-25
87D-583
87Smok/Cal-14
88F-503
88Louvl-43
88T-243

Ryan, Colin
88CapeCod/Sum-71
89Eugene/Best-13

Ryan, Connie
47TipTop
49Eureka-19
51B-216
52B-164
52T-107
53B/Col-131
53NB
53T-102
54T-136
74OPC-634CO
74T-634C

Ryan, Craig
79Vanco-5
80Vanco-15

Ryan, Dan
89SLCty-8LHP

Ryan, Duffy
81Redwd-11

Ryan, James E.
E107
E223
N172
N28
N284
N300/SC
N403
N43
WG1-15

Ryan, Jody
86Cram/PCL-117
87Wausa-3
88SnBer/Best-7
88SnBer/Cal-42
89SnBer/Best-21
89SnBer/Cal-67

Ryan, John Budd
E254
E270/2
T207

Ryan, John C.
(Blondy)
34DS-40
34Exh/4-5
34G-32
35Exh/4-6

R310
V354-73
Ryan, Ken
86Elmir-18
87Greens-6
88Lynch/Star-22
89WinHav/Star-19
Ryan, Kevin
85Anchora-26
Ryan, Mike
65T-573R
66T-419
67T-223
67T/Test/RSox-14
68T-306
69MLB/St-177
69OPC-28
69T-28
70MLB/St-93
70T-591
71MLB/St-186
71OPC-533
71T-533
72MB-302
72OPC-324
72T-324
73OPC-467
73T-467
74OPC-564
74T-564
Ryan, Nolan
68OPC-177R
68T-177R
69T-533
70MLB/St-81
70OPC-197NLCS
70T-712
70Trans/M-24
71MLB/St-162
71OPC-513
71T-513
72T-595
73K-16
73OPC-220
73OPC-67LL
73T-220
73T-67LL
73T/Comics-17
73T/Lids-45
73T/PinUps-17
74K-8
74OPC-20
74OPC-207LL
74T-20
74T-207LL
74T/DE-41
74T/Puzzles-9
74T/St-147
75Ho-58
75Ho/Twink-58
75K-26
75OPC-312LL
75OPC-500
75OPC-5RB
75OPC-7M
75T-312LL
75T-500
75T-5M
75T-7M
75T/M-312LL
75T/M-500
75T/M-5M
75T/M-7M
76Crane-52
76Ho-79
76Laugh/Jub-1
76MSA/Disc
76OPC-330
76SSPC-187
76T-330
77Ho-81
77OPC-264RB
77OPC-65
77OPC-6LL
77Pep-24
77T-234M
77T-650
77T-6LL
77T/CS-40
78Ho-83
78K-51
78OPC-105
78OPC-241RB
78OPC-6LL
78T-206LL
78T-400
78T-6M
78Wiffle/Discs-65
79Ho-101
79OPC-51
79T-115
79T-417M
79T-6LL
79T/Comics-4
80BK/PHR-9
80K-20
80OPC-303
80T-580
80T/S-20
81Coke
81D-260
81F-57
81F/St-108
81K-6
81OPC-240
81T-240
81T/HT
81T/St-173
81T/St-30
82D-13DK
82D-419
82F-229
82F/St-242M
82F/St-42
82K-11
82OPC-90
82T-167LL
82T-5M
82T-66TL
82T-90
82T/St-13
82T/St-41
83D-118
83D/AAS-23
83F-463
83K-31
83OPC-360
83OPC-361SV
83T-360
83T-361A
83T/Gloss-28
83T/Gloss40-28
83T/St-235
84D-60
84D/AAS-14
84D/Champs-39
84F-239
84F/St-82
84FunFood/Pin-109
84Moth/Ast-1
84Nes/792-470
84Nes/792-4HL
84Nes/792-66TL
84Nes/792-707LL
84OPC-66
84Ralston-14
84Seven-13W
84T-4
84T-470
84T-707
84T/Cereal-14
84T/Gloss40-15
84T/St-66
84T/Super-28
84T/Super-28
85D-60
85D/AAS-20
85D/HL-22
85F-359
85F/LimEd-30
85F/St-115
85Leaf-216
85Moth/Ast-2
85OPC-63
85Seven-1C
85Seven-3S
85T-760
85T-7RB
85T/St-58
85T/Super-23
85Woolwth-32
86D-258
86D/AAS-21
86Drake-33
86F-310
86F/HOF-5
86F/Mini-65
86F/Slug-30
86F/St-102
86Jiffy-13
86Leaf-132
86Moth/Ast-23
86OPC-100
86Pol/Ast-2
86Quaker-12
86S-141M
86S-143M
86S-182M
86S-43
86S/Dec-63M
86T-100
86T/Gloss60-45
86T/Mini-43
86T/St-24
86T/St-9
86T/Super-47
86TrueVal-26
87Class-82
87D-138
87D/HL-53
87Drake-32
87F-67
87F/Lim-38
87F/St-103
87KMart-20
87Kraft-48
87Leaf-257
87MnM's-22
87Moth/Ast-8
87OPC-155
87Pol/Ast-16
87Ralston-1
87RedFoley/St-121
87S-125
87T-757
87T/Coins-40
87T/St-27
88Woolwth-6
88Class/Red-179
88D-61
88D/Best-232
88F-455
88F/BB/AS-34
88F/Mini-79
88F/St-88
88KMart-23
88Leaf-77
88Moth/Ast-8
88Nestle-43
88OPC-250
88OPC-N
88Panini/St-288
88Panini/St-435
88Pol/Ast-20
88Score-575
88Sf-39
88T-250
88T-661TBC
88T-6RB
88T/Big-29
88T/Coins-50
88T/Mini-50
88T/Revco-8
88T/St-7
88T/UK-62
88T/WaxBox-N
89B-225
89Cadaco-46
89Class/Up/2-164
89D-154
89D/Best-55
89D/Tr-19
89F-368
89F/Up-67
89KingB/Discs-10
89Moth/R-2
89OPC-366
89Panini/St-226
89Panini/St-83
89RedFoley/St-100
89Score-300
89Score/HotSt-64
89Score/Mast-5
89Score/Tr-2
89Sf-115
89Smok/Angels-7
89Smok/R-29
89T-530
89T/Mini-15
89T/St-20
89T/Tr-106T
89T/WaxBox-K
89UD-145
89UD-669TC
89UD/Ext-774
90Class-1
90D-166
90D-659
90D-665
90D/Preview-7
90F-313
90F-636M
90Score-250
90Score-696
90Score/100St-44
90Sf-8
90T-1
90T-2M
90T-3M
90T-4M
90T-5M
90UD-34M
90UD-544
Ryan, Ray
T206
Ryan, Wilfred
(Rosy)
E121/120
E121/80
V100
W501-75
W575
Ryba, Dominic
(Mike)
54Hunter
54T-237
Ryder, Brian
81Colum-14
82Indianap-11
83Indianap-11
Ryerson, Gary
No Cards.
Rymer, Carlos
80Ander-16
Saatzer, Michael
82Redwd-10
83Nashua-7
86QuadC-30CO
Saavedra, Ed
81Watlo-27
82Chatt-4
83BuffB-20
84BuffB-22
Saavedra, Justo
80Batav-23
Saberhagen, Bret
84F/X-103
84T/X-104
85D-222
85D/HL-26
85F-212
85F/St-124
85OPC-23
85T-23
86D-100
86D-11
86D/DKsuper-11
86Drake-29
86F-19
86F/LimEd-38
86F/LL-37
86F/Mini-3
86F/Slug-31
86F/St-103
86KayBee-27
86Kitty/Disc-3
86Leaf-11DK
86NatPhoto-31
86OPC-249
86OPC-O
86Quaker-19
86S-10
86S-176M
86S-185M
86S-186M
86T-487
86T-720
86T/3D-25
86T/Gloss60-27
86T/Mini-20
86T/St-17WS
86T/St-260
86T/Super-3
86T/WaxBox-O
87Class-88
87Class/Up-116
87D-132
87D/HL-6
87F-379
87F/AwardWin-34
87F/Lim-C5
87F/Slug-36
87Leaf-261
87OPC-140
87S-145
87T-140
88Class/Red-172
88D-96
88D/AS-8
88D/Best-231
88D/PopUp-8
88F-268
88F-626M
88F/LL-33
88F/Mini-26
88F/St-32
88F/TL-32
88Jiffy-15
88Leaf-68
88Nestle-11
88OPC-5
88Panini/St-102
88Panini/St-229
88RedFoley/St-77
88Score-89
88Score/WaxBox-9
88Score/YS/II-17
88Sf-15
88Smok/Royals-16
88T-540

88T/Big-94
88T/Coins-25
88T/Gloss22-10
88T/Mini-14
88T/St-163
88T/St-254
88T/St/Backs-60
88T/UK-63
89B-111
89Class-62
89D-144
89D/Best-95
89F-291
89OPC-157
89Panini/St-352
89Score-251
89Sf-109
89T-750
89T/Big-6
89T/St-263
89Tastee/Discs-11
89UD-37
90Class-139
90D-89
90F-116
90Score-195
90Sf-94
90T-350
90T-393AS
90UD-326

Sabino, Miguel
87Sumter-3
88Greenv/Best-7
89Greenv/Pro-1170
89Greenv/Star-21
89Greenvl/Best-27

Sable, Luke
88Gasto/Pro-1002

Sabo, Chris
87Nashv-18
88D/Best-278
88D/Rook-30
88F/Slug-35
88F/U-U87
88Kahn/Reds-17
88Score/Tr-100T
88T/Tr-98T
89B-309
89Bz-18
89Class-53
89D-317
89D-4DK
89D/AS-59
89D/Best-222
89D/DKsuper-4DK
89F-170
89F-637M
89F/BBMVP's-33
89F/Excit-35
89F/Superstar-35
89F/WaxBox-C21
89K/Reds-17
89KingB/Discs-7
89KMart/DT-3
89OPC-156
89Panini/St-476
89Panini/St-64
89Score-104
89Score/HotRk-76
89Score/YS/I-10
89Sf-13
89T-490
89T/Big-251
89T/Coins-3
89T/Gloss60-40
89T/JumboR-17
89T/Mini-13
89T/St-142
89T/St-325
89T/UK-65
89ToysRUs-24
89UD-180
89UD-663ROY
89Woolwth-6
90D-242
90F-433
90Score-70
90T-737
90UD-181

Sabo, Scott
85Madis-1
85Madis/Pol-21
86Madis-19
86Madis/Pol-17
87Wmspt-20

Sabol, Tony
46Remar-13
47Remar-15
47Signal
47Smith-13

Saccomanno, Joseph
89BurlB/Pro-1600
89BurlB/Star-19

Sadecki, Ray
60T-327
61T-32
62T-383
62T/St-190
63T-486
64T-147
65OPC-10LL
65OPC-230
65T-10LL
65T-230
66OPC-26
66T-26
67T-409
68Coke
68T-494
69MB-244
69OPC-125
69T-125
70T-679
71MLB/St-163
71OPC-406
71T-406
72MB-303
72T-563
72T-564A
73OPC-283
73T-283
74OPC-216
74T-216
75OPC-349
75T-349
75T/M-349
77T-26

Sadek, Mike
74OPC-577
74T-577
75Phoen-3
76OPC-234
76T-234
77T-129
78T-8
79Pol/Giants-3
79T-256
80OPC-240DP
80Pol/Giants-3
80T-462
81D-498
81T-384

Sadler, Alan
85Beloi-21
86Stockton-24
87ElPas-24
88Stock/Cal-181
88Stock/Pro-726
89Denver/CMC-9
89Denver/Pro-44

Sadowski, Ed
59T-139
60L-113
60T-403
61T-163
62T-569
63T-527
64T-61M

Sadowski, Robert
64T-271
65OPC-156
65T-156
66T-523
78TCMA-167

Sadowski, Robert F.
62Kahn/Atl
62T-595R
63T-568

Sadowski, Ted
61Clover-24
61T-254
61T/St-174

Saferight, Harry
75Shreve/TCMA-18
76Shrev
78Colum
79Portl-21
80Richm-16
80T-683R
81Richm-24
82Toled-10

Saffell, Tom
51B-130
52Mother-36
59DF

Sagawa, Kiyoshi
89Visal/Cal-103
89Visal/Pro-1434

Sage, Henry
N172

Sager, A.J.
88Spoka/Pro-1933
89CharRa/Pro-971

Saier, Vic
14CJ-104
15CJ-104
BF2-66
D328-148
D329-152
D350/2-152
E135-148
M101/4-152
M101/5-152
T207
T222

Sain, Joe
83Wisco/LF-5

Sain, Johnny
47TipTop
48B-12
49B-47
49Eureka-21
51B-314
51FB
51T/BB-9
52BR
52T-49
53B/BW-25
53T-119
54T-205
55Rodeo
55T-193
73OPC-356CO
73T-356C
74OPC-221CO
74T-221C
78Richm
79Richm-3
80Richm-9
81Richm-1
82Richm-28
83Richm-25C
84Richm-26C
85Pol/Atl-33C
86Pol/Atl-33C
89Swell-121
D305
Exh47
R302-122

Sain, Tom
78OrlTw
79Toled-15

Saitta, Pat
87Duned-29

Sajonia, Brian
88James/Pro-1907

Sakata, Lenn
76Spoka
77Spoka
79Vanco-22
80T-668R
81D-499
81F-194
81T-287
82D-644
82F-178
82T-136
83D-205
83F-72
83T-319
84D-620
84F-19
84Nes/792-578
84T-578
85F-189
85T-81
86T-446
86Tacom-20
88SoOreg/Pro-1717
88T-716
89Modesto/Cal-288

Sakowski, Vince
83TriCit-19

Sala, David J.
87Sprin/Best-16
89Savan/Pro-367

Salaiz, David
89ColMud/Best-5
89ColMud/Pro-138

Salas, Mark
82ArkTr-11
82Nashv-20
83ArkTr-12
84Louvl-27
85D-547
85F/Up-U94
85T/Tr-101T
86D-316
86F-402
86F/St-104
86KayBee-28
86Leaf-185
86OPC-43
86S-177M
86T-537
86T/St-278
86T/St-315
87F-551
87F/U-U106
87OPC-87
87T-87
87T/Tr-107T
88Coke/WS-26
88Score-232
88Score/Tr-52T
88T/Tr-99T
89ColrSp/CMC-20
89ColSp/Pro-240
89F-511
89Score-542
89T-384
89UD-460

Salava, Randy
82Readg-18
83Readg-19
84Cram/PCL-203
85Cram/PCL-37

Salazar, Argenis
(Angel)
84D-33
84Stuart-31
85D-523
85OPC-154
85T-154
86F/Up-U100
86T/Tr-96T
87D-624
87F-380
87T-533
87T/St-259
88Berg/Cubs-18
88D-502
88D/Cubs/Bk-NEW
88F-269
88OPC-29
88Panini/St-109
88Score-330
88T-29
89Score-527
89T-642
89UD-222

Salazar, Jeff
83Peoria/LF-17

Salazar, Luis
77Salem
78Salem
80Port-9
81F-501
81T-309
81T/St-228
82D-472
82F-581
82OPC-133
82T-366TL
82T-662
82T/St-101
83D-548
83F-371
83OPC-156
83T-533
84D-356
84F-311
84Moth/Padres-24
84Nes/792-68
84OPC-68
84Smok/Padres-20
84T-68
84T/St-159
85Coke/WS-5
85D-568
85F-43
85F/Up-U95
85T-789
85T/Tr-102T
86D-302
86F-215
86T-103
87T-454
87T/Tr-108T
88F-595
88F/U-U30
88OPC-276
88Pep/T-12
88Score-284
88Score/Tr-13T
88StCath/Pro-2006
88T-276
88T/Tr-100T
89Class-72
89D-352
89F-144
89OPC-122
89Panini/St-342
89Score-316
89T-553
89T/St-276
89T/Tr-107T
89UD-136
90D-513

90Score-92
90T-378
90UD-6

Salazar, Terry
81Buffa-21

Salcedo, Luis
87Madis-24

Salcedo, Ron
84CharO-4
85CharO-11
87RochR-4
87RochR/TCMA-19
88RochR-19
88RochR-24
88RochR/CMC-16
88RochR/Gov-24
88RochR/Pro-200
89ScrWB/CMC-16
89ScrWB/Pro-707

Salee
N172

Salery, Johnny
82Wisco-9
83Wisco/LF-13

Salinas, Manual V.
87BirmB/Best-23
88Jacks/GS-18
88TexLgAS/GS-14
89Jacks/GS-13
89Tidew/Pro-1951

Salisbury, Jim
86Sumter-24
87Durhm-24

Salkeld, Bill
49B-88
49Eureka-22
50B-237

Salkeld, Roger
90Score-674DC
90T-44

Sallee, H. Slim
11Helmar-176
14CJ-123
15CJ-123
88Conlon/4-24
88Pac/8Men-82
BF2-94
D327
D328-149
D329-153
D350/2-153
E121/80
E122
E135-149
E254
E270/2
E300
M101/4-153
M101/5-153
M116
T204
T222
T3-37
V100
W514-86
W575

Salles, John
89Peoria/Ko-8P

Salmon, Chico
64T-499R
65OPC-105
65T-105
66T-594
67OPC-43
67T-43
68T-318
69MB-245
69MLB/St-99
69OPC-62
69T-62
69T/St-230
70MLB/St-156
70OPC-301
70T-301
71MLB/St-312
71OPC-249
71T-249
72MB-304
72T-646

Salmon, Timothy
88CapeCod/Sum-176

Salva, Elias
80Wausa-8

Salyer, Ron
75SnAnt

Samaniego, Art
79Elmir-5

Sambito, Joe
74Cedar
77T-227
78BK/A-10
78T-498
79T-158
80T-571
81Coke
81D-21
81F-65
81OPC-334
81T-385
81T/St-172
82D-65
82F-230
82F/St-47
82T-34
83D-244
83F-464
83OPC-296
83T-662
85D-572
85F-360
85F/Up-U96
85T-264
85T/Tr-103T
86F/Up-U101
86Moth/Ast-19
86T/Tr-97T
87D-421
87F-43
87OPC-262
87T-451
88F-364
88Score-314
88T-784
88Tucso-20

Sambo, Ramon
87Vermont-7
88Cedar/Pro-1149
89ElPas/GS-28

Samcoff, Ed
48Smith-19
49Remar

Samford, Ron
59T-242
60T-409
79TCMA-102

Samonds, Shereen
89Orlan/Best-28

Sampen, Bill
86Watertn-21
87Salem-21
89Harris/Pro-290
89Harris/Star-17

Sample, Bill
78Cr/PCL-72
79T-713R
80T-458
81D-268
81F-637
81OPC-283
81T-283
82D-69
82F-330
82OPC-112
82T-112
83D-242
83F-577
83Rang-5
83T-641
84D-403
84F-426
84Nes/792-12
84OPC-12
84Rang-5
84T-12
84T/St-352
85D-464
85F-566
85F/Up-U97
85T-337
85T/St-351
86D-539
86F-118
86F/Up-U102
86Pol/Atl-5
86T-533
86T/Tr-98T
87D-143
87F-527
87T-104

Sample, Deron
89Kingspt/Star-20

Samplinski, Rich
88CapeCod/Sum-104

Sampson, Mark
86Cram/PCL-166

Sampson, Michael
89VeroB/Star-24

Sams, Andre
78Green

Samson, Fred
87PortChar-14
89Tulsa/GS-23

Samson, William
52Park-51
53Exh/Can-54

Samuel, Amado
62T-597R
64T-129

Samuel, Juan
83Portl-2
83Readg-17
84F-47
84FunFood/Pin-68
84T/X-105
85CIGNA-1
85D-183
85D-23
85D/AAS-56
85D/DKsuper-23
85Drake-27
85F-264
85F-634IA
85F/St-44
85F/St-59
85Leaf-23DK
85OPC-265
85Seven-15E
85T-265
85T-8RB
85T/Gloss40-31
85T/St-114
85T/St-369YS
85T/Super-28
86BK/AP-10
86CIGNA-1
86D-326
86D/HL-37
86F-449
86F/LimEd-39
86F/LL-38
86F/Mini-93
86F/St-105
86KayBee-29
86Keller-4
86Leaf-196
86OPC-237
86S-94
86T-475
86T/Mini-54
86T/St-121
87D-165
87D/OD-156
87F-185
87F-642M
87F/Lim-39
87F/LL-38
87F/Mini-94
87F/St-104
87Leaf-132
87OPC-255
87S-123
87T-255
87T/Mini-29
87T/St-125
88Bz-18
88D-288
88D/AS-55
88D/Best-215
88F-314
88F/AS-10
88F/BB/AS-35
88F/Mini-101
88F/St-110
88F/TL-33
88KayBee-26
88Leaf-146
88Nestle-16
88OPC-19
88Panini/St-359
88Score-32
88Sf-96
88Sf/Gamewin-12
88T-398
88T-705
88T/Big-67
88T/Coins-51
88T/Gloss60-43
88T/Mini-66
88T/Revco-7
88T/St-120
88T/St/Backs-5
88T/UK-64
89Ames-25
89B-405
89Cadaco-47
89Class-146
89D-76
89D/Best-238
89F-581
89F/Up-102
89Kahn/Mets-7
89OPC-372
89Panini/St-152
89RedFoley/St-101
89Score-255
89Score/HotSt-26
89Score/Tr-21
89Sf-17
89T-575
89T/Big-321
89T/Coins-23
89T/Gloss60-13
89T/Hills-25
89T/Mini-29
89T/St-117
89T/St/Backs-37
89T/Tr-108T
89T/UK-66
89UD-336
90D-53
90F-215
90Score-198
90T-85
90UD-583

Samuel, Mike
81BurlB-19
82Beloi-19
84ElPas-9
85Beloi-1

Samuels, Roger
86ColumAst-23
88F/U-U131
88Phoen/CMC-8
88Phoen/Pro-70

Sanborn, Kyle
88CapeCod/Sum-112

Sanchez, Al
82OkCty-7

Sanchez, Alejandro
83Portl-22
84Cram/PCL-8
85D-43
85F-648
85F/Up-U98
86D-415
86F-236
86T-563
87Tacom-20

Sanchez, Alex
88BBAmer-13
88Knoxv/Best-1
88OPC-194
88SLAS-26
88Tacom/CMC-17
88Tacom/Pro-637
89B-245
89D-47RR
89F/Up-71
89Syrac/CMC-10
89Syrac/Pro-813
89T/Tr-109T
90D-45
90F-92
90T-563

Sanchez, Carlos
88Poca/Pro-2077

Sanchez, Celerino
73OPC-103
73T-103
74OPC-623
74T-623

Sanchez, Francisco
87Gasto-28

Sanchez, Frank
78Wausa

Sanchez, Geraldo
86Hagers-17
87Hagers-28

Sanchez, Israel
83CharR-22
85FtMyr-15
87Omaha-18
88F/U-U34
88Omaha/CMC-11
88Omaha/Pro-1496
89D-474
89T-452
89UD-326
90UD-384

Sanchez, Juan
87Clearw-22

Sanchez, Leo
84PrWill-28
85Nashua-22

Sanchez, Luis
73Cedar
74Cedar
82T-653
83D-519
83F-100
83T-623
84D-597
84F-527
84Nes/792-258
84OPC-258
84Smok/Cal-24
84T-258
84T/St-233
85D-352
85F-310

85OPC-42
85Smok/Cal-16
85T-42
86T-124

Sanchez, Orlando
80OkCty
81Louvl-24
82D-636
82F-126
82Louvl-26
82T-604
85Maine-23

Sanchez, Osvaldo
87Spoka-1
88Charl/Pro-1200
89Watlo/Pro-1786
89Watlo/Star-25

Sanchez, Pedro
75BurlB
86AubAs-22
87Ashvl-27
88Osceola/Star-23
89ColMud/Best-6
89ColMud/Pro-127
89ColMud/Star-21

Sanchez, Raul
57T-393
60T-311
61BeeHive-19

Sanchez, Rey
89OkCty/CMC-18
89OkCty/Pro-1511

Sanchez, Sammye
88LitFalls/Puc-12

Sanchez, Stan
87SnBer-6
89SnBer/Best-26
89SnBer/Cal-91CO

Sanchez, Zoilo
86Lynch-20
88Jacks/GS-2
89Jacks/GS-15

Sand, John Henry
21Exh-150
25Exh-47
26Exh-47
28Exh-23
33G-85
V354-27

Sandberg, Chuck
81Brist-11

Sandberg, Ryne
80Readg
81OkCty/TCMA-17
82RedLob
83D-277
83F-507
83OPC-83
83T-83
83T/St-328
83Thorn-23
84D-311
84D/AAS-43
84F-504
84FunFood/Pin-13
84Nes/792-596
84OPC-64
84SevenUp-23
84T-596
84T/St-45
85D-1
85D-67
85D/AAS-24
85D/DKsuper-1
85D/WaxBox-PC2
85Drake-28
85F-630IA
85F-65
85F/LimEd-31
85F/St-11
85F/St-45
85GenMills-8
85Leaf-1DK
85OPC-296
85Seven-11G
85SevenUp-23
85T-460
85T-713AS
85T/3D-7
85T/Gloss22-3
85T/Gloss40-21
85T/St-175FOIL
85T/St-34
85T/Super-1
86D-67
86D/AAS-32
86Dorman-14
86Drake-19
86F-378
86F/LimEd-40
86F/LL-39
86F/Mini-80
86F/Slug-32
86F/St-106
86Gator-23
86Jay's-15
86Jiffy-12
86Leaf-62
86Meadow/Blank-13
86Meadow/Milk-10
86Meadow/Stat-12
86OPC-19
86Quaker-13
86S-127M
86S-20
86S-51M
86T-690
86T/Gloss60-34
86T/Mini-39
86T/St-55
86T/Super-48
86TrueVal-14
87Berg/Cubs-23
87BK-18
87Class-35
87D-77
87D/AAS-13
87D/OD-75
87D/PopUp-13
87Drake-21
87F-572
87F-639M
87F-C14
87F/AwardWin-35
87F/LL-39
87F/Mini-95
87F/St-105
87F/WaxBox-C14
87Ho/St-8
87Jiffy-1
87KayBee-28
87Kraft-8
87Leaf-234
87MnM's-4
87OPC-143
87Ralston-15
87RedFoley/St-16
87S-116M
87S-197M
87S-8
87Seven-C14
87Seven-ME11
87T-680
87T/Board-30
87T/Coins-41
87T/Gloss22-3
87T/St-156
87T/St-61
88Berg/Cubs-23
88Bz-19
88ChefBoy-11
88Class/Red-169
88D-242
88D/AS-35
88D/Best-116
88D/Cubs/Bk-242
88D/PopUp-13
88F-431
88F-628M
88F-C10
88F/BB/MVP-29
88F/Excit-32
88F/Mini-70
88F/SS-C5
88F/St-80
88F/WaxBox-C10
88Leaf-207
88OPC-10
88Panini/St-234M
88Panini/St-260
88Score-26
88Score/WaxBox-12
88Sf-12
88T-10
88T/Big-16
88T/Coins-52
88T/Gloss22-14
88T/Gloss60-14
88T/St-147
88T/St-57
88T/St/Backs-6
88T/UK-65
89Ames-26
89B-290
89Cadaco-48
89D-105
89D/AS-35
89D/Best-26
89D/PopUp-35
89F-437
89F/Heroes-35
89KayBee-26
89KingB/Discs-5
89KMart/DT-24
89Mara/Cubs-23
89OPC-360
89Panini/St-233AS
89Panini/St-56
89Score-35
89Score/HotSt-54
89Score/Mast-23
89Sf-201
89T-360
89T-387AS
89T/Big-212
89T/DH-14
89T/Gloss22-14
89T/Gloss60-34
89T/HeadsUp-9
89T/St-155
89T/St-55
89T/St/Backs-38
89T/UK-67
89UD-120
89UD-675TC
90Class-27
90D-105
90D-692AS
90D/Bon/MVP-BC10
90F-40
90F-625
90F-639M
90Score-561HL
90Score-691DT
90Score-90
90Score/100St-32
90Sf-54
90T-210
90T-398AS
90UD-324

Sander, Mike
88Hagers/Star-18
89Hagers/Best-25
89Hagers/Pro-275
89Hagers/Star-15

Sander, Rick
77LodiD

Sanderlin, Rick
77Phoen
78Cr/PCL-12
79Phoen

Sanders, Al
88Elmir-10
89Elmir/Puc-19
89WinHav/Star-20

Sanders, Alexander
N172

Sanders, Deion
89Albany/Best-1
89Albany/Pro-338
89Albany/Star-23
89Class/Up/2-200
89D/Rook-6
89F/Up-53
89Score/NWest-22
89T/Tr-110T
90Class-21
90D-427
90F-454
90Score-586
90Score/100Ris-40
90Sf-221
90T-61
90UD-13

Sanders, Earl
87Duned-24
88Duned/Star-15
89Duned/Star-14

Sanders, Ken
66T-356R
69Sunoco/Pin-16
71MLB/St-451
71OPC-116
71T-116
72OPC-391
72T-391
73OPC-246
73T-246
74OPC-638
74T-638
75OPC-366
75T-366
75T/M-366
76OPC-291
76SSPC-550
76T-291
77Spoka
77T-171

Sanders, Lance
89Utica/Puc-20

Sanders, Ray
47TipTop

Sanders, Reggie
74OPC-600R
74T-600R
75OPC-617R
75T-617R
75T/M-617R
88Bill/Pro-1822
89Greens/Pro-415

Sanders, Satch
81Miami-9

Sanders, Stan
82Oneon-7

Sanderski, John
86WinHav-20
87Greens-24

Sanderson, Scott
79T-720R
80OPC-301
80T-578
81D-450
81F-166
81OPC-235
81OPC/Post-12
81T-235
82D-288
82F-206
82F/St-40
82Hygrade
82OPC-7
82OPC/Post-22
82T-7
82T/St-63
82Zeller-17
83D-446
83F-295
83OPC-54
83Stuart-17
83T-717
84D-341
84F-285
84F/X-104
84Nes/792-164
84OPC-164
84SevenUp-24
84T-164
84T/X-106
85D-266
85F-66
85Leaf-194
85OPC-373
85SevenUp-21
85T-616
85T/St-40
86D-442
86F-379
86Gator-21
86T-406
87Berg/Cubs-21
87D-447
87F-573
87T-534
87T/St-60
88Berg/Cubs-21
88D-646
88D/Cubs/Bk-646
88F-432
88Score-544
88T-311
89D-629
89F/Up-78
89Mara/Cubs-21
89T-212
89UD-342
90D-647
90F-41
90Score-488
90T-67
90UD-39

Sanderson, Shaun
89SLCty-17C

Sandling, Bob
80Elmir-14

Sandlock, Mike
53T-247
54T-104

Sandoval, Dennis
77Wausa

Sandoval, Jesus
86AppFx-20

Sandoval, Mike
87Watertn-31

Sandry, Bill
83AppFx/LF-28

Sands, Charlie
72T-538
74OPC-381
74T-381
75OPC-548
75T-548
75T/M-548
75Tucso-24
76Tucso-39

Sandt, Tommy
75Tucso-1
77T-616
78Syrac
79Portl-6

80Port-8
81Portl-21
82Buffa-18
83LynnP-23
84Cram/PCL-137
85Cram/PCL-233
86Hawai-6MG

Sanford, Ed
82ArkTr-8

Sanford, John F.
47TipTop
49B-236
50B-156
51B-145
52Mother
53Mother

Sanford, John S.
(Jack)
57T-387
58Hires-39
58T-264
59T-275
60L-54
60T-165
61P-154
61T-258
61T-383M
61T/St-84
62J-141
62P-141
62P/Can-141
62T-538
63J-110
63P-110
63T-325
63T-7LL
63T/SO
64T-414
65OPC-228
65T-228
66OPC-23
66T-23
67T-549
79TCMA-125

Sanford, Mo
89Greens/Pro-423

Sanguillen, Manny
68KDKA-35
68T-251
69T-509
70MLB/St-106
70OPC-188
70T-188
71K-13
71MD
71MLB/St-213
71OPC-480
71OPC-62LL
71T-480
71T-62LL
71T/tatt-5
72K-19
72MB-305
72OPC-225WS
72OPC-228
72OPC-60
72T-60
73K-42
73OPC-250
73T-250
73T/Lids-46
74K-15
74OPC-28
74T-28
74T/DE-22
74T/St-87
75Ho-21
75Ho/Twink-21
75OPC-515
75T-515
75T/M-515
76Crane-53
76Ho-72
76K-42
76MSA/Disc
76OPC-191LL
76OPC-220
76SSPC-571
76T-191LL
76T-220
77OPC-231
77Pep-4
77T-61
78T-58
78T-658
78Wiffle/Discs-66
79T-447
80T-148
81D-14
81F-376
81T-226
89Swell-29

Sankey, Ben
R314/Can
V355-83

Sanner, Dale
75Tucso-4
76Tucso-14

Sano, Motokuni
88Mia/Star-23

SantaCruz, Nick
88Batav/Pro-1678
89Spart/Pro-1043
89Spart/Star-21

Santana, Andres
88Clint/Pro-705
88MidwLAS/GS-2
89SanJose/Best-1
89SanJose/Cal-226
89SanJose/Pro-450
89SanJose/Star-23
89Star/Wax-87

Santana, Ernesto
87Macon-1
88Watertn/Puc-10
89StCath/Pro-2087

Santana, Jose
89AubAs/Pro-2165

Santana, Miguel
88FSLAS/Star-20

Santana, Rafael
82Louvl-27
84Tidew-16
85D-610
85F-90
85T-67
86D-319
86F-93
86OPC-102
86T-587
86T/St-102
87D-569
87D/OD-126
87F-21
87Leaf-167
87T-378
88D-633
88D/Best-273
88D/Y/Bk-NEW
88F-149
88F/U-U50
88Panini/St-344
88Score-316
88Score/Tr-54T
88T-233
88T/Big-246
88T/Tr-101T
89B-174
89D-309
89F-268
89Panini/St-407
89Score-296
89Score/NWest-11
89T-792
89T/Big-192
89T/St-313
89UD-216
90T-651

Santana, Rodolfo
80Elmir-42

Santana, Simon
77Charl

Santangelo, F.P.
88CapeCod/Sum-156
89James/Pro-2132

Santarelli, Cal
85Water-9
86Water-21

Santiago, Benito
83Miami-20
85Beaum-21
86F-644M
86LasVegas-14
87Bohem-9
87Class/Up-132
87D-31RR
87D/HL-45
87D/HL-55
87D/OD-148
87D/Rook-44
87F-429
87Leaf-31
87S-118M
87S/Rook-19
87Sf/Rook-9
87T/Tr-109T
88Woolwth-14
88Bz-20
88Class/Blue-219
88Class/Red-160
88Coke/Padres-9
88D-114
88D-3DK
88D/Best-301
88D/DKsuper-3DK
88F-596
88F/AwardWin-34
88F/BB/MVP-30
88F/Excit-33
88F/Hottest-33
88F/LL-34
88F/Mini-115
88F/RecSet-34
88F/SS-32
88F/St-125
88KMart-24
88Leaf-3DK
88Leaf-58
88MSA/Disc-15
88Nestle-12
88OPC-86
88Panini/St-402
88Panini/St-433
88RedFoley/St-78
88Score-25
88Score-654HL
88Score/YS/I-2
88Sf-22
88Sf-222
88Sf/Gamewin-10
88Smok/Padres-25
88T-404
88T-693
88T-7RB
88T/Big-12
88T/Coins-35
88T/Gloss60-30
88T/JumboR-18
88T/St-112
88T/St-2
88T/UK-66
88ToysRUs-26
89B-453
89Bimbo/Discs-3
89Cadaco-49
89Class-73
89D-205
89F-316
89OPC-256
89Panini/St-199
89RedFoley/St-102
89Score-4
89Score/HotSt-47
89Sf-22
89T-256
89T/Big-134
89T/Coins-24
89T/Gloss60-15
89T/St-101
89T/St/Backs-57
89T/UK-68
89Tetley/Discs-9
89UD-165
90D-465
90D-708AS
90F-167
90Score-454
90Score/100St-63
90Sf-115
90T-35
90UD-12TC
90UD-325

Santiago, Delvy
89Princet/Star-19

Santiago, Jose G.
56T-59

Santiago, Jose R.
65T-557
66T-203
67T-473
67T/Test/RSox-15
68OPC-123
68T-123
69MB-246
69MLB/St-16
69OPC-21
69T-21
69T/St-137
70T-708

Santiago, Mike
85Durhm-11
86Jacks/TCMA-9
88Jacks/GS-9

Santiago, Norm
86FtLaud-19
87Jaxvl-3
88WPalm/Star-22

Santo, Ron
61Bz-3
61P-196
61T-35
61T/St-9
62Bz
62J-184
62P-184
62P/Can-184
62Salada-136
62Shirriff-136
62T-170
62T/St-109
63Exh
63F-32
63J-170
63P-170
63T-252
64T-375
64T/Coins-146AS
64T/Coins-68
64T/S-58
64T/St-33
64T/SU
64Wheat/St-40
65Bz-28
65OPC-110
65OPC-6LL
65T-110
65T-6LL
65T/E-28
65T/trans-67
66Bz-39
66T-290
66T/RO-102
67Bz-39
67OPC-70
67OPC/PI-26
67T-70
67T/PI-26
67T/Test/SU-22
68Bz-15
68Bz-6
68Kahn
68OPC-5LL
68T-235
68T-366AS
68T-5LL
68T/G-19
68T/Post-21
69Citgo-13
69Kahn
69Kelly/Pin-16
69MB-247
69MLB/St-125
69MLBPA/Pin-56
69NTF
69OPC-4LL
69OPC/DE-19
69Sunoco/Pin-8
69T-420AS
69T-4LL
69T-570
69T/DE-19
69T/decal
69T/S-38
69T/St-19
69Trans-42
70Dunkin-5
70K-42
70MB-25
70MLB/St-22
70OPC-454AS
70OPC-63LL
70T-454AS
70T-63LL
70T-670
70T/PI-5
70T/S-21
70Trans-2
71MD
71MLB/St-46
71OPC-220
71T-220
71T/Coins-95
71T/S
71T/tatt-13
72MB-306
72T-555
72T-556A
73K-54
73OPC-115
73T-115
74K-7
74OPC-270
74OPC-334AS
74T-270
74T-334M
74T/St-19
74T/Tr-270T
75OPC-35
75T-35
75T/M-35
78TCMA-22
83MLBPA/Pin-32
88Pac/Leg-97
89Swell-36
Exh47
WG10-46
WG9-45

SantoDomingo, Rafael
78Indianap-17
80Indianap-22

Santop, Louis
74Laugh/Black-16
Santora, Steve
85Evrt/Cram-15
Santorini, Al
69T-592R
70OPC-212
70T-212
71MLB/St-237
71OPC-467
71T-467
72T-723
73OPC-24
73T-24
Santos, Don
86Watlo-24
87Watlo-20
Santos, Ed
77LodiD
Santos, Faustoe
85Madis-2
85Madis/Pol-22
Santos, Luis
85FtMyr-28
Santovenia, Nelson
83Memph-8
86Jaxvl/TCMA-8
87Jaxvl-5
87SLAS-5
88F/U-U103
88Indi/CMC-18
88Indi/Pro-500
88Score/Tr-96T
88T/Tr-102T
89B-361
89D-366
89D/Best-146
89F-393
89OPC-228
89Panini/St-112
89Score-346
89Score/HotRk-71
89T-228
89T/Big-98
89T/JumboR-18
89T/St-78
89ToysRUs-25
89UD-380
90D-224
90F-360
90Score-451
90Sf-162
90T-614
90UD-432
Sapienza, Rich
87Tampa-29
88Cedar/Pro-1148
Sarazen, Gene
33SK-22
Sardinha, Ed
86Elmir-19
Sarmiento, Manny
76Indianap-16
77Indianap-25
77T-475R
78T-377
79Indianap-21
79OPC-69
79T-149
80Spoka-12
80T-21
81Pawtu-10
81T-649
82Portl-8
83D-502
83F-321
83T-566
84D-200
84F-263
84Nes/792-209
84T-209
85Cram/PCL-248
Sarmiento, Wally
80Toled-12
81Toled-8
Sarni, Bill
54T-194
55B-30
55Hunter
55RM-NL9
56T-247
57T-86
79TCMA-106
Sarrett, Daniel
80Water-17
Sasser, Don
75Cedar
76Cedar
Sasser, Mackey
86Shrev-22
87Phoen-20
88D-28
88D/Mets/Bk-NEW
88D/Rook-51
88F/U-U106
88Kahn/Mets-2
88Leaf-28RR
88Score-642
88Score/Tr-30T
88T/Tr-103T
89Class-26
89D-454
89F-48
89Kahn/Mets-2
89Score-303
89Score/HotRk-82
89Score/YS/I-38
89T-457
89T/JumboR-19
89ToysRUs-26
89UD-561
90Class-78
90D-471
90F-216
90Score-510
90T-656
90UD-185
Sassone, Mike
87StPet-4
88ArkTr/GS-18
Satnat, Dave
86Salem-24
Satre, Jason
89Greens/Pro-414
Satriano, Tom
63T-548
64T-521
65OPC-124
65T-124
66T-361
67T-343
68T-238
69MB-248
69OPC-78
69T-78
69T/St-150
70MLB/St-164
70T-581
71MLB/St-330
71OPC-557
71T-557
72MB-307
Satterfield, Cory
88Hamil/Pro-1731
89Sprin/Best-18
Sattler, Bill
82Wichi-16
84Indianap-19
Satzinger, Jeff
86Macon-22
87Kenosha-17
88Orlan/Best-13
89Orlan/Best-24
89Orlan/Pro-1330
Saucier, Kevin
79OkCty
80BK/P-22
80T-682R
81F-24
81T-53
81T/Tr-827
82D-485
82F-275
82F/St-158
82OPC-238
82T-238
83T-373
Sauer, Ed
47Signal
49Eureka-196
Sauer, Henry
(Hank)
48B-45
48L-20
49B-5
50B-25
51B-22
51T/BB-49
52Dix
52NTea
52StarCal/L-80E
52T-35
53B/Col-48
53Dix
53Exh/Can-7
53NB
53RM-NL16
53T-111
54RH
54T-4
54Wilson
55T-45
55T/DH-103
56T-41
56T/Hocus-A3
56T/Pin-6
57T-197
58Hires-49
58SFCall
58T-378
59T-404
61T-481MV
74Laugh/ASG-52
75OPC-190M
75T-190MV
75T/M-190MV
88Pac/Leg-23
Exh47
R302/2-113
Saul, Jim
62Kahn
80ElPas-7MG
81Holyo-2
82Portl-23
82Portl-24
83Nashvl-18
84Nashvl-19CO
85Albany-25
86Albany/TCMA-16
89BurlB/Pro-1615
Saunders, Dennis
71OPC-423R
71T-423R
Saunders, Doug
89Clmbia/Best-20
89Clmbia/GS-23
Saunders, Mark
79Elmir-28
Saunier, Randy
82Clint-12
Sauveur, Rich
84PrWill-23
85Nashua-23
86Nashua-25
87Harrisbg-24
88Jaxvl/Best-3
88Jaxvl/Pro-986
89Indi/Pro-1228
Savage, Jack
86Bakers-24
87SnAnt-22
87TexLgAS-34
88F-650
88Tidew/CANDL-27
88Tidew/CMC-1
88Tidew/Pro-1583
89D-618
89Tidew/CMC-5
89Tidew/Pro-1971
Savage, John Robert
49B-204
Savage, John
88Reno/Cal-275
Savage, Ted
62T-104
63T-508
64T-62
66Pep/Tul
67T-552
68OPC-119
68T-119
69Sunoco/Pin-17
69T-471
70McDon-1
70T-602
71MLB/St-434
71OPC-76
71T-76
71T/Coins-44
71T/S-3
71T/tatt-7
72MB-308
Savarino, William
86Cram/PCL-51
87Modesto-2
88Modesto/Cal-75
89Huntsvl/Best-4
89Modesto/Ch-21
Saverine, Bob
63T-158R
64T-221
65T-427
66T-312
67OPC-27
67T-27
68OPC-149
68T-149
78TCMA-14
Saverino, Mike
82Danvi-23
83Peoria/LF-27
Sawatski, Carl
53T-202
54T-198
55T-122
55T/DH-93
58T-234
59T-56
60L-120
60T-545
61T-198
62J-162
62P-162
62P/Can-162
62Salada-119
62Shirriff-119
62T-106
63T-267
64T-24
Exh47
Sawkiw, Warren
88CapeCod/Sum-3
Sawyer, Eddie
49Eureka-145MG
50B-225
51B-184
60T-226
Sawyer, Rick
76SSPC-426
77T-268
Sax, Dave
79Clint
82Albuq-13
83Pol/Dodg-23
84Cram/PCL-152
84D-519
85Pawtu-15
86T-307
87D-647
87Pawtu/TCMA-25
88BuffB/CMC-22
88BuffB/Pro-1483
89Colum/CMC-26
89Colum/Pro-756
Sax, Steve
79Clint
82D-624
82F-21
82Pol/Dodg
82Pol/Dodg-52
82T-681R
82T/Tr-103T
83D-336
83F-220
83OPC-245
83Pol/Dodg-3
83Seven-2
83T-245
83T/St-329
84D-104
84F-112
84F-633
84F/St-90
84FunFood/Pin-45
84MiltBrad-22
84Nes/792-610
84OPC-144
84Pol/Dodg-3
84Seven-22W
84Smok/Dodg-3
84T-610
84T/Gloss22-14
84T/St-78
85D-418
85F-384
85F/LimEd-32
85Leaf-90
85OPC-369
85T-470
85T/St-77
86D-540
86D/HL-50
86F-143
86OPC-175
86Pol/Dodg-3
86S-60M
86S-95
86S/Rook-48M
86T-175
86T/St-72
87Class-20
87D-26DK
87D-278
87D/AAS-28
87D/DKsuper-26
87D/OD-85
87Drake-25
87F-453
87F/AS-4
87F/GameWin-39
87F/Hottest-34
87F/Mini-96
87F/RecSet-34
87F/St-106
87Kraft-38
87Leaf-203
87Leaf-26DK
87MnM's-21
87Moth/Dodg-3

87OPC-254
87Pol/Dodg-2
87S-12
87Seven-W10
87Smok/Dodg-32
87Smok/NL-1
87T-596AS
87T-769
87T/Coins-42
87T/Mini-15
87T/St-70
88D-176
88D/Best-204
88F-523
88F/Mini-85
88F/St-93
88Leaf-185
88Moth/Dodg-3
88OPC-305
88Panini/St-311
88Pol/Dodg-3
88Score-35
88Smok/Dodg-25
88T-305
88T/Big-46
88T/St-74
89B-178
89Cadaco-50
89Class/Up/2-179
89D-84
89D/Best-20
89D/Tr-23
89F-70
89F/Up-52
89F/WS-9
89OPC-40
89Panini/St-106
89RedFoley/St-103
89Score-69
89Score/HotSt-33
89Score/NWest-2
89Score/Tr-20
89Sf-58
89Smok/Dodg-99
89T-40
89T/Big-111
89T/Mini-19
89T/St-57
89T/St/Backs-39
89T/Tr-111T
89T/UK-69
89UD-53
89UD/Ext-748
90Class-149
90D-2DK
90D-78
90D/Bon/MVP-BC22
90F-455
90Score-125
90Score/100St-2
90Sf-12
90T-560
90UD-172
90UD-18TC

Sayler, Barry
83StPet-24

Sayles, Steve
83Miami-24

Scaglione, Tony
88Watlo/Pro-690
89Kinston/Star-22

Scala, Jerry
V362-28

Scales, George
78Laugh/Black-26

Scanlan, William
(Doc)
10Domino-105A
10Domino-105B
11Helmar-151
12Sweet/Pin-76
M116
S74-55
T202
T205
T207

Scanlin, Michael
87Gasto-19
88Tulsa-1

Scanlon, Bob
86Clearw-22
87Readg-20
88Maine/CMC-9
88Maine/Pro-294
89Readg/Best-8
89Readg/Pro-652
89Readg/Star-21

Scanlon, James P.
(Pat)
76SSPC-332
78T-611

Scanlon, Ken
80Ander-23
81Durhm-4
82Durhm-7
83Durhm-12

Scanlon, Steve
88Visal/Cal-161
88Visal/Pro-94

Scannell, Larry
87Elmir-5
87Elmir/Red-5
88Elmir-24
89WinHav/Star-21

Scantlebury, Pat
61BeeHive-20

Scarbery, Randy
77SnJos-18
80T-291

Scarborough, Carey
75BurlB

Scarborough, Ray
49B-140
49Royal-14
50B-108
50Drake-29
51B-39
51T/RB-42
52B-140
52Royal
52T-43
52TipTop
53T-213
79TCMA-208

Scarce, Mac
73OPC-6
73T-6
74OPC-149
74T-149
75OPC-527
75T-527
75T/M-527
76Indianap-22
77Indianap-15

Scarpace, Ken
81Cedar-17
82Water-19

Scarpetta, Dan
83Beloi/LF-25
87Denver-15
88ElPas/Best-3
88TexLgAS/GS-6
89SnAnt/Best-18

Scarsella, Les
46Remar
47Remar-2
47Signal
47Smith-3
48Signal
48Smith-6
49B/PCL-25
49Remar
R314/Can
W711/1

Scarsone, Stephen
86Cram/PCL-135
87CharWh-5
88Clearw/Star-22
89Readg/Best-4
89Readg/Pro-665
89Readg/Star-22

Schaal, Paul
65T-517R
66T-376
67OPC-58
67T-58
68T-474
69MB-249
69MLB/St-62
69T-352
69T/St-188
70MLB/St-228
70OPC-338
70T-338
71MLB/St-429
71OPC-487
71T-487
72MB-309
72OPC-177
72OPC-178IA
72T-177
72T-178A
73OPC-416
73T-416
74OPC-514
74T-514

Schacht, Al
39PB-113
40PB-116
87Conlon/2-9
R312/M
R314
V355-29

Schaefer, Bob
82Tidew-22
84Tidew-10
85IntLgAS-1
85Tidew-27
86GlenF-20
87Memph-10
87Memph/Best-1

Schaefer, Chris
88CapeCod/Sum-31
89Eugene/Best-1

Schaefer, Doug
79Phoen
80Phoen-3
81Phoen-7

Schaefer, Herman
(Germany)
09Buster/Pin-13
10Domino-106
11Helmar-76
12Sweet/Pin-63
14Piedmont/St-51
D303
D350/2-154
E101
E102
E105
E106
E90/1
E92
M101/5-154
M116
S74-40
T204
T205
T206
T207
T213/blue
T215/blue
T215/brown
T216

Schaefer, Jeff
84RochR-10
85CharO-12
85Utica-14
86MidldA-21
87SnAnt-1
88Vanco/CMC-21
88Vanco/Pro-753
89Coke/WS-25
89Vanco/CMC-24

Schaefer, Jim
79Tulsa-13
80Ashev-6

Schaefer, Steve
79Elmir-15

Schafer, Dennis
81Clint-13

Schaffer, Jim
89Hagers/Pro-282

Schaffer, Jimmie
61Union
62T-579
63T-81
64T-359
65T-313
68T-463
78TCMA-152
78TCMA-169
78TCMA-184

Schaffernoth, Joe
61T-58
63T-463

Schaive, John Jr.
82Buffa-6
83LynnP-18

Schaive, John Sr.
61T-259
62T-529
63T-356

Schalk, Ray
14CJ-61
15CJ-61
21Exh-151
25Exh-78
26Exh-78
27Exh-40
50Callahan
60F-56
61F-136
80Cram/Leg-85
80SSPC/HOF
87Conlon/2-55
88Pac/8Men-100
88Pac/8Men-43
88Pac/8Men-45M
88Pac/8Men-50
88Pac/8Men-51
88Pac/8Men-52
BF2-17
D327
D328-150
D329-154
D350/2-155
E120
E121/120
E121/80
E122
E126-8
E135-150
E210-23
E254
M101/4-154
M101/5-155
V117-3
V355-124
W501-43
W502-23
W514-60
W515-51
W516-4
W572
W573
W575

Schammel, Bill
83MidldC-1

Schang, Walter H.
(Wally)
14CJ-58
15CJ-58
21Exh-152
25Exh-101
28Exh-59
29Exh/4-29
31Exh/4-24
BF2-39
D327
D328-151
D329-155
D350/2-156
E120
E121/80
E122
E135-151
E220
M101/4-155
M101/5-156
T222
V100
V61-20
W501-27
W514-99
W515-17
W572
W573
W575

Schanz, Charley
52Mother-41
53Mother-40

Schardt, Wilbur
E254
T207

Scharein, George
47Signal

Schatter, Jim
89Hagers/Best-10

Schattinger, Jeff
81Omaha-12
82Edmon-25

Schatz, Dan
87Visal-25

Schatzeder, Dan
78T-709R
79OPC-56
79T-124
80OPC-140
80T-267
81D-248
81F-482
81OPC-112
81T-417
82D-385
82F-281
82OPC-106
82T-691
82T/Tr-104T
83F-296
83OPC-189
83Stuart-22
83T-189
84D-132
84F-286
84Nes/792-57
84OPC-57
84Stuart-7
84T-57
85D-543
85F-409
85Leaf-59
85OPC-293
85T-501
86F-259
86OPC-324
86Provigo-12
86T-324
87D-482

87F-186
87OPC-168
87T-789
88F-21
88Gator-31
88T-218
89F/Up-90
89Lennox/Ast-9
89Tucso/CMC-10
89Tucso/Pro-198
90D-594
90F-236
90Score-418
Scheckla, Roddy
88AubAs/Pro-1960
89Ashvl/Pro-946
Scheer, Ron
83Wisco/LF-2
84Visal-21
86Penin-23
87Penin-17
Scheetz, Rick
82Wisco-11
Scheffing, Bob
48L-160
49B-83
49Eureka-71
50B-168
54T-76
60Lake
60T-464C
61T-223MG
62T-416
62T-72M
63T-134
Schefsky, Steve
84Beaum-13
85Beaum-11
Scheib, Carl
49B-25
50B-213
51B-83
52B-46
52T-116
53B/Col-150
53T-57
54B-67
54T-118
Scheibeck, Frank
N172
Scheid, Rich
87FtLaud-18
88Pittsf/Pro-1372
89IowaC/CMC-9
89IowaC/Pro-1713
Scheinblum, Richie
65T-577R
68OPC-16R
68T-16R
69T-479
70OPC-161
70T-161
71OPC-326
71T-326
72OPC-468
72T-468
73OPC-78
73T-78
74OPC-323
74T-323
74T/St-148
Schell, Clyde
(Danny)
55T-79
55T/DH-81
Scheller, Rod
77LodiD
78LodiD
Schellhasse, Albert
N172
Schemer, Mike
47Sunbeam
Schenkle, William
N172
Schenz, Henry
52Mother-30
Scherer, Doug
85Cram/PCL-141
88Knoxv/Best-11
Scherger, George
73OPC-296CO
73T-296C
74OPC-326CO
74T-326C
81Water-22MG
82Indianap-2
86TexGold-CO
Scherger, Joe
82Amari-4
Scherman, Fred
71MLB/St-406
71OPC-316
71T-316
72OPC-6
72T-6
73OPC-660
73T-660
74OPC-186
74T-186
74T/Tr-186T
75OPC-252
75T-252
75T/M-252
76OPC-188
76SSPC-343
76T-188
Scherrer, Bill
80Water-7
81Water-7
84D-203
84F-482
84Nes/792-373
84T-373
84T/St-62
85Cain's-17
85F-22
85T-586
85Wendy-19
86D-516
86F-237
86T-217
87T-98
88RochR-20
88RochR/CMC-9
88RochR/Pro-209
89OkCty/CMC-3
89Tidew/Pro-1955
Schettler, Louis
M116
Scheuer, Chris
89Aug/Pro-520
Scheznayder, Wade
81Redwd-12
Schildnecht
N172
Schiller, Jon
89Everett/Star-25
Schilling, Chuck
61T-499
62Bz
62J-56
62P-56
62P/Can-56
62T-345
62T-467AS
62T/St-18
63T-52
64T-182M
64T-481
64T/Coins-103
65OPC-272
65T-272
66OPC-6
66T-6
78TCMA-183
PM10/Sm-173
PM10/Sm-174
Schilling, Curt
86Elmir-20
87Greens-2
88NewBrit/Pro-908
89D-635
89RochR/CMC-7
89RochR/Pro-1655
90D-667
90Score-581
90Score/100Ris-94
90Sf-133
90T-97
Schimdt, Eric
88Colum/CMC-8
Schimpf, Rex
82DayBe-7
83DayBe-11
Schiraldi, Calvin
84Jacks-4
85D-38
85F/Up-U99
85Tidew-5
86D-652
86Pawtu-20
86S/Rook-44
86T-210
87D-641
87F-44
87Leaf-137
87T-94
87T/HL-20
87Woolwth-20
88Berg/Cubs-32
88D-375
88D/Best-194
88D/Cubs/Bk-NEW
88F-365
88OPC-62
88Score-218
88Score/Tr-39T
88T-599
88T/Tr-104T
89D-285
89D/Best-82
89F-438
89Mara/Cubs-32
89OPC-337
89Score-321
89T-337
89T/St-56
89UD-82
90D-672
90F-168
90T-693
90UD-643
Schirm, George
C46-29
E254
T206
Schlafly, Harry
E254
T206
Schlei, George
(Admiral)
E101
E104
E105
E92
E97
M116
S74-94
T204
T205
T206
T216
T3-115
Schleighoffer, Mike
86Albuq-21
Schlesinger, Bill
65T-573R
68T-258R
Schley, Van
88SLCty-16M
89SLCty-18PPDir
Schlichting, John
85VeroB-3
86VeroB-21
Schlitzer, Victor
E90/1
Schlopy, Butch
86Watertn-22
88Aug/Pro-374
89Salem/Star-19
Schmandt, Ray
E120
E220
V100
W573
Schmees, George
52B-245
53Mother-13
V362-20
Schmelz, Heinrich
N172
Schmid, Michael
82BurlR-8
Schmidt, Augie
83Knoxv-12
84Syrac-8
85Cram/PCL-194
Schmidt, Bill
40Hughes-17
Schmidt, Butcher Boy
C46-12
Schmidt, Charles
(Boss)
10Domino-107
11Helmar-36
12Sweet/Pin-30B
12Sweet/Pin-30A
14CJ-127
15CJ-127
D350/2-157
E101
E102
E104
E105
E92
M101/5-157
M116
T205
T206
T213/blue
T213/brown
T216
T3-116
Schmidt, David F.
(Dave)
82T-381R
Schmidt, David J.
(Dave)
80Ashev-25
80Tulsa-22
82T-418R
83D-321
83F-578
83Rang-24
83T-116
84D-586
84F-427
84Nes/792-584
84Rang-24
84T-584
85D-586
85F-567
85OPC-313
85Rang-24
85T-313
86Coke/WS-24
86D-378
86F-571
86F/Up-U103
86OPC-79
86T-79
86T/Tr-99T
87D-182
87F-505
87F/U-U107
87OPC-372
87T-703
87T/Tr-110T
88D-371
88D/Best-333
88F-571
88F/Mini-2
88French-24
88OPC-214
88Panini/St-6
88Score-103
88T-214
88T/St-226
89B-5
89D-13DK
89D-215
89D/DKsuper-13DK
89F-618
89French-24
89OPC-231
89Panini/St-255
89Score-292
89T-677
89T/Big-130
89UD-447
90D-524
90F-188
90Score-30
90T-497
90UD-641
Schmidt, Eric
77Clint
78LodiD
86Albany/TCMA-21
87Albany-4
88Colum/Pol-9
88Colum/Pro-313
Schmidt, Gregg
86FtMyr-24
Schmidt, Keith
89Bluef/Star-20
Schmidt, Mike
73OPC-615R
73T-615R
74JP
74OPC-283
74T-283
75Ho-133
75K-56
75OPC-307LL
75OPC-70
75T-307LL
75T-70
75T/M-307LL
75T/M-70
76Crane-54
76Ho-84
76MSA/Disc
76OPC-193LL
76OPC-480
76SSPC-470
76T-193LL
76T-480
77Ho-43
77OPC-245
77OPC-2LL
77Pep-70
77T-140
77T-2LL
77T/CS-41
78Ho-113
78K-3
78OPC-225
78T-360

78Wiffle/Discs-67
79BK/P-16
79Ho-9
79OPC-323
79T-610
80BK/P-6
80K-2
80OPC-141DP
80T-270
80T/S-2
81Coke
81D-11
81D-590
81Drake-7
81F-5
81F-640M
81F-645M
81F/St-43M
81F/St-9
81F/St-CL3
81K-5
81MSA/Disc-28
81OPC-207
81Sqt-8
81T-206M/
81T-2LL
81T-3LL/
81T-540
81T/HT
81T/Nat/Super-13
81T/S
81T/So-60
81T/St-19
81T/St-199
81T/St-21
81T/St-254
82D-294
82D-585M
82Drake-29
82F-258
82F-637M
82F-641M
82F/St-53
82K-16
82KMart-39
82KMart-41
82OPC-100
82OPC-101IA
82OPC-339AS
82Sqt-14
82T-100
82T-101A
82T-162LL
82T-163LL
82T-339AS
82T/St-123
82T/St-3
82T/St-5
82T/St-74
83D-168
83D/AAS-57
83Drake-25
83F-173
83K-58
83OPC-300
83OPC-301SV
83OPC-342AS
83T-300
83T-301A
83T-399
83T/Gloss-8
83T/Gloss40-8
83T/St-10
83T/St-172
83T/St-270
83T/St/Box-3
84D-183
84D-23
84D/AAS-57
84D/Champs-11
84Drake-28
84F-48
84F/St-16
84F/St-35
84F/St-48
84FunFood/Pin-11
84MiltBrad-23
84Nes/792-132LL
84Nes/792-388AS
84Nes/792-700
84Nes/792-703LL
84Nestle/DT-14
84OPC-361
84OPC-388AS
84Ralston-22
84Seven-4C
84Seven-4E
84Seven-4W
84T-132
84T-388
84T-700
84T-703
84T/Cereal-22
84T/Gloss22-15
84T/Gloss40-39
84T/St-101
84T/St-117
84T/St-188FOIL
84T/Super-6
84T/Super-6
85CIGNA-4
85CircK-19
85D-61
85D/AAS-17
85Drake-29
85F-265
85F-627IA
85F-630IA
85F/LimEd-33
85F/St-17
85F/St-34
85F/St-74SA
85F/St-75
85F/St-76
85F/St-77
85F/St-78
85F/St-79
85GenMills-9
85Leaf-205
85OPC-67
85Seven-16E
85Seven-1W
85Seven-4C
85T-500
85T-714AS
85T/3D-1
85T/Gloss22-4
85T/Gloss40-23
85T/St-111
85T/St-193
85T/St-94
85T/Super-12
86BK/AP-5
86CIGNA-10
86D-61
86D/HL-36
86D/HL-4
86Dorman-8
86Drake-26
86F-450
86F/LimEd-41
86F/Mini-94
86F/Slug-33
86F/St-107
86Jiffy-17
86Keller-5
86Leaf-51
86Meadow/Blank-14
86Meadow/Milk-11
86Meadow/Stat-16
86OPC-200
86Quaker-14
86S-139M
86S-148M
86S-182M
86S-44
86S-62M
86S-68M
86S/Dec-55
86T-200
86T/3D-24
86T/Gloss60-17
86T/Mini-55
86T/St-114
86T/Super-49
86TrueVal-28
86Woolwth-30
87BK-17
87Class-62
87Class/Up-101
87D-139
87D/AAS-17
87D/HL-2
87D/OD-160
87D/PopUp-17
87Drake-23
87F-187
87F-C15
87F/AS-6
87F/AwardWin-36
87F/GameWin-40
87F/Hottest-35
87F/Lim-40
87F/LL-40
87F/McCror-37
87F/Mini-97
87F/RecSet-35
87F/Slug-37
87F/St-107
87F/WaxBox-C15
87Ho/St-13
87Jiffy-16
87KayBee-29
87KMart-31
87Kraft-30
87Leaf-122
87MnM's-3
87MSA/Discs-11
87OPC-396
87Ralston-14
87RedFoley/St-46
87S-115M
87S-156M
87S-30
87T-430
87T-597AS
87T/Board-1
87T/Coins-43
87T/Gloss22-4
87T/Gloss60-28
87T/HL-8
87T/Mini-30
87T/St-116
87T/St-160
87Woolwth-8
88Woolwth-7
88ChefBoy-14
88Class/Red-167
88D-330
88D-BC4
88D/AS-39
88D/Best-271
88D/PopUp-17
88F-315
88F-636M
88F-C11
88F/AwardWin-35
88F/BB/AS-36
88F/BB/MVP-31
88F/Excit-34
88F/Hottest-34
88F/LL-35
88F/Mini-102
88F/RecSet-35
88F/Slug-36
88F/SS-33
88F/St-111
88F/TL-34
88F/WaxBox-C11
88FanSam-19
88KayBee-27
88KingB/Disc-1
88KMart-25
88Leaf-124
88MSA/Disc-16
88Nestle-6
88OPC-321
88OPC-O
88Panini/St-234M
88Panini/St-360
88Panini/St-429
88RedFoley/St-79
88Score-16
88Score-657HL
88Score/WaxBox-13
88Sf-180
88Sf-35
88Sf/Gamewin-21
88T-600
88T/Big-88
88T/Coins-53
88T/Gloss22-15
88T/Gloss60-3
88T/Mini-67
88T/RiteAid-8
88T/St-125
88T/St-149
88T/St-9
88T/St/Backs-8
88T/UK-67
88T/WaxBox-O
89Ames-27
89B-402
89Cadaco-51
89Class-48
89Class/Up/2-153
89Crunch-16
89D-193
89F-582
89F/Superstar-36
89F/Up-131
89KayBee-27
89OPC-100
89Panini/St-153
89Panini/St-3
89Ralston-4
89RedFoley/St-104
89Score-149
89Score/HotSt-76
89Sf-21
89T-100
89T-489TL
89T/Big-220
89T/HeadsUp-24
89T/St-120
89T/UK-70
89T/WaxBox-L
89UD-406
89UD-684TC
90D-643
90T-662
90UD-20Special

Schmidt, Robert B.
(Bob)
58SFCall
58T-468
59T-109
60T-501
61P-151
61T-31
62Salada-179
62Shirriff-179
62T-262
63T-94
65T-582
79TCMA-246
84Moth/Giants-14

Schmidt, Walter
E120
V61-113
W572
W573
WG7-46

Schmidt, Willard
53Hunter
53T-168
56T-323
57T-206
58T-214
59T-171
62Kahn/Atl
79TCMA-153

Schmittou, Larry
89Nashvl-28 PRES

Schmitz, Dan
79WHave-5
81Colum-5
82Colum-16
82Colum/Pol-6
82Nashv-21
83Tidew-17
84Toled-7
85Visal-25
86Visal-18MG

Schmitz, John
47TipTop
48L-48
49B-52
49Eureka-70
50B-24
51B-69
51T/BB-41
52B-224
52NTea
52T-136
53Briggs
54T-33
55B-105
55T-159
56T-298
56T/Hocus-A16
56T/Hocus-B18
Exh47

Schneck, Dave
76Indianap-15

Schneider, Dan
63T-299R
64T-351
65T-366
67T-543
68OPC-57
68T-57
69T-656

Schneider, Jeff
80RochR-10
82Spoka-7
82T-21R
83Syrac-11

Schneider, Paul
83Wausa/LF-19
86Chatt-22
86SLAS-20
87Calgary-8
88Calg/CMC-2
88Calg/Pro-793
88SnBer/Best-2

Schnoor, Chuck
82Lynch-14

Schnurbusch, Chris
88Fay/Pro-1097
89Cedar/Best-16
89Cedar/Pro-934
89Cedar/Star-17

Schober, Dave
84Madis/Pol-3
85Madis-25TR
85Madis/Pol-23
86Madis-20
86Madis/Pol-25

87Madis-2TR
89Huntsvl/Best-19
Schock, William
(Will)
88Huntsvl/BK-17
88Madis-21
88MidwLAS/GS-54
89Huntsvl/Best-2
Schockman, Mark
85Newar-16
Schoendienst, Albert
(Red)
48B-38
49B-111
49Eureka-197
50B-71
51B-10
51FB
51T/BB-6
52B-30
52BR
52Dix
52RM-NL19
52StarCal/L-81A
52T-91
52TipTop
53B/Col-101
53Dix
53Hunter
53NB
53RM-NL12
53T-78
54B-110
54DanDee
54Dix
54Hunter
54RH
54RM-NL10
55B-29
55Hunter
55RFG-3
55RM-NL18
56T-165
56YellBase/Pin-28
57T-154
58T-190
59T-480
60Lake
60MacGregor-22
60NuCard-25
60T-335
61NuCard-425
61P-111
61T-505
62Salada-151
62Shirriff-151
62T-575
65T-556
66OPC-76MG
66T-76
67T-512
68T-294
69T-462
70OPC-346MG
70T-346
71OPC-239MG
71T-239
72OPC-67MG
72T-67
73OPC-497MG
73T-497MG
74Laugh/ASG-50
74OPC-236MG
74T-236MG
75OPC-246MG
75T-246MG
75T/M-246MG
76SSPC-300
76T-581MG
79TCMA-94
81D-431
88Pac/Leg-2
Exh47
R423-97
Schoendienst, Kevin
81QuadC-10
Schoenhaus, Ted
76Cedar
Schofield, John
86Kinston-23
87PortChar-2
Schofield, John R.
(Ducky)
54Hunter
54T-191
55Hunter
55T-143
58T-106
59T-68
60T-104
61Kahn
61T-453
62T-484
63Sugar-E
63T-34
64T-284
65OPC-218
65T-218
66OPC-156M
66T-156M
66T-474
67T-381
68T-588
69OPC-18
69T-18
70OPC-251
70T-251
71MLB/St-282
71OPC-396
71T-396
72MB-310
78TCMA-199
85T-138FS
Schofield, Richard C.
(Dick)
82Danvi-27
84D-35
84F/X-105
84Smok/Cal-25
84T/X-107
85D-329
85F-311
85Smok/Cal-13
85T-138FS
85T-629
86D-133
86F-167
86OPC-311
86Smok/Cal-13
86T-311
87D-283
87D/OD-4
87F-92
87OPC-54
87Seven-W9
87Smok/Cal-15
87T-502
87T/St-176
88D-233
88D/Best-195
88F-504
88Leaf-178
88OPC-43
88Panini/St-45
88RedFoley/St-80
88Score-274
88Smok/Angels-16
88T-43
88T/Big-204
88T/St-177
89B-46
89D-108
89D/Best-251
89F-488
89OPC-286
89Panini/St-294
89Score-16
89T-477
89T/Big-53
89T/St-174
89UD-201
90D-288
90F-144
90Score-44
90T-189
90UD-669
Schooler, Michael
86Wausa-21
87Chatt/Best-8
88Calg/CMC-9
88Calg/Pro-795
88Score/Tr-91T
88T/Tr-105T
89D-637
89D/Best-275
89F-559
89Moth/Sea-25
89Score-528
89Score/HotRk-73
89Score/YS/II-34
89T-199
89ToysRUs-27
89UD-28
90Class-79
90D-330
90F-525
90Score-149
90Sf-187
90T-681
90UD-214
Schoonmaker, Jerry
56T-216
57T-334
Schoonover, Gary
88Idaho/Pro-1836
89BurlB/Pro-1602
89BurlB/Star-20
Schoppee, Dave
81Brist-9
83Pawtu-10
Schorr, Bill
88Butte-8
Schott, Arthur Eugene
R312
W711/1
Schourek, Pete
88LitFalls/Puc-22
89Clmbia/Best-14
89Clmbia/GS-24
Schrammel, Jamie
80GlenF/C-29bb
Schreckengost, Ossie
E107
E91
T206
WG2-42
Schreiber, Bruce
89Princet/Star-20
Schreiber, Marty
84Durhm-27
85Durhm-12
86Osceola-22
Schreiber, Paul
54T-217
Schrenk, Steve
89SoBend/GS-15
Schriver, William
N172
Schroder, Bob
65T-589R
Schroeck, Bob
82ElPas-16
83ElPas-24
84ElPas-3
Schroeder, Alfred W.
(Bill)
81ElPas-13
82Vanco-3
84D-515
84Nes/792-738
84Pol/Brew-21
84T-738
85D-124
85F-594
85Gard-18
85Pol/Brew-21
85T-176
86D-211
86F-501
86Pol/Brew-21
86T-662
87D-486
87D/OD-49
87F-357
87T-302
88D-419
88F-173
88Pol/Brew-21
88Score-311
88T-12
89B-44
89D-644
89T-563
89UD-627
90D-567
90Score-362
90T-244
90UD-149
Schroll, Al
55B-319
59T-546
60L-95
60T-357
62T-102
Schrom, Ken
77QuadC
80SLCty-7
81F-425
81OPC-238R
81Syrac-21
81T-577R
82Syrac-7
83Toled-9
84D-72
84F-572
84Nes/792-11TL
84Nes/792-322
84OPC-322
84T-322
84T/St-308
85D-486
85F-288
85OPC-161
85T-161
86D-635
86F-403
86F/Up-U104
86OhHenry-18
86OPC-71
86T-71
86T/Tr-100T
87D-403
87D/AAS-53
87F-258
87F/Mini-98
87Gator-18
87OPC-171
87S-107
87T-635
87T/St-204
88D-501
88F-614
88OPC-256
88Score-574
88T-256
Schu, Rick
84Cram/PCL-209
85Cram/PCL-34
85D-448
85F/Up-U100
85T/Tr-104T
86D-570
86F-451
86OPC-16
86T-16
86T/St-122
87D-509
87F-188
87T-209
88D-432
88F-316
88French-25
88Score-448
88T-731
88T/Big-122
89D-406
89F-619
89Mara/Tigers-35
89OPC-352
89RedFoley/St-105
89RochR/CMC-23
89RochR/Pro-1642
89Score-452
89T-352
89T/Big-164
89T/Tr-112T
89UD-490
90D-599
90T-498
Schuble, Henry
33G-4
35G-1H
35G-3F
35G-5F
35G-6F
R337-411
V353-4
Schuckert, Wayne
81AppFx-12
82AppFx-17
83GlenF-19
Schueler, Ron
73OPC-169
73T-169
74JP
74OPC-544
74T-544
74T/Tr-544T
75OPC-292
75T-292
75T/M-292
76OPC-586
76T-586
77T-337
78T-409
79T-686
Schueler, Russ
87BurlEx-14
Schugel, Jeff
84Visal-14
85Visal-6
Schuler, Dave
77Watlo
78Cr/PCL-103
79SLCty-17
80SLCty-6
81SLCty-11
82Omaha-8
83Omaha-9
85Richm-8
86Omaha-19
86Omaha/TCMA-19
87Denver-11
88Vermont/Pro-941
Schulmerich, Wes
34Exh/4-6
34G-54
88Conlon/NatAS-17
Schult, Art
53T-167

58T-58
60L-123
60T-93
79TCMA-253

Schulte, Frank
10Domino-108
11Helmar-104
12Sweet/Pin-90
14CJ-101
15CJ-101
BF2-67
D328-152
D329-156
D350/2-158
E135-152
E254
E270/1
E90/3
E91
M101/4-156
M101/5-158
M116
S74-68
T202
T204
T205
T206
T207
T213/blue
T215/blue
T215/brown
T222
T3-117
W514-10
WG4-25

Schulte, Fred
28Exh-60
29Exh/4-30
31Exh/4-29
33G-112
33G-190
35BU-50
35Exh/4-16
R316

Schulte, Joe
86Ashvl-26
87Osceola-14

Schulte, John
33G-186
40PB-12
44Yank/St-23

Schulte, Mark
84ArkTr-13
86ArkTr-22
87FtMyr-12

Schulte, Todd
83BurlR-10
83BurlR/LF-2

Schultz, Bob D.
52T-401
53T-144
54B-59

Schultz, Charles
(Buddy)
78T-301
79T-532
80T-601
82ArkTr-9

Schultz, George
(Barney)
62T-89
62T/St-110
63T-452
65OPC-28
65T-28
66Pep/Tul
73OPC-497CO
73T-497C
74OPC-236CO
74T-236C
78TCMA-15

Schultz, Greg
83Albuq-18
84Cram/PCL-157
85Cram/PCL-196

Schultz, Joseph
(Dode)
47TipTop
62Kahn/Atl
69T-254
73OPC-323CO
73T-323CO
89Pac/Leg-162
E120
V61-114
W572
W573

Schultz, Scott
87Lakel-5

Schultz, Ted
76AppFx

Schulz, Harry
75Clint

Schulz, Jeff
83Butte-28
86Omaha-20
86Omaha/TCMA-6
87Omaha-23
88Omaha/CMC-15
88Omaha/Pro-1508
89Omaha/CMC-22
89Omaha/Pro-1736

Schulze, Don
81QuadC-29
83IowaC-9
84IowaC-22
84Wheat/Ind-37
85D-639
85F-454
85T-93
86OhHenry-37
86T-542
87BuffB-22
87F-259
87T-297
87Tidew-25
87Tidew/TCMA-26
88T-131
88Toled/CMC-3
88Toled/Pro-604
89Colum/CMC-6
89Colum/Pol-19
89Colum/Pro-753
89Tidew/CANDL-11

Schumacher, Hal
33G-129
33G-240
35BU-110
35BU-52
35G-1K
35G-3B
35G-4B
35G-5B
36Wheat
38ONG/Pin-26
39PB-73
40PB-85
48Swell-7
61F-137
88Conlon/NatAS-18
V355-23

Schumacher, Roy
81AppFx-11

Schumate, Jack
79Wisco-22

Schunk, Jerry
87Duned-25
88Duned/Star-16
89Knoxv/Best-23
89Knoxv/Pro-1142
89Knoxv/Star-19

Schupp, Ferdie
D328-153
E121/120
E121/80
E122
E135-153
W575

Schurr, Wayne
64T-548R
65OPC-149
65T-149

Schuster, Bill
47Signal

Schuster, Mark
79Holyo-7
80Holyo-3
81Vanco-5
82ElPas-8
84Cram/PCL-7
85Cram/PCL-185

Schwab, Ken
80Clint-8

Schwabe, Mike
88GlenF/Pro-927
89F/Up-32
89London/Pro-1375

Schwall, Don
62Bz
62J-64
62P-64
62P/Can-64
62Salada-210
62Shirriff-210
62T-35
62T/bucks
62T/St-19
63Sugar-C
63T-344
64T-558
65T-362
66OPC-144
66T-144
67T-267
78TCMA-118

Schwaner, Tom
62Pep/Tul

Schwarber, Mike
80Batav-10
81Watlo-15
82Chatt-10

Schwartz, Randy
67OPC-33R
67T-33R

Schwarz, Jeff
88WinSal/Star-19
89Hagers/Best-24
89Hagers/Pro-263
89Hagers/Star-16

Schwarz, Tom
86Visal-19
87Orlan-18
88Readg/Pro-863

Schweighoffer, Mike
85VeroB-18
87SnAnt-13
88SnAnt/Best-10

Schweitzer, Al
M116

Schwerman, Brian
77Charl
78Charl

Scioscia, Mike
77Clint
79Albuq-10
80Albuq-26
81F-131
81Pol/Dodg-14
81T-302R
82D-598
82F-22
82OPC-173
82Pol/Dodg
82Pol/Dodg-14
82T-642
83D-75
83F-221
83Pol/Dodg-14
83T-352
84F-113
84Nes/792-64
84Pol/Dodg-14
84T-64
85D-459
85F-385
85Leaf-118
85T-549
85T/St-79
86D-93
86F-144
86Leaf-87
86OPC-111
86Pol/Dodg-14
86S-167
86T-468
86T/St-68
87D-130
87D/OD-82
87F-454
87Leaf-123
87Moth/Dodg-10
87OPC-144
87Pol/Dodg-6
87S-151M
87S-67
87Seven-W12
87T-144
87T/St-73
88D-106
88D/Best-260
88F-524
88Leaf-97
88Moth/Dodg-10
88OPC-225
88Panini/St-307
88Pol/Dodg-14
88Score-53
88Sf-110
88T-225
88T/Big-72
88T/St-67
89B-342
89D-77
89D/Best-66
89F-71
89F/AS-9
89F/WS-4
89Moth/Dodg-3
89OPC-7
89Panini/St-104
89Pol/Dodg-9
89Score-121
89Sf-138
89Smok/Dodg-31
89T-669TL
89T-755
89T/Big-281
89T/St-58
89UD-116
90D-316
90F-407
90Score-398
90Score/100St-48
90Sf-163
90T-605
90UD-298

Sconiers, Daryl
80ElPas-14
81SLCty-20
82T-653R
83D-141
83T/X-99
84D-451
84F-528
84F/St-112
84Nes/792-27
84Smok/Cal-26
84T-27
85D-620
85F-312
85OPC-256
85T-604
86F-168
86SanJose-18
86T-193
87SanJose-28
88Vanco/CMC-22
88Vanco/Pro-766

Score, Herb
55Gol/Ind-26
55Salem
56T-140
57T-50
58T-352
58T-495AS
59Kahn
59T-88
60Kahn
60T-360
60T/tatt
60T/tatt-48
61T-185
61T-337M
61Union
62T-116
79TCMA-134
86Indianap-24
89Pac/Leg-126
89Swell-114
Exh47

Scott, Charles
86Watlo-25
88ColSp/CMC-9
88ColSp/Pro-1529
89ColrSp/CMC-8

Scott, Craig
89Kingspt/Star-21

Scott, Dale
88Umpire-58
89Umpires-56

Scott, Darryl
88CapeCod/Sum-34

Scott, Dick
82Colum-15
85Albany-19
87Colum-17
88Albany/Pro-1350
89Tacom/CMC-20
89Tacom/Pro-1554

Scott, Donald M.
(Donnie)
80Ashev-21
81Tulsa-13
82Tulsa-11
83OKCty-23
84OKCty-19
84Rang-43
85Cram/PCL-81
85D-544
85F-568
85T-496
85T/Tr-105T
86F-474
86RochR-19
86T-568
87ElPas-3
88ElPas/Best-2
89Denver/CMC-6
89Denver/Pro-52

Scott, Floyd
(Pete)
33G-70
V354-33

Scott, Gary
89Geneva/Pro-1877

Scott, George
66T-558R
67OPC-75
67T-75

67T/Test/RSox-16
68Bz-7
68Coke
68T-233
68T/G-22
69MLB/St-17
69T-574
69T/St-138
70MLB/St-165
70OPC-385
70T-385
71MD
71MLB/St-331
71OPC-9
71T-9
71T/Coins-98
72MB-311
72T-585
73OPC-263
73T-263
73T/Comics-18
73T/Lids-47
73T/PinUps-18
74OPC-27
74T-27
74T/DE-30
74T/St-199
75Ho-26
75Ho/Twink-26
75OPC-360
75T-360
75T/M-360
76A&P/Milw
76Ho-54
76Ho/Twink-54
76K-21
76OPC-15
76OPC-194LL
76OPC-196LL
76SSPC-237
76T-15
76T-194LL
76T-196LL
77Ho-148
77OPC-210
77T-255
78Ho-24
78OPC-12
78PapaG/Disc-15
78T-125
79OPC-340 DP
79T-645
80T-414
PM10/Sm-175

Scott, James
11Helmar-15
14CJ-26
15CJ-26
BF2-18
D329-158
D350/2-159
M101/4-158
M101/5-159
M116
T205
T206
W501-30
WG4-26

Scott, Jeff
77Ashev

Scott, Jim
86Vermont-17

Scott, John H.
75OPC-616R
75T-616R
75T/M-616R
76SSPC-131
77OPC-94
77T-473R
78T-547

Scott, John William
W515-25

Scott, Kelly
83Nashvl-19
84Colum-19
84Colum/Pol-22
85Colum-9
85Colum/Pol-19

Scott, Kevin
89AubAs/Pro-2183

Scott, L. Everett
21Exh-153
21Exh-154
D327
D328-154
D329-157
D350/2-160
E120
E121/120
E121/80
E122
E135-154
E220
M101/4-157
M101/5-160
V100
W512-7
W514-90
W515-46
W575

Scott, Mark
59HRDerby-17ANN

Scott, Mark
80Charl-2

Scott, Martin
(Marty)
79Tucso-10
81Tulsa-4
82BurlR-25MG
83Tulsa-25

Scott, Michael Warren
(Mike)
78Tidew
79Tidew-15
80T-681R
80Tidew-23
81D-37
81T-109
82D-128
82F-535
82T-246TL
82T-432
83F-554
83T-679
83T/X-100
84D-136
84F-240
84Moth/Ast-14
84Nes/792-559
84T-559
85D-258
85F-361
85Moth/Ast-18
85OPC-17
85T-17
86D-476
86D/HL-46
86F-311
86F/Mini-66
86F/St-108
86Leaf-235
86Pol/Ast-3
86S-195
86T-268
86T/St-27
87Class-81
87Class/Up-123
87D-163
87D-18DK
87D/AAS-32
87D/AS/Wax-PC13
87D/DKsuper-18
87D/OD-15
87Drake-33
87F-630M
87F-68
87F/AwardWin-37
87F/McCror-38
87F/Mini-99
87F/RecSet-36
87F/Slug-38
87F/St-108
87Ho/St-10
87Jiffy-18
87KayBee-30
87Kraft-4
87Leaf-18DK
87Leaf-258
87MnM's-18
87Moth/Ast-2
87OPC-330
87Pol/Ast-11
87S-119M
87S-120M
87S-19
87Smok/NL-5
87T-330
87T/Coins-44
87T/HL-18
87T/Mini-11
87T/St-15LCS
87T/St-35
87Woolwth-18
88ChefBoy-19
88Class/Blue-221
88D-112
88D-BC12
88D/AS-40
88D/Best-206
88D/PopUp-18
88F-456
88F-632M
88F/AwardWin-36
88F/BB/AS-37
88F/BB/MVP-32
88F/Excit-35
88F/Hottest-35
88F/LL-36
88F/Mini-80
88F/RecSet-36
88F/Slug-37
88F/SS-34
88F/St-89
88F/TL-35
88KingB/Disc-13
88KMart-26
88Leaf-54
88Moth/Ast-2
88OPC-227
88Panini/St-233
88Panini/St-289
88Pol/Ast-21
88RedFoley/St-81
88Score-335
88Score/WaxBox-18
88Sf-66
88T-760
88T/Big-140
88T/Coins-54
88T/Gloss22-21
88T/Gloss60-5
88T/Mini-51
88T/RiteAid-4
88T/St-154FOIL
88T/St-30
88T/St/Backs-26
88T/UK-68
89B-322
89Class-23
89D-69
89D/Best-94
89D/MVP-BC2
89F-367
89F/BBMVP's-34
89F/LL-34
89F/Superstar-37
89Lennox/Ast-4
89Moth/Ast-2
89OPC-180
89Panini/St-84
89RedFoley/St-106
89Score-550
89Score/HotSt-60
89Score/Mast-4
89Sf-120
89T-180
89T/Big-51
89T/Mini-14
89T/St-15
89UD-295
90Class-29
90D-207
90F-237
90F-636M
90Score-40
90Score-692 DT
90Score/100St-97
90Sf-55
90T-405AS
90T-460
90UD-125
90UD-88TC

Scott, Michael Wm.
87Greenv/Bst-28

Scott, Ralph
(Mickey)
70T-669R
72T-724R
73OPC-553
73T-553
76OPC-276
76T-276
77T-401
78Colum

Scott, Rodney
76SSPC-172
78T-191
79T-86
80OPC-360
80T-712
81D-209
81F-155
81OPC-227
81OPC/Post-2
81T-204M
81T-539
81T/St-185
82D-240
82F-207
82F/St-38
82OPC-259
82OPC/Post-14
82T-259

Scott, Tary
85Greens-3
86FSLAS-43
86WinHav-21
87NewBrit-22

Scott, Tim
83Cedar-8
83Cedar/LF-3
87Hawai-14
87SnAnt-4
88Bakers/Cal-258
89SnAnt/Best-24

Scott, Tony
76SSPC-339
78T-352
79T-143
80OPC-17
80T-33
81Coke
81D-191
81F-531
81T-165
81T/St-223
81T/Tr-828
82D-522
82F-231
82F/St-46
82T-698
83D-293
83F-465
83T-507
84D-527
84F-241
84Moth/Ast-20
84Nes/792-292
84T-292
85OPC-367
85T-733

Scranton, Jim
84Omaha-27
85Omaha-17
86Omaha-21
86Omaha/TCMA-7

Scripture, Billy
78Charl

Scrivener, Wayne
(Chuck)
77T-173
78T-94

Scruggs, Ron
86AppFx-21
87Penin-25

Scruggs, Tony
88CharlR/Star-22
89Tulsa/GS-24

Scudder, Bill
83VeroB-10
85Cram/PCL-166

Scudder, Scott
87Cedar-7
88Cedar/Pro-1157
88MidwLAS/GS-14
89F/Up-87
89Nashvl-22
89Nashvl/CMC-8
89Nashvl/Pro-1293
89Score/Tr-99
90D-435
90F-434
90Score-518
90Score/100Ris-65
90T-553
90UD-164

Scull, Angel
53Briggs
54T-204

Scurry, Rod
76Shrev
78Colum
79Portl-22
81F-380
81T-194
82D-185
82F-497
82T-207
83D-376
83F-322
83T-537
84D-235
84F-264
84Nes/792-69
84T-69
85D-142
85F-476
85T-641
86T-449
87D-374
87F-113
87OPC-393
87T-665
88Calg/CMC-10
88Calg/Pro-779
89Score-516
89UD-208

Seabaugh
E254

Seal, Mike
89Myrtle/Pro-1461
Seals, Joey
89GreatF-15
Sealy, Randy
75Shreve/TCMA-19
76Shrev
80WHave-23
Seaman, Kim
77Wausa
81Hawai-22
82Hawai-22
82Wichi-17
Seanez, Rudy
87Watlo-18
88Watlo/Pro-692
89Kinston/Star-23
90F-640
Searage, Ray
77StPet
79ArkTr-20
81Tidew-24
82Charl-10
82T-478
84Cram/PCL-30
85F-595
85Pol/Brew-41
86D-536
86F-502
86T-642
86Vanco-23
87Coke/WS-21
87F-506
87T-149
88Albuq/CMC-4
88Albuq/Pro-262
88D-429
88F-409
88T-788
89F/Up-94
89Moth/Dodg-22
89Pol/Dodg-30
90D-649
90F-408
90T-84
Searcy, Steve
86GlenF-21
87Toled-2
87Toled/TCMA-16
88Toled/CMC-4
88Toled/Pro-609
89B-95
89Class-78
89D-29RR
89F-145
89Score-627
89Score/HotRk-47
89Score/YS/II-27
89T-167FS
89UD/Ext-764
90F-615
90Score/100Ris-97
90T-487
90UD-575
Sears, Allen
83Durhm-23
Sears, Ken
44Yank/St-24
Sears, Mike
86FSLAS-44TR
86WinHav-22TR
87WinHav-19
Seaton, Tom
14CJ-100
15CJ-100
D329-159
D350/2-161
M101/4-159
M101/5-161
Seats, Dean
81Cedar-13
Seats, Tom
49B/PCL-35
Seaver, Tom
67T-581R
68OPC-45
68T-45
69MB-250
69MLB/St-170
69NTF
69T-480
69T/decal
69T/S-52
69T/St-68
69Trans-48
70K-7
70MB-26
70MLB/St-82
70OPC-195NLCS
70OPC-300
70OPC-69LL
70T-300
70T-69LL
70T/S-5
70T/SO
70Trans-4
70Trans/M-21
71Bz/Test-35
71K-2
71MD
71MLB/St-164
71MLB/St-574
71OPC-160
71OPC-68LL
71OPC-72LL
71T-160
71T-68LL
71T-72LL
71T/Coins-127
71T/S-53
71T/tatt-14
71T/tatt-14a
72K-1
72MB-312
72OPC-347KP
72OPC-445
72OPC-446IA
72OPC-91LL
72OPC-93LL
72OPC-95LL
72T-347BP
72T-445
72T-446A
72T-91LL
72T-93LL
72T-95LL
72T/Post-13
73K-46
73OPC-350
73T-350
73T/Comics-19
73T/Lids-48
73T/PinUps-19
74K-52
74Laugh/ASG-68
74OPC-206LL
74OPC-207LL
74OPC-80
74T-206LL
74T-207LL
74T-80
74T/DE-9
74T/Puzzles-10
74T/St-70
75Ho-75
75OPC-370
75T-370
75T/M-370
76Crane-55
76Ho-35
76Ho/Twink-35
76K-32
76MSA/Disc
76OPC-199LL
76OPC-201LL
76OPC-203LL
76OPC-5RB
76OPC-600
76SSPC-551
76T-199LL
76T-201LL
76T-203LL
76T-5M
76T-600
77Ho-7
77OPC-205
77OPC-6LL
77Pep-67
77T-150
77T-6LL
77T/CS-42
78Ho-149
78K-27
78OPC-120
78T-450
78Wiffle/Discs-68
79Ho-65
79K-29
79OPC-44DP
79T-100
79T/Comics-22
80BK/PHR-10
80K-49
80OPC-260
80T-500
80T/S-15
81Coke
81D-422
81D-425
81F-200
81F/St-49
81K-38
81MSA/Disc-29
81OPC-220
81T-220
81T/HT
81T/Nat/Super-14
81T/S
81T/So-107
81T/St-165
82Coke/Red
82D-148
82D-16DK
82D-628M
82F-645M
82F-82
82F/St-11
82K-8
82OPC-30
82OPC-31IA
82OPC-346AS
82Sqt-21
82T-165LL
82T-30
82T-31M
82T-346AS
82T-756TL
82T/St-36
82T/St-9
83D-122
83F-601
83OPC-354SV
83OPC-52
83T-580
83T-581A
83T/St-233
83T/X-101
84D-116
84D/AAS-53
84D/Champs-40
84F-595
84F/X-106
84FunFood/Pin-15
84Nes/792-246TL
84Nes/792-706LL
84Nes/792-707LL
84Nes/792-708LL
84Nes/792-740
84OPC-261
84Ralston-8
84Seven-8E
84T-706
84T-707
84T-708
84T-740
84T/Cereal-8
84T/St-106
84T/X-108
84TrueVal/WS-27
85Coke/WS-41
85D-424
85D/HL-1
85D/HL-30
85Drake-41
85F-526
85F/LimEd-34
85F/St-68SA
85F/St-69
85F/St-70
85F/St-71
85F/St-72
85F/St-73
85Leaf-101
85OPC-1
85Seven-12G
85T-670
85T/3D-30
85T/St-235
85T/Super-31
86Coke/WS-41
86D-609
86F-216
86F-630M
86F/HOF-3
86F/LL-40
86F/Mini-46
86F/Slug-34
86F/St-109
86Jay's-16
86Leaf-234
86OPC-390
86Quaker-32
86S-130M
86S-134M
86S-142M
86S-182M
86S-25
86S-56M
86S-67M
86S-70M
86S/Dec-52
86S/Rook-47M
86T-390
86T-402M
86T/Gloss60-22
86T/St-10
86T/St-287
86T/Super-50
86T/Tr-101T
86TrueVal-12
87D-375
87F-45
87KMart-21
87Leaf-263
87OPC-49
87S-28
87T-425
87T/St-246
Seay, Dick
78Laugh/Black-14
Seay, Mark
87SanJose-16
Sebra, Bob
83TriCit-1
85OKCty-19
86Indianap-23
87D-468
87F-331
87Leaf-213
87OPC-314
87T-479
88AAA/Pro-17
88D-458
88F-195
88Indi/CMC-3
88Indi/Pro-511
88OPC-93
88Score-337
88T-93
89ScrWB/CMC-4
89ScrWB/Pro-718
Sebring, James
T204
Secory, Frank
55B-286ump
Secrest, Charlie
59T-140
Secrist, Don
69T-654R
Sedar, Ed
83AppFx/LF-18
86Penin-24
87DayBe-19
See, Larry
82VeroB-20
84Cram/PCL-162
86Albuq-22
87Albuq/Pol-21
89Toled/CMC-14
89Toled/Pro-784
Seeburger, John
88Oneon/Pro-2050
89FtLaud/Star-25
Seeds, Robert Ira
32Orbit/un-52
33Exh/4-10
39PB-32
40PB-91
R305
R314/Can
V355-27
Seeger, Mark
81AppFx-24
Seegers, Pat
78Newar
79BurlB-3
Seelbach, Chuck
73OPC-51
73T-51
74OPC-292
74T-292
Seerey, James Pat
48L-73
Seery, John Emmett
N172
N284
WG1-35
Segelke, Herman
82IowaC-23
83Phoen/BHN-13
84Cram/PCL-10
Segrist, Kal
58Union
Segui, David
88Hagers/Star-19
89Freder/Star-21
Segui, Diego
61Union
63T-157
64T-508
64T/Coins-24
65OPC-197
65T-197
65T/E-24
65T/trans-68
66T-309
68T-517
69T-511
70OPC-2

70T-2
71MLB/St-526
71OPC-215
71OPC-67LL
71T-215
71T-67LL
72T-735
73OPC-383
73T-383
74OPC-151
74T-151
74T/Tr-151T
75OPC-232
75T-232
75T/M-232
76SSPC-423
77T-653
88Poca/Pro-2100
89Everett/Star-31

Segura, Jose
85Kingst-10
86Knoxv-19
87Syrac-9
87Syrac/TCMA-7
88Coke/WS-27
88F/U-U20
89Vanco/CMC-6
89Vanco/Pro-591

Seibert, Gib
85Cram/PCL-27
87Maine-15
87Maine/TCMA-16

Seibert, Kurt
80Toled-20
81Toled-14

Seibold, Henry
33DH-38
R316

Seidel, Dick
83Greens-12

Seidensticker, Andy
88Visal/Cal-172
88Visal/Pro-106

Seidholz, Don
78Knoxv
79Knoxv/TCMA-9

Seifert, Keith
87Watlo-21
88Watlo/Pro-678

Seilheimer, Rick
80GlenF/B-7
80GlenF/C-8
81GlenF-9
82Edmon-21

Seirra, Ernie
89SanJose/Best-30

Seitz, Charles
T206

Seitz, David
86Sumter-25

Seitzer, Kevin
83Butte-20
85FtMyr-9
86Omaha-22
86Omaha/TCMA-3
87Class/Up-139
87D/HL-26
87D/HL-47
87D/OD-207
87D/Rook-15
87F-652M
87F/Slug-39
87F/U-U108
87S-158M
87S/Rook-20
87T/Tr-111T
88Class/Blue-218
88Class/Red-159
88D-280
88D-BC17
88D/AS-27
88D/Best-175
88F-270
88F-C12
88F/AwardWin-37
88F/BB/AS-38
88F/BB/MVP-33
88F/Excit-36
88F/Hottest-36
88F/LL-37
88F/Mini-27
88F/RecSet-37
88F/Slug-38
88F/SS-35
88F/St-33
88F/TL-36
88F/WaxBox-C12
88KMart-27
88Leaf-105
88MSA/Disc-8
88OPC-275
88Panini/St-108
88Panini/St-436
88Score-6
88Score/YS/I-10
88Sf-17
88Sf/Gamewin-13
88Smok/Royals-21
88T-275
88T/Big-115
88T/Gloss60-9
88T/JumboR-9
88T/Mini-15
88T/Revco-22
88T/RiteAid-19
88T/St-261
88T/St-306
88T/UK-69
88ToysRUs-27
89B-123
89Cadaco-52
89Class-65
89D-10DK
89D-238
89D/Best-207
89D/DKsuper-10DK
89F-292
89F/Excit-36
89F/Heroes-36
89F/WaxBox-C22
89Holsum/Discs-9
89Nissen-9
89OPC-58
89Panini/St-357
89RedFoley/St-107
89Score-55
89Score/HotSt-17
89Sf-55
89T-670
89T/Big-313
89T/St-264
89Tastee/Discs-2
89UD-510
90D-85
90F-117
90Score-199
90Score/100St-88
90Sf-46
90T-435
90UD-363

Selbach, Albert
(Kip)
E107

Selby
E254

Selig, Kevin
76AppFx

Selkirk, George
34DS-88
37OPC-108
38ONG/Pin-27
39PB-25
40PB-8
V300
V355-11

Sellas, Marcelino
88CapeCod/Sum-91

Sellers, Jeff
86D/Rook-29
86Pawtu-21
87D-544
87F-46
87Leaf-158
87T-12
88D-585
88D/RedSox/Bk-585
88F-366
88Score-541
88T-653
89B-299
89D-517
89Nashvl/Pro-1270
89Score-491
89T-544

Sellers, Rick
89NiagFls/Puc-21

Sellheimer, Rick
85BuffB-5

Sellick, John
88SALAS/GS-25
88Savan/Pro-347
89Sprin/Best-14

Sellner, Scott
88Bill/Pro-1807
89Cedar/Best-17
89Cedar/Pro-925
89Cedar/Star-18

Sells, Dave
74OPC-37
74T-37

Sells, George
88CapeCod/Sum-117

Selma, Dick
66OPC-67R
66T-67R
67T-386
68T-556
69MLB/St-195
69OPC-197
69T-197
69T/decal
69T/S-62
69T/St-98
70MLB/St-23
70OPC-24
70T-24
71K-21
71MLB/St-187
71OPC-705
71T-705
72T-726
73T-632
73OPC-632

Seltzer, Randy
76AppFx
77AppFx

Semall, Paul
79Colum-3
80Wichi-15
83OKCty-16
84Cram/PCL-125
85Cram/PCL-232

Sember, Mike
79Syrac-10

Sembera, Carroll
66T-539R
67OPC-136
67T-136
68T-207
69T-351

Sementelli, Chris
89Spart/Pro-1049

Semerano, Bob
77Charl

Seminara, Frank
88Oneon/Pro-2071
89Oneon/Pro-2121
89PrWill/Star-18

Seminick, Andy
49B-30
49Eureka-146
49Lummis
49Royal-7
50B-121
51B-51
51BR-C7
51T/RB-45
52Dix
52Royal
52T-297
53B/BW-7
53Dix
53T-153
54B-172
55B-93
56T-296
Exh47
PM10/Sm-176

Semprini, John
82Jacks-9
84Chatt-12

Semproch, Ramon
58T-474
59T-197
60T-286
61T-174
61T/St-206

Sempsrott, Ed
76Watlo
77DaytB

Senne, Michael
87StPet-9
88ArkTr/GS-25
89Shreve/Pro-1840

Senne, Tim
86Visal-20
87Visal-14

Senteney, Steve
82Syrac-8
83D-52
83Tidew-10

Sentlinger, Rick
77QuadC

Seoane, Manny
76OkCty
80Wichi-21
81Evans-7

Seoane, Mitch
84Greens-25
86PalmSp/Smok-24
87MidldA-20
89QuadC/Best-25
89QuadC/GS-2

Sepanek, Rob
86FtLaud-20
87PrWill-10
88Albany/Pro-1332
89Albany/Best-9
89Albany/Pro-330
89Albany/Star-17

Sepela, Thom
86Elmir-21
87Elmir-20
87Elmir/Red-20

Seppala, L.
33SK-48

Sepulveda, Jorge
86VeroB-22

Serad, William
N172

Serafini, Rudy
83QuadC-14

Serena, Bill
50B-230
51B-246
52T-325
53B/Col-122
54B-93
55B-233

Serna, Paul
81LynnS-18
82D-567
83Chatt-2
83T-492
84Chatt-13
85Cram/PCL-79
86Wausa-23

Serna, Ramon
87ElPas-25
88ElPas/Best-7

Serra, Armando
88StCath/Pro-2037

Serrano, Andy
79Elmir-17

Serrano, Marty
77DaytB

Serritella, John
83Butte-10
83CharR-23

Serum, Gary
79T-627
80T-61
80Toled-5
82OrlTw/B-23

Servais, Scott
88T/Tr-106TOLY
89Osceola/Star-20
89Star/Wax-17
89T/Big-291

Service, Scott
88Readg/Pro-868
89F-653M
89Readg/Best-6
89Readg/Pro-657
89Readg/Star-23
90UD-35

Servoss, Bob
76Wmspt

Sevcik, John
65T-597

Severeid, Henry
21Exh-155
25Exh-116
28Exh/PCL-24
D327
D328-155
E120
E121/80
E122
E135-155
T207
V100
V61-25
W572
W573
W575

Severinsen, Al
70OPC-477R
70T-477R
71MLB/St-238
71OPC-747R
71T-747R
72OPC-274
72T-274
72T/Cloth-28

Severns, Bill
77Holyo
79Vanco-21
80Vanco-8

Severson, Rich
71MLB/St-430
71OPC-103
71T-103

Sewell, Joseph
(Joe)
21Exh-156
25Exh-85
26Exh-84
28Exh-43
28Yueng-10

29Exh/4-21
32Orbit/num-116
33G-165
61F-76
72Laugh/GF-40
80SSPC/HOF
89HOF/St-22
89Pac/Leg-125
E120
E121/120
R316
V100
V117-12
V353-89
V61-12
W501-16
W502-10
W507-46
WG7-47

Sewell, Luke
29Exh/4-22
31Exh/4-22
33Exh/4-11
33G-114
33G-163
35BU-155
35G-1F
35G-2F
35G-6F
35G-7F
38Exh/4-10
39PB-5
40PB-48
49Eureka-94
51B-322
52B-94
61F-138
E220
R312/M
R314
R316
V353-91
V355-62
W753

Sewell, T. Rip
47TipTop
49B-234
49Eureka-172
89Pac/Leg-202
Exh47

Sexton, Jimmy
75Shreve/TCMA-20
76Shrev
77SnJos-22
79T-232
80T-11
80Tucso-2
81Tacom-15
82Tacom-38
83D-449
83F-533
83T-709

Sexton, Wayne
(Twink)
79Jacks-4

Seybold, Ralph
E107
E254
E91

Seyfried, Gordon
64T-499R

Seymour, Bob
82VeroB-25

Seymour, James B.
(Cy)
C46-38
E104
E254
E91
M116
T201
T206
WG3-42

Seymour, Paul
81Batav-29

Seymour, Winston
89Salem/Star-20
89Well/Puc-21

Sferrazza, Vince
86Fres/Smk-3tr
87Shrev-23
88Shreve/Pro-1284
89Sprin/Best-26

Sferrazza, Matt
86Jaxvl/TCMA-13
87GlenF-13

Shabosky, Brian
88CapeCod-7
88CapeCod/Sum-186

Shaddy, Chris
83Knoxv-14
86Knoxv-20
87Knoxv-2
88Syrac/CMC-22
88Syrac/Pro-833
89Richm/CMC-22
89Richm/Ko-10
89Richm/Pro-824

Shade, Mike
(Mick)
83Sprin/LF-11
85Louvl-24
87Jaxvl-14
88Jaxvl/Best-2
88Jaxvl/Pro-985

Shade, Steve
86Erie-26

Shafer
11Helmar-136

Shafer, Frank T.
N172

Shafer, George
N172

Shaffer, Duane
78Knoxv
79AppFx-21
80GlenF/C-24C
80GlenF/C-25C

Shambaugh, Mike
88Boise/Pro-1611

Shamblin, Bill
87Kinston-1
88Reno/Cal-272

Shamsky, Art
65T-398R
66OPC-119
66T-119
67Kahn
67OPC-96
67T-96
68Kahn
68T-292
69MB-251
69T-221
69T/St-69
70OPC-137
70T-137
70Trans/M-23
71MLB/St-165
71OPC-445
71T-445
71T/Coins-43
72MB-313
72OPC-353
72T-353
72T/Cloth-29
78TCMA-278

Shanahan, Paul
(Greg)
74OPC-599R
74T-599R

Shanks, Howard S.
(Hank)
21Exh-157
D328-156
D329-160
D350/2-162
E120
E135-156
M101/4-160
M101/5-162
V100

Shanks, Willie
85Kingst-11
86Ventura-24

Shannon, Dan
89Hamil/Star-23

Shannon, Daniel
N172

Shannon, Maurice J.
E220

Shannon, Mike
61Union
62Kahn/Atl
64T-262R
65OPC-43
65T-43
66T-293
67T-605
68T-445
69MB-252
69MLB/St-215
69OPC-110
69T-110
69T/St-120
70MLB/St-143
70T-614
71MLB/St-283
71OPC-735
71T-735
72MB-314
78TCMA-275

Shannon, Robert
86Jamestn-22

Shannon, Thomas L.
88Rockford-32
89Rockford-32GM

Shannon, Wally
60L-93

Shannon, William P.
T206

Shantz, Bobby
50B-234
51B-227
52Dix-53
52RM-AL20
52StarCal/L-76C
52T-219
53B/Col-11
53NB
53RM-AL20
53T-225
54B-19
54T-21
55B-139M
55B-140
55Rodeo
56Rodeo
56T-261
57T-272
58T-289M
58T-419
59T-222
60T-315
61P-15
61T-379
61T-473MV
61T/St-198
62Salada-188
62Shirriff-188
62T-177
62T/bucks
62T/St-128
63T-533
64T-278
75OPC-190M
75T-190MV
75T/M-190MV
79TCMA-171
88Pac/Leg-61
89Smok/Ast-7
89Swell-131
PM10/Sm-177
PM10/Sm-178
Rawl

Shantz, Wilmer
55B-139M
55B-175
55Rodeo
56Rodeo

Sharitt, Kelly
89Oneon/Pro-2108

Sharko, Gary
89Clint/Pro-887

Sharon, Dick
74OPC-48
74T-48
75OPC-293
75T-293
75T/M-293

Sharp, Bill
74OPC-519
74T-519
75OPC-373
75T-373
75T/M-373
76A&P/Milw
76OPC-244
76SSPC-246
76T-244
77Spoka

Sharp, Gary
82BurlR-9

Sharpe, Bayard
C46-31
M116
T205
T206

Sharperson, Mike
85Syrac-19
86Syrac-22
87D-565
87D/OD-31
87Tor/Fire-27
87Tor/Fire-27
88Albuq/CMC-16
88Albuq/Pro-253
88F-525
88Pol/Dodg-27M
89Albuq/CMC-14
89Albuq/Pro-59
89B-348
89F-72
89Pol/Dodg-17
89Score-602
90D-603
90T-117

Sharpnack, Bob
86Modesto-22
87Madis-25
88Huntsvl/BK-18
89Huntsvl/Best-11

Sharsig, William J.
N172

Sharts, Stephen
85Bend/Cram-22
87Clearw-16
88Readg/Pro-865
89Readg/Best-5
89Readg/Pro-651

Shaughnessy, Francis
(Shag)
R314/Can
T206
V355-78

Shaver, Jeff
86Madis-21
86Madis/Pol-18
88Tacom/CMC-8
88Tacom/Pro-619
89Tacom/CMC-11
89Tacom/Pro-1559

Shaw, Al
T206

Shaw, Bob
58T-206
59T-159
60L-83
60T-380
61P-23
61T-352
61T/St-127
62T-109
62T/St-56
63J-154
63P-154
63Salada-7
63T-255
63T-5LL
64T-328
65T-428
65T/E-57
66T-260
67Kahn
67T-470
73OPC-646CO
73T-646C

Shaw, Cedrick
88Butte-9

Shaw, Don
67T-587R
68T-521
69OPC-183
69T-183
70OPC-476
70T-476
71OPC-654
71T-654
72OPC-479
72T-479
88SanDiegoSt-16

Shaw, Jeff
87Watlo-16
88Wmspt/Pro-1309
89Canton/Best-3
89Canton/Pro-1298
89Canton/Star-19

Shaw, John W.
N172

Shaw, Kerry
88SLCty-17
89Salin/Cal-144
89Salin/Pro-1803

Shaw, Kevin
88AppFx/Pro-140
89BBCity/Star-8
89Star/Wax-63

Shaw, Rick
82Amari-22

Shaw, Robert
C46-83

Shaw, Royal N.
T206

Shaw, Samuel E.
N172

Shaw, Scott
86FtLaud-21
87FtLaud-7
88Albany/Pro-1345
89Albany/Best-4
89Albany/Pro-317
89Albany/Star-18

Shaw, Theo
81CharR-8
84Omaha-17
85FtMyr-20
86Omaha-23
86Omaha/TCMA-20
87Memph-15
87Memph/Best-12

88Wmspt/Pro-1318
89ColSp/Pro-259

Shawkey, J. Bob
15CJ-164
25Exh-102
26Exh-103
61F-139
88Conlon/5-26
D327
D328-157
D329-161
D350/2-163
E120
E121/120
E121/80
E126-37
E135-157
E210-59
E220
M101/4-161
M101/5-163
R315-A32
R315-B32
V61-39
W501-31
W514-29
W515-9
W572
W573
W575

Shay, Dan
E91

Shea, Ed
87Watertn-4

Shea, Frank
(Spec)
48B-26
49B-49
50B-155
52B-230
52T-248
53B/Col-141
53Briggs
53T-164
54B-104
55B-207
PM10/Sm-179
R346-13

Shea, John
87Myrtle-18
88Knoxv/Best-3
89Knoxv/Best-24
89Knoxv/Pro-1140
89Knoxv/Star-20

Shea, Kevin
87VeroB-29

Shea, Kurt
88Brist/Pro-1887
89Fay/Pro-1582

Shea, M.J.
29Exh/4-24

Shea, Patrick
(Red)
E121/120
E121/80
W501-63
W575
WG7-48

Shea, Steven F.
69T-499R

Sheaffer, Danny
85Pawtu-12
86Pawtu-22
87Pawtu/TCMA-8
89ColrSp/CMC-21
89ColSp/Pro-241

Shean, David
11Helmar-105
E101
E102
E286
E90/1
E92
M116
S74-46
T202
T205

Shean, Larry
W514-116

Shearer, Ray
58T-283

Sheary, Kevin
88Rockford-33
89Rockford-33

Sheckard, James
10Domino-109
11Helmar-106
12Sweet/Pin-91
D328-158
E107
E135-158
E254
E90/1
E90/3
E91
S74-69
T202
T204
T205
T206
T215/brown
WG3-43

Sheehan, John
87Ashvl-28
88Osceola/Star-24
89Osceola/Star-21

Sheehan, Terry
78OrlTw
79Toled-10
80OrlTw-16

Sheehy, Mark
84Cram/PCL-246C
87Bakers-16C
88SnAnt/Best-25

Sheely, Earl Homer
21Exh-158
25Exh-79
26Exh-79
28Exh/PCL-25
28Yueng-37
29Exh/4-13
31Exh/4-2
33Exh/4-1
46Sunbeam
47Centen-26
E120
E121/120
E210-37
V100
V61-34
W501-46
W502-37
W572
W573
W575

Sheen, Charlie
88Pac/8Men-10

Sheets, Larry
84RochR-1
85D-36
85F/Up-U101
85T/Tr-106T
86D-350
86F-286
86S-177M
86T-147
86T/Gloss60-50
86T/St-308
87D-248
87F-479
87F/Hottest-36
87Smok/AL-10
87T-552
87T/St-229
88Class/Red-188
88D-273
88D/Best-286
88F-572
88F/AwardWin-38
88F/BB/MVP-34
88F/Excit-37
88F/Hottest-37
88F/LL-38
88F/Mini-3
88F/St-4
88French-18
88OPC-327
88Panini/St-16
88Score-219
88Sf-161
88T-327
88T/Big-26
88T/St-230
88T/UK-70
89B-16
89D-333
89F-620
89French-19
89OPC-98
89Panini/St-264
89Score-81
89T-381TL
89T-98
89T/Big-113
89T/St-239
89UD-254
90D-495
90F-189
90Score-111
90T-708
90UD-287

Sheffield, Gary
87Stockton-1
88BBAmer-22
88ElPas/Best-1
88TexLgAS/GS-26
89B-142
89Bz-19
89Class-101
89D-31RR
89D/Best-113
89D/Rook-1
89F-196
89Panini/St-364
89Pol/Brew-1
89Score-625
89Score/HotRk-10
89Score/YS/I-25
89Sf-223M
89Sf-41
89T-343FS
89T/Big-55
89T/HeadsUp-13
89T/JumboR-20
89ToysRUs-28
89UD-13
90Class-14
90D-501
90F-336
90Score-97
90Score/100Ris-20
90Sf-52
90T-718
90UD-157

Sheffield, Travis
86DayBe-25

Sheffler, Jim
89Kingspt/Star-22

Shehan, Brian
88CapeCod/Sum-38

Shelby, John
82RochR-17
83T/X-102
84D-291
84F-20
84F/St-114
84Nes/792-86
84T-86
85D-472
85F-190
85OPC-264
85RochR-13
85T-508
85T/St-204
86D-643
86F-287
86F/Mini-60
86T-309
87D-354
87D/OD-139
87F-480
87F/U-U109
87T-208
87T/Tr-112T
88D-352
88D/Best-290
88F-526
88Moth/Dodg-14
88OPC-307
88Panini/St-316
88Pol/Dodg-31
88Score-286
88T-428
88T/Big-218
89B-349
89D-314
89F-73
89Moth/Dodg-14
89OPC-175
89Panini/St-109
89Pol/Dodg-20
89Score-103
89T-175
89T/St-63
89UD-75

Sheldon, Bob
75OPC-623R
75T-623R
75T/M-623R
76OPC-626
76SSPC-256
76T-626
77Spoka

Sheldon, Dave
86AppFx-22

Sheldon, Roland
61T-541
62T-185
63T-507
65OPC-254
65T-254
66OPC-18
66T-18
69T-413

Shellenback, Frank
28Exh/PCL-26
88MinorLg/Leg-7

Shellenback, Jim
67T-592R
69T-567R
70OPC-389
70T-389
71MLB/St-549
71OPC-351
71T-351
74OPC-657
74T-657
84Toled-21
85Toled-27
87Orlan-7
88Portl/CMC-25
88Portl/Pro-644
89Portl/CMC-25
89Portl/Pro-226

Shelton, Andrew
E270/1

Shelton, Ben
88Aug/Pro-370
89Aug/Pro-511

Shelton, Harry
86Geneva-24
87Peoria-19
88CharWh/Best-21
89Peoria/Ko-26

Shelton, Mike
86Readg-24
87Readg-9
88AAA/Pro-25
88Maine/CMC-7
88Maine/Pro-282

Shepard, Jack
55T-73
55T/DH-23
79TCMA-112

Shepard, Kelvin
87Jamestn-12

Shepard, Ken
88Geneva/Pro-1656

Shepard, Larry
68KDKA-7
68T-584
69T-384
73OPC-296CO
73T-296C
74OPC-326CO
74T-326C
79Pol/Giants-8CO

Shepherd, Keith
87Watertn-15
88Aug/Pro-375
89BBCity/Star-23

Shepherd, Ron
82Knoxv-20
83Syrac-24
84Syrac-5
85F/Up-U102
86Syrac-23
87Indianap-12
87OPC-117
87T-643
88Indi/CMC-16
88Indi/Pro-524
89Louvl-34
89Louvl/CMC-22
89Louvl/Pro-1261

Sheppard, Don
89LittleSun-22

Sheppard, Phillip
84Visal-8

Shepston, Mike
79QuadC-24

Sherdel, Bill
25Exh-63
26Exh-63
E120
E126-12
V61-100
W517-6
W572

Sheridan, Bobby
87Spoka-13
89River/Cal-19
89River/Pro-1418
89Spoka/SP-22

Sheridan, Neil
52Park-16

Sheridan, Pat
81Omaha-24
82Omaha-22
83Omaha-21
84D-588
84F-357
84Nes/792-121
84T-121
84T/St-286
85D-339
85F-213
85T-359
85T/St-272
86D-155

86F-20
86Kitty/Disc-11
86OPC-240
86T-743
87Cain's-18
87Coke/Tigers-6
87F-162
87T-234
88D-522
88F-69
88Panini/St-97
88Pep/T-15
88Score-171
88T-514
89B-107
89D-417
89F-146
89Mara/Tigers-15
89Pol/Tigers-15
89Score-204
89Score/Tr-71
89T-288
89T/Big-150
89UD-652
90D-367
90F-71
90Score-509
90T-422
90UD-460

Sheriff, Dave
79WHave-29M
81LynnS-9
82Idaho-33
83Idaho-34

Sherlock, Glenn
86Osceola-23
87Colum-7
87Colum/Pol-22
87Colum/TCMA-25
88Colum/Pro-304
89Albany/Best-7
89Albany/Pro-339

Sherman, Darrell
89Spoka/SP-26

Sherman, Jack
47Signal

Sherman, Jim
83ColumAst-5
86Tucso-21

Sherman, Steve
76Cedar
77Cedar

Shermet, Dave
88AubAs/Pro-1958
89Ashvl/Pro-948

Shermeyer, Keith
77Wausa
78Wausa

Sherow, Dennis
80Memph-18
81WHave-19
82Tacom-18
82WHave-25
83Tacom-27

Sherrill, Dennis
79Colum-19
80Colum-23

Sherrill, Tim
88Savan/Pro-334
89StPet/Star-24

Sherry, Larry
60Bz-17
60Morrell
60T-105
61BB-51
61NuCard-431
61P-161
61T-412
61T-521M
61T/St-34
62BB-51
62J-111
62P-111
62P/Can-111
62T-435
63T-565
64T-474
65T-408
66T-289
67T-571
68T-468

Sherry, Norm
59DF
60T-529
61BB-34
61T-521M
62BB-34
62T-238
63T-316
77T-34MG
84Smok/SDP-21C
85Spoka/Cram-21

Shetrone, Barry
60T-348
63T-276

Shibata, Keith
88AppFx/Pro-153
88Eugene/Best-29

Shidawara, Cliff
86Phoen-23TR
87Phoen-19
88Phoen/Pro-66

Shields, Doug
88CapeCod/Sum-40

Shields, Mike
79Savan-9

Shields, Steve
81Brist-17
83Pawtu-11
84Richm-17
85Richm-9
86F-527
86Richm-20
87T/Tr-113T
88Colum/CMC-6
88Colum/Pol-10
88Colum/Pro-314
88D/Y/Bk-NEW
88Score-396
88Score/Tr-47T
88T-632
89F-269
89Portl/CMC-4
89Portl/Pro-218
89Score-578
89T-484

Shields, Tom
86Watertn-23
88Harris/Pro-836
89Harris/Pro-298
89Harris/Star-18
89Star/Wax-20

Shiflett, Chris
88Gasto/Pro-1001
89Butte/SP-14

Shiflett, Mark
83Nashvl-20
84Nashvl-20
87Memph-6
87Memph/Best-13

Shiflett, Matt
87Jamestn-25

Shikles, Larry
86Greens-22
87WinHav-4
88NewBrit/Pro-899
89NewBrit/Pro-613
89NewBrit/Star-18

Shillinglaw, Dave
86Madis-22C
86Madis/Pol-26

Shimp, Tommy Joe
80Memph-19
83Memph-10
84Tulsa-37
85OKCty-13
86OKCty-20

Shinall, Zakary (Zak)
88Bakers/Cal-259
89VeroB/Star-25

Shindle, William
N172
N300/SC

Shines, Razor
83Memph-21
84Indianap-17
85D-401
85Leaf-164
86OPC-132
86T-132
87Indianap-8
88Indi/CMC-12
88Indi/Pro-514
89Indi/CMC-12
89Indi/Pro-1219

Shingledecker, Gary
89Erie/Star-24

Shinholster, Vince
87SnBer-12

Shinners, Ralph
E120
V100
W573

Shiozaki, Kenny
88Butte-11

Shipanoff, Dave
83Knoxv-7
84Syrac-25
85Cram/PCL-28
86D-34
86F-452
86Leaf-29RR
86Portl-20
87Edmon-5

Shipke, William
T204
T206

Shipley, Craig
85Cram/PCL-155
86Albuq-23
87Albuq/Pol-22
88Jacks/GS-12
89Tidew/CMC-22
89Tidew/Pro-1961

Shipley, Joe
59T-141
60T-239
62Pep/Tul

Shippy, Greg
75Clint

Shirahata, Hiro
83SanJose-10

Shireman, Jeff
89Sprin/Best-12

Shires, Charles A. (Art)
30CEA/Pin-20
R315-C5
R316
W517-43

Shirley, Bart
66T-591R
67T-287R
69T-289

Shirley, Bob
78T-266
79T-594
80OPC-248
80T-476
81D-242
81F-495
81OPC-49
81T-49
81T/Tr-829
82D-120
82F-127
82OPC-33
82T-749
82T/Tr-105T
83F-602
83T-112
83T/X-103
84D-214
84F-141
84Nes/792-684
84T-684
85D-370
85F-145
85T-328
86D-458
86F-119
86T-213
87D-463
87F-114
87T-524
88Syrac/CMC-7
88Syrac/Pro-827
89StCath/Pro-2095

Shirley, Steve
77LodiD
78LodiD
81Albuq/TCMA-3
82Albuq-8
85Cram/PCL-235
86Albuq-24
87Omaha-14
88Indi/CMC-4
88Indi/Pro-505

Shive, Chuck
89Martins/Star-28

Shock, George
N172
WG1-70

Shocker, Urban
21Exh-159
25Exh-103
26Exh-104
28Exh-52
E120
E121/120
E126-36
E220
V100
V61-40
W501-2
W515-48
W573
W575

Shockey, Scott
88CapeCod/Sum-63
89Medford/Best-2

Shockley, John Costen
65OPC-107R
65T-107R

Shoebridge, Terry
77BurlB
78BurlB
80Holyo-9
81ElPas-5

Shoemaker, John
78LodiD
81VeroB-26
82VeroB-29
83VeroB-26
85VeroB-27
86VeroB-23CO
87VeroB-30
88FSLAS/Star-1MG
89SnAnt/Best-25

Shoeneck, Lewis
N172
WG1-36

Shoffner, Milburn
39PB-87
40PB-149
W711/1
W711/2

Shofner, Frank S.
48Sommer-9
49Sommer-15

Sholl, Derek
88Eugene/Best-25

Shombert, Otto
N172
N284

Shopay, Tom
70OPC-363
70T-363
72OPC-418
72T-418
76SSPC-401
78Colum

Shore, Eddie
33SK-19

Shore, Ernest
73F/Wild-31
87Conlon/2-56
D327
D328-159
D329-162
D350/2-164
E135-159
M101/4-162
M101/5-164

Shore, Ray
63FrBauer-24

Shore, Roy
52Park-18

Shores, Brad
86BurlEx-19tr
89AppFx/Pro-869

Shores, William
W517-7

Short, Bill
60T-142
61T-252
62T-221
67T-577
68T-536
69T-259

Short, Chris
67T-395
68OPC-139
68OPC-7LL
68T-139
68T-7LL
69MB-253
69MLB/St-178
69T-395
69T/decal
69T/S-54
69T/St-78
70K-41
70MLB/St-94
70OPC-270
70T-270
71K-75
71MLB/St-188
71OPC-511
71T-511
72MB-315
72T-665
PM10/L-35

Shorten, Charles (Chick)
D328-160
E120
E135-160

Shotkoski, David
88Huntsvl/BK-19
88Modesto-31
88Modesto/Cal-57
89Huntsvl/Best-15

Shotton, Burt
14CJ-86
15CJ-86
49Eureka-49
D327
D328-161

D329-163
D350/2-165
E135-161
M101/4-163
M101/5-165
Rawl
W514-78
Shoun, Clyde
50Remar
R423-99
W754
Shoup, Eric
88Brist/Pro-1876
Shouppe, Jamey
83DayBe-12
Shourds, Jeff
77Cedar
Show, Eric
81Hawai
82T/Tr-106T
83D-439
83F-372
83OPC-68
83T-68
83T/St-330
84D-406
84F-312
84Moth/Padres-4
84Nes/792-532
84OPC-238
84Smok/Padres-22
84T-532
84T/St-162
85D-202
85D/AAS-59
85F-44
85Leaf-137
85Moth/Padres-9
85OPC-118
85T-118
85T/St-156
86D-234
86F-334
86Leaf-111
86OPC-209
86T-762
87Bohem-30
87D-164
87D/OD-149
87F-430
87F/Hottest-37
87OPC-354
87T-730
87T/St-112
88Coke/Padres-30
88D-387
88F-597
88Panini/St-400
88Score-338
88Smok/Padres-26
88T-303
89B-446
89D-482
89F-317
89OPC-147
89Panini/St-196
89Score-254
89T-427
89T/Big-35
89UD-171
90D-559
90F-169
90Score-493
90T-239
90UD-587
Showalter, William N.
(Buck)
79WHave-7
81Colum-20
82Nashv-22
83Nashvl-21
88FSLAS/Star-27
89Albany/Best-8
89Albany/Pro-326
89Albany/Star-22
Shreve, Ben
88Geneva/Pro-1652
88Wythe/Pro-1992
Shreve, Leven
N172
Shuba, George
52T-326
53B/Col-145
53T-34
54B-202
54NYJour
55B-66
55Gol/Dodg-27
79TCMA-277
89Rini/Dodg-17
Shubert, Rich
74Gasto
77Holyo
Shuffield, Jack
83CharR-12
Shull, Mike
87PalmSp-10
Shulleeta, Mike
82QuadC-11
Shulock, John
88Umpire-39
89Umpires-37
Shultis, Chris
86Cram/PCL-22
88Boise/Pro-1613
Shumake, Brooks
86Vermont-18
Shumpert, Terry
88AppFx/Pro-142
89Omaha/CMC-18
89Omaha/Pro-1721
Shupe, Wilford
WG7-49
Siblerud, Daniel
86Columbia-23
Siddall, Joe
88James/Pro-1908
Siebern, Norm
58T-54
59T-308
60T-11
61P-82
61T-119M
61T-267
61T/Dice-16
61T/St-165
62Bz
62Exh
62J-92
62P-92
62P/Can-92
62Salada-85
62Shirriff-85
62T-127M
62T-275
62T/bucks
62T/St-57
63Bz-4
63Exh
63F-17
63J-85
63P-85
63Salada-51
63T-2LL
63T-430
63T/SO
64T-145
64T/Coins-49
64T/St-14
64T/SU
64T/tatt
64Wheat/St-41
65T-455
66OPC-14
66T-14
67T-299
68T-537
Exh47
Siebert, Dick
40PB-192
41DP-128
Siebert, Mac
89Brist/Star-26
Siebert, Paul
75Iowa/TCMA-17
75OPC-614R
75T-614R
75T/M-614R
Siebert, Rick
86Durhm-25
87Durhm-18
88Sumter/Pro-402
89Penin/Star-22
Siebert, Sonny
64T-552R
65OPC-96
65T-96
66Kahn
66T-197
66T-222LL
66T-226LL
67Kahn
67OPC-95
67T-463M
67T-95
68OPC-8LL
68T-295
68T-8LL
69MLB/St-43
69T-455
69T/St-167
70MLB/St-166
70T-597
71MLB/St-332
71OPC-710
71T-710
71T/Coins-122
72K-36
72OPC-290
72T-290
73K-14
73OPC-14
73T-14
74OPC-548
74T-548
75OPC-328
75T-328
75T/M-328
76SSPC-484
85Cram/PCL-121
87LasVegas-6
88LasVeg/CMC-25
88LasVeg/Pro-248
Siebler, Dwight
64T-516R
65T-326
66T-546
67OPC-164
67T-164
78TCMA-126
Siegel, Bob
86Wausa-24
Siegle, John H.
E101
E105
E216
E90/1
E92
Sieradzki, Al
89Bluef/Star-21
Sierra, Ruben
85Tulsa-12
86D/Rook-52
86F/Up-U105
86OKCty-21
86Rang-3
86S/Rook-16
87Class/Up-149
87D-346
87D/OD-172
87F-138
87F/Mini-100
87Leaf-225
87Moth/Rang-13
87Smok/R-17
87T-261
87T-6RB
87T/GlossRk-15
87T/St-10
87ToysRUs-24
88Class/Red-180
88D-223
88D-BC26
88D/Best-200
88F-479
88F/Excit-38
88F/Hottest-38
88F/LL-39
88F/Mini-58
88F/SS-36
88F/St-69
88KayBee-28
88Leaf-206
88Moth/R-10
88OPC-319
88Panini/St-209
88Score-113
88Score/YS/I-36
88Sf-113
88Smok/R-9
88T-771
88T/Coins-26
88T/Gloss60-4
88T/RiteAid-25
88T/St-234
88T/UK-71
89B-235
89Bimbo/Discs-6
89Class/Up/2-162
89D-48
89D/Best-111
89D/MVP-BC26
89F-532
89F/BBAS-37
89F/BBMVP's-35
89F/Excit-37
89F/Heroes-37
89Moth/R-7
89OPC-53
89Panini/St-457
89RedFoley/St-108
89Score-43
89Score/Mast-31
89Sf-189
89Smok/R-30
89T-53
89T/Big-82
89T/Coins-51
89T/Hills-26
89T/St-242
89T/UK-71
89UD-416
89UD-686TC
90Class-59
90Class-7
90D-174
90D-3DK
90D-673AS
90F-314
90F/WaxBox-C25
90Score-420
90Score/100St-85
90Sf-188
90T-185
90T-390AS
90UD-355
Sierra, Ulises
(Candy)
85Beaum-9
86Beaum-21
87Wichi-20
89F-171
89T-711
Siever, Edward
E107
Sievers, Roy
50B-16
51B-67
51FB
51T/RB-9
52T-64
53T-67
54T-245
55T-16
55T/DH-79
56T-75
56T/Pin-590F
57T-89
58T-250
59Armour-15
59Bz
59T-340
59T-465M
59T-566AS
59T-74M
60NuCard-23
60T-25
61NuCard-423
61P-26
61T-470
61T/St-128
62/Can-46
62J-46
62P-46
62Salada-66
62Shirriff-66
62T-220
62T/bucks
62T/St-169
62T/St-58
63J-177
63P-177
63T-283
64T-43
65T-574
78TCMA-242
79TCMA-206
88Pac/Leg-26
89Swell-47
Exh47
PM10/L-36
Sigler, Allen
85Cedar-25
86Cedar/TCMA-22
Siglin, W.
(Paddy)
WG7-50
Sigman, Lee
78BurlB
83ElPas-25
Sikes, Bob
82Jacks-24
83Tidew-27
84Tidew-17
Silch, Edward
N172
Siler, Mike
87Bakers-26
Silkwood, Joe
83Sprin/LF-12
84ArkTr-20
Silton
C46-24
Silva, Freddie
82Sprin-6
83StPet-12
Silva, Mark
83Nashvl-22
85Colum-24
85Colum/Pol-20

86Colum-22
86Colum/Pol-20
Silva, Ryan
86Cram/PCL-149
Silvas, Brian
81Batav-7
Silver, Keith
84Evrt/Cram-10A
86Shrev-23
Silver, Larry
78StPet
Silver, Roy
86StPet-28
87ArkTr-12
87TexLgAS-2
88Louvl-44
88Louvl/CMC-22
88Louvl/Pro-431
89ArkTr/GS-22
Silvera, Al
56T-137
Silvera, Charlie
52B-197
52T-168
53T-242
54T-96
55T-188
57T-255
73OPC-323CO
73T-323C
74OPC-379CO
74T-379C
79TCMA-266
Silverio, Francisco
86Tampa-19
87Cedar-23
Silverio, Luis
76Watlo
77Jaxvl
82Omaha-23
88FSLAS/Star-30
Silverio, Nelson
86Madis-23
86Madis/Pol-19
88Charl/Pro-1220
Silverio, Tom
72OPC-213R
72T-213R
Silverman, Aaron
52Park-2
V362-19
Silverman, Don
85IowaC-27
Silverstein, Allan
88Myrtle/Pro-1187
89Duned/Star-15
Silvestri, David
88T/Tr-107TOLY
89Osceola/Star-22
89Star/Wax-18
89T/Big-141
Silvestri, Ken
49Eureka-147
51B-256
52B-200
60T-466C
73OPC-237CO
73T-237C
74OPC-634CO
74T-634C
78Knoxv
87Portl-23
89Watertn/Star-26
Sima, Al
52T-93
53T-241
54T-216
Simcox, Larry
82DayBe-23
83ColumAst-7
Simmermacher, Bret
86Cram/PCL-114
Simmons, Al
83Miami-16
Simmons, Aloysius (Al)
21Exh-160
28Exh-56
31Exh/4-27
32Orbit/num-39
32Orbit/un-53
33CJ/Pin-20
33DH-39
33DL-2
33Exh/4-14
33G-35
34DS-2
34Exh/4-10
34Exh/4-14
35BU-34
35Exh/4-10
35G-1J
35G-3A
35G-5A
35G-6A
35Wheat
38ONG/Pin-28
50Callahn
60Exh/HOF-21
60F-32
61F-77
61GP-20
63Bz-22
69Bz/Sm
80Cram/Leg-119
80Laugh/FFeat-3
80SSPC/HOF
86S/Dec-5
88Conlon/4-25
88Conlon/AmAS-22
PR1-26
R300
R303/A
R303/B
R305
R306
R308-154
R310
R313
R314
R315-A33
R315-B33
R316
R328-17
R332-1
R337-415
R423-102
V353-35
V355-77
W517-40
Simmons, Brad
77DaytB
Simmons, Curt
49B-14
49Eureka-148
49Lummis
50B-68
51B-111
51BR-D9
52B-184
52StarCal/L-77C
52T-203
53B/Col-64
54B-79
54RM-NL12
55Armour-18
55B-64
55RFG-6
55RM-NL24
56T-290
57T-158
58Hires-28
58T-404
59T-382
60T-451
61T-11
61T/St-93
62J-167
62P-167
62P/Can-167
62T-285
62T-56LL
63T-22
64T-385
65T-373
66T-489
67OPC-39
67T-39
79TCMA-54
Exh47
PM10/Sm-180
Simmons, Enoch
89Medford/Best-26
Simmons, George
C46-75
T205
Simmons, Greg
85Beloi-17
86Beloi-21
Simmons, John
52Park-62
53Exh/Can-35
V362-5
Simmons, Nelson
83BirmB-16
84Evans-9
85F/Up-U103
86Cain's-16
86D-272
86F-238
86RochR-21
86T-121
87RochR-18
88Calg/CMC-19
88Calg/Pro-802
Simmons, Randy
88Pulas/Pro-1768
89Sumter/Pro-1110
Simmons, Ted
71OPC-117
71T-117
72OPC-154
72T-154
73OPC-85
73T-85
74K-21
74OPC-260
74T-260
74T/DE-10
74T/St-116
75Ho-95
75OPC-75
75T-75
75TM-75
76Crane-56
76Ho-113
76K-57
76MSA/Disc
76OPC-191LL
76OPC-290
76SSPC-274
76T-191LL
76T-290
77Ho-61
77OPC-196
77T-470
77T/CS-43
78Ho-65
78OPC-150
78T-380
78Wiffle/Discs-69
79Ho-44
79K-2
79OPC-267
79T-510
79T/Comics-30
80K-44
80OPC-47
80T-85
81D-308
81F-528
81F/St-120
81OPC-352
81T-705
81T/Nat/Super-15
81T/S
81T/So-63
81T/St-94
81T/Tr-830
82D-106
82F-152
82F/St-137
82OPC-150
82Pol/Brew
82Pol/Brew-23
82T-150
82T/St-201
83D-332
83F-45
83Gard-16
83OPC-284
83OPC-33SV
83Pol/Brew-23
83T-450
83T-451A
83T/St-85
84D-473
84D/AAS-58
84F-213
84FunFood/Pin-124
84Gard-17
84MiltBrad-24
84Nes/792-404AS
84Nes/792-630
84Nes/792-713LL
84Nes/792-726TL
84OPC-122
84OPC-94AS
84Pol/Brew-23
84Ralston-3
84Seven-21C
84T-404AS
84T-630
84T-713LL
84T-726TL
84T/Cereal-3
84T/Gloss22-9
84T/Gloss40-18
84T/St-193
84T/St-293
84T/St/Box-2
85D-414
85F-596
85Gard-19
85Leaf-104
85OPC-318
85Pol/Brew-23
85T-318
85T/St-294
86D-292
86F-503
86F/Up-U106
86Leaf-167
86Pol/Atl-23
86S-196
86S/Dec-62M
86T-237
86T/St-199
86T/Tr-102T
87D-537
87F-528
87Smok/Atl-13
87T-516
88D-560
88F-549
88Leaf-222
88Score-285
88T-791
89F-599
89Score-611
89UD-570
Simmons, Todd
86Beaum-22
87LasVegas-11
88F-650
88LasVeg/CMC-6
88LasVeg/Pro-240
89Denver/CMC-10
89Denver/Pro-30
89F-318
Simms, Michael
87Ashvl-17
88FSLAS/Star-21
88Osceola/Star-25
89ColMud/Best-7
89ColMud/Pro-141
89ColMud/Star-22
89Star/Wax-3
Simon, Michael
11Helmar-165
14CJ-25
15CJ-25
D322
M116
T201
T207
Simon, Richard
86AubAs-23
87AubAs-25
88Ashvl/Pro-1069
89Osceola/Star-23
Simon, Rick
74Gasto
Simon, Willie
76Wausa
Simond, Rob
80LynnS-6
81LynnS-10
Simonds, Dan
88Fresno/Cal-6
88Fresno/Pro-1230
89Freder/Star-22
89Hagers/Best-23
Simons, Doug
89Visal/Cal-95
89Visal/Pro-1435
Simons, Neil
82DayBe-15
Simonson, Bob
85Beloi-6
86Beloi-22
88Beloi/GS-9
Simpson, Danny
83TriCit-22
Simpson, Dick
63T-407R
64T-127R
65T-374R
66T-311R
67OPC-6
67T-6
68T-459
69MB-254
69T-608
Simpson, Greg
86Cedar/TCMA-9
87Vermont-6
88Cedar/Pro-1137
Simpson, Harry (Suitcase)
52B-223
52NumNum-17
52T-193
53B/Col-86
53T-150
55Rodeo
56Rodeo
56T-239
57T-225
58T-299

59T-333
60L-81
60T-180
61Union
79TCMA-79

Simpson, Joe
78Cr/PCL-63
79T-719R
80T-637
81D-168
81F-616
81Pol/Mar-15
81T-116
82D-55
82F-518
82T-382
83F-485
83T-567
83T/X-104
84Cram/PCL-115
84D-496
84F-358
84Nes/792-219
84T-219

Simpson, Wayne
70T-683R
71K-1
71MD
71MLB/St-69
71OPC-339
71OPC-68LL
71T-339
71T-68LL
71T/Coins-53
72T-762
73OPC-428
73T-428
76SSPC-599

Simpson, William
77Ashev
78Ashev

Sims, Daniel Jr.
89Idaho/Pro-2018

Sims, Duane
(Duke)
66OPC-169
66T-169
67OPC-3
67T-3
68T-508
69MB-255
69T-414
69T/St-168
70MLB/St-203
70OPC-275
70T-275
71MLB/St-114
71OPC-172
71T-172
71T/Coins-66
72MB-316
72OPC-63
72T-63
73OPC-304
73T-304
74OPC-398
74T-398
86AppFx-23
89Swell-128

Sims, Greg
66T-596R

Sims, Greg
89Aug/Pro-517

Sims, Joe Beely
86Jamestn-23
87Jamestn-8

Sims, Kinney
88Reno/Cal-278

Sims, Mark
87Spart-6
88Clearw/Star-21
89Clearw/Star-20

Sims, Mike
83Tampa-29
86Vermont-19TR

Simunic, Doug
80Memph-22
83Charl-7
84BuffB-6
84Maine-5
89AubAs/Pro-2184

Sinatro, Greg
77SnJos-8

Sinatro, Matt
81Richm-20
82D-149
82Richm-12
83D-622
83Richm-11
87Tacom-9
88Tacom/CMC-18
88Tacom/Pro-616
89Tucso/CMC-11
89Tucso/Pro-201

Sinclair, Ken
84Savan-25

Siner, Hosea John
E254

Singer, Bill
66T-288R
67OPC-12R
67T-12R
68T-249
69MLB/St-152
69OPC-12LL
69T-12LL
69T-575
69T/St-49
70K-17
70MLB/St-57
70OPC-490
70OPC-71LL
70T-490
70T-71LL
70T/CB
71MLB/St-115
71OPC-145
71T-145
72MB-317
72OPC-25
72T-25
73OPC-570
73T-570
74K-12
74OPC-210
74T-210
74T/St-149
75Ho-82
75Ho/Twink-82
75OPC-40
75T-40
75T/M-40
76OPC-411
76SSPC-188
76T-411
76T/Tr-411T
77Ho-139
77OPC-85
77T-346
77T/CS-44
87Smok/Dodg-33
88Smok/Dodg-6M
89Smok/Dodg-75

Singletary, Chico
87Savan-15

Singleton, Bert Elmer
49B-147
49Sommer-25
57T-378
59T-548
63MilSau-6

Singleton, Ken
71OPC-16
71T-16
72OPC-425
72OPC-426IA
72T-425
72T-426A
73OPC-232
73T-232
74K-48
74OPC-25
74T-25
74T/St-60
74Weston-29
75K-40
75OPC-125
75T-125
75T/M-125
76Ho-76
76K-12
76OPC-175
76SSPC-400
76T-175
77Ho-107
77OPC-19
77T-445
78Ho-75
78K-55
78OPC-80
78T-65
79Ho-135
79OPC-324
79T-615
80K-30
80OPC-178
80T-340
80T/S-11
81D-115
81Drake-12
81F-188
81F/St-103
81K-39
81OPC-281
81T-570
81T/So-17
81T/St-33
82D-105
82D-24DK
82Drake-30
82F-179
82F/St-150
82K-58
82OPC-290
82OPC-2AS
82T-290
82T-552
82T/St-136
82T/St-144
83D-257
83Drake-26
83F-73
83T-85
83T/St-28
84D-610
84F-21
84F/St-46
84F/St-55
84Nes/792-165
84OPC-165
84T-165
84T/St-206
84T/St/Box-8
85F-191
85OPC-326
85T-755
85T/St-201
89Swell-26

Singley, Joe
87Penin-6
89Utica/Puc-21

Sington, Fred
39PB-68

Sinnett, Lou
85Anchora-40

Sipe, Pat
87WPalm-8
88Jaxvl/Best-20
88Jaxvl/Pro-981
89Jaxvl/Best-8
89Jaxvl/Pro-165

Siracusa, John
75OkCty

Siriano, Rick
82Durhm-8
83Durhm-13

Sisisky, Terry
79Richm-9M

Sisk, Doug
82Jacks-10
83T/X-105
84D-615
84F-596
84Jacks/Smok-11
84Nes/792-599
84OPC-21
84T-599
85D-441
85F-91
85Leaf-187
85OPC-315
85T-315
85T/Mets/Fan-7
85T/St-103
86F-94
86T-144
86Tidew-26
87F-22
87T-404
88D-642
88F-150
88F/U-U3
88Score-227
88T-763
89F-621
89Score-264
89T-13
89UD-261

Sisk, Tommie
63T-169R
64T-224
65T-558
66EH-25
66T-441
67OPC-84
67T-84
67T/Test/PP-21
68KDKA-25
68T-429
69MLB/St-196
69OPC-152
69T-152
70MLB/St-118
70OPC-374
70T-374

Sisler, Dave
57T-56
58Hires-40
58T-59
59T-346M
59T-384
60L-64
60T-186
61P-44
61T-239
61T/St-155
62T-171
63T-284

Sisler, Dick
47TipTop
48L-143
49B-205
49Eureka-149
49Royal-19
50B-119
50Drake-10
51B-52
51BR-C8
51T/BB-8
52B-127
52Royal
52T-113
52TipTop
53B/BW-10
53Exh/Can-62
53Hunters
60HenryH-8
63FrBauer-25
64T-162M
65OPC-158
65T-158
79TCMA-152
Exh47

Sisler, George Jr.
80Colum-27
81Colum-27
82Colum-26
82Colum/Pol-xx
84Colum-24
84Colum/Pol-23
85Colum-29
85Colum/Pol-21
87Colum/Pol-23
88Colum/Pol-25GM
89Colum/Pol-25GM

Sisler, George Sr.
21Exh-161
25Exh-117
26Exh-118
27Exh-59
28Yueng-54
29Exh/4-1
40PB-179
48Exh/HOF
50Callahan
60F-13
61F-78
61F-89M
61GP-13
72K-5
72K/ATG-5
72Laugh/GF-5
73F/Wild-12
79T-411M
80Cram/Leg-108
80Laugh/3/4/5-24
80Laugh/FFeat-9
80SSPC/HOF
85Woolwth-33
87Conlon/2-58
88Conlon/4-26
BF2-43
D327
D328-162
D329-164
D350/2-166
E120
E121/120
E121/80
E122
E126-49
E135-162
E210-54
E220
M101/4-164
M101/5-166
R423-103
V100
V61-32
W501-4
W502-54
W514-101
W515-11
W572
W573
W575
WG7-51

Sismondo, Ron
83Wausa/LF-24

Sisney, Lorenzo
88Wausa/Feder-5
88Wausa/GS-5
Sisti, Sibby
41DP-42
47TipTop
49B-201
49Eureka-23
50B-164
51B-170
52B-100
52T-293
53JC-13
53T-124
54JC-13
58Union
Siuda, Matt
85Anchora-33
88Madis-22
Sivik, Mike
77AppFx
79AppFx-13
Siwy, Jim
81AppFx-10
82Edmon-3
85Maine-12
86LasVegas-15
87LasVegas-25
Sizemore, Ted
69T-552R
70MLB/St-58
70OPC-174
70T-174
71MLB/St-284
71OPC-571
71T-571
71T/Coins-65
72OPC-514
72T-514
73OPC-128
73T-128
74OPC-209
74T-209
74T/St-117
75Ho-75
75OPC-404
75T-404
75T/M-404
76Ho-70
76OPC-522
76SSPC-284
76T-522
77T-366
78OPC-118
78T-136
79OPC-148
79T-297
80OPC-46
80T-81
85SpokAT/Crm-18
Skaalen, Jim
87PortChar-24
88Tulsa-10MG
89OkCty/CMC-23
89OkCty/Pro-1508
Skaff, Francis
52Park-91
54Esskay
Skaggs, David
78T-593
79T-367
80T-211
81T-48
Skaggs, Steve
80Cedar-14
Skalski, Joe
87Wmspt-27
88ColSp/CMC-10
88ColSp/Pro-1533
89ColrSp/CMC-9
89UD/Ext-716
90Score-618
Skeels, Andy
87Spoka-7
88River/Cal-226
88River/Pro-1425
89River/Best-15
89River/Cal-12
89River/Pro-1414
Skeen, Archie
63MilSau-7
64T-428R
Skeete, Rafael
87Hagers-22
88CharlK-15
88CharlK/Pep-15
89Hagers/Best-22
89Hagers/Pro-278
89Hagers/Star-17
Skelton, John
87Kenosha-28
88Keno/Pro-1400
Skiba, Daniel
77Watlo
Skidmore, Robert Roe
71OPC-121R
71T-121R
Skiff, William (Bill)
43Centen-21
44Centen-20MG
45Centen-22MG
WG7-52
Skinner, Bob
55T-88
55T/DH-56
56T-297
57T-209
58Hires-30
58Kahn
58T-94
59Armour-16
59Kahn
59T-320
59T-543M
60Kahn
60T-113
61Kahn
61T-204
61T/St-69
62J-174
62P-174
62P/Can-174
62Salada-143
62Shirriff-143
62T-115
63FrBauer-26
63J-141
63P-141
63Sugar-B
63T-18M
63T-215
64T-377
65T-591
66T-471
69T-369
73OPC-12CO
73T-12C
74OPC-489CO
74T-489C
79TCMA-248
85T-139FS
86Pol/Atl-4C
89Tucso/CMC-25
89Tucso/Pro-203
Skinner, Joel
84D-27
85BuffB-6
85Coke/WS-22
85D-574
85F-646M
85T-139FS
85T-488
86Coke/WS-22
86D-330
86T-239
87D-545
87D/OD-240
87F-115
87T-626
88D-474
88D/Best-300
88D/Y/Bk-474
88Score-532
88T-109
89D-427
89D/Best-224
89D/Tr-22
89F-270
89OPC-127
89Score-447
89Score/Tr-76
89T-536
89UD-328
90D-73
90F-501
90T-54
90UD-369
Skinner, John
82AppFx-14
Skinner, Matt
85Newar-23
Skinner, Mike
86RochR-22
87RochR-5
87RochR/TCMA-9
Skizas, Lou
57T-83
58T-319
59T-328
60Union-15
Sklar, Joel
86LitFalls-25
Skodny, Joe
86Cram/PCL-48
87AppFx-11
88BBCity/Star-21
Skoglund, Brad
83Wisco/LF-23
Skok, Craig
79T-363
80Richm-20
Skorochocki, John
77Newar
78BurlB
81ElPas-4
82Vanco-6
Skowron, Bill
54T-239
55B-160
55T-22
55T/DH-21
56T-61
56T/Pin-30
57T-135
58T-240
58T-477AS
59T-554AS
59T-90
60MacGregor-23
60T-370
60T-553AS
61P-3
61T-371
61T-42LL
61T-568AS
62J-1
62P-1
62P/Can-1
62Salada-59
62Shirriff-59
62T-110
62T/St-91
63J-12
63P-12
63T-180
64T-445
64T/S-60
65OPC-70
65T-70
65T/E-5
65T/trans-69
66Bz-33
66T-199M
66T-590
66T/RO-4
67T-357
78TCMA-230
79TCMA-210
83MLBPA/Pin-17
88Pac/Leg-82
Exh47
PM10/L-37
WG9-46
Skripko, Joseph
85Greens-8
Skripko, Scott
86WinHav-23
87NewBrit-10
89Lynch/Star-25
Skryd, Chris
89SLCty-19
Skube, Bob
81ElPas-15
82Vanco-1
83Pol/Brew-26
85Cram/PCL-214
Skurla, John
86Fresno/Smok-23
88Shreve/Pro-1297
88TexLgAS/GS-15
89Phoen/CMC-23
89Phoen/Pro-1496
Skurski, Andy
47Signal
Slack, Bill
87Durhm-15
89Greenv/Pro-1168
89Greenvl/Best-18
Slade, Gordon
28Exh/PCL-27
Slagle, James J.
E91
T206
Slagle, Roger
77WHave
78Cr/PCL-4
80Colum-2
82Nashv-23
Slater, Bob
76QuadC
79SLCty-21
79T-703R
Slaton, Jim
72T-744
73OPC-628
73T-628
74OPC-371
74T-371
74T/St-200
75OPC-281
75T-281
75T/M-281
76A&P/Milw
76OPC-163
76SSPC-226
76T-163
77Ho-105
77OPC-29
77T-604
78BK/T-7
78Ho-14
78OPC-146
78T-474
80OPC-10
80T-24
81D-447
81F-518
81T-357
82D-80
82F-153
82Pol/Brew
82Pol/Brew-41
82T-221
83D-330
83F-46
83Gard-17
83OPC-114
83Pol/Brew-41
83T-114
84D-481
84F-214
84F/X-107
84Nes/792-772
84OPC-104
84Smok/Cal-27
84T-772
84T/St-302
84T/X-109
85D-545
85F-313
85Smok/Cal-17
85T-657
86D-402
86F-169
86Smok/Cal-17
86T-579
87F-163
87T-432
Slattery, Chris
88CapeCod/Sum-161
Slattery, Kevin
75Clint
Slattery, Mike
N172
N338/2
Slaught, Don
82Omaha-12
83D-196
83F-123
84D-419
84F-359
84Nes/792-196
84T-196
85D-496
85F-214
85F/Up-U104
85OPC-159
85Rang-4
85T-542
85T/St-279
85T/Tr-107T
86D-281
86F-572
86Leaf-155
86OPC-24
86Rang-4
86T-761
86T/St-243
87D-136
87D/OD-176
87F-139
87Moth/Rang-12
87OPC-308
87S-154M
87S-32
87Smok/R-9
87T-308
87T/St-241
88D/Best-188
88D/Y/Bk-NEW
88F/U-U51
88Score-268
88Score/Tr-19T
88T-462
88T/Tr-108T
89B-172
89D-190
89D/Best-105
89F-271
89OPC-238

89Panini/St-403
89Score-561
89Score/NWest-12
89Sf-218
89T-611
89T/Big-138
89UD-178
90D-277
90F-456
90Score-79
90T-26
90UD-152
Slaughter, Enos
41DP-40
47TipTop
48B-17
48L-127
49B-65
49Eureka-198
50B-35
50Drake-36
51B-58
51T/BB-30
52B-232
52Dix
52NTea
52RM-NL20
52StarCal/L-81D
52T-65
52TipTop
53B/Col-81
53Dix
53Hunter
53NB
53RM-NL13
53T-41
54B-62
54Dix
54Hunter
54RH
54RM-NL19
54Wilson
55B-60
55Rodeo
56Rodeo
56T-109
57T-215
58T-142
59T-155
74Laugh/ASG-53
79TCMA-240
80Cram/Leg-32
85West/2-27
86S/Dec-18
88Pac/Leg-84
89Pac/Leg-137
89Swell-65
D305
Exh47
PM10/L-38
PM10/Sm-181
R346-34
R423-96
W754
Slaughter, Garland
89Well/Puc-22
Slaughter, Sterling
64T-469R
65T-314
Slavic, Joseph
86Lakel-21
88Lakel/Star-23
Slavin, Dave
88Poca/Pro-2094
89Clint/Pro-909
Slavin, Tim
83Wausa/LF-8
Slayback, Bill
73OPC-537
73T-537
Slaymaker, Joe
75BurlB
Sleater, Lou
52T-306
53T-224
55Rodeo
58T-46
Slettvet, Doug
75QuadC
76QuadC
77QuadC
Slezak, Robert
82VeroB-11
83VeroB-12
Slider, Rachel
(Rac)
61Union
85IntLgAS-45
85Pawtu-14
Slifko, Paul
86NewBrit-22
87WinHav-20
Sline, Fred
C46-9
Sliwinski, Kevin
86Knoxv-21
87Knoxv-10
88Huntsvl/BK-20
88Tacom/CMC-20
88Tacom/Pro-626
Slocum, Ron
70T-573R
71MLB/St-239
71OPC-274
71T-274
Slocumb, Heath
86LitFalls-26
87WinSal-7
88WinSal/Star-16
89Peoria/Ko-9
Slominski, Rich
86Wausa-22
Slomkowski, Rich
89Watlo/Pro-1798
89Watlo/Star-19
Sloniger, Chris
88SLCty-5
89Mia/Star/22-17
Slotnick, Joe
86BurlEx-20
Slowik, Tad
86Peoria-21
87WinSal-11
Slusarski, Joe
88T/Tr-109TOLY
89Modesto/Cal-266
89Modesto/Ch-15
89T/Big-213
Smajstra, Craig
83AppFx/LF-10
86Water-22
87BuffB-10
88Tucso-21
88Tucso/CMC-23
88Tucso/Pro-168
89Tucso/CMC-12
89Tucso/Pro-200
Smaldone, Ed
89Geneva/Pro-1861
Small, Chris
88AubAs/Pro-1949
Small, Hank
78Richm
Small, Jeff
86Peoria-22
87WinSal-24
Small, Jim
56T-207
57T-33
61Union
D301
Small, Mark
89AubAs/Pro-2188
Small, Robert
89James/Pro-2133
Smalley, Dave
84Greens-13
Smalley, Roy Jr.
75Spoka
76OPC-657
76OPC-70FS
76SSPC-267
76T-657
76T-70M
77Ho-66
77T-66
78Ho-118
78T-471
79Ho-60
79OPC-110
79T-219
80K-13
80OPC-296
80T-570
80T/S-40
81D-487
81F-551
81F/St-55
81MSA/Disc-30
81OPC-115
81T-115
81T/So-43
81T/St-100
82D-22DK
82D-573
82F-560
82F/St-228
82OPC-197
82T-767
82T/St-207
82T/Tr-107T
83D-209
83F-397
83OPC-38
83RoyRog/Disc-11
83T-460
83T/St-96
84D-225
84F-142
84Nes/792-305
84OPC-305
84T-305
85D-622
85F-527
85F/Up-U105
85OPC-26
85Seven/Minn-6
85T-140FS
85T-26
85T/St-237
85T/Tr-108T
86D-486
86F-404
86Leaf-237
86OPC-156
86T-613
87D-443
87F-552
87OPC-47
87T-744
87T/St-282
88D-566
88F-22
88Leaf-233
88Score-606
88T-239
PM10/Sm-182
Smalley, Roy Sr.
48L-77
49Eureka-72
50B-115
51B-44
51FB
51T/BB-17
52B-64
52T-173
53B/BW-56
54B-109
54T-231
55B-252
55JC-30
57T-397
60DF-3
76OPC-70FS
76T-70M
85T-140FS
Smalls, Roberto
88Wythe/Pro-1986
89CharWh/Best-15
89CharWh/Pro-1761
Smay, Kevin
81Clint-9
Smelko, Mark
82Redwd-11
83Redwd-23
Smelser, Don
80ElPas-15
Smiley, John
85PrWill-22
86PrWill-24
87D/Rook-39
87F/U-U110
87S/Rook-21
87Sf/Rook-7
87T/Tr-114T
88D-449
88D/Best-257
88F-340
88RedFoley/St-82
88Score-287
88T-423
88ToysRUs-28
89B-413
89Class/Up/2-191
89D-329
89D/Best-157
89F-221
89OPC-322
89Panini/St-167
89Score-409
89Score/YS/I-37
89T-322
89T/Big-85
89T/St-124
89UD-516
90Class-126
90D-17DK
90D-54
90F-480
90Score-334
90Score/100St-65
90Sf-191
90T-568
90UD-387
Smiley, Reuben
88Poca/Pro-2087
89Clint/Pro-894
Smith
10Domino-110
12Sweet/Pin-77
S74-56
Smith, Adam
88Poca/Pro-2092
Smith, Al
46Sunbeam
47Signal
47Sunbeam
Smith, Alex
87Durhm-14
88Richm-30
88Richm/CMC-13
88Richm/Pro-25
89Richm/Ko-14
89Richm/Pro-841
Smith, Alphonse E.
54T-248
55B-20
55Gol/Ind-27
55Salem
55T-197
56T-105
56T/Pin-110F
57T-145
58T-177
59T-22
60T-428
61P-24
61T-170
61T-42LL
61T/St-129
62J-48
62P-48
62P/Can-48
62Salada-29
62Shirriff-29
62T-410
63J-38
63P-38
63T-16
64T-317
Smith, Anthony
T204
T205
Smith, Bernie
83Redwd-29
Smith, Bill
61BeeHive-21
Smith, Bill
83AppFx/LF-1GM
Smith, Billy Edward
76SSPC-199
78T-666
79T-237
80OkCty
80T-367
82F-400
82T-593
Smith, Billy L.
78DaytB
80Tucso-11
81Tucso-24
82T-441R
82Tucso-18
84Tor/Fire-27CO
85Tor/Fire-26CO
86Tor/Fire-28CO
87Tor/Fire-28
87Tor/Fire-28CO
88Tor/Fire-42CO
Smith, Bob E.
33G-185
35BU-47
R316
Smith, Bob G.
58T-226
59T-83
Smith, Bob W.
58T-445
Smith, Bob
61BeeHive-22
Smith, Bobby Gene
57T-384
58T-402
59T-162
60T-194
61T-316
62J-196
62P-196
62P/Can-196
62Salada-176A
62Salada-176B
62Shirriff-176
62T-531
Smith, Bobby Glen
78BurlB
79Holyo-6
80Vanco-5
81Vanco-19

Smith, Brad
88Clearw/Star-23
Smith, Brick
84Chatt-5
86Chatt-23
86SLAS-17
87Calgary-12
87Sf/Rook-5
88Calg/Pro-803
89Tucso/CMC-17
89Tucso/Pro-193
Smith, Bryan
86Bakers-25
87VeroB-24
Smith, Bryn
78Denver
80Memph-20
82Hygrade
82OPC-118R
82T-118R
83D-88
83F-297
83OPC-234
83Stuart-29
83T-447
84D-453
84F-287
84Nes/792-656
84OPC-77
84Stuart-21
84T-656
85D-209
85F-410
85Leaf-171
85OPC-88
85T-88
85T/St-90
86D-299
86F-260
86F/Mini-55
86F/Slug-35
86F/St-110
86Leaf-174
86OPC-299
86Provigo-19
86S-120
86T-299
86T/St-79
86T/Super-51
87D-159
87F-332
87Leaf-60
87OPC-281
87T-505
87T/St-83
88D-335
88D/Best-202
88F-196
88Leaf-129
88OPC-161
88Panini/St-320
88Score-356
88T-161
88T/Big-250
89B-353
89D-216
89D/Best-124
89F-394
89OPC-131
89Panini/St-116
89Score-428
89T-464
89T/Big-47
89UD-78
90D-106
90D-25DK
90F-361
90Score-419
90T-352
90UD-579
Smith, C. Bernard
71OPC-204R
71T-204R
Smith, Carl R.
(Reggie)
67T-314R
67T/Test/RSox-12
68OPC-61
68T-61
69MB-256
69MLB/St-18
69T-660
69T/St-139
70K-46
70MLB/St-167
70OPC-215
70OPC-62LL
70T-215
70T-62LL
70T/PI-20
71K-52
71MD
71MLB/St-333
71OPC-305
71T-305
71T/Coins-78
71T/S-1
71T/tatt-8
72K-35
72MB-318
72OPC-88LL
72T-565
72T-566A
72T-88LL
73OPC-40
73T-40
74OPC-285
74T-285
74T/St-118
75Ho-59
75K-3
75OPC-490
75T-490
75T/M-490
76Crane-57
76Ho-30
76Ho/Twink-30
76MSA/Disc
76OPC-215
76SSPC-278
76T-215
77OPC-223
77T-345
78Ho-30
78K-34
78OPC-57
78T-168
78Wiffle/Discs-70
79Ho-72
79OPC-243
79T-465
79T/Comics-25
80OPC-350
80Pol/Dodg-8
80T-695
81D-59
81F-111
81F/St-87
81K-36
81OPC-75
81Pol/Dodg-8
81T-75
81T/HT
81T/So-57
81T/St-178
82D-488
82F-23
82OPC-228IA
82OPC-5
82T-545
82T-546A
82T/Tr-110T
83D-611
83F-272
83OPC-282
83OPC-283SV
83T-282
83T-283A
83T/St-12
83T/St-302
87Smok/Dodg-34
88Smok/Dodg-21M
89Smok/Dodg-88
Smith, Carlos
T206
Smith, Chad
89Sumter/Pro-1108
Smith, Charles M.
M116
N172
N284
N300/SC
WG1-62
Smith, Charles W.
60DF-12
62Salada-135A
62Salada-135B
62Shirriff-135
62T-283
63T-424
64T-519
65OPC-22
65T-22
66T-358
67T-257
68T-596
69T-538
78TCMA-289
Smith, Chris W.
80Memph-21
82Wichi-18
83Phoen/BHN-22
84D-46
Smith, Dan
75Cedar
78Tidew
79Jacks-17
Smith, Dan
86Bakers-26
87Orlan-3
Smith, Dana
86Hagers-18
88CharlK-21
88CharlK/Pep-21
89Hagers/Best-21
89Hagers/Pro-286
89Hagers/Star-18
Smith, Danny
85Cedar-12
86Vermont-20
Smith, Daryl
80Ashev-19
83Tulsa-7
86Water-23
87Wmspt-12
88BirmB/Best-19
Smith, Dave
76BurlB
77Holyo
78Holyo
Smith, David A.
80Spoka-2
81LynnS-11
82Holyo-9
Smith, David Lee
(D.L.)
87RochR-14
87RochR/TCMA-14
88RochR/CMC-17
89ElPas/GS-24
Smith, David S.
(Dave)
77Cocoa
79Charl-11
81D-23
81F-71
81OPC-287
81T-534
82D-191
82F-232
82OPC-297
82T-761
83D-370
83F-466
83OPC-247
83T-247
84D-548
84F-242
84Moth/Ast-13
84Nes/792-361
84T-361
85D-548
85F-362
85Moth/Ast-21
85T-123
86D-328
86F-312
86F/St-111
86OPC-222
86Pol/Ast-11
86T-408
86T/St-31
87Class-66
87D-308
87D/AAS-30
87F-6
87F/Hottest-38
87F/St-109
87Leaf-224
87Moth/Ast-20
87OPC-50
87Pol/Ast-17
87S-94
87T-50
87T/Mini-12
88D-410
88D/Best-262
88F-457
88F/Hottest-39
88F/Mini-81
88F/St-90
88F/TL-37
88Moth/Ast-20
88OPC-73
88Panini/St-290
88Pol/Ast-22
88RochR-21
88RochR/Pro-195
88SanDiegoSt-17
88Score-365
88Sf-208
88T-520
88T/St-26
89B-317
89Class-22
89D-272
89D/Best-232
89F-369
89F/BBAS-38
89Lennox/Ast-19
89Moth/Ast-19
89OPC-305
89Panini/St-87
89Score-245
89T-305
89T/St-13
89UD-302
90Class-94
90D-88
90F-238
90Score-45
90Score/100St-19
90Sf-140
90T-746
90UD-448
Smith, David Wayne
(D.W.)
82Holyo-10
83Nashua-8
83Wausa/LF-27
84Cram/PCL-103
84Newar-11
85Cram/PCL-16
86Edmon-26
Smith, David
88Keno/Pro-1391
89Visal/Cal-117
89Visal/Pro-1448
Smith, Don
84Cram/PCL-155
85Cram/PCL-171
Smith, Donald
(Snuffy)
47Smith-16
Smith, Dwight
86Peoria-23
87Pittsf-26
88AAA/Pro-19
88IowaC/CMC-21
88IowaC/Pro-530
89B-297
89D/Best-205
89D/Rook-32
89F/Up-79
89IowaC/CMC-22
89IowaC/Pro-1708
89Mara/Cubs-18
89Score-642
89Score/HotRk-64
89T/Tr-113T
89UD/Ext-780
90Class-30
90D-393
90F-42
90Score-240
90Score/100Ris-4
90Sf-152
90T-311
90UD-376
Smith, Earl L.
28Yueng-48
E120
V100
W573
Smith, Earl S.
21Exh-162
21Exh-163
25Exh-54
26Exh-54
27Exh-27
28Exh-26
E120
E121/120
E121/80
E220
V100
W501-71
W502-48
W572
W573
W575
Smith, Ed
89SoBend/GS-28
Smith, Edward Mayo
55T-130
56T-60
56T/Hocus-A9
56T/Pin-21MG
67T-321
68T-544
69OPC-40MG
69T-40
70OPC-313MG
70T-313
Smith, Elmer E.
N172
Smith, Elmer John
21Exh-164
D328-163
E120

E121/120
E135-163
W501-109
W572
W575

Smith, F.C.
N172

Smith, Forest
(Woody)
75SnAnt
77Watlo
78Watlo
81Chatt-24

Smith, Frank T.
52B-186
52T-179
53T-116
54B-188
54T-71
55Hunter
55T-204

Smith, Frank
(Nig)
14CJ-90
15CJ-90
D303
E101
E102
E105
E254
E270/1
E90/3
E92
M116
T206
T207
T213/blue
T215/blue
T215/brown
T3-118

Smith, Freddie
81Miami-3

Smith, Garry J.
77WHave
79Colum-5
80Colum-5
81Colum-21
82Colum-14
82Colum/Pol-13

Smith, Garry
82Nashv-24

Smith, Gary
78Cr/PCL-29

Smith, Gene
81BurlB-5

Smith, George A.
V100

Smith, George C.
65T-483
66T-542
67T-444
67T/Test/RSox-18

Smith, George H.
E254
T206

Smith, George J.
N172

Smith, Greg
81VeroB-18
85Beaum-6
86Erie-27
86LasVegas-16
87Erie-11
87OKCty-19
87Peoria-14
88CLAS/Star-35
88Spoka/Pro-1932
88WinSal/Star-17
89CharlK-11
89CharRa/Pro-979
89SLAS-11
90F-643
90Score-614

Smith, Hal R.
56T-283
57T-111
58T-273
59T-497
60L-58
60L-94M
60T-84
61P-180
61T-549

Smith, Hal W.
55Esskay
55T-8
55T/DH-70
56T-62
56T/Hocus-A15
56T/Pin-3C
57T-41
58T-257
59T-227
60L-119
60L-94M
60T-48
61P-139
61T-242
61T/St-70
61T/St-94
62J-181
62Kahn
62P-181
62P/Can-181
62Salada-190
62Shirriff-190
62T-492
62T/bucks
62T/St-129
63T-153
64T-233
78TCMA-127
89Smok/Ast-12

Smith, Harry Thomas
E107
M116

Smith, Henry J.
(Hap)
T206

Smith, Hilton
78Laugh/Black-34

Smith, Jack H.
63T-496R
64T-378R

Smith, Jack
82WHave-9
83ColumAst-20
86Tampa-20
87Tampa-14
88Greens/Pro-1569
89Wmspt/Pro-643
89Wmspt/Star-20

Smith, Jack
21Exh-165
E126-51
V61-75
WG7-53

Smith, Jackie
79Knoxv/TCMA-17

Smith, James C.
(Red)
D327
D328-164
D329-165
D350/2-167
E135-164
E220
M101/4-165
M101/5-167
T222

Smith, Jed
81Louvl-30
82Louvl-28
84Louvl-10
85Louvl-10
86Louisvl-29

Smith, Jeff
75Dubuq
76Dubuq
81Redwd-6
82Redwd-12
86Beloi-23

Smith, Jim
88Eugene/Best-8

Smith, Jimmy
77Charl
79RochR-13
80RochR-17
80Tidew-20
81Portl-22
83D-402
83F-323
83T-122

Smith, Joel
88SoOreg/Pro-1697

Smith, John Francis
N172

Smith, John W.
E102
V100
W572
W573

Smith, John
(Duke)
82Madis-5

Smith, John
78Cedar

Smith, John
89Utica/Puc-22

Smith, Jon
62Pep/Tul
63Pep/Tul

Smith, Keith L.
74Gasto
77Tucso
78Cr/PCL-76
78T-710R
81D-539
81F-534

Smith, Kelly
82Phoen

Smith, Kelvin
83Clint/LF-20

Smith, Ken
79Savan-24
80Richm-18
81Richm-4
82BK/Lids-23
82Richm-23
83F-148
83Pol/Atl-11
84Richm-3
85Richm-16
86RochR-23
88Savan/Pro-332
89StPet/Star-25

Smith, Larry
83Idaho-11
85Huntsvl/BK-30
87SnBer-2

Smith, Lawrence
(Larry)
89Mia/Star/25-18
89Well/Puc-31

Smith, Lee
80Wichi-12
82D-252
82F-603
82RedLob
82T-452
83D-403
83F-508
83T-699
83Thorn-46
84D-289
84F-505
84F/St-67
84FunFood/Pin-108
84Nes/792-176
84OPC-176
84SevenUp-46
84T-176
84T/St-44
85D-311
85F-67
85F/St-105
85Leaf-128
85OPC-43
85SevenUp-46
85T-511
85T/St-41
86D-144
86D/AS/WaxBox-PC8
86F-380
86F/LimEd-42
86F/LL-41
86Gator-46
86Jay's-17
86Leaf-64
86OPC-355
86S-45
86S-55M
86T-355
86T-636M
86T/St-56
86T/Super-52
87Berg/Cubs-46
87D-292
87F-574
87F/Excit-39
87F/McCror-39
87F/Mini-101
87F/St-110
87Leaf-80
87OPC-23
87RedFoley/St-42
87S-104
87S-77M
87Seven-C16
87Seven-ME15
87T-23
87T/Mini-3
87T/St-56
88D-292
88D/AS-60
88D/Best-252
88D/RedSox/Bk-NEW
88F-433
88F/Mini-9
88F/U-U8
88OPC-240
88Panini/St-256
88Score-31
88Score/Tr-20T
88Sf-179
88T-240
88T/Gloss60-56
88T/Mini-44
88T/St-64
88T/St/Backs-33
88T/Tr-110T
89B-19
89D-66
89D/Best-84
89F-99
89OPC-149
89Panini/St-272
89RedFoley/St-109
89Score-150
89Score/HotSt-18
89Sf-148
89T-760
89T/St-251
89UD-521
90Class-137
90D-110
90F-287
90Score-37
90T-495
90UD-393

Smith, Leroy
82Readg-8

Smith, Lonnie
76OkCty
79OkCty
79T-722R
80BK/P-14
81Coke
81D-295
81F-15
81OPC-317
81T-317
82D-606
82F-259
82F-641M
82F/St-60
82OPC-127
82T-127
82T/Tr-108T
83D-91
83D/AAS-34
83F-21
83F-636
83K-30
83OPC-273
83T-465
83T-561
83T/St-283
84D-231
84D-625
84D/Champs-23
84F-335
84F/St-7
84Nes/792-186TL
84Nes/792-580
84OPC-113
84Seven-14C
84T-580
84T/St-140
84T/St/Box-5
85D-231
85F-239
85F/St-61
85F/Up-U106
85Leaf-225
85OPC-255
85T-255
85T/St-139
85T/Tr-109T
86D-399
86F-21
86F/Mini-4
86F/St-112
86Kitty/Disc-1
86Leaf-188
86NatPhoto-21
86OPC-7
86S-186M
86T-617
86T/Mini-21
86T/St-264
87D-225
87F-381
87F/McCror-40
87F/St-111
87T-69
87T/St-262
88D-527
88Panini/St-111
88Richm-5
88Richm/CMC-14
88Richm/Pro-1
88Score-263
88T-777
89B-278
89D/Best-114
89F/Up-74
89T/Big-242
89T/Tr-114T
89UD/Ext-731

90Class-52
90D-222
90F-593
90Score-399
90Score/100St-82
90Sf-65
90T-152
90UD-215

Smith, Mandy
81Wisco-19

Smith, Mark
83BirmB-7
83RochR-8

Smith, Mark
88CapeCod/Sum-146

Smith, Mike
76AppFx
82Richm-26
86Cedar/TCMA-10
87Indianap-23
87Vermont-12
88Chatt/Best-21
88Indi/CMC-7
88Indi/Pro-509
89RochR/CMC-8
89RochR/CMC-9
89RochR/Pro-1634
89RochR/Pro-1637
90T-249
90T-552

Smith, Mike
80GlenF/B-28bb
80GlenF/C-29bb

Smith, Milt
61Union

Smith, Myrl
79Tucso-2

Smith, Nick
N172

Smith, Ozzie
79Ho-102
79OPC-52
79T-116
80OPC-205
80T-393
81D-1
81F-488
81OPC-254
81T-207M
81T-254
81T/SO-68
81T/St-230
82D-21DK
82D-94
82F-582
82F/St-101
82K-6
82OPC-95
82T-95
82T/St-104
82T/Tr-109T
83D-120
83F-22
83F-636M
83K-21
83OPC-14
83T-540
83T/St-168
83T/St-180
83T/St-186
83T/St-288
84D-59
84D-625
84F-336
84FunFood/Pin-71
84MiltBrad-25
84Nes/792-130
84Nes/792-389AS
84Nestle/DT-15
84OPC-130
84OPC-389AS
84Ralston-2
84Seven-19C
84T-130
84T-389
84T/Cereal-2
84T/Gloss22-16
84T/Gloss40-17
84T/St-144
84T/St-187
85D-59
85D/AAS-28
85F-240
85F-631IA
85F/LimEd-35
85GenMills-10
85Leaf-60
85OPC-191
85Seven-16C
85T-605
85T-715AS
85T/Gloss22-5
85T/St-137
85T/St-181
85T/Super-47
86D-59
86D/AAS-8
86D/PopUp-8
86F-46
86F/LL-42
86F/Mini-10
86F/St-113
86KAS/Disc-7
86Leaf-47
86OPC-297
86Quaker-15
86S-121
86Schnucks-21
86T-704
86T-730
86T/Gloss22-16
86T/Gloss60-46
86T/St-11NLCS
86T/St-153
86T/St-46
86T/Super-53
86TrueVal-9
87BK-14
87Class-32
87D-5DK
87D-60
87D/AAS-15
87D/DKsuper-5
87D/OD-65
87D/PopUp-15
87F-308
87F/AwardWin-38
87F/Lim-41
87F/Mini-102
87F/St-112
87Ho/St-15
87Jiffy-7
87Kraft-16
87Leaf-108
87Leaf-5DK
87MnM's-24
87OPC-107
87Ralston-13
87RedFoley/St-112
87S-142
87S-79M
87Smok/Cards-17
87Smok/NL-9
87T-598AS
87T-749
87T/Coins-45
87T/Gloss22-5
87T/Gloss60-23
87T/St-162
87T/St-46
88ChefBoy-5
88Class/Blue-210
88D-263
88D-BC22
88D/AS-37
88D/AS-63
88D/Best-243
88D/PopUp-15
88F-47
88F-628M
88F/AwardWin-39
88F/BB/AS-39
88F/BB/MVP-35
88F/Hottest-40
88F/Mini-109
88F/RecSet-38
88F/St-120
88F/TL-38
88F/WS-4
88FanSam-11
88KingB/Disc-4
88KMart-28
88Leaf-115
88Nestle-5
88OPC-39
88Panini/St-235M
88Panini/St-393
88Score-12
88Score/WaxBox-14
88Sf-68
88Smok/Card-18
88T-400
88T-460
88T/Big-228
88T/Coins-55
88T/Gloss22-16
88T/Gloss60-47
88T/Mini-72
88T/St-153
88T/St-53
88T/St/Backs-12
88T/UK-72
89B-436
89Cadaco-53
89Class-58
89D-63
89D/AS-37
89D/AS-62
89D/Best-44
89D/MVP-BC14
89D/PopUp-37
89F-463
89F/Excit-38
89F/LL-35
89Holsum/Discs-3
89KayBee-28
89OPC-230
89Panini/St-186
89Panini/St-235AS
89Ralston-1
89RedFoley/St-110
89Score-80
89Score/HotSt-88
89Score/Mast-27
89Sf-105
89T-230
89T-389AS
89T/Big-110
89T/Coins-25
89T/DH-16
89T/Gloss22-16
89T/Gloss60-42
89T/HeadsUp-17
89T/Mini-36
89T/St-161
89T/St-44
89T/St/Backs-45
89T/UK-72
89UD-265
89UD-674TC
90Class-18
90D-201
90D-710AS
90F-260
90Score-285
90Score/100St-6
90Sf-16
90T-400AS
90T-590
90UD-225

Smith, P. Keith
83Nashvl-23
84Nashvl-21
85Colum-19
85Colum/Pol-22
86Colum-23
86Colum/Pol-22
87Denver-25
88Denver/CMC-14
88Denver/Pro-1261
89Vanco/CMC-13
89Vanco/Pro-578

Smith, Paul
54DanDee
54T-11
57T-345
58T-269
63MilSau-8

Smith, Peter J.
87Greenv/Bst-24
88D-571
88D/Best-197
88D/Rook-10
88F-647
88F/U-U73
88Score/Tr-84T
88T/Tr-111T
89B-269
89D-263
89F-600
89OPC-388
89Panini/St-36
89Score-207
89Score/HotRk-74
89Score/YS/I-19
89T-537
89T/St-31
89ToysRUs-29
89UD-412
90D-499
90F-594
90Score-225
90T-771
90UD-613

Smith, Peter L.
63MilSau-9
64T-428R

Smith, Phil
82DayBe-24

Smith, Randy
76QuadC

Smith, Ray
77Visal
78OrlTw
79Toled-22
80Toled-16
82Toled-11
84F-573
84Nes/792-46
84T-46
84Toled-4
85Cram/PCL-114
86Tacom-21
89Elizab/Star-29

Smith, Richard Arthur
64T-398R
65T-579

Smith, Richard H.
53Mother-3
55B-288

Smith, Rick
88Bakers/Cal-267

Smith, Rob
88Stock/Cal-192
88Stock/Pro-741
89Stock/Best-23
89Stock/Cal-168
89Stock/Pro-394
89Stock/Star-18

Smith, Robbie
86Orlan-17
87Orlan-2

Smith, Robert
21Exh-166
28Exh-3
29Exh/4-2

Smith, Ron
75BurlB
76BurlB
76Watlo
80Penin/B-20
80Penin/C-26

Smith, Ronnie
47Signal

Smith, Roy
80Penin/B-12
80Penin/C-4
83Charl-5
84Maine-3
84Wheat/Ind-33
85D-611
85F-455
85Maine-10
85Polar/Ind-33
85T-381
86D-468
86T-9
87Portl-8
88AAA/Pro-33
88Portl/CMC-6
88Portl/Pro-645
90D-273
90F-386
90Score-568
90T-672
90UD-284

Smith, Samuel
N172

Smith, Sherrod
21Exh-167
21Exh-168
25Exh-86
26Exh-85
28Yueng-31
E120
E126-22
E210-31
E220
W502-31

Smith, Steve
79Hawai-14
80Hawai-18
81Hawai-3
82Hawai-3
84Shrev/FB-18
86Beaum-23MG
86Fresno/Smok-17
87TexLgAS-13
87Wichi-9
88LasVeg/CMC-24
88LasVeg/Pro-244
89AAA/Pro-50
89LasVeg/CMC-24
89LasVeg/Pro-25

Smith, Syd
E270/1
T206
T213/brown

Smith, Terry
86Lakel-22TR
87Lakel-11

Smith, Tim
84Newar-14

Smith, Todd
86Miami-23
87Salem-26
89Medford/Best-30

Smith, Tom
81QuadC-18
83Peoria/LF-10

Smith, Tommy A.
74OPC-606R
74T-606R
75OPC-619R
75T-619R
75T/M-619R
76SSPC-530
77OPC-92
77T-14
Smith, Tommy
75Lafay
75OkCty
78Cr/PCL-31
80RochR-19
Smith, Tony
C46-32
Smith, Tracy
88Geneva/Pro-1647
89Peoria/Ko-20
Smith, Vinnie
52Mother-59
Smith, Wallace H.
T207
Smith, William G.
63T-241
Smith, Willie
65OPC-85
65T-85
66T-438
67T-397
68T-568
69MB-257
69OPC-198
69T-198
70OPC-318
70T-318
71OPC-457
71T-457
72MB-319
Smith, Willie
88Aug/Pro-377
89Salem/Star-21
Smith, Woody
88Wythe/Pro-1990
89Peoria/Ko-22
Smith, Zane
83Durhm-24
85F-651
85Pol/Atl-34
86D-565
86F-528
86Leaf-222
86OPC-167
86Pol/Atl-34
86T-167
87D-167
87F-529
87OPC-226
87RedFoley/St-73
87Smok/Atl-1
87T-544
88D-167
88D/Best-170
88F-550
88F/Mini-66
88F/St-78
88F/TL-39
88OPC-297
88Panini/St-240
88Score-410
88Sf-134
88T-297
88T/Big-193
88T/Mini-42
88T/St-40
88T/UK-73
89B-262
89D-499
89F-601
89F/Up-99
89OPC-339
89RedFoley/St-111
89Score-492
89Score/Tr-56
89T-688
89T/St-27
89UD-71
90D-460
90F-362
90Score-477
90T-48
90UD-607
Smithberg, Roger
89LasVeg/Pro-17
Smithson, Mike
81Pawtu-11
83Rang-48
83T/X-106
84D-221
84F-428
84F/X-108
84Nes/792-89
84T-89
84T/X-110
85D-316
85F-289
85OPC-359
85Seven/Minn-11
85T-483
85T/St-301
86D-147
86F-405
86Leaf-73
86OPC-101
86T-695
86T/Mini-24
86T/St-282
87D-245
87F-553
87OPC-225
87T-225
87T/St-275
88D/RedSox/Bk-NEW
88F-23
88F/U-U9
88OPC-389
88Score/Tr-59T
88T-554
89D-628
89F-100
89Score-403
89T-377
89T/Big-222
89UD-38
90D-464
90F-288
90Score-512
90T-188
90UD-610
Smoll, Clyde
87Elmir-1
87Elmir/Red-1
88Elmir-30GM
89Elmir/Puc-25
Smoltz, John
86Lakel-23
87GlenF-24
88F/U-U74
88Richm-26
88Richm/CMC-3
88Richm/Pro-23
89B-266
89Class/Up/2-174
89D-642
89D/Best-85
89F-602
89Score-616
89T-382
89T/Big-260
89UD-17
90Class-13
90D-121
90D-8DK
90D/Bon/MVP-BC12
90F-595
90Score-370
90Score/100St-35
90Sf-61
90T-535
90UD-535
90UD-84TC
Smoot, Allen
82Clint-18
Smyth, Harry
R314/Can
V355-79
Snaith, Andy
82AlexD-26
Snead, Jay
89Aug/Pro-519
Snead, Sam
51Wheat
52Wheat
Snedeker, Sean
88GreatF-20
89Bakers/Cal-181
Snediker, Jim
86WinHav-24
Snell, Dave
86Wausa-25
88Vermont/Pro-956
Snell, Nate
85F/Up-U107
85T/Tr-110T
86D-367
86F-288
86Leaf-166
86T-521
87D-396
87F-481
87T-86
88F-70
Snider, Duke
49B-226
49Eureka-50
50B-77
50Drake-5
51B-32
51T/RB-38
52B-116
52BR
52NTea
52RM-NL21
52StarCal/L-79E
52T-37
52TipTop
53B/Col-117
53Briggs
53RM-NL14
53SM
54B-170
54DanDee
54NYJour
54RH
54RM-NL16
54SM
54T-32
55Armour-19
55Gol/Dodg-28
55RM-NL19
55SM
55T-210
56T-150
56T/Pin-52
56YellBase/Pin-29
57T-170
57T-400M
58BB
58Hires-61
58T-314M
58T-436M
58T-88
59Bz
59HRDerby-18
59Morrell
59T-20
59T-468M
60BB-2
60L-37
60Morrell
60NuCard-55
60T-493
61BB-4
61P-167
61T-443
61T/St-35
62BB-4
62J-114
62P-114
62P/Can-114
62Salada-215
62Shirriff-215
62T-500
62T/St-140
63J-118
63P-118
63T-550
63T-68M
64T-155
64Wheat/St-42
76SSPC-351
79TCMA-43
79TCMA-72
80Cram/Leg-19
80SSPC/HOF
82CJ-8
83D/HOF-14
83MLBPA/Pin-33
84D-648PUZ
84West/1-24
85CircK-20
86S/Dec-32
87Nestle/DT-33
88Pac/Leg-55
89B-I10
89Rini/Dodg-4
89Smok/Dodg-27
Exh47
PM10/L-39
PM10/Sm-183
PM10/Sm-184
PM10/Sm-185
R423-95
WG9-47
Snider, Kelly
77LodiD
79Albuq-14
80Albuq-4
81Toled-15
82Toled-16
Snider, Van
83CharR-13
84Memph-9
87Omaha-4
88Nashvl/CMC-22
88Nashvl/Pro-473
89D-586
89F-172
89Nashvl-23
89Nashvl/CMC-23
89Nashvl/Pro-1281
89Score-640
89Score/HotRk-41
89Sf-177
89UD-23
Snitker, Brian
78Green
79Savan-5
83Durhm-28
84Durhm-28
86Sumter-26MG
87Durhm-6
Snoddy, Ralph
33SK-25
Snodgrass, Fred
11Helmar-137
60NuCard-54
61NuCard-454
88Conlon/3-26
D328-165
D329-166
D350/2-168
E135-165
E254
E270
M101/4-166
M101/5-168
M116
S74-95
T202
T205
T206
T207
W555
Snover, Colonel L.
E120
Snover, Don
89Pulas/Pro-1896
Snow, J.T.
88CapeCod/Sum-125
89Oneon/Pro-2112
Snuder, Kendall
87Kenosha-4
Snyder, Ben
82DayBe-8
83ColumAst-19
Snyder, Brian
81Wausa-7
82SLCty-17
83SLCty-4
84Cram/PCL-178
84Shrev/FB-19
85Cram/PCL-92
86LasVegas-17
86T-174
87LasVegas-15
88Tacom/CMC-9
88Tacom/Pro-629
89Tacom/CMC-4
89Tacom/Pro-1545
Snyder, Charles N.
N172
Snyder, Chris
88CapeCod/Sum-9
Snyder, Cory
85T-403
85Water-23
86D-29
86D/Rook-15
86F-653M
86Maine-20
86S/Rook-18
87Class/Up-110
87D-526
87D/OD-106
87F-260
87F/Excit-40
87F/Hottest-39
87F/Mini-103
87F/Slug-M5
87F/St-113
87Gator-28
87Kraft-17
87Leaf-157
87OPC-192
87S-24
87T-192
87T/Coins-24
87T/Gloss60-9
87T/GlossRk-16
87T/St-213
87ToysRUs-25
88Class/Red-184
88D-350
88D/Best-224
88F-615
88F-622M
88F/SS-37
88F/St-21
88Gator-28

88KingB/Disc-10
88Leaf-125
88OPC-169
88Panini/St-80
88RedFoley/St-83
88Score-92
88Score/YS/I-40
88Sf-29
88T-620
88T/Big-43
88T/Coins-27
88T/Gloss60-23
88T/St-208
88T/St/Backs-53
88T/UK-74
89B-89
89Class-19
89D-191
89D-8DK
89D/Best-168
89D/DKsuper-8DK
89F-412
89F/Superstar-38
89OPC-80
89Panini/St-329
89Score-52
89Score/HotSt-6
89Sf-196
89T-80
89T/Big-175
89T/St-210
89T/UK-73
89UD-170
89UD-679TC
90D-272
90F-502
90Score-10
90Score/100St-28
90Sf-3
90T-770
90UD-126

Snyder, Doug
86Osceola-24
87Osceola-9
88Visal/Cal-158
88Visal/Pro-100
89Orlan/Best-25
89Orlan/Pro-1327

Snyder, Frank
(Pancho)
21Exh-169
25Exh-38
26Exh-35
40PB-159
E120
E121/120
E121/80
E220
V61-94
W501-66
W515-44
W575

Snyder, Gene W.
59T-522

Snyder, Gerald
52B-246
54B-216
55B-74
57T-22

Snyder, Jim
76Indianap-1MG
80OkCty
81OkCty/TCMA-23
88T/Tr-112MG
89T-44MG

Snyder, Randy
89Stock/Best-17
89Stock/Cal-170
89Stock/Pro-382
89Stock/Star-16

Snyder, Russ
60L-102
60T-81
61T-143
62Salada-206
62Shirriff-206
62T-64
63J-63
63P-63
63T-543
64T-126
65OPC-204
65T-204
66T-562
67T-405
68T-504
69MB-258
69OPC-201
69T-201
70McDon-6
70OPC-347
70T-347
71MLB/St-452
71OPC-653
71T-653
72MB-320
78TCMA-136

Soar, Hank
55B-279ump

Soares, Todd
88Jaxvl/Pro-978

Sobbe, William
81VeroB-19

Sobczyk, Bob
88Beloi/GS-11
89Boise/Pro-1993

Sodders, Mike
82Toled-18
83Orlan-9
88Geneva/Pro-1642
89Peoria/Ko-10

Soden, Frank
79Richm-9M

Soderholm, Eric
73OPC-577
73T-577
74OPC-503
74T-503
75OPC-54
75T-54
75T/M-54
76K-28
76OPC-214
76SSPC-223
76T-214
77T-273
78Ho-20
78K-32
78OPC-21
78T-602
79Ho-103
79OPC-93
79T-186
80T-441
81D-106
81F-92
81T-383

Soff, Ray
81QuadC-23
83MidldC-22
84MidldC-9
86ArkTr-23
86Louisvl-26
87D-631
87F-309
87Louvl-27
87OPC-96
87Smok/Cards-1
87T-671
88Portl/CMC-7
88Portl/Pro-662
89Portl/CMC-5
89Portl/Pro-216

Sofield, Rick
77Visal
79T-709R
80T-669R
81D-592
81F-563
81OPC-278
81T-278
82T-42
82Toled-21

Softy, Mark
79WHave-16
80Wausa-9

Sohns, Thomas
80Water-16

Sojo, Luis
87Myrtle-29
88Myrtle/Pro-1189
88SALAS/GS-18
89Syrac/CMC-22
89Syrac/Pro-809
90T-594

Solaita, Tony
75OPC-389
75T-389
75T/M-389
76A&P/KC
76OPC-121
76SSPC-143
76T-121
77T-482
78T-557
79T-18
80OPC-212
80T-407

Solano, Julio
83Tucso-11
84Cram/PCL-63
85F-363
85Moth/Ast-12
85T-353
86Pol/Ast-16
87Pol/Ast-18
88Moth/Sea-24
89Moth/Sea-26

Solano, Ramon
87Fayette-6

Solarte, Jose
88James/Pro-1912

Solis, Marcelino
59T-214

Solomon, Eddie
(Buddy)
75OPC-624R
75T-624R
75T/M-624R
78T-598
79OPC-74
79T-156
80T-346
81D-16
81F-384
81T-298
82D-437
82F-498
82T-696TL
82T-73

Solseth, David
89Eugene/Best-12

Soltero, Saul
87Spoka-4
88Charl/Pro-1215
89AubAs/Pro-23
89River/Best-16
89River/Cal-31
89River/Pro-1406
89Wich/Roc/Up-9

Solters, Julius
(Moose)
34DS-85
34G-30
38G-255
38G-279
39PB-78
40PB-126
41DP-71
R313
R314
V354-77

Soma, Katsuya
83SanJose-18

Somers, P.T.
N172

Sommer, David
89James/Pro-2144

Sommer, Joseph J.
N172

Sommers, Dennis
75Lafay
82BK/Ind-10
82BK/Ind-11
82BK/Ind-12CO
82BK/Indians-10
82BK/Indians-11
82BK/Indians-12
82Wheat/Ind
83Wheat/Ind-25
85Polar/Ind-xx
88Smok/Padres-27

Sommers, Joseph A.
N172

Sommers, Scott
86Elmir-22
88Lynch/Star-23
89NewBrit/Pro-623
89NewBrit/Star-19

Sonberg, Erik
85Cram/PCL-159
89Hagers/Best-18
89Hagers/Pro-267

Songini, Michael
(Mike)
88Bill/Pro-1829
89Greens/Pro-421

Sonneberger, Steve
88Hagers/Star-20

Sontag, Alan
86Orlan-18
87Orlan-23

Soos, Charles
87Kinston-4
88Kinston/Star-20

Soper, Mike
83BurlR-11
86Colum-24
86Colum/Pol-23

Sorce, Sam
83BurlR-22
83BurlR/LF-3
85Orlan-11
86Orlan-19

Sorensen, Lary
77Spoka
78T-569
79T-303
80OPC-84
80T-154
81Coke
81D-325
81F-519
81T-379
81T/Tr-831
82D-246
82F-128
82OPC-136
82T-689
82T/Tr-111T
82Wheat/Ind
83D-363
83F-418
83OPC-48
83T-48
83Wheat/Ind-26
84D-635
84F-549
84F/X-109
84Moth/A's-14
84Nes/792-286
84Nes/792-546TL
84OPC-286
84T-286
84T-546TL
84T/St-259
84T/X-111
85D-131
85F-434
85F/Up-U108
85SevenUp-42
86F-381
86T-744
87F/U-U111
88Chatt/Best-20

Sorey, Ron
78Duned

Soriano, Hilario
77Clint

Soriano, Tony
47Remar-24

Soroko, Mark
77Tucso

Sorrel, Mike
81Cedar-14
82CharR-3

Sorrell, Billy
66T-254R
67T-341R
71OPC-17
71T-17

Sorrell, Vic
33G-15
V355-21

Sorrento, Paul
87PalmSp-11
88PalmSp/Cal-110
88PalmSp/Pro-1450
89Orlan/Best-1
89Orlan/Pro-1343
89SLAS-13
90D-626
90Score-647

Sosa, Elias
74OPC-54
74T-54
74T/St-109
75OPC-398
75T-398
75T/M-398
76OPC-364
76SSPC-558
76T-364
77T-558
78T-694
79T-78
80OPC-153
80T-293
81D-599
81F-151
81OPC-181
81T-181
82D-446
82F-208
82OPC-116
82T-414
82T/Tr-112T
83D-259
83F-342
83T-753
83T/X-107
84F-313
84Nes/792-503
84T-503
87SanJose-18
89Sumter/Pro-1093

Sosa, Jose
73Cedar
74Cedar

76OPC-591R
76T-591R
78Charl

Sosa, Miguel
80Ander-24
81Durhm-1
82Durhm-9
85IntLgAS-3
85Richm-17
86Albany/TCMA-4
86Colum-25

Sosa, Sammy
87Gasto-29
88CharlR/Star-23
89D/Best-324
89Tulsa/GS-25
90Class-140
90D-489
90F-548
90Score-558
90Score/100Ris-35
90Sf-81
90T-692
90UD-17

Sossamon, L. Timothy
(Tim)
86Cram/PCL-148
87CharWh-23
88Readg/Pro-870

Soth, Paul
77AppFx
79AppFx-1

Sothoron, Allan
21Exh-170
E120
E126-11
R312/M
W573

Soto, Ed
86DayBe-26
87Gasto-14

Soto, Jose
86Geneva-25

Soto, Mario
77Indianap-21
78Indianap-9
78T-427
79Indianap-28
80T-622
81Coke
81D-63
81F-214
81T-354
81T/HT
82Coke/Reds
82D-103
82F-83
82F/St-19
82T-63
83D-248
83F-603
83OPC-215
83T-215
83T-351
83T/St-234
84Borden-36
84D-428
84F-483
84F/St-79
84FunFood/Pin-61
84Nes/792-160
84Nes/792-756TL
84OPC-160
84Seven-13C
84T-160
84T/Gloss22-21
84T/St-51
85D-184
85D-19
85D/AAS-3
85D/DKsuper-19
85F-552
85F/LimEd-36
85F/St-116
85F/St-86
85GenMills-11
85Indianap-31
85Leaf-19DK
85OPC-131
85Seven-13G
85T-495
85T/Gloss40-37
85T/St-46
85T/Super-21
86D-184
86F-192
86F/Mini-41
86F/Slug-36
86F/St-114
86Leaf-119
86OPC-28
86S-168
86T-725
86T/Mini-42
86T/St-136
86TexGold-36
87D-82
87F-214
87Leaf-140
87OPC-11
87T-517
88T-666
88T/Big-120
89Score-588

Soto, Max
86GlenF-22

Soto, Miguel
84Savan-24

Soto, Ozzie
85Cedar-13
86Tampa-21

Soto, Tom
78Newar
79Holyo-10
81Vanco-23

Sottile, Shaun
89Pulas/Pro-1898

Souchock, Steve
52B-235
52T-234
53B/Col-91
53Glen
54B-103

Southland, Kip
87Everett-8

Southworth, Bill
25Exh-39
27Exh-32
47TipTop
49Eureka-24
51B-207
80Cram/Leg-17
E120
E121/120
E126-10
W501-89
W502-118
W514-16
W572
W754

Souza, Mark
76Watlo
79Ogden/TCMA-17
80Ogden-10
81Tacom-22

Sovern, Jeff
76Indianap-8
78Indianap-25

Sowards, Van
83Clint/LF-21
84Shrev/FB-20

Sowders, John
N172

Sowders, William J.
E223
N172
N403/Bos
N526

Spade, Robert
E254
M116
T206

Spagnola, Glen
83Cedar-5
83Cedar/LF-16
86Vermont-21
87Vermont-18
88ColAst/Best-4
89Calg/CMC-10
89Calg/Pro-527
89Wmspt/Star-21

Spagnuolo, Joe
87VeroB-3

Spahn, Warren
47TipTop
48B-18
48L-32
49B-33
49Eureka-25
49Royal-5
50B-19
50Drake-14
51B-134
51BR-B2
51T/RB-30
52B-156
52Dix
52NTea
52RM-NL22
52Royal
52T-33
52TipTop
53B/Col-99
53Dix
53Exh/Can-32
53JC-10
53NB
53RM-NL19
53T-147
54JC-21
54RH
54RM-NL11
54T-20
55Armour-20
55Gol/Braves-27
55JC-21
55RM-NL10
55T-31
55T/DH-127
56T-10
56T/Hocus-A10
56T/Hocus-B12
56T/Pin-19
57T-90
58T-270
58T-494AS
59T-40
59T-571AS
60Bz-19
60Lake
60NuCard-63
60T-230M
60T-445
60T/tatt
60T/tatt-49
61Bz-29
61NuCard-402
61NuCard-463
61P-101
61T-200
61T-47LL
61T-589AS
61T/St-47
62Bz
62Exh
62T-100
62T-312M
62T-399AS
62T-56LL
62T-58LL
62T/bucks
62T/St-150
63Bz-5
63Exh
63F-45
63Salada-8
63T-320
63T/SO
64Bz-5
64T-3LL
64T-400
64T/Coins-160AS
64T/Coins-88
64T/S-31
64T/St-57
64T/SU
64T/tatt
64Wheat/St-43
65OPC-205
65T-205
73OPC-449CO
73T-449C
79TCMA-3
80Cram/Leg-57
80Laugh/3/4/5-15
80SSPC/HOF
81Redwd-22
82CJ-3
82F/St-108M
83MLBPA/Pin-34
84West/1-19
86S/Dec-27
87Nestle/DT-32
88Pac/Leg-109
89D-588PUZ
89HOF/St-84
Exh47
PM10/L-40
R346-20

Spain, Dan
78OrlTw

Spalding, Al G.
50Callahan
75F/Pion-4
80SSPC/HOF

Spalt, Paul
88Watertn/Puc-24

Span, Brian
89CharRa/Pro-975
89Spoka/SP-15

Spangler, Al
60L-38
60Lake
60T-143
61P-114
61T-73
62J-157
62P-157
62P/Can-157
62Salada-196
62Shirriff-196
62T-556
62T/St-130
63F-39
63J-185
63P-185
63Pep
63T-77
64T-406
65OPC-164
65T-164
65T/E-53
65T/trans-70
66OPC-173
66T-173
68T-451
69MB-259
69T8-268
70T-714
72MB-321
74OPC-354CO
74T-354C
78TCMA-166
78TCMA-171
89Smok/Ast-23

Spann, Tookie
88Brist/Pro-1891
89Lakel/Star-19

Spanswick, Bill
63MilSau-10
64T-287R
65T-356
78TCMA-147

Sparks, Don
89PrWill/Star-19

Sparks, Greg
86CharRa-23
88Huntsvl/BK-21
89Salin/Pro-1819

Sparks, Joe
75Iowa/TCMA-18
81Omaha-1
82Omaha-25
83Omaha-24
86Indianap-3MG
87Indianap-4
88AAA/Pro-50
88Indi/CMC-24
88Indi/Pro-496

Sparks, Steve
88Beloi/GS-24
89Stock/Best-8
89Stock/Cal-152
89Stock/Pro-390
89Stock/Star-11

Sparks, Tully
E107
E254
M116

Sparling, Don
85FtMyr-5
87Memph-19
87Memph/Best-14

Sparma, Joe
64T-512R
65T-587
66T-267
67OPC-13
67T-13
68T-505
69T-488
70MLB/St-69
70OPC-243
70T-243
88Domino-21

Sparrow, Chris
89Idaho/Pro-2024

Speake, Bob
56T-66
57T-339
58T-437
59T-526

Speaker, Tris
10Domino-111
11Helmar-4
12Sweet/Pin-6
12Sweet/Pin-6A
14CJ-65
14Piedmont/St-52
15CJ-65
21Exh-171
25Exh-87
26Exh-86
27Exh-64
28Yung-28
33G-89
40PB-170
48Exh/HOF
50Callahan

51T/CM
60Exh/HOF-22
60F-10
61F-79
61GP-309
63Bz-24
69Bz/Sm
72F/FFeat-32
72K-11
72K/ATG-11
80SSPC/HOF
85Woolwth-34
86Conlon/1-30
87Nestle/DT-6
88Conlon/3-27
89HOF/St-41
D303
D327
D328-166
E106
E120
E121/120
E121/80
E122
E126-27
E135-166
E210-28
E220
E224
E254
E270/1
E300
E90/1
E91
E94
L1-131
M116
PM1-12
R312/M
R423-104
S74-3
S81-106
T201
T202
T205
T206
T207
T213/blue
T215/blue
T215/brown
T216
T3-36
V100
V354-29
W501-19
W502-28
W512-4
W514-102
W515-28
W516-5
W572
W573
W575
WG4-27
WG5-35
WG6-33

Speakes, Joey
88Poca/Pro-2097

Speakman, Tim
85Elmir-21

Spear, Mike
88Butte-20

Spearnock, Mike
86Cram/PCL-99
87PalmSp-1

Speck, R. Cliff
80OkCty
82RochR-6
83RochR-9
86Richm-21
87D-571
87Richm/TCMA-25
87T-269
88Colum/CMC-22
88Colum/Pol-11
88Colum/Pro-311

Speckenbach, Paul
64T-548R

Specyalski, Brian
88CapeCod/Sum-89

Speece, Byron
43Centen-22
44Centen-21
45Centen-23

Speed, Horace
75Phoen-22
76Phoen
76SSPC-112
77Phoen
79T-438
80Richm-14

Speer, V. Floyd
46Remar-18
47Remar-14
47Signal
48Signal
48Smith-18

Speier, Chris
72K-28
72OPC-165
72OPC-166IA
72T-165
72T-166A
73OPC-273
73OPC-345KP
73T-273
73T-345BP
73T/Lids-49
74K-40
74OPC-129
74OPC-335AS
74T-129
74T-335M
74T/DE-29
74T/St-110
75Ho-73
75Ho/Twink-73
75OPC-505
75T-505
75T/M-505
76Ho-82
76OPC-630
76SSPC-105
76T-630
77OPC-53
77Pep-41
77T-515
78OPC-232
78T-221
79OPC-221
79T-426
80OPC-168
80T-319
81D-329
81F-153
81OPC-97
81OPC/Post-3
81T-97
81T/St-189
82D-366
82F-209
82F/St-32
82Hygrade
82OPC-198
82T-198
82T/St-58
82Zeller-8
83D-266
83F-298
83OPC-121
83Stuart-27
83T-768
83T/St-258
84D-523
84F-288
84Moth/Giants-22
84Nes/792-678
84OPC-328
84Stuart-27
84T-678
84T/St-95
85F/Up-U109
85SevenUp-28
85T-577
85T/Tr-111T
86F-382
86Gator-28
86OPC-212
86T-212
87D-392
87F-575
87F/U-U112
87Moth/SFG-18
87T-424
87T/Tr-115T
88D-239
88F-96
88Moth/Giants-18
88Score-493
88T-329
89D-532
89F-343
89Moth/Giants-18
89Score-297
89T-94
89UD-206
90F-72
90T-753

Spence, J. Bob
71OPC-186
71T-186

Spence, Samuel
77Watlo
78Watlo

Spence, Stan
49B-102
Exh47

Spencer, Edward
(Tubby)
C46-81
E220
E254
E96
T204
T206
W514-36

Spencer, Daryl
54B-185
56T-277
57T-49
58Hires-51
58SFCall
58T-68
59T-443
60L-129
60MacGregor-24
60T-368
61P-173
61T-357
61T-451M
61T/St-95
62BB-20
62J-103
62P-103
62P/Can-103
62Salada-178A
62Salada-178B
62Shirriff-178
62T-197
62T/St-141
63FrBauer-27
63J-124
63P-124
63T-502
79TCMA-226

Spencer, George
52BR
52T-346
53T-115
55Gol/Giants-25
63MilSau-11

Spencer, Glenn Edward
33G-84
V354-37

Spencer, Jim
70OPC-255
70T-255
71MLB/St-358
71OPC-78
71T-78
71T/Coins-4
72MB-322
72OPC-419
72T-419
73OPC-319
73T-319
74OPC-580
74T-580
74T/St-239
75OPC-387
75T-387
75T/M-387
76OPC-83
76SSPC-268
76T-83
76T/Tr-83T
77OPC-46
77T-648
78BK/Y-16
78OPC-122
78T-182
79BK/Y-17
79OPC-315
79T-599
80OPC-147
81OPC-209
81T/Tr-832
82D-265
82F-107
82F/St-127
82OPC-88
82T-729
82T/St-223

Spencer, John
88Elmir-25
89Elmir/Puc-20

Spencer, Kyle
88Butte-10
89Gasto/Pro-1002
89Gasto/Star-22

Spencer, Roy
31Exh/4-31
33Exh/4-16

Spencer, Tom
76Indianap-6
78Knoxv
79Knoxv/TCMA-25
80Tucso-15
81Tucso-13
86Pittsf-22MG
88Gator-2CO
89Cedar/Best-25
89Cedar/Pro-917
89Cedar/Star-24

Sperring, Rob
76OPC-323
76SSPC-320
76T-323
77T-514
78Charl
79Charl-16

Spicer, Len
79Newar-22

Spicer, Robert
52Mother-61

Spiers, Bill
88Stock/Cal-197
88Stock/Pro-738
89D/Rook-5
89F/Up-40
89Pol/Brew-6
89Score/Tr-82
89T/Tr-115T
89UD/Ext-745
90Class-134
90D-382
90F-337
90Score-449
90Score/100Ris-55
90Sf-206
90T-538
90UD-237

Spiezio, Ed
65T-431R
66Pep/Tul
67OPC-128
67T-128
68T-349
69MLB/St-197
69T-249
70MLB/St-119
70T-718
71MLB/St-240
71OPC-6
71T-6
72MB-323
72OPC-504
72T-504

Spikes, Charlie
73OPC-614R
73T-614R
74OPC-58
74T-58
74T/DE-33
74T/St-169
75OPC-135
75T-135
75T/M-135
76OPC-408
76SSPC-531
76T-408
77T-168
78T-459
80T-294
81F-259

Spillner, Dan
75OPC-222
75T-222
75T/M-222
76OPC-557
76SSPC-119
76T-557
77T-182
78T-488
79T-359
80T-38
81F-392
81T-276
82D-411
82F-378
82OPC-1
82T-664
82Wheat/Ind
83D-137
83F-419
83OPC-278
83T-725
83T/St-59
83Wheat/Ind-27
84D-582
84F-550
84Nes/792-91
84OPC-91
84T-91
85Coke/WS-37
85F-528
85T-169
86D-122
86F-217

86T-423
Spilman, Harry
78Indianap-5
79Indianap-5
79T-717R
80T-677
81D-304
81F-209
81T-94
81T/Tr-833
82F-233
82T-509
82Tucso-11
83D-65
83F-467
83T-193
84D-258
84Moth/Ast-12
84Nes/792-612
84T-612
85Moth/Ast-19
85T-482
86T-352
87F-284
87Moth/SFG-16
87T-64
88D-607
88F-97
88Moth/Giants-16
88Score-618
88T-217
89Tucso/CMC-18
89Tucso/Pro-199
Spinks, Scipio
70OPC-492R
70T-492R
71MLB/St-92
71OPC-747R
71T-747R
72OPC-202
72T-202
73OPC-417
73T-417
74OPC-576
74T-576
75Iowa/TCMA-19
Spino, Tom
79QuadC-23
Spinosa, John
87WPalm-28
Spitale, Ben
87BurlEx-12
Splitt, Steve
77BurlB
78Holyo
79Holyo-19
Splittorff, Paul
71OPC-247R
71T-247R
72OPC-315
72T-315
73OPC-48
73T-48
74OPC-225
74T-225
74T/DE-56
74T/St-190
75OPC-340
75T-340
75T/M-340
76A&P/KC
76OPC-43
76SSPC-163
76T-43
77OPC-41
77T-534
78Ho-11
78T-638
79K-10
79OPC-90
79T-183
80OPC-214
80T-409
81D-342
81F-30
81F/St-95
81T-218
82D-464
82F-423
82OPC-126
82T-759
83D-286
83F-124
83T-316
84D-521
84F-360
84Nes/792-52
84T-52
84T/St-281
Spohrer, Al
31Exh/4-1
33G-161
35G-8L
35G-9L
R310
V353-94
Spoolstra, Scott
88Clmbia/GS-20
Spooner, Karl
55Gol/Dodg-29
55T-90
55T/DH-19
56T-83
56T/Hocus-B20
56T/Pin-53P
79TCMA-238
Sposito, Gus
85SpokAT/Crm-19
Spradlin, Jerry
88Bill/Pro-1821
89Greens/Pro-413
Sprague, Charles
N172
Sprague, Ed
69T-638
72OPC-121
72T-121
75OPC-76
75T-76
75T/M-76
76SSPC-230
Sprague, Ed Jr.
88T/Tr-113T
89B-252
89Duned/Star-16
89T/Big-40
Spratke, Ken
87Chatt/Best-12
88Memph/Best-23
89Omaha/CMC-9
89Omaha/Pro-1719
Spratt, Henry
(Jack)
T207
Spriggs, George
67T-472R
68T-314R
69T-662R
71MLB/St-431
71OPC-411
71T-411
Spring, Jack
62T-257
63T-572
64T-71
85SpokAT/Crm-20
Springer, Billy
(Steve)
84Jacks-22
85IntLgAS-13
85Tidew-16
85Tidew-17
86Tidew-27
87Tidew-11
87Tidew/TCMA-18
88Tidew/CANDL-12
88Tidew/CMC-21
88Tidew/Pro-1598
89Vanco/CMC-12
89Vanco/Pro-592
Springer, Dennis
88Bakers/Cal-260
89SnAnt/Best-20
Springer, Gary
83SanJose-6
Springer, Russell
87Anchora-27
88CapeCod/Sum-35
Sprinz, Joseph C.
48Sommer-28
49Sommer-22
Sproat, Ed
N172
Sproesser, Mark
81Redwd-18
82Redwd-13
Sprowl, Robert
(Bobby)
80Tucso-6
81T-82R
82T-441R
82Tucso-19
83ColumAst-21
Spurgeon, Fred
26Exh-87
Spurgeon, Scott
88AubAs/Pro-1948
89Ashvl/Pro-958
Squires, Mike
79T-704R
80T-466
81D-398
81F-349
81T-292
82D-39
82F-357
82F/St-188
82T-398
83D-495
83F-250
83T-669
84D-404
84F-71
84Nes/792-72
84T-72
84TrueVal/WS-29
85D-501
85F-529
85OPC-278
85T-543
89Tor/Fire-25
St.Clair, Dan
83Omaha-8
84Omaha-18
St.Claire, Ebba
52B-172
52T-393
53B/BW-34
53JC-16
53T-91
54B-128
St.Claire, Randy
85D-575
85Indianap-19
86D-463
86F-261
86Indianap-15
86Leaf-229
86OPC-89
86T-89
87F/U-U113
87OPC-366
87T-467
88D-426
88F-197
88OPC-279
88Score-397
88T-279
89Portl/CMC-11
89Portl/Pro-213
89T-666
89UD-29
90T-503
St.Claire, Steve
85Utica-23
86Jamestn-24
87BurlEx-11
St.John, Anthony
89SLCty-16
St.John, Rich
89Watertn/Star-28
St.Laurent, Jim
85BurlR-15
86DayBe-27
87TexLgAS-17
88OkCty/CMC-23
88OkCty/Pro-39
89OkCty/CMC-17
89OkCty/Pro-1524
St.Peter, William
88Geneva/Pro-1650
89CharWh/Best-6
89CharWh/Pro-1753
Stablein, George
80Hawai-15
81Hawai-15
81T-356R
82Hawai-15
Stacey, Al
89Geneva/Pro-1874
Stack, William Edward
T207
Stackhouse, Brian
86Macon-23tr
Stading, Greg
86PrWill-25
87Salem-6
Stadler, Jeff
78Cedar
Staehle, Marv
65OPC-41R
65T-41R
66OPC-164R
66T-164R
69T-394R
71LaPizza-11
71MLB/St-140
71OPC-663
71T-663
Stafford, Bill
61T-213
61T/St-199
62J-13
62P-13
62P/Can-13
62T-55LL
62T-570
63J-22
63Kahn
63P-22
63T-155
63T-331M
64T-299
65OPC-281
65T-281
WG10-21
WG9-22
Stafford, Gil
75BurlB
Stagg, Bob
47Centen-27
Staggs, Steve
78OPC-94
78T-521
Stahl, Charles
(Chick)
E107
Stahl, Garland
(Jake)
E224
E254
E270/1
E90/1
E91
L1-130
M116
S74-4
S81-105
T202
T204
T205
T206
T215/blue
T215/brown
T3-38
WG2-43
WG5-36
Stahl, Larry
66OPC-107R
66T-107R
69MB-260
69MLB/St-198
69T-271
69T/St-99
70MLB/St-120
70OPC-494
70T-494
71OPC-711
71T-711
72MB-324
72T-782
73OPC-533
73T-533
74OPC-507
74T-507
Staiger, Roy
76OPC-592R
76SSPC-560
76T-592R
77T-281
78Cr/PCL-113
79Colum-2
80Colum-9
89Tidew/CANDL-10
Stainback, G. Tucker
34DS-52
44Yank/St-25
47Signal
Stairs, Matt
89James/Pro-2141
89WPalm/Star-22
Staley, Gerald
46Sunbeam
51B-121
51T/BB-7
52B-50
52NTea
52StarCal/L-81G
52T-79
53B/Col-17
53Hunter
53RM-NL24
53T-56
54B-14
54Hunter
55B-155
57T-227
58T-412
59T-426
60T-510
60T-57M
61P-29
61T-90
61T/St-130
79TCMA-40
R423-98
Staley, Henry E.
N172

Stallard, Tracy
61T-81
62T-567
63T-419
64T-176
65OldLond-18
65T-491
66OPC-7
66T-7
Stallcup, T. Virgil
49B-81
49Eureka-95
50B-116
51B-108
52B-6
52NTea
52T-69
53T-180
Staller, George
73OPC-136CO
73T-136C
74OPC-306CO
74T-306C
Stallings, George T.
15CJ-162
D329-167
D350/2-169
M101/4-167
M101/5-169
M116
WG5-37
WG6-34
Stalp, Joe
83Cedar-10
83Cedar/LF-4
Stampel, Eric
86Lynch-21
Stamps, Jerry
75Cedar
Stanage, Oscar
11Helmar-37
12Sweet/Pin-31
14Piedmont/St-53
BF2-29
D303
D328-167
D329-168
D350/2-170
E106
E135-167
E90/1
M101/4-168
M101/5-170
M116
T202
T205
T206
T207
T216
W514-115
Stancel, Mark
86Cram/PCL-54
88Modesto-14
88Modesto/Cal-65
Standart, Rich
75Shreve/TCMA-21
76Shrev
Standiford, Mark
87Anchora-28
89Salin/Cal-139
89Salin/Pro-1801
Standley, Don
75Water
Stanek, Al
64T-99
65T-302
66T-437
Stanfield, Kevin
77Visal
79T-709R
79Toled-5
Stanfield, Mike
88Clint/Pro-713
Stanford, Don
89PrWill/Star-20
Stanford, Larry
89Oneon/Pro-2106
Stange, Albert Lee
61Clover-25
62T-321
63T-246
64T-555
65T-448
66T-371
67OPC-99
67T-99
67T/Test/RSox-19
68T-593
69MB-261
69OPC-148
69T-148
70OPC-447
70T-447
71OPC-311
71T-311
72MB-325
73OPC-131CO
73T-131C
74OPC-403CO
74T-403C
89Pawtu/Dunkin-38
89Pawtu/Pro-692
Stange, Kurt
88MidwLAS/GS-58
88Wausa/GS-10
89SnBer/Best-13
Stange, Tim
88Elmir-9
Stangel, Chris
84Evrt/Cram-18
Stanhope, Chester D.
(Chuck)
86Hagers-19
87CharO/WBTV-31
88RochR-25
88RochR/Gov-25
89Hagers/Best-17
89Hagers/Pro-269
89RochR/CMC-2
Stanhouse, Don
73OPC-352
73T-352
75OPC-493
75T-493
75T/M-493
77K-32
77OPC-63
77T-274
78OPC-162
78T-629
79T-119
80Pol/Dodg-29
80T-517
81D-557
81F-121
81OPC-24
81Pol/Dodg-26
81T-24
Stanicek, Pete
86Hagers-20
87CharO/WBTV-1
88D-541
88D/Best-294
88D/Rook-15
88F-573
88French-17
88RochR-22
88RochR/CMC-18
88RochR/Pro-205
88Score-628
88T/Tr-114T
89B-14
89D-169
89F-622
89Hagers/Star-20
89OPC-317
89Panini/St-265
89Score-236
89T-497
89T/Coins-52
89T/St-232
89ToysRUs-30
89UD-592
Stanicek, Steve
84Shrev/FB-21
86ElPas-19
87Denver-27
88Denver/CMC-22
88Denver/Pro-1266
88F-174
89ScrWB/CMC-12
89ScrWB/Pro-717
Staniland, Steve
77ArkTr
Stanka, Joe
58Union
Stankiewicz, Andy
87FtLaud-10
88Albany/Pro-1330
88EastLAS/Pro-5
89Albany/Best-15
89Albany/Pro-333
89Albany/Star-19
Stanky, Eddie
49B-104
49Eureka-26
50B-29
50Drake-22
51B-13
51T/CAS
51T/RB-48
52B-160
52BR
52RM-NL23
52T-76
53B/Col-49
53Exh/Can-9
53Hunter
54Hunter
54T-38
55B-238
55Hunter
55T-191
66T-448
67OPC-81MG
67T-81
68T-564
79TCMA-108
89Smok/Dodg-53
Exh47
R346-31
R423-105
Stanley, Bob
78PapaG/Disc-12
78T-186
79OPC-314
79T-597
80OPC-35
80T-63
81Coke
81D-456
81F-234
81OPC-296
81T-421
81T/HT
82Coke/Bos
82D-134
82F-307
82F/St-169
82OPC-289
82T-289
83D-386
83F-195
83OPC-242
83T-381TL
83T-682
84D-644
84F-409
84F/St-74
84FunFood/Pin-81
84Nes/792-320
84OPC-320
84T-320
84T/St-220
85D-91
85Drake-42
85F-169
85OPC-204
85T-555
85T/St-215
86D-91
86F-359
86OPC-158
86S-169
86T-785
86T/St-253
87D-216
87D/OD-180
87F-47
87OPC-175
87RedFoley/St-18
87T-175
87T/St-245
88D-92
88D/RedSox/Bk-92
88F-367
88OPC-369
88Panini/St-23
88Score-300
88T-573
89B-25
89D-421
89D/Best-233
89F-101
89Score-383
89T-37
89T/St-258
89UD-411
90F-289
90UD-654
Stanley, Fred
72OPC-59
72T-59
74OPC-423
74T-423
75OPC-503
75T-503
75T/M-503
76OPC-429
76SSPC-442
76T-429
77BK/Y-16
77T-123
78BK/Y-17
78T-664
79BK/Y-16
79T-16
80T-387
81D-585
81F-100
81T-281
81T/Tr-834
82D-449
82F-108
82Granny-15
82T-787
83D-197
83F-534
83T-513
Stanley, Kevin
83Butte-21
Stanley, Mickey
66T-198
67T-607
68OPC-129
68T-129
69MB-262
69MLB/St-54
69OPC-13
69T-13
69T/St-179
70MLB/St-214
70OPC-383
70T-383
71MLB/St-407
71OPC-524
71T-524
72MB-326
72OPC-385
72T-385
73OPC-88
73T-88
74OPC-530
74T-530
74T/St-180
75OPC-141
75T-141
75T/M-141
76OPC-483
76SSPC-372
76T-483
77T-533
78BK/T-21
78T-232
79OPC-368
79T-692
88Domino-22
89Swell-104
Stanley, Mike
86Tulsa-25
87D-592
87D/Rook-28
87F-647M
87OKCty-8
87S/Rook-45
87Smok/R-23
87T/Tr-116T
88D-259
88D/Best-223
88F-480
88Moth/R-11
88OPC-219
88Panini/St-199
88Score-47
88Smok/R-11
88T-219
88T/St-238
88ToysRUs-29
89D-166
89F-533
89Moth/R-22
89OPC-123
89Score-241
89Smok/R-31
89T-587
89T/St-244
89UD-579
90D-579
90T-92
Stanley, Tim
87Anchora-29
88James/Pro-1919
Stansberry
E254
Stanton, Leroy
(Lee)
72OPC-141R
72T-141R
73OPC-18
73T-18
74OPC-594
74T-594
75K-12
75OPC-342
75T-342
75T/M-342
76Ho-39
76Ho/Twink-39
76OPC-152

76SSPC-204
76T-152
77T-226
78Ho-60
78OPC-123
78T-447
79OPC-275
79T-533
87Myrtle-9
88Myrtle/Pro-1180
89Myrtle/Pro-1451

Stanton, Mike
73Cedar
75Iowa/TCMA-20
78Syrac
81F-400
82D-285
82F-379
82T-473
82T/Tr-113T
83D-433
83F-486
83T-159
84F-619
84Moth/Mar-20
84Nes/792-694
84T-694
85D-562
85F-501
85Moth/Mar-16
85T-256
85T/St-343
89Greenv/Pro-1166
89Greenv/Star-22
89Greenvl/Best-14
90D-508
90F-596
90Score-609
90Score/100Ris-29
90T-694
90UD-61

Staples, Ken
81Wisco-1
82Wisco-3

Stapleton, Dave
84T/St-221
86ElPas-20
88D-521
88D/Rook-4
88Pol/Brew-43
89Score-581
89UD-304

Stapleton, David L.
(Dave)
81Coke
81D-544
81F-236
81OPC-81
81T-81
81T/St-215
82D-208
82F-308
82F/St-76
82OPC-93
82T-589
82T/St-85
83D-200
83F-196
83OPC-239
83T-239
83T/St-35
84D-273
84F-410
84Nes/792-653
84OPC-249
84T-653
85T-322
86T-151
87T-507

Stargell, Tim
89Wausa/GS-26

Stargell, Willie
63T-553R
64T-342
65Kahn
65T-377
66EH-8
66Kahn
66OPC-99M
66T-255
66T-99
66T/RO-44
67Kahn
67OPC-140
67T-140
67T-266M
67T/Test/PP-22
67T/Test/PP-31
68KDKA-8
68OPC-86
68T-86
69MB-263
69MLB/St-188
69T-545
69T/St-89
70K-29
70MLB/St-107
70OPC-470
70T-470
70T/S-19
70T/SO
71K-68
71MLB/St-214
71OPC-230
71T-230
71T/Coins-123
71T/S-43
71T/tatt-8
72K-53
72MB-327
72OPC-343KP
72OPC-447
72OPC-448IA
72OPC-87LL
72OPC-89LL
72T-343BP
72T-447A
72T-448A
72T-87LL
72T-89LL
72T/Post-15
73K-25
73OPC-370
73T-370
73T/Comics-20
73T/Lids-50
73T/PinUps-20
74K-37
74Laugh/ASG-65
74OPC-100
74OPC-202LL
74OPC-203LL
74T-100
74T-202LL
74T-203LL
74T/DE-31
74T/Puzzles-11
74T/St-88
75Ho-135
75OPC-100
75T-100
75T/M-100
76Crane-58
76Ho-49
76Ho/Twink-49
76K-22
76MSA/Disc
76OPC-270
76SSPC-573
76T-270
77Ho-27
77OPC-25
77Pep-64
77T-460
77T/CS-45
78Ho-11
78T-510
78Wiffle/Discs-71
79Ho-104
79OPC-22
79T-55
80K-25
80OPC-319
80T-610
80T/S-1
81D-12
81D-132
81F-363
81F/St-15
81K-11
81MSA/Disc-31
81OPC-127
81T-380
82D-639
82F-499
82F/St-106M
82KMart-37
82OPC-188IA
82OPC-372
82T-715
82T-716A
83D-610
83D-8DK
83F-324
83F-634M
84West/1-6
85CircK-16
86Pol/Atl-8
87KMart-22
89HOF/St-27
89Kahn/Coop-10
89T/Gloss22-22

Stark, Clint
61Union
62Pep/Tul
66Pep/Tul

Stark, Jeff
87Spart-4
88Spart/Pro-1024

Stark, Matt
86Knoxv-22
87Tor/Fire-29
87Tor/Fire-29

Stark, Monroe
(Dolly)
39PB-106
40PB-117
T206

Starkovich, Paul
75SnAnt

Starks, Bob
76QuadC

Starr, Charles
T201
T206
T213/brown

Starr, Dick
50B-191
51B-137

Starrette, Herm
64T-239
65T-539
74OPC-634CO
74T-634C
78TCMA-194
86Pol/Brew-38C
88French-31CO

Staton, David
88CapeCod/Sum-167
89Spoka/SP-1

Statz, Arnold
(Jigger)
21Exh-172
37Wheat
88MinorLg/Leg-9
E120
E126-33
V100
V117-16

Staub, Rusty
63Pep
63T-544R
64T-109
64T/Coins-96
64T/St-88
65T-321
66OPC-106
66T-106
66T-273M
67OPC-73
67T-73
67T/Test/SU-17
68Bz-14
68Coke
68T-300
68T/3D
68T/G-28
68T/Post-22
69Citgo-15
69Fud's-11
69MB-264
69MLB/St-161
69NTF
69OPC/DE-20
69T-230
69T/DE-22
69T/decal
69T/S-48
69T/St-38
69Trans-39
70MLB/St-70
70T-585
70T/CB
70T/S-41
71Bz
71Bz/Test-40
71LaPizza-12
71MD
71MLB/St-141
71MLB/St-575
71OPC-289
71OPC-560
71T-560
71T/Coins-111
71T/GM-35
71T/S-9
71T/tatt-7
72MB-328
74OPC-475WS
74OPC-629
74T-629
75Ho-129
75OPC-90
75T-90
75T/M-90
76Crane-59
76MSA/Disc
76OPC-120
76SSPC-537
76T-120
76T/Tr-120T
77Ho-82
77OPC-88
77Pep-29
77T-420
77T/CS-46
78BK/T-22
78OPC-188
78T-370
78Wiffle/Discs-72
79Ho-56
79OPC-228
79T-440
79T/Comics-7
80OPC-347
80T-660
81Coke
81F-629
81T-80
81T/HT
81T/Tr-835
82D-56
82F-536
82F/St-82
82OPC-270
82T-270
83D-350
83F-555
83OPC-1
83OPC-51SV
83T-740
83T-741A
83T/St-14
84D-554
84D-6
84D/Champs-28
84F-597
84F/St-40
84FunFood/Pin-84
84Nes/792-430
84Nes/792-702LL
84Nes/792-704LL
84OPC-224
84T-430
84T-702
84T-704
84T/Mets/Fan-6
84T/St-287A
85F-92
85F/St-50
85OPC-190
85T-190
86F-95
86Moth/Ast-6
86S-138M
86T-570

Stauffacher, Stuart
86BurlEx-21

Stearns, Bill
83OKCty-1
86Tulsa-6MG

Stearns, Dan
N172

Stearns, Don
87SnBer-4

Stearns, John
75IntAS/TCMA-7
76OPC-633
76SSPC-546
76T-633
77T-119
78T-334
79Ho-124
79OPC-280
79T-205M
79T-545
80K-37
80OPC-41
80T-76
81D-35
81F-317
81OPC-255
81T-428
81T/So-96
81T/St-194
82D-434
82F-537
82F/St-89
82OPC-232
82T-743
83D-380
83D/AAS-25
83F-556
83OPC-212
83T-212
83T/St-264
84F-598

Stearns, Norman
78Laugh/Black-4

Stearns, Randy
87SnBer-5
Steck, Dave
76QuadC
Stedman, Tom
75Lafay
Steele, Don
75Lafay
Steele, Tim
75Water
Steele, Walt
80BurlB-20
Steele, William
11Helmar-177
T207
Steels, James
82Amari-11
83Beaum-20
84Beaum-3
85Cram/PCL-125
86LasVegas-18
87Bohem-21
87D/Rook-50
88D-360
88F/U-U64
88Moth/R-21
88OkCty/CMC-24
88OkCty/Pro-38
88T-117
Steen, Scott
86Clearw-23
Steevens, Morris
65T-521R
78TCMA-175
Stefani, Mario
89Brist/Star-27
Stefanski, Jim
82Durhm-10
Stefaro, John
84D-622
85CharO-5
87D-541
87F-652M
87T-563
88ColSp/CMC-11
88ColSp/Pro-1522
Steffen, David
80Evans-4
81T-626R
Steger, Chip
77Tucso
Steger, Kevin
81Wausa-1
83Chatt-22
Stegman, Dave
79T-706R
82Colum-13
82Colum/Pol-23
84Nes/792-664
84T-664
84TrueVal/WS-28
85Syrac-31
85T-194
86Colum/Pol-24
Steigerwald, John
75Lafay
Stein, Bill
76OPC-131
76SSPC-146
76T-131
77Ho-136
77OPC-20
77T-334
78Ho-39
78OPC-147
78T-476
79Ho-18
79OPC-372
79T-698
80OPC-121
80T-226
81D-543
81F-605
81T-532
81T/Tr-836
82D-37
82F-331
82F/St-179
82T-402
82T/St-118
83D-594
83F-579
83Rang-1
83T-64
84F-429
84Nes/792-758
84Rang-1
84T-758
85D-621
85Rang-1
85T-171
86D-403
86T-371
88LitFalls/Puc-26
89Clmbia/Best-22
89Clmbia/GS-1
Stein, John
86AppFx-24
87Bakers-9
Stein, W. Randy
79T-394
79Vanco-16
80Spoka-13
80T-613
81Spoka-24
82IowaC-24
83IowaC-10
Steinbach, Terry
84Madis/Pol-10
85Huntsvl/BK-16
86SLAS-10
87D-34RR
87D/Rook-26
87F-405
87Leaf-34RR
87S-118M
87S/Rook-22
87Sf/Rook-1
87T/Tr-117T
88Class/Red-186
88D-158
88D/A's/Bk-158
88D/Best-78
88F-294
88Moth/A's-4
88OPC-44
88Panini/St-166
88Score-82
88Score/YS/I-16
88Sf-174
88T-551
88T/Big-39
88T/Coins-28
88T/JumboR-15
88ToysRUs-30
89B-193
89Cadaco-54
89Class-69
89D-268
89D/AS-31
89D/AS-9
89D/Best-323
89D/PopUp-9
89F-22
89F-634M
89KMart/DT-19
89Moth/A's-3
89OPC-304
89Panini/St-236AS
89Panini/St-419
89Score-365
89Sf-119
89T-725
89T/Big-80
89T/Gloss22-9
89T/St-152
89T/St-165
89UD-256
90D-268
90D-637AS
90F-20
90Score-162
90Score-693DT
90Score/100St-55
90Sf-33
90T-145
90UD-246
Steinbach, Tom
85Beloi-9
Steinberg, David
83Wisco/LF-8
Steiner, Brian
88Gasto/Pro-1018
89Butte/SP-18
Steinert, Paul
84Butte-22
Steinfeldt, Harry
12Sweet/Pin-92
E107
E254
E90/3
E91
E97
M116
S74-47
S74-70
T202
T204
T205
T206
T207
T215/blue
T215/brown
W555
Steinkamp, Mike
89SLCty-13RHP
Steinmetz, Kevin
83Tampa-21
Steirer, Ricky
80ElPas-4
81SLCty-12
82Spoka-8
84Cram/PCL-102
Stellern, Mike
82AubAs-4
Stello, Dick
88Umpire-60
Stelmaszek, Rich
70T-599R
73OPC-601R
73T-601R
74OPC-611
74T-611
75OPC-338
75T-338
75T/M-338
77Tucso
78Wisco
79Wisco-23
Stember, Jeff
78Cedar
81Phoen-5
82Phoen
Stemberger, Brian
82Knoxv-9
Stemmyer, William
N172
Stengel
N172
Stengel, Casey
21Exh-173
40PB-142
46Remar-10
47Remar-8
47Signal
47Smith-1
48Signal
48Smith-20
50B-217
51B-181
52B-217
52RM-AL1
53B/BW-39
53RM-AL1
58T-475AS
59T-383M
59T-552AS
60T-227
61NuCard-461
62T-29
63T-233
63T-43M
64T-324
64T-393M
65OPC-187
65T-187
72Laugh/GF-20
80Cram/Leg-47
80Laugh/FFeat-20
80SSPC/HOF
83D/HOF-37
85West/2-35
86Conlon/1-33
89Pac/Leg-218
89Smok/Dodg-28
89Swell-130
D327
D328-168
D329-169
D350/2-171
E135-168
E220
M101/4-169
M101/5-171
R312
R423-93
W514-113
W515-24
W575
Stenholm, Richard A.
77WHave
81Colum-1
Stenhouse, Dave
60HenryH-26
62T-592R
63F-30
63J-97
63P-97
63Salada-37
63T-263
63T/SO
64T-498
65T-304
78TCMA-141
84Syrac-26
85T-141FS
86Syrac-24
87Syrac-13
87Syrac/TCMA-11
Stenhouse, Michael
82Wichi-19
84D-29
84Indianap-30
84Stuart-26
85D-376
85F-411
85F/Up-U110
85OPC-282
85T-141FS
85T-658
85T/Tr-112T
86F-406
86OPC-17
86Pawtu-23
86T-17
87Toled-19
87Toled/TCMA-5
Stennett, Matt
86AubAs-24
Stennett, Rennie
72OPC-219
72T-219
73OPC-348
73T-348
74OPC-426
74T-426
74T/St-89
75Ho-131
75OPC-336
75T-336
75T/M-336
76Crane-60
76Ho-9
76Ho/Twink-9
76MSA/Disc
76OPC-425
76OPC-6RB
76SSPC-575
76T-425
76T-6M
77Ho-101
77OPC-129
77T-35
78Ho-33
78OPC-25
78T-165
79OPC-365
79T-687
80Pol/Giants-6
80T-501
81D-72
81F-438
81OPC-257
81T-257
82D-563
82F-401
82OPC-84
82T-84
Stento, Bernie
87Elmir-28
87Elmir/Red-28
Stephan, Todd
89Penin/Star-23
Stephans, Russell
81CharR-13
83Omaha-12
84Omaha-26
85D-42
86Omaha-24
86Omaha/TCMA-10
Stephen, Louis
(Buzz)
70OPC-533
70T-533
Stephens, B.F.
N172
Stephens, Bryan
46Remar-19
V362-11
Stephens, Carl Ray
87TexLgAS-31
88Louisvl-45
88Louisvl/CMC-19
88Louisvl/Pro-422
89ArkTr/GS-23
Stephens, Darryl
82Redwd-14
83Nashua-15
Stephens, Gene
53T-248
56T-313
57T-217
58Hires-72
58T-227
59T-261
60T-363
61T-102
61T/St-105
62J-95

62P-95
62P/Can-95
62Salada-56
62Shirriff-56
62T-38
62T/St-59
64T-308
65T-498

Stephens, James W.
M116
T201
T204
T206

Stephens, Ron
88Utica/Puc-24
89Saraso/Star-22
89Star/Wax-60

Stephens, Vern
47TipTop
48L-161
49B-71
50B-2
50Drake-34
51B-92
51T/RB-4
52B-9
52RM-AL21
52StarCal/L-71D
52T-84
52TipTop
53T-270
54T-54
54Wilson
55B-109
56YellBase/Pin-30
D305
Exh47
R423-94

Stephenson, Chester
(Earl)
72OPC-61R
72T-61R
75IntAS/TCMA-4
78RochR
79Tidew-25
86Hagers-21C

Stephenson, Ed
76Baton

Stephenson, J. Riggs
21Exh-174
30CEA/Pin-9
31Exh/4-5
32Orbit/num-3
32Orbit/un-54
33DL-15
33Exh/4-3
33G-204
61F-140
80Cram/Leg-95
88Conlon/4-27
88Conlon/NatAS-19
R305
R308-170
R315-A34
R315-B34
R316
V100
V117-26

Stephenson, Jerry
65OPC-74R
65T-74R
66T-396
67T/Test/RSox-20
68T-519
69OPC-172
69T-172
71OPC-488
71T-488

Stephenson, John
64T-536R
66OPC-17
66T-17
67T-522
68OPC-83
68T-83
71OPC-421
71T-421

Stephenson, Joseph
85Greens-11

Stephenson, Phil
83Albany-15
84Cram/PCL-88
85Cram/PCL-132
86Pittsf-23
87IowaC-18
88IowaC/CMC-17
88IowaC/Pro-540
89D/Rook-36
90Score-642
90T-584

Sterling, J.C.
N172

Stevanus, Mike
86Macon-24
87Salem-22
88Salem/Star-19
88Watertn/Puc-11
89Aug/Pro-502

Steve, Harry
83SanJose-26GM
86SanJose-19
89SanJose/Cal-237

Stevens, Charles
52Mother-39
53Mother-17

Stevens, Edward Lee
47TipTop
48L-43
49B-93
49Eureka-173
52Park-25
Exh47

Stevens, J.H.
33SK-47

Stevens, John
55B-258ump

Stevens, Lee
86Cram/PCL-96
87PalmSp-12
88MidldA/GS-18
89Edmon/CMC-21
89Edmon/Pro-554
89F/Up-16
90D-449
90F-145

Stevens, Matt
89Batav/Pro-1924

Stevens, Mike
85PrWill-24
86PrWill-26
87Salem-2

Stevens, Paul
77DaytB
80WHave-7

Stevens, R.C.
58T-470
59T-282
61T-526

Stevens, Ray
87ArkTr-22

Stevens, Scott
89Utica/Puc-23

Stevens, Tony
80Elmir-22

Stevenson, Bill
85Spoka/Cram-22
86CharRa-24
88Wichi-29

Stevenson, John
78Newar
82Amari-3
84Shrev/FB-22

Stevenson, Stevie
V355-128

Stevenson, Tenoa
82Idaho-12

Steward, Charles
(Chuck)
88Fay/Pro-1092
89Lakel/Star-20

Steward, Hector
86NewBrit-23

Stewart, Carl
88Bill/Pro-1826

Stewart, Dave
77Clint
79Albuq-5
80Albuq-1
81Pol/Dodg-48
82D-410
82F-24
82Pol/Dodg
82Pol/Dodg-48
82T-213
83D-588
83F-222
83Pol/Dodg-48
83T-532
84D-343
84F-430
84Nes/792-352
84OPC-352
84Rang-31
84T-352
84T/St-360
85D-343
85F-569
85Rang-48
85T-723
86D-619
86F-453
86T-689
87D-648
87F-406
87Smok/A's-11
87T-14
87T/St-167
88Class/Red-196
88D-472
88D/A's/Bk-472
88D/Best-99
88F-295
88F-C14
88F/BB/MVP-36
88F/Mini-48
88F/Slug-39
88F/St-57
88F/WaxBox-C14
88Leaf-217
88Moth/A's-3
88OPC-353
88Panini/St-164
88Score-458
88Sf-162
88T-476
88T/Gloss60-33
88T/Mini-32
88T/Revco-29
88T/St-168
88T/UK-75
89B-188
89Cadaco-55
89D-214
89D/Best-99
89F-23
89F/Excit-39
89F/LL-36
89Moth/A's-6
89OPC-145
89Panini/St-415
89RedFoley/St-112
89Score-32
89Score-582M
89Score/Mast-14
89Sf-23
89T-145
89T/Big-101
89T/Coins-53
89T/Gloss60-45
89T/Hills-27
89T/Mini-71
89T/St-163
89T/St/Backs-27
89T/UK-74
89UD-185
90D-150
90D-6DK
90D-703AS
90D/Bon/MVP-BC3
90D/Preview-5
90F-21
90F/WaxBox-C26
90Score-410
90Score/100St-13
90Sf-194
90T-270
90UD-272

Stewart, Duncan
87Nashv-25M

Stewart, Ed
83Clint/LF-23

Stewart, Edward P.
(Bud)
48L-104
49B-173
50B-143
51B-159
52B-185
52Hawth/Pin-9
52T-279

Stewart, Glen
(Gabby)
46Remar
47Signal

Stewart, Hector
87Pawtu-11
87Pawtu/TCMA-10
89WinHav/Star-22

Stewart, James F.
64T-408R
65T-298
66OPC-63
66T-63
67OPC-124
67T-124
70T-636
71MLB/St-70
71OPC-644
71T-644
72MB-329
72T-747
73OPC-351
73T-351

Stewart, Jeff
87Wichi-17

Stewart, Joe
77Visal

Stewart, John
87Cedar-21
87Durhm-13
89SLCty-30

Stewart, Sammy
79T-206M
79T-701R
80T-119
81D-474
81F-181
81OPC-262
81T-262
82D-457
82F-180
82OPC-279
82T-426TL
82T-679
83D-203
83F-74
83OPC-347
83T-347
84D-514
84F-22
84Nes/792-59
84T-59
84T/St-25WS
85D-148
85F-192
85Leaf-98
85OPC-213
85T-469
86D-270
86F-289
86F/Up-U107
86OPC-172
86T-597
86T/St-235
86T/Tr-103T
87D-658
87F-48
87T-204
88D-596
88F-616
88T-701

Stewart, Tito
88NewBrit/Pro-905
89NewBrit/Star-5

Stewart, Vernon
(Bunky)
55T-136
55T/DH-76

Stewart, Walter C.
31Exh/4-30
33G-121
33G-146
35G-8I
35G-9I
R308-179
V353-75

Stiboro, Tom
80Batav-13

Stickels, Bob
71MLB/St-527

Stieb, Dave
80OPC-42
80T-77
81D-582
81F-414
81OPC-5
81OPC/Post-22
81T-467
81T/St-142
82D-52
82F-622
82F/St-232
82OPC-380
82OPC-53TL
82OPC/Post-6
82T-380
82T-606TL
82T/St-250
83D-507
83D-9
83D/AAS-48
83F-441
83K-36
83OPC-130
83OPC-202
83T-130
83T-202
83T/Gloss-26
83T/Gloss40-25
83T/St-127
84D-71
84D/AAS-19
84F-167
84F/St-85
84FunFood/Pin-75
84MiltBrad-26
84Nes/792-590
84Nes/792-606
84OPC-134
84OPC-289

84Seven-13E
84T-590
84T/Gloss22-10
84T/Gloss40-24
84T/St-368
84Tor/Fire-28
85D-193
85D/HL-12
85F-117
85F/LimEd-37
85F/St-110
85F/St-91
85GenMills-23
85Leaf-251CG
85Leaf-54
85OPC-240
85OPC/Post-22
85Seven-14S
85T-240
85T/3D-20
85T/Gloss22-21
85T/Gloss40-40
85T/St-191
85T/St-356
85T/Super-22
85Tor/Fire-27
86Ault-37
86D-146
86D/AAS-55
86Drake-34
86F-642M
86F-70
86F/LL-43
86F/Mini-16
86F/Slug-37
86F/St-115
86Leaf-68
86OPC-353
86S-96
86T-650
86T/3D-27
86T/Gloss60-43
86T/Mini-36
86T/St-186
86T/Super-54
86Tor/Fire-29
86TrueVal-19
87D-195
87F-238
87Leaf-72
87OPC-90
87RedFoley/St-81
87T-90
87Tor/Fire-30
87Tor/Fire-30
88D-148
88D/Best-284
88F-123
88Ho/Disc-17
88Leaf-80
88OPC-153
88Panini/St-215
88Score-76
88T-775
88T/Big-172
88T/St-191
88Tor/Fire-37
89B-239
89Class-49
89D-349
89D/AS-28
89D/Best-143
89F-244
89F/BBAS-40
89OPC-4
89Panini/St-463
89Score-197
89Sf-35
89T-460
89T/Big-128
89T/St-194
89Tor/Fire-37
89UD-383
90Class-97
90D-87
90F-93
90Score-201
90Score/100St-89
90Sf-26
90T-320
90UD-605

Stiegele, Rob
89Bluef/Star-22

Stieglitz, Al
60T-144

Stigman, Dick
59T-142
60L-85
60T-507
61Clover-26
61T-77
62T-37M
62T-532
63T-89
64T-245
64T-6LL
65T-548
66T-512
78TCMA-162

Stigman, Lee
80Holyo-25
81Vanco-20

Stiles, Will
84LitFalls-1
86Columbia-24
87Lynch-16

Stillman, Royle
76OPC-594R
76SSPC-393
76T-594R
78T-272
79Ogden/TCMA-14
79Spoka-2
80Ogden-18

Stillman, Sam
80WHave-18

Stillwell, Kurt
84Cedar-17
86F/Up-U108
86T/Tr-104T
86TexGold-11
87Class/Up-142
87D-123
87F-215
87Kahn-11
87T-623
87T/GlossRk-17
87ToysRUs-26
88D-265
88D/Best-207
88F-248
88F/U-U35
88Panini/St-276
88Score-221
88Score/Tr-4T
88Smok/Royals-23
88T-339
88T/Big-136
88T/Tr-115T
89B-120
89Class-14
89D-322
89D/AS-29
89D/Best-63
89F-293
89OPC-217
89Score-162
89Score/YS/II-42
89T-596
89T/Big-161
89T/St-266
89Tastee/Discs-8
89UD-616
90D-120
90F-118
90Score-96
90T-222
90UD-361

Stimac, Craig
79Hawai-4
80Hawai-6
81T-356R
82Charl-13

Stinson, Gorrell R.
(Bob)
70OPC-131R
70T-131R
71MLB/St-285
71OPC-594R
71T-594R
72T-679R
74OPC-653
74T-653
75OPC-471
75T-471
75T/M-471
76OPC-466
76SSPC-166
76T-466
77T-138
78T-396
79Ho-79
79OPC-126
79T-252
80OPC-305
85SpokAT/Crm-21

Stipetich, Mark
75QuadC

Stirnweiss, George
(Snuffy)
39Exh
44Yank/St-26
47TipTop
48B-35
48L-95
49B-165
50B-249
51B-21
52T-217
Exh47

Stitz, John
88Watlo/Pro-669

Stitzel, Glenn
75IntAS/TCMA-19

Stivers, Pat
88Idaho/Pro-1849

Stobbs, Chuck
52T-62
53Briggs
53T-89
54T-185
55T-41
55T/DH-44
56T-68
56T/Pin-60P
57T-101
58T-239
59T-26
60T-432
61Clover-27
61P-94
61Peters-4
61T-431
61T/St-185
62Salada-90A
62Salada-90B
62Shirriff-90
79TCMA-101
81Chatt-19C
82Chatt-24

Stock, Kevin
83BurlR-23
83BurlR/LF-22

Stock, Milt
21Exh-175
25Exh-14
52T-381
D327
D328-169
D329-170
D350/2-172
E120
E121/120
E121/80
E122
E135-169
E220
M101/4-170
M101/5-172
V100
V61-56
W501-77
W572
W575

Stock, Sterling
89StCath/Pro-2089

Stock, Wes
60T-481
61T-26
62T-442
63T-438
64T-382
65OPC-117
65T-117
67OPC-74
67T-74
70McDon-2
73OPC-179CO
73T-179C
77T-597C
78TCMA-139
78TCMA-154

Stockam, Doug
88Durhm/Star-19
89Greenv/Pro-1165
89Greenv/Star-23
89Greenvl/Best-16

Stocker, Bob
86Madis-24
86Madis/Pol-20
88Madis-23
89Huntsvl/Best-8

Stocksdale, Otis
N300/SC

Stockstill, Dave
79Wausa-5
81Tulsa-5
82Tulsa-15
83OKCty-17
84OKCty-8
85OKCty-23

Stoddard, Bob
80Spoka-1
81Spoka-18
82SLCty-18
83T-195
84D-619
84F-620
84Moth/Mar-22
84Nes/792-439
84T-439
85Cram/PCL-90
85F-502
86LasVegas-19
87F-431
87Omaha-12
88Tacom/CMC-10
88Tacom/Pro-628
89Denver/CMC-11
89Denver/Pro-31

Stoddard, Tim
78RochR
80T-314
81D-475
81F-176
81OPC-91DP
81T-91
82D-131
82F-181
82T-457
83D-581
83F-75
83OPC-217
83T-217
84D-245
84F-23
84F/X-110
84Nes/792-106
84SevenUp-49
84T-106
84T/X-112
85D-144
85F-68
85F/Up-U111
85Moth/Padres-19
85OPC-393
85T-693
85T/Tr-113T
86D-406
86F-335
86T-558
87D-497
87F-116
87OPC-321
87T-788
88D-497
88D/Y/Bk-497
88F-222
88Score-257
88T-359

Stoeckel, Jim
87SnAnt-3C

Stoerck, Scott
88Wausa/Feder-23
88Wausa/GS-23
89Wausa/GS-14

Stoker, Mike
87Ashvl-14
88Durhm/Star-20
89Durhm/Star-20

Stokes, Gus
81Clint-15
82Clint-27
83Clint/LF-1GM

Stokke, Doug
80Tucso-24

Stoll, Pete
83Sprin/LF-1TR
84ArkTr-23
85Sprin-23

Stoll, Rich
85Indianap-4
86Indianap-4

Stoltenberg, Scott
79Wisco-12

Stone, Bill
77Visal

Stone, Brian
87Beloi-9
88Stock/Cal-178
88Stock/Pro-739

Stone, Dave
88Watertn/Puc-25

Stone, Dean
54T-114
55T-60
55T/DH-17
56T-87
57T-381
59T-286
62T-574
63T-271
79TCMA-65

Stone, Eric
89Lakel/Star-21

Stone, Fred
WG2-44

Stone, George H.
69T-627
70OPC-122

70T-122
71MLB/St-22
71OPC-507
71T-507
72MB-330
72T-601
73OPC-647
73T-647
74OPC-397
74T-397
75OPC-239
75T-239
75T/M-239
76OPC-567
76SSPC-557
76T-567

Stone, George R.
12Sweet/Pin-55
E254
E90/1
E92
M116
S74-36
T205
T206
T3-119

Stone, George
86AppFx-25

Stone, H. Ron
66T-568R
68T-409R
69T-576R
70OPC-218
70T-218
71MLB/St-189
71OPC-366
71T-366
72T-528

Stone, Jeff
83Readg-20
84Cram/PCL-197
84F/X-111
85CIGNA-8
85D-624
85F-266
85F/St-119
85T-476
85T/St-116
86D-259
86F-454
86KayBee-30
86Portl-21
86T-686
87D-309
87F-189
87Maine-11
87Maine/TCMA-19
87T-532
88D-482
88F-317
88OPC-154
88RochR-26
88RochR/Gov-26
88T-154
88T/Big-146
89Moth/R-26
89OkCty/Pro-1510
89UD-486

Stone, Johnathon T.
(John)
33Exh/4-12
34G-80
35G-8H
35G-9H
37Exh/4-16
38Exh/4-16
R314
V354-89

Stone, Michael
77StPet
78Clint
78LodiD

Stone, Shawn
84PrWill-21

Stone, Steve
82Amari-17

Stone, Steven M.
(Steve)
72OPC-327
72T-327
72T/Cloth-30
73OPC-167
73T-167
74OPC-486
74T-486
74T/Tr-486T
75OPC-388
75T-388
75T/M-388
76OPC-378
76SSPC-302
76T-378
77T-17
78OPC-46
78T-153
79OPC-115
79T-227
80T-688
81D-476
81F-170
81F/St-104
81K-58
81OPC-101
81T-520
81T-5LL
81T/So-49
81T/St-1
81T/St-249
81T/St-40
82D-357
82F-182
82F/St-144
82T-419

Stoneman, Bill
68OPC-179
68T-179
69OPC-67
69T-67
70MLB/St-71
70OPC-398
70T-398
71MLB/St-142
71OPC-266
71T-266
72MB-331
72OPC-95LL
72T-610
72T-95LL
73K-23
73OPC-254
73T-254
74OPC-352
74T-352
74Weston-26

Stonikas, Bill
88AppFx/Pro-147
89BBCity/Star-24

Storey, Harvey
49B/PCL-15

Storke, Alan
E91

Stottlemyre, Jeff
81LynnS-27
81Wausa-2
82LynnS-7
83Chatt-16

Stottlemyre, Mel Jr.
86Osceola-25
87ColAst/Pro-6
87ColumAst-6
88Memph/Best-1
89B-110
89B-261FS
90T-263

Stottlemyre, Mel
65OPC-133WS
65T-550
66Bz-5
66T-224LL
66T-350
66T/RO-58
67Bz-5
67T-225
68OPC-120
68T-120
68T/3D
69Citgo-5
69MB-265
69MLB/St-79
69MLBPA/Pin-27
69NTF
69OPC-9LL
69OPC/DE-21
69T-470
69T-9LL
69T/DE-13
69T/decal
69T/S-25
69T/St-208
69Trans-28
70K-5
70MB-27
70MLB/St-250
70OPC-100
70OPC-70LL
70T-100
70T-70LL
70T/S-27
70T/SO
70Trans-13
71K-40
71MD
71MLB/St-500
71OPC-615
71T-615
71T/Coins-94
71T/S-10
71T/tatt-12
72K-50
72MB-332
72OPC-325
72OPC-492KP
72T-325
72T-492BP
73OPC-520
73T-520
74OPC-44
74T-44
74T/St-218
75OPC-183
75T-183
75T/M-183
88Kahn/Mets-30CO
88Pac/Leg-22
89B-261FS
89Kahn/Mets-30CO
WG10-22

Stottlemyre, Todd
86Ventura-25
87Syrac-11
87Syrac/TCMA-8
88D-658
88D/Rook-37
88F/U-U68
88Score/Tr-90T
88T/Tr-116T
88Tor/Fire-16
89B-242
89D-620
89F-245
89OPC-237
89Panini/St-460
89Score-453
89Score/HotRk-81
89Score/YS/II-20
89T-722
89T/Big-298
89Tor/Fire-30
89UD-362
90D-669
90F-94
90Score-554
90T-591
90UD-692

Stout, Jeff
89Aug/Pro-501

Stout, Tim
82Cedar-22

Stoval, Jerry
80Clint-5

Stovall, George T.
10Domino-112
11Helmar-65
12Sweet/Pin-19B
12Sweet/Pin-19A
14CJ-11
15CJ-11
D303
E106
E254
E90/1
M116
T201
T202
T205
T206
T207
T213/blue
T216
WG5-38

Stovey, Harry
N172
N693

Stowe
N690

Stowe, Harold
62T-291

Stowell, Steve
88Keno/Pro-1384
89Visal/Cal-97
89Visal/Pro-1444

Strahler, Mike
71MLB/St-116
71OPC-188R
71T-188R
72OPC-198R
72T-198R
73OPC-279
73T-279

Strain, Joe
78Cr/PCL-7
79Phoen
79T-726R
80OPC-280
80Pol/Giants-20
80T-538
81D-73
81F-458
81T-361
81T/Tr-837
82IowaC-9
82T-436
83OKCty-21
86Cram/PCL-180
87Everett-12
89Everett/Star-30

Straker, Les
80Cedar-17
81Water-8
83Water-8
84Albany-19
85Orlan-20
86Toled-21
87D/Rook-21
87S/Rook-46
87T/Tr-118T
88D-73
88F-24
88Score-108
88T-264
89Portl/CMC-10
89Portl/Pro-219
89Score-244
89T-101
89T/Big-90
89UD-83

Strampe, Bob
73OPC-604R
73T-604R

Strang, Sammy
E107
T206

Strange, Alan
W753

Strange, Don
89Pulas/Pro-1895

Strange, Doug
86FSLAS-45
86Lakel-24
87GlenF-10
88Toled/CMC-14
88Toled/Pro-587
89Toled/CMC-13
89Toled/Pro-782
90D-535
90Score/100Ris-63
90T-641

Strange, Kurt
88Wausa/Feder-10
89SnBer/Cal-69

Stranski, Scott
81Spoka-3
82LynnS-8
85BuffB-24
86Hagers-22
87Memph-14
87Memph/Best-10

Strathairn, David
88Pac/8Men-14

Stratton, C. Scott
N172

Stratton, Drew
88Modesto-29
88Modesto/Cal-69

Stratton, Monty
80Cram/Leg-103

Strauss, Joseph
N172
N284

Strawberry, Darryl
82Jacks-21
83T/X-108
83Tidew-28
84D-68
84Drake-29
84F-599
84F/St-104
84FunFood/Pin-8
84Jacks/Smok-12
84Nes/792-182
84OPC-182
84Seven-17E
84T-182
84T/Gloss40-29
84T/Mets/Fan-7
84T/St-385YS
84T/Super-12
84T/Super-12
85D-312
85Drake-30
85F-631IA
85F-93
85F/LimEd-38
85F/St-36
85Leaf-159
85OPC-126
85Seven-13S
85T-278FDP
85T-570
85T/3D-9

85T/Gloss22-8
85T/Mets/Fan-8
85T/St-100
85T/St-179
85T/Super-30
86D-197
86D/AAS-5
86D/HL-24
86D/PopUp-5
86Drake-16
86F-632M
86F-96
86F/Mini-21
86F/Slug-38
86F/St-116
86KayBee-31
86Leaf-131
86OPC-80
86Quaker-16
86S-60M
86S-97
86S/Rook-48M
86T-80
86T/3D-26
86T/Gloss22-19
86T/Gloss60-11
86T/Mets/Fan-8
86T/St-150
86T/St-95
86T/Super-55
87BK-19
87Class-3
87Class/Up-122
87D-118
87D-4DK
87D/AAS-12
87D/DKsuper-4
87D/HL-42
87D/HL-49
87D/OD-128
87D/PopUp-12
87Drake-1
87F-23
87F-629M
87F-638M
87F/Excit-41
87F/LL-41
87F/Slug-40
87F/St-114
87F/WS-11M
87Jiffy-17
87KayBee-31
87KMart-32
87Kraft-26
87Leaf-4DK
87Leaf-68
87MSA/Discs-1
87OPC-379
87RedFoley/St-58
87S-20
87Seven-E13
87T-460
87T-601AS
87T/Board-33
87T/Coins-46
87T/Gloss22-8
87T/Gloss60-32
87T/HL-29
87T/Mets/Fan-7
87T/Mini-26
87T/St-103
87T/St-159
87Woolwth-29
88Bz-21
88Class/Blue-209
88D-439
88D-BC20
88D/AS-34
88D/Best-182
88D/Mets/Bk-439
88D/PopUp-12
88F-151
88F-637M
88F/AwardWin-40
88F/BB/AS-40
88F/BB/MVP-37
88F/Excit-39
88F/Head-4
88F/Hottest-41
88F/LL-40
88F/Mini-97
88F/RecSet-39
88F/Slug-40
88F/SS-38
88F/St-106
88F/TL-40
88FanSam-17
88Kahn/Mets-18
88KayBee-29
88KingB/Disc-8
88KMart-29
88Leaf-220
88MSA/Disc-17
88Nestle-18
88OPC-178
88OPC-L
88Panini/St-236M
88Panini/St-347
88Score-360
88Score/WaxBox-17
88Score/YS/II-20
88Sf-155
88Sf/Gamewin-15
88T-710
88T/Big-253
88T/Coins-56
88T/Gloss22-19
88T/Gloss60-22
88T/Mets/Fan-18
88T/Mini-63
88T/RiteAid-7
88T/St-151
88T/St-96
88T/St/Backs-21
88T/UK-76
88T/WaxBox-L
89Ames-28
89B-387
89Bz-20
89Cadaco-56
89Class-108
89Class-150
89Class-8
89Crunch-7
89D-147
89D/AS-34
89D/Best-40
89D/MVP-BC6
89D/PopUp-34
89F-49
89F-632M
89F/AS-10
89F/BBAS-39
89F/BBMVP's-36
89F/Excit-40
89F/Heroes-38
89F/LL-37
89F/Superstar-39
89F/WaxBox-C25
89Holsum/Discs-10
89Kahn/Mets-18
89KayBee-29
89KingB/Discs-15
89KMart/DT-28
89Nissen-10
89OPC-300
89Panini/St-140
89Panini/St-223
89Panini/St-231AS
89Ralston-3
89RedFoley/St-113
89Score-10
89Score/HotSt-50
89Score/Mast-42
89Sf-205
89T-291TL
89T-300
89T-390AS
89T/Big-139
89T/Coins-26
89T/DH-18
89T/Gloss22-19
89T/Gloss60-8
89T/HeadsUp-6
89T/Hills-28
89T/Mets/Fan-18
89T/Mini-28
89T/St-157
89T/St-98
89T/St/Backs-53
89T/UK-75
89Tetley/Discs-5
89UD-260
89UD-681TC
90Class-33
90D-235
90F-217
90Score-200
90Score/100St-15
90Sf-146
90T-600
90UD-182

Strawn, Fla
79Tucso-13
79Tulsa-5
80Charl-14

Street, Charles
(Gabby)
10Domino-113A
10Domino-113B
11Helmar-46
12Sweet/Pin-64
12Sweet/Pin-64A
40PB-169
73F/Wild-16
88Conlon/5-27
E254
E91
M116
S74-41
T201
T202
T204
T205
T206
T207
T213/blue
T213/brown
T215/brown
T3-120

Street, Mickey
85Water-7

Streltz, Len
79ArkTr-2

Strichek, Jim
86Modesto-23

Stricker, John
N172

Strickland, Bob
86Geneva-26
87CharWh-18
89WinSal/Star-15

Strickland, George
52B-207
52T-197
54B-36
54DanDee
55B-192
55Gol/Ind-28
55Salem
57T-263
58T-102
59Kahn
59T-207
60L-30
60T-63
63Sugar-16

Strickland, Jim
72T-778R
73OPC-122
73T-122
75OkCty
76SSPC-512

Strickland, Rick
88CapeCod/Sum-49
89Oneon/Pro-2116

Strijek, Randy
88CLAS/Star-17
88Hagers/Star-21
89Hagers/Best-20
89Hagers/Pro-265
89Hagers/Star-19

Striker, Jake
60T-169

Strincevich, Nick
47TipTop
V362-17

Stringer, Lou
47Signal
49B-183
50B-187
52Mother-38

Stringfellow, Bean
87Richm/TCMA-7
88Richm-19
88Richm/CMC-4
88Richm/Pro-13

Stripp, Joe
34DS-89
34G-46
35G-1G
35G-3E
35G-4E
35G-5E
R300
V354-91

Strobel, Craig
86Hagers-23TR
87Hagers-8

Strode, Lester
(Jim)
82FtMyr-19
84Memph-14
85Omaha-7
86Omaha-25
86Omaha/TCMA-18
88Louvl-46

Strohmayer, John
71OPC-232
71T-232
72T-631
73OPC-457
73T-457

Strom, Brent
73OPC-612R
73T-612R
74OPC-359
74T-359
75OPC-643
75T-643
75T/M-643
76OPC-84
76T-84
77T-348
78T-509
80Tucso-20
81Albuq/TCMA-12
82Albuq-27
83Albuq-13
87Albuq/Pol-3CO
88Albuq/Pro-251
89Albuq/Pro-60

Stromer, Rick
83Peoria/LF-11
85Huntsvl/BK-43

Strong, Garret
75Cedar

Strong, Joe
86Modesto-24
88CalLgAS-20
88Reno/Cal-274
89Reno/Cal-245

Strong, Steve
89Lakel/Star-22

Stroud, Derrick
88Geneva/Pro-1649
89Peoria/Ko-11

Stroud, Ed
67T-598R
68OPC-31
68T-31
69MB-266
69MLB/St-108
69T-272
70MLB/St-286
70OPC-506
70T-506
71MLB/St-550
71OPC-217
71T-217
72MB-333

Stroud, Ralph
C46-58
M116
T201

Stroughter, Steve
78Cr/PCL-45
80Spoka-23
81Toled-22
82T/Tr-114T

Strube, Bob
86Kenosha-22
87Visal-5
88Visal/Cal-162
88Visal/Pro-101
89Visal/Cal-99
89Visal/Pro-1429

Strucher, Mark
82DayBe-25
83ColumAst-6
86Richm-22
87Richm/TCMA-15

Struck, J.O.
N172

Struek, Randy
87Hagers-9

Strum, John
41DP-114

Strunk, Amos
14CJ-33
15CJ-33
D327
D328-170
D329-171
D350/2-173
E104
E120
E121/120
E121/80
E135-170
E270/1
M101/4-171
M101/5-173
M116
T207
T208
T222
W501-44
W573
W575

Stryffeler, Dan
82Sprin-9
83Sprin/LF-21
84ArkTr-3
86Louisvl-27

Stuart, Marlin
52B-147
52T-208
53B/Col-120

54Esskay
Stuart, Richard L.
(Dick)
59HRDerby-19
59Kahn
59T-357
60Armour-18
60Bz-6
60Kahn
60T-402
61Kahn
61NuCard-409
61P-127
61T-126
61T/St-71
62Bz
62J-169
62Kahn
62P-169
62P/Can-169
62Salada-120
62Shirriff-120
62Sugar-D
62T-160
62T/bucks
62T/St-180
63J-137
63P-137
63T-18M
63T-285
64T-10LL
64T-12LL
64T-410
64T/Coins-12
64T/Coins-122AS
64T/S-42
64T/St-51
64T/SU
64T/tatt
650PC-280
650PC-5LL
65T-280
65T-5LL
65T/trans-29
66T-480
66T/RO-75
PM10/Sm-186
Stubberfield, Chris
86Cram/PCL-18
Stubbs, Franklin
83Albuq-1
84Cram/PCL-151
85Cram/PCL-175
85D-348
85F-386
85T-506
86D-592
86Pol/Dodg-22
86T/Tr-105T
87D-299
87D/OD-83
87F-455
87Moth/Dodg-13
870PC-292
87Pol/Dodg-10
87Seven-W14
87T-29
87T/St-72
88D-218
88D/Best-331
88F-527
88Leaf-182
88Moth/Dodg-11
880PC-198
88Panini/St-308
88Pol/Dodg-22
88RedFoley/St-84
88Score-147
88T-198
88T/Big-112
88T/St-66
89D-321
89D/GrandSlam-9
89F-74
89Moth/Dodg-11
89Pol/Dodg-13
89Score-599
89T-697
89T/Big-32
89UD-91
90D-615
90Score-478
90T-56
90UD-550
Stubing, Lawrence
(Moose)
76QuadC
80SLCty-18
81SLCty-25
82Spoka-24
84Cram/PCL-97
89T-444MG
Stuckeman, Al
75Lafay
Studeman, Dennis
87FtMyr-13
89AppFx/Pro-851
Stull, Walt
86Bakers-27
87SnBer-18
Stuper, John
82Louisvl
82Louvl-29
83D-621
83F-23
83T-363
84D-412
84F-337
84Nes/792-186TL
84Nes/792-49
84T-49
85F/Up-U112
86F-193
86T-497
Sturdivant, Dave
89PalmSp/Cal-33
89PalmSp/Pro-486
Sturdivant, Tom
57T-34
58T-127
59T-471
60T-487
61T-293
62T-179
63T-281
64T-402
Sturgeon, Bob
47TipTop
Stutzriem, Jerry
79Wausa-2
Su'a, Murphy
81BurlB-13
Suarez, Ken
66T-588R
68T-218
690PC-19
69T-19
700PC-209
70T-209
71MLB/St-383
710PC-597
71T-597
72MB-334
720PC-483
72T-483
740PC-39
74T-39
Suarez, Luis
81Wisco-9
Suarez, Nelson
81Wisco-23
Such, Dick
70T-599R
710PC-283
71T-283
Sudakis, Bill
69T-552R
700PC-341
70T-341
71MLB/St-117
710PC-253
71T-253
72T-722
730PC-586
73T-586
740PC-63
74T-63
74T/St-240
74T/Tr-63T
750PC-291
75T-291
75T/M-291
Suder, Pete
50B-140
51B-154
52B-179
52T-256
53B/BW-8
54B-99
55B-6
R346-15
Sudhoff, John
E107
Sudhoff, William
WG2-45
Sudo, Bob
85Utica-5
86BurlEx-22
87Jaxvl-19
88Sprin/Best-11
Suehr, Scott
83Peoria/LF-21
85MidldA-21
Sueme, Hal
43Centen-23
44Centen-22
45Centen-24
47Centen-28
47Signal
Suero, Williams
88Myrtle/Pro-1186
88SALAS/GS-17
89Duned/Star-17
Suetsugu, Toshimitsu
87Miami-25
Sugden, Joseph
E107
Suggs, George
10Domino-114
11Helmar-119
12Sweet/Pin-105
14CJ-113
15CJ-113
M116
T202
T205
Suhr, Gus
31Exh/4-13
33CJ/Pin-21
33Exh/4-7
33G-206
34DS-56
35BU-187
35BU-41
35G-8K
35G-9K
37Exh/4-7
38Exh/4-7
39PB-83
40PB-94
R310
R314
Suigiura, Mamoru
87Miami-27
Sukeforth, Clyde
52B-227
52T-364
Sukla, Ed
66T-417R
75Phoen-6
Sularz, Guy
78Cr/PCL-89
79Phoen
80Phoen-21
81Phoen-15
83D-605
83F-273
83Phoen/BHN-14
83T-379
84Cram/PCL-22
Sullivan, Brian
89Reno/Cal-246
Sullivan, Carl
87DayBe-2
88FSLAS/Star-49
88Tampa/Star-23
89Saraso/Star-23
Sullivan, Dan
86WinHav-25
87WinHav-9
Sullivan, Daniel C.
Scrapps
Sullivan, Dave
87Elmir-3
87Elmir/Red-3
Sullivan, Frank
55B-15
55T-106
55T/DH-22
56T-71
56T/Pin-25P
57T-21
58Hires-58
58T-18
59T-323
60T-280
61P-55
61T-281
62T-352
63T-389
79TCMA-57
Sullivan, Glenn
88WinSal/Star-18
89CharlK-10
Sullivan, Haywood
57T-336
58T-197
59T-416
60T-474
61P-56
61T-212
62J-99
62P-99
62P/Can-99
62T-184
62T/St-60
63J-92
63P-92
63T-359
Sullivan, Jack
(Twin)
T3/Box-56
Sullivan, Joe
41G-22
R312
R314
Sullivan, John L.
V100
Sullivan, John P.
65T-593R
66T-597
67T-568
76Watlo-MG
84Tor/Fire-29CO
85Tor/Fire-28CO
86Tor/Fire-30CO
87Tor/Fire-31
87Tor/Fire-31CO
88Tor/Fire-8CO
89Tor/Fire-8
Sullivan, Marc
84Pawtu-20
86D-614
86T-529
87D-643
87D/OD-187
870PC-66
87T-66
88Score-271
88T-354
Sullivan, Martin J.
E223
N172
N284
N690/2
Sullivan, Michael J.
N172
Sullivan, Mike
81Water-9
Sullivan, Mike
89Batav/Pro-1929
Sullivan, Russell
53Glen
Sullivan, Sport
88Pac/8Men-27
Sullivan, William J.
11Helmar-16
61F-141
D329-172
D350/2-174
E107
E254
E270/1
E270/2
E300
E97
M101/4-172
M101/5-174
M116
T206
T207
T3-121
WG1-16
Summa, Howard Homer
25Exh-88
26Exh-88
29Exh/4-28
V117-6
Summers, Jeff
83SanJose-22
84CharO-25
85CharO-16
Summers, John
(Champ)
760PC-299
76T-299
78Indianap-12
78T-622
79T-516
800PC-100
80T-176
81D-130
81F-466
810PC-27
81T-27
81T/So-24
81T/St-76
82D-81
82F-282
82F/St-154
82T-369
82T/Tr-115T
83F-274
83T-428
84F/X-112
84Moth/Padres-25
84Nes/792-768
84T-768
84T/X-113
85T-208

86Indianap-32
87Colum-6
89Colum/Pol-24CO

Summers, Oron Edgar
09Buster/Pin-14
E104
E254
E270/1
E90/1
M116
S74-18
T201
T202
T205
T206
T213/blue
T215/blue
T215/brown

Summers, Scott
87Greens-9

Summers, Tom
86Tampa-22

Summers, William
55B-317ump

Sunday, Billy
E223
N172
N284
N403
WG1-63

Sundberg, Jim
75Ho-100
75OPC-567
75T-567
75T/M-567
76Ho-68
76OPC-226
76SSPC-260
76T-226
77Ho-110
77OPC-185
77T-351
78BK/R-2
78Ho-79
78T-492
79Ho-97
79K-60
79OPC-53
79T-120
80OPC-276DP
80T-530
81D-385
81F-619
81OPC-95
81T-95
81T/HT
81T/St-133
82D-268
82F-332
82F/St-181
82OPC-335
82T-335
82T/St-240
83D-609
83D-7DK
83D/AAS-26
83F-580
83K-38
83OPC-158
83Rang-10
83T-665
83T/St-126
84D-178
84F-431
84F/X-113
84Gard-18
84Nes/792-779
84OPC-251
84Pol/Brew-8
84T-779
84T/St-355
84T/X-114
85D-89
85F-597
85F/Up-U113
85Leaf-78
85OPC-102
85T-446
85T/St-286
85T/Tr-114T
86D-277
86F-22
86Kitty/Disc-18
86Leaf-149
86NatPhoto-8
86OPC-245
86S-186M
86T-245
86T/St-15ALCS
86T/St-259
87Berg/Cubs-11
87D-280
87F-382
87F/U-U114
87OPC-190
87T-190
87T/St-256
87T/Tr-119T
88D-488
88D/Cubs/Bk-488
88F-434
88Score-244
88T-516
88T/Big-100
89B-227
89Moth/R-24
89Smok/R-32
89T-78
89T/Big-103
89UD-331

Sundberg, Richard
82Redwd-15

Sunderlage, Jeff
82Lynch-9
83Lynch-18

Sundgren, Scott
86BurlEx-23

Sundra, Steve
40PB-122

Sunkel, Tom
39PB-146
40PB-110

Sunker, Steve
78Clint

Sunnen, Gene
88Watertn/Puc-34

Surhoff, B.J.
86Vanco-24
87Class/Up-135
87D-28RR
87D/Rook-17
87F/U-U115
87Leaf-28RR
87S/Rook-23
87Sf/Rook-6
87T-216
88Class/Blue-202
88D-172
88D/Best-277
88F-175
88Leaf-164
88OPC-174
88Panini/St-120
88Pol/Brew-5
88RedFoley/St-85
88Score-22
88Score/YS/I-8
88Sf-57
88T-491
88T/Big-22
88T/Gloss60-49
88T/JumboR-10
88T/St-202
88T/St/Backs-57
88ToysRUs-31
89B-137
89Class-25
89D-221
89D/Best-221
89F-197
89Gard-5
89OPC-33
89Panini/St-368
89Pol/Brew-5
89Score-154
89Sf-208
89T-33
89T/St-200
89UD-343
90D-173
90F-338
90Score-74
90T-696
90UD-159

Surhoff, Rich
85Cram/PCL-49
86D-42RR
86OKCty-22
88IowaC/CMC-10
88IowaC/Pro-529

Suris, Jorge
85Spoka/Cram-23

Surkont, Max
52B-12
52T-302
53B/Col-156
53JC-11
54B-75
54DanDee
55B-83
56T-209
57T-310

Surner, Ben
82Holyo-26
83Nashua-24

Susce, George
55B-320
55Rodeo
56T-93
57T-229
58T-189
59T-511

Susce, Steve
83AlexD-21

Sutcliffe, Rick
78Cr/PCL-51
80Pol/Dodg-43
80T-544
81D-418
81F-125
81OPC-191
81Pol/Dodg-43
81T-191
82F-25
82OPC-141
82T-609
82T/Tr-116T
82Wheat/Ind
83D-72
83F-420
83T-141
83T-497
83T-707
83T/St-20
83T/St-61
83Wheat/Ind-28
84D-338
84F-551
84F/St-87
84F/X-114
84FunFood/Pin-32
84Nes/792-245
84OPC-245
84SevenUp-40
84T-245
84T/St-254
84T/X-115
85D-433
85Drake-43
85F-69
85F/LimEd-39
85F/St-89
85Leaf-139
85OPC-72
85Seven-14G
85SevenUp-40
85T-72
85T-720
85T/3D-29
85T/Gloss40-9
85T/St-35
85T/St-97
85T/Super-3
86D-189
86Dorman-17
86F-383
86F/Mini-81
86F/Slug-39
86Gator-40
86Jay's-18
86Leaf-122
86Meadow/Stat-19
86OPC-330
86S-134M
86S-149M
86S-46
86S-56M
86S-70M
86S-72M
86T-330
86T/St-61
86TrueVal-18
87Berg/Cubs-40
87D-68
87D/OD-69
87F-576
87F/Slug-41
87OPC-142
87T-142
88Berg/Cubs-40
88Class/Blue-224
88D-68
88D/AS-43
88D/Best-138
88D/Cubs/Bk-68
88F-435
88F/AwardWin-41
88F/BB/AS-41
88F/BB/MVP-38
88F/Excit-40
88F/Hottest-42
88F/LL-41
88F/Mini-71
88F/RecSet-40
88F/SS-39
88F/St-81
88F/TL-41
88KMart-30
88Leaf-91
88OPC-372
88Panini/St-257
88RedFoley/St-86
88Score-50
88Sf-27
88T-740
88T/Big-128
88T/Coins-57
88T/Mini-45
88T/Revco-9
88T/St-61
88T/St/Backs-27
88T/UK-77
89B-281
89D-223
89D/Best-138
89F-439
89Mara/Cubs-40
89OPC-394
89Panini/St-51
89Score-407
89Sf-217
89T-520
89T/St-52
89UD-303
90D-157
90F-43
90Score-450
90Sf-181
90T-640
90UD-109

Sutcliffe, Terry
81VeroB-20

Suter, Bill
80OkCty
81OkCty/TCMA-18

Sutherland, Darrell
66OPC-191
66T-191
68T-551
69T/St-59

Sutherland, Gary
67T-587R
68OPC-98
68T-98
69Fud's-12
69T-326
70T-632
71LaPizza-13
71MLB/St-143
71OPC-434
71T-434
72MB-335
72OPC-211
72T-211
73OPC-572
73T-572
74OPC-428
74T-428
74T/Tr-428T
75Ho-146
75OPC-522
75T-522
75T/M-522
76OPC-113
76SSPC-364
76T-113
77T-307

Sutherland, Harry
WG7-54

Sutherland, Leo
77AppFx
79Knoxv/TCMA-7
81D-42
81T-112R
82Edmon-11
82T-599

Sutko, Glenn
88Bill/Pro-1806
89Greens/Pro-420

Sutryk, Tom
87Penin-15

Sutter, Bruce
77T-144
78Ho-5
78K-48
78OPC-196
78T-325
79Ho-130
79K-1
79OPC-238
79T-457
80BK/PHR-11
80K-10
80OPC-4
80T-17
80T/S-32
81Coke
81D-560
81F-294
81F/St-80

81K-56
81OPC-9
81T-590
81T-7LL
81T/St-221
81T/St-32
81T/Tr-838
82D-372
82F-129
82F-631M
82F/St-28
82K-17
82OPC-260
82OPC-347AS
82Sqt-22
82T-168LL
82T-260
82T-347
82T/St-10
82T/St-130
82T/St-15
82T/St-94
83D-40
83D/AAS-41
83F-24
83K-37
83OPC-150
83OPC-151SV
83OPC-266AS
83T-150
83T-151A
83T-407
83T-708
83T/Gloss-40
83T/Gloss40-40
83T/St-166
83T/St-187
83T/St-209
83T/St-284
84D-13
84D-534
84F-338
84F/St-70
84FunFood/Pin-14
84Nes/792-709LL
84Nes/792-730
84OPC-243
84Ralston-24
84Seven-7C
84T-709
84T-730
84T/Cereal-24
84T/St-145
85D-109
85Drake-44
85F-241
85F/St-104
85F/Up-U114
85Ho/Braves-21
85Leaf-163
85OPC-370
85Pol/Atl-40
85Seven-4S
85Seven-5C
85Seven-5G
85T-370
85T-722AS
85T-9RB
85T/3D-23
85T/Gloss40-22
85T/St-135
85T/St-172
85T/Super-9
85T/Tr-115T
86D-321
86F-529
86F/Mini-106
86F/St-117
86Leaf-192
86Meadow/Stat-17
86OPC-133
86Pol/Atl-40
86S-47
86S-65M
86T-620
86T/St-37
86TrueVal-15
87F-530
87OPC-344
87RedFoley/St-125
87T-435
88T-155
89D-458
89F-603
89OPC-11
89Panini/St-39
89RedFoley/St-114
89Score-425
89T-11
89T/Big-64
89T/St-25
89T/WaxBox-M
89UD-414

Suttles, Mule

74Laugh/Black-30

Sutton, Don

66T-288R
67T-445
68OPC-103
68T-103
69MB-267
69MLB/St-153
69OPC-216
69T-216
69T/St-50
70K-8
70MLB/St-59
70T-622
71K-31
71MLB/St-118
71OPC-361
71T-361
71T/Coins-145
72MB-336
72T-530
73K-5
73OPC-10
73T-10
73T/Comics-21
73T/Lids-51
73T/PinUps-21
74OPC-220
74T-220
74T/DE-12
74T/St-50
75Ho-7
75Ho/Twink-7
75OPC-220
75T-220
75T/M-220
76Crane-61
76K-13
76MSA/Disc
76OPC-530
76SSPC-73
76T-530
77Ho-70
77OPC-24
77Pep-62
77T-620
77T/CS-47
78Ho-70
78K-57
78OPC-96
78T-310
79Ho-92
79OPC-80
79T-170
80OPC-228
80Pol/Dodg-20
80T-440
81Coke
81D-58
81F-112
81F/St-59
81Sqt-16
81T-605
81T-7LL
81T/HT
81T/St-27
81T/Tr-839
82D-443
82F-234
82F/St-43
82K-21
82OPC-305
82OPC-306IA
82T-305
82T-306A
83D-531
83F-47
83Gard-18
83OPC-145
83OPC-146SV
83Pol/Brew-21
83T-145
83T-146A
84D-414
84D/Champs-41
84F-215
84FunFood/Pin-86
84Gard-19
84Nes/792-35
84Nes/792-715LL
84Nes/792-716LL
84OPC-35
84Pol/Brew-20
84T-35
84T-715
84T-716
84T/St-300
85D-107
85D-16
85D/DKsuper-16
85F-598
85F/Up-U115
85Leaf-16DK
85Moth/A's-3
85OPC-172
85T-10RB
85T-729
85T/St-290
85T/St-7
85T/St-8
85T/Tr-116T
86D-611
86D/HL-16
86F-170
86F/LimEd-43
86F/Mini-35
86Leaf-236
86OPC-335
86S-130M
86S-175
86Smok/Cal-4
86T-335
87D-181
87F-626M
87F-93
87F/RecSet-37
87F/St-115
87Leaf-153
87OPC-259
87OPC-G
87Ralston-6
87S-156M
87S-99
87Seven-W11
87Smok/Cal-2
87Smok/Dodg-35
87T-673
87T-G
87T/HL-6
87T/St-183
87Woolwth-6
88D-407
88F-505
88Moth/Dodg-9
88Panini/St-37
88Pol/Dodg-20
88Score-105
88Sf-213
88Smok/Dodg-30
88T-575
89Score-400
89Smok/Dodg-78
89T/WaxBox-N

Sutton, Doug

89Bluef/Star-23

Sutton, Ezra

E223
N172
N284
WG1-8

Sutton, Jim

82AppFx-4

Sutton, Johnny

74Gasto
79T-676
80Ogden-13

Sutton, Mark

83BurlR-24
83BurlR/LF-21

Sutton, Rico

80Utica-33

Suzuki, Ken

88SanJose/Cal-129
88SanJose/Pro-121

Suzuki, Yasu

89Salin/Cal-135
89Salin/Pro-1814

Sveum, Dale

84ElPas-24
85Cram/PCL-209
86D/Rook-37
86F/Up-U109
86S/Rook-4
86T/Tr-106T
86Vanco-25
87D-542
87D/OD-55
87F-358
87Leaf-156
87T-327
87T/GlossRk-18
87T/St-309
87ToysRUs-27
88D-232
88D/Best-305
88F-176
88OPC-81
88Panini/St-126
88Pol/Brew-7
88Score-120
88T-592
88T/Big-44
88T/St-199
89B-139
89D-146
89F-198
89Gard-6
89OPC-12
89Panini/St-374
89Pol/Brew-7
89Score-256
89Score/YS/II-24
89T-12
89T/Big-126
89T/St-206
89UD-421
90T-739
90UD-499

Swacina, Harry

E270/1

Swaggerty, Bill

82RochR-7
83RochR-10
84RochR-17
85D-392
85F-193
85RochR-22
85T-147
86D-594
88Omaha/CMC-9
88Omaha/Pro-1498

Swaggerty, Glenn

81QuadC-25

Swail, Steve

89Pulas/Pro-1914

Swain, Rob

86WatIo-26
87Kinston-18
88CLAS/Star-36
88Kinston/Star-21
89Canton/Best-26
89Canton/Pro-1303
89Canton/Star-20

Swain, Steve

82AubAs-16

Swain, Thayer

88Butte-21

Swan, Craig

74OPC-602R
74T-602R
76OPC-494
76SSPC-558
76T-494
77T-94
78T-621
79Ho-41
79OPC-170
79T-334
79T-7LL
79T/Comics-27
80OPC-1
80T-8
80T/S-41
81Coke
81D-155
81F-319
81OPC-189
81T-189
82D-589
82F-548
82T-592
83D-254
83F-557
83OPC-292
83T-292
83T-621TL
83T/St-262
84D-441
84F-600
84F/X-115
84Nes/792-763
84T-763
84T/X-116
89Tidew/CANDL-9

Swan, Russ

86Cram/PCL-8
88SanJose/Cal-138
88SanJose/Pro-118
89Shreve/Pro-1831

Swank, Ken

82CharR-18

Swanson, Art

56T-204

Swanson, Chad

88Keno/Pro-1386
89Keno/Pro-1078

Swanson, Eric

82DayBe-16

Swanson, Evar

33G-195
34Exh/4-10
88Conlon/AmAS-23
R308-174

Swanson, Perry

82CharR-8

Swanson, Stan
72OPC-331
72T-331
72T/Cloth-31
Swartwood, Cyrus
N172
Swartz, Nick
84Omaha-7
85Omaha-3
86Omaha-26C
87Omaha-5
88Omaha/Pro-1500
Swartzbaugh, David
88CapeCod/Sum-66
89Geneva/Pro-1866
Swartzel, Parke
N172
Swartzlander, Keith
86Macon-25
Sweeney, Bill
31Exh/4-18
Sweeney, D.B.
88Pac/8Men-13
Sweeney, Ed
11Helmar-47
11Helmar-81
14CJ-112
15CJ-112
E106
E270/1
E286
E90/1
M116
T201
T202
T205
T206
T213/blue
T216
T222
WG5-39
WG6-35
Sweeney, Jim
89Geneva/Pro-1873
Sweeney, Mark
88CapeCod/Sum-59
Sweeney, Michael
89Idaho/Pro-2023
Sweeney, Peter
N172
Sweeney, William John
D303
E224
E90/1
M116
T204
T206
T207
T213/blue
T213/brown
T215/brown
Sweeney, William
(Bill)
53Mother-23
Sweet, Richard
78T-702R
79Hawai-3
79OPC-341
79T-646
80Hawai-20
81Tidew-1
83D-352
83F-487
83Nalley-6
83T-437
84D-196
84F-621
84Nes/792-211
84T-211
88Wausa/Feder-1
88Wausa/GS-1
89Osceola/Star-27
Sweetland, Lester L.
29Exh/4-12
Swenson, Mark
82Clint-31
Swenson, Mickey
82Clint-30
Swepson, Dobie
86Clint-23
88Poca/Pro-2095
Swepson, Lyle
84Evrt/Cram-2
Swetonic, Steve
R310
Swiacki, Bill
79Albuq-4
80Albuq-5
81Albuq/TCMA-6
82Tacom-9
Swift, Bill
85T-404
86D-562
86F-475
86Moth/Mar-16
86T-399
86T/Mini-46
87D-517
87F-597
87T-67
88F/U-U61
88Moth/Sea-25
88T/Tr-117T
89F-560
89Moth/Sea-17
89OPC-198
89RedFoley/St-115
89Score-219
89T-712
89T/St-228
89UD-623
90D-566
90F-526
90T-574
90UD-313
Swift, Robert V.
(Bob)
47TipTop
49B-148
50B-149
51B-214
52B-131
52T-181
54T-65
60T-470C
W753
Swift, Weldon
78BurlB
79Holyo-23
80Holyo-11
81ElPas-19
Swift, William V.
34G-57
39PB-129
R312
R313
R314
Swindell, Gary
89RedFoley/St-116
Swindell, Greg
86S/Rook-30
87D-32RR
87F-644M
87F/U-U116
87Gator-21
87Leaf-32RR
87T-319
88D-227
88D/Best-280
88F-617
88F/Slug-41
88Gator-21
88Leaf-158
88OPC-22
88Panini/St-70
88Score-154
88Score/YS/II-39
88T-22
88T/Big-156
88T/St-210
89B-76
89Class-61
89Class/Up/2-195
89D-232
89D/Best-112
89F-413
89F/LL-38
89OPC-315
89Panini/St-320
89Score-282
89Sf-4
89T-315
89T/Big-68
89T/Coins-54
89T/Mini-52
89T/St-213
89T/UK-76
89UD-250
90D-310
90D/Bon/MVP-BC24
90F-503
90Score-230
90Score/100St-11
90T-595
90UD-574
Swindle, Allen
83Tampa-22
Swingle, Russ
52Park-94
Swisher, Steve
75OPC-63
75T-63
75T/M-63
76OPC-173
76SSPC-319
76T-173
77OPC-23
77T-419
78T-252
79T-304
80T-163
81T-541
81T/Tr-840
82T-764
83D-633
83Richm-12
83T-612
86Watlo-27MG
87Wmspt-18
88ColSp/CMC-24
88ColSp/Pro-1546
89Jacks/GS-20
Swob, Tim
87Tampa-9
Swoboda, Ron
65T-533R
66OPC-35
66T-35
66T/RO-23
67OPC-186M
67T-186M
67T-264
67T/Test/SU-5
68Bz-13
68OPC-114
68T-114
68T/3D
68T/Post-17
69Citgo-18
69MB-268
69MLB/St-171
69MLBPA/Pin-57
69T-585
69T/St-70
69Trans-44
70MLB/St-83
70OPC-431
70T-431
70Trans/M-25
71MLB/St-166
71OPC-665
71T-665
72MB-337
72OPC-8
72T-8
73OPC-314
73T-314
Swoope, Bill
77Clint
78Clint
79LodiD-13
Sykes, Bob
77T-491R
79T-569
80T-223
81F-533
81T-348
82Colum-12
82Colum/Pol-38
82D-640
82F-130
82Nashv-25
82T-108
Sylvester, John
77Cedar
Sylvia, Dave
75BurlB
Sylvia, Ronald
81Redwd-7
82Redwd-16
83Nashua-9
Syverson, Dain
85Water-25
86Water-24
87Wmspt-1
Szekely, Joe
83CharR-3
85VeroB-6
87SnAnt-17
87TexLgAS-35
89Albuq/CMC-19
89Albuq/Pro-77
Szotkiewicz, Ken
71OPC-749
71T-749
Szymarek, Paul
81Shrev-12
82Phoen
Szymczak, Dave
83Nashvl-24
84BuffB-13
Szynal, Jon
89Spart/Pro-1031
89Spart/Star-22
Tabacheck, Marty
V362-23
Tabaka, Jeff
86Jamestn-25
87WPalm-5
88WPalm/Star-23
89Readg/Best-7
89Readg/Pro-663
Tabb, Jerry
78T-224
Tabeling, Bob
86Visal-21
Tabler, Pat
77FtLaud
81Colum-16
82D-529
82IowaC-10
83D-552
83F-509
84D-536
84F-552
84Nes/792-329
84T-329
84T/St-252
84Wheat/Ind-10
85D-460
85F-456
85Leaf-76
85OPC-158
85Polar/Ind-10
85T-158
85T/St-250
86D-129
86F-594
86Leaf-52
86OhHenry-10
86OPC-66
86T-674
86T/St-212
87D-254
87D/OD-107
87F-261
87F/Slug-42
87Gator-10
87Leaf-182
87OPC-77
87S-66
87T-575
87T/Mini-52
87T/St-205
88D-219
88D/AS-17
88F-618
88F-633M
88F/Hottest-43
88F/Mini-20
88F/St-22
88F/U-U36
88Gator-10
88OPC-230
88Panini/St-81
88RedFoley/St-87
88Score-23
88Score/Tr-22T
88Sf-205
88T-230
88T/Big-173
88T/St-204
88T/Tr-118T
89B-125
89D-326
89F-294
89KMart/Lead-19
89OPC-56
89Panini/St-359
89Score-391
89Sf-172
89T-56
89T/Big-67
89T/St-6
89Tastee/Discs-3
89UD-233
89Woolwth-18
90D-444
90F-119
90Score-242
90Sf-218
90T-727
90UD-142
Tabor, Greg
82BurlR-10
84Tulsa-19
85OKCty-28
86OKCty-23
87OKCty-21
88F-644
88IowaC/CMC-18
88IowaC/Pro-548
Tabor, Jim
39PB-14
40PB-36
41DP-58
49B/PCL-33
R303/A
Tabor, Scott
83BirmB-15

86Omaha-27
86Omaha/TCMA-17
Tackett, Jack
(Jeff)
85Newar-5
87CharO/WBTV-9
88CharlK-8
88CharlK/Pep-8
89RochR/CMC-17
89RochR/Pro-1645
Tafoya, Dennis
88Ashvl/Pro-1070
88AubAs/Pro-1951
89Osceola/Star-24
Tafoya, Rod
89Boise/Pro-1987
Taft, Dennie
83Clint/LF-24
Taft, Tim
88Clearw/Star-24
Tagi, Anthony
88Fresno/Cal-20
88Fresno/Pro-1234
Taguchi, Dragon
89Salin/Cal-132
89Salin/Pro-1809
Taitt, D.
29Exh/4-18
Takach, Dave
87Sprin/Best-14
88Salem/Star-20
Takacs, John
77Ashev
Talamantez, Greg
85Newar-4
86Hagers-24
87CharO/WBTV-35
88FSLAS/Star-22
89Jacks/GS-1
Talbot, Bob D.
52Mother-16
54T-229
55B-137
Talbot, Fred
65OPC-58
65T-58
66T-403
66T/RO-104
67T-517
68T-577
69T-332
70OPC-287
70T-287
72MB-338
Talbott, Shawn
86Ashvl-27
87Ashvl-18
Talford, Calvin
89Martins/Star-29
Talton, Marion
(Tim)
67T-603R
Tamargo, John
79Pol/Giants-30
79T-726R
80OPC-351R
80T-680
81D-210
81F-152
81OPC-35DP
81T-519
82Miami-22
87Lynch-22
Tamulis, Vito
39PB-139
40PB-145
41G-17
R309/2
R314
V355-101
Tanabe, Collin
82Beloi-13
Tanabe, Nori
86SanJose-20
Tanana, Frank
74OPC-605R
74T-605R
75OPC-16
75T-16
75T/M-16
76Ho-101
76K-30
76OPC-204LL
76OPC-490
76SSPC-189
76T-204LL
76T-490
77Ho-63
77K-45
77OPC-105
77T-200
78Ho-101
78K-54
78OPC-65
78OPC-7LL
78PapaG/Disc-33
78T-207LL
78Wiffle/Discs-73
79Ho-47
79OPC-274
79T-530
80OPC-57
80T-105
81Coke
81D-171
81F-276
81OPC-369
81T-369
81T/HT
81T/St-56
81T/Tr-841
82D-326
82F-309
82OPC-4
82T-792
82T/Tr-117T
83D-447
83F-581
83Rang-28
83T-272
84D-98
84F-432
84FunFood/Pin-133
84Nes/792-479
84OPC-276
84Rang-28
84T-479
85D-220
85D-9
85D/DKsuper-9
85F-570
85Leaf-9DK
85OPC-55
85T-55
85T/St-348
86Cain's-17
86D-491
86F-239
86Leaf-241
86OPC-124
86T-592
87Cain's-20
87Coke/Tigers-5
87D-152
87F-164
87F/Hottest-40
87OPC-231
87Seven-DT10
87T-726
88D-461
88D/Best-259
88F-71
88F/Slug-42
88OPC-177
88Panini/St-86
88Pep/T-26
88Pol/T-11
88Score-490
88Sf-133
88T-177
88T/St-264
89B-92
89D-90
89D/Best-91
89F-147
89Mara/Tigers-26
89OPC-299
89Panini/St-336
89Pol/Tigers-26
89RedFoley/St-117
89Score-112
89Sf-103
89Smok/Angels-9
89T-603
89T-609TL
89T/St-275
89UD-391
90Class-108
90D-180
90F-616
90Score-57
90T-343
90UD-516
Tanks, Talmage
76BurlB
Tannahill, Kevin
89Helena/SP-23
Tannehill, Jesse
T206
Tannehill, Lee Ford
11Helmar-17
E254
E90/1
M116
S74-9
T202
T205
T206
T207
Tanner, Bruce
85BuffB-25
85F/Up-U116
86BuffB-21
86F-218
87Tacom-8
88Huntsvl/BK-22
89Tacom/Pro-1540
Tanner, Chuck
55JC-18
55T-161
56T-69
57T-392
58T-91
59T-234
60L-115
60T-279
61BeeHive-23
71OPC-661MG
71T-661
72OPC-98MG
72T-98
73OPC-356MG
73T-356MG
74OPC-221MG
74T-221MG
75OPC-276MG
75T-276MG
75T/M-276MG
76SSPC-151
76T-656MG
77T-354MG
78T-494
79T-244MG
79TCMA-63
80T-5
81D-257
81F-367
81T-683R
82D-150
83D-124
83T-696
84Nes/792-291MG
84T-291
85T-268MG
86Pol/Atl-7MG
86T-351
86T/Tr-107T
87Smok/Atl-26MG
87T-593MG
88T-134
Tanner, Ed
81Batav-16
82Watlo/B-19
82Watlo/C-22
83Sprin/LF-8
84ArkTr-1
86ArkTr-24
87Nashv-19
89Nashvl-24
89Nashvl/CMC-19
89Nashvl/Pro-1287
Tanner, Mark
74Gasto
Tanner, Roy
76Watlo
77DaytB
82CharR-24
83CharR-24
Tanzi, Bobby
80Wausa-12
Tanzi, Michael
82AppFx-25
83GlenF-20
Tapais, Luis
86Kenosha-23
Tapani, Kevin
86Cram/PCL-64
87Modesto-12
88Jacks/GS-23
89Tidew/CMC-10
89Tidew/Pro-1972
90D-473
90D-476
90T-227
90UD-87
Tapia, Jose
87QuadC-7
87VeroB-2
88PalmSp/Cal-93
88PalmSp/Pro-1446
Tappe, Elvin
53Mother-48
55B-51
55T-129
55T/DH-94
58T-184
60T-457C
Tarangelo, Joseph
84Visal-23
Tarasco, Tony
89Pulas/Pro-1904
Tarchione, Travis
88CapeCod/Sum-23
89SLCty-60F
Tarin, Fernando
77QuadC
Tarnow, Greg
81QuadC-3
83AppFx/LF-21
Tarrolly, Dave
83Beloi/LF-17GM
Tartabull, Danny
82Water-14
83Chatt-6
84Cram/PCL-170
85Cram/PCL-94
85D-27
85F-647
86D-38
86D/Rook-45
86F-476
86F/Mini-99
86Moth/Mar-22
86S-178M
86S/Rook-22
86T/Tr-108T
87Class/Up-145
87D-147
87D/OD-200
87F-598
87F/U-U117
87Leaf-250
87OPC-332
87RedFoley/St-97
87S-23
87T-476
87T/Coins-25
87T/Gloss60-19
87T/GlossRk-19
87T/St-223
87T/St-306
87T/Tr-120T
87ToysRUs-28
88Class/Blue-235
88D-177
88D-5DK
88D/Best-287
88D/DKsuper-5DK
88F-271
88F/AwardWin-42
88F/Excit-41
88F/Mini-28
88F/SS-40
88F/St-34
88KayBee-30
88Leaf-190
88Leaf-5DK
88OPC-211
88Panini/St-112
88Score-106
88Score/YS/II-5
88Sf-19
88Smok/Royals-4
88T-724
88T/Big-230
88T/Coins-29
88T/Mini-16
88T/Revco-26
88T/St-257
88T/UK-78
89B-128
89D-61
89D/Best-39
89D/GrandSlam-10
89F-295
89F/BBMVP's-37
89OPC-275
89Panini/St-360
89RedFoley/St-118
89Score-105
89Score/HotSt-19
89Sf-46
89T-275
89T/Big-107
89T/Coins-55
89T/St-267
89Tastee/Discs-4
89UD-329
90D-322
90F-120
90Score-244
90Score/100St-72
90Sf-129
90T-540
90UD-656
Tartabull, Jose Jr.
86Cram/PCL-108
87Wausa-8
88RedFoley/St-88
88SnBer/Best-13

88SnBer/Cal-36
89SnBer/Best-18
89SnBer/Cal-79
Tartabull, Jose
62T-451
63T-449
64T-276
66OPC-143
66T-143
67OPC-56
67T-56
67T/Test/RSox-21
68T-555
69MB-269
69T-287
70OPC-481
70T-481
72MB-339
Tarumi, Kanenori
88Mia/Star-11
Tarver, LaSchelle
82Lynch-2
84Tidew-21
85IntLgAS-6
85Tidew-13
86Pawtu-24
87Pawtu-10
87Pawtu/TCMA-19
Tasby, Willie
59T-143
60L-100
60T-322
61P-51
61T-458
61T/St-117
62J-70
62P-70
62P/Can-70
62Salada-21
62Shirriff-21
62T-462
Tata, Terry
88Umpire-16
89Umpires-14
Tatarain, Dean
89Utica/Puc-24
Tate, Benny
R314/Can
V355-80
Tate, Chuck
86Cram/PCL-16
Tate, Edward
N172
Tate, Henry
31Exh/4-20
Tate, Lee W.
59T-544
Tate, Michael
88Boise/Pro-1606
Tate, Randy L.
76OPC-549
76SSPC-555
76T-549
78Colum
Tate, Stu
84Evrt/Cram-12
86Shrev-24
87Shrev-20
88Shreve/Pro-1295
89AAA/Pro-52
89Phoen/CMC-9
89Phoen/Pro-1491
90F-643M
Tatis, Bernie
86Knoxv-23
87Knoxv-16
87SLAS-4
88BuffB/CMC-14
88BuffB/Pro-1475
Tatis, Rafael
73Cedar
74Cedar
75Dubuq
Tatsuno, Derek
82ElPas-22
87Hawai-5
Tatum, Jarvis
70T-642R
71MLB/St-334
71OPC-159
71T-159
Tatum, Jim
85Spoka/Cram-24
86CharRa-25
87CharRa-19
88Wichi-18
Tatum, Ken
70MLB/St-180
70T-658
71MLB/St-335
71OPC-601
71T-601
72MB-340
72T-772
73OPC-463
73T-463
Tatum, Willie
88Elmir-19
89WinHav/Star-23
Taubensee, Eddie
88Greens/Pro-1558
88SALAS/GS-6
89Cedar/Best-12
89Cedar/Pro-937
89Cedar/Star-19
Tauken, Daniel
87Penin-5
Taussig, Don
62Salada-186
62Shirriff-186
62T-44
89Smok/Ast-22
Tavarez, Alfonso
85Utica-15
86BurlEx-24
Tavarez, Davis
83Clint/LF-12
84Evrt/Cram-21
Tavener, Jack
28Exh-46
29Exh/4-21
Taveras, Alejandro
75Iowa/TCMA-21
Taveras, Alex
74Cedar
77T-474R
79Albuq-15
81Albuq/TCMA-18
82Albuq-18
83Albuq-10
84Cram/PCL-153
85BuffB-12
89Beloi/Star-26M
Taveras, Frank
74OPC-607R
74T-607R
75OPC-277
75OPC-460NLCS
75T-277
75T/M-277
76OPC-36
76SSPC-583
76T-36
77T-538
78OPC-4LL
78T-204LL
78T-685
79OPC-79
79T-165
80BK/PHR-32
80OPC-237
80T-456
81Coke
81D-154
81F-320
81OPC-343
81T-343
81T/HT
81T/St-196
82D-98
82F-539
82Hygrade
82OPC-351
82T-782
82T/Tr-118T
Taveras, Marcos
88StCath/Pro-2028
89Duned/Star-18
Taylor, Andrew
86LitFalls-27
88Sprin/Best-8
89Savan/Pro-368
Taylor, Antonio S.
(Tony)
58T-411
59T-62
60L-44
60T-294
61P-118
61T-411
61T/St-59
62J-193
62P-193
62P/Can-193
62Salada-156
62Shirriff-156
62T-77
62T/bucks
62T/St-170
63J-178
63P-178
63T-366
64T-585
64T/Coins-113
64T/Coins-144AS
64T/St-9
65T-296
66T-585
67OPC-126
67T-126
68T-327
69MB-270
69MLB/St-179
69OPC-108
69T-108
70MB-28
70MLB/St-95
70OPC-324
70T-324
71K-67
71MLB/St-190
71OPC-246
71T-246
72MB-341
72OPC-511
72T-511
73OPC-29
73T-29
75OPC-574
75T-574
75T/M-574
76OPC-624
76SSPC-474
76T-624
78TCMA-133
Taylor, Ben
78Laugh/Black-12
Taylor, Bob
76Baton
Taylor, Bobbie
85Anchora-45
Taylor, Bruce
77Evansvl/TCMA-23
78T-701R
Taylor, Carl
68T-559R
69T-357
70OPC-76
70T-76
71MLB/St-286
71MLB/St-432
71OPC-353
71T-353
71T/Coins-55
73OPC-99
73T-99
74OPC-627
74T-627
Taylor, Chuck
63Pep/Tul
70OPC-119
70T-119
71OPC-606
71T-606
72OPC-407
72T-407
73OPC-176
73T-176
74OPC-412
74T-412
75OPC-58
75T-58
75T/M-58
76SSPC-346
86ColumAst-24C
87Ashvl-11C
88Ashvl/Pro-1067
89Ashvl/Pro-944
Taylor, Dan
35BU-108
35Exh/4-2
R314
V355-72
Taylor, Dave
87Beloi-25
88Stock/Cal-195
88Stock/Pro-729
Taylor, Dorn
83AlexD-30
84PrWill-6
85Nashua-24
86Nashua-26
87F/U-U118
87Vanco-24
88BuffB/CMC-9
88BuffB/Polar-5
88BuffB/Pro-1468
89AAA/Pro-9
Taylor, Dwight
82Watlo-23
83BuffB-21
84Maine-18
85Maine-28
86Omaha/TCMA-11
87Omaha-8
89ColrSp/CMC-19
89ColSp/Pro-234
Taylor, Eddie
45Centen-25
47Centen-29
Taylor, Edward
26Exh-7
Taylor, Jack
26Exh-8
27Exh-4
28Exh-4
WG3-44
Taylor, James
(Zack)
33G-152
51B-315
V353-79
W753
Taylor, Jeff
83Memph-14
86Orlan-20
88Oneon/Pro-2070
89Oneon/Pro-2101
Taylor, John W.
E107
E254
E270/1
Taylor, John
81Clint-17
82AlexD-1
82AppFx-8
83AlexD-12
Taylor, Joseph C.
(Bill)
54T-74
55Gol/Giants-26
55T-53
55T/DH-7
58T-389
Taylor, Joseph F.
54JC
55JC
Taylor, Kerry
89Elizab/Star-25
Taylor, Luther H.
(Dummy)
C46-41
E91
T206
WG3-45
Taylor, Mike
81Watlo-28
82Watlo-24
87Hawai-12
88Gasto/Pro-998
88StCath/Pro-2032
89Myrtle/Pro-1462
Taylor, Phil
86Miami-24
Taylor, Randy
77SnJos-21
Taylor, Robert D.
(Hawk)
58T-164
61T-446
62T-406
63T-481
64T-381
65T-329
68OPC-52
68T-52
69T-239
Taylor, Ron
62T-591R
63T-208R
64T-183
65T-568
66OPC-174
66T-174
67T-606
68T-421
69OPC-72
69T-72
69T/St-79
70OPC-419
70T-419
71MLB/St-167
71OPC-687
71T-687
72OPC-234
72T-234
Taylor, Sam
88CapeCod/Sum-121
89Batav/Pro-1937
Taylor, Sammy
58T-281
59T-193
60L-131
60T-162
61P-198
61T-253
61T/St-10
62J-189
62P-189
62P/Can-189

62Salada-164
62Shirriff-164
62T-274
63T-273
Taylor, Scott
88CharWh/Best-4
88Elmir-4
88Geneva/Pro-1651
89CharWh/Best-5
89CharWh/Pro-1757
89Wausa/GS-11
Taylor, Steve
78Cr/PCL-39
79Colum-20
Taylor, Terry
83Wausa/LF-9
86Chatt-24
87Calgary-17
88Calg/Pro-781
88CapeCod/Sum-137
89F-651M
89T-597
Taylor, Tommy
89Bluef/Star-24
Taylor, Wade
88FtLaud/Star-21
89PrWill/Star-21
Taylor, William
75QuadC
76QuadC
80Ashev-18
82Wausa-26
83Tulsa-5
84Tulsa-32
85Tulsa-34
86Cram/PCL-179
87OKCty-25
88OkCty/Pro-28
89LasVeg/CMC-10
89LasVeg/Pro-3
89Madis/Star-20
Taylor, William
(Will)
88River/Cal-227
88River/Pro-1419
89River/Best-17
89River/Cal-13
89River/Pro-1402
Taylor, William H.
N690
Taylor, William M.
(Joe)
58T-451
60HenryH-22
60Union-13
61Union
Taylor, William
(Ooiee)
87CharRa-6
Tayor, Fiona
85Anchora-38BG
Teahan, Jim
83Beloi/LF-19
Tebbetts, George
(Birdie)
47TipTop
50Drake-30
51B-257
52B-124
52NumNum-3
52T-282
55B-232
58T-386M
62T-588
63Sugar-18
63T-48
64T-462
65T-301
66T-552
D305
Exh47
Tebbetts, Steve
76QuadC
77QuadC
Tebeau, Oliver
(Patsy)
N172
Tedder, Scott
89Saraso/Star-24
89Star/Wax-61
Teegarden, Travis
89Bill/Pro-2040
Teel, Garett
88CapeCod/Sum-171
Teising, John
78Watlo
Teixeira, Joe
89Bluef/Star-25
Teixeira, Vince
86Cram/PCL-74
87Madis-5
88Modesto/Cal-80
89Visal/Cal-113
89Visal/Pro-1423
Tejada, Alejandro
89James/Pro-2153
Tejada, Eugenio
88Utica/Puc-10
89SoBend/GS-25
Tejada, Francisco
88Martins/Star-30
Tejada, Joaquin
86Elmir-23
87Elmir-25
87Elmir/Red-25
Tejada, Wilfredo
86Jaxvl/TCMA-18
87D-529
87Indianap-25
88Indi/CMC-19
88Indi/Pro-523
89B-468
89OPC-391
89Phoen/CMC-12
89Phoen/Pro-1489
89T-747
Tejeda, Felix
86VeroB-24
87SnAnt-15
Tekulve, Kent
76OPC-112
76SSPC-561
76T-112
77T-374
78T-84
79T-223
80OPC-297
80T-573
81Coke
81D-254
81F-362
81F/St-21
81OPC-94
81T-695
82D-311
82F-500
82F/St-73
82OPC-281
82T-485
83D-297
83F-326
83OPC-17
83OPC-18SV
83T-17
83T-18A
84D-410
84F-265
84FunFood/Pin-12
84Nes/792-754
84OPC-74
84T-754
84T/St-132
85D-479
85F-477
85F/Up-U117
85Leaf-119
85OPC-125
85T-125
85T/St-129
85T/Tr-117T
86CIGNA-4
86D-111
86F-455
86OPC-326
86T-326
87D-453
87F-190
87F/Excit-42
87F/Mini-104
87F/St-116
87OPC-86
87T-684
87T/St-118
88D-535
88D/Best-327
88F-318
88OPC-P
88Panini/St-354
88Score-425
88T-543
88T/Revco-10
88T/WaxBox-P
89F-583
89K/Reds-43
89Score-287
89T/Tr-116T
89T/WaxBox-O
89UD-207
Telford, Anthony
88Hagers/Star-22
89Freder/Star-23
Tellez, Alonzo
87SnAnt-5
Tellgren, Scott
83Toled-25
85Maine-32
Tellmann, Tom
79Hawai-23
80Hawai-14
81T-356R
82Hawai-19
83Pol/Brew-42
83T/X-109
84D-149
84F-216
84Gard-20
84Nes/792-476
84Pol/Brew-42
84T-476
84T/St-297
85Cram/PCL-150
85D-246
85F-599
85Gard-20
85T-112
85T/Tr-118T
86T-693
Temperly, Kevin
89Clint/Pro-881
Temple, Johnny
55B-31
55Kahn
56Kahn
56T-212
57Kahn
57T-9
58Kahn
58T-205
58T-478AS
59Kahn
59T-335
60Kahn
60MacGregor-25
60T-500
60T/tatt
60T/tatt-50
61Kahn
61T-155
61T/St-143
62J-38
62P-38
62P/Can-38
62Salada-52A
62Salada-52B
62Shirriff-52
62T-34
63J-189
63P-189
63Pep
63T-576
Rawl
Templeton, Chuck
79TCMA-282
Templeton, Garry
76Tulsa
77Ho-78
77OPC-84
77T-161
78Ho-43
78K-31
78OPC-51
78T-32
79Ho-127
79OPC-181
79T-350
80OPC-308
80T-587
80T/S-37
81Coke
81D-187
81F-529
81F/St-125
81K-27
81MSA/Disc-32
81OPC-144
81Sqt-12
81T-485
81T/So-82
81T/St-217
81T/St-255
82D-545
82F-131
82F/St-27
82OPC-288
82T-288
82T/St-96
82T/Tr-119T
83D-145
83F-373
83K-17
83OPC-336
83T-505
83T/St-291
84D-185
84F-314
84Moth/Padres-8
84Nes/792-615
84OPC-173
84Smok/Padres-24
84T-615
84T/St-151
85D-356
85F-45
85Moth/Padres-7
85OPC-124
85T-735
85T/St-151
86D-202
86D/AAS-30
86F-336
86F/Mini-71
86F/St-118
86Leaf-133
86OPC-90
86S-170
86T-90
86T/St-110
87Bohem-1
87D-141
87D/OD-150
87F-432
87Leaf-63
87OPC-325
87T-325
87T/St-110
88Coke/Padres-1
88D-649
88F-598
88OPC-264
88Panini/St-409
88RedFoley/St-89
88Score-189
88Smok/Padres-28
88T-640
88T/St-113
89B-455
89D-483
89D/Best-154
89F-319
89Panini/St-202
89Score-176
89T-121
89T/Big-328
89UD-297
90D-246
90F-170
90Score-336
90T-481
90UD-288
Tenace, Gene
70OPC-21R
70T-21R
71MLB/St-528
71OPC-338
71T-338
72OPC-189
72T-189
73OPC-203WS
73OPC-206WS
73OPC-360
73OPC-524
73T-524
74OPC-79
74T-79
74T/St-230
75Ho-64
75Ho/Twink-64
75OPC-535
75T-535
75T/M-535
76Ho-122
76OPC-165
76SSPC-493
76T-165
77Ho-141
77OPC-82
77Pep-39
77T-303
78Ho-125
78OPC-35
78T-240
78Wiffle/Discs-74
79Ho-19
79OPC-226
79T-435
80OPC-355
80T-704
81D-241
81F-489
81OPC-29
81T-29
81T/Tr-842
82D-152
82F-132
82F/St-26
82OPC-166
82T-631
83D-442
83F-25

83OPC-252
83T-515
83T/X-110
84D-264
84F-266
84Nes/792-729
84T-729
87Moth/A's-14
Tenacen, Francisco
86Tampa-23
87Vermont-4
88WinSal/Star-20
89WinSal/Star-16
Tenenini, Bob
80Memph-23
83Memph-17
Tener, John
N172
Tenhunfeld, Joe
88Batav/Pro-1679
Tennant, Mike
77LodiD
79Albuq-2
Tenney, Fred
D304
E103
E107
E90/1
E91
E98
M116
T204
T206
T3-122
WG3-46
Tenney, Mickey
81QuadC-8
Tepedino, Frank
70T-689
71OPC-342
71T-342
74OPC-526
74T-526
75OPC-9
75T-9
75T/M-9
Tepper, Marc
89Mia/Star/25-19
89Watertn/Star-21
Terlecky, Greg
76SSPC-299
77T-487R
Terpko, Jeff
77T-137
Terrazas, Marc
82Holyo-24
83Redwd-31
Terrell, Jerry
74OPC-481
74T-481
75OPC-654
75T-654
75T/M-654
76OPC-159
76SSPC-222
76T-159
77T-513
78T-525
79T-273
80T-98
87FtMyr-29MG
Terrell, Walt
81Tulsa-12
82Tidew-24
83Tidew-12
84D-640
84F-601
84Nes/792-549
84T-549
84T/St-110
85D-597
85F-94
85F/Up-U118
85OPC-287
85T-287
85T/St-109
85T/Tr-119T
86Cain's-18
86D-247
86F-240
86Leaf-123
86OPC-301
86T-461
86T/Mini-16
87Cain's-16
87Coke/Tigers-3
87D-275
87F-165
87Leaf-180
87OPC-72
87T-72
88D-91
88D/Best-293
88F-72
88F/Mini-24
88F/St-28
88OPC-284
88Panini/St-87
88Pep/T-35
88Pol/T-12
88RedFoley/St-90
88Score-538
88T-668
89B-445
89D-296
89D/Best-245
89D/Tr-28
89F-149
89Score-314
89Score/Tr-75
89T-127
89T/Tr-117T
89UD-475
89UD/Ext-703
90D-309
90F-457
90Score-463
90T-611
90UD-661
Terrill, James
87Everett-19
88Clint/Pro-702
89SanJose/Best-4
89SanJose/Cal-218
89SanJose/Pro-449
89SanJose/Star-24
Terrio, Tim
89Bak/Cal-208tr
Terry, Brent
88SLCty-6CO
Terry, Brett
88Utica/Puc-3
Terry, Ralph
57T-391
58T-169
59T-358
60T-96
61T-389
62J-10
62P-10
62P/Can-10
62Salada-77
62Shirriff-77
62T-48
63Bz-20
63F-26
63J-20
63Kahn
63P-20
63Salada-38
63T-10LL
63T-315
63T-8LL
64T-458
65Kahn
65T-406
66OPC-109
66T-109
66T/RO-69
67OPC-59
67T-59
78TCMA-168
88Pac/Leg-64
89Swell-31
WG9-23
Terry, Scott
81Cedar-18
82Cedar-23
83Tampa-23
87Nashv-20
87T-453
88D-647
88F/U-U121
88Louvl-47
88Smok/Card-8
88T/Tr-119T
89D-397
89F-464
89Score-397
89Smok/Cards-20
89T-686
89T/Big-31
90D-418
90F-261
90Score-235
90T-82
90UD-260
Terry, William H.
(Bill)
25Exh-40
26Exh-40
28Yueng-46
29Exh/4-9
31Exh/4-10
33CJ/Pin-22
33DL-4
33G-125
33G-20
34DS-14
34Exh/4-5
34G-21
35BU-6
35Exh/4-5
35G-1K
35G-3B
35G-4B
35G-5B
36Exh/4-5
38ONG/Pin-29
50Callahan
60F-52
61F-142
61GP-5
80Cram/Leg-9
80Laugh/3/4/5-7
80SSPC/HOF
86Conlon/1-31
88Conlon/3-28
88Conlon/NatAS-20
89HOF/St-2
E210-46
R300
R306
R311/Gloss
R315-A35
R315-B35
R316
R328-4
R337-405
V353-20
V354-53
V355-7
W502-46
W513-67
W517
Terry, William H.
N172
Terry, Zeb
D327
D328-171
E121/120
E121/80
E135-171
W501-58
W575
Terwilliger, Wayne
50B-114
51B-175
51T/RB-14
52T-7
53Briggs
53T-159
54T-73
55T-34
55T/DH-132
56T-73
59T-496
60L-134
60T-26
77Ashev
80Tulsa-24
Terzarial, Tony
88Bill/Pro-1811
Tesreau, Charles
(Jeff)
14CJ-45
15CJ-45
88Conlon/3-29
BF2-80
D328-172
D329-173
D350/2-175
E135-172
M101/4-173
M101/5-175
Teston, Phil
80Penin/C-1
Tettleton, Mickey
84Albany-22
85F/Up-U119
85Moth/A's-11
85T/Tr-120T
86D-345
86F-432
86Moth/A's-11
86T-457
87D-349
87D/OD-23
87F-407
87T-649
88D-103
88French-14
88RochR-23
88RochR/CMC-21
88RochR/Pro-202
88Score-269
88Score/Tr-31T
88T-143
88T/Tr-120T
89D-401
89D/Best-86
89F-623
89French-14
89Panini/St-259
89Score-358
89T-521
89T/Big-198
89T/St-231
89UD-553
90Class-39
90D-169
90D-5DK
90F-190
90Score-322
90Score/100St-9
90Sf-171
90T-275
90UD-297
90UD-60TC
Teufel, Tim
82Orlan/B-12
82OrlTw/A-9
83Toled-16
84D-37
84F-574
84T/X-117
85D-192
85F-290
85Leaf-97
85OPC-239
85Seven/Minn-10
85T-239
85T/St-303
86D-242
86F-407
86F/Up-U110
86OPC-91
86T-667
86T/St-280
86T/Tr-109T
87D-581
87D/OD-131
87F-24
87T-158
88D-648
88D/Mets/Bk-648
88F-152
88Kahn/Mets-11
88Score-128
88T-508
89B-382
89D-507
89F-50
89Kahn/Mets-11
89Score-58
89T-9
89UD-277
90D-618
90F-218
90Score-501
90T-764
90UD-492
Teutsch, Mark
79AppFx-15
80GlenF/B-13
80GlenF/C-3
Tevlin, Creighton J.
79Vanco-23
81Syrac-19
82Syrac-22
Tewksbury, Bob
84Nashvl-22
85Albany-11
86D/Rook-8
86F/Up-U111
86T/Tr-110T
87Colum/TCMA-9
87D-422
87F-117
87T-254
88IowaC/CMC-5
88IowaC/Pro-534
88T-593
89Louvl-35
89Louvl/CMC-11
89Louvl/Pro-1250
90D-714
Texidor, Esteban
78Holyo
Thacker, Moe
59T-474
61T-12
62T-546
Thayer, Greg
79Toled-16
Thayer, Scott
78Green
Thebo, Antonio
T206

Theilman, Harry
WG3-47
Theisen, Mike
86StPet-29
Theiss, Duane
78Richm
79Richm-16
80Ander-3
Theobald, Ron
72OPC-77
72T-77
Theodore, George
74OPC-99
74T-8
89Tidew/CANDL-8
Therrien, Ed
88CapeCod/Sum-4
Thevenow, Tom J.
31Exh/4-13
33Exh/4-7
33G-36
34Exh/4-7
35G-2B
35G-4B
35G-7B
V353-36
Thibodeau, John
69OPC-189R
69T-189R
Thibodeaux, Keith
82Buffa-8
83LynnP-8
Thielker, Dave
85CharO-6
Thielman, John
T206
Thienpont, Gregg
84Butte-23
Thies, Dave
61Union
Thies, Vernon
(Jake)
55T-12
55T/DH-40
Thiessen, Tim
86WPalm-26
Thigpen, Bobby
87Coke/WS-22
87D-370
87F-507
87Seven-C13
87T-61
88Coke/WS-28
88D-247
88D/Best-235
88F-410
88F/St-17
88F/TL-42
88Score-307
88T-613
88ToysRUs-32
89B-55
89Coke/WS-26
89D-266
89D/Best-25
89F-512
89F/BBMVP's-38
89F/Heroes-39
89F/LL-39
89OPC-368
89Panini/St-303
89Score-399
89Score/HotSt-68
89Score/YS/I-29
89Sf-207
89T-762
89T/St-305
89UD-647
90D-266
90F-549
90Score-335
90Score-694DT
90Score/100St-87
90Sf-27
90T-255
90UD-269
Thigpen, Len
89Penin/Star-24
Thoden, John
88CapeCod/Sum-106
89James/Pro-2157
Thoenen, Dick
68T-348R
Thoma, Ray
84Albany-26
85Huntsvl/BK-19
87Pittsf-1
88Pittsf/Pro-1358
Thomas, Alphonse
(Tommy)
26Exh-76
27Exh-38
29Exh/4-20
33G-169
R316
Thomas, Andres
83Ander-23
84Durhm-14
86D/Rook-10
86F/Up-U112
86Pol/Atl-14
86S/Rook-14
86T/Tr-111T
87Class-7
87D-266
87D/OD-43
87F-531
87F/Lim-42
87F/Mini-105
87F/St-117
87Smok/Atl-20
87T-296
87T/GlossRk-20
87T/St-305
87T/St-39
87ToysRUs-29
88D-627
88F-551
88OPC-13
88Score-299
88T-13
88T/Big-68
88T/St-41
89B-272
89Cadaco-57
89Class-21
89D-576
89D/Best-197
89F-604
89OPC-358
89Panini/St-43
89Score-406
89Score/YS/II-35
89T-171TL
89T-523
89T/St-26
89UD-144
90D-263
90F-597
90Score-99
90T-358
90UD-212
Thomas, Bill
83ArkTr-7
Thomas, C.L.
88Bill/Pro-1823
Thomas, Carl
87Kenosha-18
Thomas, Chester David
D327
D328-173
E121/80
E122
E135-173
T213/blue
T213/brown
W575
Thomas, Chris
83VeroB-11
Thomas, Claude
T207
Thomas, Cory
89Martins/Star-30
Thomas, Danny
77T-488R
Thomas, Dave
81Holyo-5M
Thomas, Dennis
82Readg-9
83Readg-9
Thomas, Deron
82Sprin-21
83StPet-19
84ArkTr-4
Thomas, Derrel
72OPC-457R
72T-457R
73OPC-57
73T-57
74OPC-518
74T-518
75OPC-378
75T-378
75T/M-378
76OPC-493
76SSPC-106
76T-493
77T-266
78T-194
79OPC-359
79T-679
80OPC-9
80Pol/Dodg-30
80T-23
81D-419
81F-123
81OPC-211
81Pol/Dodg-30
81T-211
82D-537
82F-26
82Pol/Dodg
82Pol/Dodg-30
82T-348
83F-223
83Pol/Dodg-30
83T-748
84D-397
84F-114
84F/X-116
84Nes/792-583
84Stuart-28
84T-583
84T/X-118
85F-314
85OPC-317
85T-448
85T/Tr-121T
86T-158
Thomas, Don
74Gasto
Thomas, Eric
75AppFx
Thomas, Frank J.
54B-155
54DanDee
55Armour-21
55B-58
55RM-NL20
56T-153
57Kahn
57T-140
58Hires-27
58Kahn
58T-409
59Armour-17
59Kahn
59T-17M
59T-490
60Kahn
60T-95
61P-193
61T-382
62J-151
62P-151
62P/Can-151
62Salada-104
62Shirriff-104
62T-7
63J-196
63P-196
63Salada-59
63T-495
64T-345
64T/Coins-73
65OPC-123
65T-123
79TCMA-24
89Pac/Leg-153
Exh47
Thomas, Frank
(Frankie)
80Holyo-5
81Vanco-6
82Vanco-2
83ElPas-22
84Cram/PCL-33
Thomas, Frank
88CapeCod-14
88CapeCod/Sum-126
90Score-663DC
90T-414
Thomas, George
61T-544
62T-525
62T/St-69
63J-34
63P-34
63T-98
64T-461
65OPC-83
65T-83
66T-277
67OPC-184
67T-184
67T/Test/RSox-22
69T-521
71OPC-678
71T-678
78TCMA-153
80K-11
Thomas, Gorman
74OPC-288
74Sacra
74T-288
75OPC-532
75T-532
75T/M-532
76OPC-139
76SSPC-243
76T-139
77Spoka
77T-439
79OPC-196
79T-376
80OPC-327
80T-623
80T/S-30
81D-326
81F-507
81F/St-77
81OPC-135
81T-135
81T/St-12
81T/St-96
82D-132
82D-26
82F-154
82F/St-134
82OPC-324
82Pol/Brew-20
82T-765
82T/St-204
83D-510
83Drake-27
83F-48
83Gard-19
83K-47
83OPC-10
83Pol/Brew-20
83T-10
83T-702
83T/St-17M
83T/St-84
83T/X-111
84D-574
84D/Champs-5
84F-553
84F/X-117
84FunFood/Pin-56
84Moth/Mar-7
84Nes/792-515
84OPC-146
84T-515
84T/St-253
84T/X-119
85F-503
85Moth/Mar-9
85OPC-202
85T-202
86D-440
86F-477
86F/AS-11
86F/St-119
86Leaf-213
86Moth/Mar-9
86OPC-347
86T-750
86T/Gloss60-48
86T/Mini-31
86T/St-216
86T/Super-56
86Woolwth-31
87F-359
87T-495
Thomas, Ira
10Domino-115
11Helmar-59
12Sweet/Pin-50A
12Sweet/Pin-50B
14CJ-34
14Piedmont/St-54
15CJ-34
E103
E104
E300
E90/1
E91
E96
M116
T201
T202
T204
T205
T206
T207
T208
T3-123
W514-97
Thomas, J. Leroy
(Lee)
61T-464
62Bz
62T-154
62T/bucks
62T/St-70
63Bz-32
63Exh
63J-30
63P-30

63T-441
63T/SO
64T-255
64T/St-99
64T/SU
64T/tatt
65OPC-111
65T-111
66T-408
67T-458
68T-438
78TCMA-231
Exh47

Thomas, Jim
83DayBe-23
84Beaum-15
86Tucso-22
87ColAst/Pro-5
87ColumAst-5
88MidldA/GS-23
89Edmon/CMC-22
89Edmon/Pro-550

Thomas, Keith
53B/BW-62
53T-129

Thomas, Keith
88Greens/Pro-1554
89Modesto/Ch-32

Thomas, Luther
(Bud)
39PB-158
40PB-42

Thomas, Mark
87Watertn-20
89Aug/Pro-507
89Well/Puc-23

Thomas, Mitch
86Salem-25
87PortChar-6
88Tulsa-4

Thomas, Orlando
87Erie-18
89Savan/Pro-349

Thomas, Randy
79ArkTr-18

Thomas, Ricky
82Idaho-28

Thomas, Rob
88Brist/Pro-1888
89Fay/Pro-1571

Thomas, Ron
88Pulas/Pro-1769
89Pulas/Pro-1889

Thomas, Roy Allen
E107

Thomas, Roy J.
78Charl
78T-711R
79T-563
80T-397
81Tacom-20
82SLCty-19
84F-622
84Moth/Mar-25
84Nes/792-181
84T-181
84T/St-348
85Cram/PCL-82
86F-478
86Moth/Mar-26
86T-626
87Calgary-13
WG3-48

Thomas, Royal Jr.
88Clearw/Star-25
88Spart/Star-20
88Spart/Star-4
89Clearw/Star-21
89Clearw/Star-26

Thomas, Stan
76OPC-148
76T-148
77T-353
78Cr/PCL-53

Thomas, Terrence
88StPet/Star-24

Thomas, Todd
86Shrev-25
87Shrev-11

Thomas, Tom
75Shreve/TCMA-22

Thomas, Tom
86Visal-22
87VeroB-14

Thomas, Tony
77Wausa

Thomas, Troy Gene
87BirmB/Best-25
88Vanco/CMC-18
88Vanco/Pro-775

Thomas, Valmy
58SFCall
58T-86
59T-235
60T-167
61T-319
79TCMA-276

Thomas, Vern
80RochR-3

Thomas, Willie
81VeroB-21

Thomason, Mel
76SSPC-600

Thomasson, Gary
74OPC-18
74T-18
75OPC-529
75T-529
75T/M-529
76OPC-261
76SSPC-107
76T-261
77T-496
78T-648
79OPC-202
79T-387
80OPC-70
80Pol/Dodg-9
80T-127
81D-534
81F-138
81T-512
86Kenosha-24

Thomasson, Hal
76Watlo
77DaytB

Thompson, Al
77Ashev

Thompson, Averett
46Sunbeam

Thompson, Bob
87Lakel-19

Thompson, Bobby L.
74Gasto
75Cedar
78BK/R-22
79T-336

Thompson, Charles
(Tim)
52Park-62
53Exh/Can-40
54T-209
57T-142
58T-57
V362-18

Thompson, Danny
71MLB/St-474
71OPC-127
71T-127
72OPC-368
72T-368
73OPC-443
73T-443
74K-35
74OPC-168
74T-168
75OPC-249
75T-249
75T/M-249
76OPC-111
76SSPC-225
76T-111

Thompson, Eugene
(Junior)
47TipTop
W711/1
W711/2

Thompson, Fay
75Dubuq
76Dubuq
78Duned

Thompson, Forrest D.
49Remar
58Remar

Thompson, Hank
50B-174
51B-89
51T/RB-32
52B-249
52BR
52T-3
53T-20
54B-217
54NYJour
54T-64
55B-94
55Gol/Giants-27
55RFG-19
55RM-NL11
56T-199
57T-109
79TCMA-150
PM10/Sm-187
R423-107

Thompson, Jason
77Ho-64
77OPC-64
77T-291
78BK/T-12
78Ho-77
78OPC-212
78T-660
79Ho-96
79K-7
79OPC-33
79T-80
80K-17
80OPC-83
80T-150
80T/S-42
81D-293
81F-278
81OPC-373
81T-505
81T/Tr-843
82D-502
82F-501
82T-295
83D-95
83D/AAS-8
83Drake-28
83F-325
83OPC-209
83T-730
83T/St-276
84D-64
84F-267
84Nes/792-355
84OPC-355
84T-355
84T/St-128
85D-322
85F-478
85Leaf-89
85OPC-22
85T-490
85T/St-125
85T/Super-56
86D-322
86F-622
86F/Up-U113
86OPC-153
86Provigo-15
86T-635
86T/St-129

Thompson, John
(Jocko)
49B-161
50B-120
51B-294

Thompson, Kelly
87Anchora-39

Thompson, Kirk
89Eugene/Best-10

Thompson, L. Fresco
29Exh/4-11
31Exh/4-3
33G-13
R314
R314/Can
R316
V353-13

Thompson, Marvin W.
78Cr/PCL-87
79Colum-12
80Colum-24
81Syrac-20

Thompson, Michael
76OPC-536
88WinHav/Star-23
89Elmir/Puc-28
89WinHav/Star-24

Thompson, Mike
73OPC-564
73T-564
76Indianap-18
76SSPC-6
76T-536

Thompson, Milt
84Richm-25
85Richm-21
86D-507
86F-530
86F/Up-U114
86T-517
86T/Tr-112T
87D-330
87D/OD-154
87F-191
87T-409
88D-236
88D/Best-296
88F-319
88F/St-112
88OPC-298
88Panini/St-363
88Score-115
88Sf-173
88T-298
88T/Big-2
89B-441
89D-313
89D/Best-212
89D/Tr-43
89F-584
89F/Up-121
89OPC-128
89Panini/St-157
89RedFoley/St-119
89Score-92
89Score/Tr-45
89Sf-169
89Smok/Cards-21
89T-128
89T/Tr-118T
89UD-317
90D-82
90F-262
90Score-49
90T-688
90UD-278

Thompson, Richard
(Rich)
81Watlo-16
82Chatt-5
83Ander-32
83BuffB-7
84BuffB-12
85F/Up-U120
85Maine-11
85Polar/Ind-41
85T/Tr-122T
86F-595
86OPC-242
86T-242
86T/St-215
86Vanco-26
88Memph/Best-2
89Indi/CMC-10
89Indi/Pro-1237
90T-474

Thompson, Rick
82AubAs-19

Thompson, Rob
89Utica/Puc-25

Thompson, Robby
86D/Rook-39
86F/Up-U115
86Moth/Giants-16
86S/Rook-25
86T/Tr-113T
87D-145
87D/OD-101
87F-285
87F/AwardWin-39
87F/Mini-106
87Leaf-64
87Moth/SFG-10
87MSA/Discs-12
87S-46
87T-658
87T/Gloss60-40
87T/GlossRk-21
87T/St-307
87T/St-91
87ToysRUs-30
88D-268
88D/Best-274
88F-98
88Leaf-120
88Moth/Giants-10
88OPC-208
88Panini/St-423
88Score-146
88Score/YS/I-28
88Sf-24
88T-472
88T/Big-83
88T/St-93
89B-473
89D-98
89D/Best-79
89F-344
89Moth/Giants-10
89OPC-15
89Panini/St-215
89RedFoley/St-120
89Score-172
89Score/HotSt-84
89Sf-78
89T-15
89T/Big-163
89T/St-87
89UD-172
90D-140
90F-73
90Score-397
90Score/100St-21
90Sf-60
90T-325

90UD-169
Thompson, Ryan
88StCath/Pro-2035
89StCath/Pro-2072
Thompson, Sam
80SSPC/HOF
E223
N172
N284
Scrapps
WG1-25
Thompson, Scot
79T-716R
80OPC-298
80T-574
81Coke
81D-519
81F-296
81T-295
82lowaC-11
82RedLob
83D-378
83T-481
84D-167
85F-621
85Moth/Giants-15
85T-646
86F-262
86Fresno/Smok-21
86OPC-93
86T-93
Thompson, Sean
88Poca/Pro-2079
Thompson, Squeezer
88Spoka/Pro-1927
Thompson, Tim
61BeeHive-24
Thompson, Tim
82Knoxv-12
83Syrac-20
84Syrac-30
Thompson, Timothy
84Visal-11
Thompson, Tom
86BuffB-22
87SnBer-23
Thompson, Tommy
47Signal
47Sunbeam
Thompson, Tommy
79ArkTr-7
81Durhm-5
82Durhm-11
82FtMyr-3
87Hawai-9
Thompson, Tommy
86Jaxvl/TCMA-19C
87Jaxvl-25
88BirmB/Best-10
88Jaxvl/Best-24
88Jaxvl/Pro-971
88SLAS-39
89BirmB/Best-27
89BirmB/Pro-104
89Tulsa/GS-1
Thompson, Tony
86LitFalls-28
Thompson, Willie
78Knoxv
79Knoxv/TCMA-26
Thomson, Bobby
48B-47
49B-18
49Eureka-124
49Royal-10
50B-28
50Drake-9
51B-126
52B-2
52BR
52Coke
52RM-NL24
52Royal
52StarCal/L-78A
52T-313
53RM-NL25
54B-201
54JC-34
55B-102
55Gol/Braves-28
55JC-34
55RFG-23
56T-257
57T-262
58Hires-46
58SFCall
58T-430
59T-429
60NuCard-10
60T-153
61NuCard-480
76Laugh/Jub-29
79TCMA-202
80Cram/Leg-115
88Pac/Leg-45
89Swell-133
D305
Exh47
PM10/Sm-188
R346-41
Thomson, Rob
88Lakel/Star-24
89London/Pro-1379
Thon, Dickie
76QuadC
78Cr/PCL-112
80T-663R
81D-290
81F-277
81T-209
81T/Tr-844
82F-235
82T-404
83D-191
83F-468
83T-558
84D-304
84D/AAS-44
84F-243
84F-634IA
84F/St-1
84Moth/Ast-7
84Nes/792-692
84OPC-344
84Seven-23W
84T-692
84T/St-64
85F-364
85Moth/Ast-9
85OPC-44
85T-44
85T/St-63
86D-572
86F-313
86Moth/Ast-26
86OPC-166
86Pol/Ast-17
86T-166
86T/St-33
87D-261
87F-70
87Leaf-196
87Moth/Ast-25
87Pol/Ast-14
87T-386
88Score/Tr-29T
88Smok/Padres-29
88T/Tr-121T
89B-400
89D-441
89F-320
89OPC-181
89Score-234
89Score/Tr-55
89T-726
89T/Tr-119T
89UD-258
89UD/Ext-704
90D-549
90F-573
90Score-142
90T-269
90UD-439
Thon, Frankie
78Cedar
80Clint-17
Thoney, John
E107
M116
T201
Thor, Audie
80Memph-30
Thoren, Rick
77AppFx
Thormahlen, H.F.
V100
Thormodsgard, Paul
78OPC-73
78T-162
79T-249
79Toled-2
80OkCty
Thornton, Al
86Elmir-24
87Elmir-13
87Elmir/Red-13
88Elmir-20
Thornton, Andre
74OPC-604R
74T-604R
75OPC-39
75T-39
75T/M-39
76Crane-62
76MSA/Disc
76OPC-26
76T-26
78OPC-114
78T-148
79Ho-93
79OPC-140
79T-280
79T/Comics-6
80K-28
80OPC-278
80T-534
80T/S-43
81D-198
81OPC-128
81T-388
81T/St-70
82D-324
82F-380
82F/St-201
82OPC-161
82T-746
82T/St-174
82Wheat/Ind
83D-211
83F-421
83F-635
83K-26
83OPC-344
83T-640
83T/Gloss-3
83T/Gloss40-3
83T/St-55
83Wheat/Ind-29
84D-25
84D-94
84D/AAS-15
84F-554
84FunFood/Pin-125
84Nes/792-115
84OPC-115
84T-115
84T/St-255
84Wheat/Ind-29
85D-468
85F-457
85F/St-32
85F/St-47
85Leaf-102
85OPC-272
85Polar/Ind-29
85T-475
85T/St-244
86D-251
86F-596
86F/St-120
86Leaf-129
86OhHenry-29
86OPC-59
86S-171
86T-336M
86T-59
86T/St-208
87D-279
87D/OD-108
87F-262
87Gator-29
87OPC-327
87T-780
88RedFoley/St-91
88Score-231
89Swell-117
Thornton, Eric
89Kingspt/Star-23
Thornton, Lou
85F/Up-U121
85Tor/Fire-29
86F-71
86OPC-18
86Syrac-25
86T-488
87Syrac-3
87Syrac/TCMA-21
89BuffB/CMC-22
89BuffB/Pro-1669
89Tidew/Pro-1954
Thornton, Woodie A.
T206
T213/brown
Thorp, Bradley S.
81VeroB-22
Thorpe, Benjamin R.
(Bob)
52T-367
Thorpe, James F.
(Jim)
33SK-6
73F/Wild-3
87Conlon/2-59
88Conlon/4-28
D350/2-176
M101/5-176
Thorpe, Michael
86Cram/PCL-111
87Wausa-19
Thorpe, Paul
86Hagers-25
87Hagers-23
88CharlK-17
88CharlK/Pep-17
89Hagers/Best-19
89Hagers/Pro-285
89Hagers/Star-21
Thorson, Brian
79Holyo-16
80BurlB-9
81Vanco-7
82Vanco-24
84Albany-9
85Huntsvl/BK-TR
88Madis-24
Thorton, John
86ElPas-21
Thoutsis, Paul
87WinHav-27
Threadgill, Chris
89PalmSp/Cal-42
89PalmSp/Pro-472
Threadgill, George
85BurlR-8
86DayBe-28
86FSLAS-46
88Tulsa-2
89Tulsa/GS-26
Threatt, Tony
83Tampa-24
Thrift, Jim
87Salem-18
Thrms, Jeff
89Boise/Pro-1988
Throneberry, M. Faye
52T-376
53T-49
55T-163
57T-356
59T-534
60L-136
60T-9
61T-282
Throneberry, Marv
58T-175
59T-326
60T-436
61P-85
61T-57
61T/St-166
63J-194
63P-194
63T-78
79TCMA-173
88Pac/Leg-48
Throop, George
76OPC-591R
76T-591R
Thrower, Keith
85Cram/PCL-128
86Tacom-22
Thurberg, Tom
77Wausa
81Louvl-25
82ArkTr-10
Thurman, Gary
85FtMyr-18
86SLAS-4
87Omaha-6
88D-44
88D/Rook-33
88F-272
88F/Mini-29
88Leaf-44RR
88Omaha/CMC-14
88Omaha/Pro-1521
88Score-631
88Score/YS/II-25
88Sf-223
88Smok/Royals-6
88T-89
89D-498
89F-296
89Panini/St-348
89Score/HotRk-24
89T-323
89UD-347
90D-416
90F-121
90T-276
Thurman, Robert
52Mother-49
56Kahn
57Kahn
57T-279
58T-34
59T-341
Thurmond, Mark
81Hawai-21

82Hawai-21
84D-505
84F-315
84Moth/Padres-26
84Nes/792-481
84Smok/Padres-25
84T-481
85D-284
85F-46
85Leaf-149
85Moth/Padres-21
85OPC-236
85T-236
86D-261
86F-337
86T-37
87Cain's-17
87D-543
87F-166
87T-361
88D-599
88F-73
88Score-382
88T-552
89French-21
89T-152
89UD-571
90D-612
90F-191
90Score-350
90T-758

Thurston, Hollis
25Exh-80
26Exh-80
28Exh/PCL-28

Tiant, Luis
65Kahn
65OPC-145
65T-145
65T/trans-30
66T-285
67T-377
68Kahn
68T-532
69Kahn
69MB-271
69MLB/St-44
69MLBPA/Pin-28
69OPC-11LL
69OPC-7LL
69OPC-9LL
69OPC/DE-22
69T-11LL
69T-560
69T-7LL
69T-9LL
69T/DE-7
69T/decal
69T/S-13
69T/St-169
69Trans-3
70K-56
70MLB/St-239
70OPC-231
70T-231
71MLB/St-475
71OPC-95
71T-95
72MB-342
73OPC-270
73OPC-65LL
73T-270
73T-65LL
74OPC-167
74T-167
74T/DE-27
74T/St-138
75Ho-102
75K-49
75OPC-430
75T-430
75T/M-430
76Crane-63
76Ho-23
76Ho/Twink-23
76MSA/Disc
76OPC-130
76SSPC-424
76T-130
77Ho-10
77OPC-87
77T-258
77T/CS-48
78OPC-124
78PapaG/Disc-23
78T-345
78Wiffle/Discs-75
79BK/Y-8
79OPC-299
79T-575
80OPC-19
80T-35
81D-231
81F-82
81Portl-23
81T-627
82OPC-160
82T-160
83D-542
83OPC-179SV
83T-178
83T-179A

Tibbs, Jay
82Lynch-19
83Lynch-16
84Tidew-15
85D-262
85F-553
85T-573
86D-262
86F-194
86F/Up-U116
86Provigo-8
86T-176
86T/Tr-114T
87D-282
87F-333
87Leaf-207
87OPC-9
87T-9
88French-53
88OPC-282
88RochR-24
88RochR/CMC-10
88RochR/Pro-201
88Score-608
88T-464
89F-624
89RochR/Pro-1633
89Score-262
89T-271
89UD-655
90F-192
90Score-480
90T-677

Tiburcio, Freddy
82Durhm-12
83Durhm-14
87Toled-11
87Toled/TCMA-6

Tidrow, Dick
72OPC-506R
72T-506R
73OPC-339
73T-339
74OPC-231
74T-231
74T/St-170
75OPC-241
75T-241
75T/M-241
76OPC-248
76SSPC-428
76T-248
77BK/Y-9
77OPC-235
77T-461
78BK/Y-6
78T-179
79OPC-37
79T-89
80T-594
81Coke
81D-551
81F-299
81T-352
82D-477
82F-604
82F/St-99
82OPC-249
82RedLob
82T-699
82T/St-27
83F-510
83T-787
83T/St-225
83T/X-112
84F-72
84Nes/792-153
84T-153

Tiefenauer, Bob
55Hunter
59T-501
62T-227
62T/St-131
64T-522
65OPC-23
65T-23
68T-269
80Penin/B-10C
80Penin/C-27C
83Readg-24
85Cram/PCL-47
86Portl-22C
87Spart-22C
88Batav/Pro-1662

Tiernan, Mike
N172
N566-176
WG1-44

Tierney, James A.
21Exh-176
21Exh-177
E120
V100
W572
W573
WG7-55

Tilden, Bill
33SK-16

Tillman, Bill
69MB-272
71MLB/St-453

Tillman, J. Bob
61Union
62T-368
63T-384
64T-112
65OPC-222
65T-222
66OPC-178
66T-178
67OPC-36
67T-36
67T/Test/RSox-23
68OPC-174
68T-174
69T-374
70T-668
71OPC-244
71T-244
72MB-343
78TCMA-172

Tillman, Ken
81Redwd-20

Tillman, Rusty
82Tidew-11
83Tidew-19
84Tidew-9
85Cram/PCL-102
86Tacom-23
88Phoen/CMC-21
88Phoen/Pro-59
89Phoen/CMC-15
89Phoen/Pro-1479

Tillotson, Thad
67T-553R

Tilmon, Pat
89Durhm/Star-21

Timberlake, Don
83Peoria/LF-13
85MidldA-12
86MidldA-22

Timberlake, Gary
No Cards.

Timko, Andy
81Miami-13

Timlin, Mike
88Myrtle/Pro-1184
89Duned/Star-19

Timmerman, Tom
70T-554
71MLB/St-408
71OPC-296
71T-296
72OPC-239
72T-239
73OPC-413
73T-413
74OPC-327
74T-327

Tincup, Frank
44Centen-23

Tingle, Darrel
87Oneon-3
88PrWill/Star-22

Tingley, Ron
81Hawai-1
82Hawai-1
85Cram/PCL-97
86Richm-23
87BuffB-11
88ColSp/CMC-12
88ColSp/Pro-1532
89ColrSp/CMC-11
89ColSp/Pro-257
89F-414
89Panini/St-316
89Score/HotRk-56
89T-721
89T/Big-37

Tinker, Joe
10Domino-116
11Helmar-107
12Sweet/Pin-93
12Sweet/Pin-93A
14CJ-3
14Piedmont/St-55
15CJ-3
48Exh/HOF
50Callahan
60Exh/HOF-23
60F-40
61F-143
63Bz/ATG-1
69Bz/Sm
80Cram/Leg-42
80SSPC/HOF
BF2-68
D303
D329-174
D350/2-177
E101
E102
E105
E106
E254
E270/1
E300
E90/1
E90/3
E91
E92
E93
E96
E98
L1-122
M101/4-174
M101/5-177
M116
PM1-13
S74-71
S81-97
T202
T204
T205
T206
T207
T213/blue
T215/blue
T215/brown
T216
T3-35
W555
WG5-40
WG6-36

Tinkey, Jim
86SanJose-21

Tinkey, Robert
87Kenosha-13
88Keno/Pro-1379

Tinkle, David
86Cram/PCL-27
87FtMyr-5

Tinning, Lyle
32Orbit/num-17
32Orbit/un-55
34G-71
R305

Tinsley, Lee
88SoOreg/Pro-1706
89Madis/Star-21

Tipton, Gordon
88CapeCod/Sum-136

Tipton, Jeff
82Madis-13

Tipton, Joe
49B-103
50B-159
51B-82
52T-134
53B/BW-13
53Briggs
54B-180

Tirado, Aristarco
86Albany/TCMA-25
86FtLaud-22
87PrWill-18
88Albany/Pro-1348
89Albany/Best-18
89Albany/Pro-331
89Albany/Star-20

Tischinski, Tom
70OPC-379
70T-379
71MLB/St-476
71OPC-724
71T-724

Tisdale, Freddie
79ArkTr-11
80ArkTr-18
81ArkTr-5

Titcomb, Ledell
N172
N338/2

Titus, John
10Domino-117
11Helmar-152
12Sweet/Pin-132B

12Sweet/Pin-132A
E254
M116
S74-105
T201
T202
T205
T206

Tjader, Jimmy
80Ashev-11

Toal, John
85Elmir-22
86Cram/PCL-7
86Greens-23
87Clint-2
87WinHav-16
89London/Pro-1365

Tobias, Grayling
80Memph-24

Tobik, Dave
79T-706R
80T-269
81T-102
82D-511
82T-391
83D-385
83F-343
83OPC-186
83Rang-41
83T-691
83T/X-113
84F-433
84Nes/792-341
84T-341
85Cram/PCL-87

Tobin, James A.
39PB-9
41G-30

Tobin, John
(Jack)
21Exh-178
25Exh-118
48Sommer-16
49Sommer-27
53Mother-45
88Conlon/5-28
E120
E126-44
E126-50
V100
V61-2
W573

Todd, Alfred
41G-28

Todd, Chuck
86Watlo-28

Todd, Jackson
78T-481
79Syrac-13
80Syrac-4
81D-31
81OPC-142
81T-142
82D-178
82F-623
82OPC-327
82Syrac-9
82T-565
86ElPas-22
87Denver-21
88Denver/Pro-1250
89Denver/CMC-24
89Denver/Pro-51

Todd, Jim
75OPC-519
75T-519
75T/M-519
76OPC-221
76SSPC-478
76T-221
77T-31
78T-333
79OPC-46
79T-103
80T-629

Todd, Kyle
86PrWill-27
87Harrisbg-13
88ColAst/Best-9

Todd, Theron
88CLAS/Star-37
88Durhm/Star-21
89Durhm/Star-22
89Star/Wax-73

Todt, Phil
25Exh-70
26Exh-71
27Exh-35
28Exh-36
29Exh/4-18
33G-86
R316
V354-39

Toerner, Sean
81Clint-20

Toft, Marv
61Union

Tolan, Bob
65OPC-116R
65T-116R
66OPC-179R
66Pep/Tul
66T-179R
67T-474
68OPC-84
68T-84
69MB-273
69T-448
69T/St-30
70MLB/St-36
70OPC-409
70T-409
71MD
71MLB/St-71
71OPC-190
71OPC-200NLCS
71T-190
71T/Coins-81
71T/tatt-12
72MB-344
72OPC-3
72T-3
73K-32
73OPC-335
73T-335
74McDon
74OPC-535
74T-535
75Ho-1
75Ho/Twink-1
75OPC-402
75T-402
75T/M-402
76Ho-42
76Ho/Twink-42
76OPC-56
76T-56
77T-188
80T-708
84Beaum-21
85Beaum-25
89Erie/Star-27

Tolentino, Jose
85Cram/PCL-127
86SLAS-6
87Tacom-17
88OkCty/CMC-14
88OkCty/Pro-41
89Tucso/CMC-13
89Tucso/Pro-183

Toler, Greg
85Cedar-15
86Cedar/TCMA-11

Toliver, Fred
82Cedar-7
83Indianap-19
86CIGNA-15
86D-612
86F-647M
86F/Up-U117
86Portl-23
87Maine-5
87Maine/TCMA-7
87T-63
88Portl/CMC-8
88Portl/Pro-664
88T-203
89B-147
89D-510
89F-126
89Score-479
89T-623
89UD-64
90T-423

Tolleson, Wayne
79Tulsa-1
80Tulsa-16
83D-573
83Rang-3
83T/X-114
84D-464
84F-434
84Nes/792-557
84Rang-3
84T-557
84T/St-358
85D-378
85F-571
85Rang-3
85T-247
86Coke/WS-1
86D-134
86F-573
86F/Up-U118
86Leaf-59
86T-641
86T/Tr-115T
87D-524
87D/OD-245
87F-118
87OPC-224
87T-224
88D-154
88F-223
88OPC-133
88Panini/St-157
88Score-117
88T-411
89D-659
89Score/NWest-9
89T-716
90Score-386
90UD-320

Tollison, Dave
88CapeCod/Sum-141

Tolman, Tim
81Tucso-20
82Tucso-8
84Cram/PCL-57
85Moth/Ast-23
86Nashv-24
86T-272
87Toled-12
87Toled/TCMA-23
88Tidew/CANDL-13
88Tidew/CMC-23
88Tidew/Pro-1584
89Syrac/CMC-14
89Syrac/Pro-815

Toman, Tom
75AppFx
76AppFx
78Knoxv

Tomanek, Dick
58T-123
59T-369

Tomaselli, Chuck
84Nashvl-23

Tomberlain, Andy
86Sumter-27
89Durhm/Star-23
89Star/Wax-74

Tomberlain, Rob
86Sumter-28

Tomlin, Dave
75OPC-578
75T-578
75T/M-578
76OPC-398
76SSPC-627
76T-398
77T-241
78T-86
79T-674
80T-126
81Syrac-22
82Indianap-25
84Cram/PCL-126
85Cram/PCL-241
86Indianap-31
87Indianap-7

Tomlin, Randy
88Watertn/Puc-12
89Salem/Star-22

Tommy, Phillip
N172

Tomori, Denny
88Butte-12

Tompkins, Ron
66OPC-107R
66T-107R
68T-247R

Toms, Tommy
76Phoen
77Phoen

Tomsick, Troy
85Durhm-13

Tomski, Jeffery
77Watlo
81Chatt-22

Tonascia, Bruce
78Green

Toney, Anthony
(Andy)
88Fay/Pro-1082
88SALAS/GS-15
89Lakel/Star-23

Toney, Chris
88Martins/Star-31

Toney, Fred
11Helmar-108
61F-80
69Bz-1
72F/FFeat-14M
72Laugh/GF-39M
D327
D328-174
D329-175
D350/2-178
E120
E121/120
E121/80
E135-174
M101/4-175
M101/5-178
W501-69
W575

Tonkin, Wyatt
(Tonk)
78Green

Tonnucci, Norm
86Knoxv-24
87Knoxv-25
88Syrac/CMC-6
88Syrac/Pro-809

Tooley, Albert
T207

Toolson, Earl
49Remar

Toporcer, George
(Specs)
21Exh-179
25Exh-64
26Exh-64
88Conlon/3-30
E120
E121/120
E126-9
V61-82
W501-79
W573
W575

Torborg, Doug
85Anchora-27
87Watertn-28
88Salem/Star-21
89Mia/Star/22-18

Torborg, Jeff
64T-337R
65T-527
66T-257
67T-398
68T-492
69MB-274
69T-353
70OPC-54
70T-54
71MLB/St-119
71OPC-314
71T-314
72MB-345
72OPC-404
72T-404
73OPC-154
73T-154
78T-351
79T-96
89Coke/WS-3
89T/Tr-120MG
90T-21

Torchia, Todd
87Spoka-21
88Charl/Pro-1209

Torchia, Tony
81Brist-8
83Pawtu-25
84Pawtu-3A
84Pawtu-3B
86NewBrit-24MG
87CharRa-17
88River/Cal-229
88River/Pro-1413
89LasVeg/Pro-27

Torgeson, Earl
49B-17
50B-163
50Drake-3
51B-99
51T/BB-34
52B-72
52NTea
52RM-NL25
52T-97
52TipTop
54B-63
55B-210
56T-147
57T-357
58T-138
59T-351
60L-122
60T-299
61T-152
Exh47

Tornay, Nine
53Mother-11

Torre, Frank
56T-172
57T-37

58T-117
59T-65
60Lake
60T-478
62T-303
63T-161
Torre, Joe
62J-152
62P-152
62P/Can-152
62Salada-152
62Shirriff-152
62T-218
62T-351M
62T/St-151
63J-156
63P-156
63T-347
64T-70
64T/Coins-118
64T/Coins-155AS
64T/S-26
64T/St-59
64T/SU
64T/tatt
64Wheat/St-44
65Bz-16
65Kahn
65OldLond-19
65OPC-200
65T-200
65T/E-12
65T/trans-31
66Bz-36
66Kahn
66OPC-130
66T-130
66T/RO-120
67Bz-36
67Kahn
67OPC/Pl-27
67T-350
67T/Pl-27
68Bz-10
68Coke
68Kahn
68OPC-30
68T-30
68T/G-31
69Citgo-11
69Kahn
69Kelly/Pin-17
69MB-275
69MLB/St-216
69MLBPA/Pin-58
69T-460
69T/S-36
69T/St-10
69Trans-49
70MLB/St-144
70OPC-190
70T-190
70Trans-3
71K-62
71MLB/St-287
71OPC-370
71OPC-62LL
71T-370
71T-62
71T/Coins-11
71T/S-61
71T/tatt-10
72K-10
72MB-346
72OPC-341KP
72OPC-500
72OPC-85LL
72OPC-87LL
72T-341
72T-500
72T-85
72T-87
72T/Post-16
73K-31
73OPC-450
73T-450
73T/Comics-22
73T/Lids-52
73T/PinUps-22
74OPC-15
74T-15
74T/St-119
75Ho-70
75OPC-209M
75OPC-565
75T-209MV
75T-565
75T/M-209MV
75T/M-565
76Crane-64
76MSA/Disc
76OPC-585
76SSPC-541
76T-585
77T-425
78T-109
78TCMA-137
79T-82
80T-259
81D-506
81F-325
81T-681MG
82KMart-20
82Pol/Atl-9MG
83D-628
83Pol/Atl-9
83T-126
84Nes/792-502MG
84Pol/Atl-9
84T-502
85T-438
86S/Dec-49M
Torrealba, Pablo
76OPC-589R
76T-589
77T-499
78T-78
79T-242
Torres, Al
89Mia/Star/22-19
Torres, Alfredo
77Charl
78Salem
80Buffa-13
81Portl-24
82Buffa-7
Torres, Angel
78Indianap-18
80Indianap-27
Torres, Felix
62T-595R
63J-27
63P-27
63T-482
Torres, Freddy
89Fay/Pro-1588
89NiagFls/Puc-22
Torres, Hector
69T-526
70OPC-272
70T-272
71MLB/St-47
71OPC-558
71T-558
72T-666
76OPC-241
76SSPC-128
76T-241
78Syrac
80Utica-11
82Knoxv-22
87Syrac-20
87Syrac/TCMA-25
88Syrac/CMC-23
88Syrac/Pro-822
89Syrac/Pro-801
Torres, Jose
83Butte-11
89Princet/Star-21
Torres, Leo
89Fay/Pro-1569
Torres, Martin
85Tigres-13
Torres, Miguel
88Oneon/Pro-2054
Torres, Phil
87VeroB-31
88SnAnt/Best-17
89ColMud/Best-27
Torres, Ray
79Knoxv/TCMA-23
80GlenF/B-8
80GlenF/C-27
81AppFx-25
81GlenF-21
Torres, Rick
88Albany/Pro-1338
89Albany/Best-11
89Albany/Pro-335
89Albany/Star-21
Torres, Ricky
84Greens-17
87PrWill-4
Torres, Rosendo
(Rusty)
72OPC-124R
72T-124R
73OPC-571
73T-571
74OPC-499
74T-499
77T-224
78Cr/PCL-118
80T-36
81Portl-25
Torres, Rudy
83Ander-17
Torres, Tony
80Holyo-24
81ElPas-18
Torrez, Mike
68OPC-162R
68T-162R
69OPC-136R
69T-136R
70OPC-312
70T-312
71MLB/St-288
71OPC-531
71T-531
73OPC-77
73T-77
74OPC-568
74T-568
75OPC-254
75T-254
75T/M-254
76Ho-139
76OPC-25
76SSPC-381
76T-25
77BK/Y-7
77Ho-13
77OPC-144
77T-365
78Ho-127
78PapaG/Disc-21
78T-645
79Ho-22
79OPC-92
79T-185
80OPC-236
80T-455
81D-216
81F-233
81OPC-216
81T-525
82Coke/Bos
82D-235
82F-310
82F/St-160
82T-225
82T-786TL
82T/St-151
83D-512
83F-197
83OPC-312
83T-743
83T/X-115
84D-556
84F-602
84Nes/792-78
84OPC-78
84T-78
84T/St-113
89Pac/Leg-168
Torrez, Peter
80RochR-21
84CharO-9
Torricelli, Tim
87Stockton-22
88Beloi/GS-14
89ElPas/GS-19
Torrienti, Christobel
74Laugh/Black-18
Tortorice, Mark
86Modesto-25
Torve, Kelvin
83Phoen/BHN-12
84Shrev/FB-23
85CharO-7
86RochR-24
87RochR-21
87RochR/TCMA-15
88Portl/CMC-15
88Portl/Pro-641
89Panini/St-380
89Portl/CMC-16
89Portl/Pro-220
89UD-177
Torve, Kenton Craig
87BirmB/Best-20
Tosca, Carlos
83Greens-27
84Greens-1
Tost, Lou
49Remar
50Remar
Toth, Paul
62Kahn/Atl
63T-489
64T-309
Touma, Tim
87WPalm-2
Toups, Tony
77Watlo
Toussaint, Daris
88Poca/Pro-2088
Toutsis, Paul
86Greens-24
Touzzo, John
85LitFalls-10
Tovar, Cesar
65OPC-201R
65T-201R
66T-563R
67T-317
68Coke
68T-420
69MB-276
69MLB/St-71
69T-530
69T/St-199
69Trans-9
70MLB/St-240
70OPC-25
70T-25
71K-18
71MD
71MLB/St-477
71OPC-165
71T-165
71T/Coins-52
72MB-347
72OPC-275
72T-275
73OPC-405
73T-405
74OPC-538
74T-538
74T/Tr-538T
75OPC-178
75T-178
75T/M-178
76OPC-246
76T-246
77T-408
78TCMA-174
Tovar, Raul
82Miami-18
83BirmB-1
86MidldA-23
Towers, Kevin
84Beaum-10
86CharRa-26
88LasVeg/CMC-8
88LasVeg/Pro-242
89Spoka/SP-23
Towey, Steve
88Myrtle/Pro-1185
89Modesto/Ch-16
Town, Randall
80Water-6
81Water-10
Townley, Jason
88Duned/Star-17
88StCath/Pro-2027
Townsend, George
N172
N690
Townsend, Howard
85Evrt/Cram-16A
85Evrt/Cram-16B
86Clint-24
87Wausa-5
88SnBer/Cal-45
89Visal/Cal-100
89Visal/Pro-1421
Townsend, James
88QuadC/GS-17
89PalmSp/Cal-48
89PalmSp/Pro-463
Townsend, John
E107
Townsend, Ken
77Clint
78LodiD
Townsend, Lee
88SnBer/Best-3
Toy, Tracy
86Watertn-24
87Macon-2
88Aug/Pro-379
Toyotoshi, Chikada
89Salin/Cal-131
Traber, Jim
85D-45
85RochR-9
86RochR-25
86S/Rook-32
87D-477
87F-482
87RochR-26
87RochR/TCMA-20
87T-484
87T/St-232
87ToysRUs-31
88French-28
88RochR-25
88T-544

89B-13
89F-625
89French-28
89OPC-124
89Score-590
89T-124
89T/St-233
89UD-294
90D-569
90F-193
90UD-268

Tracewski, Dick
64T-154
65OPC-279
65T-279
66T-378
67T-559
68T-488
69MB-277
69OPC-126
69T-126
73OPC-323CO
73T-323C
88Domino-23
88Pep/T-CO
89Mara/Tigers-CO

Tracy, James
80Wichi-2
81D-520
81F-308
82F-605
82F/St-97
82T-403
82Tucso-9
87Myrtle-16
87Peoria-27MG
88Duned/Star-18
88Peoria/Ko-29
89Chatt/Best-7
89Chatt/GS-1
89Harris/Pro-309
89Harris/Star-19

Tracy, Rich
88Batav/Pro-1685

Tracy, Rick
87SanJose-20

Traen, Tom
86Jaxvl/TCMA-5
87WPalm-20

Traffley, William
N172

Trafton, Todd
87DayBe-1
88BirmB/Best-9
89BirmB/Best-19
89BirmB/Pro-97
89SLAS-10

Tramble, Otis
82QuadC-20

Trammell, Alan
78BK/T-15
78T-707R
79OPC-184
79T-358
80OPC-123
80T-232
81Coke
81D-5
81F-461
81F/St-89
81K-51
81OPC-133DP
81T-709
81T/So-38
81T/St-75
82D-5DK
82D-76
82F-283
82F/St-155
82OPC-381
82Sqt-4
82T-475
82T/St-181
83D-207
83F-344
83OPC-95
83T-95
83T/St-66
84D-293
84Drake-30
84F-91
84F/St-14
84FunFood/Pin-40
84Nes/792-510
84OPC-88
84T-510
84T/St-266
84T/St/Box-9
85Cain's-18
85D-171
85D/AAS-44
85Drake-31
85F-23
85F/LimEd-40
85Leaf-158
85OPC-181
85Seven-15G
85Seven-8D
85T-690
85T/Gloss40-16
85T/St-18WS
85T/St-20
85T/St-258
85T/Super-25
85Wendy-20
86Cain's-19
86D-171
86D/AAS-45
86F-241
86F-633M
86F/Mini-50
86F/St-121
86Leaf-101
86OPC-130
86S-147M
86S-172
86T-130
86T/St-267
87Cain's-7
87Coke/Tigers-4
87D-127
87D/HL-51
87D/OD-216
87F-167
87F/Hottest-41
87F/Mini-107
87F/RecSet-38
87F/St-118
87Leaf-126
87OPC-209
87RedFoley/St-62
87S-188
87Seven-DT11
87T-687
87T/Mini-56
87T/St-270
88Class/Blue-231
88D-230
88D-4DK
88D-BC11
88D/AS-22
88D/Best-281
88D/DKsuper-4DK
88F-635M
88F-74
88F/AS-9
88F/AwardWin-43
88F/BB/AS-42
88F/BB/MVP-39
88F/Excit-42
88F/Hottest-44
88F/LL-42
88F/Mini-25
88F/RecSet-41
88F/SS-41
88F/St-29
88F/TL-43
88FanSam-6
88Jiffy-16
88KayBee-31
88Leaf-167
88Leaf-4DK
88Nestle-35
88OPC-320
88Panini/St-444
88Panini/St-94
88Pep/T-2
88Pol/T-13
88Score-37
88Score-651
88Sf-25
88T-320
88T-389
88T/Big-8
88T/Coins-30
88T/Gloss60-37
88T/Mini-12
88T/RiteAid-18
88T/St-273
88T/St/Backs-45
88T/UK-79
89Ames-29
89B-105
89Cadaco-58
89Class-128
89Crunch-12
89D-180
89D/Best-13
89D/MVP-BC17
89F-148
89F/AS-11
89F/BBAS-41
89F/BBMVP's-39
89F/Excit-41
89F/Heroes-40
89F/LL-40
89F/Superstar-40
89F/WaxBox-C26
89KayBee-30
89KingB/Discs-9
89KMart/Lead-22
89Mara/Tigers-3
89Master/Discs-4
89OPC-49
89Panini/St-343
89Pol/Tigers-3
89Ralston-10
89RedFoley/St-121
89Score-110
89Score/HotSt-7
89Sf-215
89T-400AS
89T-609TL
89T-770
89T/Big-123
89T/Coins-56
89T/DH-4
89T/Gloss60-25
89T/Hills-29
89T/St-281
89T/St/Backs-12
89T/UK-77
89UD-290
89UD-690TC
90Class-106
90D-90
90D/Bon/MVP-BC26
90F-617
90Score-9
90Score/100St-41
90Sf-154
90T-440
90UD-554

Trammell, Marcus
88Utica/Puc-11

Trapp, Mike
87FtMyr-4

Trautwein, Dave
89Jacks/GS-8

Trautwein, John
86Jaxvl/TCMA-7
87Jaxvl-21
87SLAS-14
88D/RedSox/Bk-NEW
88D/Rook-24
88F/U-U10
89Pawtu/CMC-9
89Pawtu/Dunkin-40
89Pawtu/Pro-685

Travels, Darren
85Utica-6
86Jamestn-26

Travers, Bill
75OPC-488
75T-488
75T/M-488
76A&P/Milw
76OPC-573
76SSPC-244
76T-573
77Ho-87
77K-9
77OPC-174
77T-125
77T/CS-49
78T-355
79OPC-106
79T-213
80T-109
81D-508
81F-525
81T-704
81T/Tr-845
82T-628

Travers, Steve
82Idaho-13

Travis, Cecil
37OPC-126
37Wheat
38Wheat
39Exh
39PB-114
40PB-16
41DP-75
41PB-48
R303/A
R313
R314
V300

Trayler, Brian
89SnAnt/Best-11

Traylor, Keith
84LitFalls-9

Traynor, Harold
(Pie)
25Exh-55
26Exh-55
27Exh-28
28Yueng-14
29Exh/4-13
31Exh/4-13
33DL-12
33G-22
34DS-27
34DS-99
34Exh/4-7
35BU-100
35BU-14
35Exh/4-7
35G-2B
35G-4B
35G-7B
36Exh/4-7
50Callahan
60F-77
61F-144
61F-89M
61GP-15
72K/ATG-8
76OPC-343AS
76T-343M
80Cram/Leg-36
80SSPC/HOF
86Conlon/1-38
86S/Dec-11
87Nestle/DT-3
88Conlon/NatAS-21
E120
E210-14
R311/Gloss
R312/M
R313
R315-A36
R315-B36
R316
R332-23
R337
V117-2
V353-22
W502-14
W513-82
W517-2
W572
WG8-46

Treadway, Andre
82Durhm-21
86Richm-24

Treadway, Doug
88WinHav/Star-24

Treadway, Jeff
86Vermont-22
87Nashv-21
88D-29
88D/Rook-17
88F-249
88F/Mini-76
88Kahn/Reds-15
88Leaf-29RR
88Score-646
88Score/YS/II-26
88Sf-225
88T/Big-214
88T/Tr-122T
89Class-54
89D-351
89D/Best-141
89F-173
89F/Up-75
89OPC-61
89Panini/St-73
89Score-86
89Score/HotRk-84
89Score/Tr-18
89Sf-107
89T-685
89T/St-139
89T/Tr-121T
89ToysRUs-31
89UD-393
90D-50
90F-598
90Score-95
90Sf-219
90T-486
90UD-141

Treadway, Steven
88CapeCod/Sum-181

Treanor, Dean
88Fresno/Cal-26
88Fresno/Pro-1236

Trebelhorn, Tom
80Port-18
81Portl-2
85Cram/PCL-215
86Pol/Brew-42C
87T/Tr-121T
88Pol/Brew-42MG
88T-224
89Pol/Brew-42

89T-344MG
90T-759MG
Trechuck, Frank
V362-6
Tredway, George
N172
Treece, Jack
44Centen-24
Trella, Steve
75Clint
Tremblay, Gary
86Pawtu-25
87Pawtu-20
87Pawtu/TCMA-12
88Pawtu/CMC-22
88Pawtu/Pro-450
89Pawtu/CMC-14
89Pawtu/Dunkin-32
89Pawtu/Pro-702
Tremblay, Wayne
79Elmir-25
85Greens-12
Trembley, Dave
86Kinston-24MG
87Harrisbg-2
88EastLAS/Pro-45
88Harris/Pro-846
89Harris/Pro-292
Tremel, William
55T-52
55T/DH-102
56T-96
56T/Pin-7
Trent, Ted
78Laugh/Black-1
Tresamer, Michael
86Cram/PCL-49
87AppFx-9
88BBCity/Star-22
89Memph/Best-22
89Memph/Pro-1197
89Memph/Star-21
89Star/Wax-45
Tresch, Dave
85Lynch-3
86Lynch-22TR
Tresh, Mickey
87PrWill-12
88PrWill/Star-23
89Penin/Star-25
Tresh, Mike
41DP-69
47TipTop
49B-166
50NumNum
Tresh, Tom
62T-31
63J-23
63P-23
63Salada-54
63T-173
63T-470
64T-395
64T/Coins-10
64Wheat/St-45
65T-440
66Bz-40
66T-205
66T/RO-59
67Bz-40
67T-289
68OPC-69
68T-69
69MB-278
69MLB/St-80
69OPC-212
69T-212
69T/St-209
70MLB/St-215
70T-698
72MB-348
88Pac/Leg-25
89Swell-52
WG10-23
WG9-24
Treuel, Ralph
80Evans-15
Trevino, Alex
77Wausa
78Tidew
80T-537
81Coke
81F-318
81T-23
81T/HT
82Coke/Reds
82D-350
82F-540
82T-368
82T/Tr-120T
83D-374
83F-604
83T-632
83T/St-232
84D-286
84F-484
84F/X-118
84Nes/792-242
84Pol/Atl-25
84T-242
84T/X-120
85D-565
85F-341
85F/Up-U122
85OPC-279
85T-747
85T/St-30
85T/Tr-123T
86F-550
86F/Up-U119
86OPC-169
86Pol/Dodg-29
86T-444
86T/Tr-116T
87D-546
87F-456
87Moth/Dodg-23
87Pol/Dodg-15
87T-173
88D-376
88Pol/Dodg-29
88Score-182
88T-512
88Tucso-22
88Tucso/CMC-16
89B-326
89Lennox/Ast-6
89Moth/Ast-17
89OPC-64
89Score-574
89T-64
89UD-262
90D-443
90F-239
90T-342
90UD-205
Trevino, Tony
88Batav/Pro-1665
88Spart/Pro-1040
89Clearw/Star-22
Triandos, Gus
55Esskay
55T-64
55T/DH-82
56T-80
56T/Pin-4
57Swift-2
57T-156
58T-429
59Armour-18
59Bz
59HRDerby-20
59T-330
59T-568AS
60Armour-19
60Bz-11
60T-60
60T/tatt
60T/tatt-51
61Bz-25
61P-69
61T-140
61T/St-106
62J-33
62P-33
62P/Can-33
62Salada-93
62Shirriff-93
62T-420
62T/bucks
62T/St-9
63T-475
64T-83
65OPC-248
65T-248
79TCMA-75
Exh47
PM10/Sm-189
Trice, Robert Lee
54T-148
55Rodeo
55T-132
55T/DH-124
PM10/Sm-190
Trice, Wally
88AubAs/Pro-1950
89Osceola/Star-25
Trillo, Manny
74OPC-597R
74T-597R
75OPC-617R
75T-617R
75T/M-617R
76OPC-206
76SSPC-316
76T-206
77OPC-158
77Pep-59
77T-395
78Ho-69
78OPC-217
78T-123
78Wiffle/Discs-76
79BK/P-14
79OPC-337
79T-639
80BK/P-5
80OPC-50
80T-90
81Coke
81D-22
81F-3
81F/St-96
81OPC-368
81T-470
81T/HT
82D-245
82F-260
82F/St-59
82OPC-220
82T-220
82T/St-122
82T/St-76
83D-294
83F-174
83F-631M
83OPC-174AS
83OPC-73
83T-398
83T-535
83T-5M
83T/St-141
83T/St-142
83T/St-268
83T/X-116
83Wheat/Ind-30
84D-575
84F-289
84F-627la
84F/X-119
84FunFood/Pin-57
84Nes/792-180
84OPC-180
84T-180
84T/Gloss22-3
84T/St-93
84T/X-121
85D-431
85D/AAS-31
85F-622
85Moth/Giants-5
85OPC-310
85T-310
86D-201
86F-551
86F/Up-U120
86Gator-19
86OPC-142
86T-655
86T/St-88
86T/Tr-117T
87Berg/Cubs-19
87D-570
87F-577
87OPC-32
87T-732
88Berg/Cubs-19
88D-516
88D/Cubs/Bk-516
88F-436
88Score-524
88T-287
89B-308
89D-608
89F-440
89Score-446
89T-66
89T/Big-295
89UD-127
Trinkle, Ken
47TipTop
49B-193
49Eureka-150
Triplett, Antonio
82BurlR-11
83BurlR-25
83BurlR/LF-6
86Tulsa-2
87SnBer-21
88Fresno/Cal-1
88Fresno/Pro-1243
Triplett, Coaker
V362-16
W754
Tripodi, Max
89SLCty-20
Trlicek, Rick
88Batav/Pro-1670
Troedson, Rich
74OPC-77
74T-77
Trombley, Mike
88CapeCod/Sum-75
Tronerud, Rick
80WHave-24
81WHave-15
84Albany-8
89Huntsvl/Best-18
Trosky, Hal
34DS-70
34G-76
35Exh/4-11
35G-1L
35G-2E
35G-6E
35G-7E
36Exh/4-11
37Exh/4-11
37OPC-113
37Wheat
38Exh/4-11
38ONG/Pin-30
40PB-50
41DP-80
41DP-87
41PB-16
41Wheat
61F-145
R303/A
R314
V300
Trott, Sam
N172
Trotter, Bill
39PB-148
40PB-54
W753
Troup, James
89SLCty-270F
Troupe, Quincy
78Laugh/Black-33
Trout, Jeff
85Orlan-12
86Orlan-21
Trout, Paul
(Dizzy)
39Exh
39PB-153
40PB-44
47TipTop
48L-10
49B-208
50B-134
51T/BB-23
52NTea
52T-39
53T-169
85T-142FS
Trout, Steve
77AppFx
78Knoxv
80T-83
81D-44
81F-345
81OPC-364
81T-552
82D-243
82F-358
82OPC-299
82T-299
82T/St-169
83D-417
83F-251
83T-461
83T/X-117
83Thorn-34
84D-533
84F-506
84Nes/792-151
84OPC-151
84SevenUp-34
84T-151
85D-198
85F-70
85Leaf-243
85OPC-139
85SevenUp-34
85T-142FS
85T-668
85T/St-43
86D-117
86F-384
86Gator-34
86OPC-384
86T-384
86T/St-57
87Berg/Cubs-34
87D-201
87F-578
87OPC-147

87T-750
88D-524
88Moth/Sea-8
88Score-342
88T-584
88T/Big-107
89Moth/Sea-24
89Score-522
89T-54

Trowbridge, Bob
58T-252
59T-239
60T-66

Trower, Don
48Sommer-10

Trucchio, Frank
83Madis/LF-30C

Trucks, Phil
76Clint
79Knoxv/TCMA-2

Trucks, Virgil
47TipTop
48L-5
49B-219
49Royal-21
50B-96
51B-104
52Dix
52T-262
53B/BW-17
53Dix
53T-96
54B-198
55Armour-22
55B-26
56T-117
57T-187
58T-277
59T-417
79TCMA-85
89Pac/Leg-120
89Swell-73
Exh47
R423-106

Trudeau, Kevin
86Watlo-29
87Portl-15
88Orlan/Best-14
89MidldA/GS-28

Trudo, Glenn
86Watertn-25TR
87Macon-21
88Aug/Pro-384

Truesdale, Fred
C46-53

Trujillo, Jose
89Hamil/Star-24

Trujillo, Louie
83Cedar-11
83Cedar/LF-12

Trujillo, Mike
83AppFx/LF-2
86F-360
86Pawtu-26
86T-687
87D-613
87Moth/Sea-25
87T-402
88T-307
88Toled/CMC-7
88Toled/Pro-593
89AAA/Pro-25
89Toled/Pro-776

Truschke, Mike
88CapeCod/Sum-24

Trusky, Ken
89Well/Puc-24

Tsamis, George
88CapeCod/Sum-80

Tschida, Tim
88Umpire-59
89Umpires-57

Tsitouris, John
60L-63
60T-497
63FrBauer-28
63T-244
64Kahn
64T-275
65Kahn
65OPC-221
65T-221
66OPC-12
66T-12
68T-523

Tsotsos, Pete
88CapeCod/Sum-26

Tubbs, Gregory Alan
87Greenv/Bst-26
88Richm-15
88Richm/CMC-15
88Richm/Pro-5
89Greenv/Pro-1152
89Richm/Pro-823

Tuck, Gary
82Tucso-25
83Tucso-24
84Cram/PCL-248
86Osceola-26CO
87AubAs-12
88Ashvl/Pro-1068
89Colum/Pol-24CO

Tucker, Bob
86VeroB-25

Tucker, Mike
81Shrev-8
82Phoen

Tucker, Scooter
89Clint/Pro-897

Tucker, Terry
62Pep/Tul-bb
63Pep/Tul-bb

Tucker, Thomas
N172
N300/unif

Tucker, Thurman
47TipTop
50NumNum
51B-222

Tucker, Vance
89CharRa/Pro-972

Tucker, William
78Green

Tuckerman, William
N172

Tudor, John
81D-457
81T-14
82Coke/Bos
82D-260
82F-311
82T-558
83D-563
83F-198
83T-318
84D-416
84F-411
84F/X-120
84Nes/792-601
84OPC-171
84T-601
84T/St-225
84T/X-122
85D-235
85D/HL-20
85F-479
85F/Up-U123
85OPC-214
85T-214
85T/Tr-124T
86D-260
86Drake-30
86F-47
86F/AS-12
86F/Mini-11
86F/Slug-40
86F/St-122
86KAS/Disc-17
86Leaf-134
86OPC-227
86S-122
86S-184M
86S-185M
86Schnucks-22
86T-474
86T-710
86T/3D-28
86T/Gloss60-53
86T/Mini-64
86T/St-20WS
86T/St-52
86T/Super-57
87Class-77
87D-170
87D/OD-63
87Drake-30
87F-310
87F/GameWin-41
87F/Mini-108
87F/RecSet-39
87F/St-119
87Kraft-22
87OPC-110
87RedFoley/St-34
87S-173
87Smok/Cards-3
87T-110
87T/St-53
88Woolwth-23
88D-553
88D/Best-212
88F-48
88F/Mini-110
88F/St-121
88F/WS-3
88Leaf-212
88OPC-356
88Score-275
88Sf-198
88Smok/Card-9
88T-792
88T/RiteAid-29
88T/St-13
88T/St-21
89Class-63
89D-195
89F-75
89Moth/Dodg-9
89OPC-35
89Panini/St-100
89Pol/Dodg-19
89RedFoley/St-122
89Score-560
89Sf-86
89T-35
89T/Mini-20
89T/St-64
89UD-66
90UD-396

Tudor, Mark
81Clint-29
82Clint-26

Tufts, Bob
80Phoen-2
81Phoen-3
82Omaha-9
82T-171R

Tuholald, Tom
89Well/Puc-25

Tujillo, Mike
89Toled/CMC-3

Tukes, Stan
89CharRa/Pro-977

Tulacz, Mike
77AppFx

Tuller, Brian
83QuadC-15

Tullier, Mike
86WinSal-25
87WinSal-19
88Pittsf/Pro-1365
89IowaC/CMC-23
89IowaC/Pro-1701

Tullish, Bill
76Cedar

Tumbas, Dave
83AlexD-15
84PrWill-27
85Nashua-25

Tumpane, Bob
82Durhm-13
83Durhm-15
84Durhm-12
85IntLgAS-2
87Richm/TCMA-16

Tunison, Rich
89Eugene/Best-16

Tunnell, Lee
82Portl-9
83T/X-118
84D-592
84F-268
84F/St-107
84Nes/792-384
84T-384
85D-288
85F-480
85F-638IA
85T-21
86F-623
86Hawai-21
86T-161
87F/U-U119
88F-49
88Louvl-48
88Score-587
89Portl/CMC-6
89Portl/Pro-217

Tunney, Gene
33SK-18

Tuozzo, John
86Columbia-25

Turang, Brian
88CapeCod-20
88CapeCod/Sum-22

Turco, Steve F.
81ArkTr-2
83StPet-25
85Sprin-18

Turek, Joseph
88Greens/Pro-1559
88SALAS/GS-8
89Cedar/Best-7
89Cedar/Pro-920
89Cedar/Star-20

Turgeon, David
87Oneon-12
88FtLaud/Star-22
89PrWill/Star-22

Turgeon, Mike
80Wichi-11
82Phoen

Turgeon, Steve
83StPet-26
85Sprin-19
86Erie-28CO

Turley, Robert
54Esskay
54T-85
55Armour-23
55T-38
55T/DH-64
56T-40
56T/Pin-31P
57T-264
58T-255
58T-493AS
59Armour-19
59Bz
59T-237M
59T-493
59T-570AS
59T-60
60L-103
60NuCard-30
60T-270
61NuCard-430
61P-5
61T-40
61T/St-200
62T-589
63T-322
79TCMA-136
88Pac/Leg-52

Turnbull, Keith
83Erie-8

Turner
N172

Turner, Col. R.
33SK-27

Turner, Jim
44Yank/St-27
52T-373C
62T-263M
63FrBauer-29
73OPC-116CO
73T-116C
W711/2

Turner, John
(Jerry)
75OPC-619R
75T-619R
75T/M-619R
76OPC-598R
76T-598R
77T-447
78T-364
79T-564
80T-133
81D-244
81F-504
81T-285
81T/St-229
82D-609
82T-736
82Wheat/Ind
83F-345
83T-41

Turner, John
86Peoria-24

Turner, Lloyd
78Watlo
79Wausa-10

Turner, Rick
82Danvi-7
83Redwd-24

Turner, Roy
WG2-46

Turner, Shane
86FSLAS-47
86FtLaud-23
87Colum-13
87Colum/Pol-24
87Colum/TCMA-18
88Maine/CMC-13
88Maine/Pro-288
89F-653M
89Readg/Best-12
89Readg/Pro-655
89Readg/Star-24
89Score/HotRk-67

Turner, Terry
10Domino-118
11Helmar-26
12Sweet/Pin-20
14Piedmont/St-56
D328-175
D329-176
D350/2-179

E135-175
E254
E270/1
E94
M101/4-176
M101/5-179
M116
S74-11
T201
T202
T205
T206
T207

Turner, Trent
88CapeCod/Sum-179

Turner, William
(Matt)
87Sumter-2
89Durhm/Star-24

Turnes, Jose
78DaytB

Turpin, Hal
43Centen-24
44Centen-25
45Centen-26

Turtletaub, Greg
88LitFalls/Puc-13

Tutt, John
84CharO-24
85Beaum-22
86LasVegas-20

Tuttle, Bill
55B-35
56T-203
57Swift-14
57T-72
58T-23
59T-459
60L-32
60T-367
61Bz-36
61Clover-28
61P-84
61T-536
61T/St-167
62J-88
62P-88
62P/Can-88
62Salada-87A
62Salada-87B
62Shirriff-87
62T-298
62T/St-80
63T-127
79TCMA-103

Twardoski, Michael
88CLAS/Star-38
88Kinston/Star-22
89Canton/Best-12
89Canton/Pro-1299
89Canton/Star-21

Twellman, Tom
74Cedar
75Dubuq
76Dubuq

Twitchell, Lawrence
E223
N172
WG1-26

Twitchell, Wayne
71OPC-692R
71T-692R
72OPC-14R
72T-14R
73OPC-227
73T-227
74K-26
74OPC-419
74T-419
74T/St-79
75OPC-326
75T-326
75T/M-326
76OPC-543
76T-543
77T-444
78OPC-189
78T-269
79OPC-18
79T-43

Twitty, Jeff
81F-49
82Richm-8

Twombly, Babe
28Exh/PCL-29

Tyler, Dave
81Brist-19

Tyler, George
(Lefty)
15CJ-146
BF2-56
D327
D328-176
D329-177
E121/80
E122
E135-176
M101/4-177
T207
T222
W575

Tyler, Mike
76Dubuq
78Charl
79Charl-7
80Port-1

Tyng, James
N172

Tyrone, Jim
74OPC-598R
74T-598R
76SSPC-604
77SnJos-7
78T-487

Tyson, Mike
74OPC-655
74T-655
74T/St-120
75OPC-231
75T-231
75T/M-231
76Crane-65
76MSA/Disc
76OPC-86
76SSPC-283
76T-86
77Pep-38
77T-599
78T-111
79OPC-162
79T-324
80OPC-252
80T-486
81Coke
81F-315
81T-294
81T/HT
81T/St-155
82D-435
82F-606
82F/St-100
82T-62

Tyson, Terry
77Watlo

Ubri, Fermin
84Jacks-24

Uecker, Bob
62T-594R
63T-126
64T-543
65T-519
66OPC-91
66T-91
67T-326

Ueda, Joe
88Fresno/Pro-1238

Ueda, Sadahito
83SanJose-16

Uhal, Bob
88LitFalls/Puc-8

Uhey, Jackie
76Clint
82ElPas-18

Uhlaender, Ted
66T-264R
67T-431
68Coke
68OPC-28
68T-28
69MB-279
69MLB/St-72
69OPC-194
69T-194
69T/St-200
70MLB/St-204
70T-673
71MLB/St-384
71OPC-347
71T-347
72MB-349
72T-614
78TCMA-161

Uhle, George E.
28Exh-44
28Yueng-11
29Exh/4-24
31Exh/4-23
33Exh/4-12
33G-100
40PB-239
61F-146
E120
E210-11
R306
V354-22
V61-16
W502-11
W572
W573
WG7-56

Ujdur, Gerry
80Evans-10
81Evans-8
81T-626R
82Evans-10
83D-600
83F-346
83T-174

Ullger, Scott
80OrlTw-21
82OrlTw/A-10
82Toled-22
84D-438
84Nes/792-551
84T-551
84Toled-12
85IntLgAS-27
85Toled-18
86Toled-22
87RochR-7
87RochR/TCMA-21
88Visal/Cal-170
88Visal/Pro-99
89Visal/Cal-118MG
89Visal/Pro-1433

Ulrich, Jeff
80Penin/B-22
80Penin/C-16
81OkCty/TCMA-26
82OkCty-17

Umbach, Arnie
66T-518R

Umbarger, Jim
76OPC-7
76SSPC-257
76T-7
77T-378
79T-518
79Tucso-24

Umbricht, Jim
60T-145
63T-99
64T-389
89Smok/Ast-9

Umdenstock, Bob
79AppFx-19
82CharR-11

Umont, Frank
55B-305ump

Umphlett, Tom
53Briggs
54B-88
55B-45
61Union

Underwood, Bobby
88Watertn/Puc-13
89Aug/Pro-500

Underwood, Pat
80OPC-358
80T-709
81D-368
81Evans-9
81F-469
81T-373
82T-133
83D-29
83Evans-10
83F-347
83T-588

Underwood, Tom
75OPC-615R
75T-615R
75T/M-615R
76OPC-407
76SSPC-461
76T-407
77T-217
78T-531
79OPC-26
79T-64
80OPC-172
80T-324
81D-108
81F-97
81OPC-114
81T-114
81T/Tr-846
82D-323
82F-109
82T-757
83D-391
83F-535
83Granny-31
83T-466
84D-253
84F-460
84F/X-121
84Nes/792-642
84OPC-293
84T-642
84T/St-335
84T/X-123
85F-194
85T-289

Unglaub, Robert
E254
E270/1
E90/1
E91
M116
T204
T206

Ungs, Mike
79Wisco-2
80OrlTw-15
81Wisco-10

Unitas, John
60P

Unser, Al
47Signal

Unser, Del
69MB-280
69T-338
70MLB/St-287
70OPC-336
70T-336
71MLB/St-551
71OPC-33
71T-33
72MB-350
72T-687
73OPC-247
73T-247
74JP
74OPC-69
74T-69
74T/St-80
75OPC-138
75T-138
75T/M-138
76OPC-268
76SSPC-535
76T-268
77OPC-27
77T-471
78OPC-216
78T-348
79OPC-330
79T-628
80BK/P-13
80OPC-12
80T-27
81D-164
81F-26
81OPC-56
81T-566
81T/HT
82D-273
82F-261
82T-713

Upham, John
67T-608R

Upp, George
(Jerry)
E90/1

Upshaw, Cecil
67OPC-179R
67T-179R
68T-286
69T-568
70OPC-295
70T-295
71MLB/St-23
71OPC-223
71T-223
72OPC-74
72T-74
73OPC-359
73T-359
74OPC-579
74T-579
74T/Tr-579T
75OPC-92
75T-92
75T/M-92
76SSPC-138

Upshaw, Lee
88Durhm/Star-22
89BurlB/Pro-1598
89BurlB/Star-21

Upshaw, Willie
76FtLaud
79OPC-175
79Syrac-4
79T-341
80Syrac-21
82D-652
82F-624
82OPC-196
82T-196

83D-558
83F-442
83OPC-338
83T-556
83T/St-128
84D-315
84F-168
84FunFood/Pin-94
84Nes/792-453
84OPC-317
84T-453
84T/St-363
84Tor/Fire-30
85D-10
85D-71
85D/AAS-52
85D/DKsuper-10
85F-118
85F-635IA
85F/LimEd-41
85Leaf-10DK
85OPC-75
85OPC/Post-14
85Seven-15S
85T-75
85T/St-358
85Tor/Fire-30
86Ault-26
86D-195
86F-72
86Leaf-128
86OPC-223
86S-98
86T-745
86T/St-188
86Tor/Fire-31
87D-367
87D/OD-30
87F-239
87Leaf-231
87OPC-245
87RedFoley/St-107
87T-245
87T/St-186
87Tor/Fire-32
87Tor/Fire-32
88D-271
88F-124
88F/U-U25
88Gator-20
88Leaf-131
88OPC-241
88Panini/St-217
88Score-279
88Score/Tr-42T
88Sf-214
88T-505
88T/St-185
88T/Tr-123T
89D-492
89F-415
89OPC-106
89Panini/St-324
89Score-188
89T-106
89UD-157

Upshur, Takashi
80Wausa-11

Upton, Jack
82IowaC-12

Upton, Thomas
52T-71

Urban, Jack E.
58T-367
59T-18

Urbanski, Bill
33DL-9
33G-212
34DS-37
34Exh/4-1
35BU-59
36Exh/4-1
37Exh/4-1
R313
R314
V355-71

Urbide, Miliciades
88Wythe/Pro-1975
89CharWh/Best-3
89CharWh/Pro-1744

Urbon, Joe
89Batav/Pro-1933

Uremovich, Mike
75Clint

Uribe, George
84Butte-24

Uribe, Jorge
86Wausa-26
88Vermont/Pro-953
89SnBer/Best-12
89SnBer/Cal-78

Uribe, Jose
81Louvl-13
84Louvl-13
85F/Up-U124
85Moth/Giants-13
85T/Tr-125T
86D-236
86F-552
86Moth/Giants-13
86OPC-12
86T-12
86T/St-87
87D-436
87D/OD-99
87F-286
87Moth/SFG-13
87OPC-94
87T-633
88D-559
88D/Best-303
88F-99
88Leaf-218
88Moth/Giants-13
88Nestle-13
88OPC-302
88Panini/St-425
88Score-165
88T-302
88T/Big-95
88T/St-91
89B-471
89D-131
89D/Best-106
89F-345
89Moth/Giants-13
89OPC-8
89Panini/St-217
89Score-56
89Sf-61
89T-753
89T/Big-258
89T/St-82
89UD-181
90D-335
90F-74
90Score-455
90Sf-79
90T-472
90UD-188

Uribe, Juan
88Beloi/GS-8

Uribe, Relito
89Duned/Star-20

Urman, Mike
88Pulas/Pro-1764
89Sumter/Pro-1109

Urrea, John
78T-587
79T-429
81D-190
81T-152

Usher, Bob
51B-286
52T-157
58T-124

Utecht, Tim
83Beloi/LF-20

Vaccaro, Sal
86Jamestn-27
87BurlEx-6
87SanJose-4

Vail, Michael
75Tidew
76Ho-55
76Ho/Twink-55
76OPC-655
76SSPC-534
76T-655
77T-246
78T-69
79T-663
80OPC-180
80T-343
81D-554
81F-311
81T-471
81T/Tr-848
82Coke/Reds
82F-84
82T-194
83D-597
83F-605
83Moth/Giants-19
83T-554
83T/X-119
84F-290
84F/X-122
84Nes/792-766
84OPC-143
84T-766
84T/X-124
89Tidew/CANDL-6

Vaji, Mark
81QuadC-24

Valasquez, Gil
89River/Cal-3

Valasquez, Ray
89Salin/Cal-123

Valdes, Ramon
88GreatF-25

Valdes, Rene
57T-337
61Union

Valdespino, Sandy
65OPC-201R
65T-201R
66OPC-56
66T-56
68T-304
69MB-281
70McDon
77WHave
85RochR-25

Valdez, Amilcar
88Bakers/Cal-241

Valdez, Angel
82Miami-17

Valdez, Efrain
88Tulsa-5
89Canton/Best-6
89Canton/Pro-1311
89Canton/Star-22

Valdez, Frank
88Keno/Pro-1393
89Gasto/Pro-1020
89Gasto/Star-23
89Visal/Cal-108
89Visal/Pro-1440

Valdez, Jose
83Peoria/LF-12

Valdez, Julio
81Pawtu-17
82D-560
82T-381R
83F-199
83T-628
85IowaC-7
86IowaC-25
87IowaC-17
88Pittsf/Pro-1357
88Wythe/Pro-1988

Valdez, Miguel
80Elmir-43

Valdez, Rafael
86CharRa-27
87CharRa-15
88Charl/Pro-1201
89River/Best-18
89River/Cal-4
89River/Pro-1398
89Wich/Roc/Up-10
89Wich/Roc/HL-6M

Valdez, Ramon
89Princet/Star-22

Valdez, Sergio
85Utica-7
87Indianap-21
88Indi/CMC-8
88Indi/Pro-501
89Indi/CMC-2
89Indi/Pro-1215
90D-405
90T-199

Valdez, Sylverio
80Utica-8
83Ander-18

Valdivielso, Jose
56T-237
57T-246
57T-246
60T-527
61Clover-29
61Peters-25
61T-557
62T-339

Valencia, Gil
89Martins/Star-31

Valencia, Jose
88Sumter/Pro-399

Valente, John
88CapeCod/Sum-2

Valentin, Eddy
89AubAs/Pro-2160

Valentin, John
88CapeCod-11
88CapeCod/Sum-138
89WinHav/Star-25

Valentin, Jose
87Spoka-23
88Charl/Pro-1198
89River/Best-19
89River/Cal-8
89River/Pro-1415
89Wich/Roc/Up-18

Valentine, Bill
80ArkTr-23

Valentine, Bobby
71OPC-188R
71T-188R
72OPC-11
72T-11
73OPC-502
73T-502
74OPC-101
74T-101
74T/DE-11
74T/St-150
75OPC-215
75T-215
75T/M-215
76OPC-366
76T-366
77T-629
78T-712
79OPC-222
79T-428
85Rang-2MG
85SpokAT/Crm-22
85T/Tr-126T
86Rang-2MG
86T-261MG
87Moth/Rang-1
87Smok/R-19MG
87T-118MG
88Moth/R-1MG
88Smok/R-8MG
88T-594
89Moth/R-1MG
89Smok/R-33MG
89T-314MG
90T-729MG

Valentine, Ellis
76OPC-590R
76SSPC-342
76T-590R
77OPC-234
77T-52
78K-19
78OPC-45
78T-185
79Ho-50
79OPC-277
79T-535
80K-21
80OPC-206
80T-395
81F-148
81OPC-244
81OPC/Post-7
81T-445
81T/So-80
81T/St-186
81T/Tr-849
82D-605
82F-541
82F/St-83
82OPC-15
82T-15
82T/St-69
83F-558
83T-653
83T/X-120
84F-529
84Nes/792-236
84OPC-236
84Smok/Cal-29
84T-236

Valentine, Fred
64T-483
66T-351
67OPC-64
67T-64
68T-248
69MB-282

Valentine, Harold
(Corky)
55T-44
55T/DH-46
79TCMA-61

Valentinetti, Vito
57T-74
58T-463
59T-44

Valentini, Vincent
80Wichi-19

Valenzuela, Fernando
81F-140
81Pol/Dodg-34
81T-302R
81T/Tr-850
82D-462
82F-27
82F-636M
82F/St-1
82F/St-108M
82F/St-111M
82K-9
82OPC-334
82OPC-345AS

82Pol/Dodg
82Pol/Dodg-34
82Sqt-20
82T-166LL
82T-345AS
82T-510
82T-6M
82T/St-11
82T/St-119
82T/St-50
83D-1DK
83D-284
83D/AAS-53
83F-224
83K-7
83OPC-40
83Pol/Dodg-34
83Seven-8
83T-40
83T-681TL
83T/Gloss-10
83T/Gloss40-10
83T/St-250
83T/St/Box-1
84D-52
84D/AAS-13
84F-115
84F/St-81
84FunFood/Pin-7
84MiltBrad-27
84Nes/792-220
84OPC-220
84Pol/Dodg-34
84Ralston-10
84Seven-9W
84T-220
84T/Cereal-10
84T/St-16LCS
84T/St-79
84T/Super-30
84T/Super-30
85D-52
85D/AAS-37
85D/HL-28
85D/HL-6
85F-387
85F/LimEd-42
85F/St-114
85GenMills-12
85Leaf-184
85OPC-357
85Seven-16W
85T-440
85T/3D-21
85T/St-71
85T/Super-52
86BK/AP-3
86D-215
86D/AAS-27
86D/HL-25
86Drake-36
86F-145
86F-641M
86F/Mini-31
86F/Slug-41
86F/St-123
86Jiffy-14
86Leaf-91
86Meadow/Blank-15
86Meadow/Milk-12
86Meadow/Stat-2
86OPC-178
86OPC-P
86Pol/Dodg-34
86Quaker-17
86S-12
86S-132M
86S-143M
86S-56M
86S-72M
86S/Dec-66
86S/Rook-47M
86T-207RB
86T-401M
86T-630
86T/3D-30
86T/Gloss60-3
86T/Mini-47
86T/St-64
86T/Super-58
86T/WaxBox-P
86TrueVal-6
87BK-20
87Class-91
87D-94
87D/AAS-54
87Drake-29
87F-457
87F-631M
87F/AS-10
87F/AwardWin-40
87F/GameWin-42
87F/Lim-43
87F/Mini-109
87F/Slug-43
87F/St-120
87Ho/St-11
87Jiffy-15
87KayBee-32
87KMart-33
87Kraft-32
87Leaf-148
87MnM's-19
87Moth/Dodg-4
87OPC-273
87Pol/Dodg-17
87Ralston-11
87RedFoley/St-57
87S-119M
87S-120M
87S-150
87Seven-W16
87Smok/Dodg-36
87T-410
87T-604AS
87T/Coins-47
87T/Gloss22-11
87T/Gloss60-53
87T/Mini-16
87T/St-75
88ChefBoy-24
88D-53
88D/Best-316
88F-528
88F/BB/MVP-40
88F/Excit-43
88F/Mini-86
88F/St-94
88KingB/Disc-19
88KMart-31
88Leaf-61
88Moth/Dodg-4
88MSA/Disc-20
88OPC-52
88Panini/St-304
88Pol/Dodg-34
88Score-600
88Sf-40
88Smok/Dodg-24
88T-780
88T/Big-18
88T/Coins-58
88T/Mini-54
88T/Revco-14
88T/St-70
88T/St/Backs-30
88T/UK-80
89B-337
89D-250
89F-76
89KMart/DT-32
89Moth/Dodg-4
89OPC-150
89Panini/St-103
89Pol/Dodg-22
89RedFoley/St-123
89Score-437
89Sf-124
89Smok/Dodg-97
89T-150
89T/St-60
89T/UK-78
89UD-656
90D-625
90F-409
90F-622
90Score-54
90T-340
90UD-445

Valera, Julio
87Columbia-26
88Clmbia/GS-11
89Jacks/GS-29
89StLucie/Star-23

Valera, Wilson
83Watlo/LF-10
85Water-2
86Lynch-23
87Lynch-26

Valez, Jose
89PalmSp/Cal-46

Vallente, Nestor
84Butte-25

Valla, Mike
88Watertn/Puc-26

Vallaran, Miguel
77LodiD

Valle, Dave
81LynnS-14
82SLCty-20
83Chatt-26
84Cram/PCL-176
85F/Up-U125
85Moth/Mar-17
86Calgary-24
87D-610
87D/OD-120
87Moth/Sea-9
87T/Tr-122T
88D-393
88F-389
88Moth/Sea-9
88OPC-83
88Panini/St-184
88Score-126
88T-583
88T/Big-210
88T/St-220
89B-208
89D-614
89D/Best-248
89F-561
89Moth/Sea-9
89RedFoley/St-124
89Score-27
89T-459
89T-498
89T/Big-56
89UD-320
90D-129
90F-527
90Score-109
90T-76
90UD-451

Valle, Hector
65T-561R
66T-314

Valle, John A.
77Evansvl/TCMA-24
78Indianap-14
79Indianap-25
80RochR-14
81RochR-17
82RochR-18
83RochR-18
84RochR-6

Valle, Tony
89Idaho/Pro-2026

Valley, Chick
77Salem
78Salem
81ElPas-16
82Vanco-18

Valo, Elmer
48L-29
49B-66
50B-49
51T/RB-28
52B-206
52T-34
53T-122
54T-145
55Rodeo
55T-145
55T/DH-85
56Rodeo
56T-3
57T-54
58T-323
60L-107
60T-237
61Peters-12
61T-186
63Sugar-17
79TCMA-148
89Pac/Leg-187

Valverde, Miguel
88Aug/Pro-361
89Salem/Star-23

Van Atta, Russ
33G-215
R312/M
R314

Van Bever, Mark
78Clint

Van Blaricom, Mark
83Butte-22
85FtMyr-10
86FtMyr-25
87Memph-12
87Memph/Best-6
88Memph/Best-3

Van Brunt, Jim
87Anchora-37bb

Van Brunt, Lefty
85Anchora-28CO
87Anchora-30CO

Van Burkleo, Ty
82Beloi-6
86PalmSp-29
86PalmSp/Smok-20
87MidldA-7

Van Cuyk, Chris
52T-53
53Mother-41

Van DeCasteele, Mike
78Tidew
79Tidew-19

Van Der Beck, Jim
75Water

Van Duzer, Donna L.
88Fresno/Pro-1249

Van Dyke, William
N172

Van Gilder, Elam
E120
E126-47

Van Gorder, Dave
80Indianap-8
81Indianap-6
82Indianap-12
83D-188
83Indianap-27
83T-322
85D-384
86D-550
86F-195
86T-143
87RochR-2
87RochR/TCMA-11

Van Haltren, George
E107
E223
N172
N403
N566-180
N690/2
WG1-17

Van Heyningen, Pat
85Newar-20

Van Horn, Dave
83Ander-24

Van Houten, Jim
85Sprin-4
87ColAst/Pro-11
87ColumAst-11

Van Ornum, John
80Pol/Giants-42

Van Robays, Maurice
47Remar-18
47Signal
47Smith-7
48Signal
48Smith-9
49B/PCL-32
49Remar

Van Scoyoc, Aaron
89Oneon/Pro-2115

Van Slyke, Andy
81Louvl-18
82ArkTr-19
84D-83
84F-339
84Nes/792-206
84T-206
84T/St-150
85D-327
85F-242
85OPC-341
85T-551
85T/St-138
86D-412
86F-48
86KAS/Disc-19
86KayBee-32
86OPC-33
86Schnucks-23
86T-683
86T/St-51
87D-417
87D/OD-161
87F-311
87F/U-U121
87OPC-33
87T-33
87T/St-51
87T/Tr-124T
88D-18DK
88D-291
88D-BC8
88D/Best-157
88D/DKsuper-18DK
88F-341
88F/LL-43
88F/Mini-105
88F/St-116
88F/TL-44
88Leaf-102
88Leaf-18DK
88OPC-142
88Panini/St-380
88RedFoley/St-92
88Score-416
88Sf-109
88T-142
88T/Big-184
88T/St-126
88T/UK-81
89Ames-30
89B-424

89Cadaco-59
89Class-111
89D-54
89D/AS-61
89D/Best-45
89D/MVP-BC10
89F-222
89F/BBAS-42
89F/BBMVP's-40
89F/Heroes-41
89F/LL-41
89F/WaxBox-C27
89KingB/Discs-19
89OPC-350
89Panini/St-173
89Score-174
89Score/HotSt-92
89Score/Mast-38
89Sf-166
89T-350
89T-392AS
89T/Big-255
89T/Coins-27
89T/DH-19
89T/Gloss60-4
89T/Hills-30
89T/Mini-32
89T/St-132
89T/St/Backs-54
89T/UK-79
89Tetley/Discs-17
89UD-537
89UD-685TC
90D-244
90F-481
90Score-440
90Score/100St-78
90Sf-101
90T-775
90UD-536

Van Stone, Paul
86Clint-25

Van Vuren, Bob
86FtMyr-26

Van Winkle, Dave
89Utica/Puc-1

Vanacore, Derek
85FtMyr-29

Vance, Clarence A.
(Dazzy)
25Exh-15
28Exh-8
29Exh/4-3
31Exh/4-3
33CJ/Pin-23
33Exh/4-2
33G-2
35G-2C
35G-4C
35G-7C
50Callahan
60F-51
61F-81
61GP-26
63Bz/ATG-28
72F/FFeat-4
72Laugh/GF-21
80SSPC/HOF
89HOF/St-73
89Smok/Dodg-29
R310
R315-A37
R315-B37
R316
R332-45
R423-109
V353-2
W517-36
W572

Vance, Gene
(Sandy)
71OPC-34
71T-34
85SpokAT/Crm-23

Vancho, Bob
89Helena/SP-18

VandeBerg, Ed
81Spoka-15
82T/Tr-122T
83D-100
83F-488
83OPC-183
83T-183
83T/St-317
84D-604
84F-623
84Moth/Mar-8
84Nes/792-63
84OPC-63
84T-63
85D-511
85F-504
85Moth/Mar-5
85OPC-207
85T-566
85T/St-336
86D-637
86F-479
86F/Up-U121
86OPC-357
86Pol/Dodg-31
86T-357
86T/Tr-118T
87D-376
87F-458
87F/U-U120
87Gator-36
87OPC-34
87T-717
87T/Tr-123T
88F-619
88OkCty/CMC-8
88OkCty/Pro-52
88T-421
89F-534
89IowaC/CMC-4
89IowaC/Pro-1710
89T-242

Vandenberg, Hy
40PB-209

Vanderbush, Walt
83Beaum-5
84Cram/PCL-229
85Cram/PCL-111

VanderMeer, John
39Exh
41DP-6
41PB-56
43MP-23
48L-53
48Swell-10
49B-128
49Eureka-96
50B-79
51B-223
60NuCard-5
61F-147
72Laugh/GF-7
74Laugh/ASG-38
76Laugh/Jub-12
80Cram/Leg-110
88Pac/Leg-30
89Swell-11
D305
Exh47
R346-46
W711/1
W711/2

Vanderwal, John
87Jamestn-14
88FSLAS/Star-23
88WPalm/Star-24
89Jaxvl/Best-25
89Jaxvl/Pro-161

Vanderwel, Bill
86Cram/PCL-84
87PalmSp-13
88PalmSp/Cal-94
88PalmSp/Pro-1457
89QuadC/Best-15
89QuadC/GS-16

Vann, Brandy
86Cram/PCL-80
87QuadC-12
88QuadC/GS-29
89PalmSp/Cal-53
89PalmSp/Pro-471

Vannaman, Tim
88SoOreg/Pro-1693
89Madis/Star-22

Vanni, Edo
47Centen-30

Vantrease, Bob
83Idaho-12

Vargas, Eddie
78Charl
80Buffa-15
81Buffa-23
82Portl-17

Vargas, Gonzalo
89StCath/Pro-2083

Vargas, Hector
87Oneon-5
87PrWill-21
88Oneon/Pro-2049
89PrWill/Star-23

Vargas, Hedi
85Cram/PCL-236
88Chatt/Best-8
89MidldA/GS-29

Vargas, Jose
86Osceola-27
86Salem-26
87Osceola-15
87PortChar-17
88ColAst/Best-8
88Tulsa-7
89Osceola/Star-26

Vargas, Julio
89Martins/Star-32

Vargas, Leonel
(Leo)
82Richm-20
83Richm-21
84Richm-12

Vargas, Miguel
87Readg-5

Vargas, Ramon
83Ander-19

Varney, Pete
76OPC-413
76SSPC-154
76T-413

Varni, Patrick
88CapeCod/Sum-182

Varoz, Brett
85Anchora-29

Varoz, Eric
86Beaum-24

Varsho, Gary
84MidldC-23
86Pittsf-24
87IowaC-23
88Berg/Cubs-24
88F/U-U81
88IowaC/CMC-22
88IowaC/Pro-535
89F-441
89Score-604
89T-613
89UD-321

Varverde, Miguel
86Watertn-26

Vasquez, Aguedo
88BBCity/Star-23
88FSLAS/Star-50
89Memph/Best-5
89Memph/Pro-1186
89Memph/Star-22

Vasquez, Angelo
85BurlR-13

Vasquez, Dennis
81GlenF-7

Vasquez, Francisco
79Elmir-18

Vasquez, George
73Cedar

Vasquez, Jesse
80BurlB-12
85Newar-22
86Hagers-26

Vasquez, Julian
89Clmbia/GS-25

Vasquez, Luis
85Elmir-23
86FSLAS-48
86WinHav-26
87NewBrit-5
88EastLAS/Pro-24
88NewBrit/Pro-889
89Nashvl-25
89Nashvl/CMC-10
89Nashvl/Pro-1285

Vasquez, Rafael
77Salem
80T-672R
80Tacom-9
81Buffa-11

Vasquez, Tony
89Cedar/Best-27

Vatcher, James
88SALAS/GS-26
88Spart/Pro-1045
88Spart/Star-21
88Spart/Star-5
89Clearw/Star-23
89Star/Wax-14

Vaughan, Charles
67OPC-179R
67T-179R

Vaughan, J. Floyd
(Arky)
33G-229
34G-22
35BU-21
35Exh/4-7
36Exh/4-7
36Wheat
37Exh/4-7
37Wheat
38Exh/4-7
39Exh
39PB-55
39Wheat
40PB-107
41DP-34
41PB-10
49Sommer-18
60F-11
61F-148
74Laugh/ASG-41
80Cram/Leg-122
88Conlon/NatAS-22
89HOF/St-21
89Pac/Leg-200
89Smok/Dodg-30
R311/Leath
R312/M
R313
R314
V354-70
V355-6
WG8-47

Vaughan, Rick
88StCath/Pro-2033
89Myrtle/Pro-1629

Vaughn, DeWayne
82Lynch-7
84Jacks-1
86Tidew-28
87Tidew-2
87Tidew/TCMA-8
88D/Rook-25
88Moth/R-24

Vaughn, Fred
47Signal

Vaughn, Greg
87Beloi-2
88BBAmer-24
88ElPas/Best-20
88TexLgAS/GS-35
89AAA/Pro-42
89Denver/CMC-23
89Denver/Pro-36
89F/Up-41
90Class-60
90D-37
90F-339
90Score-585
90Score/100Ris-30
90Sf-135
90T-57
90UD-25

Vaughn, Harry
N172

Vaughn, James
(Hippo)
11Helmar-48
14Piedmont/St-57
15CJ-176
61F-82
69Bz-1
72F/FFeat-14M
72Laugh/GF-39M
BF2-69
D327
D328-177
D329-178
D350/2-180
E121/120
E121/80
E122
E135-177
E220
E300
E98
M101/4-178
M101/5-180
T202
T205
T207
V100
W514-111
W555
W575

Vaughn, Maurice
88CapeCod-16
88CapeCod/Sum-93
90Score-675DC

Vaughn, Mike
76Clint
77Watlo

Vaughn, Randy
88Eugene/Best-10
89AppFx/Pro-850

Vaughn, Ron
89Utica/Puc-28

Vaughn, Tim
87Macon-9

Vavra, Joe
85Cram/PCL-153
86Albuq-25
89GreatF-9

Vavrock, Rob
82Madis-24

Vavruska, Paul
76Clint

Vazquez, Ed
89Kingspt/Star-24

Vazquez, Jose
89Oneon/Pro-2126
Vazquez, Marcos
88Sumter/Pro-403
89Sumter/Pro-1115
Veach
N172/PCL
Veach, Robert
15CJ-174
21Exh-180
25Exh-71
BF2-30
D327
D328-178
D329-179
D350/2-181
E120
E121/120
E121/80
E122
E135-178
E220
M101/4-179
M101/5-181
V100
V61-33
W501-5
W514-88
W572
W573
W575
Veach, William
N172
Veal, Orville
(Coot)
59T-52
61T-432
62J-68
62P-68
62P/Can-68
62Salada-84
62Shirriff-84
62T-573
Veale, Bob
62T-593R
63T-87
64Kahn
64T-501
65Bz-13
65Kahn
65OPC-12LL
65OPC-195
65T-12LL
65T-195
65T/trans-32SP
66EH-39
66Kahn
66T-238LL
66T-425
66T/RO-46
67Kahn
67T-238LL
67T-335
67T/Test/PP-23
68Bz-3
68Kahn
68KDKA-39
68OPC-70
68T-70
69Kahn
69MB-283
69MLB/St-189
69OPC-8LL
69T-520
69T-8LL
69T/St-90
70MLB/St-108
70OPC-236
70T-236
71MLB/St-215
71OPC-368
71T-368
72MB-351
72T-729
73OPC-518
73T-518
78Green
78TCMA-114
Vega, Jesus
77BurlB
78OrlTw
79Toled-20
80Toled-11
81Toled-16
83D-650
83F-624
83T-308
83Toled-17
Vegely, Bruce
89QuadC/Best-19
Veilleux, Brian
89Modesto/Cal-268
89Modesto/Ch-17
Veintidos, Juan
75OPC-621R
75T-621R
75T/M-621R
Velarde, Randy
86AppFx-26
87Albany-7
88Colum/CMC-17
88Colum/Pol-22
88Colum/Pro-324
88F-646
89AAA/Pro-19
89Colum/CMC-13
89Colum/Pol-20
89Colum/Pro-741
89Score/HotRk-18
89T-584
89T/Big-239
89UD-189
90D-630
90Score-524
90T-23
Velasquez, Al
82Readg-12
Velasquez, Guillermo
88Charl/Pro-1203
88SALAS/GS-12
89River/Best-20
89River/Pro-1394
Velasquez, Ray
85Visal-16
86Visal-23
87Clint-26
88SanJose/Cal-139
88SanJose/Pro-116
89Salin/Pro-1807
Velazquel, Ildefonso
85Tigres-9
Velazquez, Carlos
No Cards.
Velazquez, Freddy
No Cards.
Velazquez, Juan
83QuadC-17
Velez, Jose
87Gasto-25
88Gasto/Pro-1011
89PalmSp/Pro-484
Velez, Otto
74OPC-606R
74T-606R
74T/St-219
76SSPC-455
77OPC-13
77T-299
78OPC-67
78T-59
79OPC-241
79T-462
80OPC-354
80T-703
81D-391
81F-410
81OPC-351
81OPC/Post-23
81T-351
81T/So-44
81T/St-138
82D-304
82F-625
82F/St-233
82OPC-155
82OPC/Post-11
82T-155
82T/St-249
83Charl-18
Vella, Greg
88Myrtle/Pro-1183
88SALAS/GS-19
89Duned/Star-21
Velleggia, Frank
84Newar-15
Venable, Max
77Clint
78LodiD
79Pol/Giants-49
80Phoen-12
81F-443
81Phoen-6
81T-484
83F-275
83Moth/Giants-16
83T-634
84D-323
84F-385
84Indianap-28
84Nes/792-58
84T-58
85Indianap-9
86D-650
86F-196
86T-428
86TexGold-9
87F-216
87Nashv-22
87T-226
89Edmon/CMC-23
89Edmon/Pro-556
Venezia, Mike
81Redwd-8
Venger, Tad
81CharR-24
Venner, Gary
83TriCit-27
Ventress, Leroy
86Cram/PCL-145
88Batav/Pro-1666
89Spart/Pro-1044
89Spart/Star-23
Ventura, Candido
77Charl
Ventura, Jose
86Beloi-24
89SoBend/GS-16
Ventura, Robin
88T/Tr-124TOLY
89B-65
89BirmB/Best-1
89BirmB/Pro-106
89Class/Up/2-177
89F/Up-23
89SLAS-2
89T-764
89T/Big-65
90Class-5
90D-28
90F-550
90Score-595
90Score/100Ris-96
90Sf-222
90T-121
90UD-21
Venturini, Peter Paul
(Pete)
86Penin-25
87BirmB/Best-22
88BirmB/Best-11
Venturino, Phil
86MidldA-24
86PalmSp/Smok-18
87MidldA-29
88Edmon/CMC-8
88Edmon/Pro-566
Venuto, Nicholas
88SoOreg/Pro-1695
89Medford/Best-14
Veras, Camilo
86Madis-25
86Madis/Pol-21
87Madis-15
88Huntsvl/BK-23
Verban, Emil
48B-28
49B-38
49Eureka-73
Exh47
Verbanic, Joe
67T-442R
68OPC-29
68T-29
69T-541
70OPC-416
70T-416
Verdi, Frank
78Tidew
79Tidew-4
80Tidew-24
81Colum-17
82Colum-25
82Colum/Pol-26
83SanJose-1MG
84RochR-9
85RochR-24
Verdi, Mike
86SanJose-22CO
87SanJose-19
89Elmir/Puc-22
Verducci, John
85Evrt/Cram-17
86Shrev-26
87Phoen-18
Verdugo, Luis
89Mia/Star/22-20
Verdugo, Mando
88SLCty-25
89Mia/Star/25-20
Veres, David
86Cram/PCL-53
87Modesto-3
88CalLgAS-10
88Huntsvl/BK-24
88Modesto-32
88Modesto/Cal-56
89Huntsvl/Best-5
Veres, Randy
86Beloi-25
87Beloi-1
88Stock/Cal-179
88Stock/Pro-730
89ElPas/GS-17
89F/Up-42
Vergez, Johnny
33G-233
34DS-21
35BU-176
R337-401
V355-5
Verhoeff, Will
77WHave
Verhoeven, John
77T-91
78T-329
79Toled-12
81D-564
81T-603
82F-547
82T-281
Verkuilen, Mike
85Orlan-13
Verna, Cris
89SnBer/Cal-92tr
Vernon, Mickey
49B-94
50B-132
51B-65
51T/BB-13
52B-87
52NTea
52T-106
52TipTop
53B/Col-159
53Briggs
53Exh/Can-59
53RM-AL21
54B-152
54RM-AL13
55Armour-24
55B-46
55RM-AL12
56T-228
57T-92
58T-233
59Armour-20
59T-115
60T-467C
61T-134
62T-152
63T-402
76SSPC-621
79Colum-29
79TCMA-87
80Cram/Leg-78
86S/Dec-38M
89Swell-54
Exh47
Versalles, Zoilo
61Clover-30
61Peters-1
61T-21
61T/St-186
62J-86
62P-86
62P/Can-86
62Salada-51A
62Salada-51B
62Shirriff-51
62T-499
62T/St-81
63J-3
63P-3
63T-349
64T-15
64Wheat/St-46
65MacGregor-10
65OPC-157
65T-157
65T/E-33
66T-400
67T-270
68T-315
69MB-284
69MLB/St-45
69OPC-38
69T-38
69T/St-100
70MLB/St-288
70OPC-365
70T-365
72MB-352
75OPC-203M
75T-203MV
75T/M-203MV
82KMart-7
88Pac/Leg-107
Verstandig, Mark
88Spoka/Pro-1943

89CharRa/Pro-990
Veryzer, Thomas
75OPC-623R
75T-623R
75T/M-623R
76Ho-109
76OPC-432
76SSPC-367
76T-432
77OPC-188
77T-145
78OPC-14
78T-633
79T-537
80OPC-145
80T-276
81D-199
81F-390
81T-39
82D-450
82F-381
82OPC-387
82T-387
82T/Tr-123T
83F-559
83T-496
83T/X-121
83Thorn-29
84Nes/792-117
84T-117
85T-405
Veselic, Bob
80Toled-19
81Toled-9
82Toled-6
83Tucso-9
Vesely, Orece
89QuadC/GS-12
Vesling, Donald
88FSLAS/Star-51
88Lakel/Star-25
89London/Pro-1374
Vespe, Will
88CapeCod/Sum-149
89Watertn/Star-22
Vessey, Tom
81Tucso-6
Vetsch, Dave
85Visal-13
86Orlan-22
87Orlan-27
Vezendy, Gerry
65T-509R
Viau, Leon
N172
Vice, Darryl
88CapeCod/Sum-152
89Modesto/Ch-26
Vickers, Mike
78Ashev
80Tulsa-25
Vickers, Rube
C46-37
Vickery, Lou
62Kahn/Atl
63Pep/Tul
Vico, George
48L-47
49B-122
50B-150
53Mother-25
Vidal, Jose
67T-499R
68T-432R
69T-322
Vidmar, Donald
89PalmSp/Cal-50
89PalmSp/Pro-482
Viebahn
E270/1
Viebrock, Alan
76Watlo

Vierra, Joseph
88Greens/Pro-1574
89Cedar/Best-8
89Cedar/Pro-915
89Cedar/Star-21
Viggiano, Matt
88Batav/Pro-1683
Vike, Jim
86AubAs-27
Vila, Jesus
86VeroB-26
Vilella, Lazaro
84Butte-26
Villa, Jose
88StCath/Pro-2008
Villa, Mike
86Fresno/Smok-9
87Tampa-30
88Clint/Pro-719
Villaescusa, Juan
81VeroB-23
Villaman, Rafael
82Nashv-26
Villanueva, Gilbert
87CharWh-3
88Stock/Cal-188
88Stock/Pro-728
Villanueva, Hector
86WinSal-26
87Pittsf-3
88EastLAS/Pro-28
88Pittsf/Pro-1355
89IowaC/CMC-13
89IowaC/Pro-1696
Villanueva, Juan
86Lynch-24
87Lynch-2
88FSLAS/Star-24
89Jacks/GS-12
Villegas, Mike
84ElPas-8
Villegas, Ramon
85Tigres-6
Vilorio, Frank
79Toled-19
83Nashua-16
Viltz, Corey
87Jamestn-15
88WPalm/Star-25
89WPalm/Star-23
Viltz, Eski
80Cedar-7
81Water-17
82Water-15
Vincent, Mike
86Cedar/TCMA-12
87Cedar-19
Vines, Ellsworth
33SK-46
Vineyard, Dave
65OPC-169
65T-169
Vinson, Chuck
68T-328R
Vinton, William
N172
Viola, Frank
82OrlTw/B-24
82Toled-7
83D-382
83F-625
83T-586
84D-364
84F-575
84Nes/792-28
84OPC-28
84T-28
84T/St-312
85D-17
85D-436
85D/DKsuper-17
85F-291

85F/St-84
85Leaf-17DK
85OPC-266
85Seven/Minn-2
85T-266
85T-710AS
85T/Gloss40-7
85T/St-300
86D-194
86F-408
86F/St-124
86KayBee-33
86Leaf-126
86OPC-269
86S-99
86T-742
86T/Mini-25
86T/St-284
87D-196
87D/HL-24
87F-554
87Leaf-74
87OPC-310
87RedFoley/St-127
87T-310
87T/St-277
88Woolwth-19
88Woolwth-33SMVP
88ChefBoy-15
88Class/Red-183
88D-149
88D/Best-214
88F-25
88F/BB/MVP-41
88F/Mini-38
88F/RecSet-42
88F/Slug-C5
88F/St-47
88F/WS-12
88Leaf-94
88Master/Disc-2
88OPC-259
88Panini/St-134
88Score-475
88Sf-196
88Smok/Minn-1
88T-625
88T/Big-201
88T/Mini-25
88T/RiteAid-33
88T/St-25
88T/St-282
88T/UK-82
89B-150
89Bz-21
89Cadaco-60
89Class-144
89Crunch-4
89D-237
89D-23DK
89D/AS-8
89D/Best-74
89D/DKsuper-23DK
89D/PopUp-8
89F-127
89F/AS-12
89F/BBAS-43
89F/BBMVP's-41
89F/Excit-42
89F/Heroes-42
89F/LL-42
89F/Superstar-41
89F/WaxBox-C28
89Holsum/Discs-17
89KayBee-31
89KingB/Discs-14
89Master/Discs-1
89Nissen-17
89OPC-120
89Panini/St-237AS
89Panini/St-248
89Panini/St-383

89Panini/St-475
89RedFoley/St-125
89Score-290
89Score/HotSt-5
89Score/Tr-67
89Sf-10
89T-120
89T-406AS
89T/Big-140
89T/Coins-30
89T/DH-10
89T/Gloss22-10
89T/Gloss60-18
89T/HeadsUp-7
89T/Hills-31
89T/Mini-64
89T/St-153
89T/St-292
89T/St/Backs-30
89T/UK-80
89UD-397
89UD-658CY
89UD-691TC
89Woolwth-3
90Class-91
90D-353
90F-219
90Score-500
90Sf-122
90T-470
90UD-626
Viola, Lance
79Newar-23
Violat, Juan
T206
Viox, James
D329-180
D350/2-182
M101/4-180
M101/5-182
Virdon, Bill
55B-296
55Hunter
56T-170
57T-110
58Hires-45
58T-198
59T-190
59T-543M
60L-40
60T-496
61P-135
61T-70
61T/St-72
62J-175
62Kahn
62P-175
62P/Can-175
62Salada-168
62Shirriff-168
62T-415
62T/St-181
63J-142
63Kahn
63P-142
63T-55
64Kahn
64T-268M
64T-495
65Kahn
65OPC-69
65T-69
72T-661
73OPC-517
73T-517MG
75OPC-611MG
75T-611MG
75T/M-611MG
76T-147
77T-327MG
78BK/A-1
78T-279

79T-381MG
79TCMA-100
81D-384
81F-61
81T-678MG
82D-144
83OPC-6MG
83Stuart-1MG
83T-516
84Nes/792-111MG
84OPC-111MG
84Stuart-2MG
84T-111
88Pac/Leg-49
89Swell-119
Virgil, Ossie Jr.
77Spart
81OkCty/TCMA-19
82T-231
83D-606
83F-175
83T-383
84D-326
84F-49
84Nes/792-484
84T-484
85CIGNA-3
85D-82
85F-267
85Leaf-250
85OPC-103
85T-143FS
85T-611
85T/St-110
86D-137
86D/AAS-26
86F-456
86F/Up-U122
86OPC-95
86Pol/Atl-9
86T-95
86T/St-115
86T/Tr-119T
87D-67
87D/OD-45
87F-532
87OPC-183
87Smok/Atl-12
87T-571
88D-143
88D/AS-50
88D/Best-85
88F-552
88Jiffy-17
88Leaf-64
88OPC-291
88Panini/St-241
88RedFoley/St-93
88Score-129
88Sf-217
88T-755
88T/Big-148
88T/St-36
88T/St/Backs-24
89D-145
89F-605
89OPC-179
89RedFoley/St-126
89Score-111
89Sf-94
89T-179
89T/St-28
89UD-104
Virgil, Ossie Sr.
57T-365
58T-107
59T-203
61T-67
62T-327
65T-571
67OPC-132
67T-132

84Smok/SDP-26C
85T-143FS
Viskas, Steve
79QuadC-25
Visner, Joseph
N172
Vitale, Tony
86Fresno/Smok-28
Vitato, Richard
82CharR-14
83CharR-9
Vitt, Oscar
40PB-47
D327
D328-179
D329-181
D350/2-183
E121/120
E121/80
E135-179
M101/4-181
M101/5-183
T222
W501-9
W575
Vizcaino, Jose
88Bakers/Cal-240
88CalLgAS-47
89Albuq/CMC-23
89Albuq/Pro-82
90F-410
90Score-613
90UD-44
Vizcaino, Junior
87Watertn-14
88CLAS/Star-18
88Salem/Star-22
89Harris/Pro-293
89Harris/Star-20
Vizquel, Omar
86Wausa-27
88BBAmer-4
88EastLAS/Pro-37
88Vermont/Pro-946
89Calg/CMC-23
89Calg/Pro-537
89D/Best-163
89D/Rook-53
89F/Up-62
89Moth/Sea-15
89Score/Tr-105
89T/Tr-122T
89UD/Ext-787
90D-483
90F-528
90Score-264
90Score/100Ris-37
90T-698
90UD-233
Vlcek, Jim
86Salem-27
Vodvarka, Rob
83Butte-12
Voeltz, Bill
87FtLaud-16
87Oneon-19
87PrWill-16
88FtLaud/Star-23
Vogel, George
84Savan-20
Voigt, Jack
88Hagers/Star-23
89Freder/Star-24
Voigt, Paul
83Albuq-7
Voiselle, Bill
47TipTop
49Eureka-27
Exh47
Volt, David
89Beloi/Star-23
89Helena/SP-12
Vollmer, Clyde
50B-53
51B-91
52B-57
52T-255
53B/Col-152
53Briggs
53T-32
54B-136
55B-13
Vollmer, Robby
83Wausa/LF-16
Voltaggio, Vic
88Umpire-32
89Umpires-30
VonDerAhe, Christian
N172
N284
N370
Von Hoff, Bruce
68T-529
Von Ohlen, Dave
79Jacks-15
80Tidew-1
81Louvl-8
81Tidew-18
82Tidew-23
84D-205
84F-340
84Louvl-9
84Nes/792-489
84T-489
85D-412
85F-243
85F/Up-U126
85Polar/Ind-38
85T-177
85T/Tr-127T
86F-597
86Miami-25
86T-632
87F-408
87T-287
87Tacom-7
88Mia/Star-24
Vondran, Steve
89Bill/Pro-2057
Vontz, Doug
87BurlEx-29
Voorhees, Mark
77Spoka
Vosberg, Ed
84Beaum-6
85Beaum-5
86LasVegas-21
87LasVegas-24
88LasVeg/CMC-7
88LasVeg/Pro-222
89Tucso/CMC-6
89Tucso/Pro-192
Vosmik, Joe
32Orbit/num-35
32Orbit/un-56
33DH-40
33DL-20
34DS-8
34G-77
35BU-68
35G-8I
35G-9I
36Exh/4-11
36G
36Wheat
38Exh/4-9
38G-247
38G-271
39PB-107
40PB-144
41DP-144
R305
R310
R313
R314
R326-2A
R326-2B
R342-2
V355-76
WG8-48
Voss, Bill
66T-529R
68OPC-142R
68T-142R
69T-621
70OPC-326
70T-326
71MLB/St-454
71OPC-671
71T-671
72T-776
Vossler, Dan
74OPC-602R
74T-602R
Vuckovich, Pete
77OPC-130
77T-517
78OPC-157
78T-241
79T-407
80OPC-31
80T-57
81D-189
81F-547
81OPC-193
81T-193
81T/Tr-851
82D-458
82F-156
82F/St-14
82OPC-132
82Pol/Brew
82Pol/Brew-50
82T-165LL
82T-643
82T-703TL
82T/St-10LL
82T/St-202
83D-80
83F-49
83Gard-20
83K-19
83OPC-375
83OPC-394AS
83Pol/Brew-50
83T-321
83T-375
83T-394
83T/St-86
84F-217
84Gard-21
84Nes/792-505
84OPC-313
84Pol/Brew-50
84T-505
85Gard-21
85Pol/Brew-50
85T-254
86D-473
86F-504
86OPC-152
86T-737
Vukovich, George
81F-21
81OkCty/TCMA-20
81T-598
82F-262
82T-389
83D-315
83F-176
83T-16
83T/X-122
83Wheat/Ind-31
84D-468
84F-555
84Nes/792-638
84T-638
84Wheat/Ind-24
85D-276
85F-458
85Leaf-120
85Polar/Ind-24
85T-212
85T/St-249
86D-346
86F-598
86OPC-337
86T-483
86T/St-214
Vukovich, John
73OPC-451
73T-451
74OPC-349
74T-349
75OPC-602
75T-602
75T/M-602
76SSPC-43
79Ho-87
79OkCty
81F-22
83Thorn-26C
Vuksan, Jeff
79AppFx-8
81Durhm-12
Vuz, John
88Clint/Pro-693
Waag, Billy
81Buffa-14
Wabeke, Doug
81Shrev-18
Wacha, Chuck
87Greens-7
Wachs, Thomas
85LitFalls-11
86Columbia-26
87Lynch-3
Wachter, Ed
33SK-5
Wacker, Wade
89Elizab/Star-27
Wada, Hiromi
(Hank)
83SanJose-2C
86SanJose-23C
Waddell, George E.
(Rube)
48Exh/HOF
50Callahan
60F-61
61F-149
80Laugh/FFeat-11
80SSPC/HOF
86Conlon/1-35
88Conlon/5-29
E107
E254
E270/1
E91
E93
M116
T206
W555
WG2-47
Waddell, Tom
84F/X-123
84T/X-125
84Wheat/Ind-54
85D-582
85F-459
85Polar/Ind-54
85T-453
86D-94
86F-599
86OhHenry-54
86OPC-86
86T-86
86T/St-209
87Gator-54
87T-657
Wade, Ben
52T-389
53T-4
54T-126
59DF
61Union
Wade, Darrin
88Duned/Star-19
88StCath/Pro-2036
Wade, Gale
55T-196
Wade, Jake
V362-3
Wade, Scott
86NewBrit-25
87Pawtu-21
87Pawtu/TCMA-20
88Pawtu/CMC-23
88Pawtu/Pro-458
89Pawtu/CMC-15
89Pawtu/Dunkin-33
89Pawtu/Pro-695
Wadley, Tony
82Miami-7
83Idaho-13
Waggoner, Aubrey
86AppFx-27
87Penin-8
89BirmB/Best-8
89BirmB/Pro-114
Waggoner, Jimmy
89Medford/Best-25
Wagner, Charles
(Heinie)
10Domino-119
11Helmar-5
12Sweet/Pin-7
14CJ-31
15CJ-31
E91
M116
T202
T204
T205
T206
T207
T213/blue
T215/blue
T215/brown
T216
Wagner, Charlie
80Elmir-38
87Elmir-33
Wagner, Dan
87Penin-29
88BirmB/Best-13
89BirmB/Best-5
89BirmB/Pro-90
Wagner, Gary
66OPC-151
66T-151
67T-529
68T-448
69T-276
69T/St-158
70T-627
71OPC-473
71T-473
Wagner, Gerald
86Durhm-26
87Sumter-28
Wagner, Harold
47TipTop
Wagner, Hector
88Eugene/Best-6
89AppFx/Pro-849
Wagner, Jeff
83Ander-33
84Durhm-7
85Durhm-31

Wagner, John
(Honus)
14CJ-68
15CJ-68
40PB-168
47TipTop
48Exh/HOF
48L-70
50Callahan
51T/CM
60Exh/HOF-24
60F-62
61F-150
61GP-32
63Bz/ATG-10
69Bz/Sm
72F/FFeat-21
72K/ATG-9
72K/ATG-9
76OPC-344AS
76T-344M
80Cram/Leg-18
80Laugh/FFeat-1
80SSPC/HOF
83D/HOF-5
85West/2-42
86Conlon/1-55
87Nestle/DT-4
89HOF/St-14
89Pac/Leg-211
89Swell-4
BF2-92
D303
D304
D322
D328-180
D329-182
D350/2-184
E101
E102
E103
E105
E106
E107
E135-180
E224
E254
E270/1
E286
E90/1
E90/2
E91
E92
E93
E94
E95
E98
M101/4-182
M101/5-184
M116
R311/Leath
R312/M
R313
T206
W555
WG3-49
WG4-28
WG5-41
WG6-37

Wagner, Leon
59T-257
60T-383
61T-547
61T/Dice-17
62P-77
62P/Can-77
62Salada-57A
62Salada-57B
62Shirriff-57
62T-491
62T/bucks
62T/St-71
63Exh
63F-21
63J-28
63P-28
63Salada-55
63T-335
63T-4LL
64Kahn
64T-41M
64T-530
64T/Coins-130AS
64T/Coins-6
64T/S-54
64Wheat/St-47
65Kahn
65OldLond-36
65T-367
65T/E-31
65T/trans-33
66Bz-8
66OPC-65
66T-65
67Bz-8
67Kahn
67OPC-109M
67OPC/PI-24
67T-109M
67T-360
67T/PI-24
68Kahn
68T-495
69OPC-187
69T-187
78TCMA-125
78TCMA-165
Exh47

Wagner, Mark
75Clint
77T-490R
78T-598
80OPC-13
80T-29
81D-126
81F-478
81T-358
81T/Tr-852
82D-163
82F-333
82T-443
83D-268
83F-582
83T-144
84Cram/PCL-89
85T-581

Wagner, Paul
89Well/Puc-26

Wagner, Steve
78OrlTw

Wahl, Tim
88Beloi/GS-17
89Beloi/Star-24

Waid, Patrick
88SLCty-1
89SLCty-10F

Wainhouse, David
89B-358
89WPalm/Star-24

Waitkus, Ed
47TipTop
49B-142
49Eureka-151
49Lummis
50B-30
50Drake-12
51B-28
51BR-C9
51T/BB-51
52B-92
52T-158
52TipTop
54Esskay
55B-4
55Esskay
79TCMA-77
Exh47
PM10/Sm-191

Waits, M. Rick
75OkCty
76OPC-433
76SSPC-513
76T-433
77Ho-78
77Pep-16
77T-306
78OPC-191
78T-37
79Ho-35
79OPC-253
79T-484
80OPC-94
80T-168
81D-201
81F-396
81OPC-258
81T-697
82D-33
82F-382
82OPC-142
82T-573
82Wheat/Ind
83D-263
83F-422
83T-779
83T/X-123
83Wheat/Ind-32
84Nes/792-218
84T-218
85Cram/PCL-219
85D-368
85F-600
85T-59
86F-505
86T-614
86Vanco-27

Wakamatsu, Don
86Tampa-24
87Cedar-16
88Chatt/Best-12
89BirmB/Best-16
89BirmB/Pro-107

Wakana, Josh
83Tidew-25

Wakefield, Bill
62Pep/Tul
63Pep/Tul
64T-576R
65OPC-167
65T-167
66T-443
Exh47

Wakefield, Dick
47TipTop
48L-50
49B-91
50Remar
79TCMA-91

Wakefield, Tim
88Watertn/Puc-27
89Well/Puc-27

Walbeck, Matt
88CharWh/Best-1
89Peoria/Ko-15

Walberg, Bill
82Jacks-25

Walberg, George
(Rube)
32Orbit/un-57
33G-145
33G-183
R305
R313
V353-76
W517-41

Walbring, Larry
76Clint

Walden, Travis
88Clearw/Star-26

Waldenberger, Dave
89Idaho/Pro-2019

Walewander, James
86GlenF-23
87Toled-5
87Toled/TCMA-7
88Pep/T-32
88Score-571
88T-106
89D-415
89F-150
89Score-311
89T-467
89Toled/CMC-15
89Toled/Pro-770
89UD-454

Walgast, Ad
T3/Box-53

Walk, Bob
81D-393
81F-14
81T-494
81T/Tr-853
82BK/Lids-24
82Pol/Atl-43
82T-296
83D-401
83F-149
83Richm-10
83T-104
84Cram/PCL-141
85Cram/PCL-243
86D-430
86T/Tr-120T
87D-203
87F-623
87T-628
88D-514
88D/Best-269
88F-342
88Score-162
88T-349
89B-409
89D-172
89D/AS-58
89D/Best-145
89F-223
89OPC-151
89OPC-66
89Score-224
89Sf-34
89T-504
89T/St-123
89UD-438
90D-370
90F-482
90Score-21
90T-754
90UD-596

Walker, Albert
(Rube)
49Eureka-74
52T-319
53T-134
54T-153
55Gol/Dodg-30
55T-108
55T/DH-15
56T-333
57T-147
58Hires-74
58T-203
73OPC-257CO
73T-257C
74OPC-179CO
74T-179C
79TCMA-278
80BurlB-13
82Pol/Atl-54CO
83Pol/Atl-54
84Pol/Atl-54

Walker, Andy
79QuadC-20

Walker, Anthony
(Tony)
81Water-11
81Water-21
82Water-20
83DayBe-27
86F/Up-U123
86Pol/Ast-20
87F-71
87T-24

Walker, Bernie
87Cedar-25
88Chatt/Best-23
89Chatt/Best-20
89Chatt/GS-22
89SLAS-7

Walker, Cameron
(Cam)
84ElPas-22
86ElPas-23
87ElPas-18
87Wichi-25

Walker, Chico
81Pawtu-22
83Pawtu-24
84Pawtu-16
85IowaC-11
86IowaC-26
87Berg/Cubs-29
87D-539
87OPC-58
87T-695
88Edmon/Pro-561
89Syrac/CMC-23
89Syrac/Pro-792

Walker, Chris
88Batav/Pro-1677
89Clearw/Star-24

Walker, Clarence
(Tilly)
21Exh-181
D328-181
D329-183
D350/2-185
E120
E135-181
E254
M101/4-183
M101/5-185
V100
V61-6
W501-99
W515-7
W572
W575

Walker, Clifton
(Cliff)
85Bend/Cram-23
87Spart-16

Walker, Curtis
21Exh-182
E126-58

Walker, Darcy
86WinSal-27

Walker, Dennis
89Utica/Puc-26

Walker, Doak
52Wheat

Walker, Duane
80Indianap-26
81Indianap-21
82Indianap-6
83D-624
83F-606
83T-243
84D-325
84F-485

84F/St-41
84Nes/792-659
84T-659
85D-608
85F-554
85Leaf-52
85T-441
85T/St-52
86D-500
86F-574
86T-22
86Tucso-23
87Louvl-28
88Brist/Pro-1878
88Louvl-49
88Louvl/CMC-17
88Louvl/Pro-425
89Mia/Star/25-24

Walker, Ewart
(Dixie)
T207

Walker, Fred
(Dixie)
34DS-12
34G-39
35G-8E
35G-9E
39Exh
41DP-21
49Eureka-174
53T-190
55Hunter
61F-151
89Smok/Dodg-49
PM10/Sm-192
R346-45
V354-86

Walker, Frederick
15CJ-173
E254
E270/1

Walker, Gerald
(Gee)
33DH-41
34G-26
35BU-118
35G-8F
35G-9F
37OPC-110
38Wheat-4
41DP-135
41Wheat-10
R309/2
R313
R314
V300
V354-81
V355-48

Walker, Glenn
81Wausa-24
82LynnS-16
83SLCty-20
84Cram/PCL-187
86MidldA-25

Walker, Greg
80AppFx
81GlenF-16
83T/X-124
84D-609
84F-73
84Nes/792-518
84T-518
84TrueVal/WS-30
85Coke/WS-29
85D-366
85F-530
85OPC-244
85T-623
85T/St-236
86Coke/WS-29
86D-135
86F-219
86Jay's-19
86OPC-123
86S-174
86T-123
86T/St-293
87Coke/WS-17
87D-25DK
87D-59
87D/DKsuper-25
87D/OD-233
87F-508
87F/LL-42
87F/Mini-110
87Leaf-25DK
87OPC-302
87Seven-C15
87T-397
87T/St-291
88Coke/WS-29
88D-162
88D/Best-193
88F-411
88Leaf-86
88OPC-286
88Panini/St-56
88Score-93
88Sf-103
88T-764
88T/Big-105
88T/St-292
88T/UK-83
89Coke/WS-27
89D-135
89Panini/St-307
89Score-37
89Sf-19
89T-21TL
89T-408
89T/Big-4
89UD-231
90F-551
90Score-354
90T-33
90UD-350

Walker, Harry
48L-137
49B-130
49Eureka-75
50B-180
60T-468C
65T-438
66EH-3
66T-318
67T-448
67T/Test/PP-24MG
69T-633
70OPC-32MG
70T-32
71OPC-312MG
71T-312
72OPC-249
72T-249
79TCMA-261
89Pac/Leg-190
89Swell-34
Exh47
R346-39

Walker, Hugh
89AppFx/Pro-856
89B-127

Walker, J. Luke
66T-498R
67OPC-123R
67T-123R
68T-559R
69OPC-36
69T-36
70OPC-322
70T-322
71MLB/St-216
71OPC-534
71OPC-68LL
71T-534
71T-68LL
71T/S-21
72MB-353
72OPC-471
72T-471
73OPC-187
73T-187
74OPC-612
74T-612
74T/Tr-612T
75OPC-474
75T-474
75T/M-474

Walker, James
87Chatt/Best-5
88Calg/CMC-7
88Calg/Pro-791

Walker, Jerry
58T-113
59T-144
60T-399M
60T-540
60T/tatt
60T/tatt-52
60T/tatt-96
61T-85
62T-357
62T/bucks
62T/St-61
63Sugar-5
63T-413
64T-77

Walker, John
78LodiD
79LodiD-12
80Toled-9
81Toled-17

Walker, Keith
82Knoxv-7
83Syrac-12

Walker, Kurt
87Visal-8
88MidldA/GS-2

Walker, Larry
85Utica-16
86BurlEx-25
87Jaxvl-1
87SLAS-8
89Indi/CMC-23
89Indi/Pro-1239
90D-578
90F-363
90Score-631
90T-757
90UD-466

Walker, Lonnie
88LitFalls/Puc-14
89Clmbia/Best-27
89Clmbia/GS-26

Walker, Matt
86Clint-26
86Cram/PCL-186
87Everett-1

Walker, Mike
86Watertn-27
87Harrisbg-23
87Watlo-14
88Harris/Pro-850
88Wmspt/Pro-1310
89B-77
89ColSp/Pro-239

Walker, R. Tom
73OPC-41
73T-41
74OPC-193
74T-193
75OPC-627
75T-627
75T/M-627
76OPC-186
76T-186
77T-652
78Colum

Walker, Ray
88Martins/Star-32

Walker, Rich
88Batav/Pro-1681

Walker, Rod
89LittleSun-6

Walker, Steve
87SnBer-1
88BBCity/Star-24
89Memph/Best-23
89Memph/Pro-1196
89Memph/Star-23
89Star/Wax-46

Walker, William C.
29Exh/4-7
31Exh/4-7
E120
W575

Walker, William H.
33G-94
35BU-116
R313
V353-57

Walkup, James
39PB-150

Wall, Dave
81AppFx-27

Wall, Donne
89AubAs/Pro-2182

Wall, Murray
53T-217
58T-410
59T-42

Wall, Stan
76OPC-584
76T-584
77T-88

Wallace, Alex
85Anchora-30

Wallace, Brooks
81Tulsa-24

Wallace, Curtis
76Baton

Wallace, Dave
76OkCty
81VeroB-25
82VeroB-28
84Cram/PCL-245
86Albuq-26C

Wallace, Don
67T-367R

Wallace, Greg
86Miami-26

Wallace, Jim
49Remar

Wallace, Mike
74OPC-608R
74T-608R
75OPC-401
75T-401
75T/M-401
76SSPC-290
77T-539

Wallace, Roderick
(Bobby)
10Domino-120
11Helmar-66
12Sweet/Pin-56A
12Sweet/Pin-56B
14Piedmont/St-58
50Callahan
80SSPC/HOF
E107
E270/1
E90/1
E92
M116
S74-37
T201
T202
T204
T205
T206
T207
WG2-48

Wallace, Tim
83StPet-15
84ArkTr-5
86ArkTr-25
86Louisvl-28
86Peoria-25
87WinSal-15
88WinSal/Star-21
89Boise/Pro-1994

Wallach, Tim
82D-140
82F-210
82Hygrade
82OPC-191
82T-191
83D-392
83F-299
83OPC-229
83Stuart-12
83T-552
83T/St-257
84D-421
84F-291
84Nes/792-232
84OPC-232
84Stuart-14
84T-232
84T/St-94
85D-87
85F-412
85Leaf-199
85OPC-3
85OPC/Post-6
85T-473
85T/St-87
86D-219
86D/AAS-25
86F-263
86F/Mini-56
86Leaf-97
86OPC-217
86Provigo-11
86S-123
86T-685
86T-703
86T/St-82
87D-179
87D/OD-88
87F-334
87Ho/St-5
87Leaf-61
87OPC-55
87RedFoley/St-117
87S-115M
87S-72
87T-55
87T/St-80
88D-222
88D/AS-59
88D/Best-258
88F-198
88F-C15
88F/AwardWin-44
88F/BB/AS-43
88F/BB/MVP-42
88F/Mini-91
88F/St-98
88F/WaxBox-C15
88Ho/Disc-7
88Jiffy-18
88KayBee-32
88Leaf-193
88Leaf-255CG
88Nestle-23
88OPC-94
88Panini/St-327
88RedFoley/St-94

88Score-70
88Sf-151
88T-399
88T-560
88T/Big-7
88T/Coins-59
88T/Gloss60-18
88T/Mini-58
88T/Revco-6
88T/St-85
88T/St/Backs-9
88T/UK-84
89B-362
89D-156
89D/Best-34
89F-395
89KMart/DT-25
89OPC-78
89Panini/St-122
89RedFoley/St-127
89Score-220
89Sf-114
89T-720
89T/Big-215
89T/St-70
89UD-102
90D-220
90F-364
90Score-192
90Sf-182
90T-370
90UD-273

Wallaesa, John
47TipTop

Wallenhaupt, Ron
85Water-16

Waller, Casey
88CapeCod/Sum-113

Waller, Elliott (Ty)
78StPet
79ArkTr-9
82F-607
82IowaC-13
82T-51R
84Cram/PCL-60
85Cram/PCL-64
86Tucso-24
87Tucso-6
88River/Cal-233
88River/Pro-1414
88Spoka/Pro-1923
89River/Cal-30CO

Waller, Kevin
80Cedar-25
82Madis-22

Waller, Reggie
89AubAs/Pro-2168

Wallin, Craig
89SoBend/GS-1

Wallin, Leslie
88WinHav/Star-25
89Lynch/Star-20

Walling, Denny
77SnJos-17
77T-473R
79T-553
80OPC-161
80T-306
81D-144
81F-66
81T-439
82D-496
82F-236
82T-147
83D-419
83F-469
83T-692
84D-641
84F-244
84Moth/Ast-19
84Nes/792-36
84T-36
84T/St-73
85D-527
85F-365
85Moth/Ast-5
85T-382
86D-136
86F-314
86Pol/Ast-7
86T-504
87D-554
87F-72
87Leaf-159
87Moth/Ast-13
87OPC-222
87Pol/Ast-12
87T-222
87T/St-33
88D-384
88D/Best-309
88F-458
88Leaf-224
88Moth/Ast-13
88OPC-131
88Panini/St-296
88Pol/Ast-23
88Score-145
88T-719
88T/St-31
89D-279
89F-465
89Score-49
89Smok/Cards-22
89T-196
89UD-327
90D-677
90F-263
90T-462

Walling, Kendall
86Cram/PCL-192
87QuadC-25

Wallis, Joe
76OPC-598R
76T-598R
77T-279
78T-614
79T-406
80T-562

Walls, R. Lee
53Mother-56
55B-82
57Kahn
57T-52
58T-66
59T-105
60Kahn
60L-111
60T-506
61P-119
61T-78
61T/St-60
62BB-56
62T-129
62T/St-160
63J-113
63P-113
63T-11
64T-411

Wallwork, Dave
86Penin-26TR
87Penin-18
88BirmB/Best-6
89BirmB/Best-25
89BirmB/Pro-96

Walraven, Randy
78DaytB

Walsh, Dave
84Syrac-21
86Knoxv-25
87Knoxv-19
89Albuq/CMC-10
89Albuq/Pro-70

Walsh, Ed
10Domino-121
11Helmar-18
12Sweet/Pin-14
14CJ-36
14Piedmont/St-59
15CJ-36
48Exh/HOF
49Leaf/Prem-8
50Callahan
60F-49
61F-83
63Bz/ATG-7
69Bz/Sm
72F/FFeat-23
80Laugh/FFeat-34
80SSPC/HOF
85Woolwth-35
88Utica/Puc-25
89HOF/St-77
BF2-19
D329-184
D350/2-187
E224
E270/1
E286
E300
E90/1
E90/3
E98
M101/4-184
M101/5-187
M116
S81-107
T201
T202
T205
T206
WG4-29
WG5-42
WG6-38

Walsh, James C.
15CJ-144
C46-20
D327
D328-182
E135-182

Walsh, Jay
83LynnP-28

Walsh, Jim
81QuadC-11
82QuadC-25
83MidldC-4

Walsh, Joseph
N172

Walter, Craig
85FtMyr-4

Walter, Gene
83Miami-5
84Beaum-9
85Cram/PCL-112
86D/Rook-47
86F-644M
86F/Up-U124
86T/Tr-121T
87D-511
87F-433
87T-248
87Tidew-27
87Tidew/TCMA-21
88D/Mets/Bk-NEW
88F-153
88Kahn/Mets-31
89T-758
89UD-604

Walterhouse, Dick
77Salem

Walters, Alfred
D328-183
E120
E135-183

Walters, Dan
86Ashvl-28
87Osceola-8
88ColAst/Best-12
89Wich/Roc-11C

Walters, Darryel
85Beloi-13
86Stockton-25
87ElPas-21
88Denver/CMC-23
88Denver/Pro-1255
89Denver/CMC-16
89Denver/Pro-54
89ElPas/GS-29

Walters, David
86Elmir-25
87Greens-26
88Lynch/Star-24
89NewBrit/Pro-614
89NewBrit/Star-20

Walters, Ken
60T-511
61P-122
61T-394
62T-328
63FrBauer-30
63T-534

Walters, Mike
80ElPas-22
81SLCty-13
82Spoka-9
82Toled-8
83Toled-10
84Nes/792-673
84T-673
85T-187
85Toled-11

Walters, Vic
79AppFx-24

Walters, William H. (Bucky)
37Exh/4-6
38Exh/4-6
39Exh
39PB-22
40PB-73
41DP-8
41DP-96
41PB-3
41Wheat
49Eureka-97
54JC-31
55Gol/Braves-29
55JC-31
89Pac/Leg-164
Exh47
R314
V355-61
W711/1
W711/2

Walthour, B. Jr.
33SK-31

Walthour, B. Sr.
33SK-7

Walton, Bruce
86Modesto-26
87Modesto-14
88Huntsvl/BK-25
89Tacom/CMC-8
89Tacom/Pro-1546

Walton, Danny
69Sunoco/Pin-18
70McDon-73
70OPC-134
70T-134
71K-22
71MLB/St-455
71OPC-281
71T-281
71T/Coins-88
73OPC-516
73T-516
78T-263
79Spoka-4

Walton, Jerome
87Peoria-20
88BBAmer-5
88EastLAS/Pro-29
88Peoria/Ko-30
88Pittsf/Pro-1374
89B-295
89Class/Up/2-156
89D/Best-172
89D/Rook-26
89F/Up-80
89Mara/Cubs-20
89Score/Mast-2
89Score/Tr-85
89Score/YS/II-36
89T/Tr-123T
89UD/Ext-765
90Class-34
90D-285
90D/Preview-9
90F-44
90F/WaxBox-C27
90Score-229
90Score/100Ris-2
90Sf-67
90T-464
90UD-345

Walton, Jim
73OPC-646CO
73T-646C
74T-99C

Walton, Reggie
75Lafay
79Spoka-9
80Spoka-21
81F-609
81Spoka-14
82Portl-22
82T-711

Walton, Rob
88CharlK-6
88CharlK/Pep-6

Wambsganss, Bill
25Exh-72
26Exh-112
27Exh-55
72Laugh/GF-49
88Conlon/4-29
D327
D328-184
D329-185
E120
E121/120
E121/80
E122
E135-184
E220
M101/4-185
V117-29
V61-31
W501-22
W575

Waner, Lloyd
28Yueng-59
29Exh/4-14
31Exh/4-14
33Exh/4-7
33G-164
34DS-16
34Exh/4-7
35BU-157
35BU-17
35G-1E
35G-3C
35G-4C
35G-5C
39PB-89
40PB-105
41DP-119
60F-78

61F-84
72F/FFeat-35
80Cram/Leg-24
80SSPC/HOF
83D/HOF-22M
85Woolwth-36
86Conlon/1-58
89HOF/St-42
89Pac/Leg-128
89Smok/Dodg-32
PR1-27
R300
R306
R310
R312/M
R314
R316
R328-13
R332-16M
R332-2
R423-110
V353-90
W502-59
W513-73
WG8-49

Waner, Paul
28Exh-27
28Yueng-45
29Exh/4-14
31Exh/4-14
32Orbit/un-58
33CJ/Pin-24
33Exh/4-7
33G-25
34DS-83
34Exh/4-7
34G-11
35Exh/4-7
35G-1E
35G-3C
35G-4C
35G-5C
36Exh/4-7
36G
37Exh/4-7
38Exh/4-7
38Wheat
39PB-112
40PB-104
41DP-16
50Callahan
60F-76
61F-85
72F/FFeat-24
80Cram/Leg-21
80SSPC/HOF
83D/HOF-22M
86Conlon/1-8
86S/Dec-15M
88Conlon/NatAS-23
89HOF/St-45
89Pac/Leg-127
R300
R305
R306
R308-201
R310
R312/M
R314
R315-A38
R315-B38
R316
R326-10A
R326-10B
R328-2
R332-16M
R337-421
R342-10
R423-111
V353-25
V354-67
V355-2
W502-45
W513-70
W517-34
WG8-50

Wanish, John
88Bakers/Cal-261
89StCath/Pro-2086

Wanz, Doug
81Vanco-3

Wapnick, Steve
88Myrtle/Pro-1166
89Duned/Star-22

Ward, Aaron
21Exh-183
25Exh-104
E120
E121/120
E121/80
E126-7
E220
V100
W501-25
W515-20
W572

Ward, Anthony
88StCath/Pro-2034
89Myrtle/Pro-1630

Ward, Chris
75OPC-587
75T-587
75T/M-587

Ward, Colby
85Anchora-31
86Cram/PCL-89
87PalmSp-14
88MidldA/GS-11
89Edmon/CMC-10
89Edmon/Pro-568

Ward, Colin
83BirmB-19
84Cram/PCL-21
85Cram/PCL-198
86F-645M
86Shrev-27
87Phoen-9

Ward, Dan
88PalmSp/Cal-95
88PalmSp/Pro-1442

Ward, Duane
83Durhm-25
86F/Up-U125
86Pol/Atl-48
87D-45RR
87Leaf-45RR
87OPC-153
87T-153
87Tor/Fire-33
87Tor/Fire-33
88D-567
88F-125
88OPC-128
88T-696
88Tor/Fire-31
89D-543
89D/Best-216
89F-246
89OPC-392
89Score-359
89Score/YS/II-13
89T-502
89Tor/Fire-31
89UD-551
90D-307
90F-95
90Score-439
90Sf-107
90T-28
90UD-653

Ward, Gary
77Tacom
79Toled-1
80T-669R
81D-594
81T-328R
82D-571
82F-562
82F/St-229
82T-612
83D-429
83D/AAS-18
83F-627
83T-517
83T/St-92
84D-192
84F-576
84F/X-124
84FunFood/Pin-95
84Nes/792-67
84OPC-67
84Rang-32
84T-67
84T/St-303
84T/X-126
85D-342
85F-572
85Leaf-70
85OPC-84
85Rang-32
85T-414
85T/St-353
86D-20
86D-98
86D/AAS-51
86D/DKsuper-20
86F-575
86F/Mini-113
86F/St-125
86Leaf-20DK
86OPC-105
86Rang-32
86S-197
86T-105
86T/St-239
87D-427
87D/OD-242
87F-140
87F/McCror-41
87F/RecSet-40
87F/U-U122
87Leaf-177
87OPC-218
87S-91
87T-762
87T/St-235
87T/Tr-125T
88D-251
88D/Y/Bk-251
88F-224
88OPC-235
88Panini/St-160
88RedFoley/St-95
88Score-157
88Sf-125
88T-235
88T/Big-195
88T/St-303
89F-273
89F/Up-33
89Mara/Tigers-32
89OPC-302
89Score-435
89T-302
89T/Big-206
89T/Tr-124T
89UD-98
90D-621
90F-618
90Score-513
90T-679

Ward, Greg
87Savan-8
88Reno/Cal-286

Ward, John Mont.
(Montgomery)
80SSPC/HOF
89Smok/Dodg-33
E223
N172
N28
N284
N300/unif
N338/2
N566-586
N566-587
WG1-45

Ward, John F.
(Jay)
61Union
64T-116R
65T-421R
85Cedar-27
86Vermont-23MG
88CLAS/Star-1
89Wmspt/Star-24

Ward, Joseph
C46-6
T201

Ward, Kevin
86Readg-25
87Maine/TCMA-22
87Readg-12
88Maine/CMC-22
88Maine/Pro-278
89Huntsvl/Best-22

Ward, Max
87FtLaud-12
88Colum/Pro-326

Ward, Pete
63T-324R
64T-85
64T/Coins-21
64T/S-33
64T/St-8
64T/SU
64T/tatt
65Bz-8
65OldLond-37
65OPC-215
65T-215
65T/E-64
65T/trans-71
66OPC-25
66T-25
66T/RO-2
67OPC-143M
67T-143M
67T-436
68OPC-33
68T-33
69Kelly/Pin-18
69MB-285
69MLB/St-35
69MLBPA/Pin-29
69OPC-155
69T-155
69T/decal
69T/S-11
69T/St-159
69Trans-20
70MLB/St-251
70T-659
71MLB/St-501
71OPC-667
71T-667
72MB-354
78TCMA-120
81Portl-1
Exh47
WG10-47
WG9-48

Ward, Preston
50B-231
53T-173
54B-139
54T-72
55B-27
55T-95
55T/DH-97
56T-328
57T-226
58T-450
59T-176
79TCMA-111

Ward, Turner
88Colum/CMC-19
88Colum/Pol-17

Warden, Jon
69T-632
88Domino-24

Wardle, Curt
83Visal/LF-18
85F/Up-U127
86F-600
86Maine-21
86T-303

Wardlow, Jeff
88Butte-17

Wardlow, Joe
89Gasto/Pro-998
89Gasto/Star-24
89Star/Wax-39

Wardlow, Mike
77Cedar

Ware, Derek
87Duned-28

Wares, Clyde E.
(Buzzy)
86Conlon/1-14M
W754

Warfel, Brian
87Elmir-9
87Elmir/Red-9
88Elmir-26
88WinHav/Star-26

Warhop, John
10Domino-122
11Helmar-49
12Sweet/Pin-38
T206
T207
T213/blue
T215/blue
T215/brown

Warneke, Lon
32Orbit/num-4
32Orbit/un-59
33CJ/Pin-25
33DL-16
33G-203
34Exh/4-3
35BU-186
35Exh/4-3
36Exh/4-3
36Wheat
37Exh/4-8
38Exh/4-8
38Wheat
39Exh
39PB-41
40PB-114
55B-299ump
88Conlon/NatAS-24
R300
R303/A
R305
R308-194
R312/M
R314
V355-100
W754
WG8-51

Warner, E.H.
N172

Warner, Fred
80Penin/B-5
80Penin/C-8

Warner, Harry
77T-113C

80Syrac-19MG
83Visal/LF-13
Warner, Jack D.
65T-354R
Warner, Jim
47Signal
47Sunbeam
Warner, John J.
(Jackie)
65T-517R
66T-553R
Warner, John Joseph
26Exh-96
E107
Warner, John R.
33G-178
Warren, Alan
88Oneon/Pro-2066
Warren, Charlie
77Wausa
Warren, Glen
89Everett/Star-29
Warren, Marty
86AppFx-28
Warren, Mike
84D-631
84F-461
84F-639IA
84Moth/A's-20
84Nes/792-338
84Nes/792-5HL
84T-338
84T-5
84T/St-288B
85D-278
85F-435
85Moth/A's-19
85T-197
86Omaha-28
89Reno/Cal-248
Warren, Randy
88Utica/Puc-12
89SoBend/GS-17
Warren, Raymond
82BurlR-12
Warren, Ron
86Elmir-26
Warren, Travis
87Clearw-27
Warstler, Harold
(Rabbit)
39PB-120
40PB-59
41G-21
R314
Warthen, Dan
76OPC-374
76SSPC-347
76T-374
77OPC-99
77T-391
79Portl-17
80Port-26
81Buffa-12
82AlexD-20
87Chatt/Best-2
88Calg/CMC-25
88Calg/Pro-789
89Calg/CMC-25
89Calg/Pro-523
Warwick, Carl
62J-161
62P-161
62P/Can-161
62Salada-160
62Shirriff-160
62T-202
63J-190
63P-190
63Pep
63T-333
64T-179
65T-357
66T-247
WG9-49
Warwick, Clint
86Geneva-11
Wasdell, James
41DP-19
Wasem, Jim
84Evrt/Cram-24
86CharRa-28A
86CharRa-28B
88Charl/Pro-1195
Washburn, Greg
70OPC-74R
70T-74R
Washburn, Ray
62T-19
63J-168
63P-168
63T-206
64T-332
65T-467
66T-399
67OPC-92
67T-92
68T-388
69T-415
70OPC-22
70T-22
Washington, Claudell
75OPC-647
75T-647
75T/M-647
76K-2
76OPC-189
76OPC-198LL
76SSPC-489
76T-189
76T-198LL
77Ho-86
77OPC-178
77T-405
77T/CS-50
78BK/R-19
78T-67
79OPC-298
79T-574
80K-34
80OPC-171
80T-322
81F-329
81Pol/Atl-18
81T-151
81T/Tr-854
82BK/Lids-25
82D-58
82F-449
82F/St-66
82OPC-32
82Pol/Atl-15
82T-126TL
82T-758
82T/St-22
83D-249
83F-150
83OPC-235
83Pol/Atl-15
83T-235
83T/St-216
84D-310
84F-192
84Nes/792-410
84OPC-42
84Pol/Atl-15
84T-294
84T-410
84T/St-32
85D-11
85D-310
85D/DKsuper-11
85F-342
85Ho/Braves-22
85Leaf-11DK
85OPC-166
85Pol/Atl-15
85T-540
85T/St-25
86D-287
86F-531
86F/Mini-107
86Leaf-164
86OPC-303
86Pol/Atl-15
86T-675
86T/St-39
86T/Tr-122T
87F-119
87Moth/A's-15
87T-15
88D-340
88D/Best-217
88D/Y/Bk-340
88F-225
88OPC-335
88Score-579
88T-335
88T/Big-178
88T/St-301
89B-52
89D-72
89D/Best-227
89D/Tr-46
89F-272
89F/Up-17
89OPC-185
89Score-211
89Score/Tr-10
89Sf-75
89T-185
89T/Tr-125T
89T/UK-81
89UD-310
89UD/Ext-794
90D-52
90F-146
90Score-298
90T-705
90UD-395
Washington, Glenn
86QuadC-31
87PalmSp-15
88PalmSp/Cal-111
88PalmSp/Pro-1455
Washington, Herb
75OPC-407
75T-407
75T/M-407
Washington, Keith
80Penin/B-9
80Penin/C-18
82Readg-19
83Readg-21
Washington, Kraig
89CharWh/Best-4
89CharWh/Pro-1752
Washington, LaRue
77Tucso
78Cr/PCL-18
80T-233
Washington, Lozando
76Cedar
Washington, Mal
75QuadC
76Clint
Washington, Randy
81Batav-24
82Watlo/B-26
82Watlo/C-25
83Watlo/LF-1
84BuffB-20
85Water-3
86Maine-22
87BuffB-12
88ColSp/CMC-22
88ColSp/Pro-1525
Washington, Ron
78Cr/PCL-16
79Tidew-9
80Toled-6
81Toled-18
82T/Tr-124T
83D-431
83F-626
83OPC-27
83T-458
84D-391
84F-577
84Nes/792-623
84OPC-268
84T-623
85D-391
85F-292
85T-329
86D-560
86F-409
86T-513
86Toled-23
87RochR-19
87RochR/TCMA-16
87T-169
88Gator-15
88T/Tr-125T
89D-468
89F-416
89Tucso/CMC-19
89Tucso/Pro-190
89UD-519
Washington, U.L.
78T-707R
79T-157
80T-508
81Coke
81D-460
81F-34
81OPC-26
81Pol/Royals-8
81T-26
82D-160
82F-424
82F/St-203
82OPC-329
82T-329
83D-490
83F-125
83OPC-67
83Pol/Royals-7
83T-687
84D-543
84F-361
84Nes/792-294
84OPC-294
84T/St-282
85D-521
85F-215
85F/Up-U128
85OPC/Post-4
85T-431
85T/Tr-128T
86D-498
86F-264
86OPC-113
86T-113
87Vanco-25
89Well/Puc-30
Washko, Patrick
77Watlo
Wasiak, Stan
77LodiD
78LodiD
79LodiD-14
81VeroB-27
83VeroB-28
85VeroB-26
86VeroB-27
Wasilewski, Kevin
86AubAs-25
87Ashvl-12
Wasilewski, Tom
86Ventura-26
87Shrev-21
Wasinger, Mark
84Beaum-17
85Beaum-19
86LasVegas-22
87LasVegas-27
88F-100
88Moth/Giants-23
88Phoen/CMC-17
88Phoen/Pro-54
88RedFoley/St-96
88Score-283
89Colum/CMC-22
89Colum/Pol-21
89Colum/Pro-738
Waslewski, Gary
69T-438
70T-607
71MLB/St-502
71OPC-277
71T-277
72OPC-108
72T-108
Wasley, Mel
40Hughes-18
47Sunbeam
Wassenaar, Rob
88QuadC/GS-25
89Visal/Cal-98
89Visal/Pro-1425
Watanabe, Curt
80BurlB-26
Watanabe, Masahito
87Miami-12
Waterfield, Bob
52Wheat
Wathan, John
77T-218
78T-343
79T-99
80T-547
81Coke
81D-221
81F-46
81OPC-157
81T-157
82D-86
82F-425
82OPC-383
82T-429
82T/St-192
83D-86
83F-126
83OPC-289
83Pol/Royals-8
83T-6M
83T-746
83T/St-195
83T/St-196
83T/St-78
84D-466
84F-362
84Nes/792-602
84OPC-72
84T-602
84T/St-284
85D-466
85F-216
85T-308
86D-496
86F-23
86Kitty/Disc-12
86T-128
87Omaha-3
88Smok/Royals-1MG
88T-534
89T-374MG
90T-789MG

Watkins, Bob C.
70OPC-227R
70T-227R
71MLB/St-93
Watkins, Bud
58Union
Watkins, Darren
87AppFx-12
Watkins, Dave
70OPC-168
70T-168
Watkins, George
34G-53
35Exh/4-6
Watkins, Jim
81Brist-22
Watkins, Keith
88Modesto/Cal-71
Watkins, Tim
87Beloi-21
88Denver/CMC-6
88Denver/Pro-1265
89Denver/CMC-2
89Denver/Pro-41
89ElPas/GS-15
Watkins, Troy
86FtMyr-27
Watkins, William H.
N172
Watlington, Julius
52Park-83
Watson, Bob
69T-562
70OPC-407
70T-407
71MLB/St-94
71OPC-222
71T-222
72OPC-355
72T-355
72T/Cloth-32
73OPC-110
73T-110
74K-11
74OPC-370
74T-370
74T/DE-69
74T/St-39
75Ho-53
75K-6
75OPC-227
75T-227
75T/M-227
76Crane-66
76Ho-5
76Ho/Twink-5
76K-27
76MSA/Disc
76OPC-20
76SSPC-60
76T-20
77Ho-39
77T-540
77T/CS-51
78BK/A-12
78Ho-28
78OPC-107
78T-330
78Wiffle/Discs-77
79OPC-60
79T-130
80OPC-250
80T-480
81D-225
81Drake-28
81F-93
81OPC-208
81T-690
81T/HT
82BK/Lids-26
82D-108
82F-54
82OPC-275
82Pol/Atl-8
82T-275
82T/Tr-125T
83D-551
83F-151
83Pol/Atl-8
83T-572
84F-193
84Nes/792-739
84Pol/Atl-8
84T-739
85OPC-51
85T-51
86Moth/Ast-13
Watson, D.J.
87AppFx-5
Watson, Dave
89Princet/Star-23
Watson, Dejon
86FtMyr-28
88BBCity/Star-25
Watson, Frankie
88Eugene/Best-28
Watson, John Reeves
E120
W573
Watson, Milton
W514-77
Watson, Phil
77Ashev
Watson, Preston
89BurlB/Pro-1604
89BurlB/Star-22
Watson, Steve
76Cedar
83Tampa-25
Watt, Eddie
66T-442R
67T-271
68OPC-186
68T-186
69T-652
70OPC-497
70T-497
71OPC-122
71T-122
72MB-355
72OPC-128
72T-128
73JP
73OPC-362
73T-362
74OPC-534
74T-534
74T/Tr-534T
75OPC-374
75T-374
75T/M-374
86Tucso-25C
87Tucso-22
88Tucso-23
88Tucso/CMC-25
88Tucso/Pro-184
89Tucso/Pro-204
Watters, Mike
86Albuq-27
87Calgary-2
88Calg/CMC-23
88Calg/Pro-798
Watts, Bob
87Duned-3
88Duned/Star-20
89Beloi/Star-25
Watts, Brian
77Spart
Watts, Harry
63Pep/Tul
Watts, Len
86Readg-26
87Maine-3
87Maine/TCMA-20
Waugh, James
53T-178
Wauner
E254
Way, Ron
89Well/Puc-28
Wayne, Gary
86WPalm-27
87Jaxvl-22
88Indi/Pro-508
89D/Rook-27
89Score/Tr-91
90D-318
90F-387
90Score-527
90Score/100Ris-15
90T-348
90UD-372
Waznik, Allan J.
87Idaho-13
88Sumter/Pro-407
89BurlB/Pro-1612
89BurlB/Star-23
Wearing, Melvin
89Erie/Star-25
Weatherford, Brant
86Tampa-25
Weatherford, Joel
83Beloi/LF-29
Weatherly, Roy
(Stormy)
39PB-152
40PB-49
41PB-17
44Yank/St-28
Weathers, David
88StCath/Pro-2023
89Myrtle/Pro-1475
Weathers, Steven M.
75Tucso-2
76Tucso-2
77SnJos-12
Weathersby, Earl
(Tex)
28Exh/PCL-30
Weaver, D. Floyd
65T-546R
66T-231
71OPC-227
71T-227
78TCMA-176
Weaver, Earl
69T-516
70OPC-148MG
70T-148
71OPC-477MG
71T-477
72OPC-323MG
72T-323
73JP
73OPC-136MG
73T-136MG
74OPC-306MG
74T-306MG
75OPC-117MG
75T-117MG
75T/M-117MG
76T-73MG
77T-546MG
78T-211
79T-689MG
80T-404
81D-356
81F-178
81T-661MG
82D-27
83T-426
85T/Tr-129T
86T-321MG
87T-568MG
89Pac/Leg-179
89Swell-98
Weaver, George
(Buck)
73F/Wild-11
87Conlon/2-28
88Pac/8Men-107
88Pac/8Men-12
88Pac/8Men-33
88Pac/8Men-34
88Pac/8Men-40
88Pac/8Men-48M
88Pac/8Men-63
88Pac/8Men-7
88Pac/8Men-71
BF2-20
D328-185
D329-186
D350/2-188
E135-185
M101/4-186
M101/5-188
T207
W514-91
Weaver, James B.
(Jim)
68T-328R
69OPC-134
69T-134
Weaver, James D.
(Jim)
R312/M
W711/1
Weaver, James
83Orlan-3
84Toled-13
86Maine-23
87Calgary-3
88Tucso-24
88Tucso/CMC-21
88Tucso/Pro-172
89Vanco/CMC-14
89Vanco/Pro-583
Weaver, Monte
33G-111
35G-1C
35G-2C
35G-6C
35G-7C
Weaver, Roger
80Evans-1
81Evans-10
81T-626R
82Richm-9
Weaver, Trent
89Medford/Best-16
Weaver, William B.
N172
Webb, Ben
87Watertn-1
88Salem/Star-23
89Harris/Pro-311
89Harris/Star-21
Webb, Chuck
88Wausa/Feder-19
88Wausa/GS-19
Webb, Cleon Earl
D322
Webb, Dennis
81QuadC-9
Webb, Earl W.
(Billy)
31Exh/4-18
33Exh/4-9
35BU-98M
85Woolwth-37
87Conlon/2-25
Webb, Hank
73OPC-610R
73T-610R
75IntAS/TCMA-24
75OPC-615R
75T-615R
75T/M-615R
76OPC-442
76SSPC-553
76T-442
78Cr/PCL-77
Webb, James
(Skeeter)
No Cards.
Webb, Marvin
75Water
Webb, Sam
49Eureka-125
Webber, Steve
89Brist/Star-30
Weber, Charles
(Bill)
N172
Weber, Pete
87BuffB-29
Weber, Todd
88Ashvl/Pro-1078
Weber, Weston
86Cram/PCL-65
87Madis-11
88Modesto-15
89Huntsvl/Best-13
89Modesto/Ch-18
Webster, Casey
86Watlo-30
87Kinston-13
88EastLAS/Pro-43
88Wmspt/Pro-1317
89Canton/Best-5
89Canton/Pro-1318
89Canton/Star-23
Webster, Lenny
86Kenosha-25
87Kenosha-20
88Keno/Pro-1392
88MidwLAS/GS-31
89Visal/Cal-110
89Visal/Pro-1442
90Score-638
Webster, Mike
89Eugene/Best-2
Webster, Mitch
78Clint
80Syrac-12
82Syrac-23
83Syrac-25
84Tor/Fire-31
85Tor/Fire-31
86D-523
86F-265
86Leaf-253
86OPC-218
86Provigo-5
86T-629
87D-335
87D/OD-86
87F-335
87F/AwardWin-41
87F/Mini-111
87OPC-263
87S-177
87T-442
87T/St-82
88Berg/Cubs-28
88D-257
88D/Best-292
88F-199
88F/St-99
88Ho/Disc-1
88Leaf-198
88OPC-138
88Panini/St-331
88RedFoley/St-97
88Score-345
88Sf-105
88T-138
88T/Big-150
89B-296
89D-459

89D/Best-261
89F-442
89Mara/Cubs-33
89OPC-36
89Panini/St-61
89Score-71
89Sf-67
89T-36
89UD-65
90D-137
90F-45
90Score-85
90T-502
90UD-153

Webster, Ramon
67T-603R
68OPC-164
68T-164
69T-618
72MB-356
75Tucso-6

Webster, Ray G.
59T-531
60T-452

Webster, Rich
82Lynch-21

Webster, Rudy
86Cram/PCL-127
87Wausa-25
88Wausa/Feder-17
88Wausa/GS-17

Weck, Steve
85IowaC-31

Wedell, James R.
33SK-26

Wedge, Eric
88CapeCod/Sum-51
89Elmir/Puc-32

Wedvick, Jeff
86Jamestn-28
87BurlEx-16

Weeber, Mike
75Dubuq

Weekly, Johnny
62T-204
64T-256
89Smok/Ast-26

Weeks, Thomas
87Oneon-13
88FtLaud/Star-24
89PrWill/Star-24

Weems, Danny
86Sumter-29
87CharWh-13
88CLAS/Star-39
88Durhm/Star-23
89Greenv/Pro-1157
89Greenv/Star-24
89Greenvl/Best-13

Weese, Dean
88Hamil/Pro-1744
89Savan/Pro-348

Weese, Gary
75SnAnt
76Wmspt

Wegener, Mike
69Fud's-13
69T-284R
70OPC-193
70T-193
71OPC-608
71T-608
76Phoen
77Phoen

Wegman, Bill
82Beloi-4
85Cram/PCL-216
86D-490
86Pol/Brew-46
86T/Tr-123T
87D-109
87F-360
87T-179
88D-151
88D/Best-320
88F-177
88OPC-84
88Panini/St-119
88Pol/Brew-46
88Score-296
88T-538
88T/Big-244
88T/St-200
89B-135
89D-293
89F-199
89Gard-9
89OPC-354
89Pol/Brew-46
89Score-335
89Score/YS/II-9
89T-768
89UD-445
90Score-188
90T-333
90UD-629

Wehmeier, Herm
48B-46
49B-51
49Eureka-98
50B-27
51B-144
51FB
51T/BB-47
52B-150
52T-80
53B/Col-23
53T-110
54T-162
55T-29
55T/DH-131
56T-78
56T/Pin-22P
57T-81
58T-248
59T-421
79TCMA-126
Exh47

Wehner, John
88Watertn/Puc-28
89Salem/Star-24

Wehrmeister, Dave
77T-472R
80Colum-25
81Colum-23
82Colum-11
82Colum/Pol-28
82T-694
83Colum-6
84Cram/PCL-195
85BuffB-26
86BuffB-23
86F-220

Weibel, Randy
83Clint/LF-27

Weidie, Stuart
86Elmir-27
87WinHav-12
88Lynch/Star-25
89Lynch/Star-21

Weidman, George
N172

Weiermiller, Mike
82Wisco-4

Weigel, Ralph
48L-86

Weighaus, Thomas
82Wichi-20

Weik, Dick
54T-224

Weiland, Robert
34G-67
35G-8C
35G-9C

Weimer, Jacob
T206
WG3-50

Weimerskirch, Mike
88CapeCod/Sum-96

Weinberger, Gary
86Jaxvl/TCMA-17
87Jaxvl-10

Weinbrecht, Mark
80Elmir-13

Weinheimer, Wayne
88Wythe/Pro-1977
89CharWh/Best-1
89CharWh/Pro-1751

Weinstein, Bobby
55Gol/Giants-28bb

Weintraub, Phil
37Exh/4-4
V355-135

Weir, Jim
82Clint-29
83Clint/LF-5

Weis, A.J.
25Exh-24

Weis, Al
63T-537R
64T-168
65T-516
66OPC-66
66T-66
67T-556
68T-313
69MB-286
69T-269
70MLB/St-84
70OPC-498
70T-498
70Trans/M-21
71MLB/St-168
71OPC-751
71T-751
72MB-357

Weisman
E254

Weisman, Skip
83Ander-3
89Clmbia/GS-4

Weiss, Gary
80Albuq-13
81Albuq/TCMA-19
81F-130

Weiss, Jeff
87Durhm-3

Weiss, Walt
86Madis-26
86Madis/Pol-22
88D/A's/Bk-NEW
88D/Rook-18
88F-652
88F/Mini-49
88F/U-U56
88Modesto-34
88Moth/A's-11
88Score/Tr-102T
88T/Big-263
88T/Tr-126T
89B-196
89Bz-22
89Class-68
89D-446
89D/Best-155
89D/GrandSlam-3
89F-24
89F/BBMVP's-42
89F/Superstar-42
89F/WS-10
89KMart/DT-4
89Moth/A's-8
89Moth/ROY's-3
89Moth/ROY's-4M
89OPC-316
89Panini/St-412
89Panini/St-478
89Score-165
89Score/HotRk-95
89Score/YS/I-20
89Sf-116
89T-316
89T-639TL
89T/Big-305
89T/Coins-31
89T/Gloss60-50
89T/JumboR-21
89T/St-168
89T/St-326
89T/UK-82
89Tacom/Pro-1538
89ToysRUs-32
89UD-374
89UD-660ROY
89Woolwth-5
90Class-46
90D-67
90F-22
90Score-110
90Sf-74
90T-165
90UD-542

Weissman, Craig
81QuadC-26
82QuadC-13
86GlenF-24
87ArkTr-17
89ArkTr/GS-24

Weissmuller, John
33SK-21

Welaj, Johnny
V362-8

Welaj, Lou
V362-40

Welborn, Frank
86Jamestn-29

Welborn, Sam
77Spart
80LynnS-21
81Spoka-4
82SLCty-21
83Tucso-10

Welborn, Todd
85LitFalls-12
86LitFalls-29
87Columbia-29
88Jacks/GS-16
89Jacks/GS-7

Welborn, Tony
87BurlEx-4
88WPalm/Star-26

Welch
L1-132

Welch, Bryce
89Everett/Star-32

Welch, Curt
N172
N172/BC
N284/StL
N338/2
N370
N403
Scrapps

Welch, Dan
89Martins/Star-33

Welch, Doug
89Geneva/Pro-1864

Welch, Frank
25Exh-112
E120

Welch, John V.
33G-93
V353-56

Welch, Michael
(Mickey)
80SSPC/HOF
E223
N172
N338/2
N403
N690/2

Welch, Robert
(Bob)
78Cr/PCL-26
79T-318
80Pol/Dodg-35
80T-146
81D-178
81F-120
81OPC-357
81Pol/Dodg-35
81T-624
81T/HT
82D-75
82F-28
82Pol/Dodg
82Pol/Dodg-35
82T-82
83D-410
83F-225
83OPC-288
83Pol/Dodg-35
83T-454
84D-153
84F-116
84Nes/792-306TL
84Nes/792-722
84OPC-227
84Pol/Dodg-35
84T-722
85D-372
85F-388
85OPC-291
85T-291
86D-459
86F-146
86Leaf-223
86Pol/Dodg-35
86S-198
86T-549
86T/Mini-48
87D-475
87F-459
87F/LL-43
87F/St-121
87Moth/Dodg-9
87OPC-328
87Pol/Dodg-18
87Smok/Dodg-37
87T-328
88D-24DK
88D-253
88D/A's/Bk-NEW
88D/Best-134
88D/DKsuper-24DK
88F-529
88F/Mini-50
88F/U-U57
88Leaf-24DK
88Moth/A's-9
88OPC-118
88Panini/St-305
88RedFoley/St-98
88Score-510
88Score/Tr-15T
88Sf-167
88T-118
88T/Mini-55
88T/Revco-15
88T/St-73
88T/Tr-127T
89B-186
89Class-91
89D-332
89D/Best-267
89F-25
89Moth/A's-9
89Panini/St-416
89Score-308
89Score/HotSt-89

89Sf-91
89Smok/Dodg-92
89T-605
89T/St-166
89UD-191
90D-332
90F-23
90Score-159
90Sf-35
90T-475
90UD-251

Welchel, Don
81RochR-18
82RochR-8
84RochR-14
85RochR-23
86OKCty-24
88Omaha/Pro-1511

Weldin, David
89Helena/SP-21

Weleno, Doug
83MidldC-8

Welish, Scott
89CharRa/Pro-988
89Spoka/SP-16

Welke, Tim
88Umpire-55
89Umpires-53

Wellman, Bob
52Park-95
52T-41
79Jacks-6MG

Wellman, Brad
84D-265
84F-386
84Nes/792-109
84T-109
85F-623
85Moth/Giants-26
85T-409
86D-431
86F-553
86Moth/Giants-22
86OPC-41
86T-41
87Albuq/Pol-23
88Smok/Royals-24
89D-380
89Score-504

Wellman, Phil
86Durhm-27
87Harrisbg-7
88Pulas/Pro-1748C
89Pulas/Pro-1901

Wells
C46-56

Wells, David
86Ventura-27
87Syrac/TCMA-9
88D-640
88D/Best-311
88D/Rook-26
88F/U-U69
88T/Tr-128T
88Tor/Fire-36
89D-307
89D/Best-328
89F-247
89OPC-259
89T-567
89T/JumboR-22
89Tor/Fire-36
90D-425
90F-96
90Score-491
90T-229
90UD-30

Wells, Ed
34G-73

Wells, Frank
N172

Wells, Greg
(Boomer)
78Duned
79Syrac-1
80Syrac-14
81Syrac-16
82OPC-203R
82T-203R
82Toled-17

Wells, Jacob
N172

Wells, Leo
47Sunbeam

Wells, Terry
86Ashvl-29
87Osceola-1
88ColAst/Best-3
89ColMud/Pro-144
89ColMud/Star-23

Wells, Willie
74Laugh/Black-13
88Conlon/NegAS-11

Welmaker, Ray
52Mother-37

Welsh, Chris
79Colum-24
80Colum-3
82D-44
82F-584
82T-376
83D-94
83F-374
83OPC-118
83T-118
83T/X-125
84D-498
84F-292
84Indianap-4
85Rang-41
86D-464
86F-576
86T-52
86TexGold-45
87F-217
87T-592

Welsh, Jimmy D.
29Exh/4-10
R316

Wendell, Steve
88Pulas/Pro-1755
89BurlB/Pro-1616
89BurlB/Star-24

Wendelstedt, Harry
88Umpire-6
89Umpires-4

Wendlandt, Terry
84Omaha-30
85Omaha-5

Wendler, Doc
55Gol/Dodg-31

Wendt, Glenn
78Watlo

Wengert, Bill
88GreatF-17
89Bakers/Cal-188

Wenrick, Bill
88Boise/Pro-1623
88SLCty-26

Wenrick, John
88LitFalls/Puc-23
89Clmbia/Best-17
89Clmbia/GS-27

Wensloff, Charles
44Yank/St-29
47TipTop

Wenson, Paul
87Lakel-25
88GlenF/Pro-921
89Toled/CMC-8
89Toled/Pro-780

Wentz, Keith
86Cram/PCL-75

Wenz, Fred
69T-628R
71OPC-92
71T-92

Werber, Billy
34DS-61
34G-75
35Exh/4-9
35G-8G
35G-9G
36G
37Exh/4-14
38Exh/4-14
38G-259
38G-283
41DP-10
88Conlon/5-30
R313
R314
W711/1
W711/2

Werd, Norm
75SnAnt

Werhas, John
64T-456R
65T-453R
67T-514

Werle, William
48Sommer-18
49Eureka-175
50B-87
51B-64
51FB
51T/RB-33
52B-248
52T-73
53T-170
54T-144
61Union
PM10/Sm-193

Werley, Jamie
82Colum-10
82Colum/Pol-15

Werner, Dave
89Erie/Star-29

Werner, Don
76Indianap-17
77Indianap-8
78T-702R
79Indianap-22
83D-593
83OKCty-18
83T-504
84IowaC-16
86OKCty-25
87OKCty-5
88OkCty/CMC-21
88OkCty/Pro-37
89James/Pro-2150

Wernig, Pat
88Madis-25
88MidwLAS/GS-52
89Huntsvl/Best-23

Werrick, Joe
N172

Wert, Don
62T-299
64T-19
65OPC-271
65T-271
66T-253
67T-511
68OPC-178
68T-178
69MB-287
69T-443
69T/St-180
70OPC-33
70T-33
71MLB/St-552
71OPC-307
71T-307
72MB-358
78TCMA-163
88Domino-25

Werth, Dennis
78Cr/PCL-92
79Colum-10
81D-466
81F-102
81Louvl-22
81T-424R
82F-55
82T-154
82T/Tr-126T
84Louvl-30

Wertz, Vic
49B-164
50B-9
51B-176
51T/BB-40
52B-39
52BR
52RM-AL22
52StarCal/L-72D
52T-244
53B/Col-2
53T-142
54B-21
54Esskay
55B-40
55Gol/Ind-29
55RM-AL13
55Salem
56T-300
57Swift-6
57T-78
58T-170
59T-500
60T-111
61P-49
61T-173M
61T-340
61T/St-118
62Salada-60
62Shirriff-60
62T-481
63T-348
78TCMA-227
79TCMA-45
Exh47

Wesley, Tom
81Cedar-15

Wesolowski, Al
78Newar

Wessel, Troy
89James/Pro-2139

Wessinger, Jim
79Savan-26
80Richm-21

West, Bobby
89Princet/Star-24

West, Dave
84LitFalls-24
86Lynch-25
87TexLgAS-29
88AAA/Pro-41
88Tidew/CANDL-28
88Tidew/CMC-2
88Tidew/Pro-1592
89Class-134
89D-41RR
89F-51
89Kahn/Mets-46
89Score-650
89Score/YS/I-32
89Sf-45
89T-787
89Tidew/CMC-7
89Tidew/Pro-1973
89ToysRUs-33
89UD-7
90Class-68
90D-387
90F-388
90Score-573
90T-357
90UD-15

West, Joe
88Umpire-36
89Umpires-34

West, Matt
83Durhm-26
85Richm-10
86Richm-25
87Richm/TCMA-8
88Calg/CMC-8
88Calg/Pro-788
89Pulas/Pro-1902

West, Milton
N172

West, Reggie
84Cram/PCL-116
85Cram/PCL-8

West, Samuel
33G-166
35G-1F
35G-3D
35G-5D
35G-6D
36Exh/4-15
37Exh/4-15
37OPC-129
38Exh/4-15
39PB-31
40PB-22
74Laugh/ASG-40
R310
R313
V300

West, Tom
86DayBe-29
86FSLAS-49

West, W. Max
39PB-149
40PB-57
41DP-43
41PB-2
52Mother-10
53Mother-19

Westbrock, Mike
84LitFalls-3
86Lynch-26
88CLAS/Star-40
88Kinston/Star-23
89Reno/Cal-251

Westbrooks, Elanis
88Clint/Pro-716
89SanJose/Best-13
89SanJose/Cal-225
89SanJose/Pro-435
89SanJose/Star-25

Westermann, Scott
88Greens/Pro-1565

Westfall, Fred
76Wausa

Westlake, James
T206

Westlake, Wally
46Remar-8
49B-45
49Eureka-176
50B-69
51T/RB-27
52BR
52NTea
52StarCal/L-81B
52T-38
53T-192
54DanDee
54T-92
55Gol/Ind-30
55Salem
55T-102
55T/DH-13
56T-81

Exh47
Westmoreland, Claude
78Cr/PCL-21
79Albuq-21
80Albuq-11
Weston, Mickey
85Lynch-6
86Jacks/TCMA-10
88Jacks/GS-22
89RochR/CMC-6
89RochR/Pro-1638
90Score-616
90T-377
90UD-683
Weston, Tim
88Oneon/Pro-2065
89Albany/Best-29
89Albany/Pro-323
Westrope, Jack
33SK-39: jockey
Westrum, Wes
49Eureka-126
51B-161
51FB
51T/RB-37
52B-74
52BR
52Coke
52RM-NL26
52T-75
52TipTop
53RM-NL20
54B-25
54NYJour
54T-180
55B-141
55Gol/Giants-29
56T-156
57T-323
60T-469C
66T-341
67T-593
75OPC-216MG
75T-216MG
75T/M-216MG
76SSPC-113
79TCMA-46
Exh47
R423-115
Wetherby, Jeff
86Sumter-30
87Greenv/Bst-21
88Richm-22
88Richm/CMC-16
88Richm/Pro-9
89Richm/CMC-16
89Richm/Ko-22
89Richm/Pro-840
90Score-540
90Score/100Ris-44
90T-142
90UD-611
Wetteland, John
86Bakers-28
87VeroB-1
88BBAmer-28
88SnAnt/Best-21
88TexLgAS/GS-7
89Albuq/CMC-11
89Albuq/Pro-63
89Score/Tr-90
90Class-110
90D-671
90F-411
90Score-388
90Score/100Ris-25
90T-631
90UD-377
Wetzel, Tom
84Evrt/Cram-29
Wever, Stefan
82Nashv-27
83Colum-10
Wex, Gary
83Albany-8
Weyer, Lee
88Umpire-2
89Umpires-62
Weyhing, August
N172
Weyhing, John
N172
Whalen, Mike
84Newar-12
Whaley, Scott Lee
84Madis/Pol-5
85Huntsvl/BK-23
85Madis-3
85Madis/Pol-24
Whaling, Albert
15CJ-163
Whalley, Jarrell
77Spart
Wheat, Danny
83OKCty-24
85Rang-tr
86Rang-tr
Wheat, Leroy
54T-244
Wheat, Zachary D.
10Domino-123
11Helmar-89
12Sweet/Pin-78
12Sweet/Pin-78A
14CJ-52
14Piedmont/St-60
15CJ-52
21Exh-184
25Exh-16
26Exh-16
27Exh-56
60F-12
61F-1M
61F-86
80SSPC/HOF
89Smok/Dodg-34
D327
D328-187
D329-188
D350/2-186
E120
E121/120
E121/80
E122
E135-187
E220
E270/1
M101/4-188
M101/5-186
S74-57
T201
T202
T205
T206
T207
T213/blue
T215/brown
V100
V61-117
W501-97
W514-110
W515-56
W572
W573
W575
WG5-43
WG6-39
Wheatcroft, Bob
89Bluef/Star-28
Wheeler
C46-51
Wheeler, Bradley
88ElPas/Best-18
Wheeler, Ef
75AppFx
Wheeler, Ralph
78Duned
Wheeler, Rocket
85Kingst-25
86Syrac-26CO
87Myrtle-19
Wheeler, Rodney
86Clearw-24
Wheeler, Tim
82AlexD-18
82Buffa-9
83LynnP-9
84Cram/PCL-140
Wheelock, Gary
77T-493R
78SnJos-8
78T-596
79Spoka-17
80Spoka-17
87OKCty-2
Wheelock, Warren
N172
Wherry, Cliff
83Tucso-18
84OKCty-4
Whipple, Jack
45Centen-27
Whisenant, Pete
57T-373
58T-466
59T-14
60T-424
61Peters-11
61T-201
61T/St-187
83Albany-20
Whisenton, Larry
78Richm
79Richm-4
79T-715R
80Richm-4
81Richm-6
82BK/Lids-27
82Pol/Atl-28
83D-501
83F-152
83Richm-22
83T-544
84Richm-5
Whisman, Rhett
82Wisco-27
Whistler, Randy
80Ander-19
Whitacre
N172
Whitaker, Darrell
85BurlR-24
86Salem-28
87Gasto-26
88OkCty/CMC-11
88OkCty/Pro-43
88Tulsa-6
89OkCty/CMC-10
89OkCty/Pro-1516
Whitaker, Lou
78BK/T-13
78T-704R
79Ho-117
79OPC-55
79T-123
80OPC-187
80T-358
81Coke
81D-365
81F-463
81OPC-234
81T-234
82D-454
82F-284
82F/St-156
82OPC-39
82T-39
82T/St-187
83D-333
83F-348
83OPC-66
83T-509
83T/St-65
84D-227
84D/AAS-4
84F-92
84F/St-13
84F/St-30
84FunFood/Pin-78
84MiltBrad-28
84Nes/792-398AS
84Nes/792-666TL
84Nes/792-695
84Nestle/DT-2
84OPC-181AS
84OPC-211
84Seven-16C
84T-398
84T-695
84T/Gloss40-30
84T/St-196
84T/St-267
84T/St/Box-1
85Cain's-19
85D-293
85D-5
85D/AAS-42
85D/DKsuper-5
85F-24
85GenMills-24
85Leaf-5DK
85OPC-108
85Seven-16S
85Seven-1D
85T-480
85T/Gloss22-14
85T/St-183
85T/St-261
85Wendy-21
86Cain's-20
86D-49
86D/AAS-11
86D/PopUp-11
86F-242
86F/LimEd-44
86F/Mini-51
86F/St-126
86Leaf-33
86OPC-20
86S-48
86S-74M
86S/Dec-73M
86S/Rook-48M
86T-20
86T/Gloss22-3
86T/St-156
86T/St-272
86TrueVal-25
87Cain's-8
87Coke/Tigers-16
87D-107
87D/AAS-3
87D/OD-218
87D/PopUp-3
87F-168
87F/Mini-112
87F/RecSet-41
87F/St-122
87Ho/St-23
87Jiffy-11
87Leaf-78
87OPC-106
87RedFoley/St-88
87S-112M
87S-137
87Seven-DT12
87T-661
87T/Gloss22-14
87T/Gloss60-7
87T/St-153
87T/St-267
88D-173
88D/Best-315
88F-75
88Leaf-169
88OPC-179
88Panini/St-443IA
88Panini/St-92
88Pep/T-1
88Pol/T-14
88Score-56
88Sf-30
88T-770
88T/Big-99
88T/Mini-13
88T/St-270
88T/St/Backs-38
89B-103
89Class/Up/2-188
89D-298
89D/Best-35
89F-151
89Mara/Tigers-1
89OPC-320
89Panini/St-341
89Pol/Tigers-1
89Score-230
89Sf-18
89T-320
89T/Big-22
89T/Coins-57
89T/St-282
89T/St/Backs-6
89T/UK-83
89UD-451
90D-16DK
90D-298
90F-619
90Score-75
90Score/100St-71
90Sf-103
90T-280
90UD-327
90UD-41TC
Whitaker, Steve
67T-277
68T-383
69MLB/St-63
69OPC-71
69T-71
69T/St-189
70OPC-496
70T-496
Whitaker, William
N172
Whitby, William
67T-486R
White, Al
80Penin/B-16
80Penin/C-22
White, Bill
82Danvi-6
83VeroB-21
89Geneva/Pro-1884
White, Bill D.
59T-359
60T-355
60T/tatt
60T/tatt-53
61P-176
61T-232
61T-451M
61T/Dice-18
61T/St-96
62Bz
62J-158
62P-158
62P/Can-158
62Salada-115

62Shirriff-115
62T-14
62T/bucks
62T/St-191
63Bz-28
63F-63
63J-158
63P-158
63T-1LL
63T-290
63T/SO
64T-11LL
64T-240
64T/Coins-141AS
64T/Coins-78
64T/St-10
64T/SU
64Wheat/St-48
65OPC-190
65T-190
65T/E-43
65T/trans-72
66Bz-23
66T-397
66T/RO
67Bz-23
67T-290
68Bz-4
68OPC-190
68T-190
69MB-288
69T-588
72MB-359
78TCMA-12

White, Chaney
78Laugh/Black-9

White, Charles
52Park-22
54JC-24
55Gol/Braves-30
55JC-24
55T-103
55T/DH-18

White, Charlie
89Sprin/Best-17

White, Craig
89GreatF-29

White, Darrin
89Helena/SP-25

White, Dave
79AppFx-5
86SLAS-19
87Hawai-4

White, Devon
82Danvi-21
83Peoria/LF-22
85MidldA-8
86Edmon-27
87Class/Up-140
87D-38RR
87D/OD-5
87D/Rook-8
87F-646M
87F/U-U123
87Leaf-38RR
87S/Rook-24
87Seven-W13
87Sf/Rook-10
87Smok/Cal-23
87T-139
88Class/Red-178
88D-283
88D-8DK
88D/Best-227
88D/DKsuper-8DK
88F-506
88F/Excit-44
88F/Mini-12
88Leaf-127
88Leaf-8DK
88OPC-192
88Panini/St-49
88RedFoley/St-99
88Score-212
88Score/YS/I-12
88Sf-99
88Smok/Angels-13
88T-192
88T/Big-145
88T/Coins-31
88T/Gloss60-29
88T/JumboR-5
88T/St-183
88T/St-313
88ToysRUs-33
89Ames-31
89B-54
89D-213
89D/Best-27
89F-489
89OPC-344
89Panini/St-297
89Score-323
89Sf-16
89T-602
89T/Big-122
89T/St-179
89UD-110
90Class-63
90D-226
90F-147
90Score-312
90Score/100St-68
90Sf-210
90T-65
90UD-129
90UD-5TC

White, Ernie
W754

White, Foley
T206

White, Frank
74OPC-604R
74T-604R
75OPC-569
75T-569
75T/M-569
76OPC-369
76SSPC-174
76T-369
77T-117
78T-248
79OPC-227
79T-439
80OPC-24
80T-45
81Coke
81D-340
81F-44
81F/St-97
81K-34
81OPC-330
81Pol/Royals-9
81T-330
81T/So-47
81T/St-83
82D-286
82F-426
82F/St-209
82OPC-156
82OPC-183IA
82T-645
82T-646A
82T/St-193
83D-464
83F-127
83OPC-171
83Pol/Royals-9
83T-525
83T/St-169
83T/St-71
84D-222
84F-363
84FunFood/Pin-44
84Nes/792-155
84OPC-155
84T-155
84T/St-277
85D-175
85F-217
85Leaf-148
85T-743
85T/St-274
86D-130
86F-24
86F/St-127
86Kitty/Disc-13
86Leaf-54
86NatPhoto-20
86OPC-215
86S-186M
86T-215
86T/St-23WS
86T/St-263
87D-255
87D/AAS-41
87D/OD-204
87F-383
87F/AwardWin-42
87F/Mini-113
87F/St-123
87Leaf-188
87OPC-101
87S-168
87T-692
87T/St-260
88D-225
88D/Best-319
88F-273
88F/St-35
88Nestle-29
88OPC-326
88Panini/St-105
88RedFoley/St-100
88Score-79
88Sf-149
88Smok/Royals-25
88T-595
88T/Big-75
88T/St-255
88T/St/Backs-39
89B-122
89D-85
89D/Best-175
89F-297
89OPC-25
89Panini/St-356
89Score-390
89T-25
89T/Big-200
89T/St-262
89Tastee/Discs-7
89UD-350
90D-262
90F-122
90Score-372
90T-479
90UD-382

White, Fred
88Keno/Pro-1382
89Visal/Cal-102
89Visal/Pro-1446

White, G. Harris
WG2-49

White, Gary
87Clearw-17
88Spart/Pro-1044

White, Guy
(Doc)
10Domino-124
11Helmar-19
12Sweet/Pin-15
80Laugh/FFeat-15
E254
E286
M116
S74-10
S74-115
T202
T205
T206
T207
T215/blue
T215/brown

White, Harold
51B-320

White, Harry
79Newar-13

White, James
(Deacon)
N172
N284
Scrapps
WG1-27

White, Jerry
75IntAS/TCMA-1
75IntAS/TCMA-6
76OPC-594R
76SSPC-340
76T-594R
77OPC-81
77T-557
79T-494
80OPC-369
80T-724
81D-333
81F-161
81OPC-42
81OPC/Post-11
81T-42
82D-621
82F-211
82Hygrade
82OPC-386
82OPC/Post-24
82T-386
83D-602
83F-300
83OPC-214
83Stuart-19
83T-214

White, John F.
C46-4
E254
T206

White, John
82Amari-13

White, Joyner C.
(Jo-Jo)
34DS-45
35Wheat
39PB-79
40PB-84
47Centen-31
47Signal
49B/PCL-14
60T-460C
R312/M
R314
V355-74

White, Joyner M.
(Mike)
64T-492R
65OPC-31
65T-31
78TCMA-155

White, K.G.
89Bakers/Cal-199

White, Larry
81Chatt-21
82Albuq-10
83Albuq-8
83Pol/Dodg-47
84Cram/PCL-158
85Cram/PCL-168

White, Logan
84Butte-27

White, Marvin
89Butte/SP-29

White, Mike
86Bakers-29
87Bakers-12
88FSLAS/Star-25
88VeroB/Star-23
89SnAnt/Best-1

White, Mike
81LynnS-19

White, Myron
77LodiD
80Albuq-12

White, Oliver Kirby
D322
T205

White, Randy
83Greens-13
89Idaho/Pro-2034

White, Rich
80Utica-2

White, Roy
46Sunbeam

White, Roy
52T-345
53B/Col-41
53T-139
54B-34
54RH
54RM-AL14
54Wilson
55B-47
56T-168
57T-163
58Hires-53
58T-414
59T-486
60T-203
62T-494
66T-234R
68T-546
69MB-289
69MLB/St-81
69OPC-25
69T-25
69T/S-26
69T/St-210
69Trans-26
70MLB/St-252
70OPC-373
70T-373
70T/PI-14
71K-43
71MD
71MLB/St-503
71OPC-395
71T-395
71T/Coins-34
71T/GM-45
71T/S-26
71T/tatt-13
72MB-360
72OPC-340
72T-340
72T/Cloth-33
73OPC-25
73T-25
74OPC-135
74T-135
74T/St-220
75K-1
75OPC-375
75T-375
75T/M-375
76OPC-225
76SSPC-435
76T-225
77BK/Y-19
77OPC-182
77T-485
78BK/Y-19
78OPC-48

78T-16
79BK/Y-19
79OPC-75
79T-159
79TCMA-25
80OPC-341
80T-648
PM10/Sm-194

White, Sherman
51BR-B11

White, Sol
78Laugh/Black-22

White, William D.
N172

Whited, Ed
86AubAs-26
87Ashvl-24
88Greenv/Best-1
88SLAS-16
89Richm/CMC-21
89Richm/Ko-36
89Richm/Pro-837
90Score-644
90Score/100Ris-78
90T-111
90UD-447

Whitehead, Burgess
(Whitey)
34DS-51
39PB-23
40PB-92
41DP-90
41PB-28
R314
V355-59

Whitehead, Chris
88Elmir-21

Whitehead, John
R314

Whitehead, Steve
76QuadC
89James/Pro-2140

Whitehill, Earl
28Exh-47
33G-124
35Exh/4-16
35G-8H
35G-9H
36Exh/4-16
87Conlon/2-60
88Conlon/AmAS-24
R308-165
R310
R312/M
R314
R316
V355-60

Whitehouse, Len
77Ashev
78Ashev
79Tulsa-3
83T/X-126
84D-558
84F-578
84Nes/792-648
84T-648
85D-513
85T-406
85Toled-12

Whitehurst, Wally
86Madis-27
86Madis/Pol-23
88Tidew/CANDL-29
88Tidew/CMC-11
88Tidew/Pro-1589
89B-373
89F/Up-103
89Tidew/CMC-6
89Tidew/Pro-1958
89UD/Ext-737
90Score-599
90T-719
90UD-564

Whiteman, Charles
W514-119

Whiten, Mark
87Myrtle-24
88Duned/Star-21
89Knoxv/Best-26
89Knoxv/Star-21

Whitfield, Fred
62Kahn/Atl
63Sugar-27
63T-211
64Kahn
64T-367
65OPC-283
65T-283
66Kahn
66OPC-88
66T-88
67Kahn
67T-275
68OPC-133
68T-133
69MB-290
69T-518

Whitfield, Ken
85Kingst-22
86Kinston-25
89Kinston/Star-24

Whitfield, Terry
75OPC-622R
75T-622R
75T/M-622R
76OPC-590R
76SSPC-443
76T-590R
78Ho-136
78T-236
79Ho-10
79OPC-309
79Pol/Giants-45
79T-589
80OPC-361
80Pol/Giants-45
80T-713
81D-435
81F-437
81T-167
81T/So-87
81T/St-233
84F/X-125
84Pol/Dodg-45
85D-540
85F-389
85T-31
86D-337
86F-147
86Pol/Dodg-45
86T-318

Whitford, Larry
86Beloi-26

Whiting, Don
78Holyo
79Holyo-15
82ElPas-9
83Beloi/LF-14

Whiting, John
75BurlB

Whiting, Mike
86Elmir-28

Whitlock, Mike
88Beloi/GS-22
89StLucie/Star-24

Whitman, Dick
49Eureka-51
51B-221

Whitmer, Dan
79SLCty-19
80SLCty-2
82Knoxv-11
82Syrac-28
83Knoxv-9

Whitmer, Joe
83Chatt-4
84Chatt-17
85Cram/PCL-99
86Calgary-26

Whitmyer, Steve
86Water-25

Whitney, Arthur C.
(Pinky)
29Exh/4-12
31Exh/4-11
32Orbit/un-60
33DH-42
36Exh/4-1
37Exh/4-6
38Exh/4-6
38Wheat
39PB-98
R305
R313
R316

Whitney, Arthur W.
N172
N284
N338/2
WG1-71

Whitney, G.
N172

Whitney, James
N172
N284
N403

Whitshire, Vernon
R313

Whitson, Anthony
89CharWh/Best-14

Whitson, Ed
78Colum
79T-189
80Pol/Giants-32
80T-561
81D-74
81F-444
81OPC-336
81T-336
81T/St-240
82D-251
82F-402
82T-656
82T/Tr-127T
82Wheat/Ind
83D-389
83F-423
83T-429
83T/X-127
84D-528
84F-316
84Moth/Giants-26
84Moth/Padres-15
84Nes/792-277
84Smok/Padres-27
84T-277
85D-446
85F-47
85F/Up-U129
85OPC-98
85T-762
85T/St-152
85T/Tr-130T
86D-225
86F-120
86OPC-15
86T-15
86T/St-301
87Bohem-31
87D-360
87F-434
87T-155
88Coke/Padres-31
88D-81
88D/Best-322
88F-599
88OPC-330
88Panini/St-401
88RedFoley/St-101
88Score-167
88Smok/Padres-30
88T-330
88T/Big-186
88T/St-107
89B-449
89D-229
89D/Best-210
89F-321
89OPC-21
89Score-329
89T-516
89T/Big-81
89UD-453
90D-205
90D-26DK
90F-171
90Score-373
90Score/100St-69
90Sf-212
90T-618
90UD-308

Whitson, Tony
88Wythe/Pro-1984
89CharWh/Pro-1763

Whitt, Ernie
78Syrac
78T-708R
79Syrac-3
79T-714R
81D-390
81F-411
81OPC-282
81OPC/Post-20
81T-407
82D-381
82F-626
82OPC-19
82OPC/Post-3
82T-19
82T/St-247
83D-304
83F-443
83OPC-302
83T-302
83T/St-131
84D-437
84F-169
84Nes/792-506
84OPC-106
84T-506
84T/St-373
84Tor/Fire-32
85D-268
85F-119
85Leaf-181
85OPC-128
85T-128
85Tor/Fire-32
86Ault-12
86D-559
86D/AAS-48
86F-73
86Leaf-217
86OPC-136
86T-673
86Tor/Fire-32
87D-148
87D/HL-39
87D/OD-33
87F-240
87Ho/St-2
87Leaf-69
87OPC-221
87T-698
87Tor/Fire-34
87Tor/Fire-34
88D-394
88F-126
88Ho/Disc-16
88Leaf-250
88OPC-79
88Panini/St-216
88Score-168
88T-79
88T/Big-239
88T/St-187
88Tor/Fire-12
89B-248
89D-591
89D/Best-255
89F-248
89OPC-289
89Score-98
89T-289
89T/Big-224
89Tor/Fire-12
89UD-118
90D-385
90F-97
90Score-433
90T-742
90UD-148

Whitt, Mike
85Evrt/Cram-18
86Clint-27

Whitted, George
15CJ-151
21Exh-185
D327
D328-188
D329-189
D350/2-190
E121/120
E121/80
E135-188
E220
M101/4-189
M101/5-190
V100
W501-81
W514-92
W575

Whittemore, Reggie
81Brist-5
83Pawtu-19
84Pawtu-15
85Toled-19

Wichman, Mike
89Stock/Best-26M

Wick, David
82Watlo/B-10
82Watlo/C-13

Wickander, Kevin
87Kinston-2
88BBAmer-9
88EastLAS/Pro-44
88Wmspt/Pro-1315
89B-75
89ColrSp/CMC-5
89ColSp/Pro-238
90T-528

Wicker, Bob
WG3-51

Wicker, Floyd
69Fud's-14
69T-524R
71MLB/St-456
71OPC-97
71T-97

Wickersham, Dave
61T-381
62T-517
63T-492
64Det/Lids-14
64T-181
64T/Coins-105
64T/S-35
65Bz-25
65OldLond-38
65OPC-9LL

65T-375
65T-9LL
65T/trans-34
66OPC-58
66T-58
67OPC-112
67T-112
68KDKA-40
68T-288
69T-647
78TCMA-195

Wickham, Mike
89Stock/Star-26M

Wickware, Frank
78Laugh/Black-19

Widmar, Al
51B-281
52T-133
53Mother-14
74T-99C
84Tor/Fire-33CO
85Tor/Fire-33CO
86Tor/Fire-33CO
87Tor/Fire-35
87Tor/Fire-35CO
88Tor/Fire-41CO
89Tor/Fire-41

Widner, Steven
77Watlo

Widner, William
N172

Wieand, F. Ted
60T-146

Wieczorek, Chet
40Hughes-19

Wiedenbauer, Tom
77Cocoa
80Tucso-8
81Tucso-26
83DayBe-13
86Osceola-28MG
87ColAst/Pro-16
87ColumAst-16
88ColAst/Best-25
89ColMud/Best-8
89ColMud/Pro-130

Wiegandt, Scott
89Martins/Star-34

Wieghaus, Tom
80Memph-25
84Moth/Ast-18

Wielegman, Phil
86Miami-27

Wieligman, Rich
87Lakel-4
88GlenF/Pro-922
89Toled/CMC-23
89Toled/Pro-775

Wielman, Carl
D327
D328-189
D329-190
D350/2-191
E135-189
M101/4-190
M101/5-191

Wiener, Paul
79Jacks-5

Wiens, Randy
78Duned

Wiese, Phil
89Elizab/Star-28

Wieser, Dan
82Omaha-18

Wiesler, Bob
56T-327
57T-126
79TCMA-224

Wiesmiller, Bob
77Salem

Wiesner, Doug
81AppFx-29
82AppFx-29

Wietelmann, William
(Whitey)
52Mother-24
73OPC-12CO
73T-12C
76SSPC-598

Wieters, Rick
78Green
79Savan-18
80GlenF/B-12
80GlenF/C-13
81GlenF-8

Wiggins, Alan
79Clint
83D-397
83F-375
83T-251
84D-568
84F-317
84F/St-89
84Moth/Padres-10
84Nes/792-693
84OPC-27
84Smok/Padres-28
84T-693
84T/St-153
84T/St/Box-3
85D-80
85F-48
85F/St-60
85Leaf-68
85OPC-378
85T-378
85T/St-150
86D-607
86F-290
86T-508
87D/OD-138
87F/U-U124
87T/Tr-126T
88Score-291

Wiggins, Dave
81Phoen-14

Wiggins, Kevin
86Orlan-23

Wiggs, James
E107

Wight, Bill
50B-38
51B-164
52B-117
52T-177
53B/Col-100
53Glen
55B-312
55Gol/Ind-31
56T-286
57T-340
58T-237
79TCMA-131

Wihtol, Sandy
79Tacom-16
80T-665R
80Tacom-10
81Charl-7
81T-451R
83Charl-6

Wilber, Del
52B-225
52T-383
53B/BW-24
54B-178

Wilbins, Mike
75Cedar

Wilborn, Ted
80OPC-329R
80T-674R
82Phoen
83Phoen/BHN-16
86Hagers-27
87Cedar-20

Wilbur, Bob
80Utica-10

Wilburn, Fred
85MidldA-4

Wilburn, Trey
89Bill/Pro-2041

Wilcox, Milt
71OPC-164R
71T-164R
72OPC-399
72T-399
73OPC-134
73T-134
74OPC-565
74T-565
75OPC-14
75T-14
75T/M-14
76SSPC-306
77Evansvl/TCMA-25
78BK/T-11
78OPC-136
78T-151
79T-288
80OPC-204
80T-392
81D-247
81F-465
81T-658
82D-223
82F-285
82F/St-157
82T-784
82T/St-186
83D-155
83F-349
83T-457
84D-471
84F-93
84Nes/792-588
84T-588
85Cain's-20
85D-105
85F-25
85Leaf-227
85OPC-99
85Seven-6D
85T-99
85T/St-10ALCS
85T/St-17WS
85Wendy-22
86F-243
86Moth/Mar-11
86T-192

Wilcox, Steve
82Clint-11

Wild, Jerry
63Pep/Tul

Wilder, Bill
84Memph-11

Wilder, Dave
82Idaho-29
83Madis/LF-5
87Pittsf-18

Wilder, Mike
83Idaho-25
84Madis/Pol-4

Wilder, Troy
78Watlo

Wiles, Randy
78Charl

Wiley, Craig
87LasVegas-21
88Wichi-12
89NiagFls/Puc-23

Wiley, Keith
88CapeCod/Sum-11

Wiley, Mark
79Syrac-5
83RochR-25
84RochR-3
85RochR-29
88Gator-35CO

Wilfong, Rob
76Tacom
79T-633
80T-238
81D-493
81F-569
81T-453
82D-130
82F-563
82F/St-231
82T-379
82T/St-205
82T/Tr-128T
83D-612
83F-101
83T-158
84D-329
84F-530
84Nes/792-79
84Smok/Cal-30
84T-79
85D-402
85F-315
85Smok/Cal-20
85T-524
86OPC-393
86Smok/Cal-20
86T-658
87D-258
87F-94
87T-251

Wilhelm, Hoyt
52T-392
53B/BW-28
53RM-NL21
53T-151
54B-57
54NYJour
54T-36
55B-1
55Gol/Giants-30
55RM-NL12
56T-307
57T-203
58T-324
59T-349
60L-69
60T-115M
60T-395
61P-80
61T-545
61T/St-107
62J-35
62P-35
62P/Can-35
62T-423M
62T-545
62T/St-10
63Salada-39
63T-108
64T-13
65OPC-276
65T-276
66T-510
67T-422
68T-350
69JB
69MB-291
69T-565
69T/DE-11
69T/decal
69T/St-190
70OPC-17
70T-17
71MLB/St-24
71OPC-248
71T-248
71T/GM-2
72MB-361
72T-777
78Cr/PCL-100
78TCMA-100
79TCMA-270
79WHave-27
80Cram/Leg-121
82Nashv-28CO
83Nashvl-25C
84Nashvl-24C
85West/2-26
88Pac/Leg-76
89HOF/St-81
89Pac/Leg-171
89Smok/Dodg-35
89Swell-45

Wilhelm, Irvin
(Kaiser)
14Piedmont/St-61
E270/1
M116
T205
T206
T213/blue
V100

Wilhelm, James W.
79Hawai-7
80T-685R

Wilhelmi, Dave
80Clint-1
81Clint-4
84Shrev/FB-24

Wilhoit, Joe
D328-189
E135-189

Wilholte, Arnold
78Ashev

Wille, Denney
T207

Wilkerson, Bill
89London/Pro-1360

Wilkerson, Curt
82BurlR-13
82Tulsa-25
83OKCty-19
84D-99
84F/X-126
84Rang-19
84T/X-127
85D-99
85F-573
85OPC-342
85Rang-19
85T-594
85T/St-349
86D-256
86F-577
86OPC-279
86Rang-19
86T-434
86T/St-244
87D-223
87F-141
87Moth/Rang-14
87Smok/R-28
87T-228
88D-592
88F-481
88Moth/R-14
88Score-127
88Smok/R-21
88T-53
88T/Big-132
89B-292
89D-402
89D/Tr-34
89F-535
89Mara/Cubs-19
89Score-518
89T-331
89T/Tr-126T
89UD-465
90D-608
90F-46
90Score-474

90T-667
90UD-147
Wilkerson, Marty
84Omaha-12
85Omaha-20
86Omaha-29
86Omaha/TCMA-9
Wilkerson, Ron
82WHave-18
Wilkerson, Wayne
77Ashev
Wilkes, Greg
80Hawai-13
Wilkie, Aldon
47Remar-23
48Signal
Wilkins, Dean
88EastLAS/Pro-30
88Pittsf/Pro-1368
89IowaC/CMC-10
89IowaC/Pro-1690
90F-47
90Score-630
Wilkins, Eric
80T-511
80Tacom-25
81Charl-6
81T-99
Wilkins, Mark
81QuadC-28
Wilkins, Michael
88Fay/Pro-1103
89Lakel/Star-24
Wilkins, Rick
88Peoria/Ko-31
89WinSal/Star-17
Wilkins, Steve
76Cedar
Wilkinson, Bill
86Calgary-25
87F/U-U125
87Moth/Sea-26
87T/Tr-127T
88D-568
88F-390
88Moth/Sea-26
88RedFoley/St-102
88T-376
89Calg/CMC-6
89T-636
Wilkinson, Brian
89Wausa/GS-13
Wilkinson, Ray
V100
Wilkinson, Ron
82Madis-16
Wilkinson, Spencer
88Gasto/Pro-1019
89Gasto/Pro-999
89Gasto/Star-25
Wilks, Ted
47TipTop
49B-137
49Eureka-199
51B-193
52B-138
52T-109
53T-101
79TCMA-218
Will, Bob
59T-388
60T-147
61T-512
61T/St-11
62Salada-218
62Shirriff-218
62T-47
63T-58
Willard, Gerry
82Readg-11
83Charl-8
84D-520
84Wheat/Ind-16
85D-346
85F-460
85OPC-142
85Polar/Ind-16
85T-504
86D-398
86F-601
86F/Up-U126
86OPC-273
86T-273
86Tacom-24
87D-467
87F-409
87T-137
87Tacom-19
89Vanco/CMC-19
89Vanco/Pro-587
Willeford, Jerry
76Dubuq
Willett, Robert Edgar
09Buster/Pin-15
11Helmar-38
14Piedmont/St-62
E104
E254
E95
M116
S74-19
T202
T205
T206
T213/blue
T213/brown
T215/brown
Willey, Carlton
58T-407
59T-95
60Lake
60T-107
61T-105
61T/St-48
62J-155
62P-155
62P/Can-155
62T-174
63T-528
64T-84
64T/Coins-75
64T/St-44
64T/tatt
65T-401
Willhite, Nick
64T-14R
65T-284
66OPC-171
66T-171
67T-249
78Newar
Williams
E254
Williams
E254
T201
Williams, Al
73Cedar
Williams, Alberto
(Al)
80Toled-17
81T-569
82D-429
82F-564
82T-69
83D-508
83F-628
83T-731
84D-316
84F-579
84Nes/792-183
84T-183
85Colum-10
85Colum/Pol-23
85T-614
Williams, Bernie
70OPC-401R
70T-401R
71MLB/St-264
71OPC-728R
71T-728R
72T-761R
73OPC-557
73T-557
87FtLaud-21
87Oneon-4
Williams, Bernie
88CLAS/Star-19
88PrWill/Star-24
89Colum/CMC-21
89Colum/Pol-22
89Colum/Pro-736
90Class-10
90D-689
90Score-619
90T-701
Williams, Billy
61T-141
61T/St-12
62Salada-207
62Shirriff-207
62T-288
62T/bucks
62T/St-111
63Exh
63J-172
63P-172
63Salada-30
63T-353
64Bz-17
64T-175
64T/Coins-44
64T/S-52
64T/St-73
64T/SU
64T/tatt
65Bz-17
65OldLond-20
65OPC-220
65OPC-4LL
65T-220
65T-4LL
65T/E-40
65T/trans-35
66Bz-48
66T-217LL
66T-580
66T/RO-101
67Bz-48
67T-315
68Bz-14
68Kahn
68OPC-37
68T-37
69Kahn
69Kelly/Pin-19
69MB-292
69MLB/St-126
69MLBPA/Pin-59
69OPC-4LL
69Sunoco/Pin-9
69T-450
69T-4LL
69T/S-39
69T/St-20
69Trans-38
70Dunkin-6
70K-37
70MLB/St-24
70OPC-170
70T-170
70T/S-40
71Bz
71Bz/Test-26
71K-61
71MLB/St-48
71OPC-350
71OPC-64LL
71OPC-66LL
71T-350
71T-64LL
71T-66LL
71T/Coins-75
71T/GM-37
71T/tatt-12
71T/tatt-12a
72K-46
72MB-362
72OPC-439
72OPC-440IA
72T-439
72T-440A
72T/Post-21
73K-10
73OPC-200
73OPC-61LL
73T-200
73T-61LL
73T/Comics-23
73T/Lids-53
73T/PinUps-23
74K-32
74OPC-110
74OPC-338AS
74T-110
74T-338AS
74T/St-20
75OPC-545
75T-545
75T/M-545
76OPC-525
76SSPC-496
76T-525
83MLBPA/Pin-35
85CircK-18
86S/Dec-51M
87D/HL-20
88Pac/Leg-90
88T/Gloss22-22
89HOF/St-29
89Pac/Leg-184
89Swell-120
Exh47
Williams, Billy
88Umpire-3
Williams, Bob
86BurlEx-26
88CharlK-2
88CharlK/Pep-2
88Hagers/Star-25
Williams, Bruce
83Beloi/LF-9
Williams, Charles
72OPC-388
72T-388
75OPC-449
75T-449
75T/M-449
76OPC-332
76SSPC-98
76T-332
77T-73
78T-561
79T-142
Williams, Charlie
88Umpire-41
89Umpires-39
Williams, Claud
(Lefty)
88Pac/8Men-108
88Pac/8Men-11
88Pac/8Men-44
88Pac/8Men-45M
88Pac/8Men-49
88Pac/8Men-60
D327
D328-190
E135-190
W514-35
W575
Williams, Dallas
80RochR-2
81RochR-23
82Indianap-26
83Indianap-7
84Evans-12
86Indianap-26
87Indianap-22
Williams, Dan
83BirmB-3
88BurlR/Pro-1799
89Watertn/Star-23
Williams, Dana
86Pawtu-27
87NewBrit-16
87Pawtu-26
88Pawtu/CMC-21
88Pawtu/Pro-460
89Pawtu/CMC-16
89Pawtu/Dunkin-10
89Pawtu/Pro-690
90F-648M
Williams, Dave
52B-178
52T-316
53B/Col-1
53T-120
54B-9
54NYJour
55B-138
55Gol/Giants-31
79TCMA-167
Williams, Dave
85Orlan-24
Williams, Deb
40Hughes-20
Williams, Dick H.
52T-396
53T-125
54NYJour
57T-59
58T-79
59T-292
60T-188
61P-86
61T-8
61T/St-168
62J-32
62P-32
62P/Can-32
62Salada-48A
62Salada-48B
62Shirriff-48
62T-382
63T-328
64T-153
67OPC-161MG
67T-161
67T/Test/RSox-26MG
68OPC-87MG
68T-87
69T-349
71OPC-714MG
71T-714
72OPC-137MG
72T-137
73OPC-179MG
73T-179
75OPC-236MG
75T-236MG
75T/M-236MG
76SSPC-192
76T-304MG
77OPC-108MG
77T-647MG
78OPC-27MG
78T-522
79OPC-349MG
79T-606MG
79TCMA-327

81D-453
81F-149
81T-616
81T-680MG
83D-625
83T-366
84Moth/SDP-1MG
84Nes/792-742MG
84Smok/SDP-29MG
84T-742
85F/St-126MG
85Moth/SDP-1MG
85T-66MG
86D/AAS-38
86Moth/Mar-1
86T-681
86T/Gloss22-12
86T/Tr-124T
87Moth/A's-12
87Moth/Sea-1
87T-418MG
88Moth/Sea-1MG
88T-104

Williams, Don
(Spin)
84PrWill-20
85Nashua-26
86Nashua-27CO
87Harrisbg-15
88Harris/Pro-839

Williams, Don
60T-414

Williams, Dwayne
87Tampa-10

Williams, Earl
71OPC-52R
71T-52R
72OPC-380
72T-380
73JP
73OPC-504
73T-504
74OPC-375
74T-375
74T/St-130
75OPC-97
75T-97
75T/M-97
76Ho-108
76OPC-458
76SSPC-13
76T-458
77OPC-252
77T-223
78Ho-16
78T-604
89Bluef/Star-29

Williams, Eddie
85Cedar-20
86OhHenry-24
87BuffB-13
88ColSp/CMC-17
88ColSp/Pro-1547
88D-46
88F-620
88Leaf-46RR
88T-758
89Coke/WS-28
89D/Tr-29
89Score/YS/II-39
89T/Tr-127T
89UD/Ext-790
90UD-289

Williams, Edward
87Peoria-18
88Peoria/Ko-32
89Peoria/Ko-18

Williams, Edwin D.
(Dib)
33G-82
35G-1B
35G-2B
35G-6B
35G-7B
V354-36

Williams, Eric
88Geneva/Pro-1635
89CharWh/Best-2
89CharWh/Pro-1756

Williams, Flavio
88Watertn/Puc-29
89Aug/Pro-505
89Well/Puc-29

Williams, Frank
84F/X-127
84T/X-128
85D-323
85F-624
85Moth/Giants-12
85OPC-254
85T-487
85T/St-169
86F-554
86Phoen-24
86T-341
87F-287
87F/U-U127
87Kahn-47
87T-96
87T/Tr-128T
88D-512
88F-250
88Kahn/Reds-47
88Score-317
88T-773
89B-100
89D-478
89D/Best-259
89F-174
89F/Up-34
89Mara/Tigers-36
89Score-485
89T-172
89T/Tr-128T
89UD-449
90D-327
90F-620
90Score-341
90T-599
90UD-539

Williams, Fred
(Cy)
21Exh-186
25Exh-48
28Exh-24
28Yueng-52
29Exh/4-12
D327
D328-191
D329-190
D350/2-191
E120
E121/80
E122
E126-42
E135-191
E210-52
M101/4-190
M101/5-191
V100
V61-118
W501-100
W502-52
W517-18
W572
W573
W575

Williams, Fred
86Stockton-26
87Stockton-26
88ElPas/Best-19
88TexLgAS/GS-25
89Jaxvl/Best-18
89Jaxvl/Pro-172

Williams, Gary
77Jaxvl

Williams, George
63T-324R
64T-388R

Williams, Gerald
87Oneon-6
88PrWill/Star-25
89PrWill/Star-25

Williams, Glenn
77Ashev

Williams, Greg
88StCath/Pro-2019

Williams, H
86Nashua-28tr

Williams, Harold
80Ander-25
81Durhm-8
87Salem-15
88EastLAS/Pro-46
88Harris/Pro-861
89Harris/Pro-302

Williams, Jaime
88Orlan/Best-10
89Orlan/Best-2
89Orlan/Pro-1354

Williams, James A.
70OPC-262R
70T-262R
71OPC-262R
71T-262R

Williams, James A.
N172

Williams, James F.
(Jimy)
66T-544R
75Phoen-19
77SLCty
79SLCty-22
84Tor/Fire-34CO
85Tor/Fire-34CO
86Tor/Fire-34MG
87OPC-279MG
87T-786MG
87Tor/Fire-36
87Tor/Fire-36MG
88OPC-314MG
88T-314
88Tor/Fire-3MG
89OPC-381
89T-594MG
89Tor/Fire-3

Williams, James T.
E107
T206

Williams, James
82DayBe-19
83DayBe-16
84Cram/PCL-58
86Osceola-29
87Visal-1
88CalLgAS-40
88Visal/Cal-163

Williams, Jay
88Stock/Cal-203
88Stock/Pro-744

Williams, Jeff
81Miami-19
84CharO-20
86RochR-26
89Readg/Best-23
89Readg/Pro-675
89Readg/Star-25

Williams, Jerome
88Wythe/Pro-2002

Williams, Jody
87Watertn-19

Williams, John
86BurlEx-27

Williams, Ken
83AppFx/LF-14
86BuffB-24
87D/Rook-11
87F/U-U128
87Fayette-25
87Hawai-2
87S/Rook-41
88Coke/WS-30
88D-334
88D/Best-249
88F-412
88F/Mini-17
88F/SS-42
88GlenF/Pro-918
88OPC-92
88Panini/St-65
88Score-112
88Score/YS/I-6
88Sf-69
88T-559
88T/St-287
89D-337
89D/Tr-17
89Mara/Tigers-25
89Score-67
89T-34
89T/Tr-129T
89Toled/CMC-9
89Toled/Pro-763
89UD-506
89UD/Ext-714
90T-327
90UD-249

Williams, Kenneth Roy
21Exh-187
25Exh-119
26Exh-119
27Exh-58
E120
E126-48
E220
V100
V61-52
W515-26
W572
W573

Williams, Kerman
85Elmir-24
86Elmir-29

Williams, Kevin
82Orlan-1
83Orlan-4
88Modesto/Cal-59

Williams, Mark
77SnJos-6

Williams, Matt E.
82Knoxv-8
83Syrac-13
84Syrac-11
85Syrac-12
86OKCty-26

Williams, Matt
86Cram/PCL-3
87D/Rook-45
87F/U-U129
87Moth/SFG-22
87Phoen-2
87S/Rook-25
87T/Tr-129T
88Class/Blue-246
88D-628
88F-101
88Phoen/CMC-18
88Phoen/Pro-56
88Score-118
88Score/YS/I-18
88Score/YS/II-31
88T-372
89AAA/Pro-51
89D-594
89F-346
89Moth/Giants-12
89Panini/St-218
89Phoen/CMC-18
89Phoen/Pro-1485
89Score-612
89T-628
89UD-247
90Class-73
90D-348
90F-75
90Score-503
90Sf-70
90T-41
90UD-577

Williams, Matthew
87Idaho-19
88Idaho/Pro-1842
89Salin/Cal-140
89Salin/Pro-1825

Williams, Mel
83Readg-22

Williams, Mike
76Watlo
77LodiD
79Albuq-3
80Phoen-1
81Phoen-8

Williams, Mitch
86D/Rook-19
86F/Up-U127
86Rang-28
86S/Rook-20
86T/Tr-125T
87D-347
87F-142
87Moth/Rang-17
87Smok/R-7
87T-291
87ToysRUs-32
88D-161
88D/Best-279
88F-482
88F/RecSet-43
88Moth/R-17
88OPC-26
88Score-339
88Smok/R-19
88T-26
89B-283
89D-225
89D/Best-60
89D/Tr-38
89F-536
89F/Up-81
89Mara/Cubs-28
89OPC-377
89Score-301
89Score/Tr-32
89Score/YS/I-27
89Sf-151
89T-411
89T/St-247
89T/Tr-130T
89UD-95
89UD/Ext-778
90Class-23
90D-275
90F-48
90F-631M
90Score-262
90Score-695DT
90Score/100St-93
90Sf-196
90T-520
90UD-174

Williams, Paul Jr.
86Elmir-30
88WinHav/Star-27

Williams, Quinn
86Cram/PCL-131

Williams, Ray R.
78StPet
79ArkTr-3
80ArkTr-20

Williams, Ray
88Wausa/Feder-13
88Wausa/GS-13
Williams, Reggie
83VeroB-25
86Albuq-28
86D/Rook-5
86F/Up-U128
86Pol/Dodg-51
86S/Rook-19
87D-341
87F-460
87F/Hottest-42
87F/Mini-114
87F/St-124
87Moth/Dodg-15
87Pol/Dodg-9
87T-232
88ColSp/CMC-23
88ColSp/Pro-1524
89BuffB/CMC-23
89BuffB/Pro-1685
89Clint/Pro-893
Williams, Rick
73Cedar
78Charl
79T-437
80Memph-26
80T-69
80Tucso-4
81Toled-10
82Toled-9
Williams, Rob
85Utica-8
87WPalm-6
Williams, Robert E.
T207
Williams, Roger
87Pittsf-21
88IowaC/CMC-11
88IowaC/Pro-545
89IowaC/Pro-1691
Williams, Scott
85Newar-1
Williams, Slim
88Visal/Pro-96
Williams, Smokey Joe
74Laugh/Black-1
88Conlon/NegAS-12
Williams, Stan
59T-53
60BB-16
60L-109
60T-278
61BB-40
61P-162
61T-190
61T-45LL
61T/St-36
62BB-40
62J-115
62P-115
62P/Can-115
62T-515
62T-60LL
63J-122
63P-122
63T-42
64T-505
65T-404
68OPC-54
68T-54
69OPC-118
69T-118
69T/St-170
70OPC-353
70T-353
71MLB/St-478
71OPC-638
71T-638
72OPC-9
72T-9
79Colum-6
89Smok/Dodg-68
WG9-25
Williams, Steve
75Shreve/TCMA-23
86Clearw-25
87Readg-24
89Erie/Star-26
Williams, Ted
39Exh
39PB-92
40PB-27
41DP-57
41DP-81
41PB-14
43MP-24
48L-76
48Swell-16
50B-98
51B-165
51Wheat
52BR
52RM-AL23
52StarCal/L-71B
52StarCal/L-71C
52Wheat
53Exh/Can-30
54B-66A
54T-1
54T-250
54Wilson
55T-2
55T/DH-69
56T-5
56T/Hocus-A5
56T/Hocus-B7
56T/Pin-26
57T-1
58T-1
58T-321M
58T-485AS
59F/Set
60F-72
60NuCard-39
60NuCard-52
61F-152
61NuCard-439
61NuCard-452
69T-539M
69T-650
70OPC-211MG
70T-211
71OPC-380MG
71T-380
72OPC-510MG
72T-510
74Laugh/ASG-46
76Laugh/Jub-27
76OPC-347AS
76T-347M
78TCMA-260
79TCMA-10
80Cram/Leg-61
80Laugh/3/4/5-20
80Laugh/3/4/5-6
80SSPC/HOF
82F/St-237M
83D/HOF-9
83MLBPA/Pin-18
84D/Champs-14
84West/1-20
85CircK-9
85D/HOF-2
85Woolwth-38
86BLChew-8
86S/Dec-25
87Nestle/DT-18
88Pac/Leg-50
89B-I11
89HOF/St-28
89Nissen-20
89Pac/Leg-154
89Swell-100
D305
PM10/L-41
PM10/Sm-195
PM10/Sm-196
PM10/Sm-197
PM10/Sm-198
PM10/Sm-199
PM10/Sm-200
R302-101
R303/A
R346-44
R423-113
Williams, Teddy
86Cram/PCL-123
87Idaho-10
87Wausa-12
88CalLgAS-28
88SnBer/Best-4
88SnBer/Cal-38
88Sumter/Pro-419
89BurlB/Pro-1622
89BurlB/Star-25
89Wmspt/Pro-636
89Wmspt/Star-22
Williams, Tim
84Greens-14
88CapeCod/Sum-143
Williams, Tom
88CapeCod/Sum-118
Williams, Troy
86Cram/PCL-118
87Wausa-6
Williams, Walter E.
(Walt)
66Pep/Tul
67T-598R
68OPC-172
68T-172
69T-309
70MLB/St-191
70OPC-395
70T-395
70T/CB
71OPC-555
71T-555
71T/Coins-36
72MB-363
72OPC-15
72T-15
73OPC-297
73T-297
74OPC-418
74T-418
76OPC-123
76SSPC-436
76T-123
87Sumter-4
88Durhm/Star-24
89Tulsa/GS-2
Williams, William
(Billy)
89Canton/Best-8
89Canton/Pro-1317
Williams, Willie D.
82Danvi-18
Williams, Woody
47Signal
Williams, Woody
89Duned/Star-23
Williamson, Bret
87Tampa-13
Williamson, Edward
N172
N284
WG1-18
Williamson, Greg
86Watlo-31
Williamson, Kevin
87Modesto-16
Williamson, Mark
83Beaum-8
85Beaum-3
86LasVegas-23
87D/Rook-3
88D-418
88F-574
88SanDiegoSt-18
88T-571
89F-626
89French-32
89Score-592
89T-546
89T/Big-147
90D-406
90F-194
90Score-332
90T-13
90UD-173
Williamson, Mike
77Ashev
Williamson, Ray
87Watlo-22
88Kinston/Star-24
Willis, Alan
82Watlo-11
Willis, C.H.
N172
Willis, Carl
84Evans-22
87F-218
87Nashv-23
87T-101
88Vanco/CMC-4
88Vanco/Pro-762
89Edmon/CMC-3
89Edmon/Pro-567
Willis, James
54T-67
Willis, Jim
87AppFx-30
Willis, Kent
87Tampa-17
88Rockford-34
88Virgini/Star-22
89Rockford-34
Willis, Marty
89Lakel/Star-25
Willis, Mike
75IntAS/TCMA-18
75IntAS/TCMA-28
76SSPC-382
77OPC-103
77T-493R
78OPC-227
78T-293
79OPC-366
79T-688
80Syrac-7
81F-426
81OPC-324
81T-324
82OkCty-1
87Maine/TCMA-25
Willis, Ron
67T-592R
68OPC-68
68T-68
69T-273
Willis, Scott
87Cedar-3
Willis, Steve
87Anchora-31
Willis, Travis
89Geneva/Pro-1867
Willis, Vic
E104
E107
E90/1
E91
E95
M116
T206
WG3-52
Willoughby, Claude
R316
Willoughby, Jim
73OPC-79
73T-79
74OPC-553
74T-553
76OPC-102
76SSPC-419
76T-102
77T-532
78T-373
79T-266
Willoughby, Mark
86Columbia-27A
86Columbia-27B
Wills, Adrian Charles
87Greenvl/Best-8
Wills, Bump
77T-494R
78BK/R-12
78Ho-21
78OPC-208
78T-23
79OPC-190
79T-369
80OPC-373
80T-473
81D-25
81F-628
81OPC-173
81T-173
81T/HT
81T/St-134
82D-289
82F-334
82F/St-175
82OPC-272
82RedLob
82T-272
82T/St-244
82T/Tr-129T
83D-351
83F-511
83T-643
88Butte-29
89Butte/SP-24
Wills, Frank
82Omaha-10
84Omaha-5
85Cram/PCL-85
86F-480
86Maine-24
86T-419
87BuffB-23
87Gator-22
87T-551
88Syrac/CMC-11
88Syrac/Pro-830
89Syrac/CMC-5
89Syrac/Pro-794
89Tor/Fire-44
90F-98
Wills, Maury
60BB-20
61BB-30
61Morrell
61P-164
62BB-30
62J-104
62P-104
62P/Can-104
62Salada-127A
62Salada-127B
62Shirriff-127
63Exh
63F-43
63J-115
63P-115
63Salada-20
67T-570
68Bz-1

68Bz-4
68KDKA-30
68OPC-175
68T-175
69MB-293
69MLB/St-162
69OPC-45
69OPC/DE-23
69T-45
69T/DE-24
69T/decal
69T/S-49
69T/St-60
70MLB/St-60
70T-595
71Bz/Test-34
71MLB/St-120
71OPC-385
71T-385
71T/GM-29
71T/tatt-14
72MB-364
72OPC-437
72OPC-438IA
72T-437
72T-438A
75OPC-200M
75T-200MV
75T/M-200MV
77T-435M
78TCMA-70
81F-595
81Pol/Mar-14MG
81T-672MG
82KMart-2
83MLBPA/Pin-36
85Woolwth-39
87Smok/Dodg-38
87T-315TBC
88Smok/Dodg-7
89Smok/Dodg-69
Exh47

Wills, Ted
60L-56
61T-548
62T-444
65T-488
78TCMA-138

Willsher, Chris
84CharO-11

Willson, Rob
87Everett-22

Wilmet, Paul
82Lynch-10
85Sprin-30
87ArkTr-10
88EastLAS/Pro-18
88Harris/Pro-852
89OkCty/CMC-9
89OkCty/Pro-1509

Wilmont, Walter
N172
WG1-72

Wilner, Eric
85Anchora-34

Wilson, A. Parke
N566/2

Wilson, Alan
84LitFalls-20
87CharWh-4

Wilson, Archie C.
52B-210
52T-327

Wilson, Arthur Earl
10Domino-126
15CJ-148
D328-192
D329-191
D350/2-192
E135-192
E254
M101/4-191
M101/5-192
T207

Wilson, Arthur L.
(Artie)
49Remar
50Remar
52Mother-40

Wilson, Barney
75Cedar
76Cedar

Wilson, Brad
89Brist/Star-28

Wilson, Bubba
77Watlo

Wilson, Charles
R314/Can

Wilson, Chaun
88Hagers/Star-24

Wilson, Craig
85Sprin-12
87Elmir-18
87Elmir/Red-18
87StPet-2
88Louvl-50
88Louvl/CMC-15
88Louvl/Pro-439
88Lynch/Star-26
89ArkTr/GS-25
89Louvl-36
89Lynch/Star-22

Wilson, Daniel
88CapeCod/Sum-177

Wilson, Dave
81Clint-21

Wilson, David
89NiagFls/Puc-24

Wilson, Don
68Bz-13
68OPC-77
68T-77
69MLB/St-143
69OPC-202
69T-202
69T/St-39
69Trans-37
70K-62
70MLB/St-47
70OPC-515
70T-515
71MLB/St-95
71OPC-484
71T-484
71T/Coins-41
72K-51
72MB-365
72OPC-20
72OPC-91LL
72T-20
72T-91LL
73OPC-217
73T-217
74OPC-304
74T-304
75OPC-455
75T-455
75T/M-455
86Moth/Ast-10

Wilson, Doyle
87Kinston-20
88Wmspt/Pro-1324

Wilson, Earl
60T-249
61T-69
63J-83
63P-83
63T-76
64T-503
65OPC-42
65T-42
66T-575
67T-235LL
67T-237
67T-305
68Kahn
68OPC-10LL
68OPC-160
68T-10LL
68T-160
69MB-294
69T-525
70MLB/St-216
70OPC-95
70T-95
71OPC-301
71T-301
72MB-366
78TCMA-148
88Domino-26

Wilson, Eric
86Penin-27

Wilson, Gary
76Dubuq
79Charl-18
80Tucso-5
88Batav/Pro-1688
89Spart/Pro-1036
89Spart/Star-24

Wilson, George
79TCMA-189

Wilson, Glenn
81BirmB
83D-580
83F-350
83T-332
83T/St-318
84D-618
84F-94
84F/X-128
84Nes/792-563
84OPC-36
84T-563
84T/St-270
84T/X-129
85CIGNA-9
85D-609
85F-268
85OPC-189
85T-454
86BK/AP-7
86CIGNA-16
86D-285
86D/AAS-29
86F-457
86F/Mini-95
86F/St-128
86Keller-6
86Leaf-160
86OPC-318
86T-736
86T/Mini-56
86T/St-118
87D-62
87D/OD-158
87F-192
87F/Mini-115
87Leaf-146
87OPC-97
87S-166
87T-97
87T/St-117
88D-262
88D/Best-306
88F-320
88Moth/Sea-12
88OPC-359
88Panini/St-364
88RedFoley/St-103
88Score-405
88Sf-204
88T-626
88T/Big-260
88T/St-124
88T/Tr-129T
89B-423
89D-447
89D/Best-241
89F-224
89Score-106
89Sf-12
89T-293
89T/Big-284
90D-472
90F-240
90Score-346
90T-112
90UD-410

Wilson, Jack
86Phoen-25

Wilson, Jeff
83Wisco/LF-4
86Tampa-26

Wilson, Jim A.
52T-276
53B/Col-37
53JC-12
53T-208
54B-16
54JC-19
55B-253
55Gol/Braves-31
55JC-19
56T-171
57T-330
58T-163
79TCMA-130

Wilson, Jim
81Brist-6
83BuffB-14
83Pawtu-18
85IntLgAS-25
85Maine-24
86Maine-25
88EastLAS/Pro-38
88SanDiegoSt-19
88Vermont/Pro-944
89AAA/Pro-32
89Calg/CMC-22
89Calg/Pro-536

Wilson, Jimmy
28Exh-32
29Exh/4-15
31Exh/4-15
33G-37
34DS-22
34Exh/4-6
34Ward's/Pin-8
35BU-38
35Exh/4-6
35G-1E
35G-3C
35G-5C
35G-6C
36Exh/4-6
36Wheat
40PB-152
61F-88
R310
R332-30
R337-422
V353-37
V355-99
W711/2

Wilson, John F.
35BU-73
39PB-29
40PB-31
41PB-29

Wilson, John Owen
(Chief)
10Domino-125
11Helmar-138
11Helmar-166
12Sweet/Pin-122B
12Sweet/Pin-122A
12Sweet/Pin-144
14CJ-13
14Piedmont/St-63
15CJ-13
85Woolwth-41
D322
D329-192
D350/2-193
E104
E220
E224
E91
M101/4-192
M101/5-193
M116
S74-116
T202
T205
T206
T207
T213/blue
T213/brown
T215/brown

Wilson, Johnny
85Lynch-24
86Jacks/TCMA-22

Wilson, Jud
74Laugh/Black-12

Wilson, Lewis R.
(Hack)
28Exh-12
28Yueng-25
29Exh/4-5
30CEA/Pin-10
31Exh/4-5
33DH-43
33G-211
35BU-73
60F-48
61F-87
72F/FFeat-9
72Laugh/GF-27
79T-412M
80Cram/Leg-97
80Laugh/FFeat-4
80SSPC/HOF
85Woolwth-40
86Conlon/1-56
89Smok/Dodg-36
E210-25
R306
R315-A39
R315-B39
R316
R332-14
W502-25
W513-74
W517-42

Wilson, Mark
89Hamil/Star-26

Wilson, Matt
89GreatF-32

Wilson, Michael
83Toled-18
87Idaho-1

Wilson, Mike
77Clint
80Albuq-15

Wilson, Mookie
79Tidew-7
80Tidew-17
81D-575
81T-259R
82D-175
82F-542
82F/St-86
82OPC-143
82T-143
83D-56
83D/AAS-32
83Drake-29
83F-560
83OPC-55
83T-55

83T-621
83T/Gloss-2
83T/Gloss40-2
83T/St-266
84D-190
84Drake-31
84F-603
84F/St-91
84FunFood/Pin-65
84Jacks/Smok-13
84Nes/792-246TL
84Nes/792-465
84OPC-270
84T-465
84T/Mets/Fan-8
84T/St-108
85D-482
85F-95
85Leaf-122
85OPC-11
85T-775
85T/St-102
86D-604
86F-97
86Leaf-232
86OPC-315
86T-126M
86T-315
87D-487
87D/OD-129
87F-25
87F/Hottest-43
87Leaf-176
87OPC-84
87T-625
87T/Mets/Fan-8
88D-652
88D/Best-208
88D/Mets/Bk-652
88F-154
88Kahn/Mets-1
88Leaf-249
88Panini/St-348
88Score-474
88T-255
88T/Big-182
89B-386
89D-152
89F-52
89Kahn/Mets-1
89OPC-144
89Panini/St-141
89Score-302
89Score/Tr-16
89T-545
89T/Big-231
89UD-199
90D-442
90F-99
90Score-448
90Sf-128
90T-182
90UD-481

Wilson, Nigel
88StCath/Pro-2017
89StCath/Pro-2081

Wilson, Parker
80Elmir-30

Wilson, Phil
82Watlo/B-13
82Watlo/C-7
83Watlo/LF-14
85Visal-1
86Orlan-24
87Portl-9
88Portl/CMC-23
88Portl/Pro-661
89Jaxvl/Pro-171

Wilson, Randy
84Newar-22

Wilson, Ric
82Wausa-27
84Chatt-22
87Wausa-27

Wilson, Robert
(Red)
53T-250
54T-58
56T-92
57T-19
58T-213
59T-24
60T-379
61P-66
79TCMA-281

Wilson, Roger
86Miami-28
87Wmspt-21

Wilson, Sam W.
V100

Wilson, Scott
(trainer) 89SanJose/Best-17
89SanJose/Cal-234
89SanJose/Pro-454

Wilson, Steve
86Tulsa-10
87PortChar-10
88TexLgAS/GS-5
88Tulsa-8
89B-280
89D/Best-250
89D/Rook-10
89F-640M
89F/Up-82
89Mara/Cubs-44
89T/Tr-131T
89UD/Ext-799
90D-394
90F-49
90Score-531
90T-741
90UD-341

Wilson, Tack
81Albuq/TCMA-23A
82Albuq-23
84Toled-22
85Cram/PCL-195
87Edmon-10
89OkCty/CMC-22
89OkCty/Pro-1534

Wilson, Terry
89Myrtle/Pro-1474

Wilson, Tim
89Helena/SP-5

Wilson, Todd
86Cram/PCL-181

Wilson, Tom
86Tampa-27

Wilson, Trevor
86Clint-28
87Clint-27
88BBAmer-27
88Shreve/Pro-1298
89F-347
89Phoen/CMC-10
89Phoen/Pro-1481
89Score/HotRk-31
89T-783
89UD/Ext-733
90D-414
90T-408
90UD-637

Wilson, Ward
76Clint

Wilson, Wayne
84Newar-6
85Newar-11
86Hagers-28
87Hagers-16

Wilson, William D.
54T-222
55Rodeo
55T-86
55T/DH-101

Wilson, William H.
67T-402R
69T-576R
70OPC-28
70T-28
71MLB/St-192
71OPC-192
71T-192
72T-587
73OPC-619
73T-619

Wilson, Willie J.
75Watlo
79T-409
80BK/PHR-33
80OPC-87DP
80T-157
81Coke
81D-223
81F-29
81F/St-106
81K-24
81OPC-360
81Pol/Royals-10
81T-208M
81T-360
81T/So-20
81T/St-16
81T/St-247
81T/St-81
82D-448
82F-427
82F/St-207
82K-62
82OPC-230
82T-230
82T/St-189
83D-112
83D-15
83D/AAS-13
83Drake-30
83F-128
83K-23
83OPC-16
83Pol/Royals-10
83T-471
83T-701
83T-710
83T/Gloss-23
83T/Gloss40-23
83T/St-15
83T/St-161
83T/St-73
84D-175
84F-364
84F/St-94
84FunFood/Pin-82
84Nes/792-525
84OPC-5
84T-525
84T/St-280
84T/St/Box-5
85D-297
85F-218
85Leaf-110
85OPC-6
85T-617
85T/St-277
85Woolwth-42
86D-175
86F-25
86F/Mini-5
86F/St-129
86Kitty/Disc-15
86Leaf-106
86NatPhoto-6
86OPC-25
86S-124
86S-128M
86S-144M
86S-180M
86S-186M
86T-25
86T/Mini-22
86T/St-258
86T/Super-59
86Woolwth-32
87D-96
87D/OD-208
87F-384
87F/Excit-43
87F/Mini-116
87F/RecSet-42
87F/St-125
87Leaf-97
87OPC-367
87S-85
87T-783
87T/Mini-58
87T/St-261
88D-255
88D/Best-263
88F-274
88Leaf-189
88OPC-222
88Panini/St-113
88Score-102
88Sf-192
88Smok/Royals-3
88T-452
88T/Big-21
88T/Mini-17
88T/Revco-25
88T/St-263
89B-124
89D-120
89F-298
89KMart/Lead-17
89OPC-168
89Panini/St-361
89Score-28
89Sf-186
89T-168
89T/Big-136
89T/Mini-56
89T/St-268
89Tastee/Discs-5
89UD-244
90D-440
90F-123
90Score-104
90T-323
90UD-349

Wiltbank, Ben
78Salem
79Portl-4
79T-723R
81Buffa-5

Wiltse, George R.
(Hooks)
10Domino-127
11Helmar-139
12Sweet/Pin-123
14Piedmont/St-64
D303
E106
E107
E254
E90/1
E93
E95
M116
S74-96
T201
T202
T205
T206
T207
T215/blue
T215/brown
T216
W555

Wiltsie, Lew
WG3-53

Winbush, Mike
86Salem-29

Windes, Rodney
88AubAs/Pro-1955
89Ashvl/Pro-947

Windhorn, Gordon
62T-254

Wine, Robbie
86Tucso-26
87Tucso-3
88D-508
88F-459
88OkCty/CMC-22
88OkCty/Pro-42
88Score-496
88T-119
89Richm/CMC-11
89Richm/Ko-29
89Richm/Pro-843

Wine, Robert
(Bobby)
63T-71
64T-347
65OPC-36
65T-36
66T-284
67T-466
68T-396
69T-648
70MLB/St-72
70OPC-332
70T-332
71LaPizza-14
71MLB/St-144
71OPC-171
71T-171
72MB-367
72T-657
73OPC-486CO
73T-486C
74OPC-119CO
74T-119C
78TCMA-181
85Pol/Atl-7CO
86T-57MG
PM10/L-42

Winegarner, Ralph
R312

Winfield, Dave
74McDon
74OPC-456
74T-456
74T/St-100
75Ho-37
75OPC-61
75T-61
75T/M-61
76Ho-83
76OPC-160
76SSPC-133
76T-160
77Ho-44
77K-28
77OPC-156
77T-390
77T/CS-52
78Ho-63
78K-11
78OPC-78
78T-530
79Ho-125
79OPC-11
79T-30
79T/Comics-31
80BK/PHR-22
80K-32
80OPC-122
80T-230
80T/S-18
81D-364
81Drake-14
81F-484

81F/St-25
81K-21
81Sqt-19
81T-370
81T/HT
81T/St-111
81T/Tr-855
82D-18DK
82D-31
82D-575M
82Drake-31
82F-56
82F/St-110M
82F/St-113
82K-12
82OPC-352
82OPC-76AS
82Sqt-7
82T-553
82T-600
82T/St-137
82T/St-213
83D-409
83D/AAS-36
83Drake-31
83F-398
83F-633M
83K-15
83OPC-258
83RoyRog/Disc-12
83T-770
83T/Gloss-7
83T/Gloss40-7
83T/St-99
84D-51
84Drake-32
84F-143
84F/St-5
84FunFood/Pin-1
84MiltBrad-29
84Nes/792-402AS
84Nes/792-460
84Nestle/DT-6
84OPC-266AS
84OPC-378
84Ralston-7
84Seven-7E
84T-402
84T-460
84T/Cereal-7
84T/Gloss22-8
84T/Gloss40-16
84T/St-190
84T/St-319
84T/Super-27
84T/Super-27
85D-51
85D-651IA
85D/AAS-12
85D/HL-53
85Drake-32
85F-146
85F-629IA
85F/LimEd-43
85F/St-5
85GenMills-25
85Leaf-127
85Leaf-140M
85OPC-180
85Seven-3C
85Seven-3G
85Seven-5E
85Seven-5S
85Seven-5W
85T-180
85T-705AS
85T/3D-18
85T/Gloss22-17
85T/Gloss40-14
85T/St-186
85T/St-308
85T/Super-60
86BK/AP-2
86D-248
86D/AAS-15
86D/PopUp-15
86Dorman-19
86Drake-18
86F-121
86F/Mini-26
86F/St-130
86F/St-S4
86Jiffy-7
86Leaf-125
86Meadow/Blank-16
86Meadow/Stat-7
86OPC-70
86Quaker-33
86S-49
86S/Dec-74M
86T-70
86T-717
86T/3D-29
86T/Gloss22-8
86T/Gloss60-42
86T/Mini-29
86T/St-160
86T/St-298
86T/Super-60
86Woolwth-33
87Class-11
87D-105
87D-20DK
87D/AAS-2
87D/DKsuper-20
87D/OD-243
87D/PopUp-2
87Drake-5
87F-120
87F/McCror-42
87F/Mini-117
87F/St-126
87KayBee-33
87Kraft-33
87Leaf-20DK
87Leaf-70
87MSA/Discs-9
87OPC-36
87OPC-H
87Ralston-4
87RedFoley/St-28
87S-153M
87S-41
87Seven-E15
87T-770
87T-H
87T/Board-4
87T/Coins-26
87T/Gloss22-17
87T/St-152
87T/St-298
88Class/Red-170
88D-298
88D/AS-2
88D/Best-244
88D/PopUp-2
88D/Y/Bk-278
88F-226
88F/BB/AS-44
88F/BB/MVP-43
88F/Mini-44
88F/Slug-43
88F/St-53
88Jiffy-19
88KayBee-33
88Leaf-116
88Nestle-33
88OPC-89
88Panini/St-161
88Panini/St-231M
88Score-55
88Score/WaxBox-8
88Sf-7
88Sf/Gamewin-7
88T-392
88T-510
88T/Big-24
88T/Gloss22-8
88T/Gloss60-46
88T/St-159
88T/St-302
88T/St/Backs-54
88T/UK-85
89Ames-32
89B-179
89Cadaco-61
89Class-32
89D-159
89D/AS-6
89D/GrandSlam-6
89D/MVP-BC11
89D/PopUp-6
89F-274
89F/BBAS-44
89F/BBMVP's-43
89F/Excit-43
89F/Heroes-43
89F/LL-43
89F/Superstar-43
89KayBee-32
89KingB/Discs-16
89OPC-260
89Panini/St-240AS
89Panini/St-409
89RedFoley/St-128
89Score-50
89Score/HotSt-3
89Score/Mast-41
89Score/NWest-7
89Sf-24
89T-260
89T-407AS
89T/Big-314
89T/Coins-58
89T/Gloss22-8
89T/Gloss60-21
89T/Hills-32
89T/Mini-67
89T/St-149
89T/St-315
89T/St/Backs-20
89T/UK-84
89T/WaxBox-P
89Tetley/Discs-13
89UD-349
90D-551
90F-458
90Score-307
90Sf-87
90T-380
90UD-337

Winfield, Steven W.
80Memph-27
82Louvl-30
82Sprin-11
83ArkTr-8

Winford, Barry
89Butte/SP-7

Wingard, Ernest
25Exh-120
26Exh-120
27Exh-60

Wingfield, Fred
26Exh-72
27Exh-36

Wingo, Al
25Exh-95

Wingo, Ivy B.
14CJ-130
15CJ-130
21Exh-188
25Exh-32
26Exh-32
27Exh-16
BF2-72
C46-40
D327
D329-193
D350/2-194
E120
E121/120
E121/80
E122
E220
M101/4-193
M101/5-194
T207
T222
V100
V117-14
V61-83
W501-50
W514-73
W572
W575

Winkelman, George
N172

Winkler, Brad
84Greens-3
85Albany-22

Winkles, Bobby
73OPC-421MG
73T-421MG
74OPC-276MG
74T-276MG
76SSPC-624
78T-378
86Provigo-14CO

Winn, Jim
84Cram/PCL-138
85Cram/PCL-237
85T-69
86F-624
86T-489
87Coke/WS-23
87D-312
87F-624
87F/U-U126
87T-262
87T/Tr-130T
88D-409
88F-413
88OPC-388
88Portl/CMC-9
88Portl/Pro-642
88Score-462
88T-688
88T/St-288

Winningham, Herm
82Lynch-3
84Tidew-5
85F/Up-U130
85OPC/Post-8
85T/Tr-131T
86D-279
86F-266
86Leaf-153
86OPC-129
86Provigo-22
86T-448
86T/St-83
87F/U-U130
87OPC-141
87T-141
88D-581
88F-200
88Ho/Disc-4
88Leaf-242
88OPC-216
88Panini/St-332
88Score-142
88Score/Tr-43T
88T-614
88T/St-83
89D-435
89F-175
89K/Reds-29
89Score-496
89T-366
89T/Big-94
89UD-636
90D-478
90F-435
90Score-38
90T-94
90UD-589

Winslow, Daniel
81ArkTr-15

Winston, Darrin
88James/Pro-1918

Winter, George
E107

Winter, Lee
53Mother-1

Winterburn, Robert
88Boise/Pro-1631

Winterfeldt, Todd
79Wausa-3
81Tidew-7

Winters, Dan
86Lynch-27

Winters, George
WG2-50

Winters, James A.
86Penin-28
87BirmB/Best-24

Winters, Matt
83Colum-23
84Colum-22
84Colum/Pol-24
85Colum-22
85Colum/Pol-24
86BuffB-25
87Memph-7
87Memph/Best-24
87SLAS-9
88Memph/Best-19
88SLAS-1
89Omaha/CMC-21
89Omaha/Pro-1728
90F-124
90Score/100Ris-47
90UD-524

Wirth, Alan
79Ogden/TCMA-22
79T-711R
80Ogden-17
81Spoka-25

Wirth, Greg
84Newar-10

Wisdom, Allen
87Clearw-24

Wise, Brett Wayne
81VeroB-24

Wise, K. Casey
57T-396
58T-247
59T-204
60T-342

Wise, Rick
64T-561R
65T-322
67OPC-37
67T-37
68T-262
69MLB/St-180
69OPC-188
69T-188
69T/St-80
70MLB/St-96
70T-605
70T/PI-8
71MLB/St-191
71OPC-598
71T-598
71T/Coins-131
72K-23
72MB-368
72OPC-345KP
72OPC-43

72OPC-44IA
72T-345BP
72T-43
72T-44A
72T-756TR
72T/Post-14
73OPC-364
73T-364
74OPC-339AS
74OPC-84
74T-339M
74T-84
74T/St-139
75OPC-56
75T-56
75T/M-56
76K-35
76OPC-170
76T-170
77T-455
78T-572
79OPC-127
79T-253
80OPC-370
80T-725
81D-3
81OPC-274
81T-616
81T/St-232
82D-170
82F-585
82T-330
85Madis-24C
85Madis/Pol-25C
86Madis-28C
86Madis/Pol-27C
88AubAs/Pro-1963
89AubAs/Pro-2187

Wise, Sam
N172
N284
WG1-9

Wiseman, Michael
88CapeCod/Sum-174

Wiseman, Tim
85Orlan-21

Wishnevski, Bob
88Duned/Star-22
89Knoxv/Best-27
89Knoxv/Pro-1138
89Knoxv/Star-22
89SLAS-21

Wishnevski, Mike
86Chatt-25
87Calgary-16
88Calg/CMC-20
88Calg/Pro-783

Wismer, Michael
89GreatF-12

Wissel, Dick
75IntAS/TCMA-30
75IntAS/TCMA-31

Wistert, Francis
R314/Can

Witek, Nicholas
(Mickey)
47TipTop

Witherspoon, Richard
89Elmir/Puc-21

Withol, Al
77Watlo

Withrow, Mike
83GlenF-21

Witkowski, Matt
89CharRa/Pro-985

Witmeyer, Ron
89Modesto/Cal-281
89Modesto/Ch-27

Witt, Bobby
85Tulsa-18
86D/Rook-49
86F/Slug-42
86F/Up-U129
86Rang-48
86S/Rook-12
86T/Tr-126T
87D-99
87D/HL-25
87F-143
87F/Excit-44
87Leaf-112
87Moth/Rang-25
87S-39
87Smok/R-6
87T-415
88D-101
88F-483
88F-626M
88Moth/R-25
88Panini/St-198
88Score-149
88Smok/R-7
88T-747
89B-222
89Class-77
89D-461
89D/Best-279
89F-537
89Moth/R-14
89OPC-38
89Panini/St-448
89Score-463
89Score/YS/I-8
89Sf-82
89Smok/R-34
89T-548
89T/Big-191
89UD-557
90D-292
90F-315
90Score-457
90T-166
90UD-636

Witt, George
59Kahn
59T-110
60T-298
61T-286
62T-287

Witt, Hal
78StPet

Witt, Lawton
(Whitey)
D327
D328-193
E135-193
E220
V100
W515-37

Witt, Mike
82D-416
82F-473
82T-744
83D-416
83F-102
83T-53
83T-651TL
84F-531
84Nes/792-499
84Smok/Cal-31
84T-499
85D-108
85F-316
85F/St-111
85Leaf-46
85OPC-309
85Smok/Cal-1
85T-309
85T/St-195
85T/St-227
85T/Super-45
86D-179
86D/HL-38
86F-171
86F/Mini-36
86F/Slug-43
86Leaf-112
86S-53M
86Smok/Cal-1
87D-58
87D/AAS-51
87D/OD-2
87F-641M
87F-95
87F/AwardWin-43
87F/GameWin-43
87F/Lim-44
87F/Mini-118
87F/Slug-44
87F/St-127
87Kraft-47
87Leaf-111
87MnM's-17
87OPC-92
87RedFoley/St-4
87S-59
87Seven-W15
87Smok/Cal-3
87T-760
87T/Gloss60-33
87T/Mini-48
87T/St-179
88D-86
88D/AS-20
88D/Best-307
88F-507
88F-626M
88F/Mini-13
88F/SS-43
88F/St-13
88Leaf-49
88OPC-270
88Panini/St-38
88Score-81
88Sf-32
88Smok/Angels-4
88T-270
88T/Big-4
88T/St-174
88T/UK-86
89B-42
89D-372
89F-490
89OPC-190
89Panini/St-286
89RedFoley/St-129
89Score-298
89Sf-197
89Smok/Angels-19
89T-190
89T/Coins-59
89T/St-176
89T/UK-85
89UD-555
90D-580
90F-148
90Score-226
90T-650
90UD-548

Witte, Jerome
47TipTop

Wittmayer, Kurt
78OrlTw

Wockenfuss, John
76OPC-13
76T-13
78BK/T-3
78T-723
79T-231
80T-338
81Coke
81D-245
81F-472
81T-468
81T/St-79
82D-459
82F-286
82OPC-46
82T-629
83D-76
83F-351
83T-536
83T/St-64
84D-150
84F-95
84F/X-129
84Nes/792-119
84T-119
84T/St-274
84T/X-130
85D-549
85F-269
85T-39
86FSLAS-50
86Miami-29
88GlenF/Pro-917
89Toled/CMC-25
89Toled/Pro-771

Wohler, Barry
85VeroB-19
87SnAnt-8
88SnAnt/Best-2

Wohlers, Mark
89Pulas/Pro-1908
89Sumter/Pro-1099

Wohlford, Jim
73OPC-611R
73T-611R
74OPC-407
74T-407
75OPC-144
75T-144
75T/M-144
76A&P/KC
76OPC-286
76SSPC-179
76T-286
77T-622
78T-376
79T-596
80Pol/Giants-9
80T-448
81D-316
81F-440
81T-11
82F-403
82T-116
83D-524
83F-276
83Stuart-21
83T-688
83T/X-128
84F-293
84Nes/792-253
84OPC-253
84Stuart-24
84T-253
85D-585
85F-413
85Leaf-82
85OPC-4
85T-787
86D-157
86OPC-344
86Provigo-6
86T-344
87F-336
87OPC-169
87T-527

Woide, Steve
88Myrtle/Pro-1172

Wojcik, Jim
81Shrev-5

Wojcik, John
63T-253R

Wojna, Ed
83Readg-10
84Cram/PCL-231
85Cram/PCL-120
86D-505
86F-338
86LasVegas-24
86T-211
87D-589
87T-88
88Vanco/CMC-5
88Vanco/Pro-756
89ColrSp/CMC-4
89ColSp/Pro-236

Wolak, Jarry
89Utica/Puc-27

Wolf, Mike
78Knoxv

Wolf, Rick
77Wausa

Wolf, Walter
(Wally)
63T-208R
70OPC-74R
70T-74R

Wolf, William
N172

Wolfe, Donn
88StCath/Pro-2013

Wolfe, Larry
79T-137
80T-549

Wolfe, Scott
75Lafay

Wolfer, Jim
89Greens/Pro-419

Wolfgang, Meldon
D329-194
D350/2-195
M101/4-194
M101/5-195

Wolkoys, Rob
86Cram/PCL-26
87AppFx-21

Wollenburg, Jay
86Macon-26

Wollenhaupt, Ron
82Watlo/B-28
82Watlo/C-4

Wolten, Brad
87Watlo-5

Wolter, Harry
10Domino-128
11Helmar-50
12Sweet/Pin-39
M116
S74-25
T202
T205

Wolters, Mike
83ArkTr-14

Wolverton, Harry
11Helmar-51
T207

Womack, Dooley
66T-469R
67OPC-77
67T-77
68T-431
69T-594

Wong, Dave
81CharR-3
82FtMyr-14

Wong, Kaha
89Reno/Cal-257

Wood, Andre
78Duned
82Knoxv-14
83Knoxv-13

Wood, Bill
82Tucso-22

Wood, Brian
86Cram/PCL-155
88River/Cal-215
88River/Pro-1420

89Wich/Roc-23RHP

Wood, Dave
76Clint

Wood, George
N172
N284
N690
WG1-54

Wood, Jake
61T-514
62J-15
62P-15
62Salada-83
62Shirriff-83
62T-427
62T-72
62T/St-50
63T-453
64T-272
65T-547
66T-509
67T-394
78TCMA-186

Wood, Jeff
85CharO-17
87CharO/WBTV-tr
88CharlK/Pep-10

Wood, Joe
14CJ-22
15CJ-22
21Exh-189
87Conlon/2-57
88CharlK-10
BF2-7
D327
D328-194
D329-195
D350/2-196
E103
E120
E121/80
E122
E135-194
E254
E270/1
E91
M101/4-195
M101/5-196
M116
T202
T207
V100
W575
WG4-30
WG5-44
WG6-41

Wood, Johnson
81BurlB-12
82Beloi-5
84ElPas-2

Wood, Ken
50B-190
51B-209
52T-139
53B/Col-109

Wood, Mike
84Butte-5

Wood, Pete
N172

Wood, Robert Lynn
E107

Wood, Stephen
88VeroB/Star-24

Wood, Ted
88T/Tr-130TOLY
89Shreve/Pro-1842
89T/Big-308

Wood, Wilbur
64T-267
65T-478
67T-391
68T-585
69MB-295
69MLB/St-36
69OPC-123
69T-123
69T/St-160
70MLB/St-192
70OPC-342
70T-342
71OPC-436
71T-436
72K-4
72MB-369
72OPC-342KP
72OPC-92LL
72OPC-94LL
72T-342BP
72T-553
72T-554A
72T-92LL
72T-94LL
72T/Post-19
73K-9
73OPC-150
73OPC-66LL
73T-150
73T-66LL
73T/Lids-54
74K-34
74OPC-120
74OPC-205LL
74T-120
74T-205LL
74T/DE-13
74T/St-160
75Ho-68
75Ho/Twink-68
75OPC-110
75T-110
75T/M-110
76Crane-67
76Ho-99
76MSA/Disc
76OPC-368
76SSPC-139
76T-368
77T-198
78T-726
79OPC-108
79T-216
89Pac/Leg-124
89Swell-127

Woodall, Charles L.
(Lawrence)
21Exh-190
25Exh-96
28Exh-48
E120
E126-53
V61-21
W573

Woodard, Darrell
82BirmB-3

Woodard, Mike
81WHave-17
82WHave-19
83Tacom-13
85Cram/PCL-181
86D-46
86F-645M
86Phoen-26
87Phoen-10
87T-286
88Vanco/CMC-14
88Vanco/Pro-767
89Colum/CMC-12
89Colum/Pol-23
89Colum/Pro-742
89F-513

Woodbrey, Mark
75Cedar
76Cedar

Woodburn, Eugene
T207

Wooden, Mark
86Cram/PCL-129
87Wausa-16
88Vermont/Pro-939
89Wmspt/Pro-628
89Wmspt/Star-23

Woodeschick, Hal
59T-106
60T-454
61T-397
62T-526
63T-517
64T-370
64T/St-78
64T/SU
64Wheat/St-49
65OPC-179
65T-179
66T-514
67T-324
78TCMA-123
86Moth/Ast-2
89Smok/Ast-10

Woodhouse, Kevin
84Evrt/Cram-9

Woodling, Gene
48Sommer-13
51B-219
51BR-D1
52B-177
52BR
52Dix
52T-99
53B/BW-31
53Dix
53RM-AL12
53T-264
54B-209
54Dix
54NYJour
54RM-AL15
54T-101
55Esskay
55Salem
55T-190
56T-163
56YellBase/Pin-31
57T-172
58T-398
59T-170
60T-190
60T/tatt-54
61Bz-30
61P-70
61T-275
61T/St-207
62Bz
62J-71
62P-71
62P/Can-71
62Salada-96
62Shirriff-96
62T-125
62T/bucks
62T/St-101
63T-342
63T-43M
88Pac/Leg-5
89Swell-102
Exh47
PM10/L-43
PM10/L-44
PM10/Sm-201
R423-112
TCMA79-156

Woodmansee, Mark
83SLCty-12

Woodruff
E270/1

Woodruff, Pat
89Batav/Pro-1936

Woods, Alvis
(Al)
77OPC-256
77T-479R
78OPC-175
78Syrac
78T-121
79OPC-85
79T-178
80OPC-230
80T-444
81D-32
81F-422
81OPC-165
81OPC/Post-17
81T-703
81T/St-141
82D-180
82F-627
82OPC-49
82OPC/Post-5
82T-49
83F-444
83OPC-59
83T-589
84Syrac-14
85Toled-25
86Toled-24

Woods, Anthony
86Wausa-28
87Wausa-13
88SnBer/Best-5
89SnBer/Best-17
89SnBer/Cal-83

Woods, Clancy
79AppFx-7

Woods, Eric
88WinSal/Star-22
89WinSal/Star-18

Woods, Gary
76Tucso-3
77OPC-22
77T-492R
78OPC-13
78Syrac
78T-599
79Charl-5
80Tucso-22
81F-75
81T-172
82F-237
82RedLob
82T-483
82T/Tr-130T
83D-631
83F-512
83T-356
83Thorn-25
84D-144
84F-507
84Nes/792-231
84SevenUp-25
84T-231
85D-555
85F-71
85Leaf-49
85SevenUp-25
85T-46
86F-385
86LasVegas-25
86T-611

Woods, George
49B/PCL-4

Woods, Jim
60L-104
61T-59

Woods, Kelly
89Princet/Star-25

Woods, Lyle
87Anchora-41ANN

Woods, Parnell
49Remar

Woods, Preston
88CapeCod/Sum-54

Woods, Ron
69T-544R
70OPC-253
70T-253
71MLB/St-504
71OPC-514
71T-514
72OPC-82
72T-82
73OPC-531
73T-531
74OPC-377
74T-377

Woods, Tony
83QuadC-22
84MidldC-24
86Pittsf-25
87Miami-5
88Tampa/Star-24
88Wausa/Feder-22
88Wausa/GS-22

Woods, Tyrone
89James/Pro-2134

Woods, Walter
E254

Woodson, Dick
70OPC-479
70T-479
71MLB/St-479
71OPC-586
71T-586
72T-634
73OPC-98
73T-98
74OPC-143
74T-143

Woodson, George
69T-244R

Woodson, Tracy
85VeroB-2
87Albuq/Pol-24
87Moth/Dodg-22
88AAA/Pro-3
88Albuq/CMC-17
88Albuq/Pro-256
88D-499
88F/U-U98
89Albuq/CMC-16
89Albuq/Pro-75
89F-77
89Pol/Dodg-12
89Score-586
89T-306
89T/Big-92
89UD-108

Woodward, Jim
82Jacks-17

Woodward, Rob
86D/Rook-53
86F-651M
86Pawtu-28
87Class-69
87D-652
87Pawtu/TCMA-23
87T-632
88Pawtu/CMC-1
88Pawtu/Pro-448
88Score-403
89Pawtu/CMC-10
89Pawtu/Dunkin-25
89Pawtu/Pro-699

Woodward, William
(Woody)
64T-378R
65T-487
66OPC-49
66T-49
67Kahn

67T-546
68Coke
68T-476
69OPC-142
69T-142
70OPC-296
70T-296
71MLB/St-72
71OPC-496
71T-496
72MB-370
Woodworth, John
80Utica-9
82Knoxv-23
83Knoxv-21
85Syrac-10
86Syrac-27TR
Woolridge, Floyd
55Hunter
Wooten, Daryl
89AubAs/Pro-2189
Wooten, Earl
49B-189
Worden, Bill
82Danvi-20
83Redwd-25
84Nashvl-25
86Water-26
Workman, Michael
86Watlo-32
87Kinston-14
Works, Ralph
E286
T207
Worrell, Todd
81Louvl-26
84ArkTr-6
85Louvl-28
86D-43
86D/HL-29
86D/HL-54
86D/Rook-21
86F-49
86KAS/Disc-10
86S-179M
86S/Rook-35
86Schnucks-24
86T/Tr-127T
87Class-97
87D-307
87F-312
87F/AS-8
87F/AwardWin-44
87F/Hottest-44
87F/LL-44
87F/McCror-43
87F/Mini-119
87F/RecSet-43
87F/St-128
87Leaf-218
87OPC-67
87S-33
87S-77M
87Smok/Cards-2
87T-465
87T-605AS
87T-7RB
87T/Coins-48
87T/Gloss60-10
87T/GlossRk-22
87T/HL-13
87T/Mini-34
87T/St-11
87T/St-12
87T/St-310
87T/St-55
87ToysRUs-33
87Woolwth-13
88Woolwth-24
88Bz-22
88ChefBoy-8
88Class/Red-181
88D-386
88D/Best-268
88F-50
88F-C16
88F/LL-44
88F/Mini-111
88F/RecSet-44
88F/Slug-44
88F/St-122
88F/WaxBox-C16
88F/WS-5M
88KMart-32
88Leaf-229
88OPC-135
88Panini/St-386
88Score-202
88Sf-61
88Smok/Card-10
88T-715
88T/Big-149
88T/Coins-60
88T/Mini-73
88T/St-54
89B-429
89Cadaco-62
89D-82
89D/AS-60
89D/Best-243
89F-466
89F/BBMVP's-44
89F/Superstar-44
89Louvl-37
89OPC-291
89Panini/St-179
89Score-265
89Score/HotSt-94
89Sf-183
89Smok/Cards-23
89T-535
89T/Mini-37
89T/St-39
89UD-512
90D-319
90F-264
90Score-392
90Sf-165
90T-95
90UD-467
Wortham, Rich
80OPC-261DP
80T-502
81D-161
81F-347
81T-107
82Readg-10
Worthington, Al
54NYJour
55Gol/Giants-32
57T-39
58Hires-73
58SFCall
58T-427
59T-28
60T-268
62AmTract-66
63FrBauer-31
63T-556
64T-144
65OPC-216
65T-216
66OPC-181
66T-181
67T-399
68T-473
73OPC-49CO
73T-49C
79TCMA-269
Worthington, Craig
86Hagers-29
87RochR-23
87RochR/TCMA-17
88D/Rook-23
88F/U-U4
88RochR-26
88RochR-27
88RochR/CMC-19
88RochR/Gov-27
88RochR/Pro-217
89D-569
89D/Best-282
89D/Rook-25
89F-627
89French-11
89Panini/St-252
89Score-636
89Score/HotRk-6
89Score/YS/II-21
89Sf-134
89T-181
89UD/Ext-725
90Class-31
90D-141
90F-195
90Score-234
90Score/100Ris-21
90Sf-117
90T-521
90UD-444
Wortman, William
(Chuck)
D328-195
E135-195
Wortmann, Russ
82Idaho-15
Wotus, Ron
82Buffa-11
84Cram/PCL-128
86Hawai-22
87Omaha-20
89Phoen/CMC-19
89Phoen/Pro-1501
Woyce, Don
86FtMyr-29
Woyt, Boris
V362-29
Wray, James
88GreatF-13
89Bakers/Cal-189
Wren, Frank
80Memph-28
Wrenn, Luke
76Shrev
Wright, Bill
87Idaho-17
Wright, Brian
89Idaho/Pro-2009
Wright, Clyde
69T-583
70OPC-543
70T-543
71Bz
71Bz/Test-6
71JB
71K-28
71MLB/St-359
71OPC-240
71OPC-67LL
71T-240
71T-67LL
71T/Coins-60
71T/GM-18
71T/S-39
71T/tatt-14
72MB-371
72OPC-55
72T-55
73OPC-373
73T-373
74OPC-525
74T-525
75OPC-408
75T-408
75T/M-408
76OPC-559
76SSPC-258
76T-559
89Smok/Angels-6
Wright, Don
88AppFx/Pro-146
89AppFx/Pro-855
Wright, F. Glenn
25Exh-56
26Exh-56
28Exh-28
28Yueng-47
31Exh/4-4
33Exh/4-2
33G-1453
34Exh/4-2
35G-2B
35G-4B
35G-7B
R306
V353-77
W502-47
W512-5
Wright, George
50Callahan
80SSPC/HOF
Wright, George
78Ashev
80Tulsa-10
81Tulsa-1
83D-116
83F-583
83Rang-26
83T-299
83T/St-124
84D-525
84F-435
84Nes/792-688
84OPC-314
84Rang-26
84T-688
84T/St-353
85D-256
85F-574
85OKCty-16
85OPC-387
85T-443
86D-220
86F-578
86T-169
86T/Tr-128T
89HOF/St-15
89Phoen/CMC-24
89Phoen/Pro-1484
Wright, Goldie
83Redwd-26
Wright, Henderson E.
(Ed)
47TipTop
52T-368
Wright, J.P.
89Keno/Pro-1072
89Keno/Star-24
Wright, James L.
78PapaG/Disc-18
79OPC-180
79T-722R
80OkCty
80T-524
82D-490
82T-362
Wright, James R.
79T-349
80Penin/B-13
80Penin/C-7
81T-526R
82Syrac-10
86Peoria-26CO
87Pittsf-5
87Toled/TCMA-12
88IowaC/CMC-25
88IowaC/Pro-542
89IowaC/CMC-24
89IowaC/Pro-1697
Wright, Ken
71OPC-504
71T-504
72T-638
73OPC-578
73T-578
76QuadC
77QuadC
Wright, Larry
78Clint
Wright, Mark
80Batav-30
81Wisco-11
82Wisco-6
Wright, Mel
73OPC-517
73T-517C
83Stuart-25CO
Wright, Mike
79QuadC-1
Wright, Mitch
79Newar-21
Wright, Paul
82Redwd-17
Wright, Richard
(Ricky)
81Albuq/TCMA-7
82Albuq-11
83F-226
83Pol/Dodg-21
85OKCty-9
86Rang-24
86T/Tr-129T
87T-202
87Toled-6
Wright, Skipper
88Sumter/Pro-404
89BurlB/Pro-1626
Wright, Taft
40PB-186
41G-10
41PB-32
47TipTop
49B-96
Exh47
Wright, Thomas
51B-271
54T-140
55T-141
55T/DH-75
Wright, W. Henry
(Harry)
50Callahan
75F/Pion-2
80SSPC/HOF
N172
N690
Wright, William S.
T206
Wrightstone, Russell
21Exh-191
26Exh-48
27Exh-24
E120
E126-43
V61-61
W573
Wrigley, Charles
R332-9UMP
Wrona, Bill
86Beaum-25
88Wichi-21
89LasVeg/CMC-19
89LasVeg/Pro-18
Wrona, Dave
88CapeCod/Sum-39
Wrona, Rick
86WinSal-28
87Pittsf-17
89D/Rook-38
90D-512

68T-6LL
68T/G-3
68T/Post-16
69Kelly/Pin-20
69MLBPA/Pin-30
69OPC-130
69OPC-1LL
69OPC/DE-24
69T-130
69T-1LL
69T-425AS
69T/DE-4
69T/decal
69T/S-5
69T/St-140
70MLB/St-168
70OPC-10
70OPC-461AS
70T-10
70T-461AS
70T/S-29
70T/SO
71Bz
71Bz/Test-5
71MLB/St-336
71MLB/St-576
71OPC-530
71OPC-61LL
71OPC-65LL
71T-530
71T-61LL
71T-65LL
71T/Coins-58
71T/GM-40
71T/S-49
71T/tatt-2
71T/tatt-2a
72OPC-37
72OPC-38IA
72T-37
72T-38A
72T/Post-2
73OPC-245
73T-245
73T/Comics-24
73T/Lids-55
73T/PinUps-24
74Laugh/ASG-70
74OPC-280
74T-280
74T/DE-43
74T/Puzzles-12
74T/St-140
75Ho-48
75K-51
75OPC-205M
75OPC-280
75T-205MV
75T-280
75T/M-205MV
75T/M-280
76Crane-69
76Ho-149
76K-24
76Laugh/Jub-9
76MSA/Disc
76OPC-230
76SSPC-409
76T-230
77Ho-4
77OPC-37
77Pep-23
77T-434M
77T-480
77T/CS-53
78OPC-137
78PapaG/Disc-8
78T-40
78Wiffle/Discs-78
79K-45
79OPC-160
79T-320
79T/Comics-3
80K-27
80OPC-365DP
80T-720
80T/S-22
81Coke
81D-214
81D-94
81Drake-1
81F-221
81F/St-13
81K-48
81OPC-110
81T-110
81T/HT
81T/St-45
82Coke/Bos
82D-74
82F-312
82F-633M
82F/St-162
82F/St-237M
82K-43
82KMart-11
82OPC-358IA 82OPC-72
82T-650
82T-651A
82T/St-120
82T/St-155
83D-25DK
83D-326
83D/AAS-44
83Drake-32
83F-200
83F-629M
83K-9
83OPC-126SV
83OPC-4
83T-550
83T-551A
83T/Gloss-1
83T/Gloss40-1
83T/St-31
83T/St-6
84D-660
84D-LLB
84D/Champs-10
84F-412
84F-640IA
84F/St-97
84Nes/792-6HL
84T-6
84T/Gloss22-11
85CircK-17
86S/Dec-47
87KMart-11
87T-314TBC
89Kahn/Coop-11
90D-588PUZ
Exh47
PM10/Sm-203
PM10/Sm-204
WG10-48
WG9-50

Yastrzemski, Mike
84Durhm-3
85Durhm-32
86SLAS-2
87Hawai-1
88Vanco/CMC-19
88Vanco/Pro-774

Yates, Al
No Cards.

Yawkey, Tom
89HOF/St-93

Yeager, Eric
85Anchora-32
87Anchora-32

Yeager, Joseph
C46-84
E107
E270/1

Yeager, Steve
73OPC-59
73T-59
74OPC-593
74T-593
75OPC-376
75T-376
75T/M-376
76Ho-147
76OPC-515
76SSPC-83
76T-515
77OPC-159
77T-105
78T-285
79OPC-31
79T-75
80OPC-371
80Pol/Dodg-7
80T-726
81D-297
81F-129
81OPC-318
81Pol/Dodg-7
81T-318
81T/HT
82D-201
82F-29
82OPC-219
82Pol/Dodg
82Pol/Dodg-7
82T-477
83D-201
83F-227
83OPC-261
83Pol/Dodg-7
83T-555
84D-581
84F-117
84Nes/792-661
84OPC-252
84Pol/Dodg-7
84T-661
84T/St-86
85D-519
85F-390
85OPC-148
85T-148
86D-519
86F/Up-U131
86Moth/Mar-5
86OPC-32
86T-32
86T/Tr-130T
87F-599
87OPC-258
87T-258

Yearout, Mike
86Knoxv-26
87Knoxv-3

Yeglinski, John
75Lafay
77ArkTr

Yelding, Eric
85Kingst-23
86Ventura-28
87Knoxv-12
88AAA/Pro-37
88Syrac/CMC-17
88Syrac/Pro-832
89D/Rook-34
89Lennox/Ast-12
89Moth/Ast-21
89Score/HotRk-65
90D-123
90Score-411
90Score/100Ris-16
90T-309
90UD-427

Yellen, Larry
64T-226R
65T-292

Yellowhorse, Moses
21Exh-192

Yelovic, John
43Centen-25

Yerkes, Stephen
D328-196
D329-196
D350/2-197
E135-196
E224
M101/4-196
M101/5-197
T207

Yesenchak, Ed
76AppFx
77AppFx

Yett, Rich
81Wisco-12
83Orlan-15
84Toled-5
85F/Up-U131
85Toled-30
86Maine-26
86OhHenry-42
87F-263
87Gator-42
87T-134
88F-621
88Gator-42
88Score-484
88T-531
89B-79
89D-546
89F-417
89Score-467
89T-363
89T/Big-290
89UD/Ext-728
90D-509
90F-504
90Score-274
90T-689
90UD-595

Yingling, Earl
D328-197
E135-197

Yobs, Dave
85BuffB-16
86BuffB-26

Yochim, Ray
49Eureka-200

Yoder, Kris
76Wmspt
78Richm
79Savan-13

Yojo, Minoru
89Visal/Cal-115
89Visal/Pro-1424

Yokota, George
86SanJose-25

York, Anthony
47Centen-32
47Signal
49B/PCL-22

York, Jim
72OPC-68
72T-68
73OPC-546
73T-546
75OPC-383
75T-383
75T/M-383
76OPC-224
76T-224

York, Mike
86Lakel-25
87Macon-7
88Salem/Star-25
89Harris/Pro-310
89Harris/Star-23
89Star/Wax-21

York, Rudy
38Exh/4-12
38G-260
38G-284
39Exh
40Wheat-6
47TipTop
60T-456C
72F/FFeat-12
72Laugh/GF-3
74Laugh/ASG-42
85Woolwth-43
R346-27

Yoshida, Takashi
89Visal/Cal-120CO
89Visal/Pro-1430

Yoshinaga, Yoshi
89Salin/Cal-136
89Salin/Pro-1810

Yost, Eddie
49B-32
50B-162
51B-41
51T/BB-1
52B-31
52NTea
52RM-AL25
52T-123
52TipTop
53B/Col-116
53Briggs
54B-72
54RH
55B-73
56T-128
57Swift-11
57T-177
58T-173
59T-2
60T-245
61Bz-6
61P-45
61T-413
61T/St-175
62J-76
62P-76
62P/Can-76
62T-176
73OPC-257CO
73T-257C
74OPC-179CO
74T-179C
79TCMA-88
R423-117

Yost, Edgar
(Ned)
79T-708R
79Vanco-13
80Vanco-3
81T-659R
82Pol/Brew-5
82T-542
83D-458
83F-50
83Gard-21
83Pol/Brew-5
83T-297
84D-271
84F-218
84F/X-130
84Jacks/Smok-15
84Nes/792-107
84Rang-7
84T-107
84T/X-131
85D-221
85F-575
85T-777
87Greenv/Bst-12
88SALAS/GS-3
88Sumter/Pro-414
89Sumter/Pro-1095

Youmans, Floyd
84Jacks-15
86D-543
86F-267
86Leaf-210
86OPC-346
86Provigo-24
86T-732
87Class-98
87D-257
87D/HL-22
87D/OD-89
87F-337
87F/Mini-120
87F/RecSet-44
87Ho/St-6
87Leaf-206
87Leaf-65CG
87OPC-105
87S-103
87T-105
87T/Mini-19
87T/St-79
88D-56
88D/Best-314
88F-201
88Ho/Disc-9
88Leaf-66
88OPC-365
88Panini/St-321
88Score-327
88Score/YS/II-16
88Sf-108
88T-365
88T/St-82
89B-396
89OPC-91
89T-91
89UD-459
89UD/Ext-730
Young, Anthony
88LitFalls/Puc-24
89Clmbia/Best-16
89Clmbia/GS-28
Young, Bob G.
52B-193
52T-147
53T-160
54B-149
54Esskay
54T-8
55Esskay
Young, Cliff
86Knoxv-27
86SLAS-24
87Knoxv-27
88Syrac/CMC-8
88Syrac/Pro-807
89Edmon/CMC-4
89Edmon/Pro-557
Young, Curt
83Tacom-8
84Cram/PCL-85
85D-522
85F-436
85Moth/A's-22
85T-293
86T-84
86Tacom-25
87D-344
87D/OD-29
87F-410
87F/GameWin-44
87F/St-129
87Smok/A's-12
87T-519
87T/St-165
88D-97
88D/A's/Bk-97
88D/Best-323
88F-296
88F/St-58
88Moth/A's-17
88OPC-103
88Panini/St-165
88RedFoley/St-104
88Score-125
88Sf-209
88T-103
89B-184
89D-304
89F-26
89Moth/A's-14
89Score-29
89T-641
89T/Big-254
89UD-392
90D-505
90F-24
90Score-533
90T-328
90UD-4
Young, Del E.
48Sommer-27
49Sommer-21
Young, Delwyn
83Cedar-17
86Vermont-24
87BurlEx-15
87SnBer-11
88EastLAS/Pro-12
88GlenF/Pro-916
89Toled/CMC-22
89Toled/Pro-764
Young, Denton T.
(Cy)
10Domino-129
11Helmar-20
12Sweet/Pin-21A
12Sweet/Pin-21B
48Exh/HOF
50Callahan
60F-47
60NuCard-48
61F-153
61GP-33
61NuCard-448
63Bz/ATG-6
69Bz/Sm
72F/FFeat-11
72K/ATG-12
72K/ATG-12
72Laugh/GF-29
73OPC-477LL 73T-477L
75F/Pion-19
79T-416M
80Cram/Leg-91
80Laugh/3/4/5-11
80Laugh/FFeat-30
80SSPC/HOF
83D/HOF-27
84D/Champs-31
85Woolwth-44
88Conlon/4-30
89HOF/St-59
89Swell-5
BF2-31
D304
E101
E106
E107
E120
E121/120
E121/80
E122
E254
E270/1
E90/1
E92
E93
E94
E97
E98
M116
S74-12
T202
T205
T206
T215/brown
T216
W501-68
W555
WG2-51
WG5-45
WG6-42
Young, Derrick
89Clmbia/Best-3
89Clmbia/GS-29
Young, Don
66OPC-139R
66T-139R
69T-602R
70OPC-117
70T-117
89Watertn/Star-24
Young, Erik
89Watertn/Star-25
Young, Ernie
75Cedar
75Lafay
76Cedar
87Hagers-27
88Fresno/Cal-5
88Fresno/Pro-1241
Young, Floyd
WG8-52
Young, Ford
60DF-24
Young, Gerald
86ColumAst-25
87S/Rook-36
87Tucso-11
88D-431
88D/Best-318
88F-460
88Leaf-210
88Moth/Ast-3
88OPC-368
88Pol/Ast-24
88Score-442
88Score/YS/II-11
88T-368
89B-333
89D-207
89D/Best-288
89F-370
89Lennox/Ast-20
89Moth/Ast-3
89OPC-95
89Panini/St-93
89Score-97
89Score/HotSt-72
89Sf-125
89T-95
89T/Coins-28
89T/Mini-16
89T/St-23
89T/UK-86
89UD-135
90D-325
90F-241
90Score-43
90T-196
90UD-196
Young, Irving
M116
T206
WG3-54
Young, John
77ArkTr
80Indianap-31tr
81Indianap-32tr
83Sprin/LF-15
84ArkTr-22
87Nashv-24
88Nashvl/CMC-25
88Nashvl/Pro-495
88Watertn/Puc-30
89Nashvl/CMC-9
89Nashvl/Pro-1276
Young, Kenny
81Brist-14
Young, Kip
79T-706R
80Spoka-11
80T-251
81Indianap-8
82Indianap-3
Young, Larry
88Umpire-54
89Umpires-52
Young, Lemuel
(Pep)
35BU-102
39PB-102
40PB-106
D327
D328-198
D329-197
E135-198
E220
M101/4-197
R313
W514-107
W516-28
Young, Mark
88Duned/Star-24
89Butte/SP-22
89Duned/Star-25
89Myrtle/Pro-1452
Young, Matt
81Clint-12
81LynnS-12
82SLCty-22
83T/X-129
84D-16DK
84D-362
84F-624
84Moth/Mar-9
84Nes/792-235
84Nes/792-336TL
84OPC-235
84Seven-24W
84T-235
84T/St-386YS
85D-267
85F-505
85Moth/Mar-14
85OPC-136
85T-485
85T/St-340
86D-267
86F-481
86Moth/Mar-14
86OPC-274
86T-676
86T/St-220
87D-193
87F-600
87F/U-U131
87Moth/Dodg-12
87OPC-19
87Pol/Dodg-19
87RedFoley/St-123
87T-19
87T/St-218
87T/Tr-131T
88D-423
88D/A's/Bk-NEW
88F-530
88Moth/A's-21
88OPC-367
88Panini/St-306
88Score-357
88T-736
88T/St-72
90T-501
Young, Mike
82RochR-19
83RochR-22
84D-621
84F/X-131
84RochR-19
85D-367
85F-195
85T-173
86D-123
86F-291
86F/Mini-61
86S-199
86T-548
86T/St-234
87CharRa-10
87D-150
87F-483
87T-309
88D-396
88F-575
88OPC-11
88Panini/St-17
88Score-393
88Score/Tr-51T
88T-11
89ColSp/Pro-251
89D-632
89River/Best-21
89River/Cal-18
89River/Pro-1399
89Score-494
89T-731
89UD-649
Young, Norman
(Babe)
40PB-212
41DP-32
41DP-93
41G-23
41PB-27
49B-240
Young, Pete
89James/Pro-2136
Young, Ralph S.
E220
V100
W575
Young, Ray
87Duned-18
88Modesto-16
88Modesto/Cal-58
89Huntsvl/Best-24
Young, Rick
75QuadC
Young, Scott
83StPet-13
86ArkTr-26
Young, Shane
84LitFalls-10
86Lynch-28
87TexLgAS-14
88MidldA/GS-5
89MidldA/GS-30
Young, Sly
83Albany-16
Youngbauer, Jeff
79RochR-1
Youngblood, Joel
77T-548
78T-428
79OPC-48
79T-109
80OPC-194
80T-372
81Coke
81D-277
81F-331
81OPC-58
81T-58
81T/St-195
82D-613

82F-543
82OPC-189
82T-655
82T/St-65
83D-572
83F-301
83F-641
83Moth/Giants-17
83OPC-265
83T-265
83T/St-143
83T/St-144
83T/X-130
84D-480
84F-387
84Nes/792-727
84OPC-303
84T-727
84T/St-173
85D-79
85F-625
85Leaf-152
85Moth/Giants-19
85OPC-97
85T-567
85T/St-168
86D-567
86F-555
86Moth/Giants-26
86OPC-177
86T-177
87F-288
87Moth/SFG-20
87OPC-378
87T-759
88Moth/Giants-20
88Score-509
88T-418
89B-315
89K/Reds-12
89Score-539
89Score/Tr-66
89T-304
89UD-458
90Score-344

Younger, Stan
82BirmB-1
83BirmB-5
84Evans-7

Youngman, Pete
86Greens-25TR
87Greens-4
89NewBrit/Pro-601
89NewBrit/Star-25

Youngs, Ross M.
21Exh-193
61F-154
80SSPC/HOF
V100
V61-106
W573
W575

Yount, Robin
75Ho-80
75Ho/Twink-80
75OPC-223
75T-223
75T/M-223
76A&P/Milw
76Ho-11
76Ho/Twink-11
76OPC-316
76SSPC-238
76T-316
77Ho-34
77OPC-204
77Pepsi-1
77T-635
77T/CS-54
78Ho-138
78OPC-29
78T-173
79Ho-55
79OPC-41
79T-95
80OPC-139
80T-265
81D-323
81F/St-38
81K-57
81OPC-4
81T-515
81T/So-10
81T/St-244
81T/St-95
82D-510
82F-155
82F/St-135
82K-28
82OPC-237
82Pol/Brew-19
82T-435
82T/St-203
83D-258
83D/AAS-56
83Drake-33
83F-51
83F-632
83Gard-22
83K-14
83OPC-350
83OPC-389AS
83Pol/Brew-19
83T-321TL
83T-350
83T-389
83T/Gloss-5
83T/Gloss40-5
83T/St-145
83T/St-146
83T/St-150
83T/St-167
83T/St-81
84D-1
84D-48
84D/AAS-5
84D/Champs-47
84Drake-33
84F-219
84FunFood/Pin-29
84Gard-22
84MiltBrad-30
84Nes/792-10
84OPC-10
84Pol/Brew-19
84Ralston-21
84Seven-2C
84Seven-2E
84Seven-2W
84T-10
84T/Cereal-21
84T/Gloss22-5
84T/Gloss40-36
84T/St-295
84T/St/Box-6
84T/Super-29
84T/Super-29
85D-48
85D/AAS-21
85Drake-33
85F-601
85F/LimEd-44
85Gard-22
85GenMills-26
85Leaf-44
85OPC-340
85Pol/Brew-19
85Seven-16G
85T-340
85T/St-284
85T/Super-37
86D-48
86Dorman-16
86F-506
86F/LL-44
86F/Mini-103
86F/Slug-44
86F/St-131
86Jay's-20
86Jiffy-5
86Leaf-31
86OPC-144
86Pol/Brew-19
86S-42
86S-54M
86S-63M
86S-71M
86S/Dec-73M
86T-780
86T/St-197
86TrueVal-11
87Class-44
87D-126
87D/OD-58
87F-361
87F-C16
87F/McCror-44
87F/St-130
87F/WaxBox-C16
87Ho/St-25
87Kraft-23
87Leaf-67
87OPC-76
87RedFoley/St-126
87S-16
87T-773
87T/Board-9
87T/St-196
88D-295
88D/Best-183
88F-178
88F/BB/MVP-44
88F/Mini-33
88F/SS-44
88F/St-40
88Jiffy-20
88KMart-33
88Leaf-106
88OPC-165
88Panini/St-129
88Pol/Brew-19
88Score-160
88Sf-34
88T-165
88T/Big-66
88T/Coins-32
88T/Mini-21
88T/St-201
88T/UK-87
89Ames-33
89B-144
89Class-83
89Crunch-21
89D-55
89D-5DK
89D/Best-53
89D/DKsuper-5DK 89F-200
89F/Excit-44
89F/Heroes-44
89F/LL-44
89Gard-2
89KayBee-33
89KingB/Discs-13
89KMart/Lead-21
89OPC-253
89Panini/St-377
89Pol/Brew-19
89RedFoley/St-130
89Score-151
89Score/HotSt-28
89Sf-199
89T-615
89T/Big-249
89T/Coins-60
89T/Gloss60-38
89T/Hills-33
89T/Mini-59
89T/St-205
89T/St/Backs-21
89T/UK-87
89UD-285
90Class-147
90D-146
90F-340
90F/WaxBox-C28
90Score-320
90Score/100St-92
90Sf-18
90T-290
90T-389AS 90UD-567
90UD-91TC

Youse, Bob
73Cedar
74Cedar

Yuhas, John Ed
52T-386
53Hunter
53T-70
54Hunter

Yuhas, Vince
83Omaha-10
84Memph-15
84Omaha-16

Yurak, Jeff
75Cedar
76Cedar
77Holyo
78Holyo
79Holyo-28
79Vanco-18

Yurtin, Jeff
86Cram/PCL-176
88Wichi-11
89LasVeg/CMC-20
89LasVeg/Pro-20

Yvars, Sal
52T-338
53T-11
54B-78
54Hunter

Zachary, Chris
64T-23
66T-313
67T-212
70OPC-471
70T-471
73OPC-256
73T-256

Zachary, J. Tom
31Exh/4-1
33G-91
35G-8A
35G-9A
E120
E210-26
R315-A40
R315-B40
R316
V354-47
V61-3
W572
W573

Zacher, Elmer
E286

Zacher, Todd
82Clint-8

Zachry, Pat
76OPC-599R
76T-599R
77OPC-201
77Pep-57
77T-86
78OPC-172
78T-171
79K-8
79OPC-327
79T-621
80OPC-220
80T-428
81Coke
81D-275
81F-334
81OPC-224
81T/St-197
82D-254
82F-544
82F/St-88
82OPC-64
82T-399
82T/St-71
83D-560
83F-561
83Pol/Dodg-38
83T-522
83T/X-131
84D-215
84F-118
84Nes/792-747
84Pol/Dodg-38
84T-747
85F-391
85T-57
87VeroB-8
88SnAnt/Best-27

Zahn, Geoff
75OPC-294
75T-294
75T/M-294
76OPC-403
76T-403
78T-27
79K-27
79OPC-358
79T-678
80T-113
81D-532
81F-564
81T-363
81T/Tr-856
82D-164
82F-474
82T-229
83D-66
83F-103
83OPC-131
83T-547
83T/St-42
84D-402
84F-532
84Nes/792-276TL
84Nes/792-468
84OPC-153
84Smok/Cal-32
84T-468
85D-301
85D/AAS-33
85F-317
85Leaf-53
85OPC-140
85Smok/Cal-15
85SpokAT/Crm-24
85T-771
85T/St-221
86T-42

Zaksek, John
88Utica/Puc-13
89SoBend/GS-20

Zaleski, Richard
82Danvi-15
83Nashua-22
86MidldA-26TR
87Edmon-15

Zaltsman, Stan
86Erie-29
87Savan-22
88StPet/Star-25

Zambrana, Luis
81Redwd-21
82Redwd-18
83Redwd-27

Zambrano, Eduardo
(Eddie)
85Greens-13
86Greens-26
87WinHav-21
88NewBrit/Pro-895
89NewBrit/Pro-599
89NewBrit/Star-21
Zambrano, Roberto
85Greens-10
86WinHav-27
87NewBrit-20
88NewBrit/Pro-911
Zamora, Oscar
75OPC-604
75T-604
75T/M-604
76OPC-227
76SSPC-304
76T-227
78T-91
Zane, Kelly
88SLCty-8
Zanni, Dom
59T-145
62T-214
63FrBauer-32
63T-354
66T-233
Zappelli, Mark
87Anchora-33
89QuadC/Best-17
89QuadC/GS-5
Zarilla, Al
47TipTop
48L-36
49B-156
50B-45
51B-35
51T/RB-49
52B-113
52Hawth/Pin-10
52StarCal/L-73A
52T-70
52TipTop
53T-181
79Hawai-15C
Exh47
R423-118
Zarranz, Fernando
86Geneva-27
86Peoria-27
87Peoria-29
88MidwLAS/GS-29
88Peoria/Ko-33
Zaske, Jeff
82AlexD-17
84Cram/PCL-122
85Cram/PCL-249
86Hawai-23
87OKCty-26
88Tacom/CMC-6
Zauchin, Norm
55T-176
56T-89
57T-372
58T-422
59T-311
79TCMA-252
Zavaras, Clint
86Wausa-29
88Vermont/Pro-960
89Calg/CMC-11
90D-662
90T-89
Zawaski, Vince
89Star/Wax-25
89StLucie/Star-25
Zayas, Carlos
85Bend/Cram-24
87Clearw-6
88Spart/Pro-1039
89Clearw/Star-25
Zayas, Felipe
77StPet
78StPet
80ArkTr-19
81ArkTr-1
Zayas, Pedro
89Spart/Pro-1051
89Spart/Star-25
Zdeb, Joe
78T-408
79T-389
Zeber, George
78Cr/PCL-64
78T-591
Zeider, Rollie
14CJ-116
14CJ-60
15CJ-116
D328-199
D329-198
E135-199
E90/3
M101/4-198
T207
W514-32
Zeig, Robert
77WHave
79WHave-23
79WHave-29M
Zeihen, Bob
88Oneon/Pro-2058
89Star/Wax-81
Zeile, Todd E.
86Erie-30
87Sprin/Best-26
88ArkTr/GS-7
88TexLgAS/GS-2
89AAA/Pro-14
89F/Up-122
89Louvl-2
89Louvl-3
89Louvl-4
89Louvl-5
89Louvl/CMC-13
89Louvl/Pro-1267
89UD/Ext-754
90Class-90
90D-29
90D/Preview-3
90F-265
90Score-600
90Score/100Ris-6
90Sf-177
90T-162
90UD-545
Zell, Brian
80Elmir-31
Zellner, Joey
86Macon-27
87Visal-20
88Visal/Cal-148
88Visal/Pro-98
Zepp, Bill
70T-702R
71MLB/St-480
71OPC-271
71T-271
Zeratsky, Rod
86Cedar/TCMA-13
87Tampa-28
Zerb, Troy
88Batav/Pro-1690
Zernial, Gus
47Signal
50B-4
51B-262
51FB
51T/RB-36
52B-82
52BR
52RM-AL26
52StarCal/L-76A
52T-31
53B/Col-13
53Dix
53NB
53RM-AL13
53T-42
54Dix
54RH
54T-2
55RFG-2
55Rodeo
55T-110
55T/DH-123
56Rodeo
56T-45
56T/Hocus-A13
56T/Hocus-B15
56T/Pin-15
56YellBase/Pin-32
57T-253
58T-112
59T-409
79TCMA-263
Exh47
PM10/Sm-205
R423-119
Zick, Bill
88QuadC/GS-3
89QuadC/Best-4
89QuadC/GS-4
Ziegler, Bill
84Rang-tr
85Rang-tr
86Rang-tr
Ziegler, Greg
87Idaho-27
Ziem, Steve
84Durhm-23
87Richm/TCMA-9
88Greenv/Best-15
88Richm-28
89Durhm/Star-25
Zientara, Benny
49Eureka-100
Zimmer, Charles
N172
Zimmer, Don
55B-65
55Gol/Dodg-32
55T-92
55T/DH-98
56T-99
57T-284
58BB
58Hires-41
58T-77
59Morrell
59T-287
60BB-17
60T-47
61T-493
62Bz
62J-183
62P-183
62P/Can-183
62Salada-123A
62Salada-123B
62Shirriff-123
62T-478
62T/St-161
63T-439
64T-134
64T/Coins-1
64T/St-11
65OPC-233
65T-233
73OPC-12MG
73T-12MG
74OPC-403CO
74T-403C
77T-309MG
78T-63
79T-214MG
79TCMA-228
81F-230
81T-673MG
82D-195
88Berg/Cubs-4MG
88T/Tr-131MG
89Mara/Cubs-4
89Swell-23
89T-134MG
90T-549MG
Zimmerman, Brian
88LitFalls/Puc-25
Zimmerman, Eric
83AlexD-24
Zimmerman, Gerald
59T-146
60HenryH-9
61Clover-31
62J-130
62P-130
62P/Can-130
62T-222
63T-186
64T-369
65T-299
66OPC-73
66T-73
67T-501
68OPC-181
68T-181
69MB-296
73OPC-377CO
73T-377C
74OPC-531CO 74T-531C
78TCMA-117
Zimmerman, Henry
14CJ-21
15CJ-21
BF2-70
D328-200
D329-199
D350/2-199
E101
E102
E105
E106
E135-200
E224
E254
E254
E270/1
E92
M101/4-199
M101/5-199
M116
T206
T222
Zimmerman, Mike
88CapeCod/Sum-44
Zimmerman, Roy
50Remar
Zinn, Frank
N172
Zinter, Alan
88CapeCod/Sum-29
90Score-671DC
Zinter, Eddie
89Spoka/SP-2
Zipay, Ed
(Bud)
46Sunbeam
47Signal
47Sunbeam
Zipeto, Ted
86Clearw-26tr
Zipfel, M. Bud
63T-69
Zisk, John
79Wausa-11
80Wausa-10
Zisk, Richie
72OPC-392R
72T-392R
73OPC-611R
73T-611R
74OPC-317
74T-317
74T/St-90
75Ho-139
75K-25
75OPC-77
75T-77
75T/M-77
76Crane-70
76MSA/Disc
76OPC-12
76SSPC-574
76T-12
77Ho-127
77OPC-152
77Pep-27
77T-483
77T/CS-55
78BK/R-20
78PapaG/Disc-30
78T-110
78Wiffle/Discs-79
79Ho-140
79K-24
79OPC-130
79T-260
80OPC-325
80T-620
81D-28
81F-620
81F/St-105
81OPC-214
81Pol/Mar-13
81T-517
81T/So-16
81T/St-27
81T/Tr-857
82D-11DK
82D-127
82Drake-33
82F-519
82F/St-223
82K-1
82OPC-66
82T-769
82T/St-229
83D-559
83D/AAS-54
83F-489
83Nalley-3
83OPC-368
83T-368
83T/Gloss-21
83T/Gloss40-21
83T/St-116
84D-69
84D/AAS-30
84F-625
84Nes/792-83
84OPC-83
84T-83
84T/St-342
Zitzmann, William
28Exh-16
Zmudosky, Tom
84Albany-20
Zoldak, Sam
49B-78
50B-182
50NumNum
51B-114
52T-231
R423-120
Zona, Jeff
89Idaho/Pro-2029
Zosky, Eddie
90Score-665DC

Zottneck, Roger
86QuadC-32
87PalmSp-16
Zuber, William
44Yank/St-30
47TipTop
Zupcic, Bob
87Elmir/Red-31
88CLAS/Star-20
88Lynch/Star-27
89NewBrit/Pro-600
89NewBrit/Star-22
Zupka, Bill
85Elmir-25
86Greens-27
87NewBrit-3
Zupo, Frank
58T-229
Zuvella, Paul
82Richm-17
83Richm-17
84Richm-23
85F-651M
85Pol/Atl-18
86F-532
86Richm-26
86T-572
86T/Tr-131T
87T-102
88ColSp/CMC-18
88ColSp/Pro-1528
89AAA/Pro-33
89ColrSp/CMC-17
89ColSp/Pro-245
89Score-598
89UD-236
Zuverink, George
52T-199
55B-92
56T-276
57T-11
58Hires-66
58T-6
59T-219
Zwilling, Edward
(Dutch)
D329-200
D350/2-200
M101/4-200
M101/5-200
M116
Zwolensky, Mitch
82Wausa-19
83Tulsa-9
84OKCty-21
85OKCty-2
88Pittsf/Pro-1356
TEAM CARDS
Atlanta Braves
66T-326
66T/RO-115
67T-477
68T-221
69T/St/Alb-1
69T/T/Post-1
70OPC-472
70T-472
71OPC-652
71T-652
71T/tatt-5
72OPC-21
72T-21
73OPC-521
73T-521
74OPC-483
74T-483
74T/St/Alb-1
75OPC-589
75T-589
75T/M-589
76OPC-631
76T-631
77T-442
78T-551
79T-302
80T-192
81T-675
88T-549
Baltimore Orioles
56T-100
57T-251
58T-408
59T-48
60T-494
61T-159
61T/RO-85
62T-476
63T-377
64T-473
65T-572
66T-348
67T-302
68T-334
70OPC-387
70T-387
71OPC-1
71T-1
71T/tatt-10
72T-731
73OPC-278
73T-278
74OPC-16
74T-16
75OPC-117
75T-117
75T/M-117
76OPC-73
76T-73
77T-546
78T-96
79T-689
80T-404
81T-661
88T-51
N690
Boston Braves
48Exh/T-1
T200
Boston Red Sox
51T
56T-111
57T-171
58T-312
59T-248
60T-537
60T/tatt-65
61T-373
61T/RO-5
62T-334
63T-202
64T-579
65T-403
66T-259
66T/RO-109
67T-604
69T/St/Alb-3
69T/T/Post-3
70T-563
71OPC-386
71T-386
71T/tatt-2
72OPC-328
72T-328
72T/Cloth-26
73OPC-596
73T-596
74OPC-567
74T-567
74T/St/Alb-3
75OPC-172
75T-172
75T/M-172
76OPC-118
76T-118
77T-309
78T-424
79T-214
80T-689
81T-662
88T-21
R309/2
Brooklyn Dodgers
48Exh/T-13
48Exh/T-15
48Exh/T-3
48Exh/T-9
49Exh/Team
51T
52Exh/Team
55Exh/Team
56Exh/Team
56T-166
57T-324
58T-71
T200
California Angels
61T/RO-6
62T-132
63T-39
64T-213
65T-293
66OPC-131
66T-131
66T/RO-79
67T-327
68T-252
69T/St/Alb-4
69T/T/Post-4
70OPC-522
70T-522
71OPC-442
71T-442
71T/tatt
72OPC-71
72T-71
73OPC-243
73T-243
74OPC-114
74T-114
74T/St/Alb-4
75OPC-236
75T-236
75T/M-236
76OPC-304
76T-304
77T-34
78T-214
79T-424
80T-214
81T-663
88T-381
Chicago Cubs
56T-11
57T-183
58T-327
59T-304
60T-513
60T/tatt-56
61T-122
61T/RO-17
62T-552
63T-222
64T-237
65OPC-91
65T-91
66T-204
66T/RO-97
67T-354
69T/St/Alb-5
69T/T/Post-5
70T-593
71OPC-502
71T-502
71T/tatt-6
72OPC-192
72T-192
73OPC-464
73T-464
74OPC-211
74T-211
74T/St/Alb-5
75OPC-638
75T-638
75T/M-638
76OPC-277
76T-277
77T-518
78T-302
79T-551
80T-381
81T-676
88T-171
T200
Chicago White Sox
51T
56T-188
57T-329
58T-256
59T-94
60T-208
60T/tatt-66
61T-7
61T/RO-9
62T-113
63T-288
64T-496
65OPC-234
65T-234
66T-426
66T/RO-1
67T-573
68T-424
69T/St/Alb-6
69T/T/Post-6
70OPC-501
70T-501
71T-289
71T/tatt-8
72OPC-381
72T-381
73OPC-481
73T-481
74OPC-416
74T-416
74T/St/Alb-6
75OPC-276
75T-276
75T/M-276
76OPC-656
76T-656
77T-418
78T-526
79T-404
80T-112
81T-664
88T-321
T200
Cincinnati Reds
51T
56T-90
57T-322
58T-428
59T-111
60T-164
60T/tatt-57
61T-249
61T/RO-15
62T-465
63T-288
64T-403
65T-316
66OPC-59
66T-59
66T/RO-91
67T-407
68T-574
69T/St/Alb-7
69T/T/Post-7
70OPC-544
70T-544
71OPC-357
71T-357
71T/tatt-6
72T-651
73OPC-641
73T-641
74OPC-459
74T-459
74T/St/Alb-7
75OPC-531
75T-531
75T/M-531
76OPC-104
76T-104
77T-287
78T-526
79T-259
80T-606
81T-677
88T-81
N690
T200
W711/2
Cleveland Indians
48Exh/T-12
48Exh/T-2
48Exh/Team
54Exh/Team
56T-85
57T-275
58T-158
59T-476
60T-174
60T/tatt-67
61T-467
61T/RO-10
62T-537
63T-451
64T-172
65T-481
66T-303
66T/RO-67
67T-544
69T/St/Alb-8
69T/T/Post-8
70T-637
71OPC-584
71T-584
71T/tatt-7
72T-547
73OPC-629
73T-629
74OPC-541
74T-541
74T/St/Alb-8
75OPC-331
75T-331
75T/M-331
76OPC-477
76T-477
77T-18
78T-689
79T-96
80T-451
81T-665
88T-789
R309/2
T200
Detroit Tigers
56T-213
57T-198
58T-397
59T-329
60T-72
60T/tatt-68
61T-51
61T/RO-1
62T-24
63T-552
64T-67

65OPC-173
65T-173
66T-583
66T/RO-61
67T-378
68T-528
69T/St/Alb-9
69T/T/Post-9
70T-579
71OPC-336
71T-336
71T/tatt-9
72OPC-487
72T-487
73OPC-191
73T-191
74OPC-94
74T-94
74T/St/Alb-9
75OPC-18
75T-18
75T/M-18
76OPC-361
76T-361
77T-621
78T-404
79T-66
80T-626
81T-666
88T-429
N690
T200

Houston Astros
63T-312
66T/RO-7
69T/St/Alb-10
69T/T/Post-10
70OPC-448
70T-448
71OPC-722
71T-722
71T/tatt-12
72OPC-282
72T-282
73OPC-158
73T-158
74OPC-154
74T-154
74T/St/Alb-10
75OPC-487
75T-487
75T/M-487
76OPC-147
76T-147
77T-327
78T-112
79T-381
80T-82
81T-678
88T-291

Kansas City Athletics
56T-236
57T-204
58T-174
59T-172
60T-413
61T-297
61T/RO-7
62T-384
63T-397
64T-151
65T-151
66T-492
66T/RO-103
67T-262

Kansas City Royals
69T/St/Alb-11
69T/T/Post-11
70OPC-422
70T-422
71OPC-742
71T-742
71T/tatt-4
72T-617
73OPC-347
73T-347
74OPC-343
74T-343
74T/St/Alb-11
75OPC-72
75T/M-72
76OPC-236
76T-236
76T-72
77T-371
78T-724
79T-451
80T-86
81T-667
88T-141

Los Angeles Dodgers
59T-457
60T-18
60T/tatt-58
61T-86
61T/RO-13
62T-43
63T-337
64T-531
65OPC-126
65T-126
66T-238
66T/RO-13
67T-503
68OPC-168
68T-168
69T/St/Alb-12
69T/T/Post-12
70OPC-411
70T-411
71OPC-402
71T-403
71T/tatt-5
72OPC-522
72T-522
73OPC-91
73T-91
74OPC-643
74T-643
74T/St/Alb-12
75OPC-361
75T-361
75T/M-361
76OPC-46
76T-46
77T-504
78T-259
79T-526
80T-302
81T-679
82T/St-255
82T/St-256
88T-489

Milwaukee Braves
55Gol/Braves-32
56T-95
57T-114
58T-377
59T-419
60T-381
61T-426
61T/RO-18
62T-158
63T-503
64T-132
65T-426

Milwaukee Brewers
71OPC-698
71T-698
71T/tatt-7
72OPC-106
72T-106
73OPC-127
73T-127
74OPC-314
74T-314
74T/St/Alb-13
75OPC-384
75T-384
75T/M-384
76OPC-606
76T-606
77T-51
78T-328
79T-577
80T-659
81T-668
88T-639

Minnesota Twins
61T-542
61T-584
61T/RO-3
63T-162
64T-318
65OPC-24
65T-24
66T-526
66T/RO-49
67T-211
68OPC-137
68T-137
69T/St/Alb-13
69T/T/Post-13
70OPC-534
70T-534
71OPC-522
71T-522
71T/tatt-14
72OPC-156
72T-156
73OPC-654
73T-654
74OPC-74
74T-74
74T/St/Alb-14
75OPC-443
75T-443
75T/M-443
76OPC-556
76T-556
77T-228
78T-451
79T-41
80T-328
81T-669
88T-609

Montreal Expos
69T/St/Alb-14
69T/T/Post-14
70OPC-509
70T-509
71OPC-674
71T-674
71T/tatt-1
72T-582
73OPC-576
73T-576
74OPC-508
74T-508
74T/St/Alb-15
75OPC-101
75T-101
75T/M-101
76OPC-216
76T-216
77T-647
78OPC-207
78T-244
79OPC-349
79T-606
80T-479
81T-680
88T-111

New York Yankees
49Exh/Team
50Exh/Team
51Exh/Team
52Exh/Team
55Exh/Team
56Exh/Team
56T-251
57T-97
58T-246
59T-510
60T-332
60T/tatt-70
61T-228
61T/RO-2
62T-251
63T-247
64T-433
65T-513
66OPC-92
66T-92
66T/RO-55
67OPC-131
67T-131
69T/St/Alb-16
69T/T/Post-16
70OPC-399
70T-399
71OPC-543
71T-543
71T/tatt-3
72OPC-237
72T-237
73OPC-556
73T-556
74OPC-363
74T-363
74T/St/Alb-17
75OPC-611
75T-611
75T/M-611
76OPC-17
76T-17
77T-387
78T-282
79T-626
80T-424
81T-670
88T-459
T200

New York Giants
51Exh/Team
51T
54Exh/Team
55Gol/Giants-8
56T-226
57T-317
58T-19
T200

New York Mets
63T-473
64T-27
65T-551
66OPC-172
66T-172
66T/RO-19
67OPC-42
67T-42
68T-401
69T/St/Alb-15
69T/T/Post-15
70OPC-1
70T-1
71OPC-641
71T-641
71T/tatt-2
72OPC-362
72T-362
73OPC-389
73T-389
74OPC-56
74T-56
74T/St/Alb-16
75OPC-421
75T-421
75T/M-421
76OPC-531
76T-531
77T-259
78T-356
79T-82
80T-259
81T-681
88T-579

New York Team
N690

Oakland A's
65OPC-151
68T-554
69T/St/Alb-17
69T/T/Post-17
70T-631
71OPC-624
71T-624
71T/tatt-4
72OPC-454
72T-454
73OPC-500
73T-500
74OPC-246
74T-246
74T/St/Alb-18
75OPC-561
75T-561
75T/M-561
76OPC-421
76T-421
77T-74
78T-577
79T-328
80T-96
81T-671
88T-759

Oakland Oaks
46Remar
48Remar

Phila. Athletics
51T
T200

Philadelphia Phillies
50Exh/Team
51T
56T-72
57T-214
58T-134
59T-8
60T-302
60T/tatt-60
61T-491
61T/RO-14
62T-294
63T-13
64T-293
65T-338
66T-463
66T/RO-73
67T-102
68T-477
69T/St/Alb-18
69T/T/Post-18
70T-436
71T-268
71T/tatt-3
72T-397
73T-536
74T-467
74T/St/Alb-19
75T-46
75T/M-46
76T-384
77T-467
78T-381
79T-112
80T-526
81T-682
88T-669
T200

65T-443
65T-508
65T-79
66OPC-101
66OPC-183
66OPC-34
66T-101
66T-183
66T-279
66T-34
66T-363
66T-444
66T-517
67OPC-103
67OPC-191
67OPC-62
67T-103
67T-191
67T-278
67T-361
67T-454
67T-531
67T-62
68OPC-107
68OPC-192
68OPC-67
68T-107
68T-192
68T-278
68T-356
68T-454
68T-518
68T-67
69OPC-107
69OPC-214
69OPC-57
69T-107
69T-214
69T-504
69T-57
69T-582
70OPC-128
70OPC-244
70OPC-343
70OPC-432
70OPC-542
70OPC-9
70T-128
70T-244
70T-343
70T-432
70T-542
70T-588
70T-9
71OPC-123
71OPC-206
71OPC-369
71OPC-499
71OPC-54
71OPC-619
71T-123
71T-161Coin
71T-206
71T-369
71T-499
71T-54
71T-619
72OPC-103
72OPC-251
72OPC-378
72OPC-4
72OPC-478
72T-103
72T-251
72T-378
72T-4
72T-478
72T-604
72T/Cloth-5
73OPC-264
73OPC-338
73OPC-453
73OPC-54
73OPC-588
73T-264
73T-338
73T-453
73T-54
73T-588
74OPC-126
74OPC-263
74OPC-273
74OPC-414
74OPC-637
74T-126
74T-257
74T-263
74T-273
74T-414
74T-637
74T/Tr-un
75OPC-126
75OPC-257
75OPC-386
75OPC-517
75OPC-646
75T-126
75T-386
75T-517
75T-646
75T/M-126
75T/M-257
75T/M-386
75T/M-517
75T/M-646
76OPC-119
76OPC-262
76OPC-392
76OPC-526
76OPC-643
76SSPC-589--595
76T-19
76T-262
76T-392
76T-526
76T-643
76T/Tr
77OPC-124
77OPC-179
77T-208
77T-32
77T-356
77T-451
77T-562
77T/CS
78OPC-119
78OPC-183
78T-184
78T-289
78T-435
78T-535
78T-652
78T-74
79OPC-121
79OPC-242
79OPC-353
79T-121
79T-241
79T-353
79T-483
79T-602
79T-699
80OPC-128
80OPC-183
80OPC-249
80OPC-300
80OPC-67
80T-121
80T-241
80T-348
80T-484
80T-533
80T-646
81D-un
81F-641--644
81F-646--649
81F-651
81F-652
81F-654
81F-656
81F-658
81F-659
81OPC-241
81OPC-31
81OPC-331
81OPC-338
81T-241
81T-31
81T-338
81T-446
81T-562
81T-638
81T/Tr-858
82D-un
82F-647--660
82OPC-129
82OPC-226
82OPC-394
82T-129
82T-226
82T-394
82T-491
82T-634
82T-789
82T/Tr-132T
83D-un
83D/AAS-60
83D/HOF-44
83F-647--660
83OPC-129
83OPC-249
83OPC-349
83T-129
83T-249
83T-349
83T-526
83T-642
83T-769
84Cram/PCL-194
84Cram/PCL-217
84D-un
84D/AAS-60
84D/Champs-60
84F-647--660
84F/X-132
84Nes/792-114
84Nes/792-233
84Nes/792-379
84Nes/792-527
84Nes/792-646
84Nes/792-781
84Nestle/DT-23
84OPC-114
84OPC-233
84OPC-379
84T-114
84T-233
84T-379
84T-527
84T-646
84T-781
84T/Cereal-34
84T/X-132
85D-un
85D/AAS-60
85D/DKsuper-27
85D/HL-56
85F-654--660
85F/Up-U132
85Leaf-260--263
85OPC-121
85OPC-261
85OPC-377
85T-121
85T-261
85T-377
85T-527
85T-659
85T-784
85T/Tr-132T
86D-un
86D/AAS-60
86D/DKsuper-28
86D/HL-56
86D/Rook-56
86F-654--660
86F/Up-U132
86Leaf-261--264
86OPC-131
86OPC-263
86OPC-396
86T-131
86T-263
86T-394
86T-527
86T-659
86T-791
86T/Mini-66
86T/Tr-132T
87D-100
87D-200
87D-27DK
87D-300
87D-400
87D-500
87D-600
87D/AAS-60
87D/DKsuper-27
87D/HL-56
87D/Rook-56
87F-654--660
87F/U-U132
87Leaf-155
87Leaf-259
87Leaf-264
87Leaf-27
87OPC-128
87OPC-214
87OPC-264
87T-128
87T-264
87T-392
87T-522
87T-654
87T-792
87T/Mini-77
87T/Tr-132T
88D-100
88D-200
88D-27DK
88D-300
88D-400
88D-500
88D-600
88D/AS-32
88D/AS-64
88D/Best-288
88D/Best-329
88D/Best-336
88D/Rook-56
88F-654--660
88F/St-132
88F/U-U132
88Leaf-209
88Leaf-261
88Leaf-264
88Leaf-27
88OPC-253
88OPC-373
88OPC-374
88T-121
88T-253
88T-373
88T-528
88T-646
88T-776
88T/Big-126
88T/Big-216
88T/Big-28
88T/Mini-77
88T/Tr-132T
88T/UK-88
88Umpire-64
89B-481
89B-482
89B-483
89B-484
89D-100
89D-200
89D-27
89D-300
89D-400
89D-500
89D-600
89D/AS-32
89D/AS-64
89D/Best-300
89D/Best-329
89D/Best-332
89D/Rook-56
89D/Tr-56
89F-654--660
89F/Up-132
89OPC-118
89OPC-242
89OPC-247
89Swell-135
89T-118
89T-258
89T-378
89T-524
89T-619
89T-782
89T/Big-176
89T/Big-327
89T/Big-59
89T/Mini-43
89T/St/Backs-67
89T/Tr-132T
89T/UK-88
89UD-27
89UD-694--700
89UD/Ext-701
90D-100
90D-200
90D-27
90D-300
90D-400
90D-500
90D-600
90D-700
90F-654--660
90T-128
90T-262
90T-376
90T-526
90T-646
90T-783
90UD-1
90UD-10
90UD-100
90UD-12
90UD-16
90UD-18
90UD-200
90UD-24
90UD-29
90UD-300
90UD-32
90UD-36
90UD-40
90UD-400
90UD-41
90UD-48
90UD-5
90UD-500
90UD-53
90UD-60
90UD-600
90UD-62
90UD-68
90UD-7
90UD-700
90UD-73
90UD-82
90UD-84
90UD-88
90UD-91
90UD-95
90UD-99

EVEN MORE

More color superstar covers

Readers React to Ripken Card

More answers to your hobby questions

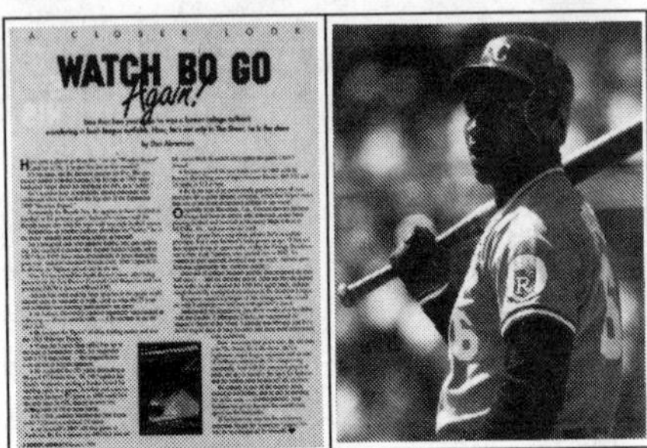
A CLOSER LOOK

WATCH BO GO Again!

More monthly profiles on the big guns in the hobby

PRICE GUIDE

Beckett Monthly Price Guide

More accurate prices to all the new sets

More hot hobby art for your autographing requests

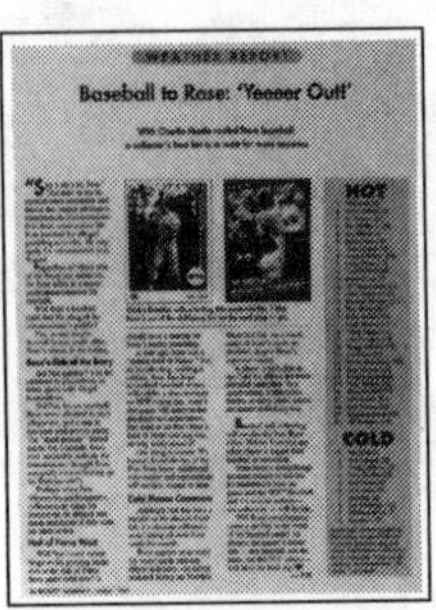
WEATHER REPORT

Baseball to Rose: 'Yeeeer Out!'

HOT

COLD

More national rankings to keep you in the know

Hit and Miss

More interaction with fellow collectors across the country

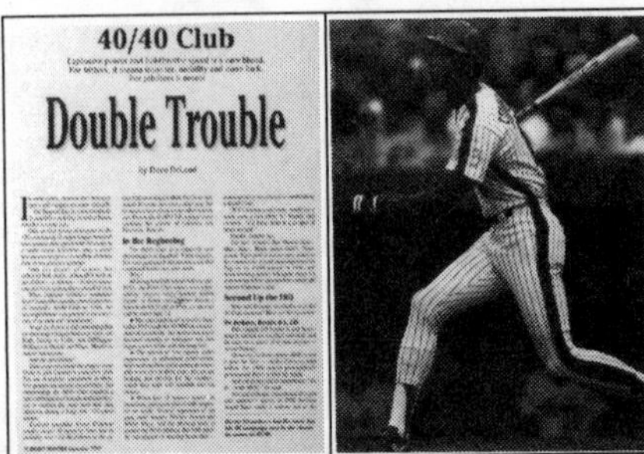
40/40 Club

Double Trouble

More informative features to help you collect better

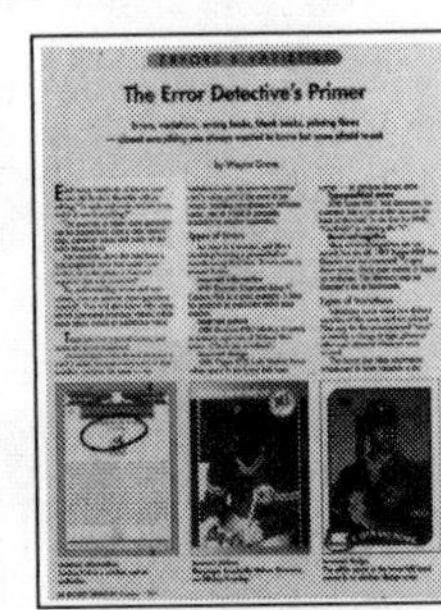
The Error Detective's Primer

More explanations to the hobby's hottest errors & variations

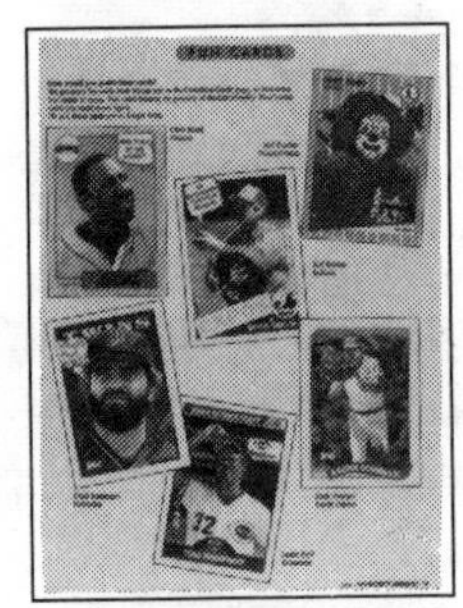
FUN CARDS

More fun for your hobby